MANUAL OF
CULTIVATED BROAD-LEAVED TREES & SHRUBS

Volume I, A–D

Written by GERD KRÜSSMANN
Translated by MICHAEL E. EPP
Technical Editor: GILBERT S. DANIELS

Timber Press
Box 1631
Beaverton, OR 97075

In cooperation with
the American Horticultural Society

PJC MIL CAMPUS LRC

Title of the German original version:
Krüssmann, Handbuch der Laubgehölze
® 1976 by Verlag Paul Parey

Berlin and Hamburg
English translation 1984 by Timber Press
Rights Reserved
Printed in Hong Kong

ISBN 0 917304-78-0

Timber Press, Beaverton, Oregon

Contents of Volume I

GENERAL

MAIN TEXT

Guide to Terminology

(alphabetical index found on pp. 33-39)

As with every technical book, a clear knowledge of the terminology must be mastered before a complete understanding of its contents is possible. Due to the wide variety of plant properties and the highly technical nature of botany, such terminology is seldom found in popular dictionaries. Hence, botanists have traditionally interpreted certain words differently as applied to their own work. Even today there exists a slight variation between the terminology of English and German botanical literature.

In gardening literature, nursery catalogues, trade magazines and many books, the botanical terms are unfortunately ill-chosen. Proper use is not possible without a complete and ongoing understanding of the often fine distinctions between botanical terms. As a result, terms such as 'lobed', 'oblong', 'creeping', etc. are used as a general description when a more exact term could have been used. In this book the terminology is detailed and representative of the most important aspects of any given species. The finer plant parts are described for a whole genus except for those species marked by important distinctions.

In the German language, the term *Laubgehoelze* is a collective term for all the angiosperms, mono- and dicotyledonous deciduous and evergreen trees and shrubs. To my knowledge only the Dutch have a similar word, *loofhoutgewassen*. The English, French and Scandinavian languages do not contain such a comprehensive word.

Within the 'Laubgehoelze' (Woody Broadleaves) are three distinct groups: Trees, Shrubs and Subshrubs. The distinction between these groups is often minute with increased age, especially if the natural growth habit has been altered (e.g. by pruning). The most important distinction between trees and shrubs is not their size but their branching character. Trees branch out at the top of a stem, shrubs at the base. Subshrubs can, under favorable growth conditions become shrubs.

Trees stand on a more or less columnar stem with a crown or, as with palms, a rosette of foliage. Occasionally multistemmed trees occur which might, in smaller sizes, be considered large shrubs (e.g. *Betula, Pterocarya, Acer, Sorbus*).

Shrubs have several branches of similar size originating at or below the ground level. They are generally smaller than trees.

Subshrubs differ from shrubs in that only the base or crown of the stem becomes woody. With several years of growth a subshrub may develop into a shrub.

All trees, shrubs and subshrubs consist of roots, stems, leaves, flower and fruit; these parts may have very different forms.

1. Roots

Roots are the downward growing portion of trees and shrubs which may be easily distinguished from underground stem parts by the lack of leaf remnants or leaf scars. There are basically two types of roots, the primary or taproot and many secondary roots. In describing the various types of plants a more detailed discussion of roots is not necessary and will therefore be avoided.

Rootlets are short aerial roots providing support for vines such as *Campsis, Hedera* and others.

2. Stems

The stem is the above ground, upright growing, woody portion upon which the crown of the tree develops; shrubs and subshrubs generally have several smaller stems.

The secondary stems arising from the main stem form the crown; the older, stronger stems are called limbs or branches while the thinner ones are referred to as twigs. For purposes of identification the current year's shoots and occasionally second year shoots are of special importance for identifying characteristics such as color, bark, pubescence, etc. The place on a branch or twig from which a leaf or new growth has arisen is called a node. Leaf buds are developed at nodes and give rise to new shoots. The buds and leaves are often characteristically arranged in each genus which will be covered further on p. 17. Internodes mark the space found between nodes and are frequently characteristic of a family or genus.

The bark is the tissue covering the stem and twigs. It is at first a smooth epidermal layer which becomes cracked and rough when stretched by the stem. With time the outer bark becomes woody with development of a corky inner bark. By steady growth the stem and branches take on a characteristic appearance typical of the species. Many trees have vertical or horizontal fissures or both in a checked pattern. There are some genera with smooth bark (*Fagus*); others with shaggy, loose bark (*Carya, Lonicera*) or flaking, patchy bark (*Platanus, Acer, Stewartia, Parrotia*). The peeling bark of *Betula*, many *Prunus* and others is striking. *Philadelphus* is remarkable because one year shoots already have peeling strips of bark, important for identification purposes. For winter identification a severed twig can provide important clues in the bark layer, cambium, wood or pith.

Under the bark lies the sap-filled cambium, a thin tissue producing phloem (food conducting) cells on the outside and xylem (water conducting) cells on the inside. Under the soft, light colored xylem is a darker, dense wood which forms the concentric annual rings in all woody plants except the monocots.

Many genera are distinct in their large pith, as in *Sambucus, Ailanthus, Rhus*, etc. Occasionally the pith is compartmentalized as with *Halesia, Juglans, Pterocarya, Forsythia*. Some genera, particularly in the new growth, have a hollow pith and are only solid at the nodes as in *Forsythia, Lonicera, Deutzia, Paulownia*.

When cleanly cut, a cross section of a twig will reveal the distinct shape of the pith, a good clue to the genus as with the following:

round	*Aesculus, Fraxinus, Prunus*
irregular	*Platanus, Rhus, Koelreuteria*
two-sided	*Aristolochia, Elsholtzia*
eccentric	*Tamarix*
triangular	*Alnus*
pentagonal	*Halesia*
hexagonal	*Acer rubrum*
three point star	*Betula*
five point star	*Populus, Quercus, Castanea*

Many cross sectional cuts should be examined. It is possible to find various shapes on the same twigs, particularly in *Rhus, Ailanthus* and *Fraxinus*. In the case of *Fraxinus* rectangular, elliptical and round pith can be found.

Also the color of the pith is an important indicator of species, as with *Sambucus nigra*, white; *S. racemosa* is, however, brown. Most often the pith is white or light colored, as *Betula* is light green, so is *Fagus* and many *Ericaceae*; *Acer, Corylus, Vitis, Sorbus, Populus* are, however, brown.

The crown and stem give a tree its particular form or growth habit. The form of the crown is dependent upon the positioning of the branches and twigs, in some ways analagous to the development of flower structure (monopodial or sympodial). We will here only briefly cover this area which is more thoroughly dealt with in a dendrology text.

Trees with monopodial development have a vertical main stem growing more strongly than the side branches throughout the height of the tree. New growth is initiated from the terminal bud until a certain height is reached, normally in the second year. Then side branches are formed which will eventually abscise (*Acer, Fraxinus, Quercus, Fagus*) (Fig. 1 I).

Sympodial development lacks a main stem. The terminal bud dies at the end of the growing period and growth resumes the following year from a lower axial bud. Side branches which continually arch upward are produced in the first and each successive year. The union of these branches will thicken with age to become the main stem (*Tilia, Ulmus*) (Fig. 1 II).

Fig. 1.I. Schematic monopodial development of a tree (branched opposite); 1-11 represents a single year's growth separated by x-x. The lower side branches are eventually cast off. The side branches add strength to the trunk. P. main stem. II. Schematic of sympodial (alternate branched) tree. G—G ground level. Other symbols as in I and Fig. 2. (Rauh)

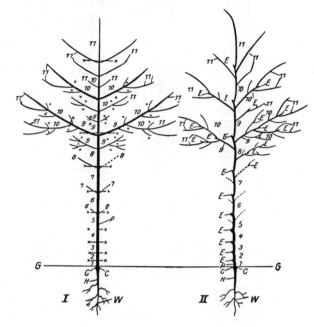

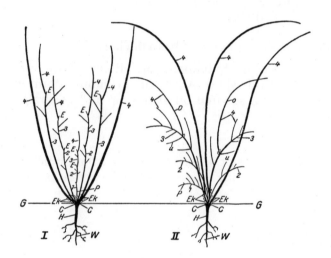

Fig. 2. Development of a shrub as with *Corylus avellana* (I) and *Sambucus* (II). W. primary root; H. hypocotyl; C. cotyledons; Ek. adventitious buds; P. primary shoot; E. stunted twigs; 1—4 each single year's growth; O. secondary branches. (Rauh)

Two distinct forms are found in the structure of shrubs:

   a)   Those with orthotropic (upright) branching, both monopodial and sympodial but in both cases with an acropetal (basal) origin (*Ribes, Rhododendron, Corylus avellana*) (Fig 2 I).
   b)   Shrubs with orthotropic branching, but mesotonal (mid zone) in origin. This group is the largest (*Sambucus, Rosa, Forsythia, Philadelphus*) (Fig. 2 II).

The branches are either regularly or irregularly arranged, opposite or alternate, whorled, paired in rows, etc. The thickness of the twigs also influences apearance (*Aralia, Gymnocladus, Salix, Betula*). The habit of mature trees and shrubs can differ from that of the juvenile plant; columnar, spherical or weeping plants show these characters especially well as young plants.

The following growth habits are the most common:

   a)   regular shapes (rounded, oval, conical, columnar)

      rounded (globusus), crown more or less round, as wide as high; small trees, of a globose form, are often dwarf forms grafted on standards (*Fraxinus excelsior* 'Nana', *Acer platanoides* 'Globosum');

      oval, crown twice as high as wide, usually wider at the base (Fig. 3e);

      conical (pyramidalis), crown widest at the base and then tapering to the top, as with many

4

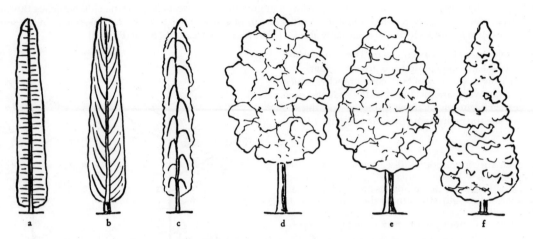

Fig. 3. Forms of crowns, a–c. columnar (a. with horizontal, b. with ascending and c. with weeping branches), d. rounded, e. oval and f. pyramidal crown.

conifers; the label 'pyramidal' is grammatically false since a pyramid has a flat base (Fig. 3f);

columnar (columnaris), crown taller than wide, generally the branches are either upright and tight against the stem or all the same length and relatively short. A particular columnar form is 'fastigiate'; having upright branches close to the stem, squared off at the top and generally without a strong leader (Fig. 3 a–c).

b) irregular shapes

These originate in: the absence of a main stem; branches of differing lengths; from branches growing in different directions; or are horizontal or weeping. Included here are pendulous or umbrella-shaped trees.

Direction of Growth of the stem or branches

upright, growing vertically (Fig. 4a);

narrowly upright, more densely and narrowly upright (Fig. 4b);

straight, generally straight growing branches as opposed to curving;

drooping, upright habit, however branch tips bend to horizontal (Fig. 4c);

nodding, upright habit, however branch tips curve downward (Fig. 4d);

deflexed, stem or branches at first upright but then making a long curve downwrd;

weeping, either the stem is vertical and the branches hang downward or the stem grows obliquely upward with branches that hang like a mane or whip; or combinations of the two (Fig. 4e);

divergent, branching at nearly right angles (Fig. 4f);

ascending, branches at first horizontal and then curving upward;

decumbent, branches start horizontally, with tips lying on the ground and curving upwards, not rooting (Fig. 6e);

procumbent, all branches and twigs lie flat on the ground, not rooting (syn. prostrate Fig. 6d);

creeping, branches and twigs lie flat on the ground, rooting at many places and in time 'creeping' from the mother plant; originally this label was only applied to herbaceous plants in which following three or four year's growth, the mother plant dies but the young rooted branches continue to grow. (Fig. 6a);

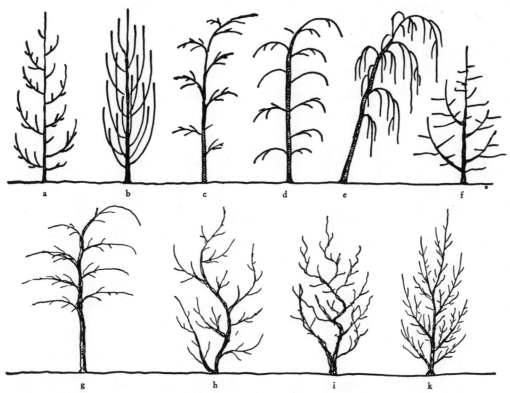

Fig. 4. Direction of Growth. a. upright; b. narrowly upright; c. drooping; d. nodding; e. weeping;
f. divergent; g. branches horizontal; h. erratic, irregular; i. twisted; k. densely branched.

rambling or climbing, with hooks, tendrils or other forms of support growing over an object; without these supports sometimes twining on the object, e.g. *Vitis, Parthenocissus, Clematis, Rosa*;

twining, climbing over objects in a corkscrew line around them, without tendrils; the direction of twining can be either right or left depending upon species;

rooting, climbing with the aid of aerial roots, *Hedera, Euonymus fortunei, Hydrangea petiolaris*;

twisted or contorted, stem and branches more or less contorted, *Salix matsudana* 'Tortuosa' (Fig. 4i);

wavy, branches curving alternately left and right (*Hedysarum, Spirea*).

Position of the Branches

alternate, sprouting alternately from one side of the stem then the other;

spiral, departing from a straight line spiraling up the stem;

opposite, branches sprouting directly opposite one another;

crosswise, branches sprouting opposite but each succesive pair turning 90° on the stem (*Rhamnus, Fraxinus*);

whorled, several branches at a node sprouting around the stem.

Branch and Stem Coverings

Bark descriptions will be based largely on young branches.

glabrous, smooth without hair, fuzz or resin;

6

resinous, coated with or secreting resin; seldom found in the woody broadleaves (*Aesculus* buds);

viscid, covered with a sticky substance (*Populus* types, *Robinia viscosa*);

furrowed, with long narrow grooves;

striped, with long narrow stripes (*Acer pensylvanicum*);

pruinose, bloomy, coated with a thin waxy film (*Rubus*, *Salix*, and *Acer* types);

(Pubescent, glandular, warty, nobby, thorny, prickly, etc. see p. 28, 7. A.)

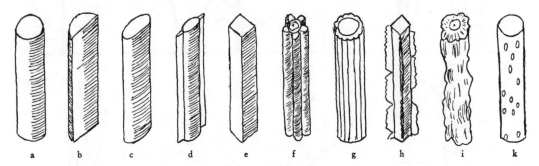

Fig. 5. Branch cross sections. a. round; b. half round; c. compressed; d. two edged; e. rectangular;
f. furrowed; g. grooved; h. winged; i. corky; k. dotted.

Branch Cross Section

As already discussed the cross section of a young branch has much significance in identification (see Fig. 5). The cross-sectional classifications are as follows:

round, practically cylindrical (Fig. 5a);

half-round, only when cut at a node (Fig. 5b);

compressed, oval in appearance (Fig. 5c);

two-edged, with two opposite wings (Fig. 5d);

rectangular, squared (Fig. 5e);

furrowed, with distinct ridges and furrows (Fig. 5f);

striped, with long thin lines down the stem (Fig. 5g);

winged, with 2 or 4 opposite corky wings (Fig. 5h);

corky, with a more or less irregular corky coating (Fig. 5i)

dotted, with noticeable lenticels (Fig. 5k).

Special Branch Forms

Most woody plants produce both long and short branches, the former generally vegetative and the latter bearing the flowers and fruit.

The long branches generally originate from a terminal bud to elongate the stem or major branch. In shrubs they can also originate from the base (*Spirea*, *Philadelphus*, *Deutzia*, *Rosa*). The foliage of these branches is generally large and lush. With some genera these vegetative branches are very characteristic and can be used alone to identify the species (*Spirea*, *Philadelphus*, *Populus*).

The short branches are the small side shoots growing off the previous year's vegetative growth. They often have characteristic foliage and carry the flowers and fruits. Such short branches only appear on

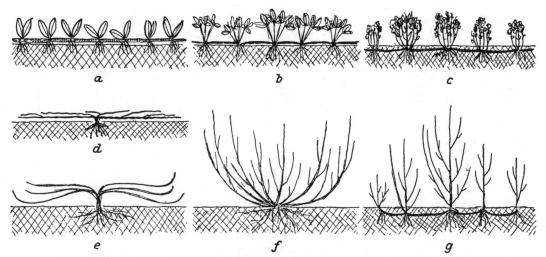

Fig. 6. Botanical terms for stolons. a. repent; b. stoloniferous (above ground); c. stoloniferous (below ground); d. procumbent; e. decumbent; f. ascending; g. soboliferous.

mature plants as opposed to juvenile growth, as with the *Araliaceae*, *Ficus* and *Euonymus fortunei*, etc. This growth is often desirable and held constant by vegetative propagation.

Thorns may be simple or branched, glabrous or pubescent, sharp, blunt, stiff or bristly (*Prunus spinosa*, *Crataegus*).

Whips are generally long, thin and flexible. Those selected for grafting (scion wood) are especially characteristic.

New growth which occurs early in the season can sometmes be distinguished from that which occurs after the initial elongation. For example, *Quercus robur* 'Prince Schwarzenberg' has normal, dark green leaves on the initial growth but white spotted foliage later in the season; *Quercus petraea* 'Laciniata' has irregular, thread-like foliage on the new growth and normal leaves later.

Phylloclades and cladodes are leaf-like flattened stems with inconspicuous axillary leaves (*Ruscus*).

Phyllodes are broad winged leaf petioles developed to reduce actual leaf surface (*Acacia*).

Stolons and Rhizomes

There still exists a qusetion as to the exact application of these terms in the botanical literature.

Stolons are generally viewed as the thin, horizontal, above or below ground stems with long internodes. Occasionally the nodes give rise to young plants with abundant leaves and roots which in turn produce more stolons (strawberries). The connecting tissue between the mother plant and offspring eventually dies. If this is the correct definition woody plants have no such organ.

Rhizomes are always identified as underground parts, usually horizontal with small scales; often thick and full of food reserves. Any above ground parts and older connecting members die annually. Therefore, no true rhizome exists among woody plants.

Buds

Winter buds are either covered with scales or naked. Position, number, size and form of the scales, presence of pubescence or resin are some of the characteristics looked for in winter observation. The number of scales is typical of a genus: *Salix*, *Platanus*, *Magnolia* have only one entire bud scale; *Alnus* and *Castanea* have two; *Fagus*, *Aesculus*, *Ribes*, *Populus*, *Quercus*, etc. have many. Plants with an opposite bud arrangement often have large terminal buds, such as *Aesculus* and *Fraxinus*.

8

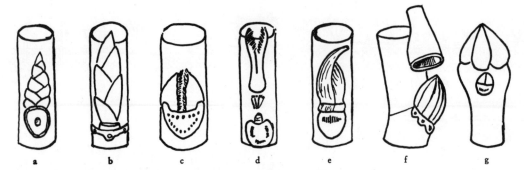

Fig. 7. Winter bud forms. a. sessile, *Orixa*; b. petiolate, *Ribies*; c. valved, *Koelreuteria*; d. naked, *Pterocarya*; e. covered, *Wisteria*; f. interpetiolar (enclosed by the petiole). *Platanus*; g. terminal bud, *Fraxinus*.

Normally each leaf axil at every node contains a single bud; in summer the small bud is hidden by the leaf petiole (*Platanus*, *Philadelphus*) and are referred to as interpetiolar buds. In some genera, however, more than one bud will be found at an axil. Such buds are serial or dual buds. They are arranged either collaterally (side by side) as with *Akebia*, *Lespedeza*, *Prunus*, *Spirea* or serially (in a column one over the next) as with *Rubus*, *Lonicera*, *Cercis*, or *Cladrastis*. The secondary leaf buds seldom develop unless the terminal bud is injured or removed.

The buds rest on the leaf 'cushion' (pulvinus), the place which swells at leaf drop in the fall and in the middle of which is found the leaf or petiole scar. From this leaf 'cushion' ridges can often be seen running lengthwise down the stem (*Populus*, *Ribes*, *Malus* etc.).

The leaf scar is normally not used in a plant description, although it is constant and distinctive to a species. A leaf scar is more difficult to use than leaves and flowers in determining species and might easily lead to mistakes.

The leaf arrangement within the bud, although seldom used, can be an important and functional clue to species for the serious observer. Here we can only show several schematic examples of the various arrangements. The cross sections shown here (Fig. 8) are distinct and oversimplified enlargements. In nature they would be much less distinct and only observable through a microscope or strong magnifying glass. One should also be aware of the presence of bud scales and lower leaves which are not shown here.

Fig. 8. Bud Arrangement in Schematic Cross Section. a. imbricate, *Syringa*; b. involuted, *Pirus*, *Malus*, *Populus*; c. revolute, *Salix*, *Ledum*, *Andromeda*; d. obvolute, *Salvia*; e. equitant, *Vaccinium*; f. convolute, *Prunus*; g. plaited, *Carpinus*, *Vitis*; h. conduplicate, *Prunus*, *Rosa*; i. multi-plaited, *Acer*.

3. Leaves

Next to the flowers and fruit, the leaf with its distinctive shape and qualities is the most important organ in the identification of a plant. It is not unusual for experts in Rhododendron, Azalea and Lilac to recognize each species flawlessly based on foliage alone since other distinctions are so scarce they defy description. The properties of the leaves are dealt with in great detail here since in practice they will prove to be the most important, through most of the year.

Leaves are normally composed of a flat, green leaf blade and a thin rod-shaped petiole. A widening of the leaf petiole is often observed where it meets the twig. Stipules are also sometimes found at this junction. The petiole and stipules will occasionally be missing. In a few cases the leaf blade will be missing and replaced by a wide petiole (Fig. 9).

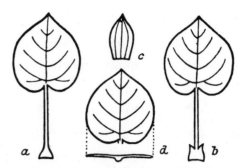

Fig. 9. a. leaf with blade and petiole; b. leaf with blade, petiole and stipules; c. scale leaf; d. leaf blade in cross section (from Troll).

Three Types of Leaves can be distinguished ranging from lower to higher levels of development:

Minor leaves: simplest form, those in most woody plants found only as scales on the winter buds;

Foliar leaves: the normal, fully opened leaves;

Higher leaves (bracts): found adjacent to the flowers and often colored, therefore resembling flower petals, as with *Cornus florida*, etc.

Leaf forms distinguished by **Properties:**

herbaceous, blades thin, as with most deciduous plants; if especially thin they will be referred to as paper thin;

leathery (coriaceus), as with most broadleaf evergreens; blades can be bent without breaking. Now and then deciduous foliage can be somewhat leathery.

succulent leaves are the rare exception among woody plants and will not be discussed here.

Leaf Duration

The active life of a leaf can vary considerably, ranging from a growing season to the life of the plant. Included are:

falling, abscising before the end of the growth period;

deciduous, abscising after the growing period, e.g. normal deciduous foliage;

semi-deciduous, falling at the beginning of the second growing season, but remaining green through the first winter;

biennial, remaining until the end of the second growing season;

evergreen, remaining through several growing seasons and never dropping all at the same time.

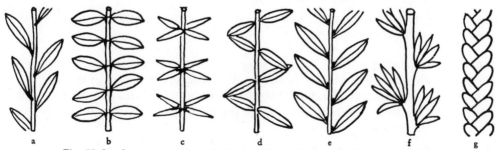

Fig. 10. Leaf arrangement. a. alternate; b. opposite; c. whorled; d. cross-wise; e. distichous; f. clustered; g. scaled.

Leaf Position (phyllotaxis)

The relation of leaves to the stem are the same as already described for branching:

alternate, occurring alternately (Fig. 10a);

opposite, leaves opposite one another (Fig. 10b);

whorled, three or more growing from a single node (Fig. 10c);

scattered, leaves widely spaced;

crosswise, leaf pairs opposite, but each successive pair turning 90°, creating four rows when looked at over some length (Fig. 10d);

distichous, leaves alternate or opposite but all the leaf blades on a single plane (Fig. 10e);

clustered, leaves several to a node (*Berberis*) (Fig. 10f);

imbricate, leaves usually small, very dense and overlapping one another (*Calluna, Cassiope*) (Fig. 10g).

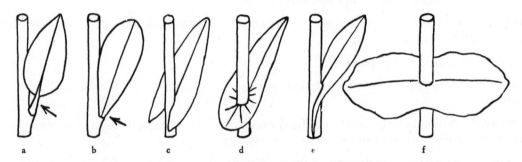

Fig. 11. Attachment of leaves. a. petiolate; b. sessile; c. stem-clasping; d. perfoliate; e. decurrent; f. connate

Attachment

sessile, seemingly without a petiole (Fig. 11b);

petiolate, with petiole (Fig. 11a);

decurrent, sessile blade, leaf base running along stem (rare in woody plants) (Fig. 11e);

stem-clasping, blade sessile, leaf base nearly surrounding stem (Fig. 11c);

connate, the leaf bases from two oppositely arranged leaves grow together to resemble a single leaf blade, in the middle of which is the stem (twining *Lonicera*) (Fig. 11f);

perfoliate, a single blade surrounds the stem (Fig. 11d);

peltate, the petiole attaches to the middle of the leaf blade rather than at the base.

Leaf Form

Leaf forms can vary somewhat within a given species, but generally not much; except when one considers the extreme divergence of *Morus, Sassafras*, etc. However, the size of the leaf in relation to its location on the stem can fluctuate considerably. Often those leaves which develop first are small, becoming larger with extension of the twig later in the season; or the form might change gradually from one leaf to the next, as with *Celtis tournefortii*.

For an overview of leaf forms, the following groups are useful (taken in part from Chittenden, *Dictionary of Gardening, Supplement*; London 1956).

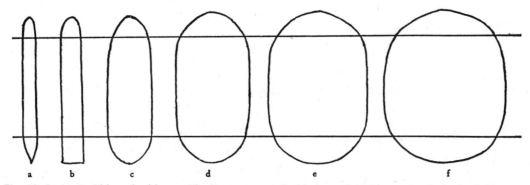

Fig. 12. Series 1: Oblong leaf forms. The lines transect the blades at the widest point. In Series 1 there are two lines between which the leaf margins are parallel.

Series 1:   Oblong leaf forms (Fig. 12)

linear, ratio of width to length, 1:12 or more, long edges parallel (Fig. 12a);

strap-form, ratio 1:6 to 8, tip rounded, sides parallel from the base up to the tip (Fig. 12b);

narrow oblong, 1:3, margins somewhat parallel (Fig. 12c);

oblong, 1:2, margins parallel for a bit in the middle (Fig. 12d);

broad oblong, 2:3, as above (Fig. 12e);

very broad oblong, 5:6, at the widest point, somewhat narrowing to the ends, both ends rounded (Fig. 12f).

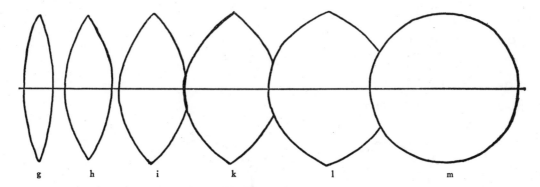

Fig. 13. Series 2: Elliptic leaf forms.

Series 2:   Elliptic or oval leaf forms (Fig. 13)

Often confused with Series 1, but easily distinguished by the fact that the widest point is found in the middle of the leaf and both ends are pointed.

The mathematical term 'ellipse' signifies a plane section of a right circular cone that is a closed curve. The botanical meaning cannot be so exact. English and American authors often use the terms 'oval' and 'elliptic' interchangeably. They also include some which we will here consider 'narrow elliptic'.

Included are:

very narrow elliptic, width to length 1:6 (Fig. 13g);

narrow elliptic, 1:3 (Fig. 13h);

elliptic, oval, 1:2 (Fig. 13i);

broad elliptic, 2:3 (Fig. 13k);

rounded, 5:6 (Fig. 13 l);

round, 6:6 (Fig. 13m);

oblate, 4:3, broader than long, rarely found, not shown.

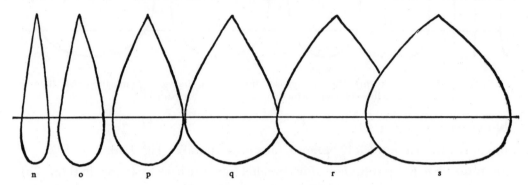

Fig. 14. Series 3: Ovate leaf forms.

Series 3:   Ovate leaf forms (Fig. 14)

Distinguished from oval or elliptical in that the broadest part is below the middle section of the leaf. The base is rounded, the tip is usually pointed.

narrow lanceolate, width to length 1:6 (Fig. 14n);

lanceolate, 1:3 (Fig. 14o);

narrow ovate, 1:2 (Fig. 14p);

ovate, 2:3 (Fig. 14q);

broadly ovate, 5:6 (Fig. 14r);

very broadly ovate, 6:6 (Fig. 14s).

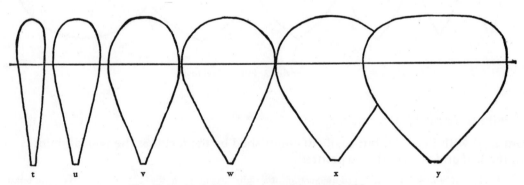

Fig. 15. Series 4: Inversely ovate (obovate) leaf forms

Series 4:   Inversely ovate (obovate) leaf forms (Fig. 15)

This series is simply the reverse of series 3, the widest part lies above the middle of the leaf blade. Also the tip is rounded while the base is pointed. The two narrowest forms are termed oblanceolate (reversed lanceolate). Included are:

narrow oblanceolate, width to length 1:6 (Fig. 15t);

oblanceolate, 1:3 (Fig. 15u);

narrow obovate, 1:2 (Fig. 15v);

obovate, 2:3 (Fig.2);

broad obovate, 5:6 (Fig. 15x);

very broad obovate, 6:6 (Fig. 15y).

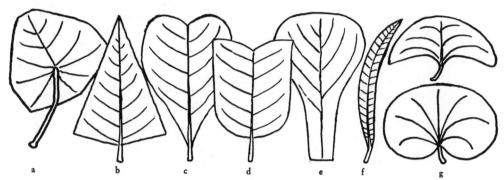

Fig. 16. Special unclassified leaf forms. a. peltate; b. triangular; c. obcordate; d. square; e. spathulate; f. falcate; g. kidney shaped; h. (top right) crescent shaped.

Other leaf forms (Fig. 16)

peltate, petiole attached in the middle of the leaf blade, not found among woody plants except one whose petiole attaches the blade near the base (*Menispermum*);

triangular, base a straight line, total form a triangle;

obcordate, reversed heart shape, as a heart standing on its point;

rectangular, rare form (*Liriodendron*);

spathulate, longer than wide, tip widely rounded, blade wide narrowing at the base;

falcate, sickle-shaped, blade a crescent curve, petiole on a point;

crescent-shaped, blade a broad crescent, petiole attached at the middle;

kidney-shaped, blade wider than long, base deeply cut.

Construction of the Leaves

In the construction of the leaves we distinguish simple from compound leaves.

Simple leaves are those composed of only one entire or lobed blade.

Compound leaves are composed of two or more blades on one petiole or at an axil. The blades are referred to as leaflets.

Most forms of the simple leaves have already been dealt with (see Fig. 12–16).

Incised simple leaves can be classified according to the depth of the incision. The groups are:

pinnately cleft, incision not reaching the middle of the blade half (Fig. 18b);

pinnately partite, incision to the middle of the blade half (Fig 18c);

pinnatisect, incision all the way to the midvein of the leaf blade (Fig. 18d);

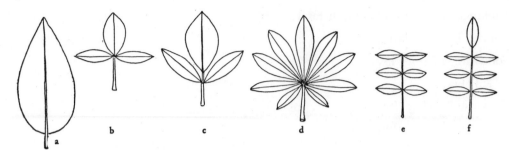

Fig. 17. Forms of leaf composition. a. entire; b. ternate; c. ternate with petioled tip blade; d. palmate; e. paired leaflets; unpaired leaflets.

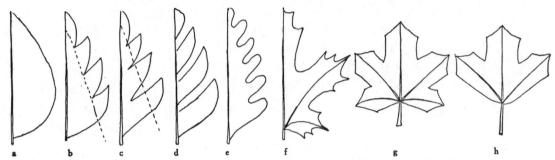

Fig. 18. Forms of leaf composition. a. entire; b. pinnately cleft; c. pinnately partite; d. pinnatisect; e. sinuate; f. lobed; g. five lobed; h. three lobed.

Compound leaves are distinguished as follows:

digitate forms, all leaflets originate from the same point, as with *Aesculus*, *Laburnum*. Instead of *digitate*, *palmate* is often used or the suffix *-foliate* as in trifoliate (Fig. 17 b–d);

pinnate forms, many leaflets attached to a common spindle or rachis; further distinguished are those with a terminal leaflet, being odd pinnate; and those without being even pinnate (Fig. 18 e–f);

multiple digitate or multiple pinnate forms, the leaflets about an axis occur in groups; the multiple fingered leaflets are generally termed 'multiple-foliate' (eg. triple –trifoliate, having three sets of three leaflets each or nine total leaflets on the leaf).

Leaf Margin

The edge of the leaf blade is either smooth and even or slightly cut. The following types of leaf margins are frequently encountered:

entire, straight line or smooth curve, not cut (Fig. 19a);

ciliate, margin having fine hairs, otherwise as entire (Fig. 19b);

serrate, teeth pointed and often curving forward (Fig. 19c);

finely serrate, teeth very fine and numerous (Fig. 19d);

deeply cut, teeth especially long, incision at least three times as long as the width of the teeth at their base (Fig. 19e);

doubly serrate, margin coarsely toothed or lobed, with these teeth further serrated (Fig. 19f);

dentate, teeth often slanted, base of incision is rounded;

The English literature often lists dentate to mean outward pointing large teeth, more similar to coarsely dentate by our description. *Serrate* refers to forward leaning teeth. Please note when consulting English references. (Fig. 19g).

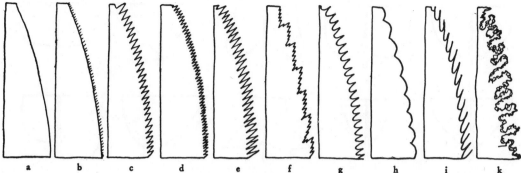

Fig. 19. Forms of leaf margins, a. entire; b. ciliate; c. serrate; d. finely serrate; e. deeply cut; f. doubly serrate; g. dentate; h. crenate; i. aristate; k. undulate

crenate, teeth rounded (Fig. 19h);

spiny, teeth coming to sharp points as in *Ilex, Berberis*; if the tip spine is especially long it is referred to as awned or aristate (Fig. 19i);

undulate, margin wavy and ragged (Fig. 19k);

lobed, deeply cut forming a few large protrusions (Fig. 18 f—h).

Blade Tip

acute, coming to less than a right angle (Fig. 20a);

blunt, greater than a right angle (Fig. 20b);

emarginate, rounded tip with angular incision (Fig. 20c);

retuse, tip having a shallow bay or dip (Fig. 20d);

apiculate, with a small, fine point on an otherwise rounded tip (Fig. 20e);

mucronulate, with a very small tip, sometimes only detectable by touch, protruding from the midrib (Fig. 20f);

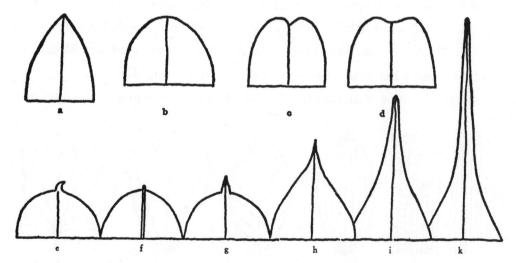

Fig. 20. Forms of blade tips. a. acute; b. blunt, obtuse; c. emarginate; d. retuse; e. apiculate; f. mucronulate; g. mucronate; h. cuspidate; i. acuminate; k. caudate

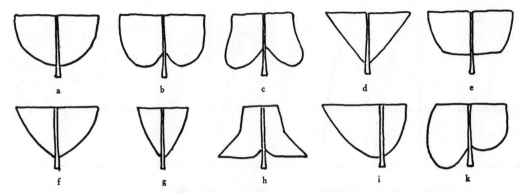

Fig. 21. Forms of the leaf bases. a. rounded; b. cordate; c. auriculate; d. cuneate; e. truncate; f. obtuse; g. acute; h. hastate; i. asymmetrical; k. oblique

mucronate, protruding tip from the midrib, flanged with small portions of the leaf blade (Fig. 20g);

cuspidate, blade makes a sudden and distinct concave curve to a fine point (Fig. 20h);

acuminate, very long narrow tip to the blade (Fig. 20i);

caudate, tip extremely long and narrow, often hanging vertically at rest (Fig. 20k).

Blade Base

The blade base is the part that attaches the blade to the petiole or the branch. They can be:

rounded, both halves form a semicircle (Fig. 21a);

cordate, semicircle with small idention (Fig. 21b);

auriculate, similar to cordate but the base halves are drawn out longer and at an angle, eared (Fig. 21c);

cuneate, blade from midway to the base straight and evenly tapered (Fig. 21d);

truncate, blade base cut straight across (Fig. 21e);

obtuse, angle formed by both halves at least 90° and generally curved (Fig. 21f);

sagittate, leaf form like an arrowhead, lobed at the base, scarce in woody plants;

hastate, similar to sagittate with basal lobes wider and pointing outward (Fig. 21h);

assymetrical, both blade halves of different size and not coinciding (Fig. 21i);

oblique, one basal half lower than the other but both blade halves similar in size (*Ulmus*) (Fig. 21k).

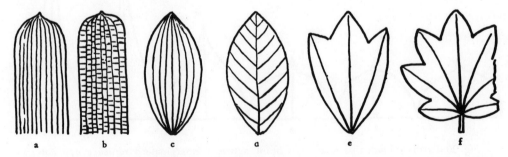

Fig. 22. Venation. a. parallel; b. checked; c. bowed (camptodrome); d. pinnate; e. and f. palmate

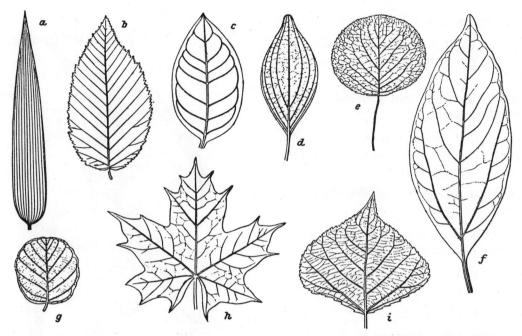

Fig. 23. Forms of venation. a. parallel in Bamboo; b. craspedrome, *Ostrya*; c. brachidodrome, *Eugenia*; d. acrodrome, *Cornus mas*; e. reticulate, *Pyrus communis*; f. camptodrome, *Cinnamomum camphora*; g. brachidodrome, *Rhamnus wulfenii*; h. palmate, *Acer platanoides*; i. uneven pinnatifed, *Populus*; b c, e. other distinct venation types (from Kerner).

Blade Venation

parallel, veins parallel or nearly so, as in the Bamboos (Fig. 22a, 23a);

checked (reticulate), as above with crossing lines forming a checked pattern, also common in the Bamboo (Fig. 22b);

bowed (acrodome), with or without distinct midrib, all major veins originate at the base and bow to the tip, most often found in the monocotyledons (*Smilax*), but also occasionally in the dicotyledons (*Viburnum davidii*) (Fig. 22c, 23d);

pinnate, most frequent form of venation, midrib with side branching veins (Fig. 22d, 23b, c, e);

palmate, branching from the base and radiating finger-like (*Acer* and many others with lobed leaves) (Fig. 22f).

The following distinctions can be made relative to the branching pattern of the side veins:

craspedrome, veins running out to the leaf margin (*Fagus, Carpinus*) (Fig. 23b);

acrodrome, veins bowed and somewhat parallel running from the base to the tip (*Cornus*) (Fig. 23d);

camptodrome, as acrodrome but not reaching to the leaf margin (*Rhamnus*) (Fig. 23f);

brachidodrome, running relatively straight toward the margin then curving to form a ring parallel to the margin (*Periploca, Myrtus, Rhamnus alaternus*) (Fig. 23g).

Upper Leaf Surface

Very often the underside of a leaf is lighter in color and more pubescent than the upper side. The leaf surface also has many distinguishing characteristics, such as:

flat, smooth and even;

18

concave, cupped as a spoon;

keeled, both blade halves come off the midrib at an angle which in cross section is 90° to obtuse;

channelled, as above but forming a semi-circle in cross section;

involute, rolled inwards with the midvein rolling up on itself (*Salix babylonica* 'Annularis', young sprouts of ferns);

revolute, leaf margin rolled slightly to the underside;

plaited, folds along the length of the blade more or less parallel to the midrib;

rugose, venation visible as deep grooves on the leaf surface;

bullate, surface blistered;

convex, cupped or curved up;

boat-shaped, as above but with blade longer than wide;

translucent, thin, transparent or nearly so.

Fig. 24. Example of heterophylly: *Eucalyptus globulus* (from Hegi); in background juvenile foliage, foreground mature leaves

Stipules

Small leaf-like structures on both sides of the leaf base, often on the petiole (*Rosa*); in many cases only short lived (*Crataegus, Prunus*), often as thorns (*Caragana, Robinia*), occasionally cirrhous or tendril-like as in *Smilax*.

Heterophylly

In many species the foliage occurs in more than one form; often the seed leaves (cotyledons) are totally different from the mature foliage. The following distinctions in leaf form can be made:

primary leaves, first leaves following the seed leaves, often simple (*Berberis*);

juvenile foliage can occasionally deviate significantly from the foliage of the mature plant (*Eucalyptus*) (Fig. 24);

summer growth may have different forms or color than the initial foliage of spring (*Quercus*);

mature foliage is most often predictable and regular except in *Sassafras, Celtis, Morus, Broussonetia*, + most of the Moraceae;

summer foliage will often differ from over-wintering foliage; *Rhododendron obtusum* has much smaller, coarser foliage in winter than in summer.

4. Flowers

A complete flower contains three elements: calyx; corolla; stamens and carpels or pistils (Fig. 25).

An incomplete flower lacks any one of these parts. On the other hand, an imperfect flower is one lacking pistils or stamens.

19

Staminate or male flowers lack pistils; pistillate or female flowers lack stamens.

Bisexual (hermaphroditic) flowers have both pistils and stamens.

Monoecious plants consistently bear both male (staminate) and female (pistillate) flowers on the same plant (*Betula, Quercus, Alnus, Corylus, Juglans*).

Dioecious refers to those plants having only male or only female flowers on a particular plant. This sexual dimorphism therefore requires two plants of opposite sex to pollinate (*Salix, Skimmia, Populus, Pernettya, Ilex*).

Polygamous plants have both single sexed and bisexual flowers on the same plant (*Acer, Ulmus, Fraxinus*).

Trioecious plants have exclusively male, or exclusively female or exclusively bisexual flowers on any given plant (*Fraxinus excelsior, Vitis vinifera*).

Fig. 25. Cross section of a flower depicting; calyx (K), corolla (C), stamen (A), and carpel (G) (from Oehlkers)

Outline of the most important sexual combinations

	male	female	bisexual	classification	
On the same plant					
flowers either	×	−	×	andromonoecious	*Chaenomeles*
flowers either	−	×	×	gymnomonoecious	*Atriplex*
flowers are all	−	−	×	bisexual	most plants
flowers either	×	×	−	monoecious	as mentioned
On different plants					
flowers either	×	−	×	androdioecous	*Dryas octopetal*
flowers either	−	×	×	gynodioecious	*Ribes*
flowers are all	×	×	−	dioecious	as mentioned
each flower form on a separate plant	×	×	×	trioecious	as mentioned

A flower is regular when its parts are of similar size and arranged so that the halves are symmetrical when divided vertically in two or more planes. If the flower cannot be divided into such symmetrical parts it is irregular.

Stamens

The stamens can be formed very differently depending upon;

a) the anthers, most with two, sometimes with four chambers from which the pollen is distributed through many splits, folds or holes (Fig. 26);

b) the filament of various lengths, forms, pubescence or occasionally its total absence.

In the absence of the filament, the anthers are borne by the connective tissue which separates the pollen chambers.

Occasionally the anthers will have some form of appendage (*Deutzia, Ericaceae*) (Fig. 26 i−p).

Staminodes are pollenless, antherless, non-functional stamens, usually found in double flowers. Often staminodes carry non-functional anther-like appendages on their tips.

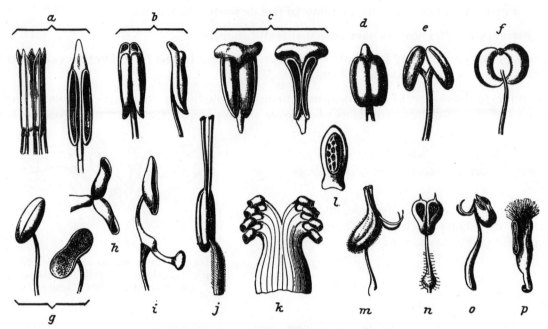

Fig. 26. Stamens. a. *Artemisia*; b. *Cassia*; c. *Platanus*; d. *Juglans*; e. *Tilia*; f. *Hypericum*; g. *Globularia*; h. *Calceolaria*; i. *Salvia*; j. *Vaccinium oxycoccus*; k. *Polygala*; l. *Viscum*; m. *Vaccinium uliginosum*; n. *Arctous alpina*; o. *Arctostaphylos uva-ursi*; p. *Vinca minor* (from Kerner, altered)

Carpel

The carpel, in most species, is a closed container with no resemblance to its leaf-like origins (*Caragana*, *Colutea*) although in some flowers it becomes green (*Rosa*, *Prunus serrulata*). The seed producing area (ovule) is completely covered and distinct from the rest of the carpel. Plants which form a carpel are referred to as Angiosperms as opposed to the Gymnosperms which include all the coniferous plants. The Gymnosperms produce a naked seed and have no pistils.

For each genus and often for whole families of plants, the number and form of the carpels is constant; some have only one carpel per flower, many more have several. The carpels can be either free standing or fused.

In its simplest form, the pistil consists of an ovary with an attached stigma. Often several stigmas are present. Frequently, a connecting element, the style, is found between the ovary and stigma.

The ovary can have one or many compartments; the chambers (locules) are normally separated by dividing walls. These chambers contain the ovules. The following types of flower receptacles can be distinguished based on the position of the ovary:

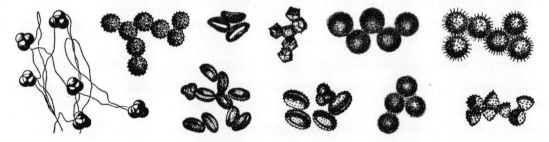

Fig. 27. Forms of pollen cells. Far left, pollen tetrad from *Rhododendron hirsutum* (50x), linked together with viscid threads; otherwise all circa 200x (from Kerner) no further discussion in text,

hypogynous, receptacle more or less arched upward, ovary stands over the petals (*Helianthemum*) (Fig. 28a);

epigynous, receptacle bowl-shaped with sunken ovary (*Philadelphus*, *Cornus*) (Fig. 28c);

perigynous, calyx, corolla and stamens on the same plane as the ovary and seem to arise from it (*Rosa*, *Prunus*) (Fig. 28b).

Fig. 28. Position of the Ovaries.
a. hypogynous; b. perigynous; c. epigynous (from Oehlkers)

Calyx

The perianth is composd of two sets of modified leaves. The outer and normally green leaves are the calyx, the inner, normally colorful set is the corolla.

The sepals make up the calyx and are the outer, protective layer while in bud. In most cases the sepals fall off after the flower opens. In many plants, however, they not only remain on the flower but are fleshy and turgid (*Morus*, *Pernettya*).

The sepals can be separate and distinct in which case the calyx is said to be polysepalous (or aposepalous); or they can fused together as a gamosepalous (or synsepalous) calyx. The calyx may also be tubular with a distinct fringe (limb). Now and then the sepals may resemble hairs or scales as in the Compositae, in which case the calyx is termed a pappus.

Corolla

Inside the calyx, if present, is found the other portion of the perianth, the corolla, composed of colorful petals.

When the sepals and petals are alike in size, color and shape, they are termed tepals (*Tulipa*, *Magnolia*).

The flowers are also categorized by the following properties:

If all the petals are separate, the flower is choripetalous; if fused it is sympetalous; if the perianth is double, the flower is dichlamydeous; if simple it is monochlamydeous; if the perianth is absent, the flower is achlamydeous.

Sometimes the petals can be differentiated into the lamina, the upper, broad portion; and the lower, more narrow, petiole-like claw as in many Caryophyllaceae and Cruciferae.

Flower Form

A cross section cut through a flower (before it has developed) in the plane which bisects every part, will reveal the order of each individual flower part. The schematic representation of these parts is referred to as a flower diagram.

A single cross section will not always reveal all the flower parts, in which case other sections must be made. The process of cross-sectioning will also reveal the relation of the flower parts which will appear as one of the following:

22

Actinomorphic (radially symmetrical), producing symmetrical halves, on at least two different cross-sectional lines.

Zygomorhic (bilaterally symmetrical), being divisible into two like halves along only a single cross sectional line.

Assymetrical (irregular), having no division which will produce symmetrical halves.

Forms of Corollas

The form of the corolla depends upon whether the petals are separate (polypetalous) or fused together (gamopetalous), and whether the flower is actinomorphic or zygomorphic. Normally, polypetalous flowers are actinomorphic, and gamopetalous are zygomorphic. There are, however, many exceptions. It is usually easy to determine the symmetry by counting the petals, the limb tips or the sepals (odd numbers being actinomorphic, even zygomorphic). Gamopetalous (fused) corollas are distinguished as follows: the tube; limb; throat; more deeply incised lobes or teeth on the very edge of the limb.

The most frequently found corollas in the woody broadleaves are as follows (Fig. 29):

rotate, also called wheel-shaped; actinomorphic; tube very short, limb very wide and flattened;

funnelform, tube, funnel-shaped opening to the outer edge, limb flared out; actinomorphic (Fig. 30 l);

salverform, actinomorphic, long narrow cylindrical corolla with a wide flattened limb (Fig. 30g);

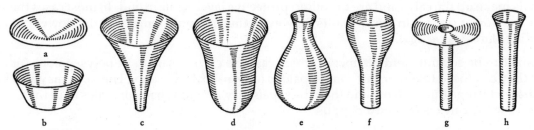

Fig. 29. Basic forms of the Corolla. a. rotate (wheel-shaped); b. cup-shaped; c. funnelform; d. campanulate (bell-shaped); e. urceolate (pitcher-shaped); f. clavate (club-shaped); g. salverform; h. tubular (from Leunis, altered)

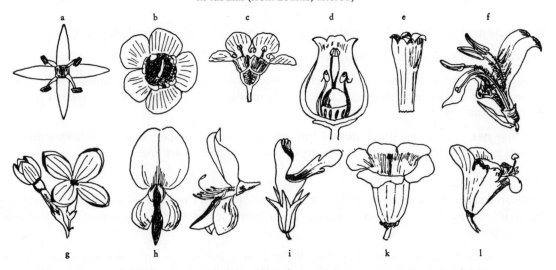

Fig. 30. Forms of Corollas. a. *Cornus mas*; b. *Ribes petr.*; c. *Ribes*; d. *Arctous*; e. *Onosma*; f. *Lonicera*; g. *Syringa*; h. *Cytisus*; i. *Stachys*; k. *Rhododendron*; l. *Rhododendron*

urceolate (pitcher-shaped), actinomorphic or if a flattened flower also zygomorphic, tube very wide at the base becoming narrow just past the middle, throat narrow, with small flared lobes (Fig. 30d);

tubular, actinomorphic, tube long, more or less cylindrical, limib absent or very narrow, somewhat flared or erect (Fig. 30d);

clavate (club-shaped), actinomorphic, tube widens toward the end, otherwise as above (Fig. 30e);

cup-shaped, actinomorphic, somewhat hemispherical without a noticeable limb (Fig. 30b−c);

campanulate (bell-shaped), actinomorphic, tube broad, as long or longer than wide, limb flared (Fig. 30k);

cruciform, 4 petals forming a cross, most actinomorphic (except *Iberis* which is zygomorphic), basic forms are found in the Cruciferae;

papilionaceous (butterfly forms), zygomorphic, composed of five petals, all separate; the large upper petal is the standard, both side petals are the wings and both lower petals, those that border the ovary are termed collectively, the keel (Fig. 30 h, l);

bilabiate, zygomorphic, limb in two parts, the upper and lower lips; upper lip often dome-like and composed of two fused lobes, the lower lip contains three lobes (Fig. 30i);

gaping, zygomorphic, also composed of two lips, with a wide open, gaping throat, upper lip arched (*Lonicera*) (Fig. 30f);

masked, 'gaping' flowers with a lower lip so upturned as to close off the throat; this must then open before pollination by insects is possible (*Antirrhinum*);

ligulate (strap-like), zygomorphic, tubular, limb split down one side, long and broad, composed of three or five lobes; typical flower of the *Compositae*. The tubular base is relatively short.

The Inflorescence

Flowers are found in one of the following arrangements:

Solitary Flowers

a) terminal, found at the end of a leafy twig on the tip, e.g., *Paeonia, Clematis;*

b) axillary, found in the axils of foliar leaves; Foliar leaves are the normal leaves. If, however, the leaves are small or colored, they are referred to as bracts. Between the foliar leaves and the flower may also be found another small, simple form of bracts called the prophylla.

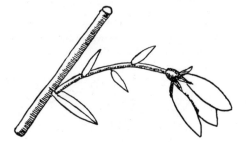

Fig. 31. Flower arising from axis of foliar leaf and three prophylla

Flowers in Inflorescences

The inflorescence is the branching system of a flower cluster. The main axis (spindel or rachis) supports the flower bearing side axes.

The inflorescence may be divided into two groups based on branching pattern:

a) racemose, having a dominant axis and flowers on short stalks;

b) cymose, having several axes of similar length forming a more or less flat clustered flower.

The following outline covers the inflorescence types in further detail.

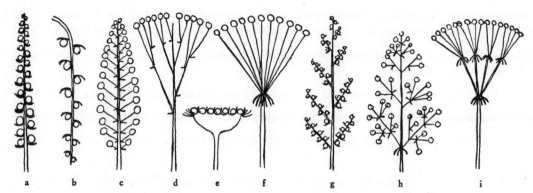

Fig. 32. Forms of Inflorescences. a. spike; b. catkin; c. raceme; d. corymb;
e. head (capitulum); f. umbel; g. compound spike; h. panicle; i. compound umbel

I. **Inflorescence racemose;** a dominant primary axis
   a) Secondary axes simple, not branched
      1. spike, primary axis long, single flowers sessile (without a stalk) (Fig. 32a)
      2. catkins, as above except hanging inverted and abscising totally (Fig. 32c)
      3. raceme, primary axis long, single flowers branching from all sides on short stalks (pedicels) of similar length (Fig. 32c)
      4. corymb, primary axis extends through the inflorescence, peduncles (stalk of a flower cluter) of varying lengths, oldest being the longest resulting in a flat cluster (Fig. 32d)
      5. umbel, primary axis shortened, all flowers single and on pedicels radiating from a central point (Fig. 32f)
      6. head, primary axis short and somewhat thickened on the upper end, single flowers sessile and densely packed (Fig. 32e)
   b) Secondary axes branched
      7. panicle, primary axis long, secondary axes as in a raceme (Fig. 32h)
      8. compound spike, primary axis long, secondary axes as in a spke (Fig. 32g)
      9. compound umbel, as an umbel, except that instead of single blooms, the secondary axes produce small umbels (Fig. 32i)

II. **Inflorescence cymose,** several secondary axes radiating from a central point and standing above the primary axis
   a) Each axis composed of only one branch (*monochasium*)
      10. sickle, all axes on single plane and new axes branching to the same side (Fig. 33d)
      11. fan-shaped, all axes on a single plane, new axes branching left then right alternately (Fig. 33c)
      12. spiral, axes on differing planes, branching constantly in the same direction.
      13. cylindrical, axes on differing planes, direction of branching alternates along axis

   b) Each axis producing two secondaries, forming a *dichasium* (Fig. 33a)

   c) Axes with more than two branches, primary axis terminating in a bloom (Pleiochasium; also termed a cyme). This category also includes the cluster or fascicle (Fig. 33b)

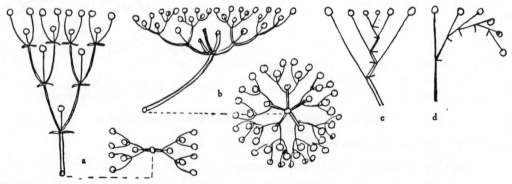

Fig. 33. Forms of Inflorescences. a dichasium, right view from beneath; b. pleiochasium (cyme), shown with all but two branch clusters cut out, lower right view from beneath with all five branches (peduncles)); c. fan, outer flowers bloom first; d. sickle; lower flowers bloom first

Flower Fragrance

Many plants including woody species have a definite scent associated with the flower. It may be pleasant or unpleasant but very noticeable and characteristic. Fragrance is also found in fruits, leaves and other plant parts. The foliage of *Rosa rubiginosa* has a very strong scent of ripe apples noticeable for a considerable distance. Many plants can be quickly identified by rubbing and then smelling a leaf as with *Orixa japonica*, *Phellodendron*, *Evodia*, *Ailanthus* and above all the unpleasant scent of *Clerodendron*.

In 1891, Kerner attempted to classify flower fragrances in scientific order by chemical properties. The comprehensive work of Kerner is still valid, though, because his book has been long out of print it is little known. Reproduced here is only an abbreviated form. He distinguished five large groups:

1. Indoloid; a heterozygous compound, originating from the disintegration of albuminous compounds and readily disseminated in the air. Belonging to the indole and skatole group of compounds, these scents are often foul smelling. Subtropical *Aristolchia* types belong to this group as well as *Calycanthus floridus*, whose spent flowers have an acidic scent.

2. Aminoid; a group of scented substances derived from ammonia when one, two or three hydrogen atoms are replaced by univalent hydrocarbon radicals. Included here is trimethylamine which carries the scent of pickled herring and is present in the flower of *Crataegus oxyacantha*, as well as *Pyrus communis*, *Mespilus*, *Sorbus* types, *Cornus sanguinea*, *Viburnum lantana* and *V. opulus*, *Castanea*, *Sambucus racemosa*, *Clematis vitalba*, *Berberis* types, *Hedera helix*. Also slightly ammonia scented are the flowers of *Ailanthus* and *Pachysandra terminalis*.

3. Benzoloid; a benzol derivative resulting from the replacement of hydrogen atoms in the benzene ring by those in the aldehyde ether or ester groups. Many readily recognizable chemicals belong to this group but since we are dealing with those related to plant material, they will go unmentioned. The scents contained in this group are pleasant and so various as to be further divided into sub-groups. The most frequently encountered sub-groups are as follows:

Lilac scented:	*Syringa vulgaris, Daphne striata* and *D. pontica*
Robinia scented:	*Robinia pseudoacacia, Cladrastis lutea, Laburnum alpinum, Spartium junceum*
Honeysuckle scented:	*Lonicera caprifolium*
Paulownia scented:	*Paulownia tomentosa, Wisteria sinensis*
Jasmine scented:	*Jasminum officinale*
Plum scented:	*Prunus domestica*
Vanilla scented:	*Daphne alpina*
Violet scented:	*Daphne laureola*

4. Paraffinoid; hydrocarbon derivative. This category includes pelargonic and valeric acid (the former closely related to the scent of *Rosa centifolia*). Among species incuded here are *Vitis vinifera*, *Gleditsia* types, *Tilia* types, *Aesculus macrostachya*, *Paeonoa*, *Sambucus nigra*, *Ruta graveolens*. Some question has been raised by Knuth as to whether or not the scents placed by Kerner into this category really belong together. It is questionable that the repulsive scent of *Ruta graveolens* should be related to the fragrance of roses.

5. Terpentoid; an isomeric alcohol derived from essential oils. Included here is neroli oil found in the flowers of *Citrus* spp., *Pittosporum tobira*, *Gardenia*, *Malus baccata*, *Magnolia liliiflora* and *obovate* as well as the flowers and foliage of *Lavendula*.

It is important to point out that although two plants may be closely related by scent, they may be totally unrelated taxonomically.

The classification of floral fragrance by Delphino into two groups (sympathetic and idiopathic scents) is given little serious consideration today and probably little known. An excerpt of this work can be found in Knuth.

Lit. Kerner, Pflanzenleben, II, 194–205 (1891) ● Knuth, Handbuch der Blutenbiologie, I, 107–115 (1898) ● Delphino, Ulteriori osservazione etc. In Atti d. Soc. Ital. d. Sci. Nat. Milano, XVI (1873) ● Troll, W., Allgemeine Botanik, 220 and 411 (1948).

5. Fruit (Fig. 34)

After pollination, the development of the fruit affects not only the seed but to a considerable extent, the flower. The walls of the ovary develop into the actual fruit; calyx, petals, sepals and stamens dry up and abscise. Occasionally the sepals will remain. Fruit types are first separated into fleshy and dry pericarp (outer covering) groups, and further subdivided by various other properties. The commonly found fruit forms of woody plants are outlined as follows:

A.   FRUIT WITH DRY COVERINGS

1.   **Indehiscent;** one seed, hull remaining closed
   a)   nut; hull thick and hard, woody, separate from the seed; with a large mark (hilum) on the base; fruit occasionally contained within a special cup (cupula) as with *Quercus, Fagus, Castanea* etc.

   b)   achene; hull thin to leathery; seed small; e.g. Compositae, *Polygonum, Clematis*

2.   **Dehiscent;** several seeds, hull split along a regular line

   c)   samara; small single seed in a leathery, thin shell surrounded by membranous 'wing', as with *Ulmus, Ptelea, Fraxinus, Ailanthus.*

   The fruit of the genus *Acer* are double samaras. However, since the ripened fruit splits into two parts it is included with the schizocarps.

   d)   follicle; originating from a single carpel and dehiscing along a single line; *Paeonia*

   e)   pod; also originating from a carpel, dehiscing along both long sides, no partitions between the seeds; Leguminosae

   f)   silicles, husk; developed from two carpels, having false partitions; Cruciferae

   g)   capsule; originating from three or more carpels; further subdivided by the method of opening; *Hypericum, Philadelphus, Rhododendron, Stewartia* etc.

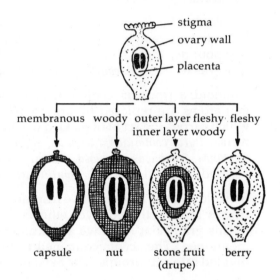

Fig. 34. Fruit formation from an ovary (from Schmeil, altered)

3.   **Split and breaking fruits**; compound fruits which divided into single seeded indehisicent parts

   h)   split fruit, schizocarp; upon ripening the fruit divides into two equal parts; *Acer*
      i)   Breaking fruit, upon ripening this fruit will break into several parts; many Leguminosae, Borraginaceae

   i)   Breaking fruit; upon ripening this fruit will break into several parts; many Leguminosae, Borraginacee

B.   FRUIT WITH FLESHY COVERINGS

4.   **Stone frutis,** drupes; one seeded fruit intermediate between nuts and berries; fleshy pulp formed from the outer ovary wall, inner ovary wall develops into a woody seed coat; *Prunus, Juglans*

5.   **Berry** (bacca); shell (epicarp) membranous or leathery, mesocarp is the fleshy pulp; several seeded, each separated by inner walls; *Vitis, Hippophae, Ribes*

C.   AGGREGATE FRUITS

Most fruits develop from a single flower, aggregate or syncarpous fruits are formed from flowers having two or more united carpels resulting in a cluster of fruits appearing as one. Three types can be distinguished according to development:

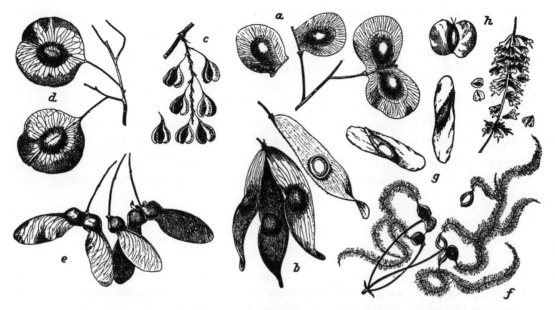

Fig. 35. Fruits and seeds with wing structures, a. *Megacarpea laciniata*; b. *Ailanthus altissima*; c. *Polygonum sieboldii*; d. *Ptelea trifoliata*; e. *Acer monspessulanum*; f. *Clematis*; g. *Cedrela sinensis*; h. *Betula pendula* (from Kerner)

6. **Aggregate with druplets:** developed from a carpel in which the ovary produces several ovules (seed producing organ) attached to a central point and forming druplets closely packed in a berry-like aggregate fruit which abscises in one piece, as in *Rubus*

7. **Aggregate with nutlets;** the flower's axis becomes cup-shaped inside of which the fruitlets with filaments attached are formed; the ovary develops a stone hard pericarp and contains only one seed; e.g. hips produced by *Rosa*; also belonging in this classification but not dealt with in this work is the genus *Fragaria* (strawberry); it should be noted that the fruitlets are easily released

8. **Aggregate with small follicles;** main axis of the flower develops into a pitcher-shape, the carpels are tightly attached to the main axis (stem) and somewhat difficult to remove; the carpels form collectively the bladder-like seed container. Two types can be distinguished:

    a) shell or follicle apple (also termed a "pome"); each carpel becomes a single follicle or shell around a seed which cannot be released so long as it is surrounded by the fleshy mesocarp. This fruit type is typical of the genera *Malus*, *Sorbus*, *Aronia*, *Amelanchier* etc. However with *Pyrus* and *Cydonia* the surrounding pulpy mesocarp contains many small hard cells giving it a more gritty consistency.

    b) nut or stone apple; mesocarp also fleshy pulp, harder at the stem attachment to the carpel; the carpel becoming woody and stone hard so that the fruitlets are like single seeded nutlets, as in *Crataegus*, *Mespilus*

D. MULTIPLE FRUIT

Not from a single flower, but developing from a whole flower cluster. Some examples are the fruits of *Morus*, *Ficus*

6. Seed

Strictly speaking, only the embryo of flowering plants together with its shell can be considered a seed. The fruit of grasses is called a *caryopsis*, the single seeded indehiscent nutlet of the Compositae is an *achene*.

The seed enclosure is either attached to the fruit wall *endocarp*, by a short stalk, *funiculus*, or unattached. When the fruit is ripe the stalk will die off separating the seed from the fruit wall. The attachment of a funiculus is normally evidenced by a dull, lighter spot on the seed coat which is properly termed the

28

hilum. The hilum has a particular form, size and color. In the Fagaceae (*Fagus, Quercus, Castanea*) and also *Aesculus* the hilum is unusually large.

A seed consists of the nucleus and its shell, the seed coat, which may be composed of one or more layers, *integuments*. The seed coat is very characteristic in a specific genus. It may be thick or thin, woody, leathery or fleshy, occasionally winged (*Paulownia, Catalpa, Bignonia*) or have a tuft of hair attached (*Populus, Salix*) (Fig. 35).

The nucleus consists of either an embryo with seed leaves (cotyledons) as in *Fraxinus, Castanea, Fagus, Acer, Quercus* or an albumen (endosperm) containing the embryo and very small cotyledons.

Now and then a fleshy appendage, termed an aril, arises from the base of the seed 'stalk' (funiculus). The aril can more or less envelop the seed coat as in *Euonymus* and *Celastrus* or be very striking as in *Taxus*.

7. The Surface of Plant Parts

The surface of the plant parts of various species have very distinct properties: glabrous or pubescent, smooth or rough, glossy or sticky, etc. Furthermore, the presence of thorns, bristles, glands, scales, tendrils, etc. can also provide characteristics useful for identification.

These characteristics may be grouped according to various hairy (trichomes), non-hairy and other types of vestiture (coverings).

A. Non-hairy Surfaces

   glabrous, the general term for a non-hairy surface;

   naked, without leaves, scales or a covering of any kind (this term is usually more widely used in describing 'Flowers' rather than 'Surfaces');

   dull, not shiny;

   glossy, shiny and very shiny;

   pulverulent, covered with a fine powder;

   farinose, similar to the above with coarser granules;

   pruinose, with a fine white or bluish waxy frosting which can be wiped clean;

   viscid, covered with a greasy exudate, not necessarily sticky to the touch;

   glutinous, coated with a more or less sticky covering;

   smooth, surface without raised areas or grooves but not glossy;

   glossy, glazed, as above but polished;

   asperous, surface punctuated with raised spots, sometimes only delectable to the touch; rough;

   scabrous, surface covered with tiny stiff points, usually detectable only by touch, seldom by sight;

   tuberculous, rough with large, visible raised points;

   warty, with rounded, more or less identical raised spots;

   lenticellate, with corky raised spots (lenticels);

   glandular, general term for a glandular surface;

   pubescent, general term for hairy surface.

B.   Pubescent (Hairy) Surfaces

Another general term for a hairy covering over a plant part is 'indumentum'. The hairs (trichomes) may be single or multicellular. They originate in the epidermis and are characteristic in terms of size and shape for a paticular species. They occasionally fulfill a specific purpose (poison hair, glandular hair). Frequently, the hairs after maturing will die, fill with air and maintain a whitish appearance.

Single Celled Hairs. An epidermal cell elongated into a hair-like, papillate form. A papille is an epidermal cell whose outer wall is extruded into a blunt cone shape. The papille may be elongated further to form a tubular or filament hair. If the hair is especially stiff it is referred to as a bristle. A particular form of the bristle is the stinging hair.

Some single celled hairs are branched. Depending upon the type of branching they may be star-shaped (stellate) or many-branched antler forms; both types occur mainly in the *Cruciferae*. The base of these hairs remains stalk-like (Fig. 36f; 38f, i—l).

Multicellular Hairs. The tubular form of single celled hairs can also be multicellular; in this case the end cell is especially long.

Fascicled or clustered hairs are trichomes which occur in groups of upright expanded epidermal cells.

Eyelash types (cilia) are those hairs which occur on the edge or perimeter of a given plant part.

Bristles are thick, stiff hairs enlarged at the base.

Poison hairs are bristles with brittle tips which break upon contact releasing an irritable secretion (Fig. 36c).

Tufted hairs are filamentous arising from two or more cells, coarse and occurring in groups.

Scaly, flat, thin cells laying on a single plane, radially arranged in a more or less round, umbrella-shaped disk on a short stalk; *Hippophae, Eleagnus* etc. For the many forms occurring in the genus *Rhododendron*, see the text (Fig. 36e, j; Fig. 38j).

Woolly or felt hair is that which is curled or twisted, often felt-like on the young leaves or internodes, not necessarily a dense layer.

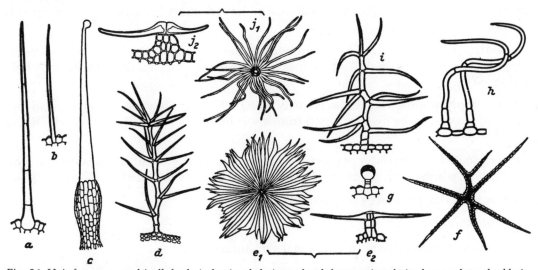

Fig. 36. Hair forms. a. multicellular hair; b. simple hair; c. glandular or poison hair; d. many branched hair of *Platanus*; e. stellate hair from *Hippophae*, seen from above and in cross section; f. single celled but branched, so-called antler-form hair of *Alyssum*; g. glandular hair; h. multicellular hair; i. multicellular, branched, so-called compound hair; j. multicellular stellate hair of *Shepherdia* seen from above and in cross section. Enlarged (from Magdefrau and Oehlkers)

Glandular forms. Include all structures originating in the epidermis which secret oil, resin, latex or similar substances; more specifically, glandular hairs, -scales or -tufts (Fig. 36g).

Glandular hairs are made of a distinctly long single or multicellular stalk usually ending in a single celled head (the actual gland) (Fig. 36d).

Glandular tufts are an elongated single cell with a multicellular head or gland group (*Rosa*).

Glandular scales consist of a long or short stalk topped by scale-like glands often layered thick in the center (*Ribes nigrum*).

An outline of glandular secretions was developed by Frey-Wyssling (Metabolism of Plants, 2nd Edition, Zurich 1949). In the same work the steps by which substances are released was summarized:

Physiological Process

Uptake	Conversion	Alienation	Elimination	Form
Resorption	→ Assimilation	→ Dissimilation	→ Excretion	Excrete
			→ Secretion	Secrete
			→ Recretion	Recrete

Recrete being any substance that passed through the plant metalolism unchanged, e.g. water, calcium salts, silicic acid, etc.

Secrete is an assimilated substance; e.g. the building block, cellulose; lignin, the bonding material; or nectar, released through specialized glands in the flower (or extrafloral as from the base of *Prunus* leaves).

Excrete is a substance which is first altered by assimilation and then released after dissimilation. The most important excrete is carbon dioxide, although primary interests here are the products of glandular hairs such as etheric oils. Further, excreta may be separated into specialized compartments (*Hypericum*, *Citrus*) or excretion cells (*Laurus*). Also included here are the 'milk tubes' of *Ficus*, *Nerium*, *Rhus* and others.

Fig. 37. Prickles (a. *Robinia pseudoacacia*) and Thorns (b−c). (*Berberis*) (from Kerner)

Armature, etc. This category differs from the trichomes in that the structures originate below the epidermis. Included here are prickles, leaf thorns, stem or leaf tendrils; whereas the stem thorns are nothing more than simple or branched, glabrous or haired short branches with sharp tips (*Prunus spinosa*, *Crataegus*).

Prickles are sharp, stiff, often hook-like outgrowths of the epidermis which originate, however, in the lower cell layers. These are the 'thorns' of the roses, whereas the 'prickles' of *Rubus* actually belong to the trichomes (Fig. 37a).

Leaf thorns are simply modified leaves, as is easily seen in *Berberis*. They are, however, also the thorns of cactus. Modified leaves can be distinguished from short branches primarily in their clustered arrangement (Fig. 37 b−c).

Leaf tendrils originate from the outer portion of a leaf, as in peas; stem tendrils, however, are leafless side sprouts on climbing plants, with holdfasts (*Parthenocissus*) or without (*Vitis*).

C.   Terminology for Hairy Surfaces (Fig. 38)

stellate, hairs star-shaped;

glandular, surface covered or with occasional glandular hairs;

glandular-hairy, as above, but hairs and glands separate;

frizzy haired, hairs curved, wavy; woolly, hair covering very thick but not appressed, hair curled but not into loops;

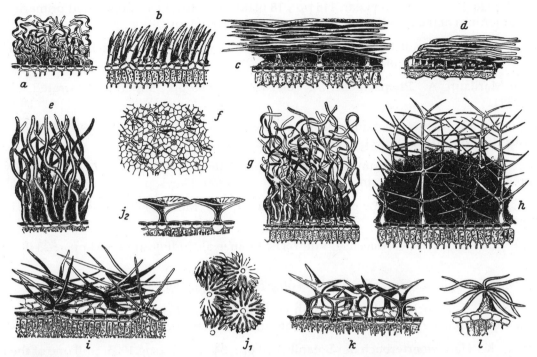

Fig. 38. Types of Hairs. a. coils of wool-hair; b. sectioned velvety; c. spindle-form hair of *Artemesia*; d. silky hair of *Concolvulus cneorum*; e. sectioned wool hair; f. stellate hair of *Alyssum*; g. ribbon-like wool hair; h. multicellular branched hair; i. clustered or fascicled hair; j. umbrella-form hair, from above and (j2) in cross section; k. stellate hair of *Aubrieta*; l. stalked hair fascicle of *Correa* (from Kerner)

tomentose, hair covering very thick, laying flat and short, very even, can't be rubbed off;

floccose, as above but indumentum tufted and easily rubbed off;

strigose, hairs straight, surface densely covered, short, brittle and stiff, a thin layer;

silky, hair straight, surface densely covered with long, soft hair, glossy;

hirsute, hair standing upright, more or less thick, most over 2 mm long, rather stiff;

hispid, hair standing upright, rough to the touch and very stiff, very dense, about 1 mm long or more;

bristle pointed, as above with hairs longer and less dense;

shaggy, hair standing upright, soft, thin, sparse and long;

velvety, hair short, soft, upright from the surface, not felty, yet tight laying;

downy, fuzzy, fine-haired, hair straight, upright, soft to the touch, seldom dense, about 1 mm long.

Literature Cited in 'Guide to Terminology'

Bischoff, W. G., Handbuch der botanischen Terminologie, Vol. 1. Nuremburg 1833. (Ahtough in many areas outdated, this is still the most comprehensive work on botanical terminology; Vol. 2 covers the taxonomy of the Cryptograms, Vol. 3 General taxonomic system and index. Richly illustrated, however, the pictures are not well arranged.)

Boros, G. Botanisches Woerterbuch. 252 pp. Zurich 1955. No illustrations.

32

Cowan, J. M., The Rhododendron Leaf. 118 pp., 18 plates. London 1950. Concerned primarily with the indumentum of the Rhododenron leaf; a very important work.

Hegi, G., Illustrated Flora of Middle Europe, I., XVII−CLVIII, 303 ill. Munich 1906. Covers the anatomy and morphology of the plants.

Kerner Von Marilaun, A., Pflanzenleben. 2 Vols. 734 and 896 pp., superbly illustrated. Leipzig 1890−1891.

Lawrence, G. H. M., An introduction to Plant Taxonomy. 179 pp., 69 ill. New York 1955. One of the best introductions to the subject; very good illustrations.

Leunis, J., Synopsis der Pflanzenkunde. 2nd edition pp 1−165, with 239 ill. Hanover 1877. Very rich and precise terminology; contains numerous lists, tables and keys; poorly illustrated.

Lubbock, J., Buds and Stipules. 239 pp., 340 ill. London 1899. Most comprehensive writing in this area; good illustrations.

Oehlkers, F., Das Leben der Gewaechse. Vol. I, Die Pflanze als Individuum. 463 pp., 523 ill. Berlin 1956.

Rauh, W., Morphologie der Nutzpflanzen. 290 pp., 236 ill. Heidelberg 1950.

Schmeil-Seybold, Lehrbuch der Botanik. 54th edition. Vol. I, 441 pp., 437 ill. Heidelberg 1950. Covers the morphology of the flowering plants and their classification.

Schneider, C. K., Handwoerterbuch der Botanik. 690 pp., 341 ill. Leipzig 1905. Still one of the most important botanical pocket dictionaries.

Stearn, W. T. (in Synge, Supplement to the Dictionary of Gardening), 'Shapes of Leaves, etc.', pp. 318−322, with ill. Oxford 1956. Contains lists of leaf forms ordered by groups, done originally by Turrill.

Troll, A., Allgemeine Botanik. 749 pp., 597 ill. Stuttgart 1948.

Alphabetical Reference to the Botanical Terminology

To facilitate the use of this book by readers of all language groups, the most frequently used botanical terms have been arranged in alphabetical order. The word is then followed by the scientific (generally Latin, but occasionally Greek) word and then by the equivalent terms in German, French and Dutch. Furthermore, in all cases where a plant part from the 'Guide to the Terminology' is illustrated, a reference number may be found in parenthesis after the word in the English column referring to the illustration number.

English (fig. no.)	Latin	German	French	Dutch
abscising	caducus	hinfaellig	caduc	afvallend
achene	achenium	Neusschen	achaine, akène	nootje
acrodrome 23d	acrodromus	spitzlaeufig (Nerven)	acrodrome	acrodroom
acuminate 20i	acuminatus	lang zugespitzt	terminé en queue	lang toegespitst
acute 20a, 21g	acutus	spitz	aigu	spits
adult leaves	folia adulta	Altersblaetter	feuilles adultes	ouderdomsbladeren
albumen	albumen	Eiweiss	albumen	eiwit
alternate	alternans	wechselstaendig	alterne	afwisselend
alternate (of leaves) 10 a	alternifolius	— (von Blaettern)	à feuilles alternes	afwisselend
angiosperms	angiospermae	Bedecktsamer	angiospermes	bedektzadigen
angle of nerves		Nervenwinkel	aisselle des nerves	nerfoksel
anther	anthera	Staubbeutel	anthère	helmknop
apex, top	apex	Blattspitze	pointe	top
apiculate	apiculatus	fein zugespitzt	apiculé	puntig
applanate	applanatus	abgeflacht	aplati	afgeplat
appressed	adpressus	angedrueckt	appresse	aangedrukt
arrow-headed	sagittatus	pfeilfoermig	sagitté	pijlvormig
ascending 6f	ascendens	aufsteigend	ascendent	opstijgend
auriculate (eared) 21e	auriculatus	geoehrt	muni d'oreillettes	geoord
awn	arista	Granne	arête	baard (van gras)
awned 19i	aristatus	grannig	aristé	met baard (van gras)
axillary	axillaris	achselstaendig, seitenstaendig	axillaire	okselstandig
bark	cortex	Rinde, Borke	écorce	bast
bearded	barbatus	Achselbart	barbé	okselbaard
berry 34	bacca	Beere	baie	bes
biennial	biennis	zweijaehrig	bisannuel	tweejarig
bilabiate 30i	bilambatus	zweilippig	bilabié	tweelippig
blade 9b	lamina	Blattspreite	limbe	bladschijf
blunt 20b, 21f	obtusus	stumpf	obtusé	stomp
boat-shaped	navicularis	kahnfoermig	naviculaire	bootvormig
brachidodrome 23c	brachidodromus	schlingenlaeufig (Nerven)	brachidodrome	brachidodroom
bract	bractea	Hochblatt	bractée	schutblad
branch	ramus	Ast	branche	tak
branchlet	ramellus	Zweiglein	petite branche	twijqje
bristle	seta	Borste	soie	borstel
bristle-pointed	setosus	borstig	seteux	borstelig
bud	gemma	Knospe	bourgeon	knop
bullate	bullatus	aufgetrieben, blasig	boursoufflé, bullé	opgeblazen
calyx	calyx	Kelch	calice	kelk
campanulate (bell-shaped) 29d	campanulatus	glockig	campanulé	klokvormig
camptodrome 22c	camptodromus	bogenlaeufig (Nerven)	camptrodrome	camptodroom
capitula (head) 32e	capitulum	koepfchen	capitule	hoofdje
capsule 34	capsula	Kapsel	capsule	doos
carpel 25f	carpellum	Fruchtblatt	carpelle	vruchtblad
catkin 32b	amentum	Kaetzchen	chaton	katje
channelled	canaliculatus	rinnenfoermig	canaliculé	gootvormig

34

English (fig. no.)	Latin	German	French	Dutch
ciliate 19b	ciliatus	gewimpert	cilie	gewimperd
cirrhous	cirrhus	Wickelranke	vrille	rank
clavate 29f	clavatus	keulenfoermig	claviforme	knodsvormig
claw	unguis	Nagel	onglet	nagel
clawed	unguiculatus	genagelt	onguicule	genageld
climbing	scandens	kletternd, klimmend	grimpant	klimmend
clustered 10f	fasciculatus	bueschelig	fasciculaire	gebundeld
coarse	grossus	grob	grossier	grof
compound	compositus	zusammengesetzt	composé	samengesteld
compressed	compressus	zusammengedraengt	comprimé	samengedrukt
concave	concavus	vertieft	concave	uitgehold
conduplicate 8h	conduplicatus	zusammengefaltet	condupliqué	samengevouwen
connate 11f	connatus	verwachsen	conné	vergroeid
connective	connectivum	Mittelband	connectif	konnektief
convex	convexus	gewoelbt	convexe	gewelfd
convolute 8f	convolutus	uebergerollt	convoluté	opgerold
cordate 21b	cordatus, cordiformis	herzfoermig	cordé, cordiforme	hartvormig
corky 5i	suberosus	korkig	subéreux, liégeux	kurkachtig
corolla	corolla	Blumenkrone	corolle	bloemkroon
corymb 32d	corymbus	Doldentraube	corymbe	schermtros
cotyledon	cotyledon	Keimblatt	cotyledon	kiemblad
craspedrome 23b	craspedromus	randlaeufig (Nerven)	craspedrome	craspedroom
creeping 6a	repens, reptans	kreichend	rampant	kruipend
crenate 19h	crenatus	gekerbt	crénelé	gekarteld
crescent-shaped 16h	lunatus	mondfoermig	luniforme	halvemaanvormig
crispate 19k	crispus	gekraust	crispé, ondulé	gekroesd
cross section	sectio transversa	Querschnitt	section transversale	dwarse doorsnede
crosswise 10d	decussatus	kreuzstaendig	décussé	kruisgewijs
crown	corona, cacumen	Krone	couronne	kroon
cuneate (wedge-shaped) 21d	cuneatus	kellfoermig	en forme de coin	wigvormig
cupulate (cup-shaped) 29b	cupulaeformis	becherfoermig	cupuliforme	bekervormig
cupule	cupula	Fruchtbecher	cupule	vruchtbeker
cuspidate 20h	cuspidatus	feinspitz	cuspidé	fijn toegespitst
cyme 33b	cyma	Scheinquirl, Trugdolde	cime, cyme	bischerm, tuil
deciduous	deciduus	abfallend	caduc	afvallend
decumbent 6e	decumbens	liegend	décombant	liggend
decurrent 11e	decurrens	herablaufend	decurrent	aflopend
decussate (deeply cut) 19e	incisus	eingeschnitten	incisé	ingesneden
deflexed	declinatus	neidergebogen	décliné	neergebogen
delicate	gracilis	zierlich	gracieux	sierlijk
dentate 19g	dentatus	gezaehnt	denté	getand
digitate	digitatus	gefingert	digité	vingervormig
dioecious	dioecus, dioicus	zweihaesig	dioique	tweehuizig
distichous (2 ranked) 10e	distichus	zweizeilig	distique	tweerijig
double	bi-, plenus (of flowers)	doppelt, gefuellt	double	dubbel-, gevuld
downy	pubescens	weichharrig	pubescent	zachtharig
drooping	cernuus	uebergebogen	penché	overgebogen
drupe	drupa	Steinfrucht	drupe	steenvrucht
dull	opacus	matt	mat	mate, dof
elliptic 13	ovalis	oval	elliptique	ovaal, elliptisch
elliptical 13	ellipticus	elliptisch	elliptique	elliptisch
emarginate 20c	emarginatus	ausgerandet	émarginé	uitgerand
enclosed/covered 7e	vestitus	bedeckt	couvert	bedekt
entire 19a	integer, -rimus	ganzrandig	entier	gaafrandig
epigynous 28c	epigynus	unterstaendig	épigyne	onderstandig

English (fig. no.)	Latin	German	French	Dutch
equitant 8e	amplex	umfassend	amplexe	omvattend
evergreen	sempervirens	immergrun	toujours vert	groenblijvend
exserted	exsertus	vorragend	saillant	eruit stekend
falcate 16f	falcatus	sichelfoermig	en forme de faux	sikkelvormig
fascicle	fasciculus	Bueschel	fascicule	bundel
fastigiate	fastigiatus	fastigiat	fastigié	fastigiaat
female flower (pistillate)	flos femineus	Stempelbluete	fleur féminin	stamperbloem
filament	filamentum	Faden	filet	helmdraad
fissured	fissura	rissig	fissurer	spleet, scheur
flagellate (whip-formed)	flagellaris	peitschenartig	flagellaire	zweepvormig
flat, plain	planus	eben, flach	plat	vlak, glad, ondiep
flexuose	flexuosus	hin und hergebogen	flexueux	zigzag gebogen
floccose	floccosus	flockig-filzig	floconneux	vlokkig, viltig
follicle	folliculus	Ballgfrucht	follicule	
fragrant	odoratus	duftend	odorant	geurend
fringed	fimbriatus	gefranst	fimbrié	met franjes
fruit	fructus	Frucht	fruit	vrucht
funnelform 29c	infundibuliformis	trichterfoermig	infundibulé	trechtervormig
furrowed 5f	sulcatus	gefurcht	silloné	gegroefd
gaping	ringens	rachenbleutig	fleur en gueule	mondvormig
geniculate	geniculatus	geknickt	genouillé	geknikt
genus	genus	Gattung	genre	geslacht
glabrous	glaber	kahl	glabre	kaal
gland	glans	Druese	gland	klier
glandulary-hairy 36g	glanduloso-pubescens	druesenhaarig	glanduleux-pubescent	klierachtig behaard
glaucous	glaucus	bereift	pruineaux	berijpt
globose	globusus	kugelig	globeux	bolvormig
glossy	lucidus, nitidus	glaenzend	brillant, luisant	glanzend
gymnosperms	gymnospermae	Nacktsamer	gymnospermes	naaktzadigen
habit	habitus	Habitus, Gestalt	forme	habitus
hair-covering	indumentum	Behaarung	pubescence	beharing
hairy	pilosus	behaart	pileux	behaard
hastate 21h	hastatus	spiessfoermig	hasté	spiesformig
herbaceous	herbaceus	krautartig, krautig	herbacé	kruidachtig
hermaphrodite	hermaphroditus	zwittrig	hermaphrodite	hermafrodiet
hilum	hilum	Nabel	hile	navel
hirsute	hirsutus	rauhhaarig	hirsute	ruwharig
hispid	hispidus	steifhaarig	hispide	stijfharig
husk	siliqua	Schote	silique	hauw
hypanthium	hypanthium	Bluetenboden	hypanthium	bloembodem
hypogynous 28a	hypogynus	oberstaendig	hypogyne	bovenstandig
imbricate 8a	imbricatus	dachziegelig	imbriqué	dakpansgewijze
incised	incisus	eingeschnitten	incisé	ingesneden
inflorescence	inflorescentia	Bluetenstand	inflorescence	bloeiwijze
involucre	involucrum	Huellkelch	involucre	omwindsel
involute (rolled inward) 8b	involutus	eingerollt	enroulé	ingerold
irregular	irregularis	unregelmaessig	irregulier	onregelmatig
jointed	articulatus	gegliedert	articulé	geleed
juvenile leaves	folia juvenilia	Jugendblaetter	feuilles juveniles	jeugdbladeren
keeled	carinatus	gekielt	caréné	gekield
kernel, stone	nucleus	Kern	noyeau	kern
kidney-shaped 16g	reniformis	nierenfoermig	en forme de rein	niervormig
lanceolate 14o	lanceatus, lanceolatus	lanzenfoermig, lanzettlich	lancéolé	lancetvormig
large, broad	latus	breit	large	breed
latex	latex	Milchsaft	laiteux	melksap

English (fig. no.)	Latin	German	French	Dutch
leaf 9a	folium	Blatt	feuille	blad
leaf base	basis	Blattgrund	base de feuille	bladvoet
leaf cushion	pulvinus	Blattkissen, Blattpolster	coussinet foliaire	bladkussen
leaf margin	margo	Blattrand	contour de feuille	bladrand
leaf scar	cicatricula	Blattnarbe	cicatrice foliaire	bladmerk
leaflet	foliolum	Blaettchen	foliole	blaadje
leathery	coriaceus	lederartig	coriace	leerachtig
leprous 36e	lepidisotus	schuelferschuppig	lepidote	schubbig
ligululate	ligula	Zungenbluete	ligule	tongetje
limb	limbus	Saum	limbe	zoom, rand
linear 12a	linearis	linealisch	linéaire	lijnvormig
lobe, loculicidal	loba	Lappen	lobe	lob
lobed 18f	lobatus	gelappt	lobé	gelobd
locule (chamber of ovary)	loculum	Faech	loge	hok
long shoot		Langtrieb	rameau longue	langlot
male flower (staminate)	flos masculus	Staubbluete	fleur mâle	meeldraadbloem
mane-like	jubatus	maehnenartig	criniforme	manenvormig
mealy	farinosus	mehlig	farineux	melig
monoecious	monoecus	einhaeusig	monoique	eenhuizig
mucronate 20g	mucronatus	stachelspitz	mucroné	gepunt
mucronulate 20f	mucronulatus	stachelspitzig	mucronulé	fijn gepunt
naked 7d	nudis	nackt	nu	naakt
narrow	angustus	schmal	étroit	smal
needle-form	acerosus	nadelfoermig	acéré	naaldvormig
nodding 4d	nutans	ueberhaengend	incliné	overhangend
not shining	opacus	glanzlos	opaque	mat, dof
nut 34	nux	Nuss	noix	noot
obcordate 16c	obcordatus	obcordat, verkehrt herzfoermig	obcordate	omgekeerd hartvormig
oblanceolate 15u	oblanceolatus	oblanzettlich	oblancéolé	omgekeerd lancetvormig
oblate	oblatus	oblat	oblate	oblaat
oblique 21k	obliquus	schief	oblique	scheef
oblong 12	oblongus	laenglich	oblong	langwerpig
obovate 15	obovatus	obovate, verkehrt eifoermig	obovate	omgekeerd eirond, eivormig
obvolute 8d	obvolutus	halbumfassend	obvoluté	halfomvattend
opposite (of foliage) 10b	oppositus, oppositifolius	gegenstaendig (bei Blaettern)	opposé	tegenoverstaand
orbiculate 13m	orbicularis	kreisrund	corbiculaire	cirkelrond
outspread	patulus	abstehend	étendre	afstaan
ovary	ovarium	Fruchtknoten	ovaire	vruchtbeginsel
ovate 14	ovatus	eifoermig, eirund	ovate	eirond, eivormig
ovule	ovulum	samenanlage	ovule	eitje
palmate 17d	palmatus	handfoermig, handteilig	palmé	handdelig, handvormig
panicle 32h	panicula	Rispe	panicule	pluim
papilionaceous (butterfly-like) 30h	papilionaceus	schmetterlingsfoermig	papilionacé	vlinderbloemig
papilla	papilla	warze	papille	wratachtig
pappus	pappus	Haarkelch	aigrette	zaadpluis
pectinate	pectinatus	kammfoermig	pectiné	kamvormig
pedate	pedatus	fussfoermig	pedatiforme	voetvormg
pedicel	pediculus	stielchen	pedicelle	steeltje
peduncle	pedunculus	Bluetenstiel	pédoncule	bloemsteel
pedunculate	pedunculatus	gestielt (Bluete)	pédoncule	gesteeld
peltate 16a	peltatus	schildfoermig	pelté	schildvormig
pendulous (weeping) 4e	pendulus	haengend	pendant	hangend
penniform 17e	pinnatiformis	fiederfoermig	penniforme	veervormig

English (fig. no.)	Latin	German	French	Dutch
perfoliate 11d	perfoliatus	durchwachsen	perfolie	doorgroeid
perianth	perianthemum	Bluetenhuelle, Perigon	périanthe	bloembekleedsel
perigynous 28b	perigynus	mittelstaendig	périgyne	halfonderstandig
petal 25c	petalum	Bluetenblatt	pétale	kroonblad
petiole	petiolus	Blattstiel	pétiole	bladsteel
petioled 11a	petiolatus	gestielt (Blatt)	petiolé	gesteeld
phylloclades	phyllocladium			
phyllode	phyllodium	Phyllodium	foliace	phyllodium
phyllotaxis	Phyllotaxis	Blattstellung	phyllotaxis	bladstand
pinnately cleft 18b	pinnatifidus	fiederspaltig	pennatifide	veerspletig
pinnately partite 18c	pinnatipartitus	fiederteilig	pennatipartite	veerdelig
pinnatisect 18d	pinnatisectus	fiederschnittig	pinnatiséqué	veervormig ingesneden
pistil	pistillum	Stempel	pistil	stamper
pistillate (see: female flower)				
pith	medulla	Mark	moelle	merg
plaited 8g	plicatus	gefaltet	plié	gevouwen
pod	legumen	Huelse	gousse	peul
poisonous	venenatus	giftig	vénéneux	vergiftig
pollen	pollen	Bluetenstaub	pollen	stuifmeel
polygamous	polygamus	vielehig	polygame	polygaam
prickle 37a	acus	Stachel	aiguillon	stekel
prickly	aculeatus	stachelig	muni d'aiguillons	stekelig
procumbent	procumbens	niederliegend	tracant	neerliggend
prostrate	prostratus	niedergestreckt	couche	neerliggend
pruinose	pruinosus	bereift	pruineux	berijpt
pubescent	pubescens	feinhaarig	pubescent	fijn behaard
pulverulent	pulverulentus	bepudert, bestaeubt	pulverulent	bepoederd, bestoven
punctate (dotted) 5k	punctatus	punktiert	ponctué	gestippeld
pungent	pungens	stechend	piquant	stekend
quadrangular 5e	quadrangulatus	vierkantig	à quatre angles	vierhoekig
raceme 32c	racemus	Traube	grappe	tros
racemose	racemosus	traubig	en grappe	trosvormig
radiate 35	radiatus	strahlig	radiaire	radiaal
receptacle	receptaculum	Bluetenboden	receptacle	bloembodem
reflexed	reflexus	zurueckgebogen	réflechi	teruggeslagen
regular	regularis	regelmassig	régulaire	regelmatig
resinous	resinosus	harzig	résineux	harsachtig
reticulate	reticulatus	netznervig	reticulé	netvormig
retuse 20d	retusus	eingedrueckt	émoussé	ingedrukt
revolute 8c	revolutus	zurueckgerollt	revoluté	teruggerold
rhizome	rhizoma	Wurzelstock	rhizome	wortelstok
rhombic	rhombicus	rautenfoermig (= rhombisch)	rhombique	ruitvormig
rooting	radicans	wurzelnd	radicant	wortelend
rotate (wheel-shaped) 29a	rotatus	radfoermig	rotacé	radvormig
rough	asper	rauh	rude	ruw
rounded 21a	rotundatus	abgerundet	arrondi	afgerond
roundish 13l	suborbiculatus	rundlich	arrondi	afgerond
rugose	rugosus	runzelig	rugueux	gerimpeld
runne 6b	sobol, stolon	Auslaeufer, Sproessling	drageon, stolon	uitloper,wortelspruit
salver-shaped 29g	hypocraterimorphus	stieltellerfoermig	hypocratériforme	schenkbladvormig
samara 35b	samara	Fluegelfrucht	samare	gevleugeld nootje
scabrous	scaber	scharf	scabre	ruw
scaly 10g	squama	Schuppe	squameux	schub
scattered	sparsifolius	zerstreut (Blaetter)	espacé	verspreid
schizocarp 35e	schizocarpium	Spaltfrucht	schizocarpe	splitvrucht
scion	vimen, virga	Rute	verger, scion	twijg, roede

38

English (fig. no.)	Latin	German	French	Dutch
seed	semen	Samen	graine, semence	zaad
semidouble	semiplenus	halbgefuellt	demi-double	half gevuld
semiterete 5b	semiteres	halbrund	demi-cylindrique	halfrond
sepals 25k	sepala	Kelchblaetter	sépales	kelkbladen
serrate	serratus	gesaegt	serré	gezaagd
serrulate 19d	serrulatus	feingesaegt	serrulé	fijn gesaagd
sessile 7a, 10b	sessilis	sitzend	sessile	zittend
shaggy	villosus	zottig behaart	poilu	donzig
shell	epicarpium	Schale	écorce	schil van vrucht opeen gehoopt
shoot	ramulus	Trieb	pousse	scheut
short branch		Kurztreib	rameau court	kortlot
shrub	frutex	Strauch	arbuste, arbrisseau	struik, heester
silky	sericeus	seidenhaarig	soyeux	zijdeachtig
simple	simplex	einfach	simple	enkelvoudig
sinuate 18e	sinuatus	gebuchtet	sinué	bochtig
slightly drooping 4c	cernuus	nickend	penché	knikkend
smooth	laevis	glatt	lisse	glad
solitary	solitaris	einzelstehend	solitaire	alleenstaand
spathulate 16e	spathuliformis	spatelfoermig	spatulé	spatelvormig
species	species (sp)	Art	espèce	soort
spike 32a	spica	Aehre	épi	aar
spindle, rachis	rhachis, rachis	Spindel	fuseau	spil
spiral	spiralis	schraubig	spiralé	spiraalvormig
spur	crus	Sporn	éperon	spoor
stamen 25a	stamen	Staubblatt	étamine	meeldraad
staminate (see: male flower)				
standard		Hockstamm	haute-tige	hoogstam
stellate 38f	stellatus	sternhaarig	étoilé	sterharig
stem	culmus	Halm (Gramineae)	tige	halm
stem-clasping 11c	amplexicaulis	stengelumfassend	amplexicaule	stengelomvattend
sticky	glutinosus, viscosus	klebrig	poisseux, visqueux	kleverig
stigma 34	stigma	Narbe	stigmate	stempel
stipule 9b	stipula	Nebenblatt	stipule	steunblad
straggly 4f	divaricatus	sparrig	divariqué	uitgespreid
strap-form 12b	loratus	riemenfoermig	loriculé	riemvormig
strap-shaped	loratus	bandfoermig	loriculé	bandvormig
striated	striatus	gestreift	strié	gestreept
strict 4b	strictus	straff	raide	opgaand
strigose 36	strigosus	striegelhaarig	à poils rudes	scherpharig
subspecies	subspecies (ssp)	Unterart	sous-espèce	ondersoort
subulate (awl-shaped)	subulatus	pfriemfoermig	subulé	priemvormig
syncarp	syncarpium	Sammelfrucht	syncarpe	vruchten
tapering	attenuatus	verschmaelert	attenue	versmald
terete 5a	teres	stielrund	cylindrique	rolrond
terminal	terminalis	endstaendig	terminal	eindstandig
terminal bud 7g		Endknospe	bourgeon terminal	eindknop
ternate 17b	ternatus	dreizaehlig	terné	drietallig
tessellate 22b	tessellatus	wuerfelnervig	tessellé	schaakbrod-vormig
thorn 37b-c	spina	Dorn	épine	doorn
thorny	spinosus	dornig	épineux	gedoornd
throat	faux	Schlund	gorge	keel
tomentose	tomentosus	filzig	tomenteux	viltig
tooth	dens	Zahn	dent	tand
toothed 19g	dentatus	gezaehnt	dente	getand
translucent	pellucidus	durchscheinend	pellucide	doorschijnend
triangular 16b	triangularis, triangulatus	dreieckig, dreikantig	à trois angles, triangulaire	driehoekig, driekantig

English (fig. no.)	Latin	German	French	Dutch
trichoma	trichoma	Haare	trichome	beharing
trifoliate	trifoliatus	dreiblaettrig	trifoliolé	driebladig
trioecious	trioecus	trioezisch	trioique	driehuizig
truncate 21e	truncatus	abgestutzt	tronqué	afgestompt
truncated	truncatus	gestutzt	tronqué	afgestompt
tube 29h	tubus	Roehre	tube	buis
tubercled	tuberculatus	hoeckerig	tuberculeux	bultig
twig (secondary branches)	ramulus	Zweig	branche	twijg
twining	volubilis	windend	volubile	windend
twisted 4i	tortus, tortuosus	gedreht	tortueux	gedraaid
two-edged 5d	anceps	zweischneidig	à deux faces	tweezijdig
umbel 32f	umbella	Dolde	ombelle	scherm
underside		Unterseite	face de dessous	onderzijde
undulate	undulatus	gewellt	ondulé	gegolfd
unisexual	unisexualis	eingeschlechtig	unisexuel	eenslachtig
upper side		Oberseite, oben	face de dessus	bovenzijde, boven
upright	erectus	aufrecht	dréssé	oprecht
urceolate	urceolatus	krugfoermig	urcéiforme	kruikvormig
-valved 7c	valvatus, -valvis	klappig	-valve	klepvormig
variety	varietas (var.)	Varietaet	variété	varieeteit
velvety	holosericeus	samtharrig	velute	fluweelhaarig
viscid	viscidus	schmierig	viscide	kleverig
warty	verrucosus	warzig	verruqueux	wrattig
whorled 10c	verticillatus	quirlig	verticille	kransstandig
winged 5h	alatus	gefluegelt	ailé	gevleugeld
wintergreen	semipersistens	wintergruen	semi-persistant	wintergroen
woolly 38	lanatus, lanuginosus	wollharig, wollig	laineux, lanugineux	wollig, zachtharig

Explanation of Symbols

To provide the reader with information relating to the use of the plants described in this work and their cultural requirements, the following symbols are used after many of the descriptions.

Light Requirements
    ○ = needs or tolerates full sun
    ◗ = needs or tolerates semishade
    ● = needs or tolerates lasting shade

Soil Requirements
    m = moist soil
    w = wet soil (most plants do not like standing water but some will tolerate it for varying lengths of time)
    d = dry soil
    S = sandy soil (light and loose)
    H = humus soil (loose, dark, organic loam)
    A = alkaline soil (even chalk soils)

Properties of the Plants
    ✧ = with ornamental flowers
    ✗ = fruit or other plant part edible or economically useful
    ∅ = especially attractive foliage or fall color
    # = evergreen foliage
    ⚭ = ornamental fruit
    Ⓕ = cultivated for timber, countries where grown are indicated

Other Symbols or Abbreviations
    N = North, S = South, E = East, W = West, M = Mid, Middle.
    Dates refer to the year of introduction into cultivation.
    × = hybrid, cross.
    HCC (with number) = color code from the Horticultural Color Chart.
    z followed by number denotes hardiness zone according to USDA Hardiness Map.

Notes on Illustrations

The abbreviation 'Fig.' always refers to illustrations within the text pages of this book. References to illustrations in other books will be found at the end of the description and are indicated by initials and numbers.

For example: DL 2: 21 = Dippel, Handbuch der Laubholzkunde, Vol. 2, Illustration #21 (or if the illustrations are not numbered, the illustration on page 21).

The list of abbreviations to the literature providing illustrations cited in this book can be found on pp. 47–49. A complete bibliography of all books used in compiling this work may be found in the last volume.
    Pl. = plate (for those found in other works). Plate 31, 43 etc. refers to those found in this book.

Synonyms

Plant names in italics at the end of a description are invalid synonyms.
The cultivars are noted with single quotes '___'

Abbreviated Temperature Conversion Chart

Fahrenheit to Celsius

°F	°C
40	4.4
35	1.7
30	− 1.1
25	− 3.9
20	− 6.7
15	− 9.4
10	−12.2
5	−15
0	−17.8
− 5	−20.6
−10	−23.2
−15	−26.1
−20	−28.9
−25	−31.7
−30	−34.4
−35	−37.2
−40	−40
−45	−42.8
−50	−45.6

Celsius to Fahrenheit

°C	°F
5	41
0	32
− 5	23
−10	14
−15	5
−20	− 4
−25	−13
−30	−22
−35	−31
−40	−40
−45	−49

Readers should note the following points relative to hardiness:

1. The majority of the plants dealt with in this book will be found in zones 4 to 8, and occasionally zone 9.
2. Areas with the same average low temperature are described by the isotherms drawn along 5°C clines.
3. Hardiness ratings of plants is given using the U. S. Dept. of Agriculture system. It is indicated in the text as ''z'' followed by a number indicating hardiness zone.

Winter hardiness ratings are only guidelines. It must be realized that microclimate plays an important role so a specific location within a zone may be warmer or cooler than the zone as a whole. Protected areas in woods, southern exposures or gardens within cities as well as careful cultivation may allow one to raise plants in a zone which is normally too cold.

Hardiness Zones and the British Isles

Very few of the trees, shrubs and other garden plants cultivated in Britain are native to the British Isles. Over the centuries they have been introduced from all over the world, though especially from cool and warm temperate climates. How well they thrive in the British Isles largely depends on the climate they evolved in.

Although all plants are closely adapted to the climate of the region in which they occur wild, few have rigid requirements of heat and cold. There are other factors that decide whether a plant will thrive, e.g. soil type and amount of rainfall, but these will be mentioned later; temperature is of primary importance.

The British Isles has an equable oceanic climate which is seldom very cold, hot or dry. As a result, a wide range of the world's plants can be grown outside providing they are sited intelligently. Undoubtedly, some of these plants would prefer more summer sun or a more definite cold winter rest, but their innate adaptability is catered for in the vagaries of our climate. There is, however, a point at which a plant's tolerance ceases. Low temperature is the most important of these tolerances. If a plant cannot survive an average winter outside it is said to be tender. If a plant survives average winters but not the exceptionally hard one it is said to be half-hardy. These terms are, of course, relevant only to the area in which one lives.

Large continental land masses, e.g. North America and Central Europe, have climates that get progressively colder winters as one proceeds northwards and further inland from the sea. North America provides a familiar example, the extreme south being almost tropical, the far north arctic. In the 1930s, the United States Department of Agriculture divided the USA into 7 hardiness zones based upon an average of the absolute minimum temperatures over a period of 20 years. Later, the system was revised and refined and 10 zones recognized (zone 1 is arctic, zone 10 tropical). More recently this Hardiness Zone system has been extended to Europe, incuding the British Isles. Gardeners in the United States and Canada soon took advantage of the hardiness zone concept and over the years, largely by trial and error, most trees and shrubs and many other plants have been assessed and given zone ratings. Nevertheless, this system, though useful, can only be considered to give approximate hardiness ratings, especially when applied to the British Isles.

Sitting as it does on the eastern edge of the North Atlantic Ocean, the British Isles occupies a unique position. Although its total length, about 650 miles (Cornwall to Orkney), lies within latitudes 50° to 60° N, it falls into zone 8! Moved into the same latitudes in North America,it would lie entirely north of the Canadian border with the tip of Cornwall level with Winnipeg (zone 2−3). Even the eastern coastal region of Canada at these latitudes is no warmer than zones 3−4. Because of the influence of the Gulf Stream the British Isles enjoys a remarkably uniform climate. Such temperature gradients as these are run east to west rather than south to north.

It is a characteristic of temperate oceanic climates to have milder winters and cooler summers than equivalent continental ones and because of their northerly position this is even more marked in the British Isles. For this reason, a number of trees and shrubs which thrive in zone 8 in USA fail to do so well in Britain e.g., *Albizia julibrissin*, *Lagerstroemia indica*, etc. Such plants may live but fail to bloom, or get cut back severely by the British winters. The factor is primarily lack of summer sun rather than absolute cold.

This lack of summer warmth brings us to the several important ancillary factors which affect a plant's hardiness. Apart from lack of damaging low temperatures a plant needs the right kind of soil, adequate rainfall and humidity, plus sufficient light intensity and warmth. As with low temperature most plants have fairly wide tolerances, though there are noteworthy exceptions. Most members of the *Ericaceae*, especially *Rhododendron* and allied genera, must have an acid soil or they will die however perfect the climate. For plants near the limits of their cold tolerance, shelter is essential. Protection from freezing winds is particularly important. This can be provided by planting in the lee of hedges, fences and walls or among trees with a fairly high canopy. Individual plants can also be protected by matting or plastic sheeting or the bases can be earthed up or mounded around with peat, coarse sand or weathered boiler ash. A thick layer of snow also provides insulation against wind and radiation frost! Plenty of sunshine promotes firm, ripened growth with good food reserves, notably a high sugar content in the cell sap which then takes longer to freeze. If the summer is poor a partial remedy is to apply sulphate of potash (at 10g/per square metre) in late summer. This will boost the amount of sugars and starches in the plant. Half-hardy plants will stand having their tissues moderately frozen providing the thawing-out is gradual. For this reason it is best to grow them in a sheltered site which does not get the first rays of the morning sun. This is especially relevant for species with tender young leaves or early flowers, e.g. *Cercidiphyllum*, *Camellia* and *Magnolia*.

Zone 9 in the USA is warm-temperate to sub-tropical with hot summers. In the British Isles it tends to have even cooler summers than zone 8, and as a result very few truly sub-tropical plants can be grown in Britain. Most of the plants in the famous so-called, sub-tropical gardens, e.g. Tresco, Logan, Inverewe, etc., are of warm-temperate origin. For the reasons set down above, in Britain, if in doubt, it is best to consider zone 8 as zone 7 and zone 9 as zone 8 for plants of unreliable hardiness.

by Kenneth Beckett

Hardiness Zones of Europe

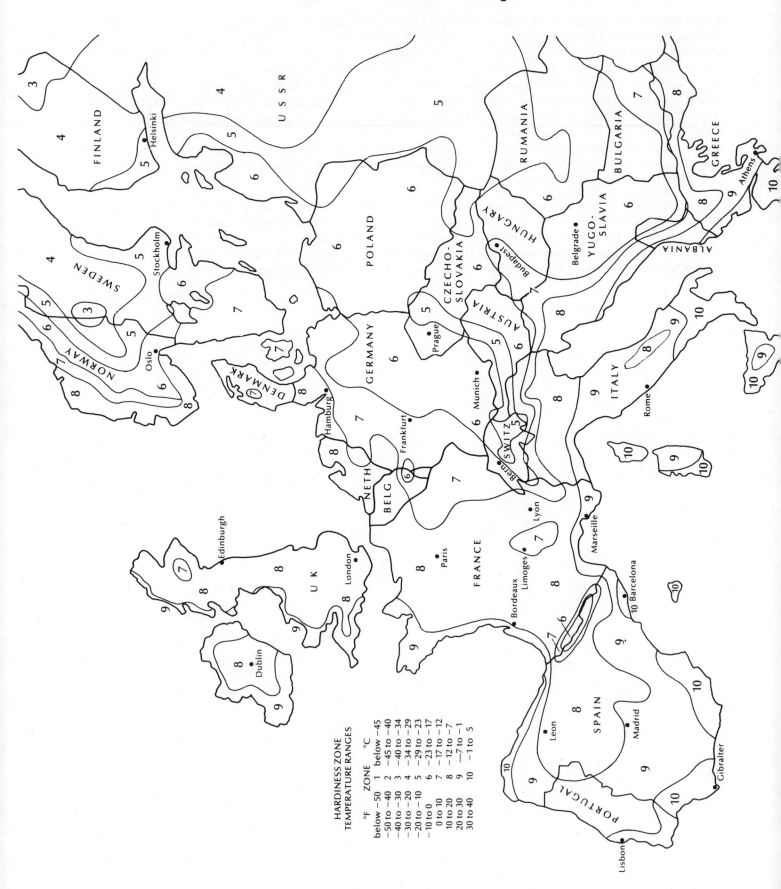

HARDINESS ZONE
TEMPERATURE RANGES

°F	ZONE	°C
below −50	1	below −45
−50 to −40	2	−45 to −40
−40 to −30	3	−40 to −34
−30 to −20	4	−34 to −29
−20 to −10	5	−29 to −23
−10 to 0	6	−23 to −17
0 to 10	7	−17 to −12
10 to 20	8	−12 to −7
20 to 30	9	−7 to −1
30 to 40	10	−1 to 5

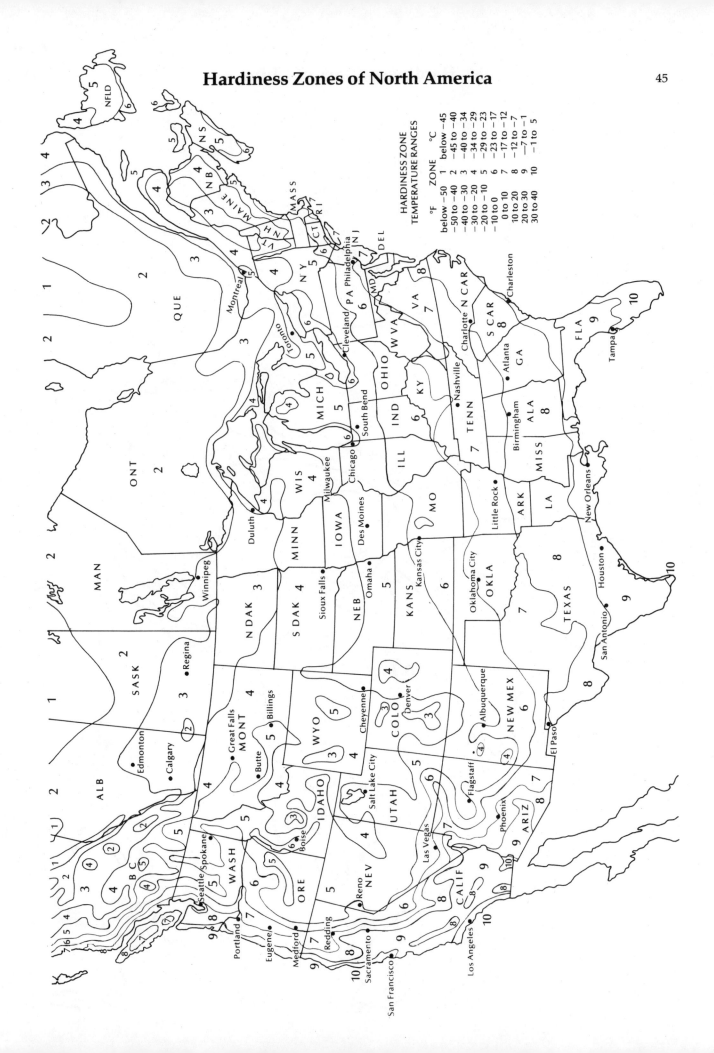

HARDINESS ZONE TEMPERATURE RANGES		
°F	ZONE	°C
below −50	1	below −45
−50 to −40	2	−45 to −40
−40 to −30	3	−40 to −34
−30 to −20	4	−34 to −29
−20 to −10	5	−29 to −23
−10 to 0	6	−23 to −17
0 to 10	7	−17 to −12
10 to 20	8	−12 to −7
20 to 30	9	−7 to −1
30 to 40	10	−1 to 5

Hardiness Zones of China

SOVIET UNION

Heilongjiang

Mongolia

Jilin

Xinjiang

Liaoning

Inner Mongolia

KOREA

Gansu

Hebei −4° C

PEOPLE'S REPUBLIC OF CHINA

Ningxia

Shanxi

Shandong

0° C

JAPAN

Qinghai

Shaanxi

Jiangsu

Tibet

Henan

Anhui

4° C

Hubei

NEPAL

SIKKIM

Zhejiang

Sichuan

8° C

BHUTAN

Hunan

Jiangxi

INDIA

ASSAM

Guizhou

Fujian

12° C

BANGLADESH

Yunnan

Guangxi

Tropic of Cancer

Guangdong

TAIWAN

BURMA

VIETNAM

LAOS

HAINAN

PHILIPPINES

THAILAND

CAMBODIA

HARDINESS ZONE
TEMPERATURE RANGES

°F	ZONE	°C
below −50	1	below −45
−50 to −40	2	−45 to −40
−40 to −30	3	−40 to −34
−30 to −20	4	−34 to −29
−20 to −10	5	−29 to −23
−10 to 0	6	−23 to −17
0 to 10	7	−17 to −12
10 to 20	8	−12 to −7
20 to 30	9	−7 to −1
30 to 40	10	−1 to 5

N. BORNEO

INDONESIA

MALAYSIA

MALAYSIA

List of Abbreviations to Other Reference Works

One or more of the following abbreviations will be found at the end of most of the plant descriptions. They refer exclusively to illustrations in the given works. Many of these abbreviations are the same as those found in American and English literature. Included in this list is the book's title and date of publication; more detailed bibliographical information may be found at the end of this work in the index volume.

AAu	Audas: Native Trees of Australia. 1947		EKW	Encke: Die schoensten Kalt— und Warmhaus-pflanzen
AB	Arnoldia; Bulletin of the Arnold Arboretum. 1911 →		ENP	Engler & Prantl: Die Natuerlichen Pflanzen-familien, 2nd Ed. 1924 →
ANZ 1—2.	Allan, H. H.: Flora of New Zealand, Vols. 1961—1970		EP	Engler: Das Pflanzenreich
Bai	Baileya (periodical). 1953		EWA	Erickson: Flowers and Plants of Western Australia
BB	Britton & Brown: Illustrated Flora of the Northern USA and Canada, 3 Vols. 1896—1898		FAu	Forest Trees of Australia. 1957
BC	Bailey: Standard Cyclopedia of Horticulture. 1950		FIO	Fang: Icones Plantarum Omeiensium. 1942—1946
BCi	Bolanos: Cistographia Hispanica. 1949		FRu	Focke: Species Ruborum 1—23. 1911 to 1914
BD	Bulletins de la Société Dendrologique de France. 1906—1939		FS	Flore des Serres et des Jardins de l'Europe, 23 Vols. 1845—1880
BFC	Clapham-Tutin-Warburg: Flora of the British Isles Illustrations, 4 Vols. 1957—1965		FSA	Coed/de Winter/Rycroft: Flora of South Africa
BFl	Barrett: Common Exotic Trees of South Florida. 1956		GC	Gardeners Chronicle. 1841 →
BIC	Bor & Raizada: Some beautiful Indian Climbers and Shrubs. 1954		GF	Garden and Forest. 1888—1897
			Gfl	Gartenflora. 1852—1938
BIT	Blatter & Millard: Some beautiful Indian Trees. 1954		GH	Gentes Herbarium. 1935 →
			Gn	The Garden (periodical)
BM	Curtis' Botanical Magazine, 1787—1947; ns(new series) 1948 →		GPN	Gram-Jessen: Vilde Planter i Norden, 4 Vols.
			Gs	Gartenschonheit. 1920—1942
BR	Botanical Register. 1815—1847		GSP	Grimm: Shrubs of Pennsylvania. 1952
BRho	Bowers: Rhododendron and Azaleas. 1960		GTP	Grimm: Trees of Pennsylvania. 1950
BS	Bean: Trees and Shrubs hardy in the British Isles, 4 Vols. 1970 →		Gw	Gartenwelt. 1897 →
			HAl	Hara: Photo-Album of Plants of Eastern Himalaya. 1968
CBa	Camus: Les Bambusées. 1913		HBa	Houzeau de Lehaie: Le Bambou. 1906 to 1908
CCh	Camus: Les Châtaigniers		HF	Schlechtendahl-Langethal-Schenck: Flora von Deutschland, 5th Edition, Hrsg. von Halier. 1880—1887
CFQ	Carvalho & Franco: Carvalhos de Portugal. 1954			
CFTa	Curtis: The endemic Flora of Tasmania, 5 Vols.		HH	Hough: Handbook of the Northern States and Canada. 1950
ChHe	Chapple: Heather Garden. 1961			
CIS	Hu-Chun: Icones Plantarum Sinicarum, Vols. 1—5		HHD	Harlow-Harrar: Textbook of Dendrology. 1941
			HHS	Harrar-Harrar: Guide to the Southern Trees. 1962
CMi	Clements: Minnesota Trees and Shrubs. 1912			
CQ	Camus: Monographie du genre *Quercus*, 6 Vols. 1936—1954		HHo	Hume: Hollies. 1953
			HHy	Haworth-Booth: Hydrangeas. 1951
CS	Camus: Monographie des Saules de France. 1904—1905		HI	Hooker: Icones Plantarum. 1836 →
			HIv	Hibbert: The Ivy. 1872
CTa	Curtis: Student's Flora of Tasmania. 1956 to 1967		HKS	Hong Kong Shrubs. 1971
CWF	Clark: Wild Flowers of British Columbia. 1973		HKT	Hong Kong Trees. 1969
DB	Deutsche Baumschule. 1949 →		HL	Hendriks: Onze Loofhoutgewassen, 2nd Edition 1957
Dfl	Dendroflora (yearbook). 1964 →			
DH	Dallimore: Holly, Box and Yew. 1908		HM	Hegi: Flora von Mitteleuropa, 13 Vols. 1908—1931
DL	Dippel: Handbuch der Laubholzkunde, 3 Vols. 1889—1893			
DRHS	Dictionary of Gardening, 4 Vols. 1951, Supplement 1969		HRh	Hooker: Rhododendrons of Sikkim-Himalaya. 1849—1851
			HS	Hao: Synopsis of the Chinese *Salix*. 1936
EH	Elwes & Henry: Trees of Great Britain and Ireland, 7 Vols. 1906—1913		HSo	Hedlund: Monographie der Gattung *Sorbus*. 1901

HTS	Harrison: Know your Trees and Shrubs. 1965
HW	Hempel & Wilhelm: Baume und Straucher des Waldes, 3 Vols. 1889–1899
IC	Ingram: Ornamental Cherries, 1948
ICS	Icones Cormophytorum Sinicorum, 4 Vols. 1972–1975
IH	L'Illustration Horticole. 1854–1896
JA	Journal of the Arnold Arboretum. 1919 →
JAm	Jones: The American species of *Amelanchier*. 1946
JMa	Johnstone: Asiatic Magnolias in Cultivation. 1955
JRHS	Journal of the Royal Horticultural Society. 1846 →
JRi	Janczewski: Monographie des Grosseillers. 1907
JRL	Jahrbuecher Rhododendron und immergrune Laubgeholz. 1937–1942; 1952 →
KD	Koehne: Deutsche Dendrologie. 1893
KEu	Kelly: Eucalypts. 1969
KF	Kirk: Forest Flora of New Zealand. 1889
KGC	Kunkel: Flora de Gran Canaria. 1974 →
KIF	Kurata: Illustrated important Forest Trees of Japan, 4 Vols. 1971–1973
KO	Kitamura & Okamoto; Coloured illustrations of Trees and Shrubs of Japan
KRA	Koidzume: Revision Aceracearum Japonicarum. 1911
KSo	Karpati: Die *Sorbus*-Arten Ungarns. 1960
KSR	Keller: Synopsis Rosarum Spontanearum Europae Mediae. 1931
KTF	Kurz & Godfrey: The Trees of Northern Florida. 1962
LAu	Lord: Shrubs and Trees for Australian Gardens. 1948
LCl	Lavallée: Les Clématites a grandes fleurs. 1884
LF	Lee: Forest Botany of China. 1935
LLC	Lloyd, C.: *Clematis*. 1965
LNH	Labillardiére: Novae Hollandiae Plantarum Specimen. 1804
LT	Liu: Illustrations of native and introduced plants of Taiwan, 2 Vols. 1960
Lu	Lustgarden (periodical). 1920 →
LWT	Li: Woody Flora of Taiwan. 1963
MB	Mitford: The Bamboo Garden. 1896
MCea	McMinn: A systematic study of the genus *Ceanothus*. 1942
MCl	Markham: *Clematis*
MD	Newsletters of the German Dendrological Society. 1892 →
MFl	Meyer: Flieder (Lilacs). 1952
MFu	Munz: A revision of the genus *Fuchsia*. 1943
MG	Moellers Deutsche Gartner-Zeitung. 1896 to 1936
MiB	Miyoshi: Die Japanischen Bergkirschen. 1916
MJ	Makino: Illustr. Flora of Japan. 1956
MJCl	Moore & Jackman: *Clematis*
MLi	McKelvey: The Lilac. 1928
MM	McMinn & Maino: The Pacific Coast Trees. 1935
MMa	Millais: Magnolias. 1927
MNZ	Metcalf: Cultivation of New Zealand Trees and Shrubs. 1972
Mot	Mottet: Les arbres et Arbustes d'ornement. 1925
MOT	Muller: The Oaks of Texas. 1951
MPW	McCurrach: Palms of the World. 1960
MRh	Millais: Rhododendrons, 2 Vols. 1917 and 1924
MS	McMinn: Manual of the Californian Shrubs. 1951
NBB	Gleason: The New Britton & Brown, Ill. Flora
NDJ	Yearbook of the Netherlands Dendrological Society. 1925 to 1961
NF	The New Flora and Silva. 1928–1940
NH	Nat. Hort. Magazine. 1922 → (see only those after 1955), from 1960–1974 titled 'American Horticulture Magazine'
NK	Nakai: Flora Sylvatica Koreana. 1915
NT	Nakai: Trees and Shrubs of Japan proper. 1927
NTC	Native Trees of Canada. 7th edition 1969
OFC	Ohwi: Flowering Cherries of Japan. 1973
PB	Hesmer: Das Pappel-Buch. 1951
PBl	Pareys Blumengartnerei, 2nd edition 1958–1960
PCa	Pertchik: Flowering Trees of the Caribbean
PDR	Poln. Dendr. Rocznik (see only after 1950)
PEu	Polunin: Flowers of Europe
PFC	Pizarro: Sinopsis de la Flora Chilena. 1959
PMe	Polunin: Flowers of the Mediterranean
PPT	Palmer, E., & N. Pitman: Trees of Southern Africa, 3 Vols. 1972
PSw	Polunin: Flowers of Southwest Europe
RBa	Rivière: Les Bambous. 1878
RH	Revue Horticole. 1829 →
Rho	Rhodora. 1899 →
RLo	Rehder: Synopsis of the genus *Lonicera*. 1903
RMi	Rosendahl: Trees and Shrubs of the Upper Midwest. 1955
RPr	Rousseau: The Proteaceae of South Africa. 1970
RWF	Rickett: Wild Flowers of the United States, 13 Vols.
RYB	Rhododendron Year Book, 1–8; from Vol. 9 Rhododendron and Camellia Year Book. To 1971
SB	Satow: The cultivation of Bamboos. 1899
SC	Sweet: Cistineae
SCa	Sealy: A revision of the genus *Camelia*. 1958
SDK	Sokoloff: Baume und Straucher der USSR, 7 Vols.
SEl	Servettaz: Monograph. Eleagnaceae
SFP	Salmon: New Zealand Flowers and Plants in Colour. 1967
SH	Schneider: Handbuch der Laubholzkunde, 2 Vols. 1904–1912
SL	Silva Tarouca: Unsere Freiland-Laubgehoelze. 1922
SM	Sargent: Manual of the Trees of North America. 1933
SME	Schwarz: Monographie der Eichen Mitteleuropas und des Mittelmeergebietes. 1936–1939
SNp	Stainton: Forests of Nepal. 1972
SPa	Sudworth: Forest Trees of the Pacific Slope. 1908

SR	Stevenson: Species of *Rhododendron*. 1947
SS	Sargent: The Silva of North America, 14 Vols. 1891–1902
ST	Sargent: Trees and Shrubs, 2 Vols. 1905 to 1913
StP	Stern: A study of the genus *Paeonia*. 1946
THe	Tobler: Die Gattung *Hedera*. 1912
TPy	Terpo: Pyri Hungariae. 1960
TY	Trelease: The Yuccaceae. 1902
UCa	Urquhart: The *Camellia*, 2 Vols. 1956 and 1960
UJD	Uehara: Japanische Dendrologie, 4 Vols. 1961
UR	Urquhart: The *Rhododendron*, 2 Vols. 1958 and 1962
VG	Viciosa: Genisteas Espanoles I–II. 1953 to 1955
VQ	Vicioso: Revision del genero *Quercus* en Espana. 1950
VSa	Vicioso: Salicaceas de Espana. 1951
VT	Vines: Trees, Shrubs and Vines of the Southwest. 1960
VU	Vicioso: Ulex. 1962
WJ	Wilson: The Cherries of Japan. 1916
WR	Willmott: The genus *Rosa*, 2 Vols. 1910 to 1914
WRu	Watson: Handbook of the Rubi of Great Britain and Ireland. 1958
WT	West-Arnold: The native Trees of Florida. 1956
YTS	Yamakai Color Guide, Flowering Garden Trees and Shrubs, Vols. 1–2. 1971
YWP	Yamakai Color Guide, Flowers of Woody Plants, 1–2. 1969.

Plant Descriptions

ABELIA R.Br. — Abelie — *Caprifoliaceae*

Deciduous or evergreen, small to medium size shrubs, twigs glabrous, pubescent or sometimes glandular; leaves opposite with petioles short, margins entire or dentate; flowers single or clustered, axillary or terminal on short side branches, occasionally as terminal panicles, small but numerous; corolla tubular-funnel or bell shaped, with straight or curved tube sometimes rounded at the base, limb regularly five lobed; stamens four, two short and two longer, attached to corolla at the base; style with bulbous stigma, calyx with 5, seldom 2—4 sepals; fruit leathery, abscises with the calyx intact. — Some 30 species, 25 from East and Middle Asia, 1 in Himalaya, 1 in Taiwan and 2 from Mexico. Most species not very winter hardy in cooler temperate zones.

Classification of the Genus (completed by Rehder)

Section I: **Euabelia** Rehd.
Twigs with dense shaggy or sparse soft indumentum or glabrous, nodes not thickened; leaf petioles neither widened at the base nor fused together; corolla bell to funnel shaped, stamen and pistils extend beyond the throat; fruit rounded;
Subsection 1: **Serratae** Rehd.
Inflorescence always composed of two flowers, each at the tip of short side branches; branches with solid narrow pith:
A. gymnocarpa; serrata; spathulata
Inflorescence single, seldom multiple, axillary often at the branch tips, many together (Subsections 2 to 4);
Subsection 2: **Uniflorae** Rehd.
Sepals 2, stamens shorter than the corolla, inflorescence single; branches thin tubular:
A. engleriana; graebneriana; koehneana; longituba; macrotera; myrtilloides; parvifolia; schumannii; tereticalyx; uniflora
Sepals 5, stamens and pistils equal to or shorter than the corolla (Subsection 3 and 4);
Subsection 3: **Rupestres** Zab.
Inflorescence axillary, 2 or more flowers at the branch tips in panicles, stamens extending at least to the limb of the corolla:
A. aschersoniana; chinensis; ionandra; rupestris
Subsection 4: **Vesaleae** Zab.
Inflorescence axillary, single to short racemes, stamen shorter than the corolla at the limb, pith in the twigs dense and narrow:
A. coriacea; floribunda

Section II: **Zabelia** Rehd.
Branches with backward leaning, bristly pubescence, seldom glabrous, nodes thickened, pith wide, dense; leaf petioles broadened at the base or connected, axillary buds covered (especially the current year's growth); inflorescence has 2—3, seldom more flowers, corolla tubular-funnelform, tube cylindrical, limb flared, anther enclosed, pistil scarcely reaching the limb, anthers pressed together;
Subsection 5: **Corymbosae** Zbl.
Inflorescences axillary, most with 3 flowers, in panicles at the branch tips:
angustifolia; buddleoides; corymbosa; triflora
Subsection 6: **Biflorae** Zbl.
Inflorescence 2 or (seldom more) multiflowered, single at the tips of short twigs, sepals 4:
A. biflora; dielsii; onkocarpa; umbellata; zanderi
Hybrids and Garden forms
A. × 'Edward Goucher' (= A. chinensis × schumannii); A. × grandiflora (= A. chinensis × uniflora)

Abelia biflora Turcz. Deciduous shrub, to 1 m high, branches reddish, pubescent, thickened at the nodes; leaves lanceolate, 2.5—4 cm long, abruptly pointed, margin shallowly serrate, somewhat leathery, upper surface dark green, glabrous, underside bright green, short stiff hairs on the midrib; flower pairs sessile, the single blooms on short pedicels, in the leaf axils, sepals 4, corolla bell-funnelform, at first bright pink, then white, somewhat haired, June. DL 1: 192 (= *A. davidii* Hance; *A. shikokiana* Mak.). Mountain forests of N. China, Manchuria. 1923. z7 Fig. 41, 42. **H**

A. buchwaldii see: **A. serrata**

A. buddleoides W. W. Sm. Very similar to *A. triflora*, but distinct in its smaller leaves and its sepals, which are only half to a third as long as the corolla tube with shorter and softer hairs on the margin. SW. China. z8 Fig. 40.

A. chinensis R. Br. Deciduous shrub, to 1.5 m high, growth wide, young twigs reddish, finely haired; leaves ovate, long, pointed, 2—4 cm long, margins serrate, base rounded, upper surface darker green than the underside, venation haired at leaf base on underside; flowers 2 or more in a cluster, axillary or terminal, 5 sepals, 4—5 mm long, half as long as the tube, corolla whitish, fragrant, funnelform, July—Sept. BMns 168 (= *A. hanceana* Martens). China, Fukien, W. Hupeh, Kiangsi, Kwangtung. 1844. *A. rupestris* Ldl. is often included here, but is somewhat different, which see. In cultivation often confused with *A. grandiflora*. z8 Fig. 41. **H**

A. × 'Edward Goucher' (Goucher) (= *A. grandiflora* × *A. schumannii*. Semi-evergreen; in growth and appearance midway between the parents; flowers somewhat larger than *A. grandiflora*, lavender-pink with orange throat, July—Sept., tube-form. Introduced before 1911 by Edward Goucher, US Dept. of Agriculture, Glenn Dale, Maryland, cultivated only in the USA. Rather hardy. z5 **H**

A. engleriana (Graebn.) Rehd. Deciduous shrub, to 2 m high, sprawling, branches pubescent; leaves ovate to elliptic-lanceolate, 2—3.5 cm long, pointed, margins somewhat serrate, top glossy green, bottom sparsely pubescent on the veins; flowers to 2, in an axil of

Fig. 40. **Abelia.** left *A. buddleoides,* right, *A. biflora* (from ICS)

clustered leaves at the ends of short branches along the previous year's growth, bell-shaped, lower corolla tubular, 2 cm long, purple-pink, June—July. Middle and West China, W. Hupeh, Szechwan. 1908. Probably one of the hardiest types; similar to *A. graebneriana,* but in all respects smaller, however more abundant and attractive flowers. z6 **H** ✥

A. floribunda Dcne. Evergreen shrub, in its native habitat 1.5—2.5 m high, in milder climates (England, Ireland) more than twice as high, young twigs reddish with soft pubescence; leaves ovate, 2—4 cm long, pointed, shallowly dentate, rough, both sides bright green and glabrous; flowers, several at the ends of short branches along the previous year's growth, pendulous, corolla funnelform, 3—5 cm long, purple-red, sepals 5, green, 8 mm long, stamen filament pubescent, June. BS 1:138; BM 4316. Mexico, Cordillera from Oaxaca, 3300 m. 1841. Most beautiful of the genus. Plate 6. z8 **# H** ⊘ ✥

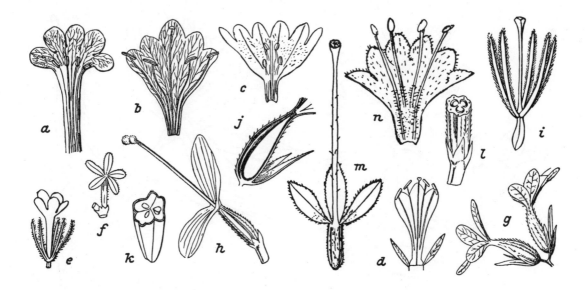

Fig. 41. **Abelia.** a. *A. rupestris* (from B.R.); b. *A. uniflora* (from Dipp); c. *A. grandiflora* (Gfl.);
d. *A. serrata* (S. & Z.); e. *A. biflora* (B.M.); f. *A triflora* (Dipp.).

Fig. 42. **Abelia.** a. *A. rupestris* (from B.R.); b. *A. uniflora* (from Dipp.); c. *A. grandiflora* (Gfl.);
d. *A. serrata* (S. & Z.); e. *A. biflora* (B.M.); f. *A. triflora* (Dipp.).

A. graebneriana Rehd. Deciduous shrub, to 3 m in its native habitat, young twigs mostly glabrous; leaves ovate to oblong, pointed, 4−5 cm long, sparsely serrate, margins often finely ciliate, upper surface somewhat sparsely pubescent, underside midrib pubescent; flowers mostly clustered on branchlet tips along previous year's growth; corolla campanulate, 25 mm long, outer pink, inner yellow sepals 2, some 8 mm long, July. Middle China, W. Hupeh, W. Szechuan. 1910. Similar to *A. engleriana*, but leaves usually much larger, margins distinctly toothed, flowers larger. z6 H ✥

'Vedrariensis'. Leaves larger, darker green; flowers larger, with large dark spot.

A. × grandiflora (André) Rehd. (= *A. chinensis* × *A. uniflora*). Shrub, semi-evergreen, 1−2.5 m high, dense growth, branches arched, finely pubescent; leaves ovate, 1.5−3.5 cm long, pointed, margins more or less shallowly serrate, upper side dark green and highly polished, under lighter and bright, underside midrib somewhat pubescent at the base, autumn color bronze-brown to purple; flowers on current year's growth, 1 to 4 in the leaf axils and branch tips, sepals 2−5, corolla funnelform, 2 cm long, white with pink, throat pubescent, July − Oct. BC 58; BS 1 Pl. 1; Gfl 1366 (= *Linnaea spaethiana* [Graebn.]). Introduced in 1886 by Rovelli in Pallanza, N. Italy as *A. rupestris grandiflora*. Practical ornamental shrub, very effective for foliage, excellent and lasting flowers. Fig. 41, 42. z5 # H ⌀ ✥

'Prostrata'. Like the type, but only 40 cm high. In USA prized as groundcover. US Plant Pat. 1431. z7

A. grandiflora × A. shumannii see: **A. × 'Edward Goucher'**

A. hanceana see: **A. chinensis**

A. ionandra Hayata. Deciduous shrub, to 1 m high; leaves sessile or with short petiole, ovate, 1−1.5 cm long, broadly pointed, base rounded, margins tiny and sparsely dentate, upper surface with sunken midrib, underside lighter with raised venation; flowers to 2, in small terminal cymes, pedicel 4−5 mm long, pubescent; calyx tube spindle shaped, 6 mm long, ribbed and pubescent, with 5 lobes, similar in size, 4−6 mm long, blunt, entire, veined, corolla long-tubular, 13 mm long, 5 lobes of similar size, outer surface pubescent. LWT 358. Taiwan; mountains of the East coast. z8

A. rupestris Ldl. According to most authors a synonym for *A. chinensis* and very slightly different; leaves alike in color on both sides (green), not as sharply pointed, base more wedge-shaped, sepals as long as the corolla tube (see *A. chinensis*). Fig. 42. H

A. schummanii (Graebn.) Rehd. Semi-evergreen shrub, 1.5 m (taller in the greenhouse), young twigs purple, softly pubescent; leaves ovate, obtuse, 1.5−3 cm long, margins entire or very shallowly dentate and ciliate, lower midrib pubescent; flowers on short side branches, most single in the leaf axils of side branches; corolla funnelform-campanulate, some 3 cm long, outer surface fine glandular, broadened at the base, pink (HCC 32/2), stamen filament pubescent at the

base, sepals 2, ovate, June−Sept. BM 8810 (as *A. longituda*), DRHS 1. Middle China. 1910. Very beautiful species. z7 H ✥

A. serrata S. & Z. Deciduous shrub, 1 to 2 m high, twigs thin, finely pubescent; leaves lanceolate, 2−4 cm long, some 1 cm wide, somewhat dentate, upper surface sparsely pubescent, mostly on the midrib, underside glabrous; flowers to 2 on small leaved side branches, terminal, corolla funnelform, 1−2 cm long, pink-white, now and then yellowish or flesh pink, outer surface pubescent, sepals 2, May−June. SZ 1:34. Japan, 700−800 m high in the mountains. 1879. Hardy but not especially ornamental and rare in cultivation. Fig. 41, 42. z6 H

var. **buchwaldii** (Graebn.) Nakai. Leaves larger, 3−5 cm long; corolla 2−3 cm long (= *A. buchwalkii* [Graebn.] Rehd.). Japan.

A. shikokiana see: **A. biflora**

A. spathulata S. & Z. Deciduous shrub, to 1m high, young twigs sparsely pubescent; leaves lanceolate to ovate, 3−5 cm long, margins unevenly serrate, glabrous above, underside softly with pubescent venation; flowers to 2 at the ends of short branches, corolla tube broadly funnelform, 2.5 cm long, cream-white, inside yellow-orange mottled, stamen filament shorter than the corolla tube, pistil longer, sepals 5, rarely 4, lanceolate, always as long as the tube. BM 6601; NT 276; SZ 34; YWP 1: 3. Japan, forests and mountains of the island Hondo. 1880. z7 Fig. 41. H

A. triflora R. Br. Deciduous shrub (occasionally semi-evergreen), upright, to 4 m in its native habitat, to 1 m in cultivation, young twigs with bristly pubescence; leaves narrowly lanceolate, long pointed, 3.5−5.5 cm long, 1−2 cm wide, base rounded, entire, leaves lower on the plant sharply dentate at the base, dark green above, lighter beneath, both sides glabrous or slightly pubescent; inflorescence 5 cm wide; flowers mostly 3, terminal on short side branches, corolla salver-shaped, tube 2 cm long, finely pubescent, tubular, limb flared 90°, 1.5 cm wide, pink, later more white, sepals 5, linear, feather haired, as long as the tube, very fragrant, June−July, ornamental even after blooming. BM 9131. NW Himalaya. 1847. Fig. 41, ·42. z6 H ✥

A. umbellata (Graebn. & Buchw.) Rehd. Deciduous shrub, 2−3 m high, wide growth, twigs bristly pubescent; leaves elliptic to lanceolate, 4−8 cm long, pointed, coarsely serrate, occasionally entire, glossy above, venation beneath haired or glabrous, petioles 5−10 mm long, swollen at the base and enveloping the bud; flowers 4−7 on a single stalk together; corolla tubular, to 1.5 cm long, pure white, June. Central and W. China, in mountain forests. 1907. z8

A. uniflora R. Br. Evergreen shrub, wide growth, 1−2 m high, branches nodding, thin, young twigs lightly pubescent; leaves ovate, pointed, 2−5 cm long, with a few shallow teeth, upper surface glossy dark green and glabrous, underside lighter and midrib pubescent; flowers 1−3 to a leaf axile at the branch tips, broadly campanulate, 2.5 cm long and wide (like small *Digitalis* flowers), outer corolla and limb white with traces of pink, inside orange, June—Sept., sepals 4 (occasionally 3–4). BM 4694; FS 824. China. 1845. Similiar to *A. grandiflora*, but easily distinguished by the sepals. Handsome and very large flowered. Fig. 41, 42. z8 # H ∅ ✤

A. zanderi (Graebn). Rehd. Deciduous shrub, 1–3 m high, upright, young twigs glabrous except for some bristles at the twig base, nodes enlarged, leaf petioles swollen at the base, covering the buds; leaves ovate to lanceolate, 4–7 cm long, pointed, base cuneate, margin occasionally somewhat dentate, mostly entire, both sides sparsely haired; flowers usually 2 on short branchlets, corolla salver-form, tube 1 cm long, outside glabrous, limb with rounded, flared lobes, pink-white, 1 cm long, sepals 4, long, glabrous, 7–10 mm long. HN 35. Middle and NW China. 1910. Variable species!! Plate 5. z6 H

'Sherwoodii'. Just 75 cm high, leaves and bloom very similar to the type. (Am. Nurseryman, 1. May 1953: 79). H ✤

Lit. Zabel, H., Ueber die Gatrtung, *Abelia*; in MD 1893: 29–31 ● Grabener, Die Gattung *Linnaea*; in Englers Bot. Yearbook. 1900: 125—145 ● Rehder, A., Synopsis of the genus *Abelia*; in Sargent, Plantae Wilsonianae I:118—129, 1913.

ABELIOPHYLLUM Nakai — OLEACEAE

Monotypic genus. Deciduous shrub, at first glance similar to *Abelia*, deviating in the flowers which appear more like *Forsythia*; branches four sided, glabrous, pith chambered; leaves opposite, simple, entire; flowers paired, in short racemes on the previous year's growth, corolla deeply cut, four lobed, ovary with two chambers containing one ovule each; fruit a rounded, flattened, some 2.5 cm wide nutlet. One species.

Abeliophyllum distichum Nakai ('White Forsythia'). Shrub, 1.5–2 m high, in native habitat, twiggy, flower resembles *Forsythia*; leaves ovate, acuminate, entire, both sides with adpressed pubescence, 3–5 cm long, petiole 2–5 cm long; flowers white, corolla 4 lobed, 15 mm wide, almond scented, inside orange, petiole and calyx brown; fruit a rounded, broad winged, 2–2.5 cm wide nutlet, flowers in May and fruit ripens in August. BMns 10. Korea, 1924. Plate 5. z4 ✤

Cultural requirements somewhat like *Forsythia*, however some winter protection is advisable. Propagation easy from cuttings.

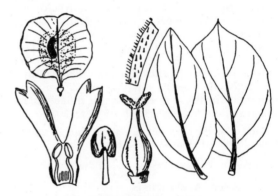

Fig. 43. *Abeliophyllum distichum.* Fruit, flower parts and leaves

ABUTILON Mill. — Flowering Maple — MALVACEAE

Tropical or subtropical herbs, shrubs or occasionally trees; leaves alternate, most cordate; flowers single and axillary or occasionally in panicles, most yellow, petals 5, campanulate, calyx 5 lobed, pistil and stamens fused into a column; fruit compound with each component having at least two seeds. — Some 100 species with only a few being garden worthy.

Abutilon darwinii Hook. f. Large twiggy shrub, in temperate zones not over 1 m high, all parts with soft silky hairs; leaves mostly 3 lobed, middle lobe longer, side lobes short, crenate, only the lower leaves 5–7 lobed, 10–15 cm long, petiole 3–6 cm long; flowers to 1–3 in an axil, campanulate, 5 cm wide, deep orange-red, with blood red veins, calyx outer surface densely tomentose, with triangular lobes. BM 5917. Brazil. 1869. Long lasting flowers. z8 ✤

A. megapotamicum St.-Hil. et Naud. Evergreen shrub, to 1.5 m high, twigs thin, long, numerous, arching; leaves long ovate, base cordate, often with 2 large lobes, margins prominently dentate, acuminate, glabrous, 5–10 cm long, petiole thin, 1–2 cm long; flowers single, axillary, hanging on long thin pedicels, corolla mimosa-yellow (HCC 602), surrounded at the base by a blood red, puffy, 5 pointed calyx (HCC 820/3), stamen filament clusters dark violet-red, longer than the corolla, May—August. FS 1599; BM 5717 (as *A. vexillarium*) (= *A. vexillarium* E. Morr.). Brazil, Rio Grande. 1864. z8 ✤

Also the cultivated form with yellow variegated foliage, **'Variegatum'.** Plate 6.

A. 'Milleri' (*A. megapotamicum* × *A. pictum*). Twigs thin, glabrous; leaves elliptic-lanceolate, deeply cordate, margins obtusely serrate, occasionally somewhat 3 lobed; flowers 1–2 axillary, bright yellow, calyx orange-brown, pistils and stamens reaching far beyond the corolla. Garden origin 1879. z8 ✤

A. ochsenii (Phil.) Phil. Shrub, to 1.5 m (in its habitat 5–6 m) resembles *A. vitifolium*, although in all parts less pubescent; leaves 3 lobed, to 8 cm long and 3 cm wide, middle lobe much longer than the side lobes, margins prominently dentate, base deeply cordate; flowers 1—3 axillary, to 6 cm wide, petals lilac-violet with a dark basal spot, May. BMns 455. Chile; Valdivia. 1961. Winter hardy in S. England. z8 ⊕

A. vexillarium see: **A. megapotanicum**

A. vitifolium (Cav.) Presl. In its habitat a tree from 5—7 m high, branches and leaves with a short white pubescence; leaves 3—5 lobed, lobes acuminate, prominently dentate, 10—15 cm long; flowers 3—4 in terminal corymbs, petiole 8—15 cm long, corolla broadly campanulate to rotate, lavender-blue, with or without venation, anthers yellow, very short, May. BM 4227 and 7328; BS 1: 171. Chile. 1837. z8 ⊕

'Album'. Flowers pure white.

Fig. 44. *Abutilon megapotamicum* (from Flore des Serres, altered)

ACACIA Mill. — Mimosa — LEGUMINOSAE

Subtropical and tropical, evergreen or deciduous trees or shrubs, some twining, few climbing with tendrils; leaves alternate, most bipinnate, leaflets small and very numerous, frequently only present in the juvenile stage, petioles often broad and leaf-like or developed into phyllodes; flowers small, in glabular heads, yellow, fruit a dehiscent pod. — 750 to 800 types, 300 with phyllodes, Australia, Polynesia, Central America, S. Africa, Sudan.

Key to the Mentioned Species

I. Leaves bipinnate;
  1. Plants without or with small thorns:
      A. baileyana, dealbata, decurrens, farnesiana, pulchella
  2. Plants with large thorns:
      A. horrida
II. Leaves phyllodes;
  1. Phyllodes needle-like:
      A. diffusa, riceana, verticellata
  2. Phyllodes short, more or less triangular, 1 or 2 veined:
      A. armata, cultriformis, decipiens, podalyriifolia, pravissima
  3. Phyllodes long, not triangular
    a) Flowers in globular heads:
      A. melanoxylon, pycnantha, retinodes
    b) Flowers in long spikes:
      A. mucronata
  4. Phyllodes decurrent, twigs therefore winged:
      A. alata

Acacia alata R. Br. Shrub, to 1.5 m high or higher, wide branches, young branches often pubescent, seldom glabrous; phyllodes short, triangular, prickly, fused together by decurrent wings on the twigs; flowers bright yellow, single or in pairs. BR 396; EWA 50. W. Australia, 1803. z8

A. armata R. Br. Kangaroo Thorn. Shrubby, densely branched, 1—3 m high and more in its habitat, twigs angular, thorns at the nodes as stipules; foliage very dense with phyllodes oblong, standing obliquely with tips curved, 15—25 mm long; flower heads single, stalked, numerous, light yellow, April. PBl 788; BM 1653 (= *A. paradoxa* DC.). Australia 1803. One of the best types, in mild areas or in cool greenhouse. In its habitat, valued as a hedge plant. Sub tropical Australia. z8 ⊕

A. baileyana F. Muell. Cootamundra Wattle. In its native habitat seldom more than 3 m, branches often pendulous, glabrous, blue-gray; leaves evergreen, bipinnate, 4—5 cm long, 4—8 petiolules containing 8—20 pairs of leaflets, these 4—8 mm long, linear, 1—2 mm wide, bluish white; flowers gold-yellow, in 8 mm wide heads, 20—30 grouped in 5—10 cm long axillary racemes, April. BM 3903; RH 1904: 336. Australia, New South Wales. 1888. Touchy, dislikes alkaline soil! (when planting in highly alkaline or chalk soils, must be grafted on *A. retinodes*). S. Africa. z8 ⊕

'Purpurea'. Phyllodes reddish. American selection.

A. cultriformis G. Don. Bushy shrub, 2m or higher; phyllodes oblique, ovate to triangular, 1.2—2 cm long, 6—12 mm wide, single veined, acute, gray-green, glabrous, prominent; very densely foliate, the branches completely covered; flowers yellow, globular, 4 mm, numerous in axillary racemes, 5—7 cm long, March to April. BMns 322. New S. Wales. 1820. z8 ⊕

A. dealbata Link. Silver Acacia. In its habitat a tree, to 30 m, in cultivation in mid regions 9—20 m high, twigs angular, dense and fine silvery pubescent; without phyllodes, leaves evergreen, bipinnate, 7—12 cm long, with 15—20 sets of 30—50 pairs of linear leaflets, these some 4 mm long and 1 mm wide, fine silvery pubescent; flowers yellow, in globular heads, grouped into large racemes, fragrant, winter through early spring, fruit a pod with seeds not interconnected by a 'string'. BS 1: 6. Tasmania, Australia. 1792. z8 ⓡ India, Japan. Plate 7. ⊕

Most popular 'Mimosa' in the Riviera; hardiest type. In Cornwall, England not uncommon as a windbreak.

Introduced in 1864 at Frankford (Castle Bocca near Cannes), since then somewhat naturalized. For the export of 'Mimosa' flowers better selections have been made for flower form, color and abundance of flowers, such as 'Mirandole', 'Tournaire', 'Gaulois' and 'Bon Acceuil', these are grafted onto seedlings of the species. The cut flowers are taken from forced plants.

A. decipiens R. Br. Shrublike, to 3 m, glabrous or rarely pubescent; phyllodes triangular or trapezoidal, 8–15 mm long, midvein eccentric and ending in a point, stipules pungent (when present); flowers in globular heads, small, pods 3–5 cm long, thick hard, curved. BM 1745 and 3244. Australia. z8.

A. decurrens (Wendl.) Willd. In its habitat a tree, to 20 m, no thorns, densely foliate, without phyllodes; twigs angular, finely pubescent; leaves bipinnate, with 15 or more sets of 30–50 paired leaflets, 3–8 mm long, green, linear, evergreen; flowers gold-yellow, to 20–30 together in panicles, February–March; fruit pods having seeds connected by a 'string', smooth. Australia, Tasmania. 1800. z7 Ⓕ S. Africa, India, Hawaii, Australia, New Zealand, Brazil. Plate 8. ⊕

A. diffusa Kerr. Shrub, 1–3 m high, glabrous, branches angular, stiff, sprawling; phyllodes upright, loose, linear, straight or sickle-form, to 5 cm long and 2–3 mm wide, with sharp point; flowers in globular heads, sulfur yellow, 5–6 mm wide, mostly 2–3 axillary on 2.5 cm long petioles, May. Tasmania. 1818. In England one of the hardiest types. z8

A. farnesiana Willd. Shrub or small tree, to 6 m high, branches brown, zig-zagged, with thin, 2.5 cm long, paired thorns, leaves and petioles finely pubescent; leaves bipinnate, petiolules in 5–8 pairs each having 15–20 pairs of linear, glossy leaflets; flowers axillary, small, stalked, gold-yellow, fragrant, in globular inflorescences 1.2 cm wide, in groups of 2–3, February–March; fruit pod twisted, inside fleshy, indehiscent. Native habitat not known for sure, presumably tropical Americas; today much used throughout tropical and subtropical regions, above all in the French Riviera where it provides a fragrant substance from the flowers. z8 ⊕

A. horrida Willd. Thorny shrub to small tree, thorns straw yellow, 5–10 cm long, stiff, sharp; leaves bipinnate (Plate 7); flowers in globular heads on 2–3 cm long stalks; pod sickle-form. S. Africa. z8

A. longifolia Willd. Golden Wattle. In its habitat a small tree, 5–9 m high, or a shrub, branches angular, glabrous; phyllodes olbong-lanceolate, 8–15 cm long, 1–2 cm wide, leaf-like, yellowish green, coarse leathery; flowers bright yellow, in 3–5 cm long cylindrical spikes, produced from the phyllode axils, March, pods 7–10 cm long. BM 1827 and 2166; AAu 95. Australia, Tasmania. 1792. Rather various type; often used in SW England. z8 Plates 2 & 7.

A. melanoxylon R. Br. Blackwood Acacia. In its habitat 18–25(–35) m high, grows broadly rounded, branches angular, pubescent, with phyllodes and true leaves;

phyllodes oblong-lanceolate, narrowing to both ends, 6–13 cm long, 2–4 cm wide, with 3–5 distinct veins; leaves in the main axils on young plants with phyllodes mixed in, bipinnate, leaflets oblong, 8 mm long; flowers yellow, fragrant, in globose heads, few in axillary racemes, April, pods flat, 5–10 cm long, often curved. BM 1659; AAu 89. Tasmania, SE Australia. 1808. z8 Ⓕ India, Chile, Argentina, Uruguay. Plates 1 & 7.

Common in SW England, one of the hardiest types. The red-brown (not black!) wood prized in Australia as the best for furniture making and as a substitute for Walnut and Mahogany. Often used in Spain and Portugal as a street tree.

A. mucronata Willd. Very similar to *A. longifolia* and often listed simply as a variety; phyllodes 3–8 cm long, but only 5 mm wide, with 3–5 rather distinctly raised veins; quite various in foliage character, flowers however, very similar to *A. longifolia*. BM 2747. Tasmania, Australia. z8

A. nemu see: **Albizia julibrissin**

A. paradoxa see: **A. armata**

A. podalyriifolia G. Don. Shrub, 2.5–3 m high, branches and twigs downy, silver-blue, phyllodes ovate to oblong, 2.5–4 cm long and 1.5–3 cm wide, with oblique prickly tips; flower heads fragrant, gold-yellow, to 20 together, axillary, phyllodes reaching beyond the racemes, flowers in winter or early spring; pods glossy or downy, 2.5–8 cm long, to 1.8 cm wide. BM 9604. Australia; Queensland. Winterhardy in Cornwall. z8 ⊕

A. pravissima F. v. Muell. Shrub or small tree, to 6 m, interesting growth habit, twigs thin and angular, glabrous; phyllodes dense on the twigs and overlapping, oblique triangular to quadrangular, 6–12 mm long and wide, distinctly veined; flowers gold-yellow, in 4 mm wide globose heads, grouped in 3–10 cm long racemes or panicles, March–April. Australia. Somewhat hardy in Ireland. z8 ⊕

A. pulchella R. Br. Evergreen shrub or small tree, densely branched, young twigs finely pubescent, with awl-shaped thorns; leaves pinnate, very small, with only one pair of petiolules having from 4–7 leaflets, 2–5 mm long, oblong, upper surface rounded, dull green; flower heads gold-yellow, globose, mostly 2 axillary, on thin, 15–25 mm stalks, spring; pods 2.5–5 cm long, 4–6 mm wide, flat, thickened at the perimeter, similar to *Laburnum anagyroides*. BM 4588. Australia. 1803. Useful for pot culture. z8 ⊕

A. pycnantha Benth. Small or medium tree or shrub, branches more or less pendulous; phyllodes leathery, flexible, sickle-form or oblong, 6–15 cm long, 2–3.5 cm wide, single veined, glossy green; flowers very fragrant, gold-yellow, in dense, globose heads, to dense, 5–7 cm long racemes, March–April; pods 5–12 cm long, 6 mm wide, individual seeds connected by a 'string'. S. Australia. Circa 1850. Appears very much like a *Eucalyptus*. z8 Ⓕ S. Africa.

A. retinodes Schlect. (incorrectly *rhetinoides*). Shrub or small tree, to 6 m, all parts glabrous, twigs angular; phyllodes lanceolate, rather thin, somewhat bowed, becoming thinner at the base, 7—15 cm long, 3 to 6 mm wide, pinnate venation; flowers bright yellow, in small globose heads, to 6—12 together in short axillary racemes, fragrant, blooms from February through fall. BM 9177; PSw 16. S. Australia, Tasmania. 1871. z8 ✧

In France noted as the *Mimose de quatre Saisons*, for its unbroken season long blooming period; too small for commercial use as cut flowers.

A. riceana Henslow. Small tree (resembles weeping willow), in its habitat to 9 m, with dense, narrow, glabrous, angular branches; phyllodes sometimes singular, sometimes 2—4 at a node, linear to awl-shaped, 2—5 cm long, deep green, often more or less curved; flowers cream-yellow, fragrant, in globose heads, grouped in narrow, 5 cm long, pendulous spikes, March—May. BM 5835. Tasmania. 1855. Very similar to *A. verticillata*, but phyllodes clustered (not whorled!). z8 ✧

A. verticillata (L'Hérit.) Willd. In its habitat a tree to 9 m, or simply a small dense shrub, young twigs distinctly angular, pubescent; phyllodes mostly to 6 in whorls, linear with needlelike tips, however not sharp, soft; flowers in 1.5—2.5 cm long, bottlebrush-like (not globose) racemes, pure yellow, in the axils of the phyllodes, April—May. PBl 1: 790; BM 110. Australia, Tasmania. 1780. z8 Plates 6 & 7. ✧

In temperate zones only useful for the cool greenhouse. All the Acacias should only be considered for frost free areas. Those that can tolerate a light frost are, *A. dealbata, longifolia* and *melanoxylon*. They may be grown in any good garden soil that is not too alkaline, *A. retinodes* and *longifolia* are somewhat more tolerant of a high pH. Many types suffer greatly from wind damage and should be protected. The roots of the Acacias have a strong odor (like raw sewage) and in transplanting provide the gardener with an unpleasant task.

The most beautiful collection of Acacias is in the garden of Tresco Abbey, Scilly Isles, SW England.

Before being introduced into the trade, every new cultivar of *Acacia* should first be registered with the international registrar, the Société Nationale d'Horticulture de France, 84 rue de Grenelle, Paris.

Lit. Jones, K. D., in Bailey, Stand. Cyc. Hort. I: 178—10, 1950, with descriptions of 67 types ● Audas, J. W., Native Trees of Australia, 84—100, 1947, with 18 Ills. ● Baglin, D., & B. Mullins, Australian Wattles; 34 pp. with 72 color photos; Sydney 1968.

ACALYPHA L. — EUPHORBIACEAE

Tropical trees and shrubs; leaves alternate, ovate, nettle-like, more or less dentate, base 3—5 veined or pinnate; flowers very small, most without or with small petals, in spikes or spike-like racemes or clusters, greenish or reddish, of little ornamental value except *A. hispida*. About 450 types in the tropics and subtropics; 3 favorite greenhouse species, grown in the open in frost free areas.

Acalypha hispida Burm. f. Shrub, to 3 m or more; leaves ovate, pointed, to 15 cm long and 9 cm wide, margins serrate, upper dark green, lighter beneath, petiole 5 cm; inflorescence 30—50 cm long, axillary, pendulous, bright red, cylindrical. BM 7632; EKW 171 (= *A. sanderi* N. E. Br.). New Guinea (?). 1896. In Germany a favorite pot plant. z10

A. sanderi see: **A. hispide**

A. wilkesiana Muell. Arg. Shrub, 2—3 m; leaves oblong, pointed, most copper-green, with many pink and red spots; flowers inconspicuous, reddish, in short, thin, upright spikes. South Sea Islands, New Hebrides. 1866. z10

Some other varieties used as pot plants:

'Godseffiana'. Grows lower; leaves evergreen, margin cream-white. New Guinea.

'Macafeana'. Leaves red, bronze and carmine marked. BC 78. 1875.

'Macrophylla'. Leaves cordate, rust-brown with lighter spots. 1876.

'Marginata'. Large leaved. olive-brown with pink margin. IH 24: 275. Fiji Islands.

'Miltoniana'. Leaves more oblong, most pendulous, irregular margins, margin white. 1911.

'Musaica'. Leaves bronze-green, with red and orange spots and markings. PBl 1:921.

'Obovata'. Leaves obovate, at first olive-green with orange-yellow margin, later bronze-green with carmine-pink margin. Polynesia. 1884.

ACANTHOLIMON Boiss. — Prickly-thrift — PLUMBAGINACEAE

Evergreen, semi-woody, cushion-form plant; twigs procumbent or ascending; leaves stiff, round or often triangular, grooved, sharply pointed; flowers in spikes or racemes, occasionally branched, stalk without leaves, flowers often hidden between the numerous, attractive bracts, petals forming a tubular ring around the 5 stamen filaments, calyx tubular, tube with 10 ribs; fruit tube-form attached to the dry calyx. — Some 120 species in Eastern Mediterranean, Asia Minor to Iran and W. Tibet, most on the mountains or in rocky wastelands. All z3

Leaves green, not blue;
  flowers pink, leaves 1—2 cm long:
    A. libanoticum

flowers red, leaves 2−3 cm long:
   A. glumaceum
flowers pink, leaves 3−4 cm long:
   A. caryophyllaceum
Leaves gray to blue gray, plant stiff;
   inflorescence 10−20 cm long, leaves 5−7 cm:
      A. acerosum
   inflorescence 10−15 cm, leaves 2−3 cm:
      A. androsaceum
   inflorescence 20−25 cm, leaves 2−3.5 cm:
      A. armenum
   inflorescence 10−15 cm long, leaves 5−20 mm:
      A. olivieri
   inflorescence 4−5 cm, leaves 15 mm:
      A. melananthum
   inflorescence 4−5 cm, flowers white:
      A. kotschyi
   leaves only 1−3 mm long, moss-like:
      A. diapensioides

Acantholimon acerosum Boiss. Cushion woody; leaves 5−7 cm long, blue-green, with depressed dots, acuminate, flat triangular, sharp, margin rough; stem protrudes beyond the foliage, flower spikes 10−20 cm long, abundant, flowers red, calyx tube with a white edge, July. West Anatolia, alpine regions. z6 # ○

A. androsaceum Boiss. Cushion thorny, sharp, gray-green; leaves needlelike, narrow, densely packed; inflorescence 10−15 cm high, flowers light pink, smaller and lighter than *A. olivieri*, bracts velvety pubescent, calyx tube softly pubescent, limb white, venation dark red, July. WS 819 (= *A. echinus* [L.] Bge.). Greece, Anatolia. 1813. z8 # d ○

A. araratii see: **A. glumaceum**

A. armenum Boiss. & Huet. Cushion hemispherical, stiff; leaves gray-white, very dense, stiff upright, 2−3.5 cm long, base 3 mm wide, flat triangular, margin rough, tip sharp, spring foliage larger than the summer foliage; inflorescence to 25 cm long, spikes unbranched, flower light pink, calyx soft fleshy, with 5 red veins, not reaching the leaf margin, calyx tube haired, August. MG 1913: 219. Armenia, Cappadocia, Syria, dry hills. z8 Plate 8. # d ○

A. caryophyllaceum Boiss. Cushion bright green, sharp, twigs long; leaves linear, triangular, rough; flower stalk longer than the leaves, to 8 cm long, in loose spikes, flower pink, bracts white on the margins, velvety pubescence, calyx tube hirsute, red venation, running to the margins. Armenia, Kurdistan. z8 # d ○

A. diapensioides Boiss. Cushion dense, grass-like; leaves only 1−3 mm long, thick obtuse triangular; inflorescence sessile in a rosette, consisting of 1−3 singled flowered spikes, bracts 4−5, ovate, brownish, fleshy. Afghanistan, high mountains of Northern Kabul and Tien Shan. z6 # d ○

A. echinus see: **A. androsaceum**

A. glumaceum (Jaub. & Spach.) Boiss. Cushion soft, green; leaves narrow awl-shaped, needlelike, very thin, triangular, 2 cm long; flower stalks reaching far past the leaves, with 1−3 velvety pubescent spikes, flowers carmine-pink (HCC 627/1), calyx tube roughly haired on the ribs, margin white, with 5 violet veins, outer bracts broadly ovate, June−July. FKS 677; MG 1913: 230 (= *A. araratii*). Armenia, Mt. Ararat. 1844. Easily cultivated, can become a weed. Plate 8. z8 # d ⊕ ○

A. kotschyi Boiss. Cushion consisting of 4−6 cm long branches; leaves blue-green, sharp, 1.5−2 cm long, linear, acuminate, very stiff; flowers in 4−5 cm long spikes with 5 to 11 white flowers arranged in two rows, calyx tube softly pubescent, venation lacking color, perimeter white, bracts wide, white, fleshy, tips prickly, July. Asia Minor, Armenia, Cicilia. Very changeable, particularly the inflorescence which is either densely packed or branched spiked. z8 #

A. libanoticum Boiss. Cushion green, consisting of 5 cm long branches, covered at the base with dark remnants of old leaves; leaves 1−2 cm long, pointed; inflorescence 4−5 cm long, often divided into 3−7 branchlets, flowers pink, calyx tube lightly coarse haired, with red veins, limb white, June−Oct. Lebanon, Anti-Lebanon Mountains. z6 # d

var. **ulicinum** (Boiss.) DC. Like the type but dwarfer, cushion denser, leaves shorter, very stiff, triangular, dark green, flowers purple-pink, in short spikes, July−Sept. Lebanon. # d

A. melananthum Boiss. Cushion of very short branches; leaves bluish, flat, lanceolate, triangular, sharp, with short prickly tips, 15 mm long, the lower leaves shorter; spike short, dense, inflorescence with 6−9 axes, flowers pink to pure white, bracts sticky, dark red, limb black to violet. Mountains of Iran. z8 # d ○

A. olivieri (Jaub. & Spach.) Boiss. Loose cushion, bluish; leaves 5−20 mm long, flat, wedge-shaped, needlelike, stiff, very hard; flower stalk 10−15 cm long, to the midpoint with light pink-red flowers, in two rows facing one side, calyx tube somewhat pubescent, perimeter red, outer bracts broadly triangular, dry membranous, June−July. BM 7506; NF 1: 116; MG 1908: 222 (= *A. venustum* Boiss.). Taurus Mts., Lesser Armenia. 1873. Most beautiful of the cultivated types. z8 # d ⊕

A. venustum see: **A. olivieri**

All species for the rock garden, prefer to be planted in deep, narrow cracks in full sun; cover during wet seasons with glass or plastic; like gravelly soil; will occasionally die for no apparent reason.

Lit. Boissier, *Plumbaginaceae*; in De Candolle, Prodromus 12, 617−696, 1848 ● Bunge, Die Gattung Acantholimon. St. Petersburg 1872.

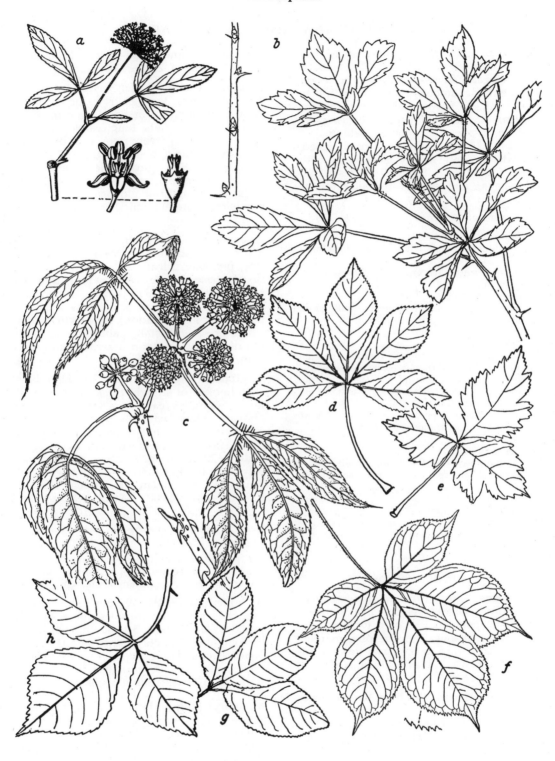

Fig. 45. **Acanthopax.** a. *A. wilsonii*; b. *A. sieboldianus*; c. *A. cimonii*; d. *A. divaricatus*; e. *A. wardii*;
f. *A. senticosus*; g. *A. sessiflorus*; h. *A. trifoliatus* (from Harms, Dippel, Nose, Harkness and original)

ACANTHOPANAX Miq. — ARALIACEAE

Deciduous shrubs or small trees, some climbing, few branches, mostly thorny; leaves alternate, 3—7 leaflets, stipules absent or weakly developed; flowers perfect or polygamous, in terminal umbels, single or multiple to large terminal panicles, flower stalk mostly unsegmented, calyx tip tiny, 5 toothed, petals 5, occasionally only 4, stamens 5, ovaries 2 chambered, seldom 3—5 chambered, pistils 2—5, free standing or partly fused; fruit a 2—5 seeded, round, mostly black berry with seeds compressed together. — Some 50 species in East Asia and Himalaya, one species reaching to the Phillipines.

Classification of the Genus (from Harms)

Section 1; **Eleutherococcus** (Maxim.) Harms
Pistils 5, fused together their whole length forming a column:
    A. brachypus, henryi, leucorrhizus, senticosus, setchuenensis, simonii
Section 2: **Cephalopanax** Baill.
Pistils 2, divided at least at the tip; flowers sessile or on very short stalks, twigs thorny:
    A. divaricatus, lasiogyne, sessiliflorus
Section 3: **Euacanthopanax** Harms
Pistils 2—5, more or less free standing or fused in a column halfway up, umbels single, leaflets 5, branches thorned:
    A. cissifolius, giaraldii, gracilistylus, rehderianus, setosulus, sieboldianus, stenophyllus, trichodon, wilsonii, yui
Section 4: **Xanthoxylopanax** Harms
Pistils only fused at the base or halfway, umbels 4—7 at the branch tips, seldom single, branches thorned:
    A. trifoliatus, wardii
Section 5: **Evodiopanax** Harms
Pistils 2—4, at the base or to the middle fused, umbels several in racemes or multiple umbels, branches lacking thorns:
    A. evodiaefolius, innovans
Section 6: **Sciadophylloides** Harms
Pistil 1, 2 indistinct lobes on the tip, very short, umbellate to racemose and either grouped in terminal panicles, branches lacking thorns:
    A. sciadophyllodes

Acanthopanax aculeatum see: **A. trifoliatus**

A. brachypus Harms. Shrub, 1 to 3 m, branches slender, glabrous, thorns recurved, sparse; leaves with 3—5 leaflets, very short petioles, 2—4 mm long or less, leaflets thin, obovate-oblong, 3—6 cm long, margins entire, glabrous, narrowing to the base; flowers unknown. China, Chainghsi, hills of Fuchien. Not yet in cultivation (?). Fig. 47. z6

A. cissifolius (Griff.) Harms. Shrub, to 3 m, branches without thorns or with sparse, short, thin, prickles; leaves with 5 leaflets, occasinally 3 to 4, petiole 5—12 cm long, glabrous or pubescent, often with single prickles, leaflets lanceolate to oblong, narrowing to a short petiolule at the base, 4—7 cm long, upper surface sparsely pubescent to glabrous, underside mainly pubescent along the midrib, margins frequently doubly serrate and ciliate; flowers in single, terminal umbels, with 3—5 usually free standing pistils; fruit

globular, 8 mm thick, black. Yunnan, Himalaya, temperate zones, 2000—4000 m. z6

A. divaricatus (S. & Z.) Seem. Shrub, 1—3 m high, branches sprawling, glabrous or at first somewhat pubescent, without or with some recurved prickles; leaves with 5 leaflets, long petioles, leaflets sessile or short stalked, sparsely pubescent or glabrous above, obovate-oblong to oblanceolate, 4—7 cm long, 2—4 cm wide, pointed, margins single or doubly serrate; flowers 3—7 in terminal umbels, most on short, pubescent stalks, August; fruit globose, 6—7 mm, black, with persistent, simple pistils. Japan; China, Hunan. 1901. Fig. 45. z6

A. evodiaefolius Franch. Shrub or tree, 3—12 m high, glabrous, lacking thorns; leaves crowded at the branch tips, petiolate, 3 leaflets, leaflets dissimilar, side ones sessile, base oblique, 5—10 cm long, thin, margins narrow dentate, distinctly ciliate, underside with red-brown clusters of hair at the base and vein axils (important for identification); flowers in terminal umbels, single or several, stalk glabrous; fruit 3—4 mm thick. Middle China, Yunnan, mountain forests; W. Szechwan, SE. Tibet. Fig. 46. z6

A. giraldii Harms. Shrub, 1—3 m high, branches thick with hooked or straight prickles, some 4—8 mm long; leaves with 3—5 leaflets, petiole 4—7 cm long, leaflets obovate-oblanceolate, 3—7 m long, doubly serrate, glabrous, somewhat pubescent only on juvenile foliage; flowers greenish, usually in single umbels, stalk 5—20 mm long, pistils 5, fused to the midpoint, July; fruit black, rounded, 8 mm thick. Middle China, Kansu, W. Szechwan, W. Hupeh, Sikang, mountain forests between 2000—3300 m. 1912. z6 Fig. 47.

var. **inermis** Harms & Rehd. Like the type, but the branches lacking thorns or nearly so, somewhat rough. Hupeh, Chianghsi. 1908. z6

var. **pilosulus** Rehd. Branches nearly thornless; leaflets oblanceolate, simple serrate, upper surface rough, short haired, underside short shaggy haired. Chianghsi, Hupeh. z6

A. gracilistylus W. W. Sm. Shrub, 2—3 m high, branches glabrous, thornless or with small hooked prickles; leaves with 5 (seldom 3—4) leaflets, petiole 5—8 cm long, leaflets oblanceolate, 3—6 cm long (= *A. hondae* Matsuda; *A. spinosus*, sensu Hance). China, widespread. z6 Very similar to *A. sieboldianus*, but with 2 thin, free standing pistils.

A. henryi (Oliv.) Harms. Shrub, to 3 m high, bark yellow-gray, branches prickly and rough, bristly; leaves with 5 leaflets, leaflets oblong, 3—6 cm long, upper surface rough, underside pubescent; flowers green, numerous, in terminal and axillary globose umbels, August—Sept.; fruit oblong, 8 mm long, black, with persistent thin pistil. BM 8316 (= *Eleutherococcus henryi* Oliv.). Middle China, Hupeh, 1901. z6

var. **faberi** Harms. Leaflets glabrous beneath, prominently

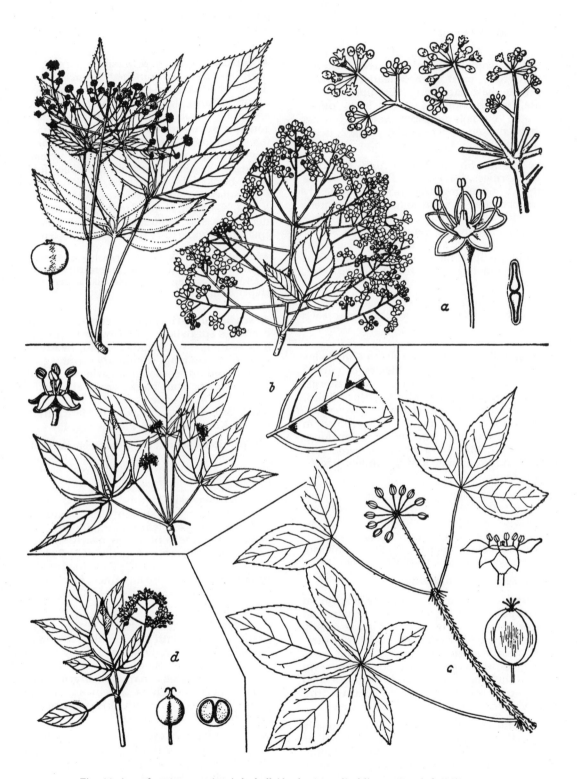

Fig. 46. **Acanthopanax.** a. *A. sciadophylloides*; b. *A. evodiaefolius*; c. *A. yui*; d. *A. innovans*.
Most 1/4 actual size (from Harms, Li and Shirasawa)

dentate; umbels small, stalk and calyx generally pubescent. Chekiang.

A. hondae see: **A. gracilistylus**

A. innovans (S. & Z.) Seem. Shrub or small tree, branches glabrous, smooth, thornless; leaves clustered on the branch tips, most with 3 leaflets, leaflets rhomboidal-ovate, base narrowing, very fine and narrowly serrate, membranous, 4–7 cm long, upper surface glabrous, vein axils pubescent beneath; flowers in loose umbels, stalked, 3–5 together, pistils 2, fused at the base. Japan. z6 Fig. 46.

A. lasiogyne Harms. Shrub, 2–6 m high, branches bright green, thornless; leaves with 3 leaflets, petiole short or long, 1.5–6 cm long, leaflets sessile or nearly so, oblong to obovate, 4–6 cm long, short pointed, base pointed, side leaflets oblique, margin nearly entire; umbels single, terminal, dense, on short stalks; flowers white, calyx and stalk densely tomentose, trichomes white, pistils 2, fused only at the base; fruit compressed, 7–9 mm long, black. China, Sikand. 1910. z6

Similar to *A. sessiliflorus*, but flower stalk is longer and pistil is free for standing; differs from *A. wardii* in the tomentose flower stalk. Fig. 47.

A. leucorrhizus (Oliv.) Harms. Shrub, to 4 m, twigs yellowish green, usually having clusters of curved prickles on the leaf petioles or nearly lacking thorns; leaflets 3–5, oblong-lanceolate, with short petiolules, leaflets 5–10 cm long, pointed, sharp doubly serrate, glabrous, leaf petiole 3–7 cm long; flowers greenish, in 4–5 cm wide umbels, July; fruit ovate, 6 mm long, black. BM 8607; BS 1: 181 (= *Eleutherococcus leucorrhizus* Oliv.). Middle and W. China, Kansu, Hupeh, Szechwan, Yunnan. z6

var. **fulvescens** Harms. Leaflets larger, to 15 cm long, veins on underside and petiolules densely pubescent. Szechwan, Yunnan. z6

var. **scaberulus** Harms & Rehd. Leaflets always 5, smaller, more lanceolate, teeth bristly tipped, veins underneath with yellowish pubescence. Chianghsi, Hupeh, Szechwan. z6

A. pentaphyllus see: **A. sieboldianus**

A. rehderianus Harms. Shrub, to 3 m, twigs thin, at first somewhat pubescent, prickles single or paired on the leaf base or sparsely scattered, stout; leaves mostly with 5 leaflets, petioles 2–7 cm long, leaflets obovate-oblanceolate, nearly sessile, narrowing to the base, 2–6 cm long, glabrous, upper surface glossy; flowers in single terminal umbels, short stalked, longer petaled flowers on the apical branchlets, pistils 4–5 fused; fruit nearly globose, black. China, Hupeh, 1200 m. z6

A. sciadophylloides Franch & Sav. Shrub, occasionally tree-like, twigs thin, glabrous, brownish in fall; leaflets 5 (occasionally 3–4), petioled, obovate to oblong, 10–20 cm long, serrate, ciliate, glabrous, dark green above lighter beneath, petiole 7–25 cm long; flowers in large, loose panicles, August–Sept.; fruit globular,

bluish black (= *Kalopanax sciadophylloides* Harms). Japan, mountainous regions. z6 Very beautiful, large leaved type. Fig. 46.

A. senticosus (Rupr. & Maxim.) Harms. Shrub, 2–5 m high, less densely branched, branches yellow-brown, dense yellowish bristles (not prickles, important for identification); leaflets 5, seldom 3, oblong-elliptic, sharp and doubly serrate, light green above, venation roughly pubescent beneath, 7–13 cm long, petiolules 0.5–2 cm long, leaf petioles 6–12 cm long; flowers yellowish (male) or pale violet to lilac (female, bisexual), several in 3–4 cm wide globose umbels, July; fruit 7 mm thick, black, juicy, bittersweet, Gfl 1863: Pl. 393; NK 16: 6 (= *Eleutherococcus senticosus* Rupr. & Maxim.). Manchuria, Korea, N. China, Hopei, Japan, Sachalin; on the fringes of deciduous and coniferous forests, but also developing thickets as understory plants, 1000–2000 m. z5 Fig. 45.

var. **subinermis** (Rgl.) Li. Branches glabrous or with few bristly prickles; leaves and inflorescence somewhat larger than with the species (= f. *inermis* Harms). Shansi, Honan, Hapei, Manchuria. z5

A. sessiliflorus (Rupr. & Maxim.) Seem. Shrub, to 4 m, branches sprawling, with few short prickles or thornless; leaflets 3 (occasionally to 5), nearly sessile, obovate, 6–15 cm long, irregularly serrate, glabrous; flowers dull red, in sessile, globose heads, mostly terminal, July–August; fruit black, broad elliptical, 10–14 mm long, in 3–4 cm wide heads. Gfl 1862: Pl. 369 (= *Panax sessiliflorus* Rupr. & Maxim.). Manchuria, N. China, Hopei, Korea. 1960. z4 Plate 9; Fig. 45.

var. **parviceps** Rehd. Low growing shrub, leaflets elliptical, 5–9 cm long, distinctly serrate; umbels usually 1–3 in a group, less than 3 cm wide; fruit ovoid, approx. 1 cm long, Hopei. 1881. z5

A. setchuenensis Harms. Shrub, 2–3 m high, glabrous, twigs yellowish, thornless or with few, straight, yellowish prickles; leaflets 3–5, oblong, 5–12 cm long, acuminate, fine toothed to nearly entire, underside gray-green; flowers in panicles of 3–7 globose umbels, the single umbels on 1–3–7 cm long stalks, July; fruit broadly elliptical, 6–8 mm thick, black, with persistent short pistil. China, Szechwan, Hupei, Shansi, 2000 m. 1904. z6 Fig. 47.

A. setosulus Franch. Shrub, 3–5 m high, rambling, branches thick with stiff bristles, a spine on the leaf base; leaves with long petioles, leaflets 5, small, some 2.5 cm long, lanceolate, sharply dentate, base margin smooth, underside venation bristly; umbels all axillary, with soft bristles. China, Szechwan. z6 Very similar to *A. sieboldianus*, but with bristly pubescence on the branches and flower stalks.

A. sieboldianus Mak. Shrub, 1–3 m high, branches wide arching, few thorns; leaflets 5 (occasionally 3 or 7), obovate-oblong, 2–9 cm long, serrate, glossy green, short petioled; flowers dioecious, greenish white, in 2–3 cm thick globose umbels, June to July;

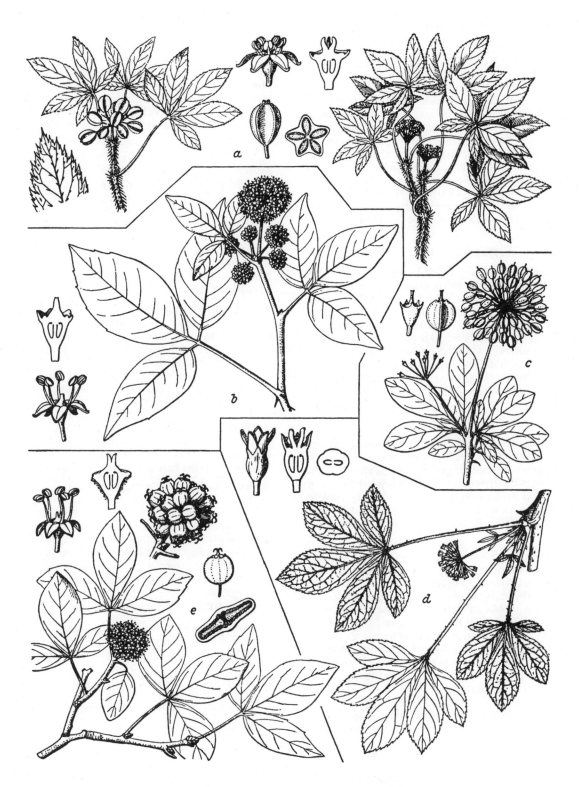

Fig. 47. **Acanthopanax.** a. *A. giraldii*; b. *A. setchuenensis*; c. *A. brachypupus*; d. *A. villosulus*; e. *A. lasiogyne*. Most 1/2 actual size (from Harms)

fruit globose, black, 6—8 mm thick (= *A. pentaphyllus* March.; *A. spinosus* Miq.). Japan; China, Anhui. 1874. z5 Fig. 45.

'Variegatus'. Grows more sparsely, leaves with white perimeter, rather rare. FS 2079; DB 1953: 52. z5

A. simonii C. Schn. Shrub, to 3 m, branches gray-brown, with few, slightly curving prickles at the leaf base; leaflets 5, oblong-lanceolate, short petioled, middle leaflet 8—12 cm long, others much shorter, sharp doubly serrate, upper surface deep green, underside blue-green, both sides with bristly spines; flowers green, insignificant, June; fruit black, in terminal globose umbels (= *Eleutherococcus simonii* Dcne.). Middle China, Hupeh, 1000—2000 m. 1901. z6 Very similar to *A. leucorrhizus*, but having bristly leaves, curving spines and inflorescences of several, short petioled umbels. Fig. 45.

A. spinosus see: **A. gracilistylus** and **A. sieboldianus**

A. stenophyllus Harms. Shrub, 2—3 m high, branches thin, glabrous or nearly so, occasionally spiny at the nodes; leaflets 3—5, petiole glabrous, 3—7 cm long, leaflets lanceolate or oblanceolate, 2—6.5 cm long, pointed, sharply single or doubly serrate, upper surface dark green, underside lighter; flowers in single and terminal umbels, stalk 0.5 cm long, glabrous, pistil 3—5, fused into a short column at the base. China, Shansi, Szechwan, 1000 m. z6 Distinguished by the exceptionally narrow leaflets and the 3—5 pistils fused at the base.

A. ternatus see: **A. wardii**

A. trichodon Franch. & Sav. Ornamental, strong branching shrub, branches thornless or with few prickles, bright green; leaflets 5, petiole with scattered small spines, leaflets nearly sessile, 5—6 cm long, 1.5—2.5 cm wide, pointed at both ends, uneven doubly serrate, teeth ending with a bristle; flowers 10-16 in terminal, long stalked umbels, pistils 2, fused nearly to the top. Japan. z6

A. trifoliatus (L.) Voss. Shrub, upright or climbing, 2—7 m high, branches gray, with scattered, strong, spines, conical shaped, broad at the base, and often recurved at the tips; leaflets usually 3 (occasionally 1—5), obovate to oblanceolate, 2—6 cm long, thin, short petioluled, pointed or obtuse, coarse or finely serrate, ciliate with short bristles, glabrous or nearly so, underside midrib often bristly; umbel glabrous, stalked, usually grouped in terminal racemes, flowers greenish, pistils usually 2, fused nearly to the middle; fruit with persistent pistil. Loddiges, Bot. Cab. Pl. 977 (as *'Panax aculeatum'*) (= *A. aculeatum* H. Witte). China; Hupeh, Yunnan, 300—1000 m; often planted as a hedge; from E. Himalaya to Japan, south to Indochina and Luzon (Philippines), widely spread. z8 Fig. 45.

A. villosulus Harms. Shrub, 1—2 m high, branches glabrous, slender, with single hooked spines at the base of short branches; leaves with long petioles, leaflets 5, sessile, oblong to obovate, distal half of leaf blade coarsely serrate, 2—6 cm long, glabrous above, loose woolly beneath; umbels single on short stalks. Middle China; E. Szechwan. Similar to *A. spinosus*, but differing in the pubescent underside of the leaf. z6 Fig. 47.

A. wardii W. W. Sm. Shrub, 1—2 m, branches gray to brown-gray, thornless or with few straight spines, usually paired under the leaf petiole base; leaflets 3, nearly sessile, ovate to oblong-obovate, 2—4 cm long, abruptly pointed, both sides glabrous and glossy, tough, margin entire or with 1—7 large teeth on either side; inflorescence of 4—7 umbels, stalk 1—2 cm long, peduncle 5—10 mm long, thin, glabrous, flowers white, October; fruit dark purple, rounded, densely packed, 7 mm wide (= *A. ternatus* Rehd.). S.W. China, Yunnan, Szechwan, Sikang, 1500—2200 m. 1905. z6 Fig. 45.

A. wilsonii Harms. Shrub, 2—3 m high, branches thin, glabrous or somewhat pubescent, thornless or with bristly spines at the nodes; leaves ornamental, leaflets 3—5, petiole glabrous, 0.5—6 cm long, leaflets oblanceolate or oblong-lanceolate, 2—5 cm long, acute or acuminate, narrowing at the base and occasionally nearly petiolate, coarsely serrate nearly to the base, glabrous, underside lighter; umbels single, terminal on 2—4 cm long stalks, pistils 3—5, fused into a short column at the base; fruit globose, black, 6—7 mm thick. China, W. Szechwan, Yunnan, 2400—4000 m. Similar to *A. sieboldianus*, but with narrower leaflets, umbels terminal, pistils fused only at the base. z5 Fig. 45.

A. yui Li. Shrub, 1 m high, branches thick, covered with thin, reflexed bristles; leaflets 3—5, petiole 4—12 cm. long, leaflets nearly sessile, 3.5—10 cm long, obovate to oblong, side leaflets often somewhat oblique and smaller, acute, base wedge-shaped, irregularly double serrate; flowers in 4 cm wide, single terminal umbels; fruits ovoid, 7 mm long, pentangular. Li, Araliaceae of China, 12 (1942). China, Yunnan. Similar to *A. giraldii*, but with tougher spines, more conical, leaflets larger, umbels larger. z6 Fig. 46.

Interesting shrubs for large open park areas, with stout thorns and long persistent, globular fruits. For sunny areas in fertile humus soil. Outside of botanic gardens, few species are available.

Lit. Harms, H., Uebersicht ueber die Arten der Gattung *Acanthopanax*; in MD 1918, 1—38, with 9 Plates ● Li, H.-L., *Acanthopanax*; in Araliaceae of China, Sargentia II, 69—90, 1942.

ACCA Berg. — MYRTACEAE

Evergreen shrubs or small trees, closely related to *Psidium*; leaves opposite, dotted; anther filament in the bud quite straight (not inward curving as with most related genera); fruit a berry. 6 species in S. America, however only the following generally found in culture.

Acca sellowiana (Berg) Burret. Evergreen shrub or small tree, branches, buds and leaf undersides tomentose with short white trichomes; leaves opposite, elliptical to ovate, 3—8 cm long, 2—4 cm wide, margin entire, apex obtuse, usually rounded at the base, upper surface glossy dark green, under white tomentose; flowers single in the lowest 2 or 4 leaf axils of the current year's growth, 3—4 cm wide, 4 petals, broad elliptic-spoon shaped, recurved at the ends, whitish with red center, sepals 4; stamens numerous, to 2.5 cm long, carmine, anthers yellow, July; fruit an ovate, 5 cm long berry, with remnants of the calyx on the tip, yellow-green, edible, tastes somewhat like a pear. BM 7620 (= *Feijoa sellowiana* [Berg] Berg). Brazil, Uruguay. 1819. Found in many botanic gardens and regularly bears fruit. z8 # ⌖ ✖

ACER L. — Maple — ACERACEAE

Deciduous or evergreen trees, occasionally small shrubs; leaves opposite, petioled, simple and usually lobed to palmate or pinnate with 3—7 leaflets; flowers usually polygamous or dioecious, small, in terminal or axillary panicles, racemes or corymbs; stamens 4—10 (usually 8); pistils or stigmas 2; fruit is 2 single seeded samaras fastened together. — Some 150 species in the northern temperate zones and in the tropical mountains; Europe, Asia, N. America, N. Africa; many species in China and Japan.

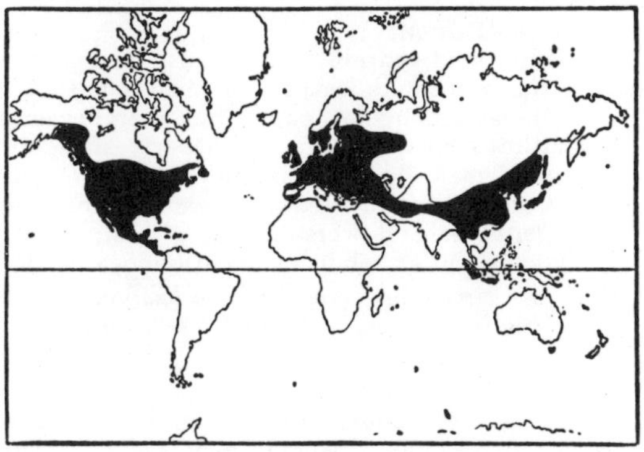

Classification of the Genus (from P. C. de Jong)*)

I. Section: **Acer**
Trees or shrubs, deciduous, occasionally evergreen (*A. sempervirens*); leaves 3—5 lobed, entire to coarsely crenate or dentate; bud scales in 5—13 pairs, imbricate, gray-brown; flowers in corymbs, terminal and axillary, in groups of 5; perianth yellowish green, flowering period frequently short and quite definite; stamens usually 8, male flowers with extended filaments; disc** extra-staminal;

A. Series **Acer**
Trees, deciduous, young twigs and buds rather thick; leaves usually 5 lobed, paper thin, margin large serrate; bud scales in 5—12 pairs; inflorescence rather large, with 25—150 flowers; fruit with ovate nutlet, occasionally somewhat keeled, with moderate tendency to parthenocarpy:
> *A. caesium, heldreichii, pseudoplatanus, trautvetteri, velutinum*

B. Series **Monspessulana** Porjark.
Trees or shrubs, deciduous or sometimes evergreen; leaves usually 3 lobed (occasionally 5), seldom simple, often leathery, margin entire or coarsely serrate; bud scales in 8—12 pairs; inflorescence with 10—50 flowers, usually on long pendulous stalks; fruit with keeled-convex nutlet, with srong tendency to parthenocarpy:
> *A. hyrcanum, monspessulanum, opalis, sempervirens*

C. Series **Saccharodendron** (Raf.) Murray
Trees, deciduous; leaves 3—5 lobed (occasionally 7), paper thin, margins entire to coarsely dentate; bud scales in 7—12 pairs; inflorescence with 10—60 flowers, stalk pendulous, terminal and frequently axillary, appearing before leaves, flowers without petals, calyx fused together; fruit with globose

Fig. 48. Distribution of the Genus *Acer*

nutlet, with strong tendency to parthenocarpy:
> *A. saccharum*

II. Section: **Platanoides** Pax
Trees and shrubs, deciduous; leaves 3—5 lobed (occasionally 7 or simple), paper thin or somewhat leathery, margin entire or sparsely dentate to serrate; bud scales in 5—8 or 8—12 pairs; flowers in corymbs, terminal or axillary, 5 flowers in a group, stamens 5 to 8, disc amphistaminal; fruit with flat nutlet, moderate tendency to parthenocarpy; seedlings with large, narrow-oblong cotyledons;

A. Series **Platanoidea**
Leaves 3—5 lobed (occasionally 7 or simple), margin entire or sparsely dentate, petiole contains a milky sap; bud scales in 5—8 pairs; inflorescence terminal, occasionally axillary, flowers with 8 stamens:
> *A. amplum, campestre, cappadocicum, catalpifolium, divergens, fulvescens, lobelii, miyabei, mono, okamotoanum, platanoides, tenellum, tibetense, truncatum, turkestanicum*

B. Series **Pubescentia** Pojark.
Leaves 3 lobed, somewhat leathery, underside blue-green, margin coarsely serrate, petiole without milky sap; bud scales in 8—12 pairs; inflorescence axillary and terminal, former partly at leafless buds, flowers with somewhat upturned petals; stamens usually 5:
> *A. pentapomicum, pilosum*

---

*) A hearty thanks is extended to Dr. P. G. de Jong for his thorough study "Flowering and sex expression in Acer L." (published 1976, Landbouwhoogeschool, Wageningen, Netherlands, 76 (2)) and for the permission to translate, summarize and quote from his systematic key.

**) The disc (being a raised, fleshy extension of the flower receptacle) can be extrastaminal (outside the stamens) or intrastaminal (between the stamens and the carpels) or amphistaminal (found on both sides of the stamens).

III. Section: **Palmata** Pax

Trees and shrubs, deciduous or (partly) evergreen, terminal buds usually or frequently stunted; leaves 3–13 lobed or unlobed, paper thin or leathery, margins serrate, occasionally entire; bud scales always in pairs; inflorescence in corymbs with flowers a cincinnus (having shortened or no peduncles or pedicels), terminal and (less often) axillary, stalk of the spent flower partly abcising, flowers 5 in a group, sepals/male red or green-red, petals usually white and involuted, stamens 8, disc extrastaminal; fruit ellipsoid-globose, never empty, slight to moderate tendency to parthenocarpy; seedlings with narrow oblong leaflets, obtuse at the tip;

A. Series **Palmata**

Trees and shrubs, deciduous, terminal buds usually stunted; leaves 5–9 lobed (occasionally to 13), nearly circular, paper thin, margins serrated; inflorescence with 5–25 flowers; stalks of the spent male flowers completley abscising, flowers occasionally with reddish petals; stamens of the spent male flowers abscising first; fruit with veined nutlet, tendency to parthenocarpy slight:

A. circinatum, japonicum, palmatum, pseudosieboldianum, pubipalmatum, robustum, shirasawanum, sieboldianum

B. Series **Sinensia** Pojark.

Trees, deciduous, terminal buds often stunted; leaves 3–7 lobed, paper thin, occasionally leathery, margin serrate, occasionally entire; inflorescence large, usually with a long stalk, 20–250 flowers, stalks of the spent flowers usually partly abscising, flowers often with somewhat reflexed sepals, petals frequently lobed, disc occasionally pubescent, in spent male flowers the anthers probably abscising first; fruit with slight tendency to parthenocarpy:

A. campbellii, erianthum, flabellatum, osmastonii, sinense, tonkinense

C. Series **Penninervia** Metcalf

Trees, sometimes evergreen, usually with terminal bud stunted; leaves simple, leathery, margin entire or serrate; all other morphological characteristics as with Series *Sinensia*:

A. cordatum, fabri, laevigatum, sino-oblongum

IV. Section: **Macrantha** Pax

Trees and frequently shrubs, deciduous; leaves simple or 3–5 lobed (occasionally to 7), often with a tail-like, drawn out tip, margin serrate; bud scales always in 2 pairs, valvate, red or green-red; inflorescence racemose or corymbose, terminal and axillary, 10–25 flowers, each with 5 petals or sepals; perianth green-yellow or reddish; stamens 8; fruit with flat nutlet, occasionally globose, tendency to parthenocarpy from moderate to weak;

A. Series **Tegmentosa** Pojark.

Small branches often with chalk white stripes, axillary buds stalked; bud scales always in 2 pairs, valvate; inflorescence in simple racemes, 10–25 flowers; perianth green-yellow or green-red, disc intrastaminal; fruit with convex nutlet, frequently rather flat, with one side convex and the other convex with a depression in the middle or concave (infertile pathenocarpic fruit); seedlings with small, elliptical cotyledons:

A. capillipes, crataegifolium, davidii, forrestii, grosseri, hookeri, laxiflorum, maximowiczii, micran-thum, pectinatum, pensylvanicum, rufinerve, sikkimense, taronense, tegmentosum, tschonoskii

B. Series **Wardiana** de Jong

Small trees or shrubs, young twigs stiffly pubescent; leaves 3 lobed, margin serrate; inflorescence upright, in corymbs, with small cincinni, secondary axes opposite; bracts very noticeable; flowers with red perianth, reflexed at the end of the blooming period; disc amphistaminal; spent male flowers lose the stamens first; fruit with rather flat nutlet:

A. wardii

V. Section: **Parviflora** Koidzumi

Trees and shrubs, deciduous; leaves 3 lobed (occasionally 5–7 or simple), paper thin, margin serrate; bud scales in 2 or occasionally 3 pairs; inflorescences large, in corymbs, long stalks with cincinni terminal and axillary, 35–400 flowers, petals 5, perianth green-white; stamens usually 8; disc amphi- or intrastaminal; end of the flowering period some weeks after general bud break; fruit with only slight tendency to parthenocarpy;

A. Series **Parviflora**

Trees, with rather thick branches; leaves large, 3–5 lobed, margin doubly serrate; bud scales always in 2 pairs; inflorescences very large, in long pendulous panicles, red-brown pubescence, 150–400 or more flowers, flowers with a small perianth, glabrous, disc intrastaminal, light rust-brown pubescence; seedlings with large, narrow-oblong cotyledons obtuse at the tip:

A. nipponicum

B. Series **Ukurunduensia** de Jong

Small trees or shrubs; leaves 3 to 5 lobed (occasionally to 7), underside pubescent, margin serrate; bud scales in 2, sometimes 3 pairs; inflorescences upright, stalk of the spent male flowers partly abcising, 50–200 flowers, flowers with narrow, white petals, twice as long as the pubescent, greenish sepals; disc lobed, partly amphistaminal, partly intrastaminal; in spent male flowers the petals and stamens abcise first; fruit with small nutlet, flat, veined, occasionally pubescent, one side convex, the other somewhat concave; seedlings with small, narrow elliptical cotyledons;

A. spicatum, ukurunduense

C. Series **Distyla** (Ogata) Murray

Trees; leaves simple, deeply cordate, margin crenate; bud scales always in 2 pairs, valvate, brownish, pubescent; inflorescence upright, red-brown haired, with 35 to 70 flowers, having pubescent sepals, disc lobed, stamens fused between the lobes; fruit with an elliptic-convex nutlet, young fruit with a rust-brown pubescence, seedlings with narrow elliptical cotyledons:

A. distylum

VI. Section: **Trifoliatae** Pax

Trees or shrubs, bark sometimes peeling; leaves pinnate, 3 leaflets, paper thin, margins nearly entire or coarsely serrate; bud scales in 11–15 pairs, gray-brown; inflorescences usually with 3, occasionally to 25 flowers (*A. sutchuenense*), racemose, sometimes corymbose, terminal and axillary, flowers with 5(–6) petals or sepals, perianth yellow-green; stamens 10–13; disc extrastaminal, sometimes amphistaminal; fruit large, hemispherical convex, with a thick, woody shell; strong tendency to pathenocarpy:

A. griseum, mandshuricum, nikoense, sutchuen-

ense, triflorum

VII. Section: **Rubra** Pax

Trees, deciduous, axillary buds, many on the flowering branches; leaves 3—5 lobed, underside blue-green, margin serrate; bud scales in 4—8 pairs, red; inflorescenses clustered-umbellate, usually with 5 flowers, axillary, from leafless buds; flowers in groups of 5, perianth red, sometimes green-red, petals and disc occasionally absent and the sepals fused (*A. saccharinum*), stamens usually 5, disc intrastaminal, flowering ends just before leaf development; fruit with small nutlet, somewhat convex or large and obovoid, ripen in early summer, slight tendency to parthenocarpy; seedlings with thick, fleshy, obovate or narrow obovate, underground cotyledons:

A. pycnanthum, rubrum, saccharinum

VII: I. Section: **Ginnala** Nakai

Shrubs or small trees, deciduous; leaves simple or 3 lobed, paper thin, margin serrate; bud scales in 5—10 pairs, gray-brown; inflorescence in terminal and axillary corymbs, with distinct bracts, flowers in groups of 5, perianth greenish white, during the flowering period somewhat rolled inwards; stamens 8, disc extrastaminal; flowering period immediately after leaf development; fruit with rather flat nutlet, elliptic, distinctly veined; seedlings with small, elliptic cotyledons:

A. aidzuense, ginnala, semenovii, tataricum

IX. Section: **Lithocarpa** Pax

Large trees, deciduous, branches rather thick; leaves large, 3—5 lobed, occasionally nearly simple, paper thin, margin fine lobed or entire, sometimes serrate; bud scales 5—8 or 8—12 pairs; inflorescences in racemes or corymbs, peduncle long, flower large, 5(—6) in a group, perianth greenish yellow; stamens 8—12, disc amphistaminal; fruit with small, keeled, convex nutlet, usually covered with stiff hairs, with strong tendency to parthenocarpy; seedlings with narrow-oblong, obtuse cotyledons;

A. Series **Lithocarpa**

Trees, dioecious; leaves 3—5 lobed, occasionally nearly simple, margin sparsely toothed to finely serrate (sometimes entire), petiole now and then contains milky sap; bud scales in 8—12 pairs, gray-brown; inflorescences racemose (occasionally partly in corymbs), axillary from leafless buds, 10—20 flowers, in groups of 5, perianth sometimes fused (in male plants of *A. diabolicum* and *A. sinopurpurascens*), usually with 8 stamens:

A. diabolicum, franchetii, sinoprupurascens, sterculiaceum, thomsonii

B. Series **Macrophylla** Pojark.

Trees, monoecious; leaves deeply 5 lobed, margin fine lobed to entire, petiole with milky sap; bud scales in 5—8 pairs, green-red, inflorescences large, in corymbs, 30—80 flowers, terminal and axillary, flowers in groups of 5—6:

A. macrophyllum

X. Section: **Negundo** (Boehmer) Maxim.

Trees or shrubs, deciduous, dioecious; leaves paper thin, compound, leaflets 3 or pinnate with 5—7 leaflets, margins entire or sparsely dentate; bud scales in 2—3 pairs; inflorescences in simple or compound racemes, axillary from leafless buds or also with 1—2 pair of smaller, quickly abcising leaves, 15—50 flowers, flowers in groups of 4, stamens 4—6, absent in female flowers; fruit with small, elliptic-globose, to rather flat, veined nutlet, tendency to parthenocarpy strong; seedlings with narrow-oblong cotyledons;

A. Series **Negundo**

Leaves pinnately compound, with 3—7 leaflets (occasionally to 9); bud scales in 2, usually in 3 pairs; inflorescences in racemes (in female plants) or in compound racemes with long pendulous stalks, flowers without petals, greenish, disc absent, wind pollinated, flowering period ends before development of leaves:

A. negundo

B. Series **Cissifolia** (Koidzumi) Pojark.

Leaves trifoliate; bud scales in 2 pairs; inflorescence in racemes with long peduncle, 15—30 flowers, in groups of 4, sepals and petals very different, greenish white or yellow; stamens 4—6; disc amphistaminal, insect pollinated; flowering period ends during the leaf development:

A. cissifolium, henryi

XI. Section: **Glabra** Pax

Trees and shrubs, deciduous; leaves paper thin, simple or 3—5 lobed (occasionally partly trifoliate), margin serrate; bud scales in 2—4 pairs; inflorescence small, in racemes or corymbs, terminal and (often exclusively) axillary, 10—25 flowers, in groups of 4—5, yellowish, disc amphi- to intrastaminal; fruit with flat, smooth nutlet, prominent venation, tendency to parthenocarpy strong; seedlings with small, obovate cotyledons;

A. Series **Glabra**

Shrubs or small trees; leaves 3 lobed (occasionally 5 or partly trifoliate); bud scales in 2—4 pairs; inflorescences in corymbs or simple racemes, terminal and axillary, flowers in groups of 5; stamens 8; disc amphi-to intrastaminal:

A. glabrum

B. Series **Arguta** (Rehder) Pojark.

Trees and shrubs, dioecious; leaves undivided or 3—5 lobed; inflorescences of male plants axillary from leafless buds, on female plants terminal and axillary from mixed buds, flowers in groups of 4; stamens 4(—6), usually absent in the female flowers; disc amphi- to intrastaminal:

A. acuminatum, argutum, barbinerve, stachyophyllum

XII. Section: **Integrifolia** Pax

Trees, usually evergreen; leaves simple or 3 lobed (occasionally compound, 5—7 lobe palmate), underside usually blue-green, margin entire or finely serrate; bud scales in 4 to 7 pairs, gray-brown; inflorescences in corymbs, with distinct bracts, terminal and axillary, with 25—75 flowers, flowers in groups of 5, perianth yellow-white, petals longer than the sepals; stamens usually 8, disc extrastaminal; fruit with convex, keeled nutlet, tendency to parthenocarpy strong; seedlings with narrow, oblong, small, acuminate cotyledons;

A. Series **Trifida** Pax

Leaves usually evergreen, simple or 3 lobed, margin entire or finely serrate:

A. albopurpurascens, buergerianum, coriaceifolium, oblongum, paxii, yui

B. Series **Pentaphylla** (Hu & Cheng) Murray

Leaves compound, 5 lobed (occasionally to 7), palmate, margin entire to serrate:

A. pentaphyllum

XIII. Section: **Indivisa** Pax

Small trees or shrubs, deciduous, terminal buds usually stunted, dioecious; leaves simple, venation pronounced, side veins parallel as with *Carpinus*, margin doubly serrate; bud scales in 9–13 pairs, brown; inflorescence racemose, axillary and terminal, from mixed buds, 10–20 flowers, in groups of 4, perianth greenish yellow, male flowers often without petals; stamens usually 6, disc amphistaminal to intrastaminal; fruit with flat, glabrous nutlet, strong tendency to parthenocarpy; seedlings with narrow-oblong, acuminate cotyledons:

A. carpinifolium

XIV. Section: **Hyptiocarpa** Fang

Trees, evergreen, occasionally deciduous; leaves simple, leathery, underside blue-green, margin entire; bud scales in 7–11 pairs; inflorescences in corymbs or simple racemes, axillary from leafless buds, flowers in groups of 5, perianth yellowish; stamens 4–6, 8 or 8–12, disc usually amphistaminal, occasionally nearly extra- or intrastaminal; fruit with large obovoid nutlet, tendency to pathenocarpy strong:

A. garrettii

Acer acuminatum Wall. In its native habitat a small tree, young twigs purple-brown, glabrous, not striped; leaves 3(–5) lobed, 6–11 cm long, base shallow cordate, lobes triangular, long caudate, doubly serrate, upperside dark green, underside lighter green, glossy, glabrous to short pubescence in the vein axils, young leaves reddish; flowers in short racemes, yellow, April; fruit 3–4 cm long, wings spread at right angles. GC 15: 68 (1881); SDK 4: 68 (= *A. caudatum* Nichols. non Wall.). W. Himalaya, mountain forests. 1825. Cultivated in England. z7

A. albopurpurascens Hayata. Evergreen tree, to 15 m, branches at first pubescent, later glabrous; leaves tough, leathery, oblong-lanceolate, 6–13 cm long, 2.5–5 cm wide, acuminate, base obtuse to wedge shaped, upperside light green and glabrous, underside reddish white to blue-green, in youth densely pubescent, base faintly 3 veined, basal vein short, somewhat elevated to indistinct, axillary veins to 7–10 pairs, branching at right angles, petiole 1.5–3 cm bluish; fruit cymose; wings nearly at right angles, 2 cm long, nutlet glabrous. LT 753 (= *A. oblongum* Wall. non DC.). China; Taiwan. z8 #

A. ambiguum see: **A. mono**

A. amoenum see: **A. palmatum** var. **amoenum**

A. amplum Rehd. Tree, in its habitat 10 to 25m, bark gray, smooth, young branches green, punctate, glabrous; leaves 3–5 lobed, 8–10 cm wide, lobes oblong, abruptly pointed, nearly leathery, upper surface glossy dark green, underside light green, glabrous, petiole 5–12 cm long, thin; inflorescence loose, 10–15 cm long; wings 3 cm long, 1 cm wide, spread at a wide angle. Middle China; Yunnan, Hupeh, Kiangsi, 700–2000 m. 1937. Presumably quite hardy. z6

var. **tientaiense** Rehd. Only 6–7 m high, like the species but leaves smaller, usually 3 lobed, lobes longer, narrower; fruit smaller, wings smaller. Middle China; Chekiang, Tien Tai

Shan; 1200 m. z6 (In Les Barres in Culture.) Hardy.

A. angustilobum see: **A. wilsonii**

A. argutum Maxim. Pointed Leaf Maple. Tree, to 8 m high, in Northern Europe usually shrubby, young twigs more or less pubescent, reddish; leaves wider than long, broadly ovate, usually 5 lobed (occasionally 7), lobes ovate, acuminate, narrow and sharp (occasionally double) serrate, upper side deep green, light green beneath, sparse gray pubescence on the veins, yellow autumn foliage, petiole 2–6 cm long; flowers greenish yellow, glabrous, distinctly 4 petalled, in pendulous, clustered racemes, April–May; fruit wings horizontal. KRA 14; ST 66. Japan, Hondo, mountain forests, to 2000 m. 1881. z6 Hardy. Plate 11; Fig. 52.

A. barbatum see: **A. rubrum**

A. barbinerve Maxim. Shrub or small tree, young twigs reddish, at first pubescent, becoming glabrous, new growth light brown; leaves 5 lobed, 6–10 cm long, coarse doubly serrate, young leaves pubescent underneath, later only on the venation, petiole 4–9 cm long; flowers yellow, in short clusters of 4–6, female in 6 cm long racemes, April; fruit wings form an obtuse angle, with the nutlet 35 mm log. ST 86; SDK 4: 68. Manchuria, in the valleys of upper Ussuri. 1867. Similar to *A. argutum*, but fruit larger and leaves larger toothed. z6 Fig. 49, 52.

A. bodinieri see: **A. mono**

A. × bornmuelleri Borb. (*A. campestre* × *A. monspessulanum*). Small tree, similar to *A. campestre*, twigs glabrous; leaves ornamental, 3–5 lobed, 5–6 cm wide, base cordate, glabrous, paper thin, upperside somewhat glossy, under eventually quite glabrous; fruit wings horizontal, with nutlet 2.5 cm long. SE Europe, Yugoslavia (Herzegovina), allegedly also in Greece. z6

A. × boscii Spach. (*A. monspessulanum* × *A. tataricum*). Medium shrub or small tree, similar to *A. tataricum*, twigs reddish green, at first pubescent, later glabrous; leaves wide obovate, at the tip usually 3 lobed, 8–9 cm long, eventually glabrous, paper thin, base round, shallowly cordate, crenate to doubly serrate, petiole thin, 4 cm long; flowers in 4 to 5 cm long, few flowered, pendulous racemes; fruit wings glabrous, curving upward, nearly parallel. Before 1834. (Fig. DL 2: 420 is wrong!) z6

A. brevilobum see: **A. nipponicum**

A. buergerianum Miq. Three Toothed Maple. In its habitat a tall tree, young branches glabrous; leaves 3 lobed, 4–8 cm wide, to 10 cm long, base cuneate from the midpoint but rounded at the point of attachment, 3 veined, lobes pointed, margin entire to slightly crenate, dark green above, blue-green beneath, pubescent only when juvenile, thin; petiole 3–7 cm long, thin; flowers yellowish, pubescent, in wide corymbose panicles, May; fruit wings upright, parallel, often touching each other, KRA 17 (as *A. trifidum*) (= *A. trifidum* Hook. & Arn.). Mountain forests of Japan, Hondo, Kiuschiu, E. China. 1890. z6 Plate 11; Fig. 49, 53.

var. **formosanum** (Hayata) Sasaki. Leaves less lobed, lobed 3, obtuse, base cordate, wings outspread. KRA 17. Formosa. z6 Fig. 53.

var. **ningpoense** (Hance) Rehd. Like the species, but lobes directed sidewards; leaves more blue-green and pubescence depressed. China, Fukien, Hupeh, 100−400 m. z6

var. **trinerve** (Siesmayer) Rehd. Shrub, 3−6 m high; leaves with 3 deep narrow lobes, these irregularly dentate to doubly serrate; fruit wings outspread. China, Kiangsi. z6

A. buntzleri see: **A. platanoides** 'Buntzeli'

A. caesium Wall. Tree, to 25 m in its habitat, bark gray; leaves 5 lobed, thin, 18 to 20 cm wide, 12−14 cm long, 5−7 veins at the base, deeply cordate, lobes caudate, double serrate, underside blue-green, eventually glabrous, basal lobes very small; flowers in large corymbs, petals and sepals of similar length, greenish white, fruit wings 4−5 cm long, spread at right angles. China; Yunnan, Szechwan, mountain forests, 2000−3000 m. z6 Ⓕ Himalaya; from the Indus River to Nepal. Fig. 53.⊘

ssp. **giraldii** (Pax) E. Murray. Tree, in its habitat to 18 m, young branches reddish, densely punctate, white striped, with triangular leaf scars, glabrous, buds many scaled; leaves usually 3 lobed, basal lobes very small, crenate, upperside deep green, glossy, underside blue-green, reticulate venation, axils along the midrib haired, 9−11 cm long, 10−13 cm wide, thick leathery, lobes ovate, pointed, base shallowly cordate, petiole 10−15 cm long, thick, red; flowers in pruinose corymbs; fruit wings 5 cm long, 2 cm wide, upright, parallel (= *A. giradlii* Pax). Middle China; W. Szechwan, Shansi, Thae-pei-san Mountains, 2400 m. z5 Similar to *A. caesium*, but points of lobes shorter, smaller at the base, fruit smaller.

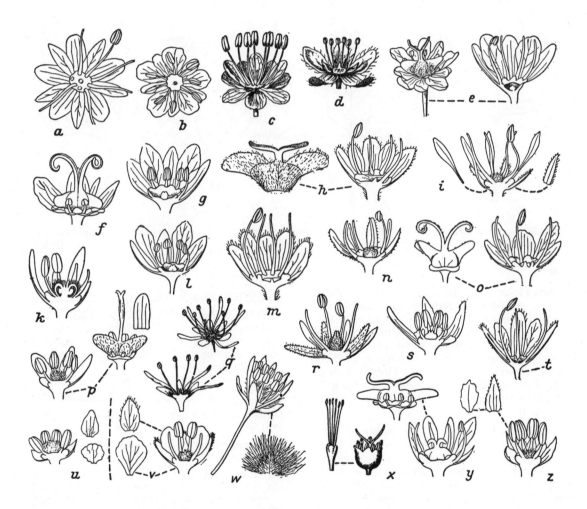

Fig. 49. **Acer** flowers, twice actual size. a. *A. thomsonii*; b. *A. capillipes*; c. *A. monspessulanum*; d. *A. circinatum*; e. *A. rufinerve*; f. *A. veitchii*; g. *A. crataegifolium*; h. *A. franchetii*; i. *A. ukurunduense*; k. *A. buergerianum*; l. *A. tegmentosum*; m. *A. sterculiaceum*; n. *A. distylum*; o. *A. stachyophyllum*; p. *A. sinense*; q. *A. spicatum*; r. *A. caudatum*; s. *A. rodustum*; t. *A. barbinerve*; u. *Campbellii*; v. *A. oviverianum*; w. *A. paxii*; ×. *A. saccharinum*; y. *A. sikkinense*; z. *a. wilsonii* (from Hempel and Wilhelm, Nicholson, Sargent, Schneider, Shirasawa)

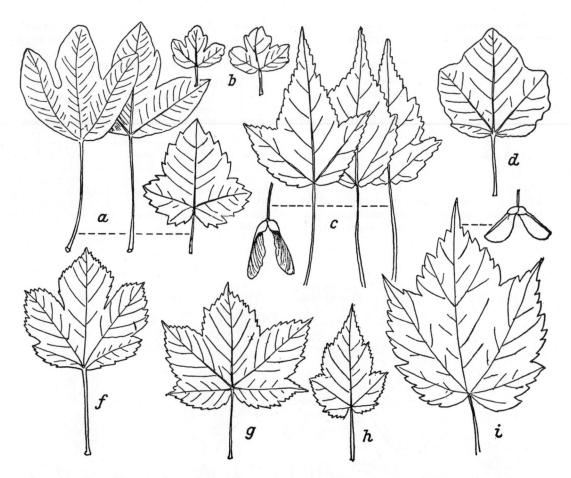

Fig. 50. a. *Acer monspessulanum* var. *bornmuelleri*, 2 mature and (right) one juvenile leaves; b. *A. monspessulanum* var. *paxii*; c. *A. pycnanthum*; d. *A. rotundilobum*; f. *A. ramosum*; g. *A. sericeum*; h. *A. veitchii*; i. *A. spicatum* (from Schwerin, Koidzumi)

A. campbellii Hook. f. & Thoms. Tree, in its habitat 18—20 m high, young twigs reddish, glabrous; leaves 5—7 lobed, 9—12 cm long, 12—15 cm wide, lobes nearly alike, ovate and caudate, sharply serrate to the tip, base rounded, not serrate, underside eventually glabrous; flowers appearing after the leaves, in slender, to 15 cm long panicles, flowers small, petals white, May; fruit wings nearly horizontally spread, some 2.5 cm long, E. Himalaya; mountain forests of Sikkim. 1934. z7 ⓕ W. Himalaya. Fig. 49.

A. campestre L. Hedge Maple. Tree, rarely to 15 m high, usually much shorter, crown rounded, twigs split or cracked, often with corky bark; leaves 3—5 lobed, lobes at obtuse angles, middle lobe often further 3 lobed, upper side dull green, underside pubescent, leaf petiole with milky sap, fall color yellow; flowers greenish, in upright, pubescent corymbs, May; fruit with horizontally spread wings, 2.5—3 cm long. HM 1856. Europe, Asia Minor. Good hedging plant, likes sandy-clay chalk soil, heat tolerant. z6 Long history of cultivation. ⓕ Yugoslavia, Denmark, USSR. Fig. 57.

Numerous variations:

(Botanical) var.	Habits of Growth	Foliage Color
var. *austriacum*	'Fastigiatum'	'Albo-maculatum'
var. *hebecarpum*	'Nanum'	'Albo-variegatum'
var. *leiocarpum*	'Pendulum'	'Laetum'
var. *tauricum*		'Postelense'
		'Pulverulentum'
		'Schwerinii'

'Albo-maculatum' (Schwerin). Leaves whitish, fruit glabrous. 1901. ⌀

'Albo-variegatum'. Leaves with large white patches, fruit pubescent. 1822. ⌀

var. *austriacum* (Tratt.) DC. Grows tree-like, leaves 5 lobed, tough to nearly leathery, lobes nearly entire, pointed, margin somewhat undulate, underside glabrous. SE. Europe, Eastern Mediterranean. z6 Fig. 51.

'Elsrijk' (C. P. Broerse). Selection from Holland (Amstelveen). 1953. Broadly conical growth, very dense, as an older tree more broadly ovate; leaves rather small, 4—6 cm, dark green. First rate small street tree.

'Fastigiatum'. Tree, branches distinctly corky, grows strictly up-right, columnar; leaves 5 lobed, underside pubescent. 1930. Found in the wild in SW. Germany.

var. **hebecarpum** DC. This is the typical form, fruit pubescent, leaves often tomentose on the underside. Fig. 51.

'Laetum' (Schwerin). Grows upright, new growth not reddish, leaves light green. 1893. ∅

var. **leiocarpon** Wallroth. A typical form but with glabrous fruit. SE. Europe.

'Nanum'. Grows upright, shrubby, dense and rounded (= 'Compactum'). 1874.

'Pendulum' (Schwerin). Branches very pendulous, leaves green. 1893.

'Postelense' (Lauche). Shrub, young leaves gold-yellow, later light green-yellow, buds and leaf petioles bright red, fruit glabrous. Found by Von Salisch in Postel near Mititsch, Silesia, Prussia (Poland), introduced into the trade in 1896 by Lauche. Best color in full sun. Fig. 51. ∅

'Pulverulentum' (Booth, ex Kirchn.). Leaves usually with a fine white dust, isolated green areas. 1859. ∅

'Schwerinii' (Hesse). Strong upright grower; leaves opening blood red, later more dull red, dark green in summer. 1897. ∅

var. **tauricum** (Kirchn.) Pax. Weaker growing, leaves 3–5 lobed, lobes blunt tipped, lobes further short lobed, 5–7 cm long and wide, underside pubescent; fruit pubescent.

'Zorgvlied' (C. P. Broerse). Dutch selection from Amstelveen. 1953. Crown narrowly ovate, similar to 'Elsrijk', but weaker growing.

A. campestre × *A. lobalii* see: **A.** × **zoeschense**

A. campestre × *A. monspessulanum* see: **A.** ˙× **bornmuelleri**

A. campestre × *A. pseudoplatanus* see: **A. ramosum**

A. capillipes Maxim. Tree, in its habitat to 12 m high, bark brown-green, white striped, young branches red, glabrous to slightly pruinose, new growth red, glabrous; leaves 3 lobed, 6–10 cm long, lobes acute, side lobes pointing outward, much shorter, doubly serrate, upperside dark green, dull, underside light green, glabrous, usually red veined, fall foliage carmine; flowers in glabrous pendulous racemes, petals greenish white, May; fruit wings usually horizontal, 2.5 cm long. ST 16; KRA 10; BS 1: 190. Japan, Hondo, mountain forests. 1892. z6 Plate 10 and 16; Fig. 49, 55. ∅ ⚭

Often confused with *A. grosseri* and cultivated under this name.

A. cappadocicum Gleditsch. Caucasian Maple. Tree, to 20 m, young twigs often pruinose, in 2nd year glossy green; leaves 5–7 lobed, 8–14 cm wide, lobes triangular, acuminate, margin entire, glossy green; underside finely reticulate, in fall a splendid gold-yellow; flowers in corymbs, light yellow, May–June; fruit with wings 3–5 cm long, widely spread. SDK 4: 51 (= *A. laetum* C. A. Mey.; *A. colchicum* Booth ex Gord.). Caucasus, Asia Minor to Himalaya. z6 Fig. 54. ∅

'Aureum'. Leaves in spring and fall yellow, otherwise bright green. 1914.

var. **cultratum** (Wall.) Bean. Pax has placed under this heading

Fig. 51. a. *Acer campestre* var. *hebecarpum*; b. *A. campestre* 'Postelense'; c. *A. capestre* var. *austriacum*; d. *A. erianthum*; e. *A. zoeschense*, with fruit; f. *A. zoeschense* 'Elongatum'; g. *A. saccharum* ssp. *grandidentatum* (Original)

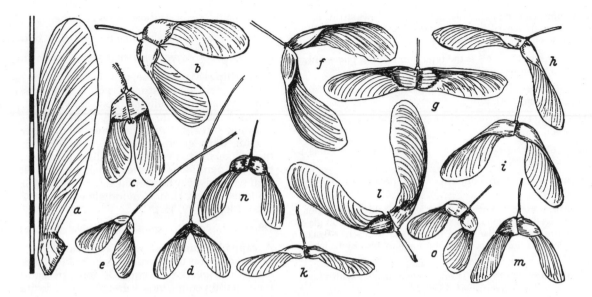

Fig. 52. **Acer** fruits. a. *A. thompsonii*; b. *A. franchetii*; c. *A. diabolicum*; d. *A. rubrum*; e. *A. pycnanthum*; f. *A. saccharinum*; g. *A. circinatum*; h. *A. barbinerve*; i. *A. stachyophyllum*; k. *A. argutum*; l. *A. stachyophyllum*; m. *A. saccharum* ssp. *nigrum*; n. *A. saccharum*; o. *A. saccharum* ssp. *grandidentatum* (Original)

all the eastern subspecies of *A. cappadocicum* from Persia to China, having much tougher leaves than the species, always only 5 lobed and bases truncate, wings of the fruit horizontal. z6 Within this group, however, the var. *sinicum* and var. *tricaudatum* can be distinguished.

var. **indicum** (Pax) Rehd. Small tree, 6–8 m high, young twigs not pruinose, reddish brown, with lenticels; leaves on both sides along midrib with silky hairs, also on the petiole; fruit wings wider and more reddish. Himalaya to Yunnan, mountain forests, 2500 m. z6 ⌀

'Rubrum'. Leaves when young blood red, later generally greening, young branches red (= *A. laetum* 'Rubrum', *A. colchicum* 'Rubrum'). 1842. ⌀

var. **sinicum** Rehd. Tree, to 20 m high, young branches reddish brown, densely punctate; leaves usually 5 lobed, base cordate to truncate, 6–10 cm wide; flowers yellow-green, in corymbs; wings twice as long as the nutlet. Himalaya to Yunnan, mountain forests, 2300–3100 m, chalk free soils, near water. z6

var. **tricaudatum** (Rehd.) Rehd. To 9 m high, bark dark gray, scaly, young twigs gray, glabrous; leaves tri-lobed, lobes caudate; fruit wings at right angles. JRHS 29, 357. W. Hupeh, 2000 to 3300 m. z6

'Tricolor' (Gouchault ex Carriere). Young twigs pink-red; young leaves at first pink, later white powdered and marbled. Rev. Hort. Belg. 1886; Pl. 1886. ⌀

A. carpinifolium S. & Z. Hornbeam Maple. Tree, to 10 m, grows broadly upright, twigs thin, glabrous; leaves long ovoid, 8–12 cm long, acute, sharply double serrate, usually pubescent on underside at the base of the veins; flowers greenish, 1 cm wide, few grouped in short racemes, May; fruit glabrous, wings at right angles, bowed inwards, 2.5–3 cm long. KRA 8. Japan, mountain forests to subalpine altitudes. 1879. z6 Plates 13 and 16; Fig. 55. ⌀

A. catalpifolium Rehd. Tree, to 20 m, bark gray, smooth, inner bark reddish brown, young twigs densely punctate; leaves ovate to long ovoid, 10–20 cm long, undivided or with 2 rounded lobes on the base, abruptly acute, underside pubescent, reticulate venation; flowers in large, loose, sessile cymes; wings spread at a very wide angle, with nutlet 4–5 cm long. FIO 129; ICS 3128 (= *A. chunii* Fang). China; W. Szechwan, Sikiang, 500–1000 m. z6 Fig. 66. ⌀

A. caudatifolium Hayata. Deciduous tree, 10–20 m, branches glabrous; leaves thin, ovate, 6 to 10 cm long, 5–8 cm wide, truncate to shallow cordate, base 5 veined, with 5–6 pair of axillary veins, margin doubly serrate, underside glabrous, flattened 5 lobed, middle lobe short ovate, acuminate, side lobes smaller and acute to obtuse, petiole 5–7 cm; flowers in racemes; fruit small, wings spread at an obtuse angle, nutlet 1.8 to 2.3 cm long and 6–7 mm wide. LT 785; ICS 3149 (as *A. kawakamii*) (= *A. kawakamii* Koidz.; *A. rubescens* Hayata; *A. morrisonense* Hayata; *A. ovatifolium* Koidz.). China, Taiwan, in mountain forests, 1800–2300 m. z8 Fig. 69.

A. caudatum Wall. ex Rehd. Tall tree, young twigs glabrous, ash gray; leaves 5 lobed, blade 7–12 cm long and wide, lobes triangular-ovate, acuminate, large and sharp double serrate to fine lobed, underside more or less yellowish brown or light brown pubescent, petiole 7–10 cm long, base finely pubescent; flowers in upright, spiked panicles, monecious, stalk and all pedicels pubescent; fruit in some 10 cm long panicles, stalk 4–6 mm, wings rising, 2.5–3 cm long with nutlet, the latter 10 mm wide. FIO 134 (= *A. papilio* King). E. Himalaya, Upper Burma. In cultivation in England. z6 Fig. 49. (See also: *A. acuminatum* and *A. multiserratum*.) ⌀

Plate 1

Acacia melanoxylon
as street tree in North Spain

Acer Griseum
in a English park

Acer macrophyllum
in its native habitat, Oregon, USA

Astelia petriei
in a garden in Ireland

Plate 2

Acacia longifolia

Actinidia kolomikta

Adenocarpus decorticans

Aethionema grandiflorum

Plate 3

Aesculus × mutabilis 'Induta',
in the Dortmund Botanic Garden, W. Germany

Aesculus × carnea

Cistus ladanifer

Aesculus neglecta 'Erythroblasta',
spring foliage

Plate 4

Berberis thunbergii 'Aurea'

Albizia julibrissin 'Rosea'

Aloe dichotoma,
in a South African garden

Atherosperma moschatum,
in a Scottish garden

Plate 5

Abeliophyllum distichum   Photo: I. E. Downward

Abelia zanderi, in the Botanic Garden at Lausanne, Switzerland   Photo: E. Hahn

Plate 6

Abelia floribunda
Archive Verlag, W. Germany

Abutilon megapotamicum
Photo: E. Hahn

Acacia verticillata
Photo: I. E. Downward

Plate 7

Acacia. a. *A. verticillata*; b. *A. longifolia*; c. *A. horrida*; d. *A. dealbata*; e. *A. melanoxylon*

Plate 8

Acantholimon glumaceum   *Acacia decurrens,* in East Portlemouth, S. England

Acantholimon armenum, cultivar   Photo: E. Nussbaumer

Plate 9

Acer trautvetteri

Archive Duetsche Baumschule, W. Germany

Acanthopanax sessiliflorus, flowers and fruit   Photo: C. R. Jelitto

Plate 10

Acer negundo var. *californicum*,
Morton Arboretum, U.S.A.

Acer negundo 'Crispum',
Belmonte Arboretum, Wageningen, Holland

Acer capillipes with fruit

Acer palmatum 'Ornatum'

Acer pseudoplatanus 'Prinz Handjery'

Acer palmatum 'Reticulatum'

Plate 11

Acer a. *A. negundo*, trifoliate, a1 quinquefoliate; b. *A. henryi*; c. *A. cissifolium*; d. *A. mandshuricum*; e. *A. griseum*
f. *A. nikoense*; g. *A. tataricum*; h1-h4. *A. ginnala*; i. *A. wilsonii*; k. *A. rotundilobrum*; l. *A. orientale*;
m. *A. argutum*; n. *A. oblongum*; o. *A. tetramerum* var. tiliifoliuim; p. *A. tetramerum* var. *betulifolium*;
q1–3. *A. buergerianum*, q3 leaf from a young plant; r. *A. oliverianum*

Plate 12

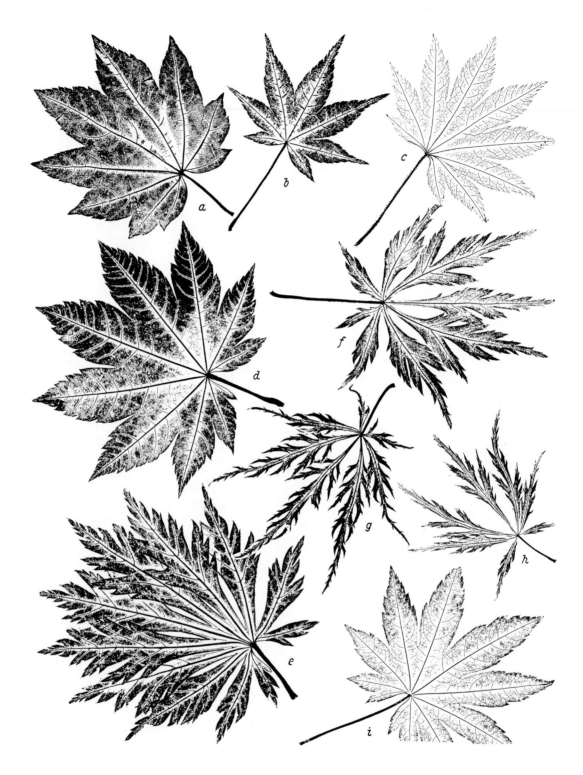

Acer. a. *A. circinatum*; b. *A. palmatum* (spp); c. *A. sieboldianum*; d. *A. japonicum*; e. (lower left) *A. japonicum* 'Aconitifolium'; f. *A. palmatum* 'Dissectum'; g. *A. palmatum* 'Rubrifolium' (green); h. *A. palmatum* 'Ornatum' (red); i. *A. pseudosieboldianum*

Plate 13

Acer carpinifolium   *Acer platanoides* in full bloom in spring

Acer negundo 'Crispum Variegatum'   *Acer negundo* 'Variegatum'

Plate 14

Acer griseum, typical bark

Acer japonicum 'Aureum'

Plate 15

Acer glabrum in native habitat in the Rocky Mountains
Photo: US Forest Service

Acer saccharum in native habitat in Pisgah National Forest,
N. Carolina   Photo: US Forest Service

Plate 16

Acer. a. *A. rufinerve;* b. + b1 *A. grosseri;* c. *A. pensylvanicum;* d. *A. laxiflorum;* e. + e1 *A. davidii;* f. + f1 *A. crataegifolium;* g. *A. capillipes;* h. *A. carpinifolium*

var. **prattii** Rehd. Tree, 6—12 m high, young twigs gray, at first silky haired, later glabrous; leaves 5—7 lobed, lobes caudate, densely serrate, upperside dark green, underside sparsely tomentose, trichomes gray, 8—10 cm wide, thin, however also somewhat tough, petiole 5—10 cm long, densely pubescent; flowers in terminal corymbs, small, greenish, fruit similar to the type. FI0 134 (= *A. caudatum* var. *prattii* Rehd.). China; Szechwan, Yunnan, 3000—4000 m. z6 ⌀

var. *ukurundense* see: **A. ukurundense**

A. cinnamomifolium see: **A. coriaceifolium**

A. chienii see: **A. taronense**

A. chloranthum see: **A. taronense**

A. chunii see: **A. catalpifolium**

A. circinatum Pursh. Small tree, often only a shrub, frequently multistemmed, twigs glabrous, pale green to brown, frequently whitish pruinose; leaves 7—9 lobed, 6—12 cm wide, cordate, lobes ovate, very acute, sharp and often double serrate, upperside light green, underside at first pubescent, fall foliage splendid red; flowers rather large, male and female together, sepals purple, petals whitish (however also a type with yellowish petals and sepals), May; fruit wings horizontal, to 4 cm long, 1 cm wide. SPa 183 and 184. North America, from British Columbia to N. California, along river banks in fertile soil. 1826. z6 Plate 12; Fig. 49, 52. ⌀

The leaf serves as a pattern for the insignia of Majors and Lieutenant Colonels in the U. S. Army.

A. cissifolium (S. & Z.) K. Koch. Small tree, 12 m high, occasionally a shrub, bark gray, smooth, young twigs pubescent, later glabrous; leaves trifoliate, leaflets petioled, ovate, 5—8 cm long, acute, large and unequally sharp serrate, ciliate, upperside dark green, under light green, orange-red in fall, petioles red, 5—8 cm long, glabrous; flowers small, yellowish, appearing after leaf development, in terminal, pubescent, upright racemes, April (In Europe nearly always only female plants in culture); fruit wings nearly at right angles, 2.5 cm long. KRA 15. Japan; mountain forests. 1875. z6 Hardy. Plate 11; Fig. 56. ⌀

ssp. *henryii* see: **A. henryi**

A. colchicum see: **A. cappadocicum**

A. cordatum Pax. Shrub to tree, 3—9 high, bark gray, smooth, branches gray, glabrous, pruinose; leaves oval, unlobed, 6 cm long, 3.5 cm wide, acute with short tip, base cordate, three veined, fine serrate, upperside glossy green, underside blue-green, slightly pubescent at the base, petiole 1—1.5 cm long; flowers in glabrous, stalked, reddish corymbs, small; fruit wings wide spread. EP IV, 163: 6; ICS 3142. China, Hupeh. z6 Fig. 69, 74. ⌀

A. coriaceifolium Lév. Tree, twigs pubescent and tomentose; leaves evergreen, oblong, 8 to 15 cm long, 2.5—5 cm wide, three veined, margins entire, underside gray or yellowish tomentose, petiole reddish; flowers in terminal, tomentose corymbs, petals 5; fruit 2.5—5 cm long, obtuse angled or upright, tomentose. ICS 3143 (as

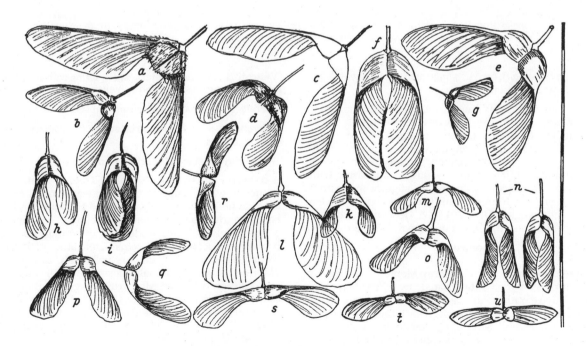

Fig. 53. **Acer** fruits. a. *Macrophyllum*; b. *A. pseudoplatanus*; c. *A. caesium*; d. *A. hybridum*; e. *A. heldreichii*; f. *A. trautvetteri*; g. *A. spicatum*; h. *A. ginnala*; i. *A. ginnala* f. *aidzuense*; k. *A. tataricium*; l. *A. velutinum* m. *A. buergerianum* var. *formosanum*; n. *A. buergerianum*; o. *A. paxii*; p. *A. ukurunduense*; q. *A. nipponicum*; r. *A. oliverianum*; s. *A. sinense*; t. *A. wilsonii*; u. *A. erianthum* (Original)

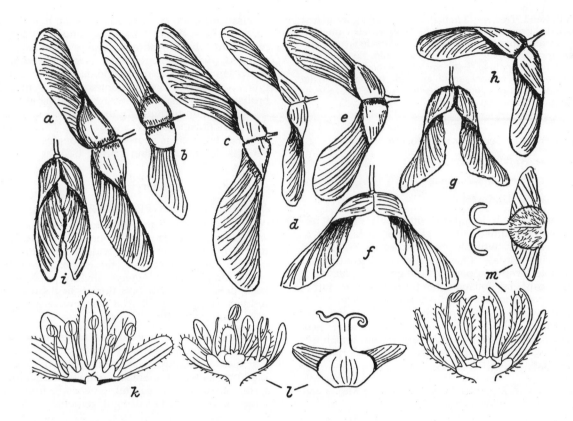

Fig. 54. **Acer** fruits. a. *A. lobelii*; b. *A. miyabei*; c. *A. platanoides*; d. *A. mono* var. *mayri*, another form/. Acer flowers.
k. *A. mono* (from PAX, male); l. *A. lobelii* (from Schneider, left male, right female); m. *A. miyabei* (from Schneider,
lower male, upper female)

A. cinnamomifolium) (= *A. cinnamomifolium* Hayata). S. China; Yunnan. z8 Fig. 66. #

A. × coriaceum Bosc ex Tausch. (*A. monspessulanum* × *A. pseudoplatanus*). Shrub, branches gray-brown, thick, glabrous; leaves tri-lobed, nearly cordate, 5—8 cm wide, lobes often rounded to triangular, uneven and sparsely serrate, upperside glossy green, under bluish green, pubescent at first, later glabrous; flowers appearing with the leaves in short, glabrous to slightly pubescent corymbs, yellowish green; fruit glabrous, wings 2.5 cm long, at acute angles. DL 2: 204 (= *A. creticum* F. Schmidt; *A. parvifolium* Tausch). Origin unknown. 1790. z6

A. crassipes see: **A. nipponicum**

A. crataegifolium S. & Z. Hawthorn Maple. Small tree, to 10 m, upright, bark white striated, twigs reddish, glabrous; leaves rather divergent, usually ovate, base truncate to cordate, 5—8 cm long, with 1—2 small lobes on either side, unevenly serrate, upperside dark green, underside lighter with pubescent vein axils at first; flowers appearing with the foliage, 5—8 in glabrous, short racemes, yellowish white, May; fruit 2—3 cm long, wings nearly horizontal. DL 2: 193; KRA 3. Japan, mountain forests, Hondo, Kiuschiu. 1862. z6 Plate 16; Fig. 49, 55.

'Veitchii'. Leaves first to break bud in spring with attractive pink and white tones. 1881. Found by Veitch.

A. crataegifolium × *A. pensylvanicum* see: **A. × veitchii**

A. creticum see: **A. × coriaceum, A. orientale** and **A. sempervirens**

A. dasycarpum see: **A. saccharinum**

A davidii Franch. David's Maple. Tree, to 15 m, younger branches white striped, glabrous; leaves oval, 8—15 cm long, acute, always undivided and without basal lobes, base rounded to somewhat cordate, not 3—5 veined, uneven deeply serrate, underside of young leaves red-brown pubescent on the veins, later rather glabrous, fall color yellow and red; flowers yellowish, in pendulous, glabrous racemes, female racemes larger and longer stalked than the male, May; fruit wings at right angles or obtuse, to 3 cm long. ST 83; JA 1933: 213; FIO 138 (= *A. laxiflorum* var. *ningpoense* Pax.). Middle China; Yunnan, Hupeh, Szechwan, 1200—3000 m, in lime free soil. 1879. z6 Plate 16; Fig. 55, 69. ⌀ &

'Ernest Wilson'. Crown round, dense and compact, internodes to 6 cm long; leaves to 11.5 cm long, to 7 cm wide. *Baileya* 1957: 31. China, W. Hupeh, W. Yunnan. 1907. In culture at the Botanic Garden of Edinburgh.

'George Forrest'. Tree, with open crown, strong growing, internodes to 10 cm long; leaves to 18 cm long and 13 cm wide. *Baileya* 1957: 30. Yunnan. 1921. In culture at the Botanic Garden of Edinburgh.

var. *horizontale* see: **A. grosseri**

A. decandrum see: **A. garrettii**

A diabolicum Blume ex K. Koch. Horned Maple. Round crowned tree, to 10 m, young branches pubescent, later glabrous, red-brown; leaves with dense white pubescence on both sides at first, later sparsely pubescent except on the veins; flowers yellow, male in fascicles, female in racemes of few flowers, pendulous, April—May, before the leaves; fruit wings upright, parallel, 3—4 cm long, nutlet with bristly hairs. KRA 33. Japan, mountain forests. 1880. z6 The name *diabolicum* comes from the two horn-like curved stigmas between the nutlets on the inner base at the point of wing attachment. Plate 19; Fig. 52.

f. **purpurascens** (Franch. & Sav.) Rehd. Like the type, but flowers, young fruits and foliage purple-red at bud break (= *A. purpurascens* Franch. & Sav.). Japan, Nikko Mountains. 1878. z6 Plate 19.

A. × dieckii Pax (*A. lobelii* × *A. platanoides*). Natural hybrid. Tree, 15—18 m; leaves 3—5 lobed, usually with 2 small basal lobes, 10 cm long, 12 cm wide, upper side dark glossy green, underside lighter with brown pubescence in the vein axils, fall foliage yellow-gold, lobes broadly triangular, margin entire, with short obtuse tips; flowers in yellow corymbs; fruit glabrous, wings spread wide, 4 cm long. DH 2: 213 (as *A. platanoides integrilobum*) (= *A. platanoides* var. *integrilobum* Zabel). In culture since 1886. z5 Plate 18.

A. distylum S. & Z. Linden Leaved maple. Tree, to 15 m, young branches softly pubescent; leaves look like Linden leaves, ovate, 10 to 15 cm long, deeply cordate, blade tip acuminate, finely serrate, underside light green, glossy, glabrous, petiole 3—4 cm long, pubescent at first; flowers yellow, in small, nodding panicles, style of the pistil split to the base, June; fruit in upright panicles; wings upright, inclined together, 3 cm long. KRA 2. Japan, the island of Nippon. 1879. Similar to *A. davidii*, but with leaves broader and fruits upright. z7 Fig 49, 55, 74. Ø

A. divergens Koch ex Pax. Shrub, leaves usually 5 or only 3 lobed, 2—3 cm wide, deeply lobed, lobes broadly ovate, margin entire, acute tips or nearly obtuse, base truncate to nearly cordate, underside with reticulate venation, glabrous; wings horizontal, ends curving upward, 2.5 cm long, 1 cm wide. Gfl 1898: 123; SDK 4: 53. Trans-Caucasus. 1932. Hardy. z5 Fig. 59. Ø

A. × durettii Pax (= *A. monspessulanum* × *A. psuedoplatanus*). Natural hybrid. Tree, to some 12 m high or more, young branches glabrous; leaves tri-lobed, base often with two more lobes, 5—12 cm wide, 6—9 cm long, upperside light green, glabrous, underside pubescent along the veins, lobes large, triangular, margin irregularly serrate, petiole red; flowers greenish yellow, in pubescent, stalked corymbs, 5—8 cm long. Origin unknown. Hardy. In culture since 1892. Only slightly garden worthy. z6

A. erianthum Schwer. Shrub or small tree, young twigs green, nearly completely glabrous; leaves 5 lobed, thin, 6—12 cm long, lobes triangular, acute, coarsely serrate, upperside dark green, glabrous, under somewhat lighter, slightly pubescent, distinct white pubescence in the vein axils on both sides; flowers appear after the foliage, yellowish, in slender panicles, 5—10 cm long, ovary densely yellow tomentose; fruit in 5—10 cm long panicles, wings to 3 cm long, horizontal. ST 80; FIO 133; ICS 3134. China, Szechwan, Hupeh, 2000 to 3000 m. 1901. z6 Fig. 53.

A. fabri Hance. Tree, in its habitat to 18 m, bark smooth, gray, young twigs thin, red at first, then gray-green, glabrous; leaves oblong, red at first, 5—15 cm long, 3—4 cm wide, acuminate, margin entire or finely serrate, base broadly cuneate (most important distinction from *A. cordatum*), both sides glossy green, underside lighter and veined, leathery, petiole 2—3 cm long; flowers in upright racemes; wings of fruit 3 cm long, reddish, at an obtuse angle with each other. ICS 3144; FIO 138. Middle China to Hong Kong, Mid and E. Himalayas. z8 Fig. 69. (See also: *A. fargesii*.) Ø

A. fargesii Rehd. Very similar to *A. fabri*, however young branches beautiful red; leaves more lanceolate, only 4—8 cm long, underside light green, without reticulate venation, likewise not three veined, red when first leaved out; flowers red, petiole glabrous, panicles 5 cm long; fruit red, wings 2 cm long, at right or obtuse angles. DRHS 21; JRHS 1904: 94 (= *A. fabri* var. *rubrocarpum* Metcalf [Rehd.] Fang). China, Hupeh, Szechwan, 1000—2000 m. 1902. z8

A. flabellatum Rehd. Small tree, 6—9 m, young branches gray, with thin stripes; leaves 7 lobed, lower lobes very small, base cordate, lobes ovate, coarsely serrate, acuminate, upper side deep green, underside lighter, glossy, venation slightly pubescent, petiole 4—5 cm long, slightly pubescent; wings 2 cm long, brown-red, at wide angles apart. ICS 3133; FIO 132. China; Hupeh, Szechwan, lime free soils, 1800—2600 m. z5

var. **yunnanense** (Rehd.) Fang. Small tree, young twigs thin, reddish, glabrous; leaves 5—7 lobed, lobes ovate, abruptly acuminate, finely serrate, silky pubescence along the veins on both sides; flowers dark blue-green, in narrow corymbs; fruit wings wide apart, reddish. Yunnan; 3000 m. z6

A. floridanum see: **A. rubrum**

A. forrestii Diels. Tree, 7—12 m high; leaves cordate-ovate, 7—8.5 cm long, 5—6.5 cm wide, tri-lobed, upper side glabrous, dark green, underside lighter and bluish, glabrous except for tufts at the vein axils, the three lobes with caudate tips, margin doubly serrate, petiole 2—2.5 cm long; inflorescence appears with the leaves, in short stalked, simple, 6—7 cm long, 1.2 to 1.4 cm wide racemes, glabrous; flowers brown-green, petals and sepals narrower than the very similar *A. sinense*. BS 1: 199. Hupeh, Szechwan, z6
(Note: The plant distributed by the Edinburgh Botanic Garden as *Acer forrestii* is actually *Acer davidii* 'George Forrest'.)

A. franchetii Pax. Tree to 6 m high, resembles *A. diabolicum*, young branches glabrous; leaves tri-lobed, oc-

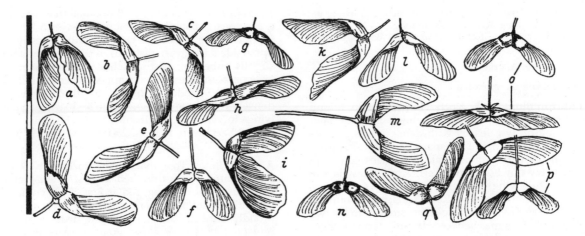

Fig. 55. **Acer** fruits. a. *A. rufinerve*; b. *A. pensylvanicum*; c. *A. micranthum*; d. *A. tegmentosum*; e. *A. davdii*; f. *A. tschonoskii*; g. *A. capillipes*; h. *crataegifolium*; i. *A. glabrum*; k. *oblongum*; l. *A. distylum*; m. *A. carpinifolium*; n. *A. pseudosieboldianum*; o. *A. japonicum*; q. *A. palmatum* (Original)

casionally with additional 2 basal lobes, 8—12 cm long, nearly cordate, lobes directed forward, triangular, short acute, irregular and sparsely serrate, light green, underside pubescent or glabrous, vein axils pubescent, petiole 4—10 cm long, pubescent; flowers yellow-green, short stalked corymbs of few flowers, pubescent, April—May; fruit wings to 5 cm long, spread at right angles or nearly upright, nutlets pubescent. ST 87; ICS 3152; FIO 141. Middle China, Yunnan, Szechwan, Hupeh, Honan, lime free soils, but also adaptable, 1600—3500 cm. 1901. z6 Fig. 49, 52, 75.

A. × freemanii E. Murray (= *A. rubrum* × *A. saccharinum*). Growth habit intermediate between the parents; bark silver-gray, twigs gray; leaves smaller than *A. saccharinum*, usually rather deeply lobed, but the lobes not so long. 1933 from Oliver Freeman, of the U. S. National Arboretum, Washington D.C. (later also found in the wild.) z3

A. fulgens see: **A. rubrum** var. **tomentosum**

A. fulvescens see: **A. longipes**

A. garrettii Craib. Small, dioecious tree, branches bluish to reddish; leaves evergreen, oblong-elliptic, 7—15 cm long, 2.5—7.5 cm wide, underside usually blue-green, margin entire, petiole often thickened at the leaf blade; flowers in axillary corymbs, petals 5, anthers 10—12; fruit wings upright, 2.5—7.5 cm long, the pair unequal in size, often reddish. ICS 3147 (= *A. decandrum* Merrill). S. China; Hainan Island, Kwangtung. z8 Fig. 66.

A. ginnala Maxim. Amur Maple. Shrub or small tree, to 6 m high, crown broad, branches thin, glabrous; leaves tri-lobed, 4—8 cm long, 3 to 6 cm wide, some leaves also unlobed, middle lobe distinctly longer than the side lobes, sharp or coarsely double serrate, upper side glossy dark green, under light green, glabrous, light red in fall, often whitish marbled; flowers yellowish white, fragrant, in long stalked panicles, end of May; fruit wings parallel to

acute angled, some 2.5 cm long. KRA 18; DB 1954: 49. Middle and N. China, Jpan, Manchuria. 1860. z7 Ⓕ in the USSR and the USA. Often used as windbreak or snow fence. Plate 11; Fig. 53.

var. **aidzuense** (Franch.). Leaves darker green, thin-membranous, wings nearly parallel and sometimes overlapping. 1879. Fig. 53.

'Albovariegatum'. Leaves irregular and blotched with large white areas. 1910.

'Durand Dwarf' (Harkness). Dwarf form, some 50—60 cm high, many branched, twigs red; leaves smaller than the type. 1955. Very suitable for low hedges. In cultivation in USA.

'Pulverulentum' (Schwerin). Leaves very much white marbled and powdered. 1896. ∅

var. **semenovii** see: *A. semenovii*

A. giraldii see: **A. caesium**

A. glabrum Torr. Small tree, to 8 m, quite glabrous, twigs red-brown; leaves 3—5 lobed, often also trifoliate, lobes acute or acuminate, sharply double serrate, upper surface glossy green, under lighter to blue-green, beautiful yellow in fall, petiole red; flowers greenish yellow, in corymbs, May; fruit wings nearly upright to parallel, often a clear pink in summer. SPa 185—187; BB 2377. North America, Rocky Mountains, gravelly slopes, river banks and mountain forests, also understory in deep shade. z4 Plate 15; Fig. 55.

var. **douglasii** (Hook.) Dipp. Shrub or small tree, 5—6 m high, branches strictly upright, thin; leaves usually three lobed, 5—10 cm wide, lobes short acute, deeply serrate, middle lobe broadly ovate, upper side dull dark green, under light green; fruit wings wider than the type, upright, spread outward. SM 615; NTC 247. Alaska to British Columbia, gravelly banks of mountain streams. z4 Plate 19.

f. **rhodocarpum** Schwer. Young fruit bright red until ripe.

A. granatense see: **A. opalus**

A. griseum (Franch.) Pax. Paperbark Maple. Tree, to 12 m, bark quite smooth, cinnamon brown, peeling, can stain when touched, young twigs at first shaggy pubescent, later rather glabrous; leaves trifoliate, the middle leaflet to 5 cm long, side leaflets 3 cm, oblong, each side having 3–5 large teeth, upper side dark green, under practically blue-green, petiole and midrib pubescent, fall color purple-red; flowers yellow, few, pendulous, stalk pubescent; fruit wings 3.5 cm long, nearly at right angles. EP IV, 163, 5 (= *A. nikoense* var. *griseum* Franch.). Middle China; Szechwan, Shansi, Hupeh, Honan. 1901. Hardy. z6 Plate 1, 11 and 14; Fig. 56. ∅ ⚭

Of the trifoliate types, without doubt this is the most attractive for its foliage and bark.

A. grosseri Pax. Small tree, often only a shrub, 6–9 m, quite glabrous, bark gray-green, white striped, young twigs gray-green; leaves triangular-ovate, base cordate, to 7 cm long, nearly as wide as long, occasionally 3 lobed, side lobes small, quite short pointed, directed outward, dense and sharply double serrate, fresh green, underside at the base with a light brownish pubescence, petiole 2–4 cm long; flowers and fruit in 5–7 cm long, pendulous racemes; wings some 2 cm long, nearly horizontal, slightly curved. JA 14: 219 (= *A. davidii* var. *horizontale* Pax). N. and Middle China, Honan, Shansi. 1927. z6 Plate 16. ∅ ⚭

var. **hersii** (Rehd.) Rehd. Like the type, but with leaves longer ovate, 3(–5) lobed (the lower lobes insignificant), lobes ovate, acuminate, about half as long as the middle lobe, fall color red; fruit wings nearly horizontal. JA 14: 221 (= *A. hersii* Rehd.). Eastern Middle China. 1923. z6 Hardy and attractive. Plate 17. ∅ ⚭

A. heldreichii Orph. Greek Maple. Tree, to 15 m, branches brown-gray, glabrous; leaves appearing late in spring, 5 lobed, 8–12 cm wide, lobes cut nearly to the base, paper thin, upper side glossy dark green, underside light yellow-green, glabrous, yellow-gold in fall; flowers yellow, in upright corymbs, end of May; wings 4–5 cm long, spread on an arch-like curve. EH 206. Balkan; mountain forests of Greece, Bulgaria, S. Serbia. 1879. z6 Leaves nearly as deeply lobed as *A. platanoides* 'Pal-

matifidum'. Ⓕ Yugoslavia. Plate 19; Fig. 53.

A. henryi Pax. Tree, to 10 m, young twigs at first pubescent, soon glabrous; leaves trifoliate, petiole 5–10 cm long, leaflets elliptic, middle 5–10 cm long, acuminate and sparsely dentate, base cuneate, margin entire, both sides green, underside pubescent only on the veins; flowers sessile in slender, pubescent spikes, before the leaves, May; fruit red at first, in 10–15 cm long, pendulous racemes, wings at an acute angle, 2 cm long, red fall foliage. LF 213 (= *A. cissifolium* ssp. *henryi* [Pax] E. Murray). Middle China, Hupeh, Szechwan. z6 Plate 11; Fig. 56. ∅

var. **intermedium** Fang. Leaflets with margins entire or somewhat toothed on the tip; fruit in long racemes, wings some 45° spread, otherwise like the type. Hupeh, 600–3000 m.

A. hersii see: **A. grosseri**

A. heterophyllum see: **A. sempervirens**

A. × **hillieri** (*A. miyabei* × *A. campestre*). Hybrid developed in 1928 by Hillier Nursery in Winchester, England, but apparently scarce in cultivation.

A. hispaniceum see: **A. opalus**

A. hiterophyllum see: **A. orientale**

A. hookeri Miq. Tree, in its habitat 12 to 15 m, young twigs red, glabrous, buds break red; leaves long ovate, unlobed, 10–14 cm long, paper thin, abruptly acuminate to caudate, sharply serrate, base cordate or ovate, petiole 2–4 cm long; flowers small, yellow-green, appearing with the foliage, in 10–15 cm long, slender racemes; fruit 2 cm long, wings at right angles or somewhat obtuse. E. Himalaya, Sikkim, Bhutan, mountain forests, 2600–3300 m. Similar to *A. davdii*. z8 Fig. 59. ∅

var. **majus** Pax. Leaves larger, more leathery, larger toothed, teeth abruptly pointed. Sikkim. # ∅

A. × **hybridum** Bosc. (*A. opalus* × *A. pseudoplatanus*). Tree, 12–15(–20) m, crown rounded, young branches glabrous, dense with brown lenticels; leaves 3 lobed, base cordate, 4–8 cm long, somewhat unevenly large serrate, upper side dark green, veins pubescent; flowers yel-

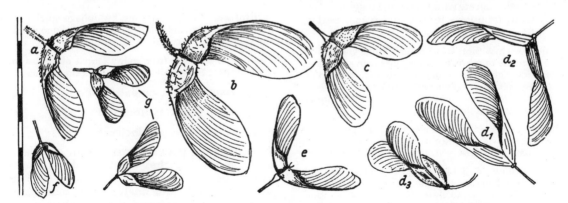

Fig. 56. **Acer** fruit. a. *A. griseum*; b. *A. nikoense*; c. *A. triflorum*; d. *A. negundol*; d₁ *negundo* Type; d₂ *negundo* f. *rectangulum*; d₃ *negundo* var. *californicum*; e. *A. mandschuricum*; f. *A. henryi*; g. *A. cissifolium* (Original)

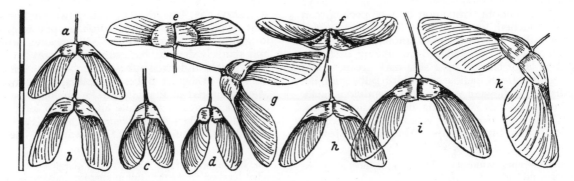

Fig. 57. **Acer** fruit. a. and b. *A. orientale*; c. *A. monspessulanum* ssp. *cinerascens*; d. *A. monspessulanum* ; e. *A. campestre*; f. *A. zoeschense*; g. *A. hyracanum*; h. *A. opalus*; i. *A. opalus* var. *obtusatum*; k. *A. opalus* var. *tomentosum* (Original)

lowish, appearing after the foliage, in 8—12 cm long, pendulous racemes, May; fruit wings 2.5 cm long, nearly parallel upright or sloping together, narrowing at the base. Origin unknown, however in cultivation before 1834. z6 Plate 19; Fig. 53, 57.

A. hypoleucum Hayata. Small tree, young branches thin, tomentose at first, soon glabrous and blue-green; leaves evergreen, membranous to leathery, oblong to elliptic-oblong, some 8 cm long, 3—4 cm wide, obtuse to acute, base round to obtuse, margin entire or slightly wavy, upper surface green, underside bluish white, densely tomentose, base lightly 3 veined, with 5—6 paired veins, petiole 2—3 cm, thin, tomentose; fruit clusters cymose, wings nearly at right angles, 17 mm long and 6 mm wide. LT 755. China, E. Taiwan. z8 #

A. hyrcanum Fisch. & Mey. Balkan Maple. Small tree, 5—9 m, also occasionally a large shrub, branches dark gray-brown, at first pubescent, soon becoming glabrous; leaves 5 lobed, acute, 5—10 cm wide, coarsely dentate, the upper lobes incised at right angles, upper surface fresh green, lower surface blue-green and pubescent along the veins, basal lobes usually small and ovate, petiole to 10 cm long, red; flowers yellow-green, in glabrous, short stalked corymbs, appearing with the leaves; fruit glabrous, with upright, falcate wings, inclined together, 3 cm long. N. Balkan; mountain forests of Croatia, Serbia, Bosnia, Montenegro. 1865. z6 Fig. 57.

var. **keckianum** Asch. & Sint. To 3.5 m high, trunk gray; leaves smaller, open cordate to nearly truncate, lobes with a few large teeth, upper side light green, underside densely pubescent. Lebanon, 1700—1900 m. Together with *Cedrus, Quercus libani, Ostrya carpinifolia, Juniperus drupacea*; outside of the forests, found usually as a stunted shrub. z6

ssp. **stevenii** (Pojark.) E. Murray. Leaves dark blue-green on the upper side, lighter with pubescent venation beneath, lobes caudate-acuminate. SDK 4: 64 (= *A. stevenii* Pojark.). Krim.

ssp. **tauricolum** (Boiss. & Bal.) Yaltirik. Tree or shrub, bark brown; leaves larger than var. *keckianum*, slightly cordate, upperside darker green, under eventually quite glabrous, petiole long, red, venation underneath reddish (= *A. tauricolum* Boiss. & Bal.; *A. hyrcanum* var. *reigassei* Boiss.). W. and N. Lebanon, 1600—1800 m, W. Syria, Turkey.

A. ibericum see: **A. monspessulanum**

A. insigne see: **A. velutinum**

A. italum see: **A. opalus**

A. japonicum Thunb. Full Moon Maple. Small tree or shrub, 5—7 m in the wild, seldom taller, twigs glabrous; leaves rounded, with 7—11 long oval, acutely tipped lobes, 8—14 cm long and wide, lobes doubly serrate, bright green, silky pubescent when young, carmine red in fall; flowers large, purple, in long stalked clusters before the leaves, April—May; fruit pubescent at first, wings at right angles to horizontal, to 2.5 cm long, stalks pubescent. KRA 24; DL 2: 220. N. Japan, mountain forests. 1864. z6 Plate 12; Fig. 55, 58. ⌀

'Aconitifolium'. Leaves 10—15 cm wide, deeply incised, with 9-11 pinnatisect lobes, light green, brown-red to carmine in fall. KRAPl. 25, 7(= f. *filicifolium* Hesse, f. *parsonii* Veitch). 1888. Plate 12. ⌀

'Aureum'. Shrub, small, weak grower, in Europe seldom over 3 m high; leaves always gold-green, veins and petiole reddish, young twigs striated. 1888. Best planted in semishade as foliage will easily scorch. Plate 14. ⌀

'Microphyllum'. Leaves much smaller, particularly than the species. KRA 25, 6. 1888. ⌀

'Vitifolium'. Like the species, but foliage much more deeply lobed, carmine in fall. JRHS 29: 335. 1882. Somewhat between the species and 'Aconitifolium'. ⌀

The plants released from many Dutch nurseries under this name appear to be little different from the species.

A. kawakamii see: **A. caudatifolium**

A. komarovii see: **A. tschonoskii**

A. laetum see: **A. cappedocicum**

A. laevigatum Wall. Tree, similar to *A. oblongum*, bark gray, young branches unlobed, oblong, semi-decid-uous, coarse-leathery, 5—15 cm long, 4—5 cm wide, margin entire or quite finely serrate, acuminate, underside light green, strong reticulate venation, petiole 1.5 cm long, not red; flowers yellow, in glabrous corymbs, 5—10 cm long, April; fruit wings 3—4 cm long, at right angles or obtuse. Wallich, Pl. As. Rar. 2: 104; ICS 3145; FIO 137. Middle China to Hong Kong, mountain forests, 1500-3300 m, Nepal, widely dispersed throughout Szechwan. z8 Fig. 66 # Ø

var. **salweenense** (W. W. Sm.) J. M. Cowan ex Fang. Tree, 6−9 m high in its habitat, young twigs whitish gray, glabrous, however densely pubescent at first; leaves leathery, long oval, 8 cm long, 3.5 cm wide, acuminate, base rounded, margin entire or finely serrate, both sides glossy green, glabrous, new foliage red at bud break, with thick silky white pubescence, petioles 1−2 cm long, upper side flat, thick white pubescent at first; flowers light yellow-green, in terminal panicles; fruit wings 2.5 cm long, 1 cm wide, at a wide angle apart (= *A. salweenense* W. W. Sm.). Tibet, Yunnan, 3000 m. z8 #

A. lasiocarpum see: **A. ukurundense**

A. laxiflorum Pax. Tree, 6−12 m in the wild, young branches reddish, glabrous; leaves ovate-triangular, usually 3 lobed, side lobes very small, middle lobe longer and acuminate, margins irregular and finely serrate, 8−9 cm long, base nearly cordate, 5 veined, upper side dark green, underside lighter with brownish vein axils, thin, but somewhat leathery, petiole 3−6 cm long, reddish; flowers brownish green, in 10 cm long, slender, pendulous, racemes, appearing with the leaves in May; fruit wings right angled to nearly horizontal, 3 cm long. ICS 3150; FIO 138. High mountains of Szechwan (Mt. Omei), Yunnan, Tibet, 900−3300 m. 1906. z6 Plate 16; Fig. 69. Ø

var. *longilobum* see: **A. taronense**

var. *ningpoense* see: **A. davidii**

A. leucoderme Small. Shrub or tree, to 8 m, bark light gray or light brown, crown rounded, twigs thin, glabrous; leaves 3(−5) lobed, lobes nearly triangular and usually with 2 large teeth, base nearly cordate or truncate, upper side dark yellow-green, underside lighter and whitish soft pubescent (important distinction); flowers yellow, few in short clusters, April; fruit wings wide spread with the pubescent (later glabrous) nutlets 2 cm long. SS 624 (= *A. saccharinum* var. *leucoderme* [Small] Sarg.). Southern USA, N. Carolina to Florida and Alabama. 1902. z6

A. leucoderme × *A. saccharum* see: **A. × senecaense**

A. lipskyi see: **A. turkestanicum**

A. litseifolium Hayata. Evergreen tree, very closely related to *A. albopurpurascens*, but young twigs glabrous; leaves oblanceolate, coarse, 10−17 cm long, 3−5 cm wide, short pointed, base cuneate to truncate, upper side light green and glabrous, under white and glabrous, with short basal, 10−12 paired axillary veins, petiole 1.5−2 cm long; fruit cluster cymose, fruit wings 2 cm long, at obtuse angles. ICS 3146. China; Formosa, in mountain forests. z8 Fig. 66 #

A. lobelii Ten. Tree, 15−18 m, compact when young, later narrowly upright, nearly columnar, young twigs with bluish white pruinose; leaves usually 5 lobed, 10−15 cm wide, lobes acuminate, base cordate or truncate, upper side dark green, glabrous, underside more bluish green and eventually glabrous, except for gray tufts in the vein axils; flowers small, yellow, in corymbs appearing with the foliage, May; fruit to 3 cm

Fig. 58. a. *Acer japonicum*, with three different fruits; b. *A. palmatum* var. *heptalobum*; c. *A. sieboldianum*; d. *shirasawanum* (from Koidzumi)

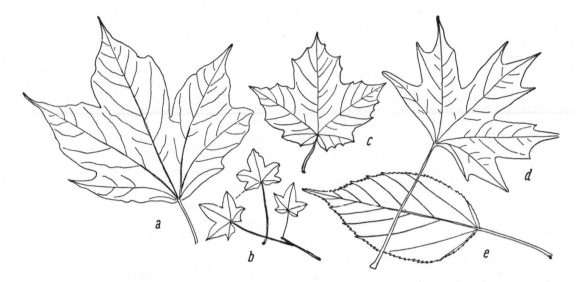

Fig. 59. a. *Acer lobelii*; b. *A. divergens*; c. *A. saccharum* ssp. *nigrum*; d. *A. truncatum*; e. *A. hookeri* (Original)

long, wings nearly horizontal. DL 2: 215. S. Italy, mountain forests around the Gulf of Naples. z6 Fig. 54, 59.

Resembles *A. platanoides*, but grows nearly columnar, young twigs pruinose and later striated white. In cultivation in England before 1844.

A. lobelii × *A. platanoides* see: **A. × dieckii**

A. longipes Franch. Tree, in the wild to 10 m, bark stays smooth, young twigs green, glabrous; leaves at bud break reddish, usually 3 (occasionally 5) lobed, 10–15 cm wide, margin entire, acuminate, also unlobed, ovate leaves, underside light green and softly pubescent; flowers in loose, nearly sessile cymes, after the leaves, May–June; fruit wings at right angles, nutlet 3 cm long. FIO 128 (as *A. fulvescens*) (= *A. fulvescens* Rehd.). W. China; Szechwan, Hupeh, Honan. 1900. Quite hardy in zone 6. Very similar to *A. lobelii*, but without pruinose twigs. Fig. 54.

A. macrophyllum Pursh. Oregon or Bigleaf Maple. Tree, 15–25 m, occasionally taller, in Northern Europe only a tree-like shrub, young twigs glabrous; leaves very large, 5 lobed, 20–30 cm wide, middle lobe usually further 3 lobed, lobes with a few, large, obtuse teeth, upper surface glossy dark green, underside lighter, pubescent at first, coarse, orange in fall; flowers yellow, fragrant, in 10–20 cm long, narrow, nodding panicles, appearing with the leaves in May; fruit at right angles, to 7 cm long, nutlets bristly haired, fruit also in whorls of 3. SPa 182. W. North America, Alaska to S. California. 1812. Outstanding shade tree of the large coniferous forests of the West Coast. One of the most beautiful of all the maples. z6 Plate 1 and 19; Fig. 53. ⚭ ∅

'Tricolor' (Schwerin 1893). Leaves patchy white, patches at first pink to red. ∅

A. mandshuricum Maxim. Shrub, also a small tree, occasionally to 10 m, twigs glabrous; leaves trifoliate, leaflets oblong-lanceolate 5 to 10 cm long, 2.5–3.5 cm wide, acute-acuminate, middle leaflet much longer petioled than the side ones, margins obtuse serrate, upper side dark green, underside blue-green, quite glabrous except for the pubescent midrib, red fall color as early as August, petiole 5–10 cm long; flowers greenish yellow, usually only 3 together, May; fruit wings obtuse or right angled, 3 cm long. NK 10. Southeast Manchuria, mountain forests of Ussuri, Korea. 1904. Often harmed by a late frost. z6 Plate 11; Fig. 56.

A. × martinii Jordan (*A. monspessulanum* × *A. opalus*). Natural hybrid. Small tree, young twigs brown, glabrous; leaves 3 lobed, some 7 cm long and wide, occasionally with 2 small basal lobes, lobe triangular, coarsely serrate, upper side glabrous and rugose, underside blue-green, wooly pubescent at bud break, later glabrous; flowers appear with the foliage, 7–11 in 5 cm long racemes, yellowish; fruit wings wide angled (= *A. × peronai* Schwerin; *A. perrieri* Chabert). N.E. Spain, S. France, Italy (Apennines, near Valombrosa), Switzerland, Yugoslavia. 1895. z6

Leaves more pointed than *A. opalus* and 3 lobed, differs from *A. monspessulanum* in the rugose upper surface and dentate margin.

A. maximowiczianum Miq. is the botanically correct name for **A. nikoense** Maxim. Even so, the latter name is retained to avoid confusion with *A. maximowiczii*.

A. maximowiczii Pax. Small, quite glabrous, tree; leaves resemble those of *A. tschonoskii*, but 3–5 lobed, 5–8 cm long, middle lobe tip caudate, others acute-acuminate, sharply double serrate, upper side dark green, underside blue-green, glabrous except for the gray vein axils; flowers in upright, many flowered racemes, greenish yellow; fruit short stalked, wings wide angled to nearly horizontal. ST 84; JA 1933: 217; FIO 140 (= *A. urophyllum* Maxim.). Middle China, Szechwan, Kansu, Hupeh. *A. forrestii* grows in the same area but is distinctly hardier. z6

A. mexicanum see: **A. negundo** var. *mexicanum*

A micranthum S. & Z. Shrub or small tree, twigs red-brown, glabrous; leaves 5 (occasionally 7) lobed, 5–8 cm wide, lobes acuminte, deeply double serrate, both sides glabrous or underside with some pubescence at the vein axils, bright red or yellow fall color; flowers greenish white, very small, in 3–5 cm long racemes, May; fruit wings at an obtuse angle, 2 cm long. KRA 12; SDK 4: 53. Japan; mountain forests. 1864. Resembles *A. tschonoskii*, but flowers and fruit smaller. z6 Fig. 55, 63.

A. microphyllum see: **A. opalus**

A. mirabile see: **A. wardii**

A. miyabei Maxim. Tree, 12–15 m high, round crowned, twigs with rough, corky bark, young twigs pubescent at first; leaves 5 lobed, 10–15 cm wide, base deeply cordate, lobes sharply acute, blunt toothed and slightly lobed, upper side dark green and pubescent when young, underside blue-green, pubescent as are the petioles, with milky sap; flowers yellowish green, few together in 5–7 cm long, stalked corymbs, May; fruit velvety pubescent, wings horizontal and bowed, 2.5 cm long. KRA 31. N. Japan; Yezo on river banks together with *A. mono*. 1895. z5 Fig. 54.

A. miyabei × *A. campestre* see: **A. hillieri**

Fig. 60. *Acer mono* and forms. a. Species; b. f. *dissectum*; c. var. *savatieri*; d. var. *tricuspis* (= *A. tenellum*); e. var. *ambiguum*; f. var. *latilobum* (from Koidzumi)

A. mono Maxim. Tree, to 10 m high, twigs glabrous, yellow-gray in the 2nd year; leaves 5–7 lobed, nearly cordate, 8–15 cm wide, lobes triangular, margins entire, apiculate and acuminate, both sides green and glabrous except for pubescent venation beneath; flowers appearing with the foliage, greenish yellow, in 4–6 cm wide corymbs, April–May; fruit horizontal to somewhat upright, fruit wings at right angles, not narrowing at the base, 2–3 cm long. DL 2: 216; KRA 32; FIO 128 (= *A. pictum* Thunb; *A. pictum* var. *mono* Maxim.). China, Manchuria, Korea. 1881. z6 Fig. 54, 60. ∅

f. **ambiguum** (Pax) Rehd. Shrub or tree, twigs rough with gray lenticels, glabrous; leaves 5 lobed, 9–14 cm wide, underside light gray, short, soft pubesent, middle lobe much larger, lobes entire; flower and fruit unknown. DL 2: 218 (= *A. ambiguum* Dipp.; *A.pictum* var. *paxii* Schwer.). Origin unknown, supposedly Japan. 1892. Fig. 60.

f. **dissectum** Wesmael. Leaves deeply incised, narrow and acuminate, middle lobe usually somewhat narrowed at the base, underside glabrous (= *A. pictum* var. *angustilobum* Makino). 1907. Fig. 60. ∅

var. **latilobum** (Koidz.). Leaves smaller, 4–5 cm long and wide. 5 lobed (partly 3 lobed), base truncate, seldom rounded, lobes widely triangular, abruptly acute; fruit wings nearly horizontal. Japan. Fig. 60.

'Marmoratum'. Shrubby, leaves with fine white spots and pulverulent, usually more white than light green. 1881. Originated in Pallanza, Villa Taranto, 1958. ∅

var. **mayri** (Schwerin) Nakai. Tree, to 25 m in the wild, bark smooth, young branches densely blue pruinose, quite glabrous, yellowish or red-brown in the 2nd year; leaves rounded, thin, 3–5 lobed, base rounded, lobes with entire margins, broad ovate, abruptly short acute, both sides green, underside glabrous with reticulate venation; flowers greenish white, in 4–6 cm wide corymbs, April–May; fruit wings usually upright and curved inward to slightly spread, 3 cm long. Japan; Ezo Island. 1916. z6 Hardy. Resembles *A. cappadocicum*. Fig. 54.

var. **savatieri** (Pax) Nakai. Leaves 7– (partly 5) lobed, base deeply cordate, lobes broadly triangular, abruptly acute; fruit wings nearly horizontal to obtuse angled. Yezo. Fig. 60, 54.

'Tricolor'. Leaves large and irregularly white speckled, occasionally an entire half-blade white (= *A. pictum* 'Variegatum'). ∅

var. **tricuspis** (Rehd.) Rehd. Tree, to 7 m; leaves 5–6 cm long and wide, 3 lobed, side lobes short, acute to obtuse, base cordate, the smallest leaves unlobed, ovate, upper side glossy green; fruit wings widely spread. LF 216 (= *A. tenellum* Pax; *A. bodinieri* Lév.). Middle China, Yunnan, Szechwan, Schansi. z6 Fig. 60.

A. monspessulanum L. Montpellier Maple. Small, dense tree, 6–8(–10) m high, rounded crown, branches glabrous; leaves 3 lobed, obtuse, small, 3.8 cm wide, margin entire or finely serrate, tough and leathery, upper side glossy dark green until leaf drop, underside bluish green, base cordate, both sides quite glabrous; flowers yellow-green, in pendulous, many flowered corymbs or loose racemes, end of April; fruit usually an attractive red, wings glabrous, upright, often overlapping, 2–2.5 cm long. HM 1858 (= *A.*

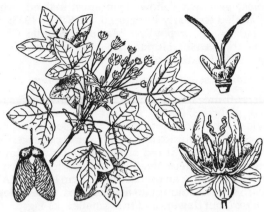

Fig. 61. *Acer monspessulanum.* Upper male flower, lower female flower (from Hempel & Wilhelm)

trilobatum Lam.). Mediterranean area, Spain to the Caucasus, north to the Rhine and Mosel Rivers, dry gravelly slopes. 1739. z6 Ⓕ Yugoslavia. Fig. 49, 57, 61.∅

The following geographical subspecies and forms, seldom found in cultivation are:

ssp. **cinerascens** (Boiss.) Yaltirik. Normally only a shrub, resembles *A. orientale*, bark olive-green with black patches, leaf size and form variable, young twigs pubescent, later glabrous; leaves 3 lobed or often with 2 additional small lobes at the base, 2–6 cm long, ornamental, deep green, lobes obtuse, margin entire or crenate, underside pubescent; flowers appearing with the foliage, April–May; fruit wings upright, nearly parallel, 1.5-3 cm long. MD 1898: 47. z6 Asia Minor. Prefers a dry climate. Fig. 57.

The following 3 varieties are found within subspecies *cinerascens:*

var. **boissieri** Schwer. Leaves small, some 2 cm long, both sides always pubescent. MD 1898: 49. S. Iran mountains, 1800–2000 m.

var. **bornmuelleri** Schwer. Similar in appearance to *A. monspessulanum*, 2–5 cm long, upper side totally glabrous, petiole and undersides of young leaves densely pubescent. Fig. 50.

var. **paxii** Schwer. Leaves to 1.5 cm long, 2 cm wide, both sides nearly completely glabrous. S. Iran mountains, hot, dry southern exposures, 2700—3000 m Fig. 50.

f. **commutatum** (Presl) Borb. Leaf lobes with entire margins, rounded, somewhat more deeply incised than the species, wings bowed crosswise over one another (= *A. rumeliacum* Borb.). Balkan; Istria, Serbia, Banat.

f. **hispanicum** Schwer. Mature leaves pubescent beneath, also the young twigs and petioles, lobes entire. Spain.

var. **ibericum** (Willd.) Leaves large, middle lobe (also occasionally the side lobes) further short lobed in the middle (= *A. ibericum* Bieb.). West Asia, Banat.

f. **illyricum** (Jacq. f.) Spach. Leaves 3 lobed, lobes triangular, cuspidate, base rounded. Balkan, Asia Minor.

f. **liburnicum** Pax. Lobes dentate, leaves much smaller, frequently with short, distinct basal lobes. Balkan and Asia Minor.

f. **maroccanum** Schwer. Leaves 3 lobed, lobes rounded, base cuneate, margin entire. Morocco, mountain forests, 1400–2000 m. z6

ssp. **turcomanicum** (Pojark.) E. Murray. Leaves red-brown pubescent beneath (= *A. turcomanicum* Pojark.). Turkmenia; Kopet-dagh. 1932.

A. monspessulanum × *A. opulus* see: **A. martinii**

A. monspessulanum × *A. pseudoplatanus* see: **A. × coriaceum** and **A. × durettii**

A. monspessulanum × *A. tartaricum* see: **A. × boseii**

A. morrisonense see: **A. caudatifolium**

A. multiserratum Maxim. Tree, to 15 m, bark yellow-gray, peeling in thin scales, young twigs gray, densely dentate, glabrous; leaves 5–7 lobed, acuminate, base cordate, distinctly serrate, upper side deep green, underside densely brown silky pubescent, very thin, petiole 4–10 cm long, glabrous; flowers in terminal racemes, greenish, small; fruit wings at right angles, some 2 cm long with nutlet (= *A. caudatum* var. *multiserratum* [Maxim.] Rehd.). China; Yunnan to Kansu, 2500–3000 m. z6

A. neapolitanum see: **A. opulus**

A. neglectum see: **A. × zoeschense**

A. negundo L. Boxelder. Tall, often multistemmed tree, 10–15 m, crown wide, nodding, twigs completely glabrous, often also pruinose, usually green; leaves pinnate, 3–5 (occasionally 7–9) leaflets, leaflets long oval, 5–10 cm long, cuspidate, distinctly serrate, terminal leaflet often further 3 lobed, upper side light green, underside lighter and often thinly pubescent; flowers yellow-green, dioecious, female flowers in long pendulous racemes, male in dense clusters,

March–April; fruit wings curved inward, acute angled, yellow-white, in long racemes, usually sterile, in Northern Europe. BB 2380; HM 1863A. Eastern and Middle USA, along the shores of permanent bodies of water, never in a pure stand. 1688. z2 ⓕ USA, Canada, Czechoslovakia, USSR, Romania, Italy, Bulgaria, Yugoslavia, India. Plate 11; Fig. 56.

In addition the following cultivars:

A. Young branches pruinose, not pubescent;
Foliage colored:
'Argenteo-limbatum'
'Argenteo-marginatum'
'Argenteo-notatum'
'Aureo-maculatum'
'Aureo-variegatum'
'Chrysophyllum'
'Crispum Variegatum'
'Discolor'
'Elegans'
'Guttatum'
'Luteo-pictum'
'Lutescens'
'Rubescens'
'Variegatum'
'Versicolor'

Foliage green:
'Angustifolium'
'Crispum'
'Giganteum'
'Petiolatum'
var. *pseudo-californicum*
var. *violaceum*'

Growth habit:
'Nanum'

B. Young branches not pruinose, glabrous:
Foliage colored:

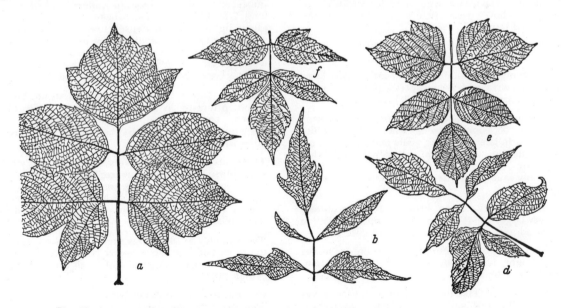

Fig. 62. *Acer negundo* cultivars. a. 'Giganteum; b. 'Angustifolium'; d. 'Nanum'; e. 'Lutescens'; f. 'Quinatum' (from Schwerin)

'Aureo-limbatum'
'Aureo-notatum'
'Auratum'
'Insigne'

Foliage green:
    f. *heterophyllum*
    f. *quinatum*

C. Young branches densely tomentose:
    var. *californicum*
    var. *glaucum*
    var. *interius*
    var. *mexicanum*
    var. *texanum*
    'Odessanum' (gold)

'Angustifolium' (Dieck). Branches pruinose, leaves green, leaflets 5, leaf form quite variable, usually very narrow, tip long drawn out. Fig. 62.

'Argenteo-limbatum' (Schwerin). Very strong growing, branches pruinose, leaflets with a wide white perimeter, mostly green. Male. 1893. ⊘

'Argenteo-marginatum' (Deegen). Very strong growing, branches pruinose; leaflets with a narrow perimeter band, only wider on young leaves. Male. 1888. ⊘

'Argenteo-notatum'. Very strong growing, strongest grower of all the white variegated forms, twigs pruinose, dark violet in fall; leaves dark green with white specks, soft pink at bud break. Before 1893. ⊘

'Auratum' (Spaeth). Strong growing, twigs green, not pruinose; leaves normal, but gold-yellow in color, becoming lighter in fall, petiole usually reddish. Female. 1891. Originated from 'Aureo-limbatum'; see 'Odessanum'! ⊘

'Aureo-limbatum'. Twigs green, tips however a light olive color; leaflets with a wide and regular yellow border. Female. Before 1893. ⊘

'Aureo-maculatum'. Twigs white pruinose; leaves with large and small gold-yellow specks. Before 1893. Oldest of the yellow variegated forms. ⊘

'Aureo-notatum'. Twigs dark green, not pruinose; leaflet with gold-yellow specks. Female. Before 1893. ⊘

'Aureo-variegatum' (Spaeth). Twigs pruinose, leaflets long, acute, dark green with gold-yellow specks, the yellow parts dislike too much sun (= f. *bicolor* Pax z.T.). 1887. ⊘

var. californicum (Torr. & Gray) Sarg. Tree, twigs tomentose; leaflets 3, occasionally to 5, when young, white tomentose beneath, later becoming white pubesent, 4–8 cm long, ovate, acute; fruit with upright, occasionally somewhat overlapped wings, SPa 188; SS 97. S. California, valleys, river banks, generally found with *Alnus, Salix, Platanus*. Plate 10; Fig. 56. ⊘

'Chrysophyllum'. Very strong grower, twigs pruinose; leaflets 5, very large, 14–16 cm long, oval-elliptic, 3 lobed to nearly 3 toothed, yellow colored. Male. Before 1892. ⊘

'Crispum'. Strong grower, young twigs pruinose; leaves green, very bright, leaflets bowed convex on the margin. Female. 1825. Plate 10. ⊘

'Crispum Variegatum'. Like the green form, but the leaves more or less broad yellow bordered. Common in the parks of Holland. Plate 13.

'Discolor'. Fast growing, twigs white pruinose; leaves large, light yellow when young, later generally greening. Female. Before 1893.

'Elegans' (Schwerin). Twigs white pruinose, very light green; leaves with a narrow yellow border, border sharply delineated, lighter yellow than with 'Aureo-limbatum' (= 'Aureo-marginatum' Dieck). Female. Of French origin. Before 1885. ⊘

'Giganteum' (Schwerin). Leaves unusually large. Fig. 62.

'Glaucum'. Young twigs finely pubescent; leaves green. Only male known to occur. Before 1894.

'Guttatum' (Schwerin). Twigs green, pruinose; leaflets oblong, light green, with a lighter green spot in the middle. Female. 1893.

'Heterophyllum' (Spaeth). Young wood green, not pruinose; leaflets ovate, without drawn out tip (as with the pruinose form 'Angustifolium'), however with many various leaf forms, border assymetrical, usually entire and lighter colored than the leaf blade, seldom dentate. Female. 1883.

'Insigne'. Young twigs green, not pruinose; leaflets green, middle yellowish green. Female. Originated from 'Aureo-limbatum'. 1893.

var. interius (Britt.) Sarg. Young twigs with short, lighter pubescence, occasionally nearly completely glabrous; leaflets 3, thin petiole, underside glabrous or with shaggy pubescence along the midrib. BT 665. W. North America. 1914.

'Luteo-pictum'. Young branches brownish violet, darker pruinose in fall; leaflets cuspidate, dull dark green, with a lighter, yellow-green patch in the middle.

'Lutescens'. Young twigs green, brownish on the tip, slightly pruinose; leaflets 5, broad ovate, only slightly longer than wide, light green, becoming yellow in summer. Male. 1893. Fig. 62.

var. mexicanum Wesmael. Tree, young twigs only slightly pubescent, leaves compound, leaflets 3, all elliptic, 6–8 cm long, 2.5–3 cm wide, base cuneate, rather tough, upper side green, lighter beneath, densely tomentose, regularly densely serrate, acuminate; female flower in long racemes, male in clusters, petiole long, white pubescent; fruit glabrous, wings wide spread, 2.5–3.5 cm long (= *A. mexicanum* [DC]. Pax). Mexico; Guatemala; in the mountains. z6

'Nanum' (Dieck). Very weak growing shrub, young twigs green, pruinose, in the 2nd year usually with a beautiful brown, cracked bark; leaflets assymetrical, somewhat branched, margin partly toothed, partly glossy and bowed downward. 1885. Fig. 62.

'Odessanum' (H. Rothe). Very strong grower, young twigs with dense whitish pubescence; leaflets normal, light gold-yellow in the sun, remaining green in shade. Brought into the trade by H. Rothe, Odessa, in 1890, often confused with the glabrous branched 'Auratum', which is the least desirable of the two. ⊘

'Petiolatum'. Shrub, twigs green, pruinose; leaves as with the type, but with much longer petioles (often 18 cm to the first pair of leaflets), total leaf to 40 cm long, pendulous. Female. 1893.

var. pseudo-californicum Schwer. Standard for the green branched types, never brown or violet colored, densely white pruinose, strong grower.

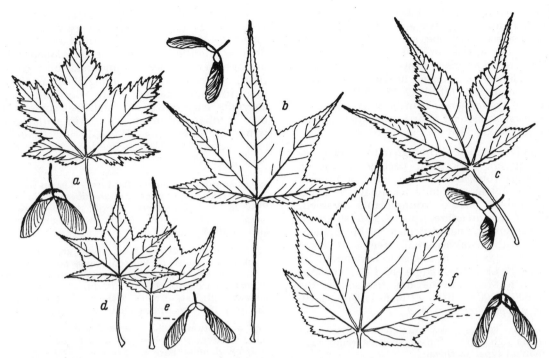

Fig. 63. a. *Acer tschonoskii*; b. *A. oliverianum* var. *nakaharae*; c. *A. micranthum*; d. *A. oliverianum* var. *formosanum*; e. *A. oliverianum* var. *trilobatum*; f. *A. nipponicum* (from Koidzumi)

'Pseudo-crispum'. Young twigs brown-green, violet-white pruinose in fall, first leaves normal until summer, then the lower pairs of leaflets become curled and undulate, the upper pairs remain normal. Male. Schwerin. 1901.

'Quinatum'. Branches green, not pruinose, leaves compound, 5 leaflets. Male and female in culture. 1893. Fig. 62.

f. **rectangulum** Pax. Fruit wings at right angles to obtuse. Fig. 56.

'Rozineckianum'. Twigs green, densely white pruinose; leaves with short petioles, leaflets nearly round. Originated before 1900 in Czechoslovakia.

'Rubescens' (Schwerin). Young twigs brownish green, later violet, pruinose, the youngest 4—6 leaves on the branch are reddish. Female. 1893.

'Subintegrilobum' (Schwerin). Very strong growing, young twigs green, thickly white pruinose; leaves light green, leaflets nearly entire. Male. 1901.

var. **texanum** Pax. Young banches blue tomentose; leaflets 3, broadly elliptic, pubescent beneath when young, eventually totally glabrous, irregularly serrate; fruit with fine pubescence. Texas.

'Variegatum' (Bonamy). Rather weak grower, twigs pruinose; leaflets with wide and irregular white border, green in the middle, blade predominantly white, young leaves edged pink. Female. FS 1781-2 (= f. *bicolor* Pax). The oldest white variegated cultivar and the most common. Plate 13. ⌀

'Versicolor' (Dieck). Young twigs green, white pruinose; leaflets dark green, at first with a wide light green border, but becoming pale in the sun and appearing totally yellowish green, only the shaded leaves are patterned. Male. 1885.

var. **violaceum** (Kirchn.) Jager. Strong grower, branches brown-green, eventually nearly violet-black, blue pruinose, glabrous; leaflets 3—11 (normally 5—7), underside usually softly pubescent. Midwest USA.

A. nevadense see: **A. opalus**

A. nigrum see:. **A. saccharum**

A. nikoense Maxim. Nikko Maple. Tree, to 15 m high, bark not flaky, branches until 2nd year with a rust-yellow pubescence; leaves compound, leaflets 3, ovate to elliptic-oblong, 5—12 cm long, middle leaflet stalked, axillary leaflets sessile, margins entire or occasionally obtusely dentate, upper side dull green, underside gray-green with scattered pubescence, practically scarlet-red in fall; flowers usually 3 in a group, yellow, May; fruit wings nearly parallel, 4.5 cm long. BM ns 387; KRA 30 (= *A. maximowiczianum* Miq., non *A. maximowiczii* Pax.). Japan, mountain forests of Kiusui and Nippon. 1881. Completely hardy. z6 Plate 11; Fig. 56. ⌀

var. *griseum* see: **A. griseum**

var. **megalocarpum** Rehd. Leaflets oblong, to 10 cm long, 5 cm wide, margin crispate or wavy, upper side glossy dark green, whitish green beneath, densely pubescent; flowers 2—5 in dense tomentose clusters; nutlet nearly 1 cm thick, wings 4 cm long, wide apart, with reddish spots. China, W. Hupeh, 1500 to 1800 m. z6

A. nipponicum Hara. Tree or shrub, young twigs and inflorescence at first with fine brown pubescense, but soon glabrous; leaves usually 5 lobed, deeply cordate, 10—15 cm long and wide, lobes acute, broadly ovate, middle lobes largest, basal lobes small, short cuspidate and sharply double serrate, underside pubescent when young, otherwise light green; flowers appearing with the leaves, in dense, long spikes, 10—20 cm long; fruit wings at obtuse angles. MD 1912: 359; KRA 1 (al *2. parviflorum*) (= *A. parviflorum* Franch. & Sav.; *A. crassipes* Pax; *A. brevilobum* Rehd.). Japan; mountain forests of Hondo and Sikoku. 1900. z6 Fig. 53, 63. ∅

A. oblongum DC. Tree, 8—15 m high in the wild, occasionally evergreen, bark gray, peeling in uneven scales, twigs glabrous, new foliage red at bud break; leaves oval-lanceolate, very long acuminate, 5—12 cm long, occasionally 3 lobed on young plants, 3 veined, tough leathery, margin entire, upper side fresh green, underside gray-green, finely reticulate, glabrous; flowers appearing with the leaves, small, greenish, in short panicles; fruit wings at right angles to horizontal, 2.5 cm long. KRA 29; LF 214; ICS 3141; FIO 135. Himalaya; from Kashmir to Middle China, lime free soils in the mountains, 600—2000 m. 1901. z7 Plate 11; Fig. 55, 69, (See also: *A. albopurpurascens*) # ∅

var. **concolor** Pax. Leaves glossy blue-green on the upper side, underside light green, glossy, axillary veins more numerous than the type. Szechwan.

var. **latialatum** Pax. Fruit wings 3 cm long, 1.5 cm wide at the middle. W. Hupeh.

A. obtusatum see: **A. opalus**

A. okamotoanum Nak. Tree, very similar to *A. mono*, young twigs however becoming red-brown (not yellow), then gray-brown, not split; leaves 7 lobed; fruit wings 3.5—4.5 cm long, curving together or at right angles. NK 1: 7. Korea. 1917. Hardy. z5

A. oliverianum Pax. Smaller tree, to 9 m in its habitat, young branches glabrous; leaves 5 lobed, 5—10 cm wide, base truncate to nearly cordate, lobes ovate, acuminate, finely serrate (somewhat like *A. palmatum* var. *palmatum*), both sides equally bright green and glabrous, glossy, reticulate venation; flowers small, whitish, in long stalked corymbs, appearing with the leaves in April—May; fruit with wings 2.5 cm long, horizontally spread, ST 77; KRA 20; ICS 3131; FIO 130. China; Yunnan, Hupeh. 1901. z6 Plate 11; Fig. 49, 53, 75. ∅

ssp. **formosanum** (Koidz.) Murray. Deciduous tree, to 20 m, twigs reddish, glabrous; leaves oval to nearly broad globular, some 7 cm long and 9—10 cm wide, both sides glabrous, base cordate, with 5 vein pairs, palmate, 5 lobed, lobes rather similar, triangular-lanceolate, middle lobe some 5—7 cm long and 1.5—2 cm wide, all irregularly or coarsely double serrate, petiole 2—2.5 cm, glabrous; flowers in terminal cymes, petals 5, yellow, round; fruit wings set at obtuse angles, with nutlet 2.5 cm long. LT 759; KRA 20 (= *A. serrulatum* Hayata). China; Taiwan, common and the tallest species of the genus in Taiwan. z7 Fig. 63.

For var. *nakaharae* Koidz. and var. *trilobum* Koidz see Fig. 63.

var. *tutcheri* see: **A. tutcheri**

A. opalus Mill. Italian Maple. Tree, 10 to 12 m high, young twigs glabrous; leaves very variable, obtuse 5 lobed, 6—10 cm wide, lobes short and wide, bluntly dentate, middle lobe often further 3 lobed, upper side dark green and glabrous, underside blue-green and at first pubescent, soon becoming glabrous; flowers yellow, in short stalked, many flowered, pendulous corymbs, each flower on a stalk 2—4 cm long, floriferous, at foliar bud break, April; fruit with right angled wings, 2.5—4 cm long. HM 1861 (= *A. italum* Lauth; *A. opulifolium* Vill.). SW. Switzerland, SE. France, 1752. z6 Fig. 57. ∅

ssp. **hispanicum** (Pourret) E. Murray. Leaves small, 5 lobed, 2.5—7.5 cm wide, underside often pubescent along the veins. PSw 26 (= *A. hispanicum* Pourret; *A. granatense* Boiss.; *A. nevadense* Boiss. ex Pax). Spain, in the mountains; SW. France, in the Pyreenes. z6

var. **microphyllum** (Kirchn.). Dwarf growing, bark nearly black, twigs short, brown-red; leaves nearly circular, 3 cm wide, 5 lobed, upper side glabrous and dark green, lighter beneath, base with clusters of pubescence, tip of the lobes usually with 3 short teeth. MD 1894: 83 (= *A. microphyllum* Kirchn.). 1865. z6 Appears to be known only in cultivation.

ssp. **obtusatum** (Willd.) Gams. Shrub or small tree; leaves wide, to 10 cm, 5—7 lobed, lobes short, never pointed, margin sparsely dentate, base more or less cordate, upper side glabrous, underside gray-green, softly pubescent, petiole thick; flower stalk pubescent at first, later glabrous; fruit 3 cm long, wings at right angles to nearly acute. DL 2: 208; HM 1861 (= *A. obtusatum* Visiani). Croatia, Dalmatia, Bosnia, Serbia, Herzegovina, Rumelia, Pindus; in Italy appearing only in Calabria and Sicily. 1805. z6 Fig. 57. ∅

var. **tomentosum** (Tausch) Rehd. Leaves to 16 cm wide, lobes short and rounded, underside tomentose, cordate, margin indistinctly crenate; flower stalk pubescent; fruit wings short, wide, spreading. DL 2: 210 (= *A. neapolitanum* Ten.; *A. opalus* var. *neapolitanum* Henry). Italy, open mountain forests near Naples. 1805. z6 Fig. 57.

A. opalus × *A. pseudoplatanus* see: **A. × hybridum**

A. opulifolium see: **A. opalus**

A. × *opulus* var. *obtusatum* × *A. monspessulanum* see: **A. × rotundilobum**

A. orientale L. Shrub or small tree, twigs brownish, few bud scales; leaves evergreen, tough leathery, distinctly unlobed to shallowly 3 lobed, 2.5—5 cm wide, upper side dark green, underside olive-green, margin entire or sparsely serrate, petiole 6—25 mm long; flowers in terminal, rather upright corymbs, petals 5, yellow-green, March; fruit with 2 cm long wings, at acute to horizontal spread, light red at first, ripe in August—Sept. (= *A. creticum* L.; *A. syriacum* Boiss. & Gaillardot; *A. willkommii* Wettst.; *A. hiterophyllum* Wild.). Syria, Lebanon, Cypress. In England, very hardy and evergreen. z8 Plate 11; Fig. 57, 64. See also: *A. sempervirens*.

In the mountains to 800 m, usually in small groups and shrubby growing with *Platanus, Oleander, Arbutus andrachne, Juniperus oxycedrus* etc.

Fig. 64. Upper row *Acer sempervirens*; middle row *Acer orientale*; a. and b, in the lower row were earlier classified by Pax as f. *rotundifolium* and f. *cuneifolium* respectively (Original)

A. osmastonii Gamble. Tree, twigs olive to reddish brown, few bud scales; leaves simple to 3 lobed, 7—15 cm long, margin serrate, base round to cuneate, petiole 2.5 cm; flowers in terminal corymbs, petals 5, cream-yellow to yellow; fruit wings upright or spread, 25 mm. Himalaya; Sikkim. 1908. z6 Earlier erroneously identified as a hybrid of *A. campbellii* and *A. laevigatum*.

A. ovetifolium see: **A. caudatifolium**

A. palmatum Thunb. Shrub or small tree, seldom over 8 m high, twigs glabrous, thin, bright red; leaves deeply (past the middle) 5—11 lobed, 5—10 cm wide, lobes oval-lanceolate, cuspidate, finely double serrate, fresh green, underside lighter, pubescent at the vein axils, carmine-red in fall; flowers small, purple, in small corymbs, June; fruit wing spread at obtuse angles, 1—2 cm long. KRA 26—28; DL 2: 222 (= *A. polymorphum* S. & Z.). Korea, Japan, on all the islands. 1820. z6 Quite variable and well distributed in many cultivars. Plate 12; Fig. 55. ∅

Synonyms of the Cultivars of *A. palmatum* cross referenced to the Japanese names (from E. Murray)
(varieties from other species are noted as such)

'Akai-washino-o'	=	**'Dissectum Orantum'**
'Aoba'	=	**'Caudatum'**
'Aoba-fuké'	=	**'Volubile'**
'Aoki'	=	**'Versicolor'**
'Ayaigasa'	=	*Acer sieboldianum*
'Chishio'	=	**'Sanguineum'**
'Hageromo'	=	**'Sessilifolium'**
'Hazeroino'	=	**'Sessilifolium Hazeroino'**
'Itaya'	=	belongs to *Acer japonicum*
'Koshimino'	=	**'Sessilifolium'**
'Matsugai'	=	**'Argenteo-marginatum'**
'Matsukaze'	=	**'Dissectum'**
'Murasame'	=	*Acer shirasawanum*
'Okushimo'	=	**'Crispum'**
'Sangokaku'	=	**'Corallinum'**
'Senkaki'	=	**'Corallinum'**
'Shigarayama'	=	**'Bicolor'**
'Shishigashira'	=	**'Crispum'**
'Tanabata'	=	**'Atropurpureum'**
'Tsukubane'	=	**'Linearilobum'**
'Tsuru-nishiki'	=	**'Laciniatum'**
'Washino-o'	=	**'Dissectum Rubrum'**
'Yezo-nishiki'	=	**'Sinuatum'**

Classification of the Varieties and Cultivars

1. Leaves medium large, deep 5 lobed, occasionally 7—9 lobed, lobes narrow, oblong-lanceolate, large and biserrate to deeply serrate:
   = var. *palmatum*
   a) Leaves green, normally developed:
      'Autumn Glory' var. *coreanum*, var. *palmatum*, var. *pubescens*
   b) Leaves green, irregularly developed:
      'Crispum', 'Shishigashira', 'Volubile'
   c) Leaves red:
      'Atropurpureum', 'Atropurpureum Novum', 'Bicolor', 'Bloodgood', 'Nigrum', 'Oshio beni', 'Roseo-marginatum', 'Rubricaule', (only the veins red), 'Sanguineum'
   d) Leaves with white areas, also pink at bud break:
      'Argenteo-marginatum', 'Pulverulentum', 'Tricolor', 'Versicolor'
   e) Leaves yellowish:
      'Aureum'
   f) Bark coral red:
      'Corallinum'

2. Leaves large, 7 (occasionally 5 or 9—) lobed, lobes oval-oblong, widest in the middle, fine and regularly biserrate:
   = var. *heptalobum*
   a) Leaves green, lobes incised to ⅓ of the blade:
      'Brevilobum', 'Osakazuki', var. *amoenum*
   b) Leaves green, incised almost to the base:
      'Cuneatum', 'Elegans', 'Laciniatum', 'Sinuatum'
   c) Leaves red or reddish, solid colored:
      'Hessei', 'Laciniatum Purpureum', 'Nicholsonii', 'Sanguineum'
   d) Leaves red or green, with pink or white specks:
      'Reticulatum', 'Saintpaulianum'
   e) Leaves yellow, partly irregular:
      'Flavescens', 'Lutescens', 'Rufescens'

3. Leaves incised to nearly the base, lobes 5—7, linear, narrow, needle-like caudate tipped, very finely and sparsely serrate:
   = 'Linearilobum'
   a) Leaves green:
      'Linearilobum'
   b) Leaves red:
      'Crippsii', 'Linearilobum Atropurpureum', 'Vanhouttei'
   c) Leaves yellow-green:
      'Villa Taranto'

4. Leaves 5—7(—9) lobed, incised nearly to the base, lobes pinnatisect and deeply serrate:
   = 'Dissectum'
   a) Leaves green:
      'Dissectum', 'Dissectum Paucum'

b) Leaves green, white and pink dotted:
   'Dissectum Variegatum'
c) Leaves red or reddish when young:
   'Dissectum Rubrifolium', Dissectum Rubrum',
   'Spring Fire'
d) Leaves always red:
   'Dissectum Crimson Queen', Dissectum Garnet',
   'Dissectum Nigrum', 'Dissectum Ornatum', 'Red
   Pygmy'

5. Leaves deeply incised, all short stalked:
   green:
     'Sessilifolium'
   white variegated:
     'Sessilifolium Hazeroino'

var. **amoenum** (Carr.) Ohwi. Leaves larger than the species,
6–10(–12) cm wide, 7(–9) lobed, lobes often incised to the
middle of the blade and regularly serrate; fruit wings 2–2.5 cm

long, with nutlet; flowers April–May (= A. amoenum Carr.; A.
palmatum ssp. septemlobum Koidz.). Japan; in the mountains.
Quite variable and frequently planted.

'**Argenteo-marginatum**' (Koch 1869). Leaves medium sized,
deeply 5 lobed, margin irregularly with a wide pink border,
soon fading to white (= 'Albo-marginatum'; 'Matsugai').

'**Atropurpureum**' (Van Houtte 1857). Leaves medium size,
deeply 5 lobed, lobes narrow, oblong-lanceolate, coarsely biserrate, nearly black-red and remaining so until fall. FS 1273 (=
'Tanabata', the name of a star). Fig. 65.

'**Atropurpureum Novum**' (Koster 1914). Grows denser than
the above; leaves large, 8–12 cm, with 5–7 lobes, dull dark
brown, also the foliage of the 2nd year twigs is larger than that
of 'Atropurpureum', and remaining on the tree longer than
'Bloodgood'.

'**Aureum**' (Nicholson 1881). Grows bushy; leaves rather small,

Fig. 65. *Acer palmatum*. a. var. *linearilobum*; b. 'Osaka-zuki'; c. 'Nicholsonii;, d. 'Oshio-beni'; e. 'Hessei'
(large and small leaves); f. 'Cuneatum'; g. 'Atropurpureum'; h. var. *heptalobum*; i. 'Reticulatum' (Original)

5−7 cm, 5−7 lobed, gold-yellow, margin somewhat red, good yellow color throughout the summer with no sunscald problem.

'Autumn Glory' (de Belder 1954). Selection for especially good fall foliage, light red, however, during the growing season green and seldom deviating from the species.

'Bicolor' (Siebold 1864). Leaves medium sized, deeply 5 lobed, blood red at bud break, later greening and with some large red specks (= 'Shigara-jama', from the mountain Shigara).

'Bloodgood' (Bloodgood Nurseries, USA). Selection of 'Atropurpureum', but slower growing; leaves 6−10 cm wide, with 5(−7) lobes, slightly serrate, rather deeply incised, dark brown-red, also on the 2nd year twigs.

'Brevilobum' (Hesse ex Schwerin 1893). Leaves very large, 7 lobed, lobes incised to ⅓ of the blade, short, widest at the base, nearly triangular, yellow at bud break, later green.

'Caudatum' (Schwerin 1893) Leaves rather large, 5 lobed, green, lobes long and tips caudate, coarsely serrate, upper side dull lustrous (= 'Aoba', in English "Green").

'Corallinum' (Veitch 1904). Coral Bark Maple. Shrub, to 3 m high, bark of the young twigs a light coral red, especially in winter; leaves 5 lobed, only 4−6 cm long, deeply incised, light green, light pink-red at bud break, orange to light red fall color (= 'Senkaki'; or 'Sangokaku').

var. **coreanum** Nakai. Leaves 5−7 lobed, some 5 cm wide, lobes lanceolate, caudate tipped, doubly serrate; fruit wings to 12 mm long. Geographical form from S. Korea. Fall color an intense carmine and lasting longer than most other maples.

'Crippsii' (Hillier 1928). Of the 'Linearilobum'; lobes nearly grass-like, entire margins, bronze red. Ornamental but a sensitive, weak growing form.

'Crispum' (Siebold ex André 1870). Growth narrow and strictly upright to columnar; leaves small, 5 lobed, dark green, margins rolled upward. IH 43 (= 'Okushimo', English "frost in the ground").

Cuneatum (Schwerin 1893). Leaves large, 7 lobed, the outer pair of lobes much shorter than the middle ones, green, incised to nearly the middle of the blade. Fig. 65.

'Dissectum' (Thunberg 1784). Growth dense, branches often twisted, hemispherical crown, to some 3 × 3 m, usually lower; leaves 5−7(9) lobed, incised nearly to the base, lobes pinnate and deeply serrate, green (× *A. palmatum* var. *dissectum* [Thunb.] Miq.; *A.palmatum* 'Dissectum Viride'; 'Matsukaze'). Plate 12.

'Dissectum Atropurpureum' see: **'Dissectum Ornatum'**.

'Dissectum Crimson Queen' (Cascio 1965). Growth wide and low, otherwise scarcely different from the other red foliage types, somewhat finer, older leaves dark red, 8−13 cm wide.

'Dissectum Flavescens' (Hillier 1928). Leaves like "Dissectum', but young leaves a beautiful yellow-green, on the 2nd year branches yellow-green to orange. As a young plant less branched than the green form.

'Dissectum Garnet' (Guldemond 1960). Growth and foliage like that of 'Dissectum', very dark brown-red and remaining so for the entire summer, somewhat coarser serrate. The best of the red foliage 'Dissectum' forms.

'Dissectum Nigrum' (Waka 1938). Grows denser than the green 'Dissectum' form; leaves very dark brown-red, but somewhat coarser serrate, not turning green (= 'Dissectum Atrosanguineum').

'Dissectum Ornatum' (Siesmayer 1888). Grows 2 to 4 m wide and nearly as high, but usually smaller; leaves as on 'Dissectum', at first brown-red, later light brown-green, the 2nd year growth a dark brown-red (= 'Dissectum Atropurpureum'; 'Akai-washino-o', in English "red Eagle tail"). The most common but not the best red 'Dissectum' form. Plates 10 and 12.

'Dissectum Paucum' (Boskoop 1962). Grows like 'Dissectum', but somewhat wider and taller; leaves dark green, much larger, often reddish. Often used as a rootstock for the other forms. Only slightly ornamental.

'Dissectum Rubrifolium' (Miquel 1865). Growth habit and leaves like 'Dissectum', but brown-red tips at bud break, soon becoming green, 2nd year growth also at first brown-red, soon green (= 'Rubellum'; 'Washino-o', in English "Eagle tail"). Plate 12.

'Dissectum Rubrum' (Barron 1875). Grows like 'Dissectum'; leaves brownish red, later green, larger than on 'Dissectum Rubrifolium'. Good fall color. Rare in cultivation.

'Dissectum Variegatum' (Lawson 1874). Habit and foliage like 'Dissectum', deep lobed, green, lobes partly pink, later white speckled, the colored portions of the lobes curved sickle-shape (= 'Friderici-Guillelmi'; 'Roseopictum'). Not an exceptional form.

'Elegans' (R. Smith 1874). Large, wide shrub, 4−6 m high, branches remaining green for several years; leaves large, 7−12 cm, 7 lobed, incised nearly to the base, coarsely biserrate, light green, leaves pink on 2nd year branches, later becoming green, orange to yellow fall color (= 'Septemlobum Elegans').

'Flavescens' (Veitch 1876). Leaves small, distinctly 7 lobed, base cuneate to truncate, lobes narrow, coarsely serrate, blistery bumps between the veins, leaves cupped, dirty yellow when young, turning dark green.

var. **heptalobum** Rehd. Leaves large, 7 (occasionally 5 or 9) lobed, lobes oval-oblong, widest at the middle, very finely and regularly biserrate. KRA Pl. 26, 7-8 (= *A. palmatum septemlobum* K. Koch). Fig. 58, 65.

'Hessei' (Schwerin 183). Shrub, 4−5 m high and wide, with rather short, thick branches; leaves large, incised nearly to the base, 7 lobed, coarse and deeply biserrate, always dull brown, not greening, brown form of 'Elegans' (= 'Elegans Purpureum'; 'Septemlobum Elegans Purpureum'). Fig. 65.

'Laciniatum' (Siesmayer 1888). Leaves resemble 'Elegans', but with narrower lobes, not as coarsely serrate, lush growing foliage incised nearly to base, the lowest pair of lobes standing horizontally, young leaves dull yellow with brown-red border (= 'Tsuru-nishiki', in English "twisted multicolor").

'Laciniatum Purpureum' (Boskoop 1962). Dense growing shrub, to 3 m high and wide; leaves large, 8 to 12 cm, 7 lobed, deeply incised, coarsely biserrate, brown-red, soon becoming a dirty green, also on the 2nd year twigs. Rare in cultivation, over-shadowed by 'Hessei'.

'Linearilobum' (Miquel 1867). Large, upright shrub; leaves medium sized, 5−7 cm, incised nearly to the base, with 5−7 linear, very narrow, needle-form acute lobes, very finely and sparsely serrate, fresh green, lobes on 2nd year wood, wider and more serrate (= 'Lineare'; 'Scolopendrifolium'). Fig. 65.

Fig. 66. **Acer**. a. *A. coriaceifolium*; b. *A. catalpifolium*; c. *A. garrettii*; d. *A. laevigatum*;
e. *A. litseifolium*; f. *A. paxii* (from ICS)

'Linearifolium Atropurpureum' (Nicholson 1881). Like the above cultivar, but only 3 m high and 1.5 m wide; leaves somewhat larger, the lineal lobes not or scarcely serrate, brown-red, lobes on second year wood wider and coarsely serrate. FS 1273 (= 'Atrolineare'; 'Scolopendrifolium Rubrum'). Problem prone, out performed by 'Red Pygmy'.

'Lutescens' (Hillier 1928). Leaves 7 lobed, very glossy, butter-yellow in fall (= 'Heptalobum Lutescens').

'Nicholsonii' (Schwerin 1893). Very similar to 'Laciniatum', the lowest pair of lobes likewise horizontal, but cordate on the base (very straight on 'Laciniatum') and with red leaves, soon turning green, the same on the 2nd year wood; red fall color. Fig. 65.

'Nigrum' (Hillier 1928). Leaves 7 lobed, deep purple.

'Osakazuki' (Yokohama 1898). Strong grower, to 5 m high and 4 m wide; leaves large, 6–10 cm, 7 lobed, dark green, usually incised to near the middle, finely serrate, young leaves pink-brown, then yellow-brown, finally green, orange

and carmine fall color. Classified under var. *heptalobum*. Very useful form. Fig. 65.

'Oshio-beni' (Yokohama 1898). Leaves brown-red, 9 lobes, very deeply incised, more dull brown in summer. Fig. 65.

var. **palmatum.** The type of this species. KRK 26: 1–6. For description see p. 87.

var. **pubescens** Li. Shaggy white pubescence on young twigs, later glabrous; leaves to 5 cm long, veins on both sides with long pubescence, likewise the blade and petiole. LT 757. Taiwan; in mountain forests, at 1600 m.

'Pulverulentum' (Schwerin 1896). Leaves medium size, 5 lobed, coarsely punctate and pulverulent. Occasionally encountered as a mutation on 'Versicolor' and held constant by grafting.

'Red Pygmy' (C. Esveld 1967). Dwarf growth, to 70 cm in some 10 years, seldom over 2 m high at maturity; dark leaved form of 'Linearilobum'; leaves 5 lobed, the lobes 3–7 cm long, 2–3 mm wide, margins nearly entire, dark red-brown, later more brown-green, 2nd year growth lighter red, lobes shorter, wider, 3—5 cm long, 5—13 mm wide, serrate, but in the following years returning to normal size lobes. Found in Italy.

'Reticulatum' (André' 1870). Leaves medium size, light gray-green to whitish yellow, but with all venation remaining dark green. Plate 10; Fig. 65.

'Roseomarginatum' (Van Houtte 1865). Grows strongly upright, 4—6 m; leaves rather small, 4—6 cm, 5—7 lobed, deeply incised, margin irregularly serrate and notched, dark pink, later becoming lighter, but never white. FS 1566.

'Rubricaule' (R. Smith 1874). Leaves medium size, 5 lobed, lobes coarsely serrate, widest in the middle, light green, petiole and veins remaining red (= 'Rubrinerve').

'Rufescens' (Siesmayer 1888). Growth wide and strong, to 4 m high; leaves large, 7—9 cm, 7—9 lobed, rather deeply incised, yellow-green, fox-red in fall (= 'Heptalobum Rufescens').

'Saintpaulianum' (Schwerin 1896). Leaves large, 7 lobed, dark red as with 'Sanguineum', with numerous gold-yellow specks, but not on every leaf.

'Sanguineum' (Lemaire 1867). Shrub, widely branched, 3—4 m high; leaves large, 8—12 cm, 7 lobed, deeply incised, finely serrate, exactly like var. *heptalobum*, but red-brown. IH 526; RH 1867: 391 (= 'Rubrum'; 'Rubro-latifolium'; 'Purpureum'; 'Septemlobum Rubrum').

'Scolopendrifolium, see: **'Linearilobum'**.

'Senkaki' see: **'Corallinum'**.

'Septemlobum' see: var. **heptalobum**.

'Sessifolium' (Sieb. & Zucc. 1845). Upright shrub, grows like the species; leaf petiole 6 mm long, leaves small, 4—6 cm, 5 lobed, irregularly developed, divided nearly to the base, lower part of the leaflets drawn out to a thin stalk, margin very coarsely serrate, green (= 'Hagoromo', in English "Winged Rock"). Of little ornamental value.

'Sessilifolium Hazeroino' (Boom 1965). Like 'Sessilifolium' but with white variegated leaves.

'Shishi-gashiri' (Yokohama 1896). Growth broadly columnar, with thick, knotty branches, 3—4 m high; leaves very small, 2—4 cm, dark green, 5 lobed, lobe halves split and slightly overlapped, then curved under in claw-like fashion or cupped like a snail shell (= 'Cristatum'). Ornamental and very effective.

'Sinuatum' (Schwerin 1893). Leaves large, 7 lobed, incised to the base, lobes narrowing considerably to the base, rounded between the lobes, green, otherwise like var. *heptalobum* (= 'Yezonishiki').

'Spring Fire' (Van Gelderen 1969). Growth very slow, upright, to 2 m; leaves small, 4—6 cm, 5—7 lobed, deeply incised and serrate, light fire red at first, soon changing to wine red, eventually nearly green or dirty green (= 'Purpureum' Kruessmann). From the Villa Taranto Botanic Garden in Pallanza, Italy. Originally disseminated as 'Purpureum'.

'Tricolor' (Nicholson 1881). Leaves medium size, 7 lobed, green with red, pink and white specks at the same time, symmetry of blade distinguishes it from 'Versicolor'.

'Vanhouttei' (Schwerin 1893). Leaves deeply 5 lobed, margin deep and irregularly serrate, as with 'Linearilobum', but red.

'Versicolor' (Van Houte 1861). Growth strong and tall, as with the species; leaves medium size, 5 lobed, fresh green with large specks, at first light pink, later white, colored parts slow to develop and therefore leaf blade is asymmetrical. FS 1498; Gfl 1363 (= 'Aoki').

'Villa Taranto' (Van Gelderen 1969). Shrub, densely branched, to 3 m high, slow growing; leaves 5—7 lobed, lobes linear, incised to the base, finely serrate, yellow-green to light brown, 2nd year branches fire red, and leaves with lobes wider and serrate. Found in the Villa Taranto Botanic Garden, but also long in cultivation at the Kalmthout Arboretum (Belgium).

'Volubile' (Schwerin 1893). Leaves medium size, 5 lobed, middle lobe twisted either completely or just on the tip, light green at bud break, later becoming dark green, older leaves with a wide yellow-green stripe on both sides of the midrib on each lobe (= 'Aoka-fuké', in English "green blade-speckled").

A. palmifolium see: **A. saccharum**

A. papilio see: **A. caudatum**

A. parviflorum see: **A. nipponicum**

A. parvifolium see: **A. × coriaceum**

A. paxii Franch. Tree, to 9 m high in the wild, resembles *A. buergerianum*, but evergreen; leaves oval-oblong, 3 lobed on the tip, 5—7 cm long, 3—4 cm wide, lobes short acuminate, base 3 veined, round, upper side light green and glossy, underside blue-green, tough and leathery, petiole 2—4 cm long, thin; flowers small, whitish, appearing with the leaves, April—May; ovary long and densely pubescent, fruit 3 cm long, wings form a wide angle. EP IV, 136: 3; ICS 3140. Middle China; Yunnan, mountain forests. In cultivation at the Royal Botanic Garden, Kew (England). z8 Fig. 49, 53, 66. #

A. pectinatum Wall. ex Nichols. Tall, deciduous tree, young branches glabrous, reddish to brownish or gray; leaves 3—5 lobed (5 lobed leaves often have very small basal lobes), blade 7.5—14 cm long and wide or somewhat wider, lobes triangular to oval, acuminate to caudate, finely and sharply serrate to biserrate, teeth drawn out to awn-like tips, midrib and venation on the underside at first covered with a rust colored powder, later more or less glabrous except for the basal vein axils; flowers in racemes; fruit in dense racemes, 7—10 cm long, on 4 to 10 mm long stalks; wings wide angled to horizontal, 2—2.5 cm long, 5—10 mm wide. Himalaya; from Nepal east to Upper Burma, probably to Yunnan. Commonly cultivated in England. Often confused with *A. caudatum*, but easy to distinguish by the awn tipped teeth and pruinose underside of the young foliage. z6 ∅

A. pensylvanicum L. Striped, Snake-bark Maple, Moosewood. Tree or tree-like shrub, 6—12 m high, wide crowned when growing in the open, twigs smooth, green with white stripes, never pruinose; leaves obovate, 3 very short, sharp acuminate, doubly serrate lobes at the blade tip, 12—18 cm long, underside with rust-yellow soft pubescence at first, later only at the vein axils, clear yellow fall foliage, leaf petiole with brown-yellow pubescence; flowers yellowish, in glabrous, pendulous racemes, following the leaves; fruit with sickle-form curved, upright wings. HH 386-387; SS 84; BB 2378 (= *A. striatum* DuRoi). NE. USA, E. Canada. 1755. z4 Plate 16 and 17; Fig. 55. ∅ ⚭

In its natural habitat often only a shrub, shade loving and usually near water, companion plant of *Betula lutea, Tsuga, Picea, Carya, Fagus.*

'Erythrocladum' (Spaeth). Young twigs a lively carmine-red in winter. Before 1904. ∅
Seedlings will occasionally occur with yellow or white speckled foliage and are named 'Aureovariegatum' and 'Albovariegatum' respectively. The leaves are often asymmetrical as a result of the slower developing variegated areas.

A. pentaphyllum Diels. Tree, to 10 m, bark ash gray, branches wide spreading, young twigs thin, brown; leaves compound, 4—7, usually 5, leaflets, oblong-lanceolate, 5—7 cm long, 1.5 cm wide, obtuse, margin entire or serrate, often also rolled inwards, upper side fresh green, underside bluish, lowest leaflets nearly sessile, others stalked to 6 mm long, leaf petiole reddish, 4—7 cm long; flowers in corymbs, but so far not observed; fruit wings wide spread, to 2 cm long, nutlet pubescent, 5 mm wide. ICS 3157. SW. China, Szechwan, Yalung Valley. 1929. Outside of its native habitat, a very rare tree. z6 Fig. 75. ∅

A. pentapotamicum. J. L. Stewart. Small tree or shrub, bark smooth, gray; leaves 3 lobed, quite variable in size, from 3—10 cm long and 5—15 cm wide, lobes incised to the middle of the blade, narrowing at the tip, obtusely serrate, base truncate to cordate, both sides gray-green and underside eventually glabrous except for the vein axils; flowers in short corymbs, petals 5; fruit wings 2.5 cm long, at acute angles, nutlet glabrous (= *A. regelii* Pax.). NW. Himalaya; Afghanistan, Turkestan, W. Pakistan, in dry, open forests. (A. "pentapomicum" is simply a printing error!) In cultivation in England. z6 Ⓕ W. Pakistan.

A. × peronai see: **A. × martinii**

A. perrieri see: **A. × martinii**

A. pictum see: **A. mono**

A. pilosum Maxim. Small tree, 6—9 m high, twigs thin, reddish or gray, dotted; leaves 3 lobed, 4—10 cm wide, base slightly cordate, lobes oval-oblong, acuminate, middle lobe much longer and with parallel margins, nearly entire or sparsely coarse serrate, tough leathery, upper side dark green and glossy, underside lighter and gray pubescent, at least on the veins, petiole 3 to 6 cm long, red, pubescent; flowers yellow-green, small, in clusters. NW. China; Kansu, Shansi. 1911. Hardy. z6 So far not in cultivation.

A. platanoides L. Norway Maple. Tree, to 30 m high, crown dense, oval, bark dark gray, finely ridged, not peeling, twigs glabrous; leaves 5 lobed, 10—18 cm

wide, lobes acuminate, sparsely serrate, dark green above, glossy beneath, vein axils pubesent, yellow fall color; flowers yellowish green, in many flowered, upright corymbs, on the red foliage varieties often reddish yellow, appearing before the leaves, April; fruit pendulous, wings nearly horizontal, 3—5 cm long, nutlet flat. HM 1851. Europe to the Caucasus. Long history of cultivation. Many cultivars. z3 Ⓕ Romania, Czechoslovakia, Netherlands, USSR. Plates 13 and 18; Fig. 54, 68. ∅

Outline of the Cultivars

A. Growth Habit
Branches pendulous:
   'Almira', 'Pendulum'
Columnar:
   'Cleveland', 'Columnare', 'Emerald Queen', 'Erectum', 'Olmsted'
Globose:
   'Globosum', 'Charles F. Irish'
Grows Dwarf:
   'Pygmaeum'

B. Leaf forms
1. Leaves green, normally developed;
   a) Foliage at bud break pale reddish:
      'Acuminatum', 'Columnare', 'Erectum', 'Incumbens'
   b) Young leaves dotted red:
      'Adspersum', 'Latifolium'
   c) Young leaves red-brown:
      'Globosum', 'Laetum', 'Rufescens'
2. Leaves off color;
   a) Leaves dark red:
      'Crimson King', 'Faassens Black', 'Goldsworth Purple', 'Reitenbachii', 'Royal Red', 'Rubrum', 'Schwedleri'
   b) Leaves white colored:
      'Albescens', 'Albovariegatum', 'Bicolor', 'Drummondii', 'Pictum', 'Pueckleri', 'Walderseei'
   c) Leaves yellow colored:
      'Aureovariegatum', 'Buntzelii'
3. Leaves bumpy or blistery:
   'Roseo-bullatum', 'Undulatum'
4. Leaves symmetrical, divided nearly to the base, long and deeply incised and dentate:
   'Dissectum', 'Palmatifidum'
5. Leaves crispate on the margin:
   a) Leaf base rounded:
      'Cucullatum'
   b) Leaf base cuneate:
      'Argutum', 'Laciniatum', 'Plicatum'
6. Leaves asymmetrical, margin irregularly incised (partly colored):
   'Albodentatum', 'Dilaceratum', 'Heterophyllum Variegatum', 'Irregulare', 'Wittmackii'
7. Leaves 3 lobed, often cupulate:
   'Stollii'

'Acuminatum' (Schwerin). Leaves normal green, lobes narrow and drawn out to an acute tip. 1893. Fig. 68.

'Adspersum' (Schwerin). Leaves normal, however thick when young with small red, sharply defined specks. 1893.

'Albescens' (Dieck). Leaves normal, cream-white at bud break, but shortly becoming green, and later in summer and fall mature foliage is reddish, not white. 1885.

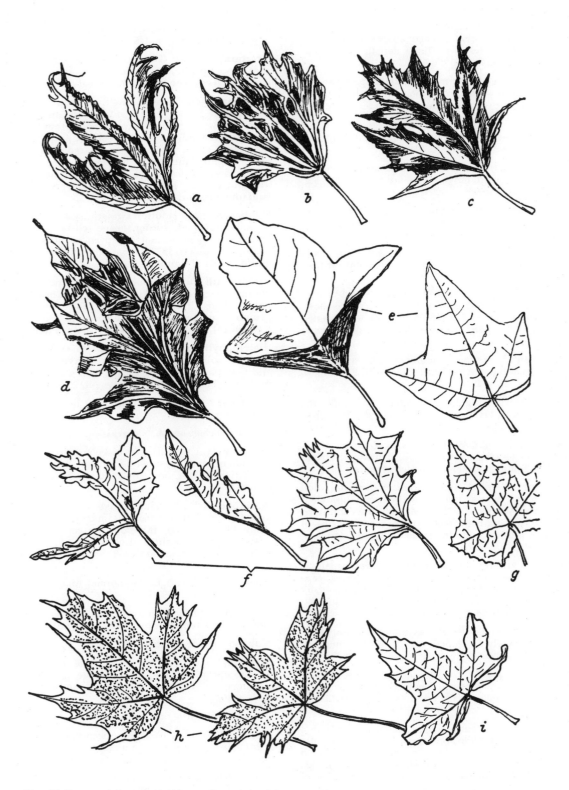

Fig. 67. Forms of *Acer platanoides*. a. 'Laciniatum'; b. 'Cucullatum'; c. 'Argutum'; d. 'Plicatum'; e. 'Stollii', left with cup; f. 'Dilaceratum', 3 leaves; g. 'Albodentatum'; h. 'Heterophyllum Variegatum'; i. 'Aureovariegatum' (h. from Boom, others from Schwerin)

'Aibodentatum', New foliage normal; leaves on summer branches are 3 lobed, margin notched, a few summer leaves also unlobed, white pulverulent, finely dentate, white, August leaves again normal. 1893. Fig. 67.

'Albovariegatum'. Leaves normal, speckled, specks at first light pink, later clear white, leaves sometimes half white and green or completely white or white with green centers or gray-green (= *quadricolor* Dieck). 1822. ∅

'Almira'. Umbrella-shaped canopy, low. A selection from H. E. Scanlon Cleveland, Ohio, USA. 1948.

'Argutum' (Schwerin). Leaves green, deeply incised, margin generally curved inward, but the lobes not rolled. 1893. Fig. 67.

'Aureovariegatum'. Leaves normal, only faintly reddish at bud break, large gold-yellow specks. Originated in Moscow before 1893, but common in England as early as 1838. Fig. 67.

'Bicolor' (Schwerin). Leaves normal, green, speckled, specks on the branch tips, large and light yellow (not pink) at first, very soon paling to pure white. 1893.

'Buntzelii'; (Wittmack). Leaves at bud break red-brown, speckled, specks orange-brown at first, later gold-yellow, venation remaining red (= *buntzleri* Wittmack). 1880. Named for Max Buntzler, Garden Director of Berlin-Niederschoene-weide.

'Charles F. Irish'. Large tree, globular crown; leaves somewhat smaller than the species. A selection of H. E. Scanlon, Cleveland, Ohio, USA. 1948.

'Cleveland'. Grows upright, oval, dense; leaves like the species. A selection of H. E. Scanlon, Cleveland, Ohio, USA. 1947.

'Columnare' (Carrière). Growth narrowly columnar, dense, slow, stays low; leaves normal, small, lightly red at bud break. 1855 by Simon Louis Frères in Metz, France.

'Crimson King' (Barbier). Leaves remain dark red, dull glazed, youngest leaves dark brown-red and wrinkled. American Plant Patent Nr. 735 (= *A. platanoides schwedleri nigrum* Barbier). Originally raised from seed by Tips in Belgium, then introduced to the trade by Barbier, Orléans, France. 1946. ∅

'Cucullatum' (Carrière). Leaves rounded, base usually 7 veined, lobes small, curved downward, blade convex, cap-like, somewhat bubbled out between the major veins; habit normal, tree-like (10 m tall in Westfalenpark, Dortmund, W. Germany). 1866. Plate 18, Fig. 67. ∅

'Dilaceratum' (Dieck). Leaves very asymmetrical, quite variable, some completely developed, see Fig. 67; the abnormal margin yellowish. 1885.

'Dissectum'. Weak grower, young twigs smooth, red-brown; leaves divided nearly to the base, deeply toothed, new foliage brownish, mature foliage dark green (= var. *palmatum* K. Koch). 1869. Fig. 68.

'Drummondii'. Leaves normal, light green, margin with a very wide and regular white border, partly yellowish white, soft pink at bud break, middle gray-green. MD 1910. (shown somewhat atypically with the white border too narrow). 1903 from Drummond, introduced to the trade in Stirling, Scotland. Fig. 68. ∅

'Emerald Queen' (McGill). Growth strictly upright, quickly develops a strong stem, young branches ascending, later developing a wide crown. Introduced in 1963 by A. McGill & Son, Fairview, Oregon, USA.

'Erectum' (Slavin). Growth narrowly pyramidal, branches short and upright, very similar to 'Columnare', but with larger, darker green leaves. In cultivation in USA since 1931.

'Faassens Black' (Tips). Growth moderately strong; leaves dark purple-brown, upper side glossy, margin somewhat curved upward, young leaves smooth (not wrinkled), fall color an outstanding red; inflorescence purple-red except for the yellow-green petals; fruit stalk red. Found in Herkde-Stad, Belgium. Introduced in 1936 by Tips. Previously distributed as *A. platanoides* 'Globosum Purpureum'. Since 1946 distributed by the Faasen-Hekkens Nursery in Tegelen, Holland under its current name. ∅

'Globosum' (Van Houtte). Growth broader than high, very densely branched, spring foliage red-brown; lower leaves light red, others normal, sharp and acutely dentate (= f. *compactum* Paillet). 1873. Frequently found but nearly always grafted on a tall standard. Plate 18.

'Goldsworth Purple' (Slocock). Leaves normal, black-red, young leaves very wrinkled, totally light brown-red, much lighter than 'Crimson King' and 'Faassens Black', dull if pruinose, no particular fall coloration. Introduced to the trade in 1947 by W. C. Slocock of Woking, England. ∅

'Heterophyllum Variegatum'. Leaves asymmetrical, 10–12 cm wide, lobes of uneven size and varying form, teeth long and very narrow, spring foliage light green, margin at first pink, later becoming light yellow. ND 20: 10c-d. Fig. 67.

'Incumbens'. Leaves normal, base deeply cordate, lobes overlapping. 1886..

var. *integrilobum* see: **A. × dieckii**

'Irregulare' (Schwerin). Leaves asymmetrical, often one side of blade normal, the other deformed, slightly crenate, varying with each leaf, not variegated. 1893. Commonly grown. Fig. 68.

'Laciniatum' (Sutherland). Leaves deeply lobed, very long and acutely dentate, margins and lobes curled under in "claw-like" fashion, therefore the common name "Eagle Claw Maple" ("Griffes du Procureur", "Vogelkrallena-horn"); growth pyramidal. 1683. Not unusual. Plate 18, Fig. 67.

'Laetum' (Schwerin). Leaves normal, totally light green, later becoming darker. 1893.

'Latifolium'. Leaves normal, but much larger than the species, large red spots on spring foliage. Dieck 1885.

'Lobergii' see: 'Palmatifidum'.

Meyering' (J. Meyering 1958). Selection from Holland; growth upright, strong; spring foliage light brown, soon becoming green, beautiful orange-red to red-brown in fall.

'Natorp'. Very weak grower, small-leaved sport of 'Schwedleri'. Little horticultural value.

'Olmsted' (Scanlon 1952). American selection; slow grower, columnar to narrowly pyramidal, well branched. Good tree for narrow streets; much used in Holland.

'Palmatifidum' (Tausch). Leaves incised to the base, lobes deeply dentate, very similar to 'Dissectum', but with mature foliage remaining light green, young branches yellow-green, later rough and yellow-brown, very strong growing, branches occasionally twisted. Known since 1829 by this

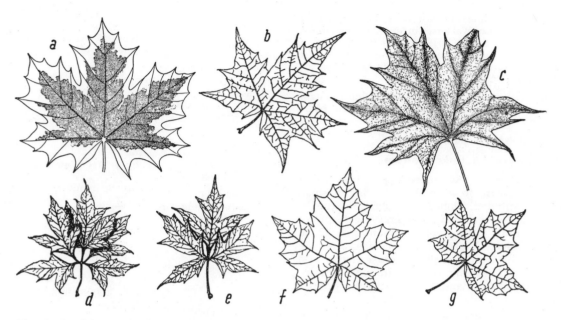

Fig. 68. Leaf forms of *Acer platanoides*. a. 'Drummondii'; b. 'Acuminatum'; c. 'Walderseei'; d. 'Palmatifidum' (= 'Lorbergii'); e. 'Dissectum'; f. the typical species; g. 'Irregulare' (from Boom, Schwerin)

name, but in 1878 given the name 'Lorbergii' for a plant found by Lorberg. Fig. 68.

'Pendulum' (Niemetz). Branches strictly weeping. Found around 1900 by Niemetz in Timisoara, Romania. Not in cultivation.

'Pictum' (Hesse). Very strong grower; leaves normal, pink pulverulent spring foliage, later evenly white pulverulent. 1891. Similar to 'Walderseei', but less consistent. Not in cultivation.

'Plicatutm' (Schwerin). Leaves 5 lobed, base cuneate, lobes long triangular, margin entire, blade folded between the major veins both upward and under. Found before 1893 in the castle garden of Janow, Pomerania. Fig. 67.

'Pueckleri' (Spaeth). Leaves normal, variegated in red, pink, gray, brown and white tones on the spring foliage, but the mature foliage only white variegated. 1885. (as "Reichsgraf von Pückler"). Ø

'Pygmaeum' (Schwerin). Dwarf, a year's growth only a few cm long; leaves only 3.5—5 cm long. 1893. Long in cultivation at Spaeth Nursery, Berlin, W. Germany.

'Reitenbachii'. Leaves and growth habit normal, spring foliage reddish green with numerous dark red specks (twigs of young grafted plants red), turning blackish red in late summer and remaining so until fall, also the venation underneath; petals, flower stalk and outside of calyx red; leaf margin somewhat bowed upward. Found by Reitenbach at his Manor Plicken near Gumbinnen, W. Germany, 1874. Later erroneously listed by Rehder as a synonym to *A. platanoides* 'Rubrum'. Ø

'Roseo-bullatum' (Schwerin). Spring foliage normal, then later leaves with pink blister-like bumps, rest of the blade remains dark green. Before 1893.

'Royal Red' (Holmason). American selection; supposedly a

stronger grower with darker red leaves than 'Crimson King'; from its use in Holland, little difference has been observed. 1964.

'Rubrum' (Herder). Leaves normal green, becoming dark red in fall, inflorescence green. Gfl 1867: Pl. 545 (see note on 'Reitenbachii'). No longer in cultivation.

'Rufescens' (Schwerin). Leaves normal, spring foliage dark red-brown, soon becoming green. 1893.

'Schwedleri' (K. Koch). Spring foliage blood red; leaves later dark red-green to olive green, upper side glossy, margin somewhat revolute, petiole and venation remaining red, generally an effective red in early summer. Found by Carl Heinrich Schwedler, head gardener for Prince Hohenlohe, in Slawentitz, Upper Silesia, Prussia (Poland). 1864.

'Stollii' (Spaeth). Leaves usually 3 lobed, margins entire, very much resembling *Hedera*, often with cone-shaped base, growth pyramidal (= *A. platanoides* 'Oekonomierat Stoll'). A seedling of 'Schwedleri' germinated by Spaeth, Berlin. 1888. Plate 18, Fig. 67. Ø

'Summershade'. Upright, fast growing selection, very dark foliage. US Plant Patent Nr. 1748. Introduced by Princeton Nursery, USA. 1957. Said to succeed in hot dry areas where the species would fail to thrive.

'Superform Miller'. Growth strong and strictly upright; young leaves at the branch tips always dark green, never brownish. Introduced in 1968 by Milton Nursery in Milton-Freewater, Oregon, USA.

'Undulatum' (Dieck). Leaf blade welled up between the veins, medium size, margin crispate, teeth short, acute. From seed by Dieck of Zoschen, introduced to the trade in 1885.

'Walderseei' (Spaeth). Strong grower; leaves somewhat irregular, incision between lobes relatively shallow, spring foliage gray-green with trace of pink or brown, developing leaves with numerous fine white dots on the blade. Found in 1900 in the park of Count Waldersee in Mesendorf and introduced to the trade by Spaeth in 1904. Resembels 'Pictum', a weaker grower, although having more consistent color. A large tree in the Tannenhoft Arboretum in Schmalenbeck near Hamburg. Fig. 68. Ø

'Wittmackii' (Schwerin). Leaves asymmetrical, margin notched, occasionally dentate, young leaves colored, blade green, margin yellow, teeth red. Before 1893.

A. polymorphum see: **A. palmatum**

A. pseudo-laetum see: **A. turkestanicum**

A. psepudoplatanus L. Sycamore Maple. Tree with a broad arched crown, to 40 m, bark peeling in small flakes; leaves rounded, 5 lobed, 8—16 cm wide, tough, upper side dark green, underside gray-green, pretty gold-yellow in fall; flowers yellow-green, in 8—12 cm long, many flowered, pendulous racemes, after the leaves, May; fruit wings usually at obtuse angles. HM 1848. z6 ⓕ West Germany, Austria, Italy, Czechoslovakia, Romania, Netherlands, New Zealand. Fig. 53. Ø ✿

Mid-European mountains, north to the Harz; Crimea, Caucasus. Prefers a deep humus soil, tolerates alkaline or sandy-clay soil, dislikes excessive moisture or dryness. Superior park tree.
There are many cultivars to this species often found in older parks.

Outline of the Cultivars

A. Leaves distinctly 5 lobed;
  1. Leaves green;
    a) Leaves symmetrical, base broadly cordate:
      'Erectum', 'Jaspideum', 'Latifolium', 'Laxum', 'Negenia', 'Pyramidale', 'Rotterdam', Serotinum', var. *tomentosum*
    b) Leaves asymmetrical:
      'Heterophyllum'
    c) Leaves bullate:
      'Concavum', 'Neglectum', 'Rugosum'
    d) Blade base deeply cordate, basal lobes overlapping:
      'Clausum'
    e) Leaves deeply 5 lobed:
      'Palmatifidum', 'Serratum'

  2. Leaves off colored:
    a) Leaves green, but light red on the branch tips:
      'Cupreum', 'Metallicum', 'Opulifolium'
    b) Leaves yellowish, those in shade greenish:
      'Flavescens', 'Worleei'
    c) Leaves gold-yellow speckled, young leaves brown:
      'Aucubifolium', 'Aureo-variegatum', 'Brilliantissimum'
    d) Leaves speckled straw-yellow, young leaves reddish:
      'Leopoldii', 'Limbatum', 'Tricolor', 'Variegatum', 'Zebrinum'
    e) Leaves light green, very densely dotted light yellow:
      'Bicolor', 'Luteo-virescens'
    f.) Leaves purple-red on the underside:
      + upper side not speckled:
      'Atropurpureum', 'Purpurescens', 'Purpureum'

      ++ upper side gold-yellow or light yellow speckled:
      'Nervosum', 'Nizetii', 'Prinz Handjery', 'Pseudo-Nizetti'

B. Leaves 3 lobed:
  1. Leaves green:
    'Cruciatum', 'Trilobatum', 'Vitifolium'
  2. Leaves colored:
    a) Leaves green, young leaves blood red:
      'Rafinesquianum'
    b) Leaves yellow:
      'Albertii'
    c) Leaves very light green, new leaves yellow-green:
      'Laetum', 'Spaethii'

C. Leaves triangular:
  1. Leaves green:
    'Argutum', 'Opizii'
  2. Leaves yellow:
    'Corstorphinense'
  3. Leaves speckled white, new leaves pink
    'Annae', 'Discolor', 'Insigne', 'Pulverulentum', 'Simon Louis Frères'

D. Leaves with crispate margin:
  'Crispum'
E. Leaves incised to the base, 3 lobed:
  'Ternatum', 'Purpureo-digitatum'
F. Fruit wings bright red:
  f. *erythrocarpum*

(Some cultivars are based on variation in form and spread of the fruit wings, but they have little garden importance and are therefore omitted here.)

'Albertii' (Dippel). Leaves shallowly 3 lobed, especially the young leaves, basal lobes very small, others large, broadly ovate, at first light orange to yellow, later leaves in sun speckled white-yellow, branches very thick, light gray, buds thick. 1892.

'Annae' (Schwerin). Leaves nearly triangular, lobes long, speckled white, without powdery white surface, new foliage dark brown, specks blood red, then pink and finally white, blade otherwise light green, specks few, but large. 1893.

'Argutum' (Schwerin). Leaves nearly triangular, light green, the lobes long acuminate, deep and sharply serrate. 1893.

'Atropurpureum' (Spaeth). Leaves normal, 5 lobed, upper side dark green, red-brown in spring, underside deep red, total leaf appears deep red with backlighting, fruit wings dark red (see 'Purpurascens'). 1883. Referred to as 'Spaethii' in Holland. Plate 20. Ø

'Aucubifolium' (Nicholson). Leaves normal, 5 lobed, green, entire blade surface covered with pea size, round, yellow specks. England 1881.

'Aureo-variegatum'. With few large yellow specks, otherwise like 'Aucubifolium', with specks much larger. Introduced into the trade in 1885 by Dieck as var. *bicolor*.

'Bicilor' (Spaeth). Leaves normal, 5 lobed, new foliage light green, then becoming straw yellow, later densely white pulverulant. 1880.

'Brilliantissimum' (Clark). Very similar to 'Prinz Handjery', but with underside green, not red, upper surface gold-yellow at first, later light yellow specks running to pink; weak grower, only 2—3 m high, conical, therefore usually grafted

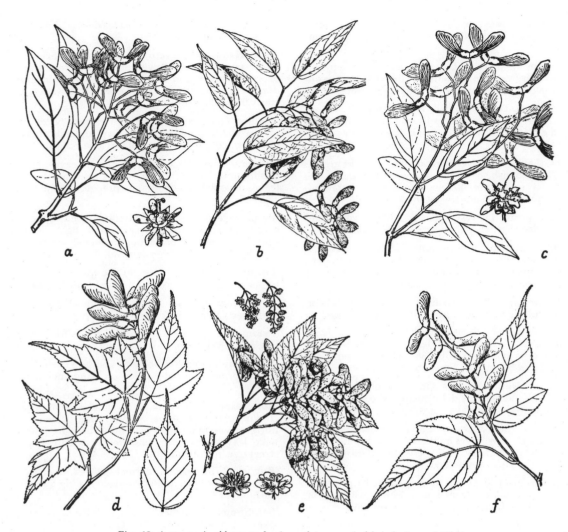

Fig. 69. **Acer.** a. *A. oblongum*; b. *A. cordatum*; c. *A. fabri*; d. *A. caudatifolium*;
e. *A. davidii*; f. *A. laxiflorum* (from ICS)

on standards. Known since 1905 in England and not uncommon today.

'Clausum' (Schwerin). Leaves normal, 5 lobed, green, basal lobes widely overlapping. 1893.

'Concavum' (Schwerin). Leaves 5 lobed, margins generally bowed upward, gold-yellow in the sun, leaves much smaller than those of 'Worleei' (= 'Luteo concavum'). 1893.

'Corstorphinense' (Sutherland). Leaves often only 3 lobed, especially when young, lobes triangular, light yellow, later becoming green, leafs out 8—10 days before the other forms. Found 1679, in Corstorphine near Edinburgh, Scotland where the original tree still stands. ⊘

'Crispum' (Schwerin). Leaves asymmetrical, usually 5 lobed, lobes twisted and crispate, venation usually yellowish. 1893.

'Cruciatum' (Schwerin). Leaves nearly distinct 3 lobed, green, both side lobes standing at right angles from the petiole, forming a cross. 1893.

'Cupreum' (Behnsch). Leaves normal, 5 lobed, green, young foliage light copper-red. 1885.

'Discolor' (J. Miller). Leaves small, 3 lobed, lobes triangular, yellowish pink in spring, later becoming pure white, major veins green, eventually leaves becoming green with white pulverulence; weak growth (= *A. pseudoplatanus punctatum*). 1826.

'Erectum' (Doorenbos). Growth narrowly upright, all branches directed stiffly upward; leaves normally 5 lobed, base rather flat (!). Found in 1935 in "Nachtegaalplein", The Hague, Holland and originally distributed under that name.

f. **erythrocarpum** (Carr.) Pax. Leaves like the type, but somewhat smaller, upper side glossy, fruit wings bright red. RH 1864, Bavarian alps, common. Plate 19. ⊗

'Euchlorum' (Spaeth). Leaves deep dark green, deeply 5 lobed, underside light gray-green, petiole yellow. 1878. Plate 19. ⊘

'Flavescens' (Schwerin). Leaves 5 lobed, new foliage light yellow-green, later light yellow in full sun, light green in shade. 1893.

'Heterophyllum' (Schwerin). Leaves usually asymmetrical, deeply lobed, very variable, sometimes 4 lobed or 2 leaves on one petiole, occasionally gray specked, margin serrate. 1896.

'Insigne' (Spaeth). Leaves 3 lobed, lobes triangular, rather small, reddish at first, later white pulverulent, mostly on the middle of the blade and along the veins, colored only on the surface. 1883. ⌀

'Jaspideum' (Lavallée) Leaves normal, 5 lobed, light green, glossy, bark yellowish, a vertical yellow stripe under the buds. In cultivation since 1877 in the Segrez Arboretum, France, introduced into Germany by Dieck, 1895.

'Laetum' (Schwerin). Leaves shallowly 3 lobed, very light green, new foliage lighter, yellow-green, not speckled. 1893.

'Latifolium' (Schwerin). Leaves normal, 5 lobed, but distinctly larger than the species, base broadly cordate, underside very pale green. Found by Reuter, head gardener on the Pfauen Islands near Potsdam, before 1896.

'Laxum' (Schwerin). Leaves normal, 5 lobed, leaf petiole bent at the base resulting in the leaves hanging vertically. 1896.

'Leopoldii' (Vervaene). Leaves normal, 5 lobed, new foliage copper-pink and yellow, later very dense with light yellow to yellow-white dots and specks. IH 1864: Pl. 411. Named for King Leopold I. of Belgium by Vervaene. ⌀

'Limbatum' (Schwerin). Leaves normal, 5 lobed, margins fading to yellow (not sharply delineated) and colored in the same fashion between the major veins. 1901.

'Luteo-virescens' (Simon Louis). Leaves normal, 5 lobed, light yellow-green, new leaves light green with straw-yellow speckles, specks rather large. 1887. Resembles 'Tricolor', but the latter with brownish new foliage.

'Metallicum' (Schwerin). Leaves normal, 5 lobed, upper side smooth, glossy metallic, green, young leaves yellowish at first, later coppery, then olive and finally green. 1893.

'Negenia' (N.A.K.B. 1948). Dutch selection. Tree, very stable, strong grower, crown broadly pyramidal; leaves large, deep green, totally flat, margin somewhat upturned at the blade tip, petiole red. Fruit set sparse. Much planted in Holland as a street tree.

'Neglectum' (Schwerin). Leaves very large, only slightly incised, margin irregular and sparsely dentate, tip occasionally curved downward. 1893.

'Nervosum' (Schwerin). Weak grower, conical, densely branched; leaves very small, 5 lobed, lobes acuminate, upper side totally yellow-pink with wide green veins, underside orange to pink; summer foliage normal sized, green, upper side occasionally somewhat yellow speckled, underside red.

'Nizetii' (Makoy). Leaves normal, 5 lobed, red brown at bud break, later dark green, richly speckled, specks always red to orange, underside dark red. 1887. ⌀

'Opizii' (Ortmann). Leaves 3 lobed, lobes triangular, base semi-circular, occasionally slightly cordate, margin crenate. 1852.

'Opulifolium' (Kirchn.). Leaves 5 lobed, upper side a nice dark green, white-green beneath, somewhat smaller than the species, more constant, more acutely lobed, petiole long, red, vein axils pubescent. 1864.

'Palmatifidum' (Duhamel). Leaves deeply 5 lobed, nearly the same as *A. heldreichii*. 1755.

'Prinz Handjery' (Spaeth). Weak grower, shrubby; leaves 5 lobed, new foliage and twigs at first brick red, later generally becoming green and densely yellow-gray pulverulent, underside pale violet-red. 1883. Very popular variety and still in cultivation. Plate 10. ⌀

'Pseudo-Nizetii' (Schwerin). Differs from 'Nizetii' in the pale orange specks on the young leaves, underside light reddish, not deep red, otherwise normal, 5 lobed. 1893. ⌀

'Pulverulentum' (Jacques & Herincq). Leaves similar to 'Aucubifolium', but with many fine gray-white dots, youngest leaves on long branches a slight orange, without large specks. 1847. ⌀

'Purpurascens'. Leaves distinctly 5 lobed, upper side dark green, underside at bud break usually light green, then red speckled, generally becoming totally red, appears olive with back lighting; fruit wings light violet. 1886.

'Purpureo-digitatum' (Hesse). Leaves distinctly trifoliate, upper side green, becoming purple beneath. 1898. ⌀

'Purpureum' (Clark). English selection from 1828. Leaves dark green above, dark purple beneath; seed wings green.

'Pyramidale'. Like earlier introductions from Nicholson in England. 1881. Perhaps = 'Erectum'?

'Rafinesquianum' (Nicholson). Leaves 3 lobed, large, blood red in spring, otherwise green (= 'Sanguineum' Schwerin). 1881.

'Rotterdam' (H. W. Vink 1944). Dutch selection. Large trees, crown broadly columnar when young, later more broadly upright, with more or less ascending branches, twice as tall as wide; leaves dark green, base deeply cordate. Important as a street tree in Holland.

'Rugosum' (Schwerin). Normal, 5 lobed, dark green leaves, fine and densely wrinkled above, creating a rough texture. 1901.

'Serotinum' (Endlicher). Normal, 5 lobed leaves with both sides green, leafing out much later than the species, but very fast growing. From the Vienna Botanic Garden. 1843.

'Simon Louis Frères' (Deegen). Very weak grower, often only shrub-like; leaves nearly 3 lobed, delicate pink at bud break, later distinctly white specked, only slightly green, green parts usually pale (= 'Webbianum'; 'Quadricolor'). In England since 1881 and also encountered today. ⌀

'Spaethii' (Schwerin). Like 'Laetum', but with very large, light yellow specks, new foliage a clear light green. 1893. ⌀

"Spaethii" (in the Dutch nurseries) is the generally used name for 'Atropurpureum' (Spaeth 1883), propagated only by grafting.

'Ternatum' (Schwerin). Leaves trifoliate, leaflets frequently petiolate, both sides green. 1893.

var. **tomentosum** Tausch. Leaves normal, 5 lobed, coarse, somewhat leathery, coarsely deeply cut serrate, base often cordate, softly pubescent beneath; fruit wings to 2 cm wide, rounded at the tip (= *A. villosum* Presl; *A. pseudoplatanus villosum* Parl.). Mediterranean, mountain forests of Dalmatia, Calabria, Sicily.

'Tricolor' (Kirchn.). Leaves normal, 5 lobed, similar to 'Leopoldii', but larger, less densely yellow speckled, more prominently green, young leaves more reddish brown. Moscow Arboretum. 1864. ⌀

'Trilobatum' (Lavallée). Leaves large, 3 lobed, slightly cordate when young, later with base more truncate to cuneate, lobes long, not rounded, margins parallel. Segres Arboretum, France.

'Variegatum'. Leaves normal, 5 lobed, very numerous white-yellow specks large and small, only little green, new growth faintly reddish yellow (= albo-variegatum). Growth stronger than 'Leopoldii', but less attractive in color. ⌀

'Vitifolium' (Tausch). Leaves shallowly 3 lobed, large, base usually deeply cordate, lobes broad rounded. 1829.

'Worleei' (Ohlendorf). Leaves normal, 5 lobed, sinuses large rounded, lobes slightly dentate, new growth dark orange, later gold-yellow (not speckled, rather monochrome), then generally becoming green in summer, also the shaded foliage is green, petiole red. Named by von Ohlendorf in Hamburg before 1893 and not by Rosenthal as is almost always erroneously listed. Better than 'Corstorphinense'. ⌀

'Zebrinum' (Schwerin). Like 'Nervosum', but with leaves green beneath, not red. 1901.

A. psuedo-sieboldianum (Pax) Komar. Korean Maple. Small tree, very similar to A. japonicm and A. sieboldianum, but with young twigs white pruinose, leaves 9−11 lobed (A. sieboldianum, 7−9 lobed; A. japonicum, 7−11 lobed), base cordate, lobes oblong-lanceolate, doubly serrate, glossy green above, fine silky pubescence beneath, only slightly at first, petiole 3−6 cm long; flowers reddish, stalk glabrous, sepals ciliate, inflorescence at first softly pubescent, later glabrous; fruit glabrous. NK 1, 4; ICS 3129 (= A. sieboldianum var. mandschuricum Maxim.). Manchuria, Korea. 1903. Hardy. z5 Plate 12; Fig. 55. ⌀

A. pubipalmatum Fang. Small tree, twigs tomentose, later glabrous; leaves deeply 5−7 lobed, 5−7.5 cm wide, margin doubly and sharply serrate, base truncate to nearly cordate, venation gray pubescent beneath, petiole pubescent, 2.5−5 cm long; flowers in shaggy pubescent corymbs, petals 5, sepals purple, petals cream-yellow; ovary pubescent, fruit wings at a wide angle, to 2.5 cm long, pubescent. E. China; Szechwan. Not in cultivation? z6

Fig. 70. Acer rubrum. a. Species; b. var. drummondii; c. var. trilobum from Sargent, ½ actual size)

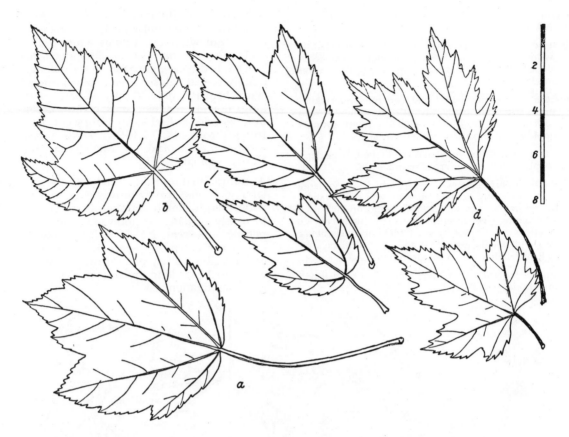

Fig. 71. *Acer rubrum*. a. Species; b. var. *drummondii*; c. var. *trilobum*; d. var. *tomentosum* (Original)

A. purpurascens see: **A. diabolicum**

A. pusillum see: **A. semenovii**

A. pycnanthum K. Koch. Tree, very similar to *A. rubrum*, but much smaller, twigs bluish; leaves 3−7 cm wide, 5−9 cm long, but occasionally almost simple, usually 3 veined, venation partly pinnate, obtuse tipped, obtusely doubly serrate, base rounded to slightly cordate, blue-green beneath, petiole thin, to 6 cm long; flowers appear before the leaves, red, in clusters, stalk threadlike, glabrous; fruit upright or acutely spread, glabrous. KRA 16 (as *A. rubrum*) (= *A. rubrum* mak. non L.). Japan; Hondo. 1915. z6 Fig. 50, 52. ⊕ ∅

A. ramosum Schwerin (? *A. campestre* × *A. pseupdoplatanus*). Small upright tree, strong branching, twigs dark brown; leaves rounded, 3−5 lobed, 5−9 cm wide, lobes doubly serrate, base nearly cordate, dark green above, veins deep, light green underside, glabrous, with brown haired vein axils, petole 7 cm long; flowers yellow (like *A. pseudoplatanus*); fruit glabrous, wings at obtuse to horizontal spread, 2−2.5 cm long. MD 1894: 83. Only known in cultivation. z6 Fig. 50.

A. regelii see: **A. pentapotamicum**

A. reginae-amaliae Orphan. ex Boiss. is probably only a subspecies of *A. hyrcanum*, endemic to Greece and W. Turkey. Adapted to dry soils with small leaves, but otherwise like *A. hyrcanum*. z6

A. robustum Pax. Similar to *A. palmatum*, but taller and easy to distinguish by its much larger fruits; tree, young twigs often pruinose, otherwise red-brown; leaves 7−9 lobed, 7−10 cm wide, outline round, lobes ovate, acute, finely and sharply serrate, lowest lobes very small, base cordate, both sides glossy green, white vein axils beneath, reddish fall color; flowers dark red, in terminal corymbs; fruit with nearly horizontal or slightly curved wings, 4 cm long and 1 cm wide. Middle China; Yunnan, Hupeh, 1100−2000 m. 1907. Presumably hardy. z6 Fig 49.

A. × rotundilobum Schwerin (= *A. × opulus* var. *obtusatum* × *A. monspessulanum*). Shrub or small tree, twigs reddish with gray lenticels, pubescent at first, new growth blood red; leaves rounded, 3 lobed, 5−7 cm long, lobes rounded, weakly dentate to nearly entire, leathery, dark green above, light green beneath, both sides glabrous, petiole 5 cm long. MD 1894: 83. Only known in cultivation (Les Barres). z6 Plate 11; Fig. 50.

A. rubescens see: **A. caudatifolium**

A. rubrum L. Red Maple. Tree, in its habitat to 40 m high, open crown, twigs glabrous, bright red in the first year, with numerous small lenticels; leaves 3–5 lobed, 6–10 cm long, usually longer than wide, lobes triangular-ovate, unevenly notched serrate and acute, dark green above, bluish beneath, carmine and orange in fall; flowers attractive, dark red, with petals, anthers reaching far past corolla, before the leaves, March–April; fruit wings at acute angle, already ripe in June. HH 391 and 392; BB 2373; HM V/l, 269. Eastern N. America; by rivers, low areas, swamps, avoiding alkaline soils; grows together with *Alnus, Thuja, Carpinus* and *Larix*. 1656. Hardy. z3 ℗ USA; S. Africa. Fig. 52, 70, 71. See also: *A. pycnanthum*. ∅ ✧

'**Albo-variegatum**', leaves white speckled, and 'Aureovariegatum', leaves yellow speckled, both occur occasionally as chance seedlings, coloring not consistent. Neither are important.

var. **barbatum** (Michx.) Lauche. Tree, 15–18 m high, crown dense and rounded, bark light gray, shallowly furrowed, young twigs thin, light red brown, glabrous, rough with many lenticels; leaves 3–5 lobed, wider than long, 4–8 cm long, lobes acute or obtuse, base truncate or slightly cordate, margin wavy, lobes with 1–2 teeth, old dried foliage remains on the tree until the following spring; flowers yellowish green, appearing with the foliage, long stalked, in small terminal clusters; fruit pubescent when young, wings brownish, paper thin, 2–3 cm long, rather upright. WT 132; Rho 1942: 725 (= *A. barbatum* Michx.; *A. floridanum* [Chapm.] Sarg.). Coastal plains from Virginia to Florida. z6

'**Columnare**'. Grows upright, broadly columnar, to 20 m high. GF 1894: 65.

In addition, two American selections: 'Armstrong', growth narrowly columnar, found in 1949 in Windsor, Ohio by Newton Armstrong and introduced into the trade in 1955 by Scanlon; 'Bowhall', growth somewhat tighter, pyramidal, but crown somewhat irregular (both portrayed in the Proc. Plant Propagators Soc. 1, 30–31, 1951). USA.

var. **drummondii** (Nutt.) Sarg. Tree, young twigs coral red, densely tomentose; leaves usually 3 lobed, base rounded to cordate, light green above with red venation, underside silvery and pubescent, petiole pubescent; flowers larger than the species, bright red; fruit red, wings bowed inward. SS 95; Gfl 1374; SM 640. Flood plains in Arkansas, Texas to W. Lousiana. Sensitive plant in cultivation. z6 Fig. 70, 71. ∅ ໑

'**Gerling**'. Growth broadly conical, named in honor of J. Gerling, Director of the Durand-Eastman Parks in Rochester, N.Y., introduced to the trade in 1951 by Scanlon.

'**Globosum**'. Dwarf growing, dense, rounded, blood red.

'**October Glory**' (Princeton). American selection. Leaves glossy green, fall foliage an intensive red. US Plant Pat. No. 2116. 1964.

var. **pallidiflorum** K. Koch. Leaves like the type, yellow in fall; flowers light yellow, occasionally with red anthers, abundant flowers (= *A. rubrum* 'Hybridum'). Only the female known. Hardy. z6

'**Red Sunset**' (Cole). American selection with dense, upright growth habit with especially intensive red fall foliage. 1968.∅

'**Sanguineum**'. Shrubby, twigs light red; leaves somewhat smaller than the type, dark green above, intense blue-green beneath, frequently more pubescent, base deeply cordate, blood red fall foliage; flowers deep carmine red (= *A. rubrum coccineum* Kirchn.). Disseminated from the Jardin des Plantes in Paris. 1877. Only the female known. ∅ ໑

'**Scanlon**' Grows conically. US Plant Patent No. 1722. Selection from Scanlon, introduced to the trade in 1948.

'**Schlesingeri**' (Sargent). Leaves to 12 cm long, and larger than the species, base nearly truncate, intense red, regular fall foliage, petiole red. Found in the garden of a Mr. Schlesinger, USA by Prof. Sargent; brought into the trade by Spaeth, Berlin in 1888 and still propagated. Only female plants known. ∅

'**Tilford**'. Globose form. Selection from Scanlon, introduced in 1949. Named in honor of Dr. P. Tilford, Wooster, Ohio, USA.

var. **tomentosum** (Desf.) K. Koch. Usually only shrubby, twigs thin, dark red-brown; leaves smaller than the species, more deeply lobed, sharper and more deeply serrate, very dark green above, woolly pubescent beneath, petole red; flowers dark red (= *A. fulgens* hort.; *A. tomentosum* Desf.). Only the male known, only in cultivation. z6 Fig. 71. ✧

var. **trilobum** Torr. & Gray. Leaves oval, 3 lobed, lobes acute, coarsely serrate on the upper half of the blade, tough, blue-green beneath and usually pubescent; flowers yellow; fruit much smaller than the species, yellow-brown. SM 523 (as var. *tridens*) (= var. *tridens* Wood; *A. semiorbiculatum* Pax). Coastal regions of the Eastern United States, from New Jersey to Florida and Texas. z6 Fig. 70, 71.

'**Wageri**' (K. Koch). Twigs pendulous; leaves large, deeply 5 lobed; flowers red (= var. *pendulum* Lav.). 1869. Named for Sir Charles Wager, not "Wagneri"! Only the female known.

A. rubrum × *A. saccarinum* see: *A.* × **freemanii**

A. rufinerve S. & Z. Tree, to 10 m high, twigs and buds and first pruinose, glabrous, white striped in winter; leaves 3 lobed, 6–12 cm long, side lobes pointing outward, less sharply serrate, dark green above, venation beneath brown pubescent at first, becoming glabrous, carmine in fall (those resembling *A. pensylvanicum* light yellow); flowers greenish, in upright, rust-red pubescent racemes, soon after the foliage, May; wings spread at obtuse angles, 2 cm long. KRA 9; DL 2: 192; Gsch 2: 36. Japan; mountain forests on Nippon, to 2500 m. 1879. Hardy. z6 Plate 16; Fig. 49, 55. ∅

'**Albolimbatum**' (Hook. f.). Leaves with a broad border of white specks. BM 5793. Japanese cultivar. 1869. Not as hardy as the species. ∅

A. rumeliacum see: **A. monspessulanum**

A. saccharinum L. Silver Maple. Tree, 15–20 m, in its habitat to 40 m, twigs often pendulous at the tips; leaves deeply 5 lobed to 5 parted, 8–14 cm wide, lobes acute, deep and doubly serrate, middle lobes further 3 lobed, light green above, silvery white beneath, yellow in fall; flowers greenish, without petals, in small clusters, February-March; fruit wings sickle-formed, at wide angles apart, 3–5 cm long, abscising singly, ripe in June. HH 388-390; HM V/1: 268; SS 2: 93; DB 1956: 166 (= *A. dasycarpum* Ehrh.). N. America, Quebec to Florida, west to Minnesota, Kansas, Oklahoma. z3 Fig. 44, 52, 72. ∅

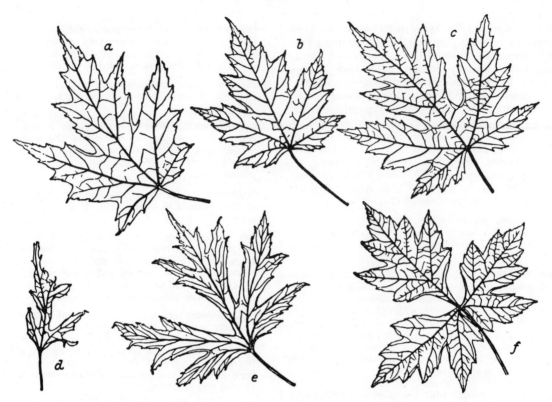

Fig. 72. Forms of *Acer saccharinum*. a. 'Curvatum'; b. species; c. 'Palmatum', d. 'Dissectum';
e. 'Heterophyllum'; f. 'Pseudoternatum' (from Schwerin)

Occurs in low areas and flood plains, together with *Salix*, *Betula*, *Alnus*, *Quercus*, *Acer rubrum* and *A. nigrum*, not a forest tree. Sap contains sugar. Good park tree, but unfortunately easily damaged by wind.

Outline of the Cultivars of *A. saccharinum*

1. Leaves 5 lobed, incised to the middle of the blade, base more or less cordate, fully developed leaves green;
   a) Growth normal:
      'Macrophyllum'. 'Sanguineum'. 'Palmatum'
   b) Growth strictly upright:
      'Pyramidale'
   c) Growth low, shrubby:
      'Arbuscula' (shrubby), 'Nanum' (globose)
   d) Other forms:
      'Monstrosum' (branches thick, compressed, internodes short), 'Serpentinum' (branches bowed back and forth)
2. Leaves deeply incised, base cuneate or truncate, occasionally cordate, basal lobes very small, blade practically 3 lobed, mature foliage green;
   a) Leaves distinctly 3 lobed:
      'Longifolium', 'Trilobatum'
   b) Leaves 3 parted:
      'Tripartitum', 'Pseudoternatum', 'Dissectum'
   c) Other variations:
      'Curvatum' (blade asymmetrical), 'Pendulum' (weeping habit)
3. Leaves incised nearly to the base, lobes long and narrow, blade green;

a) Leaves symmetrical, lobes now and then narrow to nearly thread-like:
   'Wieri' (growth pendulous, lobes only occasionally thread-like), 'Schwerinii' (growth upright, lobes usually thread-like), 'Borns Graciosa;
b) Leaves asymmetrical, grows upright:
   'Heterophyllum'
4. Leaves when fully developed not pure green, rather yellowish, reddish or speckled:
a) Blade develops normally;
   + White variegated forms:
      'Albo-variegatum', 'Lacteum', 'Pulverulentum'
   ++ Yellow variegated forms:
      'Aureo-variegatum', 'Bicolor', 'Citreo-variegatum'
   +++ Whole blade reddish or yellowish:
      'Rubellum (reddish), 'Lutescens' (yellowish)

b) Blade deformed:
   'Crispum' (welled up between the major veins), 'Dilaceratum' (Lobes shredded, gray and yellow striped), 'Wagneri' (small leaved, white colored)

'Albo-variegatum' (Spaeth). Leaves normal, 5 lobed, with large, white, or at the branch tips pink specks (= 'Juehlkei' Jurrissen). 1883.

'Arbusculum' (Reuter). Leaves normal, 5 lobed, growth shrubby, multistemmed; leaves reddish in fall. Found on the

Pfaue Islands near Potsdam, E. Germany. Before 1893. Typical properties retained only by propagation of cuttings as grafted plants are too strong growing.

'Asplenifolium' (De Bie-van Aalst 1925). Dutch Selection. Large tree, rather upright growth, branches long and limp, but not as wide as the very similar 'Wieri' and also less pendulous; leaves very deeply incised, veins closer together.Ø

'Aureo-variegatum' (Willkomm). Leaves normal, 5 lobed, dark yellow specked, specks on the young leaves at the branch tips orange. Before 1881.

'Bicolor' (Schwerin). Mature foliage dull yellow-green speckled, specks not visible on the young leaves. 1901.

'Borns Graciosa' (Born). Strong grower, upright; leaves lobed nearly to the base, 10–16 cm long, lobes only 1–2 cm wide and irregularly coarsely serrate or occasionally lobed. DB 11: 21. From Georg Born, Rosenheim, W. Germany, introduced to the trade in 1959. Very winter hardy.

'Citreo-variegatum' (Schwerin). New growth and spring foliage light green, never reddish, mature foliage light green with light yellow specks. MD 1896, Pl. 2. 1893.

'Crispum (Kelsey). Leaves deformed, deeply incised, deeply serrate, blade arched upward between the major veins, parallel to the veins, light green, veins light yellow, twigs very thin (= *A. virginianum cristatum*). From USA. Before 1894.

'Curvatum' (Schwerin). Leaves 3 lobed, with 2 small basal lobes, base truncate, horizontal, asymmetrical, midvein bowed to the right or left, axillary veins curved accordingly, young leaves occasionally white variegated on the tip; weak grower. Before 1893. Fig. 72.

'Dilaceratum' (Schwerin). Leaf blade completely deformed, margin often irregularly split and shredded, often with gray and yellowish stripes, otherwise dark green. Before 1901.

'Dissectum'. Leaves small, deeply 3 lobed or 3 parted, with white border, otherwise like Fig. 72.

'Elegant'. So called in Holland; moderate height, branches ascending, slightly pendulous; leaves rather small, only incised halfway into the blade. 1969. Presumably originated at Spaeth, Berlin.Ø

'Heterophyllum (Ellwanger & Barry). Leaves asymmetrical, 5 lobed, lobes forming obtuse angles, 2nd year growth often symmetrical and then resmbling 'Palmatum', therefore with 2 leaf forms; growth nearly conical upright. From USA. Before 1881. Fig. 72.

'Lacteum'. (Schwerin). Leaves normal, whitish covered ("as if dipped in milk"; Schwerin), venation green, margins dentate with white tipped teeth, often long drawn out. Before 1893.

var. *leucoderme* see: **A. leucoderme**

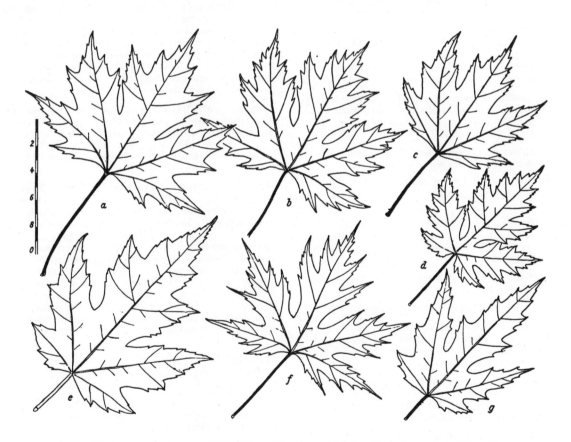

Fig. 73. *Acer saccharinum.* a. 'Monstrosum'; b. 'Pyramidale'; c. 'Sanguineum'; d. 'Tripartitum'; e. Lutescens'; f. 'Wieri'; g. 'Longifolium'

'Longifolium' (Spaeth). Leaves more 3 lobed, lobes very long stretched out, basal lobes very small, horizontal, base usually cuneate or cut straight across, seldom slightly cordate (= f. *cuneatum* Pax). 1892. Fig. 73. Ø

'Lutescens' (Spaeth). Leaves normal, 5 lobed, new growth a nice orange, later whole leaf yellowish, more intense in the sun. Gartenzeitung 1883: Pl. 5. 1881. Fig. 73. Ø

'Macrophyllum' (Kirchner). Normal leaves, as with the species, 5 lobed, but distinctly larger, appearing to be smaller with age. Moscow. 1864.

'Monstrosum' (Simon). Leaves normal, 5 lobed, green, red at bud break, fall color light reddish, twigs compressed, sometimes even pressed flat, annual growth short and squat. Before 1893. Fig. 73.

'Nanum' (Schwerin). Leaves normal 5 lobed, weak grower, rounded. Dwarf form. Before 1893.

'Palmatum'. Leaves 5 lobed, the 3 middle lobes very large, deeply incised, basal lobes much smaller, the whole leaf somewhat larger and wider than the species, light green (= f. *pavia* Kirchn.) Moscow. 1864. Fig. 72.

'Pendulum' (Van Houtte). Leaves deeply incised beside the middle lobe, more 3 lobed, light green, twigs very strongly pendulous; differing from the similarly weeping 'Wieri' in the leaf form. From England. 1875. Ø

'Pseudoternatum' (Schwerin). Leaves distinctly 3 parted, especially on the long twigs, light green, lobes not touching. Before 1893. Fig. 72.

'Pulverulentum' (Spaeth). Leaves normal 5 lobed, densely covered with fine white dots, like powder, on the newest foliage, pink at first, and again becoming pink in the fall with midrib then red; weak grower, wider than the species. 1883.Ø

'Pyramidale' (Spaeth). Leaves sharply 5 lobed, more deeply incised than the species, margins often curved upward, middle of the blade often lower; growth broad columnar. 1885. Still widely planted. Plate 17; Fig. 73.

'Rubellum' (Schwerin). Leaves normal 5 lobed, always reddish, fall foliage blood red, very white beneath. 1901.

'Sanguineum' (Schwerin). Leaves normal 5 lobed, like the species, but with new foliage blood red, mature leaves very dark green. 1893. Fig. 73. Ø

'Schwerinii' (Beissner). Leaves asymmetrical, lobes nearly thread-like, coarsely dentate; growth upright, ornamental. From the nursery of the Count Schwerin circa 1900. Different from 'Wieri', which see.

'Serpentium' (Schwerin). Twigs bowed back and forth, bent at about every 50 cm. 1893.

'Trilobatum' (Schwerin). Leaves distinctly 3 lobed. 1901.

'Tripartitum' (Transon). Leaves very large, larger than the species, light green, 3 lobed nearly to the base, middle lobe very wide, side lobes partly overlapping, young twigs with very large, white lenticels. 1893. Fig. 73.

'Wagneri' (Lebas). Leaves very small, very narrow, outline irregular, deeply incised, border very thin and white; very weak grower (= var. *dissectum* Pax; f. *heterophyllum argenteomarginatum* Hort. belg.). From Belgium. 1868. Ø

'Wieri' (Ellwanger & Barry). Leaves symmetrical, lobes long and narrow, sharply serrate, becoming more narrow on leaves formed after midsummer, often nearly thread-like;

strong grower, branches very attractive and broadly pendulous. Found by Wier in 1873 (see index to authors). Very attractive park tree. Fig. 73. Ø

A. saccharophorum see: **A. saccharum**

A. saccharum Marsh. Sugar Maple. Tall tree, occasionally to 40 m in its native habitat, bark gray, furrowed; leaves 3 to 5 lobed, 8 to 14 cm wide, with many small and only 1—2 large teeth, dull green above, gray-white beneath, glabrous, a bright red and orange in fall; flowers campanulate, greenish yellow, on thread-like, pubescent, 3—6 cm long stalks, in nearly sessile, fasicled corymbs, before the leaves, April; fruit wings nearly parallel upright or at acute angles. HH 379; EP IV/163: 14; BB 2375 (= *A. palmifolium* Borkh.; *A. saccharophorum* K. Koch). 1753. Hardy z3 Ⓕ USA. Plates 15 and 19; Fig. 52. Ø

The most valuable North American hardwood tree; frequently found on high ground with *Fagus, Tsuga, Prunus, Betula lenta*. The source of maple syrup. The sap is collected in March; it flows very thinly as its content is only 3% sugar.

f. glaucum (Schmidt) Pax. Leaves blue-green beneath, base cordate (= *A. saccharophorum* f. *glaucum* Rousseau).

ssp. grandidentatum (Nutt. ex Torr. & Gray) Desmarais. Shrub or tree, to 12 m, bark dark brown, twigs glabrous, red-brown; leaves 3—5 lobed, 5—8 cm wide, shallowly lobed with open sinuses, lobes acute to obtuse, margin entire or with 3 small side lobes, glossy green above, soft bluish pubescent beneath, especially on the veins; flowers yellowish, in short stalked, pendulous clusters, April; fruit wings at right angles, 2.5—3 cm long. SM 519 (= *A. grandidentatum* Nutt.). Western N. America, Rocky Mountains, Utah to New Mexico, by mountain streams. 1885. z3 Fig. 51, 52.

'Newton Sentry'. Growth narrow columnar, without a distinct trunk, with few, short, ascending side branches, strong grower; leaves dark green, tough, leathery, wavy margin as with *A. nigrum*. Baileya 2, 31B. Introduced 1885 as "*A. saccharinum columnare*" by F. L. Temple of Shady Hill Nurseries, Cambridge, Mass., USA.

ssp. nigrum (Michx. f.) Desmarais. Tree, to 25—40 m in its native habitat, rounded with age, bark black, deeply fissured, twigs pubescent at first; leaves usually 3 lobed, pendulous, 10—14 cm wide, lobes acuminate, with few short teeth or wavy margin, dull green above, gray-green beneath, sparsely pubescent, denser pubescence on the veins, bright yellow fall foliage; flowers yellow-green, in pendulous nearly sessile umbellate panicles, April; fruit wings nearly at right angles. DL 2, 206; HH 382 (= *A. nigrum* Michx. f.). Eastern and Middle N. America, on alkaline soils. 1812. z5 Resembles *A. saccharum*, but with leaf underside and petiole pubescent; also used in sugar production. Grows together with *Acer rubrum, A. saccharinum, A. negundo, Quercus alba, Carya*. Fig. 52, 59.

var. rugelii (Pax) Palm. & Steyerm. Leaves more leathery, wider than long, usually 3 lobed, slightly cordate, underside lighter or bluish and pubescent, lobes with entire margins, tough. SM 515; SS 2: 91. West Alleghany Mountains. 1903. z6

'Slavin's Upright'. Narrow upright form. Nat. Hort. Mag. 1950: 103 ill. Found in New York.

var. schneckii Rehd. Leaf petiole and underside densely shaggy pubescent. Indiana, Illinois, Missouri. 1913.

'Temple's Upright'. Growth broad columnar, without main stem, densely branched; leaves thin, light green, margin flat, not wavy, as with *A. saccharum*. Baileya 2, 31A. Introduced to the trade in 1887 by F. L. Temple as "*A. saccharinum monumentale*". Often used as a street tree in the USA. Plate 19.

A. salweenense see: **A. laevigatum**

A. schneiderianum Pax & Hoffm. Tree, often confused with *A. campbellii*, to 6 m, young twigs dark gray; leaves 3—5 lobed, base rounded to nearly cordate, thin, lobes obovate, short acuminate, finely serrate, petiole 5 cm long, dull red; flowers small, yellow-green, in terminal panicles. Szechwan, 2800 m. z6

A. schoenermarkiae see: **A. sterculiaceum**

A. semenovii Reg. & Herd. Sparse open shrub, very closely related to *A. ginnala*, but with smaller leaves, less glossy, deeper 3—5 lobed, middle lobe shorter, not whitish colored in fall; fruit wings nearly at right angles. ICS 3138; GC 1881: 3 (= *A. ginala* var. *semenovii* [Reg. & Herd.] Pax; *A. pusillum* Schwerin). Turkestan, mountain forests near Alatau and Ili regions, in very dry areas. z6

A. semiorbiculatum see: **A. rubrum** var. **trilobum**

A. sempervirens L. Cretan Maple. Deciduous shrub or small tree, 3—5 m, seldom 9—10 m high, sparsely branching, young twigs glabrous, occasionally also fine tomentose; leaves very changeable, partly ovate, partly blunt three lobed, 2—5 cm long, margin entire or slightly crenate, tough leathery, both sides bright green, occasionally somewhat lighter beneath, both sides glabrous, often semi-deciduous; flowers few, in upright corymbs, some 2 cm long, light yellow, appearing with the foliage; fruit wings parallel upright or at acute angles, 1—1.5 cm long. EP IV: 163 (= *A. orientale* auct. non L.; *A. creticum* L.; *A. heterophyllum* Willd.; *A. virens* Thunb.). East Mediterranean. 1752. z7 Fig. 64.

Because of the various leaf forms many varieties have been named, presumably based on herbarium materials.

A. × senecaense B. Slavin (= *A. leucoderme* × *A. saccharum*). Wide crowned tree; leaves in form and size intermediate between those of *A. grandidentatum* and *A. saccharum* var. *schneckii*. Nat. Hort. Mag. 1950: 103—107 with ill. z6

A. × sericeum Schwerin (= *A. pseupdoplatanus* × ?). Small tree; leaves 5 lobed, thin to tough, to 9 cm long, 11 cm wide, cordate, glossy and yellowish green above, densely white tomentose beneath, the large lobes irregularly double serrate; flowers in short racemes, twice as long as wide. MD 1894: 49. Originated in cultivation. Before 1894. z6 Fig. 50.

A. serrulatum see: **A. oliverianum**

A. shirasawanum Koidz. Small tree, closely related to *A. palmatum* and *A. sieboldianum*; leaves usually 11 lobed, lobes acuminate and sharply double serrate, 6 cm long and wide, base cordate, petiole glabrous; flowers pale yellow to white, sepals reddish outside; ovary shaggy pubescent, fruit horizontal, the wings slightly upturned, 2 cm long. KRA Pl. 22; Baileya 1954: fig. 31. Japan; Hondo. 1876. Hardy. z6 Fig. 58.

A. sieboldianum Miq. Small tree, very similar to *A. japonicum*, but with twigs remaining densely soft pubescent, also the leaf petiole and flower stalks; leaves rounded, 7—9 lobed, 5—8 cm wide, lobes oval-oblong, acuminate,, sharply serrate, underside with venation pubescent, fall color red; flowers small, yellowish, on long, nodding stalks, in corymbs, May; fruit wings at obtuse angles, 1.5 cm long. KRA Pl. 21; DL 2: 219. Japan; mountain forests of Nippon and Kiusiu, 1879. Hardy. z6 Plate 12; Fig. 58. Ø

var. *mandschuricum* see: **A. pseudo-sieboldianum**

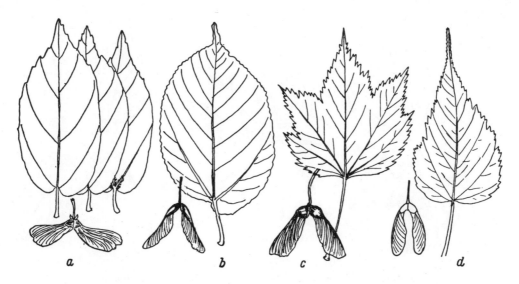

Fig. 74. a. *Acer cordatum*; b. *A. distylum*; c. *A. ukurunduense*; d. *Stachyophyllum* (from Pax, Koidzumi)

A. sikkimense Miq. Closely related to *A. davidii*. A tree in its habitat; leaves oval-oblong, 10–18 cm long, 8–9 cm wide, tough leathery, always glabrous, with margins entire or finely serrate, abruptly short acuminate, base deeply cordate, 3 veined, petiole 3–4 cm long; flowers apearing with the foliage in 5 cm long spikes, at fruiting time to 15 cm long; wings 2 cm long, nearly at right angles. E. Himalaya; Sikkim; E. China, and especially Yunnan; mountain forests at 2500–3000 m. 1880. z7 Fig. 49. Ø

A. sinense Pax. Tree, to 9–10 m in its habitat, bark rough, gray, twigs green, glabrous, thin, new growth reddish; leaves 5 lobed, 9–11 cm wide, base somewhat cordate, basal lobes acute, the others oval-oblong, acuminate, crenate margin at the apical end of the blade, thin, glossy green above, blue-green beneath, venation gray pubescent, petiole 3–5 cm long, pubescent, usually red; flowers in 5–10 cm long panicles, greenish-white, appearing with the foliage, May; fruit wings at obtuse angles apart, 3 cm long. ST 78; ICS 3132. China; Hupeh, Szechwan. 1901. z6 Fig. 49, 53, 75.

var. **concolor** Pax. Leaves somewhat larger, both sides green, wings horizontal. JRHS 29: 351. Szechwan.

A. sino-oblongum Metcalf. Small tree, twigs thin, reddish; leaves oblong, 6 cm long, 2 cm wide, short acuminate, base broad cuneate, margin entire, glossy green above, lighter beneath, tough leathery, petiole 2 cm long, reddish, round; flowers small, yellow-green, in terminal panicles; fruit wings 15 mm long, 8 mm wide, at acute angles. China; Kwantung. z6 #

A. sino-purpurescens Cheng. Tree, 6–9 m high, twigs gray; leaves 5 lobed, base slightly cordate, 5 veined, basal lobes very small and acute, the upper ones oval-oblong, acuminate, margin wavy, deep green above, glossy, lighter beneath, somewhat gray pubescent along the veins, thick leathery, petiole thin, 3.5 cm

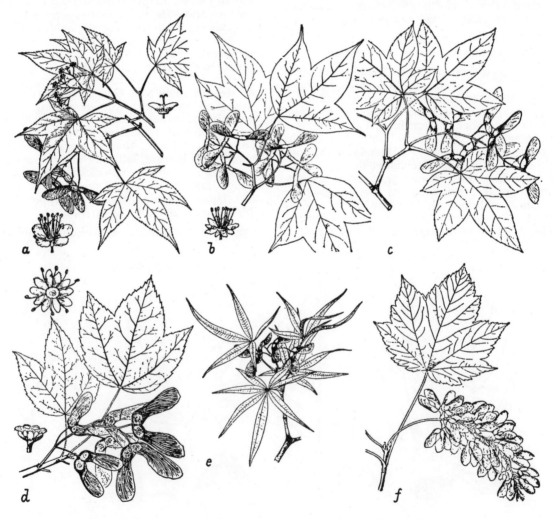

Fig. 75. **Acer.** a. *A. oliverianum*; b. *A. wilsonii*; c. *A. sinense*; d. *A. franchetti*; e. *A. pentaphyllum*; f. *A. ukurunduense* (from ICS)

long, channeled above; flowers reddish, long stalked, in terminal racemes; fruit large, nutlet triangular, 1 cm wide, wings with nutiet 4 cm long, 1 cm wide, reddish, at wide angles apart. China; Chekiang, Tien-Mu-Shan. z6

A. spicatum Lam. Usually shrubby, 6 m, occasionally a small tree in its habitat, young twigs red-brown, gray pubescent, later glabrous; leaves 3 (occasionally 5) lobed, 6−12 cm long, cordate, lobes large or unevenly deeply serrate, yellow-green above, pubescent beneath at least when young, orange and red in fall; flowers greenish, small, in 8−15 cm long, upright racemes, after the leaves May−June; fruit wings at nearly right angles, 1.5−2 cm long, red in fall. SS 82 to 83; HH 384. Eastern N. America. 1750. z2 Fig. 50, 53.

Grows in forests, usually moist, rocky areas, all over the East near water and nearly always shrubby.

A. stachyophyllum Hiern. Small tree, dioecious, twigs brownish, bud scales valvate; leaves ovate, 5−7 cm long, margin deeply serrate to small lobed, underside gray pubescent at first becoming glabrous, petiole 5 cm long; female flowers in terminal racemes with 2 leaves, flowers 4 parted, yellowish, male flowers axillary, without leaves, stamens 4; fruit wings forming acute angles, 2.5−5 cm long. EP IV/163, 7 AB; SDK 4: 68 (as *A. tetramerum*); JRHS 1904: 94 and 97 (as *A. tetramerum* var. *lobulatum*) (= *A. tetramerum* Pax with all varieties and forms). Himalaya to Central China. 1901. z6 Fig. 52, 74.

A. sterculiaceum Wall. A tree in its habitat, twigs brownish, tomentose when young, later less densely tomentose; leaves 3−5 lobed, paper thin, 14−20 cm wide, lobes coarsely serrate, base cordate, usually 5 veined, both sides densely tomentose when young, later glabrous above and deep green, remaining gray-green beneath, tomentose; flowers appearing before or with the foliage, yellowish-green; fruit in long pendulous racemes, often branched at the base, densely tomentose, wings rather upright. DL 2: 190 (= *A. villosum* Wall.). W. Himalaya, mountain forests from Cashmere to Nepal, 2300−3000 m. 1830. z8? Fig. 49.

ssp. **franchetti** (Pax) E. Murray. Leaves 3 lobed, base cordate; fruit wings 2.5−5 cm long. EP IV: 163: 13 (= *A. schoenermarkiae* Pax). SW. China; Yunnan, mountain forests. 1889.

A. stevenii see: **A. hyrcanum**

A. striatum see: **A. pensylvanicum**

A. sutchuenense Franch. Tree, to 10 m in the wild, twigs gray-brown, dotted; leaves 3 parted, rachis 5−10 cm long, flat above, leaflets oval-oblong, 6−10 cm long, 3−4 cm wide, short acuminate, irregularly serrate, glossy yellowish green above, bluish beneath, reticulate venation, gray hairs at the vein axils, rather coarse, short petioled; flowers many, yellowish green in terminal, 4 cm long corymbs; fruit in upright stands, wings upright, parallel, curved, 2.5 cm long. ST 112. Middle China, E. Szechwan. 1907. z6

Very similar to *A. henryi*, but with young twigs glabrous and

leaflets toothed.

A. taronense Hand.-Mazz. Small, wide crowned tree, twigs thin, glabrous, gray-brown and pruinose at first, later reddish brown; leaves broadly ovate, 5 lobed, 4−10 cm long and wide, lobes triangular-ovate, apex caudate, side lobes only half as long as the middle lobes, both basal lobes small, pointing outward, dark green above, venation beneath brown woolly pubescent, margin doubly serrate; fruit in 5−8 cm long racemes, petiole thin, 5 mm, wings usually at right angles (= *A. laxiflorum* var. *longilobum* Rehd.; *A. chienii* Hu & Cheng; *A. chloranthum* Merrill). Himalaya; NE. Burma, China; Yunnan and Szechwan. 1924. z6

A. tataricum L. Tatarian Maple. Shrub or occasionally small tree; leaves not lobed (except on young plants), broadly ovate, 5−10 cm long, acute, irregularly double serrate, bright green above, not glossy, light red in fall, underside with pubescent venation when young, later becoming glabrous; flowers greenish white, in upright, long stalked panicles, May; fruit usually with parallel wings, 2−3 cm long, red. HM 1846. SE. Europe, Balkans, Hungary, Asia Minor to Armenia, Elbrus Mountain, sunny, brushy areas. 1759. z4 Ⓕ Romania, USSR. Plate 11; Fig. 53. ∅ ⚭

'**Aureo-variegatum**' (Schwerin). Leaves dark yellow variegated. 1901. Occuring occasionally as chance seedlings.

var. **incumbens** Pax. Like the species, but fruit wings curving inward and overlapping, fruit not pubescent; leaves normal. E. Bulgaria.

A. tauricolum see: **A. hyrcanum**

A. tegmentosum Maxim. Small tree, young twigs glabrous, light green at first, later lightly striped, buds stalked; leaves green from bud break (unlike the related *A. capillipes* which is red!), usually 3 lobed, 7−16 cm long, often with 2 small basal lobes, irregularly double serrate, lobes acuminate, glabrous beneath, base usually rather cordate, petiole 3−8 cm long; flowers in 7−10 cm long, nodding racemes, May; fruit with nearly horizontal, 3 cm long wings, fruit stalk 8 mm long, thin, NK 1: 13; SDK 4: 62. Manchuria, Korea, mountain forests in the lower Amur and Ussuri River areas. 1892. Hardy. z5 Fig. 49, 55. ∅

A. tenellum see: **A. mono**

A. tetramerum see: **A. stachyophyllum**

A. thomsonii Miq. A large tree in its habitat; leaves thin, usually 3 lobed, 15−20 cm long and wide, base cordate, side lobes small, margins entire, light green beneath, venation pubescent at first, later glabrous; flowers many in simple racemes; fruit with acute angled wings, 8−10 cm long, glabrous. E. Himalaya, Sikkim, mountain forests at 2000−3000 m. z8 Fig. 49, 52. ∅ ⚭

A. tibetense Fang. Tree, twigs purple to brown, bud scales few; leaves 5 lobed, 5−10 cm wide, lobes ovate, apex caudate, margin entire, base rounded, gray-yellow tomentose beneath, petiole 5−7 cm, flowers in corymbs, terminal, petals 5, yellow-green; fruit wings nearly horizontal, 2.5—5 cm long. SE. Tibet. z6

var. **slendzinskii** Raciborski. Fruit wings at right angles, fruit not pubescent; leaves normal, usually unlobed. 1888.

var. **torminaloides** Pax. Leaves always 3 lobed, somewhat similar to *Sorbus torminalis*; seemingly between *A. tataricum* and *A. ginnala*, but not a cross! Armenia. Occasionally found in cultivation. z6

A. tomentusum see: **A. rubrum** var. **tomentosum**

A. tonkinense Lecompte. Tree, young twigs olive to purple or gray-brown; leaves leathery, broad 3 toothed to shallowly 3 lobed, 9—15 cm wide, lobes acute, margins entire, base rounded to nearly cordate, vein axils pubescent beneath, petiole thick, some 2.5 cm long; flowers 5 parted, in terminal panicles; fruit wings nearly horizontal, 2.5 cm long. JRHS 1975: 497. China; Kwangsi, Yunnan; North Vietnam. z8

A. trautvetteri Medwed. Caucasian Maple. Broad crowned tree, to 16 m high, bark gray, smooth, young twigs dark red-brown, glabrous, foliar buds very thick; leaves deeply 5 lobed, cordate, 10—15 cm wide, lobes oval-oblong, acuminate and irregularly serrate and finely lobed, deep glossy green above, blue-green beneath, venation pubescent on young leaves; flowers in long stalked, upright corymbs, after the leaves, May; fruit wings parallel, often overlapping, 4—5 cm long, bright red. DL 2: 202; SDK 4: 56. Caucasus. 1866. Hardy. z6 Plate 9 and 19; Fig. 53. ⊘ ⌘

Characteristic tree of ancient Colchis, in subalpine regions at the timber line, 1800—2500 m. Bud scales at bud break bright red; distinguished from the very similar *A. heldreichii* in the lobe sinuses which go only to the middle of the blade, and from *A. velutinum* in the blue undersides and much narrower lobes; terminal shoot almost always dying out.

A. trifidum see: **A. buergerianum**

A. triflorum Komar. Three Flowered maple. Tree, to 8 m in the wild, resembles *A. nikoense*, but with leaflets smaller, sessile, young twigs soon becoming glabrous, with many small lenticels; leaflets 3, oval-oblong to lanceolate, margins entire or with a few large teeth, blue-green beneath, somewhat pubescent only along the midrib; flowers always in threes, on short stalks with 2 leaves, May; fruit with dense pubescent nuts 3—4 cm long, wings obtuse angled. NK Pl. 11; ICS 3154. Korea, Manchuria. 1923. z6 Fig. 56.

A. trilobatum see: **A. monspessulanum**

A. truncatum Bge. Small tree, 5—8 m high, twigs glabrous, new growth brown-red; leaves deeply 5 lobed, 6—10 cm wide, base truncate to slightly cordate, lobes acuminate, usually with entire margins or middle lobe further 3 lobed, both sides light green, glossy, glabrous, red fall color, petiole with milky sap. 3—7 cm long; flowers yellow-green, in 6—8 cm wide, upright corymbs, after the leaves, May; fruit wings obtuse to right angled, 3 cm long. ST 76. N. China, forest tree. 1881. Hardy. z6 ⓕ N. China. Fig. 59.

A. tschonoskii Maxim. Shrub or small tree, usually not over 5 m, twigs glabrous, usually green, buds stalked;

leaves oval, usually 5 (occasionally 7) lobed, 5—10 cm wide, lobes ovate, sharply double serrate, young leaves with rust-brown pubescence on the venation beneath. Fall foliage a beautiful yellow; flowers to 6-10 in 5 cm long racemes, greenish white, May; fruit wings at right angles to obtuse and curving inward, 2.5—3 cm long. ST 17; KRA 13. Japan, mountain forests of Nippon, Hondo, Hokkaido, widely spread. 1892. Hardy. z6 Fig. 55, 63.

var. **rubripes** Komar. Tips of leaf lobes caudate, petiole and young twigs red; fruit wings wider spread. NK 14; ICS 3151 (as *A. komarovii*) (= *A. komarovii* Pojark.). Korea, Manchuria. 1917. z5

A. turcomanicum see: **A. monspessulanum**

A. turkestanicum Pax. Tree, young twigs fox red, glabrous, bud scales few; leaves 5—7 lobed, 10—20 cm wide, lobes acuminate, margin entire, base cordate to truncate, pubescent vein axils beneath, petiole 5—12 cm; flowers in upright, terminal corymbs, petals 5, yellow-green; fruit wings 2.5—5 cm long, broad sickleform. SDK 4: 51 (= *A. lipskyi* Rehd.; *A. pseudo-laetum* Radde-Fomin). NE. Afghanistan; Turkestan, Pamir-Alai and Tien Shan, mountain forests. z6

A. tutcheri Duthie. Small tree, twigs glabrous, bud scales few; leaves 3 lobed, 5—10 cm wide, leathery, the lobes triangular-ovate, finely serrate, base rounded to nearly truncate, vein axils pubescent beneath, petiole 2.5 cm; flowers in terminal corymbs, yellowish; fruit wings 2.5 cm long, at obtuse angles (= *A. oliverianum* var. *tutcheri* [Duthie] Metcalf). S. China; Kwantung, 300—900 m. z6

A. ukurundense Trautv. & Mey. Small tree or shrub, 3—6 m, young twigs reddish gray, appressed pubescence; leaves 5—7 lobed, small, 5—8 cm wide, densely gray tomentose beneath, lobes deeply incised, coarsely dentate, petiole slightly pubescent; inflorescence large and dense; fruit wings small, acute angled. KRA 19; ICS 3136 (= *A. caudatum* var. *ukurunduense* [Trautv. & Mey.] Rehd.; *A. lasiocarpum* Lév. & Vaniot). Manchuria to Hupeh, 600 m. Before 1906. z6 Fig. 49, 53, 74, 75.

A. urophyllum see: **A. maximowiczii**

A. vanvolxemii see: **A. velutinum**

A. × veitchii Schwerin. Presumably *S. crataegifolium* × *A. pensylvanicum*. Small tree, twigs dark green-white striped, pruinose; leaves oval-oblong, 7—10 cm long, slightly lobed, greenish beneath, whitish pubescent at first, petiole 3—5 cm long; flowers appearing with the leaves, greenish, in 4 cm long, upright racemes. MD 1894: 83. Origin unknown. 1890. Found in cultivation by Veitch. Hardy. z5 Fig. 49, 50.

A. velutinum Boiss. Tall tree, winter buds acute; leaves 5 lobed, very large, some 15 cm wide, base nearly cordate, lobes ovate and coarsely serrate, bright green above, bluish and densely pubescent beneath; flowers in upright, 8—10 cm long panicles, yellowish green, after the leaves, May; fruit wings at right to obtuse angles, 4 cm long; fruit remaining pubescent. SDK 4: 56 (= *A. insigne* Boiss. & Buhse; *A. insigne* var. *velutinum* Boiss.). Caucasus, N. Persian Mountains. 1873. Hardy. z5 Fig. 53. ∅

f. **glabrescens** (Boiss. & Buhse) Rehd. New growth brownish pink; leaves glabrous and more blue-green beneath; fruit pubescent when young. MD 1932: 13.

var. **vanvolxemii** (Mast.) Rehd. Buds break later than the type; leaves to 30 cm wide, blue-green beneath, venation pubescent; wings horizontal. DL 2: 432 (= *A. vanvolxemii* Mast.; *A. insigne* var. **vanvolxemii** [Mast.] Pax). E. Caucasus, mountain forests of the lower regions. Very rapid growth. z6 ∅

f. **wolfii** (Schwer.) Rehd. Leaves to 25 cm long and 23 cm wide, glabrous and purple-red beneath. 1905. Propagated readily from seed of native trees. Named for Prof. Egbert Wolf, Petersburg. ∅

A. villosum see: **A. psepudoplatanus** var. **tomentosum** and **A. sterculiaceum**

A. virens see: **A. sempervirens**

A. virginianum cristatum see: **A. saccharinum** 'Crispum'

A. wardii W. W. Sm. Tree, 6—10 m high; leaves 3 lobed, round, base 3 veined, lobes wide and long with thread-like apexes, side veins branching at right angles, glossy yellow-green above, blue-green beneath, vein axils with stiff, brown pubescence, somewhat leathery; flowers small, greenish brown, in panicles, stalk with lanceolate bracts; fruit wings at wide angles, curved inward (= *A. mirabile* Hand.-Mazz.). Yunnan, Tibet, 3300 m. z5

A. willkommii see: **A. orientale**

A. wilsonii Rehd. Large tree, young twigs glabrous, thin, yellow-green; leaves 3 lobed, 8—10 cm wide, often with small basal lobes, lobes with margins entire or somewhat serrate, oval-oblong, blue-green beneath and glabrous, vein axils with white pubescence, petiole 3—6 cm long; flowers greenish yellow, in terminal panicles; fruit brown-yellow, wings ovate, horizontally spread, 2 cm long. ST 79; ICS 3135 (= *A. angustilobum* Hu). China, Yunnan, Hupeh. 1907. z7 Plate 11; Fig. 49, 53.

A. yuii Fang. Small tree, young branches reddish to gray-brown, bud scales imbricate and ciliate; leaves 3 lobed-triangular, 5—7.5 cm wide, tip acute, margin entire to open wavy, base rounded, dark green above, yellow-green beneath and with yellow pubescence at the vein axils, petiole reddish, 2.5—5 cm long; flowers

in corymbs, wings at obtuse angles, 2.5 cm long. W. China, Szechwan. z5

A. × zoeschense Pax. (*A. campestre × A. lobelii*). Very near *A. campestre*, young twigs finely pubescent; leaves 5 lobed, 8—12 cm wide, cordate, lobes acuminate, dark green above, glossy, lighter beneath, pubescent at first, later glabrous; flowers in upright, pubescent corymbs, yellow-green, after the leaves, May; fruit with glabrous, horizontal, 3 cm long wings. DL 2: 214; EH 205 (= *A. neglectum* Lange). z6 Fig. 51, 57. ∅

'Annae' (Schwerin). Leaves dark red at bud break, later generally turning olive green, coloration somewhat like that of *A. platanoides* 'Schwedleri' (= *A. neglectum annae* Schwerin). 1908. Frequently used in Holland. ∅

'Elongatum' (Schwerin). Leaves 3 lobed, lobes long and narrow acuminate, side lobes further lightly lobed, margin wavy, veins and petiole red. 1911. Fig. 51.

'Friderici' (Schwerin). New growth whitish yellow; leaves later a constant gold-yellow, petiole and venation red (= *A. neglectum friderici* Schwerin). 1908. Named for Duke Friedrich Von Baden. ∅

Although the genus *Acer* is distributed over a very large area, for cultivation of the various species some attention must be paid to the location and soil type. Those forms with long acuminate to caudate blade tips seem well adapted to areas with frequent and heavy rain showers. The evergreen types are not winter hardy in most temperate zones and must be overwintered in greenhouses. In general, all species of *Acer* prefer a deep, nutrient rich, humus soil. Many species have attractive fall foliage, but only in those areas with sufficient humidity in the air.

Lit. Pax, F., Monographie der Gattung *Acer*; in Engler, Bot. Jahrb. **6**, 287—374, 1885; **7**, 177 to 263, 1885/86; **11**, 72—83, 1889 ● Pax., F., Aceraceae'; in Engler, Pflanzenreich IV, 163, 1—89, 1902 ● Schwerin, F., Beitrage zur Gattung *Acer*, in Mitt. DDG 1894—1896; 1899—1902 ● Koidzumi, G., Revisio Aceracearum Japonicarum. Jour. Coll. Sci. Tokyo **32**, **1**, 1—75, 1911 ● Fang, W.P., A Monograph of Chinese Aceraceae; in Contrib. Biol. Lab. Sci. Soc. China, Botan. Ser. **11**, 1—346; Peking 1939 ● Bailly, F., Die rotblattrigen Formen des Spitz-Ahorn; Dtsch. Baumsch. 1957, 299—301 ● Mulligan, B.O., Maples cultivated in the United States and Canada. Publ. of Am. Ass'n of Bot. Gard. and Arboretums 1958, 1—56 ● Kochno, M.A., Introduktsia kleniw na Ukraini. 171 pp., 50 ill. and maps; Kiev (1968; only 500 copies printed) ● Grootendorst, H. J., *Acer*; Keuringsrapport van de Regelingscommissie Sierbomen N.A.K.B.; in Dendroflora **6**, 3—18, 1969 ● Van Gelderen, D.M., Japanese *Acer*; in Dendroflora **6**, 19—36, 1969 ● Murray, A. E., A Monograph of Aceraceae. 332 pp. Ann Arbor. 1970.

The following work was, unfortunately, not seen: Veitch, J. H., Far Eastern Maples; in JHRS 1904, 327—360, figs. 75—103.

ACIPHYLLA Forst. — Spear Grass — UMBELLIFERAE

Actually a perennial with long, sharp, acute leaves and an attractive inflorescence, which gives the impression of a subshrub; leaves in rosettes, stellate, thick, pinnate or only 3 parted; flowers in umbels, densely clustered or in panicles or spikes (dioecious female plants occasionally also having male flowers, while the reverse

has, to date, not been observed). — 36 species in New Zealand and Australia.

Aciphylla aurea W. R. B. Oliv. Yellow-green, 1 m high and wide; leaves simple to irregularly double pinnate, to 70 cm long, stipules to 27 × 0.5 cm, sharp pointed

apex, pinnate, compound leaflets, in 2—4 pairs, 20 ×
0.7 cm, upright, margin finely serrate, secondary
leaflets rather small; inflorescence thick, furrowed, 80
cm, usually with linear bracts along the whole length.
New Zealand, in the mountains. 1974. Cultivated in the
Edinburgh Botanic Garden. z6

A. colensoi Hook. f. "Wild Spaniard", Tamarea
(Maori). 60—80 cm high, leaves 30—60 cm long, 15—200
mm wide, blue-green, dagger shaped with needle
sharp tips, grouped in a hemispherical "cushion of
knives"; flowers in stiff upright racemes, with foliate
leaves, greenish yellow, flowering time in its habitat
November—December. New Zealand, both islands.
1875. Completely winter hardy in Scotland. z6 Plate

21.

A. squarrosa Frst. Spear Grass. Kuri-Kuri (Maori).
Lower than the previous species, leaflets narrower,
more gray, only 3—4 mm wide; flowers whitish, inflorescence to 2 m high. NF 6: 121. New Zealand,
mountainous areas of the North island. z6 Grown in
England.

The mentioned species are quite hardy to zone 5. An excellent
choice for dry areas in the rock garden (xerophytes!). Propagation by seed. Young plants have soft, somewhat pendulous
leaves; the stiffer blades develop with increasing age. In New
Zealand the young plants have been overgrazed by sheep and
therefore are becoming rather scarce. The mentioned species
contain a fragrant resin which is collected by young girls for
use in ceremonial herb pillows.

ACRADENIA Kippist — RUTACEAE

Monotypical genus; closely related to *Boronia*.

Acradenia frankliniae Kippist. In its habitat, a tall
shrub or small tree, young branches green, angular,
with reddish oil glands and pubescent when young;
leaves opposite, 3 parted, short petioled, leaflets oblanceolate, blunt, more or less crenate, 2—7 cm long,
coarse and leathery with prominent glands; inflorescence a terminal cyme, flat, open and glandular-
pubescent, calyx 5—7 parted, sepals small, rounded,

fleshy, petals 5—7, ovate, some 6 mm long, white, overlapping, outer pubescent, May; fruit a compartmentalized capsule, each chamber single seeded, outer shell
woody and with crossing wrinkles. BM 9187. Tasmania, at Macquarie Harbour and on the river banks of
the West coast. 1845. z8

Only of botanical interest. In England seen occasionally in the
nurseries of milder regions.

ACTINIDIA Lindley — ACTINIDIACEAE

Deciduous, twining, glabrous, bristly haired or
tomentose (indumentum of simple or stellate hairs)
vine; pith solid or chambered; winter buds very small,
hidden in the enlarged petiole base; leaves simple, alternate, usually long petioled, dentate or serrate, occasionally with entire margin; flowers white, yellow or
reddish, polygamous or dioecious, usually 4—5 parted,
in axillary "mock" umbels, occasionally single, sepals 5
(occasionally 2—4), petals 5 (occasionally 4), thin, stamens numerous, yellow, brown or purple, in female
flowers usually a short filament and sterile anthers,
pistils many (15—30), free standing, radiating outward,
becoming longer after flowering, in male flowers very
rudimentary; fruit a glabrous or pubescent, round or
oblong, many seeded berry. — 40 species in E. Asia,
from Sachalin and E. Siberia, Japan and China to
Himalaya and Malaya, although most species in China.

Positive indentification is difficult, not only because of male
and female plants being distinctive, but the foliage types on a
single plant can be quite variable.

Outline of the Sections (from LI)

Section 1: **Strigosae** Li

Shoots and leaf petioles with long, stiff bristles, leaves
more or less bristly, berries speckled:
   A. henryi, holotricha, strigosa

Section 2: **Maculatae** Dunn.
Shoots and petioles usually glabrous, leaves glabrous,
fruit speckled:
   A. callosa, coriacea, rubicaulis, venosa

Section 3: **Leiocarpae** Dunn.
Shoots and leaf petioles glabrous, leaves glabrous, fruit
not speckled:
   *A. arguta, kolomikta, melanandra, polygama, purpurea,
   tetramera*

Section 4: **Stellatae** Li
Plants more or less tomentose, indumentum stellate on
leaf undersides, fruits glabrous or pubescent, speckled:
   A. chinensis

Important Characteristics of the Mentioned Species

Species	Pith, young twigs	Anthers	Fruits	Remarks
arguta	chambered, white to brown	dark red	greenish-yellow	leaves glossy on both sides
callosa	chambered, orange	yellow	green, red dotted	leaves thick
chinensis	chambered whitish-yellow	yellow	green with brown tomentose	leaves with stellate pubescence
coriacea	solid, yellowish white	yellow	brown, dotted	
fairchildii	chambered, white	yellowish	green	
hemsleyana	chambered	yellow	brown tomentose	
henryi	chambered	yellow	?	
holotricha	chambered, white	yellow	?	
kolomikta	chambered, brown	yellow	yellowish-green	leaves of male plants partly pink-white
melanandra	chambered, whitish	black-red	red-brown pruinose	leaves bluish beneath, completely glabrous
polygama	solid, white	yellow	yellow, tough	leaves of male plants yellow to silvery
purpurea	chambered, white	purple-red	purple	leaves glabrous on both sides
strigosa	chambered, whitish	yellow	?	
tetramera	chambered, brown	yellow; flowers 4 parted	yellow, then brown	pith narrow
venosa	chambered, white	yellow	brown, white dotted	

Actinidia arguta (S. & Z.) Planch. ex Miq. Twining to 7 m high, twigs glabrous, young twigs occasionally finely pubescent, pith narrow, light pink to white, chambered; leaves membranous to paper thin, elliptic-ovate to broadly ovate, 8–12 cm long, 4.5 to 7.5 cm wide, short acuminate, base rounded to slightly cordate, usually oblique, margin sharply serrate, glabrous and dull above, color the same beneath, glabrous to bristly or brown tomentose, with or without white pubescent vein axils, petioles 4–8 cm long; flowers white, in axillary mock-umbels, staminate flowers often numerous, pistillate flowers 1–3 or more, June, sepals 5, ovate, limb ciliate, glabrous or fine pubescent outside, petals white, base brown, often uneven, 7–12 mm long, stamens numerous, filaments thin, anthers purple; ovaries glabrous, fruit ovoid to oblong, green-yellow, 2–2.5 cm long, glabrous, edible (sweet/sour). ICS 3409. Japan, Korea, China. z5 Plate 22, 23; Fig. 76, 78.

The species includes 3 geographical varieties:

var. **arguta**. Leaves membranous to paper thin, elliptic-ovate to broadly ovate, 8–12 cm long, 4.5–7.5 cm wide, base rounded to slightly cordate, underside glabrous or venation bristly, new growth otherwise totally glabrous; inflorescence finely pubescent, flowers white, anthers purple, June. BM 7497 (as *polygama*) (= *A. arguta* [S. & Z.] Planch.; *A. giraldii* Diels; *A. megalocarpa* Nakai). China, Manchuria, Korea, Japan. z5 Plate 22, 23; Fig. 76, 78.

var. **cordifolia** Dunn. Leaves more papery, broadly ovate, 4–9 cm long, 5–10 cm wide, base distinctly cordate, venation clearly bristly; inflorescence brown tomentose, flowers white, anthers purple (= *A. cordifolia* Miq.). Japan and Korea, in thickets. z5

var. **rufa** (S. & Z.) Maxim. Leaves more membranous, ovate to broad ovate, 6–10 cm long, 5–10 cm wide, base cordate to truncate, glabrous to pubescent vein axils beneath, young twigs, leaves and inflorescence rusty tomentose (= *A. rufa* Planch.). Japan, Korea, Liukui.

Within *A. arguta* is also found a Russian Section by Mitschurin, cultivated for its fruits and all being very winter hardy. These varieties are, as yet, virtually unknown in the western world. They are listed in Soviet fruit literature as:

'**Podsnaja**' (= late ripening). Fruitful, sweet, ripening late September. ✕

'**Rannaja**' (= early ripening). Fruitful, sweet, mid-August. ✕

'**Uroshainaja**' (= fruitful). Very fruitful, very sweet, fruiting at an early age. ✕

A. callosa Lindl. Vine, twining to 7 m high, twigs glabrous, young branches dark gray or red-brown tomentose, with distinct, long, yellow lenticels, pith solid, light orange; leaves papery, obovate to ovate-elliptic, 5–13 cm long, 2.5–6.5 cm wide, acuminate, base rounded to somewhat cuneate, usually oblique, finely serrate or crenate to nearly entire, glabrous or tomentose at vein axils on both sides; flowers to 1–5 axillary, white, sepals ovate, 6 mm, June; fruit oval-oblong, gray-green, 3–4 cm long, 4 mm wide, petals 10 mm long, 7 mm wide, filament thin, anther yellow, fragrant, long, gray or brown dotted. ICS 3412. S. China to Java. Quite variable. z7

var. **callosa.** Petiole and calyx completely glabrous; leaves glabrous, also not tomentose in the axils beneath, usually obovate to oval-elliptic, 3–13 cm long, 2.5–6. cm wide; flowers April–May. S. China, Indochina, N.E. India to Malaysia. Quite variable, especially the leaf form and margin. z6 Plate 22; Fig. 78.

A. chinensis Planch. "Yang-tao" (in China). Twining to 8 m high, easily distinguished from the other species by the brown-red tomentose young branches with whitish to yellowish, very wide, solid pitch; leaves thin or thick, on sterile branches broad ovate to elliptic, short acuminate, on fertile twigs usually rounded, apex rounded, 6–17 cm long and equally wide, margin finely dentate (teeth found at the vein ends), dark green above, dense whitish stellate pubescence

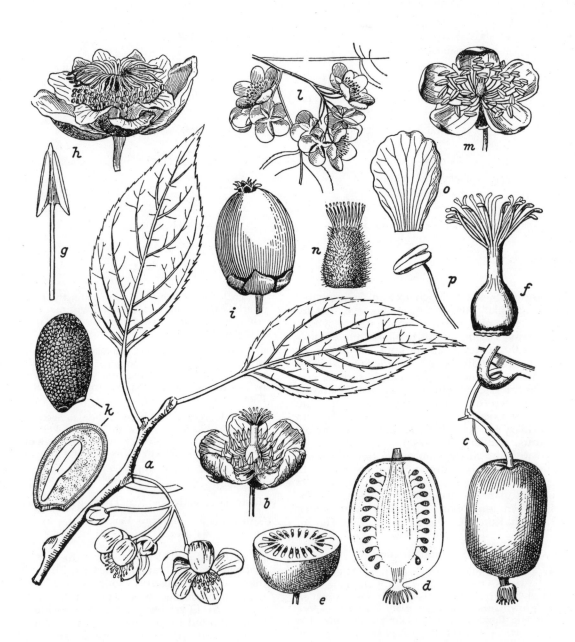

Fig. 76. **Actinidia.** *A. polygama* (a. branch with flowers, b. flower, c, d, e. fruit, f. ovary, g. stamen); *A. strigosa* (h. flower, i. fruit, k. seed exterior and in longitudinal section); *A. arguta* (l. inflorescence); *A. holotricha* (m. flower, n. ovary, o. petal, p. stamen) (from Baillon, Bolle, Finet & Gagnepain, Gilg, Lavallée)

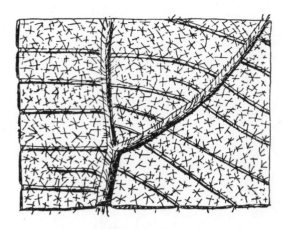

Fig. 77. *Actinidia chinensis*, underside of a leaf, × 3
(Original)

beneath (important for identification), petiole 3.5−7.5 cm long, pubescent; flowers orange-yellow, female flowers somewhat smaller, sepals 5 (or only 3−4), some 8−10 mm long, petals 1.5 cm long, June; fruit 3−5 cm long, some 3 cm wide, yellow-green, pubescent, very sweet, edible. FIO 14. China, grows all over the country but especially in the Yangtse Valley. 1900. Most beautiful type. Fruit sold in European markets as "Kiwi". z7 Plate 20, 22; Fig. 77. ∅ ✗

var. **chinensis.** Leaves thick, usually rounded, apex often emarginate, usually with bristly venation beneath; twigs and petiole softly pubescent when young; later glabrous. BM 8538; SL 87; DB 1951: 125. China, over all except the northern parts, in forests and thickets, 200−2300 m. 1900. ✗

var. **setosa** Li. Leaves thinner, usually ovate, apex acute or short acuminate, rough bristly above, twigs and leaf petiole dense bristly. Taiwan, 1300−2600 m.

A. coriacea Dunn.   Twining to 10 m high, twigs reddish brown, glabrous or nearly so, pith solid, firm, white to yellowish; leaves thick leathery, oblong to oblong-ovate, 10−16 cm long, 3−5 cm wide, acuminate, base acute to cuneate, usually oblique, margin more or less sparsely sharp dentate and finely serrate, tips of the teeth reddish glandular, both sides glabrous, deep green above, lighter beneath, with 6−7 paired veins, petole 1.5−2.5 cm long; flowers reddish, single or 2-4 on short leafless branches, petals rounded, red with whitish or yellowish margin, 7−10 mm long, filament red, anthers yellow, May−June; fruit ovate, 2 cm long, brown with white dots. BM 9140; FIO 14; ICS 3416. China; Szechwan, Kweichow, Sikang. 1908. z6 Fig. 78. ∅

A. × fairchildii Rehd. (= *A. arguta × chinensis*). Characteristics are intermediate between the parents. The only hybrid between these 2 species. Originated in Washington, 1923. Jour. Hered. 1927. Fig. 7.

A. hemsleyana Dunn. Twining to 10 m high; the twigs in 2 forms: one long, bowed, and most importantly dense bristly when young, with narrow leaves, the other, short side branches, finer rough haired and bristly, with leaves and flowers; leaves thin, oval-oblong to lanceolate-oblong, 8−13 cm long, 2.5−4.5 cm wide, occasionally also to 20 cm long and 10 cm wide, finely serrate, both sides glabrous or with rust-brown pubescence beneath, along the veins, deep green above, more bluish beneath, base cuneate, never cordate; flowers greenish, with 5 petals, June; fruit oval-oblong, to 2.5 cm long, 1.5 cm wide, brown pubesent to glabrous. E. China; Chekiang, Fukien, in underbrush. z6 Fig. 78.

A. henryi (Maxim.) Dunn. Luxuriant twining vine, twigs lightly striped, more or less bristly, young twigs brown shaggy pubescent, pith small, whitish chambered; leaves thin, oblong-ovate, 8−14 cm long, 3−6.5 cm wide, acuminate, base more or less cordate, margin finely serrate, deep green above, lighter beneath, both sides glabrous except for the finely bristled 8-10 paired veins, petiole 1−2.5 cm long, brown pubescent; flowers 10 or more in axillary groups, stalk with dense shaggy red pubescence, petals white, ovate, 6 mm long, anthers yellow. Kew Bull. 1916: 1 (= *A. callosa* var. *henryi* Maxim.). China, Yunnan. z6

A. holotoricha Finet & Gagnep. High twining, twigs and petioles slack, brown bristly, pith white, chambered; leaves thin, broad oblong-ovate, 9−13 cm long, 6−7.5 cm wide, short to long acuminate, base rounded or flat, finely and sharply dentate, venation more or less bristly on both sides, petiole 5−8 cm long, somewhat bristly pubescent; flowers yellow (?), petals 10 mm long, May−June; ovary rounded, densely pubescent, fruit unknown. SW. China; NE. Yunnan, 1400−2000 mm. z6 As yet not well known. Fig. 76.

A. kolomikta (Maxim. & Rupr.) Maxim. Weak climbing, in cultivation seldom over 2 m, to 7 m high in the wild, twigs usually dark brown, glabrous, pith chambered, brown; leaves thin, oblong to ovate, 6−15 cm long, 3−12 cm wide, acuminate, irregularly serrate, base always distinctly cordate, with 6-8 paired veins, both sides usually glabrous, part of upper blade half whitish on male plants, becoming pink sometime after June (important distinction); flowers 1−3, some 1.5 cm wide, white, fragrant, June; fruit globose, 2 cm long, yellow-green (erroneously referred to as "blue-black" in some literature), sweet, edible. E. Siberia, Manchuria, Korea, Japan, W. China. z5 Plate 2 and 23; Fig. 78. ∅

var. **gagnepainii** (Nakai) Li. Leaves larger, usually 6−15 cm long, 5−12 cm wide, venation on both sides usually somewhat bristly pubescent, petiole usually brown tomentose; flowers May−June (= *A. gagnepainii* Nakai). W. China, in thickets; 1800−3600 m. z5 The statement by Nakai, that the leaves of this variety are never white or pink colored, has been refuted by Li (Li, l.c. 20).

var. **kolomikta.** Leaves usually small, somewhat narrower, some 6−11 cm long, 3−8 cm wide, both sides nearly completely glabrous. BM 9093. E. Siberia, Sachalin, Manchuria, Korea, Japan; in thickets, 150−1600 m. 1877. z3 Most typical of the species. Plate 2 and 23.

Fig. 78. **Actinidia.** a. *A. arguta*; b. *A. callosa*; c. *A. kolomikta*; d. *A. coriacea*;
e. *A. hemsleyana*; f. *A. melanandra* (from ICS)

Both varieties show color on the female plant which is much less intense than on the male.

In addition the following selections are from the USSR:

'Anansja Mitschurina'. To 4 m high, fruit form quite variable, broad oval to ovate, ribbed, dark green, solid fleshy, sweet, refreshing, ripening late August. Mitschurin, Sel. Writings, p. 596, Pl. 1925. ✖

'Klara Zetkin'. To 3 m high, fruit pale green, oblong-elliptical, light striped, some 3.5 cm long, juicy, very sweet, when overripe nearly translucent. Mitschurin, S. Writings, p. 598, Pl. 1926. ✖

A. melanandra Franch. Vine, to 7 m, twigs reddish, finely white pubescent and bluish when young, pith chambered, more or less whitish; leaves thin, elliptic or ovate to oblong-ovate or oblong-lanceolate, 6–9 cm long, 3–4 cm wide, acuminate, base cuneate or rounded, often uneven, very fine serrate, teeth appressed, both sides glabrous except for small brown pubescent vein axils, bluish beneath, with 4–6 paired veins, petiole 2.5–3 cm long; flowers 3–5 or single, white, sepals 5 (occasionally 4), petals 4, white (occasionally brown at the base), oblong, 1.2 cm long, stamen filament black-red, June–July; fruit ovate, reddish brown, pruinose, without dots, 2–3 cm long. ICS 3413 (= *A. rufa* var. *parvifolia* Dunn). China; Hupeh, Szechwan. 1910. z6 Plate 22; Fig. 78.

A. polygama (S. & Z.) Maxim. Vine, twining to 5 m high, twigs glabrous, pith solid, wide, white; leaves thin, membranous, often the whole blade white or yellowish white or only on the upper half, or with a yellow patch (important for identification), ovate, 7–12 cm long, 4.5–8 cm wide, acuminate, base acute to rounded, rarely slightly cordate, margin finely serrate, somewhat lighter beneath and the 6–7 paired veins somewhat bristly pubescent, petiole 2–4.5 cm long; flowers white, single or in clusters of 2–3, with 5 (now and then somewhat uneven) sepals, 5 oblong-ovate petals, 12–13 mm long, fragrant, anthers yellow or brown, June; fruit ovate, yellow, somewhat translucent, with a beak-like extension on the tip, 2–3 cm long, bitter. z6 SDK 4: 116; ICS 3410. ∅

This species is very often confused with, but is easily distinguished from *A. kolomikta* by its totally different pith.

var. **lecomtei** (Nakai) Li. Leaves generally glabrous beneath, occasionally somewhat bristly pubescent; anthers brown. W. China; Schensi, Hupeh, Szechwan. z6

var. **polygama**. Leaves beneath always more or less bristly pubescent on the veins; anthers yellow (= *A. volubilis* [S. & Z.] Planch.; *A. repanda* Honda). Sachalin, Manchuria, Korea, Japan; developing thickets in the mountains. 1891. z6 Fig. 76.

A. purpurea Rehd. A vine, in the wild twining to 20 m high, in cultivation to 7 m, young twigs glabrous, new growth finely pubescent, gray, pith white, chambered; leaves tough, elliptic to broad ovate, 8–12 cm long, 4.5–6.5 cm wide, acuminate, base acute to rounded and usually oblique, margin finely serrate, appressed, dull green and glabrous above, somewhat lighter beneath, tomentose along the veins; flowers in axillary cymes, the female usually in 3's, the male flowers many, white, some 15–20 mm wide, anthers black-red, June; ovaries "bottle shaped", fruit oval-oblong, 2–2.5 cm long, purple, glabrous, "beaked", sweet. China; Hupeh, Szechwan, Yunnan and others. 1908. z6 Very similar to *A. arguta*, but leaves longer, narrower, teeth always appressed and fruits purple.

A. rubricaulis Dunn. High climbing, twigs red-brown, completely glabrous, with lenticels, pith solid, dense, whitish; leaves tough, oblong-lanceolate to oblong-ovate, 8–10 cm long, 1.2–3.8 cm wide, acuminate, base cordate, usually oblique, somewhat sparsely serrate, teeth often glandular, both sides completely glabrous, dark green above, much lighter beneath, with 6–7 paired veins, petiole 1–2.5 cm long; flowers usually on short side branches, usually single or the higher ones in clusters to 5, whitish, petals 5, often uneven, oblong, 7.5 mm long, anthers yellow; fruits ovoid, 1.6 cm long, yellow, with persistent, reflexed sepals. SW. China: only in S. Yunnan, in mountain forests from 1500–2300 m. 1906. z6

A. strigosa Hook f. & Thoms. Twining vine, twigs red-brown, with light lenticels, densely bristled and brown pubescent at first, pith wide, whitish, chambered; leaves tough, ovate to oblong-ovate, 7–13 cm long, 4–7 cm wide, acuminate, base rounded, often oblique, margin coarsely dentate, both sides equal in color, venation light bristly beneath, with 5–7 paired veins; flowers 2–4 in cymes, white, petals obovate, 8 mm long, anthers yellow; ovaries rounded, densely pubescent. India: Sikkim, E. Himalaya. z6 Fig. 76.

A. tetramera Maxim. Twining to 13 m high in the wild, twigs gray to red-brown, pith narrow, chambered, brown; leaves tough, often with white or pink specks (resembling *A. polygama*), narow oblong-ovate, some 5–10 cm long, 2.5–4 cm wide, acuminate, base oblique cuneate, margin finely serrate, both sides glabrous or the 6–8 paired veins beneath lightly bristled; flowers in clusters of 2–3 or single, sepals 4 (rarely 5), petals 4 (rarely 5) (important for identification), white, often pink tinged, anthers yellow, June; fruit ovoid, 1.5–2 cm long, brown, glabrous, without lenticels. W. China. Resembles *A. polygama*, but easily distinguished from all other species by the 4 parted flowers. z5 ∅

A. venosa Rehd. Vine, climbing 6–9 m high, twigs purple-brown, with whitish lenticels, finely tomentose when young, soon becoming glabrous, pith wide, white, chambered; leaves thin, ovate to ovate-oblong, some 5–15 cm long, 3–6 cm wide, acuminate, base usually rounded to cordate, margin finely serrate, dark green above, somewhat lighter beneath, more or less finely tomentose when young, soon becoming glabrous, venation distinctly reticulate with 7–11 paired veins; flowers 1–7 in axillary, brown pubescent cymes, yellowish white, June–July; fruit ovoid, brown, glabrous, 1.5 cm thick. W.China. 1908. z6 Easily recognizable by its abundant and distinctly raised reticulate venation.

Beautiful, usually very luxuriant growing vine with conspicuous foliage, especially on *A. kolomikta, polygama* and *chinensis*; the flower and fruit are, however, not always satisfactory. The Russian fruit-types are not readily usable in the West for fruit. Needs a fertile, humus soil; prefers semishade but in the proper soil can also thrive in full sun.

Lit. Li, Hui-Lin, a taxonomic review of the genus *Actinidia*; in Jour. Arnold Arboretum 33: 1–61, 1952 ● Mitschurin, I.W., Selected Writings (German Version); 7. Beih. Sowj. Wiss. Berlin 1951.

ACTINODAPHNE — LAURACEAE

Evergreen, tropical trees, very closely related to *Litsea* Lam.; leaves alternate, occasionally nearly whorled, tough leathery, venation pinnate; inflorescence umbellate, surrounded at first by fugacious imbricate bracts, stalked or sessile; flowers small, corolla tube in 6 sections, occasionally persistent, tube short; stamens 9, in 3 circles, the outer 6 without glands, the anthers pointing inward, 4 chambered; fruit a berry, with the persistent receptical on the base. — Some 100 species in the tropics from Asia and Malaysia.

The very best for cultivation is from S. Japan (Honshu, Shikoku, Kyushu); *Actinodaphne lancifolia* (S. & Z.) Meissn. KIF: 1: 66. Not winter hardy. z8 # ∅

ADENANDRA Willd. — RUTACEAE

Evergreen shrubs; leaves alternate or opposite, small, dotted with glands; flowers usually single or several on the branch tips, white or pink; alternating 5 staminodes with 5 true stamens, the latter shorter. — Some 25 species in S. Africa.

Adenandra fragans Roem. et Schult. Shrub, erect, 50—70 cm high, glabrous; leaves oblong, blunt, 2—4 cm long, dark green above, whitish beneath and with glandular, finely dentate margin; flowers pink, in terminal clusters, fragrant, May—June. BM 519 (as *Diosma fragans*). Cape of Good Hope 1812. z8 # ✤

A. umbellata Willd. Evergreen shrub, 60 cm or higher, erect growing; very dense foliage, linear-oblong to obovate-oblong, 1—2 cm long, aromatic, pronounced glandular dots; flowers usually single terminal or also in the higher leaf axils, 2.5—3 cm wide, petals obovate, inside white with a pink-red midstripe on the lower half, outside red, June. RCA 25. S. Africa, mountains on the Cape, 300—1200 m. 1790. z8 #

A. uniflora Willd. Shrub, 50—70 cm high, erect, twigs thin, dense foliage; leaves linear, acuminate, 1—2 cm long, 3 mm wide, dark green above, glossy, lighter beneath with translucent dots, ciliate; flowers single, white, but all the petals with a pink midstripe, anthers purple brown, April—June; leaves and flowers fragrant. BM 273 (as *Diosma uniflora*); RCA 25; HTS 17. S. Africa. 1775 z8 # ✤

Besides the above species, others may be found in the mildest areas of the British Isles, especially in botanic gardens, and generally over-wintered in a cool greenhouse.

ADENOCARPUS DC. — LEGUMINOSAE

Deciduous or semi-evergreen shrubs, twigs more or less pubescent; leaves 3 parted, leaflets small; flowers yellow, in terminal racemes, calyx 2 lipped (size of calyx teeth important for identification), standard petal circular, flared out, keel petals bowed inward, as long as the standard; pods sessile, linear, sticky-glandular, many seeded. — About 20 species in the Mediterranean region, Asia Minor, N. and W. Africa.

Adenocarpus anagyrifolius Coss. & Balansa. Deciduous, dense shrub, 1—1.5 m high and wide, young branches strictly upright, somewhat furrowed, glabrous or nearly so; leaves 3 parted, tightly packed, petiole 1—3 cm long, leaflets sessile, elliptic to obovate, 1—3 cm long, 0.7—2 cm wide, margin entire, glabrous; flowers gold-yellow, 1.5 cm long, in dense terminal, 10—20 cm long racemes, June; pod 5—6 cm long, 6 mm wide, distinctly warty. Morocco, Atlas Mountains, 1000-3000 m. z8 ✤

A. complicatus (L.) Gay. Deciduous, strong branched shrub, 20—70 cm high, twigs thin, pubescent at first, soon glabrous and whitish; leaflets lanceolate to oblong, often also folded, appressed pubescent beneath, 6—12 mm long; flowers gold-yellow, standard petal reddish, in terminal, elongated racemes, May—June; calyx glandular. BM 1387 (as *Cytisus divaricatus*); VG 62. Portugal, Spain, SW. France, S. Italy. z8 d ✤ ○

A. decorticans Boiss. Sparse, deciduous shrub, occasionally a small tree in its habitat, bark on trunk and older branches white, peeling, young twigs tomentose; leaves closely spaced, leaflets linear, 8—18 mm long, margin rolled up, pubescent; flowers gold-yellow, in dense, upright, 3—6 cm long racemes, June; pods 3—5 cm long. BM 48 ns; PSw 19; VG 58. Spain. 1879. Plate 2; Fig. 79. z8 d ✤ ○

A foliolosus DC. Semi-evergreen shrub, some 1 m high, very densely branched, pubescent only when young; leaflets small, pubescent, tightly packed; flow-

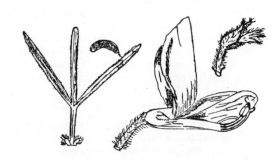

Fig. 79. *Adenocarpus decorticans* Leaf in cross section, flower, calyx (from B.M.)

ers yellow, standard pubescent, May—June, in dense, terminal racemes, points on the lower calyx lip all of equal length; pod glandular when young, eventually glabrous. BM 426 (as *Cytisus foliolosus*); BFCa 165—166; KGC 24. Canary Islands. 1629. z8 # d ✤ ○

A. hispanicus (Lam.) DC. Deciduous, small, sparse shrub, 0.5—1 m, bark split, young branches softly pubescent; leaves tightly packed, 3 parted, leaflets lanceolate, tough, glabrous above, silky white pubescent beneath, plaited at first; flowers many in terminal racemes, yellow, standard obovate and bordered, outside somewhat pubescent, calyx glandular and pubescent, June to July; pod protruding, to 3 cm long. VG 57. Spain, Portugal. 1816. z8 ✤

A. telonensis Robert. Low shrub, young twigs at first pubescent, later glabrous and whitish; leaves in clusters, leaflets to 3, obovate, both sides glabrous, margin occasionally ciliate; flowers yellow, May—June, in a few flowered, short stalked racemes, nearly capitate, calyx teeth of similar length; pod glandular, 2—4 cm long. VG 59 (= *A. grandiflorus* Boiss.). Portugal, Spain, S. France, Morocco. z8 d ✤ ○

A. viscosus (Willd.) Webb & Berth. Semi-evergreen, small shrub, 0.3—1 m, young branches pubescent; leaves 3 parted, very tightly packed, sessile, leaflets linear-lanceolate, gray-green, pubescent, plaited; flowers orange-yellow, in tight, terminal racemes, calyx glandular and pubescent, middle tooth of the lower lip longer than the side lips, April; pod dense glandular and viscid. BFCa 164. Tenerife. 1825. z8 ◇

These species are only for experienced gardeners. Prefer very warm, dry areas in the rock garden, tolerate poor soil; must be overwintered in a greenhouse. Good for tub planting.

ADENOSTOMA Hook. et Arn. — ROSACEAE

Evergreen shrubs, occasionally at small tree in the wild, with "heather-like" foliage; leaves alternate, clustered, very numerous, linear, margin entire, resinous; flowers small, white, some 5 mm wide, with 5 petals and 10—15 stamens, calyx tube with 5 glands on the apex, fruit a small nutlet with persistent calyx tube. — 2 species in California.

Adenostoma fasciculatum Hook. et Arn. In California "Chamiso". Diversely branching shrub, 0.5—3 m high, with thin, sraight twigs, dense with small, clustered leaves; flowers in 5—10 cm long panicles, white, February—July. MS 210. Typical shrub of the coastal hills of California, developing dense, impenetrable thickets ("Chaparral"). Hardiest type. Fig. 80. z8 # ○

A. sparsifolium Torr. Shrub, 0.5—6 m high; leaves alternate (not clustered), bark yellow-green, later reddish and shredding on older trunks; flowers white, seldom pink, fragrant, in loose, 2—6 cm long panicles, July—August. MS 212. California, in the chaparral from Santa Barbara County south. z8 # ○

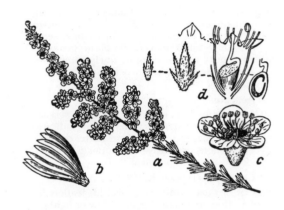

Fig. 80. *Adenostoma fasciculatum*.
a. branch, reduced; b. leaf cluster; c. flower; d. flower in longitudinal section, ovary and 2 bracts (from Torrey)

Easily propagated by cuttings. For sunny areas, well drained soils and frost free winters.

Fig. 81. *Adhatoda vasica* (from ICS)

ADHATODA Mill. — ACANTHACEAE

Tropical shrubs; leaves opposite, margins entire; flowers white to purple; calyx 5 lobed, corolla comprised of a short tube with a long, 2 lipped limb; stamens 2, short spurred; bracts protruding, frequently much longer than the calyx. — From some 20 species in tropical Africa and Asia, only the following species is commonly found in gardens of the Mediterranean region.

Adhatoda vasica Ness. Shrub, erect, to some 2.5 m high, strong branching; leaves elliptic, 10—15 cm, short petioled; flowers in terminal spikes, nearly as long as the leaves, the single flowers some 3 cm long, white, lower lip pink veined, July. BM 861. India. 1699. z9 Fig. 81. ◇

AESCULUS L. — HIPPOCASTANACEAE

Deciduous trees or shrubs; leaves opposite, palmately compound with 4−9 leaflets, long petioled, serrate; flowers many in upright, terminal panicles; calyx campanulate to tubular, with 4−5 teeth, petals 4−5, dissimilar; fruit a leathery capsule with 1−3 seeds; seeds large, with wide hilum scar. — 13 species, including 1 in SE. Europe, 5 in E. Asia and India, 7 in N. America, plus a number of hybrids.

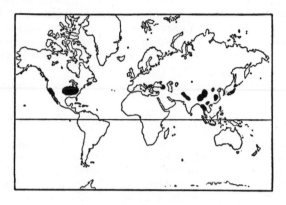

Fig. 82. Range of the genus *Aesculus*

Outline of the Genus (with the hybrids)

Section **Parryanae** Wiggins

Small trees or shrubs; winter buds not viscid; leaflets 5−7 (occasionally only 1−3), sessile, tomentose or woolly beneath, margins entire; calyx campanulate, sepals fused midway, the 5 lobes uneven and blunt; petals 4−5, with stalked glands on the margin, finely tomentose on the back; fruit tomentose and warty (not prickly):

A. parryana

Section **Aesculus**

Tall tree, winter buds viscid; leaflets 5−7, sessile; flowers white, limb of the petal and veins yellow, fading to brown; petals 4 or (usually) 5, wide, claw shorter than the 5 lobed calyces; stamens protrusive; fruit prickly or warty:

A. hippocastanum, turbinata

Section **Calothyrus** (Spach) K. Koch

Trees or shrubs; winter buds viscid; leaflets 5−9, long petioled; flowers white, cream-yellow or light gray-pink; calyx usually 2 lipped, upper lip with 3 slits, lower lip seldom 2 pointed; petals 4 or 5, nearly even length, their stalks not reaching past the calyx; teeth stamens 5−7, glabrous; fruits pear-shaped, smooth:

A. assamica, californica, chinensis, indica, wilsonii

Section **Macrothyrsus** (Spach) K. Koch

Shrubs or small trees; winter buds not viscid; leaflets 5−7, stalked; inflorescence 20−30 cm long, columnar; flowers white, with 4−5 nearly even petals; stamens 3 to 4 times as long as the petals, straight; fruit smooth:

A. parviflora

Section **Pavia** (Mill.) Persoon

Shrubs or large trees; winter buds not viscid; leaflets distinctly stalked; calyx with 5 blunt, short lobes; flowers yellow or red, petals 4, sometimes striped, their stalks reaching past the calyx teeth, the limbs of the 2 side petals erect, those of the upper ones pointing outward:

A. flava, glabra, pavia, silvatica

Aesculus arguta see: **A. glabra**

A. assamica Griff. Tropical, tall tree; leaves large, leaflets 5−7, oblong-lanceolate, acuminate, finely serrate, base cuneate and somewhat narrowing, short stalked, both side green and glabrous; flowers in racemes, on axillary panicles with attractive velvety pubescence, petals white, pink at the base, calyx tubular, stamens very protruding; fruit obovoid, smooth, brown, leathery, 4 cm (= *A. punduana* Wall.). India. z8

A. × arnoldiana Sarg. (*A. glabra* × *A. hybrida*). Tree, leaflets elliptic, often finely and doubly serrate, glabrous beneath except for the pubescent midrib; calyx campanulate, yellow, petals yellow, upper reddish, stamens as long or longer than the petals; fruit short

prickled and warty. Originated in the Arnold Arboretum, 1900. z5

A. atrosanguinea see: **A. woerlitzensis**

A. austrina see: **A. pavia**

A. buckleyi see: **A. glabra**

A. × bushii Schneid. (*A. glabra* × *A. pavia*). Tree, branches and petioles pubescent, leaflets fine serrate, pubescent beneath; petals yellow and pink, stamens longer than the petals; fruit somewhat warty. Arkansas, Missouri. 1901. z5 ⊕

A. californica (Spach) Nutt. California Horsechestnut. Shrubby in its habitat, 3−4 m high, rarely a small tree, crown broad and round, wider than high, trunk short, twigs glabrous, winter buds viscid; leaves very small, usually 5(−7) parted, oblong-oval, 8−14 cm long, sharply serrate, gray-green pubescent only when young, somewhat metallic in appearance, petiolules 1−1.5 cm long; flowers in dense, narrow, 8−20 cm long panicles, petals even length, white to pink, fragrant, stamens protruding, May−June; fruit somewhat fig-shaped, 5−7 cm long, rough, but not prickly. SPa 189; BS 1: 251; BM 5070; FS 1312 (= *Pavia californica* Hartw.). California. 1855. Dry, gravelly soil. z7 Plate 26; Fig. 83, 85. ⊕

A. × carnea Hayne. Red Flowering Horsechestnut (*A. hippocastanum* × *A. pavia*). Tree, to 20 m high, winter buds slightly viscid, new growth not woolly; leaflets usually 5, nearly sessile to short stalked, cuneate-oblong, doubly and bluntly serrate, somewhat glossy above, 8−15 cm long, somewhat smaller and darker than *A. hippocastanum*, petals light red, glandular and shaggy on the margin; fruit globose, 3−4 cm wide, slightly prickly. FS 2229; BR 1056 (= *A. rubicunda* Loisel.). Originated circa 1818. A. tetraploid and therefore comes true from seed. One of the most beautiful of the genus. Fig. 83. z3 See also: *A. × plantierensis*. ⊕

'Aureo-marginata'. Leaves yellow bordered.

'**Briotii'.** Inflorescence somewhat larger than the type, petals much darker, light blood red, pistil not pubescent or only pubescent to the middle, fruit soft prickly. RH 1878: Pl. 370. Originated 1858 in the Trianon, Versailles, France. Plate 3 and 25. ⊕

'**Marginata'.** Leaves variegated, margin wide dark green, middle light green, both separated by an irregularly wide, yellow band (= *fol. marginatis*).

'**Pendula'.** Twigs more or less pendulous. In Kew Gardens since 1902.

A. chinensis Bunge. Chinese Horsechestnut. Tree, to 20 m in its native habitat, bark gray-brown, rough, branches thick, stiff, glabrous, winter buds viscid, leaf scar very large; leaflets (5−)7, narrow oblong to obovate, 12−20 cm long, 4−6 cm wide, drawn out to a fine point, shallow and evenly dentate, petiolulus 3−4 mm long; flowers in 20−35 cm long panicles, 5−10 cm wide at the base, flower stalk glabrous, petals 5, white, stamens somewhat longer than the petals, calyx campanulate with 5 teeth, fruit somewhat flattened sphere, thick shelled, rough, not warty, seeds 2−2.5 cm wide, hilum covering nearly half the surface. CIS 86; Jour. Arnold Arboretum 1962: Pl. 2. N. China. 1877 and 1912. Susceptible to damage by a late frost! Earlier, *A. turbinata* was erroneously included under this heading in cultivation. z6 Fig. 83. See also: *A. turbinata* and *A. wilsonii*

A. × dallimorei Sealy. (Periclinal-Chimera from *A. hippocastanum* with *A. flava*). Tree, older branches somewhat reddish green, young twigs thick, gray-green, winter buds not viscid, some 2 cm long, 1 cm thick; leaflets 5, with rust-red woolly tufts at the base, partly sessile, some with 5−7 mm long petiolules, usually broad elliptic, acuminate, base cuneate, 10−25 cm long, 5−11 cm wide, irregularly and bluntly double serrate, deep green above, silvery beneath, loose white pubescence; flowers in 20−23 cm long, erect panicles, axis green, upper portion finely pubescent, otherwise loose brown woolly, usually male, occasionally bisexual flowers, calyx campanulate, 10−13 cm long, green, evenly 5 lobed, tube pubescent and glandular, petals 4, in 2 dissimilar pairs, somewhat spread apart, usually white with dark red spot, but some flowers always green-yellow with dark yellow spot. Found by Dallimore in Bidborough, Kent, England, 1955. Fruit and seed as yet unknown. z5

A. discolor see: **A × hybrida**

A. × dupontii Sarg. (*A. silvatica × A. pavia*). Tree, leaflets oblong-obovate to elliptic, with 18−25 paired veins, sharply serrate, light green and glabrous beneath except for the pubescent tufts in the vein axils, calyx narrow campanulate, red, petals yellow or slightly reddish, stamens shorter than the petals; fruit smooth. Originated after 1820. z5

var. **hessei** Sarg. (*A. silvatica × A. pavia*). Leaflets elliptical or elliptic-obovate, panicles tighter, petals yellow, turning red. 1909.

A. flava Soland. Sweet Buckeye. Tree, to 20 m high, with wide spreading, rounded crown, bark deep brown, winter buds not viscid; leaflets 5, oblong to narrow-elliptic, 10−15 cm long, finely serrate, dark green above, light green beneath, pubescent at first (often brownish), later glabrous, deep yellow in fall, abcising early; flowers in 10−15 cm long, velvety pubescent panicles, petals 4, light green-yellow, stripes brown-red to purple, stamens 7, shorter and hidden by the petals, calyx and flower stalk with stalked glands (!!), May−June; fruit globose, 5−6 cm thick, without prickles, poisonous to humans. DB 1954: 161; BB 2384; GTP 296 (= *A. octandra* Marsh., *A. lutea* Wangenh.). N. America, Pennsylvania to Georgia and Illinois, in river valleys and hillsides. 1764. z4 Plate 25; Fig. 83, 85.

f. **vestita** (Sarg.) Fernald. Young twigs and leaf undersides densely pubescent. Ohio Valley and W. Kentucky. 1893.

f. **virginica** (Sarg.). Fernald. Flowers red, pink to yellowish. W. Virginia.

A. georgiana see: **A. silvatica**

A. glabra Willd. var. *glabra*. Tree, 10−30 m, bark rough and markedly split, new growth dull red-brown; leaflets 5, elliptic-obovate, 8−12 cm long, finely serrate, light green, pubescent beneath at first, later glabrous, orange fall color; flowers pale yellow-green, of little merit, 2−3 cm long, in 10−15 cm long panicles, petals 4, rather even length, stamens 1/3 longer than the petals, May; fruit nearly globose, 3−5 cm thick, short prickled, poisonous to humans. SS Pl. 67−68; BB 2382; GTP 295 (= *A. ohioensis* DC.). E. USA. River banks and low land. 1809. z4 Easily distinguished from all other species by the unpleasant odor from a broken twig; distinguished from the similar *A. flava* by its rough bark, less pubescent leaves, longer stamens and prickly fruits. Plate 25, 24; Fig. 83, 84, 85.

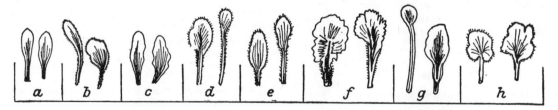

Fig. 83. **Aesculus** flower petals. a. *A. chinensis*; b. *A. indica*; c. *A. californica*; d. *A. flava*; e. *A. glabra*; f. *A. carnea*; g. *A. pavia* var. *discolor*; h. *A. hippocastanum*

Fig. 84. *Aesculus glabra* (from Guimpel)

var. **arguta** (Buckl.) Robinson. Known as a shrub to 2 m high, however recently seen as a small tree, to 6 m (Harkness, in Phytologia 4: 175, 1955), often low-hanging from the weight of the fruits, twigs thin, pubescent; leaflets 7−9, lanceolate, 6−12 cm long, sharply and doubly serrate, pubescent beneath at first, later glabrous, acuminate; flowers light yellow, petals nearly even length, oblong-obovate, tapering to needle-like tip, outside soft pubescent, stamens usually 7, pubescent, May; fruit rounded, 1−3 seeded, seed brown, 2.5 cm thick. BB 2383; ST 198 (= *A. arguta* Buckl.). E. Texas. 1909. z6 Often misidentified in cultivation. Tolerates dryness and competition from taller trees. ✥

var. **leucodermis** Sarg. Tree, to 20 m, especially attractive for its white or white striped bark; leaflets slightly tomentose beneath; flowers later than the species. Missouri. 1901.

var. **monticola** Sarg. Leaflets 6−7, young leaves with soft pubescent midrib beneath, later becoming glabrous; fruit rounded, to 2 cm wide, usually with only 1 seed. Oklahoma. 1922.

f. **pallida** (Wiild.) Schelle. Leaflets remaining pubescent beneath. USA; Midwest. 1809.

var. **sargentii** Rehd. Tree, to 8 m (mistakenly described by Rehder as only a shrub); leaflets 6−7, apex longer acuminate, heavier pubescence beneath, double dentate, petiole brown pubescent (= *A. buckleyi* Bush). Ohio to Oklahoma. 1895.

A. × glaucescens Sarg. (= *A. flava* × *A. silvatica*). Shrubby, usually not over 2−3 m high, only rarely a small tree, young twigs pubescent at first; leaflets 5, to 20 cm long, 5−8 cm wide, light green, midrib pubescent above, blue-green with axillary tufts beneath, petiole glabrous; flowers to 3 cm long, yellow, stamens usually shorter than the petals, calyx campanulate, limb glandular; fruit 3−4 cm wide. ST 196. Georgia, USA. 1914. z5 ∅

A. harbisonii see: **A. × mutabilis**

A. hippocastanum L. Common Horsechestnut. Tree, to 25 m high, crown tall oval, very densely branched, twigs glabrous, lower branches usually pendulous, winter buds resinous, new growth with thick brown woolly pubescence; leaflets 5−7, blunt doubly serrate, 10−25 cm long, brown woolly when young; flowers white, yellow-red speckled, 2 cm wide, in 20−30 cm long, erect panicles, calyx tubular-campanulate, 5 parted, pistil not pubescent, May−June; fruit to 6 cm thick, prickly, with 1−2 large seeds. HM 1868 to 1869; BB 2381. Native to the mountains of N. Greece, Albania, Bulgaria. Brought from Constantinople to Vienna in 1576 by Clusius and from here soon distributed over all of W. and Middle Europe. z3 Ⓕ Romania. Fig. 83, 85. ∅ ✥

'**Albovariegata**'. Leaves white variegated. Known since 1770.

'**Aureovariegata**'. Leaves yellow speckled, of little merit. Occasionally in cultivation.

'**Baumanii**'. Flowers full, white, sterile. JH 1855: Pl. 50 (= 'Plena'). Introduced to the trade by Baumann, 1819. Found as a sport of a plant in Geneva, Switzerland. Very popular today as a park and street tree; flowers lasting longer than those of the species. ✥

'**Crispa**'. Growth tightly pyramidal; leaflets short and wide. 1838.

'**Digitata**'. Dwarf form, leaves small, leaflets 3 (to 5), linear, deep green, petiole somewhat winged; flowers not known (= *A. hippocastanum pumila* Dipp.). Presumably from France. Before 1864. Occasionally still found today. Plate 25.

'**Incisa**'. Leaflets 5, smaller than the type, margin nearly frayed, doubly serrate (= *A. hippocastanum* 'Henkelii' Henkel). Known in cultivation since 1840 and still growing in Kew, England but of little value. ('Henkelii' presumably remaining green later in the fall, otherwise not particularly different.) Plate 25.

'**Laciniata**'. Leaflets narrow, often needle-like, deeply incised, not dense (= *A. hippocastanum asplenifolia*). Known since 1844, from France. Plate 25.

'**Memmingeri**'. Grows as a tree; leaflets thick whitish yellow pulverulent and striped. Cultivated since 1855, but origin unknown. Named for Gustav Memminger, a noted gardener from Verdum, great uncle of Otto Froebel, Zurich. Plate 23. ∅

'**Monstrosa**'. Very weak irregularly pyramidal growth, twigs short, compressed, banded, with many foliar buds; leaves more or less normal, but very small. 1.5 m high at the Botanic Garden of Kiel, W. Germany.

'**Pendula**'. Branches pendulous even on young plants.

'**Praecox**'. Leafing out 2 weeks earlier than the species, flowers 10−14 days earlier. 2 large trees in Kew. Not recommended where there is danger of a late frost.

'**Pyramidalis**'. Growth narrowly upright, weak, dense crown, branches at 45° angle from the stem. Before 1900.

'**Schirnhoferi**'. Normal growth; flowers full, yellowish red. Originated in Austria. ✥

'**Tortuosa**'. Twigs twisted.

'**Umbraculifera**'. Dwarf form, growth shrubby, globose and very dense, known only as top-grafted tree. Before 1884.

A. × hybrida DC. (*A. flava* × *A. pavia*). Probably a natural hybrid. Large tree; leaflets 5, inversely ovate-

Plate 17

Acer saccharinum 'Pyramidale' with typical crown form in the Dortmund Botanic Garden, W. Germany

Acer grosseri var. *hersii* in Copenhagen Botanical Garden, Denmark

Acer pensylvanicum at leaf drop in autumn in the Tervuren Arboretum, Brussels, Belgium

Plate 18

Acer. a. *A. platanoides* 'Globosum'; b. *A. platanoides*; c. *A. platanoides* 'Cucullatum';
d. + e. *A. platanoides* 'Stollii'; f. *A. platanoides* 'Laciniatum'; g. *A. dieckii*

Plate 19

Acer. a. *A. saccharum;* b. 'Temples Upright'; *c. A. pseupdoplatanus* 'Auchlorum'; d. *A. macrophyllum;* e. *A. diabolicum;* f. *A. glabrum* var. *douglasii'*; g. *A. diabolicum* var. *purpurascens;* h. *A. trantvetterii;* i. *A. pseudoplatanus* f. *erythrocarpum;* k. *A. heldreichii;* l. *A. hybridum*

Plate 20

Actinidia chinensis in the Gothenburg Botanical Garden, Sweden
(note the varying leaves on the same plant)

Acer pseudoplatanus 'Atropurpureum'
in the Aarhus Botanical Garden, Denmark

Plate 21

Arctostaphylos media
in Edinburgh Botanic Garden

Artemisia procera
in Dortmund Botanic Garden

Aciphylla colensoi in Edinburgh Botanic Garden, Scotland

Plate 22

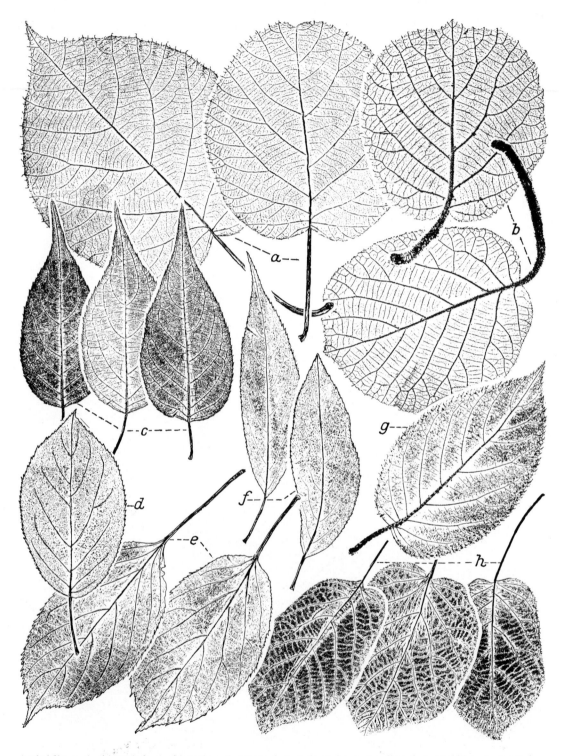

Actinidia. a. *A. chinensis*; b. *A. chinensis*; c. *A. arguta*; d. *A. melanandra*; e. *A. callosa*; f. *A. giraldii*; g. *A. arguta*; h. *A. kolomikta* (material from the Leiden Botanic Garden, Holland [a], botanic gardens in Dortmund [b. g. h], Munich [e] and Gothenburg, Sweden [c. d. f]

Plate 23

Actinidia kolomikta
in Munich Botanic Garden

Aesculus hippocastanum 'Memmingeri'
in Dortmund Botanic Garden

Actinidia arguta, male flower, in Berggarten Hannover-Herrenhausen

Plate 24

Aesculus turbinata
Photo: Dr. Watari, Tokyo

Aesculus glabra
in its native habitat in Ohio, USA
Photo: US Forest Service

Aesculus parviflora in Charlottenlund Botanic Garden, Copenhagen

Plate 25

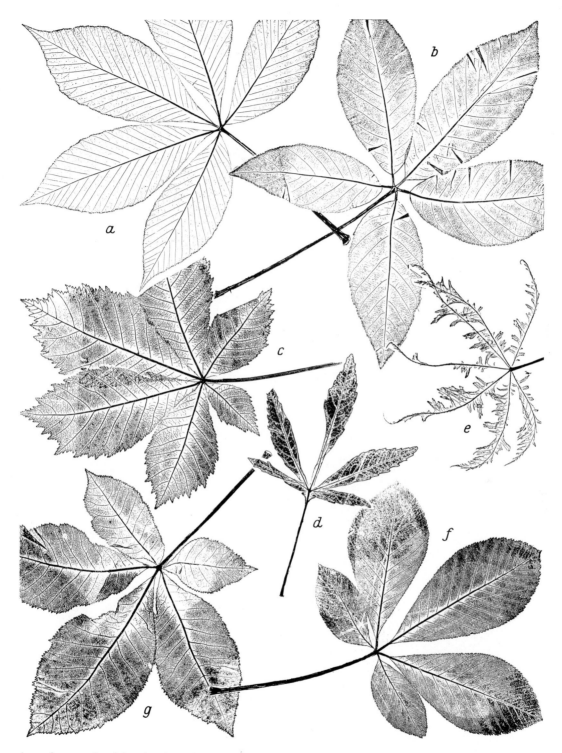

Aesculus. a. *A. glabra*; b. *A. pavia*; c. *A. hippocastanum* 'Incisa'; d. *A. hippocastanum* 'Digitata'; e. *A. hippocastanum* 'Laciniata'; f. *A. flava*, spp.; g. *A. carnea* 'Briotii' (from material in the US National Arboretum, Washington [a, b], Kew Gardens [c. d. e. f. g])

Plate 26

Aesculus. a. *A. wilsonii*; b. *A. californica*; c. *A. indica* (all from Kew Gardens)

Plate 27

Aethionema grandiflorum

Photo: C. R. Jelitto

Aethionema armenum 'Warley Rose'

Photo: E. Hahn

Plate 28

Albizia julibrissin
Photo: E. Hahn

Albizia julibrissin in Les Barres Arboretum, France

Akebia quinata on Madre Island, Lake Maggiore, Italy

Plate 29

Alnus incana 'Laciniata'
in Dortmund Botanic Garden

Andromeda polifolia
Photo: C. R. Jelitto

Anthyllis montana in Lyon Botanic Garden, France

Plate 30

Alnus incana in flower and fruit
Photo: C. R. Jelitto

Alnus japonica
in Kalmthout Arboretum, Belgium

Alnus maximowiczii

Photo: Dr. Watari, Tokyo

Plate 31

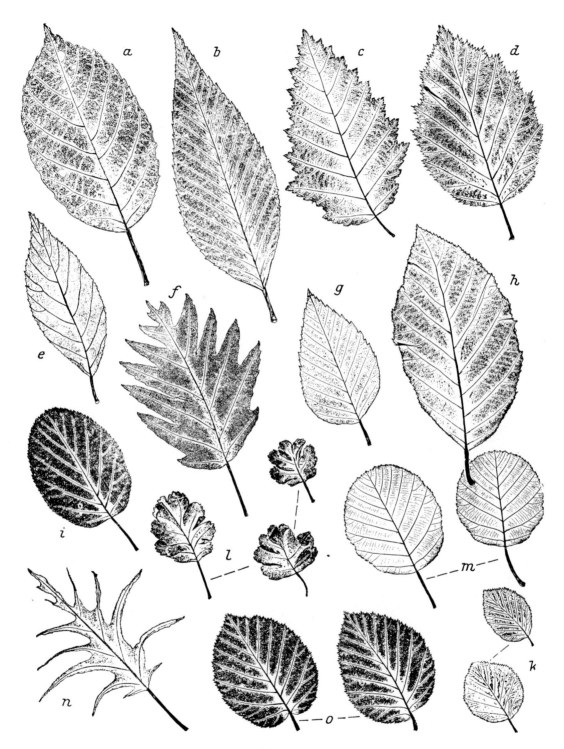

Alnus. a. *A. maritima*; b. *A. firma* var. *multinervis*; c. *A. tenuifolia*; d. *A. sinuata*; e. *A. japonica*; f. *A. glutinosa* 'Laciniata'; g. *A. firma*; h. *A. rugosa*; i. *A. elliptica* 'Itolanda'; k. *A. viridis* f. *microphylla*; l. *A. glutinosa* 'Incisa'; m. *A. rugosa* var. *emersoniana*; n. *A. glutinosa* 'Imperialis'; o. *A. viridis*

Plate 32

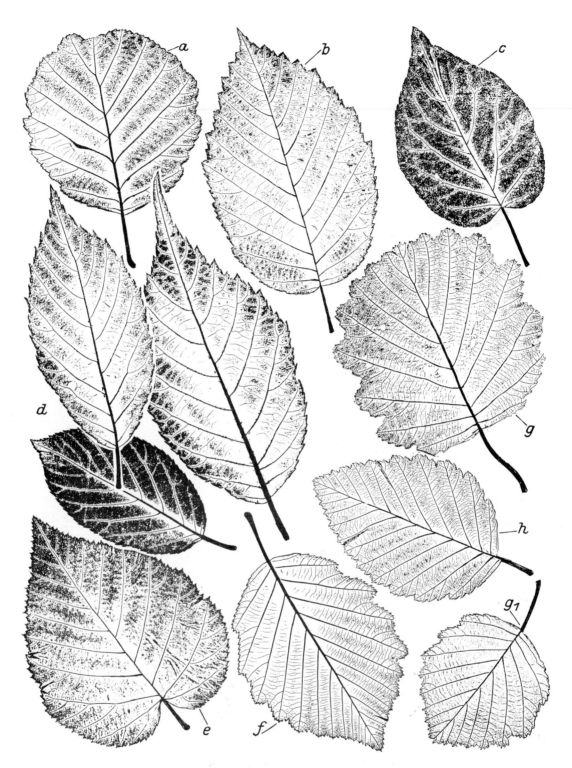

Alnus. a. *A. glutinosa*; b. *A. subcordata*; c. *A. cordata*; d. *A. spaethii* (3 leaves), lower leaf from a short branch; e. *A. maximowiczii*; f. *A. incana*; g. + g₁ *A. hirsuta* var. *sibirica*; h. *A. rubra*

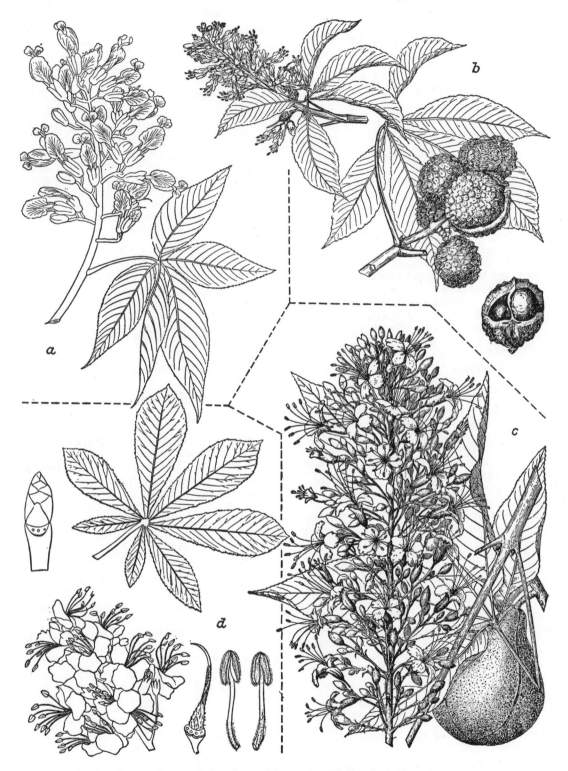

Fig. 85. **Aesculus.** a. *A. flava*; b. *A. glabra*; c. *A. californica*; d. *A. hippocastanum*
(from Sudworth, Illick, Gimpel)

oblong, 10—15 cm long, acuminate, finely crenate, pubescent venation beneath; flowers yellow and reddish, in 10—16 m long panicles (but also pale yellow to red, several cultivars), petiole and calyx glandular, stamens shorter than the petals, shaggy pubescent at the base, May—June; fruit globose. BR 310 (as *A. discolor*) (= *A. versicolor* Wender.; *A. lyonii* hort.). USA, native of the Alleghany Mountains. Before 1815. z5 ✧

Distinguished from *A. flava* by the bicolored or reddish flowers and the glandular and pubescent petal margin (as with *A.pavia*).

var. **purpurascens** A. Gray. Natural hybrid; flowers purple-red. Alleghany Mountains, USA.

A. indica (Cambess.) Hook. Indian Horsechestnut. A tree in its habitat, to 30 m, with short, very thick trunk, bark peeling in long strips; leaves 7 parted, new growth and petioles remaining red through spring, leaflets obovate-lanceolate, to 20 cm long, both sides glabrous, glossy green; flowers in 20—30 cm long, thin panicles, petals 4, uneven, the upper longer, white, with red-yellow patch on the base, the shorter light pink, June to July, 4—6 weeks after *A. hippocastanum*; fruit rough, not prickly. BM 5117; FS 1538; BS 1: 259. N. India. Prefers rich humus soil, in wooded areas. z7 ⑫ India (Kashmir). Plate 26; Fig. 83. See also: *A. wilsonii*. # H ⬦ ✧ ◐

A. lutea see: **A. flava**

A. lyonii see: **A. × hybrida**

A. macrostachya see: **A. parviflora**

A. × marylandica Booth (*A. glabra × A. flava*). Small tree; leaflet tough, ovate-lanceolate to oblong-elliptic, finely serrate. 10—15 cm long, 3—4 cm wide, glossy green above, light yellow-green beneath, venation and axils with rust yellow pubescence; flowers yellow. Origin unknown. Before 1864. z5

A. michauxii see: **A. silvatica**

A. mississippiensis Sarg. (*A. glabra × A. pavia*). Tree; leaflets oblong-obovate, finely doubly serrate, underside glabrous except for the vein axils, occasionally with a slight reddish fall coloration along the veins, calyx narrow campanulate; flowers dark red and yellow, stamens usually longer than the petals; fruit somewhat warty. Missouri. 1913. z5

A. × mutabilis (Spach) Schelle (*A. pavia × A. silvatica*). Tree; leaflets oblong-elliptic, pale green beneath, shaggy pubescent; calyx narrow campanulate to tubular, red, petals red and yellow; flowers in 10—15 cm long panicles (= *Pavia mutabilis* Spach; *A. pavia mutabilis* Spaeth). 1834. z5 ✧

'Harbisonii'. Leaflets bluish beneath, shaggy pubescent when young; calyx tubular, flowers light red, in 15—20 cm long panicles, May—June (= *A. harbisonii* Sarg.). Originated in the Arnold Arboretum from wild collected seed of *A. silvatica*. 1905. ✧

'Induta' (*A.pavia* var. *discolor* × *A. neglecta*). Large but slow growing shrub; leaves blue-green beneath with dense shaggy pubescence; flowers pink with yellow markings, very

abundant, May—June (= *A. rosea nana* Hesse). 1905, by Hesse-Weener. Plate 3. ✧

'Penduliflora' (*A. pavia* var. *discolor* × *A. neglecta*). Leaflets lanceolate, pale green beneath and softly pubescent; calyx tubular, reddish, petals yellow, flowers in 14—16 cm long, loose, somewhat pendulous panicles (= *A. humilis × A. lutea* Spaeth). 1902. ✧

A. × neglecta Lindl. (= *A. flava × A. silvatica*). Tree, to 20 m; leaflets 5, obovate-oblong, 10—15 cm long, simple or doubly serrate, yellowish green beneath, glabrous except for the venation, petiolules 3—8 mm long; calyx narrow campanulate, outside finely pubescent (but not glandular as with the similar *A. flava*!), petals very uneven, light yellow, red veined at the base, stamens with lower half shaggy pubescent, May—June; fruit globose, 2—3 cm wide, usually single seeded. BR 1009. USA, N. Carolina. 1826. z5 See also: *A. neglecta*.

(Although *A. neglecta* Lindl. [1826] is usually recognized as a synonym for *A. silvatica* Bartr. [1791], original herbarium materials demonstrate that Lindley's material is not purely *A. silvatica*, but rather a hybrid of *A. flava × A. silvatica*.)

'Erythroblasta' (Spaeth). New growth a good carmine-red, later becoming green; flowers reddish yellow, otherwise quite like the species. NF 8: 58. Originally found by Behnsch and distributed by Spaeth as *A. pavia fol. roseis*. Large specimen in the Botanic Garden of Munich-Nymphenburg. Plate 3. ⬦

Differing from *A. silvatica* in its glandular calyx and inflorescence.

A. octandra see: **A. flava**

A. ohioensis see: **A. glabra**

A. parryi A. Gray. Shrub or small tree, 1—6 m; leaves tough, leaflets 5—7, occasionally only 1—3, sessile or very short stalked, obovate to more oblong, 4—11 cm, obtuse or rounded, margin entire or nearly so, brown tomentose or woolly beneath; flowers in 8—20 cm long by 5 cm wide panicles, petals 4 or 5, cream white, base orange, later brown, calyx 4—9 mm, campanulate, tomentose, stamens prominent, May; fruit obovate to globose, 2—3 cm wide, light brown, tomentose and somewhat warty. GF 3: 356. Mexico; Baja California. z8

A. parviflora Walt. Stoloniferous shrub, to 10 m wide and (rarely) to 4 m high; leaflets 5—7, oblong, 8—20 cm long, acuminate, crenate, nearly sessile, finely gray pubescent beneath; flowers white, 1 cm long, in 20—30 cm long panicles showing above the foliage, stamens 3—4 cm long, whitish red, July—August; fruit inversely oval, 3—4 cm long. DB 1954: 163; BB 2385 (= *A. macrostachya* Michx.). N. America, S. Carolina to Alabama and Florida. Practical, completely hardy, late flowering species. z5 Plate 24. ✧

f. **serotina** Rehd. Leaves lightly pubescent beneath or also slightly glabrous and blue-green; blooms 2—3 weeks after the species, inflorescence longer. Jour. Arnold Arb. 1928: 30. Alabama. 1919.

A. pavia L. Red Buckeye. Shrub to small tree, usually 1—4 (rarely to 12 m) high and 2(—5) m wide, twigs glabrous, winter buds not viscid; leaf with 5−7 leaflets, petiole 3-17 cm long, leaflets oblong to oblanceolate, 6−17 cm long, 3−6 cm wide,thin to tough, margin irregularly serrate, base entire, glabrous to densely tomentose beneath; inflorescence 10−25 cm long, flowers red, but also yellow-red or yellow, calyx tubular-campanulate, with 5 points, glandular and pubescent, the single flowers some 3 cm long, with 4 uneven petals, inclining together and with margins glandular, stamens usually 8, as long as the petals, June; fruit oval, 3.5−6 cm thick, outside smooth, light brown. NBB 2: 511 (= *A. pavia* var. *atrosanguinea* Hort.; *A. pavia* var. *nana* Dipp., *A.pavia* var. *whitleyi* Hort.) Southern USA, North Carolina to Mississippi. 1711. z5 Plate 25. ⊕

var. **discolor** (Pursh) Torr. & Gray. Shrub (or tree, to 10 m), twigs finely soft pubescent; leaflets 5, short stalked, elliptic to oblong, 8−18 cm long, acuminate, finely crenate, dark green above, glossy, whitish tomentose beneath; flowers in pubescent, 15−20 cm long panicles, calyx red or yellow with trace of red, petals glandular ciliate on the margin, yellow with trace of red, very uneven, leaning together, shorter than the stamens, May to June; fruit inversely egg-shaped, 3−6 cm long, with 2 yellow-brown seeds. BR 310 (= *A. discolor* Pursh). SE. USA. 1812. z5 Fig. 83, 86. ∅ ⊕

The red flowering *A. discolor* var. *mollis* (Raf.) Sarg. (= *A. austrina* Small) is no longer treated as a separate taxon. SS 622. SE. USA. 1905.

var. **pavia.** Flowers scarlet to yellow-red, calyx narrow tubular. USA, Texas, eastern half. ⊕

var. **flavescens** (Sarg.) Correll. Flowers yellow. USA., Texas, Edward County and Edwards Plateau. ⊕

'Koehnei'. Dwarf form of var. *discolor*; flowers red and yellow. 1893, already in cultivation and erroneously referred to as "*A. humilis* Lodd. by Koehne. ⊕

'Humilis'. Dwarf form with red flowers in small panicles; often grows nearly procumbent, therefore usually grafted on a standard and called "*Pavia pendula*'. BR 1018. In the trade since 1826 as *Pavia humilis* Lindl. ⊕

A. × plantierensis André (*A. hippocastanum* (female) × *A. carnea*). Large tree; leaflets usually 7, not stalked (as with *hippocastanum*), but blade distinctly ribbed and uneven (as with *A. carnea*), inflorescence like *A. hippocastanum* in form and size, but flower delicate pink, sterile; fruit prickly, but undeveloped, triplolid (= *A.

Fig. 86. *Aesculus pavia* var. *discolor* (from Sargent)

carnea f. *plantierensis* [André] Rehd.). Originated by Simon Louis Frères, 1894, in Plantières near Metz, France. Recently separated from *A. carnea* because of the chromosome number (Phytologia 1953:282). z4 ⊕

A. punduana see: **A. assamica**

A. rosea nana see:**A. × mutabilis**

A. rubicunde see:**A. × carnea**

A. silvatica Bartr. Shrub, 1−1.5 m, twigs glabrous; leaflets 5, narrow obovate, 10−15 cm long, half as wide, soon glabrous; flowers 2.5−3 cm long, in 12−15 cm long panicles, to 7 cm wide at the base, calyx pubescent, red above,petals yellow, later red, ciliate, May to June; fruit globose, seed 2.5 cm wide. ST Pl. 197; BC 134 (= *A. georgiana* Sarg.; *A. neglecta* var. *georgiana* [Sarg.] Sarg.). SE. USA. 1905. z5

var. **lanceolata** (Sarg.) Sarg. Leaflets lanceolate to oblanceolate; flowers light red. SM 707. Georgia. 1917.

var. **pubescens** (Sarg.) Sarg. Tree, 10 m, leaflets soft pubescent beneath; petals without glands, flowers yellow and red, May−June. N. Carolina to Georgia and Alabama. 1905.

var. **tomentosa** Sarg. Growing to 5m (or more?); leaflets gray tomentose or dense shaggy beneath; flowers light red (= *A. michauxii* Hort.). S. Carolina. 1880. Slow growing.

A. splendens Sarg. Shrub, 3−4 m high, twigs thin, pubescent; leaflets 5, lanceolate to oblanceolate, 10−15 cm long, slightly stalked, gray pubescent beneath; flowers in 15−25 cm long panicles, petals scarlet, calyx tubular, light red, stamens longer or shorter than the petals, May; fruits rounded, smooth. ST Pl. 200. SE. USA. Hardy! Most beautiful of the "buckeye" group. z5 ⊕

Although this is surely a form or hybrid of *A. pavia*, the specific name remains unchanged.

A turbinata Bl. Japanese Horsechestnut. Tree, to 30 m, occasionally to 40 m in its habitat, narrowly upright and slow growing, winter buds strongly resinous; leaves very large (largest of the genus), leaflets 5−7, cuneate-oblong, 20−30 cm long, serrate, bluish beneath, frequently with pubescent venation; flowers in 15−25 cm long panicles, petals yellowish white with red spots, June (2−3 weeks after *A. hippocastanum*); fruit pear-shaped, rough or warty, 5 cm wide. BM 8713; KIF 1: 85(= *A. chinensis* Hort.). Japan. 1880. z6 Plate 24. ∅

var. **pubescens** Rehd. Like the type, but leaflets more or less pubescent beneath.

A. versicolor see: **A. × hybrida**

A. wilsonii Rehd. Tree, to 25 m, branches thickly pubescent, bark light gray, flaking; leaflets 5−7, obovate to oblanceolate, 15−20 cm long, acuminate, tightly and finely serrate, young leaves with thick gray pubescence beneath, eventually glabrous, with some 22 paired veins; flowers in 25−35 cm long panicles, fragrant, flower stalk pubescent, petals 5, white, the upper ones with a yellow sap stain, 1.5 cm long, calyx tubular, 5 toothed, stamens very long, June; fruit rounded, 3 valved, 3.5 cm wide, prickly. LF 218; FIO 56 (= *A. chinensis* Diels non Bunge; *A. indica* Pamp. non Hook.). China, Szechwan, Hupeh. 1908. Very similar to *A.chinensis*, but leaves larger, leaflets longer stalked, base rounded to slightly cordate and underside at first with much thicker pubescence. z6 Plate 26. ∅

A. woerlitzensis Koehne. Tree, leaflets oblong-obovate, 10—16 cm long, yellowish green beneath, sparsely pubescent on the midrib, with 17—20 paired veins; flowers red, side petals with oblong-obovate blade and cuneate base, calyx tubular, in 10—20 cm long racemes, May—June. Origin unknown, presumably Woerlitz. 1910.

var. **ellwangeri** Rehd. Small tree, leaflets 12 to 18 cm long, slightly pubescent beneath when young, differing from the type in the 20—27 paired veins; flowers an intense red, calyx narrower, widening above the middle (= *A. pavia whitleyei* Ellw. & Barry; *A. atrosanguinea*). Introduced by Ellwanger & Barry, USA. 1901. z6 In culture in N. American arboreta. ✧

Very similar to *A. pavia*, but easily distinguished by the shaggy ciliate petals.

With the exception of the noted types, all the *Aesculus* are winter hardy, usually fast growing and very attractive in flower. All prefer a deep humus soil. Some of the more unusual tpes will fill out better if planted in somewhat protected or wooded areas.

The positive identification of species, especially the red flowering species and varieties, is not easy and requires careful examination of the flowers.

Lit. Bush, B.: Notes on *Aesculus* species; in Amer. Midl. Nat. **12**, 19—36, 1930 ● Hardin, J.W.,: A Revision of the American Hippocastanaceae; in Brittonia **9**, 145—195, 1957 ● Hardin, J.W.: Studies in the Hippocastanaceae. II. Inflorescence structure and distribution of perfect flowers; in Amer. Journ. Bot. **43**, 418—424, 1956 ● Hardin, J.W.:III. A hybrid swarm in the Buckeyes; in Rhodora **59**, 45—51, 1957 ● Hardin, J.W.: IV. Hybridization in *Aesculus*; in Rhodora **59**, 185—203, 1957 ● Hardin, J. W.: V. Species of the Old World; in Brittonia **12**, 26—38, 1960 ● Hardin, J.W.: The status of Lindley's *Aesculus neglecta*; in Rhodora **62**, 127—129, 1960 ● Henssen, K.J.W.: De *Aesculus*-collectie in de Botanische Tuinen en het Belmonte Arboretum van de Landbouwhoogeschool te Wageningen; in Jaarb. Ned. Dendrol. Ver. **22**, 36—47, 1963 ● Pax. F.: Hippocastanaceae; in Engler & Prantl, Nat. Pfl. Fam. III (5), 273—276, 1895 ● Yeo, P.F: The identity of *Aesculus neglecta* and *A. neglecta* 'Erythroblastos'; in Baileya **8**, 59—61, 1960.

AETHIONEMA R. Br. — CRUCIFERAE

Small subshrubs, perennials with woody basal branches or annuals; leaves alternate, margins entire; flowers very similar to those of *Iberis*, but with all the petals of even length, pink, red or white, seldom yellowish; fruit a dehiscent silicle, winged or not winged with 1—2 seeds in each chamber. — Some 40(—70) species in the Mediterranean Region to Asia Minor, most in Turkey.

Aethionema armenum Boiss. Growth dense and bushy, unbranched twigs, 10—12 cm high; leaves linear-oblong, acute; flowers pink, seldom white, in dense racemes, flowering through fruit set, May—June. E. Anatolia and Transcaucasia. z6 The following forms are probably of this species:

'**Warley Rose**' (Willmott). 15—20 cm high, wide growing; leaves with reddish limb; flowers dark pink with stripes (HCC 628/), sterile, May—August (= *A.* × *warleyense* Bergm.; *A.* 'Warley Hybrid'). Originated, 1912, by Miss E. A. Willmott in Warley Place, near London, England. This variety is somewhat variable in appearance from one specimen to the next. Plate 27. **d** ✧ ○

'**Warley Ruber**' (Willmott). A broader type, not as attractive as the former, and a weak grower; flowers more purple-red (not dark red, as it is often described!). **d** ✧ ○

A. coridifolium DC. Some 15—20 cm high, many branched, flowering shoots not branched; leaves linear to lanceolate, blue-green, 2 cm, tightly packed at the base of the twigs; flowers lilac-pink, on dense, short, compressed branches at the tips, petals some 2.5 times as large as the calyx, June; silicles oval, 6—8 mm long, incised 1—2 mm deep. BM 5952. Lebanon, Turkey, Cilicia, Antitaurus; in the mountains. 1871. z6 ✧

A. grandiflorum Boiss. & Hohen. 25—35 cm high, twigs densely branched, thin, glabrous, ascending, woody at the base; leaves linear-lanceolate, some 2 cm, obtuse, blue-green, smooth, distributed along the whole length of the twigs(!); flowers large, pink, in 5—7 cm long, 2.5 cm wide racemes, fragrant, petals 3—4 times as large as the calyx, May—August; silicles somewhat wider than long, rounded, 1 cm wide, wings entire or lightly serrate. WS 509 (= *A. pulchellum* Boiss. & Huet.). Transcaucasia, E. Anatolia, N. Iran and Iraq. 1879. z6 Prettiest type and frequently seen in cultivation, but often under other names, such as *A. antilibani*, *A. persicum*, *A. amoenum*, *A. kotschyi*. Plate 2 and 27. ✧

A. iberideum (Boiss.) Boiss. Erect, 15 cm, branching out from the base, leaves usually opposite, broad ovate, acute, generally narrower at the base of the branch, margin rough; flowers white, rather large, in small terminal racemes, May; silicles cordate, with entire margin, netted wings. Turkey. z6 **d** ✧ ○

Attractive, but sensitive dwarf shrubs for the rock garden, prefer full sun, alkaline, gravelly/sandy clay soils. Protect from excessive moisture in winter. After a few year's growth the long branches should be pruned back. Seeds itself readily. Also propagated from cuttings. Suitable for pot culture.

Lit. Boissier, E.: Flora Orientalis, I, 1867.

AGAPETES D. Don ex G. Don — ERICACEAE

Evergreen, semi-epiphytic shrubs with smooth or bristly twigs; leaves alternate, nearly sessile; flowers single axillary or several in cymes, attractive, beautifully colored; calyx tube spherical to hemispherical, 5 winged or 5 ribbed; corolla tubular, 5 sided, limb with 5 short, erect or reflexed poits; 10 stamens, anthers with spurs on the backside; fruit a 5 winged berry. — 80 species in E. Himalaya, Sikkim, Khasi, in the mountains from 1000 to 2500 m; to N. Australia.

Agapetes buxifolia Nutt. Small, evergreen shrub, some 1.5 m high, twigs wide spreading, pubescent; leaves small, elliptic-oblong, 2.5—3 cm long, some 1.2 cm wide, margin crenate on the upper third of the blade, glossy green; flowers tubular, 1 or 2 in a leaf axil, waxy, bright red, 2.5 cm long, April; fruit a white berry. BM 5012; JRHS 25: 67. Bhutan. z8 # ☺

A. rugosum (Hook.) Sleum. Shrub, 30—90 cm high, grows rather stiffly upright; leaves oval-lanceolate, 7—10 cm long, acuminate, dentate, reddish new growth, nearly sessile, base somewhat cordate, deep green and very rugose above, lighter beneath; flowers 2.5 cm long, pendulous, white with purple marbling, several at a node, angles deep red, limb narrow and green, March—May; fruit globose, red, 8 mm thick. BM 5198; FS 1145 (= *Pentapterygium rugosum* Hook.). Khasi Mountains. 1880. Hardier than *A. serpens*, but rarer in cultivation. z8 # ☺

A. serpens (Klotzsch) Sleum. Shrub, 0.5—0.7 m high, but by training as much as 3 m high, rootstock bulbous, thickened, twigs long pendulous; leaves 2 parted, closely spaced, lanceolate, 1.2 cm long, nearly sessile; flowers numerous, hanging from the leaf axils along the branch, calyx green, 5 sided, corolla light red, with darker, V-shaped marks, some 2 cm long, January—April. BM 6777; DRHS 1523 (= *Pentapterygium serpens* Klotzsch). W. China. 1881. z8 Fig. 87. # ☺

A. 'Ludgvan Cross' (Talbot) (*A. rugosum* × *A. serpens*). Growth habit intermediate, not so stiff as *A. rugosum*, but branches also not so long and pendulous; leaves ovate, acuminate, 2.5—3.5 cm long, flowers more carmine red, with the V mark white, limb green-white; fruit pale purple. Developed by Miss G. Talbot, Ludgvan Rectory, Cornwall, England, before 1938. z8 Fig. 87. # ☺

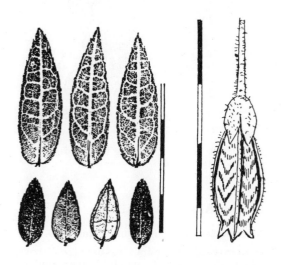

Fig. 87. *Agapetes serpens* (small leaves and flower); 'Ludgvan Cross' (large leaves) (Original)

All species and cultivars very nice, for protected areas in milder regions, walled gardens or cool greenhouse. Always plant it near a walkway to encourage close inspection of the beautiful flowers. Prefers a rich, humus soil somewhat like Azaleas.

AGAVE L. — AGAVACEAE

Rosette-form plant, sometimes developing a short stem with age; leaves more or less sword-like, fleshy or tough, ending in a sharp thorny apex, margin usually with hooked teeth; flowers either in clusters or cymes on a huge central shaft (sometimes 8 m high) or in loose panicles or racemes; perianth nearly funnelform, usually greenish or brownish. — Out of approximately 300 species from S. USA to S. America, only a few are occasionally found in cultivation. ⌀

Agava americana L. Century Plant. Rosette very large, the single leaves 1—1.5 m long or longer, to 20 cm wide, tough, leathery, gray-green to light gray, terminal thorns short but sharp, 3 cm, the marginal teeth dark brown, short, curved forward or back; inflorescence 5—8 m high, with 25—30 branches, flowers green, with yellow anthers, June—August. Mexico; naturalized in the Mediterranean area. circa 1580. z8 # ⌀

A. fourcroydes Lem. Henequen-Agave. Develops a trunk, 1—2 m high, stoloniferous; leaves stiff spreading, to 1.4 m long, 10—12 cm wide, leathery-fleshy, blue-green, marginal teeth hooked, terminal thorn conical, sharp, 3 cm long; inflorescence 6—7 m high, many plantlets in the panicles. PBl. 353 (= *A. ixtlioides* Lem.). Yucatan. 1864. z8 # ⌀

A. parryi Engelm. Virtually without a trunk; rosettes 50—60 cm wide, many leaved; leaves acute-oblong, 25—30 cm long, 5—10 cm wide, blue-green, terminal thorn grooved, margin toothed; inflorescence candelabra-formed, 2.5—3.5 m high, flower red outside, inside yellow, 6 cm long. SW. USA. 1873. One of the most winter hardy types. z8 # ⌀

Lit. Berger, A.: Die Agaven; Jena 1915.

Fig. 88. *Ailanthus altissima*. branch (b), leaf (a), inflorescence (3), male flower (c), female flower (d), in longitudinal section (f), fruit cluster (g) (from Engler, Nose)

AILANTHUS Desf. — Tree of Heaven — SIMAROUBACEAE

Deciduous trees; leaves very large, alternate, pinnately compound, unpleasant smelling; lower leaflet blade with some large marginate teeth, each with a gland; flowers small, numerous, in large, usually terminal, branched panicles, petals 5—6, stamens 10, male flowers without pistils; fruit winged (like *Fraxinus*), but with the seed in the middle. — Some 10 species in E. India, E. Asia and N. Australia.

Ailanthus altissima (Mill.) Swingle. Tree of Heaven. Tree, to 25 m high, often 2 stemmed, bark longitudinally striped, smooth, with characteristic white grooves, young twigs very thick, pithy, red-brown, with dense fine pubescence, velvety; leaves 40—60 cm long, leaflets to 10-15 pairs, stalked, 7—12 cm long, ovate-lanceolate, finely ciliate, bluish beneath, glabrous or occasionally lightly pubescent; flowers insignificant, greenish, in 10—20 cm long panicles, June—July; fruits 3—4 cm long, numerous, light brown. DB 1954: 43 (= *A. glandulosa* Desf.; = *A. cacodendron* Schinz & Thell.). China. 1751. z5 Ⓕ Germany, Austria, Yugoslavia, Romania, Italy; India, New Zealand, China, Argentina, Uruguay. Fig. 88. ∅

Tolerates smoke and industrial pollution very well, is not particular as to soil type and therefore a good urban tree. Quite vigorous.

'Aucubaefolia' (Dieck). Leaves always yellow dotted. Ori-ginated in the Zoeschen Arboretum. Before 1889.

f. **erythrocarpa** (Carr.) Rehd. Leaves dark green above, more bluish beneath, fruit red (= *glandulosa rubra* Hort.). Before 1867. Grows slowly, but supposedly more winter hardy than the species. ⚥

'Pendulifolia'. Growth upright; leaves pendulous, much longer than the type, to 90 cm long. RH 1906: 205, Pl. Before 1889.

var. **sutchuenensis** (Dode) Rehd. & Wils. Young twigs glabrous, red-brown, glossy; leaf petiole and stipules purple-red, leaflets not ciliate, narrower at the base, not so unpleasant smelling, white, some 13 cm long, 5 cm wide, long stalked, petiolule and rachis purple-red; inflorescence more upright; fruit cluster to 40 cm long. BD 1907: 192, fig. a (= *A. sutchuenensis* Dode). W. China, W. Hupeh, Szechwan. Circa 1897. z5 ∅

'Tricolor' (Purpus). Young leaves pink and white speckled. Occasionally seen in seedlings but not constant.

A. giraldii Dode. Tree, to 12 m, usually single stemmed, bark gray, bark of younger branches brown, finely pubescent; leaflets in 16—20 pairs, 7—15 cm long and 3 cm wide, lanceolate, closely set, margin wavy, only 1 tooth at the base, dark green above, pale green beneath, both sides loosely pubescent, leaves on younger plants to 100 cm long, but much smaller on older plants, very thin, petiole

15 mm long; inflorescence 20—30 cm wide. BD 1907; 191, fig. W. China, Szechwan. Circa 1893. z6 Ø

var. **duclouxii** (Dode) Rehd. Young twigs light orange; leaf petiole green, leaflets generally silver-gray pubescent on the venation beneath, otherwise more glabrous or like the species (= *A. duclouxii* Dode). Szechwan. Ø

A. vilmoriniana Dode. Tree, 5—15 m high, young twigs more green, pubescent and with numerous small prickles on the young twigs (important for identification); leaves 50—100 cm long, leaflets oblong-lanceolate, with 2—4 large teeth, some 12 cm long and to 4 cm wide, dark green above and sparsely pubescent, dense silver-gray pubescence beneath, petiolules 5—10 mm long, pubescent; rachis often reddish, also often prickly; inflorescence to 30 cm long, greenish-yellow; fruit 5 cm long, twisted propeller-like, 1 cm wide. RH 1904: 184. China, W. Hupeh. 1897. Somewhat more sensitive in cultivation than *A. altissima*. z6 Ø

All species good for solitary plantings in parks, very adaptable to soils, good winter hardiness, fast growing and free of disease problems.

Lit. 18 Titles presented in Jour. Arnold Arboretum **43**, 180—181, 1962, which see.

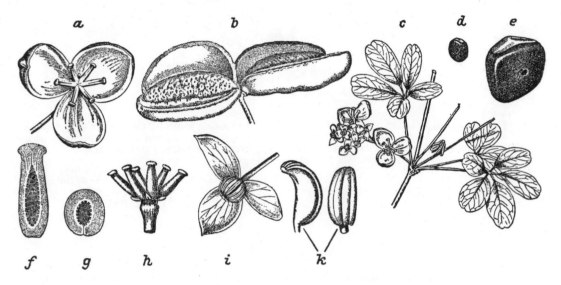

Fig.89. *Akebia quinata*. a. female flower, b. fruit, opened, c. twig with female and male flowers, d. seed, e. enlarged, f. and g. ovary in longitudinal and cross section, h. gynoecium, i. male flower, k. stamen from the side and front (from Lavallée)

AKEBIA Dcne. — Akebia — LARDIZABALACEAE

Deciduous to semi-evergreen vines, twigs glabrous; leaves alternate, palmately compound, with 3—5 leaflets, these with petiolules, apex emarginate; flowers in short, alternate racemes, perianth 3 parted, brown-violet, petals absent; male flower with 6 distinct stamens, anthers bowed inward; female flowers with 3—9 ovaries and 6 or 9 staminodes; fruit a cucumber-like, many seeded, wide opening berry; seeds black. — 5 species in Japan, China and Korea.

Akebia longiracemosa Matsum. Leaves 5 parted, long petioled, leaflets oblong to more obovate, wide at the apex, emarginate and with a small tip, base obtuse; male flowers 25—30 in long racemes, stalk 5 mm, leaves on flowering branches linear; sepals 3, some 3 mm long and 2 mm wide, glabrous; female flowers only few together. LWT 60. Taiwan, in the mountains. z6

A. × pentaphylla (Mak.) Mak. (= *A. quinata* × *A. trifoliata*). Intermediate between the parents; leaflets 3—5, margins entire or somewhat crenate. 1902.

Coming from the same general areas as the parents, but also hybridized in cultivation. z5

A. quinata (Houtt.) Dcne. To 10 m high or higher, twining, fast growing, twigs glabrous, violet-purple; leaflets 5, ovate-elliptic, 3—6 cm long, margin entire, tough fleshy, long stalked, evergreen or deciduous, dark green above, blue-green beneath; flowers violet-brown, fragrant, on thin stalks, female 2—3 cm wide, male much smaller, more pink, May; fruit light violet, pruinose, 5—10 cm long. BM 4864; FS 1000; YTS 1: 73. Middle China to Japan and Korea. 1845. z5 Plate 28; Fig. 89, 90. Ø ⚘

A. trifoliata (Thunb.) Koidz. To 6 m high, twining; leaflets 3, broad-ovate, 3—7 cm long, margin wavy or shallowly crenate, dark green above, lighter beneath; female flowers chestnut-brown, 2—2.5 cm wide, male flowers smaller, light purple, numerous, May; fruit cucumber-formed, 7—15 cm long, 3—5 cm thick, light purple, tasty! BM 7485; GW 13: 438 (= *A. lobata* Dcne.).

Fig. 90. **Akebia.** a. *A. trifoliata*; b. *A. quinata*

Middle China to Japan. Before 1890. z5 Fig. 90. ⌀ ⚭

var. **australis** (Diels) Rehd. Leaves more oval to ovate-oblong, tough leathery, usually entire margins. ICS 1512 (= *A. chaffanjonii* Lev.). China.

var. **clematifolia** Ito. Leaves broadly ovate, margin entire, thin, 8—9 cm long. Japan.

Fast growing vines, climb readily on a trellis or into other plants; does equally well in sun or partial shade. Some winter protection for young plants is advisable, otherwise perfectly hardy.

Lit. Shimizu, T.: Taxonomic study of the genus *Akebia*, with special reference to a new species from Taiwan; Quart. Jour. Taiwan Mus. **14,** 195—202, 1961.

AKOCANTHERA

Akocanthera venenata see: **Carissa akocanthera**

ALANGIUM Lindl. — ALANGIACEAE

Deciduous or evergreen trees and shrubs; leaves alternate, large, margins entire or lobed (nearly maple-like); flowers perfect, whitish, some species also fragrant, in axillary clusters, calyx small, campanulate, petals 4—10, linear, usually slightly reflexed, stamens

Fig. 91. **Alangium.** a. *A. platanifolium* var. *genuinum*;
b. *A. platanifolium* var. *macrophyllum*; c. *A. chinense*

4—30, pistil simple, elongated; fruit a single seeded, small round drupe. 17 species in tropical and subtropical Asia (centered in India), Africa and Australia.

Alangium chinense (Lour.) Harms. Tree, to 9 m; leaves evergreen, ovate, 9—20 cm long, base usually oblique, margin entire or somewhat lobed, usually asymmetrical, acuminate; flowers yellow, 2 cm long, petals and stamens usually 6, July to August. CIS 94; ICS 3700; EP IV, 220b: 1, 5 (= *Marlea begoniifolia* Roxb.). E. Africa, S. and E. Asia. 1826. Distributed widely and quite variable. z7 Fig. 91. ⌀

A. platanifolium (S. & Z.) Harms. In its habitat, a tree, twigs pithy, pubescent at first, later glabrous; leaves deciduous, broad oval, 10—20 cm long and wide, with 2—7 (usually 3—5) large, acute lobes, lobes triangular-oblong, margins entire, deep green above, somewhat pubescent beneath; flowers white, fragrant, 3 cm long, petals and stamens usually 6, 1—4 in the leaf axils of the current year's growth, June—July; fruit ovoid, 12 mm long, thin shelled. CIS 95; ICS 3701; EP IV, 220b: 6 (= *Marlea platanifolia* S. & Z.). Middle China to Japan. 1879. z7 ⌀

var. **genuinum** Wang. Leaves incised to at least the middle of the blade. Japan, in the forest; Middle China, Szechwan, N. Shansi. Fig. 91.

var. **macrophyllum** (S. & Z.) Wang. Leaves lobed, incised less than 1/3 of the way into the blade, base more or less cordate. Middle China, Korea, Japan. Fig. 91.

Only occasionally in cultivation in Europe, and hardy only in the warmest regions. Freezes back in a cold winter. Very ornamental foliage.

Lit. Wangerin, W.: *Alangiaceae*; in Engler, Pflanzenreich, IV, 220b, 1—25, 1910.

ALBIZIA Durazz. — Silk Tree — LEGUMINOSAE

The original spelling comes from Durazzini, Mag. Tosc. 3(4), 11 Pl. 1772, although the name is taken from Cavaliere Filippo Degl'Albizzi and in many works is spelled with "zz".

Deciduous, tropical or subtropical trees or shrubs with doubly pinnate, large leaves; leaflets numerous and small; flowers in stalked, axillary heads or in bottle brush formed spikes; fruit pods strap-like. — Some 100—150 species in the tropics and subtropics, generally fast growing (*A. moluccana* Miq., chosen as a shade tree in tea plantations has, in one year, grown 2.5 m!).

Albizia julibrissin Durazz. Silk Tree. Beautiful, tree in S. Europe and S. USA, crown broad spreading, branches angular, glabrous; leaves with 8—24 pinnae, each with 40—50 sickle-shaped, oblong, oblique, 1 cm long leaflets, folding up at night; flowers light pink, in stalked heads at the ends of the higher branches, June—August. KIF 1: 75; FS 2199 (= *Acacia nemu* Willd.). Iran to Japan, but much planted in the Mediterranean area, Cornwall, England and S. USA. 1745. z8 Plate 4 and 28. Ø ✧

'Ernest Wilson'. Growth wide; flowers pink and white, from the end of June to the end of September, flowers abundantly. JA 28: 33. Originated 1918 in the Arnold Arboretum as a seedling from seed collected by Ernest H. Wilson in Seoul, Korea. 1968. Extraordinarily winter hardy. ✧

var. **rosea** Mouill. Shrubby, flowers a strong pink. FS 2199 (as *Acacia nemu*). Distinctly winter hardy. Ø ✧

A. kalkora (Roxb.) Prain. Small tropical tree, to 9 m, stem to 30 cm, very similar to *A. lebbeck*, but leaflets more oblong and narrower; flowers pink, in small heads, the stamens some 2.5 cm long; fruit pods on stalks to 15 cm long. FIO 92. India, SW. China. z8 ✧

A. lebbeck (L.) Benth. Women's Tongues (named for the rustling of the dry fruit pods). Tall tree, smooth trunk, gray, wide crowned, resembling *Sophora:* leaves doubly pinnate, with 2—4 paired pinnae, each with 12—14 leaflets, oval-elliptic, blunt on both ends, 3 cm long; flowers greenish yellow to white, fragrant, in globose heads; pods to 30 cm long. GF 7: 235; LWTP 60. Tropical Asia, N. Australia, but also naturalized throughout the tropical world. 1823. z8 Ⓕ Trop. Asia; Cameroon. Ø ✧

A. lophantha (Willd.) Benth. Shrub to small tree, seldom taller than 6 m; leaves with 14—24 pinnae, each with 40—60 leaflets, these 6—8 mm long, linear, silky pubescent beneath; flowers yellowish, many in bottle brush panicles, often 2 panicles together, flowers in summer (or in winter in the greenhouse). BM 304ns; EKW 214. W. Australia. 1803. Usually seen only in botanic gardens. z8 Ø ✧

A. procera (Roxb.) Benth. Tall tree; leaf rachis nearly completely glabrous, pinnae 6—10, each with 12—16 leaflets, these oblique-oblong, 2.5—3.5 cm long, glabrous; flowers greenish white, in few flowered, nearly sessile heads. LWTP 61. Trop. Asia and Australia. z9 Ⓕ India. ✧

Culture as with *Acacia*; which see.

Lit. Britton & Rose: N. Amer. Fl. **23**, 43—48, 1928; *Albizzia*.

ALECTRYON Gaertn. — SAPINDACEAE

Tall trees; leaves alternate, leaflets alternate, pinnately compound, without stipules; flowers usually unisexual, in axillary or terminal, many flowered panicles; calyx 4 or 5 lobed, inside pubescent, lobes uneven, petals absent; fruit a more or less woody capsule; seed covered with a fleshy aril. — Some 20 species in Hawaii, Pacific Islands, New Guinea, Australia and New Zealand.

Alectryon excelsus Gaertn. Tall tree, to 10 m, twigs thick, with nearly black bark, branches, leaflets, inflorescence and young fruit with rust red pubescence at first; leaves pinnately compound, 10—40 cm long,

Fig. 92. *Alectryon excelsus* (from Adams)

petiole 8 cm, leaflets 8—12, 5—10 cm long, oval-lanceolate, acuminate, wavy and coarsely crenate to entire margins; flowers, up to 30 cm long panicles, anthers very large, dark red; fruit capsule somewhat woody, 8—12 mm, winged above; seed black, globose, glossy, in a scarlet-red fleshy aril. KF 92—93; MNZ 1. New Zealand. In cultivation in England at Tresco Abby; Scilly Isles. z8 Fig. 92. ⊕ ⚭

ALEURITES Forst. — EUPHORBIACEAE

Tall evergreen trees with milky sap; leaves alternate, often deeply lobed and of variable form, long petioled, without stipules, palmate venation, with extra-floral nectaries on the blade base and at the apex of the major veins; flowers small, white, usually monoecious, in loose, terminal fascicles; sepals 2—5, petals 5; fruit drupe-like, large, with a thick shelled, poisonous seed. — 5 species in tropical Asia. Cultivated for oil content.

Aleurites cordata (Thunb.) R. Br. Small tree, 3—6 m high, bark gray-brown, branches thick, glabrous, with lenticels; leaves simple, oval, base cordate, 5 veined, apex acute or 3 lobed, glossy green above, lighter beneath with reticulate venation, both sides glabrous, paper thin; flowers white, in terminal cymes; fruit 2 cm high and wide, drupe-like. KTF 123; SDK 4: 32. SW. Asia. z6 Ⓕ Japan; S. Dalmatia.

A. fordii Hemsel. Tung Oil Tree. Tree, 3—7 m, twigs somewhat whorled; leaves dark green, simple, long petioled, 10—25 cm long and wide (not including petiole); flowers reddish white, spring; fruit dark green at first, brown when ripe, a flattened sphere, 5—7 cm wide, with 3—5 large seeds. Middle Asia. z6 Fig. 93. ∅ ⚭

Tung oil is obtained from the seeds and shells of the fruit and used in the paint and varnish industry as a drying agent.

Fig. 93. *Aleurites fordii*

Seeds and leaves are very poisonous to men and animals.

Occasionally found in southern botanic gardens. Very fast growing, but will defoliate in a frost.

Lit. Dickey et al: The Genus *Aleurites* in Florida; Bull. 503, Univ. Fla. Agr. Exp. Sta. 1952, with ill. of all 5 species.

ALGHAGI Desv. — LEGUMINOSAE

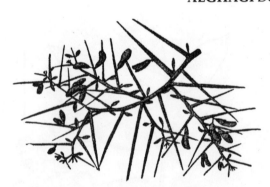

Fig. 94. *Alhagi maurorum* (from Taubert)

Thorny, deciduous, low desert shrubs; leaves alternate, small, oblong, margins entire; flowers small, red, few in axillary racemes with thorned rachis; calyx campanulate, 5 toothed; pod terete, constricted between the seeds. — 5 species from Greece and Egypt to Himalaya, especially in desert areas.

During the hot summer some plants are uprooted by the wind after which they release a honey-like yellow sap. This sap congeals overnight to a granular consistency and is collected by the natives and used as a food ("manna"). Plants are also collected for firewood and grazed by camels.

Alhagi camelorum Fisch. Camel Thorn. Completely glabrous, stiff shrub, very thorny, 20—50 cm high, thorns 1—2.5 cm long; leaves elliptic to oblanceolate, 15—20 mm long, margins entire, glabrous; flowers lilac-red, bisexual, in few flowered racemes, June—July; fruit an irregular pod with 1—3 seeds, 1—2.5 cm long. Asia Minor to Himalaya; also naturalized in the desert areas of California, USA. 1876. z8 Fig. 94. **d** ○

A. maurorum Medic. Shrub 50—75 cm high, branches finely pubescent, thorny; thorns larger than *A. camelorum*; leaves more ovate-oblong; flowers with purple middle, reddish border, July. Egypt, Iran. z8 **d**

Only of botanical interest. For very dry, sunny areas in summer and over-wintered dry in a greenhouse. Young plants very sensitive to excessive moisture.

Lit. Keller, A. B., & K. K. Shaparenko: material fuer die systematisch-okololgische Monographie der Gattung *Alhagi*; Sovetsk. Bot. 3—4, 150—185, fig. 17. 1833 (not seen in Russia).

ALLAMANDA L. — APOCYNACEAE

(Linnaeus wrote *Allemandra*; the above spelling is, however, preferred.)

Tropical, evergreen shrubs or vines; leaves in whorls, alternate or opposite, with axillary glands at the base; flowers large, funnel-form, with wide limb in 5 parts, in bud stage corolla sections twisted, lower portion of corolla tubular, flared at the apex; calyx with 5 lanceolate lobes; fruit an ovate, prickly, dehiscent, bivalvate capsule. — 15 species in tropical S. America and W. Indies. Common in the frost free gardens of the world.

Allamandra cathartica L. Evergreen, vining shrubs, to 6 m high, very strong growing; leaves in whorls to 4, obovate, acute on both ends, 10—14 cm long, 2—4 cm wide, margin somewhat wavy, glabrous except for the usually pubescent midrib; flowers gold-yellow with whitish throat markings, 5—7 cm wide, tube not swollen, in cymes, June—October. BM 4411 (as *A. aubletii*); DRHS 74. Brazil. 1785. The varieties are more common in cultivation than the species. z9 # ✧

var. **grandiflora** (Hook). Raffill. Less vigorous growth, lower, branches thinner, wavy; leaves smaller, thinner, oval-lanceolate; flowers numerous, to 10 cm wide, corolla sections nearly circular, lemon yellow. DRHS 74 (= *A. grandiflora* Hook.). 1844. # ✧

var. **hendersonii** (Bull) Raffill. Very strong grower; leaves larger, thick, leathery, smooth, usually in whorls of 3 or 4; flowers larger, to 10 cm wide, orange-yellow, with 5 white spots on the throat, outside brownish in bud, corolla sections thick and waxy, broad oval. PBl 2: 380; EKW 28 (= *A. hendersonii* Raffill). Common. ✧

var. **nobilis** (T. Moore) Raffill. Branches reddish; leaves 3-4, nearly sessile, 15—20 cm long, oblong-lanceolate, abruptly acuminate, more pubescent beneath; flowers pure gold-yellow, 10—12 cm wide, with a lighter spot at the base of each corolla section, fragrant (resembling *Magnolia*), July. BM 5764; FS 1832 (= *A. nobilis* T. Moore). 1867. # ✧

var. **schottii** (Pohl) Raffill. Strong grower, young branches and leaf petioles somewhat pubescent, older branches warty; leaves 3—4 in whorls, broadly lanceolate, glabrous on both sides; flowers very large, yellow, throat darker and brown striped. BM 4351 (= *A. schottii* Pohl). ✧

Only cultivated in frost free areas or under glass.

ALNIPHYLLUM Matsum. — STYRACACEAE

Deciduous trees or shrubs; leaves simple alternate, petioled, serrate; flowers complete, in terminal or axillary racemes, white or pink, attractive; calyx campanulate, 5 toothed, softly pubescent, petals 5, imbricate, connate (fused) at the base; stamens 10, in 2 whorls, 5 being shorter, filaments at the base fused into a thin column; ovaries 5 chambered, each chamber with 5—8 ovules; stigma in 5 sections; fruit a woody capsule, dehiscent with 5 valves; numerous seed, small, irregularly winged. — 8 species in SW. China and Formosa.

Alniphyllum fauriei Perk. Tree, 8—10 m high, young branches stellate pubescent, soon becoming glabrous; leaves oblong-lanceolate to ovate-lanceolate, 6—12 cm long, 2.5—4 cm wide, acuminate, base cuneate, margins irregularly glandular toothed, eventually glabrous above, sparsely stellate pubescent beneath; flowers white, 1.5 cm, in racemes, May. Formosa, in forests. z8

A. fortunei (Hemsl.) Perk. Tree, to 10 m high, bark gray, smooth, young twigs gray, thick silky and brown pubescent; leaves variable in size and shape, oblong to ovate, 8—16 cm long, 5—11 c wide, acute to obtuse, base cuneate, glossy green above with stellate pubescence, pale green beneath, reticulate venation, thick silky pubescence, tough leathery, petiole 1—2 cm long; flowers white, some with red blush, 10—15 in axillary racemes, corolla some 2.5 cm long, with deeply incised lobes; fruit capsule 2 cm long. EP 30 (IV, 241): 14; LF 260. China; Yunnan, and Szechwan; mountain forests. z6 Fig. 95. H⌀ ✧ ◑

A. hainanense Hayata. Resembles *A. pterospermum*, but leaves paper thin, much larger stellate pubescence, stamen column glabrous outside, inside thick pubescent. HFF 3: 40. Formosa; Hainan. z8 H⌀ ✧ ◑

Fig. 95. *Alniphyllum fortunei*. a. twig, 1/3 actual size; b. corolla, in cross section; c. ovaries and calyx; d. and e. ovaries in vertical and cross section; f. fruit; g. seed (from Perkins)

A. pterospermum Matsum. Tree or shrub, 5—10 m high, young twigs brown; leaves oblong, 15 cm long, 5 cm wide, acuminate apex, finely serrate, dark green above, stellate pubescent beneath, thin, leathery; flowers yellowish white, in terminal racemes; fruit 15 mm long, chestnut brown, April. HFF 3: 40. Formosa; China, Kwangtung. z8 H Ø ✧ ◐

Very beautiful flowering shrubs or trees. Highly recommended for milder areas. Flowers and foliage oustanding.

Lit. Perkins, J.: *Styracaceae*; in E. P., Heft 30 (IV. 241), 1907 ● Hu, H. H.: Some interesting new genera and species of *Styracaceae* in China; in New Flora and Silva 12, 148, 158, 1942.

ALNUS B. Ehrh. — Alder — BETULACEAE

Deciduous trees and shrubs with stalked winter buds; leaves alternate, serrate or dentate; flowers monoecious, in male and female catkins; male catkins longer, each flower axis with 3 flowers and 4 parted calyx; female catkins short, each flower axil with 2 flowers and without a calyx; fruit small, flat, narrow winged nutlet, grouped in woody cones. Around 35 species in the Northern Hemisphere, but in the Americas extending southward to Peru. Generally moisture loving plants.

Outline of the Genus

Subgenus I: **Alnaster** (Spach) Endl.
　　Winter buds sessile, with 2 or more uneven scales; flowers in terminal catkins even in fall, overwintering in bud, but appearing in early spring with the foliage:
　　　　A. crispa, firma, fruticosa, maximowiczii, pendula, sinuata, viridis
Subgenus II: **Gymnothyrsus** (Spach) Regel
　　Winter buds stalked, with 2—3, nearly equal size scales, naked male and female catkins overwintering on similar twigs, usually appearing before the leaves;
　　●Leaves folded in the winter buds, usually slightly lobed, with veins straight:
　　　　A. aschersoniana, glutinosa, hirsuta, incana, jorullensis, matsumurae, oblongifolia, pubescens, purpusii, rhombifolia, rubra, rugosa, serrulata, silesiaca, tenuifolia
　　●●Leaves not folded in the bud stage, irregularly and sparsely serrate, never lobed, veins bowed:
　　　　A. cordata, elliptic, japonica, koehnei, maritima, orientalis, spaethii, spectabilis, subcordata, trabeculosa
Subgenus III: **Clethropis** (Spach) Regel
　　Male flowers in racemes of 10—15, very long, thin catkins in the leaf axils:
　　　　A. nepalensis, nitida
Subgenus IV: **Cremastogyne** (Winkl.) Schnd.
　　Male and female catkins single in the leaf axils, the male long stalked, the female naked:
　　　　A. cremastogyne, lanata

Alnus alnobetula see: **A. viridis**

A. × aschersoniana Call. (*A. serrulata × incana*). Small tree, young twigs faintly pubescent or nearly glabrous; leaves broad oval or broad elliptical, 5—9 cm long, 4—5 cm wide, with short, blunt apex, base more or less cuneate, gray or bluish-green beneath, nearly tomentose yellowish pubescence, coarsely serrate, petiole 1—2 cm long; fruit cones grouped 6—8, short stalked or sessile. SH 1: 71, b, c. Occurring with the parents. First observed in Germany (1867); Brandenburg. z5

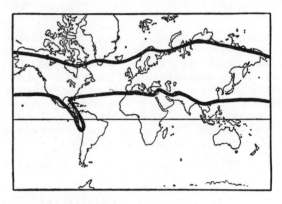

Fig. 96. Distribution of the genus *Alnus*

A. barbata see: **A. glutinosa**

A. californica see: **A. rhombifolia**

A. cordata (Loisel.) Desf. Italian Alder. Tree, 10—15 m high, young twigs more or less viscid, brown-red, somewhat angular and with lenticels, glabrous; leaves broad rounded, base cordate, 5—10 cm long, acute, finely serrate, viscid when young, later leathery, glossy deep green above, glabrous, lighter beneath, venation yellow-brownish pubescent, with axillary tufts, petioles 2—3 cm long; cones grouped 1—3, stalked. BM 8658; EP IV, 61: 26 (= *A. cordifolia* Ten.). Italy, Corsica. 1820. One of the loveliest Alders, leaves somewhat resembling those of *Pyrus*. Plate 32. z6 Ⓕ France Ø

'**Purpurea**'. Leaves at the branch tips purple-brown. Originated 1927 in Kornik, Poland. Ø

A. cordifolia see: **A. cordata**

A. cremastogne Burkill. A tree in it habitat, 18—30 cm high, with smooth gray bark, twigs rather thin and at wide angles from the branch, finely pubescent when young, soon becoming glabrous and dark red; leaves obovate to ovate, 7—11 cm long, acute, base cuneate, irregularly serrate, dark glossy green above, light green and brownish pubescent beneath, with 8—11 paired veins, petiole 1—2 cm lng; fruit cones single in the leaf axils, on 5—8 cm long, thin stalks (important for identification), male catkins 3—5 cm long, only 3 mm thick, usually several together. LF 83; MD Pl. 17; EP IV. 61: 28, ICS 772. China, Szechwan; frequently planted at the edges of rice paddys. 1908. Distinguished from all the other alders by its long stalked fruits. z7 ⓕ China. Fig. 99, 100.

A. crispa see: **A. viridis**

A. × elliptica Requien. (*A. cordata* × *A. glutinosa*). Tree, to 20 m (possibly taller); leaves broad or rounded elliptic, apex nearly always rounded or obtuse, base rounded (not cordate!), regularly toothed, not lobed, dark green and glossy above, glabrous except for axillary tufts beneath; fruit cones in groups of 3−5, some 2 cm long, 1 cm wide (smaller than those of *A. cordata*). MD 1918: Pl. 19, fig. 6. Corsica, found at the mouth of the Salenzara River. 1828. z5

'Itolanda'. Very strong grower, grows like the species, leaves elliptic, when on long branches much larger than those of *A. cordata*, veins slightly curved, cones in 3's. DB 1956: 224. Introduced 1935 by S. G. A. Doorenbos, of The Hague, Netherlands. Found as a chance seedling and propagated by grafting. The name "Itolanda" is taken from Italy and Olanda (Holland), the native countries of both parents. Plate 31. ⌀

A. fiekii see: **A. × silensiaca**

A. firma S. & Z. Shrub or tree, to 3 m high, young twigs viscid, glabrous, later gray-brown, glabrous; leaves oval-oblong to oval-lanceolate, generally acuminate, 5−12 cm long, with 12−15 paired veins, sharply and irregularly serrate, venation pubescent beneath, petiole 1.5−2 cm long; fruit cones single, elliptic to nearly globose, some 2 cm long; male catkins grouped 1−2, March−April. EP IV, 61: 24; KIF 1: 3 (= *A. sieboldiana* Matsum.). Japan. 1862. Very attractive shrub with striking foliage. ⓕ Japan. z6 Plate 31; Fig. 100. ⌀

var. **hirtella** Franch. & Sav. Growth stronger, more tree-like, twigs pubescent; leaves oval-oblong to oval-lanceolate, 5−12 cm long, with 10−16 paired veins; fruit to 2.5 cm long. DRHS 81; BM 8770 (= *A. yasha* Matsum.). 1893. ⌀

var. **multinervis** Reg. Small tree, 5−10 m high, young twigs deep brown, pubescent at first, although soon becoming glabrous; leaves oblong-lanceolate, acuminate, 5−12 cm long, margins irregularly and sharply serrate, with 18−26 paired veins, base rounded or cuneate; cones some 1−1.5 cm long, 3−5 in 5−6 cm long, pendulous racemes, seed nearly as broad winged as the fruit. MD Pl. 10; KIF (= *A. multinervis* Call.; *A. pendula* Matsum.). Japan, Hondo. 1862. ⓕ Japan, Korea. Plate 31. ⌀

A. fruticosa Rupr. Shrub, young twigs red-brown, older ones gray, with few lenticels; leaves broadly ovate, 3−5 cm long, always narrowing to the tip, with 7(−9) paired veins, glabrous beneath, petiole 0.5−1 cm long; fruit cones 1 cm long. SH 1: 66h (= *A. viridis* var. *sibirica* Regel p.p.). Siberia. 1888. Only slightly different than *A. viridis*. z3

A. glutinosa (L.) Gaertn. Common, European or Black Alder. Tree, to 25 m, often multistemmed, open crowned, bark brown-black, young twigs strongly viscid, glabrous; leaves rounded or obovate, apex rounded or emarginate, 4−10 cm long, with 5−6 paired veins, margins coarsely double dentate, glabrous beneath except for the rust-yellow pubescent vein axils, remaining green far into the fall; cones grouped 3−5, distinctly stalked; flower catkins appearing late March

to early April. HW 2, 12; HM Pl. 85. Europe to Caucasus and Siberia, N. Africa. In cultivation since ancient times; ⓕ Germany, Holland, Romania, Yugoslavia, Czechoslovakia, Soviet Union. z3 Plate 32; Fig. 97.

Prefers a deep, moist, humus soil but also excellent for sandy or gravelly areas. Tolerates excessive moisture, but not stagnant water; develops many adventitious roots; not suitable for strongly alkaline soil. In addition to the species, the following varieties are grown:

'Angustiloba'. Distinguished from the similar 'Laciniata' by the more deeply incised leaves, narrower lobes, very acute, margin entire. Sov. Bt. Tidskr. 51, 1957: Pl. 3.

'Aurea'. Weaker growing than the species, young bark orange; leaves yellow, especially in spring. Found in 1860 at the Vervaene nursery in Ledeberg near Ghent, Belgium. ⌀

var. **barbata** (C. A. Mey.). Ledeb. Leaves oval-oblong, finely toothed, pubescent beneath (= *A. barbata* C. A. Mey.). Caucasus, Iran. 1870.

var. **denticulata** (C. A. Mey.) Ledeb. Leaves broad elliptic to obovate, obtuse, 5−10 cm long, margin uneven finely double serrate, somewhat lobed only on the long branches, with 7−9 paired veins, base narrowing, seldom rounded. Asia Minor, Caucasus. 1759? Fig. 98.

f. **graeca** Call. Leaves smaller than the type, usually very thick, leathery, 2.5−3.5 cm long. Greece; Naxos, Euboea.

'Imperialis'. Weak grower, slow, large open shrub with slender branches; leaves narrower than the species, deeply incised, lobe narrow, acute, usually with entire margins. Lu 37−38: Pl. 19. Before 1859. Plate 31; Fig. 98. ⌀

'Incisa'. Growth very weak, slowly mounding to a low dense shrub, although observed in England as a 12 m high tree; leaves very small, rounded, obtuse lobed, more or less deeply incised, often distinctly resembling *Crataegus oxycantha*. Lu 37−38: Pl. 21. (= *A. glutinosa* 'Oxycanthifolia'). 1800. Known only in cultivation. Plate 31; Fig. 98. ⌀

f. **lacera** (Mela) Mela. Shrub or small tree, twigs at a wide angle; leaves oblong to oval, 4−7 cm long, 2−4 cm wide, each side of the upper blade half with 5−6 large, oblong, deeply toothed lobes, often overlapping each other. Sov. Bot. Tidskr. 51: Pl. VI. Found in Finland before 1892. Fig. 98.

'Laciniata'. Resembles 'Imperialis', but not so deeply and narrowly lobed, lobes often without teeth, acute to sharp acuminate. Lu 37−38: Pl. 18. Found in a garden near St. Germain, France, 1819, where presumably, all the plants in Europe have originated. Also found in Finland and Sweden. Plate 31; Fig. 98. ⌀

'Lobulata'. Leaves usually rounded, margin distinctly, deeply lobed, lobes obtuse. Lu 37−38: Pl. 17. Found in Finland, 1895. Fig. 98.

'Maculata'. Leaves somewhat white spotted, otherwise like the species.

'Minutifolia'. Shrub, to 4 m high; leaves nearly circular, margin crenate, 1.5−2.5 cm long and wide. Lu 37−38: Pl. 22. Found 1889 in Aland, Scandinavia. Fig. 98.

f. **parvifolia** (Ktze.) Call. Leaves rounded, small, 3−5 cm long and wide, otherwise like the species. Occasionally found with the species throughout Europe.

'Pyramidalis'. Growth narrowly pyramidal; leaves rather short and wide, dark green (= f. *fastigiata* Beissner; f. *pyramidalis birkiana* Spaeth). 1880.

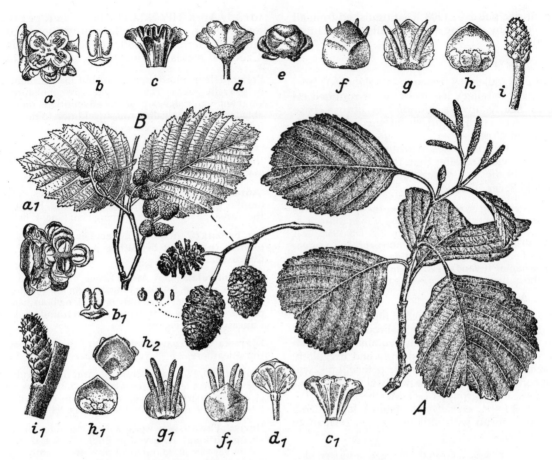

Fig. 97. **Alnus.** A. *Alnus glutinosa*, twig (a. male flower, b. anthers; c. fruit scales; d. bract and prophylla of the male flower from outside; e. from inside f.—h. flower from outside and inside; i. female inflorescence); B. *A. incana* (a1 to i1 analogous to a. thru i.) from Hempel & Wilhelm, Kerner)

'Quercifolia'. Leaves obovate, base cuneate, rounded at the apex, apical blade half with 3—4 rounded lobes on each side, 4—8 cm long, 3—7 cm wide, venation reddish, usually without axillary pubescence beneath. Lu 37—38: Pl. 20. Found in Sweden (W. Gotland). Fig. 98.

'Rubrinerva'. Strong grower, rather conical, twigs glossy viscid when young, red-brown; leaves rounded to obovate, base cuneate to rounded, 6—12 cm long, apex more or less emarginate, otherwise margin simple to double blunt toothed, dark green, with light or dark red veins and leaf petioles. Found in E. Germany in 1870. ∅

'Sorbifolia'. Tree, growth weak, open crowned; leaves oblong to elliptic, both blade halves with 6 deep, oblong, crenate lobes (= *A. glutinosa* f. *sorbifolia* Dipp.). 1892. Very similar to f. *lacera*.

A. hirsuta (Spach.) Rupr. Tree, to 20 m high, strong growing and broadly pyramidal especially when young, bark black-brown, split, older twigs gray pruinose, glabrous, young twigs reddish, shaggy pubescent at first, soon becoming glabrous, winter buds pubescent; leaves broad ovate, 8—14 cm long, acute, coarsely double serrate and slightly lobed, dark green above, blue-green beneath, brownish pubescent; cones 3—4, short petioled to sessile, 2.5 cm long. KIF 1: 32; MD 1918: Pl. 20, 23 (= *A. tinctoria* Sarg.; *A. incana* var. *hirsuta* Spach). Japan, Manchuria; moist areas. 1879. Very closely related to *A. glutinosa*, but with larger leaves and much larger fruits. ℗ Japan. z6

var. **mandschurica** Call. Leaves broadly elliptic, to 10 cm long, 8 cm wide, with short, blunt tips, margin with short, distinctly rounded lobes, base rounded, sparsely pubescent above, the 8—10 paired veins rather thickly pubescent beneath, otherwise slightly blue-green to light green (= *A. mandschurica* [Call.] Hand.-Mazz.). Manchuria. z6 Fig. 99.

var. **sibirica** (Spach) Schnd. Young twigs always glabrous or nearly so; leaves pubescent only on the venation beneath. SH 2: 557 f—h; ICS 770 (= *A. sibirica* Fisch.). Japan and NE. Asia. z3 Plate 32.

A. hybrida see: **A. × pubescens**

A. incana (L.) Moench. American Speckled or Gray Alder. Tree, to 20 m high, bark light gray and smooth, young twigs gray and pubescent; leaves broad ovate, 4—10 cm long, dark gray-green above, whitish gray and pubescent or also glabrous beneath; cones 4—8, sessile or short stalked; flower catkins longer and more limp than those of *A. glutinosa*, March, female catkins pendulous at flowering time. HW 2: 16; HM Pl. 85 (= *incana* var. *typica* Beck.). Europe, Caucasus. Very variable species, growing equally well in dry or moist areas. Ⓕ Germany z2 Plate 30, 32; Fig. 97.

From the countless varieties available, only the following are noted:

'Angermannica'. Leaves normal size, oval to broad oval, margin incised to the midrib, each side usually with 6 lobes, these with obtuse tips, upper margin of the lobes entire, lower lobes regularly and finely serrate, base cordate. Lu 37—38: Pl. 25. Found in 1909 in Angermanland, Sweden. Fig. 98.

'Angustissima'. Blades very deeply incised, the lobes nearly thread-like at the apex. Lu 37—38; Pl. 31—32. Found in Sweden, Norway and Finland. Most elegant of the laceleaf forms. Fig. 98. ⊘

'Arcuata'. Very similar to 'Chamaedryoides', but with young twigs distinctly bowed back and forth; leaves equally large, rounded to broad ovate, acute, sharp double serrate. Sov. Bot. T. 51, 1957, Pl. 10. Found in Sweden, 1887.

'Aurea'. Young twigs always yellow, orange-red in winter; leaves more or less yellow, pubescent beneath; young catkins orange. Much more common than the yellow form of *A. glutinosa*. ⊘

f. **blyttiana** Call. Leaves ovate to broadly elliptic, obtuse, margin with short, rounded lobes, 2.5—3 cm long, green beneath or somewhat bluish, more or less faintly pubescent, with 7—8 paired veins; fruit cones sessile. Finland, Norway. 1911.

'Bolleana'. Leaves more or less lemon-yellow speckled, the spots irregular, large and small throughout. Before 1904 from the Schwerin Arboretum, E. Germany.

'Chamaedryoides'. Leaves small, elliptic-oval, with small apex, 3.5—4.5 cm long, large and blunt lobe serrate, teeth triangular and appressed, base somewhat toothed to entire. Lu 37—38: Pl. 23. Found in Sweden, 1898. Fig. 98.

'Coccinea'. Twigs orange-red; leaves only slightly yellowish toned, broad ovate, blue-green beneath, glabrous.

'Darlecalica'. Leaves broadly elliptic, sinuses a narrow V to U shape, the lobes straight to bowed out from the blade, acute, linear-triangular, margins lacking teeth. Lu 37—38: Pl. 28. Found in Sweden, 1926. Very attractive foliage. Fig. 98. ⊘

'Falunensis'. Resembles 'Laciniata', but with leaves much more regular in form, the lobes narrower, incision seldom going to the midrib, lower margin of the lobes dense and regularly serrate, upper margin sparsely serrate to entire. Sov. Bot. Tids. 51: Pl. 27. Found, 1889, in Dalarna, Sweden.

var. *glauca* see: **A. rugosa**

var. *hirsuta* see: **A. hirsuta**

var. **hypochlora** Call. Leaves elliptic or broadly ovate, ab-

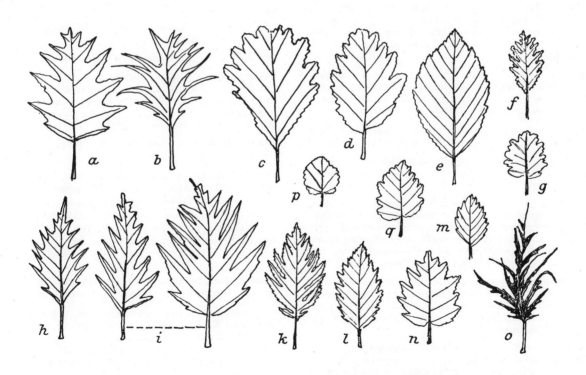

Fig. 98. *Alnus glutinosa*-Forms. a. 'Laciniata'; b. 'Imperialis'; c. 'Quercifolia'; d. 'Lobulata'; e. var. *denticulata*; f. f. *lacera*; g. 'Incisa'; p. Minutifolia'. — *A. incana*-forms. h. 'Darlecarlica'; i. 'Laciniata'; k. 'Sempipinnata'; l. 'Lobata'; m. 'Chamaedryoides'; n. 'Angermannica'; o. 'Angustissima' q. 'Pinnata'

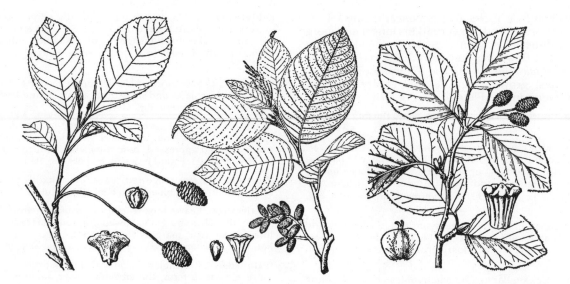

Fig. 99. Left *Alnus cremastogyne*; middle *A. nepalensis*; right *A. hirsuta* var. *mandschurica* (from ICS)

ruptly acuminate, margin with slightly rounded lobes, green beneath, slightly pubescent to nearly glabrous, with 8—10 paired veins; fruit cones sessile, 1—1.5 cm long. Found with the species from Finland to Italy.

'Laciniata'. In appearance, very similar to *A. glutinosa* 'Laciniata', but leaves somewhat longer, narrower, longer acuminate, often quite variable in leaf form, usually each blade half with 8 lobes, base usually truncate. Lu 37—38: Pl. 26—27. (= *A. incana* f. *acuminata* [Regel] Call.). Found occasionally in Scandinavia. 1861. Commonly cultivated in Europe. Plate 29; Fig. 98. Ø

'Lobata'. Leaves ovate-oblong, lobes acute, lobes incised to nearly the midrib, serrate, lobes and teeth becoming smaller toward the apex, base truncate. Lu 37—38: Pl. 24. Found at various locations in Scandinavia, since 1858. Fig. 98.

f. **microphylla** Call. Leaves like the species, but only 3—5 cm long, 2.5 cm wide. Occurring with the species in the wild.

'Monstrosa'. Low shrub, growth wide, flat, with banded twigs. Originated by Spaeth before 1892 and disseminated from that nursery.

'Orbicularis'. Leaves nearly circular, 3—4 cm long and wide, occasionally somewhat plaited (folded), margin irregularly serrate (nearly entire), young leaves with both sides densely tomentose, later gray-green beneath and remaining thinly pubescent, with 5—6 distinctly prominent paired veins; fruit cones small, sessile. MD 1918; Pl. 16. E. Germany. 1892.

'Oxycanthoides'. Leaves nearly quadrangular with 4—5 large teeth on each side, obliquely triangualr, becoming smaller near the blade apex, base cordate. Sov. Bot. Tid. 51: Pl. 11. Found in Sweden in 1920. Very characteristic and quite distinctively leaved form.

f. **parvifolia** Regel. Leaves very small, rounded, only 1—1.5 cm long and wide, gray or gray-green beneath, with 5—7 paired veins; fruit cones usually sessile or short stalked. Finland. 1865.

'Pendula'. Usually seen in the garden with a vertical stem; twigs short or broadly arching, pendulous, very picturesque.

Originated in the Van Der Bom Nursery, Holland before 1900, and distributed at first as *A. incana* "*pendula nova*". Not unusual.

'Pinnata'. Leaves deeply incised, only 2—3 cm long, lobes narrow and acute, gray beneath, densely pubescent. Lu 37—38: Pl. 29 (= *A. incana incisa* Dipp.; *A. incana lobulata* call.). Sweden. Fig. 98. Ø

'Pinnatipartita'. Leaves sharply and deeply incised. Lu 37—38: 5. Finland. Ø

ssp. *rugosa* see: **A. rugosa** and **A. serrulata**

'Semipinnata'. Leaves usually with 1—2 distinctly free "leaflets" at the base, blade deeply incised nearer the apex (¾ or ⅔ into the blade) so that the leaves appear to be pinnate, lobes with nearly parallel margins, sharply serrate. Lu 37—38: Pl. 29. Found in Dalarna, Sweden in 1956. Fig. 98. Ø

'Variegata'. Leaves more or less whitish speckled, otherwise like the species. Rarely seen.

A. japonica (Thunb.) Steud. Japanese Alder. Shrub or tree, to 25 m high, conical habit, young twigs lightly pubescent or glabrous; leaves ovate to oval-lanceolate, 6—10 cm long, acuminate, tough leathery, sharply and irregularly serrate, glossy dark green above, glabrous, lighter beneath, somewhat pubescent in the vein axils, otherwise glabrous; cones 2—6 stalked, 1.5—2.5 cm long. GF 345; KIF 2: 7. Japan, Korea, Taiwan, Manchuria. Before 1880. Very dense foliage species. ⓕ Soviet Union, China, Japan. z5 Plate 31, 30.

var. **koreana** Call. Leaves broadly ovate, 3—5.5 cm long, apex short and blunt, teeth large, broad obtuse, base broad and round, dull green above with dense short pubescence, dense shaggy pubescence on the venation beneath, with 7—8 paired veins, petiole 1—1.5 cm long, pubescent. Sh 2: 555 m. Korea.

var. **minor** Miq. Leaves elliptic, smaller than the type, some 4—6.5 cm long, acuminate, sharp and short toothed, sparsely pubescent above, loose short pubescence beneath, with 7—8 (—10) paired veins; fruit cones 1—2. Japan.

A. jorullensis H. B. K. Leaves oblong elliptic, 6−9 cm long, distinctly short acuminate, margins nearly entire, glabrous above, yellowish beneath, petiole 0.5 cm long, usually with 7 paired veins; flowers on leafy twigs. MD 1918: Pl. 71 fig. 18. Mexico. Ⓕ Costa Rica, Argentina. z6

A. × **koehnei** Call. (*A. incana* × *subcordata*). Tree, young twigs always pubescent, usually thick, hispid; leaves nearly always elliptic, 6−9 cm long, glabrous above or sparsely pubescent, thick hispid pubescence especially on the venation beneath, base rounded, margins usually regularly dentate as with *A. subcordata*; cones short stalked to nearly sessile. MD 1918: Pl. 19. Origin unknown. Before 1892.

A. lanata Duthie. Tree, 15−18 m high, bark yellow-gray, smooth, young twigs brown, hispid pubescence, with white lenticels; leaves obovate, 8−14 cm long, 5−9 cm wide, apex short, base rounded to cuneate, apical blade half irregularly serrate to dentate, tomentose above, dull green, dense brown woolly pubescence beneath, petiole densely pubescent; catkins 3−5 cm long, 2 mm thick, yellow-brown and densely pubescent; fruit cones with stalks 4 cm long, single. China, Szechwan, 1600−2500 m. 1908. z5 Performance in cultivation not known.

A. mandshurica see: **A. hirsuta**

A. maritima (Marsh.) Muhl. Beach Alder. Shrub, occasionally a tree, twigs pubescent at first, later glabrous and dull orange to reddish brown; leaves obovate, acute, seldom obtuse, 6−10 cm long, dark green above, glossy, light green beneath, glabrous; cones 2−4, short stalked; male catkins gold-yellow, in September (important for identification). BB 1224; SS 458; MD 1918: Pl. 11 (= *A. oblongata* Mill.). USA, Delaware to Oklahoma. 1878. Interesting in that it blooms in the fall and therefore easily recognized. z6 Ⓕ Phillipines. Plate 31. ⌀ ✤

A. matsumarae Call. Tree, related to *A. hirsuta*; young twigs yellow-brown, glabrous, lenticels orange; leaves rounded obovate to nearly circular, 7 cm long, distinct and deeply concave at the apex, doubly dentate, small lobed, dull green above, gray and short pubescence beneath, with 8−9 paired veins; fruit obovate to elliptic. MD 1918: Pl. 15; KIF 2: 8. Japan; Hondo. 1914. Hardy. z6

A. maximowiczii Call. Shrub or tree, to 10 m, young twigs light brown, angular, glabrous; leaves broad and rounded ovate, 7−10 cm long, short acuminate, base broad rounded to somewhat cordate, densely finely dentate, teeth alternately pointing forward and back, not lobed, glabrous above, dark green, lighter beneath, glabrous, but midrib often distinctly spotted, with 8−11 paired veins; fruit in groups of 4−5. MD 1918: Pl. 9; KIF 2: 9. Japan, Sachalin, very common in the mountains. Hardy. z5 Plate 30, 32. ⌀

Very similar to *A. viridis*, but easily distinguished by the fringed teeth and cordate leaf base.

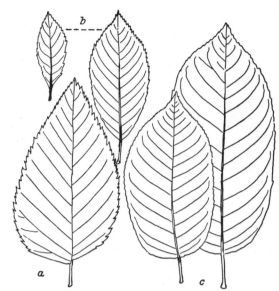

Fig. 100. a. *Alnus firma*; b. *A. cremastogyne*; c. *A. nepalensis* (from Winkler)

A. mitchelliana see: **A. viridis**

A. mollis see: **A. viridis**

A. multinervis see: **A. firme**

A. nepalensis D. Don. Nepal Alder. Tree, 9−12 m high, bark dark gray, young twigs gray-brown, with many white glands; leaves obovate, 11 cm long, 7 cm wide, acute, base cuneate, very evenly dentate, dull green and glabrous above, lighter beneath, reticulate venation, somewhat pubescent, with 10−18 paired veins; male catkins 8−10 cm long, yellowish brown, 10 or more in dense terminal clusters, very beautiful while flowering in the fall. ICS 767; EP IV, 61: 25. Himalaya; SW. Yunnan, 1200−1500 m. 1880(?). z7 Ⓕ Himalaya region. Fig. 99, 100. ⌀ ✤

A. nitida (Spach) Endl. Tree, to 30 m in its habitat, bark blackish and eventually flaking in square patches, young twigs yellow-brown, somewhat pubescent at first, soon becoming completely glabrous; leaves very thin, ovate to oval, 8−14 cm long, usually acuminate, sparsely finely dentate, base usually distinctly narrowing, seldom rounded, dark green above, glossy, glabrous, light green beneath, usually glabrous, with 5 paired veins; male catkins 10−15 cm long, usually grouped in 5, flowering in September, female fruit cones 3−5 together, erect. BM 7654; MD 1918: Pl. 13. India, Himalaya. 1882. Very beatiful, for wet spots. z6 Ⓕ India, Punjab. ⌀ ✤

A. oblongata see: **A. maritima**

A. oblongifolia Torr. Tree, to 10 m, young twigs red-brown, glabrous; leaves oblong-ovate, the highest more lanceolate, 5.5−7 cm long, acute, distincty narrowing to the apex and the base, sharp and usually double serrate, dark green above, glossy, glabrous, underside glabrous or somewhat pubescent; cones 3—6, sessile or short stalked. SS 457; MD 1918: Pl. 20. N. America, USA., Arizona to California. z6

A. occidentalis see: **A. tennifolia**

A. oregona see: **A. rubre**

A. orientalis Dcne. Tree, to 15 m, young twigs red-brown, somewhat angular, glabrous, with orange lenticels; leaves ovate to oval, large and irregularly dentate, 4—12 cm long, obtuse, base rounded, dark green above, glabrous, glossy, lighter beneath, glabrous except for the small axillary tufts, with 8—10 paired veins, petiole 2—3 cm long; cones 2—3 together, rounded, to 2.5 cm long and nearly as wide; seeds obovate, slightly thick winged. MD 1918 Pl. 12. Syria, Cyprus, Cicilia. 1924. Ⓕ In the Near East. z6

Very attractive species, resembles *A. cordata*, but only rarely cordate at the base; distinguished from *A. subcordata* by the glabrous underside of the leaves.

A. pendula see: **A. firma**

A. × pubescens Tausch (*A. glutinosa* × *A. incana*). Tree, young twigs more or less pubescent; leaves not viscid, obovate to ovate, seldom short acuminate, 3—6 cm long, some 2.5 cm wide, slightly wavy lobed, with 7—8 paired veins, dark green above, light green to blue-green beneath, pubescent to lightly tomentose, petiole 1—2 cm long. MD 1918: Pl. 20 (= *A. spuria* Call.; *A. hybrida* A. Br.). Frequently found in Europe with the parents, also in nursery seed beds (usually unnoticed) and appearing as a blending of the parents. z3

A. × purpusii Call. (? *A. rugosa* × *A. tenuifolia*). Tree, young leaves thickly rust colored tomentose, buds thickly pubescent; leaves usually ovate, obtuse, 3—6 cm long, short and bluntly lobed, with usually 8 paired veins, venation beneath dense red-brown tomentose (important for identification), petiole 0.5—1 cm long, brown tomentose; fruit cones very short stalked or sessile, form of the fruit scales a blending of the parents. Found in 1887 by C. A. Purpus in British Columbia and later also in Montana, Missouri and Washington. z3

A. rhombilfolia Nutt. White Alder. Tree, 9—25(—30) m, crown broadly rounded, growth open, ends of the branches pendulous, young twigs somewhat pubescent at first, but soon becoming glabrous; leaves ovate, oval to rounded, 6—10 cm long, usually acute, narrowing to the base, uneven to doubly usually finely serrate, dark green and glossy above, also pubescent when young, later only underside pubescent and yellowish; catkins 2—7 together, before the leaves; fruit cones grouped 3—7, 1.5 cm long. SPa 115—116; MD 1918: Pl. 19. (= *A. californica* hort.). W. USA, along permanently flowing mountain streams. 1885. True species quite rare in cultivation; in Europe often confused with *A. rubra* Bong. z5 ⊘

A. rubra Bong. Red Alder, Oregon Alder. Narrow

pyramidal tree, some 10—15 m high, branches slightly pendulous, young twigs angular, not pubescent or only at the branch tips, viscid when young, dark red, winter buds red, glandular bud scales; leaves ovate to oval, 7—12 cm long, slightly lobed and crenate, margin somewhat rolled up, with 12—15 paired veins, petiole 1.5—3 cm long, venation and petiole orange-brown, dark green above, gray or blue-gray beneath, occasionally also somewhat red-brown pubescent; female catkins red, March; fruit cones barrel shaped, nearly 3 cm long, grouped 6—8, sessile or on orange-red stalks. SPa 118; SS 454; MD 1918: Pl. 20 (= *A. oregona* Nutt.). Alaska to California, in a band within 70 kilometers along the coast. 1884. Ⓕ New Zealand. z6 Plate 32.

In addition, a cultivar with deeply incised leaves, 'Pinnatisecta'; with 5—7 narrow lobe pairs. Jour. For. 37 ill. 1939.

A. rugosa (DuRoi) Spreng. Smooth Alder. Usually a shrub, occasionally a small tree, to 6 m, young twigs glabrous or slightly rust-brown pubescent, now and then somewhat viscid; leaves ovate to broadly elliptic or obovate, acute or obtuse, 5—12 cm long, doubly serrate and often slightly lobed, finely serrate, narrowing to the base, never rounded, glabrous above, gray-green to blue-green beneath, usually only the 10—12 paired veins brownish pubescent, rarely the entire surface; female catkins, erect (important for identification), fruit cones grouped 4—10, the highest sessile, the lowest stalked. GSP 104; Rho 1945: Pl. 977 (= *A. incana* ssp. *rugosa* DuRoi). E. North America. 1769. z5 Plate 31. See also: *A. serrulata*

var. **americana** (Regel) Fern. Leaves broadly elliptic to ovate, 7—10 cm long, 5—7 cm wide, apex short, very slightly round lobed, base broadly rounded, blue-gray to blue-green beneath, venation more or less densely short pubescent, 10—12 paired veins, petiole 0.5—1 cm long, pubescent. MD 1918: Pl. 21; RMi 109 (= *A. incana* var. *glauca* Loud.). Eastern N. America.

f. **emersoniana** Fern. Leaves rounded to circular, 3—5 cm long and wide, very slightly lobed or sharply entire and finely serrate, gray tomentose beneath, with 7—9 paired veins. USA., Massachusetts. Plate 31.

'Tomophylla'. Leaves deeply and irregularly incised. Rho 1945, Pl. 982.

A. serrulata (Ait.) Willd. Hazel Alder. Shrub, 2—4 m high, or a tree to 6 m, twigs glabrous or soon becoming so, buds glabrous, more or less viscid; leaves obovate, apex short, obtuse, 5—9 cm long, evenly and finely serrate, base usually cuneate, with 8—9 paired veins, dark green above, glabrous, distinctly pubescent vein axils beneath, petiole 0.5—1 cm long, glabrous; fruit cones 3—4 together, usually very short stalked. GSP 107. Eastern N. America. z5

This species was known earlier as "*A. rugosa* (Du Roi) Spreng.", and *A. incana* ssp. *rugosa* DuRoi.

A. siberica see: **A. hirsuta**

A. sieboldiana see: **A. firme**

A. × silesiaca fiek (= *A. serrulata* × *A. glutinosa*). Young twigs weakly pubescent to glabrous; leaves usually rounded-elliptic or indistinctly obovate, 6—8 cm long, apex usually obtuse, base usually rounded, occasionally lightly cordate, finely serrate, scarcely lobed, glabrous above, lighter beneath, usually rust-brown pubescent only on the 10—12 paired veins; fruit cones 4—8. MD 1918: Pl. 20 (= *A. fiekii* Call.). Found first in Schlesien, E. Germany, 1888. z5

A. sinuata (Regel) Rydb. Sitka Alder. Shrub or also a tree, to 10 m high, crown narrow, branches usually short and horizontal, young twigs finely pubescent at first, soon glabrous, with many lenticels; leaves ovate, acute, 6—9 cm long, double toothed and shallowly lobed, with some 9 paired veins, light green above, underside more pale and glossy, glabrous or with midrib and vein axils pubescent, young leaves viscid; male catkins 10—12 cm long, April—June, appearing with the leaves; fruit cones 3—6 together. SS 727; SPa 119—120 (= *A. sitchensis* Sarg.). Western N. America, Alaska to California. 1903. z5 Plate 31. ∅

A. sitchensis see: **A. sinuata**

A. × spaethii Call. (*A. japonica* × *A. subcordata*). Tree, 15—20 m, very fast growing; young twigs sparsely softly pubescent, with few lenticels, buds glabrous, bud stalks 1—2 mm long; leaves lanceolate to ovate, 6—16 cm long, 3—6 cm wide, somewhat leathery, with short tips, sharp and unevenly coarsely serrate, dark green above and somewhat glossy, new growth purple-brown to dark violet and young foliage retaining a colored middle stripe, usually glabrous beneath; with 8—11 paired veins; cones usually in 4's, some 1.5 cm long. Dfl 9: 7. Found in the Spaeth Arboretum, Berlin. 1908. z5 Plate 32. ∅

A. × spectabilis Call. (*A. incana* × *A. japonica*). Resembles *A. japonica*; young twigs brown, glabrous; leaves broad oval to oval or obovate on the same twig, 5—7(—10) cm long, apex either acute or obtuse to round or somewhat emarginate, base narrow, margin acute or blunt toothed, dark green above, not glossy, light green beneath and glabrous except for the 8—9 lightly pubescent paired veins; fruit cones 3—9, sessile to short stalked. MD 1918: Pl. 14. Before 1904. Only known in cultivation. z5 ∅

A. spurie see: **A. × pubescens**

A. subcordata C. A. Mey. Caucasian Alder. Tree, to 15 m, young twigs softly pubescent, angular toward the apex, buds stalked; leaves ovate to oval, 5—16 cm long, short acuminate, serrate, base rounded to lightly cordate, dark green above, glabrous, lighter beneath with the midrib and 8—10 paired veins softly pubescent, new growth brown-red; holds its foliage very late in the fall; male catkins 4—5 in groups, often blooming as early as December, some 15 cm long; fruit cones 1—5, nodding. SH 1: 69. Caucasus, Iran. 1860. Very attractive, quite winter hardy species. z6 Plate 32. ∅

A. tenuifolia Nutt. Round crowned tree, 7—10 m high, young twigs slightly pubescent at first, later glabrous,

winter buds red, stalked, pubescent; leaves oval to ovate, 5—10 cm long, 3—6 cm wide, acute, shallowly to obtusely lobed and dentate, base rounded to slightly cordate, with some 10 paired veins, these terminating in the lobe tips, dark green with pubescent venation above, lighter to blue-green and more or less pubescent beneath; male catkins 4—6 cm long, March; fruit cones 3—5, narrowly ovate. SPa 117; SS 445. Western N. America, from British Columbia to California. 1880. z6 Plate 31.

var. **occidentalis** (Dipp.) Call. Leaves larger, 8—10 cm long, on young twigs sometimes to 15 cm long and 12 cm wide, distinctly acute, lobes acute, with 10—12 paired veins, petiole 2—2.5 cm long. DL 2: 72 (as *A. occidentalis*) (= *A. occidentalis* Dipp.). British Columbia to Oregon. 1891. z6

var. **virescens** (Wats.) Call. Leaves only 3—6 cm long, light green to yellowish green beneath, obtuse, usually with short obtuse lobes, 8 paired veins, petiole usually light yellow. MD 1918: Pl. 20. Found together with the species. z6

A. tinctoria see: **A. hirsuta**

A. trabeculosa Hand.—Mazz. Tree, to 7 m, bark smooth, scaly or deeply furrowed, young twigs gray; leaves obovate, quite variable in size, 5.5—7.5 cm long, 3.5—5 cm wide, tough leathery, short acuminate, base cuneate, irregularly serrate, both sides dark green and glabrous, lightly pubescent only on the venation and the 2 cm long red petiole; cones oblong, 2 cm long, 1 cm thick, 1—2 on 2 cm long stalks; male catkins dark green, 6—7 together, 4—6 cm long, somewhat viscid. CIS 16; KIF 3: 6; ICS 769 (= *A. jackii* Hu). SE. China. 1926. Presumably winter hardy. z6

A. viridis (Chaix) DC. Green Alder. Multistemmed shrub, 0.5—2.5 m high, occasionally prostrate, bark smooth, dark gray, twigs clustered together, more or less pubescent; leaves ovate to elliptic, 3—6 cm long, acuminate, base broadly cuneate, irregularly sharply serrate, with 5—10 paired veins, bright green above, lighter beneath, pubescent when young; male flower catkins erect at first, later pendulous, April—May; fruit cones 3—5 in racemes, yellow-brown, 1 cm long. HW 2: 14; HM Pl. 85 (= *A. alnobetula* Hartig). Mountains of Europe. 1820. Ⓕ Romania, Austria, (N. Tyrol). z6 Plate 31.

var. **pumila** Cesati. Dwarf shrub, 0.2—0.5 m high; leaves only 1—1.5 cm long, with 6 paired veins, glabrous beneath; fruit only 3—8 mm long. MD 1918: Pl. 18 (= var. *parvifolia* Dipp.; var. *brembana* [Rota] Call.). Tyrol to N. Italy. z6

var. *sibirica* see: **A. fruticosa**

ssp. *crispa* (Ait.) Turrill. Often a prostrate shrub or to 3 m high, young twigs glabrous to sparsely pubescent; leaves ovate to broadly elliptic, 3—8 cm long, base rounded to slightly cordate (most important distinction from the similar *A. viridis*), finely and densely serrate, with 5—10 paired veins, young leaves somewhat viscid and aromatic, fresh green; cones 3—6, stalked. RMi 109; BMns 382 (= *A. crispa* [Ait.] Pursh; *A. mitchelliana* M. A. Curt.). N. America, Labrador to N. Carolina; cool and moist areas in the mountains. 1782. z3

ssp. **crispa** has the following forms:

'**Grandifolia**'. Leaves larger than the type, 6 to 11 cm long, 5—9 cm wide, with 6—10 paired veins, veins and petiole pubescent beneath. ND 20: Fig. 3a, 1957. In the same region as the species.

'**Laciniata**'. Leaves deeply incised. SH 1: Fig. 667.

'**Microphylla**'. Leaves much smaller, rounded. Plate 31.

f. **mollis** (Beck) Call. Leaves 3—5 cm long, both sides densely white pubescent when young, with 5—7 paired veins. Bavaria to Italy. z6

var. **mollis** (Fern.) Fern. Young twigs pubescent; leaves larger, pubescent beneath; cones to 2 cm long (the species only 1—1.5 cm long). GC 77: 41 (= *A. mollis* Fern.). Newfoundland to Lake Winnepeg, south to Massachusetts. 1897. z2

var. **repens** (Wormsk.) Call. Prostrate grower; leaves 3—5 (—7) cm long, with 5—7(—9) paired veins, completely glabrous beneath; male catkins shorter than those of the species. MD 1918, Pl. 18. Greenland. z1

A. yasha see: **A. firma**

Most of the Alders are not completely winter hardy, but they are fast growing in heavy soil and in moist areas. Nearly all of them bloom with long catkins in early spring except 3 species which bloom in the fall; *A. maritima, nitida* and *nepalensis*. Propagation is usually easy by seed, except of course, for the variegated and laceleaf types, which should be grafted on the appropriate species.

Lit. Winkler, H.: *Alnus*; in Engler, Pflanzenreich, IV, 61, 101—134, 1904 ● Callier, A.: *Alnus*-Formen der europaeischen Herbarien und Gaerten; in Mitt. DDG **27**, 39—185, 1918 ● Fernald, M. L.: Eastern North American representatives of *Alnus incana*; in Rhodora **47**, 333—361, 1945 ● Hylander, N.: Om flikbladiga och smabladiga former av klibbal och graal; in Lustgarden **37—38**, 85—119, with Pl. 17—32, 1957 ● Hylander, N.: On cut-leaved and small leaved forms of *Alnus glutinosa* and *A. incana*; in Svensk Bot. Tidskr. **51**, 437—453, with 28 Pl., 1957.

ALOE L. — LILIACEAE

Plants without or with up to 9 m high stem; leaves usually in a rosette or in a loose spiral, usually very succulent, clasping the stem, margin toothed, often hornlike, upper leaf surface monochrome or speckled; inflorescence simple or branched, flowers in simple or branched racemes; perianth tubular, usually red, but also pink, yellow or orange. — About 275 species in tropical and S. Africa, 42 in Madagascar, 12—15 in

Arabia. Only one species will be covered here:

Aloe dichotoma L.f. Treelike, 8—10 m high, with a thick stem and repeatedly forked branching; leaves arranged in an open spiral, lanceolate, gray-green with yellowish margin, tiny toothed, 15—25 cm long, 5—7 cm wide; flowers yellow, in a branched inflorescence. S. Africa. z9 Plate 4.

ALOYSIA Ort. & Palau ex Pers. — VERBENACEAE

Shrubs and subshrubs or perennials; leaves opposite or in whorls of 3, margins entire, dentate or lobed, often very aromatic; flowers small, resembling *Lantana*, in heads or spikes, usually white, pink or lilac; corolla 4 lobed, oblique or 2 lipped; calyx 2—4 toothed. — 37 species in the Americas from California, USA , to Chile.

Aloysia chamaedryfolia Chamisso. Rambling shrub, twigs 4 sided, pubescent; leaves opposite, acute ovate, large toothed, margin curled up, glossy above, more or less tomentose beneath, very aromatic; flowers small, lilac-pink, in 7—15 cm long panicled spikes, June—August. Brazil, Argentina. z8 ⊕

A. triphylla (L'Hérit.) Britt. Lemon Verbena. Shrub, deciduous, to 2.5 m high (in favorable conditions to 5 m), branched striped and somewhat rough; leaves in whorls of 3(—4), lanceolate, short stalked, 7—10 cm long, acuminate, base cuneate, margins entire or somewhat toothed at mid-blade, glandular spots beneath, very strong lemon scent; flowers small, lilac, in terminal, 10—15 cm long, pubescent, large panicled spikes, August. GC II, 11: 301; BM 367 (as *Verbena triphylla*) (= *Lippia citriodora* [Ortega] Kunth.). Chile, Argentina. 1784. z8 ⊕

Thrives in any soil in full sun; notable for the wonderful lemon scented foliage, but very susceptable to frost damage. Easily propagated by cuttings.

ALSOPHILA

Alsophila australis see: **Cyathea australis**

ALYSSUM L. — CRUCIFERAE

Low, often fast growing annuals, perennials or sub-shrubs (only the latter considered here); leaves with stellate pubescence or silvery scales, alternate, simple, margins entire or dentate; flowers yellow or white, in long terminal racemes or corymbs; petals entire or somewhat emarginate; filaments toothed or with nectar glands on both sides at the base; fruit an elliptic to circular silique with flat seeds. — Some 150 species in Europe, mostly in the Mediterranean region. d ○

Alyssum argenteum Vitm. To 40 cm high, subshrub, branches thin, ascending, fleshy (not rigid), woody only at the base; leaves obovate to lanceolate, gray-green above, silver-white beneath; surest identification characteristic is the silvery-white ripe fruit, thick with 14—40 radiating stellate hairs hiding the epidermis. Italian Alps. (Those plants in cultivation under this name are generally *A. murale* W. & K.; almost always confused except in the latest literature!) z6 **d**

A. montanum L. 10—20 cm high, stalk ascending or upright, woody only at the base; leaves obovate to lanceolate, acute to obtuse, gray with stellate pubescence, especially dense beneath, 2—3 cm long; flowers gold-yellow, fragrant petals emarginate on the tips, April—May; inflorescence elongated at fruiting time, fruit circular to elliptic, 5—8 mm long, slightly convex, with brown, narrow, membranous margined valves,

dense stellate pubescence, each chamber with 2 seeds. HF 1385; HM 827. Middle and S. Europe; on dry chalk slopes, and sandy grasslands. 1713. z6 **d** ⊕ ○

A. murale W. & K. 25—60 cm high, woody only at the base, total plant with gray-green stellate pubescence; leaves oblanceolate, 1.5—2—3 cm long, acute or obtuse, cuneate, short petioled, denser stellate pubescence beneath; flowers small, yellow, several in terminal, corymbs, 5—15 cm wide, May—July; fruit usually rounded, with 6—13 radiating, sparse stellate hairs (epidermis always visible between the hairs), only one winged seed in each chamber. HF 1384 (erroneously as *A. argenteum* Vitm.) (= *A. argenteum* Boiss. non Vitm.). SE. Europe to S. Russia and Syria. 1777. See notice after *A. argenteum* Vitm. z6 **d** ⊕ ○

A. saxatile L. see: **Aurinia saxatilis** (L.) Desv.

A. spinosum see: **Ptilotrichum spinosum**

All species very attractive in sunny areas in the rock garden, easy to cultivate, abundant flowers; for sandy, gravelly soil; propagated easily by seed. For information on the other somewhat woody species, such as *A. alpestre* L., *A. serpyllifolium* Desf., *A. moellendorfianum* Aschers and *A. wulfenianum* Bernh., see the following literature.

Lit. Bailey: Manual of cult. plants, 444, 1949 (for nomenclature) ● Schlechtendahl and Langethal: Flora on Deutschland, 5th edition, 14: Pl. 1380—1390.

AMELANCHIER Medic. — ROSACEAE

Deciduous shrubs or small trees; winter buds with many scales, acute; leaves simple, alternate, petioled, margins entire or sharply serrate; stipules small, abscising; flowers white, in simple, often foliate racemes on the previous year's growth; calyx tube campanulate, with 5 short, blunt teeth; petals 5, obovate to lanceolate; stamens 10—20; pistils 2—5, partly connate or distinct; carpels 5, occasionally 2—4, connate, tip of the ovary wide or narrow, semi-epigynous or totally so; each seed chamber of the developed fruit half subdivided by an incomplete partition; sepals remaining

on the fruit; fruit pulp not gritty; fruit a pea-size, berry-like pome with 4—10 seeds, purple to dark red, juicy and sweet, or dry and tasteless. — 25 species, nearly all in N. America, 1(—2) in Europe to Asia Minor, 1 in E. Asia.

The separation of species is not easy; first observe the new growth (gray, white, red, glabrous or pubescent), then the flowers, the ovaries, pistils, form and margins of the leaves. Positive identification in the dormant season is only possible with a few prominent species.

Key to the Identification of Flowering Plants
(edited and completed by Jones)

● Pistils all distinct, 5, calyx not surpassing the corolla:
   A. ovalis

●● Pistils connate, at least to just below the midpoint (*A. utahensis* distinct nearly to the base);
1. Pistils normally 5 (rarely 4); stamens 20; fruit purple-black, glabrous, usually juicy and edible, 10 chambered;
   2. Ovary glabrous on the tip;
      3. Sepals more or less pubescent, at least on the inside;
         4. Petals 3—9 mm long; racemes upright; young leaves densely white tomentose; mature leaves elliptic to oval, finely serrate and acute or more obtuse and apiculate, base rounded to somewhat acuminate;
            5. Racemes 2.5—6 cm long, on leafy twigs, lower flower stalks 5—10 mm long; petals oblanceolate; pistils 4 mm long, lower half connate; anthers 1 mm long; young leaves green; shrub, fastigiate branched, alder-like, 3—8 m high, open bushy growth:

A. canadensis

5. Racemes 1—3 cm long, compact, without leaves, early flowers on 1—3 mm long stalks; petals elliptic; pistils 2—3 mm long, connate less than halfway up; anthers 0.5—0.7 mm long; low stoloniferous shrub, only 0.20—1 m high, in forests:
     A. obovalis

4. Petals of opened flowers 12—25 mm long;
   6. Leaves short acuminate, base cordate or rounded, blade usually ovate to obovate, finely serrate; racemes loose, becoming erect or pendulous, 4—12 cm long; trees or shrubs;
      7. Leaves at flowering time half unfolded, nearly or completely glabrous or only sparsely pubescent, bronze-red; sepals lanceolate, acuminate; racemes nearly or completely glabrous; fruit sweet and juicy, lowest fruit stalk usually 2.5—5 cm long, sepals reflexed:
         A. laevis
      7. Leaves at flowering time just unfolded and half developed, copper-red, white silky pubescent beneath; sepals 3—5 mm long, triangular-lanceolate; racemes silky pubescent at first, soon glabrous; fruit sweet and juicy, with erect sepals, lowest fruit stalk usually 2.2—3.3 cm long:
         A. lamarckii
      7. Leaves at flowering time hardly developed, thick white tomentose beneath; sepals oval-lanceolate, abruptly acuminate; racemes silky pubescent; fruit somewhat dry, powdery, tasteless, abcising early, lowest fruit stalk 1—2.5 cm long:
         A. arborea
   6. Leaves obtuse or acute at the apex, not acuminate; racemes erect or ascending, 2—5 cm long; shrubs 1—3 m high;
      8. Petals 16—25 mm long, 5—7 mm wide past the middle; pistils 3—4 mm long; anthers 1—1.5 mm long; leaf blade thin, green, oval, 2.5—5 cm long, when fully developed:
         A. cusickii
      8. Petals 12—16 mm long, 3—4 mm wide over the middle; pistils 2—2.5 cm long; anthers 0.8 mm long; leaf blade tough, pale green, rounded, 1.5—3 cm long:
         A. basalticola

3. Sepals, hypanthium and flower stalk completely glabrous, blue-green; total plant glabrous; petals 8—12 mm long:
     A. pumila

2. Ovary tomentose at the tip, usually very thick, occasionally only a few trichomes;
   9. Leaves with a lasting soft pubescence or finely tomentose, at least on the underside; petals 5—11 mm long;
      10. Sepals lanceolate to triangular-lanceolate; hypanthium and flower stalks sparsely pubescent to glabrous; leaves with 7—9 paired side veins; previous year's growth usually brown and glabrous; hypanthium narrowed at the upper margin of the fruit:
         A. pallida
      10. Sepals linear or narrow lanceolate to linear-spathulate; inflorescence usually more or less densely woolly; leaves with 11—13 paired side veins; previous year's growth often remaining softly pubescent, gray; hypanthium at the fruit not or only slightly narrowed:
         A. utahensis
   9. Leaves eventually completely glabrous or with some soft pubescence, never remaining pubescent; young leaves glabrous or soon becoming glabrous or also floccose, at least on the underside.
      11. Leaves at flowering time more or less floccose or tomentose beneath;
         12. Petals 4—10 mm long; low, stoloniferous shrub, 0.2—2 m high; leaves usually with 7—9 paired side veins, venation irregular and bending before reaching the finely dentate margin:

            A. spicata
         12. Petals some 15 mm long; shrub or tree, to 12 m, leaves with 9—10 paired side veins, terminating at the fine margin; finely serrate nearly to the base; base nearly always rounded, never cordate:
            A. asiatica
         12. Petals mature, 11—22 mm long; shrub or small tree, 2—6 m high; leaves with 11—13 regular, distinctly parallel paired veins, usually terminating in the coarsely dentate margin:
            A. sanguinea
      11. Leaves when half developed or at flowering time not densely tomentose, both sides becoming glabrous or nearly so;
         13. Leaves finely serrate, usually 6—10 teeth per centimeter, some 20—40 teeth on each side of the blade, leaves larger on flowering and fruiting twigs;
            14. Flowers 3—12 in racemes; petals oblanceolate, 8—13 mm long, leaf blade usually round or somewhat cordate at the base;
               15. Leaves usually elliptic or somewhat obovate, unfolded and more than half developed and dull

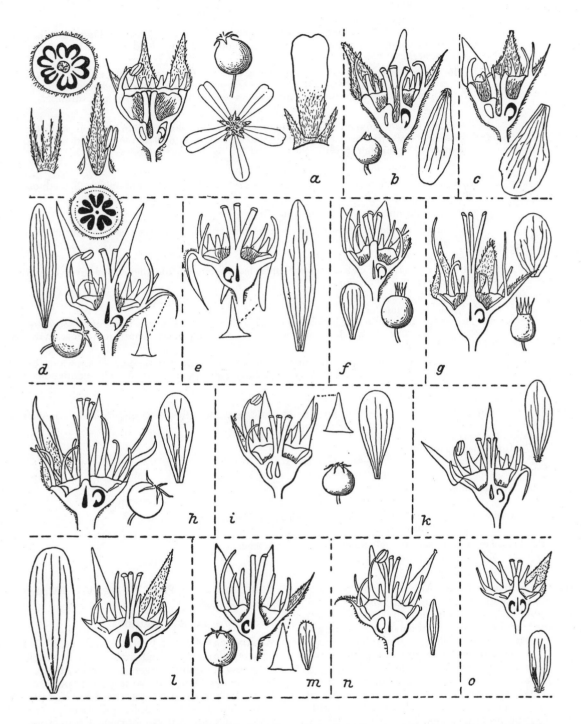

Fig. 101. **Amelanchier**, flower parts and fruit. a. *A. ovalis*; b. *A. ovalus* var. *cretica*; c. . *ovalis* var. *integrifolia*; d. *A. asiatica*; e. *A. asiatica* var. *sinica*; f. *A. spicata*; g. *A. bartramiana*; h. *A. canadensis*; i. *A. alnifolia*; k. *A. florida*; l. *A. cusickii*; m. *A. utahensis*; n. *A. pallida* var. *siskyouensis*; o. *A. pallida* (mostly from Schneider)

green and glabrous at flowering time, obtuse or acute at the apex, rounded on the base; shrub, 0.3−1 m high, with stolons, open branched:
    A. fernaldii

15.   Leaves ovate or oval;
    16.   Racemes 2−4 cm long; leaves ovate, short acuminate, unfolded and more than half developed and completely glabrous or nearly so at flowering time; slender, 1−3 m high shrub:
        A. neglecta

    16.   Racemes loose, 4−7 cm long; leaves oval, acute, unfolded, but not yet fully developed at flowering time, sparsely floccose-tomentose or also more or less glabrous beneath, sometimes petals pubescent until abscising; growth rank or nodding, 2−3 m high shrub:
        A. interior

14.   Flowers usually grouped 2−3 (or single), one terminal, the others in leaf axils of the higher leaves; blade glabrous, flat, oval, acute at both ends; petals oval, 6−9 mm long; multi-stemmed, fast open grower, 0.3−5 m high shrub:

      A. bartramiana

13.   Leaves coarsely serrate, usually not more than 2−5 per centimeter and only 5−20 teeth on each blade half;

    17.   Petals 6−10 mm long, 2−3.5 mm wide;
        18.   Petals completely glabrous; older leaves rather thin, pale green beneath; shrub, only 30−90 cm high:
           A. gaspensis

        18.   Petals inside the claw pubescent; older leaves somewhat leathery, blue-green beneath; shrub or small tree, 2−4 m high:
           A. alnifolia

    17.   Petals 12−25 mm long;
        19.   Petals 12−15 mm long (seldom shorter), 3−3.5 mm wide; sepals triangular-lanceolate, 2−2.5 mm long; pistil 2−2.5 mm long; anthers 0.5−0.7 mm long; ovary densely tomentose on the tip:
           A. florida

        19.   Petals 16−25 mm long, 5−7 mm wide; sepals lanceolate, acuminate, 3−3.5 mm long; pistil 3−4 mm long; anthers 1−1.5 mm long, ovary nearly glabrous on the tip or only slightly tomentose at the pistil base:
           A. cusickii

1.   Pistils 4, 3 or 2 (rarely 5); stamens 10−15(−18); petals 5−10 mm long; racemes erect or ascending, 2−4 cm long; fruit usually small, 3−8 chambered, often brown and dry before ripe;
    20.   Petals oblanceolate;
        21.   Mature foliage glabrous;
           22.   Hypanthium sparsely pubescent outside:
               A. florida var. *humptulipensis*

           22.   Hypanthium glabrous:
               glabrous forms of *A. atahensis*

        21.   Leaves more or less pubescent or tomentose, at least the underside:
           A. utahensis

    20.   Petals oval or obovate; leaves finely pubescent (rarely glabrous):
        A. pallida

Amelanchier alnifolia Nutt. Alder Leaved Serviceberry. Shrub or small tree, 2−4 m high, also occasionally lower, twigs softly tomentose at first, soon becoming completely glabrous and red-brown; leaves tough, oval to rounded or nearly 4 sided, tomentose beneath only when young, soon becoming completely glabrous, fully developed at flowering time, 2−5 cm long, with 8 to 13 paired veins, curving just before reaching the coarsely dentate margin, teeth 2−20 on each side of the blade, 2−5 per centimeter; flowers small, white, fragrant, 5−15 in erect racemes, May; fruit 1−1.5 cm thick, rounded, purple-black, pruinose, edible, sweet, juicy. BB 1989; JAm Pl. 2; SS 196; CWF 231. Along river banks in moist thickets and forests of Northwestern N. America. 1918. ⓕ USA; used in windbreaks for erosion control. z5 Plate 34; Fig. 101, 102. See also: *A. florida*. ⌀ ⚭ ✵

A. amabilis see: **A. sanguinea**

A. arborea (Michx. f.) Fern. Small tree, 5−20 m high, or an irregularly branched shrub, usually single stemmed or a few together, never in clumps, twigs ascending, gray-brown, smooth, young twigs pubescent at first, later becoming glabrous and brown, striped; leaves with dense white woolly pubescence at first, light green, usually not developed at flowering time (bud scales may have abscised), 4−10 cm long, ovate to oval, short acuminate, base cordate or round, tough, dark green and glabrous above, lighter and eventually completely glabrous beneath, with 11−17 paired veins spaced unevenly and bending before reaching the dentate margin, teeth sharp and fine, 6–10 per centimeter, 50–60 on each blade half, dentate nearly to the base which is distinctly cordate; flowers 2–2.5 cm wide, white, fragrant, grouped 4–10 in pendulous racemes, very early, usually before the leaves, March–April; fruit 6–10 mm thick, purple, tasteless and dry, ripening June, abscising early, with protrudent calyx teeth. JAm Pl. 1, 8 (= *A. canadensis* var. *botryapium* T. & G.). Eastern N. America, Canada. Ⓕ USA; planted for erosion control. z4

A. asiatica (S. & Z.). Endl. Shrub or tree, to 12 m, twigs thin, upright at first, later horizontal or pendulous, pubescent at first, then becoming glabrous, gray-brown; leaves ovate, 4–7 cm long, acute, base usually round to slightly cordate, margin finely serrate nearly to the base, whitish or yellowish tomentose beneath at first, but soon becoming glabrous on both sides, dark green above, rather tough, fall foliage reddish-orange; flowers at first in upright, later nodding, 3–6 cm long, dense woolly racemes; corolla 3 cm wide, petals ovate-oblong, mid-May; fruit blue-black. KIF 4: 13; YTS 1: 49. Japan, China, Korea. 1865 z5 Plate 35; Fig. 101, 102. ∅ ✿

var. **sinica** C. Schnd. Leaves smaller, seldom over 5 cm long, only serrate on the upper half, slightly tomentose when young, both sides soon becoming glabrous; inflorescence usually completely glabrous; fruit smaller, blue-black. CIS 31; LF 171 (= *A. sinica* [Schnd.] Chun.). China; Hupeh, Szechwan, 300–2400 m. 1920. z5 Fig. 101.

A. bartramiana (Tausch.) M. Roem. Shrub, multi-stemmed, broad and open growing, 0.5 to 3 m high, twigs thin, glabrous, brown; leaves completely glabrous in new growth, half developed at flowering time, oval to elliptic or obovate, 3–6 cm long, usually acute at both ends, with 10–16 paired veins spaced irregularly, somewhat red-brown at first, later dark green, pale green beneath, sharply and finely dentate, 6–10 teeth per centimeter, 20–40 on each side nearly to the middle; flowers single or to 3 together, petals only 6–9 mm long (very easily distinguished by both of these characteristics), May; fruit nearly black, pruinose, with protrudent, occasionally reflexed calyx tips, 10–15 mm thick, ripening July. BB 1990 (as *A. oligocarpa*) (= *A. oligocarpa* M. Roem.). Eastern N. America, mountain forests, cold swamps or wet rocky soil. 1800. z5 Plate 35; Fig. 101, 102. ∅ ✿

A. basalticola Piper. Shrub, 1–3 m high, current year's branches brown, glabrous; leaves fully developed before the flowers, initially pale green, glabrous and becoming bluish, coarse, rounded, 1.5–3 cm long, with 10–13 paired veins, teeth small, sharp, 5–15 on either side, 4–6 per centimeter, dentate nearly to the base; flowers grouped 4–8 in 2–4 cm long, glabrous panicles; petals white, 12–16 mm long, narrow; fruit globose, dark purple, 9–12 mm thick, juicy. JAm Pl. 3. Grows over basalt rock in the river valleys of SE. Washington State, USA. z5

A. botryapium see: **A. canadensis** and **A. lamarckii**

A. canadensis (L.) Med. Shrub, 2–8 m high, stem thin, upright, fastigiate branching, in dense, bushy clumps, with stolons, twigs gray, glabrous; leaves thin, nearly exactly elliptic, at flowering time initially light green and (while less than half grown!) thickly white tomentose beneath, though soon becoming fully glabrous, except for the midrib and petiole, blade 3.5–5 cm long, 1.5–2.5 cm wide, acute or rounded, base rounded to (rarely) somewhat cordate, with 9–13 paired veins, unevenly spaced, margin with 25–40 shallow, sharp teeth on either side, 6–11 per centimeter; flowers in 2.5–6 cm long, erect racemes, whitish pubescent at first, appearing with the foliage, petals oval to oblanceolate, obtuse, 3–9 mm long, 2–3 mm wide, stamens around 20, April–May; fruit globose, 7–10 mm thick, purple-black, bluish pruinose, sweet, juicy, edible; sepals on the fruit usually erect, seldom horizontal. BB 1896 (as *A. botryapium*); JAm Pl. 2, 9, 10 (= *A. botryapium* Borkh.; *A. intermedia* Spach; *A. oblongifolia* Roem.). Eastern N. America, mainly in swamps and in lowland forests from Newfoundland to Georgia, especially in coastal areas. 1623. z4 Plate 35; Fig. 101, 102. See also: *A. arborea*, *A. laevis* and *A. lamarckii*.

This species seldom found in Europe, outside of some botanic gardens. Has little garden merit.

A. confusa Hylander. Shrub, growth habit like that of *A. spicata*; leaves elliptic to broadly ovate, 3–5.5 cm long, 2–3.5 cm wide, widest in the middle, acute, base rounded, occasionally slightly cordate, upper third irregularly serrate, light green above, light bluish green beneath, at first whitish silky pubescent, usually already fully opened at flowering time and glabrous; flowers 3–8 cm long racemes with 6–8 flowers, these 2.5–3.5 cm wide, petals obovate, May–early June; fruit 7–9 mm thick, ripening in July, calyx fully reflexed (Fig. 22 to 23 by Schroeder 1972). Origin unknown. Planted in Sweden since 1830 and naturalized in S. Sweden. z5 See also: *A. lamarckii*

A. crenata see: **A. utahensis**

A. cusickii Fern. Shrub, 1–3 m high, of many rod-like, bowed stems, young branches reddish and somewhat glossy at first, later becoming gray; leaves oval, thin, totally glabrous at first, later tough leathery, fully developed at flowering time, 2–5.5 cm long, acute or rounded, base round to slightly cordate, with 7–10 paired veins, both sides with 3–15 sharp teeth, usually especially distinct only on the upper half, 3–6 per centimeter; flowers large, grouped 3–8 in 2–5 cm long racemes, petals obovate to oblanceolate, 16–25 mm long (important for identification, largest flowers of all!), 5–7 mm wide, April; fruit globose, red at first, then blue-black, juicy, edible, 1 cm thick. JAm Pl. 3, 20. NW. USA, on basalt rock along rivers. 1934. Quite distinct from other species with its large flowers. z5 Fig. 101. ✿ ⚭ ✕

A. fernaldii Wieg. Low, stoloniferous, irregularly branched shrub, 0.3–1 m high, growing in large clumps, twigs glabrous, gray or brown; leaves rather thin, at flowering time either undeveloped or half open and totally glabrous, dull green, later elliptic to obovate, both sides glabrous, dark green above, lighter beneath, 5–8 cm long, obtuse, base rounded, with 7–13 irregularly paired veins, each side with 15–35 sharp teeth nearly to the base, 4–10 per centimeter; flowers small, in erect or ascending racemes, early June; fruit red at first, then purple-black, juicy. JAm Pl. 1, 4. SE. Canada, wet forests, edges of swamps, moist sand dunes or on limestone. Found in only a very small area. z5

A. florida Lindl. Slender, 1.5 m high shrub, also occasionally a tree, 10–12 m high, branches upright, young twigs red-brown at first, tomentose, but soon becoming glabrous; leaves thin, fully developed at flowering time, oval to oblong, tomentose at first, especially beneath, later becoming glabrous and fresh green above, lighter beneath, 3–4 cm long, rounded, base acute to slightly cordate, with 8–12 paired veins, usually terminating at the margin, each side with 5–20 triangular, outward pointing teeth in the apical half, 4–6 per centimeter; flowers white, 2–3 cm wide, fragrant, in 4–8 cm long, upright racemes of 5–15 flowers, May; fruit black, pruinose, 10–13 mm thick, juicy, edible. JAm Pl. 2; SPa 162 (as *A. alnifolia*) (= *A. oxyodon* Koehne; *A. alnifolia* var. *florida* Schneid.). NW. USA, in open forests, on hills and in the mountains, near the coast. 1826. z6 Fig. 101, 102. ✦ ⊘ ⌘ ✗

var. **humptulipensis** Jones. Leaves and flowers smaller; leaves 2–3 cm long, usually oval, finer toothed; flowers grouped 5–9 in 2–4 cm long racemes, petals 6–10 mm long; fruit 5–7 mm thick. Washington State, USA; Humptulips Prairie. z6

A. gaspensis (Wieg.) Fern. & Weatherby. Low branched shrub, 30–90 cm high, growing in dense thickets, new shoots somewhat tomentose, but soon becoming totally glabrous; leaves oval to rounded, 3–6 cm long, fully developed at flowering time, thin, rounded above, base cordate, with 6–13 evenly spaced paired veins, terminating at the margin, with 5–20 sharp, upturned teeth, on each side to just past the middle, 3–6 per centimeter; flowers small, 5–15 in ascending or upright racemes from 3–6 cm long, petals 6–9 mm long; fruit blue-black, globose, 8–10 mm thick. JAm Pl. 19; BR Pl. 1171 (as *A. sanguinea*). Canada; Quebec, Gaspé Island. z4

A. × *grandiflora* see: **A. lamarckii**

A. interior Nielsen. Low shrub or 8 m high tree; leaves ovate to broad oval or elliptic, fully developed at flowering time, then green and sparsely pubescent beneath, soon becoming glabrous, 3–7 cm long, acute, base round to nearly cordate, eventually with both sides totally glabrous, with 8–11 paired veins, margin finely and evenly serrate to the base with 2–30 teeth on either side, 5–6 per centimeter; flowers 7–12 in 3–7 cm long racemes, May; petals 8–13 mm long, obtuse; fruit

globose, purple-black, pruinose, 6–8 mm thick, sweet, juicy, edible. JAm Pl. 1 and 7. Central USA; Minnesota; open, dry forest, sandy forests on slopes or wooded river banks. z3

A. intermedia see: **A. canadensis**

A. laevis Weig. Allegheny Serviceberry. Tree, 10 to 13 m high, or only a broadly branched shrub, bark longitudinally split with age, twigs thin, glabrous; leaves tough, ovate to oval, initially glabrous and bronze-red, often longitudinally folded and bluish-red at flowering time, eventually totally glabrous and somewhat bluish, dark green, 4–6 cm long, short acuminate, base rounded to lightly cordate, with 12–17 paired veins, unevenly spaced, finely and sharply serrate nearly to the base, both sides 35–45 teeth, 6–8 per centimeter; flowers many in 4–12 cm long pendulous racemes, very attractive, glabrous, May; petals 12–22 mm long; fruit globose, purple to nearly black, 16–18 mm thick, pruinose, sweet, juicy, edible, calyx reflexed. BB 1985 (as *A. canadensis*); SM 351. 1870. One of the loveliest and most valuable species; under various names in the nursery trade. z4 Plate 35. See also : *A. lamarckii* ✦ ⊘ ⌘ ✗

Frequently found in cultivation, often confused with *A. lamarckii*, but with beautiful red spring foliage fully open and glabrous at flowering time, otherwise flowers 1–2 weeks before *A. lamarckii*.

A. lamarckii F. G. Shroed. Large shrub or small tree, to 10 m high, usually without stolons, wide branching, young twigs silky pubescent; leaves elliptic, with short apex, 4.5–8.5 cm long, 2–5 cm wide, finely serrate, base rounded to slightly cordate, young leaves copper-red at flowering time, silky pubescent, folded (not yet fully opened!), petiole usually remaining pubescent; flowers 6–10 in loose racemes, white, petals 9–14 mm long, 2.5–5 mm wide, petiole 1.5–2.5 cm long, April–May; fruit purple-black, sweet and juicy, with erect calyx tips, stalk usually 2–3.5 cm long. DB 1969: 208-211 (= *A. botryapium* DC.; *A. canadensis* K. Koch, non [L.] Med.; *A. canadensis* var. *botryapium* Koehne; *A. laevis* Clapham, Tutin & Warburg; *A. confusa* Schmeil & Fitschen, non Hylander; *A.* × *grandiflora* Rehd.). Eastern Canada; presumably brought over to France in the second half of the 19th century, disseminated from there and today, naturalized in NW. Germany and Holland. This species one of the most frequently found in Northern European nurseries and gardens, next to *A. laevis*; fall color a glorious yellow to carmine red. z4 Plate 33, 35. ⊘ ✦ ✗

'Rubescens'. Like the species, but with purple-pink flower buds, soft pink-white in full bloom. 1920. Found as a seedling in the Durand-Eastman Park in Rochester, N.Y., USA. ✦ ⊘

A. mormonica see: **A. utahensis**

A. neglecta Egglest. Shrub, 1–3 m high, with thin stems; leaves at flowering time somewhat half developed and nearly totally glabrous, tough, lighter beneath, 5–6 cm long, short acuminate, base round to slightly cordate, with 7–11 paired veins, margin with

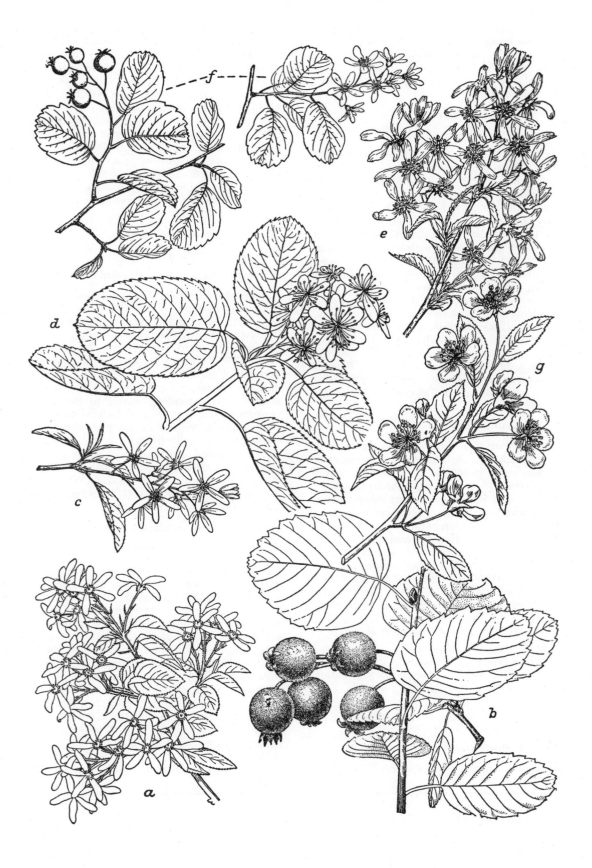

20—30 fine sharp teeth on each side, 7—9 per centimeter, nearly to the base; flowers 7—10 in 2—4 cm long, upright to ascending racemes, totally glabrous axis; petals narrow oval, 8—10 mm long; fruit 8—10 mm thick, purple-black, juicy, globose. JAm Pl. 1, 5. NE. USA, New England States. z4

A. oblongifolia see: **A. canadensis**

A. oligocarpa see: **A. bartramiana**

A. obovalis (Michx.) Ashe. Shrub, 0.2—1.5 m high, short branched, open columnar habit, twigs thin, soon becoming glabrous; leaves oval to elliptic or lightly obovate, developing after the flowers and at first whitish tomentose beneath, later nearly totally glabrous, finally coarse, 1—3 cm long, acute or also obtuse, base acute or round, dark green above, lighter beneath, with 7—9 paired veins with uneven spacing, margin sharply and finely serrate nearly to the base, 20—30 teeth on each side, 6—9 per centimeter; flowers in 1—3 cm long dense, upright, nearly totally leafless, but white tomentose branches, 4—10 together, petals only 6—7 mm long, May; fruits 6—8 mm thick, globose, nearly black, sweet, juicy, edible, in 2—3 cm long, erect fruit clusters, erect calyx tips, fruit stalks only 3—8 mm long, the basal 8—11 mm long. JAm 49 (= *A. stolonifera* Wieg.); JAm Pl. 8, 22, 23; Rhodora 1941: Pl. 672. Eastern USA; Pennsylvania to S. Carolina. 1833. Of little value and seldom true in cultivation. Fall color yellow. Plate 35; Fig. 102. z5

A. oreophila see: **A. utahensis**

A. ovalis Med. Shrub, 1.5—3 m high, multistemmed, stems narrowly upright, stoloniferous, tomentose at first, later becoming glabrous, dark brown; leaves ovate to oval, round on both ends, sharply serrate (rarely entire), white woolly beneath when young, later becoming totally glabrous, 2.5—4.5 cm long; flowers 3—8 in white tomentose, erect racemes, petals oval-oblong, May; pistil not reaching beyond the calyx (important for identification); fruits dark blue, nearly black, pruinose, globose, edible, but tasteless; sepals pointing outward. HM 1073; BM 2430 (= *A. vulgaris* Moench; *A. rotundifolia* Dum.-Cours.). Only native European species, especially in mountainous Central and S. Europe. In cultivation since circa 1596. z5 Plate 35, 34; Fig. 101, 102. See also: *A. spicata* ✧ Ø

ssp. **cretica** (Willd.) Maire & Petitmengin. Leaves smaller, racemes shorter and with fewer flowers; young branches, leaves, calyces and petioles densely white tomentose. Greece, Crete, in the mountains. Fig. 101.

ssp. **integrifolia** (Boiss. & Hoh.) Bornm. Leaves tougher, more bluish green, still tomentose beneath at fruiting time, margin usually entire. Armenia, Kurdistan. Fig. 101.

A. oxyodon see: **A. florida**

A. pallida Greene. Shrub, 1—3(—8) m high, twigs up-

right or ascending or (especially in dry locations) also sparsely branched, multistemmed, occasionally more or less pendulous; leaves oval to elliptic or rounded, rather tough, leathery, both sides dull green, usually somewhat lighter beneath, both sides finely tomentose, occasionally completely glabrous, 2—4 cm long, with 7—9 paired veins, margins often entire or with a few small teeth at the apex; flowers grouped 4—6 in 3—4 cm long, somewhat corymbose inflorescences, petals 8—11 mm long, sepals shaggy pubescent on both sides; fruit globose, purple-black, 4—6 mm thick, juicy. JAm Pl. 3, 21 (= *A. siskiyouensis* Schneid.; *A. subintegra* Schneid); California, Siskiyou County, USA, moraines, rocky forests, river banks, thickets. Fig. 101. z5

A. prunifolia see: **A. utahensis**

A. purpusii see: **A. utahensis**

A. rotundifolia see: **A. ovalis** and **A. sanguinea**

A. sanguinea (Pursh) DC. Shrub, loose upright, 1—3 m high, single stemmed or multistemed columnar, young twigs reddish or gray; leaves oval to rounded, developing with or before the flowers, at first densely white to yellowish tomentose beneath, later becoming glabrous, 2.5—7 cm long, acute or obtuse, base rounded to somewhat cordate, with 11—13 paired veins, straight and closely spaced, margin on each side with 20—30 sharp teeth extending nearly to the base, 4—6 per centimeter; flowers 4—10 in 4—8 cm long, ascending to pendulous racemes, rachis pubescent, May; petals white, occasionally light pink, 11—22 mm long; fruit broad rounded, purple-black, pruinose, sweet, juicy, edible. BB 1988 (as *A. rotundifolia*); JAm Pl. 17, 18 (= *A. rotundifolia* Roem.; = *A. amabilis* Wieg.). Eastern N. America, S. Canada, forests, thickets, in groups. 1824. z4 See also: *A. gaspensis*

A. simica see: **A. asiatica**

A. siskiyouensis see: **A. pallida**

A. spicata (Lam.) K. Koch. Low, columnar, 0.3—2 m high shrub; leaves usually oval, broad ovate or rounded, developing with or before the flowers, densely white tomentose beneath, 2.5—5 cm long, acute, base rounded to slightly cordate, both sides eventually totally glabrous, with 7—9 paired veins, margin with 20—30 fine and even teeth extending to the base, or lower 1/3 without teeth, 5—8 per centimeter; flowers 4—10 in short, dense, erect, 1.5—4 cm long racemes, April; petals 4—10 mm long, oblanceolate, white or occasionally light pink; fruit rounded, purple-black, pruinose, 6—8 mm thick, sweet, juicy, edible, stalk 1—3 cm long. JAm Pl. 2, 12, 13—16; GSP 186 (= *A. humilis* Wieg.; *A. ovalis* Borkh. non Med.). Forests, dunes, rocky areas, riverbanks of Northeastern N. America. 1800. Until recently this species was er-

---

Fig. 102. **Amelanchier** a. *A. asiatica*; b. *A. flolrida*; c. *A. obavalis*; e. *A. candensis*; f. *A. alnifolia*; g. *A. bartramiana* (from Sudworth, Sargent, Lauche, Illinck, Sieb. & Zucc., Gard. and Forest)

roneously considered a hybrid between *A. canadensis* and *A. ovalis*. z4 Fig. 101.

A. stolonifera see: **A. obovalis**

A. subintegra see: **A. pallida**

A. utahensis Koehne. Shrub or small tree, 0.5—5 m high, abundantly branched, grows in clumps, current year's wood gray tomentose, often remaining so into the 2nd and 3rd year; leaves usually small, rounded to oval, usually gray-green and finely tomentose on both sides, developing with or before the flowers, 0.5—3 cm long, rounded to emarginate, base round to cuneate, with 11—13 paired veins, margin with 3—10 large teeth on each side at the apex, 3—5 per centimeter; flowers 3—6 in 2—3 cm long, erect or ascending racemes, rachis tomentose; petals linear, 7 mm long; fruit 6—10 mm thick, rounded, purple-black, often dry when ripe, leathery and tasteless. JAm Pl. 3 (= *A. purpusii* Koehne; *A. mormonica* Schneid.; *A. prunifolia* Greene; *A. crenata* Greene; *A. oreophila* A. Nelson). Generally the most common species in the mountain and desert regions of Western N. America. Dry areas, slopes and banks. 1900. Quite variable. z3 Fig. 101.

A. vulgaris see: **A. ovalis**

Most species highly recommended for their beautiful, early flowers and the generally splendid orange-red fall foliage. Fruits quickly eaten by the birds, also once used as a substitute for currants (although more grainy), particularly in Holland.

In the past, the nomenclature has been very confused; therefore, the work of Jones is very important, as well as that of F. G. Shroeder for this species native to NW. Europe.

Lit. Browicz, K.: Distribution of woody *Rosaceae* in W. Asia. VII. Genus *Amelanchier*; Arboret. Kornickie 1971, 5—26 ● Fernald, M. L.: Another century of additions to the Flora of Virginia. Rhodora **43**, 559—629 ● Hylander, N.: Nagra anmaerkningar om de i Sverige odlade och foervildrade *Amelanchier* arterna, saeskilt *A. confusa* Hyl. Lustgarden **45**/**46**, 266—277, 1966 ●Jones, G. M.: American Species of *Amelanchier*; Illin. Biol. Monogr. **20 (2)**, 1946 ● Nielsen, E. L.: A taxonomic study of the genus *Amelanchier* in Minnesota; Amer. Midl. Nat. **22**, 160—206, 1939 ● Schroeder, F.—G.: Zur Nomenklatur der Gattung *Amelanchier*; Taxon **17**, 633 to 634, 1968 ● Schroeder, F.—G.: *Amelanchier lamarckii*, ein neuer name fuer einen alten Zierstrauch; Dtsch. Baumsch. 1969, 288—291 ● Schroeder, F.—G.: *Amelanchier*-Arten als Neophyten in Europa; Abh. Naturw. Ver. Bremen **37 (3)**, 1969, 287—419 ● Weaver, R. E. jr.: The Shadbushes; in Arnoldia **34**, 22—31, 1974 ● Wiegand, K. M.: The genus *Amelanchier* in Eastern North America. Rhodora **14**, 117—161, 1912.

× **AMELASORBUS** Rehd. — ROSACEAE

Generic hybrids between *Amelanchier* and *Sorbus*. Distinguished from *Amelanchier* in the partially incompletely pinnate leaves and the panicled flowers; from *Sorbus* in the partially simple, partially lobed or incompletely pinnate leaves, panicled flowers with 5 pistils; fruit with distinctly developed but incomplete partition.

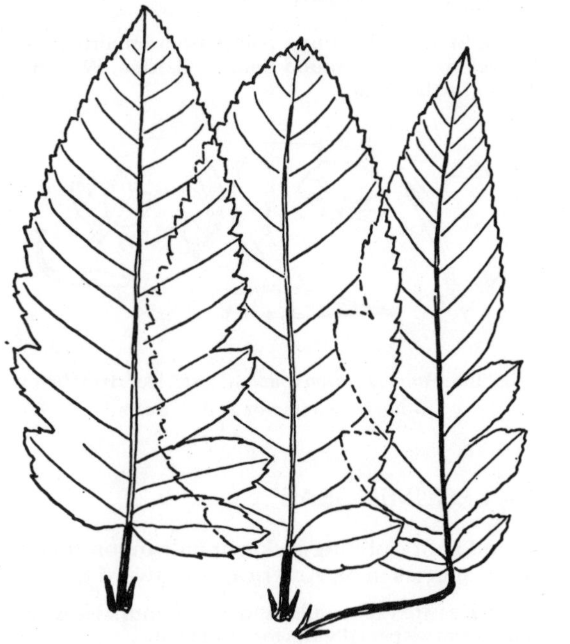

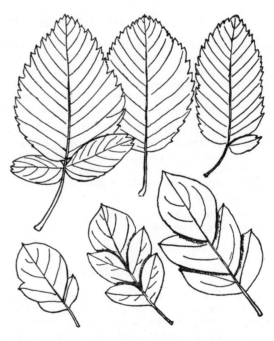

Fig. 103. × *Amelasorbus raciborskiana*, somewhat reduced (from material in the Kornik Arboretum, Poland)

Fig. 104. Upper row × *Amelasorbuis jackii*; lower row × *Amelasorbus hoseri* (from material in the Kornik Arboretum, Poland)

× **Amelasorbus hoseri** Wroblewski. Source unknown, presumably a hybrid of × Sorbopyrus auricularis × Amelanchier sp. Shrub, leaves oval-oblong, 4–7 cm long, 2–4 cm wide, incompletely pinnate, usually with 2 leaflets on either side, point of attachment wide, terminal leaflet large, margin completely entire, a tiny apex on each leaflet, underside remaining thinly gray tomentose. Originated around 1936 in Kornik, Poland; original plant now dead. Existence in cultivation today unknown. Fig. 104.

× **A. jackii** Rehd. (Amelanchier florida × Sorbus scopulina). Strong grower, upright shrub, 2.5 m; leaves ovate to elliptic, among them always some incompletely pinnate leaves, 4–10 cm long, larger toothed than Amelanchier florida, margin often somewhat wavy, slightly pubescent at first, soon becoming glabrous; flowers in 5 cm long panicles, white, petals oblong, May; fruit globose, pea-size, dark red, blue pruinose, dry, tasteless. Bk 7: 57; fig. 2 (1952). Found in the mountains of Idaho among the parents, 1925. z3 Fig. 104. ✤

The assumption by Rehder, that this plant is not found in cultivation, is no longer valid; in recent years it has been distributed by some Dutch nurseries and has proven itself a useful ornamental shrub, although not fruiting as well in cultivation as is reported in native stands.

× **A. raciborskiana** Wroblewski (Amelanchier asiatica × Sorbus sp. ex sect. Sorbus). Tree, young twigs reddish, pubescent, bud elongated, white pubescent at first, later becoming glabrous; leaves ovate-oblong, 10–12 cm long, basal part of the blade deeply lobed or with 2–3 paired leaflets, margin serrate, dark glossy green above, petiole and midrib reddish; flowers and fruit thus far not observed. Arb. Kornik. III; 79 (1958). Developed by Wroblewski in the Korni Arboretum, Poland, in 1934. z3 Fig. 103. ⌀

Both plants of first class botanical interest, and useful as ornamentals; A. jackii has attractive flowers, both species have attractive foliage, but they are scarcely available outside of Poland. Both fully winter hardy.

AMICIA Kunth — LEGUMINOSAE

Shrubs, leaves alternate, paired pinnae with few leaflets, these translucent punctate, stipules large, abcising; flowers rather large, in axillary racemes or solitary; calyx with 2 large upper tips, the side points small; anthers equal in size; a narrow, flattened pod. — 8 species, from Mexico to Argentina.

Amicia zygomeris DC. Medium sized, very strong growing, upright shrub, to 2.5 m, twigs hollow, greenish, pubescent as is the petiole; leaves pinnate, with 4 leaflets, obcordate, mucronulate, dotted, the large, swollen stipules purple toned; flowers 5–6 in short, axillary racemes, yellow, turning purple, October. BM 4008. Mexico. 1826. z9 ✤ ⌀

AMMODENDRON Fisch. ex DC. — LEGUMINOSAE

Deciduous shrubs, resembling Halimodendron, twigs thorny with thorny leaf rachis and stipules; leaves alternate, even pinnate, with only 2 leaflets; flowers in terminal racemes; keel petals distinct, anthers distinct, ovary very short-stalked; fruit with winged seams, indehiscent, with 1–2 seeds. — 5 species in Asia Minor.

Ammodendron conollyi Bge. Shrub, leaves gray-green, silvery beneath, leaflets oblanceolate, some 3 cm long; flowers violet-black, June; otherwise as in Fig. 105. SDK 4: 11. Transcaspian; desert sand dunes. Ⓕ Soviet Union; used for dune planting around the Caspian Sea. z6 **d S** ○

Thus far only cultivated in Soviet botanic gardens; also available there, A. argenteum and A. eichwaldii, for illustrations of

these see SDK 4: 11. Young plants from imported seed are doing well in the Dortmund Botanic Garden, W. Germany; worthy of further trial.

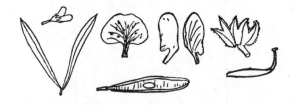

Fig. 105. *Ammodendron conollyi*. Left, leaf; fruit below; otherwise a flower and its parts

AMORPHA L. — Bastard Indigo — LEGUMINOSAE

Deciduous shrubs or subshrubs, rarely perennials; leaves alternate, unevenly pinnate, leaflets numerous, stipules awl shaped, abcising; flowers small, blue-violet, black-purple or brownish, with yellow anthers, seldom white, in dense terminal racemes or grouped racemes, with only one petal (standard), wings and keel petals absent; anthers uneven length, tubular con-

nate; pod short, oblong, sickle or half-moon shaped. — Some 20 species in N. America, southward to Mexico.

Many species are very similar and only identifiable with sufficient material, especially flowers and fruit.

Amorpha brachycarpa Palmer. To 1 m high, very similar to the well-known A. nana; leaflets 21–45, elliptic oblong, base rounded to somewhat cordate; flowers bluish purple, in 10−25 cm long panicles; lower calyx teeth as long as the tube. Missouri. 1920. Hardy. z2

A. californica Nutt. Shrub, 1−2 m high, very similar to *A. fruticosa*, twigs and leaf rachis glandular bristly pubescent, with scattered punctate glands, leaflets 11−27, fresh green, broad oval to elliptic, 2−3 cm long, often with small prickly tips, both sides softly pubescent, whole leaf 10−25 cm long; flowers reddish-purple, May−July, calyx teeth 1/3−1/4 as long as the tube; pods 8 mm long. MS 268. S. California, in wooded canyons near the coast, and to 1500 m in the mountains. z7 Fig. 106. **d S**

A. canescens Pursh. Lead Plant. Fine twigged sub-shrub, 25−70 cm high, twigs angular, densely gray pubescent; leaves nearly sessile (lowest pair of leaflets very close to the stem), with 21−42 leaflets, these oval-elliptic, 7−20 mm long, both sides densely gray pubescent; flowers blue, in dense, short stalked, 10−15 cm long racemes, June-August; pods 4 mm long. BM 6618; NBB 2: 409 (= *A. canescens* Nutt.). Understory plant of dry prairies and the plains of Middle N. America. 1812. Good for the rock garden. ⑮ USA, planted for erosion control. z2 Fig. 106. **d S** ✧

A. croceolanata S. Wats. Shrub, to 3 m, young twigs shaggy brown-yellow pubescent; leaflets 13−23, ob-

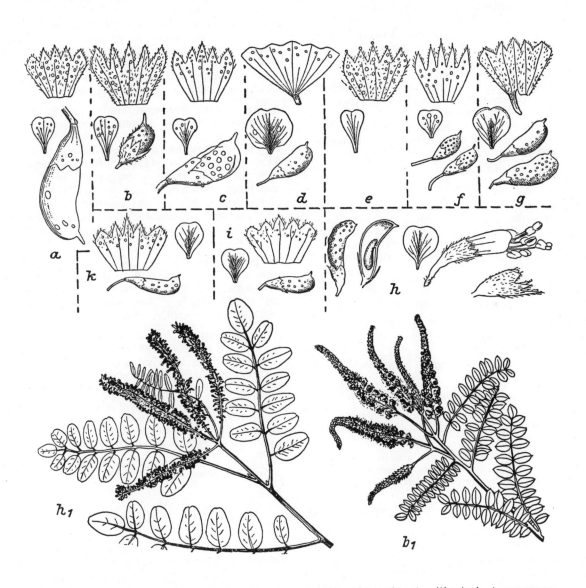

Fig. 106. **Amorpha.** Upper bisected calyx, banner petal and fruit beneath. a.*A. californica*; b. *A. canescens*; c. *A. cyanostachya*; d. *A. glabra*; e. *A. herbacea*; f. *A. nana*; g. *A. virgata*; h. *A. fruticosa*; i. *A. fruticosa* var. *tennessensis*; k. *A. fruticosa* var. *angustifolia*; h1 twig of h.; b1 twig of b. (from Schneider, except h1 and b1)

long, 2—5 cm long, rounded on both ends, yellow-brown tomentose at first, eventually only shaggy pubescent beneath, and on the calyx; flowers purple, July—August. NBB 2: 411 (= *A. fruticosa* var. *croceolanata* Mouillef.). 1812. Hardy. z6

A. cyanostachya M. A. Curtis. Shrub, to 2 m high; leaflets 11—25, oval, 1—2.5 cm long, rounded at both ends, distinctly glandular punctate beneath; flowers blue, usually solitary, in 5—15 cm long racemes; pods distinctly glandular punctate (= *A. caroliniana* sensu Rydb. non Croom). USA; N. Carolina to Florida. 1848. z7 Fig. 106. d S ⊕

A. fruticosa L. Bastard or False Indigo. Shrub, to 3 m high, twigs softly pubescent or nearly glabrous; leaves to 30 cm long, leaflets 11—25, the lowest pair some 1 cm from the node, 2—4 cm long, elliptic; flowers brown-violet to blue, in 15—20 cm long racemes, June—August; calyx teeth usually not longer than 1/3 of the tube; pods usually with 2 seeds, bowed, 7—9 cm long. BB 2101; HM 1442; BM 604ns (= *A. pubescens* Schlechtd. non Willd.). Eastern and Southeastern N. America, hills, moist areas and river banks. 1724. Used by the early settlers as a substitute for Indigo as a blue dye. Ⓕ Italy, Czechoslovakia, USA, Japan; used in windbreaks for erosion control. z5 Fig. 106. d S ⊕

In addition, the following varieties:

'Albiflora'. Flowers white. 1894.

var. **angustifolia** Pursh. Twiggy, 1.5—5 m high; leaflets 9—27, oval to oblong, distinctly pointed on both ends, 2—4 cm long; racemes 5—20 cm long; pods 6—7 mm long, bowed, usually 2 seeded. BM 2112 (as *A. nana* sensu Sims non Nutt.) (= *A. fragrans* Sweet). USA; Iowa to Montana, on river banks. z3 Fig. 106

'Corulea'. Flowers light blue. 1838.

'Crispa'. Leaflets with distinctly crispate margin.

var. **emarginata** Pursh. Leaflets wider than the species, emarginate at the apex or obtuse (= *A. emarginata* Sweet). 1827.

f. **humilis** (Tausch) Palmer. Dwarf form, usually winter killed to the ground every year. 1838.

'Lewisii'. Flowers larger than the species. Loddiges Catalogue 1830.

'Pendula'. Branches prostrate or arching downward, otherwise like the species. 1869.

var. **tennessensis** (Kunze) Palmer. To 6 m high, strongly pubescent, leaflets somewhat longer, calyx teeth more blunt, fruit pods longer. Southeastern USA, river banks and stream

sides. Fig. 106. z5

A. glabra Poiret non Boyt. Shrub, to 2 m high, twigs reddish, often somewhat pubescent, strongly branched; leaves 7—15 cm long, leaflets very thin, 9—19, oval to oblong or ovate, 3—5 cm long, obtuse, base rounded; flowers blue, grouped in racemes, 6—15 cm long, calyx teeth very short, May—June; pods 7—8 mm long, back side straight (= *A. montana* Boynt.). N. Carolina to Georgia and Alabama; dry mountain slopes. 1800. z6 Fig. 106. d S

A. herbacea Walt. Shrub, to 1.5 m high, twigs finely pubescent, brown-red, striped; leaves projected outward, 4—16 cm long; leaflets 11—37, elliptic to oblong, venation reticulate and black dotted beneath, leaflets generally becoming smaller toward the leaf base; flowers white to violet-purple, grouped in fine pubescent racemes, June—July; pods only 4—5 mm long, with distinct, black glands. SDK 4: 16 (= *A. pubescens* Willd.; *A. pumila* Michx.). USA; N. Carolia to Florida, in sterile sandy soil. 1820. z6 Fig. 106. d S

A. nana Nutt. Shrub, reaching over 50 cm high in cultivation, often only 10—40 cm high in the wild, twigs nodding, glabrous; leaves to 10 cm long, leaflets 13—19, lowest pair very near the base, elliptic, 5—12 mm long, fresh green, punctate beneath; flowers purple, single, in 6—8 cm long racemes, fragrant, June—July; pods 5 mm long, somewhat glandular. BB 2112 (= *A. microphylla* Pursh). Middle and Southern N. America, hills and prairies, often developing wide heath-like expanses. 1811. Ⓕ USA, planted for erosion control. z4 Fig. 106. d S ⊕

A. paniculata Tor. & Gray. To 4 m high, twigs tomentose; leaflets 15—19, oval-oblong, 3—8 cm long, tomentose beneath; inflorescence to 40 cm long, calyx soft pubescent, July. Arkansas to Texas, moist areas and salt marshes. 1926. z7 d S

A. virgata Small. To 2 m high, often smaller, twigs red-brown; leaflets 9—19, oblong to ovate, both ends round or apex somewhat emarginate, tough leathery, margin eventually rolled inward, somewhat pubescent beneath. Georgia to Mississippi. 1923. z8 Fig. 106. d S

Amorpha species have little to offer as ornamentals, but they are all easy to grow, summer blooming, attract bees and, more recently, planted in the USSR for soil stabilization and windbreaks. Easily propagated by seed.

Lit. Palmer, E. J.: Conspectus of the Genus *Amorpha*; in Jour. Arnold Arboretum 12, 157—197, 1931.

AMPELOPSIS Michx. — VITACEAE

Deciduous climbers, having tendrils; twigs with lenticels and white pith; leaves alternate, simple or compound, usually with long petioles; flowers small, greenish, usually 5 parted, in long stalked cymes, opposite the leaves and without tendrils; fruit a 1—4 seeded berry. — Some 20 species in Atlantic N. America, in Mexico, Near East, S. and especially E. Asia.

Often confused wth *Vitis* and *Parthenocissus*, but easily distinguished by a few characteristics:

Vitis:	Bark frayed, pith brown
Ampelopsis:	Bark not frayed, pith white. Tendrils without holdfasts
Parthenocissus:	Tendrils with holdfasts

KEY (completed by Rehder)

● Leaves not compound; undivided or lobed;

    Leaves whitish to bluish beneath, tough;

        Fruit light yellow or light blue or whitish:
            A. humulifolia

        Fruit dark violet or blue:
            A. bodinieri or *A. vitifolia*

    Leaves green beneath, thin;
        Blade not or shallow lobed, fruit bluish to greenish:
            A. cordata

        Blade 3−5 lobed, fruit eventually blue:
            A. brevipedunculata

●● Leaves compound, occasionally also partly simple;

    Leaves 3−5 parted, simple and 3 lobed;

        Blade sections serrate or pinnatifid, lower leaves often simple;

            Middle leaflet short stalked, fruit dark blue:
                A. delavayana

            Middle leaflet sessile, cuneate, fruit orange, also often bluish before ripening:
                A. aconitifolia

            Blade sections at least partly pinnate, rachis broad winged, pinnae jointed:
                A. japonica

    Leaves pinnate or bi-pinnate, leaflets stalked;

        Flowers 5 parted, fruit purple:
            A. arborea

         Flowers 4 parted, fruit light red:
            A. orientalis

        Whole plant bluish, leaves 40−60 cm long:
            A. megalophylla

         Leaves purple beneath, to 30 cm long:
            A. chaffanjonii

Ampelopsis aconitifolia Bge. Lush growing, twigs thin, glabrous; leaves 5 parted, long petioled, leaflets lanceolate, 4−7 cm long, pinnatifid, often pinnatisect, both sides fresh green; fruit globose, pea size, bluish at first, eventually yellow, orange or brownish. RH 1868: 10; DL 2: 269−270 (= *Vitis dissecta* Carr.) N. China, Mongolia. 1868. z5 Fig. 107. ⌀ ⚭

var. **glabra** Diels. Leaves usually only 3 parted, lower leaves often 3 lobed, blade sections rhomboid, lobed and large toothed. RH 1867: 451 (as *Ampelopsis palmiloba*) (= *A. rubricaulis* Carr.; *A. aconitifolia* var. *palmiloba* Rehd.). Fig. 108. ⌀ ⚭

A. arborea (L.) Koehne. Strong grower, twigs thin, with numerous tendrils; leaves bi-pinnate, 10−20 cm long, petiole 1−4 cm long, much shorter than the internodes; leaflets ovate-rhombic, 1−4 cm long, acute, terminal leaflet stalked, the others nearly sessile, all large toothed, dark green and glabrous above, venation beneath pubescent when young; flowers 5 parted, August; fruit dark purple, 8 mm thick (seldom sets fruit in N. Europe). BB 2404 (= *A. bipinnata* Michx.). S. USA. 1700. z7 to 8. Fig. 107. ⌀ ⚭

A. bodinieri (Lév. & Vent.) Rehd. Strong grower, climbing to 6 m, young twigs reddish, glabrous; leaves tough, triangular-ovate and unlobed or broad ovate and shallow lobed, 7−15 cm long, velvety pubescent above when young, later dark, glossy green, bluish beneath; fruit dark blue, ripening October (= *A. micans* Rehd.; *Vitis repens* Veitch; *V. flexuosa wilsonii* Veitch). Middle China. 1900. Hardy. z5 ⌀ ⚭

var. **cinerea** Rehd. Leaves often 3−5 lobed, both sides or only the underside gray tomentose. 1907. ⌀ ⚭

A. brevipedunculata (Maxim.) Trautv. Lush climbing vine, young twigs roughly pubescent at first; leaves broad cordate, to 12 cm long, acute, 3 lobed, large toothed, dark green above, lighter and pubescent beneath, violet-brown in spring, basal sinus wide; inflorescence short and dense, not protruding beyond the foliage; fruit rounded, pea size, blue-green to light blue, eventually blue to lilac colored, in September−October. BC 191; DL 2: 267; Gn 85: 557 (= *A. heterophylla* var. *amurensis* Planch.). Japan, Manchuria, N. China. 1868. z5 Fig. 107. ⌀ ⚭

'Citrulloides'. Leaves more deeply and narrowly lobed, with wide, open sinuses, middle lobe narrowed at the base and at or beyond the middle, side lobes often further lobed, therefore the entire leaf appears 5 lobed (= *A. citrulloides* Lebas; *Vitis citrulloides* Dipp.). 1875. ⌀

'Elegans'. Leaves smaller than the type, white and greenish-yellowish-white variegated, youngest leaves often also pink colored. Gn 54: 5 (= *A. tricolor* hort.; *Vitis heterophylla* var. *iegata* Nichols.; *V. elegantissima* Jaeger). Before 1847. Often used as a potted plant. Fig. 108. ⌀

var. **maximowiczii** (Regel) Rehd. Twigs and leaves less pubescent, leaves deeper 3−5 lobed, basal sinus rounder, petiole longer. Gfl 22: 765; BM 5682 (as *A. humulifolia*); NK 12: 15, Pl. 3 (as *A. heterophylla*). China, Japan, Korea. 1860. z5 Fig. 108. ⌀ ⚭

A. chaffanjonii (Lév.) Rehd. Closely related to *A. megalophylla*. Total plant glabrous; leaves pinnate, to 30 cm long, with 5−7 leaflets, leaflets oval to oblong, 4−10 cm long, acuminate, sparsely dentate, glossy green above, purple beneath, splendid fall color; fruit pea-size, red at first, eventually black (= *A. watsoniana* Rehd. & Wils.; *Vitis leeoides* Veitch; *Vitis chaffanjonii* Lév.). China. 1900. z5 ⌀ ⚭

A. cordata Michx. High climbing, branches nearly glabrous; leaves usually ovate, acuminate, not or indistinctly 3 lobed, 5−10 cm long, base cordate, slightly serrate, thin, green beneath with lightly pubescent venation, petiole shorter than the blade, flower stalk 4−8 cm long; fruit pea size, bluish or blue-green, ripening September. BB 2408; HM 1909 (= *Vitis indivisa* Willd.). N. America, Virginia to Ohio and Illinois, Florida, Texas and Mexico. 1796. z4 Fig. 107. ⌀ ⚭

A. delavayana Planch. Strong growing, young twigs usually reddish and pubescent; leaves usually 3 lobed and some 3 parted, 5−12 cm long, coarsely crenate, acuminate, base cordate, dark green and nearly glabrous above, light green and generally pubescent beneath; the middle segment elliptic-oblong, cuneate,

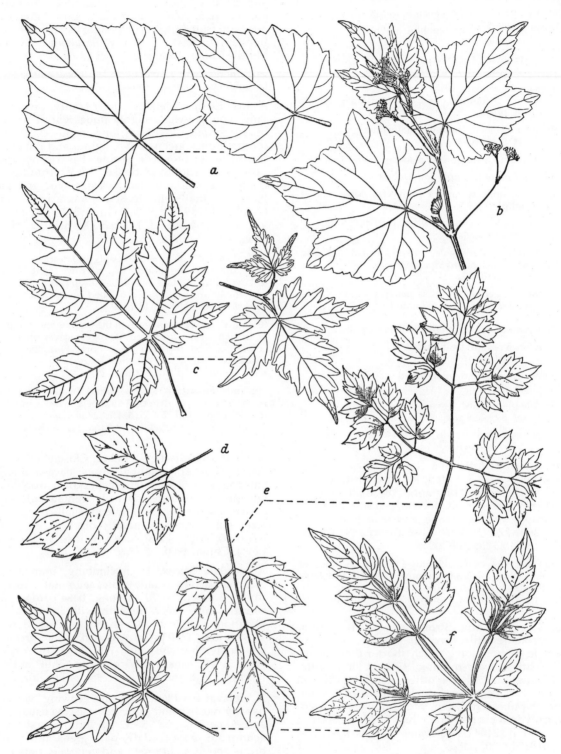

Fig. 107. **Ampelopsis** a. *A. cordata*; b. *A. brevipedunculata*; c. *A. aconitifolia*; d. *A. orientalis*, basal pinna; e. *A. arborea*, lower basal pinna; f. *A. japonica* (from Dippel)

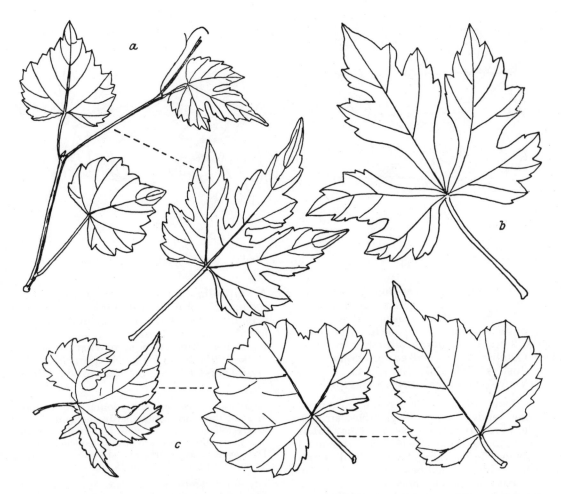

Fig. 108. **Ampelopsis** a. *A. brevipedunculata* var. *maximowiczii*; b. *A. aconitifolia* var. *glabra*; c. *A. brevipedunculata* 'Elegans'

side segments very unequal; fruit cluster on 2–3 cm long stalk; fruit small, blue-black. Gn 89: 272 (= *Vitis delavayana* Franch.). Middle China. 1900. Hardy. z5 Fig. 109. ⌀

A. humulifolia Bge. High growing, young twigs glabrous, occasionally also long haired; leaves broadly ovate, 7–10 cm long, 3–5 lobed, lobes often only slightly distinct, acute to acuminate, coarsely dentate, base truncate to lightly cordate, glossy green and glabrous above, bluish white beneath, glabrous or pubescent; fruits only a few together, 6–8 mm thick, usually light yellow with bluish blush or solid yellow or light blue, October. RH 1886: 2; Gn 7: 199. N. China. 1868. Hardy. z5 ⌀

This species is often confused with *A. brevipedunculata* var. *maximowiczii*, but easily distinguished by its much coarser leaves with whitish undersides and the yellow-blue fruit.

A. japonica (Thunb.) Mak. Ornamental and creeping, with bulbous rhizomes, branches glabrous; leaves 3–5 parted, leaflets partly pinnate, partly pinnatifid, mid-dle pinnae 4–10 cm long, others much smaller, rachis broad winged, leaflets ovate-oblong, acute, sparsely and coarsely dentate, dark green, glossy; fruit 5–7 mm thick, light violet, darker dots, September–October. DL 2: 271; Gfl 1867: Pl. 531 (= *A. serjaniaefolia* Bge.). N. China, Japan. 1867. Easily recognized by its winged midrib and partly pinnate leaves. z7 Fig. 107. ⌀

A. leeoides (Maxim.) Planch. Branches glabrous, with lenticels; leaves always bi- or tri-pinnate, 12–30 cm long, glabrous or nearly so, leaflets stalked, ovate to oblong, occasionally rather narrow, 4–7 cm long, with teeth appressed, basal 3 parted or lobed, base acute; tendrils 2 branched; inflorescence finely pubescent, large, usually terminal, flowers short stalked, green-yellow, July–August; fruit globose, red. Japan, in forests and thickets. (In cultivation in Europe?) z7 ⌀

A. megalophylla Diels & Gilg. Climbing to 10 m high, twigs glabrous, thick, with large winter buds, internodes very long; leaves long petioled, bi-pinnate, smaller ones pinnate, 20–50 cm long, outstanding

Fig. 109. **Ampelopsis** Left, *A. orientalis*; middle, *A. megalophylla* (only in part); right, *A. delavayana* (from Schneider)

blue-green, leaflets ovate, to 10 cm long, coarsely crenate, glossy green above, blue-green beneath, veins terminating in the toothed margin; flowers in abundantly branched umbellate panicles; fruit teardrop shaped, 8 mm thick, purple at first, then black, September—October, in long stalked, 10—15 cm wide, pendulous clusters. BM 8537; Gn 65: 45 (= *Vitis megalophylla* Veitch). W. China. 1894. z5 Fig. 109. ∅

A. orientalis (Lam.) Planch. Climber or a loose open shrub with few tendrils, branches glabrous, striped; leaves simple, bi- or tri-pinnate, petiole somewhat as long as the internodes, leaflets 9—15, ovate, rhomboid to obovate-oblong, 2—7 cm long, large toothed, terminal leaflet often with rounded base; flowers 4 parted; fruit red, like currants (= *Vitis orientalis* Boiss.). Asia Minor, Syria. 1818. Good for pot culture. z6 Fig. 107, 109. ∅ ⚭

A. vitifolia (Boiss.) Planch. Closely related to *A. bodninieri*, but without tendrils, also glabrous; leaves broadly ovate, 4—7 cm long, undivided or lightly 3 lobed, coarsely dentate with acuminate, triangular teeth, base truncate or somewhat cordate; cymes thin stalked. SH 2: 213 k-l (= *A. aegirophylla* Planch.; *Vitis persica* Boiss.). Iran, Turkestan to NW. Himalaya. 1885. z6 ∅

Ampelopsis species are rarely found in cultivation, although most of them are winter hardy and quite interesting. The lovely foliage and fruit, with its occasionally blue-green or orange-yellow tones, are both conspicuous and decorative. The species may be propagated by seed or cuttings, the variegated forms only by cuttings.

Lit. Suessenguth, K.: *Vitaceae;* in Engler-Prantl, Nat. Pfl. Famil. Bd. 20d, 313—315, 1953.

AMYGDALUS see: **PRUNUS**

ANAGYRIS L. — LEGUMINOSAE

Deciduous shrubs, somewhat resembling *Laburnum*; leaves 3 parted, stipules connate; flowers in short racemes on short side branches; calyx cup-shaped with 5 somewhat even teeth, all petals distinct and erect, standard petal distinctly shorter than the wing and keel petals (important for identification), anthers completely distinct; pods long, flat, many seeded. — 2 species in the Mediterranean area, Asia Minor, Canary Islands.

Anagyris foetida L. Shrub, to 3 m high, upright, foul smelling (when crushed), young twigs with compressed pubescence, leaflets oblong, acute or somewhat emarginate, 4—8 cm long, dark green above, gray-green from pubescence beneath; flowers grouped 5—20, yellow, standard petal with brown patch, not fragrant, April—May; fruit 10 cm long, to 2 cm wide, curved. S. Europe, Asia Minor; forming dense thickets. 1750. z8 Fig. 110. **d** ○ ⚙

Fig. 110. *Anagyris foetida.* Twig, flowering branch, calyx, petals (from Lauche)

A. latifolia Brouss. ex Willd. Semi-evergreen shrub, 3—5 m high in its habitat, young twigs undulating, knotty, glabrous; leaves trifoliate, petiole 2—3 cm long, leaflets short stalked, thick, elliptic-lanceolate, to 5 cm long, 1.5 cm wide, deep green above, more bluish beneath; flowers few in axillary, short racemes, yellow, standard much shorter than the wing, calyx cupshaped, with 5 large teeth, October—February; pods to 10 cm long, brown. KGC 20. Canary Islands. Rather rare in the wild, but of great garden merit. z9 ✤

ANDRACHNE L. — EUPHORBIACEAE

Low shrubs or subshrubs or perennials; leaves alternate, margins entire, with small stipules; flowers usually monoecious, small, yellowish-green, male in axillary fascicles, female single; petals smaller than the sepals; anthers shorter than the sepals; female flowers often without petals; pistils 3, with 2 slits; fruit a loculicidal capsule. — 22 species in N. America, Asia, Africa and S. Europe.

Andrachne colchica Fisch. et May. Deciduous shrub, some 60 cm high, finely branched, twigs nodding, glabrous, foliage dense; leaves oval, obtuse, margin somewhat thickened, base rounded, 0.8—2 cm long; petals filamentous and much shorter than the sepals, July to August; fruit globose, 5 mm thick, light brown. SL 99. Asia Minor, Caucasus. Before 1900. z6

A. cordifolia (Dcne.) Muell. Arg. Shrub, to 1 m high; leaves ovate to oblong, 2—5 cm long, base rounded, occasionally also cordate, underside softly pubescent; petals spathulate, flowers also somewhat larger than the above species; fruit flattened globular, 6 mm thick. NW. Himalaya, China. z6

A. fruticosa L. Flowers greenish white, leaves 2.5—4 cm long. BM 1862. S. China. Greenhouse shrub. Not winter hardy in temperate zones. z8

A. phyllanthoides (Nutt.) Muell. Arg. Shrub to 1 m high, only the young, angular twigs pubescent, otherwise glabrous; leaves elliptic, 1—2 cm long, obtuse or emarginate, usually both sides with scattered pubescence; flowers 5—6 mm wide, sepals oblong, petals of male flowers narrow obovate, somewhat shorter than the sepals, dentate, female flowers not dentate, July—August; fruit some 8 mm thick. BB ed. 2; 2: 453 (= *A. roemeriana* Muell. Arg.; *A. reverchonii* Coult.). N. America; USA; Missouri to Arkansas and Texas. 1899. z7

A. telephioides L. Low subshrub, twigs very thin, glabrous, whole plant blue-green, very densely branched; leaves obovate to elliptic, acute, some 6 mm long; flowers 4 mm wide, usually solitary, axillary, sepals white margined, June—August. Mediterranean region to Afghanistan. z8

All the mentioned species are only of botanical interest or for collectors. The winter hardy species will tolerate a wide range of soils, but prefer a sunny location. Only *A. telephioides* requires a dry, alkaline soil. Propagates readily from seed.

Lit. Pojarkova, A. J.: Icrementa ad monographiam generum *Andrachne* L. et *Leptopus* Dcne.; Notulae Syst. Herb. Inst. Bot. Komarov. **20**, 251—274, 1960. With aerial maps (in Russian).

ANDROMEDA L. — ERICACEAE

Evergreen, creeping, low shrubs; leaves narrow, margins entire, short petioled, alternate; flowers in terminal, nodding umbels; calyx small, 5 lobed, corolla globose-urceolate (pitcher-shaped), with 5 short, reflexed tips; filaments 10, anthers with 2 thin awns, opening at the apex; fruit a nearly globose, small capsule, 5 chambered; seed numerous, small, oval, smooth. — 2 species in the colder areas of the Northern Hemisphere.

A. × *acuminata* see: **Leucothoe topulifolia**

A. × *axillaris* see: **Leucothoe axillaris**

A. calyculata see: **Chamaedaphne**

A. ferruginea see: **Lyonia ferruginea**

A. glaucophylla Link. 10—30 cm high, mat forming, twigs blue-green; leaves oblong-linear, 2—3.5 cm long,

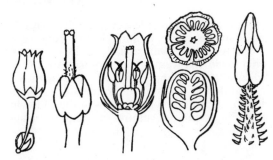

Fig. 111. *Andromeda polifolia.* Flower, ovary, flower in longitudinal section, fruit in longitudinal and cross section, anther (from Lauche)

white tomentose beneath; flowers whitish-pink, peduncle under 1 cm long (during the flowering period), calyx whitish, May—June. BB 2767; PAr 337. Northern N. America, in peat bogs together with *Vac-

cinium spp., *Ledum, Chamaedaphne calyculata, Sarracenia*, etc. The foliage is poisonous, especially for sheep. Much less common in cultivation than the following species. z2 # ⊕

var. **latifolia** (Ait.) Rehd. Like the species, but with wider leaves, oblong.

A. ligustrina see: **Lyonia ligustrina**

A. lucida see: **Leucothoe populifolia, Lyonia lucida**

A. ovalifolia see: **Lyonia ovalifolia**

A. polifolia L. Bog Rosemary. Creeping, usually not over 10 cm high, occasionally to 20 cm, twigs thin, erect, little branched; leaves often pointing in one direction, linear, 3—5 cm long, margin rolled under, dark green above, blue-green or light green beneath; flowers grouped 3—5 at the branch terminals, white to light pink, calyx reddish, May—July. GSP 395. N. Europe, N. Asia, N. America. 1786. Typical plant of the *Sphagnum* peat bog.

In North German bogs rather rare, but common in Scandinavia, especially Lapland. z2 Plate 29; Fig. 111. # **H w** ⊕

In addition the following cultivars originate in Japan:

'**Compacta**'. Grows densely compact and enclosed, foliage dense; leaves pea-green, distinctly blue-green beneath; flower luminous pink, May—June (= 'Nana'). ⊕

'**Compacta Alba**'. Compact grower; flowers pure white. Found in the mountains north of Tokyo. Introduced 1959. ⊕

'**Grandiflora Compacta**'. Grows compactly, foliage blue-green; flowers coral-pink. GC 1965 (I) :473. Found in the wild in Japan; propagated in Boskoop, Holland. ⊕

'**Major**'. Like the species, but taller growing, leaves wider and more gray. ⊕

'**Minima**'. Prostrate, some 7—8 cm high; leaves linear thread-like, 12—15 mm long, deep green above, blue-green beneath; flowers light pink, May—June (= 'Ericoides'). Found in the mountains of N. Japan. ⊕

A. populifolia see: **Leucothoe populifolia**

A. racemosa see: **Leucothoe racemose**

The leaves are (or were) used in Russia to make tan and black dyes; they contain Andromedotoxin ($C_{31}H_{51}O_{10}$) and can cause dizziness, cramps and vomiting in humans.

The plants will tolerate some dryness in culture if provided a cool, sandy humus soil and a semishaded location. In culture the leaves are generally somewhat larger than in the wild.

A large number of plants are found in nursery catalogues under the name "Andromeda"; the following is a list of the valid names for those plants. The descriptions for those species may be found elsewhere in this work.

Andromeda

acuminata Ait.	= *Leucothoe populifolia*
— *arborea* L.	= *Oxydendron arboreum*
— *axillaris* Lam.	= *Leucothoe axillaris*
— *calyculata* L.	= *Chamaedaphne calyculata*
— *catesbaei* Walt.	= *Leucothoe fontanesiana*
— *floribunda* Pursh.	= *Pieris floribunda*
— *formosa* Wall.	= *Pieris formosa*
— *japonica* Thunb.	= *Pieris japonica*
— *mariana* L.	= *Lyonia mariana*
— *nana* Maxim.	= *Arcterica nana*
— *nitida* Sims.	= *Zenobia pulverulenta* f. *nitida*
— *racemosa* L.	= *Leucothoe racemosa*
— *recurvata* Buckl.	= *Leucothoe recurvata*
— *speciosa* D. Don	= *Zenobia pulverulenta* f. *nitida*

Lit. Ingram, J.: Studies in the cultivated *Ericaceae*. 3. *Andromeda*; Baileya **11**, 37—38, 1963 (lacks descriptions of the cultivars).

ANEMOPAEGMA Mart. ex Meissn. — BIGNONIACEAE

Climbing tropical plants; leaves opposite, with 3 or 5 leaflets, margins entire, terminal leaflet often absent or forming a tendril; flowers usually white or yellowish, seldom purple, in racemes; calyx truncate or with 5 tiny teeth; corolla somewhat 2 lipped, limb with 5 tips, these rounded or emarginate; anthers 4. — Some 30 species in tropical America, of these the following is occasionally found in culture in Mediterranean climates.

Anemopaegma chamberlaynii (Sims) Bur. & Schum. Strong growing, tropical vine; leaves ovate, acuminate, tapering to the base, glossy above, lighter beneath; flowers luminous yellow, large, tubular or funnel-form, with relatively short, protruding limb; in axillary racemes, September. BR 741 (as *Bignonia aequinoctalis*); FS 235 (= *A. racemosum*). Brazil. 1879. z9 # ⊕

ANNONA L. — ANNONACEAE

Evergreen or deciduous shrubs or small trees; leaves alternate, in 2 rows, without stipules; flowers not in the leaf axils, often opposite a leaf or terminal, solitary or grouped, calyx 3 parted, petals usually 6, in 2 rings, the inner ring often much smaller or absent; stamens and pistils numerous, the latter eventually developing into an aggregate fruit, many chambered, fleshy, edible, epidermis scaly, veined or smooth. — Some 120 species

in the warmer regions, mainly America. Of the 5 species described *A. cherimola, muricata* and *squamosa* have the most importance economically. The culture is very much like that of the *Citrus* although *Annona* grows best and develops its most flavorful fruit in high areas. In Europe it is only grown commonly on Madeira Island, Portugal.

Annona cherimola Mill. Cherimoya. Small tree, to 6 m high, young twigs yellow tomentose; leaves oval-lanceolate, not punctate, remaining velvety pubescent beneath, strongly aromatic; flowers usually solitary, opposite the leaves, nodding, fragrant, outer petals linear-oblong, 3 cm long, outer greenish yellow to reddish brown, inner light yellow or whitish with purple basal spot, July; fruit nearly globose to cordate, 10 cm long, exterior covered with U-shaped deep scales, fruit pulp white, pleasantly sour. BM 2011 (as *A. tripetala*). Peru. 1739. z9 # ✕

A. glabra L. Alligator Pear. Small tree, 10—12 m high, often smaller, young twigs glabrous; leaves oval-oblong, glabrous, glossy green; flowers 2, opposite the leaves, fragrant, outer petals yellowish or greenish-yellow, with a deep red basal spot inside, inner petals narrower, dark red or red spotted inside, July; fruit cone shaped, round at the tip, some 7 cm long, green-yellow, smooth, fruit pulp cream-white, not edible. BM 4226 (as *A. palustris*); BC 211. Peru; USA, Florida; W. Africa. 1739. z9 #

A. muricata L. Soursop, Prickly Annona. Large shrub, 4—5 m high; leaves obovate to oval-lanceolate, 12—20 cm long, dark green, leathery, glossy, underside red-brown pubescent at first, later becoming glabrous, concave punctate in the axils of the major veins, unpleasant smelling; flowers solitary, outer petals thick, fleshy, ovate, green outside, yellow and spotted inside, inner petals smaller; fruit acute ovate, very large, weighing to 2 kilograms, dark green, epidermis diamond patterned, every diamond with a small, fleshy, reflexed thorn in the middle, unpleasant smelling, fruit pulp white, juicy, sour, too sour to eat raw, but excellent mixed in drinks, ice cream, etc. BC 209. Trop. America, West Indies. 1656. z9 # ✕

A. reticulata L. Ox Heart. Deciduous shrub, 4—6 m high, twigs red-brown pubescent at first, later becoming glabrous; leaves lanceolate, acute, somewhat punctate, glabrous; flowers in fascicles on the current year's wood, nodding, not axillary, outer petals narrow-oblong, fleshy, olive-green or yellowish outside, inside

ANOPTERUS Labill. — SAXIFRAGACEAE

Evergreen shrubs or small trees; leaves alternate, oblong, tough leathery, without stipules; flowers white, in terminal racemes, calyx with 6—9 persistent teeth, petals and stamens 6—9; fruit an oblong, bivalvate capsule, seed winged. — 1 species in Australia and 1 in Tasmania.

Anopterus glandulosus Labill. 2—4 m high in its habitat, also occasionally a small tree; leaves bunched at the ends of the branches, projected outward, lanceolate-elliptic, 7—17 cm long, 2—4 cm wide, tough to thick, glossy, glandular serrate; flowers in 7—15 cm long, somewhat pendulous racemes, April—May; petals usually 6, white, occasionally a trace of light pink, calyx 6 pointed. LHN 112; CFTa 44. Tasmania. 1823. z8 Fig. 112. # ◗ ⊕

often reddish and with purple basal spot; fruit ovate, 7—12 cm wide, smooth, surface with a net-like diamond pattern, reddish-brown on the sunny side or when ripe, ripening early winter, weight some 500g, sweet tasting, but without exceptional quality. BM 2911; BC 213. Trop. America. 1619. In tropical America, Cuba and elsewhere erroneously referred to as "Cherimoya" (*A. cherimola*) which is totally different in appearance and much preferred. z9 ✕

A. squamosa L. Custard Apple, Sweet Sop. Large deciduous shrub, 4—6 m high, irregularly branched, young twigs undulate, pubescent at first; leaves nearly in 2 rows, oblong-lanceolate, acute to short acuminate, finely pubescent at first, later becoming nearly completely glabrous, light green, punctate on both sides, petiole pubescent; flowers 2—4 in fascicles, opposite the leaves, occasionally solitary, resemblig those of *A. reticulata*, greenish-yellow outside, inside reddish at the base, inner petals very small, keeled on the outside; fruit about the size of an orange, globose to cordate, yellow-green and large scaled (like a pine cone) and usually pruinose, fruit pulp white, grainy, very sweet and pleasant tasting, seed dark brown to black. BM 3095; BC 214. Trop. America. 1739 z9 ⓕ India. ✕

A. triloba see: **Asimina triloba**

All species need a deep peaty soil and warm night temperatures. Propagated by seed, which will germinate in about 4 weeks and grow vigorously for 6—7 years. Cultivars propagated by cleft grafts on *A. reticulata*.

Lit. Movry-Toy-Wolff: Miscellaneous Tropical and subtropical Florida Fruits; 96 S. Univ. Florida Agr. Exp. Serv. Bull. 109 (1941).

Fig. 112. *Anopterus glandulosus* (from Curtis)

Very beautiful flowering shrub for milder climates. Somewhat resembes *Clethra arborea*, but growth stiffer, flowers larger. In cultivation in many botanic gardens.

ANTHYLLIS L. — LEGUMINOSAE

Evergreen or deciduous shrubs or perennials; leaves alternate, pinnate or tri-foliate or simple; flowers small, papilionaceous corolla, grouped in attractive terminal or axillary heads, fruit pods ovate to linear, with 1 or more seeds, calyx persistent, swollen after petal fall. — 50 species in Europe, N. Africa and Asia Minor.

Anthyllis barba-jovis L. Jupiters Beard. Evergreen shrub, growth narrowly upright, becoming 2—3 m high, totally silver-gray silky pubescent; leaves pinnate, with 9—19 leaflets, linear-oblong, 1—2 cm long, all rather even-sized, gray, especially silky pubescent beneath, often rolled inward at the base; flowers light yellow, in axillary, globose heads, about 2.5 cm wide, May—June. BM 1927. Mediterranean region. 1640. Very attractive plant for its foliage, but must be over-wintered in a greenhouse, flowers in March. z8 Fig. 115. # **d** ○ ∅

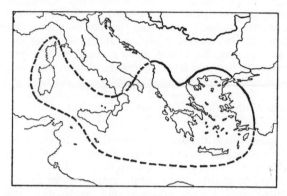

Fig. 114. Distribution of *Anthyllis hermanniae* (from Rickli)

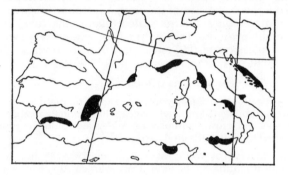

Fig. 113. *Anthyllis barba-jovis* (from Rickli and Fenaroli, completed)

A. cytisoides L. Shrub, to 60 m, twigs woody, upright, straight or undulating, not thorny, finely gray or whitish tomentose, lower leaves simple, the higher tri-foliate, terminal leaflet narrow elliptic, much larger than the others; flowers solitary or 2—3 in an axil, oval-elliptic bracts, inflorescence a spike, yellow, calyx 4.5—7 mm long, shaggy pubescent, with 5 even-sized teeth, all shorter than the tube; single seeded. PMe 69. S. and E. Spain, Balearic Island, S. France. z6 ✤

A. hermanniae L. Bushy, deciduous shrub, 40—50 cm high, twigs bent and growth erratic, undulating here and there, short gray pubescent, with thorny tips; leaves generally simple (rarely tri-foliate), linear-obovate, 1—2.5 cm long, rounded apex, tapering to the base, more or less appressed silky pubescence, especially berneath; flowers grouped 3—5, axillary, in short stalked fasicles, about 8 mm long, gold-yellow, June (April in its native habitat). BM 2576. Corsica to Asia Minor. 1700. Very pretty for sunny rock gardens. z6 Fig. 115. **d** ○ ✤

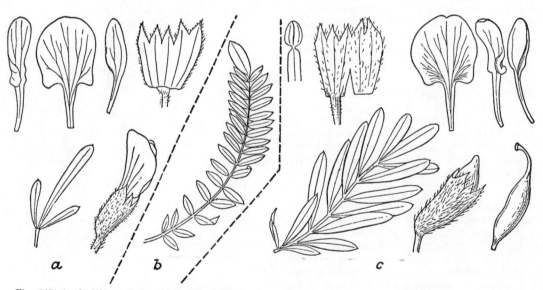

Fig. 115. **Anthyllis**. a. *A. hermanniae*, leaf, flower, flower parts, enlarged; b. *A. montana*, c. *A. barba-jovis*, leaf, flower with parts, fruit (from Schneider)

var. **aspalathi** (DC.) Rouy & Foucaud. Total plant more thorny, less pubescent, inflorescence with 1–3 flowers (= *A. spiniflora* L, Hér.; *Aspalathus cretica* L.). Crete. 1910. z7

A. montana L. Subshrub, growth mat-like, base woody, with many twigs about 10 cm high, very dense with long pubescence; leaves 3–8 cm long, pinnate, with 13–31 leaflets, these linear-oblong, 6–12 mm long, sessile, densely whitish pubescent above, thinner pubescence beneath; flowers pink-red with darker middle, many in hemispherical, 3–4 cm wide, long stalked heads, June. BMns 333. S. and SE. Europe, mountains from Spain to the Balkans. 1759. z6 Plate 29; Fig. 115. **d** ○ ⊕

Quite a variable species distinguished by its 3 rather similar subspecies and 2 cultivars:

'**Atropurpurea**'. Flowers black-purple. ⊕

ssp. **jacquinii** (A. Kern.) Hayek. Terminal leaflet hardly differing from the others in form and size; calyx tube and calyx teeth each 3–4 mm; corolla pink; bracts usually longer than the flowers (= *A. jacquinii* A. Kern.). E. Alps and mountains in the Balkan Peninsula. z6 ⊕

ssp. **hispanica** (Deegen & Hervier) Cullen. Terminal leaflet rounded above, form somewhat differing from that of the side leaflets. S. Spain. z8 ⊕

ssp. **montana**. Terminal leaflet hardly differing from the others in form and size; calyx tube and calyx teeth each 4–5; corolla purple; bracts normally not surpassing the flower. Alps, from France to Austria and the Apennines. z6 ⊕

'**Rubra**'. Dark pink, darker than the species. ⊕

All species for very sunny and warm areas, the latter two species especially for the rock garden. All tolerate very poor, gravelly soil. Dislike moisture in winter. All propagated easily from seed or cuttings.

ANTIRRHINUM L. — SCROPHULARIACEAE

Herbaceous perennials, seldom shrubs; leaves simple, opposite, the higher leaves frequently also alternate; flower bisexual, irregular, calyx 5 parted, corolla 2 lipped, base broader on one side, the lower side of the corolla throat arched up so as to be nearly closed, with 4 viable stamens, the 5th replaced by a gland; fruit a capsule. — Some 40 species in Pacific N. America and W. Mediterranean region; only a few actually shrubby. Some others woody at the base, but they will not be covered here.

Antirrhinum sempervirens Lapeyr. Low, soft pubescent shrublets, often procumbent, twigs sparse, to 20 cm long; leaves narrow-elliptic to oblong, usually opposite, pubescent, petiole 3–7 mm; flowers white to yellowish, lilac striped, with orange-yellow spotted throat, 1–1.5 cm long, 5–6 mm lanceolate calyx tips, June–September; fruit capsule 6 mm, glandular pubescent. PSw 138. Central Pyrenees. For shady locations on lime soils. z7 ⊕

A. speciosum Gray. Evergreen, wide branched shrub, 0.5–1.5 cm high, twigs green, glabrous or softly pubescent; leaves alternate or 3 together, ovate-oblong, 2.5–3.5 cm long, thick, leathery, margins entire, both sides usually totally glabrous and dark green, petiole short; flowers axillary and terminal, some 2.5 cm long, nice red, March–June. MS 604 (= *Gambelia speciosa* Nutt.). S. California, on the islands aong the coast. z8 Fig. 116. # **d** ○ ⊕

Fig. 116. *Antirrhinum speciosum* (from McMinn)

Little cultivated, but highly regarded in California as a very desirable, long-flowering shrub, requiring little care and easily propagated from seed and cuttings. Requires a well drained soil.

Lit. De Wolf, G. P.: Notes on cultivated **Scrophlariaceae**. 2. *Antirrhinum* and *Asarina*; Baileya **4**, 55–58, 1956, with ill.

APHANANTHE Planch. -- ULMACEAE

Deciduous or evergreen trees or shrubs; leaves simple, alternate, petiolate, with stipules, serrate, ordered in 2 rows, with straight veins terminating in the toothed margin (the closely related genus *Celtus* has veins bending before reaching the margin); flowers always unisexual, monoecious, appearing with the foliage, the male flowers axillary at the base of the young twigs,

female flowers in the leaf axils of the higher leaves; calyx 4 parted (rarely 5), stamens 5, pistils 2; fruit a small, ovate drupe. — 3 to 4 species in Asia and Australia (including 1 in China) and another in Mexico.

Aphananthe aspera (Thunb.) Planch. Tree, to 20 m, crown dense and rounded, bark gray-brown, flaking in fine scales, young twigs red-brown, silky pubescent, with white lenticels; leaves ovate-oblong, 5–9 cm long, acuminate, 3 veined at the base, serrate, venation on both sides rough pubescent, base oblique, tough leathery, dark green above, lighter beneath, petiole 5 mm long; flowers greenish, April–May; fruit globose-ovate, 8 mm thick, black, somewhat appressed pubescent. LF 117–118; KIF 1: 56; LWT 30 (= *Celtis muku* Sieb.; = *Homoceltis aspera* Bl.). Japan, Korea, E. China. 1880. z7 Fig. 117.

Of much botanical interest, otherwise of little garden merit; very fast growing, but usually not hardening off well in the fall and so freezing back in the winter.

APOLLONIAS Nees. — LAURACEAE

Evergreen trees or shrubs; leaves alternate, loose, open, venation pinnate; buds naked; flowers small, in axillary or nearly terminal panicles; calyx funnel-form, 6 incised, persistent, 9 fertile anthers, 3 staminodes; fruit an ovate berry, with 6 calyx sections on the base. — 1 species in the Canary Islands and Madeira, and 1 in the E. Indies.

Apollonias canariensis Nees. Barbusano. Usually a tall shrub, but also a tree from 15–30 m, with rough bark on older plants; leaves alternate to nearly opposite, leathery, glabrous, variable in size, usually 6–8 cm long, 3 cm wide, oblong to elliptic, glossy above, petiole thick and short; flowers greenish, fragrant,

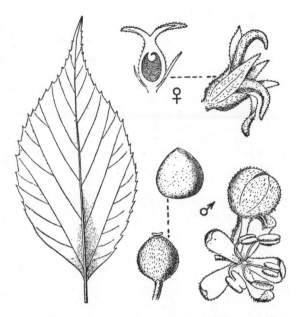

Fig. 117. *Aphananthe aspera*, Leaf, Flower and Fruit (from Blume)

usually 3 in 2–7 cm long panicles; fruit ovate, 1–1.5 cm long, in short cups. BFCa 14, 132; KGC 15 (= *A. barbujana* [Cav.] Bornm.). Canary Islands. z9 # ∅

Cultivated much like *Laurus*.

ARALIA L. — ARALIACEAE

Deciduous shrubs, occasionally small trees, twigs with stout pith, usually thorny; leaves alternate, petiolate, simple to 3-pinnate, without stipules; flowers in umbels, usually grouped in large terminal panicles or cymes; stamens 5, pistils usually 5, distinct or connate at the base; fruit a small berry-like drupe, globose with fleshy exterior, with 2–5 tightly packed "stones". — Some 35, usually weedy species in the temperate zones of the Northern Hemisphere in N. America, Asia and Australia.

Aralia chinensis L. Medium sized shrub, 2–5 m, occasionally a tree to 8 m high, stem usually somewhat prickly; leaves large, 2–3 pinnate, 40–80 cm long, coarse, not prickly or with single prickles, glossy or somewhat rough above, pubescent beneath especially along the veins, acuminate, densely serrate; flowers in large, 25–40 cm long, terminal, pyramidal panicles, with a long main axis, side axes 20–35 cm long, stalks of a single umbel 1–4 cm long, individual flower pedicels 4–6 mm long, flowers white, August–September; fruit globose, 2–3 mm thick. LF 248 (= *A. chinenesis* var. *canescens* Koehne). Manchuria to Yunnan and Szechwan. 1865. z5 Plate 36. **H** ◑ ✧ ∅

This species is nearly always mislabeled in cultivation; and most often *A. elata* is delivered in its place. Distinguished from the more common and similar *A. elata* by the less prickly stem, lower growth habit and nearly sessile leaflets.

var. **dasyphylloides** Hand. Mazz. Leaflets dense yellow bristly above, dense rough bristly-tomentose beneath, especially along the veins, petiole 2–3 mm long. Kiangsi, Hunan, Kwangsi, Kwangtung.

var. **nuda** Nakai. Leaflets smaller than the species, somewhat longer petioled, bluish beneath and glabrous except for the sparsely pubescent midrib; inflorescence finely pubescent, with main axis soon becoming glabrous. 1919.

A. elata Seem. Shrub, to 5 m high, branches usually prickly; leaves large, bipinnate, 40–80 cm long, often prickly, usually with 1 pair of prickles on each branching of the main axis, leaflets thin, glabrous, venation on both sides pubescent when young, acuminate, 5–12 cm long, coarsely and widely serrate; inflorescence a terminal cyme with short rachis and umbel-like protruding side axes, stalk axils pubescent; petals white, August; fruit globose, pentagonal, 3 mm thick, pistils 5, reflexed. NK 16: Pl. 16; BS 223 (= *A. chinensis* var. *mandschurica* [Maxim.] Rehd.). E. Siberia, Manchuria, Korea, Japan. 1830. Much more frequently cultivated than *A. chinensis* and very decorative. z3 Plate 36; Fig. 118. **H** ◑ ✧ ∅

'**Aureo-variegata**'. Leaflets wide, yellow variegated. Commonly seen in Dutch botanic gardens. ∅

'**Pyramidalis**'. Grows narrowly upright; leaves smaller than the species, less outspread, leaflets smaller. 1917.

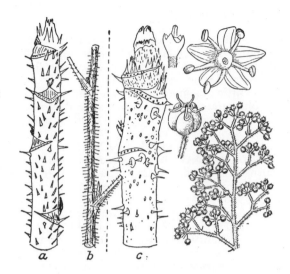

Fig. 118. *Arfalia. a. Twig of A. spinosa*, b. *A. hispida*,
c. *A. elata* with flowers (latter from Shirasawa)

'Variegata'. Leaflets irregularly broad white or gray-white margined. IH 33: 609. Popular variegated form. Plate 47. ⌀

A. hispida Vent. Stoloniferous subshrub, 0.5—1 m high, twigs thin, dense with needle-fine, soft bristles, woody only at the base; leaves petiolate, the highest usually sessile, 10—40 cm long, usually bipinnate, leaflets usually sessile, ovate to lanceolate, acute, coarsely serrate, 3—5 cm long, light green and smooth above, lighter beneath with bristly venation; flowers white, June—July; fruit globose, 8 mm thick, black-red, somewhat pentagonal. BB 2629; GSP 341; BM 1085. Newfoundland to Manitoba, Great Lakes area. 1788. Of slight ornamental value. z3 Fig. 118. **H ◑**

A. japonica see: **Fatsia japonica**

A. nudicaulis L. Subshrub wih far reaching rhizomes; originating from the usually 10 cm long stem are the 20—30 cm long, 3—5 parted leaves, leaflets sessile or short stalked, oval to ovate, 5—12 cm long, acuminate, finely serrate, usually soft pubescent beneath; flowers

greenish, in 2—3 umbels, May—June; fruit globose, dry yet 5 ribbed, purple-black. BB 2628; CWF 338. Newfoundland to Manitoba, Carolina and Missouri; in forests. 1731. z3 **H ◑**

A. sieboldii see: **Fatsia japonica**

A. spinosa L. Hercules' Club, Devil's Walking-stick (in USA). Tall shrub or tree, to 10 m, twigs, stem and leaves prickly, twigs very thick and stiff, to 2.5 cm thick, gray-yellow; leaves 2—3 pinnate, to 70 cm long and 60 cm wide, leaflets ovate, acute, base rounded, 3—8 cm long, sessile, deep green above, glabrous, lighter beneath and often soft pubescent; flowers white, in large, terminal panicles, June—August; fruit ovate, pentagonal, with persistent pistils, in pyramidal clusters; sought after by birds. BB 2626; GTP 307. S. USA; New York to Florida and Texas, in low areas along river banks but only in spotty groups. 1688. z4 Fig. 118. **H ◑ ✧**

The Aralias prefer cool, sandy to humus soil in sunny to semishady areas. Very decorative with thick, prickly stems, large leaves and the whitish inflorescence from midsummer to fall.

The following outline will help the reader to distinguish the very similar *A. chinensis* and *A. elata*:

	A. chinensis	*A. elata*
Leaves	Bipinnate, often prickly	2—3 pinnate. not or only slightly prickly
Leaf margin	Teeth rather large, and widely spaced	Teeth fine, close spaced, often appressed
Inflorescence	Main axis shorter than the side axes, latter 30—45 cm long, inflorescence broad umbrella form	Main axis longer than the side axes, former 25—40 cm long; inflorescence conical

Lit. Li, Hui-Lin: The *Araliaceae* of China, 101—116, Jamaica Plain 1942 (Sargentia II) ● Smith, A.: *Araliaceae*; in North American Flora, 28 B, 3—41, 1944.

ARAUJIA Brot. — ASCLEPIADACEAE

Evergreen, twining shrubs; leaves opposite, simple; flowers white or pink, corolla tube swollen at the base, limb 5 lobed, covered in the bud stage, corolla with 5 scales attached to the middle of the tube; pollen waxy, clumped in every pollen sac; veins often 2-beaked at the tip; fruit a pod; the seeds having long silky pubescence at the tip. — 2 or 3 species in S. America.

Araujia sericofera Brot. Evergreen, high twining shrub, 5 m high or more, young twigs finely soft pubescent; leaves opposite, oval-oblong, acute, base broad cuneate to truncate, 5—10 cm long, 2—5 cm wide, light

green, short tomentose beneath, petiole 1—3 cm; flowers grouped 2—8 in some 5 cm long panicles, situated opposite the leaves, corolla white, swollen at the base, 1.5 cm long, 0.8 cm wide, limb with 5 flared points, September; fruit a large, furrowed, 12 cm long and 5—7 cm thick pod, widest at the base, tapering to the tip, with several deep longitudinal furrows; seed small, but with a 2.5 cm long fasicle of silky hairs at one end. BM 3201; BR 1759 (= *A. albens* Mart.) S. America. 1830. z9 Plate 36. **# ✧ ⚭**

Requires a rich, fertile soil and a sunny location.

ARBUTUS L. — Strawberry Tree — ERICACEAE

Evergreen trees or shrubs with flaking, reddish, brown or white-gray bark; leaves alternate, petiolate, serrate or entire; flowers white, pink, or greenish, pitcher shaped, in terminal, erect or pendulous panicles, calyx persistent; fruit berry-like, with mealy pulp, smooth or grainy-bumpy, 5 chambered, many seeded. — Some 20 species in the Mediterranean region, W. Europe, Asia Minor, N. and Middle America.

Arbutus andrachne L. Grecian Strawberry Tree. In its habitat tree-like, in Northern Europe (as with all the following species) only for container planting; bark red-brown, flaking, young twigs finely glandular pubescent; leaves ovate to oblong, 5—10 cm long, margins entire or occasionally serrate (often both on same twig), dark green above, glabrous, lighter beneath, often also yellow-green, margin often finely ciliate, tough leathery; flowers white, in dense, erect, 10 cm long panicles, March—April; fruit 1—1.5 cm thick, globose, fine warty-grainy, orange-red. DL 1: 225; BM 2024 (= *A. integrifolia* Lam.). Greece, Orient. 1724. Rare in cultivation, most often incorrectly labelled *A. andrachnoides*. z8 Plate 42. # ✧ ⚭

A. × andrachnoides Link (*A. andrachne* × *A. unedo*). Hybrid Strawberry Tree. Intermediate between the parents. Shrub (in England becoming a large shrub or small tree, to 7 m), bark, very attractive red; leaves ovate to lanceolate, acute, 4—10 cm long, gradually narrowing to the base, margin always finely serrate, more or less pubescent beneath; flowers pitcher shaped, ivory white, in terminal, leafy, somewhat pendulous panicles, in fall or spring; fruit some 1.5 cm thick, but seldom developing, not as rough as *A. unedo*. BR 619 (= *A. hybrida* Ker; *A. serratifolia* Lodd.). Found wild among the parents in Greece, but also allegedly hybridized by Osborn in Fulham, England about 1800. Occasionally the plant will favor one or the other parents in appearance. z8 Plate 37, 41, 42. # ✧ ∅ ⚭

A. arizonica (A. Gray) Sarg. Tree, 10—15 m, stem with gray to white bark; leaves oblong-lanceolate, 4—8 cm long, margins entire, base cuneate, glabrous, underside lighter than above; flowers white, in loose, 5—7 cm long, erect panicles, March—April; fruit round to oblong, deep orange-red. GF 4: 54 (= *A. xalapensis* var. *arizonica* A. Gray). Mountains of SW. USA, from New Mexico to S. Arizona to Northern Mexico. z6 Fig. 119. # ✧ ⚭

A. canariensis Lindl. Shrub to small tree, 2—7 m high; leaves oblong-lanceolate, rather soft, serrate, occasionally somewhat pubescent on the midrib beneath, otherwise glabrous and bluish; flowers greenish white, occasionally somewhat tubular, rounded-pitcher shaped, in terminal, leafy, glandular, erect panicles, May—June; fruit red, grainy-warty. BM 1577; KGC 36 (= *A. procera* Soland.) Canary Islands. 1796. z8 #✧⚭✖

A. menziesii Pursh. Madrona. A tree in its habitat, to 20 m high, with thick stem and completely exfoliating bark, stem eventually completely smooth and cinnamon-brown; leaves ovate, 5—12 cm long, obtuse, margins entire or somewhat serrate, dark glossy green above, blue-green beneath, with scattered pubescence; flowers white, in terminal, erect, rather pyramidal panicles, some 7—20 cm long, May; fruit globose, orange-red, some 1 cm thick. SPa 200; BNns 275 (= *A. procera* Dougl.). NW. America, coastal regions from SW. British Columbia to California. z8 Plate 37; Fig. 119. # ✧ ∅ ⚭

A. unedo L. Strawberry Tree. A large shrub or tree in its habitat, to 10 m, bark rough and scaly, twigs glandular pubescent when young; leaves elliptic-oblong, 5—10 cm long, acute, serrate, very glossy above, both sides glabrous; flowers white to light pink, in 5 cm long and equally wide, pendulous panicles, flowering along with ripened fruit, October—December; fruit to 2 cm thick, globose, orange-red, exterior very grainy, edible, but tasteless. HF 2040; HM 2675—2676. In cultivation for ages. SW. Ireland toAsia Minor. z8 Plate 42; Fig. 119. #✧ ⚭ ✖

'Compacta'. Grows much denser, lower, fewer flowers.

'Integerrima'. Leaves always entire (not serrate), but with form varying from elliptic to oblong or lanceolate. BM 2319.

'Quercifolia. Leaves with irregular, large teeth, especially at the apex.

'Rubra'. Flowers deep pink, fruit somewhat smaller than the species. BMns 203 (= var. *Croomei* hort.). Found in 1835 in Glengariff, Ireland. Should be significantly more winter hardy.

A. xalapensis H. B. K. Shrub, 2.5—5 m high; leaves oval to ovate-oblong, margin entire to crenate, glabrous or pubescent beneath; flowers reddish, corolla abruptly narrowing above the middle. BM 4595; SS 5:232. Mexico. z8 Fig. 119. # ✧ ⚭

In colder regions only used as tub plants, however in warmer regions succeeds in open areas. Very beautiful with the colorful contrasts of flower, fruit, leaves and bark. Prefers a nutrient rich soil, lime free (with the exception of *A. unedo* which tolerates alkaline soils). Propagated from cuttings or seed.

Fig. 119. **Arbutus**. a. *A. unedo*; b. *A. arizonica*; c. *A. mensiesii*; d. *A. xalapensis*. — **Ardisia**. e. *A. japonica*; f. *A. crispa*, fruit, cross section, enlarged (from Baillon, Sargent, Sudworth and Kerner)

ARCTERICA Cov. — ERICACEAE

A monotypic genus, which would otherwise be included in *Cassiope* or *Pieris*, but differing from *Pieris* in the 2–3 whorled leaves, and from *Cassiope* in the form of the leaf. 1 species in NE. Asia, Bering Strait.

Arcterica nana Mak. Growth habit cushion-form, the fine twigs pubescent, flat to the ground, cushion 5–10 cm high; leaves in whorls of 3, seldom 2, ovate some 1 cm long, margins rolled inward, petioled, leathery, both sides completely glabrous, glossy above; flowers rounded-pitcher shaped, with 5 short, erect tips, white, fragrant, in terminal fascicles or racemes, grouped 3–8, April–May, often flowering again in fall; stamens 7–10. JRHS 1935: 153 (= *Pieris nana* [Maxim.] Mak.; *Andromeda nana* Maxim.; *Arcterica oxyococcoides* Cov.). NE. Asia, Bering Strait, N. Japan. z3 Fg. 120. # H ⊕

For semi-shaded areas in the rock garden, acid soil, well drained, addition of peat helpful; fully winter hardy; effective in mass plantings.

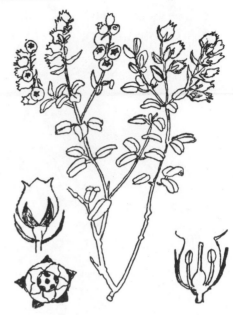

Fig. 120. *Arcterica nana* (from Chittenden)

ARCTOSTAPHYLOS Adans. — Bearberry — ERICACEAE

Evergreen shrubs, partly procumbent, in their habitat large shrubs or small trees, twigs often very curvy and with smooth, reddish or brownish bark on the older stems or rough and scaly, twigs densely foliate; leaves alternate, simple, occasionally sessile, usually entire and obtuse, often appearing the same on both sides; flowers in terminal panicles or racemes, small, nodding, corolla pitcher shaped (urceolate) or campanulate, with 4–5 tips; calyx 5 parted with broad tips, distinct; stamens 8–10, enclosed; ovary with 4–10 chambers, fruit a smooth or warty, globose, berry-like drupe with 4–10 (usually 5) nutlets. — Some 70 species in N. and Middle America, mostly in California, 1 species over the entire Northern Hemisphere.

Arctostaphylos alpinus see: **Arctous alpinus**

A. andersonii A. Gray. Shrub, erect, 1–4 m high, with a distinct stem or branching from the base, bark smooth, dark red-brown, young twigs thick and short pubescent, interspersed with stiff bristles, often with glandular heads; leaves oblong to oblong-ovate, 3–7 cm long, pale or dark green, glabrous above, glabrous to glandular beneath, acute, with basal lobes, margins entire, finely serrate nearer the base, sessile or nearly so; flowers in large, sessile panicles with pubescent and glandular rachis, corolla white to pink, 6–7 mm long, December–January; ovaries densely glandular, with divisible fruits. MS 490; BM 280 ns. USA, California, near Santa Cruz, sandy or gravelly slopes. Quite variable and therefore not easy to identify. z8 Plate 48. # ⚭

A. canescens Eastw. Upright shrub, 1–2 m high, usually much smaller, growth dense and gnarled, older stems with dark red, smooth bark, young twigs densely white tomentose, also the young leaves; leaves ovate to oblong to rounded, projected outward, 2–4 cm long, becoming much less pubescent with age, petiole 5–8 mm long, pubescent; flowers in short, dense panicles with white tomentose rachis; corolla pink, 8–9 mm long; ovaries densely white pubescent, not glandular, December–January; fruit flattened-spherical, 8 mm thick, brown, nutlet divisible. MS 476. USA, California, dry and gravelly mountainsides. z7 #

A. columbiana Piper. Shrub, upright, branching from the base or single stemmed, 1–3 m high, bark red-brown, smooth, young twigs white tomentose and pubescent; leaves ovate to oblong, tomentose when young, later becoming rather glabrous, acute, 2–7 cm long, base rounded to obtuse, petiole 3–7 mm long; flowers in terminal, dense, tomentose-bristly pubescent panicles, March–May; corolla white, 6 mm long; ovaries densely white pubescent, pubescence often glandular; fruit light red, flattened sphere, usually white pubescent and sticky, 8 mm thick. MS 473; NF 11: 100; CWF 378. N. California to British Columbia. Often confused with *A. tomentosa*! z7 #

A. edmundsii J. T. Howell. Low shrub, only 0.5 m high, but 3 m wide or more from the rooting branches, young branches with erect pubescence; leaves elliptic to ovate or rounded, apex rounded and mucronulate,

Fig. 121. *Arctostaphylos* a. *A. uva-ursi*; b. *A. tomentosa*; c. *A. pungens*; d. *A. manzanita* (from Bot. Mag., Schroeter)

some 2.5 cm long, without stomata on the upper side; flowers pink, in small, dense racemes; fruit brown. California, only in Monterey, at the mouth of the Little Sur River. Best of all the low growing types. z8 # ✤

A. glauca Lindl. Shrub, upright, 1.5−7 m high, with short, distinct stem and usually flat-rounded crown, bark smooth, dark red, young twigs usually blue-green and often somewhat glandular pubescent, but usually glabrous; leaves round to broad ovate, obtuse to acute, 2.5−4.5 cm long, petiole short, thick, leaves and petiole glabrous, blue-green; flowers in dense, wide, short panicles, corolla white, 7−8 cm long, ovaries glandular viscid, March−April; fruit round to oblong, 12−15 mm wide, glandular-viscid, with firm pit. MS 450. S. California, hills and mountains. z8 #

A. hookeri G. Don. Shrub, low or mat-forming, 15 cm high to nearly 1 m, side branches rooting upon contact with the ground, bark smooth, dark red-brown, young twigs pubescent or finely gray pubescent on the tips; leaves ovate to elliptic, 1.5−2.5 cm long, glossy, glabrous, thin, acute; flowers few, in small, tight, terminal fascicles, corolla white to pink, 4 mm long, March−April; ovaries glabrous; fruit light red, 6 mm thick, glossy. MS 450. Central California, on the hills along the coast. z8 #

A. manzanita Parry. Shrub, upright, 2−4.5 m high, twigs curving here and there, chocolate-brown, finely

pubescent when young; leaves broad ovate, 2.5−5 cm long, obtuse, mucronate, margin entire, gray-green, leathery, glabrous or finely pubescent; flowers in 3 cm long, dense, pendulous panicles, corolla urceolate, white to pink, some 1 cm long, April−May; fruit plate-like, glabrous, brown. MS 456; BM 8128. USA, California; along the north coast often developing huge, impenetrable thickets of plants to 6 m high. 1897. Leaf color quite variable, from light green to gray green. z8 Fig. 121. # ✤ ⚭ ✂

A. × media Greene (*A. columbiana* × *A. uva-ursi*). Irregularly growing shrub, main stem horizontal, with some 25 mm long, vertical branches; leaves obovate, obtuse, to somewhat acute, some 2.5 cm long, tapering to the base, more or less softly pubescent beneath; flowers in short, compact, terminal racemes, corolla white to pink, urceolate, April; fruits flattened-globose, 6 mm wide. NF 11: 100; CWF 386. USA, Washington State, dry rocky areas. Among the parents. z7 Plate 21. #

A. myrtifolia Parry. Growth low, irregular, side branches often procumbent and rooting, 0.5−1 m high, usually very curvy, bark dark red, with gray waxy coating, young twigs scaly and with erect glandular bristles; leaves elliptic to narrow ovate, usually acute, 5−15 mm long, base obtuse to acute, light green and glossy above, petiole 2 mm long, somewhat bristly;

inflorescence small, rachis pubescent, corolla white to pink, 4 mm long, ovaries pubescent; fruit oblong, 4 mm long, greenish, divisible into 4—5 "fruitlets". MB 444. USA, California. z8 #

A. nevadensis A. Gray. Evergreen, often mat-like shrub, branching irregular, twigs rooting upon contact with the ground, branches upright, 15—40 cm high, bark of older stems smooth, brown to deep red, young twigs distinctly gray pubescent, later becoming viscid; leaf forms quite various, narrow lanceolate, or elliptic to oblanceolate, oval or broad obovate, apex with a distinct, small tip (very important for identification!), 2 to 2.5 (—3.5) cm long, light green, glabrous to sparsely pubescent, petiole 5 mm; inflorescence compact, many flowered, erect, flower stalks pubescent, corolla white to pink, 5 mm long, ovaries glabrous; fruit globose, dark brown. MS 451; BS 1: 319. California; Sierra Nevada, in the higher mountains. z6 #

The plant cultivated under this name in N. Europe is most often actually *A. uva-ursi* or one of its varieties, in any case, not *A. nevandensis*.

A. nummalaria A. Gray. Grows mat-like to hemispherical, branches either somewhat ascending, 2—6 m high, or upright and to 1 m high, twigs soft pubescent and with white bristles, very densely foliate; leaves elliptic to ovate, 1—1.5 long, dark green, glossy, distinctly veined beneath, margin entire to ciliate, round, base somewhat cordate; inflorescence small, flowers 4 parted, corolla white, 4—5 mm long, ovaries sparsely pubescent; fruit oblong, 3—4 mm long, greenish, pits divisible into 4—5 nutlets. MS 445. California, Mendocino coast, dry areas. z6 #

A. patula Greene. Shrub, upright, 1—2 m high, multistemmed, developing a regular crown, bark smooth, chocolate-brown, young twigs with tiny glandular hairs, the glands yellow-green; leaves directed outward, broad oval to oblong or rounded, 2.5—5.5 cm long (usually 4 cm), thick, fresh green, obtuse, base usually rounded, petiole 6—10 mm long, thickly fine pubescent; flowers in loose, wide panicles, rachis with typical yellow-green glands, corolla pink, 5—8 mm long, ovaries glabrous, March—May; fruit dark brown, flat-round, 8—10 mm thick, pit partly divisible. MS 463. California, Sierra Nevada. Quite variable. z6 #

A. pumila Nutt. Shrub with mat forming growth habit, twigs somewhat ascending, young twigs finely pubescent; leaves obovate, variable in size, usually 1.5—2 cm long and 8 mm wide, dull green above or somewhat glossy and glabrous, slightly tomentose beneath; flowers in short, dense racemes, with pubescent rachis, corolla white, 4 mm long, ovary glabrous; fruit 5 mm thick, glabrous, nutlets all divisible. MS 447. California, sandy hills around Monterey Bay. z8 #

A. pungens H. B. K. Upright shrub, 2—3 m high or only 60 cm high and wide growing, young twigs somewhat gray pubescent to tomentose; leaves oblong to elliptic or narrow ovate, apex sharp, some 2 cm long, light green above, glabrous; inflorescence short and thick, rachis thickened at the tip, corolla white, 5 mm long, ovaries glabrous; fruit 5—6 mm thick, rounded or somewhat irregular, brown-red. MS 458; BM 3927 (= *A. montana* Eastw.). SW. USA to Mexico. 1840. z8 Fig. 121. # ⌀

A. rubra see: **Arctous ruber**

A. stanfordiana Parry. Upright shrub, 1.5—2.5 m high, twigs long, thin, dark red, glabrous or finely pubescent; leaves usually oblanceolate or narrow ovate, 3—6 cm long, pointing upward, light green and glossy; flowers in terminal, elongated panicles with reddish, finely pubescent rachis, corolla whitish-pink to pink, usually 4—5 mm long, narrow urceolate, with tightly packed sepals, ovaries glabrous; fruit light red, glabrous, usually asymmetrical, 5—7 mm wide, pit divisible. MS 448, 543. USA, California, mountains from 300—1000 m. z6 #

A. tomentosa (Pursh) Lindl. Shrub, open branched, upright, 1—2.5 m high, usually single stemmed, bark long peeling, remaining striped, young twigs white tomentose; leaves oblong to broad elliptic or broad ovate, 2.5—4.5 cm long, glabrous above and glossy, dense white tomentose beneath, petiole short, tomentose; inflorescence a short sessile, wide panicle with dense tomentose rachis, corolla white, 5—6 mm long, March—May, ovaries densely white pubescent, not glandular; fruit flat-globose, 8—10 mm wide, brown-red, finely pubescent. MS 479 (= *A. cordifolia* Lindl.). California, pine forests or dry hillsides on Monterey Bay. 1835. z8 Fig. 121. # ⌀

A. uva-ursi (L.) A. Gray. Common Bearberry. Procumbent shrub, all branches rooting, mat-forming flat to the ground, young twigs to 50 cm long, glabrous or soon becoming so; leaves obovate, tough leathery, 1—3 cm long, apex obtuse to slightly emarginate, generally tapering to the base, ciliate, dark green above, lighter beneath; flowers 3—12 in short, terminal, pendulous racemes, corolla urceolate, white with pink tips, 5—6 mm long, inside pubescent, April—May; fruit globose, scarlet-red, pea size, mealy, glossy. CWF 386; HF 2042; HM 2670. Northern hemisphere. 1800.

In Russia, Scandinavia and Iceland the foliage, which contains tannin, is used to treat fine leathers; also protected as a medicinal plant (an extract of the foliage is used in treating problems of the bladder, liver and urinary tract); and the Indians are said to have smoked the leaves. z4 Plate 48; Fig. 121 # ✖

Aside from the species there are 2 geographical varieties:

var. **adenotricha** Fern. & McBride. Young twigs and petiole long haired, sticky, black glands among the hairs. N. America; Quebec to Saskatchewan, British Columbia, Montreal and Colorado. z3

var. **coactilis** Fern. & McBride. Pubescence on the twigs and leaf petioles persistent, short, fine, dense, but without glands. Newfoundland to Yukon, south to Virginia, Illinois, British Columbia, coast of N. California. z3

Plate 33

Amelanchier lamarckii in full bloom

Amelanchier lamarckii
in Dortmund Botanic Garden

Atraphaxis caucasica in Vienna Botanic Garden, Austria

Plate 34

Amelanchier alnifolia in its habitat in Deerlodge National Forest, Montana
Photo: US Forestery Service

Amelanchier ovalis in Berlin Botanic Garden

Photo: C. R. Jelitto

Plate 35

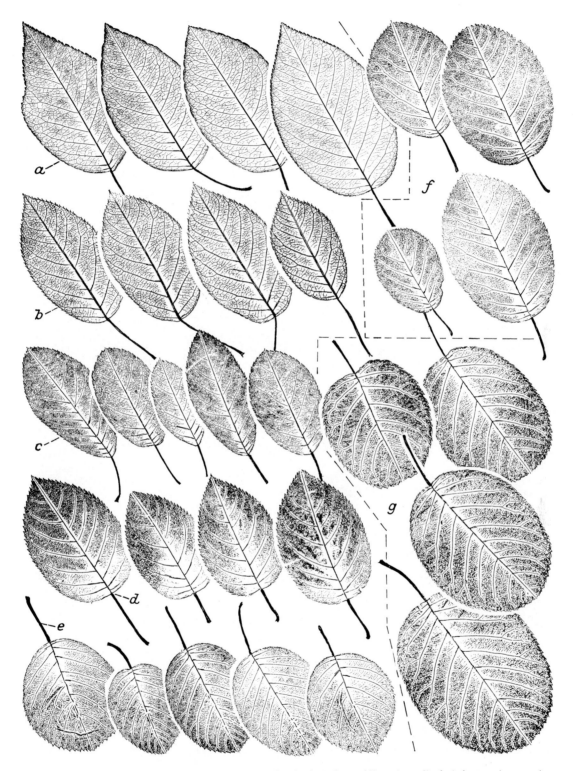

Amelanchier. a. *A. asiatica*; b. *A. laevis*; c. *A. canadensis*; d. *A. lamarckii*; e. *A. ovalis*; f. *A. bartramiana*; g. *A. obovalis* (Material gathered by the author from the US national Arboretum and Morton Arboretum)

Plate 36

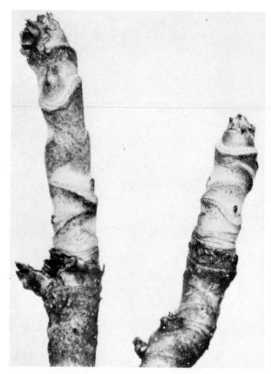

Aralia chinensis in winter (Archives)

Arauja sericofera in Lyon Botanic Garden, France

Aralia elata in its native habitat Hokkaido, Japan

Photo: T. Nitzelius

Plate 37

Arbutus × andrachnoides
in a garden in Scotland

Arbutus menziesii
as a street tree in Seattle, USA

Azara lanceolata

Betula nigra in winter

Plate 38

Berberidopsis corallina
in Benmore, Scotland

Clerodendrum trichotomum
in Locarno, Southern Switzerland

Berberis × *stenophylla* 'Pink Pearl'
in Cornwall, England

Brachyglottis repanda
on the Scilly Isles, England

Plate 39

Buddleia salviifolia

Calluna vulgaris 'H. E. Beale'

Calluna vulgaris 'Multicolor'

Calluna vulgaris 'Sunset'

Plate 40

Callicarpa bodinieri 'Profusion'

Callistemon phoeniceus

Camellia × williamsii 'Donation'
in the Hillier Arboretum, England

Camellia × williamsii 'Inspiration'
in the Hillier Arboretum

Plate 41

Arbutus andrachnoides, ×2, in Berlin Botanic Garden   Photo: C. R. Jelitto

Plate 42

Arbutus unedo, fruit
Photo E. Hahn

Arbutus unedo,
older trunk in Kew Gardens, London

Arbutus andrachne, older trunk in Kew Gardens,
London   Photo: Dr. Hondelmann

Arbutus menziesii in Kew Gardens, London

Plate 43

Artemisia stelleriana
in Copenhagen Botanic Garden, Denmark

Arundo donax 'Variegata'
in Les Barres Arboretum, France

Arundo donax, growing wild in Gerona Province, Spain

Plate 44

Arundinaria humilis
in Copenhagen Botanic Garden, Denmark

Arundinaria viridi-striata var. *vagans*
in Pitt White, S. England (Bamboo Garden)

Arundinaria simonii
on Madre Island, Lake Maggiore, Italy

Arundinaria simonii
Photo: News Crops Research Branch, USA

Plate 45

Arundinaria graminea in Japan   Photo: Dr. Watari, Tokyo

Asimina triloba, fruit (Archiv)   *Asimina triloba*, flower (Archiv)

Plate 46

Atriplex halimus in Lisbon Botanic Garden, Portugal

Astragalus angustifolius in the rock garden   Archivbild

Plate 47

Aucuba japonica 'Picturata'
Photo: E. Hahn

Aralia elata 'Variegata'
Photo: E. Hahn

Azara. a. *A. petiolaris*; b. *microphylla*, twig and 2 small leaves; c. *A. integrifolia*; d. *A. dentata*

Plate 48

Arctostaphylos andersonii
in the Edinburgh Botanic Garden, Scotland

Argania spinosa
in native habitat near Agadir, Morocco

Arctostaphylos uva-ursi in native habitat in the Alps   Photo: C. R. Jelitto

A. viscida Parry. Upright shrub, 1–4 m high, usually multistemmed from the base, bark deep red, smooth, twigs and petiole thin, glabrous, blue-green, often also glandular; leaves pale-bluish, rounded or ovate to elliptic, 2–4 cm long, abruptly short acuminate, base round to truncate, petiole 5–8 mm long; flowers pink to white, corolla 6 mm long, ovaries glabrous or also glandular; fruit small, dark red, 6–8 mm wide, flat-round, glabrous to very glandular, pit completely divisible. MS 465 (= *A. pulchella* Howell). California, Sierra Nevada, developing into a dense bush. z6 #

In colder open areas only *A. uva-ursi* is generally acceptable as a groundcover. The Californian species are very attractive with their beautiful bark and foliage but unfortunately too

tender in all but the milder regions or for greenhouse culture. All species propagated by cuttings in late summer, under glass, without difficulty or also by seed as with the other *Ericaceae*.

Precise and unquestionable descriptions of this genus are very difficult because of the great variability of most species. Most garden books are lacking in this area and therefore only the following works can be recommended.

Lit. Adams, J. E.: A systematic study of the genus *Arctostaphylos*; in Jour. Elisha Mitchell Scie. Soc. **56**, 1–62, 1940 ● Eastwood, A.: A revision of *Arctostaphylos*; Leaflets West. Bot. **1**, 105–127, 1934 ● McMinn, H. E.: *Arctostaphylos*; in Ill. Manual Calif. Shrubs, 382–421, figs. 443–497, Berkeley 1951.

ARCTOUS (A. Gray) Niedenzu — Black Bearberry — ERICACEAE

Very closely related to *Arctostaphylos* but differing in the deciduous foliage and its totally different anatomical structure from that of the Arbuteae group (not covered in great detail here; for further explanation see: Hegi, Fl. Middl. Eur., V: 1663), ovaries 4–5 chambered, berry-like, juicy drupe with 4–5 nutlets. — 3 species, circumpolar.

Arctous alpinus (L.) Niedenzu. Deciduous, creeping shrublet, 10–15 cm high; leaves oblanceolate, 2–3 cm long, generally tapering to the base, finely serrate and ciliate, reticulate venation on both sides, fresh green, bright red in fall (at least in the higher mountains of N. Norway, where it forms masses); flowers urceolate, 3–4 mm long, white with pink trace, corolla tips ciliate, April–June; fruit pea-size, red at first, black or blue-black in the following year. HM 2673 and Pl. 206; HF 2041; PEu 88 (= *Arctostaphylos alpinus* Spreng.). N. Europe, N. Asia, N. America. 1789. z3 Fig. 122.⊕ ∅ ⌘

A. ruber (Rehd. & Wils.) Nakai. Like the previous species, but with leaves usually obovate, lighter green;

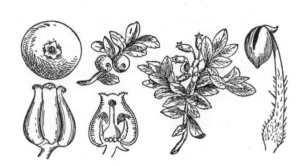

Fig. 122. *Arctous alpinus* (from Schroeter)

corolla narrower, limb entire; fruit light red. NT 1: 217; CWF 375 (= *A. crythrocarpa* Small; *Arctostaphylos rubra* Fern.). N. America, Korea, W. China. z3

Substantially more delicate in cultivation than the creeping *Arctostaphylos* types; requires a cool, moist, gravelly northern exposure. Very scarce in cultivation.

ARDISIA Swartz — MYRSINACEAE

Evergreen trees or shrubs, rarely subshrubs; leaves alternate, seldom opposite or 3-whorled, simple, short petioled, margins entire or serrate, glandular punctate; flowers small, white or red, in terminal or axillary racemes or panicles; calyx and corolla 5 parted, stamens 5, ovaries rounded, unilocular; fruit a small, globose, fleshy drupe with 1 seed, covered by a leathery seed coat. — Some 400 species in the tropics and subtropics, but few in Africa.

Ardisia crispa (Thunb.) A. DC. Shrub, 60–120 cm high, twigs sparse, open; leaves oblong-lanceolate, tapering to both ends, thick leathery, 5–10 cm long, margin crisped-crenate, dark glossy green above, lighter and punctate beneath; flowers in terminal, usually 4–5 flowered umbellate racemes, white or reddish, fragrant, June; corolla 12 mm wide, petals ovate, acute; fruit globose, scarlet-red, ripening in winter. YTS 2: 109; BM 1950 (= *A. crenulata* Lodd.). E. Indies. 1809. A very popular and marketable plant in the past because

of its red fruit. Must be over-wintered in a cool greenhouse. z7 Fig. 119. # ⊕ ∅ ⌘

43 cultivars have been developed and are described in UJD **3**, 579–591.

'Alba'. Like the species but with white fruit.

'Variegata'. Leaves somewhat deformed, margin wide or narrow white marked, young leaves reddish. HTS 25. In cultivation in New Zealand. Attractive.

A. japonica (Thunb.) Bl. Shrub, only 25–40 cm high, procumbent, with upright branching, young twigs red-brown, softly pubescent; leaves clustered at the branch tips, oval-ovate, coarsely dentate, 5–7 cm long, dark green above, glossy, lighter and distinctly veined beneath; flowers white to light red, fragrant, in short, few flowered, pendulous racemes, August–September; fruit globose, light red, 6 mm thick, very ornamental. China, Japan, in the mountains. 1830. z8 Fig. 119. # ∅ ⌘

57 cultivars developed and described, all with latin names (Nakai) in UJD 3, 591–605.

A. pusilla A. DC. Stoloniferous, stem prostrate and rotting, young twigs rust-brown shaggy pubescent; leaves in whorls 3–5, all along the branch, ovate, 2–5 cm long, 1.2–2.5 cm wide, coarsely serrate, young leaves pink at first; flowers about 12 in racemes, white, calyx green; fruit red, somewhat smaller than *A. japonica*. NH 1958: 266; UJD 3: 606. S. China, Kwang-tung; Japan, forests in Ise Bay and on Yakushima Island. 1957. z6 # Ø ⊗

The latter 2 species are prominent groundcovers in very mild areas, especially *A. pusilla*. *A. crispa* has only recently been introduced into cultivation.

ARDUINA

Arduina grandiflora see: **Carissa macrocarpa**

ARGANIA Roem. & Schult. — SAPOTACEAE

Monotypic genus, without ornamental value but a tree of economic important in its native habitat. Morocco.

Argania spinosa (L.) Maire. Ironwood Tree. Evergreen tree or large shrub, to 10 m high (usually only 5–6 m) and to 10 m wide, crown dense, broad rounded, trunk with rough, cracked bark, resembling that of *Pyrus*, twig short, stout thorny; leaves alternate, often clustered, oblong to spathulate, 2–4 cm long, 1 cm wide, tough leathery, margins entire, deep green above, lighter beneath, completely glabrous; flowers small, inconspicuous, sessile, in small fascicles in the leaf axils, petals 5, connate campanulate at the base, yellowish-green, April; fruit "olive to pigeon eye-size", yellow, hard pit with 3 seeds, seed coat fleshy (= *A. sideroxylon* Roem. & Schult.). Morocco, especially in the SW, on limestone, sand or gravelly soil. z9 Plate 48. # ○ ⊗

The normally diagonal trunk and rough bark allows goats to climb into the crown, despite the thorns, to eat the leaves and fruits. The hard, indigestable seeds are valued for their oil content.

ARGYROLOBIUM Eckl. & Zeyh. — LEGUMINOSAE

Usually perennial, subshrubs, or rarely shrubs; whole plant silky-shaggy pubescent; leaves alternate, trifoliate, with distinct stipules; inflorescence racemose to umbellate, with small prophylla and bracts; calyx campanulate, the 5 tips much longer than the tube; corolla yellow to reddish, wing petals obovate, distinct; stamen tube usually closed; pods linear, flat; seed without hilum bulge. — Some 70 species, most in S. Africa, only 12 in the Mediterranean region.

Argyrolobium linneanum Walp. Subshrub, 10–30 cm high, branches ascending, thinly silky pubescent; leaflets ovate-lanceolate, some 1 cm long, 4 mm wide, dark green above, glabrous, appressed silky pubescence beneath; flowers 1–4 in terminal heads, May–June; corolla bright yellow, standard petal pubescent outside; pods 2–3 cm long, flat, slightly curved, silky pubescent. HM 1313 (= *A. argenteum* Willkomm. non Eckl. & Zeyh.). Mediterranean region, north to Garda Lake, Italy. z7 ○ ⊕

Xerophytic plant for dry limestone screes or rocky crevices; for the rock garden.

ARISTOLOCHIA L. — Dutchman's Pipe — ARISTOLOCHIACEAE

Twining or upright perennials or vines; leaves simple, seldom lobed; flowers 1–2, axillary, ornamental, often unpleasant smelling; perianth bulging, usually long and curved tubular, limb oblique 3 lobed; anthers 6, fused with the columnar style which terminates in a 3–6 lobed stigma; ovary oblong, 6 chambered; fruit an oblong, usually from bottom to top dehiscent 6 valved, many seeded capsule. — Around 350 species in the temperate and tropical zones.

Aristolochia altissima Desf. A subshrub, totally glabrous, branches reaching 2–2.5 m each year; leaves ovate, base cordate, glabrous and glossy, petiole some 1–2 cm long; flowers some 2.5–4 cm long, yellow-brown with darker lines, tube generally funnel-form to the limb, yellow inside, June–August; fruit oblong, 3 cm long. BM 6586. Sicily, Algieria. Very beautiful; eas-ily identified by the *Smilax*-like appearance. z8 ⊕ Ø

This species is often included under *A. sempervirens* by many authors.

A. californica Torr. Subshrub, 1.5–3 high, woody only at the base, branches more or less silky pubescent; leaves ovate, base cordate, 4–12 cm long, both sides remaining softly pubescent, petiole 1.5–3 cm long; flowers solitary, pendulous, curved U-shape, tube much inflated, some 5 cm long, the 3 small limb tips purple, March–April; fruit a 6 sided capsule, 3–7 cm long. MS 81. USA, California, hills along the coast. 1877. z8

A. heterophylla Hemsl. Subshrub, young branches becoming some 2.5 m high, like the leaves, finely and softly pubescent; leaves narrow or broad ovate, base

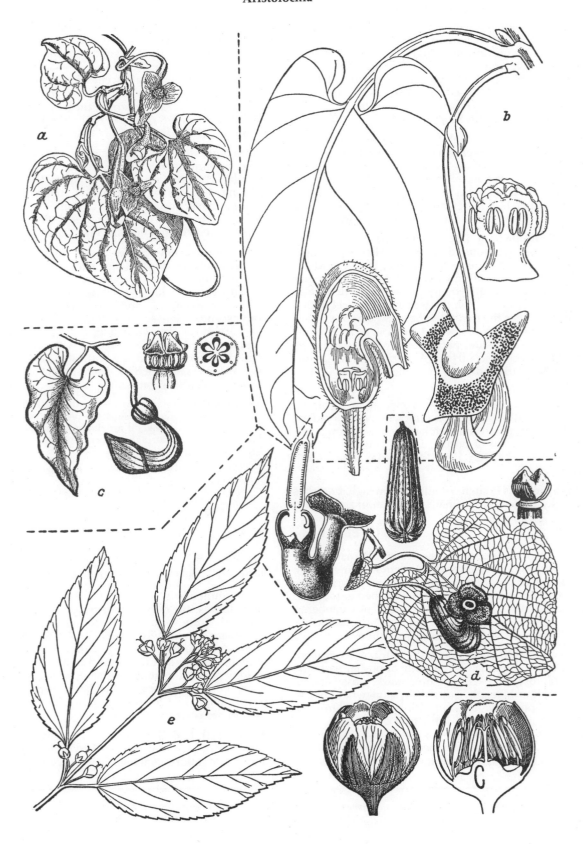

cordate, occasionally with a small lobe on each side of the base, 3.5—10 cm long, acute, dull green, petiole 1.5—2.5 cm long; flowers solitary, 5 cm long, bowed U-shape, pubescent, yellow outside, limb tips "dirty purple" to black, throat gold-yellow, June; fruit 6 sided, 5 cm long. BM 8957; ICS 1091 (= *A. setchuensis* Franch.). W. China, Hupeh. 1904. Very beautiful, but touchy species in cultivation. z8 ✧ ∅

A. kaempferi Willd. High twining, woody, branches softly pubescent; leaves ovate, base cordate, occasionally also shaped like an arrowhead (sagittate), quite variable, 7—15 cm long, silky pubescent beneath; flowers solitary, softly pubescent, outside, yellow, limb 2 lipped, upper lip emarginate, narrow, purple inside, June—July. Japan. 1854. Should be winter hardy. z6

A. macrophylla Lam. Dutchman's Pipe. Twining to 10 m high, stem glabrous, dark green, also older stems remaining conspicuously dark green; leaves cordate-ovate, obtuse, 10—30 cm long, dark green above, glabrous, lighter beneath, thinly pubescent at first, then glabrous; flowers 1—2 in the leaf axils, pedicel with a small leaf under the middle, tube very curved, yellow-green outside, glabrous, with 3 equal sized limb lobes, 1.5—2 cm wide inside, purple-brown, June. BB 1283; BM 534 (= *A. sipho* L'Hér.; *A. durior* Hill.). Eastern USA. 1783. Bark and roots aromatic. z6 Plate 49; Fig. 123. ∅

A. manchuriensis Komar. Very similar to *A. macrophylla*, but with young twigs pubescent; leaves pubescent beneath, perianth much larger, to 5 cm long, yellowish, with trace of purple, limb 3 cm wide, purple brown. NK 21: 1; ICS 1088. Manchuria, Korea. 1909. Hardy. z5

A. moupinensis Franch. Twining to 4 m high, branches soft silky pubescent at first, later becoming glabrous;

leaves cordate, usually acute, 6—15 cm long, sparse pubescence above, denser beneath, petiole 2.5—5 cm long, pubescent; flowers solitary, pendulous on a 5 cm long pedicel, some 3 cm long, U-shaped, tube somewhat compressed, pubescent outside, greenish, limb with 3 widespread lobes, these yellow with brown spots, greenish to the margin, throat yellow, June; fruit 7 cm long, with 6 ribs. BM 8325; ICS 1090. W. China, Moupin. 1903. Hardy. z5 Fig. 123.

A. sempervirens L. Evergreen, usually prostrate, but also twining, smaller and weaker growing than the similar *A. altissima*, twigs angular; leaves cordate-oblong, 3—10 cm long, acuminate, tough membranous, glossy above; flowers curved U-shape, with only 1 limb lobe, purple-brown outside, May. BM 1116. Crete. 1727. Rare in cultivation. z8 Fig. 123. # ∅

A. tomentosa Sims. Shrub, 5—7 m high twining, young twigs, flowers and foliage very woolly tomentose; leaves broad ovate to rounded, apex rounded, base usually cordate, 10—16 cm long, often equally as wide, dull green above and eventually with scattered pubescence, denser persistent pubescence beneath; flowers purple-brown inside, the 3 limb lobes yellow and wrinkled (rugose), pedicel without bracts, June; fruit 5 cm long, cylindrical with ribs. BB 1284; BM 1369 (= *A. angulisans* Michx.). Eastern USA. 1799. Hardy, but rare in cultivation. z5 Fig. 123. ∅

The woody species are all winter hardy but seldom in cultivation outside of botanic gardens; the subshrub species are only for milder areas. All good for climbing on walls, fences, arbors, etc., but requiring support. The pipe-shaped flowers are very unique.

Lit. Pfeifer, H. W.: *Aristolochia*; Ann. Miss. Bot. Gard. **53**, 115—196.

ARISTOTELIA L'Hér. — ELAEOCARPACEAE

Evergreen or deciduous shrubs; leaves alternate or opposite, simple, margins entire or dentate; flowers few in axillary or terminal corymbs, often polygamous; calyx 4—5 parted; petals 4—5, apexes lobed or toothed; stamens distinct, pubescent; fruit a 2—4 chambered berry. — Some 5 species in the southern temperate zones; Australia, New Zealand, Peru, Chile.

Aristotelia chilensis (Molina) Stuntz. Evergreen shrub, to 3 m high; leaves partially opposite, partially alternate, ovate, 5—10 cm long, dark glossy green above, lighter beneath, but glossy, somewhat pubescent venation; flowers usually 3 in axillary or terminal fascicles, greenish white, June; fruit 6 mm thick, reddish at first, then black. PFC 83 (= *A. macqui* L'Hér.). Chile. In Chile, the fruit is occasionally made into a wine which is said to have medicinal properties. z8

Fig. 123. # ∅ ✧

'variegata'. Leaves white variegated.

A. penduncularis (Labill.). Hook. f. Shrub, 2—4 m high; leaves not quite opposite, often alternate or 3-whorled, quite variable in form, usually broad-ovate, lanceolate or narrowly elliptic, 2—7 cm long, normally undivided, but occasionally with 3—4 narrow paired pinnae, margins serrate; flowers axillary, 1—3 together, on long pendulous stalks, petals 4, white, 3 lobed at the apex, orange spotted at the base, September; fruit purple-pink, 1—1.5 cm long, CTa 25; LNH 155; CFTa 12. Tasmania. 1818. z8 # ∅ ⚭

A. serrata (J. R. & G. Forst.) W. R. B. Oliver. Deciduous shrub or ornamental tree, to 7 m high, twigs, young leaves and inflorescence softly pubescent; leaves oppo-

---

Fig. 123. **Aristolochia**. a. *A. tomentosa*; b. *A. moupinensis*; c. *A. sempervirens*; d. *A. macrophylla*. **Aristotelia**. e. *A. chilensis* (from Bot. Mag., Bot. Reg., Baillon, Lauche)

site, ovate, base cordate, 5—10 cm long, deeply and sharply irregularly dentate, petiole 2.5—4 cm long; flowers small, many in 5—10 cm long, axillary panicles, light pink, dioecious, May; fruit dark red to nearly black, pea-size. BM 7868; KF 113 (= *A. racemosa* Hook. f.). New Zealand. 1873. z8

All the mentioned species are quite easy to cultivate and very attractive, but only for the mildest areas; those not mentioned are rarely found in cultivation.

Lit. Moore, H. E.: Some Notes on Cultivated *Elaeocarpaceae;* in Baileya **1**, 113, 1953.

AROMADENDRON Blume — MAGNOLIACEAE

Of the 3 species in this genus, 2 are from Malaysia. The 3rd species, *Aromadendron yunnanense* Hu, was found in Yunnan in 1936 and as yet has never been officially introduced into cultivation. The small flowers are simi-

lar to those of *Magnolia stellata*, the leaves some 15—20 cm long, oval-elliptic, acute on both ends. For further details, see Pl. 103 in the Jour. RHS, 1938.

ARONIA Med. — Chokeberry — ROSACEAE

Deciduous shrubs; leaves alternate, simple, margins crenate, with blackish glands on the midrib above; stipules small, abcising; flowers white or pale pink, in small corymbs, petals 5, widespread, stamens numerous, anthers purple, pistils always 5, connate at the base; fruit a small pome, with persistent calyx tips. — 3 species in N. America.

Distinguished from *Sorbus* by the always simple leaves with a glandular midrib above, always 5 pistils connate at the base and persistent calyx tips.
- Leaves (on both sides) and inflorescence glabrous:
     A. melanocarpa
- Leaves pubescent beneath, also the inflorescence;
  +Fruit red:
     A. arbutifolia
  ++Fruit black-red:
     A. prunifolia

Aronia arbutifolia (L.) Pers. Shrub, 1.5—2 m high, young twigs tomentose; leaves elliptic to oblong or obovate, 4—8 cm long, acute to acuminate, glabrous above except for the glandular midrib, deep green, gray tomentose beneath, fall color fire-red; flower 1 cm wide, reddish-white, 9—20 in small, dense, gray tomentose umbellate panicles, May—June; fruit pea-size, bright red, late ripening and persisting to December. BM 3668; NBB 337; GSP 181 (= *Sorbus arbutifolia* Heynh.). Eastern USA. 1700. z5 Fig. 124. ✧ ∅ ⚭

'Erecta'. Grows srictly columnar, 1—2 m high; leaves 4—5 cm long, with especially good fall color. ∅

f. **macrophylla** (Hook.) Rehd. Growth taller, occasionally a small tree, to 6 m high; leaves 5—9 cm long. Southern USA. 1918. Hardy. z5 ∅

var. **pumila** (Schmidt) Rehd. Lower than the species, leaves smaller, fruit darker red (= *Pyrus depressa* Lindl.) z5

Fig. 124. **Aronia**. left, *A. melanocarpa;* middle and right, *A. arbutifolia* (from Garden and Forest; Dippel)

A. melanocarpa (Michx.) Ell. Shrub, only 0.5 to 1 m high, with stolons, young twigs nearly completely glabrous; leaves elliptic to obovate or oblong-oblanceolate, often abruptly acuminate, 2—6 cm long, deep glossy green above, lighter and glabrous beneath, fall foliage brown-red; flowers pure white, 1.5 cm wide, in glabrous umbellate panicles, May; fruit pea-size, glossy, black, ripening August—September, abscising soon thereafter. BM 9052; NBB 337; GSP 178 (= *A. nigra* Dipp., *Sorbus melanocarpa* Heynh.). Eastern USA. Around 1700. z3 Fig. 124 ⌀

var. **elata** Rehd. Growth stronger, to 3 m high; leaves oblong-obovate, acute; flowers and fruit larger. BC 382. ⚭

var. **grandifolia** (Lindl.) Schneid. To 2.5 m high; leaves obovate to broad obovate; flowers and fruit larger. BR 1154 (= *Pyrus grandifolia* Lindl.).⊕ ⌀ ⚭

A. prunifolia (Marsh.) Rehd. To 4 m high, resembles *A. arbutifolia*, but with inflorescence somewhat looser, calyx more or less densely tomentose, calyx tips virtually without glands; fruit to 1 cm thick, dark red to black-red, early ripening. BR 1006 (= *A. floribunda* Spach; *A. atropurpurea* Brit.). Eastern USA. Red fall color; not as good as *A. arbutifolia*. Somewhat intermediate between the other 2 species, but not a hybrid. z5 ⌀ ⚭

'Brilliant'. Selection with especially bright fall color; fruit dark red. ⌀

Cultural requirements minimal, prefer cool, moist soil, only *A. melanocarpa* will tolerate dryness and light soil.

Lit. Hardin. J. W.: The enigmatic Chokeberries (*Aronia*, Rosaceae); in Bull. Torrey Bot. Club **100**, 178—184. 1973.

ARTEMISIA L. — COMPOSITAE

Perennials, subshrubs or shrubs, rarely tree-like, fragrant; leaves alternate, rarely simple and unlobed, usually palmate or pinnately compound; flowers in racemes or panicles made up of many flowered heads, perianth with imbricate sepals, without ray flowers; disc flowers bisexual, the marginal flowers often female; fruitlet without a pappus. — Some 400 species in the Northern Hemisphere and in S. America.

Because of the limited number of species covered here, an outline of the taxonomic sections is not given. For the European species, see Hegi, Fl. v. M. Eur., for the American species, Rydberg, Fl. of the Rocky Mts.

Artemisia abrotanum L. Eberraute. Subshrub, upright, to 1 m high, twigs somewhat pubescent at first, then becoming glabrous; leaves 2—6 cm long, bipinnately cleft, tips narrow and glandular punctate, glabrous above, gray pubescent beneath; flower heads numerous, in leafy, axillary racemes; heads globose, pubescent, 4—5 mm wide, yellow, nodding, July—October. HF 3006; NBB 3: 391. S. Europe, Spain, Dalmatia. 1548. Whole plant with a refreshing fragrance. z6 Fig. 125.

A. absinthium L. Wermut. Subshrub, to 1 m high, stalks upright, abundant foliage; leaves silky pubescent on both sides, lowest petiolate, tripinnate; heads in strong branched panicles, short stalked, nodding; outer perianth oblong-linear, inner ovate with a broad, membranous margin, July—September. HF 3001; NBB 3: 393. Northern temperate zone. Good choice as understory for open, dry pine stands. z5 Fig. 125.

A. alba Turrill. Subshrub, 0.3—1 m high, banches upright or ascending, glabrous to downy-tomentose, not silvery-glossy; leaves 2—4 cm long, petiolate, stipulate with several small lobes, from the base of the petiole 5—8 cm long, tripinnate with only a few pinnae, the higher leaves only singly pinnate; flowers nearly always in simple, tight panicles, heads short stalked, yellow, disc florets bisexual, August—September. HF 3001 A; HM VI: 365 (= *A. comphorata* Vill.; *A. lobelii* All.). S. Europe, N. Africa; on dry, warm gravelly slopes, over limestone or chalk. 1820. Whole plant with a camphor-like fragrance. z7 Fig. 125.

A. arborescens L. Upright shrub, 1—2 m high, twigs glossy gray pubescent; leaves long petioled, 3-pinnatisect, long stalked, sections linear, acute or obtuse, eventually dark green and glabrous above, soft silky pubescent and somewhat glossy gray-green beneath; flowers in spikes or panicles, September; heads large, nodding at first, then upright, green-yellow. JRHS 89: 180. Eastern Mediterranean region, to S. Italy and Corsica. z8 Fig. 125.

A. austriaca Jacq. Subshrub, 0.2—0.6 m high, branches often thinly gray tomentose-downy at the base, often turning to red; leaves bipinnate, sections rather linear, some 1 mm wide, with the elongated stalk some 4—5 cm long; flowers numerous in dense, short panicles or racemes, July—September; heads reddish-yellow. HF 3008; HM VI: 351 (= *A. nivea* Redow.; *A. orientalis* Willd.; *A. repens* Pall.). Southeastern Europe to Siberia, in the steppes. z4 Fig. 125.

A. cana Pursh. Upright shrub, 0.3—0.6 m high, stem many branched, whole plant densely gray-white pubescent; leaves linear-oblong-lanceolate, acute at both ends, 2.5—5 cm long, margins entire, rarely with 2—3 teeth; flowers in terminal, leafy panicles, July—September. BB 4018. USA, Nebraska and Colorado to N. Dakota. 1800. z3 Fig. 125 ⌀

A. pontica L. Subshrub, only slightly woody, main stem creeping, stalks ascending, 40—60 cm high, gray downy-tomentose, especially in the upper portion, more glabrous and red-brown at the base; leaves bipinnate, apical sessile, basal stalked, 3—4 cm long, dull gray-green above, pubescent, gray tomentose beneath; flowers yellow, glabrous, in narrow, branched, leafy racemes, August—September. HF 3007; HM VI: 352; NBB 3: 391. Middle Europe, steppes and dry areas. z6 Fig. 125.

A. procera Willd. Shrub, 1—2.5 m high, growth upright at first, then spreading laterally; leaves bipinnately

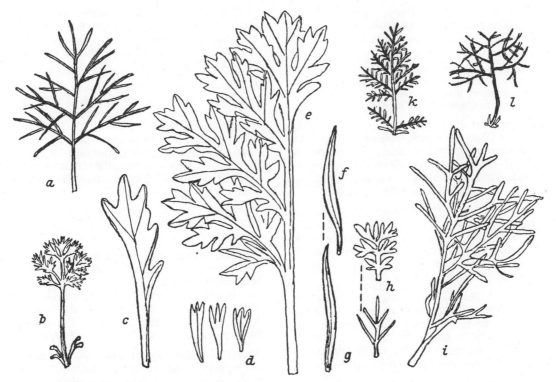

Fig. 125. **Artemisia.** a. *A. abrotanum*; b. *A. austriaca*; c. *A. stelleriana*; d. *A. tridentata*; e. *A. absinthium*; f. *A. cana*; g. and h. *A. frigida*; i. *A. arborescens*; k. *A. pontica*; l. *A. alba*

cleft, 5—8 cm long, sections threadlike, pubescent when young, later dark green above, gray pubescent beneath; flowers yellow-green, in compound, terminal spikes, heads yellow-green, small, September—October. S. Europe to the Caucasus and Siberia. 1800. z4 Very similar to *A. abrotanum*, but grows taller, wider and with involucre glabrous. Plate 21.

A. sacrorum Ledeb. Subshrub, to 1.5 m high, whole plant gray pubescent; leaves ovate, bipinnate, the pinnae comb-like incised, long petioled, 4—7 cm long, sections linear, petiole and midrib winged; flowers in large, terminal, 20—40 cm long panicles, August—September. S. Russia to Siberia and NE. Asia. 1828. z4

A. stelleriana Bess. Subshrub, 30—70 cm high, the branches prostrate to ascending, sterile branches lying on the ground, entire plant white tomentose; leaves obovate in outline, 3—10 cm long, pinnatisect with oblong, obtuse lobes, older leaves somewhat green; flowers of little merit, July—August. BB 4009; NBB 3: 391. NE. Asia, Eastern N. America, sandy sea coasts. 1870. z6 Plate 43; Fig. 125. ∅

A. suavis Jordan. Stalks grassy, ascending; plant very closely related to *A. alba*; leaves broadly ovate in outline, lower leaves bipinnate, sections nearly parallel, green to gray-green, petiole with stipules at the base; flower heads protruding far past the basal leaf, involucre gray, heads pendulous. S. France. 1904. Whole plant with a sweet-spicy fragrance. z8

A. tridentata Nutt. Shrub to 3 m high, occasionally a tree in very favorable conditions, to 6 m; twiggy, very strongly aromatic, leaves silver-gray, leaflets sessile, narrow spathulate, with 3, occasionally 7 teeth at the apex; flower heads small, very numerous, nearly sessile, in large, dense, 30—50 cm long panicles, August—September. BB 4017. NW. USA, dry plains, gravelly soil. 1895. z6 Fig. 125. ∅

A. tridentata has been subdivided into several geographical varieties by Jepson and McMinn. See McMinn. Ill. Man. of Calif. Shrubs, 107—109, with ill.

All species more or less subshrubs with the few exceptions mentioned above. All prefer a sunny area in dry, light, sandy-gravelly, alkaline soil. Because of their strong fragrance these plants are quite popular, despite their somewhat unattractive appearance.

Lit. See the notes before *A. abrotanum*.

ARUNDINARIA Michx. — BAMBUSACEAE

Tall subshrub or also a woody, rhizomatous grass to 10 m high; stems upright, terete (rod-like), hollow; axillary twigs several at every node; soon branching out across the ground; branches with persistent stem sheath; leaf sheath rough bristly; spikelets 2−8 flowered; pistil short, with 3 stigmas. — Some 10 species in E. and S. Asia and N. America.

The distinction between the Bamboo species is very difficult and the classification is mainly based on flower characteristics. Unfortunately the plants seldom bloom in cultivation and only after a long interval, usually dying after flowering. As a result taxonomy has not been extensively studied.

Arundinaria angustifolia Houzeau. Growth upright, stalks 60−80 cm high, 2−8 mm wide, rhizomes fast growing, quickly developing thickets, side branches upright; leaves 5−15 cm long, some 8 mm wide, acuminate, both sides glossy, with 4−8 veins (= *Bambusa vilmorinii* Latour-Marliac). Japan. 1875. z6 H ◑ ∅

A. chino (Franch. & Sav.) Mak. Growth upright, stalks 100−180 cm high, green, turning purple, rhizomes creeping; leaves 7 to 20 cm long, 4−18 mm wide, dark green, dull yellow speckled, with 6−14 veins. CBa 17 (= *Pleioblastus maximowiczii* Nakai). Japan. 1876. Species of little importance. z6 H ◑

A. gigantea (Walt.) Chapm. To 9 m high, stem sections reddish; leaves to 30 cm long and 5 cm wide, rounded at the base, underside either finely pubescent or glabrous, margins finely dentate, with 12−28 veins. BB 2, 1:295; CBa 14 (= *A. macrosperma* Michx.). Southeastern USA, common in the swamps, rarely cultivated in Europe. z7 H ◑

A. graminea (Bean) Mak. Closely related to *A. hindsii*, but with thinner stems and narrower leaves; stems to 3 m high, yellowish, 6−12 mm thick, nodes spaced 7−15 cm apart, hollow, densely branched and leafy toward the top; leaves narrow, 10−20 cm long, 1−1.2 cm wide, with 4−8 veins (= *Pleioblastus graminea* Nakai). Japan. 1877. Hardy and attractive. z5 Plate 45. H ◑ ∅

A. hindsii Munro. To 4 m high, stems to 2.5 cm thick, hollow, dark olive-green, pruinose at first, internodes to 20 cm long, side branches very numerous and cluttered, developing especially large clusters at the higher nodes; leaves usually directed upward, to 20 cm long, 1−2 cm wide, dark green above, blue-green and distinctly reticulate venation beneath, with 8−12 veins. RH 1921: 367; SB 7 (= *Bambusa gracilis* Hort.; *B. erecta* Hort.). Japan. 1875. z8 H ◑ ∅

A. humilis Mitford. Stems 0.5−0.7 m high, very thin, forming dense stands, with only a few, long branches, stem-parts reddish at first, rhizomes divergent; leaves 5−18 cm long, 8−20 mm wide, fresh green on both sides, margins dentate; with 6−10 veins. CBa 5 (= *Arundinaria fortunei viridis* Hort.; *Sasa humilis* [Mitf.] Camus; *Pleioblastus humilis* [Mitford] Nakai). Japan. z8 Plate 44. H ◑ ∅

A. simonii C. & A. Rivière. To 8 m high in its habitat, in cultivation in N. Europe seldom taller than 3 m, stems hollow, 2−3 cm thick, the outer stems arching, stem sheath reddish at first; leaves 10−30 cm long, 1−3 cm wide, acuminate, fresh green above, frequently with narrow white stripes, underside blue-green on one half, nearly green on the other half; veins 8−14. SB 17; CBa 17 (= *Pleioblastus simonii* [Carr.] Mak.). Japan. 1862. z7 Plate 44. H ◑ ∅

'Variegata'. Like the species, but the smaller leaves more frequently white striped. BM 7146 (= *A. simonii* var. *striata* Mitford).

A. tecta (Walt.) Muehl. Stalks 1−3 m high, hollow, branched at the higher nodes, stem branches persistent, pubescent; leaves narrow oblong, 12−25 cm long, 15−30 mm wide, softly pubescent beneath, with 12−14 veins. BB 2, 1: 195; CBA 14 (as *A. macrosperma*) (= *Bambusa pumila* Mitf.). Eastern USA. Good hardiness, but not a very valuable species. z5 H ◑

A. viridi-striata (Regel) Mak. Stalks some 100−120 cm high, thin, reddish, green, hollow; leaves 10−20 cm long, green and gold-yellow striped, softly pubescent beneath, 1−3 cm wide. CBa 6 (as *Sasa auricoma*) (= *Pleioblastus viridi-striata* [Reg.] Mak.; = *A. auricoma* Mitf., *Sasa auricoma* E. G. Camus). Japan. 1870, z8 H ◑ ∅

var. **vagans** (Gamble) Mak. Stalks 0.1−0.2 m high, very strong grower and soon becoming a weed; leaves 5−12 cm long, 8−25 mm wide, both sides pubescent, denser beneath, veins 6−10 (= *A. pygmaea sensu* Nichols.; *A. vagans* Gamble). Japan. 1892. z8 Plate 44. H ◑ ∅

Arundinaria species are easily distinguished from the other winter hardy bamboo species by the stalks which are always terete and never flattened on one side such as, for example, *Phyllostachys*. All species prefer locations with semi-shade, and protection from cold north or west winds; a humus soil over a clay base is especially ideal. Planting is best done in spring; propagation is easily done by division.

Lit. Camus, E. G.: *Les Bambusees*; Text volume and Atlas. Paris 1913 ● Rivière, A. & C.: *Les Bambous*; Paris 1878 ● Pfitzer, E.: Die in Deutschland kultivierten *Arundinaria*-Arten; in DDG 1907, **221** to **223** ● For further literature see *Bambusaceae*, p. 100.

ARUNDO L. — GRAMINEAE

Perennial grasses with woody basal stems; leaves flat and wide; inflorescence (not developing in North Europe) dense, often very long, either tight or widening panicles; further details on the flowers will be unnecessary. — 12 species in tropical and subtropical Asia, 1 in the Mediterranean region.

Arundo donax L. To 5 m in its habitat, in cultivation in N. Europe to 3 m high; stalks 4−6 cm thick, foliate the whole length and originating from the fleshy, nearly knobby rhizomes; leaves alternate, numerous, lorate (strap-like), 5−7 cm wide, 30−70 cm long, blue-green, smooth, with rough margins; inflorescence 30−50 cm long, reddish at first, later white, September. S. Europe; in cultivation for ages. z7 Plate 43. ○ ∅

'Variegata'. Remaining somewhat smaller, often only 1 m high; leaves with broad white stripe. FS 1425 (= 'Versicolor';

'Picta'), Much more difficult to grow than the species. z7
Plate 43. ○ ∅

Found all over the Mediterranean region both planted and
wild. The long stalks are dried and used for various purposes.
Growing in any good garden soil, but requiring abundant
moisture for full, lush development.

ASCLEPIAS

Asclepias fruticosa see: **Gomphocampus fruticosa**

ASCYRUM L. — GUTTIFERAE

Shrubs or subshrubs, very closely related to *Hypericum*,
but with flowers 4 parted; twigs with 2 ridges, glabrous; leaves deciduous, opposite or in whorls, rarely
alternate, sessile, simple, margins entire, black dotted
beneath or deeply punctate visible from both sides;
flowers complete, with 4 yellow, usually somewhat
oblique or twisted, petals; sepals 4, in 2 pairs, the outer
set distinctly larger, collapsing together after blooming
to cover the fruit capsule; stamens numerous; fruit a
single chambered capsule, dehiscing along the 2−4
valves; seeds not winged. — 5 species in N. America
and Himalaya.

Ascyrum hypericoides L. St. Andrew's Cross. Deciduous shrub, 80 cm high, densely branched; leaves
densely packed, linear-oblong to oblanceolate, 1−2 cm
long, smaller leaves clustered in the leaf axils; flowers
terminal and axillary, some 1.5 cm wide, yellow, outer
sepals ovate, some 1 cm long, inner sepals much smaller and narrower, June−September; 2 very short

pistils. BC 400 (= *A. crux-andreae* L.) Southern N.
America on sandy, dry soil. z7 Fig. 126. **d S** ○ ✧

var. **multicaule** (Michx.) Fern. Only 10−30 cm high, stem
nearly horizontal to upright; leaves oblong to oblanceolate,
1−2 cm long; outer sepals oval to ovate, 1−2 cm long, petals
forming a cross. BB 2: 2443 (as *A. hypericoides*). Southern N.
America. Short lived. z7 **d S** ○ ✧

A. stans Michx. Shrub, upright, to 80 cm high, usually
with only one or few stems, these lightly winged;
leaves oval to broad oblong, obtuse, tough, 1−4 cm
long, some oriented outward, some upright; flowers
few, terminal, 3−4 cm wide, petals forming a cross,
gold-yellow, July−August; outer sepals nearly crossing, inner lanceolate; pistils 3−4. BB 2: 2442. Dry sandy
soil in Eastern N. America. z5 Fig. 126. **d S** ○ ✧

Both species quite hardy but living only a few years; always
propagated by seed. Prefers a light, sandy, acid soil,
otherwise treated like *Hypericum*. Interesting for its cruciform
flowers.

ASIMINA Adans. — PawPaw — ANNONACEAE

Evergreen or deciduous shrubs, occasionally also small
trees; leaves alternate, simple, margins entire; flowers
usually large, hermaphroditic, solitary or few in axillary groups, nodding, short stalked; 3 sepals, abcising
and smaller than the 6 petals; inner petals smaller and
usually upright; stamens numerous; carpels 3−15; fruit
a large, many seeded berry. —8 species in N. America.

Asimino triloba (L.) Dun. To 12 m high in its native
habitat, stem often branched low, bark dark gray,
young twigs red-brown pubescent; leaves obovate,

Fig. 126. **Ascyrum.**
Left, *A. stans,*
right *A. hypericoides*
(after Grimm)

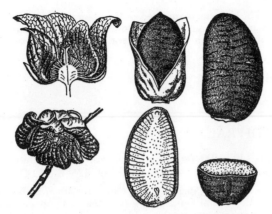

Fig. 127. *Asimina triloba*. Flower (natural size); seed with and without aril; seed cut longitudinally and across (after Baillon, Sargent)

10—25 cm long, short acuminate, generally tapering to the base, underside strongly pubescent when young; flowers appearing with the foliage or shortly before, solitary on 1 cm long, thick, rust-brown pubescent

pedicels, dirty purple-brown, often greenish at first, campanulate, May; fruit usually in whorls of 3, 5—15 cm long, green-yellow at first, then brown, edible; pulp somewhat banana-like, ripening September—October; seeds numerous, oval, flat, 2—2.5 cm long. BS 1: 346 (= *Annona triloba* L.). Eastern USA, New Jersey to Texas and Florida. z6 Plate 45; Fig. 127.

In the southern states of the USA has some economic value for its fruits. Requires, however, the best of soil. Interesting in cultivation as the only winter-hardy representative of the large tropical family, Annonaceae.

A. speciosus Nash. Upright shrub, to 1.5 m, twigs stiff; leaves elliptic to obovate or ovate, tough leathery, 5—8 cm long, white tomentose beneath at first, finally becoming glabrous; flowers 1—4 at a node, pedicel densely pubescent; calyx 8—12 mm long, outer petals 3—7 cm long, oblong, white or cream-yellow, very attractive, inner petals only half as long, spring; fruit oblong, 4—8 cm long, 1—2 cm thick, yellow-green MD 1933: 73. USA, Florida to Georgia. z8 ✧ ∅

Lit. Uphof, J.C. TH.: Die nordamerikanischen Arten der Gattung *Asimina*; DDG **45**, 61—76, 1933, with complete descriptions of the other species and ill.

ASPARAGUS L. — LILIACAE

Upright or climbing shrubs, some slightly woody, most with needlelike or linear phylloclades; usually inconspicuous flowers at the phylloclade base, white, yellow to greenish, solitary or grouped 2—4, frequently unisexual; fruit a berry. — Some 300 species in the Old World, usually in dry areas. Some species found in the trade in the warmer regions.

Asparagus acutifolius L. To 1 m high, stem woody, brown, bowed here and there, somewhat erratic; "leaves" reverting back to hard scales, the lower with sharp thorny tips, phylloclades ("leaves") narrow, twisting, 5—10 mm long, sharp acuminate, in clusters of 4—12 at a node, 0.5 mm thick, twigs and side branches with sparse pubescence; flowers very small, greenish-yellow, campanulate, inconspicuous, 5 mm long, August—December; fruit carmine-red to black. PMe 431; PEu 168. Throughout the Mediterranean area, in dry places, in hedges and especially on chalk soils. 1640. z9

A. aphyllus L. Similar to the above species, but with glabrous stem, rough, not climbing, strongly branched and angular, phylloclades thorny, in fascicles of 2—6,

0.5—1.5 mm wide. Spain, Sardinia, Sicily and Eastern Meditteranean. z9

A. stipularis Forsk. Stems upright, strongly branched, twigs very stiff, pointing outward, thorns short, phylloclades solitary or also in pairs, 2—3 cm long and 1—1.5 mm wide, thorny tipped, pointing radially out from the stem; flowers singular or in pairs, whitish, February—March. Mediterranean region. z9

A. umbellatus Link. Subshrub, twigs thin and wire-like, furrowed and strongly branched, the side branches pendulous, densely covered with stiff, nearly thorny, triangular phylloclades, in clusters of 10—20, some 12 mm long; flowers small, white, fragrant in fascicles of 12; fruit yellow to deep red. BM 7733; DRHS 195. Canary Islands and Madeira. z9

In frost-free areas the well-known foliage plant, *A. densiflorus* (Kunth) Jessop 'Sprengeri', better known as *A. sprengeri* Regel, can be grown.

Lit. Huttleston, D.G.: The names of three commonly cultivated ornamental asparaguses; in Baileya **17**, 58—63, 1970.

ASTEALIA Banks & Soland — LILIACEAE

Actually not shrubs, plants forming a rosette (somewhat like *Yucca* and *Beschorneria*, also found within this work); rhizomes short and thick, with lineally-keeled leaves, crowded, sheathed near the base and silky pubescent or scaly; flowers small, dioecious, few or many, usually in panicles on a long stalk; perianth with 6 lobes, persistent, tubular connate at the base or also

distinct, outspread or reflexed; stamens of the male flowers 6, fastened at the base of the lobes, stamens becoming staminodes in the female flowers; fruit a berry. — 25 species, usually in New Zealand, some in Australia, Tasmania, New Guinea and South Sea Islands to Hawaii. In cultivation in milder areas and very ornamental. Require rich humus soil. Positive identification of the species only possible with the fruit capsule and seed in hand.

Astelia banksii A. Cunn. Plant very dense, tough rosette; leaves 100−250 cm long, 3−4.5 cm wide, lower half ascending, upper half nodding, leathery, margins curled with age; above the sheath narrow, keeled and folded, apex long and tapering narrower, sheath wide, both sides covered with dense, glossy white scales, blade bluish-green and glabrous above, silvery beneath, base densely silky; male flowers slender, with 25−30 cm long panicles of numerous, greenish flowers, female inflorescence shorter and thicker; berries ovoid, 3 chambered, purple-black (= *A. latifolia* Jacques). New Zealand. z8 ⌀

A. chathamica (Skottsb.) L. B. Moore. Plant tough rosette; leaves 60−200 cm long, 4−10 cm wide, keeled near the sheath, but otherwise the blade only slightly keeled, sheath base white, scaly on both sides, blade silvery-metallic above, silky gray-green beneath; inflorescence large and upright; fruit 10 × 10 mm in size, nearly globose, orange. Chatham Island, on wet, peaty soil. z8 ⌀

A. nervosa Hook. f. Bushy plant, often developing large columnar, stem 1−2(−3) cm thick; leaves 50−150 cm long, 2−4 cm wide, stiff, bowed outward and very tough, strongly keeled over the sheath, sheaths to 8 cm wide at the base, thickly scaled, blade green above with dense translucent scales, underside with a persistent film of white or brownish scales over a thin tomentose layer; inflorescence erect, scaly, flowers from light greenish-brown to deep chestnut-brown; fruit broad ovate, 8−15 × 2.5−4.5 cm in size, from orange to nearly red, until fully ripe surrounded by a fleshy calyx (= *A. montana* [Kirk] Cockayne; *A. cockaynei* Cheesem.). New Zealand; subalpine forests and grasslands. z8 ⌀

A.petriei Cockayne. Plant dense, broad rosette, stem 2−2.5 cm thick; leaves 25−80 cm long, 2−6.5 wide, bowed, but stiff and leathery tough, not folded above the sheathed base, sheaths 7 cm wide at the base, white, only slightly scaly, blade not acuminate, light green above, midrib reddish, white beneath, with very dense, persistent, short scales, keeled; male panicles 4−20 cm long, loose, female panicles only 3 × 3 cm or less and densely packed; fruit inversely conical, 2 × 1 cm, but usually smaller and wider, yellow-orange, in a fleshy shell. New Zealand, in the mountains. z8 Plate 1.

ASTERANTHERA Hanst. — GESNERIACEAE

Climbing shrub from the temperate rain forests of Chile and neighboring parts of Argentina, very closely related to *Mitraria* and *Sarmienta*, but differing from them in the flower form which more closely resembles *Columnea*. Differing from *Columnea* in the undivided disc ring (which on *Columnea* is made up of irregular but distinct glands). — Only 1 species.

Asteranthera ovata (Cav.) Hanst. Evergreen shrublet, climbing on stems and into trees by means of aerial roots, to 3 m high, weakly rooting at the nodes, twigs whitish pubescent; leaves opposite, usually rounded, 1 to 3.5 cm long, obtuse, each side with usually 3 obtuse crenate teeth, bristly pubescent, thickish; flowers solitary, axillary, usually in pairs, corolla tubular at the base, limb outspread, 5 pointed, red, 2.5 cm long, June; anthers in stellate bundles. BMns 15; BS 1: 348. Chile. 1926 z8 #✤

Needs a rich, organic soil in a cool place with something on which to climb (tree or old stem).

ASTERISCUS Mill. — COMPOSITAE

Low shrubs or subshrubs; leaves opposite, margins entire or sparsely dentate, thin or also succulent; flowers in rather large, solitary heads, terminal, with ray and disc florets, outer perianth like foliate leaves, obtuse; base of inflorescence with tiny scale-like leaves; pappus composed of very small scales. — 5 species on the Canary Islands; placed by many authors in *Odontospermum*.

Asteriscus intermedius Webb. Resembles *A. sericeus*, but with silvery twigs (not gray), leaves narrower and longer, not grouped at the branch ends. BFCa 91. Canary Islands; Lanzarote. z9 ✤

A. sericeus L.f. Shrub, 30−50 cm high, very densely branched, the older branches dark gray to blackish; leaves in tight rosettes at the branch tips, 3−5 cm long, broad oblanceolate, dense silver silky pubescence on both sides, aromatic; flower heads solitary, terminal, 3−3.5 cm wide, gold-yellow, sessile, February−May. PBl 2: 740; BFCa 274 (= *Odontospermum sericeum* [L.f.] Schultz Bip.). Canary Islands; Fuerteventura. 1779. z9 Plate 49.✤ ⌀

A. stenophyllus Link. Small, densely branched shrub, 15−40 cm high, twigs gray; leaves densely covering the branches, linear, dense gray pubescence; flower heads some 2 cm wide, ray florets light yellow to gold-yellow. BFCa 275, Canary Islands; Grand Canary on the dry east slopes. z9 ✤

In culture occasionally as *A. sericeus*; must be over-wintered in a cool greenhouse in temperate zones.

ASTRAGALUS L. — LEGUMINOSAE

Perennials, annuals or subshrubs, usually densely branched; pubescence quite variable; leaves even or uneven (because of thorned rachis) pinnate, rarely with only 1 or 3 leaflets; leaflets always entire; stipules distinct or fused to the petiole or beneath; flowers whitish, yellowish, purple or violet, in axillary racemes, spikes or heads; calyx tubular, campanulate or teardrop shaped, with uneven teeth; standard petal erect, narrow; wing petals oblong, keel appressed; ovary sessile or stalked, usually with many ovules; pods very diverse, often divided into 2 long chambers and opening at the end, or also 1 chambered, membranous and remaining closed. — Some 2000 species in the Northern Hemisphere, but only a few in culture.

Astragalus angustifolia Lam. Thorny, globose subshrub, 20 cm high, stiff cushion-like; leaves with 3—20 paired, narrow-lanceolate, leathery leaflets, densely white pubescent, later becoming nearly glabrous; flowers whitish-yellow, grouped 3—8 in short stalked racemes, July—August. PBl 882 (= *A. olympicus* Pall.; *A. leucophyllus* Willd.). Greece, Asia Minor. z6 Plate 46. **d** ○ ✧

A. austriacus Jacq. Subshrub, 30 cm high, woody at the base, wide branching, woody part crooked, much branched, glabrous; leaves 5—8 cm long, with 7—10 paired pinnae, leaflets 1 cm long, linear, emarginate, basal leaves more obovate; flowers 8—20 in curving racemes on a 10 cm long stalk, lilac, July—August; calyx short campanulate, pubescent, teeth triangular; wing tips 2 cleft. HM 1477; HF 2435 (= *A. dichopterus* Pall.). Spain to Siberia; dry areas in the mountains, fields and meadows. z5 **d** ○

A. depressus L. Woody, some 10 cm high, nearly conical growing subshrub, twigs seldom longer than 10 cm; leaves 5—10 cm long, with 19—27 pinnae, leaflets oval-ovate-rounded, 6—8 mm long, very blunt to emarginate, glabrous above, appressed pubescent beneath; flowers whitish to bluish, in short racemes, with 6—14 flowers on a 2—3 cm long shaft, May—June; pods 2 cm long, nearly cylindrical, 2 chambered. HM 1464 (= *A. leucophaeus* Sm.). Dry, rough, steep south facing slopes in the high mountains of Spain to Asia Minor. z6 **d** ○ ✧

A. exscapus L. Rosette-form subshrub, woody only at the base, twigs usually only 1 cm long, very rarely longer, usually with a very long and finger-thick taproot, rosette middle and stem with 2—4 mm long, whitish pubescence; leaves consistent, 15—25 cm long, with 12—19 pairs of oval-ovate, 1—2 cm leaflets with both sides densely silky pubescent; inflorescence with 3—9 flowers, nearly sessile, flowers 2.5 cm long, light yellow, May—July; pods 2 cm long, nearly 1 cm thick. HM Pl. 167. Spain, N. Italy to Crimea, open, dry woods, alkaline soils. Very difficult to transplant. z6 **d** ○

A. massiliensis (Mill.) Lam. Deciduous shrub, to 30 cm high, very thorny, whitish, older branches densely covered with stiff, thorny, sharp 2.5—6 cm long leaf

Fig. 128. *Astragalus masiliensis* (from Kerner)

rachises; leaves pinnate, with 6—12 paired leaflets, these oblong-elliptic, 3—6 mm long, obtuse, silky pubescent on both sides; flowers white, usually 3—8 in racemes, sometimes as long or shorter than the leaves, July; calyx tubular, 6 mm long, appressed pubescent, teeth rather short, at most 1/3 as long as the calyx tube; corolla some 1.5 cm long, standard petal ovate; fruit pod 1 cm, appressed pubescent. BS 1: 349 (= *A. tragacantha* L.p.p.). NW. Mediterranean region, sunny areas in gravelly soil near the sea. 1640. z6 Fig. 128. ✧

A. monspessulanus L. Subshrub, growth rosette-like, stem woody at the base, 10—15 cm high, thin, light green, at first with sparse forked hairs, later becoming glabrous, densely surrounded with stipules; leaves all 10—20 cm long, with 8—20 paired leaflets, leaflets ovate to lanceolate, somewhat pubescent beneath; flowers 10—12 in nearly capitate inflorescences on 10—15 cm long stalks, the leaves seldom surpassing the flowers, violet-blue; calyx as long as the corolla, tubular, with 5 unevenly long teeth; April—June; fruit pods to 3 cm long, rod-round, 3 mm thick, curved. BM 375; HM 185. Spain, S. France, SE. Europe; slopes, gravelly open conifer stands. Very nice. z6 **d** ○ ✧

A. sempervirens Lam. Subshrub, 10—15 cm high, branching espalier-like, woody, stalks and leaves with simple, white woolly pubescence, twigs with thorny leaf rachises; leaves 3—6 cm long, with 6—10 paired pinnae, leaflets 1 cm long, 2 mm wide, gray-green, prickly tipped; flowers 5—8 in capitate racemes, light pink to whitish, July—August; calyx teeth awl-shaped, as long as the keel petals; pods ovate, white, erect. HM 1486; HF 2445 (= *A. aristatus* L'Hér.). Pyrenees to the Balkans; dry slopes in the high mountains; on limestone. z6 ○

The botanical name is misleading, as the plant is not evergreen.

A. sirinicus Ten. Very similar to *A. massiliensis*, but growing much denser; calyx teeth relatively longer, to half as long as the calyx tube, calyx pubescence erect; flowers yellow or reddish, either with long, rather erect pubescence or nearly glabrous (= *A. tragacantha* L.p.p.). Mountains of Corsica, Sardinia, Apennines and Balkans. z6

A. tragacantha L. By modern interpretation, this name is simply doubtful nomenclature (nomen ambiguum), Linné (Linnaeus) was presumably referring to 2 other species; *A. massiliensis* and *A. sirinicus*, which see.

Although very attractive and usually perfectly hardy plants for the rock garden, they are rarely found in cultivation because of difficulties in culture. Most species require gravelly, limestone soil in warm sunny locations.

Lit. Barneby, R.C.: *Pugillus Astragalorum*; I. Leafl. W. Bot. **3**, 97—114; 1944; II. Proc. Calif. Acad. Sci. ser 4, **15**, 147—170, 1944; III-IV. Leafl. W. Bot. **4**, 49—63, 65-147, 228-238, 1944-1946; **5**, 1—9, 1947; VII. Amer. Mdl. Nat. **37**, 421—516, 1947; VIII-IX. Leafl. W. Bot. **5**, 25—35, 82—89, 1947—1948.

ASTRAPAEA

Astrapaea wallichi see: **Dombeya wallichii**

ATHEROSPERMA Labill. — ATHEROSPERMATACEAE

Monotypic genus rather closely related to Calycanthaceae; perianth not, as with other genera of the Atherospermataceae, consisting of sepals and petals, but rather a whorl of "tepals" (similar to *Magnolia*) and ovary with a number of pistils, each with its own style; leaves without reticulate venation; anthers with dehiscent valves; fruit dry, feather-like.

Atherosperma moschatum Labill. Black Sassafras. Evergreen tree, to 45 m high in its habitat (in England to only 8 m), stem straight, bark smooth, gray, crown narrowly conical and very densely branched, young twigs finely pubescent; leaves opposite, short petioled, lanceolate, 5—10 cm long, 1—3 cm wide, acute to acuminate, each side with some teeth on the apical half or also entire, leathery tough, dark green above, smooth and glossy, underside more or less bluish to white and short tomentose, with a peppery fragrance; flowers dioecious, solitary axillary, male flowers 2 cm wide, with 8 tepals in 2 whorls, white and silky pubescent, anthers usually 12, female flowers smaller, greenish, denser and longer pubescence, February; fruit 1 cm wide, feathery. BMns 43; LNH 224 (= *A. integrifolium* A. Cunn.). Tasmania, in forests together with *Eucalyptus*; SE. Australia. z8 Plate 4. # ✧ Ø

Cultivated in the British Isles in protected areas of the milder regions in good, fertile soil. Propagation easy from cuttings.

ATRAPHAXIS L. — Shrubby Buckwheat — POLYGONACEAE

Low, deciduous, strongly branched shrubs with or without thorns; leaves small, alternate or in fascicles at the nodes, with distinct, membranous sheath; flowers bisexual, small, white or light pink, solitary or several in the leaf axils, to grouped in terminal racemes; perianth 4—5 parted, both outer parts smaller and inconspicuous, the inner larger; anthers usually 6—8, filaments widened and connate at the base; ovary compressed or triangular; fruit a 2 or 3 sided nutlet, later covered by the enlarged inner petals. — 25 species in Central Asia, Asia Minor, Greece, N. Africa, in deserts and steppes.

Atraphaxis billardieri Jaub. & Spach. Shrub, 30—50 cm high, often also procumbent, thornless or also somewhat thorny, young twigs glabrous, gray; leaves narrow ovate to lanceolate, 3—8 mm long, margins entire, green, glabrous, distinctly reticulate venation; flowers with 5 sepals, the inner 3 ovate to cordate, erect, pink-red, June; fruit triangular. BM 8820. Greece, Asia Minor, Syria. z6 Fig. 129. d ○

A. caucasica (Hoffm.) Pavlov. Shrub, 50 cm high, often procumbent, twigs thornless or with few thorns, young twigs light green, fine glandular; leaves oval or obovate to rounded, 1—2.5 cm long, narrowing to both ends, margin wavy, dull green; flowers pink-white, with 5 sepals, 3 persistent and later becoming dark pink, in 2—4 cm long racemes, June; fruit triangular. BM 1065 (= *A. buxifolia* Jaub. & Spach.). Transcaucasia to Turkestan. z6 Plate 33; Fig. 129. d ○

A. frutescens (L.) Eversm. Shrub, 30—60 cm high, twigs erect, thin, gray-white, thornless; leaves oblong-lanceolate to oval, quite variable, 0.8—3 cm long, gray-green, margin wavy; flowers whitish, grouped 2—5 together in small fascicles, those clustered in terminal racemes, August—September; fruit 6 mm wide, pink, triangular (= *A. lanceolata* Meisn.). SE. Europe and Caucasus to Turkestan and Siberia. ℗ China, as a soil stabilizer. z3 Fig. 129. d ○ ⚭

var. **virgata** Regel. Twigs thinner, whiter. Turkestan.

A. muschketowii Krassn. Shrub, 1.5—2.5 m high, densely branched, bark very cracked and peeling, young twigs light brown-yellow, thornless; leaves oblong-elliptic, 3—8 cm long, light green, margin crisped; flowers white, 1 cm wide, ovary and anthers pink, sepals 5, in 3—5 cm long, leafy, short, terminal racemes, May—June; fruit triangular. BS 1:335; BM 7435 (= *A. latifolia* Koehne). Middle Asia, Tian Shan region. Most beautiful species of the entire genus. z5 Fig. 129. d ○ ✧ ⚭

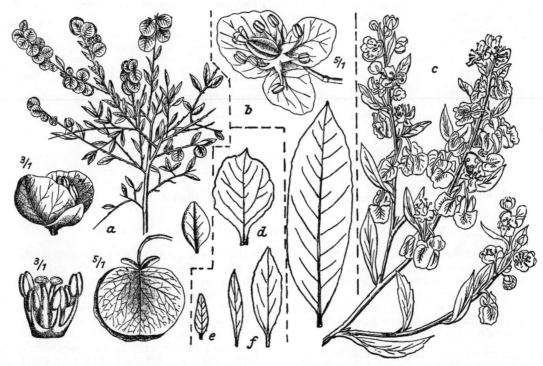

Fig. 129. **Atraphaxis.** a. *A. spinosa*, twig with mature perianths, single flower, stamens and ovary, fruit with petals, leaf; b. *A. mucshketowii*, flower and leaf; c. *A. frutescens*, twig; d. *A. caucasica*; e. *A. billardieri*; f. *A. frutescens* (from Dammer, Bot. Reg.)

A. spinosa L. Desert shrub, 30—50 cm high, stiff branches, whitish, very thorny and twiggy; leaves ovate-oval, 5—10 mm long, blue-green; flowers 8 mm wide, whitish-pink, sepals 4, both inner ones remaining rounded, long retaining their pink color, August; fruit 2 winged. BM 1065 (as *Polygonum crispulum*). Asia Minor, SE. Europe, Orient; dry areas. Deserts. z6 Fig. 129. **d** ○

As desert plants they require only sandy, gravelly soil, and especially dryness and full sun. Although *A. muschketowii* is very attractive in the rock garden, these species are only practical for the collector.

ATRIPLEX L. — CHENOPODIACEAE

Deciduous shrubs or subshrubs, somewhat covered with gray scales or powder; leaves usually alternate, rarely opposite, lanceolate-obovate-ovate, gray pulverulent or scaly or smooth, without pubescence; flowers unisexual, among them also occasionally perfect flowers, clustered in terminal spikes or panicles; male flowers with 3 to 5 parted calyx, female flowers with 2 large bracts, but without a calyx; bracts usually dentate; fruit a nutlet with a thin shell, enclosed by the bracts. — Some 200 species in the temperate zones and in the subtropics, usually weedy.

Atriplex canescens (Pursh) James. Shrub, to 1.5 m high, fast growing, twigs more or less silver-gray; leaves linear-lanceolate, 2—5 cm long, gray-green; flowers yellowish, very small, July—September; fruit bracts 1.5 cm long, deeply dentate. BB 1385; MS 106 (= *A. occidentalis* D. Dietr.). Western N. America, from British Columbia to California; dry, alkaline soil or saline areas. Evergreen in milder regions. z7 Fig. 130. **d** ○ ∅

A. confertifolia (Torr.) S. Wats. Nearly evergreen shrub, to 1.5 m high, open branched, often more or less thorny, twigs terete, gray-white scabby; leaves oval-obovate-circular, 5—20 mm long, short-petioled, both sides scabby gray-green, thickish; flowers yellowish-green, small, in rounded, dense fasicles in the leaf axils, May—August; fruit bracts broad-oval to rounded, 1 cm wide. MS 101 (= *A. spinosa* D. Dietr.). Western N. America, from Oregon to New Mexico. z7 Fig. 130. **# d** ○ ∅

A. halimus L. Shrub, to 2 m, semi-evergreen (in milder areas), branches and twigs gray-white scaly and pulverulent, very stoutly branched; leaves ovate, rhombic or oblong, 2—5 cm long, acute, bluish or white-gray, pulverulent, occasionally with some teeth, petiole short; flowers greenish, in large, terminal, 20 cm long panicles, perianth somewhat reddish, July—September; fruit bracts kidney shaped, margins entire. S. Europe; coast of the Mediterranean. z8 Ⓕ S.

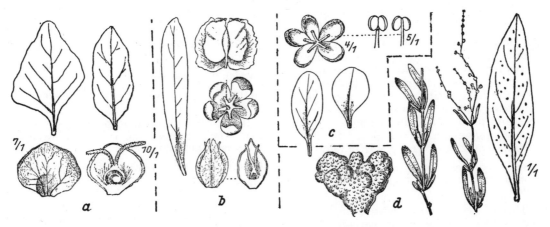

Fig. 130. **Atriplex.** a. *A. halimus*, leaves, flower, fruit; b. *A. canescens*, leaf, flowers, fruit; c. *A. confertifolia*, leaves, flower, stamens; d. *A. portulacoides*, twigs, leaf, fruit (from Fiori, Schneider)

Tunisia, for stabilizing sand dunes Plate 46; Fig. 130. **d** ○∅

A. nuttallii S. Wats. Shrub, 30—60 cm high, densely branched, twigs rather stiff, terete, nearly white; leaves oblong, linear-oblanceolate, 2—5 cm long, margin entire, sessile, pale green; flowers yellowish, the male in terminal spikes, the female in axillary heads, often dioecious, June—September; fruit bracts ovate to rounded, deep and irregularly dentate, 3—4 mm long. BB 1384. W. Canada to Idaho; inland plains and dry areas. Hardy. z6 **d** ○∅

A. portulacoides L. Shrub, to 50 cm, branches thin, more or less procumbent; leaves obovate-oblong, thickish, opposite (important for identification!), some 1 cm long, yellowish or gray-green, silvery pulverulent; flowers very small, greenish, in terminal panicles, August. Coast of England, Denmark to Mediterranean; on saline soils and beach fronts. Of little merit in cultivation. z6 Fig. 130. **d** ○

All the mentioned species are of primary use along the sea coast, as they require a saline soil. *A. halimus* is often found along the Mediterranean shores but usually much grazed by livestock. They are quite appealing in appearance with the silver-gray powdery coating, if given the proper cultural requirements.

AUCUBA Thunb. — CORNACEAE

Evergreen shrubs; leaves opposite, margins entire or somewhat dentate, leathery, glossy; flowers dioecious, 4 parted, small, reddish or greenish, in terminal panicles; male flowers with 4 petals, stunted ovary and 4 stamens, female flowers without stamens, panicles short; fruit a single seeded, berry-like drupe, with persistent calyx and pistil. — 3 or 4 species in China, Japan and Western Himalaya.

Aucuba chinensis Benth. Evergreen shrub, 2—3 m high; leaves quite variable in form, usually oblong to oval, 8—20 cm long, sharply acuminate, margins entire or dentate toward the apex, very leathery tough, dull gray-green above (very important for identification!), more blue-green beneath; inflorescence 10 cm long, with scattered, brown pubescence, petals longer and narrower than those of *A. japonica* with caudate tips; fruits red, ovate. LWT 282. China: Hupeh, Szechwan, Yunnan, Formosa. 1901. z8 Fig. 131. # ◑∅

f. **angustifolia** Rehd. Leaves quite narrow, 7—20 cm long, only some 1.5—4 cm wide. #∅

Fig. 131. **Aucuba.** a. *A. japonica*, leaf and petal; b. *A. japonica* 'Longifolia'; c. *A. chinensis*, petals; d. *A. himalaica*, leaf and flower (from Wangerin, Flore des Serres; a. and b. original)

f. **obcordata** Rehd. Leaves distinctly cuneate, generally tapering from the apex to the petiole. # Ø

A. himalaica Hook. & Thoms. Shrub, 2—3 m high, young twigs pubescent at first, though soon becoming glabrous; leaves narrow ovate-lanceolate, acuminate, cuneate at the base, much finer and wider toothed on the basal half of the blade (relative to the other species), 15—20 cm long, leaf petiole usually violet; inflorescence densely pubescent, petals lanceolate, acuminate; fruit some 1.3 cm long, orange or bright red, glossy. FS 1271; HAL 101. E. Himalaya, 2500 m. z6 Fig. 131. # ◑ Ø

(There exists some controversy as to whether the plant in cultivation is actually *A. himalaica* or is confused with *A. japonica* 'Longifolia'.)

A. japonica Thunb. Evergreen, upright shrub, 2—2.5 m high, branches thick, green, glabrous; leaves leathery, narrow oval to more elliptic, 8—20 cm long, acute, margins sparsely and coarsely dentate, glossy green on both sides; flowers of the male plants in erect, terminal, 10 cm long panicles, with 4(—5) reddish petals, female flowers in much smaller inflorescences, March—April; fruit 1—1.5 cm long, elliptic, red, usually many in clusters. KIF 3: 57. Japan; in evergreen brushy forests; Formosa, Korea. 1783. z7 Fig. 131. # ◑ Ø

In addition to the species a number of cultivars are in the trade, many only available in one sex:

'**Bicolor**'. Leaves green with a large spot in the middle, without small speckles, margin large toothed. Ø

'**Concolor**'. Leaves totally green (typical), male and female (= *viridis*).

'**Crassifolia**'. Leaves totally green, especially thick and leathery.

'**Crotonifolia**'. Leaves very dense and finely yellow punctate, female. HTS 31. Most popular form in Belgium. Ø

'**Dentata**'. Leaves green, only 4—8 cm long, with 1—2 very large teeth on each side.

'**Grandis**'. Green, leaves very large, wide, very glossy, female.

'**Hillieri**'. Leaves very large, deep green, very glossy, fruit dark carmine; fast growing. Introduced by Hillier Nursery, Winchester, England.

'**Leucocarpa**'. Fruit yellowish-white. From Japan. ⚭

'**Limbata**'. Leaves very large, large toothed, green with yellow limb (= *sulphurea*).

'**Longifolia**'. Leaves green, oblong-lanceolate, 8—15 cm long, sharply acuminate, abundant fruiting (= *angustifolia*, *salicifolia*). Plate 49; Fig. 131. Ø ⚭

'**Luteocarpa**'. Leaves broad elliptic, sparsely dentate, somewhat yellow punctate; fruit yellow. ⚭

'**Nana**'. Dwarf growing; leaves smaller, abundant fruiting (or = '*Rotundifolia*'?).

'**Picturata**'. Leaves oval-oblong, with a large yellow patch in the middle, surrounded by small yellow dots (= *latimaculata*, *picta*, *aureomaculata*). Plate 47. Ø

'**Variegata**'. Leaves dense yellow punctate, dots of unequal size, male and female (= *maculata*, *punctata*). Plate 49. Ø

Most *Aucuba* species are quite winter hardy even in less than favorable conditions, although as may have been presupposed, semi-shade to shady locations, under tall trees, out of the winter sun and a well mulched soil are advisable. Otherwise treated like *Rhododendron*.

AURINIA Desv. — CRUCIFERAE

Formerly classified with *Alyssum*. Recent work has set this genus as separate. Leaves in dense, basal rosettes, erect, seldom shorter than 5 cm, usually 7—15 cm long, margin sinuate, dentate or pinnatisect, fleshy and swollen at the base; leaves along the stem only half as long, more sparsely distributed; flower buds globose, calyx cup-shaped, sepals more or less horizontally widespread; stigmas distinctly 2 lobed. — 7 species, from Middle and S. Europe to Asia Minor.

Aurinia saxatilis (L.) Desv. To 30 cm high, with erect, branching stalks; leaves in rosettes, the lowest spathulate, 10 cm long, lanceolate to obovate, margins entire or somewhat curving toothed, narrowing at the petiole, soft gray stellate tomentose, leaves on the stalk less numerous, only 1—2 cm long; inflorescences in corymbs, flowers gold-yellow, petals spathulate, somewhat emarginate, April—May; fruit clusters somewhat elongated, siliques with 2 seeds in each chamber. HF 1382 (= *Alyssum saxatile* L.). Middle Europe, highlands of N. Balkan, S. Russia, Asia Minor; sunny limestone slopes. 1680. z6 Plate 50. d ○ ✦

Widely disseminated in gardens and often found in the rock garden. Also available, the following cultivars:

'**Citrinum**'. Flowers lemon-yellow (HCC 602/1). 1894. d ○ ✦

'**Compactum**'. Only to 15 cm high, otherwise like the species. Introduced by Vilmorin, 1872. d ○ ✦

'**Dudley Nevill**'. Dark cream-yellow. From English gardens. d ○ ✦

'**Plenum**'. Flowers gold-yellow, double, sterile, darker yellow than the others. d ○ ✦

'**Tom Thumb**'. Only 7—10 cm high in bloom, all other parts small. Very nice. In English gardens. d ○ ✦

'**Variegatum**'. Weaker growing; leaves yellow-white variegated. 1865. Ø

Lit. Dudley, T.D.: Ornamental Madworts (*Alyssum*) and the correct name of the Goldentuft *Alyssum*. Arnoldia 1966, 33—45.!!

AZALEA see under RHODODENDRON

The Azaleas are only a subgenus of *Rhododendron*. In most cases the specific epithet remains unchanged. For example, *Azalea albrechtii* is found alphabetically as **Rhododendron albrechtii**, *Azalea calendulacea* as **R. calendulaceum**, and *Azalea nudiflora* as **R. nudiflorum**, etc.

The better known Azalea forms and varieties, however, which do not share the same specific epithet are as follows:

Azalea	= **Rhododendron**
amoena	**obtusum 'Amoenum'**
daviesii	**viscosepalum 'Daviesii'**

indica	**simsii**
kaempferi	**obtusum** var. **kaempferi**
ledifolia	**mucronatum**
macrantha	**indicum** (L.) Sweet
mollis Andr.	**japonicum**
mollis × *sinensis*	**kosterianum**
pontica	**luteum**
rhombica	**reticulatum**
rustica 'Flore pleno'	**mixtum**
sinensis	**molle**
Yodogawa	**yedoense**

A. procumbens see: **Loiseleuria procumbens**

AZARA Ruiz. & Pav. — FLACOURTIACEAE

Evergreen, twiggy shrubs, also small trees in their habitat; leaves alternate, occasionally also paired at the nodes (also in that case one leaf large and one small), margins entire or serrate, often with stipules, stipule often as large as the corresponding leaf, therefore making the impression of paired leaves (but not opposite!), bitter tasting; flowers usually in corymbs, fragrant, corolla absent, sepals 4—6, connate only at the base, with numerous, yellow stamens; fruit a many seeded, small berry. — 11 species in S. America, from S. Bolivia and Brazil to Chile and Argentina, on both sides of the Andes.

Azara dentata Ruiz & Pav. Shrub, to 2m, in its habitat also to 3 m high or a small tree, twigs terete, eventually red-brown, gray tomentose; leaves leathery, 1—3 at a node, the largest oval or ovate, to 3 cm long, fine toothed, dark glossy green above, tomentose beneath, the other leaves much smaller; flowers gold-yellow, in short, many-branched corymbs, fragrant, May—June. BR 1788. Chile, Concepcion. 1830. Tolerates dryness well. z8 Plate 47. # ☼

A. integrifolia Ruiz & Pav. Low shrub, although in the milder parts of England reaching 5—10 m high, twigs reddish-brown, with lenticels, young twigs gray-tomentose at first, later becoming sparsely pubescent; leaves oval, to 2 cm long, grouped 2—3, nearly sessile, usually entire, tough; flowers gold-yellow with dark anthers, very numerous, fragrant, sepals somewhat reddish outside, February—March; fruit pea size, lilac-white. BM 9620. Chile, near Llolli. 1832. z8 Plate 47. # ☼

var. **brownae** (Phil). Bean. Primarily differing from the species in the larger leaves, to 6 cm long and 3 cm wide, apical ¼ dentate, more obovate. Chile, Cordilleras. z8 # ☼

'Variegata'. Leaves smaller, rounder, middle dark green, margin white, a narrow pink zone between. Originated around 1870 in Kew Gardens, London. Very tender. z8 # ☼ Ø

A. lanceolata Hook. f. Tall shrub or small tree in milder areas, young twigs densely brown tomentose; leaves lanceolate to narrow oval, 2—6 cm long, coarsely and evenly dentate, glossy and light green on both sides; flowers gold-yellow, very large, 5—7 together, in small, axillary corymbs, slightly fragrant, April—May; fruit pea size, lilac to white, porcelain-like in appearance, with persistent calyx. BM 9374; NF 5: 227; BS 1: 362; PFC 101. Chile; moist areas of the forest. 1926. Probably the most beautiful of the genus. z8 Plate 37, 50. # ☼ ⚛

A. microphylla Hook. f. Small shrub, to 5 m high in mild areas, twigs dense and dark tomentose, later becoming glabrous, pinnately branched; leaves in 2 opposing rows, obovate, the larger leaf to 2.5 cm long, the smaller ½ as large, obtuse, somewhat dentate or entire, dark glossy green; flowers with greenish sepals and yellow stamens, very small, vanilla scented. February—April; berries small, orange-red, globose. SH 2: 240. Chile. 1861. Hardiest species. z8 Plate 47. #

'Variegata'. Leaves with irregularly wide white-yellow border, otherwise like the species; weaker grower, slight winter hardiness. Originated around 1916. As a young plant, resembling *Cotoneaster horizontalis* 'Variegatus'. # Ø

A. petiolairs Johnst. Upright growing shrub, in its native habitat also a small tree, *Ilex*-like in appearance, twigs reddish, glabrous; leaves ovate or oval, 4—8 cm long, leathery tough, margins prickly saw-toothed, dark green above, light green beneath; flowers nearly "mimosa"-like, cream-yellow, with very long stamens, April—May, very attractive in flower. BM 5178; PFC 101 (= *A. gilliesii* Hook.). Chile. 1859 z8 Plate 47. # ☼ Ø

A. serrata Ruiz. & Pav. Shrub, 3—4 m high in its habitat, resembles *A. dentata* (and often confused with such), but with soft pubescent twigs, leaves larger, 3—5 cm long, not tomentose beneath, frequently totally glabrous; flowers in globose, axillary umbels, yellow, on 3 cm long, thin, pubescent stalks. Chile. z8 # ☼

All species should only be considered for very mild, practically frost free areas, otherwise overwintering in the greenhouse is necessary. Very splendid with the Mimosa-like flowers in early spring. All species prefer a deep, moist humus soil.

Lit. Lawrence, W.: *Azara*; in New Flora and Silva **5**, 226—228, 1933.

BACCHARIS L. — Bush Groundsel — COMPOSITAE

Deciduous or evergreen shrubs, occasionally also small trees or perennials; young twigs glabrous, often somewhat sticky and lepidote (crusty scales); leaves alternate, simple, usually coarsely dentate; flowers dioecious, in many-flowered small heads, grouped in terminal or axillary panicles; fruit compressed, usually 10 ribbed; male flowers with often feathery pappus "brush" at the tip, female flowers with strap-like corolla. — Some 400 species in N. and S. America, many of those leafless and xerophytic, with green, occasionally winged stems; only a few moderately winter hardy.

Baccharis genistelloides Pers. Upright shrub, branches several winged, running spirally on the young twigs; leaves usually stunted; flowers of little merit, gold-yellow, with strong honey scent, December—February. EKW 131. S. Brazil to N. Patagonia. Occasionally in botanic gardens, but of little garden worth. z8

A. halimifolia L. Deciduous shrub, to 3 m high, many branched, branches somewhat angular; leaves obovate to oblong, short petioled, 2—7 cm long, gray-green, acute, sparsely dentate, on flowering branches margins entire, resinous; flowers white, in heads of 3—5, these grouped in large panicles, August—Septemer, very attractive in flower; fruit 1 mm long, with 8 mm long, white pappus. BB 3834. N. America, Massachusetts to Florida and Texas, salt marshes. 1683. Very hardy. z5 Plate 51; Fig. 132.

B. patagonica Hook. & Arn. Evergreen, twiggy shrub, 2—3 high, twigs angular, sticky at first; leaves obovate, sessile, 0.8—2 cm long, with a few large teeth, dark green above, both sides dense rough scaly (lepidote); flowers yellowish-white, heads usually solitary, sessile, axillary, May—June; pappus 1 cm long. Patagonia, Straight of Magellan. 1880. z8 #

B. pilularis DC. Evergreen, mat-forming shrub, 15—30 cm high, becoming 2.5 m wide; leaves obovate-cuneate, 6—12 mm long, dark green, glabrous, with few large or sinuate teeth or entire; flower heads solitary axillary, male flowers yellowish, female flowers whitish, pappus of the female flowers later becoming some 1 cm long, July—September. MS 696. California, on sandy hills and dunes near the coast. Valuable, soil stabilizing groundcover. z8 Ⓕ Planted in California for erosion control.

Fig. 132. *Baccharis halimifolia* (from Hoffmann, Schmidt)

B. salicina Torr. & Gray. Shrub, some 1 m high, densely branched, twigs glabrous, sticky; leaves nearly sessile, narrow lanceolate, 2—4 cm long, obtuse, slightly or not dentate, tough, more or less distinctly 3 veined; flowers white, May—June. BB 3833. N. America, Kansas and Colorado to W. Texas. Most durable species. Hardy. z4

No soil preference, but all grow well on the seacoast; not especially ornamental, but the white pappus fruits on *B. halimifolia* are very attractive in the fall.

BAILLONIA

Baillonia juncea see: **Diostea juncea**

BALLOTA L. — LABIATAE

Subshrubs or perennials; leaves opposite, without stipules; flowers many in axillary whorls; calyx funnelform, 10 veined, with 5 broad ovate, acuminate, more or less even sized teeth; upper lip of the corolla somewhat concave; corolla tube shorter than the calyx, with a pubescent ring inside; stamens 4, parallel, outer pair longer; nutlet oblong, rounded at the apex. — 35 species in Europe, Mediterranean region and Asia Minor.

Ballota frutescens (L.) Woods. Small, twiggy, shrublet, 15—30 cm high, globose, bushy, erect, twigs very thin, pubescent, with a pair of small, thin, 6—12 mm long prickles at the nodes; leaves opposite, ovate, some

2.5 cm long, the upper leaves with 3—9 large crenate teeth, the lower with margins entire, dull green, both sides softly pubescent; flowers white, small, 2—3 in a leaf axil, July—August (= *B. spinosa* Link). S. France, Italy. z8

For sunny areas in the rock garden, but with little garden merit.

BAMBUSACEAE — BAMBOO

Bambusa erecta see: **Arundinaria hindsii**

While it not the intention of this book to provide more than an alphabetical listing of the genera, the Bamboo are examined here (as will the Palm genera later) only in order to put them into proper perspective.

The Bamboos are grasses, comprised of 45 genera distributed throughout the tropics and subtropics, and displaying the following properties:

Stalks perennial, woody, often tall; leaf blade flat, usually broad, thin, narrowing to rod-like at the base and arising from the sheath; spikelets with 2 or several empty "glumes" (dry bracts), often branched and loosened; stamens 3—6 to many; fruit a nutlet (caryopsis).

Key to the Most Important Genera

A. Stalks terete; pistil short and with 3 stigmas, or pistils 2;
   a) Side branches single at the nodes, seldom 2;
      ● Leaf sheaths with rough stiff bristles:
         Sasa
      ●● Leaf sheaths without bristles or with curved smooth bristles:
         Pseudosasa
   b) Side branches several at a node;
      ● Inflorescence without large foliate leaves under the spikelet and panicle stalks;
         + Stem sheath persistent:
            Arundinaria
         + + Stem sheath abscising;
            * Pistil 1, with 3 stigmas; stems 4—15 m high;
               z6 Leaves with 5—6 paired veins; leaf sheath with erect bristles:
                  Semiarundinaria
               z7 Leaves with 2—4 paired veins; leaf sheath with curved bristles:
                  Sinarundinaria
            ** Pistil 2; stems to 2 m high:
               Chimonobambusa
      ●● Inflorescence with large (abscising) foliate leaves under the spikelet and panicle stalks; leaves with 12—15 paired veins:
         Thamnocalamus

B. Stalks more or less flattened on one side of the node; pistil long, stigmas 3;
   a) Leaves lanceolate to linear-lanceolate; stalks straight or slightly bowed, 3—8 m high:
      Phyllostachys
   b) Leaves ovate-lanceolate to oblong-ovate; stalks bowed here and there, 1 to 2 m high:
      Shibataea

The identification of the various genera and species is usually very difficult, especially since preferred soil type and location

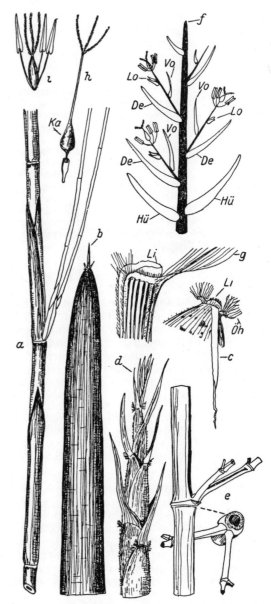

Fig. 133. **Bambusaceae.** a. stem with sheaths and 2 side branches; b. single stem sheath; c. apex of a stem sheath; d. young cane sprouting; e. stem parts with branching, stalk flattened on one side; f. schematic of an inflorescence; g. leaf base; h. ovary with stigma and style, flower with sessile stigmas and 3 stamens. De. flowering glume, HU. empty glume, Ka. caryopsis, Li. ligule, Lo. lodicule, Oh. auricle, Vo. palea

are more or less consistent throughout. The flowers are seldom developed in cultivation which therefore eliminates that possible distinguishing characteristic, so that the available plant parts must be carefully compared for positive identification.

Herewith a cross reference to Bamboo terminology in English, Latin, and German:

English	Latin	German
Auricle	Auricula	Ohrchen
Branch sheath	Vagina rami	Zweigescheide
Bristle	Cilium	Wimper
Caryopsis	Caryopsis	Karyopse (Kornfrucht)
Culm bud	Turio	Stockknospe
Culm sheath	Vagina	Scheide
Empty glume	Gluma	Huellspelze
Flowering glume	Glumella exterior	Deckspelze
Internode	Merithallium	Internodium
Leaf sheath	Vaginella	Scheidchen
Ligule	Ligula	Blatthaeutchen
Lodicule	Glumellula	Lodiculae
Palea	Glumella interior	Vorspelze
Partition	Leptum	Scheidewand
Rhachilla	Rhachilla	Spindelchen
Root-spine	Spino-radix	Wurzeldorn
Spikelet	Spicula	Ahrchen

Lit. Camus, E. G.: Les Bambusées; Paris 1913. Text Volume and Atlas with 101 plates; in the text p. 197 is a list of the most important Bamboo collections in Europe ● Freeman-Mitford, A. B.: The Bamboo Garden; London 1896 (especially interesting historically, but not botanically as the plant descriptions are somewhat erroneous) ● Houzeau De Lehaie, J.: Le Bambou, son étude, sa culture, son emploie; Mons, Belgique, 1906−1908 (a periodical which was published for only 2 years; very important) ● Houzeau De Lehaie, J.: Die in Deutschland angepflanzten, mittlere Wintertemperaturen vertragenden Arundinaria-Arten; in Mitt. DDG 1907, 223−227 ● McClure, F. A.: New Species in the Bamboo genus Phyllostachys and some nomenclatural notes; in Journ. Arnold Arboretum 19−56, 180−196 — McClure, F. A.: Bamboos of the genus Phyllostachys under cultivation in the United States; Agricultural Handbook No. 114; Washington D.C. 1957 ● McClure, F. A.: Bambusoideae (Gramineae IV); in Engler/Prantl, Die Natuerlichen Pflanzenfamilien; in preparation ● Pfitzer, E.: Ueber die Gattungsunterschiede von Arundinaria Michx.; Thamnocalamus Munro und Phyllostachys Sieb. & Zucc. in nicht bluehendem Zustand; in Mitt. DDG 1902, 473−476 ● Pfitzer, E.: Die in Deutschland kultivierten Arundinaria-Arten; in Mitt. DDG 1907, 221−223 ● Rivière, A. & Ch.: Les Bambous, végétation, culture, multiplication; Paris 1878 ● Satow, E.: The cultivation of Bamboos in Japan; Tokyo 1899. With many very beautiful color plates ● Young, R. A.: Bamboos for American Gardens. I-V; in Nat. Hort. Mag. 1945: 171−196, 274−291; 1946: 40−64, 257-283, 352−365 ● Young, R. A.: Bamboos for northern Gardens; in Journ. Arnold Arboretum 1946, 29−42.

BANKSIA L.f. — PROTEACEAE

Evergreen trees and shrubs, usually with very beautiful foliage; leaves very divergent in form, usually dark green above, white or dark brown tomentose beneath, margin dentate or thorny; flowers in cylindrical or oblong, dense spikes or catkins, very attractive; fruit a woody follicled capsule, originating from the gradually developing woody bracts; seed winged. — Some 50 species in Australia.

Banksia baueri R. Br. Rounded shrub, 1−2 m high; leaves cuneate, apex rounded, large toothed; inflorescence very large, cylindrical, white woolly pubescent, with awn-like tips, May−June. HTS 56. W. Australia. z8 # ✧ ∅

B. baxteri R. Br. Shrub, 2−3 m high, growth open and wide; leaves oblong, 15−20 cm long, tomentose beneath, blade with 4−8 triangular, sharp tipped sections on either side, incised to the midrib, forming a zig-zag pattern with each other, 2−2.5 cm long and to 2 cm wide, both upper sections usually flat tipped; inflorescence globose, greenish-yellow at first, later brownish, December−May. EWA 64. ★ W. Australia. z8 # ✧ ∅

B. coccinea R. Br. Slender, upright shrub, 2−4 m high (occasionally higher); leaves obovate to oblong, 3−6 cm long, tough, finely dentate, venation reticulate; flowers scarlet-red and white, in cylindrical, 6 cm high and wide, dense spikes, bracts subulate, perianth woolly. BMns 630; EWA 61; HTS 57. ★ W. Australia, distributed over open wasteland on deep sandy soil. z8

Plate 51. # ✧ ∅

B. collina R. Br. Shrub, 1.5−2.5 m high, twigs thin, gray; leaves linear, 5−7 cm long, 1 cm wide, truncate, gradually widening at the petiole, distinctly dentate, dark green above, silvery beneath; inflorescence cylindrical, large, greenish, with red-brown pistils, bracts obtuse, tomentose at the tip, December−March. HTS 55. Australia. 1822. z8

B. ericifolia L. Shrub or small tree, in its habitat to 3 m high; leaves densely crowded, linear, 12 mm long, margins entire, involute; flowers orange, in cylindrical spikes, 10 cm long, although occasionally reaching to 25 cm long. BM 738. ★ Australia, New South Wales. z8 Plate 51. # ✧ ∅

B. goodii R. Br. Shrub, 60 cm high, branches at times prostrate, thick, tomentose; leaves narrow-oblong, deeply sinuate-dentate, with long, oblique triangular teeth, coarse veined beneath and with tomentose "dimples"; inflorescence oblong-ovate, reddish and white. HTS 58. Australia. z8 # ✧ ∅

B. integrifolia L. f. Shrub, 2.5−3 m high; leaves oblong-cuneate, to 15 cm long, 2.5 cm wide, margins entire, dark green above, white tomentose with reticulate venation beneath; flowers greenish-white, in loose cylindrical spikes, 10 cm long, 5−6 cm wide. HTS 60; BM 2770. ★ Australia. 1824. z8 # ✧ ∅

B. marescens R. Br. Shrub, 1.5−2 m high, twigs pubescent; leaves oblong, 2.5−3.5 cm long, 1.2 cm

Fig. 134. *Banksia serrata*, fruit cluster (from Baillon)

wide, dentate, apex truncate, tapering to the base, white punctate beneath, finely pubescent, flat; flowers yellowish-green, in 10—25 cm long, cylindrical, dense spikes, January—March. BM 2803 (= *B. praemorsa* Andr.). Australia. 1794. z8 # ⊕ ∅

B. marginata Cav. Shrub, 1.5—2 m high; leaves cuneate, apex truncate, margin dentate with some short thorns, dark green above, silvery white tomentose and reticulate venation beneath, 3—5 cm long, 12 mm wide; flowers greenish-yellow, in 2—7 cm long, ovate spikes, flowering throughout the year. BM 1947 (as *B. australis microstacya*). ★ Australia. 1822. z8 # ⊕ ∅

B. media R. Br. Shrub, to 1.8 m high, twigs tomentose-pubescent; leaves cuneate to parallel sided; apex truncate, cuneate taper at the base, 5—8 cm long or longer, 1—2 cm wide, with a short petiole, margin dentate, flat, finely pubescent beneath; flowers yellow, in oblong or cylindrical. 7—15 cm long spikes. HTS 62; BM 3120. ★ Australia. 1824. z8 #   ⊕ ∅

B. ornata F. v. Muell. Shrub, 1—2 m high; leaves

sparsely arranged, oblong-lanceolate, apex somewhat truncate, 5—10 cm long, regularly dentate; flowers pale yellow, in 5—14 cm long, 5—8 cm thick spikes, more gray at the apex, September—January. HTS 54. SW. Australia. z8 # ⊕ ∅

B. prionotes Lindl. Small tree, 4—8 m high, branches tomentose; leaves linear, 20—30 cm long, 1.5—2.5 cm wide, coarsely and evenly serrate, deep green above, tomentose beneath with reticulate venation, nearly snow-white in the "dimples"; inflorescence oblong-ovate, 7—15 cm long, flowers yellowish-brown and woolly, buds white. HTS 63. ★ Australia. z8 # ⊕ ∅

B. serrata. L. Shrub, 3—5 m high in its habitat, young twigs tomentose-pubescent; leaves oblong-lanceolate, leathery tough, 7—14 cm long, deeply dentate, white beneath, midrib brownish woolly; flowers red, in oblong to cylindrical, erect, terminal spikes. BR 1316 (as *B. undudulata*). Australia. z8 Fig. 134. # ⊕ ∅

B. speciosa R. Br. Shrub, about 1.5 m high; leaves 20—35 cm long, linear, 12 mm wide, both margins pinnately incised, pointed and with a thorny point, above deep green, underside silver-white, midrib red-brown woolly; flowers greenish-yellow with red pistils, with fleshy terminals 10—12 cm long and 7—10 cm wide, long, ovate, spikes, summer. HTS 61; BM 3052. ★ (= *B. grandidentata* Dum. — Cours non *B. speciosa* Lindl.!). Australia. z8 # ⊕ ∅

B. spinulosa Sm. Shrub, to 1.5 high; leaves narrow-lanceolate-linear, 3—8 cm long, incised and 3 toothed at the apex, often only 2—3 small teeth near the tip, margin finely thorny dentate, dark green above, tomentose beneath; flowers yellow, larger than those of *B. ericifolia*, in ovate, 5—7 cm long spikes, occasionally more cylindrical and longer, August. BMns 498; HTS 65. ★ Australia. 1788. z8 # ⊕ ∅

All *Banksia* species, except in the mildest areas, must be overwintered in a cool greenhouse at 5—8°C; they prefer a lime free, humus soil, with good water retention, and should never be allowed to dry out. Banksias are found in many botanic gardens.

Lit. Bosse, J. F. W.: Vollst. Handbuch der Blumengaertnerei, 3rd Edition., 426—430; with descriptions of 44 species (1859) ● Baglin, D., & B. Mullins: Australian Banksias; N. Sydney 1940, including 40 color photos (denoted in the above section with a ★)

BAROSMA Willd. — RUTACEAE

Low, evergreen shrubs; leaves opposite or alternate (occasionally within the same species), very strongly scented when crushed, with oil glands on the underside and at the margin sinuses; flowers in axillary racemes; calyx 5 parted, petals 5, stamens 5, alternating with 5 staminodes; fruit a 5 chambered capsule. — Some 30 species in S. Africa.

Barosma foetidissima Bartl. & Wendl. Shrub, 0.5—1 m high; leaves grouped in 3's, linear, 6—12 mm long, 1—2

mm wide, obtuse, thickened at the margin, glandular and rolled inward; flowers on the ends of the short branches, about 10 together, in 1.5—2.5 cm wide umbels, petals white to light pink. S. Africa. z10 # ⊕

B. pulchella Bartl. & Wendl. Shrub, to 1 m high, twigs very thin and softly pubescent, densely foliate; leaves ovate, 4—12 mm long, margin thickened, dentate but teeth tiny and glandular, glabrous; flowers in fascicles near the branch tips, 1—2 axillary, purple, 8 mm wide,

petiole very thin, 12 mm. BM 1357 (as *Diosma pulchella*). S. Africa. 1787. z10 # ✧

Both of the above, and the remaining species, only winter

hardy in frost free climates, otherwise overwinter in a cool greenhouse. They prefer a sandy, humus soil. The foliage fragrance is very strong and unpleasant, especially in the greenhouse.

BAUERA Banks ex Andr. — BAUERACEAE

Small evergreen shrubs; leaves opposite, trifoliate, in whorls appearing to consist of 6 leaflets; flowers solitary axillary, often grouped at the branch tips; calyx 4—10 segmented, as many petals as calyx segments, white to purple, stamens few to many; fruit a bi-valved capsule, each valve further split. — 3 species in temperate E. Australia and Tasmania.

Bauera rubioides Andr. Shrub, 30—60 cm high, up-

right or also prostrate; leaves oblong-lanceolate, acute, margin finely crenate, 6—12 mm long; flowers light red, pink or white, with slender pedicel, petals elliptic, obtuse, much longer than the reflexed calyx tips, spring. BM 715; DRHS 241; NF 3: 98. Australia; New South Wales. 1793. z9 Plate 52. # ✧

Culture simple, full sun in summer, overwinter, however, in a cool greenhouse.

BAUHINIA L. — LEGUMINOSAE

Tropical evergreen trees and shrubs, many also climbing with peculiarly formed, flattened or twisting branches, partly also with tendrils; leaves consisting of 2 leaflets connate at the base and appearing 2 lobed, occasionally also both leaflets nearly distinct, petiole elongated in a short, but characteristic "awn" between the leaflets; flowers in simple or terminal panicles or also axillary racemes; petals 5, somewhat uneven, usually tapering to a "claw", oblong, outspread, the 2 upper petals usually further apart than the 3 lower ones; stamens usually 10, occasionally reduced to 3 and then sterile; fruit a long, flat, dehiscent or indehiscent pod. — Around 300 species in the tropics; some in the completely frost free areas of the Mediterranean and the Black Sea, occasionally in gardens; often seen in the botanic gardens, where the flowers, due to their size, always leave the impression of huge Geraniums or Orchids. The wood from many species is called "ebony". The number and fertility of the stamens is very important for the determination of species.

Bauhinia acuminata L. Shrub, 1.5—2 m high; leaflets ovate, acuminate, lightly cordate at the base, connate below the middle, parallel 4 veined, folding up at night; flowers white, 5—7 cm wide, petals broadly ovate, seldom "clawed"; fertile stamen long and nearly distinct, the other 9 sterile, short and connate, May—September. BM 7860. India, Burma, Malaysia, China. 1808. One of the best species for its garden merit, flowering readily as a small plant. z9 Plate 52. ✧

B. densiflora Franch. Deciduous, loose, somewhat climbing shrub, 2—3 m high; leaves incised to 1/3 their length, each half kidney-shaped, 2.5—7 cm wide and 2—4 cm long, glabrous above, pubescent beneath, petiole 12—20 mm long; flowers white, only 12 mm wide, grouped 6 in short, pubescent racemes, June; petals narrow-obovate. W. China; Szechwan. 1908. In cultivation in England (Cornwall), but without garden merit. z9 ✧

B. galpinii N. E. Br. Shrub, semi-climbing, 1.5 to 3 m high; leaves nearly circular to broad oblong, 2 lobed, split 1/5 to 1/2 their length, 3—7 cm long, light green, 7

veined, petiole 8 mm long; flowers 6—10 in racemes, with a leaf opposite, flowering from spring to fall; petals carmine or scarlet-red, 5, all equal in size, some 3 cm long, claw as long as the nearly circular, somewhat acuminate blade; 3 fertile stamens; pod 7—15 cm long, seeds dark brown. BM 7495; MCL 105. Tropics and S. Africa. 1895. z9 ✧

B. purpurea L. A tree in its habitat, in cultivation only a shrub, to 2 m; leaves somewhat cordate at the base, leathery tough, glabrous, split 1/3 to 1/2 their length, each leaflet broadly ovate, obtuse, 4—5 veined; flowers few, grouped in axillary and terminal fascicles, fragrant, petals lanceolate, acute, from nearly white to purple and also dappled, the 3—4 fertile stamens very long, abundantly flowering in summer; pods to 30 cm long. ICS 2402; BIT 3; SNp 35 (= *B. triandra* Roxb.) India, Burma, China. 1778. z9 ✧

B. variegata L. A tree in its habitat, 6 m or more, similar in habit to *B. purpurea*; leaves 7—10 cm wide, somewhat wider than long, split to 1/3 or 1/4 their length, both leaflets obtuse and 5 veined, petiole 2.5—5 cm long; flowers grouped about 7 in loose, terminal racemes, petals 5, obovate-oblong, clawed, veined, pink with red and yellow markings, the lowest petal larger, wider above the middle, with intense carmine-red markings, June; pods 30—60 cm long. PCa 92; BM 6818; MCL 9; BIT 1. India. 1690. z9 ✧

var. **candida** Roxb. Low, usually not over 1.5 m (to 6 m in its native habitat), flowers large, white with attractive green markings, fragrant. BM 7312 (= *B. alba* Buch.-Ham.). Tropical Asia. 1893. z8 ✧

B. yunnanensis Franch. Shrub, more or less climbing, strong growing, glabrous, totally blue-green, stem cylindrical, tendrils flattened; leaves leathery tough, small, both halves oblique elliptic, 3—4 veined, 4 cm long, base rounded; flowers many in pendulous racemes, pink-white with purple stripes. FIO 199; BM 7814; ICS 2395. China; Yunnan. Probably the hardiest type; hardy in open areas in the milder regions such as England. z8 Plate 52. ✧

While *B. purpurea* and *B. variegata* can be counted among the most popular and beautiful flowering trees in India, they can only be cultivated in frost free areas. They require no particular soil or care where they are winter hardy. As for greenhouse culture, long term success is uncertain.

BEAUMONTIA Wall. — APOCYNACEAE

Tall tropical evergreen trees or tall-growing vine, twining habit; leaves opposite, thin, often with small glands in the axils; flowers very attractive, white and very fragrant; calyx 5 parted; corolla funnel-form, with short tube, without throat scales, limb with 5 wide lobes, disc comprised of 5 lobes or scales. — 15 species in China and Indomalaysia.

Beaumontia grandiflora (Roxb.) Wall. High twining vine, young twigs pink toned, rust-brown pubescent; leaves broad ovate, with small tips, margin wavy, smooth and glossy above, softly pubescent beneath, pubescence rust-brown at first; calyx with 5 large, ovate, wavy sepals, red at the tips; corolla tube large, white, green outside at the base, darker inside, tube short, limb campanulate and 5 lobed, in many flowered, axillary and terminal corymbs on the previous year's wood. SNp 115; BIT 206; MCL 104. India. 1820. z9 #⊕

Only for totally frost free areas with high summer temperatures. Given these conditions, one can expect abundant winter blooming. Requires a sunny area with good soil and should be cut back after the major flower display.

BEJARIA Mutis ex L. corr. Zea ex Vent. — ERICACEAE

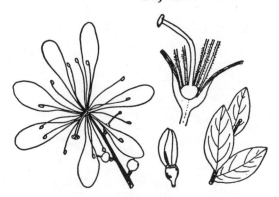

Fig. 135. *Bejaria racemosa* (from Uphof)

Evergreen shrubs, resembling *Ledum*; leaves entire, leathery, densely arranged; flowers in racemes or corymbs; corolla split to the base, and with 6—7 distinct petals, these far apart; seed with a long wing. — 30 species in the tropics and subtropics, mostly in S. America, 3 in Mexico and one in N. America (= *Befaria* Mutis ex L.).

Bejaria racemosa Muehl. Evergreen shrub, 1—2 m high in its native habitat, twigs often coarsely pubescent, brown; leaves oval-lanceolate, 4—6 cm long, sessile, glabrous; flowers in viscid terminal panicles or racemes, some 15—20 cm long, July; fruit a small, rounded, dehiscent capsule. MD 1924: 210. N. America, Georgia to Florida, in Pine groves of the coastal plains. 1810. z8? Fig. 135. # ⊕

Some further species have been known in cultivation, but no information can be found as to their existence in garden culture today. For further information on these species please refer to:

B. coarctata Humb. & Bonpl. (BM 4433; DRHS 256); *B. glauca* Humb. & Bonpl.(BM 6893; and the var. *tomentella* BM 4981); *B. ledifolia* Humb. & Bonpl. (FS 194).

BENTHAMIA

Benthamia fragifera see: **Cornus capitata**

BENZOIN

Benzoin aestivale see: **Lindera benzoin**

B. obtusilobum see: **Lindera obtusiloba**

B. odoriferum see: **Lindera benzoin**

B. praecox see: **Lindera praecox**

B. touyunense see: **Lindera megathylla**

B. trilobum see: **Lindera triloba**

B. umbellatum see: **Lindera umbellata**

BERBERIDOPSIS Hook. f.— FLACOURTIACEAE

Monotypic genus. Evergreen shrub, leaves alternate, simple, evergreen, smooth, petiolate; flowers many in terminal and axillary, pendulous, long stalked racemes; perianth spiral, without a distinct difference between sepals and petals; 9—15 "tepals", all colored and imbricate, gradually getting larger to the inside; floral axis ring-like, thick, with 7—10 distinct stamens on the inner margin; fruit a many-seeded berry; ovary one chambered. — One species in Chile.

Berberidopsis corallina Hook. f. Evergreen, thin branched, somewhat vining shrub, in milder areas and as an espalier reaching 5 × 5 m; leaves cordate, tough, thin, 6—10 cm long, margin thorny dentate, glabrous, dark green above, bluish beneath, flowers nearly hemispherical, some 2 cm wide, deep red, long stalked, in pendulous racemes, July—September. FS 2157; BM 5343. Chile, in the forest near Valdivia. 1862. z8 Plate 38; Fig. 136. #

Gorgeous plant for covering a wall, but needs protection even in England. Prefers semi-shady wooded areas and humus soil, free of limestone. Very impressive in full bloom.

BERBERIS L. — Barberry — BERBERIDACEAE

Evergreen or deciduous thorny shrubs, in mild areas developing into large shrubs or small trees, wood and inner bark yellow; leaves alternate, simple, in clusters, on long shoots often developing 3 parted thorns and with only one normal leaf; flowers solitary or in fascicles, umbels, racemes or panicles, normally yellow, seldom orange; sepals 6, petals 6 (often smaller than the sepals), the latter usually with 2 nectar glands; 6 stamens, the anthers with valves opening upward; ovaries one chambered, with 1 to several ovules; stigma sessile or on a short style; fruit a red to black berry with 1 to several seeds. — Some 450 species in Europe, N. Africa, America, E. and Middle Asia.

Outline of Genus
(Schneider and Rehder)

● I.   **Leaves evergreen or semi-evergreen**
Sec. 1:   **Buxifoliae** (Schneid.) Rehd.
   Leaves evergreen, small, margins entire; flowers solitary or in fascicles of 2—5; stigmas sessile:
      B. antoniana, buxifolia, chillanensis, empetrifolia, linearifolia, montana, stenophylla

Ser. 2:   **Actenacanthae** (Schneid.) Rehd.
   Leaves evergreen or semi-evergreen, usually dentate; flowers solitary, in fascicles or umbellate panicles; style short or absent:
      B. actinacantha, congestiflora, hakeoides, heterophylla

Ser. 3:   **Ilicifolia** (Schneid.) Rehd.
   Leaves evergreen, dentate; flowers in racemes, ovaries with distinct styles:
      B. comberi, darwinii, ilicifolia, lologensis, ruscifolia, valdiviana

Ser. 4: **Wallichianae** (Schneid.) Rehd.
   Leaves evergreen, elliptic to narrow-lanceolate; flowers singular or in fascicles of 2—25; styles very short or absent; fruit purple-violet to black:
      B. acuminata, atrocarpa, bergmanniae, bristolensis, calliantha, candidula, cavalieri, centiflora, chenaultii, chrysosphaera, 'Concal', coxii, dumicola, frikartii, gagnepainii, helenae, hookeri, hybrido-gagnepainii, hypokerina, incrassata, insignis, interposita, julianae, kawakamii, lempergiana, levis, manipurana, mentorensis, phanera, pruinosa, recurvata, replicata, sanguinea, sargentiana, soulieana, subcoriacea, sublevis, taliensis, triacanthophora, vanfleetii, veitchii, verruculosa, vilmorinii, wallichiana, wintonensis, wisleyensis, wokingensis, xanthoxylon

Fig. 136. *Berberidopsis corallina*
(after Hooker)

●● II.   Leaves deciduous (except Ser. 8)
Ser. 5:   **Angulosae** (Schneid.) Rehd.
   Leaves deciduous; flowers usually grouped 1—3, seldom to 5; styles absent or very short; fruit red or pink:
      B. aemulans, anglosa, capillaris, circumserrata; concinna, consumilis, diaphana, dictyophylla, faxoniana, johannis, macrosepala, morrisonensis, orthobotrys, parisepala, sibirica, spraguei, suberecta, temolaica, tischleri, tsangpoensis, tsarongensis, yunnaninsis

Ser. 6:   **Polyanthae** (Schneid.) Rehd.
   Leaves deciduous or semi-evergreen; flowers in panicles, often grouped in short dense racemes; fruit red, with distinct styles:
      B. aggregata, arido-calida, carminea, edgeworthiana, gyalaica, parvifolia, polyantha, pratti, rubrostilla, wilsoniae

Ser. 7: Tinctoriae (Schneid.) Rehd.
Leaves deciduous, obovate to oblong; flowers in corymbs
or simple racemes; fruit usually with a distinct style:
> B. anniae, aristata, beaniana, chitria, coriaria, floribunda,
> forrestii, francisi-ferdinandi, jamesiana, kewensis, lepto-
> clada, liechtensteinii, marcracantha, pallens, potaninii, sik-
> kimensis, spaethii, umbellata

Ser. 8: Asiaticae (Schneid.) Rehd.
Leaves evergreen or semi-evergreen, light green to
whitish beneath; flowers in racemes or fascicles; style
short:
> B. asiatica, glaucocarpa, lycoides, lycium

Ser. 9: Initegerrimae (Schneid.) Rehd.
Leaves deciduous, petiolate, lanceolate to broad obovate,
margins entire or serrate, usually gray-green with reticulate venation on both sides; flowers in dense, elongated
racemes; fruit red, with sessile stigma:
> B. iliensis, nummularia, turcomanica, vernae

Ser. 10: Heteropodae (Schneid). Rehd.
Leaves deciduous, petiolate, usually with margins entire;
flowers fascicled or in corymbs; ovules 2−6; fruit blue-
black:
> B. heteropoda, notabilis, sheriffii

Ser. 11: Tschonoskyanae (Schneid.) Rehd.
Similar to the above series, but with only 2 ovules, fruit
red, nearly sessile:
> B. mouillacana, oblonga, silva-taroucana, virgetorum

Ser. 12: Sinensis (Schneid.) Rehd.
Previous year's wood more or less reddish to brown;
leaves deciduous, lanceolate to obovate, usually with
margins entire or sparsely dentate; flowers in (often only
short) racemes, fascicles, seldom solitary; ovules 1−2;
fruits usually red, stigma sessile:
> B. boschanii, bretschneideri, canadensis, chinensis, cratae-
> gina, cretica, declinata, dielsiana, durobrivensis, fendleri,
> graminea, henryana, hispanica, jaeschkeana, koreana, lax-
> iflora, lecomtei, lepidifolia, media, meehanii, minuti-
> flora, mucrifolia, oritrepha, ottawensis, para-virescens,
> poiretta, quelpartensis, rehderiana, reticulata, sieboldii,
> stearnii, thibetica, thunbergii, virescens, zabeliana

Ser. 13: Dasystachyae (Schneid.) Rehd.
Leaves wide, rounded at the base, long petioled; flowers
in dense, erect racemes; ovules 1−2; fruit red, with sessile
stigma:
> B. dasystachys, honanensis, kansuensis

Ser. 14: Brachypodae (Schneid.) Rehd.
Leaves and the dense racemes pubescent:
> B. brachypoda, gilgiana, giraldii, mitifolia

Ser. 15: Vulgares (Schneid.) Rehd.
Previous year's branches gray-yellow or gray, grooved;
leaves deciduous, serrate or dentate; flowers many in
long, pendulous racemes; ovules 2−3; fruits red or purple, usually pruinose, stigma sessile:
> B. aetnensis, amurensis, dictyoneura, emarginata, mekon-
> gensis, provincialis, regeliana, vulgaris

Table of the *Berberis* cultivars
and the species to which they belong

This list contains no cultivars with Latin names, also ex-
cluded are descriptive names such as 'Nana', 'Compacta',
'Gracilis', etc.; included here are only those which have been
given 'fancy' names.

'Amstelveen'	frikartii
'Apricot Queen'	lologensis
'Auricoma'	ottawensis
'Aurora'	carminea
'Autumn Cheer'	carminea
'Bagatelle'	thunbergii
'Barbarossa'	carminea
'Barresiana'	pruinosa
'Bountiful'	carminea
'Brilliant'	stenophylla
'Brouwer's Green'	thunbergii
'Buccaneer'	carminea
'Chealii'	rubrostilla
'Chenault'	hybrido-gagnepainii
'Chenault Compact'	hybrido-gagnepainii
'Cherry Ripe'	rubrostilla
'Comber's Apricot'	linearifolia
'Comet'	wilsoniae
'Coral'	wilsoniae
'Cornish Cream'	stenophylla
'Crawleyensis'	rubrostilla
'Crawley Gem'	stenophylla
'Crimson Bead'	aggregata
'Dart's Improvement'	verruculosa
'Dart's Superb'	julianae
'Decora'	ottawensis
'Electra'	thunbergii
'Emperor'	suberecta
'Etna'	stenophylla
'Ferax'	wilsoniae
'Fernspray'	gagnepainii
'Fireball'	wilsoniae
'Fireflame'	carminea; darwinii
'Firefly'	wilsoniae
'Flamboyant'	amurensis
'Flame'	darwinii
'Genty'	hybrido-gagnepainii
'Gertrud Hardyzer'	lologensis
'Gold'	darwinii
'Golden Ring'	thunbergii
'Green Carpet'	thunbergii
'Green Mantle'	gagnepainii
'Green Ornament'	thunbergii
'Haalboom'	candidula
'Harlqeuin'	thunbergii'
'Highdown'	lologensis
'Hilde'	hybrido-gagnepainii
'Jewel'	linerifolia
'Joke'	wilsoniae
'Jytte'	candidula
'Kelleriis'	thunbergii
'Kugowski'	gagnepainii
'Kobold'	thunbergii
'Lombart's Red'	julianae
'Minikin'	hybrido-gagnapainii
'Mrs. Kennedy'	frikartii
'Nymans'	lologensis
'Orangeade'	wilsoniae
'Orange King'	linearifolia
'Parkjuweel'	media
'Phoenix'	linearifolia

'Pink Pearl'	*stenophylla*
'Pink Queen'	*thunbergii*
'Pirate King'	*carminea*
'Red Bird'	*thunbergii*
'Red Chief'	*thunbergii*
'Red Pillar'	*thunbergii*
'Red Tears'	*koreana*
'Red Wonder'	*thunbergii*
'Robin Hood'	*gagnepainii*
'Rose Glow'	*thunbergii*
'Rosetta'	*thunbergii*
'Ruby Watson'	*aggregata*
'Rusthof'	*gagnepainii*
'Select'	*hybrido-gagnepainii*
'Silbertoft Coral'	*aggregata*
'Silver Beauty'	*thunbergii*
'Sparkler'	*carminea*
'Special' see:	'Green Ornament'
'Stafa'	*frikartii*
'Stonefield Dawn'	*aggregata*
'Stonefield Surprise'	*wilsoniae*
'Stonefield Mauve'	*beaniana*
'Superba'	*ottawensis*
'Suzanne'	*ottawensis*
'Telstar'	*frikartii*
'Terra Nova'	*hybrido-gagnepainii*
'Tom Thumb'	*wilsoniae*
'Tottenham'	*hybrido-gagnepainii*
'Triumph'	*darwinii*
'Unique	*orthobotrys*
'Vermillion'	*thunbergii*
'Verrucandi'	*frikartii*
'Wallich's Purple'	*interposita*
'Yellow Beauty'	*lologensis*

Note: The plates with leaf illustrations were largely completed from material furnished by Leslie W. Ahrendt, for which, once again, many thanks are due.

Berberis actinacantha Martelli. Semi-evergreen shrub, about 1 m high, branches long and thin, twigs sparse, dark red, pubescent, thorns 3 parted or also widened leaf-like; leaves broadly obovate, 1–3 cm long, both sides with 1–3 thorny teeth, often with long petioled primordial leaves at the twig base; flowers 3–6 in fascicles, gold-yellow; fruit blue-black. BR 31: 55. Chile. 1925. Mainly of botanical interest. z7 Plate 65; Fig. 138.

B. acuminata Franch.is, according to Ahrendt, not in cultivation; what is generally found in fact under this name are:

    B. gagnepainii var. **lanceifolia** Ahrendt (= *B. acuminata* sensu Stapf in BM 8185);
    B. veitchii Schneid. (= *B. acuminata* sensu J. H. Veitch, non Franch.).

B. aemulans Schneid. Deciduous shrub, very similar to *B. diaphana*, but to 1.5 m high, young twigs red, glabrous, angular, thorns in 3's, about 1.5 cm long, often mixed with single thorns; leaves obovate, round at the apex, with a small prickly tip, tapering to the base, 2.5–5 cm long, thorny dentate or entire, totally glabrous, dark green above, blue-green beneath; flowers 1–3, light yellow; fruit to 1.5 cm long, orange-red. BMns 179. W. China. 1908. Hardy. z5 (?)

B. aetnensis Presl. Deciduous shrub, 0.5–0.7 m high, twigs stiff, curved, angular, glabrous, yellow; leaves obovate, 0.8–2 cm long, partly bristly dentate, with 10–15 thorns on each side, partly entire, both sides gray-green; thorns 3 parted, over 2.5 cm long; flowers gold-yellow, in dense, short racemes, grouped 7–15 together, May–June; fruit red. Sicily, Sardinia, Corsica. Beautiful for the rock garden. z7 ⊕

B. aggregata C. Schneid. Deciduous shrub, 1.5 m (rarely to 3 m), young twigs brown, finely pubescent, angular, thorns thin, 3 parted, 1–3 cm long; leaves obovate, thorny dentate, apex rounded, base cuneate, blue-green beneath; flowers light yellow, 6 mm wide, in short, upright, nearly globose, 3 cm long panicles, May–June; fruits ovate, 5–6 mm thick, cinnamon red, pruinose. BM 8722 (= *B. geraldii* Veitch). z6 Fig. 137.

The following hybrids may be included here:

'Crimson Bead' (A. R. Ahrendt 1942). Berries numerous, in pendulous panicles, oblong, dark carmine, 5 × 4 mm in size.

'Ruby Watson' (Ahrendt 1942). Twigs dark brown-red, finely pubescent, leaves persistent, berries ruby-red, 4–6.5 mm long, 4–5.5 mm wide.

'Sibbertoft Coral' (Stanley 1942). Berries ovate, large, numerous, red, bluish pruinose, to 7 mm long, 5 mm wide. Somewhat susceptable to frost damage. z6 Plate 53.

'Stonefield Dawn' (Ahrendt 1940). Leaves light yellowish-green, fruit globose, 4–5 m thick, carmine red.

var. **prattie** see: **B. prattii**

B. amurensis Rupr. Deciduous shrub, narrowly upright, to 3.5 m high, twigs furrowed, gray in the 2nd year, thorns 3 parted, 1–2 cm long; leaves elliptic to oblong, 3–8 cm long, obtuse or acute and finely bristly serrate, venation reticulate, both sides light green, seldom bluish beneath; flowers 10–25 in long, pendulous racemes, petals slightly emarginate on the apex, May; fruit elliptic, 1 cm long, bright red, often pruinose. NK 21: 5; SH 1: 200 k–m, (= *B. vulgaris* var. *amurensis* Regel). NE. Asia. Before 1860. z6 (?)

'Flamboyant'. Leaves ovate to elliptic, 3–5 cm long, fresh green above, lighter beneath to somewhat bluish, fall color bright red (= *B. rugidicans* 'Flamboyant'). From French nurseries. ⊘

var. **japonica** see: **B. regeliana**

B. angulizans see: **B. canadensis**

B. angulosa Hook. f. & Thoms. Deciduous shrub, some 1 m high, twigs upright, furrowed, dense with short dark brown pubescence when young, some thorns simple, some 3–5 parted, stout, to 1.5 cm long; leaves obovate, 1.5 to 4 cm long, margins entire or with 1–3 thorny teeth on each blade half, dark green above, whitish beneath; flowers solitary, rounded, to 1.5 cm long, scarlet red, edible, slightly sour. BM 7071. Himalaya. 1844. z6 Fig. 144.

B. anniae Ahrendt. Evergreen shrub, resembling *B. potaninii*, but with leaves 4–6 cm long, oblong, with 5–8 thorns on each blade half; flowers in fascicles of 3–6, peduncles 1–1.5 cm long; fruit light red, 1 cm long. z6 Plate 61. #

Fig. 137. From left to right: *Berberis brachypoda*; *B. aggregata* (2); *B. wilsoniae* (after ICS)

B. × antoniana Smith (*B. buxifolia* × *B. darwinii*). Evergreen shrub, some 1—1.2 m high, young twigs densely pubescent; foliage 2 cm long, 1 cm wide, margins usually entire, without veins, glossy deep green above, yellow-green beneath; flowers solitary, gold-yellow, pedicel 2—4 cm long; fruits 8 mm thick, globose, blue pruinose, with 2.5 mm long style. Originated in Newry, N. Ireland. z6

B. aquifolium see: **Mahonia aquifolium**

B. arido-calida Ahrendt. Deciduous shrub, very closely related to *B. parvifolia*, but with leaves wider, larger, some 1.5 cm long, 1 cm wide, with 3—6 teeth on each blade half; fruit oblong, some 5mm long. China, Kansu. 1912. z6

B. aristata DC. Deciduous shrub, to 3 m high, twigs attractively pendulous, glabrous, round, yellow-brown at first, later becoming gray; leaves persisting well into winter under favorable conditions, obovate, grouped 3—6 in clusters, 3—6 cm long, with 3—5 large thorns on either blade half or entire, both sides green or underside whitish or yellow-green; flowers yellow, reddish outside, grouped 10—15 in 5—10 cm long racemes, May; thorns simple or 3 parted, to 3 cm long; fruits fusiform, to 1 cm long, red, bluish pruinose, with short style. BS 1: 267. NW. Himalaya. Around 1820. One of the largest and loveliest of the deciduous species in Europe. *B. chitria* or *B. floribunda* Wall. are often cultivated under this name. z6 Plate 58; Fig. 58, 138. ⊕ ∅ ⚭

var. **coriacea** see: **B. coriaria**

B. asiatica Roxb. Evergreen, strong growing shrub, to 3 m high; branches thick, stiff, often twining, not or slightly furrowed, thorns rather small; leaves rounded-obovate, 4—8 cm long, with 1—4 thorns on each blade half, leathery tough and hard, dark green with distinctly reticulate venation above, whitish beneath; flowers yellow, in clustered umbels grouped 18—24; filaments about 1.5 times as long as the anthers, May—June; fruits ovate to nearly globose, 8 mm wide, red, later black but ripening reddish. Himalaya. 1820. z8 Fig. 138. # ⚭

Always misidentified and usually confused with *B. chitria* or *B. aristata* in European cultivation.

B. atrocarpa Schneid. Evergreen shrub, 1—1.5 m high, resembling *B. gagnepainii* var. *lanceifolia*, but not so multistemmed and with more side branches, leaves not so strongly undulate; branched rigid, glabrous, thorns 3 parted, stiff, 3—6 cm long; leaves lanceolate, tough, flexible, to 8 cm long, venation indistinct, with 5—10 teeth on each blade half, pale yellow-green beneath, in clusters of 6—12, petiole 5—10 mm long; fruits small, ovate, black, not pruinose, with a style. BM 8857 (= *B. levis* sensu Schneid.). China, W. Szechwan. 1908. z6 Plate 56. #

B. beaniana Schneid. Deciduous shrub, growth narrowly upright and dense, to 2 m high, young twigs glabrous, red-brown at first, later gray, thorns 3 parted, 2 cm long; leaves elliptic-lanceolate, acute, 2—4 cm long, venation reticulate, 6—14 closely spaced teeth on each blade half, glossy green above, blue-green beneath; flowers 6 mm wide, grouped 10—20 in 4 cm long panicles, deep yellow, June; fruits about 1 cm long, narrowly ovate, purple, pruinose, stigma sessile. BM 8781. China, W. Szechwan. z6

Including:

'**Stonefield Mauve**' (Ahrendt). Leaves deciduous, thorny, fruit oblong-elliptic, 8 × 6 mm, dark red, distinctly lilac colored when ripe, style absent. ⚭

B. bergmanniae Schneid. Evergreen shrub, to 2 m high, growth dense and bushy, internodes 2–3.5 cm long, twigs angular, gray-yellow, glabrous, thorns to 3 cm long; leaves elliptic, 4–7 cm long, with 3–8 prominent teeth on each blade half, leathery tough, somewhat glossy above, lighter and very glossy beneath; flowers in fascicles of 8–15, yellow, May–June; fruits ovate, with short style, black, dense blue-white pruinose, stalk reddish. W. China. 1908. Closely related to *B. julianae*. z6 Plate 57. # ∅

var. **acantophylla** Schneid. Leaves to 10 cm long, 3 cm wide, each blade half with 6–10 large thorny teeth, teeth often triangular and *Ilex*-like. Otherwise like the species. Cultivated in Kew Gardens, London. Plate 57. # ∅

B. boschanii Schneid. Deciduous shrub, very closely related to *B. lecomtei*; thorns to 1.8 cm long; leaves obovate, 1–2 cm long; fruit ellipsoid, coral-red, 6 mm long. China, W. Szechwan. 1908. z6

B. brachypoda Maxim. Deciduous shrub, to 2 m high, twigs furrowed in the first year, pubescent, gray-yellow, thorns 3 parted, 1–2.5 cm long; leaves oval to obovate, 3–6 cm long, acute, each blade half with 15–30 teeth, green beneath, both sides pubescent, denser beneath; flowers in dense, narrow racemes, 5–8 cm long, with 15–30 flowers, light yellow, to 1 cm wide, pendulous, May; fruits elliptical, 1 cm long, deep red, slightly pruinose, in dense, pendulous racemes. Middle and NW. China; Kansu. Around 1880. z6 Plate 62; Fig. 137. ⚭

B. bretschneideri Rehd. Deciduous shrub, to 4 m high, sprawling growth habit, twigs usually rod-like, red-brown in the 2nd year, thorns 1–3 parted, to 15 mm long; leaves obovate, 3–8 cm long, obtuse, densely bristly dentate, bright green above, more bluish beneath with reticulate venation; flowers light yellow, 10–15 in 5 cm long racemes, May; fruits elliptical, 1 cm long, purple, somewhat pruinose. Japan. 1892. Resembles *B. vulgaris*, but easily distinguished by the red-brown rod-like twigs and lighter flowers. z6

B. × bristolensis Ahrendt (*B. calliantha* × *B. verruculosa*). Evergreen shrub, closely resembling *B. calliantha*, but with more elliptic leaves, 2–4 cm long, each side with 5–10 thorny teeth. (Personally unfamiliar to me.) z6 Plate 54. # ∅

B. buxifolia Lam. Evergreen shrubs, 1–3 m high and wide, twigs brown, pubescent, striped, thorns 3 parted or simple, to 1.5 cm long; leaves obovate to elliptic, 1–2.5 cm long, prickly tip, otherwise entire; flowers 1–2, orange-yellow, petiole 2.5–3 cm long, reddish, May–June; fruit rounded, black-red, blue pruinose, on protruding stalks. BM 6505 (= *B. dulcis* Sweet). S. Chile. 1830. Very hardy and attractive, seldom found in cultivation; cultivars are much more common. z6 Fig. 139. # ∅

'Aureomarginata'. Leaves yellow margined. #

'Nana'. Growth very dense, seldom taller than 30 cm, thorns very small; leaves rounder than the type; flowers infrequently. Gs 1932:27 (= *B. dulcis* nana Carr.). Very good low hedging plant. z5? # ∅

'Pygmaea'. Juvenile form with thin, thornless twigs; leaves elliptic to ovate, gray-green beneath, petiole very thin, unequal, seldom longer than the blade, margin often thorny (= *B. pygmaea* Koehne). # ∅

'Spinosissima'. Like the species, but with thorns to 3 cm long, longer than the leaf blade. #

B. calliantha Mulligan. Evergreen shrub, somewhat similar to *B. hookeri*, but only 60–80 cm high (usually only 30 cm); twigs angular, thorns 3 parted; leaves elliptic to oval, 2.5–6 cm long with 5–8 thorned teeth on each side, dark glossy green above, waxy white beneath; flowers pale yellow, grouped 1–3, 2 cm wide, May; fruits ovate, 1 cm long, blue-black, but thick gray pruinose. BS 1: 374; BMns 584. SE. Tibet. 1925. Very beautiful species. z7 Plate 54. # ∅ ⚭

B. canadensis Mill. Deciduous shrub, seldom over 1.3 m high, twigs thin, elegantly pendulous, slightly angular, red-brown, glabrous, densely branched, thorns 3 parted, thin, usually not over 1 cm long; leaves obovate, 2–5 cm long, sparsely thorny dentate, often with only 2–4 thorns on either side or margins entire, bright green above, gray-green beneath, fall color a splendid scarlet-red and green; flowers yellow, grouped 6–15 in 3–5 cm long racemes, May to June; fruits 1 cm long, elliptic, deep red, not pruinose. BB 1641; GSP 134 (= *B. caroliniana* Loud.; = *B. angulizans* Massias). Eastern N. America. 1759. z5? Plate 58. ∅ ⚭

The species name is misleading since the plant does not thrive in Canada but rather in the southern Appalachians.

B. candidula Schneid. Evergreen shrub, 30–50 cm high, growth dense and tight, rounded, twigs outspread and usually somewhat upturned, not or scarcely warty (as the somewhat similar *B. verruculosa*); leaves elliptic, 2–3 cm long, margin involuted, with only few, small teeth, dark green above, very glossy, white beneath; flowers gold-yellow, solitary, small, May; fruit ovate, without a style, dense white pruinose. China, W. Hupeh. Very popular, good hardy species; often atypical in the nursery. z6 Plate 54. See also: *B. × frikartii*. # ✧ ∅

Included here are 3 cultivars, presumably hybrids of *B. candidula* × *B. gagnepainii*:

'Gracilis' (Haalboom, around 1957). Growth taller and looser than *B. candidula*, twigs thin, smooth; leaves light green; flowers 2–3, occasionally to 4 together. #

'Haalboom' (Haalboom 1955). Growth strong and upright, to 1 m high; leaves elliptical, 2–4.5 cm long, 0.8–1.2 cm wide, glossy fresh green above, blue-white beneath; flowers usually 3–4 together. Dfl 9: 12. #

'Jytte' (from Denmark). Growth more or less globose, dense, branch tips often stiffly upright; leaves narrow elliptic, 2–3 cm, glossy dark green above, white beneath. Dfl 9:12. Resembles 'Haalboom', but leaf undersides whiter. #

B. capillaris Ahrendt. Closely related to *B. angulosa*,

Fig. 138. From left to right: *Berberis aristata*; *B. actinacantha*; *B. asiatica*
(from Bot. Reg. and DeLessert)

but the leaves gray-green above, underside gray; shrub, deciduous, 0.3–1 m high, mature branches glabrous, dark red to purple; leaf margins entire, 2–4 cm long, 1–2 cm wide; flowers solitary, 1.5 cm wide(!), gold-yellow, May; fruits to 18 mm long and 9 mm wide, scarlet red. Burma; NW. Yunnan. 1939. z8

B. × carminea Ahrendt (*B. aggregata* × *B. wilsoniae*). Deciduous shrub, some 1 m high, twigs yellow, furrowed, glabrous, thorns 3 parted; leaves obovate, to 3 cm long and 0.8 cm wide, with 2–4 teeth on each side, venation reticulate, undersides gray-blue; flowers in 2.5–5 cm long panicles, flower stalk 2–8 mm long; fruit ovate, 8 mm long, 5 mm wide, carmine-red, with a style. JRHS 1942: 44. Originated in Wisley Gardens, England. Before 1942. z6 ⊕ ⊗

In addition the following hybrids; for further descriptions please refer to the key on p. 232:

'Aurora' (Wisley Gardens). Medium size shrub.

'Autumn Cheer' (Wisley Gardens 1938).

'Barbarossa' (Watson & Sons 1942). Medium size shrub.

'Bountiful' (A. R. Ahrendt 1938).

'Fireflame' (Wisley Gardens 1942). Growth dense and tall; leaves very small. Sensitive. z7

'Pirate King' (Waterer, Sons & Crisp 1937). Growth tall, branches attractively pendulous.

'Sparkler' (Wisley Gardens 1938).

B. caroli-hoenghensis see: **B. vernae**

B. caroliniana see: **B. canadensis**

B. cavalieri Lev. Evergreen, upright shrub, to 1 m high,

similar to *B. julianae*, twigs also yellow, but less angular, thorns 1–3 cm long; leaves grouped 2–4, elliptic-lanceolate, 2–6 cm long, very tough. China, Kwei-chow. # z6

This species falls between *B. julianae* and *B. bergmanniae* and is not completely known. Plants in cultivation under this name are usually *B. lempergiana*.

B. centiflora Diels. Evergreen shrub, 0.5 to 1.5 m high, bark of the twigs gray, thorns small; leaves leathery, obovate to oblanceolate or oblong, 3–4 cm long, green above, more yellowish beneath, margin with short, upturned teeth; flowers numerous, over 20, solitary or in racemes, fascicled, long stalked, sepals equal sized; fruits with sessile stigmas. China, Yunnan. z6 Plate. # ⊕

B. × chenaultii Chenault see: **B. hybrido-gagnepainii.**

B. chillanensis (Schneid.) Sprague. Deciduous shrub, some 1–3 m high, young twigs gray to gray-brown, usually short pubescent, thorns simple, 3 parted or totally absent, 4–8 mm long; leaves obovate, narrow, 8 mm wide, to 15 mm long, margins entire; flowers solitary, 1–1.5 cm wide, orange-yellow, stalk somewhat longer than the petals; fruit 8 mm long, rounded, black, with distinct style, reddish pruinose. NF 5: 16; BS 1: Pl. 1 (= *B. montana* var. *chillanensis* Schneid.) S. America, Andes of Chila and Peru. Very beautiful species. z7 Plate 65.

var. **hirsutipes** Sprague. Like the species, but becoming 4–5 m high (in its habitat), long shoots very dense short brown tomentose, thorns at the twig tips usually simple, at the base 3 parted; leaves 5–13 mm long, 2–5 mm wide, deep green; petals orange, stamens somewhat shorter than the petals, flower stalk pubescent. BM 9503. Argentina, Andes. 1925.

B. chinensis Poir. Deciduous shrub, to 3 m high, branches and twigs furrowed or angular, brown-red, thorns simple or 3 parted, to 18 mm long; leaves oblanceolate, 2–4 cm long, acute, margin entire or with 5–10 fine teeth on either side, bright green above, green or light bluish beneath; flowers grouped 10–12 in some 7 cm long racemes, 6–8 mm wide, May; fruits elliptic, 1 cm long, deep red, often pruinose, style absent (= *B. sinensis* Desf.; = *B. guimpelii* Koch). Caucasus. 1808. z6

B. chitria Hort., non Lindl. Deciduous shrub, to 3 m high, branches terete, pubescent, sometimes somewhat furrowed, thorns usually simple, to 3 cm long, new growth bronze-brown; leaves often semi-evergreen, obovate, elliptic or oblanceolate, 4–8 cm long, each blade half with 4–9 teeth, both sides green with finely reticulate venation; flowers in 15 cm long pendulous racemes, light yellow, May; fruits oblong, bright red, pruinose, August–September, with a style. BR 729; BM 2549 (as *B. aristata*). Himalaya, Nepal. z8 Plate 63.

B. chrysophaera Mulligan. Evergreen shrub, low, resembles *B. candidula*, but looser and shrubbier growth; twigs slightly furrowed, glabrous, reddish, thorns 3 parted, some 1.2 cm long; leaves oblanceolate, 1.5 to 4 cm long, clustered 3–7, indistinct venation, with some fine teeth, dark glossy green above, white beneath; flowers solitary, yellow, 1.2 cm wide, April–May, stalk 2.5 cm long; fruits blue-violet, erect. JRHS 1940: 77. SE. Tibet. 1933. z6 Plate 65. #

B. circumserrata Schneid. Deciduous, upright shrub, 0.7–1 m high, young twigs furrowed, yellowish or reddish, thorns simple to 3 parted, to 2.5 cm long; leaves obovate, 4 to 5 cm long, each side with 15–40 thorned teeth, base cuneate, apex rounded, tough reticulate venation, splendid red in fall, whitish beneath; flowers grouped 1–3, yellow, 1 cm wide, May; fruits elliptic, to 1.5 cm long, red-orange. NW. China, Shansi, Honan. z6 Plate 63.

var. **subarmata** Ahrendt. Thorns smaller and thinner; leaves elliptic to obcordate, with 15–20 thorns on either side, blood red fall color (Farrer Nr. 238). W. China. Plate 63.

B. comberi Sprague & Sandwith. Evergreen shrub, to 1 m high, growth very stiff, with stolons, no thorns on the twigs, twigs gray, glabrous; leaves ovate-rounded, 2–4 cm long, *Ilex*-like, leathery tough, with some large teeth on either side, light glossy green above, blue-gray beneath, distinctly veined; flowers grouped 2–3, very short stalked, orange-yellow, fragrant, April; petals and sepals 5 each (not 6). S. America, Andes of Chile. 1925. Notable for its lack of thorns and 5 parted flowers. z8 #⊕∅

B. 'Concal' (*B. concinna* × *B. calliantha*). Intermediate between the parents. Low growing, compact; leaves evergreen, ovate, some 3 cm long, thorny toothed, blue-white beneath; flowers numerous, lemon-yellow,

with 15 petals. Developed by C. Ingram of Benenden, England. 1948. z6

B. concinna Hook. f. Deciduous shrub, growth dense, some 60 cm high, twigs red at first, furrowed, then gray, thorns 3 parted, to 2 cm long; leaves obovate, 1–3 cm long, sparse thorny toothed, with 3–5 teeth on either side, white with reticulate venation beneath, beautiful red fall foliage; flowers grouped 1–2, gold-yellow, May; fruits oblong, 1.5 cm long, red, not pruinose, style absent. BM 4744. Sikkim. Around 1850. Good winter hardiness. z5? Fig. 139. ∅⌀

'Coral Gem' (*B. concinna* × ?). To 1 m high, compact; red fall color; fruit pear shaped, bright red. ∅⌀

B. congestiflora Gay. Very similar to *B. hakeoides*; dense, evergreen shrub, young twigs softly pubescent, eventually becoming nearly glabrous, light yellow; leaves thinner, ovate, 1–2.5 cm long and nearly as wide, base slightly cordate, petiole 2–5 cm long, margin thorny toothed with 6–20 thorns, rounded at the apex, both sides with reticulate venation, dull gray-green above, lighter beneath, more gray and pruinose; flowers grouped 8–10, in dense corymbs; fruits globose, hilum absent, blue, pruinose, 4–5 mm. PFC 35. Chile; Valdivia. # z6

B. consimilis Schneid. Deciduous shrub, resembling *B. faxoniana*, but with stouter thorns; leaves obovate, 2 cm long, 1 cm wide, with 8–14 teeth on either side; inflorescence 4–6 cm long; purple, style absent. China, W. Szechwan. Before 1916. z5?

B. coriaria Royle ex Lindl. Strong growing, evergreen shrub, to 2 m high, twigs glabrous and light yellow when mature, thorns 3 parted, some 2.5 cm long, thick; leaves obovate, 2–5 × 1–1.5 cm large, margins entire, both sides green; flowers in stiff racemes, with 10–25 flowers; each some 1.5 cm wide, yellow, petal tips emarginate (!); fruits ovate, bright red, not pruinose, 1.5 cm long. BR 720 (= *B. aristata* var. *coriacea* [Lindl.] Schneid.). W. Himalaya; Kumaon. 1835. z6

B. coxii Schneid. Evergreen shrub, upright, 1–1.5 m high, young twigs yellow-brown, rounded, later becoming gray, thorns 8–15 mm long; leaves grouped 3–4, elliptic to obovate, 2.5–5 cm long, with 6–12 small teeth on each wide, very glossy and dark green above, whitish beneath; flowers grouped 2–7, light yellow, some 1 cm wide, May; fruits obovate, black, somewhat pruinose, with 3–4 seeds. E. Himalaya, Upper Burma. 1919. z6 Plate 65. # ∅

B. crataegina DC. Deciduous shrub, over 1 m high, nodding-erect, the twigs slightly furrowed, brown, thorns usually simple; leaves oblong-ovate to obovate, somewhat leathery, 2.5–4 cm long, margins entire or with a few small teeth, glossy green above, lighter beneath to bluish-green, with prominent venation; flowers in umbel-like racemes, yellow, grouped 6–20 together, June; fruits oval, deep red. SH 1: 197 r–t. Asia Minor. 1835. Whether in cultivation is uncertain.

B. cretica L. Deciduous, strong growing shrub, quite

Fig. 139. From left to right: *Berberis buxifolia; B. empetrifolia; B. concinna; B. hakeoides* (from Bot. Mag., Bot. Reg. and Loddiges)

low, often procumbent, crooked, thorns 3 parted, very stout, 1–2.5 cm long, somewhat longer than the leaves; leaves obovate to oblanceolate, 1–2 cm long, tough, usually with entire margins or with single thorned teeth, bright green above and somewhat glossy, lighter beneath and somewhat veined; flowers few in fascicles, very short stalked; fruits black-red, nearly globose, with distinct style, somewhat prui- nose. SH 1: 194 d–f. Greece, Spain, Crete, in the mountains. 1703. z8

B. darwinii Hook. Evergreen shrub, 1–2 (to 3.5) m high, growth very dense, branches brown, finely pubescent, thorns short, 3–7 parted; leaves leathery tough, obovate, 1–3 cm long, with 1–3 thorned teeth on each side (nearly like tiny *Ilex* leaves), glossy above and dark green, light green beneath; flowers gold-yellow, somewhat reddish, 15–25 together in 4–10 cm long, pendulous racemes, April–May; fruits ovate, blue- green to black, with long style. BM 4950; FS 663. Chile to Patagonia. Very beautiful species. z7 Plate 53, 65.

In addition, several cultivars in England, most from T. Smith, Daisy Hill, and W. J. Marchant, Wimborne, Dorest:

'Fireflame'. Leaves 2.5 cm long, 0.6 cm wide; flowers 13–18 mm wide. Smith 1937. # ✧

'Flame'. Only 1.5 m high; leaves 1.8 cm long, 1.4 cm wide; flowers a strong orange-red. Marchant 1937. # ✧

'Gold'. Only 1–1.5 m high; flowers an intensive gold-yellow and very numerous, flowers from February to May in milder regions. Marchant 1934. # ✧

var. **magellanica** Ahrendt. Tall growing; flowers grouped 5–10, pure orange, 8–11 cm wide. Argentina, Strait of Magellan. 1944. #

'Nana'. Only 0.8–0.9 m high and wide; leaves dull green,

margins entire, much smaller than the species; flowers few. Smith 1908. #

'Pendula'. Twigs wide arching; leaves 1.8 cm long, 8 mm wide; flowers very reddish, 8–11 mm wide. Smith 1932. #

'Prostrata'. Only 0.4–0.5 m high; leaves dull green, margin dentate; very abundant flowering, buds reddish. Smith 1914. #

'Rubens'. Like the species but with very red buds, flowers an intense yellow, going into red. Watson, Ireland. # ✧

'Triumph' (Van Klaveren 1962) (*B. darwinii* female × ? *B. koreana*). Growth strictly upright, densely branched, rather compact, to some 1 m high, thorns 5 (to 7) parted, 5–10 mm long; leaves evergreen, broadly elliptic, to 3 cm long and 1.5 cm wide, frosted glossy dark green above, somewhat blue-green beneath. Presumably sterile. Good winter hardiness. z5 #

B. dasystachya Maxim. Deciduous shrub, upright, to 4 m high, twigs light red-brown, rod-like, thorns simple, to 1.5 cm long; leaves rounded-elliptic, 2.5–5 cm long, rounded at the apex, with 25–40 fine teeth on either half, both sides dull green, petiole 1–5 cm long (good identification characteristic); racemes slender, 3–6 cm long, erect, often with up to 40 solitary flowers, April– May; fruits globose, coral-red, not pruinose, style ab- sent, 8 mm thick. NF 1: 39. China; Kansu, Szechwan. 1915. Very Hardy. z5 ✧ ⚭

B. declinata Schrad. Deciduous shrub, presumably *B. canadensis* × *B. vulgaris*. Upright, branches brownish or also yellowish with traces of violet; leaves obovate, nearly entire or sparsely serrate, gray beneath; flowers in stalked umbels, some 6 cm long, small, petals some- what emarginate; fruits oval-elliptic, blood red, 1 cm long. Origin unknown. Before 1906. z4

B. diaphana Maxim. Deciduous shrub, 1 to 2 m high,

twigs glabrous, yellow, furrowed, thorns to 3 cm long; leaves obovate, 2–4 cm long, rounded at the apex, cuneate at the base, with 5–10 small teeth on each blade half, distinctly reticulate venation and light blue-green on the underside, fall color scarlet-red; flowers in fascicles of 1–5, rich yellow, long stalked, to 1.5 cm wide, May; fruits ovate, light red, not pruinose, with small style, translucent. BM 8224 (as *B. yunnanensis*). W. China, Kansu. 1894. z5 Plate 63. ⌀ ⚭

B. dictyoneura Schneid. Deciduous shrub, resembling *B. seiboldii*; young twigs reddish at first, later becoming gray; leaves elliptic to oblong-obovate, 2 cm long, thorny toothed, distinct reticulate venation, gray-green beneath; flowers grouped 4–7 in 2–3 cm long racemes, petiole 2–4 mm long; fruits obovoid, 8 mm long, red. China. W. Szechwan. 1910. z6 Plate 62.

B. dictyophylla Franch. Deciduous shrub, some 15 m high, twigs red, whitish pruinose, rod-like, thorns 3 parted, stiff, to 3 cm long; leaves elliptic, densely reticulate venation, 2 cm long, 1 cm wide, margins entire, white pruinose beneath, beautiful red fall foliage; flowers 1.5 cm wide, usually singular in each leaf cluster, light yellow, May; fruits ovate, light red, 1 cm long, with distinct style (= *B. dictyophylla* var. *albicaulis* Hesse). China; Yunnan. 1886. Rare in cultivation; usually produced under this name is var. *approximata* (with thorny toothed leaves). z6 Plate 64; Fig. 145. ⌀ ⚭

var. **approximata** (Sprague) Rehd. Twigs furrowed, shorter internodes, thorns 1.5–2 cm long; leaves smaller, 0.6–1.5 cm long, usually with 3–6 small thorned teeth on each side; flowers smaller; fruits thick white pruinose. BM 7833 (as *B. dictyophylla*). China; E. Szechwan. ⌀ ⚭

var. **epruinosa** Schneid. Twigs more angular, completely lacking pruinose coating, reddish; leaves bluish or completely green on the underside. Yunnan. 1910. ⚭

B. dielsiana Fedde. Deciduous shrub, 2–3 m high, resembles *B. henryana*; twigs red, somewhat angular, thorns simple or 3 parted, to 3 cm long; leaves ovate-oblong, 2.5–7 cm long, acute, margin finely thorny toothed, underside green; flower racemes branched at the bottom, 4–6 cm long, with 10–20 flowers; fruits ovoid, bright red, with short style. China; W. Szechwan. 1908. z5? ⌖ ⚭

'Compacta'. To only 1.5 m high, twigs shorter, stiffer, very dense, shorter internodes; leaves somewhat blue-green. Introduced to the trade by Hesse, Weener, W. Germany.

B. duleis see: **B. buxifolia**

B. dumicola Schneid. Evergreen shrub, some 1 m high, very dense, twigs arching downward somewhat, bark red at first, later becoming yellow, round or nearly so, thorns 1–3 cm long, 3 parted; leaves 3–5 together, elliptic-lanceolate, acute, 4–7 cm long, new growth brownish, later dark green above, lighter beneath, distinctly veined, with 20–40 long teeth on either blade half, teeth pointing outward; flowers grouped 8–12, light yellow, 8 mm wide; fruits ellipsoid, purple-black, slightly pruinose, with style. MD 1942; Pl. 2. W. China, Yunnan. 1914. z8 Plate 56. #

B. × durobrivensis Schneid. (*B. canadensis* × ? *B. poiretii*). Resembles *B. poiretii*. Deciduous shrub, to 2 m high, but young twigs redder, thorns very small; leaves more obovate-oblong, finely serrate; flowers in racemes, but flowers at the base solitary and longer stalked. Before 1906.

B. edgeworthiana Schneid. Deciduous shrub, some 1 m high, resembling *B. aggregata*, but with leaves elliptic to lanceolate, 1.5–3 cm long, tough, acute, with 3–8 small teeth on either blade half, distinct reticulate venation, underside green; inflorescence 2–3 cm long; fruits oblong, 1 cm long, red, with sessile stigma. NW. Himalaya. 1919. Very attractive shrub, especially for its bright red berries. z5? ⚭

B. × emarginata Willd. (*B. vulgaris* × *B. sibirica*). Deciduous shrub, 0.5–1 m high, twigs pendulous, angular, yellowish or reddish, thorns 3 (–5–7) parted, sometimes longer than the leaves; leaves obovate-oblong, 2–4 cm long, bristly serrate, underside gray; flowers in short, dense racemes, only slightly protruding past the foliage clusters, petals deeply emarginate, May; fruits oblong, 1 cm long, deep red, somewhat pruinose (= *B. vulgaris* var. *emarginana* Gord.). S. Europe to Himalaya. z3 ? ⚭

B. empetrifolia Lam. Evergreen shrub, only 20–30 cm high, prostrate grower, but taller in the wild, young twigs brown, furrowed; leaves linear, prickly tipped, to 2.5 cm long, margins rolled inward, therefore seldom 0.3 cm wide, dark green above, lighter beneath; flowers 1–2 in the foliage clusters, gold-yellow, May; fruits black, pruinose, globose, style absent. BR 26: 27. Chile to Tierra del Fuego. Very nice species for the rock garden; seldom found outside botanic gardens. z7 Fig. 139. #

B. faxoniana Schneid. Deciduous shrub, some 1.2 m high, thorns thin, to 8 mm long; leaves obovate, some 2.5 cm long, with 4–8 thorned teeth on either side, distinctly reticulate venation, gray-blue beneath; inflorescence nearly umbellate, to 3 cm long, flowers 1.2 cm wide; fruits ellipsoid, 1 cm long, reddish, with short style. China, W. Szechwan. Before 1916. z6

B. fendleri A. Gray. Deciduous shrub, some 1.5 m high, twigs nearly rod-like, thin, red-brown, glossy as if lacquered (important for identification), thorns 1 cm long, 3–5 parted; leaves lanceolate, 2–4 cm long, margin entire or sparsely thorned serrate, glossy above, light green beneath, venation reticulate; flowers grouped 6–10 in 3–5 cm long racemes; light yellow inside, outside orange, May; fruits rounded, 5 mm thick, red. GF 1888: 72. NW. America. z7 Very rare in cultivation.

B. floribunda G. Don. Tall shrub, to 3 m, twigs drooping, green, glabrous, light yellow pruinose, rounded, thorns absent or simple to 3 parted, 4–10 mm; leaves elliptic to slightly ovate, 2.5 × 1–2 cm, base drawn into the 1–3 mm long petiole, margin entire, but large toothed on the long summer twigs, dull green above,

Plate 49

Aucuba japonica 'Variegata'
in Dortmund Botanic Garden, W. Germany

Aucuba japonica 'Longifolia'
in Nantes Botanic Garden, France

Arıstolochia macrophylla
in the Park of Versailles, France

Asteriscus sericeus
in Tuebingen Botanic Garden, W. Germany

Plate 50

Azara lanceolata in Lochinch, Scotland

Aurinia saxatilis in an alpine garden

Plate 51

Banksia coccinea

Baccharis halimifolia
in Brissago Botanic Garden, Tessin, S. Switzerland

Banksia ericifolia with 2 inflorescences   Photo: Australia, News and Information Bureau, Canberra

Plate 52

Bauhinia acuminata
in Batumi Botanic Garden, USSR

Bauera sessiliflora
Photo: Australia News and Information Bureau,
Canberra

Bauhinia yunnanensis
in Sotchi Dendrarium, USSR

Broussonetia papyrifera in fruit,
in Tiflis Botanic Garden, USSR

Bupleurum spinosum
in Hannover-Muenden Botanic Garden, W. Germany

Plate 53

Berberis darwinii at Lismore Castle, Ireland

Berberis 'Sibbertoft Coral' (a. *B. aggregata*)   Photo: I. E. Downward

Plate 54

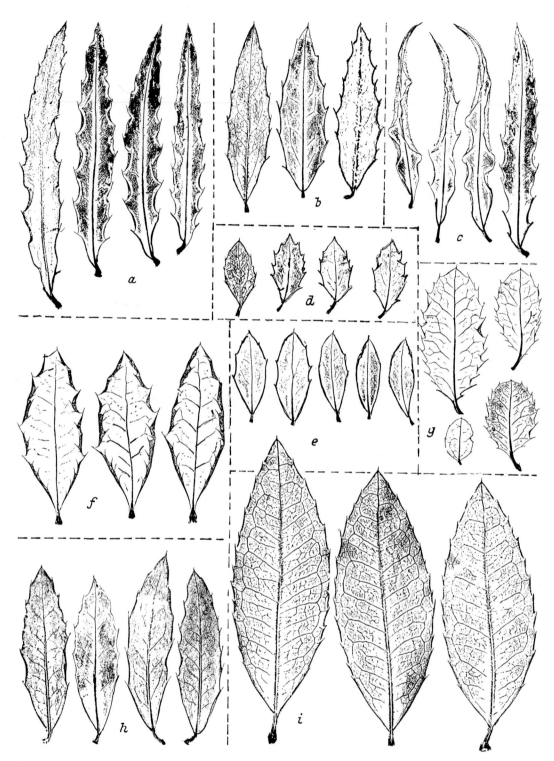

Berberis. a. *B. gagnepainii* var. *lanceifolia*; b. *B. gagnepainii* var. *subovata*; c. *B. gagnepainii* var. *filipes*; d. *B. verruculosa*; e. *B. candidula*; f. *B. calliantha*; g. *B. bristolensis*; h. *B. hybrido-gagnepainii* 'Terra Nova'; i. *B. manipurana*

Plate 55

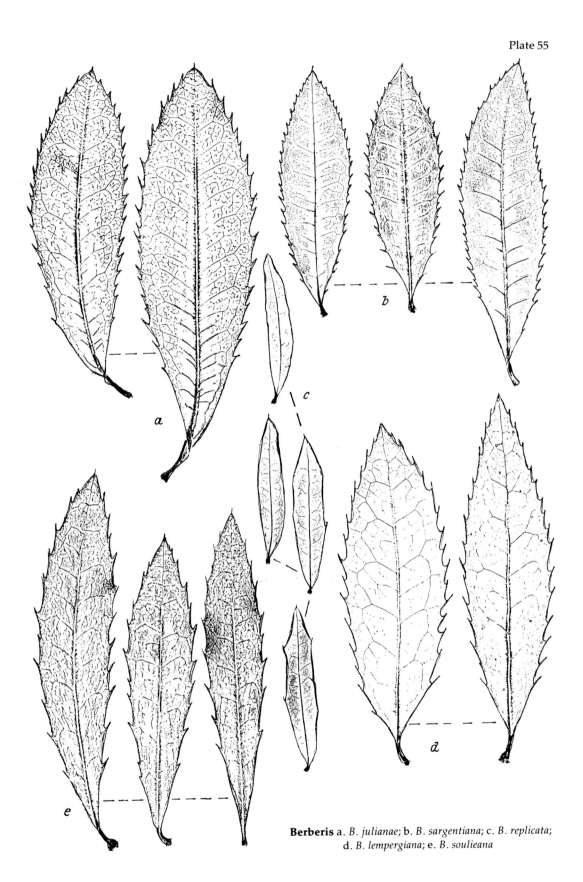

Berberis a. *B. julianae*; b. *B. sargentiana*; c. *B. replicata*; d. *B. lempergiana*; e. *B. soulieana*

Plate 56

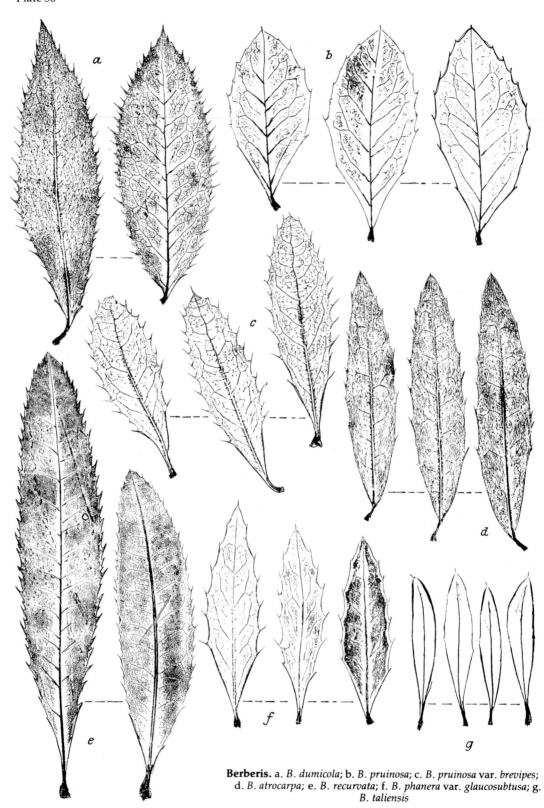

Berberis. a. *B. dumicola*; b. *B. pruinosa*; c. *B. pruinosa* var. *brevipes*;
d. *B. atrocarpa*; e. *B. recurvata*; f. *B. phanera* var. *glaucosubtusa*; g.
B. taliensis

Plate 57

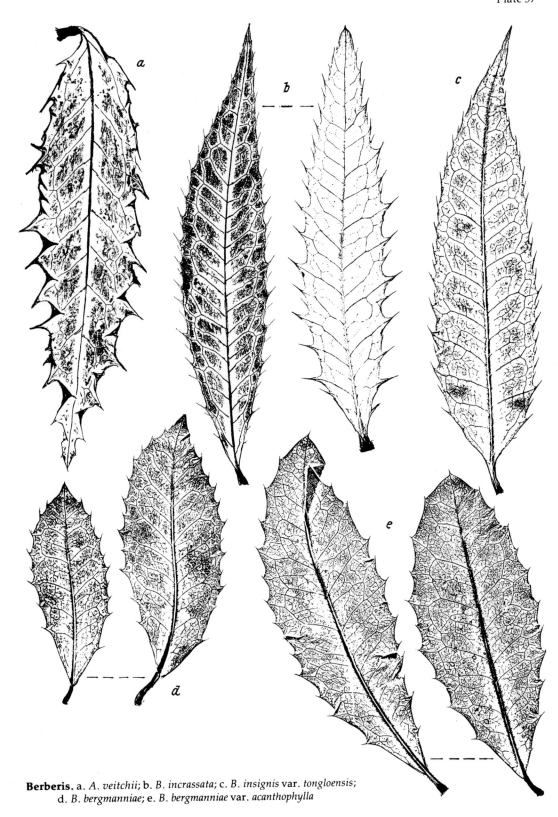

Berberis. a. *A. veitchii*; b. *B. incrassata*; c. *B. insignis* var. *tongloensis*;
d. *B. bergmanniae*; e. *B. bergmanniae* var. *acanthophylla*

Plate 60

Berberis montana   Photo: I. E. Downward

Berberis lologensis 'Nymans'   Photo: I. E. Downward

Plate 57

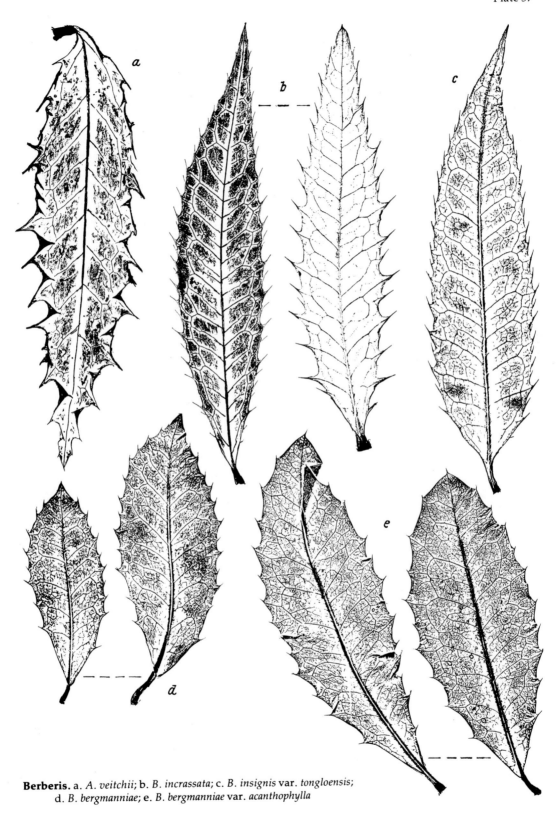

Berberis. a. *A. veitchii*; b. *B. incrassata*; c. *B. insignis* var. *tongloensis*;
d. *B. bergmanniae*; e. *B. bergmanniae* var. *acanthophylla*

Plate 58

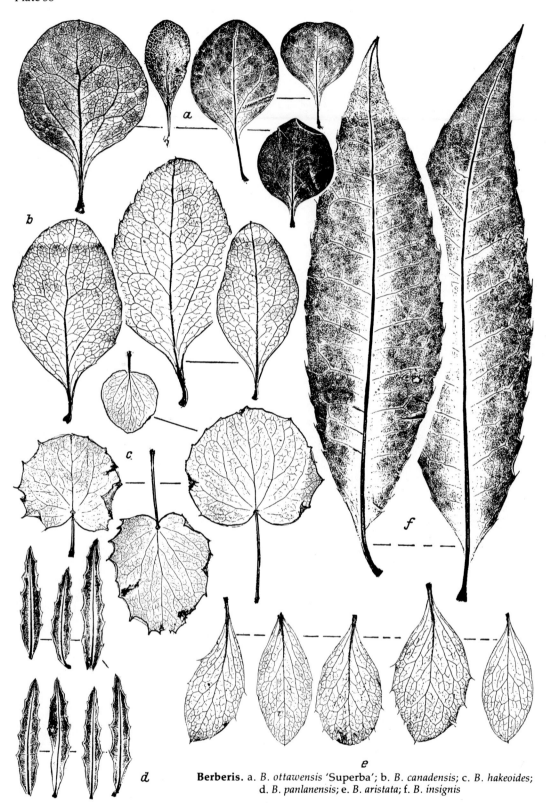

Berberis. a. *B. ottawensis* 'Superba'; b. *B. canadensis*; c. *B. hakeoides*;
d. *B. panlanensis*; e. *B. aristata*; f. *B. insignis*

Plate 59

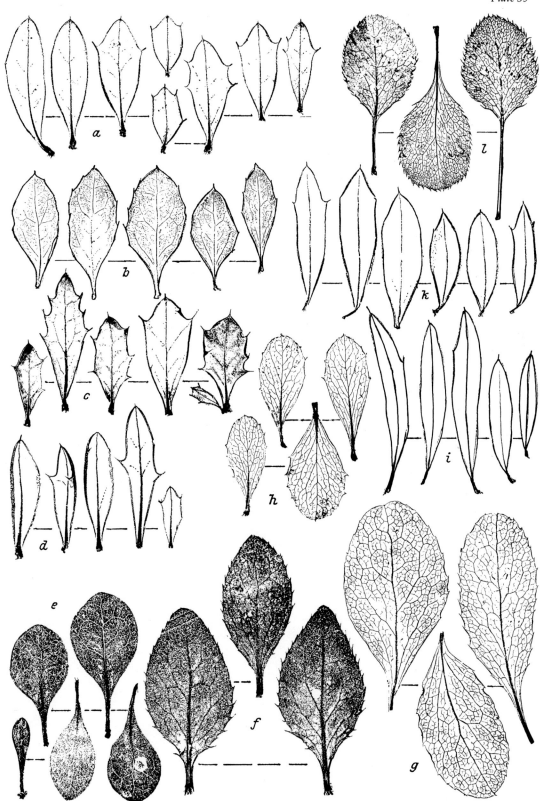

Berberis. a. *B. lologensis*; b. *B. media* 'Parkjuweel'; c. *B. lologensis* 'Yellow Beauty'; d. *B. lologensis* 'Highdown'; e. *B. thunbergii* 'Atropurpurea'; f. *B. vulgaris* 'Atropurpurea'; g. *B. regeliana* h. *B. suberecta*; i. *B.linearifolia*; k. *B. linearifolia* 'Orange King'; l. *B. honanensis*

Plate 60

Berberis montana   Photo: I. E. Downward

Berberis lologensis 'Nymans'   Photo: I. E. Downward

Plate 61

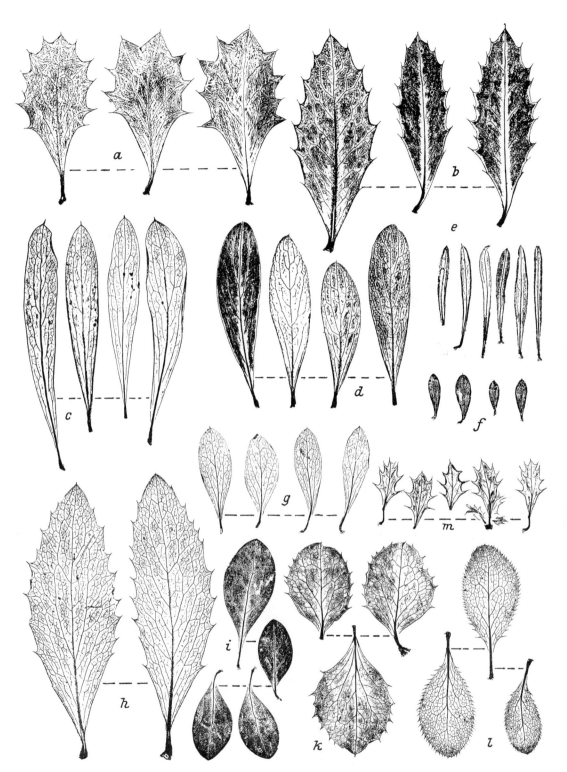

Berberis. a. *B. liechtensteinii;* b. *B. anniae;* c. *B. lycium;* d. *B. lycioides;* e. *B. lepidifolia;* f. *B. graminea;* g. *B. thibetica;* h. *B. glaucocarpa;* i. *B. lecomtei;* k. *B. mekongensis;* l. *B. zabeliana;* m. *B. minutiflora*

Plate 62

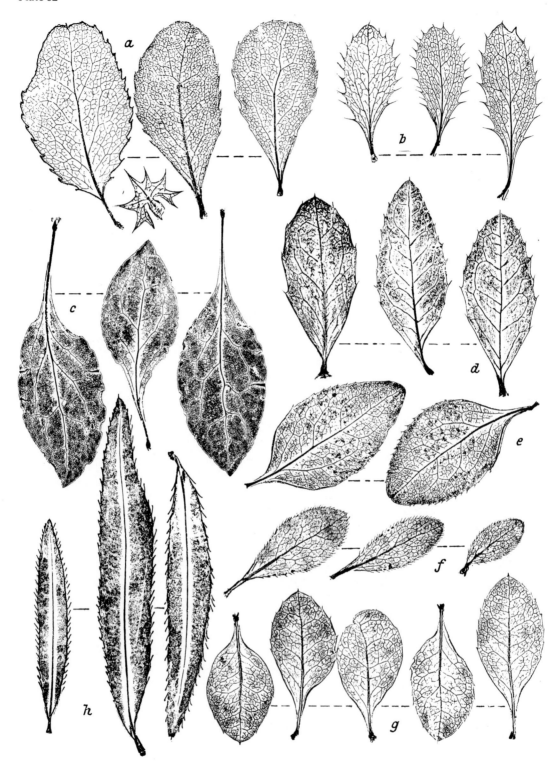

Berberis. a. *B. koreana*; b. *B. dictyoneura*; c. *B. virgetorum*; d. *B. centiflora*; e. *B. brachypoda*; f. *B. quelpartensis*; g. *B. mentorensis*; h. *B. sublevis*

Plate 63

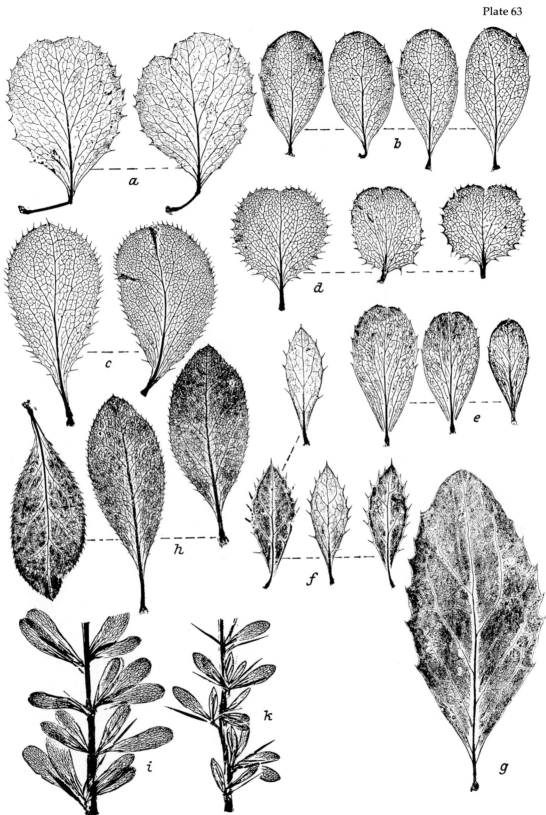

Berberis. a. *B. macrosepala*; b. *B. diaphana*; c. *B. circumserrata*; d. *B. circumserrata* var. *subarmata* (Farrer 238);
e. *B. temolaica*; f. *B. sikkimensis*; g. *B. chitria*; h. *B. umbellata*; i. *B. wilsoniae*; k. *B. wilsoniae* var. *subcauliata*

Plate 64

Berberis thunbergii 'Erecta'
in Dortmund Botanic Garden, W. Germany

Berberis dictyophylla
in Wageningen Arboretum, Holland

Berberis thunbergii 'Minor' in Wageningen Arboretum, Holland

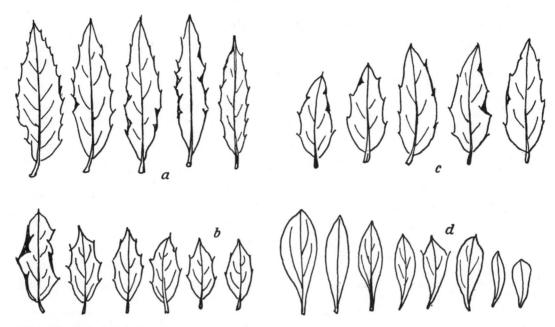

Fig. 140. *Berberis hybrido-gagnepainii* 'Terra Nova' (a) and 'Tottenham' (c), *B. frikartii* 'Staefa' (b) and *B. johannis* (d) (Original)

lighter beneath and yellow-green; flowers 15—25 in racemes; fruits broad ellipsoid, dark red, eventually nearly purple and blue pruinose, to 7.5 × 5 mm large. Nepal, high in the mountains. 1905. z4?

B. forrestii Ahrendt. Deciduous shrub, to 1.8 m high, twigs attractively drooping, thornless or with only short, weak thorns, young twigs red; leaves oblong-obovate, margins entire, to 6 cm long, gray above, gray pruinose beneath; flowers in umbellate racemes, to 12 cm long; fruits oval-oblong, 1 cm long, bright red. China; Yunnan. 1910. Closely related to *B. pallens* and occasionally confused with it. z6

B. francisci-ferdinandi Schneid. Deciduous shrub, to 3 m high, elegantly drooping, young twigs angular on strong branches, otherwise more rod-like, reddish, thorns usually simple, to 2.5 cm long; leaves oval, 2—7 cm long, acuminate, margin finely thorny toothed (occasionally nearly entire), green beneath, usually somewhat glossy; flowers yellow, 8 mm wide, in to 12 cm long, narrow, pendulous racemes (best distinction), May; fruits ellipsoid, to 1.2 cm long, scarlet red, with very short style. BM 9281. W. China. 1900. z6 Fig. 144. ✧ ⚭

B. × frikartii Schneid. ex van de Laar. (*B. candidula* × *B. verruculosa*). Evergreen shrub, 1—1.5 m high, dense, young twigs more or less densely warty, broownish-yellow, thorns 3 parted, 1.2—1.5 (2) cm long, yellowish-green to light brown; leaves elliptic, leathery tough, 1.5—3 cm long, glossy green above, gray-white beneath, margin with 2—4 sharp teeth on either side, often slightly rolled inward; flowers light yellow, 1—2 together, often partly abscising, May—June; fruit oval-oblong, green, blue-white pruinose. z6 The typical

plant of this hybrid is 'Staefa'.

Containing the following cultivars: all originating in Holland (except 'Staefa'):

'Amstelveen' (Broerse, around 1960). Growth compact and low, to some 1 m high, twigs outspread and attractively drooping; leaves resembling *B. candidula*, but somewhat shorter, flatter, lighter above, glossy, blue-white to white beneath (= *B. candidula* 'Amstelveen'.). Selected by C. P. Broerse in Amstelveen. Good winter hardiness and fast growing. #

'Mrs. Kennedy' (Haalboom, arond 1960). Practically no difference from 'Telstar'. #

'Staefa' (Frikart, around 1928). The typical plant of the hybrid; for description, see above (= *B. × chenaultii* 'Staefa'; *B. × hybrido-gagnepainii* 'Staefa'). Found by Karl Frikart in Staefa, Switzerland. Still in cultivation as the best winter hardy form. Fig. 140. #

'Telstar' (Van den Oever, around 1960). Growth low and compact, to 1.2 m high, twigs attractively sidespread; leaves wider than those of *B. candidula*, flatter, glossy green, bluish-white beneath; resembling 'Amstelveen', but somewhat larger. Dfl 9: 12 (= *B. candidula* 'Telstar'). Introduced by M. Van Der Oever & Zonen, Haaren, Netherlands. Winter hardiness very good. #

'Verrucandi' (Hardijzer, before 1952). Practically identical to 'Telstar' in growth and leaf (= *B.* 'Ruhm von Hirschstetten'; *B. frikarii* 'Typ Timm' 1969). Selection by J. G. Hardijzer; Boskoop, Holland, and introduced as *Berberis* 'Verrucandi'. #

B. gagnepainii Schneid. Evergreen shrub, leaves 5 cm long and 1 cm wide. The typical species from W. China is not in culture. The plant found by this name in gardens is its variety *lanceifolia*, see below. z6 #

'Fernspray' (Jackman 1955). To 1.5 m high, compact; leaves light green, very long and narrow, margin wavy. Selected by G. Jackman & Son, Woking, Surrey, England from var. *lanceifolia* and mainly disseminated in England.

'Green Mantle' (Darthuizer Boomkw. 1967). Selected from seedlings of var. *lanceifolia* with numerous nodding twigs and very narrow gray-green leaves.

var. **filipes** Ahrendt. Leaves lanceolate, 4–6 cm long, some 8 mm wide, with 6–10 teeth on either side; flower stalk very thin, some 2.5–4 cm long. Plate 54. #

var. **lanceifolia** Ahrendt. Evergreen shrub, to 1.5 m high, twigs round, yellow, lightly pubescent, thorns thin, 3 parted, 1–2 cm long; leaves lanceolate, indistinctly veined, with 6–20 large teeth on either blade half, margin slightly wavy, dull green above, glossy yellow-green beneath, 3—10 cm long, 1–2 cm wide; flowers gold-yellow, 3–7 together, some 1 cm wide, May–June; fruits ovate, 1 cm long, blue-black pruinose, style absent. BMns 504. China, W. Hupeh. 1903. z6 Plate 54. # ∅

var. **subovata** Schneid. Only to 1 m high, twigs more yellow; leaves more oblong-ovate, 4–6 cm long, 1–1.5 cm wide, with 10–12 fine teeth on either side, margin scarcely wavy; flowers grouped 1–6, stalk 2 cm long. W. Szechwan, Yunnan. Plate 54.

In addition there are 3 common hybrids with *B. gagnepainii* as the principal parent. The second parent is unknown, but it is not *B. verruculosa* and so these hybrids cannot be included under B. × *hybrido-gagnepainii*. #

'Klugowski' (Klugowski, around 1960). Shrub to 1 m high, growth very dense; leaves narrow lanceolate, to 5 cm long, dark green above, blue-green beneath; slow grower (= B. 'Klugowskiana'; *B. hybrida* 'Typ Klugowski' (Hort.). Originated by Alfons Klugowski in Flein, near Heilbronn, W. Germany. #

'Robin Hood' (Broerse 1965). Growth more or less globose, low, some 1 m high; leaves narrow elliptic, to 4.5 cm long and 1 cm wide, dull dark green above, blue-green beneath, old leaves turning a dark red and abscising in the fall. Dfl 9: 16C (= *B. hybrido-gagnepainii* 'Robin Hood'). #

'Rusthof' (Van Drie, around 1958). Growth rather open, to 1 m, twigs upright drooping at the tips; leaves elliptic, 3–5 cm long, dull, dark green above, blue-green beneath. Found in the 'Rusthof' Cemetary in Amersfort, Netherlands by C. Nan Drie. #

B. geraldii see: **B. aggregata**

B. gilgiana Fedde. Deciduous shrub, to 2 m high, sprawling habit, twigs furrowed, yellowish or reddish-brown, finely pubescent, thorns usually 3 parted, 0.5–2.5 cm long; leaves elliptic-oblong, 3–5 cm long, tapering to the base, sparsely serrate or nearly entire, dull green above, gray-green and pubescent beneath; flowers light yellow, in dense, short racemes, stalk pubescent; fruits oblong, dark red, slightly pruinose, 1 cm long. China, Shansi. 1910. z6

B. giraldii Hesse. Deciduous wide-growing shrub, resembling *B. mitifolia*; to 2 m high, twigs somewhat angular, yellow-brown or dark brown, thorns usually simple, 3 cm long; leaves ovate-oblong to rhombic, 4–10 cm long, finely serrate, reddish at first, later be-

coming deep green and glabrous above, light green beneath, venation reticulate and finely pubescent; flowers in 10 cm long, pendulous racemes, light yellow, 9 mm wide; fruits purple, ellipsoid. China, Shansi. Around 1935. z6 Seldom true; those in cultivation usually mislabeled *B. suberecta*. (from Ahrendt).

B. glaucocarpa Stapf. Semi-evergreen shrub, very similar to *B. lycioides*, but with toothed leaves, elliptic, 6–8 cm long, with 8–12 large teeth on either side; flower racemes stiffer with short stalk, fruits thicker, more oblong, blue-black. Himalaya, Punjab. z6 Plate 61.

B. graminea Ahrendt. Deciduous shrub, very ornamental, twigs purple, glabrous; leaves oblanceolate to obovate, 1–2 cm long, 3 to 5 mm wide, with thorny tips, white beneath; fruit red, style absent. Yunnan. 1937. z6 Plate 61.

B. guimpelii see: **B. chinensis** and **B. × laxiflora**

B. gyalaica Ahrendt. Deciduous shrub, closely related to *B. aggregata* var. *prattii*, 2–3 m high, twigs thin and drooping, brown, furrowed, pubescent, thorns thin, 3 parted, some 1 cm long; leaves elliptic, 6–15 mm long, with 3–4 teeth on either side, bluish beneath; panicles of 20–30 flowers, some 5–7 cm long, axis brown, pubescent, stalk 2–3 mm long; fruits ovate-oblong, often somewhat deformed, 1 cm long, blue-black, blue pruinose, style absent. BMns 22. SE. Tibet. 1924. Very beautiful, relatively new species. z5? ⊕ ⚭

B. hakeoides (Hook. f.) Schneid. Evergreen shrub, growth narrowly upright, somewhat stocky, grows to 3 m in its native habitat, branches not very twiggy, furrowed, glabrous; leaves usually paired, very changeable, rounded to cordate, 2–4 cm wide and long, tough, dark green above, bluish beneath, margin thorny toothed, petioles at the basal end of the twigs to 3 cm long, becoming shorter to sessile toward the apex, thorned, flattened leaf-like; flowers gold-yellow, 8 mm wide, grouped 10–20 in hemispherical clusters, April to May; fruits blue-black, with 1 seed. BM 6770 (as *B. congestiflora hakeoides* Hook. f.). Chile. 1861. z8 Plate 58; Fig. 139. # ∅ ⊕

B. helenae Ahrendt. Evergreen shrub, some 1 m high, twigs rounded, very warty, yellow, glabrous; leaves elliptic, 2–5 cm long and 1 cm wide, acute, with 6–9 small thorny teeth on either side, glossy yellow-green above, gray-pruinose beneath and with papillae; flowers 6–10 in fascicles, on 3–4 cm long stalks, the individual blooms some 1 cm wide, June; fruit ovate, 1 cm long, 7 mm wide, purple, heavily lilac pruinose, style absent. Origin unknown, possibly a hybrid. In culture at Wisley Garden, England. z6 #

B. henryana Schneid. Deciduous shrub, to 3 m high, twigs somewhat angular, yellow to brown, thorns simple to 3 parted, to 3 cm long; leaves elliptic, 2–5 cm long, obtuse, margins entire or somewhat thorny toothed, fresh green above, gray-green beneath, pruinose, petiole to 1 cm long; flowers to 1 cm wide,

Fig. 141. From left to right: *Berberis heteropoda*; *B. hookeri*; *B. sieboldii* (from Bot. Mag., Dippel, Garden and Forest)

10–20 in 6 cm long racemes, May; fruits ellipsoid, 1 cm long, dark red, somewhat pruinose. Middle China. z6

B. heterophylla Juss. Semi-evergreen shrub, to 0.7–1.5 m high in its habitat, stoloniferous, twigs crooked, unevenly spaced, abundantly branched, thirns 3 parted, 1.5–2 cm long, internodes 1.5 cm long; leaves 1–3 cm long, in 2 forms, either narrow oblong and entire or obovate and with 3–5 *Ilex*-like, large thorns; flowers solitary, orange-yellow, petals and sepals nearly globose curved inward, April–May; fruits pea size, black, pruinose. SH 1: 195 t–w. Chile to Tierra del Fuego. Very beautiful species, rare. z8 ⊕ ⊘ ⌘

B. heteropoda Schrenk. Deciduous shrub, to 2 m high, growth broad and open, twigs rod-like, brown, glossy, thorns simple to 3 parted, to 2.5 cm long, sometimes absent; leaves broad ovate to oval, rounded at the apex, to 2.5 cm long, abruptly tapering for the basal 2 cm long, red petiole, entire or finely thorny toothed, gray-green above, more bluish beneath; flowers orange-yellow, 1.2 cm wide, fragrant, usually grouped 15 in long, pendulous racemes, with 2 short secondary racemes of 3–4 flowers each, May; fruits ovate, black, 1 cm thick, pruinose, stigma sessile. GF 1895: 455. Turkestan. z6 Fig. 141. ⌘

B. hispanica Boiss. & Reut. Deciduous, upright shrub, 1–1.5 m high, growth open, twigs dark red, thorns simple to 3 parted, 1–2 cm long; leaves elliptic to obovate, entire or with some sparse teeth, 0.8–2.4 cm long, tapering to the base; flowers orange-yellow,

grouped 6–15 in fascicles or short racemes, May; fruits ovate, blue-black, 6 mm long. PSw 8. SE. Spain, Morocco, Algeria, in the mountains. z6

B. honanensis Ahrendt. Deciduous shrub, leaves elliptic, 2–3 cm long, with 20–30 small teeth on either side, easily distinguished by the 1–3 cm long petiole. N. China, Honan. z6 Plate 59.

B. hookeri Lem. Evergreen shrub, some 0.7 m high, twigs angular, thorns 3 parted, some 2 cm long, yellowish; leaves 3–5 together, elliptic, 4–6 cm long, 1–2 cm wide, thin, venation reticulate, each blade half with 7–15 large teeth, glossy green above, white pruinose beneath; flowers grouped 3–6 in fascicles, petiole straight, 2–2.5 cm long, petals with entire margins, flowers to 1.8 cm wide, greenish-yellow, May; fruits oblong, 1.3 cm long, blackish-purple, style absent, only slightly or not at all pruinose, usually 3 seeded. BM 4656, 9153; NF 1:60 (as *B. wallichiana*). Himalaya; Sikkim, Bhutan. 1848. z6 Fig. 141. # ⊘

This winter hardy species is quite variable and therefore, often confused; the primary distinguishing characteristic is that the underside of the leaf is often green.

var. **latifolia** Hook. & Thoms. is not in cultivation. Garden plants by this name are usually *B. manipurana*; which see.

var. **viridis** Schneid. Like the species, but with leaves always green beneath; fruits somewhat smaller. # ⊘

B. × **hybrido-gagnepainii** Suring. (*B. gagnepainii* × *B. verruculosa*). A group of hybrids, intermediate between the parents; usually growing more luxuriantly than *B. verruculosa*.

The cultivar 'Terra Nova' has been erroneously described by Duringar as a hybrid of *B. candidula* and *B. gagnepainii* despite the rought warty twigs, which are a sure mark of *B. verruculosa* (and not *B. candidula*). The name *hybrido-gagnepainii* has been officially accepted since 1929.

'Chenault'. Shrub, to some 1.5 m high, to 2 m wide, twigs somewhat warty; leaves narrowly oblong, 2–3.5 cm long, very glossy above, bluish beneath, thorny toothed; flowers gold-yellow, 1.5 cm wide (= *B. chenaultii* Chenault). 1926, originated in Orléans, France by Chenault. # ∅

'Chenault Compact' (Hardijzer, arond 1952). Grows more compactly than 'Chenault', twigs more prominently drooping; leaves smaller (= *B. chenaultii* 'Compacta'). # ∅

'Genty' (Hardijzer 1966). Growth wide and compact, to 1 m high, twigs upright; leaves 2–5 cm long, narrow, dull green above, blue-white beneath. # ∅

'Hilde' (Haalboom, around 1953). Growth wide and compact, to 1.2 m high, branches sprawling, twigs purple-red at first; leaves small, 1–3 cm long, glossy green above, dull blue-gray beneath. Dfl 9: 20D. # ∅

'Minikin' (Hardijzer 1970). Dwarf form, growth very compact, to some 50 cm high, but becoming 80 cm wide; leaves small and somewhat twisted, 1–2 cm long, fresh green above and glossy white beneath. Originated in Boskoop, Holland by Hanno Hardijzer. Very nice. # ∅

'Select' (Haalboom, around 1953). Growth loosely upright, twigs straight at first, then spreading; leaves 2–4 cm long, 0.8–1.5 cm wide, somewhat glossy above, dull blue-gray beneath. Without great ornamental value; outperformed by 'Wallich's Purple'. # ∅

'Terra Nova' (Keessen 1969). Growth low, densely branched, twigs finely warty, internodes short; leaves 6–12 at an internode, lanceolate, 3.5–4 cm long, somewhat glossy above, green or also bluish beneath, each blade half with 3–12 small thorns. Found by W. Keessen, Aalsmeer, Holland. Plate 54; Fig. 140. # ∅

'Tottenham' Tall, branches nodding; leaves more ovate, to 4 cm long and to 1.3 cm wide, with 2–4 (6) thorns on either blade half, both sides green, somewhat glossy above, often becoming red in fall. Originated around 1930 by Ruys, Dedemsvaart, Holland. Fig. 140. #

B. hypokerina Airy-Shaw. Evergreen shrub, growth narrowly upright or also wide-procumbent, 0.5–0.7 m high, twigs reddish, glabrous, thorns not observed; leaves solitary, oblong-oval, to 5 cm long and 5 cm wide, very rigid and leathery tough, deep green above, silver-white beneath, margin with some 12 very large *Ilex*-like thorned teeth, a number of leaves becoming scarlet-red in the fall; flowers abundant, light yellow, 1 cm wide, in fascicles, June; fruits small, black-violet, with thick, white pruinose coating, style absent. Upper Burma, at altitudes of 3000 to 3500 m. 1926. z8 Plate 66; Fig. 144. # ⊕ ∅

B. ilicifolia Forrest. Evergreen shrub, irregular growth, to 2 m in its habitat, twigs deeply furrowed, yellow; leaves nearly *Ilex*-like, 3–5 cm long, obovate, with few large thorns on either blade half, very glossy and dark green above, light green beneath; flowers orange-yellow, 1.5 cm wide, several in dense, short racemes; fruits steel-blue, reverse pear-shaped. BM

4308; FS 291. S. Chile. 1791. Very rare in cultivation. z8 Fig. 143 # ∅ ⚭

B. iliensis Popof. Deciduous shrub, resembling *B. turcomanica* var. *itegerrima*, but with flower stalk only some 8 mm long, fruits smaller, style present. Turkestan. 1936. z6

B. incrassata Ahrendt. Evergreen, low shrub, twigs glabrous, rounded, reddish thornless; leaves narrow lanceolate, 5–15 cm long, large toothed, gray-green above, glossy light green beneath, solitary on young twigs, however clustered on older banches; flowers some 1.5 cm wide, light yellow, 15–30 in short stalked, dense fascicles, flower stalk very thin at the base, much thicker nearer the flower; fruits globose, blue-black. MD 1942, Pl. 6. N. Burma. 1931. z7 Plate 57. # ∅

B. insignis Hook. & Thoms. Evergreen, *Ilex*-like shrub, to 1.5 m high, young twigs round, with slender thorns or thornless (important for identification), fox-red; leaves solitary or grouped in 3's, thin leathery, 5–12 cm long, elliptic-lanceolate, with 12 to 20 small, thorned teeth on either blade half, deep green above, yellow-green and veined beneath, both sides glossy; flowers 10–20 in fascicles, light gold-yellow, petals emarginate; fruits oval, black, 8 mm long, not pruinose, style absent. Sikkim. 1848. z8 Plate 58. # ∅

var. **tongloensis** Schneid. Twigs yellowish or gray-yellow; leaves narrower, finer and narrower thorny toothed. Sikkim. 1902. Often under the species name in cultivation. Plate 57. # ∅

B. × interposita Ahrendt (*B. hookeri* × *B. verruculosa*). Very similar to *B. hookeri*, distinguished by the smaller, less distinctly veined leaves, the groups of 1–2 flowers with 15 mm long stalk; fruits 1 cm long, 6 mm thick. z6 # ∅

Included here (from Van De Laar) the following form:

'Wallich's Purple' (Keessen, around 1950). Densely branched, to 1.5 m high, twigs more or less drooping; leaves broad-elliptic, 2–3.5 cm long, 0.8–1.2 cm wide, with 3–6 thorned teeth on either blade half, young leaves a pretty copper-red tone, later glossy green above, dull blue-green beneath. Dfl 9: 20B (= *B. wallichiana purpurea* Hort.). Originated by W. Keessen in Aalsmeer, Holland. Very valuable garden form, earlier classified under *B. × hybrido-gagnepainii*. # ∅

B. jaeschkeana Schneid. Deciduous shrub, to 1m high, twigs angular, yellow, pubescent, thorns to 2 cm long; leaves elliptic to obovate, 2–2.5 cm long, with 3–4 teeth on either half, both sides green; flowers in 3 cm long umbels; fruits obovoid, not pruinose, style absent. Kashmir. 1865. z6

B. jamesiana Forrest & W. W. Smith. Deciduous shrub, to 2 m high, twigs round, glabrous, red, thorns 3 parted, to 3.5 cm long; leaves rounded to obovate, 2.5–5 cm long, entire or finely thorny toothed toward the apex, venation reticulate, both sides dull green; flowers in 5–10 cm long racemes, orange-yellow, petiole 8–12 mm long, flowers only 5 mm wide, June; fruits globose, coral-red, somewhat translucent, very

Fig. 142. *Berberis jamesiana* (from ICS)

bright and attractive. BM 9298. NW. Yunnan. 1913. z6 Fig. 142.

B. jamesonii Lindl. Evergreen species with large leaves and flowers in panicles. Indigenous to Peru. Not found in cultivation. Plants under this name are usually *B. hookeri*. z6? Fig. 132. #

B. johannis Ahrendt. Deciduous shrub, to 1.5 m high, very closely related to *B. tsarongensis* and *B. yunnanensis*, but with twigs reddish at first, later becoming yellow, somewhat furrowed, thorns to 1.5 cm long; leaves obovate, to 2 cm long and 1 cm wide, margins entire, blue-green beneath; flowers grouped 4—10 in 2—3.5 cm long racemes or corymbs; fruits narrow oblong, often somewhat narrowed in the middle, 1.2 cm long, scarlet-red, not pruinose, style absent. BMns 57. SE. Tibet, 1924. z6 Fig. 140. ⊕ ∅ ⌀

B. julianae Schneid. Evergreen shrub, to some 2.5 m high, growth upright, twigs furrowed, yellowish at first, later gray-yellow, thorns stout, 3 parted, nearly 4 cm long, very stiff; leaves obovate, to 10 cm long and to 2.5 cm wide at the upper half, with 12—20 thorny teeth on either side, leathery tough, upper surface dark, glossy green, pale green beneath, seldom glossy, veins widely spaced; flowers pure yellow, 8—15 in fascicles, occasionally reddish outside, 1 cm wide, stalk to 1.5 cm long, May—June; fruits oblong, blue-black, pruinose, 8 mm long, with short style. BM 9283 (as *B. xanthoxylon*). Middle China, W. Hupeh. 1907. z6 Plate 55; Fig. 146. # ∅ ⊕

One of the nicest and hardiest of the evergreen species, but unfortunately often erroneously identified in cultivation and confused with the less hardy *B. sargentiana* or *B. manipurana* (according to Ahrendt).

'Dart's Superb' (Darthuizer Boomkw. 1967). Growth moderately tall, branches outspread, leaves smaller than the species. Selected from seedlings of the species; probably a hybrid. #

'Lombarts Red' (Lombarts 1953). Growth habit and foliage like a vegetatively propagated clone of *B. julianae*, but with the leaf undersides lilac-pink to wine-red. Without particular garden merit. #

B. kansuensis Schneid. Deciduous shrub, to 4 m high in its habitat, twigs light red, thin, thorns usually simple, to 1.5 cm long; leaves broadly elliptic to rounded, 3—5 cm lng, sparsely serrate, occasionally also entire, long petioled, fresh green above, blue-green beneath, petiole 1—3 cm long; flowers 8 mm wide, in dense, erect racemes; fruits ellipsoid, 7 mm long, coral red. NW. China, Kansu. 1910. z5? ⊕ ⌀

B. kawakamii Hayata. Evergreen shrub, growth upright, strongly branched, to 1.8 high, young twigs angular, yellowish to yellow-gray, thorns 1—2 cm long; leaves 2—4 together, elliptic to obovate or lanceolate, 3—7 cm long, leathery tough, light green above, lighter and somewhat glossy beneath, with 10—20 fine teeth on either side; flowers grouped 5—15, small, yellow, sepals 1 cm long, very narrow, red on the back side, petals only 0.5 cm long; fruits oval, 8 mm long, dark blue. BM 9622; LWT 62. Taiwan, forested mountain slopes of the Kagi Province. Hardy. z6 Plate 65. #

B. kewensis Schneid. Deciduous shrub, closely related to *B. aristata*, but with angular twigs, red-brown; leaves narrow elliptic to obovate, 3—5 cm long, blue-green with reticulate venation beneath, thorny serrate; flowers 1 cm wide, in 4—8 cm long racemes; fruits oval-oblong, dark violet, pruinose, 1 cm long, with short style. Origin unknown. 1889. z6 ⌀

B. 'Klugowskiana' see: **B. gagnepainii**

B. koreana Palibin. deciduous shrub, to 1.5 m high, twigs reddish, furrowed, thorns on the long shoots often 5 parted, the simple thorns usually flattened leaf-like, gradually changing to simple, normal thorns; leaves obovate to oval, apex rounded, 3—7 cm long, gradually tapering to the long petiole, densely thorny serrate, deep red in fall; flowers many in 4—5 cm long, pendulous racemes, May; fruits ovate, bright red, 8 mm long. NK 21: 7. Korea. 1905. Quite hardy and very attractive. z4 Plate 62. ⊕ ∅ ⌀

'Red Tears' (Lombarts 1958). Growth wide and strong, 1.5—2 m high, twigs outspread, thorns to 3 cm long, 3 parted, occasionally 5 parted to leaf-like; leaves broad elliptic, 4—7 cm long, dull blue-green, lighter beneath; fruits in 10 cm long pendulous racemes, oblong, 12 × 7 mm, splendid red, holding its color a long time. Dfl. 9: 30 D. Probably a hybrid of *B. vulgaris*. ∅

B. latifolia see: × **Mahoberberis**, × **Neubertii**

B. × laxiflora Schrad. (*B. ? chinensis* × *B. vulgaris*). Deciduous shrub, young twigs gray-brown at first, later becoming grayer, thorns simple to 3 parted; leaves obovate-oblong, 2—5 cm long, entire to sparsely finely serrate; flowers usually in sessile, 4—8 cm long racemes. Originated before 1838. z5 ✥ ⚭

var. **langeana** Schneid. Young twigs reddish-brown, gray-brown in the second year; leaves obovate-oblong, 2—6 cm long, sparsely toothed (= *B. guimpelii* Hort. non Koch.). Origin unknown.

B. lecomtei Schneid. Deciduous shrub, twigs red, glabrous, angular; leaves oblong-obovate, obtuse, entire, 3—4 cm long, gray-green beneath; flowers in fascicles, nearly umbellate racemes, to 2 cm long, flowers 8 mm wide; fruits ellipsoid, carmine, not pruinose, style absent. W. China, Yunnan. 1887. Hardy. z5? Plate 61.

B. lempergiana Ahrendt. Evergreen shrub, very closely related to *B. julianae*, but with leaves more gray-green, widest in the middle, 6—10 cm long, 2—2.5 cm wide, with 15—25 thorns on either half, underside glossy; flowers larger, with distinct style, with 2—3 seeds. BMns 90. China. 1935. z6 Plate 55. # ∅

B. lepidifolia Ahrendt. Decidous shrub, some 1.5 m high, young twigs furrowed, glabrous, brown, thornless or with simple, 3—4 mm long thorns; leaves linear-oblanceolate, 2—4 cm long, 3—4 mm wide, entire, distinctly veined, gray-blue beneath; flowers in small umbels; fruits ovoid, 8 mm long, red, bluish pruinose, with a short style. Yunnan. 1923. z6 Plate 61. ∅

B. leptoclada Diels. Deciduous shrub, resembling *B. francisce-ferdinanda*, but with young twigs red and pruinose; leaves obovate to oblong, 1—2 cm long, obtuse and with a small prickly tip, otherwise entire or with some thorned teeth, reticulate venation; flowers few in racemes, stalk 1 cm long, thin; fruits with a short style. W. China. 1928. z8 ∅

B. levis Franch. Evergreen species not in cultivation; plants by this name in the garden are either *B. atrocarpa* or *B. soulieana*. W. China, Yunnan. z6 #

B. levis see: **B. atrocarpa**

B. liechtensteinii Schneid. Attractive, evergreen shrub, very closely related to *B. potaninii*, but with leaves obovate, 3—5 cm long, tough with 4—7 very large, coarse thorns on either blade half; flowers in short racemes; fruits red, globose, 8 mm thick. W. Szechwan. 1908. z6 Plate 61. # ∅

B. linearifolia Phil. Evergreen shrub, 0.7—1.5 m high, but seldom more than 1 m in cultivation, growth open, young twigs distinctly furrowed, yellow, thorns 3 parted, 1—1.5 cm long; leaves oblanceolate, 3—5 cm long, tip thorny acuminate, margin rolled inward, dark glossy green above, bluish beneath; flowers nearly 2 cm wide, 4—6 in fascicles, orange-red, May; fruits ovate, black, bluish pruinose, with distinct style, some 1.2 cm long. BM 9526. Chile, Andes. 1925. An abundantly flowering, beautiful, very hardy species. z6 Plate 59. # ✥ ∅

Including several cultivars:

'Comber's Apricot'. Buds orange, opening apricot-yellow. # ✥

'Jewel'. Leaves narrower than the species; buds deep orange,

opening dark orange-yellow. Originated by C. J. Marchant, 1937. Very attractive. # ✥

'Orange King'. Strong growing selection; leaves narrower, somewhat darker; flowers somewhat larger, more red-orange. # Plate 59. ✥

'Phoenix'. Buds intensive red, opening deep orange-red. Introduced to the trade in 1958 by C. Ingram. The darkest of the cultivars. # ✥

B. × lologensis Sandwith (*B. darwinii* × *B. lineaerifolia*). Evergreen shrub, intermediate between the parents, twigs scarcely furrowed; leaves partly oblanceolate, with 1—5 large thorns on either side, margin partially entire, apex thorned acuminate, in clusters of 5—8; flowers somewhat larger than those of *B. darwinii*, but more orange-yellow; fruits ovate, dark purple. On Lake Lolog, Argentina, occurring among the parents. 1927. z6 Plate 59. # ✥ ∅

In addition, several cultivars:

'Apricot Queen'. Growth narrowly upright; flowers orange. # ✥

'Gertrude Hardijzer' (Hardijzer 1961). Slender and upright, resembling *B. lologensis* in habit and leaf, but holds its leaves better; flowers dark orange. Selection from Hanno Hardijzer, Boskoop, Holland. # ✥

'Highdown' (F. Stern). Growth lower, much broader than the species, thorns curved claw-like (good I.D. characteristic); leaves more linear, glossier; flowers more yellow, not orange. Plate 59. # ✥

'Nymans'. Flowers especially abundant. Introduced by Messel, Nymans, England. Plate 60. # ✥

'Yellow Beauty'. Young twigs reddish; young leaves light green, later glossy green; flower gold-yellow; fruits blue pruinose. Plate 59. # ✥

B. lycioides Stapf. Semi-evergreen shrub, to 2.5 m high in its habitat, twigs round, thorn simple or 3 parted, to 1.8 cm long; leaves in clusters of 4—6, narrow obovate to oblanceolate, entire or with 1—3 thorned teeth on either half, 4—6 cm long, glossy dark green above, often somewhat blue-green beneath; flowers in 6—8 cm long pendulous racemes to panicles, yellow; fruits ovate, purple-black, dense white pruinose, 1 cm long. BM 9102. NW. Himalay, Jaunsar. Around 1892. Gorgeous! z5? Plate 61. ✥ ∅ ⚭

B. lycium Royle. Deciduous or semi-evergreen shrub, to 3 m high, twigs rod-like, yellow, not pubescent, gray in the 2nd year, thorns 3 parted, to 2 cm long; leaves oblanceolate, 2—5 cm long, either acute or obtuse and mucronate, margins entire or with few teeth, light green above, bluish green beneath; flowers gold-yellow, 10—20 in long racemes, May—July; fruits elliptic, 8—12 mm long, purple, pruinose, with distinct style. BM 7075. Himalaya, Kashmir to Nepal. Around 1835. z6 Plate 61; Fig. 143. ✥

B. × macracantha Schrad. (*B. aristata* × *B. vulgaris*). Deciduous shrub, to 4 m high, twigs furrowed to round, gray-yellow in the 2nd year, thorns to 3 cm long; leaves obovate, to 6 cm long, sparsely thorny

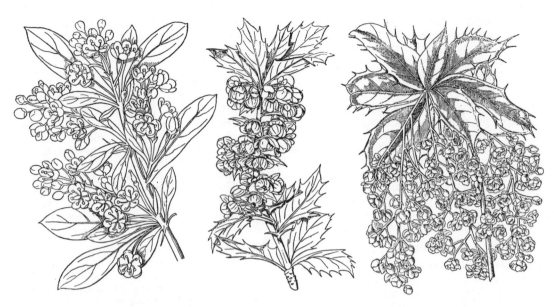

Fig. 143. From left to right: *Berberis lycium*; *B. ilicifolia*; *B. jamesonii* (from Bot. Mag., Illustr. Hortic.)

serrate; flowers yellow, grouped 10—20 in racemes, May; fruit elliptic, purple, usually without a style. z5? ⊕

B. macrosepala Hook. Deciduous shrub, closely related to *B. concinna*, but with brown twigs; leaves obovate, 5 cm long, 3—4 cm wide, rounded at the apex, base broadly cuneate, with 5—10 teeth on either half; flowers to 1.5 cm wide, petals all equal size, stalk to 2.5 cm long. SE. Tibet, Sikkim. 1849. z6 Plate 63. ⊕

B. manipurana Ahrendt. Evergreen shrub, 1—2.5 m high, twigs angular, thorns 1.3—3 cm long; leaves elliptic, rather tough, 2—7 cm long, nearly entire or with 8—12 small thorny teeth on either blade half, very glossy above with reticulate venation, dull green beneath, not pruinose; flowers grouped 6—15, 1—1.5 cm wide, petals somewhat emarginate, pedicels 1—1.6 cm long; fruits oblong, with sessile stigma, with 3—5 locules, black, pruinose. Manipur, Assam. 1882. Not unusual in cultivation but often under other names such as: *B. hookeri latifolia*, *B. knightii* or *B. xanthoxylon*. z6? Plate 54. # ∅

B. × media Grootend. (*B. hybrido-gagnepainii* 'Chenault' × *B. thunbergii*). Semi-evergreen shrub, some 0.8 m high, open growing, rounded, young twigs red-brown, thorns 3 parted, 2—3 cm long; leaves oblong-ovate, 1.5—3 cm long, 0.8—1.2 cm wide, with 2—4 small teeth on either blade half, very glossy above, green beneath; flowers never observed. z6 # ∅

'Parkjuweel' (Van Eck 1956). Typical of the species. Originated by W. H. Van Eck, Boskoop, Holland. Plate 59. ∅

B. × meehanii Schneid. (*B.? chinensis* × *B. amurensis*). Deciduous shrub, very closely related to *B. laxiflora*, but with angular young twigs, brown in the first year, grayer in the 2nd year, thorns usually simple, to 2 cm

long; leaves obovate to elliptic, 2.5—4 cm long, dense and fine serrate, reticulate venation beneath; flowers in 4—9 cm long racemes; fruits ellipsoid, red, somewhat pruinose. Origin unknown, but disseminated from the Meehan nursery (USA) as "*B. concinna*". Before 1927. z5?

B. mekongensis W. W. Smith. Deciduous shrub, leaves broadly elliptic to nearly rounded, 3 cm long, nearly 2 cm wide, very glossy green on both sides, each blade half with 5—15 teeth; flowers in 3—5 cm long racemes, stalk 0.5—1.5 cm long; fruits ellipsoid, 1.5 cm long, red, not pruinose, style absent. Yunnan. 1914. z6 Plate 61. ∅

B. × mentorensis L. M. Ames (*B. julianae* × *B. thunbergii*). Deciduous shrub, with the appearance of *B. thunbergii*, but more upright, to 2 m high, twigs glabrous, brown, angular; leaves elliptic, 2—4 cm long, very tough, with 0—3 small thorns on either half, thorns simple (on the branch tips) to 3 parted; flowers light yellow, grouped 1—2 together; fruits ellipsoid, red (according to Wyman, USA; in Europe, however, fruits not observed). Originated in USA, 1924 and introduced to the trade by Wayside Gardens, Mentor, Ohio. Good hardiness. Effective for its scarlet red fall foliage. z5 Plate 62. ∅

B. minutiflora Schneid. Deciduous shrub, twigs brown, furrowed, pubescent, thorns 4—8 mm long, 3 parted; leaves obovate, 1.5—2 cm long, entire or with some small thorns on the leaves of long shoots, blue-green beneath; flowers 8 mm wide; fruits ovate, red, not pruinose, style absent. Yunnan. 1932. z6 Plate 61.

B. mitifolia Stapf. Deciduous shrub, to 2 m high, twigs finely furrowed, gray, pubescent, thorns simple or 3 parted, 1—2.5 cm long; leaves obovate to oblong, 3—6 cm long, entire or finely thorny serrate; light green and finely pubescent above, venation pubescent beneath; flower 8 mm wide, in dense, pubescent racemes, occasionally branched at the base; outer sepals red and finely pubescent; fruits ellipsoid, 1 cm long, carmine-red. BM 9236. W. Hupeh. 1907. z6 ⚭

B. montana Gay. Deciduous, ornamental shrub, 1–2 m high, twigs furrowed, glabrous, red, thorns simple or 3 parted, 1–1.5 cm long; leaves grouped 3–7, oblanceolate, 1.5–2 cm long, 8 mm wide, entire, apex rounded; flowers grouped 2–4 in stalked umbels or fascicles, flowers singular some 2 cm wide, yellow and light orange, May; fruits black, ellipsoid, reddish pruinose and with a distinct stigma. JRHS 1950: 88. Andes of Argentina and Chile. Very meritorious species for its large flowers, but variable. z6 Plate 60. ⊕ ⚭

var. *chillanensis* see: **B. chillanensis**

B. morrisonensis Hayata. Deciduous shrub, some 0.7 m high, twigs dark red, distinctly furrowed, glabrous, thorns 1.5–2.5 cm long, 3 parted; leaves obovate, 2.5 cm long, with 4–7 thorns on either blade half, slightly bluish beneath; flowers 2–5 in fascicles, light yellow, some 1.2 cm wide, June; fruits ovate, bright red, somewhat translucent, 1 cm long, not pruinose, with a short style. BM 9017. Taiwan. 1918. Good fall color, bright red and yellow. z6 ⊘ ⚭

B. mouillacana Schneid. Deciduous shrub, very similar to *B. silva-taroucana*, but with twigs red (not yellow), leaves narrowly obovate, glossy green beneath (not blue-gray); inflorescence shorter, fruits 8 mm long. W. Szechwan. z5? 1908

B. mucrifolia Ahrendt. Deciduous shrub, small, 30–60 cm high, twigs yellowish or tending to gray, finely pubescent when young, angular and finely furrowed, thorns 3 parted, thin, to 2 cm long; leaves narrowly elliptic to obovate, 2 cm long, glabrous, yellowish green beneath, generally (in cultivated plants) entire, thorned only at the apex; flowers singular, 8 mm wide; fruits light red, globose or more oblong, 6 mm long, but not very abundant, with distinct style. BMns 643. Himalaya; Nepal. 1956. z5? ⊕

B. neubertii see: × **Mahoberberis**, × **Neubertii**

B. × notabilis Schneid (*B. heteropoda* × ? *B. vulgaris*). Deciduous, tall growing shrub, twigs lightly furrowed, gray-brown when young; leaves obovate to oblong, nearly always finely serrate; flowers in long racemes of 14–20 blooms, but the individual flowers quite small; fruits oblong-oval, dark red, pruinose. Around 1895. z5? ⊕ ⚭

B. nummularia Bge. Deciduous shrub, some 3 m high, twigs reddish, pruinose when young, round, red-brown in the 2nd season, thorns usually simple, 2–3 cm long; leaves oblong, obovate or oblanceolate, 2–4 cm long, apex usually rounded, usually with only a few small teeth on either blade half or entire, thin, bluish-green with reticulate venation on both sides (important for identification); flowers 5 mm wide, many in 3–5 cm long, dense racemes; fruits oval, red, 5–6 mm long,

with 2–3 seeds, stigma sessile. Turkestan, N. Iran. Before 1878. Hardy. z6 ⊕

B. oblonga (Rgl.) Schneid. Deciduous shrub, to 2 m high, twigs round or somewhat grooved, glossy, thorns simple to 3 parted, 5–15 mm long; leaves very uneven, obovate to elliptic, 2–6 cm long, entire or sparsely dentate, gray-green above, bluish beneath; flowers 1 cm wide, to 50 in many flowered panicles; fruit oblong, black-red, pruinose, with short style, usually only a single seed. Turkestan. Around 1874. z6 ⊕ ⚭

B. oritrepha Schneid. Deciduous shrub, closely related to *B. thunbergii*, but with light red twigs, thorns longer, coarser; leaves with reticulate venation, margin partly bristly serrate, bluish beneath; flowers 3–6 in umbel-like racemes, often nearly sessile. N. China. 1911. z5

B. orthobotrys Schneid. Deciduous shrub, 1 m high, young twigs glabrous, dark, thorns 3 parted, slender, 8 mm long; leaves obovate to oblong, 1.5–3 cm long, 5–12 mm wide, margin usually finely dentate, glabrous, distinct reticulate venation beneath; flowers yellow, grouped 5–12 in corymbs, some 2.5 cm long, and so numerous that the branch is virtually hidden from view, May; fruits ovate, red, 1 cm long, persisting to November (=*B. vulgaris* var. *brachybotrys* Hook. f.) Kashmir, Afghanistan. Very worthy flowering shrub. z6

var. **canescens** Ahrendt. Leaves narrower, gray, pruinose beneath; fruits red, some 10 × 6 mm in size (= B. 'Unique'). Kashmir. 1940.

'Auricoma' (Croux). Growth upright; foliage purple-brown. Introduced by Croux, Chatenay-Malabry, France.

B. × ottawensis Schneid. (*B. thunbergii* × *B. vulgaris*). Deciduous shrub, resembling *B. thunbergii*, but with twigs usually yellow-brown, seldom reddish, usually a much stronger grower; leaves obovate, to 3 cm long, partly entire, partly finely dentate; flowers in shorter or longer stalked racemes of 5–10 blooms (important distinction from *B. thunbergii*), or in stalked umbels; fruits ovate, red. Spaeth catalogue, 1930: 200 (as *B. thunbergii*) (= *B. thunbergii pluriflora* Koehne). 1893. In cultivation for a long time but first recognized as a hybrid in 1923. z4? ⊕ ⊘ ⚭

Including:

'Decora' (Haalboom, around 1953). Broad bushy growth, to 1.75 m high, ornamental; leaves somewhat like those of 'Superba', but somewhat smaller, dull bluish purple-red. Smaller than 'Superba' in all aspects; rare on cultivation. ⊘

'Superba' (Ruys 1943). Growth particularly strong, to 2 m high and wide, twigs deep red-brown, thorns on the long shoots often 3 parted and to 15 mm long, on other twigs simple; leaves usually round, to 5 cm long (with petiole), often somewhat serrate on long shoots; flowers partly in stalked umbels, partly in fascicles or both together, peduncle to 3 cm long, pedicels to 1 cm; flowers yellow with red; fruits ovate, light red (= *B. thunbergii atropurpurea superba* Ruys). Introduced to the trade by Ruys, Dedemsvaart, Holland, but in cultivation before 1943. Plate 58. ⊕ ⊘

'Suzanne' (Brouwers, around 1965). Very much resembles 'Decora', but more narrowly upright; leaves more acuminate. Selected by Brouwers in Groenekan, Holland.

B. pallens Franch. Deciduous shrub, resembling *B. chinensis*, but not in cultivation. Yunnan.

B. panlanensis Ahrendt. Evergreen shrub, only 0.3—0.4 m high, growth dense, twigs yellow-green, furrowed, very angular, internodes very short (7—14 mm), thorns 3 parted, 8—16 mm; leaves linear-lanceolate, 1—2.5 cm long, with 3—6 appressed teeth on either blade half, margin slightly rolled, gray-green above, yellow-green beneath, both sides lacking distinct venation; flowers normally solitary, 1 cm wide, petals pale green, yellow, outside not rddish; fruits black, not pruinose, style absent. W. Szechwan. 1908. Often erroneously labeled as *B. sanguinea*, which is not in cultivation. z6 Plate 58. # ∅

B. para-virescens Ahrendt. Deciduous shrub, very closely related to *B. virescens*, but 2—3 m high, twigs dark red, somewhat furrowed, thorns 5—15 mm long; leaves 1—3 cm long, obovate, somewhat gray beneath; inflorescence with 4—8 flowers; fruits red at first, then dark blue or dark purple, eventually nearly black, not pruinose, oblong, style absent, 9 mm long, 6 mm thick, with 3—4 locules. BM 7116 (as *B. virescens*) (= *B. virescens macrocarpa* Hort.). Sikkim. Before 1880. z6 Fig. 144.

B. parisepala Ahrendt. Deciduous shrub, abundantly branched, to 2 m high, very closely related to *B. angulosa*, foliage very dense, young twigs brown, densely pubescent, furrowed, thorns 3 parted, thin, 1—2.5 cm long; leaves obovate or broadly elliptic, 1.5—3 cm long, normally entire, but occasionally a leaf with 3—4 large teeth on either blade half, very glossy green above, lighter beneath, tough; flowers 2 cm wide, singular, the 6 sepals very large, outer and inner whorls equal size (important for identification), emarginate; fruits ellipsoid, 12 mm long, 9 mm wide, bright red, with distinct stye. BMns 119. N. Assam. 1928. z6 ⊕∅⚭

B. parvifolia Sprague. Deciduous shrub, closely related to *B. wilsoniae*, but with twigs yellow and pubescent, low growing, thorns 3 parted, yellow, to 1.5 cm long; leaves ovate, 5—15 mm long, usually sparsely thorny dentate, bluish beneath; flowers yellow, 6 mm wide, in fascicles of 2—10, June; fruit ellipsoid, 6 mm long, red, pruinose, 8 mm long. W. Szechwan. 1896. z5

B. phanera Schneid. Evergreen shrub, closely related to *B. verruculosa*, but 1—2 m high, twigs nearly round, yellowish, somewhat warty, thorns 1—3 cm long; leaves grouped 3—5 together. W. China. The species is not yet in cultivation, but the following variety is. z6 #

var. **glaucosubtusa** Ahrendt. Leaves to 5 cm long and 1 cm wide, very similar to *B. gagnepainii*, but the leaves finer toothed, margin not rolled inward, blue-green beneath; locules only 2. W. China. z6 Plate 56. #

B. poiretii Schneid. Deciduous shrub, some 1 m high, grows very elegantly with nodding branches, somewhat angular, glabrous, glossy, thorns usually simple, small, 8 mm long; leaves oblanceolate, 3—5 cm long, entire, green on both sides; flowers light yellow, reddish outside, grouped 8—15 in pendulous racemes, end

of May; fruits oval-oblong, 1 cm long, light red. BS 1: 285. N. China, Amur River area. 1862. Rarely true to name in cultivation; usually *B. chinensis* Poir. instead. z5 Fig. 145.

B. potaninii Maxim. Evergreen shrub, resembling *B. anniae* or *B. liechtensteinii*; 1 m high, twigs nearly round, glabrous, reddish, thorns to 4 cm long; leaves tough and rigid, 2.5 cm long, 8 mm wide, without distinct venation, with 1—2 large teeth on either blade half, underside green; flowers in 2 cm long inflorescences; stalk 3 mm long; fruits oblong, 1 cm thick, red, with short stalk. Kansu. 1914. z6 # ∅

B. × provincialis (Audib). Schrad. (*B. vulgaris* × ? *B. sibirica*). Deciduous shrub, very closely related to *B. sibirica*, but with twigs furrowed, yellow-brown, more gray-brown in the 2nd year; leaves obovate-oblong to narrow oblong, 1 to 2.5 cm long, fine bristly serrate, green with reticulate venation beneath; flowers in 1—3 cm long racemes in groups of 6—12, often nearly umbellate; fruits 8—9 mm long, red, with sessile stigma. Before 1830. z3?

B. prattii Schneid. Deciduous shrub, to 3 m high, twigs reddish with white pubescence when young, eventually becoming yellowish and nearly glabrous, thorns rather thin, simple or 3 parted, some 12 mm long; leaves usually in clusters of 10, obovate to oblong, rounded at the apex, 1—3 cm long, tapering cuneate at the base, entire or with few marginal thorns, dark glossy green above, gray beneath; flowers 5 mm wide, in many flowered erect, 10—20 cm long panicles, summer; fruits ovate, salmon-red, 8 mm long, with short, persistent style. BMns 286 (= *B. aggregata* var. *pratti* [Schneid.] Schneid.) W. China. 1899. z5 Plate 65.

var. **laxipendula** Ahrendt. Flower panicles more pendulous, some 10 cm long or usually shorter, but looser and wider than the species; berries somewhat larger and with longer style. ⚭

var. **recurvata** Schneid. Leaves oblong-obovate, often entire, panicles more cylindrical, longer stalked, panicle axis at fruiting curving downward; fruits 5 mm long, nearly globose, scarlet red. W. China. z5 ⚭

B. pruinosa Franch. Evergreen, in cold areas often the only evergreen shrub, some 1.5 m high, growth open, twigs round, yellowish, new growth often somewhat reddish, thorns tough, rigid, 2.3—4 cm long; leaves in spring often brownish, elliptic to oblong, 3—6 (8) cm long, with 2—6 large teeth on either blade half, leathery tough, dull gray-green above, white pruinose beneath, venation indistinct on both sides; flowers in short, stalked (important for identification) fascicles of 8—25, light yellow, medium sized, petals emarginate, May; fruits oval-oblong, 6—7 mm long, blue-black, thickly white pruinose, style absent. Yunnan. 1883. z6 Plate 56. # ⊕ ∅

'Barresiana'. Leaves to 6 cm log and 2.5 cm wide, margin more finely dentate, green underneath; flowers grouped 3—6, petals not emarginate; fruits smaller. From the Les Barres Arboretum, France. 1907. # ∅

var. **brevipes** Ahrendt. Leaves narrower, more coarsely

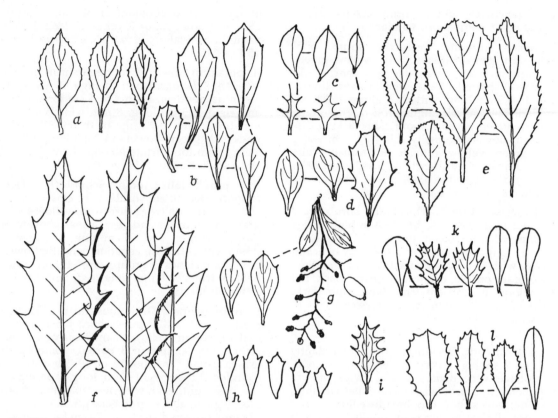

Fig. 144. **Berberis.** a. *B. francisci-ferdinandi*; b. *B. angulosa*; c. *B. tsarongensis*; d. *B. paravirescens*; e. *B. vulgaris*; f. *B. hypokerina*; g. *B. sherriffii*; h. *B. stenophylla* 'Irwinii'; i. *B. sibirica*; k. *B. vernae*; l. *B. yunnanensis*

dentate, teeth pointing outward; flowers shorter stalked, only some 5–8 mm long. Yunan. 1937. Plate 56. # ⌀

'Viridifolia'. Leaves larger, wider, glossy green on both sides (not pruinose); fruits wider. # ⌀

B. pygmaea see: **B. buxifolia**

B. quelpartensis Nakai. Deciduous shrub, resembling *B. sieboldii*; leaves obovate to oblong or oblanceolate, 3–5 cm long, margin totally finely serrate or nearly to the base; flowers grouped 8–12 in 2–3 cm long racemes, stalk 4–6 mm long, Quelpaert (Saishu), S. Korea. Around 1935. z6 Plate 62. ⌀

B. × recurvata Ahrendt (*B. atrocarpa* × *B. sargentiana*). Evergreen shrub, closely related to *B. sargentiana*, but with leaves somewhat more coarsely dentate, with only 8–15 thorny teeth on either side, flower stalk 5–10 mm long, fruits 6–7 mm long, with style. Frequently found in gardens as *B. sargentiana*. z6 Plate 56. #

B. regeliana Koehne. Deciduous shrub, very similar to *B. amurensis*, but with leaf undersides gray-white pruinose; plant 1.5 m high, twigs yellow-gray, angular, furrowed; leaves obovate, to 6 cm long and 4 cm wide, rounded at the apex, margin on either blade half with 20–40 fine teeth, dull green above, gray-white beneath; inflorescence with some 6–10 flowers, 1 cm wide; fruits red, oblong, 10 mm long, 5 mm thick, red, somewhat bluish pruinose at the base. GF 3:249 (= *B. amurensis* var. *japonica* [Regel] Rehd.). Japan. 1865. Frequently erroneously labeled, *B. koreana* or *B. sieboldii*. z6 Plate 59. ⌀

B. × rehderiana Schneid. (*B. canadensis* × *B. fendleri* ?). Small, round, deciduous shrub, twigs thin, red-brown, slightly angular, thorns 3–5 parted; leaves obovate-oblong, 2–3 cm long, thorny dentate; flowers 8–15 in stalked racemes; fruits globose, 5–6 mm thick, glossy, very persistent. z6 ⚭

B. replicata W. W. Smith. Evergreen shrub, to 1 m high, twigs attractively arching, totally glabrous, yellowish when young, thorns 3 parted, 1.5 cm long; leaves narrow lanceolate, 2–4 cm long, usually only fine prickly tipped, margin distinctly rolled, seldom with a few thorny teeth, dark green above, not glossy, whitish beneath; flowers in fascicles of 3–10, stalk 8–12 mm long, light yellow, May; fruits oblong, red at first, then black, 1 cm long. BM 9076. W. Yunan. 1912. Very attractive species. z6 Plate 55. # ✥ ⌀

B. reticulata Bijhouwer. Deciduous shrub, very closely related to *B. koreana*, but twigs purple-brown in the 2nd year; leaves obovate to oblong-obovate, 2–4 cm long, finely thorny serrate, gray-green beneath with reticulate venation; flowers in umbel-like racemes of 3–8 together, with the short axis 1.5−2 cm long; fruits oval, 7−10 mm long, red, lightly pruinose. N. China. 1910. z5?

B. × rubrostilla Chitt. (*B. wilsoniae* × ?). A group of cultivars mostly 90−150 cm high, twigs upright or also nodding, red-brown, angular, thorns usually 3 parted, some 2 cm long, yellow-brown; leaves lanceolate to spathulate, entire or also thorny serrate, fresh green above, blue-green beneath; flowers grouped 2−4 in some 2 cm long racemes, light yellow, June; fruits usually ovate, scarlet red, to 1.5 cm long, not pruinose, style absent. z6

Ahrendt classified the following cultivars here, which together with the *B. carminea* forms make up the, so-called, "Wisley Hybrids". On the other hand, Van De Laar considers them all varieties of *B. rubrostilla*, whereby *B. carminea* is reduced to cultivar rank. But, for practical purposes it is sufficient to use the cultivar names with no mention of the species.

'Chealii' (Cheal 1937). Berries dark red, oval-oblong, some 1 cm long and 8 mm wide, style absent. ⚭

'Cherry Ripe' (A. R. Ahrendt 1951). Shrub, 1.5 m high, young twigs green at first, eventually red, densely warty; leaves obovate, 1.5−2.5 cm long, 1 cm wide, dull green above, gray pruinose beneath; berries cream-white at first, eventually cherry-red, broad oval, 9 × 7 mm, style absent. ⚭

'Crawleyensis' (Cheal 1942, named by Ahrendt). Leaves oblanceolate, to 4 × 1 cm in size, margin with 4−8 fine thorns on each blade half; flowers 5−7 in umbels; berries broad oval, bright red, to 1.7 cm long and 5 mm thick. One of the most beautiful garden forms for fruit. ⚭

B. rugidicans see: **B. amurensis**

B. ruscifolia Lam. Evergreen shrub, very closely related to *B. ilicifolia*; twigs yellow, round, glabrous, thorns 3 parted, some 12 mm long; leaves elliptic-lanceolate, with 2−4 large teeth on either half, both sides evenly green colored, 3−5 cm long; flowers grouped 4−5, 6 mm wide, petiole 6−8 mm long; fruits blue-black, ovate, 6−7 mm long, with style. Chile, Argentina. 1925. z6 Plate 65. # ∅

B. sanguinea Franch. Evergreen shrub, to 2 m high in its native habitat, twigs gray-yellow, angular, thorns 3 parted, 1−2.5 cm long; leaves grouped 3−7, linear to linear-lanceolate, 2−6 cm long, either half with 6−20 teeth, both sides green; flowers usually 2−4, outside very red (hence the name), May; fruits blue-black, ellipsoid. W. China. This species is not in cultivation but is consistently confused with the very similar *B. panlanensis*, with pale yellow flowers. #

B. sargentiana Schneid. Evergreen shrub, sometimes only semi-evergreen in cultivation, to 1.5 high, twigs quite round, red at first, later yellow, thorns 3 parted, tough, 1−3 cm long; leaves oblong-elliptic (widest at the middle), 4−10 cm long, with 15−25 fine thorny teeth on either half, leathery tough, glossy, dark green above, yellowish-green with distinct reticulate venation beneath; flowers in fascicles of 2−6, light yellow, May−June; fruits oval-oblong, 6−7 mm long, blue-

black, seldom pruinose, stigma sessile. W. Hupeh. 1907. Often confused with *B. julianae*. z6 Plate 55; Fig. 146. # ∅

B. sherriffii Ahrendt. Deciduous shrub, resembling *B. gyalaica*, but with twigs not pubescent, leaves entire, occasionally with a small thorn on one side, narrow obovate, 1.5−2 cm long, distinctly reticulate venation; flowers 10−20 in elongated, to 5 cm long panicles; fruits oblong, 6−8 mm long, red, stigma sessile. SE. Tibet. 1938. z6 Fig. 144.

B. sibirica Pall. Deciduous shrub, rounded, seldom over 0.5 m high, twigs furrowed, yellow, pubescent, thorns 3−11 parted, thin, 3−8 mm long; leaves lanceolate to obovate, to 2.5 cm long, with 4−6 teeth on either blade half, both sides a bright green; flowers usually solitary, seldom in pairs, 12 mm wide, light yellow, pendulous, May; fruits ovate, 7 mm long, green, stigma sessile, red, not pruinose. Siberia. Around 1773. Resembles *B. aetnensis*, but flowers single and thorns many-parted. z3? Fig. 144 ∅

B. sieboldii Miq. Deciduous shrub, 0.5 to 1 m high, closely related to *B. vulgaris*, but shorter and leaves ciliate-bristly; twigs dark red, glabrous and angular, thorns 3 parted, 8−12 mm long; leaves oblong-elliptic, 3−6 cm long, red in spring, light green beneath, dense ciliate-bristly, fall color wine-red; flowers light yellow, 3−7 in umbel-like racemes, May; fruits globose, 5 mm thick, light red, glossy. GF 3: 38. Japan. z5? Fig. 141. ✧ ∅ ⚭

B. sikkimensis Ahrendt. Deciduous shrub, densely thorny, to 1.5 m high, young twigs dark gray, pubescent, furrowed, thorns 3 parted, 1−2 cm long; leaves grouped 5−8, obovate to oblanceolate, 2−3.5 cm long, 7−11 mm wide, thorny dentate, with 4−6 (to 9) thorns on either blade half, leathery, dark green above, usually bluish beneath; flowers 4−9 in long stalked, 4−5 cm long racemes, yellow, outer sepals red, 1−1.2 cm wide, May; fruits oblong, 1.5 cm long, dark purple, with distinct style. BMns 173. Sikkim. Around 1924. z5? Plate 63. ✧ ⚭

B. silva-taroucana Schneid. Deciduous shrub, to 2 m high, twigs glabrous, yellow, furrowed, thorns small, to 8 mm long, usually simple or absent; leaves obovate, 2 to 5 cm long, obtuse, tapering to the 2 cm long petiole, entire or with few thorns, dark green above, bluish with reticulate venation beneath; flowers yellow, 8 mm wide, grouped 8−10 in 3−7 cm long racemes, each flower with 1−2 cm long pedicel; fruits ovate, 1 cm long, scarlet-red, stigma sessile. W. China. Around 1908. z5? ✧ ∅ ⚭

B. sinensis see: **B. chinensis**

B. soulieana Schneid. Evergreen shrub, to 1.5 m high, bushy, twigs gray, occasionally angular, stiff, thorns 3 parted, 2.5−3.5 cm long, very stiff and sharp; leaves narrow lanceolate, widest just above the middle, tough, at wide angles to the stem, 4−10 cm long, 8−15 m wide, pale green beneath, more or less distinctly reticulate venation, with 12−20 thorns on either blade

Fig. 145. From left to right: *Berberis dictyophylla*; *B. polyantha*; *B. poiretti* (from ICS)

half; flower in fascicles of 3−10, occasionally light reddish outside; fruits ovate, with short style, black, thick lilac pruinose. China, Kansu, Shansi. 1897. Often incorrectly labeled. z6 Plate 55. # ∅

B. × spaethii Schneid. (*B. chitria* × ?) Shrub, very similar to *B. chitria*, but the twigs not quite rod-like round, not pubescent; leaves elliptic to oval-oblong, finely thorny serrate, light green to gray beneath; fruits purple-red, pruinose. Origin unknown. Around 1902. z6

B. spraguei Ahrendt. Decidous shrub, to 1.5 m high, twigs green at first, later becoming dark red, eventually yellow, thorns absent or weak, 2−8 m long; leaves obovate, veined, some 3 cm long, 1.2 cm wide, with 5−10 thorny teeth on either blade half, gray-green beneath; flowers in loose racemes, 8 mm wide, racemes 3 cm long; fruits oblong, 8 mm long, bright red, not pruinose, style absent. NW. Yunnan. Around 1930. z6

B. stearnii Ahrendt. Deciduous shrub, upright, 1.5−2 m, young twigs terete, greenish, later red-brown, not warty, thorns simple to 3 parted, 1 cm long; leaves obovate, usually entire, occasionally with 1−4 thorns on either half, to 3 × 1 cm in size, fresh green above, gray pruinose beneath; flowers 1 cm wide, outside red at first, inside yellow, appearing with the young, fresh green, red patterned leaves, and then very ornamental, April. China; Yunnan. 1938. z6

B. × stenophylla Lindl. (*B. darwinii* × *B. empetrifolia*). Evergreen shrub, in appearance somewhat intermediate or at times favoring one of the parents; flowers yellow to orange, more or less racemose, flowers in groups of 4−10(14); fruits pea size, globose, black, blue-black pruinose, style only 1−1.5 mm long. For the typical hybrid, see *B. stenophylla* 'Stenophylla'. z6

The following list of cultivars was developed by: T. Smith,

Daisy Hill Nursery, Newry; Messrs. Cheal, Crawley, Sussex; and others; all of England. z7-8 (for all cultivars):

'**Autumnalis**' (Smith). 1 m high; leaves entire, margins rolled; flowers yellow, petals emarginate, longer than the inner sepals, flowering in the fall. 1929. # ☉

'**Brilliant**' (Smith) 1 m high; leaves 2.5 to 3.5 cm long, 1 cm wide, light green above, some abscising in fall and then scarlet-red; flowers in groups of 4-8, deep orange, outside not reddish, inner sepals 4 mm long. 1909. # ☉

'**Coccinea**' (Smith). Very similar to 'Brilliant', but with dark green leaves, somewhat bluish; buds intense orange-red, inner sepals 6 mm long. 1920. # ☉

'**Compacta**'. Only 40−60 cm high; leaves narrow, otherwise like 'Stenophylla'; flowers grouped 7−15, orange, petals longer than the inner sepals. 1910. # ☉

'**Corallina**' (Smith). 0.7−1.2 m high; flowers deep yellow, petals shorter than the inner sepals; buds coral-red, nice contrast with the flowers. 1912. # ☉

'**Corallina Compacta**' (Smith). Like 'Corallina', but only 30 cm high; flowers deep yellow, but with petals longer than the inner sepals. 1930. # ☉

'**Cornish Cream**' (Treseder). Mutation with cream colored flowers. Orginated in Treseder's Nursery, Truro, Cornwall. # ☉

'**Crawley Gem**' (Cheal). 50 cm high, growth wide and attractively nodding; leaves wide, dull green; flowers 7−14 in racemes, red outside, petals longer than the inner sepals. 1930. # ☉

'**Diversifolia**' (Smith). Shrub, 0.7−1.5 m high; leaves grouped 5−6 together, 4−5 cm long, some only 1 cm long, blade flat, margin with 1−3 thorns on either side; flowers orange, petals longer than the inner sepals. 1905. # ☉

'**Etna**' (Hillier). Seedling of 'Irwinii'; leaves very glossy; flowers extraordinarily abundant, intense orange, April (= *B. hillieri* Hillier). # ☉

'**Glauca**' (Smith). Under 1 m high; leaves dull blue-green; flowers orange, petals shorter than the inner sepals. 1933. #

'**Gracilis**' (Smith). Some 1 m high, twigs nodding; leaves narrow, margin with 1 thorn on either side; flowers light yellow, petals longer than the inner sepals. 1907. ✜

'**Gracilis Nana**' (Smith). Like 'Gracilis', but only 30 cm high with very dense growth. 1909. #

'**Irwinii**' (Smith). Growth similar to *B. darwinii*, only 0.5–1.2 m high; leaves wide, with 3 teeth; flowers orange (= *B. irwinii* Bijhouwer). 1903. Fig. 144. # ✜ Ø

'**Latifolia**' (Smith). Large shrub, 2–3 m high; leaves entire, rolled inward, 4 cm long, 0.7 cm wide; flowers gold-yellow, petals entire. 1903. # ✜

'**Pendula**' (Smith). Growth like 'Stenophylla', but the twigs somewhat longer and more pendulous; leaves 1.8 cm long, with 1 thorn on either blade half, dark green above; flowers in short racemes, reddish outside (= *B. darwinii pendula* Smith). 1932. # ✜

'**Picturata**' (Smith). Leaves white variegated on young twigs; flowers orange. # Ø

'**Pink Pearl**'. Sport. Leaves very small and white variegated; flowers very small, pink, like pearls, but frequently reflexed on the typical plant; occasional straight green leaves should be pruned out. In cultivation at Treseder. Plate 38. # ✜

'**Reflexa**' (Smith). Leaves with 3 thorned teeth, rolled inward, thorns claw-like along the stem. 1906. #

'**Rigida**' (Smith). Shrub, 0.7—1 m; leaves narrow, like those of 'Stenophylla', dark green; flowers 4–7 in racemes, orange, petals shorter than the inner sepals. 1906. Poor bloomer. #

'**Semperflorens**' (Smith). 0.6–1 m high; young leaves bronze-brown, later light green; flowers numerous, dark yellow, petals shorter than the inner sepals; buds coral-red; major flowering period in the spring, but with some flowers in the fall. 1930. # ✜

'**Stenophylla**; (Fisher & Holmes). The typical hybrid; shrub, 2–3 m high, twigs thin, nodding, red-brown, somewhat pubescent; leaves narrow lanceolate, 1.5–2 cm long, prickly tipped, margin rolled, dark green above, bluish white beneath; flowers gold-yellow, 1 cm wide, grouped 2–6 together, May; fruits pea size, blue-black, pruinose. Originated around 1860 by Fisher & Holmes, Handsworth near Sheffield, England. One of the most beautiful *Berberis* types. # ✜

B. subcoriacea Ahrendt. Evergreen shrub, very closely related to *B. sargentiana* and *B. recurvata*, but (compared to the latter) with longer flower stalks, 1–2 cm long, fruits larger, 12 mm long and 8 mm thick. z6 #

B. suberecta Ahrendt. Deciduous shrub, very similar to *B. rubrostilla*, but growth narrowly upright, twigs glabrous; leaves oblong-obovate, 2–3 cm long, with 1–5 small, outward pointing thorns on either blade half; fruits ovate-oblong, dull pink, with short style (= *B. rubrostilla erecta* Hort; = *B.* 'Tali Range'). Yunnan. 1919. z6 Plate 59. ⚭

'**Emperor**' (Chittenden 1938). Twigs finely pubescent, thorns yellow, 8–13 mm long; leaves some 2.5 × 1.5 cm, margin with 2–7 small thorns, although thorns absent on long shoots, fresh green above, gray pruinose beneath; flowers grouped 3–6 in fascicled racemes; fruits oval-oblong, 12 × 10 mm, dull

red, with short, distinct style. ⚭

'**Unique**' see: **B. orthobotrys** var. **canescens.**

B. sublevis W. W. Smith. Evergreen shrub, some 1 m high, somewhat stiff, twigs very furrowed, glabrous, thorns 3 parted, 3 cm long; leaves lanceolate, thin, grouped 1–6, 3–7 cm long, margins entire or with 10–15 small teeth on either blade half, dull green above, light green and glossy beneath; flowers to 12 in loose fascicles, stalk 1.5–2.5 cm long, light orange-yellow, fragrant, 1 cm wide; fruits 8 mm long, black, not pruinose, with style. Assam, Manipur, W. Yunnan. 1913. z6 Plate 62. #

B. taliensis Schneid. Evergreen shrub, closely related to *B. replicata*, some 0.3–0.5 m high, twigs thick, furrowed, yellow-brown, thorns 3 parted, some 1 cm long; leaves grouped 3–6, leathery, lanceolate to oblanceolate, 2–4 cm long, margin somewhat rolled, dark green above, somewhat glossy, bluish beneath; flowers light yellow, grouped 3–6; fruits black-purple, oblong, 12 mm long, somewhat pruinose. W. China, NW. Yunnan. 1922. z6 Plate 56. # ⚭

B. temolaica Ahrendt. Deciduous shrub, some 1.5 m high, twigs red at first, whitish pruinose, later darker to nearly black, round; leaves obovate, 3–4.5 cm long, with 3–7 large teeth on either half, dull above, gray-green and somewhat pruinose, white pruinose beneath; flowers light yellow and somewhat pruinose, 1.5 cm wide; fruits ovate, 1 cm long, white pruinose, with style. SE. Tibet. z5? Plate 63.

B. thibetica Schneid. Deciduous shrub, confused with *B. poiretii*, but to 2 m high, twigs angular and with 2.5 cm long, 3 parted thorns; leaves obovate to oblong, 1–3 cm long, entire or with few teeth; flowers yellow, 5–7 in umbels on 2.5–3.5 cm long stalks, May; fruits oblong, 1 cm long, red, with short style. W. China. z5? Plate 61. ⚭

B. thunbergii DC. Deciduous shrub, densely branched, some 1m high, twigs angular, red-brown, thorns simple; leaves partly ovate, spathulate or oblong, entire, 1–3.5 cm long, fresh green, bluish or green beneath, wonderful scarlet-red and orange in the fall; flowers 1–2 (5) in fascicles, yellow, often somewhat reddish outside, May; fruits elliptic, red, 8 mm long, style absent. BM 6646. Japan. z5 ✜ Ø ⚭

One of the most popular *Berberis* species for hedges and specimen planting. Including the following cultivars:

Outline of the Garden Varieties of *B. thunbergii*

● Growth normal
    Leaves green:
        'Brouwers Green', large leaved
        'Erecta', growth narrowly upright
        'Green Carpet', growth very broad
        'Green Ornament', deep green
        var. *maximowiczii*, twigs rod-like
        'Vermillion', fall foliage vermillion

    Leaves red or brown:
        'Atropurpurea', most common form

Fig. 146. From left to right: *Berberis julianae*; *B. sargentiana*; *B. virgetorum* (from ICS)

'Electra', narrowly upright, red
'Golden Ring', narrow yellow margined
'Red Chief', narrow leaved, 2 m high
'Red Wonder', similar to 'Atropurpurea'

Leaves pink variegated:
'Harlequin', small leaved
'Pink Queen', slightly white variegated
'Rose Glow', very white variegated
'Rosetta', slightly white variegated

Leaves green with white:
'Kelleriis', growth strong
'Silver Beauty', growth weak

●● Dwarf growing

Leaves green:
'Kobold', to 40 cm high
'Minor', to 50 cm high

Leaves yellow:
'Aurea'

Leaves red to brown:
'Atropurpurea Nana', to 40 cm
'Bagatelle', to 25 cm

'Atropurpurea' (Léon Renault 1913). Grows like the species; leaves purple-red to red-brown, bright carmine in late fall; fruits like those of the species. Comes true from seed. For further information on this cultivar see Kruessmann: Die Geschichte der *Berberis thunbergii* 'Atropurpurea'; in Dtsch. Baumschule 1964: 143. ∅

var. *atropurpurea* see: **B. × ottawensis**

'Atropurpurea Nana' (Van Eck 1942). Chance seedling; growing only 40(60) cm, but becoming 60–70(100) cm wide, multistemmed and densely branched, thorns very small; leaves dark purple-brown (= *B. thunbergii* 'Crimson Beauty', 'Crimson Pygmy' [in USA]; 'Little Favourite' in England; occasionally 'Kleiner Favorit' in Germany). Originated by B. Van Eck in Boskoop, Holland. ∅

'Aurea'. Like the species, but leaves lemon-yellow to gold-yellow, but only yellow-green if in a shady location; very

slow growing. Originator unknown; in cultivation in USA before 1950. Plate 4. ∅

'Bagatelle' (Van Klaveren 1971) (*B. thunbergii* 'Kobold' female × 'Atropurpurea Nana'). Dwarf form, very slow growing, growth flat-hemispherical, twigs very short and dense, probably not over 40 cm high (6 year plant only 22 cm high); leaves brown-red, later black-red, some 2 cm long at first, summer leaves only half as long, ovate. Originated by K. W. Van Klaverin, Boskoop, Holland. Like 'Kobold', but with red-brown foliage.

'Brouwers Green' (Brouwers 1965). Like the species, but larger and holding its green leaves longer; growth wide upright, thick branched; leaves round-elliptic, rather large, light green, fall color more or less yellow.

'Electra' (Van Drie, around 1955). Growth dense and broad to 1.5 m high, twigs red-brown, thorns simple; leaves round to elliptic, light green, fall color yellow and orange to fire-red (= *B. thunbergii* 'Vuurrood'; *B. × ottawensis* 'Electra'). Originated by C. Van Drie, Amersfoort, Holland. Noteworthy for its fall color. ∅

'Erecta' (Horvath 1935). Growth very narrowly upright, but later separating; leaves very light green, abscising early. Brought into the trade by the Cole Nursery, Painesville, Ohio in 1936. Plate 64.

'Golden Ring' (Lombarts, around 1950). Large leaved selection of *B. thunbergii* 'Atropurpurea'; all leaves with a narrow yellow edge. Selected by P. Lombarts, Zundert, Holland. ∅

'Green Carpet' (Schiphorst 1956). Growth wide, but to 1 m high, twigs long arching; leaves broadly elliptic to round, green, fall foliage orange-yellow to red. Selection of A. E. Schiphorst, Wageningen, Holland.

'Green Ornament' (Van Drie 1953). Growth dense and upright, to 1.5 m, twigs thick; leaves round-elliptic, 1.5–3 cm long, somewhat brownish at first, later yellowish-green, eventually deep green and remaining so long into the fall, fall color eventually brownish-yellow and greenish; good fruiter, fruits red, very glossy (= *B. thunbergii* 'Speciaal'; *B. ottawansis* 'Green Ornament'). Selection of C. Van Drie, Amersfoort, Holland.

'**Harlequin**' (Hardijzer 1969). Red leaved form, fine textured; leaves small, pink, white and gray speckled (× *B. thunbergii* 'Rosa II'). Developed by H. Hardijzer, Boskoop, Holland. Ø

'**Kelleriis**' (D. T. Poulsen). Wide bushy growth habit; leaves green, white speckled and punctate, resembling 'Silver Beauty', but larger, pink fall foliage, white specks persisting into fall. Selected by D. T. Poulsen in Kelleriis, Denmark. Ø

'**Kobold**' (Van Klaveren 1960). Green dwarf form, seldom over 40 cm high, very densely branched, broad globose; leaves dark green and remaining so until leaf drop. Developed by K. W. Van Kalveren, Boskoop, Holland.

var. **maximowiczii** (Rgl.) Regel. Twigs more rod-like; leaves narrower, acute, underside light green and glossy (= *B. maximowiczii* Regel).

'**Minor**'. Only reaching 50 cm high, multistemmed; leaves very light green, 1 cm long, oblanceolate; in all parts smaller than the species. 1898. Plate 64.

'**Pink Queen**' (Veerman 1965). Wide growth habit, to 1.25 m high; young leaves nearly red, later becoming more brown with pink-red and gray and white specks and stripes, pretty carmine-red in fall. Introduced to the trade in 1958 by the Veerman brothers in Boskoop under the name *B. thunbergii* 'Atropurpurea Rosea'. Far the best of the "pink colored" cultivars ('Harlequin' and 'Rose Glow'). Ø

var. *pluriflora* see: **B. × ottawensis**

'**Red Chief**' (Schiphorst 1965). Tall shrub, can become 2 m high, wide branching and more or less nodding; leaves attractive purple-brown-red, lanceolate to obovate, 4 × 1.2 cm; only few fruits. Selected in 1942 by A. E., Schiphorst in Wageningen, but not introduced into the trade until 1965. Very nice cultivar. Ø

'**Red Pillar**' (Lombarts 1958). Growth narrowly upright (like 'Erecta'), to 1.5 m, but leaves brown-red. Originally brought to the trade by P. Lombarts from a group of upright growing, brown leaved plants, but cloned in 1968 by Jac. Schoemaker in Boskoop, Holland. Ø

'**Red Bird**' (Willis Nursery). Canadian selection f *B. thunbergii* 'Atropurpurea' with dense habit and bright red leaf color. Presumably not grown in Europe. Ø

'**Red Wonder**' (Schiphorst, around 1967). Selection of 'Atropurpurea' with finer, more compact growth habit than the normal seedling. Ø

'**Rose Glow**' (Spaargaren 1957). Growth broadly upright, to 1.5 m high; leaves bright red-brown to carmine-pink, later duller brown-red with pink, gray and white coloration (= *B. thunbergii* 'Ida'). Selected by J. Spaargaren in Boskoop; disseminated by Lefeber, Boskoop, Holland. This is the earliest of 3 pink toned cultivars, but will be out-performed by the more recent 'Pink Queen'. Ø

'**Rosetta**' (Hardijzer 1971). Very similar to 'Harlequin', but larger in all respects; leaves have less white variegation (= *B. thunbergii* 'Rosea VI').

'**Silver Beauty**' (Van Leeuwen, around 1911). Growth weak, young twigs brown-red (on the similar 'Kelleriis', green!); leaves green with white specks and dots (= *B. thunbergii* 'Argenteomarginata'). First disseminated in the USA; but surpassed today by the stronger growing 'Kelleriis'. Ø

'**Vermillion**' (Jackman 1952). Habit very dense and compact, to some 1 m high; leaves medium sized, green intense vermillion-red in fall (= *B. thunbergii* 'Afterglow'). Selected

for its fall color by G. Jackman & Son, Woking Surrey, England. Ø

B. tischleri Schneid. Deciduous shrub, closely related to *B. diaphana*, 2–3 m high, young twigs reddish, thorns 3 parted, 1.5–2 cm long; leaves grouped 3–8 together, obovate, 1.5 to 5 cm long, usually finely and regularly dentate, occasionally entire; flowers 3–10 in pendulous racemes 5–10 cm long, each flower on a 2.5 cm long pedicel, June; fruits oblong, red, bluish pruinose, with distinct style. W. China, W. Szechwan. 1910. z5? ✧

B. triacanthophora Fedde. Evergreen shrub, 1–1.5 m high, twigs reddish, later red-brown, thin, gracefully drooping, thorns 3 parted, 1–2.5 cm long; leaves 3–4 together, linear-lanceolate, thin leathery, margin somewhat bowed, 2–7 cm long, to 1 cm wide, with 5–15 teeth on either blade half, light green above, blue-green beneath; flowers whitish-yellow, grouped 3–5, somewhat salmon-red outside, nearly globose; fruits ellipsoid, glossy black, lightly pruinose, 8 mm long. Middle China, W. Hupeh. This species (according to Ahrendt) is not found in cultivation; plants under this name are actually *B. wisleyensis*. z6 #

B. tsangpoensis Ahrendt. Closely related to *B. concinna*, but easily distinguished by the thin, yellow twigs, the leaves with reticulate venation and the fruits with 12–15 locules; growth wide, twigs horizontally spreading, thorns 3 parted, 1–4 cm long; leaves evergreen, to 2 cm long and 1 cm wide, obovate, with 1–2 thorns on the margin; fruits ovate, to 13 mm long and 10 mm wide, partly whitish at first, eventually lighter or darker red and very attractive; some leaves also with good fall color. SE. Tibet. 1938. z6 ⚭

B. tsarongensis Stapf. Deciduous, glabrous shrub, 2–3 m high, young twigs red, then brown, thin, with simple or 3 parted, 1–2 cm long thorns; leaves usually 3–5 together, obovate to oblanceolate, entire or with 1–5 large teeth on either blade half; flowers yellow, some 8 together in fascicles, 6–8 mm wide; fruits ovate, dark red, lightly pruinose. BM 9332. NW. Yunnan. 1917. z6 Fig. 144. ✧ Ø ⚭

B. turcomanica Karelin. Deciduous shrub, to 3 m high, twigs nearly round or somewhat furrowed, usually reddish and pruinose when young, thorns simple to 3 parted; leaves quite variable, obovate to oblong, 2.5–4 cm long, tapering to a 1–2.5 cm long petiole, entire or somewhat thorny toothed, blue-green with reticulate venation on both sides; flowers 12–25 together in dense, 4–7 cm long racemes, light yellow; fruits ellipsoid, dark red, pruinose, 9 mm long. SH 1: 198 r–v. Turkestan and N. Iran to Armenia. 1880. z6 ⚭

var. **integerrima** (Bge.) Schneid. Like the species, but with papillae (minute conical protuberances on the epidermis), while the type is without these papillae.

B. umbellata wall. Semi-evergreen, densely branched shrub, to 3 m high in its habitat, completely glabrous, bright red young twigs, later brownish, thorns 3 parted, 1–2 cm long, light yellow; leaves on the juvenile twigs grouped 3—5, on older branches grouped to 10, elliptic to ovate, 3—6 cm long, very sparsely dentate, thin leathery, dark green above, bluish beneath; flowers in 1—2 stalked umbels each with 2—7 flowers, yellow, stalks red, May; fruits oblong, somewhat bowed, 1.5 cm long, purple, slightly pruinose, stigma sessile. BMns 145. Nepal. 1848. z7 Plate 63. ✧ ∅ ⚭

B. valdiviana Phil. Evergreen, somewhat stiffly growing shrub, to 3—5 m high in its habitat, young twigs smooth, brown, thorns few, often absent, otherwise 3 parted, 1—2.5 cm long; leaves usually elliptic to ovate, usually 2—5 cm long; leathery, entire or with 2—4 small teeth on either half, deep green and glossy above, light green beneath; flowers deep orange, only 5 mm wide, globose, but 12—20 in pendulous, 3—5 cm long racemes; fruits globose, 6 mm thick, black, light blue pruinose. BMns 139; BS 1: 405. Chile. 1925. z8 Plate 65. # ✧ ∅

B. × vanfleetii Schneid. (*B. veitchii × B. vulgaris*?). Shrub, evergreen, twigs round; leaves elliptic, acute, with 8—12 thorny teeth on either side, thin leathery; flowers in umbel-like racemes; fruits dark red, pruinose. Before 1915. z5? #

B. veitchii Schneid. Evergreen, upright, but outwardly projecting shrub, to 1.5 m high, twigs red (to nearly violet-red), thorns 3 parted, 1—4 cm long; leaves grouped 2—5 together, narrow lanceolate, dark green above, light green beneath, 3—10 cm long, margin on either half with 10—24 large teeth, thorns undulating up and down; flowers whitish yellow, brownish outside or reddish, in fascicles of 4—8, stalk 2—3.5 cm long, May; fruits oblong to ellipsoid, 9—12 mm long, black, blue pruinose, stigma sessile. Middle China. W. Hupeh. 1900. Very frequently seen in cultivation under the label "*B. acuminata*". z6 Plate 57, 65. # ∅

B. vernae Schneid. Deciduous shrub, 1 (2) m high, twigs red, glabrous, angular, thorns usually simple; leaves oblanceolate, some also spathulate, 1—3 cm long, usually entire, green with slightly reticulate venation on both sides; flowers yellow, in dense, 3—4 cm long, pendulous racemes, individual flowers small, abundant, May; fruits globose, red, 5 mm thick, style absent. BM 9089 (= *B. caroli-hoanghensis* Schneid.). NW. China, Kansu. One of the prettiest deciduous species and quite hardy; named in honor of Verna Berger, daughter of the past curator of Italy's La Mortola, A. Berger. z5? Fig. 144. ✧ ⚭

B. verruculosa Hemsl. & Wils. Evergreen shrub, some 1—1.5 m high, but very slow growing, twigs widely spaced and curved downward, brown-yellow, densely warty (verrucose), thorns 3 parted, thin, 1—2 cm long; leaves ovate or elliptic, tapering to both ends, 15—25 mm long, with 2—4 thorns on either half, glossy green above, blue-green beneath; flowers grouped 1—2, gold-yellow, May to June; fruits black, blue pruinose, somewhat bottle-shaped, 12 mm long, style absent. BM 8454. W. Szechwan. 1904. Hardy and beautiful. z6 Plate 54. # ✧ ⚭

Including the selection **'Dart's Improvement'** (Darthuizer Boomkw. 1967), distinguished by its more wavy leaves. Attractive. #

B. × vilmorinii Schneid. (*B. diaphana × B. pruinosa*). Evergreen, very similar to *B. pruinosa*, but with yellow twigs, furrowed, leaves smaller, less tough and with more (smaller) teeth, 6—10 on either blade half, bluish beneath; inflorescence nearly umbellate, few flowered, flowers 1 cm wide, stalks 8—12 mm long; fruits 1 cm long, dark red, not pruinose, style absent. 1905. z6 #∅

B. virescens Hook. f. Deciduous shrub, to 3 m high, twigs thin, glossy yellow-red, thorns simple or 3 parted, thin, 1—2 cm long; leaves oblong to obovate, to 3 cm long, prickly tipped, sparsely dentate or entire, dull green above, whitish beneath, brownish-scarlet in fall; flowers light yellow, in corymbs, May—June; fruits ovoid, 1 cm long, light red, not pruinose, with style. Himalaya, Sikkim. 1849. z5? Often confused with the very similar but black fruited *B. paravirescens* (BM 7116, as *B. virescens*).

B. virgetorum Schneid. Deciduous, tall shrub, confused with *B. silva-taroucana*, but thorns longer; leaves 7—10 cm long, elliptic to ovate, cuneate, tapering to the 2 cm long petiole, entire; fruits oblong, 8 mm long, red. Kiangsi. 1935. z6 Plate 62; Fig. 146.

B. vulgaris L. Common Barberry. Deciduous shrub, usually not over 2 m tall, twigs very furrowed, brownish yellow in the 1st year, later more white-gray, thorns 3 parted, seldom simple, 1—2 cm long; leaves obovate to elliptic, 2—4 cm long, tapering to the 1 cm long petiole, dark green, greenish beneath, venation not reticulate, margin finely dentate; flowers yellow, in 5—7 cm long, pendulous racemes, abundant flowering, May; fruits oblong, blood-red, to 12 mm long, ripening October. HF 1094. Europe, N. America, Middle Asia. In cultivation for ages. z3 Fig. 144. ✧ ∅ ⚭

var. *amurensis* see: **B. amurensis**

var. *emarginata* see: **B. × emarginata**

Included here are various cultivars with deviant fruits or foliage:

'Alba'. Fruits white or yellowish white.

'Asperma'. Fruits seedless. Used (according to Uphot) in the production of *Confiture d'epine veinette* (barberry preserves) in Rouen, France, but fruits are only produced on older plants. GC 128: 122 (= *B. thunbergii* var. *enuclea* West.; *B. thunbergii* var. *apyrena* Schrad.) ⚭

'Atropurpurea'. Leaves dark red, underside somewhat pruinose. Frequently used as an understock because its red color makes the basal sprouts easier to recognize. Plate 59. ✧ ∅ ⚭

'Dulcis'. Fruits sweet or only slightly sour (= *edulis* Jaeg.). ⚭

'Lutea'. Fruits light yellow. ⚭

'Marginata'. Leaves white bordered (= *argenteomarginata* Usteri). ∅

'Variegata'. Leaves yellow bordered (= 'Aureomarginata').

B. wallichiana DC. Evergreen shrub, to 2 m high, thorns 3 cm long; leaves lanceolate to oblong-lanceolate, widest just past the middle, 5−9 cm long, 1−2 cm wide, acute at both ends, some 15−30 teeth on either half, light green beneath; flowers in fascicles of 6−8, yellow; fruits single seeded. Nepal. This species has never been in cultivation; the plant listed under this name in BM 4656 is actually *B. hookeri,* as are most plants by this name in cultivation. #

var. *purpurea* see: **B. × interposita**

B. wilsoniae Hemsl. & Wils. Deciduous shrub, bushy, some 1 m high, very dense, twigs angular, brown-red, pubescent at first, thorns thin, 3 parted, 1−2 cm long; leaves lanceolate, to linear-oblong, tough, gray-green with reticulate venation on both sides, 1−3 cm long, thorned apex, persistant, eventually scarlet-red; flowers small, light yellow, grouped 2−6, May−June; fruits globose, with short style, salmon-red. BM 8414. W. Szechwan. Gorgeous species! z6 Plate 63; Fig. 137.⊕ ∅ ⚭

Included here are the following "Wisley Hybrids":

'Comet' (Wisley)   **smithiana** (J. Smith)
'Coral' (Wisley)   **'Stonefield Suprise'** (Ahrendt)
'Ferax' (Wisley)   **'Tom Thumb'** (Sidney Morris)
'Fireball' (Wisley)
'Firefly' (Wisley) Ill.
  in JRHS 1942, 44

For more exact descriptions, see the key at the end of this section.

var. **stapfiana** (Schneid.) Schneid. Twigs always glabrous, thorns shorter, leaves more obovate-ovate, more whitish-gray beneath; fruits more elliptic, deep red, pruinose. BM 8701 (= *B. stapfiana* Schneid.). W. China. 1896. z6

var. **subcaulialata** (Schneid.) Schneid. Twigs glabrous, more furrowed, but less thorny; leaves larger, greener, with 2−3 thorns at the apex, whitish beneath; flowers 8−10 together, appearing in June−July; fruits globose, yellow-red, pruinose ripening in November. BM 8656. W. Szechwan. 1908. z6 Plate 63. ⊕ ∅ ⚭

The Darthuizer Boomkwekerijen (Nursery) in Leersam, Holland in 1972 offered no less than 13 cultivars which they had developed from 1960 to 1969. Previously the Boskoop area had only produced 2 cultivars worthy of mention.

'Joke' (1967). Growth wide and openly upright; berries salmon colored and carmine, very large and numerous. Very winter hardy. ⚭

'Orangeade' (1969). Low growing, wide; berries carmine and orange, otherwise as large and numerous as 'Joke'. Somewhat less hardy. ⚭

B. × wintonensis Ahrendt (*B. bergmanniae* × *B. replicata?*). Evergreen, dense shrub, slightly over 1 m high; leaves oblong-elliptic, 5 cm long, 1 cm wide, weakly veined, margin with 9−12 thorned teeth on each blade half, underside green; flowers 1 cm wide, petiole 6−12 mm long; fruits obovoid, 8 mm long, black, blue pruinose, very abundant flowering and fruiting, with style. z6 # ⊕

B. × wisleyensis Ahrendt. Evergreen shrub, to 1.5 m high, twigs red, somewhat angular, later pale yellow, round to somewhat angular, not warty, thorns 3 parted, 1.5−3.5 cm long; leaves linear-lanceolate, 2−5.5 cm long, with 6−15 teeth on either half, thin leathery, dull gray-green above, blue-green beneath, both sides without distinct venation; flowers 2−6, stalk 1−1.5 cm long; fruits oblong, some 1 cm long, black, somewhat pruinose. Origin not certain, but known before 1939. This is the plant often disseminated as *B. triacanthophora.* z6 # ∅

B. × wokingensis Ahrendt (*B. candidula* × *B. gagnepainii* var. *lanceifolia*). Evergreen shrub, resembling *B. × chenaultii,* but with flowers solitary, stalk shorter, only 3−6 mm long, fruits smaller; leaves lanceolate, 2−4 cm long, abundantly thorned on the margin, less glossy above, whitish beneath, but occasionally also becoming green. z6 # ∅

B. xanthoxylon Hassk. Evergreen species indigenous to Java, not in cultivation. That usually found under this name is *B. manipurana.* The plant described in BM 9238 as *B. xanthoxylon,* should be identified as *B. julianae!* #

B. yunnanensis Franch. Deciduous shrub, resembling *B. diaphana,* but to 2 m high, twigs red at first, later brown, thorns to 3 cm long, yellow; leaves somewhat smaller, obovate, to 5 cm long, usually entire or sparsely dentate, gray-green beneath, scarlet-red in fall; flowers in fascicles of 3−8, gold-yellow, to 18 mm wide; fruits ellipsoid, light red, 1 cm long, not pruinose, style absent. Yunnan. 1886. z6 Fig. 144.⊕ ∅ ⚭

B. zabeliana Schneid. Deciduous shrub, closely related to *B. sieboldii;* leaves elliptic-obovate, 2.5−3.5 cm long, both sides with reticulate venation, margin finely thorny; flowers heavy in loose, pendulous racemes. Kashmir. z6 Plate 61. ⊕

The "Wisley Hybrids" (Key from Ahrendt, simplified)

1. Panicles long; locules 1−2:
     B. 'Stonefield' — Resembling *B. pratti,* but leaves persistent, entire; fruits larger (7−8 mm), softer, scarlet-red (HCC 19).
2. Panicles short; locules 1−2; inflorescence always shorter than *B. aggregata,* also shorter bracts;
   a) Twigs light yellow, finely pubescent, leaves deciduous like *B. aggregata:*
     B. 'Stonefield Dawn' — Leaves pale yellow-green; berries globose, 4−5 mm thick, carmine (HCC 21).
   b) Twigs light yellow, but glabrous; leaves deciduous:
     B. 'Crimson Bead' — Fruits oblong, 4.5−5 × 3.5−5 mm, carmine (HCC 22a)
     B. 'Sibbertoft Coral' — Fruits ovoid, 6−7 × 5−6.5 mm, carmine (HCC 21). Plate 53.
   c. Twigs dark red and finely pubescent like *B. wilsoniae;* leaves persistent:
     B. 'Ruby' — Fruits ovoid, 5.5−6.5 × 4.5−5.5 mm, ruby red (HCC 22/1).
3. Panicles short; locules 3−5; flowers longer stalked than *B. aggregata* (with shorter bracts); twigs glabrous;
   a) Panicles sessile or like those of *B. aggregata;*
     ● Twigs light yellow, leaves entire, narrow (1:3.5−4), semi-evergreen:

B. 'Buccaneer'   Fruits globose, 9 mm wide, style usually absent, partly whitish, eventually glossy red (HCC 20).

●● Twigs dark red; leaves entire, wider (1:2.5−3):

B. 'Barbarossa'   Leaves semi-evergreen, fruits oblong to ovate, 6.5−7 mm, scarlet (HCC 19).
B. 'Bountiful'   Leaves semi-evergreen, fruits globose to round-oblong, 7.5−8.5 mm, scarlet-red (HCC 19), flowers large, 10 mm wide.
B. 'Pirate King'   Leaves deciduous, fruits globose, 5.5−6.5 mm, light scarlet (HCC 19/1).

b) Panicles with 1−3 cm long stalk;
   ● Twigs light yellow, leaves deciduous:

B. × carminea   Leaves narrow (1:4), thorny, fruits ovoid, 8−9 × 6.5 to 7 mm, carmine (HCC 21).
B. 'Sparkler'   Leaves wider (1:2.5), entire, fruits oval-conical, tangerine-red (HCC 17/1).

●● Twigs dark red, leaves entire, deciduous:

B. 'Aurora'   Leaves narrow (1:4), fruits globose-ovate, 8.5 × 8 mm, vermillion (HCC 18).
B. 'Autumn Cheer'   Leaves wide (1:2.5), fruits oblong-ovate, 6−7 × 5 to 6 mm, scarlet (HCC 19).
B. 'Fireflame'   Leaves narrow (1:3.5), fruits ovate, 6.5 × 5.5 mm, carmine (HCC 21).

4. Inflorescence with few flowers, fascicled or nearly racemose, flowers and fruits small, locules 3−5;
   a) Twigs finely pubescent as with *B. wilsoniae*, fruits small, globose, 4−5 mm, carmine (HCC 21);
      ● Twigs yellow, shrub to 1 m high, inflorescence sessile, leaves narrow (1:4):
B. 'Tom Thumb'
      ●● Twigs red, shrub, 1 m high, inflorescence with 1.5−2.5 cm stalk; leaves wider, semi-evergreen;
B. 'Stonefield Surprise'
   b) Twigs glabrous and dark red, as with *B. wilsoniae subcaulialata* and *B. wilsoniae stapfiana*; leaves semi-evergreen, except 'Firefly', which is deciduous;
      ● Leaves very narrow (1:5−6):

B. 'Ferax'   Fruits oblong-ovate, 5−6 × 3−3.5 mm, scarlet (HCC 19).
B. smithiana   Fruits oval-rounded, 6 × 5 mm.

      ●● Leaves wider (1:2.5−3);
       * Leaves small, 6−8 mm wide:

B. 'Comet'   Fruits oval-rounded, 6−6.5 mm, scarlet (HCC 19).
B. 'Coral'   Fruits oval-oblong, 5−5.5 × 4−5 mm, carmine (HCC 21).
B. 'Firefly'   Fruits oval-conical, 7−8 × 6−7 mm, vermillion (HCC 18).
    ** Flowers larger, 9−11 mm wide:
B. 'Fireball'   Fruits oval-conical, 7−8 × 6−7 mm, vermillion (HCC 18).

5. Plants very similar to the Series *Angulosae*, with large flowers and fruits, but also showing traces of *B. aggregata* or *B. wilsoniae*, distinguished by the short flower stalks; locule 3−5;
   a) Twigs glabrous, leaves narrow (1:3−4), flowers large, 1.5 cm wide:

B. × rubrostilla   Inflorescence 3−5 mm long, fruits ovate, glossy (HCC 19), 15 × 9−10 mm.
B. × rubrostilla   'Chealii' Fruits dark purple-red, 9−11 × 6.5−7 mm.
B. × rubrostilla   'Crawleyensis' Flower stalks 1−5−3 cm long, fruits glossy, scarlet, 15−17 × 5−6 mm.

   b) Twigs finely pubescent, leaves wider (1:2−2.5), flowers small, 7−9 mm wide:
B. 'Cherry Ripe'   Leaves entire, flower stalk 2−4 mm long, fruits glossy, geranium-red (HCC 20).
B. 'Emperor'   Leaves with thorned margin, inflorescence sessile or with 1−2 cm long stalk, fruits dull geranium-red (HCC 20), oblong-ovate, 10−12 × 90 mm.

6. Flowers in panicles like those of Nr. 2, but with 5−7 locules, as in Nr. 5; twigs glabrous, dark red, leaves entire, fruits scarlet (HCC 19):
B. 'Autumn Beauty'   Leaves usually deciduous, wide (1:2−2.5), with rounded apex, flowers 8−9 mm wide, fruits ovate, 9 × 8 mm.
B. 'Knockvale Scarlet'   Leaves usually evergreen, narrow (1:4.5−6), with acute apex, flowers 10−12 mm wide, fruits ovate, 7 mm.

Breeders of the *Berberis* Hybrids

Wisley Gardens, England; mainly forms of *B. × carminea* and *B. × rubrostilla*; see under these names; 12 cultivars.

Mrs. A. R. Ahrendt, Stonefield, Watlington, Oxfordshire, England, 7 cultivars.

Watson & Sons, Killiney, Dublin, Ireland, 3 cultivars.

Cheal, Lowfield Heath, Crawley, Sussex, England, 3 cultivars.

C. Smith, Caledonian Nursery;, Guernsey, England, 1 cultivar.

Lady Beatrix Stanley, Sibbertoft Manor, Leicestershire, England, 1 cultivar.

Sidney Morris, Earlham Hall, Norwich, England, 1 cultivar.

Waterer, Sons and Crisp, Bagshot, Surrey, England, 1 cultivar.

T. Smith, Newry, Northern Ireland (*stenophylla* and *darwinii* Hybrids).

The genus *Berberis* contains some of the most beautiful ornamental shrubs. Many have not only attractive flowers, but good foliage, abundant bright fruits and often gorgeous fall color. The deciduous types prefer sunny areas, while the evergreen varieties require semishade and humus soil. Soil requirements are minimal. The uses of this genus in the landscape are manifold. The nomenclature of *Berberis* in the nursery trade is a matter of great concern and controversy. Many of these disputes will, hopefully, be resolved through comparisons with the plates of typical plants found in this book.

Lit. Ahrendt, L. W.: An analysis of the Wisley Hybrid *Berberis*; in Journ. RHS 1942, 129—135, with 4 plates ● Ahrendt, L. W.: The *Berberis stenophylla* Hybrids; in Jour. RHS 1949, 36—40 ● Ahrendt, L. W.: *Berberis*; in Chittenden, Dictionary of Gardening, 1951, 264—271; alphabetical listing with 5 ill. ● Ahrendt, L. W.: *Berberis* and *Mahonia*; a taxonomic Revision; in Journ. Linn. Soc. London **57**, 1—410, 1961 ● Bean, W. J.: Trees and Shrubs, 8th edition; vol. I (A—C), 1970 ● Schneider, C.: Die Gattung *Berberis*; in conjunction with DDG 1905, 451—464 (systematic arrangement) ● Schneider, C.: Die *Berberis*; der Section Wallichiane; in conjunction with DDG 1942, 1—60, with 6 plates. ● Usteri, A.: Das Geschlect der Berberitzen; in conj. with DDG 1899, 81—98 (only of historical interest; arranged systematically) ● Van De Laar, H. J.: *Berberis*; in Dendroflora 9, 9—35, with ill.; 1972.

BERCHEMIA Necker — RHAMNACEAE

Deciduous, twining climber with alternate, petiolate, entire leaves with pinnate venation; stipules small, abscising; flowers perfect, small, 5 parted, in terminal panicles, white; fruits an oblong drupe, leathery-fleshy, with crusty 2 chambered pit. — 22 species in S. and E. Asia, N. America and E. Africa. Closely related to *Paliurus* and *Zizyphus*, but these 2 genera have 3 veined leaves.

Berchemia flavescens Wall. Vine, 1.5—2 m high, climbing; twigs glabrous or with erect dark pubescence; leaves 5—15 cm long, 2.5—6.5 cm wide, tapering to the base, metallic green above, lighter and nearly glabrous beneath, with 9—16 paired veins; flowers white, in pyramidal, 3—10 cm long panicles, terminal, on the current year's wood; fruits cylindrical, 8 mm long. Himalaya, Tibet, W. China. 1904. z5?

B. giraldiana Schneid. Vine, 5—6 m high, climbing, closely related to *B. racemosa*; leaves ovate-oblong, 3—7 cm long, acute or acuminate, base rounded to lightly cordate, often gray or bluish beneath, with 9—11 paired veins; flowers white, in terminal panicles, some 20 cm long, flower buds round with abrupt tip, June—July; fruits oblong, 8 mm long, red at first, eventually black. SH 2: 182 m—n. China: Hupeh, Szechwan, Shansi. 1911 z6 ⚭

B. lineata DC. Vine, resembling *B. scandens*, but much more elegant; leaves oval-ovate, 1—3 cm long, 3—15 mm wide, usually rounded at both ends, deep green above, gray-white beneath with usually 9 paired veins; flowers white, in terminal and axillary fascicles, sepals linear, erect, enclosing the other floral parts; fruits oblong, 8 mm long, eventually blue-black. China, Taiwan, N. India. z8

B. racemosa S. & Z. Weak climber, to some 4 m high; leaves ovate, somewhat cordate at the base, 3—6 cm long, dark green above, lighter or bluish beneath, 6—8 paired veins; flowers greenish white, in large, terminal, to 15 cm long panicles, July—August; fruits elliptic, 8 mm long, red for a long time, finally turning black, ripening in the 2nd year. Japan, Taiwan. 1888. z6 Plate 66. ⚭

B. scandens (Hill) K. Koch. Climbing, to 5 m high; leaves oval, base round, not cordate, 4—7 cm long, apex often terminating in a small bristly tip, margin usually wavy, with 9—12 paired veins; flowers greenish-white, in 2.5—5 cm long racemes at the ends of the short axillary branches and in a terminal panicle, June; fruits oblong, dark blue to black, 8 mm long. BB 2390 (= *B. volubilis* [L.f.] DC.). Southern USA. 1714. z7

Unpretentious, twining climbers for the collector; thriving in any garden soil, but *B. scandens* requires a protected area. The most attractive is *B. racemosa*, which is also quite hardy; *B. lineata* is very rare; fruits usually ripen early in the 2nd year.

Lit. Hatusima, S.: On the genus *Berchemia* from Japan; Korea and Formosa; in Jour. Geobot. 7, 44—47, 69—70, 1958 ● Suessenguth: *Rhamnaceae*; in Engler-Prantl, Nat. Pflanzenfam. **20d**, 141 to 145, 1953.

BERCHEMIELLA Nakai — RHAMNACEAE

This genus is distinguished from Berchemia by the following: tree-like habit, inflorescence panicled or racemose, flowers in fascicles; sepals with a short beak in the middle, disc thick, flattened, surrounding half the ovary; style abscising at the base; seed pit uniloculed. — One species in Japan, one in China, W. Hupeh (*B. wilsonii* [Schneid.] Nakai). Not yet in cultivation.

Berchemiella berchemiifolia (Mak.) Nakai. Small tree, twigs reddish-brown, glabrous, with lenticels; leaves thin, oblong to oval-oblong, 7—12 cm long, 3—5 cm wide, acuminate, base acute to round, occasionally oblique, entire or somewhat undulate, with 6—7 paired veins, these with thin pubescence in the vein axils beneath; inforesences in the upper leaf axils, flowers few, small, singular, 3—4 mm wide, June; drupe oblong, 7—8 mm (= *Berchemia berchemiifolia* [Mak.] Koidz.). Japan; mountains of Honshu, Shikoku, seldom; Korea, China. z6

BESCHORNERIA Kunth — AGAVACEAE

Succulent desert plant with somewhat woody stem and leaves in rosettes resembling those of *Yucca*; leaves bluish, white, juicy, but not as thick as *Agave*, without the hard terminal and marginal thorns; inflorescence a shaft with a raceme or panicle, flowers with colorful bracts, tubular, reddish and green, segments long and narrow, stamens shorter than the segments, filaments seldom thick. — About 10 very similar species in Mexico, of which only one is sufficiently hardy for milder temperate regions.

Beschorneria pubescens Berger. Resembles (the more frequently planted) *B. yuccoides*, but with leaves larger and broader, rough near the apex on the underside, margin somewhat sharper toothed; flower shaft light red, bracts ovate, flowers with green to yellow soft pubescence. Mexico. z9 # ⊕ ∅

B. tubiflora Kunth. Leaves grouped 10−15 in rosettes, 30 cm long, 2.5 cm wide, somewhat gray-green, very rough; trunk some 1 m high, unbranched, red-brown, flowers 2−3 in the axils of the bracts, reddish-green, nodding, some 2 cm long, bracts "hat"-like, ovate, usually purple toned, May. BM 4642. Mexico. z9 #⊕ ∅

B. yuccoides Hook. f. Stem seldom visible; leaves to 20 in rosettes, 50 cm long, 5 cm wide, rough beneath, blue-gray, lanceolate, short acuminate, only 2 cm wide at the base; flower shaft 1 m high, inclined at an angle, rhubarb-red, about finger thick, unbranched, the bracts pink-red, flowers light green, tubular, pendulous, some 4 cm long, April−May; fruits fig shaped. BM 5203. Mexico. Around 1859. z8 Plate 67. ⊕ ∅

Also occasionally found in cultivation are the following species, with reference to available illustrations:

B. bracteata Jacobi (BM 6641), **B. dekosteriana** K. Koch (BM 6768), **B. tonellii** Jacobi (BM 6091) and **B. wightii** (BM 7779), all from Mexico.

Best handled like *Agave*, if possible, frost free in winter, very sunny, dry areas in summer; quite hardy in the milder areas of Europe and North America with very showy flowers.

BETULA L. — BIRCH — BETULACEAE*)

Deciduous trees or shrubs; leaves alternate, petiolate, usually ovate, serrate, dentate or lobed; flowers monoecious, male catkins long cylindrical, dense, naked over winter, but already markedly developed in the fall, female catkins on the tips of the shorter side branches, positioned under the male, covered in winter by bud scales, smaller than the male; stamens 2, seldom 3; primary, secondary and tertiary bracts (or prophylls) of the female flowers 3 lobed or 3 cleft, abscising bud scales connate; fruit a single seeded, thin membranous, 2 winged nut. — About 60 species in the North temperate and arctic zones.

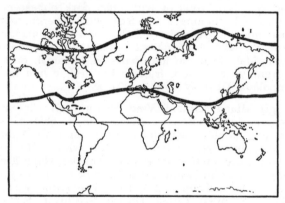

Fig. 147. The range of the genus *Betula*

*) *Betulaceae* has been given preference as "nom conserv." by Little in 1949, although Corylaceae is older and more valid; recently subdivided by many authors (Hutchinson, Hjelmquist) into Betulaceae and Corylaceae (as followed in this work). The reasons for using Corylaceae instead of Betulaceae are the results of work by A. Rehder: Notes on some cultivated trees and shrubs; in Journ. Arnold Arb. **27**, 169−170, 1946.

In the years from 1934 to 1958 some 30 species were named by Russian botanists (Vassiliev, Sukatchev, Baranov, Krylov, Litvinov, Popov); found in Siberia, Mongolia, Sachalin, Central Asia and on the Kola Peninsula. They are not yet in cultivation and therefore not included in this work. A compilation of these species, without desciptions may be found in: Fontaine, Geslacht *Betula* (1970). For further study of these species the reader must refer to the Russian literature.

Systematic Classification

● Leaves with 7 or more paired veins, these more or less indented above

Series 1: **Acuminatae** Regel
Catkins cylindrical, pendulous, in racemes or singular, 4−11 cm long; fruit wings much wider than the nutlets; leaves 7−14 cm long:
B. alnoides, luminifera, maximowicziana

Series 2: **Costatae** Regel
Catkins singular, 2−5 cm long, fruit wings not or only slightly wider than the nutlets:
B. albo-sinensis, alleghaniensis, chinensis, corylifolia, costata, delavayi, ermanii, forrestii, globispica, grossa, jacquemontii, lenta, medwediewii, nigra, potaninii, raddeana, schmidtii, utilis

●● Leaves with 3−7 paired veins

Series 3: **Excelsae** Koch
Usually trees, seldom shrubs; fruit wings wider than the nutlets:
B. aurata, borealis, coerulea, coerulea-grandis, concinna, coreacea, davurica, eastwoodiae, fennica, hornei, intermedia, koehnei, microphylla, minor, occidentalis, papyrifera, platyphylla, populifolia, pubescens, turkestanica, verrucosa

Series 4: **Humiles** Koch

Shrubs; leaves small, with 2−5 paired veins; fruit wings much smaller than the nutlets:
B. borggreveana, fruticosa, glandulifera, glandulosa,

hallii, humilis, jackii, michauxii, middendorffii, nana, pumila, purpusii, sandbergii

Key to the more common species (from W. J. Bean)

1.	Leaves with 7 or more paired veins	2
	Leaves with 3–7 paired veins	17
2.	Leaves with usually 10 or more paired veins	3
	Leaves often with fewer than 10 paired veins	12
3.	Young twigs glabrous	4
	Young twigs more or less pubescent	6
4.	Leaves 7–13 cm long, base deeply cordate:	
	B. maximowicziana	
	Leaves 3–7.5 cm long	5
5.	Bark light gray to nearly white:	
	B. corylifolia	
	Bark orange to orange-red:	
	B. albo-sinensis	
6.	Twigs pubescent and glandular:	
	B. utilis	
	Twigs not glandular	7
7.	Shrub; twigs shaggy pubescent, leaves 2–3.5 cm long:	
	B. potaninii	
	Trees; leaves 5–12 cm long or more	
8.	Twigs pubescent	9
	Twigs nearly glabrous; leaves doubly serrate	10
9.	Bark peeling; leaves usually cordate, venation pubescent:	
	B. alleghaniensis	
10.	Marginal teeth large; veins in 10–15 pairs:	
	B. grossa	
	Marginal teeth fine	11
11.	Blade base more or less cordate; 9–12 paired veins:	
	B. lenta	
	Blade base usually rounded; 10–16 paired veins:	
	B. costata	
12.	Young twigs glandular	13
	Young twigs not glandular	15
13.	Petiole not over 1 cm long:	
	B. schmidtii	
	Petiole 1–2 cm long	14
14.	Young twigs pubescent at first:	
	B. jacquemontii	
	Young twigs glabrous except on the glands:	
	B. ermanii	
15.	Leaves whitish beneath	
	B. nigra	
	Leaves light green beneath	16
16.	Shrub or small tree; leaves 2–5 cm long; bark gray:	
	B. chinensis	
	Shrub twigs thick; leaves 6–12 cm long, buds viscid:	
	B. medwediewii	
17.	Shrubs	18
	Trees	23
18.	Low, wide, branches erect, 40–80 cm high:	
	B. nana	
	Growing taller	19
19.	Branches glandular	20
	Branches not glandular	22
20.	Young twigs pubescent	21
	Young twigs not pubescent:	
	B. glandulosa	
21.	Leaves 15–30 mm long:	
	B. humilis	
	Leaves 2–5 cm long, midrib pubescent beneath:	
	B. fruticosa	
22.	Leaves rounded to obovate, large toothed:	
	B. pumila	

	Leaves ovate, margin crenate:	
	B. × intermedia	
23.	Young twigs glandular and pubescent	24
	Young twigs neither glandular nor pubescent	25
24.	Leaves ovate, base rounded, 2.5–4.5 cm long, venation pubescent beneath:	
	B. raddeana	
	Leaves narrow ovate, 4.5–7 cm long, both sides pubescent at first, bark rough and brown:	
	B. davurica	
25.	Young twigs glabrous and glandular	27
	Young twigs without glands or nearly so	26
26.	Leaf base round to slightly cordate, twigs softly pubescent:	
	B. papyrifera	
	Leaf base cuneate, twigs velvety pubescent:	
	B. pubescens	
27.	Bark white or whitish, peeling; leaf petioles 1.5–3cm long	28
	Bark brown, tight; leaf petiole 5 to 15 mm long, plants often shrubby:	
	B. occidentalis	
28.	Leaves glabrous; base cuneate:	
	B. verrucosa	
	Leaves truncate at the base	29
29.	Leaves glabrous:	
	B. populifolia	
	Leaves more or less pubescent beneath, at least when young	30
30.	Twigs densely glandular; bark reddish or dull white, peeling:	
	B. papyrifera var. *humilis*	
	Twigs less glandular; bark white; leaves fresh green above:	
	B. platyphylla var. *japonica*	

Betula acuminata see: **B. alnoides** and **B. cylindro-stachya**

B. alaskana see: **B. papyrifera**

B. alba see: **B. pubescens** and **B. verrucosa**

B. albo-sinensis Burkill. Chinese Red Birch. Tree, 18–25 m high, normally much smaller in cultivation, bark orange or red-orange, peeling, quite thin, young bark bluish pruinose, young twigs glandular pubescent, eventually deep brown and glabrous; leaves ovate, 4–7 cm long, acuminate, uneven and doubly serrate, yellow-green above, lighter beneath, with 10–14 paired veins; fruit cones 3–4 cm long. ICS 780; CIS 103 (= *B. utilis* var. *sinensis* [Franch.] Winkl.). W. China; Shansi, W. Yunnan, Kansu, Szechwan. 1901. Very desirable for its beautiful bark color, but seldom true in cultivation. z6 Plate 71; Fig. 157.

var. **septentrionalis** Schneid. Normally becoming taller than the species, to 30 m, bark orange-brown to yellow-orange or orange-gray, the peeling bark persisting on the trunk, twigs thin, red-brown, glandular; leaves obovate or oblong-ovate, 5–9 cm long, venation silky pubescent beneath, with axillary pubescence; fruit scales with very long, narrow middle lobes. W. China; Szechwan. 1908. z6 Plate 71.

B. alleghaniensis Britt. Yellow Birch. Tree, 20–30 m high, growth wide, bark like that of *Prunus padus*, peeling, yellowish to gray (very important for identification), crisped or curled, twigs pubescent, bitter scented, light olive-green; leaves ovate-oblong, 8–12 cm long, coarsely serrate, dull green, with 9–11 paired veins, ciliate, at first silky pubescent beneath, fall color yellow; fruit catkins 3 cm long, thick. BB 1216; GTB 139 (= *B. lutea* Michx.). Eastern N. America, moist and swampy areas. 1800. ⓕ USA; little used. z2 Plate 68, 78; Fig. 148, 155. **m d** ∅

var. **fallax** Fasset. Very similar to the species, but differing especially in the bark, which is often tight, and therefore more like *B. lenta*. Found in the range of the species. Plate 78.

var. **macrolepis** Fern. Fruit scales 8–12 mm long (only 5–8 mm on the species), otherwise like the species. **m**

B. alnoides Buch.-Ham. ex Don. Tree, to 40 m tall, bark reddish-brown, twigs purple-red, glandular, glabrous, pendulous; leaves oblong-elliptic, some 10 cm long, 4 cm wide, variable in size, acute or acuminate, base round, thin, unevenly doubly serrate, glabrous on both sides, venation brown tomentose beneath, petiole 2 cm long, red, pubescent; fruit catkins several, 5–7 cm long, fruit scales lightly pubescent. HAL 140; ICS 773; CIS 101; SNp 146 (= *B. acuminata* Wall.). China; Szechwan, Yunnan. 1901. z7 ⓕ India. Fig. 150, 154.

B. alpestris see: **B. × intermedia**

B. × aurata Borkh. (*B. pubescens × B. verrucosa*). Hybrid occurring among the parents, usually only shrubby, occasionally a small tree, characteristics quite variable; growth habit more like *B. pubescens*, but with finer twigs, young twigs more or less pubescent and glandular; leaves usually rhombic, 4 to 5 cm long, finely dentate (= *B. hybrida* Bechst.). z2

B. beeniana see: **B. × hornei**

B. bhojpathra see: **B. utilis**

B. borealis Spach. Low shrub, 0.25–1.5 m, very closely related to *B. pumila*, but with ovate to broadly ovate leaves, 2–3 cm long, 1–2 cm wide (to 5 cm long and 4 cm wide on long shoots), deep, sharply and doubly

Fig. 148. *Betula alleghaniensis* (fruiting twig, twig with male catkins, fruit scales, seed, winter buds); *B. lenta* (same parts) (from Illinck)

crenate serrate, pubescent at first, later quite glabrous. Rho 1945: 973 (= *B. pumila* var. *borealis* Regel). N. America. z4

B. borggreveana Zabel (*B. papyrifera* × *B. pumila*). Growth shrubby, young twigs densely pubescent; leaves ovate to ovate-oblong to rounded, 3.5—7.5 cm long, base rounded, coarsely serrate, densely pubescent when young, later glabrous, resinous punctate beneath, petioles 8—14 mm long. SH 1:59 r 2—3 (*B. excelsa* sensu Schneid. non Ait. nec Willd.). Originated in cultivation in 1872 at Forst Botanic Garden, Hannover-Muenden, W. Germany. z2

B. callosa Notoe. Small or low tree, but always single stemmed, with rigidly upright growth, bark glossy, yellowish to brown-red or black-red, young twigs thick, short tomentose with scattered tiny glands, in the 2nd year glabrous and glandular; leaves broadly ovate, short acuminate, 3—4 cm long, with 4—7 paired veins, irregularly serrate, underside pubescent at first, later totally glabrous; female catkins ovate, erect, 1.2 cm wide, 2.3 cm long; fruit scales finger-like, totally different from all the other European Birchs. Sv. Bot. Tidskr. 1945: Pl. 4. Scandinavia (subalpine zone) and tundra, also on Iceland. z2 Plate 71.

B. carpinifolia see: **B. grossa** and **B. lenta.**

B. chinensis Maxim. In its habitat 1.5—3 m (in Korea to 9 m high) tall shrub, bark reddish-gray, young twigs thin, silky pubescent; leaves ovate, 4 cm long, acute, rounded at the base and oblique, serrate, dull green above, lighter beneath, glabrous, with 7—10 paired veins, these pubescent beneath, petiole 7—10 mm long; male catkins ovate, 1—2 cm long; fruits scales with 3 narrow, forward pointing tips. CIS 106; ICS 786; EP IV, 61: 19 G—J (= *B. exalata* S. Moore). N. China, Japan, Korea. 1906. z4 Fig. 149, 150.

var. *delavayi* see: **B. delavayi**

B. × coerulea Blanchard. (*B. coerulea-grandis* × *B. populifolia*). Blue Birch. Tree, to 10 m, usually lower, twigs thin, ascending, with many small, light lenticels, new growth somewhat shaggy pubescent, later becoming glabrous and red-brown, trunk bark white with pink, glossy, seldom divisible in layers; leaves ovate, acuminate, base cuneate or rounded, 4—6 cm long, sharply and doubly serrate, upper surface eventually dull blue-green, yellowish-green beneath; male catkins 1—3, to 5 cm long, female catkins 2.5 cm long, pubescent, cylindrical, pendulous. SM 198. Northeastern USA, Canada, widely disseminated. 1905. z3 ∅

B. coerulea-grandis Blanchard. Tree, to 10 m, twigs glabrous, a few resin glands; leaves triangular-ovate, acuminate, 6—8 cm long, base usually rounded, usually sharp and doubly serrate, blue-green above, yellow-green beneath, venation pubescent at first, but soon glabrous, petiole 1.5—2.5 cm long; fruit catkins cylindrical, pubescent, 2.5—3 cm long, 8—10 mm wide. Sm 198 A. N. America and Canada, together with *B. coerulea.* 1905. Very similar to *B. coerulea*, but leaves

Fig. 149. *Betula chinensis* (from ICS)

larger, fruit catkins somewhat larger and much thicker. z3 Plate 78. ∅

B. concinna Gunnarsson. Tree or shrub, 2 or multi-stemmed, bark dark brown to nearly black, not flaking, inner bark red-brown, young twigs brown, furrowed, not glossy, with rather large, yellow-brown lenticels, winter buds acuminate, very viscid; leaves elliptic to ovate, acute, firm, fine veined, pubescent when young, soon becoming glabrous; middle tip of the fruit scales distinctly longer than the side points. Gunnarsson, Mon. Scand. Betul. Pl. 1, 4, 28, 30. S. Sweden. z4

B. cordifolia see: **B. papyrifera**

B. coriacea Gunnarsson. Tree or shrub, 2 or multi-stemmed, bark yellow-brown to gray, slightly flaking, inside dark yellow-brownish, winter buds short, thick, obtuse, viscid; leaves thick, leathery, broad elliptic to ovate, with obtuse apex, thick reticulate venation, gray-green beneath; middle tip of the fruit scales slightly longer than the side points. Gunnarsson, Mon. Scand. Betul. Pl. 1, 4. N. Sweden. z3

B. corylifolia Rgl. & Maxim. Tree, to 20 m high, bark gray or whitish, young twigs glabrous, reddish brown, with some warts; leaves elliptic to obovate, 4—6 cm long, coarsely doubly serrate with triangular teeth (important for identification), bluish beneath(!), with 10—14 distinct silky pubescent paired veins; fruit catkins erect, 3—4 cm long, somewhat curved; fruit scales pubescent, 12—15 mm long, with very narrow, erect tips. KIF 2: 11; EP IV, 61: 17. Japan; higher mountainous areas of Honshu Island. Nearly always incorrectly labelled in gardens! z5? Fig. 150, 155. ∅

B. costata Trautv. Tree, 12—24 m high, ornamental growth habit, bark light yellow to gray-yellow, paper thin, peeling, older bark scaly, young twigs pubescent, brown, with many round glands, eventually glabrous;

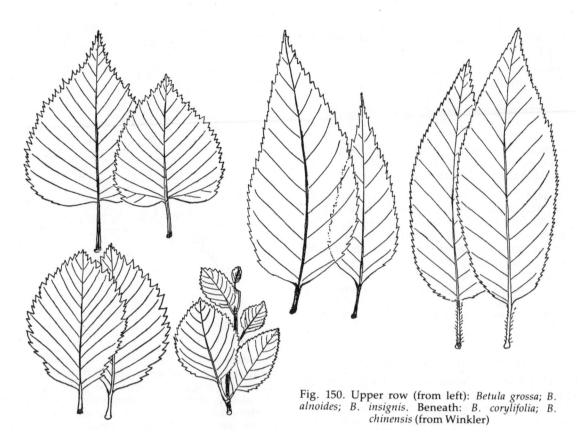

Fig. 150. Upper row (from left): *Betula grossa; B. alnoides; B. insignis*. Beneath: *B. corylifolia; B. chinensis* (from Winkler)

leaves ovate, 5—8 cm long, with cuspidate apex, leathery tough, base rounded to slightly cordate, finely and sharply double serrate, with 10—16 ridged (plaited), prominent vein pairs, often somewhat pubescent above, light green beneath, glandular-warty, petiole 8—15 mm long; fruit catkins elliptic, 2 cm long; middle tip of the fruit scales twice as long as the side tips. NS 33: 19; ICS 783. Manchuria, Korea, in the mountains. 1880. z6 Fig. 151, 154. ⌀

B. cylindrostachya Lindl. apud Wall. Tall tree, bark yellowish-gray, young twigs gray-brown, with many glands; leaves obovate, 8 cm long, to 5 cm wide, acute or short acuminate, base rounded, uneven, margins coarse and simply or doubly serrate, tough to nearly leathery, venation yellowish tomentose beneath with axillary pubescence, glabrous above, petiole 2 cm long, brown-red, pubescent; female catkins 6 cm long, 3 mm wide, usually in fascicles of 3—4; fruit scales oblong-spathulate, glandular pubescent (= *B. acuminata* var. *cylindrostachya* [Lindl.] Winkl.). Yunnan to India. z7?

B. dahurica see: **B. davurica** and **B. minor**

B. davurica Pall. Black Birch. Tree 5—9 (to 20 m), trunk with dense peeling, gray-brown, eventually often totally ray bark, nearly like that of *B. nigra* (very important for identification), young twigs dark gray with white glands; leaves ovate-rhombic, to 6 cm long, acute, cuneate at the base, unevenly serrate, glandular

punctate beneath, with 6—8 paired veins, these pubescent on both sides; fruit catkins 2—2.5 cm long. LF 81; CIS 107; KIF 2: 12 (= *B. dahurica* Regel; *B. wutaica* Mayr; *B. maackii* Rupr.). Manchuria, N. China, Korea. Ⓕ USSR. z5 Plate 67, 71; Fig. 155.

B. delavayi Franch. Small tree or only a shrub, somewhat intermediate between *B. potaninii* and *B. chinensis*, bark dark gray, branching horizontally, young twigs dark gray, with many white glands; leaves ovate-elliptic, 2—4 cm long, to 2 cm wide, acute, base cuneate, unevenly and doubly serrate, teeth long, fresh green on both sides, with 10—14 indented vein pairs, these pubescent beneath; fruit catkins 1.5—2 cm long, to 1 cm thick; fruit scales dense glandular pubescent. ICS 785; EP IV, 61: 19 m (= *B. chinensis* var. *delavayi* Schneid.). W. China; Kansu, Szechwan, Yunnan. 1919. Hardy. z4? Fig. 152.

var. *forrestii* see: **B. forrestii**

B. dentata see: **B. verrucosa**

B. × eastwoodiae Sarg. (*B. glandulosa* × *B. papyrifera* var. *humilis*). Yukon Birch. Sm 208. N. America; Alberta, Yukon, Alaska. Very scarce in cultivation. z2

B. ermanii Cham. Erman's Birch, Gold Birch, Russian Rock Birch. Tree, to 20 m high, crown wide spreading, open, bark yellow-white (but tending to white or reddish), peeling, young branches orange-brown, young

Fig. 151. *Betula costata* (from Dippel)

twigs glandular-warty, glabrous; leaves triangular-cordate, 5–10 cm long, apex cuspidate, coarsely serrate, with 7–11 paired veins, dark green above, glandular beneath, venation occasionally pubescent; fruit catkins erect, ovate-ellipsoid, 2–3 cm long, 1–1.5 cm thick; tips of the fruit scales oblong. ICS 784; KIF 1: 34; NK 2: 16. NE. Asia (entire forests in Sachalin), Japan, Korea. 1880. Extraordinarily variable! z6 Plate 69, 77; Fig. 155, 157. ∅

var. **japonica** (Shirai) Koidz. Leaves triangular-ovate, with 14–15 paired veins, base more or less truncate; fruit scales with narrow middle lobe and wider side lobes (= *B. nikoense* Koidz.; *B. bhojpattra* var. *japonica* Shirai). Japan; Honshu. z6

var. **subcordata** (Regel) Koidz. Leaf base slightly cordate. (According to Schneider this is actually a mixture of forms from the mainland and Japan, all differing from the species in one way or another [Bean, 8th edition], only the above described variety, *japonica*, is distinctly different). The plant under this name in cultivation (also as var. *nipponica* Maxim.), has more or less glandular young twigs and leaf petioles, leaves with 10–14 paired veins, base distinctly cordate and with 4 cm long fruit catkins. Japan; Honshu. 1903. Beautiful park tree. z6 ∅

B. exaltata see: **B. chinensis**

B. excelsa see: **B. borggraveana**

B. × fennica Doerfl. (*B. nana × B. verrucosa*). Shrub, to 3m high, upright, twigs glandular, short pubescent when young; leaves small, broad ovate, 1.5–2.5 cm long, glandular punctate beneath. SH 1: 58 g–g 4. Finland. 1886. z3 Plate 77. ∅

B. fontinalis see: **B. occidentalis**

B. forrestii (W. W. Sm.) Hand.-Mazz. Shrub, to 5m, occasionally a small tree, bark dark brown, polished appearance, young twigs dark and rather rough with numerous, white glands; leaves ovate to oblong-ovate, 3–6 cm long, to 3 cm wide, base cuneate, irregularly doubly serrate, dull green above, lighter beneath, both sides finely silky pubescent; fruit catkins to 3 cm long; fruit scales densely silky pubescent (= *B. delavayi* var. *forrestii* W. W. Smith). W. China. 1919 Hardy. z6

B. fruticosa Pall. Shrub Birch. Shrub, 1–2 m high, young twigs often only slightly glandular; leaves acute, ovate to broadly elliptic, base cuneate, 2–5 cm long, with 5–6 paired veins, margin finely serrate, midrib somewhat pubescent beneath; middle tip of the fruit scales somewhat smaller than the side tips. ICS 788; NK 2: 15 (as *B. gmelinii*) (= *B. smelinii* Bge.). NE. Asia, N. China. z5? Fig. 155.

B. glandulifera (Regel) Butler. Shrub, to 2 m high, twigs thin, with a few resin glands, pubescent; leaves obovate to rounded, 2–5 cm long, acute, serrate or crenate, lower young veins pubescent, later with a few resin glands, venation reticulate; fruit catkins to 2 cm long, cylindrical. RMi 107 (= *B. pumila* var. *glandulifera* Regel). USA; Ontario to British Columbia. z4

B. glandulosa Michx. Shrub, to 2m high, twigs with dense resin glands, but not pubescent; leaves rounded to broadly elliptic, 2–25 mm long, rounded, crenate dentate, glabrous beneath, glandular-punctate; fruit catkins 1.5–2 cm long, erect. BB 1217 (= *B. nana* var. *intermedia* Regel). N. America, Greenland. 1880.

Fig. 152. *Betula delavayi* (from ICS)

Resembles *B. nana*, but the twigs densely glandular warty, leaves longer petioled. For moist areas. z3 Plate 77; Fig. 155.

B. globispica Shiras. Tree, to 20 m high, bark nearly white, peeling, young twigs gray-yellow or gray-brown, with thick lenticels; leaves ovate to nearly circular, but with a short apical tip, 4–7 cm long, unevenly and sharply serrate, with some 10 paired veins, venation and midrib pubescent beneath; petiole 5–15 mm long, with erect pubescence; fruit catkins ovate, 2.5–3.5 cm long; fruit scales with linear, ciliate tips, 13–15 mm long. KIF 2: 13; EP IV, 61: 19 d–f. Central Japan; rare. 1896. Hardy. z5? Plate 77; Fig. 155. ∅

B. gmelinii see: **B. fruticosa**

B. grossa S. & Z. Tree, to 25 m high, closely related to *B. lenta*; bark black-gray, smooth, becoming grooved on older trees, twigs yellow-brown at first, later red-brown, glabrous, somewhat pubescent at first, with few lenticels; leaves oval-oblong, 5–10 cm long, base cordate, coarsely doubly serrate, 2 teeth between each vein pair, glandular with veins silky pubescent beneath; fruit catkins solitary, nearly sessile, rounded, 2.5 cm long; fruit scales pubescent, middle tip narrow oblong, protruding beyond the side tips, 7–8 mm long. KIF 1: 35; EP IV, 61: 18 D–F (= *B. carpinifolia* S. & Z.). Japan, in the mountains. 1896. Only rarely in cultivation but hardy. z5 Fig. 150, 155. ∅

B. hallii Howell. Small shrub, growth narrowly upright, conical, young twigs velvety pubescent and somewhat glandular; leaves obovate to nearly circular, 2.5–3 cm long, base cuneate, margins crenate, both sides with resin glands, venation pubescent beneath; tips of the fruit scales nearly even length, obtuse (= *B. pumila* var. *fastigiata* Rehd.). USA, Oregon to Alaska and Yukon. 1898. z4

B. × hornei Butler (*B. nana* × *B. papyrifera*) Shrub, 1–2 m high, young twigs purple-red, glabrous, with resin glands, older branches with thin, gray, peeling bark; leaves wide diamond shape to elliptic, to 4 cm long and wide, margin irregularly crenate to lobed, with 4–5 paired veins, deep bronze-green above, yellowish-green beneath, petiole 1–1.5 cm; fruit catkins 15 mm long, about 1 cm thick (= *B. beeniana* Nelson). Alaska. Probably not in cultivation. z2

B. humilis Schrenk. Shrub, 0.5–2 m high, bark black-brown, young twigs quickly becoming glabrous, with large resin-warts; leaves elliptic to oval-elliptic, obtuse or barely acute, 1.5–3 cm long, irregularly serrate, glabrous and green on both sides, with 4–5 paired veins; fruit catkins erect, 5–15 mm long; fruit scales with 3 nearly equal tips. HM 480; HW 122; GuB 6. Middle and N. Europe, N. Asia to the Altai mountains. 1818. z2? Plate 77; Fig. 155.

B. hupehensis see: **B. luminifera**

B. hybrida see: **B. × aurata**

B. insignis Franch. Tree, 9–12 m high, bark dark gray, young twigs fox-red, with numerous, white glands, glabrous; leaves ovate-lanceolate, acute or acuminate, 8–9 mm long, irregularly doubly serrate, 12–14 paired veins pubescent beneath, otherwise glabrous on both sides, base oblique and cuneate to round, petiole 1–2 cm long, red-brown, pubescent; fruits catkins 4–6 cm long, nearly cylindrical, to 1.5 cm thick, erect; middle tip of the fruit scales twice as long as the side tips, all 3 with stiff pubescence. CIS 105; ICS 781; EP VI, 61: 19 A–C. China; Hupeh, Szechwan, Sikang. z5 Fig. 150.∅

B. × intermedia (Hartm.) Thomas (*B. nana* × *B. pubescens*). Shrub, 1–2 m high, branches short, straggly, twigs brownish or brown-green, usually without glands, slightly pubescent when young, soon becoming glabrous, with white lenticels; leaves diamond shape or ovate, 8–25 mm long, usually doubly serrate, glandular punctate on both sides; middle tip of the fruit scales wider than the side tips. SH 1: 58 e; HF 950. N. Europe, Switzerland, occurring naturally. z3 Fig. 153.

var. **alpestris** (Fries) Winkl. Shrubby, twigs occasionally slightly pubescent, always without glandular warts; leaves rounded to ovate, crenate, always glabrous, reticulate venation benath; fruit scale tips erect, side tips usually wider and shorter; seed wings very narrow. SH 1: 58 e4–e5 (= *B. alpestris* Fries). N. Europe, Iceland, Greenland. z3 Fig. 153.

B. × jackii Schneid. (= *B. pumila* × *B. lenta*). Shrub, bark aromatic like that of *B. lenta*; leaves ovate to elliptic, 3–5 cm long, with 7 paired veins, glabrous; fruit catkins oblong, 1.2–1.8 cm long, to 1.2 cm thick; middle tip of the fruit scales longer than the erect side tips. GF 8: 243; SH 1: 59 a–a1. Originated in the Arnold Arboretum. z3

B. jacquemontii Spath. White Barked Himalayan Birch. Tall tree, bark white, peeling, young twigs pubescent with resin glands and warty; leaves ovate, base round or somewhat cuneate, 5–7 cm long, with 7–9 paired veins, unevenly serrate (highest leaves often doubly serrate), both sides usually totally glabrous, glandular punctate beneath, petiole 1.5–2 cm long; fruit catkins cylindrical, singular, on long, pubescent stalks; fruit scales with linear middle tips. BS 1: 20; EH 270 (= *B. utilis* var. *jacquemontii* Henry). W. Himalaya. 1880. Often confused with *B. utilis*. z6 Plate 67.

B. japonica see: **B. platyphylla** with varieties.

B. kenaica see: **B. papyrifera**

B. × koehnei Schneid. (*B. papyrifera* × *B. verrucosa*). Large tree with open crown, twigs slightly nodding, bark white even on young branches; leaves triangular-ovate, resembling those of *B. papyrifera*, but more finely serrate and more acuminate, to 9 cm long, tough membranous, deep green above, quickly becoming glabrous, much lighter beneath, scattered pubescence on the 5–7 paired veins, petiole 1–2.5 cm long. SH 1: 59 d–d1. 1905. Very garden worthy, but rare. z2 ∅

B. lacinata see: **B. verrucosa**

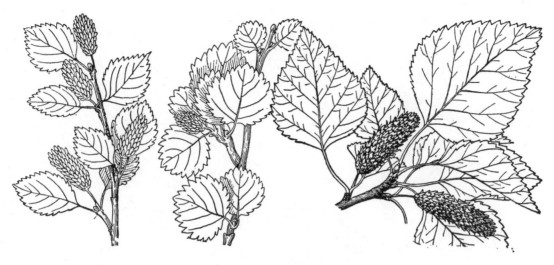

Fig. 153. From left to right: *Betula intermedia*; B. *intermedia* var. *alpestris*; *B. papyrifera* var. *kenaica* (from Reichenbach, Sudworth)

B. latifolia see: **B. papyrifera**

B. lenta L. Sweet Birch. Tree, to 25m high, growth narrowly and regularly upright, bark dark red-brown, very fissured, but not peeling, young bark purple-brown, aromatic, glabrous or nearly so (important distinction from *B. alleghanienesis*); leaves oblong-ovate, 6–12 cm long, acuminate, sharply doubly serrate, with 9–12 paired veins, glossy green, young leaves at first silky pubescent beneath, fall color gold-yellow; fruit catkins nearly sessile, erect, oval-oblong, 2–3.5 cm long, fruit scales not pubescent (important for identification!), side tips wider than the middle tip. BB 1215; SS 448 (*B. carpinifola* Ehrh.). Eastern N. America. 1759. Attractive Birch but not as worthy as *B. alleghaniensis*. Ⓕ Germany in trial plots. z3 Plate 68; Fig. 148, 155. ∅

B. luminifera Winkl. Tree, 5–26 m high, bark of older stems yellow-gray, not peeling, young twigs brown, more or less brown pubescent; leaves ovate, 6–10 cm long, base round to nearly cordate, coarsely and unevenly serrate, teeth acuminate, with 10–13 paired veins, deep green above (reddish at first), lighter beneath, finely tomentose or nearly glabrous, with many glossy resin glands; fruit catkins singular, 4–10 cm long, 5 mm thick, erect (like candles, hence the name!), fruit scales oblong, side tips absent or rudimentary (important for identification!). ICS 774; CIS 102; EP IV, 61: 23 A–C (= *B. hupehensis* Schneid., *B. wilsoniana* Schneid.). Central China; Szechwan, W. Hupeh. 1901. Gorgeous species. z5 Plate 78; Fig. 154. ∅ ⚭

B. lutea see: **B. alleghaniensis**

B. lyalliane see: **B. papyrifera**

B. maakii see: **B. davurica**

B. mandshurica see: **B. platyphylle**

B. maximowicziana Regel. Monarch Birch. Fast growing tree, to 30 m high, branches open, bark orange-gray-white, peeling, thin, twigs dark red-brown, glabrous; leaves broadly cordate-ovate, 8–14 cm long, acute, doubly serrate, pubescent on young trees, but later becoming glabrous, with 10–12 paired veins, vein tips protruding past the margin, fall color gold-yellow, often with red venation; fruit catkins in clusters of 3–4, cylindrical, some 7 cm long. KIF 1: 36; EP IV, 61: 22 D–F (= *B. maximowiczianii* Regel). Japan. 1888. Quite hardy; nearly Linden-like with its large leaves. One of the loveliest Birches. z5 Plate 79, 80; Fig. 155. ∅

B. medwediewii Regel. Transcaucasian Birch. Small, Alder-like, erect shrub (when young), also a tree in its habitat, to 20 m, shrubs with gray-yellow, peeling bark, branches thick, stiff, with very large, green, viscid buds; leaves on shrubs broad elliptic, 8–11 cm long, unevenly doubly serrate, deep green above, light green beneath, with 8–11 paired veins, glabrous or somewhat pubescent; leaves on mature trees much smaller, twigs also less stiff; fruit catkins stalked, erect, 2–4 cm long; middle tip of the fruit scales twice as long as the side tips. SL 122; BM 9569. Transcaucasus. Introduced in 1906 by Spaeth, Berlin. Hardy. z5 Plate 69, 78; Fig. 155. ∅

B. michauxii Spach. Dwarf, about 0.5 m high, very similar to *B. anna*, strongly branched, young twigs tomentose; leaves fan shape, cuneate at the base, some 1 cm long, deeply crenate; fruit catkins 1–1.2 cm long, ovate-oblong; fruit scales not cleft, oblong, or the lower ones 3 lobed. EP IV, 61: 20 A–C (= *B. terrae-novae* Fern.; *B. nana* var. *michauxii* Regel). N. America; Labrador, Newfoundland. z3

B. microphylla Bge. Tree, bark yellowish, young twigs pubescent with dense resin glands; leaves obovate to rhombic-ovate, base cuneate, entire, otherwise coarsely and unevenly serrate, 2.5–3 cm long, some 2

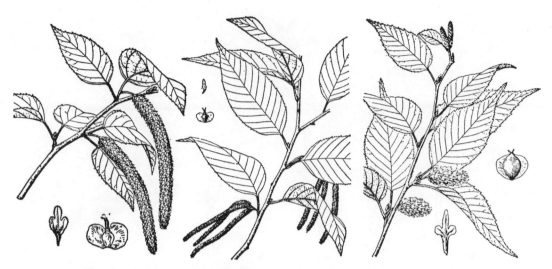

Fig. 154. From left to right: *Betula luminifera*; *B. alnoides*; *B. costata* (from ICS)

cm wide, with about 5 paired veins, usually glabrous beneath, but glandular, petiole pubescent, some 1 cm long; fruit catkins oblong-cylindrical, nearly sessile, 2 cm long, side tips of fruit scales erect and somewhat shorter than the middle tip. Regel, Mon. Betul. Pl. 7; DL 2: 80. Middle Asia; Altai Mts. The plant usually found in gardens under this name is *B. middendorfii*. z4?

B. middendorffii Trautv. & Mey. Shrub, 1–3 m high, sparsely branched, twigs with resin glands and fine pubescence or also totally smooth and glabrous; leaves ovate, 2–4 cm long, coarsely serrate, base usually round, yellow-green beneath; fruit catkins 1.5–2 cm long; fruit scales with erect, nearly equally long tips. SH 1: 56 m. E. Siberia, Amur region. 1904. z3 Plate 77.

B. minor (Tuckerm.) Fern. Dwarf, intermediate between *B. occidentalis* and *B. papyrifera*, short trunk, more shrubby; leaves ovate or oval-elliptic, glabrous, 3–5 cm long, with 7–8 paired veins. Rho. 1945: Pl. 963 (= *B. dahurica* var. *americana* Regel). Eastern USA, Mount Washington in New Hampshire. z4

B. nana L. Dwarf Birch. Shrub, prostrate or also ascending, about 0.5 m high (rarely to 1 m), current year's twigs brown, densely pubescent, never warty; leaves small, nearly circular, apex rounded, 5–15 mm long, coarsely crenate, somewhat viscid when young and pubescent beneath; fruit catkins ovate, nearly sessile, 7–10 mm long, erect; with 2 paired veins, normally yellow-green in fall, but sometimes dark red in Northern Europe; fruit scales glabrous, tips nearly equal in length, middle tip widest. BB 1218; HM 84. N. Europe, N. America, moist and swampy areas in the mountains. 1789. Tolerates dry areas in the rock garden. z2 Plate 77, 80. Ø

var. *intermedia* see: **B. glandulosa**

var. *michauxii* see: **B. michauxii**

B. nigra L. River Birch. Tall, usually multistemmed, ornamental tree, trunk with thick, peeling but not exfoliating, black-red bark, young twigs pubescent, young bark red-brown to yellow-brown; leaves oval-rhombic, 8 cm long, base cuneate, doubly serrate, glossy green above, gray or blue-gray and pubescent beneath, yellow in fall, with 7–9 paired veins; fruit "cones" cylindrical, pubescent; fruit scales narrow, the 3 tips nearly equal in length and erect. BB 1214; GTB 140; SS 452 (= *B. rubra* Michx.). Eastern USA, river banks, swamps, flood plains; however, thriving also in dry areas in cultivation. 1736. z5 Plate 37, 68, 79; Fig. 155. Ø

B. neoalaskana see: **B. papyrifera**

B. obscura Kotula. The Sand Birch. Closely related to *B. verrucosa*, trunk bark not white, rather dark brown, younger branches fox-red, occasionally nearly white, young twigs pubescent or also glabrous. Beskid Mountains, Silesia (Poland). Quite variable species. z4 Plate 72.

B. occidentalis Hook. Water Birch. Tree-like shrub or also a small tree, 4–5 m high (rarely to 12 m), grows upright at first in cultivation, later branches long nodding, bark remains tight, black-brown, not peeling (important distinction), young twigs with many resin glands; leaves broadly ovate, rounded to slightly cordate at the base, acuminate, 3–5 cm long, sharply and doubly serrate, glabrous above, dark green, somewhat viscid, somewhat pubescent beneath, soon becoming glabrous, with 3–5 paired veins; fruit catkins 2–3 cm long, 5–10 mm thick; fruit scales pubescent or glabrous, all tips acute, side tips ascending, somewhat shorter than the middle. SPa 114 (as *B. fontinalis*) (= *B. fontinalis* Sarg.). Western N. America. 1874. z5 Fig. 155. Ø var. **fecunda** Fern. More tree-like; leaves ovate to elliptic, 5–6 cm long, base broadly cuneate, venation beneath pubescent when young; fruit catkins cylindrical, 3–5 cm long, fruit scales with ascending, side tips lobed at the base. Sm 207 (as *B. fontinalis* var. *piperi* Sarg.) (= *B. piperi* Brit.; *B. fontinalis* var. *piperi* [Brit.] Sarg.). USA; Washington, Montana. 1903. z5

B. odorata see: **B. pubescens**

B. papyrifera Marsh. Paper Birch. Tree, to 30 m high, very often multistemmed, bright white bark, young twigs red-brown, pubescent, later glabrous, somewhat glandular; leaves ovate, 4–10 cm long, with 6–10 paired veins, acuminate, coarsely and usually doubly serrate, dull green above, glabrous, usually pubescent on the venation beneath; fruit catkins cylindrical, 3–5 cm long, usually pendulous; fruit scales pubescent, side tips somewhat shorter than the middle and erect or pointing outward. SS 451; BB 1212; GTB 144 (= *B. papyracea* Ait.; *B. latifolia* Tausch). N. America. 1876. One of the most beautiful of the white barked species. ℗ USA; Greenland. z4 Plate 68, 79. ∅

Including a number of varieties:

var. **commutata** (Regel) Fern. Tree, reaching 40 m, largest birch species in the world, bark reddish-brown to orange or also whitish, peeling, young twigs yellow-brown, warty and pubescent; leaves ovate to broad ovate, acute or acuminate, base rounded or usually deeply cordate, 7–10 cm long, to 12 cm on young plants, doubly serrate, with 7–10 paired veins, light or dark green, rather thin; fruit catkins 3–4 cm long, fruit scales ciliate on the margin. SM 203 (as *B. papyrifera* var. *occidentalis* Sarg.); Rho 1945, Pl. 965; SS 725 (= *B. papyracea* var. *occidentalis* Dipp.; *B. papyrifera* var. *lyalliana* [Koehne] Schneid.; *B. lyalliana* Koehne). NW. USA, in moist areas. 1885. z5 Plate 79; Fig. 155. m ∅

var. **cordifolia** (Regel) Fern. Small tree, bark white to dark brown, thin, peeling, crown wider than the species, also often only a shrub, young twigs pubescent; leaves broadly ovate, base slightly cordate, 3–7 cm long, doubly serrate, venation long haired beneath; fruit scales pubescent or glabrous. SM 200; SS 724 (= *B. cordifolia* Regel). Labrador to Minnesota. 1876. z3 ∅

var. **humilis** (Regel) Fern. & Raup. Tree, 8–10 m high, occasionally to 25 m high, bark dull white to reddish-brown, separating into thin layers, young twigs glabrous, but with dense resin glands; leaves triangular-ovate, base usually truncate, thin, 4–8 cm long, coarsely serrate, with 4–5 paired veins, dark green above, light green beneath, young leaves viscid; fruit catkins some 3 cm long, on 2 cm long stalks, fruit scales ciliate only on the upper margin. SPa 113 (as *B. alaskana*); SM 205 (as *B. alaskana*); SS 726 (= *B. alaskana* Sarg.; *B. neoalaskana* Sarg.). NW. USA to Alaska. 1905. z4

var. **kenaica** (Evans) Henry. Small tree, 7–10 m high, bark white, with orange or brown stripes, young twigs softly pubescent, more or less glandular; leaves ovate, acute, to 5 cm long, base broadly cuneate, with 5–6 yellowish paired veins, petiole yellow, dull green above, yellow-green beneath; fruit catkins 2.5 cm long, fruit scales ciliate, otherwise glabrous. SS 723; BSPa 112; SM 204 (= *B. kenaica* Evans). Coast of Alaska. 1897 z4 Fig. 153.

var. **papyrifera**. The typical form, description same as the species *B. papyrifera* above. SM 199; Rho 1945: Pl. 967 (as var. *pensilis*) (= *B. papyrifera* var. *pensilis* Fern.). Eastern N. America. 1750. z4 Fig. 155.

var. **subcordata** (Rydb.) Sarg. Small tree, 6 to 10 m high, bark silver-gray with blue-red stripes, young twigs glabrous or also pubescent, occasionally somewhat glandular; leaves broad-ovate, acute, cordate at the base, or rounded, glabrous, 5–6 cm long, unevenly serrate, teeth directed forward, glabrous; fruit catkins 2.5–3 cm long, pendulous, fruit scales pubescent and ciliate. SM 201 (= *B. subcordata* Rydb.). N. Rocky Mountains. 1918. z3 ∅

B. pendula see: **B. verrucosa**

B. piperi see: **B. occidentalis**

B. platyphylla Sukatchev. Manchurian Birch. Tree, 10–20 m high, light-open crowned, young twigs thin, dark gray to reddish, densely covered with white resin glands; leaves triangular-ovate, short acuminate, base cuneate and somewhat oblique, with 5–7 paired veins, coarsely serrate, 4–6 cm long, deep green above, lighter beneath and with brownish, small glands, otherwise both sides glabrous; buds break very early, often 3 weeks before all the other Birches (important distinction!); fruit catkins 3 cm long; middle tips of the fruit scales triangular and smaller than the wider, outspread side tips. NK 2: 13; KIF 1: 37 (= *B. mandschurica* [Regel] Nakai). Manchuria, Korea. Having merit especially for its very early bud break. ℗ SSR (Kamchatka); Japan (Hokkaido). z5 Plate 71. ∅

In addition, the following geographical varieties:

var. **japonica** (Miq.) Hara. Bark pure white, twigs glandular-warty; leaves triangular-ovate, 4–7.5 cm long, to 6 cm wide, truncate at the base or also somewhat cordate, glabrous beneath or frequently finely pubescent and with axillary pubescence; fruit catkins singular, to 5 cm long. CIS 108; LF 82 (= *B. japonica* Sieb.; *B. tauschii* [Regel] Koidz.; *B. mandschurica* var. *japonica* [Miq.] Rehd.). Japan, Manchuria, N. China. 1902. z4 Plate 69. ∅

var. **rockii** (Rehd.) Rehd. Tree, 6–9 m high, bark silver-gray to bluish, crown oblong and pointed; leaves triangular to ovate, 3.5 cm long, 3 cm wide, acute, base cuneate, irregularly coarsely serrate, glabrous on both sides, petiole 3 cm long, red-brown; fruit catkins deeply 3 cleft, bluish-brown, connate only at the base, very slightly pubescent (= *B. japonica* var. *rockii* Rehd.). E. Tibet, Szechwan, in the mountains from 3300–3400 m. z4

var. **szechwanica** (Schneid.) Rehd. Szechwan Birch. Tree, 5–12 m high, bark white to silver-gray or somewhat reddish, thin peeling, branches sparsely arranged, young twigs dark gray or reddish-brown; leaves triangular to ovate, to 6 cm long and 5 cm wide, short acuminate, base cuneate, irregularly serrate, tough to leathery, deep green above, lighter beneath, both sides glabrous, glandular beneath, petiole 2–3 cm long; fruit scales arrow-shape (sagittate) (= *B. japonica* var. *szechwanica* Schneid.). W. China, Szechwan, Yunnan, Sikang. 1872. Easily recognized by the leaves which are densely glandular beneath and persist until late fall. z4 Plate 71. ∅

B. populifolia Marsh. Gray Birch. Tree, 10–20 m high, very often multistemmed, crown thin, conical, bark gray-white, not peeling, young twigs glabrous, thin, somewhat pendulous, bowed, very rough from many warts; leaves triangular, apex cuspidate, 6–8 cm long, coarsely and doubly serrate, viscid when young, glossy green, light yellow in fall, with 6–9 paired veins; fruit

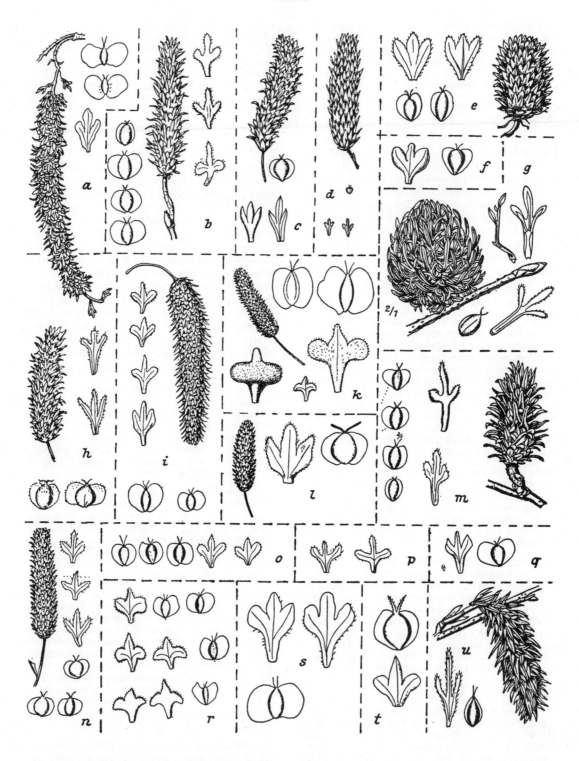

Fig. 155. **Betula**, fruits, seeds and fruit scales. a. *B. maximowicziana*; b. *B. ermanii*; c. *B. utilis*; d. *B. medwediewii*; e. *B. alleghaniensis*; f. *B. lenta*; g. *B. globispica*; h. *B. nigra*; i. *B. papyrifera*; k. *B. populifolia*; l. *B. glandulosa*; m. *B. grossa*; n. *B. pumila*; o. *B. fruticosa*; p. *B. humilis*; q. *B. occidentalis*; r. *B. verrucosa*; s. *B. papyrifera commutata*; t. *B. davurica*; u. *B. corylifolia* (from Shirai, Regel, Sargent, Schneider)

catkins cylindrical, 3 cm long, widely spaced, pubescent, fruit scales as wide as long, middle tip very small. BB 1211; GTB 142; SS 450. Eastern N. America. 1750. Tolerates dry, poor to nearly sterile soil; but having little garden merit. Short lived. z3 Plate 79; Fig. 155.

'Laciniata'. Leaves pinnate-like deeply lobed.

'Pendula'. Pendulous habit, otherwise like the species.

'Purpurea' (Ellw. & Barry). Young leaves red or bluish-red, later deep green. Originated in the USA in 1892.

B. potaninii Batal. Shrub, to 3 m high, bark dark and rough, branches often procumbent, young twigs dense brown pubescent; leaves ovate, acuminate, 2–4 cm long, unevenly and sharply serrate, glabrous above and with 10–20 indented vein pairs (best I.D. character), venation beneath rust-red, long silky pubescent; fruit catkins singular, 2 cm long, 1 cm thick, middle tip of the fruit scales twice as long as the side tips and with long white glandular hairs at the apices (= *B. wilsonii* Bean). W. China, in the mountains to 3000 m. Very characteristic, easily recognizable species. Rare in cultivation (Mount Usher, Ireland). z4 Ø

B. pubescens Ehrh. Tree, usually not over 20 m high, bark white, peeling in thin strips, trunk at the base with rough, black bark, twigs stiff, ascending, never pendulous, young twigs pubescent, not warty; leaves thin, soft, more or less pubescent on both sides, often shaggy when young, ovate-elliptic to rhombic, with straight tips, 3–5 cm long, unevenly doubly serrate, petiole pubescent; fruit catkins 2.5–3 cm long, fruit scales pubescent, middle tip somewhat longer than the curved side lobes. HM Pl. 84; HW 24–25 (= *B. odorata* Bechst., *B. alba* L.p.p.). Middle Europe to Siberia; prefers moist, swampy areas. In cultivation for ages. ⓕ Poland, USSR (W. Siberia). z2 Plate 72.

In addition, a number of varieties:

'Aurea'. Young leaves yellow, densely pubescent.

var. **carpatica** (Waldst. & Kit.) Koch. Tree or shrub, young twigs and leaves pubescent only at first, bark glossy yellow to reddish-brown, trunk knotty; leaves rhombic eventually only pubescent in the vein axils. HM 480 f–g. Middle and S. Europe, to Romania, usually developing large stands in the heath moors. z2 Plate 72.

var. **glabra** V. N. Andrejeff. Young sprouts and leaves nearly glabrous, wings of the nutlets far surpassing the tip. Ukraine.

'Incisa'. Leaves ovate to triangular, base round to truncate, with 3–4 coarsely serrate lobes on either blade half. Sv. Bot. Tidskr. 51, 1957: Pl. 2. Found in Sweden. 1914.

'Integrifolia'. Leaves ovate, obtuse, base round to lightly cordate, margin occasionally somewhat lobed, but completely entire, deep green above, much lighter beneath. Sv. Bot. Tidskr. **51**, 1957: Pl. 18 (= t. *integrifolia* [Larss.] Hylander). Found in 1865 in Vaermland, Sweden. Very pretty Birch, but rarely in cultivation.

'Murithii'. Trunk knotty, bark gray, branches and twigs slanting upright; leaves short petiolate, widest under the middle, coarsely doubly serrate. Switzerland.

'Urticifolia'. Tree, leaves ovate to rhombic, deeply and sharply serrate or also doubly serrate, usually acuminate-cuspidate, base cuneate, or rounded; fruit catkins longer than those of the species, wings of the nutlets wider than the species. GuB 7; Sv. Bot. Tidskr. 51, 1957: Pl. 24–25. N. Europe, widely found in the wild. Ø

B. pumila L. American Dwarf Birch. Shrub, 1(–5) m, twigs densely tomentose, but not glandular; leaves rounded to broadly elliptic, 1–3 cm long, obtuse, coarse crenately toothed, usually dense pubescent and whitish beneath, venation reticulate, eventually often nearly glabrous, with 4–6 paired veins; fruit catkins erect, stalked, 1.5–2.5 cm long, middle lobe of the fruit scales longer than the side lobes. BB 1219. NE. America, Labrador to Ohio, swampy areas. z2 Fig. 155.

var. *borealis* see: **B. borealis**

var. *fastigiata* see: **B. hallyi**

var. *glandulifera* see: **B. glandulifera**

B. × purpusii Schneid. (*B. alleghaniensis × B. glandulifera*). Tree or shrub, 3–6 cm high, bark gray-brown, not peeling, inner bark aromatic, young twigs thinly pubescent, with few resin glands; leaves ovate to oblong or elliptic, with 5–7 paired veins, 3–6 cm long, dull green above and glabrous, much lighter and soon becoming glabrous beneath, often glandular punctate, usually unevenly and sharply crenate-serrate, tough; fruit catkins 1.5–2.8 cm long, 1 cm thick, wings somewhat narrower than the nutlet. RMi 107. NE. USA 1900. z3? Plate 67.

B. raddeana Trautv. Tree or large shrub, bark silver-gray, young twigs densely velvety through the 2nd year, with few scattered warts; leaves ovate, 3–4.5 cm long, acute, base rounded, with 6–7 paired veins, venation pubescent beneath, coarsely and unevenly serrate; fruit catkins ellipsoid, 2–4 cm long, tips of the fruit scales erect, middle lobe twice as long as the side lobes, linear. GF 1887: 384. Caucasus. 1924 z5 Fig. 156.

B. rubra see: **B. nigra**

Fig. 156. *Betula raddana* (from Regel)

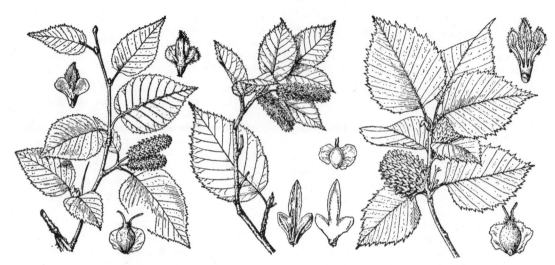

Fig. 157. From left to right: From left to right: *Betula utilis*; *B. albo-sinensis*; *B. ermanii* (from ICS)

B. × sandbergii Brit. (*B. glandulifera* × *B. papyrifera*). Shrub, occasionally tree-like, 2(−10) m high, bark brown, not flaking, young twigs rust-brown pubescent, becoming glabrous in the fall with visible glands, bark not aromatic; leaves rhombic-ovate, with 4−5 paired veins, 2.5−5 cm long, larger on sterile twigs, somewhat unevenly crenate dentate, tough and thick, dull green, lighter beneath and finely glandular punctate; fruit catkins erect, 2−2.5 cm long, 5−7 mm thick, seed wings as wide or wider than the nutlet. RMi 107; Rho 1928: Pl. 170. NE. America. 1914. z3?

B. schmidtii Regel. Tree, to 30 m, bark black to gray, deeply furrowed, with small, thick plates, branches thick, young twigs glandular pubescent, later becoming glabrous, brown; leaves ovate, acuminate, 4−8 cm long, unevenly and finely serrate, light green, with 9−10 paired veins, petiole 4−8 mm long; fruit catkins stiff and erect, usually solitary, 2.5−3 cm long; fruit scales ciliate, tips linear, nutlets not winged. KIF 2:14; NK 2: 19. Japan, Korea, Manchuria. z5 Ⓕ Far Eastern USSR; wood very hard. Plate 77.

B. subcordata see: **B. papyrifera**

B. tauschii see: **B. platyphylla**

B. terrae-novae see: **B. michauxii**

B. turkestanica Litvin. Tree, closely related to *B. pubescens*, bark yellowish or whitish, young twigs pubescent and glandular; leaves ovate, base cuneate or round, pubescent only when young, later pubescent only on the veins, but without pubescent vein axils; fruit catkins to 2.5 cm long; side lobes of the fruit scales only half as long as the middle and erect. Turkestan. z6 Plate 78.

B. utilis D. Don. Himalayan Birch. Tall tree, bark light gray to cream-white, paper thin and peeling, twigs long silky pubescent and with many glands, red-brown in fall; leaves ovate, cuspidate apex, 5−8 cm long, base rounded or broadly cuneate, leathery, unevenly ser-rate, with 10−14 paired veins protruding above, pubescent petioles and vein axils beneath, fall color gold-yellow; male catkins to 12 cm long, fruit catkins 2.5−3.5 cm long, cylindrical, fruit scales pubescent, middle lobe much longer and rounded above. EH 269; HAL 151; SNp 145 (= *B. bhojpathra* Wall.). Himalaya, Kashmir, in the mountains from 3300 to 4300 cm. A tree with handsome bark, especially in winter, but marginally hardy in European cultivation. The name *utilis* (useful) comes from the many uses given the tree (bark as paper, wood for building, branches as cables, etc.). z7 Fig. 155, 157. ⵁ

var. *jacquemontii* see: **B. jacquemontii**

var. **prattii** Burkhill. Tall tree, 20−27 m, bark rough, more flaking, orange-brown to orange-gray; leaves ovate, to 6 cm long, base round, irregularly and doubly serrate, both sides glabrous, but midrib pubescent beneath; fruit catkins singular, 3.5 cm long, 1 cm thick, long stalked, fruit scales reddish, ciliate, side lobes widened, spathulate. W. China; Yunnan, Szechwan, Kansu. 1908. Hardier than the species. z6

var. *sinensis* see: **B. albo-sinensis**

B. verrucosa Ehrh. Sand Birch, European White Birch. Tree, to 20 m high, bark white, peeling, but soon becoming fissured and black, young twigs thin, usually pendulous, glabrous, with many resin glands; leaves triangular, 3−7 cm long, finely acuminate, coarsely doubly serrate, viscid when young, glabrous, petiole 2−3 cm long; fruit cones cylindrical, 2−3 cm long, middle lobe small, acute, side lobes large, wide rounded. HW 15; HM Pl. 84 (= *B. alba* L.p.p.; *B. pendula* Roth). Europe, Asia Minor. In cultivation for ages; popular park tree in Europe. Ⓕ Denmark, Aust., Czech., Netherlands, USSR. z2 Plate 72; Fig. 155.

Many cultivars:

'Birkalensis'. Tall tree; leaves triangular, both sides with 3−4 simple teeth sometimes incised nearly to the midrib. Found in Finland in 1877, occasionally seen in gardens. Plate 72. ⵁ

'Darlecarlica'. Tall, elegant tree; leaves deeply lobed, 4−8 cm

Plate 65

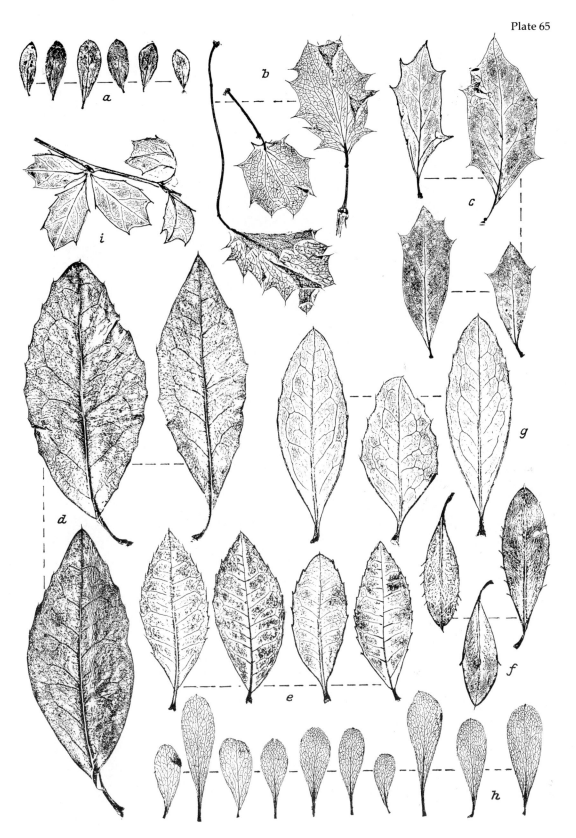

Berberis. a. *B. chillanensis*; b. *B. actinacantha*; c. *B. ruscifolia*; d. *B. valdiviana*; e. *B. kawakami* var. *formosana*; f. *B. chrysosphaera*; g. *B. coxii*; h. *B. prattii*; i. *B. darwinii*

Plate 66

Berberis veitchii
in Wageningen Arboretum, Holland

Berberis hypokerina
Knighthayes Court, Devon, England

Berchmeia racemosa in flower in Japan   Photo: Dr. Watari, Tokyo

Plate 67

Beschorneria yuccoiaes
in the Bell Garden, Ireland

Betula davurica
in the Central-Botanic Garden, Kiev, Ukraine, USSR
Photo: Hinrich Kordes

Betula jacquemontii
in the Wageningen Botanic Garden, Holland

Betula purpusii
in the Wageningen Botanic Garden, Holland

Plate 68

Betula alleghaniensis
in its hative habitat in New York, USA
Photo: US Forest Service

Betula alleghaniensis, trunk with characteristic bark
in the Dortmund Botanic Garden, W. Germany

Betula papyrifera
in its habitat in Wisconsin, USA
Photo: US Forest Service

Betula nigra, typical bark development
in the Trompenburg Arboretum, Holland

Plate 69

Betula medwediewii
in the Dortmund Botanic Garden, W. Germany

Betula platyphylla var. *japonica* in its native habitat,
Japan   Photo: Dr. Watari, Tokyo

Betula ermanii in its habitat in Japan   Photo: Dr. Watari, Tokyo

Plate 70

Betula verucosa 'Youngii', grafted on a standard, in the Dortmund Botanic Garden, W. Germany

Betula verrucosa 'Fastigiata' in a North American nursery

Betula verrucosa 'Tristis' in Westerstede, W. Germany

Betula verrucosa 'Gracilis' in a park in Orleans, France

Plate 71

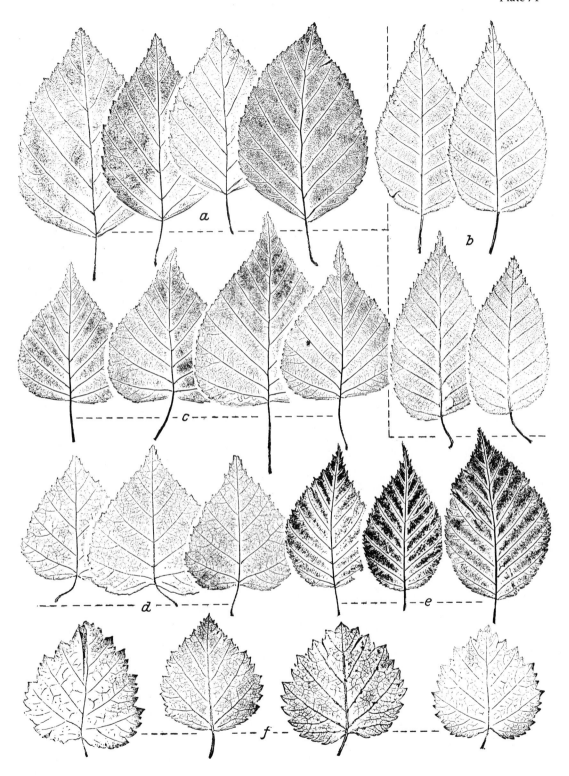

Betula. a. *B. davurica*; b. *B. albo-sinensis* var. *septentrionalis*; c. *B. platyphylla*; d. *B. platyphylla* var. *szechuanica*; e. *B. albo-sinensis*; f. *B. callosa*

Plate 72

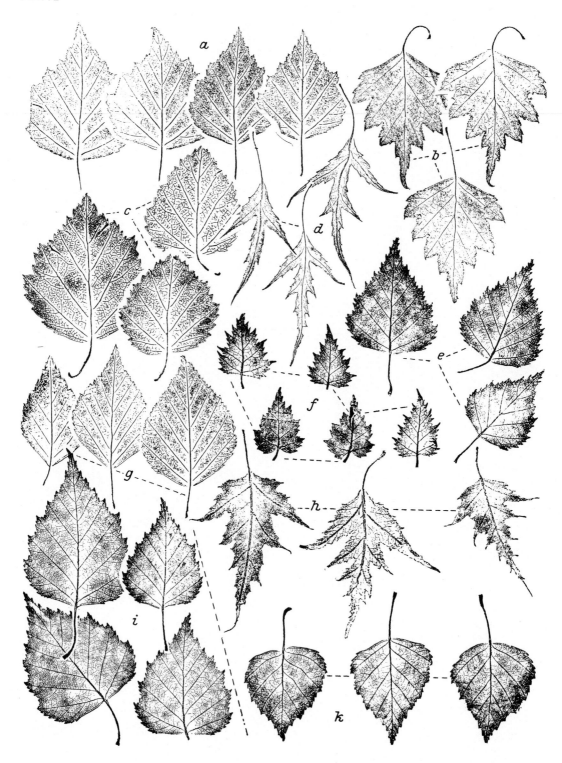

Betula. a. *B. obscura*; b. *B. verrucosa* 'Birkalensis'; c. *B. pubescens* var. *carpatica*; d. *B. verrucosa* 'Gracilis'; e. *B. verrucosa* 'Tristis'; f. *B. verrucosa* 'Viscosa'; g. *B. pubescens*; h. *B. verrucosa* 'Dalecarlica; in *B. verrucosa*; k. *B. verrucosa* 'Youngii'

Plate 73

Camellia japonica 'Gloire de Nantes'
in the Hillier Arboretum, England

Ceanothus thyrsiflorus
in Kew Gardens, London, England

Cercis chinensis
in the Les Barres Arboretum, France

Cercis racemosa
in the Les Barres Arboretum

Plate 74

Cestrum elegans

Clematus koreana f. *lutea*
in the Dortmund Botanic Garden, W. Germany

Chaenomeles speciosa 'Simonii'
in Cornwall, England

Clerodendrum bungei

Plate 75

Clematis fruticosa
in the Nikita Botanic Garden, Crimea

Clematis 'Vyvyan Pennell'

Clianthus puniceus
in a garden in Southern England

Cornus capitata in fruit in the Villa Taranto
Botanic Garden, Pallanza, North Italy

Plate 76

Cornus alternifolia 'Variegata'

Cornus controversa 'Variegata'
in the gardenof Dunloe Castle, Ireland

Cornus florida with pink flowers
in a garden in N. America

Cornus nuttallii

Plate 77

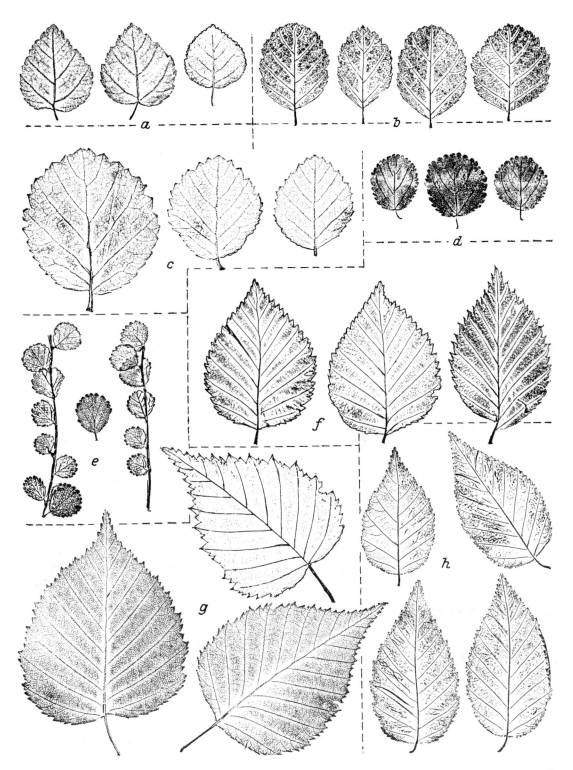

Betula. a. *B. fennica;* b. *B. humilis;* c. *B. middendorffii;* d. *B. glandulosa;* e. *B. nana;* f. *B. globispica;* g. *B. ermanii;* h. *B. schmidtii*

Plate 78

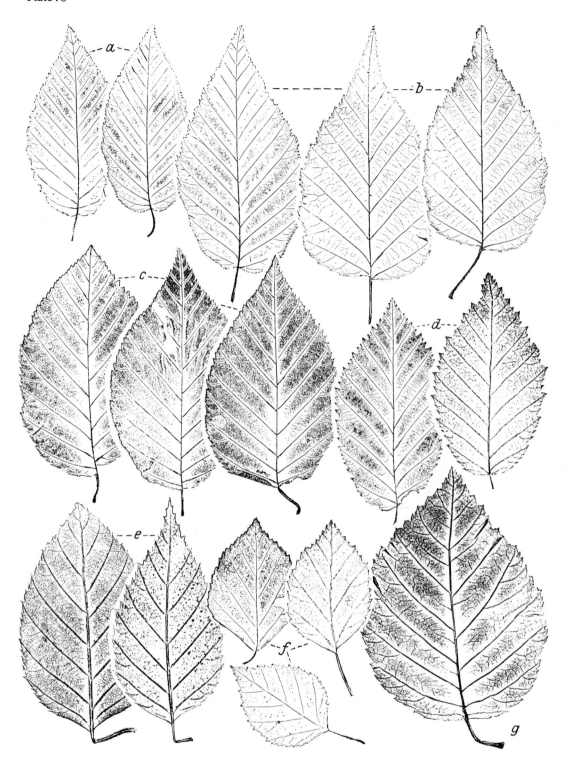

Betula. a. *B. lenta*; b. *B. coerulea-grandis*; c. *B. alleghaniensis*; d. *B. allegheniensis* var. *fallax*; e. *B. luminifera*; f. *B. turkestanica*; g. *B. medwediewii*

Plate 79

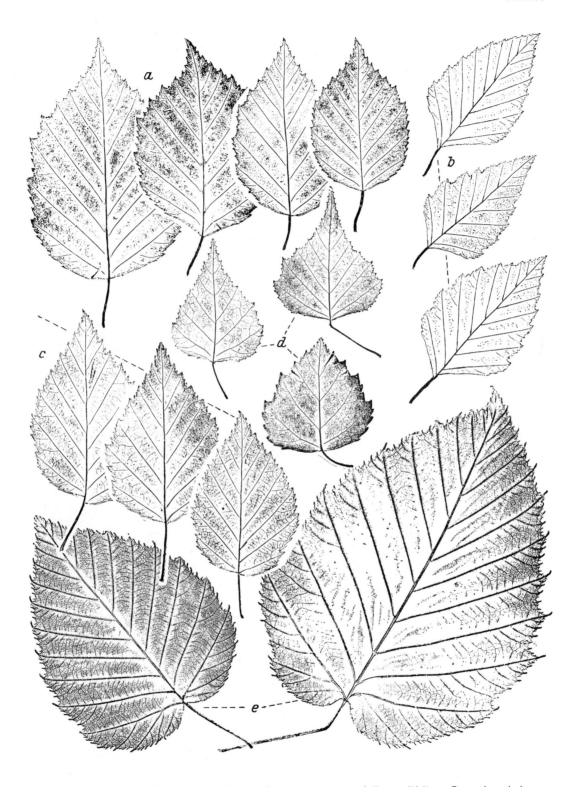

Betula. a. *B. papyrifera*; b. *B. nigra*; c. *B. papyrifera* var. *commutata*; d. *B. populifolia*; e. *B. maximowicziana*

Plate 80

Betula maximowicziana, male flower catkins
Photo: C. R. Jelitto

Betula nana, twigs
Archivbild

Bischofia trifoliata
in the Suchumi Botanic Garden, USSR

Boehmeria nivea 'Candicans'
in the Dortmund Botanic Garden, W. Germany

long, lobes irregularly serrate, middle lobe lanceolate, petiole 2.5—4 cm long, leaves and ∅ anch tips pendulous (= *B. laciniata*). First found in a forest near Lilla Örnaes in Dalecarlien, S. Sweden, 1767. Plate 72.

'Fastigiata'. Growth narrowly columnar upright (like a very narrow 'Lombardy Poplar'), twigs twisting; leaves normal, deep green, abscising late. Plate 70.

'Gracilis'. Grows tree-like, but seldom over 5—6 m high, without a dominant leader, branches weeping in wide arches, twigs very thin, clustered like a 'pony tail' at the ends of the branches; leaves deeply lobed, finer than 'Darlecarlica'; much rarer in gardens than the latter (= *B. verrucosa elegans gracilis* Hort.; *B. laciniata gracilis pendula* Hort.). First recognized in Moscow in 1888. Plate 70, 72. ∅

'Obelisk' (A. van der Bom 1956). Columnar with many strong, straight branches, bark an attractive pure white; foliage somewhat persistent. Found in the wild near Arras, N. France. Introduced to the trade by V. D. Bom.

var. oycoviensis (Bess.) Dipp. Shrub, twigs densely glandular; leaves ovate to broad oval-rhombic, base usually broadly cuneate, acute, coarsely doubly or irregularly serrate, 1.5—3 cm long, the upper leaves 3—3.5 cm long, petiole 1—1.5 cm long; fruit catkins 1.5—2 cm long. Galicia, NE. Hungary, valley of Oycow. Found in 1809.

'Purple Splendour' (Belcher, USA). Growth upright at first, 2nd year branches pendulous; young leaves purple, later deeper green, bark white in the 2nd year. US plant patent 2107. Chance seedling found by D. Belcher, Powell Valley Nurseries, Gresham, Oregon, USA. ∅

'Purpurea'. Leaves dark red, more bronze-green in fall.

'Tristis'. Tall tree, always (even on young plants) with a straight leader, side branches lengthen rapidly and arch widely, crown tall ovate; leaves normal. 1904. Plate 70, 72. ∅

'Viscosa; (Chenault). Shrub or seldom a small tree, much branched, twigs and leaves very viscid; very dense foliage, nearly triangular, often somewhat bowed, 2—3 cm long, coarsely doubly serrate to lightly lobed (= *B. dentata viscosa pyramicalis* Hort.). Brought into the trade by Chenault in 1912. Plate 72. ∅

'Youngii'. Markedly weeping form; usually grafted on a standard with an umbrella-like crown, or grafted low and trained up with support, thus becoming conical, twigs thin, thread-like; leaves triangular, long acuminate, usually doubly serrate, base broad cuneate. Plate 70, 72. ∅

B. wilsoniana see: **B. luminifera**

B. wilsonii see: **B. potaninii**

B. wutaica see: **B. davurica**

The following Scandinavian *Betula* forms are covered and illustrated by Hylander (1957):

	Pl.	
B. verrucosa f. *serrata* (Morner) Neum.		1
— f. *subdalecarlica* Lindb. f.		2
— f. *crispa* (Rchb.) Holmberg		3—5
— f. *dalecarlica* (L.f.) C. Hartm.		6—7
— f. *serratolobulata* Hyl.		8
— f. *lobulata* (C. Anders.) Larss.		9
— f. *bircalensis* mela.		10
— f. *irregularis* Holmberg		10—11
— f. *subarbuscula* Hyl.		12
— f. *arbuscula* Fr.		13—14
— f. *palmeri* (Gunnarss.) Hyl.		15
— f. *sellandii* Holmboe		16—17
B. pubescens f. *integrifolia* (Larss.) Hyl.		18
— f. *incisa* A. Helmsb.		19—20
— × *verrucosa* nm. *incisa* (Brenn.) Hyl.		21
— × *verrucosa* nm. *lamiifolia* Hyl.		22
— × *verrucosa* nm. *rigida* (Gunnarss.) Hyl.		23
— × *verrucosa* nm. *urticulifolia* (Loud.) Hyl.		24—25
— × *verrucosa* nm. *hjelmqvistiana* Hyl.		26—27
— × *verrucosa* nm. *mirabilis* Hyl.		28

The birches are generally adaptable to many soil types, however, they prefer a light sandy soil. Many will tolerate moist areas, even swamps. Most need sunny locations in open space for best development. Very decorative in winter for their ornamental bark.

Lit. Butler, B.; The western American birches; in Torrey Bot. Club Bull. 3, **36**, 421—440, 1909, ill. ● Fernald, M. L.: Some North American *Corylaceae* (Betalaceae). I. Notes on *Betula* in eastern North America; in Rhodora **47**, 303—329, 1945, ill. ● Fontaine, E. J.: Het geslacht *Betula*; in Belmontiana **13**, 99—180, 170 ● Gunnarsson, J. G.: Monografi oever Skandinaviens *Betulae*; Malmoe 1925; with 32 plates ● Hylander, N.: On cut-leaved and small-leaved forms of Scandinavian birches; in Svensk. Bot. Tidskr. **51**, 417—436, 1957, with 28 plates ● Regel, E.: Monographia Betulacearum hucusque congitarum; Mém. Soc. Natur. Moscow **13**, 1861 ● Winkler, H.: *Betula*; in Engler, Pflanzenreich IV, **61**, 56—101, 1904.

BIGELOWIA DC.

Bigelowia graveolens see: **Chrysothamnus graveolens**

BIGNONIA L. — BIGNONIACEAE

Evergreen, high climbing vines; leaves opposite, with paired opposite leaflets and 3 parted tendrils, terminating in holdfasts; flowers solitary or grouped, axillary, large, corolla tubular, large, throat more campanulate, limb 2 lipped, flared; seed elliptic, winged, several in a linear capsule. — 1 species in N. America.

Bignonia capreolata L. High climbing, occasionally to 20 m, glabrous vine; leaflets paired, oblong-lanceolate, somewhat rigid, 5—10 cm long, blunt acuminate, entire, base cordate; flowers 2—5 in stalked cymes; corolla tube orange-red, inside somewhat lighter, 4—5 cm long, May—June; calyx campanulate, with 5 ovate lobes; fruit a 15 cm long, flat, thin pod. Bureau, Monogr. Bign. Pl. 6 (= *B. crucigera* L. p. p.; *Doxantha capreolata* Miers). SE. USA. 1710. z8 ⊕

'Atrosanguinea'. Leaves longer and narrower; flowers deep

purple-brown, the limb tips short and oval-triangular. BM
6501 (= *B. atrosanguinea* Hort.). Fig. 158.

Needs a protected 'practically frost' free area. Develops
beautifully in good soil. In greenhouse culture requires good
ventilation during the summer.

Remarks: The earlier genus *Bignonia*, by Bentham & Hooker
included about 150 species which were later subdivided into a
number of new genera by Schumann (in Engler & Prantl).
Therefore garden literature occasionally still cites a *Bignonia*
from the old classification. Following is a list reflecting the
modern nomenclature:

Bignonia australis	— **Pandorea pandorana**
B. callistegioides	— **Clytostoma callistegioides**
B. capensis	— **Tecomaria capensis**
B. chamberlaynii	— **Anemopaegma chamberlaynii**
B. cherere	— **Phaedranthus buccinatorius**
B. chinensis	— **Campsis grandiflora**
B. grandiflora	— **Campsis grandiflora**
B. ignea	— **Pyrostegia ignea**
B. jasminoides	— **Pandorea jasminoides**
B. lactiflora	— **Distictis lactiflora**
B. pandorana	— **Pandorea pandorana**
B. purpurea	— **Clytostoma purpureum**
B. radicans	— **Campsis radicans**
B. rugosa	— **Anemopaegma rugosum**
B. speciosa	— *Clytostoma callistegioides*
B. tweediana Lindl.	— **Doxantha unguis-cati**
B. unguis-cati	— **Doxantha unguis-cati**
B. variabilis	— **Pleonotoma variabilis**
B. venusta	— **Pyprostegia ignea**

Fig. 158. *Bignonia capreolata* 'Atrosanguinea' (from Bot. Mag.)

BILDERDYKIA Dumort. — POLYGONACEAE

B. aubertii (L. Henry) Moldenke see: **Polygonum aubertii**

B. baldschuanica (Regel) D. A. Webb see: **P. baldschuanicum**

Bildderdykia is occasionally found in garden literature for the
vining *Polygonum* species. According to C. W. Willis' "Dictionary", both have been replaced by **Fallopia** Adans.

BILLARDIERA Sm. — PITTOSPORACEAE

Twining vines, stem very thin; leaves evergreen, alternate, usually lanceolate, entire; flowers solitary or
several at the branch tips, pendulous, somewhat
campanulate, 5 petals, usually connate on the basal
half, normally yellow, 5 sepals; fruit an edible berry
with numerous seeds. — 9 species in Australia, usually
as understory plants.

Billardiera longiflora Labill. Twining to several meters
high, twigs finely pubescent when young or
completely glabrous; leaves narrowly elliptic to
oblanceolate, 1.5—4.5 cm long, obtuse, tapering to a
fine petiole; flowers solitary, pendulous, greenish-
yellow, often later turning pink, 1.5—3.5 cm long, July;
fruits usually blue (but also with red and white forms),

Fig. 159. *Billardiera longiflora* from Curtis)

ovate to nearly globose, 2 cm long, ripening in October. BS 1: 436; CTa 16. Tasmania. 1810. For milder areas. z8 Fig. 159. # ⚭

B. scandens Sm. Similar to the above, but with leaves oval-lanceolate, 2.5 cm long, margin undulate, glabrous above, scattered pubescence beneath; flowers greenish, light yellow or lilac, 1.5—2.5 cm long, petals flared (somewhat campanulate); fruit 1.5 cm long, cylindrical, green or yellow, occasionally red, pubescent. DRHS 279; BC 554. Tasmania. More demanding than the previous species. z8 #

Useful as vines for walls in mild areas. Need well drained soil and semishade. Propagated from cuttings.

BISCHOFIA Blume — BISCHOFIACEAE

Tropical trees, leaves alternate, 3 parted (trifoliate), stipules abscising early; flowers dioecious or monoecious, axillary panicles; sepals 5, imbricate; petals absent; ovaries 3 chambered, with 2 ovules in each chamber; style linear, entire; fruit a globose drupe (= *Bischoffia* Blume). — 2 species in India, China, Taiwan and Polynesia.

Bischofia trifoliata Bl. A tree in the wild, ovate crowned; leaves trifoliate, leaflets on petiolules, elliptic, acuminate, 3—6 cm long, crenate, dark green, later becoming more bronze-green, red before leaf drop; flowers yellowish-green, short stalked, not very conspicuous, appearing just after the new leaves, March—April; fruit ripening early the following year, globose, 1 cm. HKT 14; HI 844 (= *B. javanica* Bl.). Tropical India, S. China, Polynesia; frequently found in forests on moist, shady slopes. Also planted as an ornamental. z9 Ⓕ S. China. Plate 80.

BOEHMERIA Jacq. — URTICACEAE

Subshrubs, shrubs or small trees; leaves without stinging hairs, alternate or opposite, petioled, equal or unequal blade halves or 2 lobed; flowers monoecious or dioecious, singular or in axillary panicles; female flowers with tubular-convex, 2—4 toothed perianth, male flowers with 4—5 parted perianth; fruit an indehiscent achene with a crusty shell. — Some 50 species in the tropics, also in N. America and E. Asia.

Boehmeria nivea (L.) Gaud. "Ramie". Subshrub, to 2 m high, multistemmed, stems usually not branched, white-gray pubescent at the apex, base glabrous; leaves opposite, all of similar form and both blade halves even, broadly ovate, 8—15 cm long, coarsely crenately dentate, dark green and gritty above, snow-white beneath, short tomentose, petiole 5—15 cm long; flowers monoecious, in 5—15 cm long, pendulous panicles of numerous globose heads. China, Japan. z7 ∅

'Candicans'. Like the species, but the twigs short pubescent; leaves greenish beneath, not white. Plate 80.

Of economic importance in China and Japan (as well as other areas) in the production of cloth and cordage. Also used to produce a fine machine oil.

In cultivation, best handled as a perennial, cut back in fall, tolerates −15°C without protection. Needs good garden soil.○

Lit. Karpawiczowa, L.: Rami (*Boehmeria nivea*); 42 pp. Warsaw 1954.

BOENNINGHAUSENIA Reichb. ex Meissn. — RUTACEAE

Subshrubs, closely related to *Ruta* and *Dictamnus*; with translucent glands; leaves alternate, 2 or 3 pinnate-trifoliate, leaflets entire; flowers in compound panicles, with leafy base, flowers with 4 small sepals, connate at the base, 4 petals, 6—8 stamens; fruits originate from 4 carpels, connate at the base, later a valvate capsule, dehiscent on the ventral side. — 2 species in E. Asia and India; occasionally found in botanic gardens.

Boenninghausenia albifloora (Hook.) Reichb. Deciduous subshrub, 50—80 cm high, young twigs hollow, all parts glabrous; leaves alternate, 2 to 3 pinnate-trifoliate, 7—15 cm long, long petioled, leaflets numerous, from 7—50 or more, obovate to elliptic, apex rounded, entire, from 2.5 × 1.5 cm to only 6 × 4 mm in size, with translucent oil glands, short stalked or sessile, unpleasant smelling if crushed; flowers in loose panicles, to 30 cm long and 20 cm wide on the current year's wood, the individual flowers small, about 1 cm long, pure white, with 4 long petals, yellow patterned at the base, July—August. BS 1: 437 (= *Ruta albiflora* Hook.). E. Asia, from Himalaya to Japan. 1885. z8 Fig. 160. ✥

Fig. 160. *Boenninghausenia albiflora* (from ICS)

Beautiful ornamental plants, culture somewhat like that of *Fuchsia*, for good garden soil, not too dry, tolerates alkalinity; propagates readily from cuttings or seed.

BOTRYOSTEGE Stapf — ERICACEAE

Monotypical genus; very closely related to *Tripetaleia* and usually classified as such, but differing in the relatively few flowered inflorescences in simple racemes, distinctly leaf-like subtending bracts, 5 distinct, oblong sepals and sessile capsules (distinctly stalked on *Tripetaleia*). — Japan.

Botryostege bracteata (Maxim.) Stapf. Deciduous shrub, many branched, 1–1.5 m high, young twigs red-brown, somewhat striped, glabrous; leaves alternate, obovate, 2.5–6 cm long, 1 to 2 cm wide, usually rounded with small tip (mucronulate), both sides glabrous, but with ciliate margin when young; racemes with 3–8 flowers, 6–10 cm long, flowers greenish white, with 3 oblong, reflexed, 8–10 mm long petals, in the axils of 1 cm long bracts or subtending leaves, July–August; fruit a 3 valved capsule. BS 1: 438; MJ 772 (= *Tripetaleia bracteata* Maxim.). Japan, generally found in the higher mountains of Honshu and Hokkaido. 1877. z6 ⊕

Cultivated like Azaleas; fully winter hardy, without great ornamental value, but of botanical interest for its flowers with only 3 petals.

BOUGAINVILLEA Comm. ex Juss. — NYCTAGINACEAE

Shrub or vine, with or without thorns; leaves alternate, ovate to more elliptic-lanceolate, stalked, entire; flowers axillary or terminal, grouped 1–3 together, each with persistent stalk, often with colorful bracts, flowers bisexual; perianth tubular and slightly bowed, narrow spindle-like below the middle, then narrow funnelform; stamens 7–8 (5–10), very uneven, seldom reaching past the corolla; aggregate fruit spindle shape to pear shape, surrounded by the persistent bracts. — 18 species in S. America, but only 3 in cultivation. Positive identification is difficult because of the considerable variability of the species and hybrids, especially *B. glabra* and *B. speciosa*.

Key (from Pancho & Bardenas)

Perianth, leaves and twigs glabrous to more or less pubescent, the hairs 0.8mm or less in length;
● Perianth, leaves and twigs glabrous, except for the undersides of the flared limb; tube less than 1 mm wide:
      B. peruviana
●● Perianth, leaves and twigs finely pubescent, 1 mm wide or wider;
      + Leaves broadly ovate; bracts orange, yellow, purple, scarlet or carmine; very crispate on the margin:
      B. × buttiana
      ++ Leaves nearly evenly elliptic; bracts white, purple to violet-purple, spent flowers becoming lighter or not; less crispate on the margin:
      B. glabra
Perianth, leaves and twigs pubescent, hairs 1.3 mm long or longer; bracts pink, purple or red:
      B. spectabilis

Bougainvillea × buttiana Holttum & Standley (*B. peruviana × B. glabra*). Climbing shrubs; leaves broad ovate, 11.5 cm long and 8 cm wide, acuminate, underside lighter, glabrous, midrib somewhat pubescent; bracts purple, 3.5 cm long and nearly as wide, glabrous except for the fine pubescent venation; corolla tube to 2.2 cm long, narrowing past the middle, the lower portion widest at just past its midpoint, 2 mm wide, angular, pubescent. Bai 1959: 95. z9 # ⊕

The following are a few of the many cultivars:

● Bracts orange or yellow

'Golden Glow. Sulfur-yellow. Possibly a yellow mutation of 'Mrs. Butt'.

'Louis Wathen'. Orange-yellow to reddish.

'Mrs. McClean'. Apricot-orange to reddish-orange.

●● Bracts purple, carmine, scarlet or deep red

'Miss Luzon'. Scarlet to garnet-red.

'Miss Manila'. Carmine.

'Mrs. Butt'. Purple (= 'Crimson Lake'; 'Presas'). The 'type' of the hybrids.

'Pigeon Blood'. Dark brown-red.

'Scarlet Queen'. Amaranth-purple.

B. glabra Choisy in DC. Leaves nearly evenly elliptic, to 13 cm long and 6 cm wide, both sides glabrous or sparsely pubescent, most cultivars with foliage glossy above, others dull, much lighter beneath with elevated, lightly pubescent venation; bracts white to purple, spent flowers fading or not; corolla tube distinctly swollen, 5 sided, with short, upward curving pubescence, summer flowering. BC 605; BIC 267; Bai 1959: 96. Brazil. 1861. z9 Widely used as a pot plant, landscape plant in frost free areas.

Also containing many cultivars with the most popular being:

● Bracts persisting after the flowers

'Snow White'. White.

'Formosa'. Light purple-pink, tube 5–6 mm wide, semi-climber.

'Lady Huggins'. Light amaranth-pink, tube 3 mm wide. Lightest colored form.

'Sanderiana'. Purple, bracts rather triangular. Most common form in cultivation.

'Penang'. Violet purple, bracts more elliptic (= 'Dwarf Gem'). Darkest form.

'Variegata'. Leaves white variegated.

●● Bracts abscising after blooming.

'Cypheri'. Dark pink, bracts very large, inflorescence large.

'Pink Beauty'. Light mallow-pink.

'Magnifica'. Strong purple, leaves very glossy.

'Mrs. Leano'. Intensive red. Blooms in the driest part of summer. Very beautiful form.

B. peruviana Humb. & Bonpl. Leaves broad ovate, to 10.5 cm long and 8 cm wide; bracts light magenta-pink, lightly wrinkled, to 3.5 cm long and 2 cm wide, venation not green; corolla tube slender, glabrous except for the underside of the flared lobes. Bai 1959: 27. S. America; Peru, Columbia, Ecuador. Often found in gardens under the names 'Lady Hudson', 'Princess Margaret Rose' and 'Ecuador Pink'; these not differing from one another or from the species. z9 # ⊕

B. spectabilis Willd. Stronger growing than the other species, twigs with large, hook-like thorns, leaves ovate, to 10 cm long and 6 cm wide or larger, densely tomentose on both sides; bracts purple; corolla tube less distinctly angular, often covered with erect pubescence, March—June. Bai 1959: 98. Brazil. 1892. z9 # ⊕

Including 2 cultivars:

'**Lateritia**'. Bracts brick-red, to 3.5 cm long or less. IH 466.

'**Thomasii**'. Bracts pink.

The culture of *Bougainvillea* in the landscape is very simple. They need only full sun, warm summers and frost free winters. They are not particular as to soil type.

Lit. Pancho, J. V., & E. A. Bardenas: *Bougainvillea* in the Phillippines; Baileya 7, 91—101, 1959; with descriptions of many cultivars.

BOUVARDIA Salisb. — RUBIACEAE

Evergreen shrubs or perennials; leaves opposite or in whorls, simple, stipules growing from both sides of the petiole; flowers terminal, 3 on a peduncle or in corymbs on 3 branched stalks; perianth funnel form or tubular, tube long, velvety outside, limb with 4 short, flared lobes; stamens 4, tube jointed, carpels 2, style with 2 stigmas; fruit a capsule. — Some 50 species in tropical America; but generally hybrids in cultivation. Most hybridizing has been done in S. England where *B. ternifolia* is hardy. These plants, however, have been somewhat 'out of fashion' for the past 50 years and therefore not widely cultivated.

Bouvardia longiflora H.B.K. Glabrous shrub, to 90 cm, well branched; leaves opposite, oblong, acute, cuneate at the base; flowers white, 4—8 cm long, tube form, very fragrant, limb flared wide, solitary or 2—3 in the axils of the highest leaves, or grouped in terminal corymbs, August—October. BM 4223; FS 123; HTS 81 (= *B. humboldtii* hort.). Mexico. 1827. z9 # ⊕

B. ternifolia (Cav.) Schlect. Small shrub, 0.5—1 m; leaves in whorls of 3 or 4, occasionally also opposite, lanceolate to oval-lanceolate, glabrous above, pubescent beneath; flowers scarlet-red, pubescent, some 2.5 cm long, in corymbs, May—November. BM 3781 (as *B. splendens*) (= *B. triphylla* Salisb.; *B. jacquinii* H.B.K.). Mexico to Arizona and Texas, on dry soil in the mountains. 1794. z9 # ⊕

Frost free winters required.

BOWKERIA Harv.— SCROPHULARIACEAE

Evergreen shrubs, very closely related to *Scrophularia*, but becoming woody. Characteristics as mentioned in the species description. — 8 species in S. Africa, but only the following in cultivation.

Bowkeria gerardiana Harvey. Evergreen shrub, upright, becoming 1—2 m high or more, twigs with fine gray pubescence; leaves sessile, in whorls of 3, oval-lanceolate, long acuminate, dentate, 10—15 cm long, 4—6 cm wide, dull green, somewhat pubescent on both sides; flowers in small, axillary cymes; corolla resembling that of *Calceolaria*, but pure white, 2 lipped, 2 cm wide, upper lip 2 lobed, lower lip 3 lobed, July to August; inflorescence very viscid. BM 8021 (= *B. triphylla* hort. non Harvey). Natal. 1890. z9 # ⊕

Only for very mild areas.

BRACHYCHITON Schott & Endl. — STERCULIACEAE

Evergreen tree, resembling *Sterculia*; leaves alternate, stipules abscising; flowers monoecious or polygamous, usually in panicles; calyx more or less deeply 5 lobed, petaloid, petals absent; filaments grouped in a column on the male flowers, the anthers grouped in 5 bundles and forming a globose head; female flowers with 5 pubescent carpels; fruit composed of 5 beaked woody follicles. — 11 species in Australia, some in cultivation in warmer climates.

Brachychiton acerifolium F. v. Muell. "Flame Tree". Large forest tree in its habitat; leaves long petioled, broad 5—7 lobed, 20—30 cm wide, the lobe oblong-lanceolate to nearly diamond shape; flowers campanulate, scarlet-red, in loose racemes or small panicles; calyx 2 cm long, glabrous, broad lobed; fruits composed of long stalked follicled capsules. MCL 10; SDK 4: 115. Australia; New South Wales. z9 # ⊕

B. discolor F.v. Muell. A tall tree in its habitat, to 12 m or more, twigs and leaves thinly pubescent; leaves irregularly 5 to 7 lobed, 10—15 cm wide, base broadly cordate, underside lighter to white; flowers grouped 1—3, calyx broad funnel-form, 3 cm long, deeply 6 lobed, pink inside, outside rust brown pubescent, August. MCL 11; LAu 18; AAu 152; BM 6608. Australia. 1858. z9 # ⊕

B. populneum (Cav.) R. Br. "Kurrajong". Tree, 6—15 m high; leaves variable in form, some ovate and simple, some lanceolate or (most) 3(−5) lobed, the middle lobe longer than the side lobes, all long acuminate, petioles long and thin; flowers in irregular, some 10 cm long, axillary panicles; calyx broadly campanulate, some 1.5 cm wide, yellowish white to green, red punctate in the middle. SDK 4: 115 (= *B. diversifolium* G. Don). E. Australia. 1824. z9 # ✧

A forest tree in its habitat, also used as a street tree; occasionally found in warmer climates as a park tree.

BRACHYGLOTTIS J. R. & G. Forst — COMPOSITAE

Monotypic genus; evergreen tall shrub, or in its habitat, also a small tree; leaves alternate, large, sinuate or shallowly dentate; flowers in heads, these grouped in large panicles; ray florets not conspicuous. — New Zealand.

Brachyglottis repanda J. R. & G. Forst. Evergreen shrub, to 6 m or more in its habitat, twigs stiff, widespread, easily broken; leaves broad ovate in outline, from 5 × 5 to 20 × 25 cm in size, obtuse, base obliquely cordate to truncate, irregularly sinuate margin, deep green above, densely white tomentose beneath; flowers tiny, only 4 mm long and wide, greenish-white, but in terminal, 25 cm long and 30 cm wide panicles, spring. BM 8037. New Zealand. 1890. z8 Plate 38; Fig. 161. # ✧ ⌀

'**Purpurea**'. Leaves purple above, white beneath, otherwise like the species. Found in the wild in New Zealand. z8 # ⌀

'**Variegata**'. Leaves dark green, irregular, yellow-green, gray-green, and cream yellow markings in the middle. MNZ 14. z8 # ✧ ⌀

var. **rangiora** (Buchan.) Allan. Differing from the species in the 35 cm long and 30 cm wide leaves, blade more leathery tough, glossier above, margin not so irregularly sinuate; involucre with purple scales. MNZ 14 (= *B. rangiora* Buchan.). New Zealand; on the coast along Cook Straight. z8 # ✧ ⌀

Frequently planted in milder areas and very impressive; prefers dry locations but protected from the wind, which easily damages the leaves.

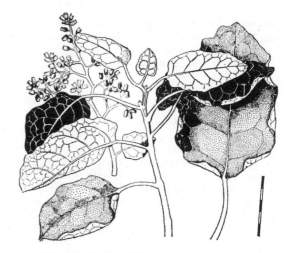

Fig. 161. *Brachyglottisrepanda* (from Adams)

BROUSSONETIA L'Hér. — Paper Mulberry — MORACEAE

Deciduous trees or shrubs; leaves with milky sap, alternate, large, serrate, entire or lobed, often various forms on the same twig; stipules small, abscising; flowers dioecious, male flowers in 4 part perianths, grouped in pendulous catkins, the anthers releasing pollen with a small explosion; female flowers in pitcher shape (urceolate) perianths, style with filamentous stigma; aggregate fruits in globose heads. — 7—8 species in E. Asia and Polynesia.

Broussonetia kazinoki Sieb. Shrub, to 2 m high, but usually much lower, twigs thin, reddish, pubescent only at first, soon completely glabrous (important distinction); leaves ovate, 5—20 cm long, long acuminate, finely serrate, occasionally also 2—3 lobed, rough above, weakly pubescent beneath at first, but soon becoming glabrous, leaf petiole 1 to 2 cm long; fruits red, pubescent. KIF 4: 3 (= *B. sieboldii* Bl.). Korea, Japan. 1884. z7 Fig. 162.

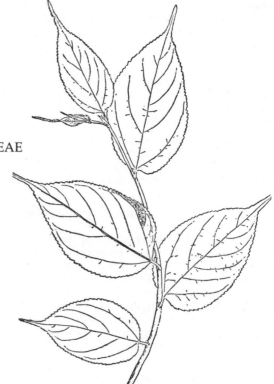

Fig. 162. *Broussonetia kazinoki* (from Ser.)

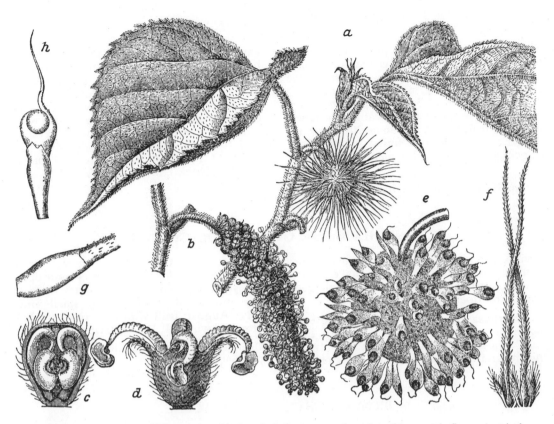

Fig. 163. *Broussonetia papyrifera*. a twig with female inflorescence, b male catkin, c male flower just before opening, d opened, e fruit cluster, f female flowers, g ovary, h single fruit (from Shirasawa, Kerner)

B. papyrifera (L.) L'Hér. A tree in its habitat, to 15 m, only a shrub in European cultivation, to some 3 m, multistemmed, branches gray-red, thick, rigid, pithy, soft pubescent; leaves broad ovate, short acuminate or also 3 lobed, especially on young plants, 7—20 cm long, rough above, soft pubescent beneath, gray-green, petiole 3—10 cm long; flowers in May; fruits globose, orange-red to scarlet, 2 cm wide, unpleasantly sweet. KIF 4: 4; BS 1: 411. Japan, China, 1750. z8 Ⓕ India; Phillippines. Fig. 163. ∅

'Billardii' (Billard, around 1860). Resembles 'Laciniata', but a stronger grower and more upright. RH 1866: 420; 1878: 374.

Originated by Billard in Fontenay-aux-Roses, France.

'Cucullata'. Leaves large, unlobed, irregular, convex.

'Laciniata'. Very weak growing shrublet; leaves usually consisting only of a tiny remnant of a blade at the tip of the midvein. RH 1878: 374. Before 1866. z7

'Macrophylla'. Leaves especially large, normally undivided, cordate at the base. ∅

'Variegata'. Leaves white variegated. ∅

Attractive specimen plants; not particular as to soil type.

BRUCKENTHALIA Reichenb. — ERICACEAE

A genus closely related to *Erica*, but distinguished by the stamens which are basally connate and fused to the corolla; flowers in dense, terminal spikes without bracts. — 1 species in SE. Europe and Asia Minor.

Bruckenthalia spiculifolia (Salisb.) Reichenb. Evergreen shrublet, 10—20 cm high, twigs thin, erect, very dense foliage; leaves opposite or grouped 5 in whorls, at wide angles to the twig, 3—5 mm long, faintly pubescent; flowers light pink, many in terminal, dense 2—3 cm long spikes, July—August; stamens completely enclosed. BS 1: 443; BM 8148. SE. Europe, primarily Romania. 1880. z6 Plate 81. W# **H** ⊙

Uses and cultural requirements like those of *Erica*.

BRUGMANSIA Pers.

Brugmansia candida see: **Datura candida**

BRUNFELSIA L. — SOLANACEAE

Evergreen trees or shrubs; leaves simple, oblong, often glossy; flowers solitary or in terminal clusters or cymes, attractive and beautiful, frequently also fragrant; corolla salverform, with long, narrow tube and very wide, flat limb composed of 5 round, perpendicular lobes; 4 stamens, fused with the throat of the tube, anthers all equal; fruit a berry. — Some 30 species in tropical America, but only one found in frost free gardens. Species as a container plant in botanical gardens.

Brunfelsia pauciflora (Cham. & Schlechtend.) Benth.

var. *calycina* (Benth.) Hook. Evergreen shrub, 1.5—2 m high, well branched and multistemmed from the base; leaves short petioled, elliptic to oval-elliptic, 7—10 cm long, acute, glossy green, lighter beneath; flowers salverform, some 4 cm wide, violet colored on the 1st day, lilac on the 2nd and on the 3rd day white to nearly white (therefore the English name "Yesterday, today and tomorrow"), March—April. MCL 61; BM 4583; HKS 13 (= *B. calycina* Benth.; *Franciscea calycina* [Benth.] Hook.). Brazil. 1850. z9 # ✧

BRUNNICHIA Banks ex Gaertn. — POLYGONACEAE

Deciduous vine, very closely related to *Polygonum*, but twigs terminating in forked leaf tendrils; flowers with persistent calyx, surrounding the ovary and enlarged wing-like until fruit ripening. — Only 1 species.

Brunnichia chirrhosa Gaertn. Vine, climbing to 5 m high (going to the tops of tall trees in its habitat), like climbing buckwheat in appearance, but with twigs terminating in tendrils, twigs glabrous, slender and

furrowed except for the nodes; leaves alternate, ovate, acute, 5—10 cm long, entire, base more or less cordate, glossy dark green above, glabrous; terminal panicles, the individual flowers very small and greenish, July—August; fruit with a narrow, nearly 2 cm long, attached wing. HI 1382. SE. USA. 1787. z6? ✧

Of little ornamental value, but of botanical interest for its peculiar fruits.

BRYANTHUS Gmel. — ERICACEAE

Monotypic genus, earlier included in the genus *Phylodoce*, but distinguished from this and *Loiseleuria* by the 4 sectioned corolla, 4 parted flowers and 8 stamens. — 1 species in N. Japan, Kamchsatka and on the neighboring islands.

Bryanthus gmelinii Don. Evergreen shrublets, mat-like, only some 3—8 cm high, twigs wiry; leaves linear, sparsely finely dentate, 2—3 mm long (very fine and

moss-like), white tomentose beneath; corolla rotate, pink-red, the 4 petals very tiny, only 3—4 mm wide, flowers solitary, terminal, sepals 4, June; fruit a dry capsule. NT 1: 25. z6 W# **H**

Only recently in cultivation; best grown in humus and sphagnum and over wintered in a cold frame. Excellent plant for collectors.

BUCKLEYA Torr. — SANTALACEAE

Deciduous, parasitic shrub; leaves opposite, sessile to short petioled, entire, privet-like in appearance; flowers dioecious; male in small terminal and axillary umbels, with 4 stamen filaments; female flowers solitary, at the ends of short twigs, with 4 small, inconspicuous sepals and club-shape (clavate) calyx tube; with 4 erect bracts immediately beneath the sepals; fruit an elliptic drupe. — 2 or 3 species in N. America, China and Japan.

Buckleya distichophylla (Nutt.) Torr. To 4 m tall, deciduous, privet-like, but ornamental shrub, leaves 2 ranked (distichous), sessile, ovate-lanceolate, 2—6 cm long, long acuminate, margin finely ciliate; flowers small, greenish, inconspicuous, May; fruits ellipsoid, greenish-yellow to dull orange, 1.5 cm long. GF 3: 237. N. America; N. Carolina and Tennessee. 1842. z7 Plate 81.

Exceptionally rare in cultivation, but quite winter hardy. Only specimens in Germany are in the Dortmund Botanic Garden, where some have been cultivated since 1953. The seed was placed on the main root of a containerized *Tsuga canadensis*. Development was slow but consistent, becoming some 1 m high in 1970 and since then producing fruit.

B. lanceolata (S. & Z.) Miq. Shrub, more or less short haired; leaves opposite (not 2 ranked!), ovate, caudate apex, 4—8 cm long, 1.5—3 cm wide; flowers greenish; fruits small, 7—10 mm long, the oblanceolate bracts yellow-green, to 3 cm long, erect. YWP 2: 74. Japan; Honshu, in mountain forests. z7

Lit. Harkness, B.: A trip to Tennessee for *Buckleya*; in Asa Gray Bull. 1953, 297—298.

BUDDLEIA L. (= BUDDLEJA L.) — Buddleia, Butterfly Bush — BUDDLEIACEAE

Deciduous or evergreen shrubs, occasionally also small trees in their native habitat, some subshrubs or only herbaceous; twigs usually 4 sided, leaves normally opposite (*B. alternifolia* is alternate!), lanceolate to ovate, long acuminate, entire or serrate, usually rather large, normally woolly or pubescent, short petioled; flowers in long panicles, heads or false spikes; calyx campanulate, 4 lobed; corolla either short tubular or campanulate to nearly rotate or long cylindrical, with plate-like, 4 lobed limb; stamens 4; fruit a 2 valved capsule with numerous, very small seeds. — Some 100 species, mostly tropical or subtropical and evergreen, especially in E. Asia, and deciduous; only *B. globosa* in S. America.

Key to the most important species and hybrids in cultivation (from Bean)

1. Leaves alternate:
    B. alternifolia
    Leaves opposite — 2
2. Flower heads globose, terminal — 3
    Flowers in racemes or panicles — 4
3. Flowers yellow:
    B. globosa
    Flowers only yellowish with pink tones:
    B. × weyeriana
4. Flowers some 2.5 cm wide:
    B. colvilei
    Flowers much smaller — 5
5. Flowers orange-yellow; leaves entire, white beneath:
    B. madagascariensis
    Flowers not yellow — 6
6. Flower tube curved — 7
    Flower tube straight — 8
7. Leaves 5—10 cm long; flowers purple-violet:
    B. lindleyana
    Leaves 7—15 cm long; flowers pale lilac:
    B. japonica
8. Stamens reaching to near the mouth of the tube — 9
    Stamens reaching to the middle of the tube — 13
9. Tube about twice as long as the width of the limb; twigs 4 sided:
    B. forrestii
    Tube at least 3 times as long as wide — 10
10. Panicles about as long as wide — 11
    Panicles narrow — 12
11. Leaves lanceolate, large toothed:
    B. crispa
    Leaves ovate or with base hastate:
    B. pulchella
12. Twigs, rachis and corolla usually white, woolly:
    B. nivea
    Twigs quickly becoming glabrous:
    B. albiflora
13. Ovary glabrous — 14
    Ovary pubescent — 15
14. Flowers nearly sessile; corolla tips erect:
    B. asiatica
    Flowers distinctly stalked; tips flared outward:
    B. davidii
15. Inflorescences on short branches of the previous year's wood — 23
    Inflorescences at the tips of leafy twigs — 16
16. Panicles many flowered, spike-form — 17

Panicles of few flowers, wider inflorescence — 18
17. Flowers densely packed in upright panicles:
    B. fallowiana
    Flowers in looser, bowed panicles; leaves glabrous above:
    B. stenostachya
18. Leaves auriculate (eared) at the base — 19
    Leaves not auriculate at the base — 20
19. Leaves convex, stellate pubescence above:
    B. salviifolia
    Leaves glossy above, white tomentose beneath:
    B. auriculata
20. Leaves long petioled, with rounded teeth — 21
    Leaves short petioled to sessile, entire — 22
21. Inflorescence compound, with or without small bracts:
    B. crispa
    Inflorescence only 7 cm long, on the current year's wood, with long bracts:
    B. caryopteridifolia
22. Leaves elliptic-lanceolate, inflorescence nearly cylindrical:
    B. heliophila
    Leaves narrow-lanceolate, long acuminate, panicles pyramidal:
    B. officinalis
23. Flowers in dense, globose heads:
    B. tibetica
    Flowers in elongated clusters — 24
24. Flowers in loose, open clusters:
    B. farreri
    Flowers in tight, dense clusters:
    B. sterniana

Buddleia albiflora Hemsl. Deciduous shrub, to 3 m in its habitat, seldom over 2 m in cultivation, growth broad, twigs slightly angular, erect, soon becoming glabrous; purple; leaves lanceolate, long acuminate, 10—20 cm long, unevenly dentate, dense silvery-tomentose beneath; flowers in 20—50 cm long panicles, faintly pubescent, corolla barely twice as long as the calyx, lilac inside, throat orange colored, July—September. ICS 4696 (= *B. hemsleyana* Koehne). Middle and W. China. 1900. Resembling *B. davidii*, but less attractive. z6 Fig. 166 ⊕

B. alternifolia Maxim. Deciduous shrub, growth strong, 2—4 m high in cultivation, a small tree in its habitat, to 6 m, twigs very long and thin, wide spreading and attractively pendulous; leaves alternate, lanceolate, 3—10 cm long, dull dark green above, whitish scabby beneath; flowers in 2.5 cm wide, dense fascicles along the previous year's branches, bright purple-lilac, June. BM 9085. NW. China. 1915. Very attractive and quite hardy. z6 Plate 85. ⊕

'**Argentea**' (Hillier, before 1939). Differing from the species in the silver-white pubescent leaves. ⊘

B. asiatica Lour. Evergreen shrub, twigs rod-like rounded, white or yellowish tomentose; leaves narrow lanceolate, 10—20 cm long, white tomentose beneath; flowers white, in terminal, 15 cm long panicles, very fragrant, February—April. BM 6323; ICS 4698; LWT

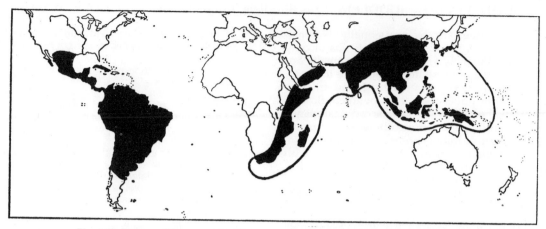

Fig. 164. Range of the genus *Buddleia* (from R. J. Moore, revised and completed)

309. E. India. Landscape use limited to the mildest areas, otherwise a greenhouse plant. z8 # ✧

B. auriculata Benth. Evergreen shrub, 1–2 m high, growth loose and open, twigs thin, scabby at first, later glabrous; leaves lanceolate to ovate-oblong, 5–10 cm long, long acuminate, white tomentose beneath, dull green above, wrinkled, leaf petioles auriculate; flowers in axillary and terminal, rounded, 2.5 cm wide and 3–5 cm long panicles, very fragrant, cream-white, inside yellow, corolla tube densely pubescent outside, calyx gray tomentose, September–January. BM 9409. S. Africa. Easily cultivated, but in colder areas only flowering in a cool greenhouse. z8 Plate 70. # ✧

B. candida Dunn. Shrub, 2–3 m high, entire plant densely white woolly-tomentose, young twigs twisted-round, light brown tomentose at first; leaves narrow lanceolate, rather tough, distinctly rugose above, white tomentose, base abruptly drawn out into the 1 to 1.5 cm long petiole; flowers in long, loose, bowed spikes, violet. E. Himalaya (cultivated by Hillier). z8 ✧ ⌀

B. caryopteridifolia W. W. Sm. Deciduous shrub, to 2 m high, but becoming much wider, young twigs thick white woolly, also the leaf undersides, petiole and calyx; leaves on long shoots ovate, base cordate, large and unevenly dentate, 7–15 cm long, half as wide, white tomentose beneath, yellow-brown tomentose above at first, later becoming glabrous, leaves on the previous year's wood much smaller, tapering to the base; flowers lilac, in 7 cm long, slender panicles, very fragrant, on the previous year's wood, May–June. W. China. 1913. z8 ⌀

B. colvilei Hook. f. Shrub, in its habitat a small tree, young twigs rust-brown woolly at first; leaves oval-lanceolate, acuminate, finely dentate, 7–20 cm long, glabrous above, underside at first brown tomentose, later becoming glabrous; flowers in slightly drooping, some 15–20 cm long and 7–8 cm wide, panicles, corolla some 2.5 cm long, equally wide, carmine-red or pink; calyx campanulate, with short tips, June. BM 7449;

BS 1: 449; FS 1487; HTS 84. Himalaya. 1849. This species has the largest flowers of all *Buddleia* species in cultivation. Gorgeous! z8 Fig. 166. ✧

'**Kewensis**'. Flowers especially intense carmine-red.

B. crispa Benth. ex Wall. Deciduous shrub, 1–1.5 m high, young twigs woolly; leaves ovate-lanceolate, 5–12 cm long, coarsely dentate, base cordate or truncate, woolly on both sides; flowers in 7–10 cm long panicles, fragrant, corolla lilac with white throat, tube 8 mm long, equally wide at the limb, July–August. BM 4793: FS 958; ICS 4699 (= *B. paniculata* C. B. Clarke). N. India. 1850. z8 Plate 82.

B. davidii Franch. Deciduous shrub, 3 to 5 m high, very strong grower, twigs elongating to 2 m in one season, generally freezing back in cold winters, rod-like to slightly angular, finely pubescent; leaves oval-lanceolate, 15–25 cm long, narow panicles, fragrant; calyx pubescent, corolla 3–4 times as long (or more) as the calyx, lilac, throat orange colored, July–October. BM 7609; Add 2: 45. China. 1896. z6 The species is still in cultivation but far surpassed by the many cultivars. The flowers are much sought after by butterflies in summer (hence the common name). Fig. 166.

Very little hybridizing was done between the years 1900 and 1920. In the 1920's and subsequently the following gardeners concerned themselves with the improvement of the species, principally by selection:

Ebben Roeland, Cuyk an der Maas, Holland
Good & Reese, Inc., Springfield, Ohio, USA
Lemoine, V., Nancy, France
Nonin, A., Chatillon-sous-Bagneux, France
Schmidt, Paul, Youngstown 12, Ohio, USA
Schoemaker, Jac., Boskoop, Holland
Tarnok, Sigmund, Nature Gardens, Slidell, Louisiana, USA
Watsons & Sons, Wm., Killiney, Ireland
Winzer Paul A., Emmaus, Penn., U.S.A.

'**African Queen**' (Schoemaker). Dark violet, HCC 735, rather short panicles, 18–22 cm long. 1959. ✧

'**Alba**'. Often occurring as a chance seedling, normally of little merit, white flowers; leaves narrow.

'**Amplissima**' (Lemoine). Dark violet, spent flowers much lighter, panicles in groups of 3—5, some 20 cm long; less than 2 m high. Before 1911.

'**Black Knight**' (Ruys). Flowers blackish-violet, HCC 934, abundant. 1959. ✥

'**Border Beauty**' (Schiphorst 1962). Dark violet-lilac, abundant bloomer; medium size shrub, strongly branched. A. E. Schiphorst, Wageningen, Holland. ✥

'**Burgundy Medium**'. Flowers deep and shining purple-red, color holds well, panicles 20 cm long; leaves deep, dark green.

'**Cardinal**' (Ebben). Deep purple-red, panicles to 20 cm long; leaves light green; medium strong grower, wider than high. Originated from 'Royal Red' by colchicine treatments. ✥

'**Carminea**' (Watsons). Deep lilac-pink; remaining low.

'**Charming**' (Winzer). Pink, HCC 31/2, throat ring orange, panicles long, narrow, loose, strong grower, more upright. Surpassed by 'Fascination'.

'**Dubonnet**' (Schmidt). Dark violet, HCC 34/1, throat ring light orange, panicles to 35 cm long; fruits dull red; strong upright grower. Around 1940. ✥

'**Empire Blue**' (Good & Reese). Violet-blue, HCC 37, best blue to date, panicles 25—30 cm long; strong grower, well branched, some 2 m high. Around 1941. ✥

'**Fascination**' (Schmidt). Cattleya-pink, HCC 629/2, panicles about 30 cm long, occasionally to 80 cm long, 6—8 cm wide; very strong grower. Best pink form. 1940. Sometimes labeled 'Fascinating' in American nurseries. Plate 84. ✥

'**Flaming Violet**' (Schmidt). Deep purple, HCC 31, panicles very large, tight; narrow, upright habit. 1945.

'**Fortune**' (Schmidt). Soft lilac, HCC 634/1, throat orange, fruit clusters and twigs reddish, panicles to 40 cm long; to 2 m high, open branched. 1936. Very often incorrectly labeled. ✥

'**Fromow's Purple**' (Fromow, before 1949). Dark purple-violet, in very large panicles. Surpassed by 'Royal Red' in garden merit. Breeder: Fromow, Windlesham, Surrey, Eng.

'**Harlequin**'. Sport of 'Royal Red'; lower growing, leaves white variegated, new growth yellow variegated; flowers reddish-purple. DB 1965: 112 (= 'Variegated Royal Red'). From England, before 1964.

'**Ile de France**' (Nonin). Violet, HCC 633, panicles to 70 cm long, throat ring yellow, fruit clusters dull red, flowers abundant; leaves light green; very well branched. Around 1930. ✥

'**Imperial Purple**'. Purple-violet with orange colored ring, flowers abundant, panicles 20 cm long, to 7 cm wide; strong grower. ✥

var. **magnifica** (Wils.) Rehd. & Wils. Deep purple-pink, throat ring deep orange, corolla tips reflexed. Collected by Wilson in China for Veitch, 1900. z6

var. **nanhoensis** (Chitt.) Rehd. Only 1—1.5 m high, twigs thin, sparse; leaves lanceolate, to 12 cm long, usually only 5—8 cm; flowers soft lilac, late. Found by R. Farrer in the Nan-ho Valley, Kansu, China and introduced 1914. z6 ✥

'**Nanhoensis Alba**' (H. C. Heps, Belgium, 1967). Differing from the variety by its small, pure white inflorescences; leaves narrow-lanceolate; growth quite low. ✥

'**Opéra**' (Croux). Growth wide and low; flowers violet-lilac, with large orange-red 'eyes', panicles very large. ✥

'**Orchid Beauty**' (Schmidt). Pure mauve colored, panicles very tight; growth wide, low. 1940. Improvement upon var. *magnifica*. ✥

'**Peace**' (Schmidt). Panicles white, very dense, to 55 cm long, 5 cm wide, throat ring yellow; leaves very large and dark green; fruit clusters light green; strong grower. 1945.

'**Pendula**'. (Lemoine). Flowers lilac, HCC 633/2; branches broadly pendulous; leaves very narrow.

'**Pink Pearl**'. Pale lilac-pink, throat ring orange, panicles usually fragmented, to 30 cm long, poor color; growth very compact, scarcely over 1 m high.

'**Purple Prince**' (Schmidt). Deep violet, HCC 33, to 30 cm long, tight, lower portion very thick. 1945. Distinct improvement over 'Ile de France'. ✥

'**Royal Purple**' (Good & Reese). Deep purple; panicles medium size, smaller than 'Flaming Violet' and less effective. Occasionally erroneously listed as 'Royal Red' in the trade.

'**Royal Red**'; (Good & Reese). Purple-red, HCC 30; panicles to 50 cm long, lower portion occasionally fragmented, upper parts very thick; fruits dull red. GC 1928: 50. 1941. The best red form. ✥

'**Royal Red Superior**'. Purple, distinctly less red than 'Royal Red'; a stronger grower. ✥

'**Salicifolia**'. Growth very low and wide; leaves very narrow-lanceolate; flowers pale lilac, like var. *nanhoensis* and a very similar plant.

'**Serotina**' (Lemoine). Like var. *veitchiana*, but very late, blooming in September; growth wider than tall.

var. **superba** (De Corte) Rehd. & Wils. Resembling var. *magnifica*, but with longer panicles; blooming a week later, purple-violet, corolla tips not reflexed. 1909. z6

'**Variegata**'. Leaves white variegated. Less attractive than 'Harlequin'. Originated in England.

var. **veitchiana** (Veitch) Rehd. Panicles heliotrope (moderate purple), dense and large, 30 cm long, bright orange throat ring, earliest to bloom. 1893 (Vilmorin), 1903 (Veitch). z6

'**White Bouquet**' (Tarnok). Pure white, orange throat ring, panicles to 30 cm long, normally bent in the middle; low growing. 1942. Obsolete.

'**White Cloud**'. Flowers white, in small panicles.

'**White Profusion**' (Schmidt). Pure white; long stout panicles. 1945. Most attractive and best white form. ✥

var. **wilsonii** (Wils.) Rehd. & Wils. Leaves long and narrow; inflorescences wide and arching, to 70 cm long, individual flowers small, lilac-pink, corolla tips not reflexed. 1900.

B. fallowiana Balf. f. & W. W. Sm. Deciduous shrub, some 1.5—2 m high, twigs densely white tomentose; leaves oblong-lanceolate, long acuminate, 10—15(—20) cm long, white tomentose above at first (like the twigs), later dark green and glabrous, white tomentose beneath; flowers in erect, terminal, 20—40 cm long panicles, in dense fascicles on the main axis, very fragrant, August—September; stamens attached to the corolla tube at the middle (important distinction from

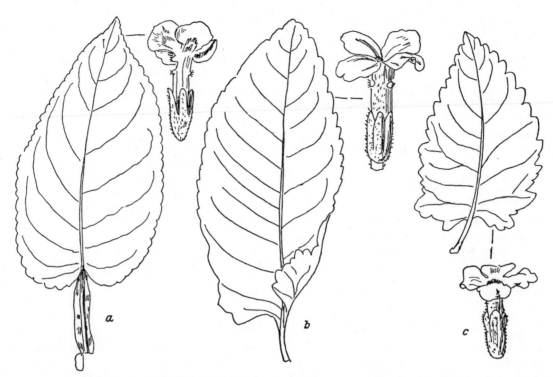

Fig. 165. **Buddleia**. a. *B. tibetica*; b. *B. farreri*; c. *B. sterniana* (from JRHS, revised)

the very similar *B. nivea yunnanensis*, which has stamens attached just below the tube opening). BM 9564; NF 1: 99. W. China, Yunnan. 1915. Usually freezing back every year, but if covered, regenerating well and flowering on young wood. z8 ⌀

'Alba'. Flowers milk white, otherwise like the species. 1920. Very attractive. z8 Plate 82. ⊕ ⌀

In addition, the 3 hybrids of *B. fallowiana* and *B. davidii* originated by the Earl of Stair in Lochinch, Scotland before 1940. All showing better winter hardiness than *B. fallowiana*. Brought to the trade by Messrs. W. J. Marchant, Wimborne, Dorset and the Sunningdale Nurseries, England. A third form was introduced by Hillier, Winchester, England; and lastly one form from Ireland. z7-8

'Glasnevin'. Growth strong, wide; leaves white tomentose on the underside; flowers dark lilac, intermediate between 'Lochinch' and 'West Hill' in color tone. z7-8 ⊕

'Lochinch' (Stair; introduced by Sunningdale 1959). To 2 m high and wide or wider, well branched, young twigs white tomentose; leaves green above, white tomentose beneath; flowers a strong lilac-blue, in 3 branched, fragrant, terminal, long panicles, August to October. z7-8 ⊕

'West Hill' (Hillier 1971). Broad upright shrub, 2–3 m high, well branched; leaves at first gray pubescent above, later nearly glabrous and green, persistent white tomentose beneath; flowers pale lilac, fragrant, in 10–30 cm long, very narrow, bowed panicles, August–October. These plants were earlier erroneously distributed as "*B. fallowiana*". ⊕

B. farreri Balf. f. & W. W. Sm. Deciduous shrub, 2–3 m high, young twigs densely white tomentose; leaves

ovate, those at the branch tips with cordate bases, otherwise cuneate, 7–20 cm long, at first white pubescent above, later dull green, white tomentose beneath; flowers in loose fascicles, in 20 cm long, terminal panicles, on the previous year's wood, April–May; corolla tube pink-lilac, very narrow, some 8 mm long, stamens to the middle of the tube; calyx white woolly. BM 9027; JRHS 1947: 430 (= *B. tibetica* var. *farreri* Marquand). China, Kansu. 1918. z7 Plate 84; Fig. 165. ⌀

B. forrestii Diels. Deciduous shrub, 1 to 2 m high, young twigs rod-like to slightly flattened, scarcely angular, green, somewhat stellate pubescent-tomentose only at first; leaves obovate to oblanceolate, acuminate at both ends, 9–15 cm long (occasionally to 20 cm), blunt toothed, dull dark green above, pale green beneath and dense, finely stellate pubescent-tomentose; flowers in 7–15 cm long, usually only terminal panicles of few flowered fascicles; corolla tube some 1 cm long, 5 mm wide, pink-lilac at first, later yellow-brown, inside orange, tips erect, remaining lilac, August–September. BMns 93 (= *B. taliensis* W. W. Sm.). China, NW. Yunnan. Before 1910. Very attractive, but often mistakenly described species. z7 ⊕

B. globosa Hope. Semi-evergreen shrub, 2–5 m high, twigs yellowish, sparsely tomentose; leaves elliptic-ovate to lanceolate, 8–20 cm long, acuminate, blunt toothed, somewhat rugose, yellowish tomentose beneath; flowers small, attractive yellow, in some 2 cm wide, globose heads, fragrant, usually grouped in small, terminal panicles, June. BM 174; PFC 39. Chile,

Peru. 1774. In colder areas best in a cool greenhouse. z8 Fig. 166. ⊕

B. heliophila W. W. Sm. Deciduous shrub, 2—3 cm high, young twigs rod-like, densely gray tomentose at first, but very soon becoming glabrous; leaves lanceolate or elliptic, long acuminate, tapering to the base, 7—12 cm long, entire, thin, deep green above, thickly white tomentose beneath at first, soon becoming glabrous and bluish, nearly sessile or petiole 5 mm long (important!); flower buds formed at the tips of the short side branches in the fall, developing in the leaf axils, brown tomentose, 3—8 in stalked fascicles, fragrant, grouped in 8—15 cm long panicles, around May—June; corolla tube narrow, 1 cm long, 1.5 mm wide, limb 8 mm wide, lilac-pink, outside (as with the calyx) finely pubescent, tube orange inside. BMns 193; ICS 4701. China, NW. Yunnan. 1913. z8 ⊕

B. hemsleyana see: **B. albiflora**

B. × 'Hotblackiana' (Hotblack) (*B. davidii* var. *veitchiana × B. forrestii*). Resembling the former in appearance, especially the flowers, but the coloration is deep lilac and yellow-brown as with the latter; very early flowering. Gw 1955, Nr. 17, cover photo. Developed before 1952 by H. S. Hotblack, Deakes, Cuckfield, Sussex, England. z7? ⊕

B. × hybrida Farquhar. (*B. asiatica × B. davidii*). Resembles *B. davidii*, but with leaves densely white tomentose beneath, finely serrate; inflorescence slender, corolla tube pubescent outside. Before 1918. z8

'Eva Dudley'. Pale lilac-pink, throat orange. ⊕

B. × intermedia Carr. (*B. japonica × B. lindleyana*). Very similar to *B. lindleyana*; leaves oval-oblong, 8—15 cm long; flowers violet, panicles drooping to pendulous, calyx teeth ovate-lanceolate. RH 1873: 151. Around 1870. z8

'Insignis'. Twigs 4 winged; leaves 6—8 cm long, often arranged in whorls of 3, lanceolate; flowers violet-pink, in erect, dense, 10—15 cm long panicles. RH 1878: 330 (= *B. insignis* Carr.). Around 1875.

B. japonica Hemsl. Deciduous shrub, upright, open branched, twigs 4 sided and winged, red-brown; leaves narrow lanceolate, 10—20 cm long, sparsely dentate, brownish tomentose beneath when young; flowers in nodding, dense, tomentose, terminal panicles, corolla tube bowed, July—August, pale lilac, 1.2 cm long, woolly outside (as with the calyx); fruits abundant, ovate, 8 mm long, brown, with persistent calyx and corolla tube. IH 1870: 25; NT 1: 428 (= *B. curviflora* André). Japan. 1865. Of little garden merit; short lived, must be replaced by new seedlings every few years. z8 Fig. 166.

B. × lewisiana Everett (*B. asiatica × B. madagascariensis*). In general, only for the greenhouse. Twigs white tomentose; leaves lanceolate, dull green, white tomentose beneath, to 17 cm long; flowers in dense, terminal, to 20 cm long panicles, saffron-yellow, HCC 7 (= *B. × madagasiatica* Pike). Winter blooming. z8 #

'Margaret Pike'. The type of the above hybrid. Breeder: V. A. Pike, Threshers Field, Chiddingstone, Kent, England. Before 1953. Plate 83.

B. lindleyana Fort. Deciduous shrub, some 2 m high, well branched, twigs glabrous, 4 sided, narow winged, yellow-brown; leaves ovate, 5—10 cm long, acuminate, seldom dentate, glabrous, light green beneath; flowers in erect panicles, 10—20 cm long, corolla tube bowed, 2 cm long (important for identification!), purple-violet, outside somewhat scabby, limb tips triangular, July—August. FS 112; BR 32:4; ICS 4702. E. China. 1840. z8 Plate 82; Fig. 166.

B. longifolia see: **B. pterocaulis**

B. madagascariensis Lam. Evergreen, loose growing shrub, twigs tomentose; leaves lanceolate, entire, base cordate to round, 15 cm long, yellowish to white tomentose beneath; flowers in 15 cm long, terminal, panicles, orange-yellow, corolla tube thin, 12 mm long, 8 mm wide at the limb, January—May. BM 2824. Madagascar. 1827. z9 # ⊕

B. × madagasiatica see: **B. × lewisiana**

B. nivea Duthie. Shrub, to 3 m high, upright, twiggy, leaf undersides and inflorescences white floccose-tomentose; leaves ovate-lanceolate, 10—20 cm long, acuminate, coarsely dentate, eventually dark green above, underside eventually brownish tomentose; flowers in compound, terminal panicles, 15 cm long, corolla tube dense woolly outside, with prominent purple limb tips, August—September. BS 1: 273. W. China. 1901. Very attractive foliage plant. Often confused with *B. fallowiana*. z7 Plate 85; Fig. 166. ∅

var. **yunnanensis** (Dop) Rehd. & Wils. Like the species, but with less floccose indumentum, more yellow-brown, leaves also pubescent above; flowers larger, inflorescences solitary. W. China. 1908. z7 ∅

B. officinalis Maxim. Semi-evergreen, some 1.5 m high shrub, twigs dense gray woolly; leaves narrow lanceolate, long acuminate, usually entire, 7—15 cm long; flowers in pyramidal, terminal panicles, lilac with yellow throat, fragrant, October to winter. BM 8401; ICS 4703; HI 1972. China; Hupeh and Szechwan. 1908. For greenhouse culture only. z8 Plate 84. #

B. paniculata see: **B. crispa**

B. × pikei Fletcher (*B. alternifolia × B. caryopteridifolia*). Deciduous shrub, to some 1.5 m high, straggly grower (divaricate), twigs, leaves and flowers stellate pubescent; leaves usually opposite, but some also alternate or in whorls of 3, ovate-oblong, to 15 cm long, irregularly lobed to coarsely dentate; flowers in leafy, terminal panicles, purple-pink, throat orange, very fragrant, September. z7 ?

'Hever Castle'. The type of the cross. Resembling *B. alternifolia*, but looser growing. JRHS 1954: 4. Originated 1950 at Hever Castle, England. Plate 83. ⊕

B. pterocaulis A. B. Jacks. Closely related to *B. forrestii*; medium size shrub, leaves longer, long acuminate;

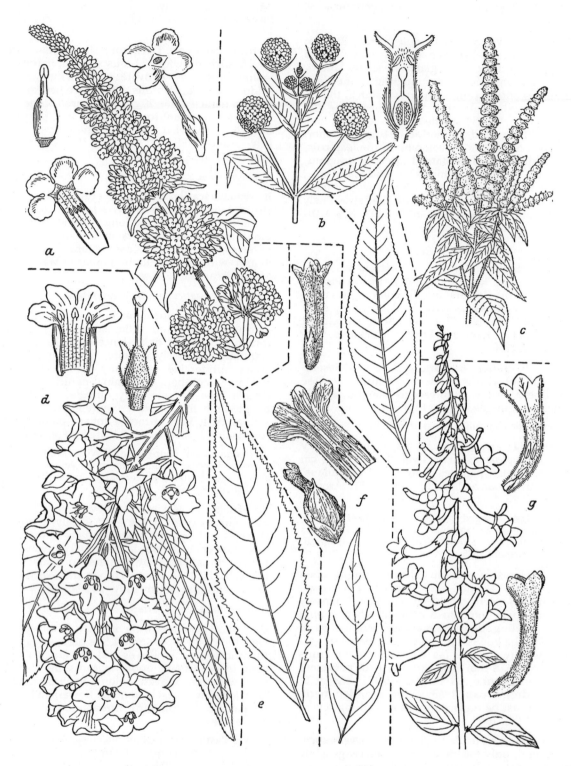

Fig. 166. **Buddleia.** a. *B. davidii*; b. *B. globosa*; c. *B. nivea*; d. *B. colvilei*; e. *B. albiflora*; f. *B. japonica*; g. *B. lindleyana* (from Solereder, Koehne, Schneider, Gard. Chron. and Bot. Mag.)

flowers in long, cylindrical panicles, but a less attractive lilac (= *B. longifolia* Gagnep. non H. B. K.). Himalaya, Upper Burma; Yunnan. z7

B. pulchella N. E. Br. Low shrub, some 0.5 high, twigs rod-like round, white woolly; leaves evergreen, lanceolate, some also hastate, 7–10 cm long, white woolly beneath; flowers gray-white with orange 'eye', in loose, terminal and axillary, 5–7 cm long and equally wide panicles, fragrant. S. Africa; Natal. 1894. z8

B. salvifolia (L.) Lam. Semi-evergreen shrub, to 4 m in its habitat, much lower in N. European gardens, twigs thin, 4 sided, whitish or brown tomentose; leaves lanceolate, nearly sessile, base cordate, 3–10 cm long, upper side *Salvia*-like rugose and stellate pubescent; flowers in 7–15 cm long, terminal panicles on the current year's wood, lilac to white, orange throat, fragrant, July. HTS 82. S. Africa. 1783. z8 Plate 39, 82. #

B. stenostachya Rehd. & Wils. Deciduous shrub, to 2.5 m high, resembles *B. nivea*, but less floccose-tomentose; leaves oblong-lanceolate to oblong-ovate, long acuminate, somewhat dentate or entire, 10–20 cm long, white woolly beneath; flowers usually in narrow, terminal panicles with 2 side panicles, composed of dense, small corymbs, the whole inflorescence 15–40 cm long; corolla tube lilac with orange throat, densely pubescent both inside and out, August–September; stamens attached to the tube in the upper portion. Amer. Jour. Bot. 36: 512 (1949). China, W. Szechwan. 1908. z7

B. sterniana Cotton. Deciduous shrub, strongly branched, 1–2 m high, twigs thin, white pubescent at first, later becoming glabrous; leaves ovate, coarsely dentate, base cordate, 5–8 cm long, eventually glabrous above, densely white pubescent beneath; flowers in axillary, dense, cylindrical, 3–6 cm long clusters (totally different than all the other species!), lilac with large orange 'eyes', April. JRHS 1947: 76. China. 1922. z6 Fig. 165. ⊕

B. tibetica W. W. Sm. Deciduous shrub, 2 m high or more, twigs terete, finely tomentose; leaves broad lanceolate, to 10 cm long, crenate, base cordate, always finely gray pubescent above, white tomentose beneath, coarse reticulate venation, leaf petioles on long shoots broad winged (important for identitication!); flowers in dense, globose, sessile fascicles, purple at

first, later nearly white, fragrant, March–April. JRHS 1947: 429. Tibet. 1931. The earliest flowering of the (relatively) hardy species. z7 Fig. 165. ⊕

B. × weyeriana Weyer (*B. davidii* × *B. globosa*). Deciduous shrub, resembling *B. globosa*, but with flowers gray-yellow to gray or violet, in globose heads, grouped in dense, terminal panicles, July–October; leaves lanceolate, to 20 cm long. Breeder: W. Van De Weyer, Smedmore House, Corfe Castle, Dorset, England. 1914.

'Elstead Hybrid'. Flowers light apricot, throat brown. ⊕

'Golden Glow' (Weyer). Strong grower; flowers pale yellowish-orange with a trace of lilac. HTS 85. ⊕

'Moonlight' (Weyer). Flowers cream-yellow with a trace of lilac-pink and a dark orange throat. ⊕

'Sungold' (P. G. Zwijnenburg 1966). Inflorescences partly globose, but acute on the apex, flowers a good orange. A sport of 'Golden Glow' with much better color, found by Zwijnenburg, Boskoop. ⊕

B. × whiteana R. J. Moore (*B. asiatica* × *B. alternifolia*). Intermediate between the parents; leaves lanceolate, 4–12 cm long, 1 to 2 cm wide, dark green and glabrous above, lighter beneath, as much opposite as alternate or in whorls; flowers in long, narrow, terminal panicles, lilac to orange; Amer. Jour. Bot. 36: 512 (1949). z6

The **Buddleias** include some of the best summer flowering shrubs, as well as the less hardy, spring flowering types (only to be considered for the mildest areas). Since they generally continue to grow up to the first frost, the new growth is usually frozen back. This is, however, of little consequence since most species bloom on the current years growth. The flowers are very attractive to butterflies. All species prefer full sun and good garden soil. Propagation is easily done from cuttings.

Lit. Cotton, A.D.: The spring-flowering *Buddleias*; in JRHS 1947, 247–437 ● Gagnepain, F.: Revision des *Buddleia* d'Asie; in Not. Syst. Lecomte **2**, 182 to 194, 1912 ● Grootendorst, H. J.: *Buddleia*; Keuringsrapport; in Dendroflora **9**, 38–42, 1972 ● Moore, R. J.: Cytotaxonomic studies in the *Loganiaceae*. I. Chromosome number and phylogeny; in Amer. Jour. Bot. **34**, 527–538, 1947; III. Artificial hybrids in the genus *Buddleia* L.; **36**, 511–516, 1949 ● Marquand, C. V. B.: Revision of the old world species of *Buddleia*; in Kew Bull Misc. Inf. 1930, 177–208 ● Norman, E. M.: *Buddleia*; in Gentes Herbarum **10**, 47–114 ● Solereder, H.: *Loganiaceae*; in Engler-Prantl, Nat. Pflanzenfam. **4**, 19 to 30, 1895, including a supplement from R. Pilger in Vol. **3**, 291–292, 1907.

BUGLOSSIS see: **LITHOSPERMUM**

Since this generic name is not officially differentiated from *Lithospermum*, the older classification will be used.

Lit. Imgram, J.: Studies in the cultivated Boraginaceae; 1. *Lithospermum* and related genera; in *Baileya* **6**, 96–99, 1958.

BUMELIA Sw. — SAPOTACEAE

Deciduous shrubs, trees in their native habitat, with milky sap; twigs often thorny; leaves alternate, simple, tough, abscising very late; flowers small, short stalked, in the leaf axils, white, inconspicuous; corolla 5 cleft, campanulate, stamens 5, also with 5 leaf-like staminodes; ovaries 5 chambered; style filamentous; fruit a single seeded, fleshy, globose or oblong berry. — 25 species in SE. N. America.

Bumelia lanuginosa (Michx.) Pers. Tree, to 8 m, usually only a shrub in cultivation, in colder climates, rounded, twigs erect, thorny, thin, flexible; leaves alternate or fascicled, elliptic to narrow lanceolate, entire, sinuate, tough, glossy green above, lighter and brown woolly beneath when young, 3–8 cm long; flowers white, small, in fascicles on the previous years wood, June–July; fruit black, 1.2 cm long, juicy. WT 177; BB 2830. SE. USA. z7 ? ℗ USA, in windbreaks. Fig. 167.

B. lycioides (L.) Pers. Tree, to 8 m, a shrub in European culture, twigs nearly never thorny, glabrous; leaves elliptic, 5–13 cm long, bright green above, lighter beneath and silky pubescent at first, on young plants very similar to peach leaves in size and form, abscising late; flowers many, in fascicles, June–August; fruit black, ellipsoid, 1 cm long, but seldom developed in colder climates. BB 2829. SE. USA. Hardiest species. z6 Fig. 167.

B. tenax (L.) Willd. A tree in its habitat, a shrub in cultivation, very thorny branches, twigs with appressed pubescence and glossy; leaves evergreen, deciduous in colder climates, oblanceolate to spathulate, 4–6 cm long, entire, glabrous above, reticulate venation, dark green, underside with dense yellowish white, appressed silky hairs; flowers numerous, small, white, July; fruit small, oval, blue-black. WT 178. SE. USA. z7

This genus has little value in the garden; likes good soil and warm weather, best covered in winter (with the possible

Fig. 167. **Bumelia.** Upper row, *B. lanuginosa*; lower row, *B. lycioides* (from Sargent)

exception of *B. lycioides*). Branches may be killed back in winter, but re-sprout well in the spring.

Lit. Clark, R.B.: A revision of the genus *Bumelia* in the United States; in Mo. Bot. Gard. Ann. 1942, 155–182 ● Cronquist, A.: Studies in the *Sapotaceae*. III. *Dipholis* and *Bumelia*; in Jour. Arnold Arboretum 1945, 435–471.

BUPLEURUM — UMBELLIFERAE

Annuals, perennials, seldom shrubs; leaves deciduous, rarely evergreen, alternate, the base stem-clasping on many species; flowers in simple or compound umbels; calyx indistinctly toothed; petals wide, bowed inward at the tips; disc flat, entire, style short, much thickened at the base; fruit flattened longitudinally, aggregate fruits with 5 ribs. — Some 100 species in Europe, Asia, Africa and N. America.

Bupleurum fruticosum L. More or less evergreen shrubs, to 1.5 m high, twigs glabrous; leaves narrow elliptic to ovate-oblong, sessile, 5–8 cm long, leathery-tough, entire, bluish-green on both sides; flowers greenish-yellow, small, in numerous, long stalked, erect, compound umbels, 7–10 cm wide, July–August. BMns 408. S. Europe. 1596. z8 Plate 86. # ⊘

B. spinosum Gouan. Sparsely branched, low thorny shrub, to some 30 cm high, older branches stiff, leafless, persisting several years; basal leaves linear-subulate (awl-shaped), with 3–5 veins, distinct on the underside, evergreen, stem leaves similar but smaller. S. and E. Spain. Cultivated only in botanic gardens; interesting but of little ornamental value. z7 #

Of interest only to collectors; need very warm locations and good winter protection. *B. fruticosum* will attract wasps.

BURSARIA Cav. — Australian Boxwood — PITTOSPORACEAE

Evergreen shrubs or small trees; leaves simple, alternate; flowers small, in terminal panicles; sepals 5, petals 5, small, stamens 5; fruit a 2 chambered, thin walled capsule, with only 1 seed in each chamber. — 3 species in Australia.

Bursaria spinosa Cav. Evergreen shrub or small tree (in S. England to 5 m high), short side branches totally covered with thorns; leaves obovate, 2–4 cm long, apex rounded or incised, base cuneate; often grouped in clusters; flowers usually in 10 to 15 cm long, terminal panicles, fragrant, white, July–August, the individual flowers some 1 cm wide, petals 5 mm; fruit a pouch-like capsule, brown, 5–10 mm long. BM 1767; DRHS 334. Australia. 1793. z8 # ⊕

Pretty shrub for very mild areas.

BUTIA Becc. — Butia Palm — PALMAE

Low to medium sized feather palm, stem usually short and thick, covered with stiff, old petiole bases for a long time; leaves bowed, gray-green; leaf petiole with flat teeth or prickles along the thin margins and usually more or less fibrous; fruits 3 celled or (by the abortion of 2 cells) only single celled, globose to ovate, small, but often in large clusters weighing up to 35 kilograms. — 9 species in tropical and subtropical S. America; of those, the following 2 occasionally found in southern botanic gardens.

Butia capitata (Mart.) Becc. Stem 2—6 m high, some 20—25 cm thick, with deep rings, densely covered with old leaf petiole bases; leaves palmately compound, erect and then nodding, 2—3 m long, about 100 pinna on either side, partly grouped 2—3 together, leathery, gray-green, leaf petiole to 8 cm wide or more at the base, edged with prickles and teeth; fruits oblong-ovate, some 2.5 cm long, yellow to red, fleshy, fibrous. MPW 31 (= *Cocos australis* hort.). E. Brazil. Rather variable species. z8 Plate 86. #⌀

B. yatay (Mart.) Becc. Yatay Palm. Grows taller than the former, 5—8 m high, stem to 30 cm thick, densely covered with persistent old petiole bases; leaves pinnate, 2.5—3 m long, bowed, petiole with fibrous fringe and thorns on the lower portion, the longest leaves having some 50—60 pinnae on either blade half, more densely arranged on the lower portion of the blade, linear-lanceolate, the uppermost nearly thread-like, stiff, the middle leaflets much wider, blue-green beneath; fruit to 5 cm long. MPW 32 (= *Cocos yatay* Mart.). Brazil, Argentina. z8 #⌀

Slow growing palms, but very steadfast in suitable climates. (z10)

Lit. Bailey, L. H.: The Butias; in Gentes Herb. **4**, 16—49,1936.

BUXUS — Boxwood — BUXACEAE

Evergreen, small trees or shrubs with opposite, short petioled, small, leathery, entire, usually glabrous leaves; flowers inconspicuous, small, unisexual, monoecious, without petals, in dense, axillary clusters, usually 1 pistil and several stamens together; fruit a globose, 3 valved capsule, each valve with 2 horns and 2 black, glossy seeds. — 70 species in W. Europe, Mediterranean region, E. Asia, NW. India, tropical and S. Africa and Central America.

Buxus balearica Lam. Balearic Boxwood. Dense bushy shrub or small tree, upright, twigs nearly glabrous; leaves oval-oblong, leathery tough, 2—4 cm long, 1—2 cm wide, dark green, not as glossy above as *B. sempervirens*, light green beneath, obtuse to emarginate at the apex; female flowers sessile, male flowers stalked. DH 3: 42. S. Spain, Baleares. 1780. z8 Fig. 168, 172. #⌀

B. harlandii ·Hance. Shrub, low, young twigs somewhat pubescent, but soon glabrous; leaves narrow obovate to oblanceolate, emarginate at the apex, margin slightly curled inward, 2—3 cm long, 5—6 mm wide, very glossy above, dull beneath, petiole 1—2 mm long; male flowers distinctly stalked, ovary glabrous. HBu 20 and Pl. 20, 22 (= *B. microphylla* var. *japonica* Rehd. & Wils.). China, Hong Kong. Existence in cultivation unknown, but in any case, scarcely winter hardy. Not to be confused with "*B. harlandii* hort." z8 Fig. 170, 172. #

Fig. 168. *Buxus balearica* (from Nouv. Duhamel)

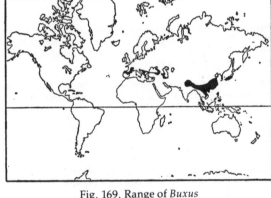

Fig. 169. Range of *Buxus* (only the European and Asiatic species)

B. henryi Mayr. Shrub, twigs nearly rod-like round; leaves oval-oblong to lanceolate, 5—7(—11) cm long, 15—25 mm wide, long acuminate, short petioled; flowers stalked, with erect style and reflexed stigma. GC 1912: 182. China; W. Hupeh. z6 Fig. 170.

B. microphylla S. et Z. Shrub, to 1 m high, compact, occasionally also procumbent, twigs glabrous, sharply angular; leaves usually oblanceolate, 8—25 mm long, rounded or emarginate at the apex, cuneate at the base, widest above the middle; male flowers with rudimentary pistils, as long as the calyx. HBu 23 and Pl. 18 and 27. Japan, Kiusiu, to date not seen in the wild; presumably originated in cultivation. 1860. Distinctly hardier than *B. sempervirens*! z6 Fig. 172. #

var. **aemulans** (Rehd. & Wils.) Hatusima. Differing in the oval-lanceolate to lanceolate, acute leaves and short stamens. China. Classified under ssp. *sinica*. z6 #

Fig. 170. **Buxus**. a. *B. microphylla* var. *sinica*; b. *B. henry*; c. *B. harlandii* (from ICS)

'Compacta' (Appleby 1928). Slow grower, only 30 cm tall in 30 years, very tolerant of frost and dryness (= *B. microphylla* var. *compacta* Rehd.). Found as a seedling by Samuel Appleby, in Baltimore, Md., USA. 1912 z5 #

'Green Pillow' (Appleby). Resembles 'Compacta', but with longer leaves. Planted in great numbers in the garden of President John F. Kennedy, 1962. #

var. **insularis** (Nakai) Hatusima. Twigs eventually glabrous; leaves somewhat larger and thicker. Probably only an island form of ssp. *sinica*. #

var. **intermedia** (Kanehira) Li. Shrub, leaves lanceolate to ovate, 2.5—3 cm, 8—15 mm wide; fruit capsule to 1 cm thick. LWT 170 (= *B. intermedia* Kanehira). Taiwan. z6 #

var. **japonica** (Muell. Arg.) Rehd. & Wils. Taller than the species, usually 3—5 m in its native habitat, to 2 m in European culture, fewer branches, twigs thicker; leaves tougher, leathery, usually ovate to ovate-elliptic, only seldom obovate or lanceolate, usually 1—1.5 cm long. HBu 24 and Pl. 18, 2. Japan, widely planted. That cultivated in German nurseries as "*B. harlandii*", is very likely this plant. z6 Fig. 170. # Ø

var. **koreana** Nakai. Lower, denser shrub, 25—60 cm, young twigs and leaf petioles somewhat pubescent; leaves ovate to ovate-oblong, 1—1.8 cm long, side veins indistinct on both sides, margin markedly curved downward. HBu 26 and Pl. 26, 1. Korea; China. 1919. z5 #

f. **major** (Makino) Hatusima. Especially large leaved form; leaves to 3.5 cm long. Form of var. *japonica*. #

'Rubra'. Garden form with orange-yellow leaves (= f. *rubra* Makino Hatusima). Under var *japonica*. #

var. **sinica** Rehd. & Wils. Shrub, 1—6 m high in the wild, wide grower, twigs and leaf petiole more or less pubescent; leaves light green, ovate to obovate, 1 to 3.5 cm long, margin slightly rolled inward, venation distinct above. HBu 25 and Pl. 22, 1. China, Japan, Taiwan. 1900. A rather variable form with a wide range in Middle and N. China. z5

'Sunnyside'. An especially frost hardy selection, remaining green during the entire winter. Introduction of Sunnyside Nurseries in Troy, Illinois, USA. Belongs in var. *koreana*. z5 #

'Wintergreen' (Scarff 1940). Low growing, globose, also holding a good green color throughout the winter, very frost hardy. Selected in 1940 at the Scarff Nurseries, New Carlisle, Ohio, USA and introduced to the trade in 1960. Also belonging in var. *koreana*. #

B. sempervirens L. Shrub or small tree, to 8 m (to 16 m in the Caucasus), twigs somewhat pubescent at first, later glabrous, olive-green, angular, foliage dense; leaves ovate to oval-oblong or oblong-elliptic, obtuse or emarginate at the apex, 1.5—3 cm long, leathery, dark green above and very glossy, lighter beneath, widest at or slightly below the middle; flowers yellow, inconspicuous, April—May. HW 3: 29. S. Europe, N. Africa, Asia Minor. In cultivation for ages. z6 Fig. 171. #

Quite variable in nature and therefore presenting many garden varieties:

Review of the Forms

Strong growing to tree-like, leaves dark green:
    'Agram', var. *arborescens*, 'Handsworthiensis', 'Pyramidalis', 'Rotundifolia', 'Undulifolia'
Strong grower, leaves blue-green:
    'Bullata', 'Glauca'
Growth pendulous, leaves green:
    'Pendula' (also variegated)
Weak growing to dwarf, leaves green:
    'Angustifolia', 'Myosotidifolia', 'Myrtifolia', 'Prostrata', 'Rosmarinifolia', 'Suffruticosa'
Leaves white or yellow variegated:
    'Arborescens Variegata', 'Argenteo-variegata', 'Aureopendula', 'Aureo-variegata', 'Elegans', 'Marginata', 'Notata'

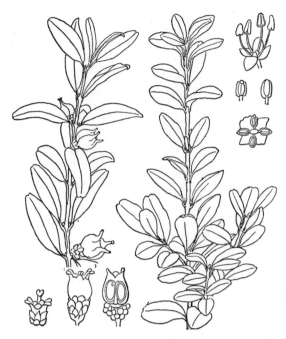

Fig. 171. *Buxus sempervirens*. Left, fruiting twig; lower left, fruit in longitudinal section and female flower (far left); at right, sterile twig; upper right, male flower and its parts (from Nose)

'Agram'. Growth narrowly upright; leaves average to large, elliptic to oblong, deep green and glossy. Collected from the wild by E. Anderson in the Vardar Valley, Macedonia, near Skopje, Yugoslavia. #

'Angustifolia'. Growth very dense, compact; leaves lanceolate, 25—35 mm long, obtuse, usually 2 ranked on an even plane, deep green, often somewhat blue pruinose (= 'Longifolia'; 'Salicifolia'). Very common. Also a yellow variegated form. Fig. 172. #

var. **arborescens** L. The species, with tall, tree-like growth habit; leaves ovate, twice as long as wide. #

'Arborescens Variegata'. To 1.5 m high, dense and compact; leaves dark green, medium size, somewhat variable in form, lighter green striped and irregular yellowish-white border. #

'Argenteo-variegata'. Leaves ovate to elliptic-oblong. 12—25 mm long, white variegated (= 'Argenteo-marginata'). #

'Aureo-pendula'. Growth tall, bushy, but with side branches very attractively drooping; leaves some 20 mm long, 8 mm wide, yellow or only yellow bordered. Very popular and common in England. #

'Aureo-variegata'. Growth strongly pyramidal and open; leaves ovate to elliptic-oblong, yellow and green speckled, young leaves usually yellow, later greening (= 'Aureomaculata'; 'Aurea'). #

'Bullata'. Growth tall and wide, but rather stiff, less attractive than other forms; leaves broad ovate to obovate, blistery (bullate), to 3.5 cm long, 2 cm wide, emarginate apex, dark blue-green, leaf petiole pubescent. Gw 33: 151 (= 'Macrophylla'; 'Latifolia'). Fig. 172. # Ø

'Elegans'. Weak grower; upright; leaves narrow, often somewhat deformed, white margined (= 'Elegantissima'). Frequently cultivated in French nurseries. # Ø

'Glauca'. Strong grower, upright, rather rigid; leaves ovate to oval-oblong, 2—2.5 cm long, obtuse, excellent blue-green, but not bullate. Gw 33: 151. # Ø

'Handsworthiensis'. Strong grower, upright, dense bushy, seldom tree-like; leaves broad ovate, usually emarginate, to 4 cm long, deep green, margin somewhat "boat-like" bowed upward. Gw 33: 152 (= 'Handsworthii'; 'Navicularis'). Originated by Fisher Son & Sibray, Handsworth Nursery, near Sheffield, England. # Ø

'Marginata'. Strong grower, narrow and stiffly upright; leaves deep green with yellow edge, broadly ovate, often peculiarly deformed at the apex, often rounded or sinuate (= 'Aureo-marginata'; 'Aureo-limbata'). #

'Myosotidifolia'. Growth rather dwarf, reaching some 30 cm high in 10—12 years, very densely branched; leaves very small, the largest about 12 mm long and 3 mm wide, green. #

'Myrtifolia'. Low, dense bushy shrub, becoming some 1—1.2 m high, loosely branched, slow growing; leaves ovate to oval-rhombic or narrow oblong, 6—18 mm long, 4—8 mm wide, obtuse to acute, gray-green, but also yellow and white margined (= 'Leptophylla'). #

'Notata'. Tall growing, to 4 m; leaves medium size, dark green, with distinct yellow apex, especially on older specimens (= 'Gold Tip'). #

'Pendula'. Growth tall, with a dominant leader, branches thin, pendulous, very graceful habit; leaves reverse oval-oblong, 2 cm long, obtuse. #

'Pyramidalis'. Pyramidal growing, upright, rigid, not attractive; leaves usually ovate-oblong, some 2—2.5 cm long, obtuse or somewhat emarginate, deep green. Fig. 172. #

'Rosmarinifolia'. Low, dense bushy shrub; leaves linear-lanceolate, 8—15 mm long, 3—6 mm wide, obtuse or acute, margin rolled inward. Not winter hardy. z7 Fig. 172. #

'Rotundifolia. Growth tree-like or tall shrubby; leaves rounded-obovate to broad ovate, to 25 mm long and 15 mm wide, rounded or emarginate, base usually broad cuneate. Also a yellow variegated form. Fig. 172. #

'Suffruticosa'. Low shrub, eventually becoming 1 m tall, very dense; leaves ovate or obovate, 1—2 cm long, emarginate (= 'Humulis'; 'Nana'). The popular border boxwood. #

'Undulifolia'. As strong growing as the type; leaves also similar but with margin very sinuate. #

B. wallichiana Baill. Small shrub, some 1 m high in culture, but tree-like in the wild, young twigs remaining densely pubescent; leaves lanceolate to ovate-lanceolate, usually 4—5 cm long, 7—10 mm wide, widest in the middle, dark green, petiole and midrib pubescent; flowers in dense, axillary clusters, anthers yellow, April. BS 1: 464. India; NW. Himalaya. 1850. z8 Fig. 172. #

The *Buxus* species and especially the cultivars are collectively very serviceable and winter hardy, except *B. balearica*, *wallichiana* and the rarely cultivatd *B. harlandii*. They thrive equally well in sun or shade and tolerate dryness. Propagated easily from cuttings:

Lit. Baldwin, J. T., Jr.: The Korean Boxes; in Amer. Nurseryman 5/15/75, 7, 39—47 ● Dallimore, W.: Holly, Box and Yew, 207—231; London 1908 ● Hatusima, S.: A revision of the asiatic *Buxus*; in Jour. Dept. Agr. Kyusyu Imp. Univ. **6**, 261 to 342, with 26 ill., 12 pl. and 3 maps; (most important work) ●

Lancaster, R.: The common box in Britain (series with 6 pp. total); in Gard. Chron. 1968 (May and June) ● Wagenknecht, B. L.: Registration List of Cultivar names in *Buxus*; Amer. Boxwood Society, 1965.

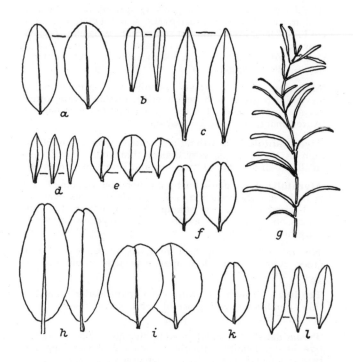

Fig. 172. **Buxus.** A. *B. sempervirens* 'Bullata'; b. *B. harlandii*; c. *B. wallichiana*; d. *B. microphylla*; e. *B. microphylla* var. *sinica*; f. *B. sempervirens* 'Pyramidalis'; g. *B. sempervirens* 'Rosmarinifolia'; h. *B. balearica*; i. *B. sempervirens* 'Rotundifolia'; k. *B. sempervirens* (wild); l. *B. sempervirens* 'Angustifolia'

CAESALPINIA L. — LEGUMINOSAE

Deciduous shrubs, also trees in the wild, many species climbing by hooks, partly thorny; leaves alternate, bipinnate, with stipules; flowers not papilionaceus, in terminal, often panicled racemes; calyx with short tube, 5 toothed, petals 5, rather equal, clawed (unguiculate); stamens 10, protruding markedly; fruits an ovate to lanceolate, usually flattened pod. — Some 60 species in the tropics and subtropics.

Caesalpinia gilliesii Wall. Shrub, a small tree in its native habitat, young twigs glandular pubescent; leaves bipinnate, some 20 cm long, with 9—11 pinnae, each composed of numerous leaflets, leaflets some 8 mm long, oblong, glabrous; flowers in upright, rigid, terminal, 30 cm long racemes, with 30—40 individual flowers, corolla plate-like, gold-yellow, some 3.5 cm wide, stamen filaments scarlet-red, to 7 cm long, flower stalk 2.5 cm long, pubescent, July—August. BM 4006 (= *Poinciana gilliesii* Hook). Argentina, especially the Mendoza Province. z8 Plate 86. ○ ✧ ∅

C. japonica S. et Z. Shrub, very thorny, some 2 m high, tends to climb with hooks, twigs not pubescent, with 6—8 mm long, blackberry-like prickles; leaves bipinnate, some 30 cm long, with 3—8 paired pinnae, each pair of pinnae with 12—20 oblong leaflets, some 20 mm long, 1 erect and 2 curved prickles on every leaf petiole, in addition several smaller scattered prickles; flowers in 30 cm long, terminal racemes, with 20 to 30 individual flowers, corolla plate-like (rotate), 3.5 cm wide, light yellow, the smallest petal red striped, stamen filament red, June—July. BM 8207; BS 1: 24. Japan. 1881. z8 ○ ✧ ∅

C. sepiaria Roxb. Tall, thorny climbing shrub, forming impenetrable thickets, very similar to *C. japonica*, but with twigs and inflorescence softly pubescent, thorns short, stout hooked; leaves 25—45 cm long, wth 6—8 paired pinnae, each with 8—12 pairs of oblong, obtuse leaflets; flowers in simple, axillary racemes, yellow. FIO 93; HAL 66c. India, Burma, Himalaya, in the mountains to 1800m. 1857. z9 ✧

For illustrations of further species, see: *C. crista* L. (ICS 2427); *C. minax* Hance (ICS 2428); *C. nuga* Ait. (ICS 2429); *C. sappan* L. (ICS 2430); *C. pulcherrima* Sw. (ICS 2432; DRHS 346) and *C. szechuenensis* (FIO 94).

All 3 species very beautiful; require well drained, loam soil; in colder areas best used in tub plantings, but the latter two are very thorny making them hard to handle.

CALCEOLARIA L. — Slipperworts — SCROPHULARIACEAE

Herbaceous or shrubby; leaves usually opposite or in whorls, rugose and pubescent, simple or incised; corolla divided nearly to the base, the lower portion larger and often swollen "slipper"-like, the upper part often widened pouch-like; stamens 2(−3); fruit a many seeded capsule. — Some 300 to 400 species in S. America, Mexico, New Zealand; and many hybrids in cultivation.

Calceolaria integrifolia Murray. Evergreen subshrub, 0.5−1 m high, upright, sparsely branched, twigs light brown, somewhat viscid when young; leaves oblong to lanceolate, 2−5 cm long, distinctly dentate, very rugose and deep green above, usually gray or brownish pubescent beneath, petiole winged; flowers many in corymbs, corolla yellow, some 1.2 cm wide, August to frost. BR. 744 (= *C. rugosa* Ruiz et Pav.). Chile. 1822. Popular garden plant. z8 # **H** ○ ✧

'Angustifolia'. Leaves lanceolate, densely pubescent beneath; inflorescence on long stalks. BM 2523.

'Viscosissima'. Leaves oblong, dull, very rugose, glandular pubescent, underside not rust-brown; main axis of inflorescence shorter. BM 3214.

C. sinclarii see: **Jovellana sinclarii**

C. violacea see: **Jovellana violacea**

For best effect, replant young plants in groups each year, since older plants will loose their character. They prefer sunny areas in good garden soil.

CALDCLUVIA D. Don — CUNONIACEAE

Monotypic genus, earlier included with *Weinmannia*. For characteristics, see the description of the species.

Caldcluvia paniculata (Cav.) D. Don. Evergreen shrub or small tree, 4−6 m high; leaves simple, oblong-lanceolate, tapering to both ends, 5−12 cm long, short petioled, margin sharply serrate and resembling those of *Castanea sativa*, but much thicker and tougher; flowers small, white, in some 5 cm wide, axillary cymes, May−June; fruit a many seeded, leathery capsule. Chile. 1831. In cultivation in Logan, Scotland. z8 # ✧ ⊘

CALICOTOME (CALYCOTOME) Link. — LEGUMINOSAE

Deciduous shrub, low growing, thorny, twigs occasionally opposite, leaves trifoliate, petiolate, without stipules, leaflets sessile, small; flowers singular or fascicled, calyx tear-drop shaped, without calyx teeth, standard petal erect, keel petal curved, shorter than the wings; fruit a linear-oblong, dehiscent pod. — 7 species in the Mediterranean region, all species hardy in cultivation only to z8.

Calicotome infesta (Presl) Guss. Thorny, dense shrub, 1−2 m high, very similar to *C. spinosa*, but the leaves gray-green with appressed pubescence; flower stalk with 3 lobed bract, the middle lobe largest, all lobes obtuse, pod with 3 ribs down the dorsal side. PMe 55. Spain to Greece, Morocco and Tunisia; on sunny slopes and cliffs, on acid soil. z8 ○

C. spinosa (L.) Link. Shrub, to 1.5 m high, glabrous, all branches terminating in sharp thorns; leaflets obovate, 8−12 mm long, glabrous or somewhat pubescent beneath; flowers solitary or to groups of 4, 1 cm long, yellow, May−July; pods 2−3 cm long, 2 winged on the upper seam. HF 2311; PSw 17; VG 54. S. Europe. z8 Fig. 173, 174. **S** ○

C. villosa (Poir.) Link. Only 1 m high, very similar to *C. spinosa*, but young twigs with short silky pubescence; leaflets narrow elliptic, to 13 mm long, silky pubescent beneath; flowers yellow, March−June; fruits, flower stalk and calyx distinctly erect, shaggy pubescent; fruits distinctly angular winged. SH 2: 36a-f; PEu 51;

Fig. 173. right, *Calicotome spinosa*; left, *C. villosa* (from Taubert, Sibthorp)

VG 56. S. Europe, N. Africa, Corsica. 1893. z8 Fig. 173. **S** ○

CALLIANDRA Benth. — LEGUMINOSAE

Evergreen shrubs or also small trees; leaves alternate, bipinnate, the pinnae and leaflets paired, leaflets oblique; inflorescence globose or hemispherical, with very small calyx and corolla, stamens very numerous, to 4 cm long, red, purple, pink or white. — Some 100 species in Madagascar, milder parts of Asia and America. Occasionally found in frost free Mediterranean gardens and very attractive.

Calliandra haematocephala Hassk. Loosely growing shrub, blooms as a young 0.5—1 m tall plant, although becoming 6—7 m high in warm climates; leaves with 2 pinnae, each with 5—10 paired leaflets, each 2—3 cm long, oblique oblong-lanceolate; flowers in 5—7 cm wide globose heads, corolla small, pink, stamen filaments 2.5—3 cm long, bright carmine, anthers black, February. BM 5181; MCL 62; HKS 15. Native habitat unknown, probably America. z9 # ✿

C. tweedii benth. Shrub or also a small tree; leaves bipinnate, with 2—7 paired pinnae, each pinna with numerous, overlapping, narrow oblong, 6—8 mm long leaflets, silky pubescent when young; flowers in hemispherical heads, 5—7 cm wide, each on 5 cm long, pubescent stalks, axillary; stamens 3 cm long, red. BM 4188; MCL 52. S. Brazil. z8 # ✿

Suitable in frost free areas only, in colder areas for the greenhouse and then kept warm.

Lit. Cowan, R. S.: Correct name of the Powder-puff tree; in Baileya **11**, 94—98, 1963.

Fig. 174. *Calicotome spinsosa*, sterile twig (From Kerner)

CALLICARPA L. — Beautyberry — VERBENACEAE

Evergreen or deciduous shrubs, sometimes a tree in its habitat; leaves opposite, dentate, often stellate pubescent; flowers small, in axillary cymes; calyx campanulate, short, 4 toothed (rarely 3); corolla tubular only at the base, limb broad 4 lobed; stamens 4, prominent; fruit a small, berry-like drupe with 2—4 seeds. — Some 40 species in the tropics and subtropics from Asia, Australia, N. and Central America, only a few in cultivation.

Key

- Main inflorescence axis longer than the leaf petiole; leaves glabrous or only slightly pubescent beneath (*C. shirasawana* somewhat clustered pubescence and glandular);
  - Leaves crenate-serrate in the upper half:
    - *C. dichotoma*
  - Leaves finely serrate nearly to the base:
    - *C. japonica, C. shirasawana*
- •• Main inflorescence axis shorter than or as long as the leaf petiole;
  - Leaves with clustered pubescence or becoming glabrous beneath:
    - *C. bodinieri*
  - Leaves tomentose beneath, not glandular:
    - *C. mollis*

Leaves tomentose and glandular beneath:
C. americana

Callicarpa americana L. Deciduous shrub, to 2 m high, young twigs tomentose; leaves oval-oblong, acuminate at both ends, 7—13 cm long, obtuse, softly pubescent above, tomentose beneath and yellow glandular; flowers glabrous, light blue, very small, glabrous outside, June—July; fruits 4 mm thick, violet, in small, nearly sessile fascicles. BB 3563. SE. USA. 1724. Forests, moist thickets and bordering swamps. z7 Plate 87. ⊗

'Lactea'. Like the species, but with fruits white. ⊗

C. bodinieri Lév. Shrub, to 2 m high, young twigs scabby pubescent; leaves elliptic to oblong, 5—12 cm long, long acuminate, clustered pubescence beneath becoming glabrous; flowers many in 2.1 cm wide and some 12 mm long stalked cymes, lilac, July—August; fruits violet, 3—4 mm wide, September to October. ICS 5124. Central and West China. Less frequently used in cultivation than its varieties. z6 Fig. 176. ⊗

var. **giraldii** (Hesse) Rehd. Differing from the species in the glabrous upper leaf surface, clustered pubescence with yellow glands beneath; inflorescence less pubescent. MD 1912: 366; BM 8682. Central and W. China. 1900. Very well known

Fig. 175. **Callicarpa.** a. *C. japonica*; b. *C. mollis*; c. *C. bodinieri* var. *giraldii*; d. *C. dichotoma*
(from Shirasawa, Hesse; the twig drawn by Eiselt)

and widely planted; good hardiness. z6 Plate 87; Fig. 175. ⚭

'Profusion' (T. van Veen & Zonen). Selection from seedlings of var. *giraldii*; growth the same, branch tips and young leaves dark brown; fruits violet (HCC 033/1), 3−4 mm thick, grouped 30−40 together, abundantly fruiting even on young plants. Plate 40. ⚭

C. dichotoma (Lour.) K. Koch. Shrub, to 1.5 m high, young twigs scabby pubescent; leaves elliptic to obovate, 3−7.5 cm long, apical half crenate-serrate, light green beneath, yellow glandular-punctate, nearly glabrous, petiole 2 to 4 mm long; flowers in 1−2 cm wide and 5−12 cm long stalked cymes, corolla pink, with 5 mm long stamens, anthers splitting open at the tip, August; fruits 3−4 mm thick, lilac-violet. NK 14: Pl. 5; NT 1: 451; ICS 5126 (= *C. purpurea* Juss.; *C. gracilis* S. et Z.; *C. koreana* Hort.). Korea, E. and Central China. 1857. Only cultivated in Japan, occasionally naturalized in E. USA. z6 Plate 87; Fig. 175, 176. ⚭

C. japonica Thunb. Shrub, 1.5 m high, young twigs tomentose at first, but soon becoming glabrous; leaves elliptic to ovate-lanceolate, long acuminate, 5−12 cm long, finely serrate to the base, glabrous beneath, but glandular; flowers in 1.5−3 cm wide, many flowered, 5−10 mm long stalked cymes, corolla whitish to light pink, anthers opening by a pore at the tip (see *C. dichotoma*), August; fruits 4 mm thick, violet. NT 1: 453; ICS 5128. Japan. Around 1845. z6 Plate 87; Fig. 175, 176. ⚭

var. **angustata** Rehd. Leaves oblong-lanceolate, 5−12 cm long, 1−3 cm wide. NT 1: 456 (= *C. longifolia* Hemsl.). Central China. 1907. Plate 87. ⚭

'Leucocarpa'. Like the species, but with white fruits (= f. *albobacca* Hara). 1845. Occasionally occurring as a chance seedling. ⚭

C. mollis S. et Z. Resembles *C. bodinieri*, but often only a subshrub, twigs quite densely and white pubescent; leaves elliptic to oblong-lanceolate, long acuminate, 5−10 cm long, dull green above, thick stellate pubescent beneath, dentate; flowers pink, stamens as long as the corolla and its lobes, July; fruits dull lilac. NT 1: 57; NK 14: Pl. 9. Japan, Korea. 1863. z7−8 Fig. 175. ⚭

C. rubella Lindl. Deciduous shrub, to 3 m high, growth open, twigs softly pubescent and glandular; leaves oblong-lanceolate to more obovate, slender acuminate, 10−15 cm long, shallowly dentate, base cordate, densely pubescent beneath and glandular, seldom stalked; flowers pink or lilac, 3 mm wide, very numerous in stalked, 2.5 cm wide fascicles, calyx pubescent, corolla tips erect; fruits globose, 3 mm thick, bright purple-pink. BM 9340; JRHS 87: 116; HTS 93. China; Burma, Assam. 1821. z9 ⚭

C. × shirasawana Mak. (*C. japonica* × *C. mollis*). Intermediate between the parents, but with leaves elliptic to ovate-lanceolate or ovate-oblong, 5−12 cm long, 2−4 cm wide, serrate, clustered pubescent beneath and loosely glandular; flowers lilac, calyx distinctly lobed; fruits violet. NT 1: 462. Originated in Japan before 1895. ⚭

For good garden soil; best planted in groups to insure good pollination and best fruit development. Most species have an attractive yellow and violet fall coloration.

Accurate distinction of the *Callicarpa* species is impossible without a good magnifying lens and careful examination.

Lit. Moldenke, H. N.: Monograph of the genus *Callicarpa*, as it occurs in America and in cultivation; in Fedde. Repert. Sp. Nov. **39**, 288–317; **40**, 38–131, 1936 (contains 28 wild species, one indigenous to America [*C. dichotoma*] and those existing in cultivation).

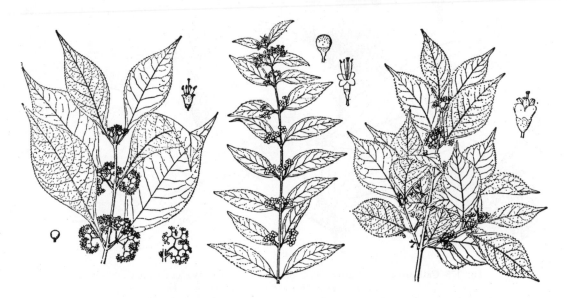

Fig. 176. From left to right: *Callicarpa bodinieri, C. dichotoma, C. japonica* (from ICS)

CALLIGONUM L. — POLYGONACEAE

Closely related to *Atraphaxis* (in appearance more similar to *Ephedra*), but with leaves linear or totally absent and replaced with short branches; fruits winged and bristly; flowers small and inconspicuous, but fruit attractively colored. — Some 80 species in Asia Minor, N. Africa, S. Europe, Central Asia.

Calligonum aphyllum Schneid., *C. caput-medusae* Schrenk, *C. polygonoides* L. and *C. eriopodum* Bge. are

typical shrubs of the asiatic desert and in recent years offered on the seed exchange lists of Russian botanic gardens. See also, *C. junceum* (ICS 552) and *C. mongolicum* (ICS 553); China.

Despite repeated seedings in the Dortmund Botanic Garden, no plants have been produced. Whether in cultivation in Central or W. Europe is unknown. ⓕ Several species used in the USSR as dune stabilizers on the Caspian Sea. **S** ⚭

CALLISTEMON R. Br. — Bottlebrush — MYRTACEAE

Evergreen shrubs, also tree-like in their habitat; leaves alternate, entire, lanceolate or linear or terete, with oil or resin glands, fragrant when crushed; flowers in dense cylindrical spikes, terminal at first, but later appearing axillary on leafy twigs; calyx teeth 5, petals 5, abscising; stamens very numerous, not connate, filaments on most species carmine or scarlet; fruit a woody capsule, persisting for several years. — 25 species in Australia and New Caledonia.

The very similar genus *Melaleuca* is distinguished by the connate stamen filaments which in *Callistemon* are all distinct.

Key

1. Leaves lanceolate   2

	Leaves linear or cylindrical	6
2.	Stamen filaments red	3
	Stamen filaments greenish-yellow:	
	C. falignus	
3.	Leaves with pinnate venation	4
	Leaves indistinctly veined; inflorescence loose:	
	C. phoeniceus	
4.	Flower spikes dense	5
	Flower spikes loose, anthers dark:	
	C. citrinus	
5.	Flower spikes 7–12 cm long, pubescent, stamen filaments connate:	
	C. speciosus	
	Flower spikes short, 5–10 cm, stamen filaments distinct, anthers yellow:	

C. coccineus
6. Leaves linear   7
   Leaves awl-shaped and terete   9
7. Stamen filaments red:
      C. salignus
   Stamen filaments greenish-yellow:
      C. rigidus
8. Leaves with pinnate venation:
      C. rigidus
   Leaves concave, vein only 1 or absent:
      C. linearis
9. Leaves 12—25 mm long, stamen filaments yellow:
      C. sieberi
   Leaves longer than 25 mm   10
10. Leaves usually over 5 cm long, stamen
    filaments yellowish-green, over 12 mm long:
       C. pinifolius
    Leaves under 3 cm long, stamen filaments red,
    8 mm long:
       C. brachyandrus

Callistemon brachyandrus Lindl. Tall shrub, also a small tree in its native habitat; young leaves silky, older leaves glabrous, circular, stiff, with prickly tips, 2—3.5 cm long, 1 mm thick, with a groove above; spikes 3 cm long, rachis and flowers pubescent at first, later becoming glabrous, petals greenish, 4 mm, filaments red or pink, only 6—8 mm long (!!), anthers gold-yellow, August-September; fruit globose, 6—7 mm wide. BMns 316. Australia, New South Wales. z9 #⊕

C. citrinus (Curt.) Skeels. Shrub to 3 m, twigs erect or wide spreading; leaves lanceolate, 2.5—7.5 cm long, some 6 mm wide, acute, red when young, midrib and axillary veins elevated; flowers in 5—10 cm long, loose spikes, filaments 2.5 cm long, dark scarlet-red, anthers darker, June; capsule ovate. MCL 13; EKW 273; PBl 1: 177 (= *C. lanceolatus* [Sm.] DC.; *Metrosideros citrina* Curt.; *M. semperflorens* Lodd.). Australia. 1788. z9 #⊕

The epithet "*citrinus*" is derived from the lemon scent of the crushed foliage.

'Splendens'. Differing from the species in that the glossy carmine red stamen filaments are twice as long. BM 9050; HTS 90. Good flowering even on small plants. Most beautiful of the entire genus. z9 ⊕

C. coccineus F. Muell. Shrub, 1.5—4 m high, glabrous, young twigs silky pubescent; leaves narrow lanceolate, 2—6 cm long, acute at both ends, 3—5 mm wide, stiff, prickly, both sides glandular punctate, midrib and margin thickened; flower spikes 5—10 cm long, 3—5 cm wide (stamen filaments enclosed), stamen filaments carmine, anthers greenish-yellow, June—August; fruit capsule globose-flattened on one end (= *C. rugulosus* DC.). S. Australia. z9 #⊕

C. linearis (Sm.) DC. Shrub, to 2 m high, twigs silky pubescent when young; leaves linear, to 12 cm long, only 2.5 mm wide, with 1 groove above; inflorescence 7—12 cm long, flowers very densely arranged, stamen filaments carmine, to 2.5 cm long, anthers darker, July (= *Metrosideros linearis* Sm.). New South wales. 1788. z9 #⊕

C. phoeniceus Lindl. Shrub, 1.5—3 m high, growth wide; leaves narrow lanceolate, prickly tipped, stiff, 5—10 cm long, 4—6 mm wide, midrib elevated, margin thickened; inflorescence 6—10 cm long, to 5 cm wide, stamen filaments to 2.5 cm, scarlet-red. EWA 149. W. Australia. z9 Plate 40. #⊕

C. pinifolius DC. Tall shrub, leaves needle-like, furrowed above, 7—12 cm long, 1.5 mm wide, new growth pale lilac and silky pubescent, soon becoming completely glabrous; inflorescence 5—7 cm long, to 5 cm wide, stamen filaments yellow-green, anthers yellow. BM 3989. New South Wales. z9 #⊕

C. rigidus R. Br. Shrub, 2—2.5 m high, twigs finely pubescent when young; leaves linear to more lanceolate, flat, stiff, sharp pointed, to 15 cm long, 6 mm wide, not furrowed above; flowers in very dense, 7—10 cm long and 5 cm wide spikes, stamen filaments dark red, anthers dark brown, March—July. BR 393; BMns 619 (= *C. linearifolius* DC.). New South Wales. 1815. z9 #⊕

C. salignus (Sm.) DC. Shrub, to 3 m, in its habitat a small tree to 9 m, bark papery, new growth soft pink, silky pubescent; leaves linear to more lanceolate, thin, but tough, 5—10 cm long, 4—8 mm wide, acute at both ends, dull green, midrib elevated; inflorescence 3—7 cm long, 3 cm wide, light yellow to light pink (some cultivars also red or white), June. BM 1821; HTS 91 (= *Metrosideros saligna* Sm.). SE. Australia. 1788. z9 #⊕

var. **viridiflora** F. v. Muell. Leaves only 2.5—5 cm long, thicker, veins not elevated; stamens green or greenish-yellow. BM 2602 (= *viridiflorus* [Sims] Sweet). Tasmania z9 #⊕

C. sieberi DC. Shrub, to 5 m high in its habitat, stem dark gray-brown; leaves linear, thick, stiff, densely arranged on the branch, to 2.5 cm long and 2.5 mm wide, often half round in section, furrowed above; flower spikes narrow, 2—4 cm long, stamens yellow, only some 1 cm long, July—August. BS 1: 472 (= *C. pithyoides* Miq.). SE. Australia. z9 #⊕

C. speciosus (Sims) DC. Shrub, a small tree in its habitat, twigs stiff, brown, striped; leaves densely arranged, linear-elliptic, 3—10 cm long, 10—12 mm wide, acute, tapering to the base, midrib elevated, side veins indistinct; flower spikes 7—12 cm long, 5—6 cm wide, stamen filaments 2.5 cm long, bright carmine-red, anthers gold-yellow, abundant flowers only on older plants, May—June; fruit capsule densely white pubescent outside. BM 1761; EA 65 (= *Metrosideros speciosa* Sims). W. Australia. 1823. The plant often cultivated under this name is actually a form of *C. citrinus*. z9 #⊕

C. viminalis Cheel. Tree-like in its habitat, twigs nodding; leaves linear-oblong, stamen filaments red, 2 cm long. MCL 13. Australia. Very similar to *C. speciosus*, but differing in the pendulous branches. z9 #⊕

Frequently found in southern botanic gardens. Prefers heavy soil in sunny areas; water requirements minimal but some helpful in summer. Most species bloom only on older plants, except *C. citrinus* 'Splendens'. Hard pruning of fruiting twigs promotes flowering.

CALLUNA Salisb. — Heather — ERICACEAE

Evergreen shrubs separated from *Erica* by their colorful calyces, which are longer than the 4 parted corolla; calyx and corolla also persisting after the flowers; fruit a 4 valved capsule. — 1 species in nearly all of Europe and NE. Asia Minor.

Calluna vulgaris (L.) Hull. The typical plant of the European heath and moor. Shrub, from 20—100 cm tall, twigs procumbent, often rooting and ascending; dense foliage, leaves ovate-oblong, 1—3 mm long, opposite, decussate, awl-shaped at the base, more or less glabrous or pubescent; flowers usually pink-lilac, in dense, 20 cm long racemes, June—November, in the wild from July—August. HM Pl. 207; HF Pl. 2022 (= *Erica vulgaris* L.). In cultivation for centuries and available in many varieties. z5 # S H ✥

Despite the many cultivars available it is an extremely difficult species for scientific hybridization; most of the garden varieties have been found in the wild or occurred as chance seedlings. The selections have, with few exceptions, all been found in England. The more prominent specialists are: Maxwell & Beale, Broadstone, Dorset, England; James Smith & Son, Darley Dale, Derbyshire, England; J. W. Sparkes, Beechwood Nurseries, Beoley, Redditch, Worchester, England.

Nomenclature of the following cultivars is taken from T. L. Underhill, Heaths and Heathers (1971). There are actually many more cultivars available from the specialist nurseries than are listed here. The largest inventory of Calluna on the European continent is available at Darthuizer Boomkwekerijen in Leersum, Holland with 86 varieties (1972).

Outline of the Cultivars

● Those with erect growth habit, flowers always simple (not double);
1. Leaves green, flowers lilac to purple:
   'Barnett Anley', 'C. W. Nix', David Eason', 'Elegantissima Walter Ingwersen', 'Hiemalis'
2. Leaves green, flowers pink to carmine:
   'Alportii', 'Alportii Praecox', 'Beechwood Crimson', 'Darkness', 'E. Hoare', 'Goldsworth Crimson', 'Hookstone', 'October Crimson', 'Tib', 'Underwoodii'
3. Leaves green, flowers white:
   f. *alba*, 'August Beauty', 'Elegantissima', 'Hammondii', 'Kit Hill', 'Long White', 'Mair's Variety', 'October White', 'Serlei', 'Spicata'
4. Leaves yellow to orange:
   'Alba Carlton', 'Aurea', 'Beoley Gold', 'Christina', 'Golden Feather', 'Gold Haze', 'Hammondii Aureifolia', 'Rosalind', 'Serlei Aurea'
5. Leaves bronze, brown to red:
   'Blazeaway', 'Bognie', 'Cuprea', 'Darleyensis', 'Fred J. Chapple', 'Hammondii Rubrifolia', 'Multicolor', 'Orange Queen', 'Robert Chapman', 'Serlei Purpurea', 'Spitfire', 'Spring Torch', Sunset', 'Tricolorifolia', 'Winter Chocolate'
6. Leaves white variegated or gray woolly:
   'Argentea', 'Hirsuta Typica', 'Silver Knight', 'Silver Queen', Sister Anne', 'Spring Queen'

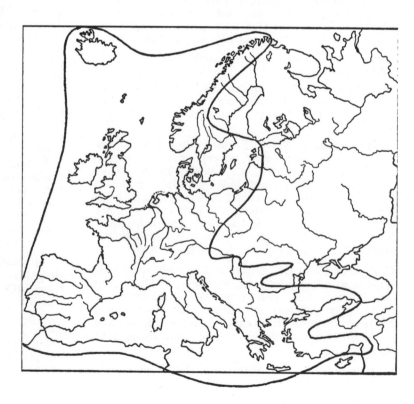

Fig. 177. Range of the genus *Calluna* (from Underhill)

●● Those with dwarf growth habit; flowers simple (not double);
    7. Leaves green:
        'Alba Pumila', 'Elkstone White', 'Foxhollow Wanderer', 'Foxii', 'Foxii Nana', 'Gnome', 'Hibernica', 'Humpty Dumpty', 'Kupharldtii', 'Minima', 'Mrs. Pat', 'Mrs. Ronald Gray', 'Mullion', 'Rigida', 'Roma', 'Tenuis', 'Tom Thumb'
    8. Leaves yellow:
        'Alba Aurea', 'Golden Carpet', 'John F. Letts', 'Lambs Tails', 'Prostrate Orange'
●●● Those with double flowers;
    9. Flowers pink to purple:
        'Carl Roeders', 'County Wicklow', 'Elsie Purnell', 'H. E. Beale', 'J. H. Hamilton', 'Joan Sparkes', 'Peter Sparkes', 'Plena'
    10. Flowers white:
        'Alba Plena', 'Else Frye', 'Ruth Sparkes'

f. **alba** (West.) Braun-Blanquet. The wild form with white flowers, style white or greenish; leaves remaining fresh green in winter.

'Alba Aurea'. Growth prostrate, to 10 cm high; leaves yellow at first, later greenish-yellow, spring growth green; flowers pure white, August.

'Alba Carlton' (S. H. Ward, Malton). 40–60 cm high; flowers pure white, very numerous, as compared to the other cultivars, also blooming on the side branches, August–September (= 'Carlton').

'Alba Plena' (A. Lamken 1934). Growth broad, upright; flowers pure white, somewhat larger and more densely arranged than those of 'H. E. Beale', September–October. Found in a moor near Oldenburg, W. Germany. ⊕

'Alba Praecox' (Arends 1938). Prostrate, 10–20 cm high, twigs erect; flowers white, July to August (= 'Alba Pumila').

'Alportii'. Growth strong, to 1 m high, more or less gray-green pubescent; flowers red to red-violet, August–September. From England.⊕

'Alportii Praecox' (Arends 1938). Like 'Alportii', but only half as high; foliage more gray-green; blooming 3–4 weeks earlier, purple.

'Argentea'. Growth wide and low; leaves fresh green, branch tips white in winter; flowers violet, in small inflorescences.∅

'August Beauty. To 30 cm high, twigs curved to the ground; flowers white, August–September.

'Aurea'. Leaves remaining gold-yellow; flowers light violet, not particularly attractive. ∅

'Barnett Anley' (B. L. Anley, Woking, Surrey, before 1960). Compact upright, 30–60 cm; foliage fresh green, reddish on the sunny side; flowering branches 25–30 cm long, flowers purple, simple, August–September. ⊕

'Beechwood Crimson' (J. W. Sparkes). Growth upright; foliage dark green; flowers dark carmine. Improvement on 'C. W. Nix'.

'Beoley Gold' (J. W. Sparkes, before 1968). 40–45 cm high; foliage bright yellow, gold tones on the sunny side; flowers white, August–September. ∅

'Blazeaway' (J. W. Sparkes). Resembles 'Robert Chapman', but flowering 2 weeks earlier; 45–55 cm high; foliage turning orange and red in winter; flowers lilac, August–September. ⊕ ∅

'Bognie'. 30 cm high; foliage bronze, not as well colored as 'Cuprea', but with gold tones; flowers August-September. Found in the wild in Scotland.

'Carl Roeders' (H. Westermann, Bispingen-Borstel 1970). Growth upright; flowers double, violet-pink, better color than 'H. E. Beale', very early and long lasting flowers. ⊕

'Christiana' (Rijnbeek 1970). Growth dense, upright, to 50 cm; foliage yellow-green, yellow in winter; flowers white, September–October. ∅

'County Wicklow' (Maxwell & Beale). Wide branching, but upright; flowers dense, double, true pink, in full inflorescences, from mid-August (= 'Camla'). ⊕

'Cuprea'. Growth upright; small leaved, leaves red-brown in winter, yellow-green in summer, better color than 'Aurea'; flowers violet. ∅

'C. W. Nix' (Maxwell & Beale). To 60 cm high; flowers violet-red, darker than 'Alportii' and flowering later. Weak growing descendent of 'Alportii'. ⊕

'Darkness' (Pratt). Growth dense and upright, to 30 cm; flowers very densely spaced, carmine-purple, August–September. Flower color somewhat brighter than that of 'Alportii'. ⊕

'Darleyensis' (J. Smith and Son, Darleydale). Nest-like growth habit, erratic branching, 45–50 cm; foliage dark bronze in winter; flowers pink-red, August-September.

'David Eason' (Maxwell & Beale). To 30 cm high; flowers bud-like, remaining closed, pink-lilac to nearly violet, holding its color well over a long period, September–November. ⊕

'E. Hoare' (Maxwell & Beale). Dark red descendant of 'Alportii', some 30 cm high; August–September.

'Elegantissima'. Growth broad, ascending, to 50 cm; foliage gray-green; flowers pure white, August–September. Originated in Holland. ⊕

'Elegantissima Walter Ingwersen'. To over 30 cm high, branches grow very long in a single season; leaves deep green; flowers pink-lilac (not white, as is often erroneously listed), in very long inflorescences. Very late and not always totally hardy, originated in Portugal. Introduced by Ingwersen, Engand, 1928. z7 ⊕

'Elkstone White' (J. Ravenscroft, Nantwich, England around 1950). Growth cushion-like, only 15 cm high; fresh green; flowers white, July–August.

'Elsie Frye' (Frye, Seattle, USA 1940). 20 cm high; foliage similar to 'Alba Elegans', but darker green and somewhat smaller; flowers white, double, but the first flowers usually single.

'Elsie Purnell' (J. W. Sparkes, before 1963). Sport of 'H. E. Beale', but somewhat lighter and later; to 70 cm high; pink-red, September–October. ⊕

'Foxhollow Wanderer' (Letts). Growth wide and mat-like, only 15 cm high, very strong grower, dense; foliage fresh green; flowers purple, August to October.

'Foxii'. Develops into a small, medium green cushion, 7–15 cm high; normally not flowering, or only 1 or 2 branches with purple flowers in August to September.

'Foxii Nana'. Normally not over 7 cm high and cushion-like, to 45 cm wide, then eventually to 20 cm high; foliage deep green; flowers purple, August–September.

'Fred J. Chapple' (Chapple, before 1961). Growth compact and upright, between 40—80 cm high; foliage normally medium green, but variable with green, yellow, pink and copper tones, pink-red at the branch tips, much better than 'Tricolorifolia' and 'Hammondii Rubrifolia' and recognized by its yellow speckled foliage in summer; flowers purple, August—September.

'Gnome' (J. W. Sparkes). To 20 cm high, resembles 'Humpty Dumpty', but denser and with greenish-yellow branch tips, like a dwarf conifer in appearance; occasionally some flowers in September to October, white.

'Golden Carpet' (Letts). Very slow growing, only 5 cm high, developing into a gold-yellow carpet, with orange and red tones in winter; flowers purple, August—September. ⌀

'Golden Feather' (J. W. Sparkes, before 1967). Branches featherlike, to 45 cm high; foliage gold in early summer, then orange for the rest of the year; flowers lilac, August—October. Notable for its foliage.

'Gold Haze' (J. W. Sparkes, before 1963). Long branched, to 70 cm high; foliage remaining a light gold-yellow the whole year; long shoots with white flowers, August—September.⌀

'Goldworth Crimson'. Strong grower, to 60 cm high; foliage deep green; flowers dark violet-red, very late, September—November. ⊕

'Hammondii'. Very strong grower, 60—80 cm high; foliage an attractive deep green, the young twigs somewhat lighter, especially in winter; flowers in very long spikes, pure white, August—September (= 'Alba Hammondii'). Excellent for cut flowers. Plate 88.

'Hammondii Aureifolia'. Very strong grower, 45—90 cm high, rather densely branched; foliage a fresh gold-yellow in spring, in good contrast with the older green foliage; white flowers in August—September (= 'Hammondii Aurea'; 'Aureifolia').⌀

'Hammondii Rubrifoia'. New growth in spring a beautiful red; flowers lilac. Seedling of the former.⌀

'H. E. Beale' (Maxwell & Beale). Growth strong, sparsely upright to 60 cm high; flowers densely packed, in long, branched inflorescences, very full, pink, medium light, September—October. Found in the New Forest, England. Lasts well as a cut flower. Plate 39, 89. ⊕

'Hibernica'. Growth prostrate, 15 cm high; flowers abundantly, light pink, very late, October—November (= 'Autumnalis').

'Hiemalis'. Growth narrowly upright, 30 cm; leaves very dense; flowers pale violet, mid-September—November, the last flowers usually freezing back. JRHS 67: 106. Found in 1938 in Hyères, S. France, where the plant was in full bloom in mid-January. Introduced into culture by T. Johnson, Conway, N. Wales.

'Hirsuta Typica'. Very strong grower, to 60 cm high; foliage very dense, gray; flowers pale lilac, August—September (= 'Incana').

'Hookstone'. Growth narrowly upright, to 60 cm high; flowers pure pink, spent flowers darker, August—September.

'Humpty Dumpty' (J. W. Sparkes, before 1965). Growth nest-like, 15—20 cm high, looks like a dwarf conifer from a distance; fresh green, flowers white, August—September, few flowers.

'J. H. Hamilton' (Maxwell & Beale 1935). Growth wide and compact, some 25 cm high; inflorescence wide, flowers very densely arranged, full, salmon-pink. Found on Mount Maughan in Yorkshire, England. Probably the most beautiful cultivar of all. ⊕

'Joan Sparkes' (Sparkes). Growth loose and open; flowers double, orchid-purple, HCC 31/3. Supposedly originated as a mutation on a normal branch of 'Alba Plena'. ⊕

'John F. Letts' (Letts). Compact grower, resembling 'Sister Anne', 10—15 cm high; foliage soft yellow in summer, later with orange and red in fall and winter; flowers pale lilac, August—September. ⌀

'Kit Hill' (Maxwell & Beale). To 25 cm high; flowering branches very curved, branches spreading laterally, flowers white, very late.

'Kuphaldtii' (Kuphaldt Hesse-Weener 1932). Growth procumbent, with long, zigzag branches, laying over one antoher, dark green; flowers lilac, August—September (= 'Decumbens').

'Lambs Tails' (J. W. Sparkes). Growth wide, but only 10 cm high, twigs very wide ("like small lamb's tails"), gold-yellow with a trace of yellow, especially in winter; flowers pink, August—September.

'Long White'. Growth upright, loose, 45 cm; foliage fresh green; long white inflorescences, September—October. Very vigorous grower. ⊕

'Mair's Variety'. Strong grower, to 75 cm high; flowering twigs to 30 cm long, flowers pure white, August—September. GC 138: 105. Very durable.

'Minima'. Growth grass-like, some 10 cm high, twigs very thin and ornamental, light green; inflorescence short, with only few, violet flowers. ⌀

'Mrs. Pat' (Maxwell & Beale). Dwarf, branch tips on new growth pink; flowers lilac. Very attractive. ⌀

'Mrs. Ronald Gray' (Dr. R. Gray). Creeping, grass-like, branches growing horizontally along the ground, light green; flowers reddish, August—September. Very attractive between stepping stones, tolerates foot traffic well. ⌀

'Mullion' (Maxwell & Beale). Growth dense, grass-like, twigs feathery; flowers violet-pink. One of the best cushion forms.

'Multicolor'. Height to some 30 cm; normal foliage yellowish-green, twig tips red in winter, often over the entire plant, not only the sunny side, new spring growth copper-red, very attractive in contrast to the old leaves; flowers pale lilac, August—September. Plate 39. ⌀

'October Crimson' (J. W. Sparkes). Upright, 45 cm; foliage a good green; flowers in long spikes, carmine, October.

'Orange Queen' (J. W. Sparkes, before 1965). Foliage pale green in summer, yellow with orange tones in winter, new growth red; flowers in 10 cm long spikes, August—September, pink-purple.

'October White'. Flowers in very long, erect spikes, 60 cm, pure white, October—November. Excellent cut flower.

'Peter Sparkes' (Sparkes). Like 'H. E. Beale' in habit and flower, but darker pink, HCC 527/3—627/3. ⊕

'Plena'. Medium sized, twigs erect; flowers double, violet-pink. Weak grower. ⊕

'Prostrate Orange' (J. W. Sparkes). Some 20 cm high; foliage yellow-green in summer, reddish in winter, stronger orange than 'Orange Queen'; few flowers, pink, August—September.

'Rigida'. Low growing, narrowly upright, twigs nearly angular, fresh green; flowers white (= 'Tetragona').

'Robert Chapman'. Growth broad, upright, to 45 cm, twigs of various length, very dense, gold-brown, coppery in winter; flowers purple-pink, August—September.

'Roma' (Maxwell & Beale). Weak grower, some 15 cm high, very dense; flowers deep pink. Plate 88. ⊕

'Rosalind' (Underwood). Growth upright, to 45 cm; foliage a bright gold-yellow, older plants often with many green lower branches, occasionally also red branches; flowers lilac, August—September.

'Ruth Sparkes' (J. W. Sparkes, 1958). Sport of 'Alba Plena'; growth compact, 20 cm high; foliage gold-yellow; flowers full, pure white, August—September. Occasionally reverting back to the green foliage, simple flowering form.

'Serlei'. Old cultivar, growth upright, to 60 cm, vigorous; foliage emerald-green, twigs long, with white flowers from September—November. Its name is often mistakenly spelled (= 'Searle', 'Searly', 'Serlii', 'Shirley' etc.).

'Serlei Aurea'. Sport of 'Serlei', 45 cm high; foliage remaining gold-yellow the entire year; flowers white, August—September.

'Serlei Purpurea'. Growth bushy, to 60cm high; flowers lavender-purple, September—October.

'Silver Knight' (J. W. Sparkes). Very similar to 'Silver Queen', but more compact, usually not over 30 cm; foliage silvery woolly; flowers pink-lilac, August—September.

'Silver Queen'. Growth 30 cm high, total plant dense silver-gray with long pubescence; flowers lilac, August—September. ∅

'Sister Anne'. Growth carpet-like on the ground, densely silver-gray pubescent, reddish-gray in winter; flowers violet-pink, September. Found in Cornwall, SW. England. 1929. ∅

'Spicata'. Old cultivar, 30 cm high; flowers abundantly, pure white, August—September (= 'Alba Spicata').

'Spitfire' (R. E. Hardwick, Newick, Sussex). Good yellow foliage type, 30 cm high; winter color red, especially intense on the sunny side; flowers pink, August—September.

'Spring Cream' (J. W. Sparkes). Growth upright, to some 45 cm; foliage fresh green with cream-white branch tips, August—September.

'Spring Torch' (J. W. Sparkes). Growth to 30 cm; foliage fresh green, twig tips vermillion-red in spring; flowers pink, August—September.

'Sunset'. Growth loose, 15—20 cm high; foliage yellow-orange with darker tips, redder in winter (more markedly than 'Robert Chapman'); few flowers, pink, August—September. Plate 39. ∅

'Tenuis'. Growth loose, prostrate, some 15 cm high, twigs irregularly twisted; leaves dark green; flowers deep lilac to violet, very early, June—July. ⊕

'Tib' (Maxwell & Beale). Growth upright to 30 cm high; flowers dense and double, nearly as violet-red as 'Alportii', August—September. Found in 1934 in Scotland. ⊕

'Tom Thumb'. Only 15 cm high, very dense, nearly moss-like; leaves gold-green; flowers pink, August—September. Very attractive. ∅

'Tricolorifolia' (James Smith, Darleydale). To 60 cm high; foliage dark green-bronze in winter, branch tips light green, in summer bronze, red and gray, best in April—May; flowers pink but only a few flowers.

'Underwoodii' (G.E. Underwood, Woking, England before 1960). Growth to 30 cm high; foliage dark green, somewhat lilac toned in winter; flowers in 15 cm long spikes, remaining in the bud stage and not opening, ivory-pink at first, then silvery pink, finally purple, September—November. ⊕

'Winter Chocolate' (J. W. Sparkes). Growth 30 cm high; foliage green and orange in summer, chocolate-brown in winter, new spring growth red, August—September. ∅

All forms prefer a sandy, acid, peat soil for best development; older plants become somewhat unattractive and should be pruned back severely in the spring, before bud break.

Lit. Beijerinck, W.: Die geographische Verbreitung von *Calluna vulgaris*; in Rec. Trav. Bot. Néerl. **33**, 341—350, 1936 ● Beijerinck, W.: Uebersicht der bis jetzt bekannten Formen von *Calluna vulgaris*; in Rec. Trav. Bot. Néerl. **34**, 445—470, 1937 ● Beijerinck, W.: *Calluna*; a monograph of the Scotch Heather; 180 pp., 29 plates, Amsterdam 1940 ● Chapple, F. J.: The Heather Garden; 180 pp. London 1951 ● Letts, J. F.: Handbook of hardy Heaths and Heathers; 127 pp., privately printed, 1966 ● Maxwell, D. F.: The low Road; 105 pp., 7 color plates, London 1917 ● Johnson, A. T.: Hardy Heaths; 127 pp., London 1956 ● Honelmann, W.: Die winterharten Gartenheiden; in Deutsche Baumschule 1956, 166—173 ● Underhill, T. L.: Heaths and Heathers; *Calluna, Daboecia* and *Erica*; 256 pp., Newton Abbot, 1971 ● Van De Laar, H.: Heidegaerten; with 84 colored ill., Berlin 1876.

CALODENDRUM Thunb. — Cape chestnut — RUTACEAE

Evergreen trees; leaves opposite or in whorls of three, simple, glandular; flowers in terminal panicles, with 5 sepals, 5 long narrow petals, stamens 10, including 5 staminodes (petaloid), ovary 5 chambered; fruit a large, 5 valved capsule, thick and warty exterior, seed black, angular. — 2 species, one well distributed in S. Africa, the other in the tropics.

Calodendrum capense (L.f.) Thunb. Cape chestnut. Tall and wide crowned tree in its habitat (where it is one of the most popular street trees), trunk gray, smooth even on older trees, branches opposite, young twigs pubescent; leaves opposite, entire, 5—20 cm long, 3—10 cm wide, elliptic to oblong, midrib very thick, blade with oil glands (easily visible with back lighting), usually deciduous, in favorable conditions evergreen; inflorescence to 18 cm long and 15 cm wide, terminal; calyx soon abscising, petals 3 cm long, 4 mm wide, pink with lilac, red or purple markings, July; fruit 3.5 cm

thick, the black seeds about the size of hazel nuts.
BMns 34; MCL 14; PPT 984 (= *Dictamnus capensis* L.f.).
S. Africa. 1789. z9 # ✧

Occasionally found in gardens located in warm climates. Tolerates occasional light frost but them blooms poorly.

CALOPHACA Fisch. — LEGUMINOSAE

Low, deciduous, glandular-pubescent shrubs or herbaceous plants; leaves alternate, odd pinnate, with up to 25 short stalked leaflets; papilionaceous corollas yellow or violet, singular or in racemes; calyx tubular, acute dentate; standard petal erect, margin reflexed, slightly auriculate at the base, wing petals oblong, as long as the keel petal; pod cylindrical, not swollen. — 10 species; southern USSR to Burma and China, in dry areas.

Calophaca crassucaulis (Baker) Komar. Subshrub, twigs erect, short, thick, densely covered with the persistent old leaf rachises; leaflets 21—25, linear-oblong, 4—6 mm long, pubescent; flowers solitary, 2 cm long, yellow to red, stalk 1 cm long; calyx very oblique, densely shaggy pubescent; standard pubescent outside. W. China, Himalaya. 1932. z6

C. grandiflora Regel. Small, procumbent shrub, less pubescent than *C. wolgarica*; leaves 10—20 cm long, with 21—27 ovate tipped, 2.5 cm long leaflets; flowers light yellow, 2.5—3 cm long, grouped 12 or more together in erect, 20 cm long racemes, June—July; pods oblong, with 1—2 seeds. Turkestan. 1886. z6 Fig. 178. **S** ○ ✧

C. wolgarica (L.f.) Fisch. Procumbent shrub, rarely to 1 m high, young twigs very glandular-pubescent; leaves 5—8 cm long, leaflets 11—17, rounded, 15 mm wide, with bristly tips, pubescent beneath; flowers gold-yellow, 2.5—3 cm long, 4—6 in glandular, axillary racemes, June—July; pods 2—3 cm long, glandular-pubescent. S. Russia, along the Volga River; Turkestan. 1786. z6 Fig. 178. **S** ○ ✧

Beautiful, very hardy plants, best suited to very sunny, dry spots in the rock garden; branches pendulous when top-grafted, as is often done.

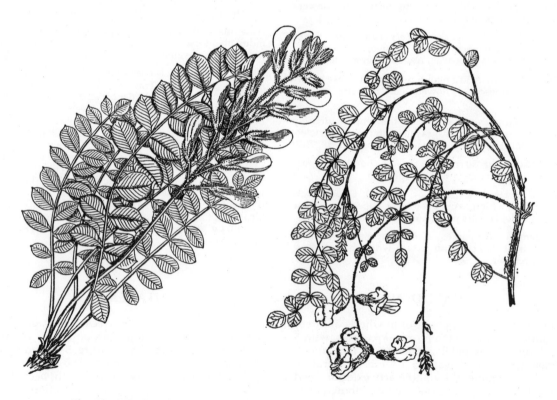

Fig. 178. **Calophaca.** Left, *C. grandiflora*; right, *C. wolgarica* (from Gartenflora and Browicz)

CALOTHAMNUS Labill. — MYRTACEAE

Evergreen shrubs, very closely related to *Callistemon*, but the stamen filaments not distinct, clustered 4—5 together, the flowers all directed to one side, not completely around the branch; leaves very distinctive, sometimes long and nearly cylindrical, sometimes flat, alternate. — 25 species, all in W. Australia.

Calothamnus asper Turcz. Small, bushy shrub, branches thick, but completely covered with erect, linear, 12—25 mm long and 2 mm wide, stiff, rough leaves; spikes short, dense with 4 parted flowers; stamen filament bundles red, 2—2.5 cm long. W. Australia. z9 # ✤

C. quadrifidus R. Br. Shrub, 0.5—1 m high, twigs glabrous or pubescent; leaves narrow, twisted or slightly flattened, heather-like, glandular-punctate, densely arranged, 1.5—2.5 cm long; flowers in fascicles under the new spring growth, 4 parted, stamen filament bundles intense carmine, anthers yellow, June—July. BM 1099. W. Australia. z9 # ✤

For cultural requirements see: *Callistemon*.

Color ills. of further species: *C. homalophyllus* F.v.M. (EWA 101); *C. pinifolius* F.v.M. (EWA 94); *C. rupestris* Schau. (EWA 134) and *C. validus* S. Moore (EWA 91; BMns 614).

CALYCANTHUS L. — Spicebush — CALYCANTHACEAE

Deciduous shrubs with aromatic bark, buds free or covered by the petiole base, leaves opposite, entire, usually rough above; flowers solitary, terminal on short side branches; perianth composed of numerous dark red-brown tepals; stamens in several spiralling circles, with only the outer 12 fertile; ovaries to 20; fruit an elliptic capsule with many brown seeds. — 4 species in N. America and 1 from China.

● Buds hidden in the leaf petiole base;
  + Leaves glabrous beneath:
      C. fertilis
  ++ Leaves densely pubescent beneath;
     * Base cuneate:
       C. floridus
    ** Base round to cordate:
       C. mohrii
●● Buds not hidden in the leaf petiole base:
      C. occidentalis

Calycanthus chinensis Chen & S. Y. Chang (1957), with ivory white flowers, from China, probably not in cultivation (ICS 804). ✤

C. fertilis Walt. Shrub, 1—3 m high, twigs only slightly aromatic, with short pubescence when young, buds hidden; leaves ovate-elliptic, rough and glossy dark green above, at first finely pubescent beneath, soon becoming nearly totally glabrous and blue-green, acute, 5—15 cm long; flowers greenish purple or reddish brown, 3—5 cm wide, slightly fragrant, June—July; fruit 5—7 cm long, contracted at the top, abundant, seed bean-like, GSP 140; BB 1651 (= *C. glaucus* Willd.). SE. USA. 1806. Often confused with *C. floridus*, which is much less common in the garden and produces little fruit. z6 Plate 89; Fig. 179. ✤

var. **laevigatus** (Willd.) Bean. Leaves more elliptic-oblong, light green and glossy beneath. BR 481 (= var. *ferax* Rehd.; *C. laevigatus* Willd.).

'**Nanus**'. Dwarf shrub, leaves ovate to elliptic or oblong, green beneath, 4—8 cm long. ND 1: Pl. 48.

'**Purpureus**'. Leaves very reddish beneath, otherwise like the species. Disseminated from Holland around 1933. ✤ ∅

C. floridus L. True Spicebush. Shrub, 1—3 m high, twigs, roots and leaves having a strong fragrance of cloves, especially the dried bark; young twigs very tomentose, later olive-brown; leaves oval to ovate to oblong, often rounded at the apex, not always acuminate, 5—12 cm long, gray-green beneath and remaining densely pubescent (very important for identification!); flowers dark red-brown, 4—5 cm wide, fragrance resembling strawberries, June—July; fruit obovoid, 6—7

Fig. 179. *Calycanthus fertilis* (from Guimpel)

cm long, very narrowed at the top, seldom developing in N. Europe. BM 503. SE. USA. 1726. The seeds are poisonous to cattle and sheep, as are those of *C. fertilis*. z5 ⊕ ∅

Mrs. Henry Type'. Flowers distinctly larger than those of the species and much more numerous. Found by Mrs. J. Norman Henry, in Philadelphia; grown at the Morton Arboretum, Lisle, Ill. ⊕ ∅

'Ovatus'. Leaves ovate to ovate-oblong, rounded at the base to somewhat cordate. SH 1: 222b (= *C. ovatus* Ait.).

C. mohrii (Small) Pollard. Shrub, to 1 m high, very similar to *C. floridus*, twigs pubescent; leaves more broad elliptic, base broad cuneate to somewhat cordate, 7—15 cm long; flowers purple, 5—6 cm wide, June—July; fruit only slightly narrowed at the top. SE. USA. 1908. z6 ⊕

C. occidentalis Hook. & Arn. Shrub, 1.5 to 3 m, twigs aromatic, buds always free (important for identification!); leaves ovate to oblong-lanceolate, 8—20 cm long, acute, finely scabrous above, green and glabrous beneath; flowers purple-brown, quickly wilting from the apex inward and then becoming rust-yellow, 5—7 cm wide, very fragrant, June—August; fruit ovate-campanulate, not narrowed at the top, 4—5 cm long. BM 4808; MS 111; FS 1113 (= *C. macrophyllus* Hort.). California. 1831. Few flowers. z7 ⊕

C. praecox see: **Chimonanthus praecox**

All species prefer sunny, although somewhat protected areas in deep, fertile, moist soil; they will over-winter better if the twigs are permitted to "harden off" in the summer.

CALYCOCARPUM Nutt. — MENISPERMACEAE

Deciduous, strong growing, twining vines; leaves alternate, palmately lobed; flowers dioecious, greenish, in long, pendulous panicles; sepals 6, petals absent; stamens about 12, as long as the sepals; ovaries 3, with stellate stigma; fruit a drupe, with flat pit, concave on one side. — Only 1 species; Southern USA.

Calycocarpum lyonii (Pursh) Nutt. Climbing vine twining into the crowns of trees, young twigs glabrous or somewhat pubescent; leaves long petioled, deeply palmately lobed, rounded in outline, 12—20 cm wide, base deeply cordate, lobes usually entire; flowers greenish, in 10—20 cm long panicles, May—June; fruit a 2.5 cm long, rounded-oblong, black drupe. BB 1674. S. USA. 1879. Hardy. z6 Fig. 180. ∅

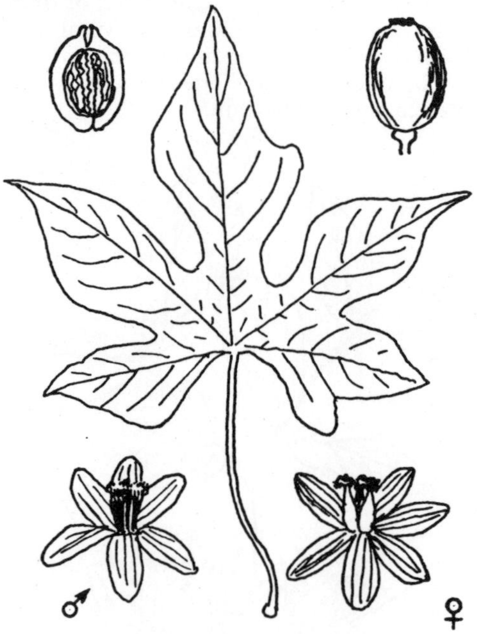

Fig. 180. *Calycocarpum lyonii*

CAMELLIA L. — THEACEAE

Evergreen shrubs, also trees in their native habitat; winter buds with imbricate scales; leaves alternate, without stipules, simple, short petioled, margin serrate; flowers bisexual, axillary, usually solitary, occasionally 2—3 together, white, pink, red or multicolored; sepals 5, persistent, often immediately subtended by several imbricate bracts; petals 5—12, slightly connate at the base; stamens numerous, connate at the base or in a column to half their length; style filamentous, connate at the base; fruit a loculicidal, woody capsule with persistent central axis and few seeds. — Some 82 species in tropical and subtropical SE. Asia, China, Japan and India.

Only those species found in gardens will be covered here, as most plants used in the milder areas are cultivars of *C. japonica*. Only in relatively recent years have other species (*C. sasanqua*, *C. cuspidata*, *C. saluensis*, etc.) been introduced.

Camellia cuspidata (Kochs) Veitch. Evergreen shrub, growth upright, to 1.5 m high, thin branched when young, young twigs glabrous to finely pubescent, yellowish to gray; leaves elliptic to oval-lanceolate, long acuminate, base rounded or cuneate, 5—8 cm long, finely and evenly serrate, smooth above, deep green, occasionally reddish, lighter beneath, finely punctate; flowers solitary at the ends of short branches or in the leaf axils, pure white, simple, 3 cm wide, March—April. BM 9277. W. China. The hardiest type by far, but only slightly decorative. z7 Fig. 182, 184. #

C. hongkongensis Seeman. Tall shrub, twigs thick, glabrous; developing leaves of an unusual bluish-brown tone, oblong to elliptic, 7—12 cm long, 2—3 cm wide, short acuminate, sparsely and finely dentate, appearing nearly entire, leathery tough; flowers nearly sessile, some 5 cm wide, dark carmine, styles 3, distinct, stamens 2.5 cm long; ovary dense tomentose. JRHS 74: 80; KHT 18. Hong Kong. 1874. z8 Fig. 182

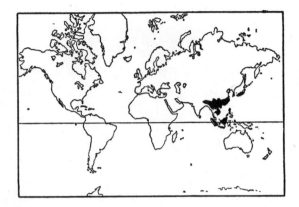

Fig. 181. Range of *Camellia*

Characteristics of the More Important Species

Camellia	cuspidata	japonica	reticulata	saluenensis	sasanqua	× williamsii
twigs	glabrous, thin, thin, yellowish to gray	glabrous	glabrous. stiff	pubescent at first, then glabrous, with dense foliage	glabrous or pubescent very thin	glabrous, thick
leaves	elliptic, long, acuminate, 5—8 cm	broad elliptic, short acuminate, 5—8 cm	broad elliptic, short acuminate, 8—11 cm	oblong-elliptic, usually obtuse, 3—6 cm	elliptic, margin margin crenate, 3—5 cm	elliptic, 6—8 cm
flowers	short stalked, simple, white	nearly sessile, quite variable in form, color and size	sessile, simple, pink to red	sessile, simple, white to pink	sessile, simple, 6—8 petals, white to pink	sessile, simple to semi-double, white to red
ovaries	glabrous	glabrous	tomentose	tomentose	tomentose	tomentose
style	3 cleft	3 cleft	3 cleft	3 cleft	3 cleft or 3 distinct styles	3 cleft
stamens	connate only at the base	connate to ½—⅔ of its length	½—¾ connate	⅔—¾ connate	spread widely apart	½—¾ connate, densely pubescent

C. japonica L. Evergreen shrub, densely branched, growth tall, a small tree in its habitat, 7—10 m (also in milder areas under favorable conditions); leaves broad elliptic or ovate, 5—8 cm long, short and usually obtusely tipped, slightly serrate, totally glabrous, often with scattered dots (corky warts) beneath, dark green above, very glossy, lighter beneath; flowers of the wild species red, simple, 3—4 cm wide, but on the many cultivars (see the list at the end of this section) rather various in form, size, fullness and color, from white or pink to deep red or multicolored, March—May; seed to 2.5 cm long, half as wide. LF 231; HCa 1. Japan, Korea. 1739. z8 Fig. 182. # ⊕ ⊘

Including many cultivars listed at the end of this section.

ssp. **rusticana** (Honda) Kitamura. "Snow Camellia". Shrub, 2—5 m high in its habitat, although usually procumbent; leaf petiole 5—8 mm long, often pubescent above; perianth of sepals and bracts shorter, some 1.5—1.7 cm long, inside glabrous to densely silky pubescent, flowers 4—5 cm wide, red, simple to semidouble, filaments only connate 2—3 mm over the petals. Japan; Honshu, in the mountains at 500—1000 m, often growing under *Fagus sieboldii*. 1954. Unusually winter hardy. z7 ⊕

C. oleifera Abel. Medium sized shrub, twigs roughly pubescent, seldom totally glabrous; leaves narrow to broad elliptic or more oblanceolate to obovate, sharply acuminate, 3—8 cm long, 2—3 cm wide, leathery tough and serrate; flowers nearly sessile, small, white, with 5—7 petals, stamens 1—1.5 cm long, erect, clinging tightly together, October to December; ovary tomentose. BMns 221; HKS 19. China. 1820. Cultivated for the oil content of its fruits. z8 Fig. 182.

C. reticulata Lindl. Evergreen shrub, a tree in its habitat, to 10 m, young branches stiff, glabrous, gray, winter buds to 1.2 cm long; leaves elliptic to broad obovate, often abruptly acuminate, leathery tough,

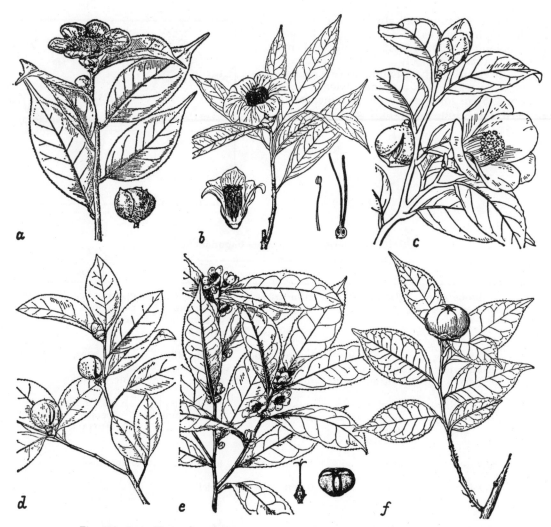

Fig. 182. **Camellia.** a. *C. cuspidata*; b. *C. hongkongenis*; c. *C. japonica*; d. *C. oleifera*;
e. *C. sinensis*; f. *C. yunnansis* (from ICS)

8—11 cm long, finely and evenly serrate, dark dull
green above, glabrous beneath with reticulate venation; flowers solitary, pink-red, to 7 cm wide, with 5—8
petals; also with semidouble garden forms. BM 9397
('Shot Silk'). W. China, Yunnan, in the mountains at
1500—2700 m. z8 Plate 91. # ✥

6 cultivars covered in UCa II.

C. saluenensis Stapf. Evergreen shrubs, 2—3 m high,
very dense foliage, young twigs pubescent at first;
leaves elliptic, acuminate, finely and regularly serrate,
with a small black gland at the tip of each tooth, 3—6 cm
long, deep green above, light green beneath,
glossy on both sides, glabrous except for the somewhat
pubescent midrib beneath; flowers solitary or in 2's, at
the ends of the previous year's branches, light pink
with darker lines or white, 5 petals, March—April;
fruits woody, with 3 seeds, 2.5 cm wide. W. China;
Yunnan. 1924. z7 Plate 90. # ✥

'**Macrophylla**' (BM 9505) = *C. williamsii*; which see.

C. sasanqua Thunb. Evergreen shrub, a small tree in its
habitat (and in mild climate), twigs very thin, glabrous
or pubescent; leaves elliptic, 3—5 cm long, regularly
crenate, on cultivars more or less leathery tough; flowers simple, with 6—8 petals, white to pink, also double
on the cultivars, January—March. BM 5152. Japan;
Liukiu Island. 1811. z8 # ✥

C. sinensis (L.) O. Ktze. Tea plant. Evergreen,
cultivated in tea plantations (Fig. 183), as a low shrub
with very dense foliage; leaves elliptic, short stalked,
5—10 cm long, cuneate, obtuse to open serrate, glossy
dark green above; flowers nodding on short, thick
stalks, small, white, with 7—8 petals, sepals persistent.
BM 998; 3148 (= *C. thea* Link; *C. theifera* Griff.; *Thea
sinensis* L.). China; Yunnan. In cultivation for centuries. z8 Fig. 182.

var. **assamica** (Mast.) Kitamura. Becoming a tree if allowed to grow; leaves larger, thinner, more sharply acuminate, 7–15 cm long, 3.5–6 cm wide, sparsely and indistinctly dentate to obtuse wavy serrate (= *Thea sinensis* L.). S. China, Indochina, Thailand, Burma, Assam. Many intermediate forms and hybrids of this variety and the species have been propagated. This variety originated in and for growing in tropical tea plantations, such as Ceylon and Assam. z8

C. tsai Hu. Twigs moderately thick, pendulous, with more or less densely appressed pubescence; leaves short petioled, oblong or more lanceolate to oblong-elliptic, caudate apex, 7–9 cm long, 2–3 cm wide, thin, finely serrate, glossy dark green above, lighter beneath, somewhat shaggy pubescent along the midrib; flowers white, 2–3 cm, 5 petals, very abundant, stalk with 4–5 persistent bracts, glabrous or silky pubescent like the calyx. HI 3430. W. China. 1924. z8 # ⊕

C. × williamsii W. W. Sm. (*C. japonica* × *C. saluenensis*). Tall shrub, with dense foliage, leaves and twigs resembling those of *C. japonica*, the flowers (especially the tomentose ovaries) resembling *C. saluenensis*; leaves elliptic to broad elliptic, 6–8 cm long, deep green and very glossy above, light green beneath, with brown corky warts, but also glossy, margin shallowly serrate; flowers simple or semi-double, white to deep pink; November–May. BM 9505 (as *C. saluenensis* f. *macrophylla*). Developed around 1930 by J. C. Williams at Caerhays Castle, Cornwall, England. 8 # ⊕

Including some cultivars listed at the end of this section.

C. yunnanensis (Pitard ex Diels) C. Stuart. Evergreen shrub, 1.5–7 m high, twigs light brown, pubescent, later brown with flaking bark; leaves short petioled, elliptic to broad ovate, obtuse, base broad cuneate, 4–7 cm long, 1.5–3 cm wide, leathery tough, serrate to finely serrate; flowers quite variable in size, 2–4 cm long, white, with 8–12 petals; fruit capsules 3–4 cm thick. China; Szechwan, Yunnan. z8 Fig. 182.

List of the Major Cultivars

a) Forms of *C. japonica*

'Adolph Audusson'. Strong grower, dense, upright; leaves large; flowers dark red, very large, semidouble. RYB 11: 43; UCa I. French introduction. Around 1875.

'Alba Plena'. Slow growing, bushy; leaves sharply acuminate, finely serrate; flowers white, large, regularly double. HCa 6. Very old cultivar. Introduced from China, 1792.

'Alba Simplex'. Flowers simple, large, white. RYB 8: 35 ('Snow Goose').

'Althaeiflora'. Pink, occasionally also white speckled, large flowering peony-form.

'Anemoniflora'. Strong grower, upright; flowers pink-red, medium size, semidouble peony-form; middle-early.

'Angelo Cocchi'. Flowers white, red striped, regularly double; middle-early.

'Are-jishi'. Strong grower, loose, upright; leaves large, glossy, acute, coarsely serrate; flowers deep blood-red, large, dense peony-form, irregular, petals wavy; early. Japan.

'Baronne Leguay'. Flowers dark pink, very large flowering, semi-peony-form, with irregular, erect petals in the center; middle early.

'Campbellii' = **'Margherita Coleoni'.**

'Coquetti'. Growth upright; flowers blood-red, dense, slow to open; late.

'Compton's Brow White'. Strong grower; leaves light green; flowers medium size, simple, pure white, stamens gold-yellow.

'Comte de Gomer'. Growth medium high, compact; flowers soft pink, with carmine specks and stripes, large and regularly double.

'Contessa Lavinia Maggi'. Strong grower; flowers pure white, red striped, regularly double, flowers abundant. HCa 49; FS 1525.

'Donckelarii'. Slow grower, bushy, rather erect; flowers red, white marbled in various tones, very large, semidouble, good

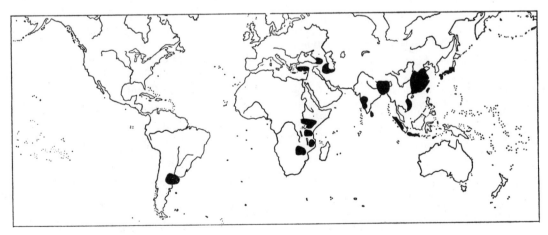

Fig. 183. Cultural range of *Camellia sinensis* (tea) (from Schutt 1972)

plant, abundant flowering. UCa I; HCa 96. Introduced before 1834 from the Orient by Von Siebold for Donckelar, then Head Gardener of the Louvain Botanic Garden, Belgium.

'Duchesse de Caze'. Strong grower, upright, compact; flowers pink-red, darker veined, limb white, medium size, double peony-form; middle early.

'Duchess de Rohan'. Strong grower, upright; flowers almond-pink, medium size, peony-form; middle late.

'Elegans' (Chandler). Growth slow and wide; leaves large, glossy; flowers pink and white, very large, anemone-form, incompletely double, outer petals large, center composed of petaloid staminodes and stamens; early to middle early. RYB 13: 58; UCa I; HCa 101 (better known than 'Chandleri elegans'). Breeder: A. Chandler, Vauxhall, England. Around 1822.

'Fred Sander'. Strong grower, upright, dense; flowers carmine, large, semidouble, petals wavy and fringed, with many yellow stamens; middle early to late. Breeder: F. Sander & Fils, Brugge, Belgium. Before 1913.

'Gauntlettii'. Strong grower, upright; flowers abundantly, flowers white, very large, semidouble waterlily-form to loose peony-form, petals wide, stamens yellow; middle early. UCa I.

'Giardino Schmitz. Slow grower and compact; flowers pink-red, medium size, regularly double, petals curved inward.

'Gloire de Nantes'. Growth upright, dense medium size; leaves deep green, glossy; flowers pink-red, large semi-double, early. RYB 11: 44. Plate 73.

'Grandiflora Alba' = 'Gauntlettii'.

'Haku-rakuten'. Strong grower, upright; flowers white, large, semi-peony-form, petals wavy, numerous petaloid staminodes and stamens; middle early. HCa 147.

'Imbricata Rubra'. Flowers light red, white speckled, large, regularly double.

'Italiana'. Flowers red, small, regularly double.

'Jupiter'. Growth narrowly upright; flowers scarlet-red, occasionally white speckled, medium size, semidouble.

'Kimberley'. Strong grower, upright, dense; flowers carmine, red filaments, cup-form, simple; middle early. HCa 156. Somewhat "touchy" in cultivation.

'Lady Clare'. Strong grower, bushy, loose; leaves large, deep green, attractive; flowers deep pink, very large, semidouble; early to middle early. HCa 165. Prefers a protected location.

'Lady de Saumerez'. Flowers light red, white speckled, semidouble.

'Lady Vansittart'. Slow growing, bushy; leaves Ilex-like; flowers white, pink striped, large, semidouble, petals wide, limb wavy. HCa 243; UCa II. Introduced 1887 from Japan.

'Latifolia'. Strong grower, bushy; leaves wide; flowers deep red, medium size to large, semidouble; late. Breeder: Guichard, Nantes, France.

'Lotus' = American name for 'Gauntlettii'.

'Magnoliiflora' ('Hagoromo' in Japan). Growth medium high, dense; leaves light green; flowers soft pink, medium size, semidouble. UCa 251. From Japan.

'Marchioness of Exeter'. Strong grower, loose, wide; flowers light pink, dense peony-form, often somewhat white variegated, outer petals crisped, inner erect, occasionally reflexed; early to midseason.

'Margherita Coleoni'. Strong grower, upright; flowers deep pink, rosette-form or regularly double to simple (= 'Campbellii'). From France.

'Marguerite Gouillon'. Strong grower, bushy; flowers soft pink, darker striped and speckled, medium size, full peony-form; middle-early (= 'Duc d'Orléans').

'Mathotiana'. Strong grower, dense, upright to broad; flowers scarlet-red, very large, regularly imbricate, somewhat loose. RYB 12:46; HCa 229. Breeder: M. Mathot, nursery in Belgium.

'Mathotiana Alba'. Strong grower, upright; flowers white, occasionally with pink tones, large, regularly double; late. UCa II.

'Mme. Canaert d'Hamale'. Sport from 'Cup of Beauty'; flowers light pink with darker shades.

'Nagasaki' ('Mikenjaku' in Japan). Weak grower, becoming wider than high; leaves wide, deep green; flowers pink-red, white marbled, outer petals and some of the inner, small and lying flat in the center, very large, semidouble. RYB 10: 29, HCa 252.

'Nobilissima'. Growth narrowly upright; flowers white with yellowish appearance, harmed by excessive rain, medium size, dense peony-form, often with petaloid staminodes and some stamens; early to midseason. HCa 312.

'Optima'. Growth bushy and upright; large flowering, soft pink with red specks; middle-early.

'Paolina Guichardina'. Flowers pink, somewhat red veined, medium size, regularly double, with large outer and long inner petals; middle-early.

'Peach Blossom'. Growth medium high, compact; flowers medium size, semidouble, light pink, somewhat darker than 'Magnoliiflora'.

'Principessa Baciocchi'. Flowers carmine, with white, medium size, regularly double; middle-early. HCa 266. Italian introduction.

'Principessa Clothilde'. Flowers white to pink, red striped, large, loose rosette-form, double.

'Professore Giovanni Santarelli'. Flowers white, with dark pink to dark red specks and stripes, medium size, regularly double.

'Rubescens Major'. Growth bushy and compact; large flowered, double, carmine red with darker veins.

'Sode-Gashuki' = 'Gauntlettii'.

'Splendens'. Large flowering, semidouble, red; late.

'Tricolor' (Siebold). Strong grower, dense, upright; flowers waxy white, with carmine stripes, medium size, somewhat cup-form, semidouble; middle-early. UCa I; HCa 309. Imported by Von Siebold from Japan in 1834.

'Yours Truly'. Sport of 'Lady Vansittart'; growth slow, bushy; leaves wavy; flowers medium size, semidouble, pink, darker striped, white margined.

b) Forms of C. × williamsii

'Donation'. (C. saluenensis × C. japonica 'Donckelarii'). Pink,

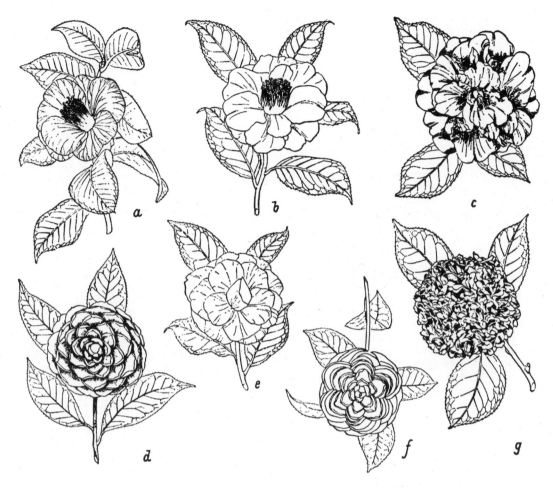

Fig. 184. Flower forms of *Camellia japonica*. a. simple; b. semidouble; c. incompletely double; d. regularly imbricate; e. incompletely imbricate; f. ranked; g. irregular (from H. Vogel)

large flowered, semidouble. HCa 396; UCa II. Breeder: Clarke. Before 1941. Plate 40.

'Elizabeth Rothschild (*C. saluenensis* × *C. japonica* 'Adolphe Andusson'). Flesh pink, semidouble.

'Francis Hanger' (*C. saluenensis* × *C. japonica* 'Alba simplex'). Growth upright; white, yellow stamens bundled in the middle, medium size. Breeder: Hanger. Before 1953.

'J. C. Williams'. Light to dark pink, medium size, simple, abundant, February—March. HCa 387; UCa 1. Breeder: J. C. Williams. Before 1942.

'Mary Christian. Dark pink, medium size, simple, very similar to 'J. C. Williams'. JRHS 1948: 80. Breeder: Williams. Before 1942.

'Pink Wave' (Seedling of 'J. C. Williams'). Pink-red, simple. Found as a seedling in Windsor Great Park, England. Before 1957. Plate 91.

'St. Ewe'. Pink-red, medium size, simple, broad cup-form. HCa 395; RYB 22: 11. Breeder: Williams. Before 1947.

c) Other Hybrids

'Cornish Snow' (*C. saluenensis* × *C. cuspidata*). White, occasionally with a trace of pink, small, simple, early and very abundant bloomer. Breeder: Williams. Before 1948.

'Inspiration' (*C. reticulata* × *C. saluenensis* ?). Growth upright; flowers pink, semidouble, good flowerng. Plate 40.

'Salutation' (*C. saluenensis* × *C. reticulata*). Soft pink, very large, simple to semidouble. JRHS 1948: 69. Breeder: Clarke. Before 1936 (Steph. Clarke, Borde Hill, Sussex, England).

Only cultivated as landscape plants in milder regions. Otherwise requiring a cool greenhouse in winter. Camellias will tolerate temperatures down to −7°C.

Lit. Since the *Camellia* literature is unusually extensive, only the major modern works will be mentioned: Urquhart, B. L.: The Camellia (1), 20 Pl. and text, Sharpthorne 1956; (2) 16 Pl. and text; 1960 ● Hertrich, W.: Camellias in the Huntingdon Gardens; 3 vols., San Marino, Calif., 1955–1958 ● Hume, H. H.: Camellias in America; Harrisburg 1955; notable for its extensive and accurate cultivar descriptions ● Sealy, J. R.: A revision of the genus *Camellia*; London 1958; one of the more modern monographs of the genus, with excellent illustrations ● Tourje, E. C.: *Camellia* Culture; New York 1958; compendium of 55 specialists ● The *Camellia*, its culture and nomenclature, 4th ed., Pasadena 1954; contains a very extensive cultivar list, published by the South. Calif. Camellia Society, who have also published the "Camellia Review" since 1939.

CAMPHOROSMA L. — CHENOPODIACEAE

Evergreen or deciduous, aromatic shrubs or only herbaceous plants with heather-like foliage; leaves alternate, needle-like, terete (round) or semi-terete (half-round); flowers small, inconspicuous, axillary, but grouped in spikes; calyx campanulate, 4 toothed; stamens 4, style with 2(−3) stigmas; fruit enclosed within the campanulate calyx. — 11 species in the Eastern Mediterranean region to Middle Asia.

Camphorosma monspeliaca L. Heather-like subshrub, to 0.5 m high, twigs procumbent, aromatic, woolly pubescent; leaves terete, clusters of smaller leaves in the axils of the larger, 4−8 mm long, awl-shape, softly pubescent; flowers in dense, oblong spikes; style red; seeds black, July. Mediterranean region to Middle Asia. z8 #

Only to be considered in milder areas especially along a coastline.

CAMPSIDIUM Seem. — BIGNONIACEAE

Evergreen vine, climbing without tendrils or aerial roots; leaves opposite, odd-pinnate; flowers tubular, orange, in terminal, loose, short racemes; calyx teardrop shape, 5 toothed, without glands; corolla tubular, somewhat swollen, straight, with 5 short, equally large limb lobes; stamens 4, the two longer ones with anthers protruding past the corolla; fruit a narrow, many seeded capsule. — 1 species in Chile and one in the Fiji Islands.

Campsidium valdivianum Seem. Climbing to 15 m high in its habitat, twigs angular, glabrous; leaves glabrous, 10−15 cm long, with usually 11−13 sessile, elliptic-oblong, 2−4 cm long leaflets, these serrate near the apex to nearly entire; flowers grouped 6−10 in pendulous racemes, corolla some 3 cm long, orange, pubescent from the throat to the base, May; capsule narrow elliptic−oblong, 7−10 cm l ong. FS 2142; BM 6111 (as *C. chilense*) (= *C. chilense* Reissek & Seem.; *Tecoma valdiviana* Phil.). 1870. z9 # ⊕

For culture see: *Campsis*

CAMPSIS Lour. — Trumpet-creeper — BIGNONIACEAE

Deciduous vines climbing by means of aerial roots; leaves opposite, odd-pinnate, leaflets serrate; flowers in terminal panicles or cymes, the stalks cruciform-opposite; calyx thick, leathery, corolla campanulate to wide funnelform, basal portion somewhat curved and widened; stamens 4; fruit a long, bi-valved dehiscent capsule; seed flat, winged. — One species in E. Asia and one in N. America.

Campsis	Aerial roots	Leaflets	Calyx teeth
grandiflora	absent or only a few	7−9, always glabrous beneath	long, lanceolate, nearly as long as the tube
radicans	present	9−11, midrib pubescent beneath	short, triangular, much shorter than the tube
× tagliabuana	present	7−11, venation pubescent beneath	long, lanceolate, but much shorter than the tube

Campsis grandiflora (Thunb.) Schumann. Vine, climbing 3−6 m high, without or with only few aerial roots; leaflets 7−9, oval-lanceolate, serrate, glabrous, 4−7 cm long, long acuminate; flowers in loose, terminal, large panicles; calyx deeply 5 cleft, teeth nearly 2 cm long; corolla tube flared, very funnelform, 5−6 cm wide at the limb, tangerine-red, inside a deep yellow, August−September. DL 1: 20; FS 1124; BIC 36 (= *C. chinensis* Voss). China, Japan. 1800. Much rarer in cultivation than the others, also much more difficult to grow. z7 Plate 89; Fig. 185. ⊕

'Thunbergii'. Tube much shorter, limb reflexed, orange, flowering time later, more winter hardy. ⊕

C. radicans (L.) Seem. Climbing to 10 m high, numerous aerial roots; leaflets 9−11, elliptic, 3−6 cm long, serrate, midrib always pubescent beneath; flowers 4−12 in terminal clusters on the current year's wood; calyx campanulate, with 5 short teeth; corolla tube long tubular-funnelform, 5−7 cm long, orange to light orange, inside yellow, corolla limb scarlet-red, 3−4 cm wide, July−September; fruit 8−10 cm long. BB 3366; GSP 441; BM 485 (= *Tecoma radicans* Juss.). SE. USA. 1640. The flowers can cause a skin irritation on susceptible persons. z5 Fig. 185.⊕

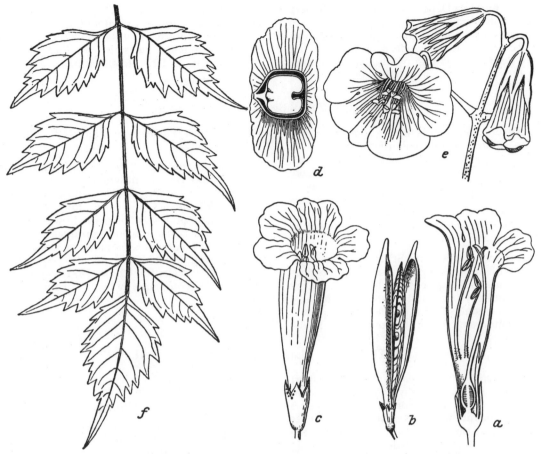

Fig. 185. **Campsis.** a—d C. *radicans*; e—f C. *grandiflora* (from Baillon, Dippel)

'Flava'. Leaves lighter green; flowers orange-yellow to pure yellow (= 'Yellow Trumpet'). Before 1842. ⊕

'Praecox'. Flowers scarlet-red, blooms in June (= 'Sanguinea praecox'). Before 1864. ⊕

'Speciosa'. Only weakly climbing or shrubby, but long branched; leaves abruptly long acuminate; flowers small, orange-red, limb 3 cm wide. Before 1902. ⊕

C. × tagliabuana (Vis.) Rehd. (= C. *grandiflora* × C. *radicans*). Intermediate between the parents and much more frequently found in European gardens; growth usually more shrubby and less climbing, erratic habit; flowers in loose panicles, corolla 5—6 cm wide, orange outside, scarlet-red inside. HR 1928: 310 (= C. *hybrida* Zab.). Originated in 1858 by De Visiani in the Tagliabue Nursery in Lainate, near Milan, Italy. z5

In addition several forms, most developed by Simon Louis Freres in Plantieres near Metz and Sahut, Montpellier, France.

'Coccinea'. Flowers bright red. ⊕

'Mme Galen' (Sahut, Montpellier 1889). Leaves to 45 cm long, leaflets to 15 together, ovate, distinctly acuminate, coarsely dentate, pubescent along the venation beneath, leaves of the flowering branches smaller and with fewer leaflets; individual flowers to 8 cm long and 7 cm wide, with 5 round limb sections, tube orange outside (HCC 014), jasper-red inside (HCC 018), darker shades along the veins. BMns 198. ⊕

Although climbing by aerial roots, it is advisable to provide support, preferably along a warm southern wall. Like *Clematis*, they would prefer to have their roots shaded in a fertile soil. A severe pruning each year is helpful since, like grape vines, they bloom on the current year's wood. Valuable summer and autumn blooming plants with outstanding funnelform flowers.

CAMPTOTHECA Dcne. — NYSSACEAE

Deciduous tree with alternate, simple, entire leaves; flowers unisexual or bisexual, sessile, solitary or in axillary or terminal panicles; calyx cup-form, 5 toothed; petals 5 valvate; stamens 10, white, uneven, in 2 circles; fruits samara-like, sessile, sides unequal, grouped in globose heads (capitula). — Only 1 species.

Camptotheca acuminata Dcne. Tree, to 20 m high, bark light gray, smooth, branches thick, at wide angles to the stem, twigs gray-green, glabrous; leaves oval-oblong, to 12 cm long and 9 cm wide, acuminate, entire, but sparsely dentate on young plants, base rounded, dark green above, lighter beneath with venation dense silvery silky pubescent, with 8—12 raised paired veins; flowers with white, prominent stamens, in axillary, 2 cm wide, globose capitula, stalk 3 cm; samara 2.5 cm long, 8 mm wide, glossy brown. FIO 15; ICS 3699; CIS 41. SW. China, Tibet, to elevations of 2000 m. z8? ⌀

Rare in cultivation.

CAMPYLOTROPIS Bge. — LEGUMINOSAE

Deciduous shrubs, low, resembling *Lespedeza*, but flower stalks solitary in the axils of the subtending leaves, the latter persistent or abscising; flower stalk segmented beneath the calyx (not so on *Lespedeza*); leaves trifoliate, middle leaflet thin stalked; flowers usually purple, in racemes, clustered in large panicles at the branch tips; calyx campanulate, 5 parted, both upper teeth connate; pod single seeded. — Some 40 species in Europe and Asia.

Campylotropis falconeri (Prain) Schindler. 1 m high, twigs striped with appressed pubescence; leaflets obovate, 1—4 cm long, softly pubescent beneath; flowers purple, in dense, 5—20 cm long panicles, August—September, flower stalks 2—5 mm long; bracts persistent; pods 7—9 mm long, dense silky pubescent. BR 32: 28 (= *Lespedeza dubia* Schindler). NW. Himalaya. 1920. z8? **d** ○ ✥

C. macrocarpa (Bge.) Rehd. 1 m high, twigs nearly round, silky pubescent when young; leaflets elliptic to oblong, 2—5 cm long, obtuse and usually emarginate, the middle leaflet 3—5 mm, long stalked, glabrous above, silky pubescent beneath; flowers purple, some 1 cm long, in axillary racemes grouped in panicles at the branch tips, August to September; pods elliptic, some 1.5 cm long. SH 2: 69 h-l, 70 a (= *Lespedeza macrocarpa* Bge.). N. and Central China. 1871. Very similar to *Lespedeza thunbergii*, equally beautiful and yet hardier. z5 **d** ○ ✥

For culture see: *Lespedeza*.

CANTUA Juss. ex Lam. — POLEMONIACEAE

Evergreen trees and shrubs; leaves alternate, short petioled, simple, flowers usually many in terminal corymbs, occasionally solitary; corolla tubular, with 5 short, ovate or obovate limb lobes; stamen filaments joined at the base of the tube, protruding beyond the tube; fruit a leathery, many seeded capsule. — 11 species in the Andes of Ecuador, Peru and Bolivia.

Cantua buxifolia Juss. Ornamental shrub, to 1 m high, more or less pubescent; leaves elliptic to lanceolate, entire, occasionally finely serrate, pubescent or glabrous, 2 cm long on flowering branches, larger on the others; flowers 5—8 hanging from horizontal shoots, tube some 6 cm long, yellow striped, limb purple, April—May. BM 4582; FS 650; HTS 120 (= *C. dependens* Pers.). Andes of Peru, Bolivia and Chile. 1849. z9

C. pyrifolia Juss. Shrub or tree; leaves usually clustered, elliptic to oblong, 4—5 cm long, occasionally somewhat dentate on the apical half; flowers about 15 in dense, erect racemes, terminal; calyx usually 3 toothed, corolla tube-form, yellow, about twice as long as the calyx, limb lobes white, March. FS 383; BM 4386; HTS 121. Ecuador, Peru, Bolivia. 1846. z9

Only winter hardy and easily cultivated in frost free areas; otherwise must be over-wintered in a cool greenhouse.

CAPPARIS L. — CAPPARIDACEAE

Deciduous or evergreen shrubs or trees, often climbing with hooks; leaves simple, alternate; flowers usually with 4 cruciform petals, 4 sepals, many stamens, filaments reaching far beyond the petals; ovary long stalked; fruit a berry. — Some 250 species in the tropics and subtropics outside of N. America.

Capparis spinosa L. Deciduous shrub, thorny, prostrate, 0.3—0.7 m high, twigs with prickles (hardened stipules); leaves ovate to nearly circular, 1.3 cm long, glabrous, green to gray-green, thick; flowers light pink or whitish, stamen filaments violet, anthers yellow, June—August; fruits green, to 5 cm long when ripe. PEu 31. S. Europe. z8 Fig. 186. **d** ○

The young, pea size flower buds are collected and prepared as the spice "capers". The shrub has little ornamental value; the other species are cultivated as greenhouse plants.

Fig. 186. *Capparis spinosa* (from Baillon)

CARAGANA Lam. — Peashrub — LEGUMINOSAE

Deciduous shrubs or small trees; leaves alternate, evenly pinnate, rachis often persistent and thorny, leaves often clustered; stipules small, membranous and abscising or persistent and thorny; flowers usually yellow (seldom whitish or pink), solitary or fascicled, attractive; pod linear, cylindrical or inflated. — Some 80 species, from Southern Russia to China, Manchuria and Himalaya.

Key to the Major Species

● Leaves with (2) 3–9 paired leaflets;
   + Rachis abscising;
      * Stipules short, not thorned:
         C. arborescens
      ** Stipules longer, always thorned:
         C. boisii, decorticans, microphylla
   ++ Rachis persistent, prickly;
      * Stipules membranous, not thorned, flowers pale yellow:
         C. brevispina, gerardiana, jubata, sukiensis, tangutica
      ** Stipules only membranous at first, thorned after the flowers are spent:
         C. franchetiana, maximowicziana
●◗ Leaves with 2–4 paired leaflets, short branches always with 2 paired leaflets:
      C. spinosa
●●● Leaves always with 2 paired leaflets;
   + Leaflet pairs densely spaced:
         C. aurantiaca, densa, frutex
   ++ Leaflet pairs distinctly spaced further apart:
         C. sinica

Caragana arborescens Lam. Shrub, to 6 m high, growth narrowly upright, young twigs pubescent, bark green, later yellow-green; leaflets 8–12, elliptic, to 2.5 cm long, with a small prickly tip, light green; flowers 1–4, light yellow, May; pod cylindrical, somewhat pubescent. HM 1457; BM 1886. Siberia, Manchuria. 1752. Ⓕ in CSSR, USSR, USA and Canadian windbreaks. z2 Fig. 187.

'Albescens'. New growth whitish-yellow, turning green eventually. Occasionally found among seedlings. ∅

'Lorbergii'. Leaflets 10–14, linear-lanceolate, to 3.5 cm long, only 5 mm wide; petals narrow. Originated in the Lorberg nursery before 1906. ∅

'Nana'. Dwarf cultivar, twigs short, twisted. Before 1875.

'Pendula'. Actually a creeping form, but normally top grafted on a standard; strong grower, branches tightly arching and then growing directly downward. Before 1856.

'Sericea' (Pelkwijk). Leaflets 8, both sides densely silky pubescent when young, also the flower stalk and calyx; pods narrow, 3–3.5 cm long.

'Walker' (C. arborescens 'Pendula' × C. arborescens 'Lorbergii'). Growth procumbent; leaflets very narrow, like those of 'Lobergii'. Best top grafted on a standard; also propagated by cuttings. Breeder: Prof. John Walker, Canada; introduced to the trade by Fopma, Boskoop (regional trade association), Holland.

C. aurantiaca Koehne. Shrub, to 1 m high, twigs long and thin, very numerous; leaflets 4, very densely spaced, rachis only 1 to 2 mm long, leaflets oblanceolate, 1–1.5 cm long, light green, underside lighter yet, glabrous, distinctly veined; flowers solitary, orange-yellow, on 8 mm long pedicels hanging from the previous year's branches, May; calyx campanulate, margin pubescent; ovary always glabrous (important for identification!). BS 1: 493. Central Asia, mountain valleys. 1887. One of the most beautiful of the Caraganas; hardly distinguishable from the similar C. pygmaea when not in flower. z5 Fig. 187. ⊕

B. boisii Schneid. Closely related to C. arborescens; some 1.5 m high, but usually much wider; leaflets 10–12, obovate to narrow obovate, 12 mm long, silky pubescent and whitish beneath when young, stipules dense and thorned, 8–10 mm long; flowers singular, yellow, calyx teeth longer than those of C. arborescens, ovaries and young fruit pubescent. VFr 57; SDK 4: 21 (= C. arborescens var. crasse-aculeta [Bois] R. J. Moore). China; Szechwan. 1904. z6 Fig. 187.

C. brevifolia Komar. Shrub, to 1.5 m high, closely related to C. grandiflora; leaf rachis and stipules thorned; leaflets narrow obovate to obovate-oblanceolate, 2–6 mm long, acute; flowers 1.5–1.8 cm long, stalk to 5 mm long; calyx often pruinose, with triangular thorned teeth. ICS 2540. NW. China, Kashmir. 1925. z6

C. brevispina Royle. Shrub, to 2m high, young twigs pubescent; leaflets 10–14, elliptic to oblong, 8–25 mm long, rounded at the apex, rachis 3–7 cm long, thorned, stipules thorny, 6 mm long; flowers 2 to 4 on one stalk (important for identification!), yellow, June; pods 5 cm long, silky outside, inside shaggy pubescent. SNp 12 and 34 (= C. triflora Lindl.). NW. Himalaya. 1849. z6 Fig. 187.

C. decorticans Hemsl. Shrub or small tree, bark greenish, shredding; stipules thorny, brown, leaflets 6–12, oval-elliptic, to 1.5 cm long, with thorny tips, with appressed pubescence and reticulate venation, rachis thorned; flowers grouped 1–2, May, stalk 2 cm long; calyx campanulate, thorny toothed. SH 2: 59 r–s2 (as C. prainii). Afghanistan. 1879. z6 Fig. 187.

C. densa Komar. Shrub, to 2.5 m high, densely branched, twigs glossy brown, bark patchy, internodes 1 cm long; leaflets to 4, densely spaced on a thorny, persistent, 7 mm long rachis, narrow oblanceolate, with long prickly tips, 8–16 mm long; flowers solitary, some 2 cm long, yellow, stalk 1 cm long, densely pubescent; calyx tubular, glabrous, teeth triangular; ovary glabrous. Middle China, mountain valleys. 1926. z6 Fig. 187.

C. franchetiana Komar. Shrub, to 3 m high, twigs light brown, rather smooth, pubescent when young; leaflets 10–16, narrow obovate to lanceolate, 7–12 mm long, dull green above, lighter beneath, margin and midrib pubescent; flowers 1–2 on a 2 cm long stalk with 3 prophylls and bracts, pale yellow with wine-red; calyx teeth triangular-lanceolate, nearly as long as the calyx tube; pods pubescent, 3—4 cm long. ICS 2550. SW. China. 1914. z6 Fig. 187.

C. frutex (L.) K. Koch. Shrub, upright 1—3 m high, stoloniferous, twigs thin, yellowish and glabrous; leaves petiolate, leaflets 4, obovate, nearly palmate, 2 cm long, dark green, soft, petiole and stipules somewhat thorny; flowers grouped 1—3, large, yellow, May to June; pods somewhat compressed, glabrous. BC 791 (= *C. frutescens* DC.). S. Russia to Turkestan and Siberia; in the steppes. 1752. Useful for dry areas. z2 Fig. 187.

'Biflora'. Flowers always in 2's, therefore much more floriferous and attractive.

'Globosa' (Skinner 1949). Seedling selection; growth compact and globose. Amer. Nurseryman, 4/1/1971.

'Latifolia'. Rachis to 18 mm long, always abscising; leaflets to 3.5 cm long, 1.5 cm wide, glossy dark green above; flowers to 2.5 cm long, petiole to 2.5 cm long. SH 2: 64 t—v.

'Macrantha'. Leaflets to 2.8 cm long; flowers to 3 cm long, calyx broader than that of the type, rachis abscising. SH 2: 64 w—y.

C. fruticosa (Pall.) Steud. Shrub, to 2 m high, upright, very similar to *C. arborescens*, but with leaflets 10—14, oblong-obovate, 1.5—2.5 cm long, rounded or acute, base cuneate, stipules only slightly thorny or membranous; flowers solitary, larger than those of *C. arborescens*, stalk longer and pubescent; calyx pubescent, teeth very short; pods 2—3 cm long (= *C. redowskii* DC.). Korea, Amur region. z5 1817.

C. gerardiana (Royale) Benth. Shrub, to 1 m high, densely branched, compact, twigs angular, glossy brown, densely woolly pubescent when young, internodes 1—2 cm; leaflets 8—12, obovate-oblanceolate, to 2 cm long, gray-green, silky pubescent, rachis thorny, to 5 cm long; flowers solitary, yellowish-white, short stalked, April to May; calyx tubular, 1 cm long, pubescent, teeth triangular; pods shaggy pubescent, 2—3 cm long. S. Tibet; alpine zone of the Himalayas. Before 1870. Very beautiful shrub with thin, but long haired twigs, for full sun. z5 Fig. 1871. ∅

C. grandiflora (Bieb.) DC. Very closely related to *C. aurantiaca*. Shrub, to 1 m high, rachis persistent, 4—7 mm long; leaflets oblong-obovate, apex rounded and with small thorned tips, glabrous or pubescent; flowers nearly 3 cm long, basal portion of the stalk segmented; calyx tubular, widened at the base. SH 2: 64 e—h. S. Russia and the Caucasus to Turkestan. 1823. Very hardy. z5 ⊕

C. jubata (Pall.) Poir. Shrub, to 1m high, sparsely branched, growth irregular, twigs short, thick, covered with dense, shaggy, thorned rachises, these 3 cm long and bowed; leaves densely arranged, leaflets usually 4—6, oblong-lanceolate, 1 cm long; flowers reddish-white, singular, May—June; pods 2 cm long, hairy. FS 2013; DRHS 338; ICS 2546. E. Siberia to W. China and

Turkestan; on moist slopes in the high mountains at 3000—4000 m. 1796. Very peculiar, erratic growing plant, quite winter hardy. z3 Fig. 187. ∅

'Columnaris'. Growth very columnar, to 2 m high; otherwise like the species (= 'Fastigiata'). Originated as a seedling in the Bergianska Traedgarden, Stockholm, Sweden. Before 1933. Plate 96. ∅

C. maximowicziana Komar. Shrub, to 1.5 m high, growth dense and wide, twigs red-brown, thin, peeling, rachis thorned, short; leaflets 4—6, oblong-lanceolate, 5—10 mm long, thorned-acute, light green; flowers yellow, 2.5 cm long, short stalked, May—June; calyx tubular, glabrous, with very short teeth; ovary pubescent only on the ventral seam. China, Tibet. 1910. Ornamental shrub with attractive leaves and flowers. z2 Plate 92. ⊕ ∅

C. microphylla Lam. Shrub, 1.5—2 m (3 m) high, young twigs silky pubescent; leaflets 12—18, oval to obovate, 5—8 mm, emarginate, gray-green, silky at first; flowers yellow, grouped 1—2, short stalked, May—June; calyx cylindrical, short toothed; pods 3 cm long. BC 790; ICS 2553 (= *C. altagana* Poir.). Siberia, N. China. 1789. Easily distinguished by its wide growth habit and numerous small leaflets. z2 Fig. 187. ∅

'Megalantha'. Leaflets larger, to 1.2 cm long, more round-obovate, less pubescent, light green; flowers to 3 cm long; pods to 4 cm long. SH 2: 60c. Originated in cultivation.

C. oreophila W. W. Sm. Shrub, 0.7—1 m high, bushy growth, twigs woolly, rachis woolly at first, later completely glabrous and thorny; leaves 2.5—3 cm long, with usually 16 leaflets, these oblong to obovate, 5—7 mm long, silky pubescent; flowers solitary, orange with brown, 2 cm long; calyx tubular, woolly, toothed; pods woolly. W. China. 1914. Hardy. z4

C. pekinensis Komar. Closely related to *C. decorticans*. Shrub, to 2 m high; stipules thorny, 5—10 mm long, leaflets 6—12, obovate, 8—12 mm long, gray pubescent on both sides; calyx tubular, long pubescent, teeth short; pods silky pubescent. ICS 2552. NE. China. 1923. Hardy. z5

C. pygmaea (L.) DC. Shrub, to 1 m high, also frequently procumbent, twigs rod-like, glabrous; leaf rachis 5—8 mm long, persistent or abscising, stipules short, thorny, leaflets 4, linear-oblanceolate, to 1.5 cm long, prickly tipped; flowers solitary, yellow, 2 cm long, stalk 1 cm long, May—June; calyx narrowly campanulate, teeth triangular (very important for identification!); wings with very small "ears" (auriculate); pods tubular 2—3 cm long, glabrous. BR 1021; SL 62. NW. China, Siberia. 1751. Plants in cultivation under this name often actually belong to *C. aurantiaca*; which see. z4 Fig. 187.

C. sinica (Buc'hoz) Rehd. Shrub, to 1 m high, growth sparse, twigs angular, yellow-brown, older twigs shredded; leaflets 4, in 2 distinctly separate pairs, obovate, dark green, glossy, 1—3.5 cm long; flowers solitary, 3 cm long, light yellow, spent flowers dark brown,

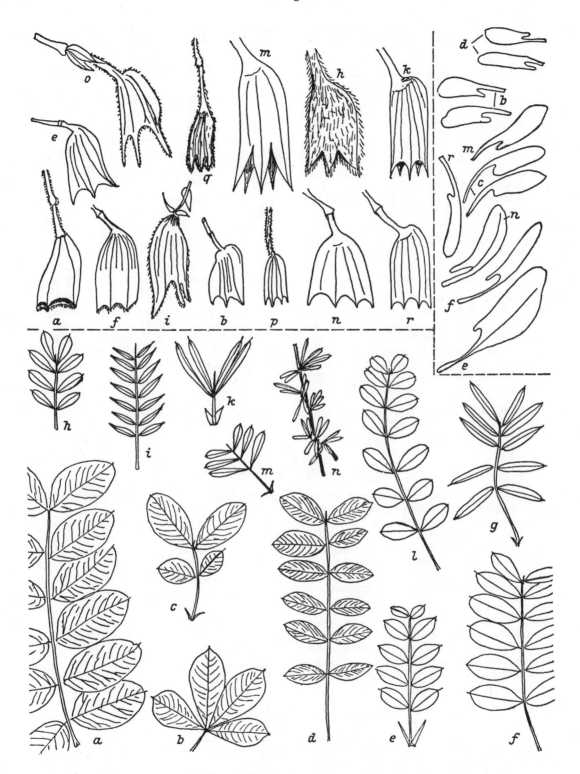

Fig. 187. **Caragana,** Leaves, calyxes and petals. a. *C. arborescens*; b. *C. frutex*; c. *C. sinica*; d. *C. brevispina*; e. *C. decorticans*; f. *C. boisii*; g. *C. jubata*; h. *C. gerardiana*; i. *C. sukiensis*; k. *C. spinosa*; l. *C. microphylla*; m. *C. tragacanthoides*; n. *C. aurantiaca*; o. *C. franchetiana*; p. *C. densa*; q. *C. tangutica*; r. *C. pygmaea* (partly from Ter Pelkwijk)

May—June; calyx campanulate, 5 toothed. HM 1458; SL 133; ICS 2545 (= *C. chamlagu* Lam.). N. China. 1773. z6 Fig. 187.

C. × sophorifolia Tausch. (*C. arborescens* × *C. microphylla*). Like *C. arborescens*, but leaflets usually 12, more elliptic-oblong, 8—15 mm long, with small prickly tips, cuneate at the base; pods some 2 cm long (= *C. cuneifolia* Dipp.). Before 1816.

C. spinosa (L.) DC. Shrub, 0.7—1.5 m high, growth loose, twigs without side branches, very thorny on the 7—45 mm long, stiff rachises; leaflets 4—8 on long shoots, linear-oblanceolate, 1.5—2 cm long, only 4 leaflets on short branches, 1.5 cm long, rachis only 7 mm long; flowers solitary, 2 cm long, light yellow, occasionally somewhat brown; calyx tubular, teeth short, triangular. Siberia. 1775. The Chinese around Peking often place the branches at the tops of the clay garden walls to discourage anyone from climbing over them (according to Pallas). z3 Fig. 187.

C. sukiensis Schneid. Shrub, resembling *C. gerardiana*. 1 m high, twigs long and nodding, pubescent; leaf rachises 2.5—3.5 cm long, persistent, hard, pubescent, leaflets 10—14, narrow oblong-oblanceolate, distinctly parallel venation, silky pubescent beneath, 6—8 mm long; flowers yellow, 2.5 cm long, singular; calyx tubeform; pod 1.5 cm long, somewhat pubescent. NW. Himalaya. 1919. Very hardy. z4 Plate 92; Fig. 187.

C. tangutica Maxim. Shrub, to 1 m high, growth wide, sprawling, twigs red-brown, older ones flaking, younger pubescent; leaflets usually 6, broad elliptic to obovate, with prickly tips, dark green above, gray-green beneath, 1 cm long, rachis thorny, persistent, 1.5—3.5 cm long; flowers yellow, 3 cm long, solitary; ovary very pubescent. ICS 2547. China, Kansu. z4 Fig. 187.

C. tibetica (Schneid.) Komar. Low growing shrub, densely branched, to 25 cm high; rachis persistent, thorny, whitish, glabrous, closely spaced on short internodes, stipules membranous, leaflets 6—12, linear-oblong, 5—10 mm long, silky pubescent; flowers light yellow, 2.5 cm long; standard petal emarginate. ICS 2549. W. China. 1927. z4

C. tragacanthoides (Pall.) Poir. Shrub, 0.3 to 0.5m high, wide and very twiggy, twigs very thorny with the numerous, persistent, bowed, 3 cm long rachises; leaflets 4—10, obovate, 8—15 mm long, cuneate at the base, with appressed pubescence; flowers to 3 cm long; pods 2.5—3 cm long, half surrounded by the campanulate calyx. NW. China to Altai and NW. Himalaya. 1816. Hardy. z4 Fig. 187.

All the Caraganas need a location in full sun. They prefer a dry, alkaline, light soil. They are not easily transplanted because of their relatively few, long roots. *Caragana arborescens* is an excellent hedging plant in windy locations.

Lit. Komarow, V. L.: Generis *Caraganae* Monographia; in Act. Hort. Petropol. **29**, 177—288, Pl. 1 to 20, 1901 (a short outline of these mentioned species and groups may be found in Schneider, Ill. Handbuch Laubholzkde., II, 1012—1016) ● Ter Pelkwijk, A. F.: Overzicht van de in Nederland gekweekte *Caragana*-soorten; in Jaarb. Ned. Dendr. Ver. **15**, 36 to 51, 1946.

CARICA L. — Papaya — CARICACEAE

Evergreen, tropical trees, containing milky sap; leaves alternate, palmately lobed, long petioled; flowers dioecious, white, yellow or greenish; male flowers on long stalks, axillary, funnelform, with 10 stamens joined to the throat, female larger and with 5 distinct petals, ovary with 5 lobed stigma, sessile in the leaf axils. — Some 45 species in tropical America, but cultivated all over the tropical world for their fruits.

Carica papaya L. Papaya. Short lived, fast growing, usually single stemmed small tree, 3—4 m high, stem some 15 cm thick; leaves nearly circular, deeply palmate 7 lobed, the lobes oblong, acute, entire or with some large teeth, thin, limp, yellow-green; flowers appear when plant is only 70—100 cm high (often only a few months old); fruits hang from the leaf axils, obovate or elliptic, size quite variable (numerous cultivars!), from 10—50 cm long, pulp light to dark orange, with numerous small, black seeds. BM 2898. S. America. 1690. The cultivars are grafted and bear fruit unusually quickly. They will continue to bear for about five years and are then replaced with new plants.

Culture is only possible in frost free areas with warm temperatures. They are commonly seen in the conservatories of larger botanic gardens.

Lit. Thursby, I. S.: The fruitfull Papaya; in Florida Agric. Ext. Service Bull. **134**, 1—20, 1948 ● Wolfe, H. S., & S. J. Lynch: Papaya Culture in Florida; in Florida Agric. Ext. Service Bull. **113**, 1—36, 1944.

CARISSA L. — APOCYNACEAE

Evergreen shrubs or small trees, some strongly branched and thornless or with stout simple or forked branched thorns; leaves opposite or decussate, leathery thick; flowers solitary or in dense cymes, axillary, pure white or with outside pink, very fragrant; calyx 5 parted, with or without glands at the base, corolla plate-like with a cylindrical tube, 5 petals; stamens connate under the tip of the tube; fruit a globose or ellipsoid berry. — 35 species in tropical Africa and Asia.

Carissa akocanthera Pichon. Evergreen shrub, to 4 m high, twigs rounded, green; leaves ovate to elliptic, to 10 × 5 cm in size, leathery, glossy, entire, glabrous; flowers in short stalked, axillary clusters, very attractive, white to pink, February—April, very fragrant; berries black-red, 2 cm long, very poisonous, as is the total plant. PBl (I.) 2: 217; RH 1880: 370 (= *Akocanthera venenata* [Thunb.] Don). South Africa, Cape. 1787. A gorgeous shrub in flower, but only cultivated in warmer climates. z9

C. macrocarpa (Eckl.) A. DC. Natal plum. Very dense and shrubby growing, never developing a stem, 4 m, branches and twigs with stout, forked, 3.5 cm long thorns; leaves 3—5 cm long, ovate, deep green, base rounded; flowers white, solitary, to 5 cm wide, very attractive, fragrant, May; fruits somewhat the size of plums, acute, 3—5 cm long, dark red, ripening in summer, very thin shelled, edible, tastes somewhat like raspberries. BM 6307; MCL 63 (= *Arduina grandiflora* [E. Mey.] A. DC.). S. Africa. 1862. z9

Cultivated in its native habitat and in California, USA. for its fruit, especially the cultivar 'Fancy'. In California 2 procumbent forms have been developed, thornless with smaller, ovate leaves and more globose fruits ('Cascade' and 'Tomlinsonii').

Lit. Lawrence, G. H. M.: The cultivated species of *Carissa*; in Baileya 7, 87—90, 1959; with 1 ill.

CARMICHAELIA R. Br. — LEGUMINOSAE

Shrub, leafless or with leaves quickly abscising; twigs (phylloclades) widened, green; leaves consisting of 3—5 leaflets, these small, unlobed; flowers in short, fascicled racemes, small, but usually very numerous, often fragrant; standard petal circular and usually reflexed, wings somewhat sickle-shape oblong, keel oblong, curved inward; pods small, oblong to circular, when the seeds are ripe, they and the pod flaps will abscise leaving the string-like "frame"; seeds 1—2, black or red. — Some 41 species in New Zealand.

Carmichaelia australis R. Br. Shrub, 1—3 m high, upright, densely branched, twigs flat; leaves (only on seedling!) 2.5 cm long, consisting of 5 cuneate, soon abscising leaflets; flowers lilac, 12 in small racemes, June—July; calyx campanulate, with small, triangular teeth; pods oval, 1 cm long, with 1—4 red seeds, but usually single seeded. LNz 75 + 76; BM 8972. New Zealand. 1825. z8

C. enysii Kirk. Shrub, leafless, 15—30 cm high, very densely branched, twigs green, thin, flattened when young; flowers small, solitary or in fascicles of 6 together, violet, July; calyx campanulate, lower portion and stalk silky pubescent; pods 6—8 mm long, single seeded. New Zealand. 1892. z8 Fig. 188.

C. flagelliformis Colinso. Shrub, 1 m high, twigs erect, thin, flattened when young; flowers lilac-red, very small, 1—3 small racemes in each leaf axil, each raceme with 3—7 flowers, June, flowers abundantly; pods 6—12 mm long, usually with 2 seeds. New Zealand. z8

C. grandiflora (Benth.) Hook. f. Deciduous shrub, well branched, to 1.5 m, young twigs flattened, distinctly furrowed, glabrous, leafy when young, until summer (obcordate, 1—1.5 cm long, grouped 3—5, glabrous); flowers 6 mm long, grouped 5—12 in 2.5 cm long racemes, lilac, with violet venation, fragrant, June—July, petiole glabrous; pods oblong, to 1 cm long, drawn out to a long "beak", seeds 2—4, red with black dots. PRP 6 (= *C. australis* var. *grandiflora* Benth.). New Zealand. z7—8?

C. monroi Hook. f. Dwarf shrub, 5—15 cm high, twigs very densely arranged, erect, to 20 cm wide, nest-like, twigs 2—4 mm wide, flat; flowers in small racemes,

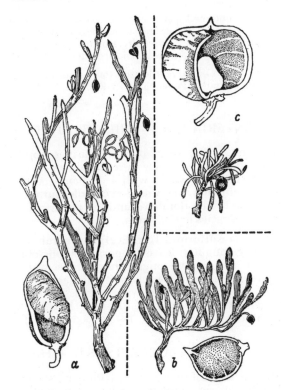

Fig. 188. **Carmichaelia**. a. *C. petriei*; b. *C. enysi*; c. *C. orbiculata* (from Adams)

white, purple veined; fruit black-brown, seeds yellow, black spotted. New Zealand. z8 Plate 92. New Zealand. Fig. 188.

C. orbiculata Col. Shrub, to only 8 cm high, small nest-like, twig stiff, erect, 2—3 cm long, 2—3 mm thick, striped, quite densely arranged; flowers purple, keel petal greenish-white; fruits nearly circular, 4—5 mm, seeds olive-green, black spotted. New Zealand. z8 Fig. 188.

C. petriei T. Kirk. Stiffer, more sparsely branched shrub, 50—150 cm high, young twigs glabrous, slightly furrowed, somewhat flattened, later becoming nearly round; flowers 3 mm long, 3—8 together in 2—3 cm long racemes, purple-violet, fragrant, often grouped in dense fascicles; calyx with short, triangular teeth, silky pubescent, as is the flower stalk; pods some 1 cm long, thick, with 2—3 seeds. New Zealand. z8 Plate 92; Fig. 188.

C. williamsii Kirk. Shrub, 0.7—2 m high, twigs 6—12 mm wide, finely striped, glabrous, finely appressed pubescent when young; flowers much larger than those of the other species, *Genista*-like to 2.5 cm long, cream-yellow, turning to green, standard petal somewhat reddish, April, solitary or 2—6 in fascicles; pods rounded, 2 cm long. New Zealand. 1925. More delicate in cultivation than the other species, but much more ornamental. z8 ⊕

The above mentioned species can only be used in the gardens of the mildest areas and otherwise must be over-wintered in a cool greenhouse. They all require a light soil and full sun. Found in most warm climate botanical gardens.

Lit. Simpson, G.: A revision of the genus *Carmichaelia* (Cockayne Memorial Paper No. 1); T.R.S.N.Z. **75**, 131—187, 1945.

CARPENTERIA Torr. — PHILADELPHACEAE

Evergreen shrubs, twigs opposite; leaves opposite, simple, entire; flowers few in terminal cymes; sepals and petals 5(—7); ovaries with 5—7 chambers; fruit a leathery dehiscent, many seeded capsule, surrounded at the base by the floral axis and the persistent calyx lobes. — 1 species in California.

Carpenteria californica Torr. Evergreen shrub, to 2 m high, twigs angular; leaves opposite, elliptic-oblong, 4—10 cm long, entire, bright green above, glabrous, blue-green beneath, sparsely soft pubescent; flowers white, fragrant, 5—7 cm wide, petals in a rotate arrangement, June—August. BM 6911; MS 137; MCL 186. California. 1880. z8 Fig. 189. # ⊕ ∅

Fig. 189. *Carpenteria californica* (from Dippel)

'Ladham's Variety'. Strong growing clone; flowers to 8 cm wide, flowers abundantly. 1924. Cultivated by Hillier.

Pretty shrubs for very mild areas in fertile, clay soil. Soil must be well drained, especially in winter.

CARPINUS L. — Hornbeam, Ironwood — CORYLACEAE

Deciduous trees or only shrubs, with gray, smooth or scaly bark; leaves 2-ranked, simple serrate, with 7—14 paired veins; male flowes in pendulous catkins, appearing in spring; fruit a ribbed nutlet with a 3 lobed or deeply toothed bract. — Some 35 species from Europe to E. Asia, N. and Central America.

Section 1: **Distegocarpus** (S. & Z.) Sarg.
　　Leaves with 20—34 paired veins; bracts of the male flowers ovate-lanceolate, distinctly stalked; fruit cluster imbricate, bracts thin; nutlet covered by pericarp lobes; bark of trunk scaly.
　　　　Included here are *C. cordata*, *C. fangiana* and *C. japonica*

Sections 2: **Eucarpinus** Sarg.
　　Leaves with 7—15 paired veins; bracts of the male inflorescence broad ovate, nearly sessile; fruit cluster loose; bracts parchment-like; nutlets in the fruit distinct; bark of trunk smooth.
　　　　Included here are all the other species

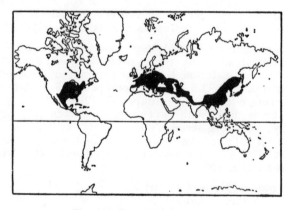

Fig. 190. Range of *Carpinus*

Fig. 191. *Carpinus betulus*, fruit cluster
(from Kerner)

Carpinus betulus L. Hornbeam, Musclewood, Iron-wood. Tree, to 20 m, occasionally taller, bark smooth, trunk often somewhat twisted or spiraling; leaves oval-oblong, to 12 cm long, rounded to cordate base, with 12–14 paired veins, glabrous, gold-yellow in fall; bracts on the fruit 3 lobed, side lobes only ½ – ⅓ as long as the middle lobe, 3–5 veined on the base; nutlet oval, somewhat compressed, ribbed. HW 2: 12; HF Pl. 83. Europe to Iran. In cultivation for ages. Ⓕ Yugoslavia. z5 Plate 94; Fig. 191. ∅

Including many garden forms:

'Albo-variegata'. Leaves white specked.

var. **angustifolia** (Medwed.) O. Radde. Leaves oblong, apex more drawn out; bract lobes sharply acuminate; nutlets coni-cal, sharply ribbed, apex acuminate.

var. **carpinizza** (Host) Neilr. Leaves smaller, with only 7–9 paired veins, often cordate at the base; fruit bracts entire. Romania. z6

'Columnaris'. Growth narrow at first, columnar, later nearly oval, very densely branched, round topped, slow growing. Introduced by Spaeth in 1891. ∅

'Cucullata'. Growth broad, columnar; leaves pale colored in spring. Before 1904.

'Fastigiata'. Regular conical, fast growing, always with a long apical leader, tree-like (= 'Pyramidals'; 'Erecta'). Before 1883. Most common cultivar.

'Horizontalis'. Round crowned, branches nearly horizontal. Found around 1900 in the nursery of Simon Louis in Metz, France and introduced to the trade through Jouin.

'Incisa'. Leaves narrow, deeply lobed, lobes acute, occasion-ally also entire (= 'Asplenifolia'; 'Heterophylla'; 'Laciniata'). Before 1789. Plate 94. ∅

'Marmorata'. Leaves white marbled (= 'Albomarmorata'). Before 1867. Probably brought into the trade by C. De Vos, Hazerswoude, Holland.

var. **parva** O. Radde. Leaves ovate, small, pubescent from the base to the middle; nutlet ovate, inflated in the middle, crowned with perianth tips, apex pubescent.

'Pendula'. Very weak growing, hemispherical, twigs hori-zontal at first, then ascending. Plate 96.

'Punctata'. Leaves white pulverulent and punctate.

'Purpurea'. Young leaves more or less intense reddish-green, later greening. Before 1873.

'Quercifolia'. Leaves narrower than those of 'Incisa', lobed serrate, lobes rounded. Before 1783. Plate 94. ∅

'Variegata'. Leaves speckled yellow, irregular (= 'Aureo-variegata'). Before 1770. Common in cultivation.

C. caroliniana Walt. American Hornbeam. Tree, to 10 m high, twigs attractively nodding; leaves acute ovate, 6–10 cm long, more blue-green, sharply and doubly serrate, venation and vein axils pubescent beneath, fall color a splendid scarlet-orange; fruit bracts 5–7 veined at the base. BB 1207; GTP 147 (= var. *virginiana* [Marsh.] Fern.; in Rho 1936. Pl. 349; *C. americana* Michx.). Eastern N. America. 1812. Slow growing. z2 Plate 94; Fig. 192. 194. ∅

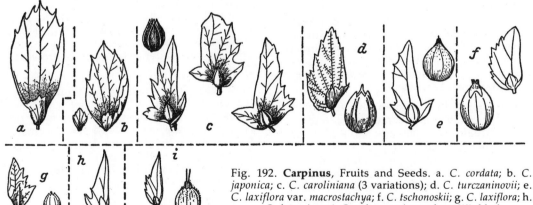

Fig. 192. **Carpinus**, Fruits and Seeds. a. *C. cordata*; b. *C. japonica*; c. *C. caroliniana* (3 variations); d. *C. turczaninovii*; e. *C. laxiflora* var. *macrostachya*; f. *C. tschonoskii*; g. *C. laxiflora*; h. *C. fargesiana*; i. *C. polyneura* (most from Winkler)

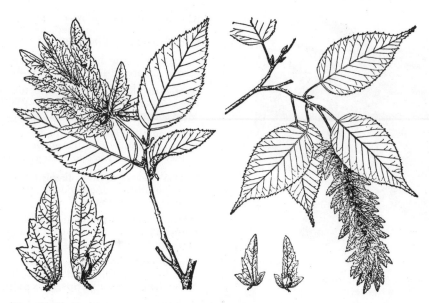

Fig. 193. Left, *Carpinus laxiflora* var. *macrostachya*; right, *C. fargesiana* (from ICS)

'Ascendens'. Growth broad, columnar, multistemmed, without a dominant leader; leaves long acuminate, 6–10 cm long. NH 1955: 111. Originated in Rochester, New York, USA, 1918, but not yet in the trade.

C. cordata Bl. Tree, to 15 m high, very slow growing, scaly bark, winter buds very large, young twigs slightly pubescent at first, soon becoming glabrous; leaves broadly cordate, unevenly doubly serrate, 7–12 cm long, with 15–20 paired veins, venation thinly pubescent beneath; fruit catkins 6–8 cm long. CIS 111; KIF 2: 13; LF 79; EP 61: 8. Japan, NE. Asia. 1879. One of the most beautiful *Carpinus* types, but very little known. Quite winter hardy. z6 Plate 94. Fig. 192, 195. ∅

var. **chinensis** Franch. Young twigs more pubescent; leaves smaller and narrower. SH 2: 558 f. China; E. Szechuan. 1901. z6

C. exima Nakai. Tree, to 9 m, trunk gray; leaves ovate to oblong, base rounded to truncate, long acuminate, doubly serrate, 7–10 cm long, with 14–18 paired veins, venation silky pubescent beneath, upper leaf surface softly pubescent; fruit catkins 5–7 cm long, fruit bracts half-ovate, 3.5 cm long, 1.3 cm wide, venation pubescent; nutlets glandular punctate, pubescent at the apex. NK 2: Pl. 8. Korea, 1921. z6

C. fangiana Hu. Tree, to 18 m, smooth bark, twigs thin, oblong to more lanceolate, long acuminate, base somewhat obliquely cordate, to 27 cm long and 8 cm wide, dense and irregularly doubly serrate, with 24–34 paired veins; fruits in up to 45 cm (!) long and 4 cm thick, "tail-like" clusters. FIO 1; CIS 109 (= *C. wilsoniana* Hu). China; S. Szechwan to S. Kweichow. Unknown whether or not in cultivation, but by far the most beautiful of the genus and known since 1929. z6 Fig. 195.

C. fargesiana Winkl. Small tree, to 6 m high, bark gray, smooth, young twigs dark gray, with distinct lenticels; leaves oblanceolate to obovate, 6 cm long, 3 cm wide, short acuminate, base rounded, unevenly serrate, both sides glabrous; female inflorescence a small raceme; nutlets nearly sessile, flat, ovate, somewhat pubescent and glandular on the apex, otherwise glabrous. EP 61: 10g; CIS 118 (= *C. jedoensis*, Franch. non Maxim.). China; Szechwan, Kweitschau. Not to be confused in *C. fargesii* Franch. (= *C. laxiflora* var *macrostachya*)! Fig. 192, 193.

C. henryana (Winkl.) Winkl. Tree, to 15 m high, young twigs silky pubescent; leaves narrow ovate-lanceolate, base usually round to slightly cordate, simple or doubly serrate, long acuminate, to 6 cm long, glabrous above, underside silky pubescent on the 12–16 paired veins, petiole 8 mm long, densely pubescent; fruit catkins slender, to 5 cm long, fruit bracts obliquely ovate, large toothed, some 1.5 cm long; nutlets dark brown, ovate, with 6–8 ribs. CIS 124 (= *C. tschonoskii* var. *henryana* Winkl.). Central China; Szechwan. 1907. z5 Very hardy, dense foliage, fast growing.

C. japonica Bl. Japanese Hornbeam. Tree, to 15 m high, bark scaly, light gray-brown, young twigs pubescent; leaves reddish in spring and softly pubescent on both sides, acute oval-oblong, 5–10 cm long, unevenly and coarsely serrate, with 20–24 paired veins; fruit catkins 5–6 cm long, bracts ovate, large toothed, inflexed enclosing nutlet; nutlets 4 mm long. EP 61: 8c; GF 6: 365; KIF 1: 38. Japan. 1895. Very beautiful and hardy. z5 Plate 94; Fig. 192. ∅

C. laxiflora (S. & Z.) Bl. Tree, to 15 m; leaves elliptic, abruptly cuspidate, base oblique rounded to nearly cordate, doubly serrate, 4–7 cm long, with 7–15 paired

Plate 81

Bruckenthalia spiculifolia in the Dortmund Garden, W. Germany

Buckleya distichophylla, 3 year plant, parasitic on the roots of *Tsuga canadensis*; in the Dortmund Botanic
Garden, W. Germany (now 1.5 m high)

Plate 82

Buddleia lindleyana
in the Tbilisi Botanic Garden, Georgia, USSR

Buddleia salviifolia
in its habitat in S. Africa

Buddleia crispa
in the Malahide Castle Gardens, Ireland

Buddleia fallowiana 'Alba'
in the Malahide Castle Gardens, Ireland

Plate 83

Buddleia × lewisiana 'Margaret Pike'   Photo: I. E. Downward

Buddleia × pikei 'Hever Castle'   Photo: I. E. Downward

Plate 84

Buddleia officinalis
in the Malahide Castle Gardens, Ireland

Buddleia farreri
in the Malahide Castle Gardens, Ireland

Buddleia davidii 'Fascination' in the Dortmund Botanic Garden, W. Germany

Plate 85

Cercidiphyllum japonicum 'Pendulum',
the original Japanese tree

Buddleia auriculata in Kew Gardens, England

Buddleia alternifolia in the Geneva Botanic Garden, Switzerland

Photo: Archiv Schweiz. Gartenbau-Blatt

Plate 86

Bupleurum fruticosum in flower
in the Lisbon Botanic Garden, Portugal

Butia capitata
in the Suchumi Botanic Garden, USSR

Caesalpinia gilliesii in the Lisbon Botanic Garden, Portugal

Plate 87

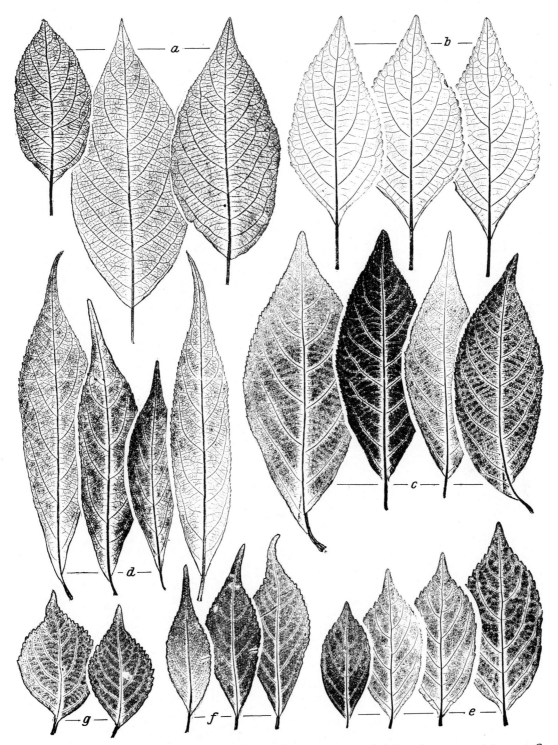

Callicarpa. a. *C. bodinieri* var. *giraldii*; b. *C. americana*; c. *C. japonica*; d. *C. japonica* var. *angustata*; e. –g. *C. dichotoma* (from various sources)

Plate 88

Calluna vulgaris 'Roma' in the Dortmund Botanic Garden, W. Germany

Calluna vulgaris 'Hammondii' in the Dortmund Botanic Garden, W. Germany

Plate 89

Calycanthus fertilis, fruits, somewhat enlarged
Photo: Dr. Pilat, Prag

Campsis grandiflora
in the Garden Pina de Rosa, Sta. Cristina, Spain

Calluna vulgaris 'H. E. Beale'
Archivbild

Camellia oleifera
in the Hillier Arboretum, England

Plate 90

Camellia saluenensis

Photo: I. E. Downward

Plate 91

Camellia reticulata 'Shot Silk'   Photo: I. E. Downward

Camellia williamsii 'Pink Wave'   Photo: I. E. Downward

Plate 92

Caragana maximowicziana
in the Copenhagen Botanic Garden, Denmark

Caragana sukiensis
in the Glasnevin Botanic Garden, Dublin, Ireland

Carmichaelia petriei
in the Crathes Castle Garden, Scotland

Carmichaelia monroi
in the Edinburgh Botanic Garden, Scotland

Plate 93

Cassia didymobotrya,
Cristina Hotel Garden, Algeciras, Spain

Cassia marylandica
in the Hamburg Botanical Garden, W. Germany

Casuarina equisetifolia
in San Marroig, Majorca, Spain

Close-up of the tree at left

Plate 94

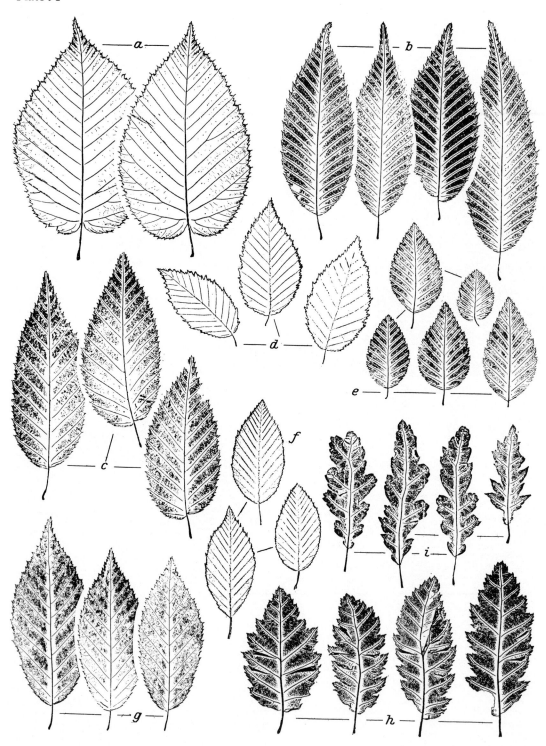

a. *C. cordata*; b. *C. japonica*; c. *C. caroliniana*; d. *C. orientalis*; e. *C. turczaninowii*; f. *C. polyneura*; g. *C. betulus* 'Incisa'; i. *C. betulus* 'Quercifolia'

Plate 95

Carpinus orientalis
in the mountains near Dubrovnik, Yugoslavia

Carpinus cordata
in a forestry test plot in Kyoto, Japan

Cassinia fulvida
in the Malahide Castle Gardens, Ireland

Cassinia vauvilliersii 'Albida'
in the Malahide Castle Gardens, Ireland

Plate 96

Carpinus betulus 'Pendula' in the Jardin des Plantes, Paris, France

Carya illinoensis
in the Apalchicola National Forest, Florida, U.S.A.
Photo: US Forest Service

Caragana jubata 'Colunaris'

Photo: Bergianska Traedgarden, Stockholm

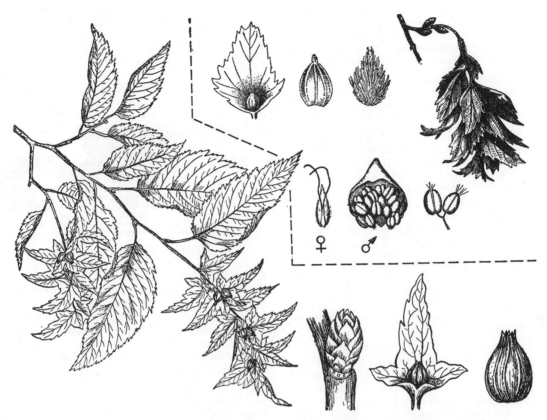

Fig. 194. **Carpinus** Above: *C. orientalis*, fruit clusters, single fruit, seed, involucral leaf of a female flower, with flowers and stamens beneath; lower and left: *C. caroliniana*, fruiting twig, winter buds, singular fruit, seed (from Illinck, Hempel & Wilhelm)

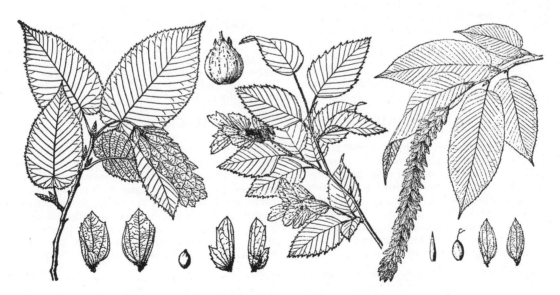

Fig. 195. From left to right: *Carpinus cordata*; *C. turczaninovii*; *C. fangiana* (from ICS)

veins, with axillary pubescence beneath; fruit clusters
to 7.5 cm long, loose, fruit bracts some 1.5 cm long,
usually 3 lobed, middle lobe narrow and serrate on one
side; nutlets 3 lobed, middle lobe narrow and serrate on
one side; nutlets with some resinous dots. KIF 1: 39;
CIS 15. Japan. 1914. Rarely in cultivation. z6 Fig. 192 ⊘

var. **macrostachya** Oliver. Leaves larger, to 10 cm long, 5 cm
wide; fruit catkins twice as long, to 15 cm, stiffer, fruit bracts
to 2.5 cm long (= C. fargesii Franch.). China. 1900. Much more
frequent in cultivation, hardy, fast growing. Fig. 192, 193. ⊘

C. orientalis Mill. Oriental Hornbeam. Shrubby, to 5 m
high, very dense and ornamentally branched; leaves
oval-elliptic, acute and doubly serrate, scabrous, 3—5
cm long, dark green above, glossy, only the midrib
pubescent beneath, with 10—14 paired veins; fruit
catkins 3—6 cm long, fruit bracts ovate, asymmetrical, 2
cm long, 1.3 cm wide, coarsely and irregularly serrate,
but not lobed; nutlets 4 mm long, ovate, with lighter
ribs. HW 2: 34; SH 1: 140; EP 61: 10j (= C. duinensis
Scop.).   SE. Europe, Asia Minor. 1739.   z6
Ⓕ Yugoslavia. Plate 94, 95; Fig. 194, 196. ⊘

'Calcarea'. Leaves leathery, nearly sessile, venation widely
spaced, petioles woolly pubescent.

'Grandifolia'. Leaves larger, elliptic; fruit clusters dense, to 8
cm long, nutlets undeveloped.

C. polyneura Franch. Elegant tree to 7 m high, stipules
persisting after leaf drop and throughout the winter;
leaves ovate, acuminate, 3—6 cm long, scabrous bristly
serrate, base round to slightly cordate, 15—20 paired
veins; fruit bracts ovate, with very uneven sides, 2 cm
long, acute, large toothed; nutlets ovate, 4 mm long.
CIS 123. W. China, Szechwan, Hupeh. 1889. One of the
most beautiful Carpinus species, quite winter hardy and
worthy of wider cultivation. z5 Plate 94; Fig. 192. ⊘

C. tschonoskii Maxim. Tree, to 15 m high, twigs softly
pubescent at first; leaves acute oval-elliptic, finely serrate, to 9 cm long, both sides pubescent at first, later
pubescent only on the 12—14 paired veins; fruit catkins
5—7 cm long, fruit bracts narrow ovate, serrate on one
side, silky pubescent on the veins and at the base. KIF
2: 16; CIS 117; EP 61: 10g (= C. yedoensis Maxim.; C.
fauriei Nakai). China, Szechwan; originated in Japanese horticulture. 1894. Fig. 192. ⊘

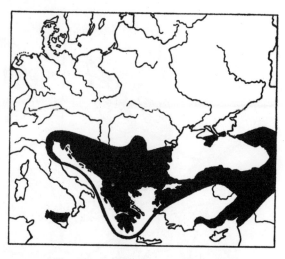

Fig. 196. Range of *Carpinus orientalis*

C. turczaninowii Hance. Shrub or tree-like, to 5 m,
young twigs and leaf petioles finely tomentose;
stipules linear, persisting throughout the winter,
leaves broad ovate, 3—5 cm long, doubly serrate, with
10—12 paired veins, pubescent beneath and with tufts
at the vein axils; fruit bracts ovate, deeply incised
serrate on one side; nutlets resin dotted. EP 61: 10 a—c;
BS 1: 29; CIS 116 (= C. paxii Winkl.; C. stipulata Winkl.).
N. China, Korea. 1905. z5 Plate 94; Fig. 192,195. ⊘

var. **ovalifolia** Winkl. Leaves larger, 3—6 cm long, ovate to
ovate-oblong, occasionally doubly serrate, not lobed at the
base, EH Pl. 205. W. China. 1889. Hardy.

All the Carpinus species are valuable, attractive park trees,
and some good lumber trees; many will tolerate shady locations. Wide tolerance to soil types. The East Asiatic species
are quite winter hardy. Especially attractive as single
specimens.

Lit. Winkler, H.: in Engler-Prantl, Pflanzenreich, IV, 61,
24—43, 1904, with many illustrations ● Radde-Fomin, O.:
Beitraege zur Systematik der Gattung Carpinus in Russland;
in Mém. Cl. Sc. Phys. Math. Acad. Sc. Ukraine, **15**, 51—107,
1929, summarized in DDG 1932, 31—33 ● Lee, S. C.: Forest
Botany of China; Shanghai 1935, 243—261, with descriptions
of 24 Chinese species.

CARRIEREA Franch. — FLACOURTIACEAE

Deciduous trees; leaves alternate, long petioled, simple, serrate; flowers dioecious, in racemes or panicles;
sepals 5, large, petals absent; stamens numerous,
shorter than the sepals; ovaries unilocular, rudimentary in staminate flowers, with numerous seed
chambers (ovules); styles 3—4, 3 lobed, short and at
wide angles; fruit a woody dehiscent capsule opening
at both ends; seeds winged. — 3 species in S. and W.
China and Indochina, but as yet only one in cultivation.

Carrierea calycina Franch. Tree, to 20 m high in its
habitat, somewhat resembling Idesia polycarpa, crown
broad and flat, young twigs glabrous and glossy or also
somewhat pubescent; leaves elliptic, obovate to round

elliptic, 6—16 cm long, 5—8 cm wide, often acuminate,
base round or slightly cordate, crenate-serrate, each
tooth with a sessile gland, glossy green above, lighter
beneath, both sides glabrous; flowers 4—7 in terminal
racemes on short side branches; sepals broad cordate-
ovate, some 3 cm long, cream-yellow with a trace of
green, arranged in a cup-form, fragrant, June—July;
fruit spindle shaped, 5 cm long. BMns 53; FIO 73. W.
China; Hupeh, Szechwan. 1908. z8 Fig. 197. ✜ ⊘

Experience in cultivation as yet very limited within England;
flowers only on older plants; needs winter protection and
fertile soil. Only for the collector.

CARYA Nutt. — Hickory — JUGLANDACEAE

Usually large deciduous trees with alternate, odd-pinnate, somewhat aromatic foliage; leaflets 3–17, opposite, serrate; flowers monoecious; male flowers in pendulous catkins, female flowers 2–10 in spikes; fruit a smooth, occasionally somewhat winged angular nut.— Some 25 species in NE. USA, 3 species in China. Fig. 198.

Easily distinguished from *Juglans* by the non-chambered pith of the young twigs and the smooth-shelled nuts. For positive identification of the species the fruits and winter twigs are necessary; the leaves alone are not sufficient.

The difficulty arises in that only very sight deviations in form or size of the fruits, more or less apparent pubescence of the leaves and other relatively minor variations led many authors to establish a new species, especially C. S. Sargent and W. W. Ashe. Since the North American dendrology is still being revised, it appears unnecessary to include those species and varieties which are unclear.

Section 1. **Pacania** (Raf.) Rehd.
Winter buds light colored, with 2–3 crosswise arranged, paired valvate scales; leaflets 5–17, usually lanceolate and often sickle shaped, bowed; fruits with winged seams, nut usually thin-shelled:
    C. aquatica, brownii, cathayensis, cordiformis, illinoensis, lecontei, myristiciformis

Section 2. **Eucarya** C. DC.
Winter buds dark colored, more than 6 imbricate scales; leaflets 3–9, never sickle-shaped, terminal leaflet larger than the others, usually obovate; fruits not or seldom winged; inner shell of the nut thick walled:
    C. glabra, laciniosa, lanei, ovata, pallida, texana, tomentosa

Key to the most important *Carya* species

1. Buds very dark yellow, slender, acute, terminal leaflet sessile; leaves to 25 cm; leaflets usually 9:
    C. cordiformis
Buds light green and/or brown, ovate, terminal leaflet petiolate or nearly sessile; leaflets 3–7, rarely 9   2

2. Larger leaves 20–30 cm long, rachis glabrous, leaflets 5 or 3, rarely 7; terminal leaflet nearly sessile:
    C. glabra
Larger leaves 45–70 cm long, rachis pubescent, at least at first; terminal leaflet with 1 to 4 cm long petiole   3

3. Leaflets 5, seldom 7; stalk of terminal leaflet thick; shoots dark purple-brown, becoming glabrous; leaves often thick and oily, yellowish-green, ciliate; bark peeling on young trees:
    C. ovata
Leaflets 7, seldom 5 or 9, stalk of the terminal leaflet thin; shoots green-brown or yellow-reddish, with dense pubescences; leaves thin, stiff, parchment-like, dark green   4

4. Twigs stiff pubescent; leaves coarsely serrate; shoots yellow with dark pink; bark smooth or fine plaited:
    C. tomentosa
Twigs softly pubescent, leaves crenate; shoots green-brown, bark with peeling plates, later exfoliating:
    C. laciniosa

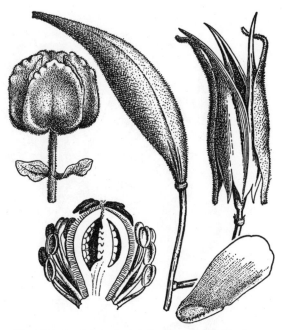

Fig. 197. *Carrierea calycina*, flower, longitudinal section, fruit, dehiscent fruit, seed (from Franchet)

Carya aquatica (Michx. f.) Nutt. Water Hickory. Tree, usually not over 20 m high, bark light brown, peeling in long thin plates, young twigs glandular or sparsely tomentose at first, eventually deep brown; leaflets 7–13, lanceolate, long acuminate, 8–12 cm long, yellow tomentose when young, later glabrous; fruits ovate, 3–4 cm long and wide, often grouped 3–4; nut 4 sided, red-brown, somewhat rugose, kernel bitter. HHD 64; SS 344; SM 172; KTF 23. SE. USA, especially along river banks and swamps of the Mississippi Valley. 1800. z6 Fig. 200.

C. × brownii Sarg. (*C. cordiformis* × *C. illinoensis*). Very simlar to *C. illinoensis*, but usually with only 11 leaflets (or only 9); fruit more ovate, nut flattened, 3–4 cm long (ovate on *C. illinoensis*, but not flattened). 1909.

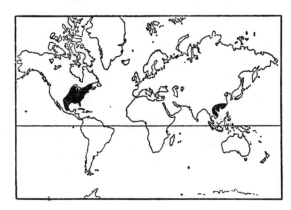

Fig. 198. Range of *Carya*

284   Carya

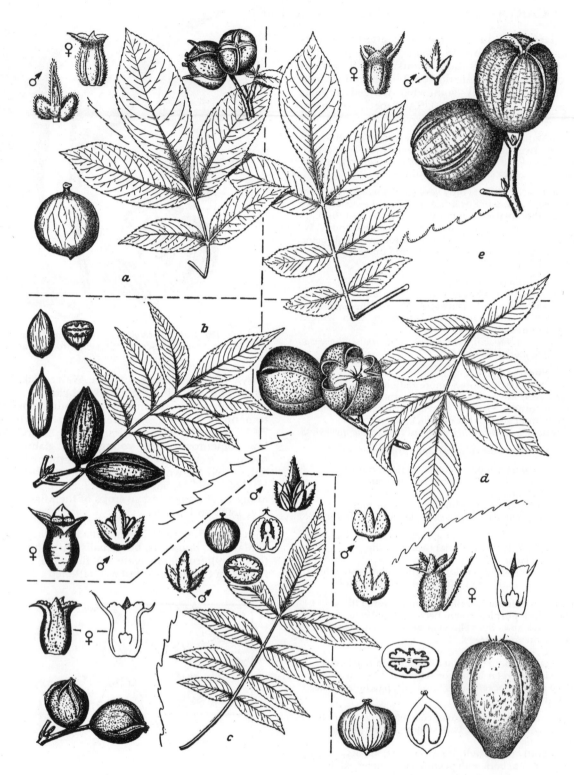

Fig. 199. **Carya.** a. *C. glabra;* b. *C. illinoensis;* c. *C. cordiformis* d. *C. glabra* var. *megacarpa;*
e. *C. laciniosa* (from Sargent)

C. cathayensis Sarg. Tree, to 20 m, young twigs densely covered with orange-yellow scales; leaflets 5—7, oval-lanceolate, short stalked, 10—14 cm long, yellow pulverulent beneath, midrib pubescent; fruits obovoid, 4 winged; nuts ovoid, indistinctly 4 sided, 2.5 cm long, kernel sweet. LF 75; ICS 383. E. China. 1917. z6

C. cordiformis (Wangh.) K. Koch. Bitternut. Tree, to 30 m high, fast growing, thin scaly bark, young twigs rust-brown pubescent at first, eventually glabrous and glossy, buds yellow glandular; leaflets 5—9 (usually 9), oval-lanceolate, acuminate, serrate, 8—15 cm long, light green and pubescent beneath; fruit globose, 2—3 cm thick, 4 sided above the middle; nut broad ovate, flattened, thin-shelled, gray, smooth, abruptly coming to a sharp point, kernel bitter. HHD 61; EH 170; SM 171; KTF 24 (= *C. amara* Nutt.; *C. minima* [Marsh.] Brit.). Northern N. America, usually in low areas, river banks and swamps z5 Plate 97; Fig. 199, 200.

C. glabra (Mill.) Sweet. Pignut. Tree, to 20—30(—40) m high, bark dark gray, finely grooved, tighter, young twigs glabrous or soon glabrous; leaflets 3—7, usually 5, oblong-lanceolate, acuminate, 8—15 cm long, glabrous, sharply serrate, the lowest pair of leaflets smaller; fruit pear-shape or globose, usually slightly winged near the tip; nut 2.5 cm long, not angular, brownish, thin-shelled, kernel bitter. HHD 74; EH 172; SM 181; KTF 28 (= *C. porcina* Nutt.). E. USA. 1779. Commonly found on dry, fertile slopes. ⓕ USA. z5 Plate 97, Fig. 199.

var. **megacarpa** (Sarg.) Sarg. Coast Pignut Hickory. Mainly differing in the fruit, 3—5 cm long, some 3 cm wide, obovoid, somewhat flattened, outer shell opening sooner, inner shell thick. SM 182 (= *C. megacarpa* Sarg.; *C. ashei* Sudw.; *C. austrina* Small). Fig. 199.

C. illinoensis (Wangh.) K. Koch. Pecan. Tree, 30(50) m high, bark light brown to gray, deep and irregularly furrowed, twigs pubescent when young, buds pubescent, yellow; 11—17 leaflets, lanceolate, somewhat sickle-shape, 5—17 cm long, long acuminate, finely dentate, tomentose and glandular beneath when young, later glabrous; fruits 3—10 in spikes, acute-oblong, 3—8 cm long, outer shell slightly 4 winged; nut smooth, light brown, thin-shelled, sweet. HHD 66; SS 338; SM 169 (= *C. pecan* [Marsh.] Engl. & Graebn.; *C. oliviformis* Michx.). USA. Mississippi Valley. ⓕ USSR (Azerbeijan). z6 Plate 96; Fig. 199.

Cultivated for centuries and an important nut tree in N. America; nuts collected from both wild and grafted varieties. Many cultivars available; see descriptions and illustrations in Blackmon, G. H., Pecan Growing in Florida; Fla. Agr. Expt. Sta. Bull. 437: 1947. The pecan is the state tree of Texas, USA.

C. laciniosa (Michx. f.) Loud. Big Shellbark. Tree, 30—40 m tall, bark peeling in long strips (often 60—80 cm long), young twigs thick and stiff, orange, pubescent at first, finally glabrous; leaflets usually 7—9, oblong-lanceolate, 10—20 cm long, terminal leaflet obovate, acuminate, serrate, pubescent beneath; fruits rounded-elliptic, to 7 cm long; nut flattened, indis-

tinctly 4 sided, thick-shelled, acute at both ends, yellow or reddish; kernel sweet. HHD 70; SS 348; SM 177 (= *C. sulcata* Nutt.). E. USA; in swamps and flood plains. 1804. Easily distinguished from all the other species by the thick twigs. ⓕ USA. z6 Plate 97; Fig. 199.

C. × lanei Sarg. (*C. cordiformis* × *C. ovata*). Resembles *C. ovata* but with dark gray bark, not grooved, terminal bud 1 cm long, the outer scales glabrous, abcising, the inner bud scales lepidote, yellow; leaflets 5, lanceolate to oblanceolate; fruit ovate; nut flattened, somewhat obovoid, thin shelled, kernel large, sweet. W. New York. 1913. z5

C. × lecontei Little. Bitter Pecan. (*C. aquatica* × *C. illinoensis*). Tree, 20(30) m high, round crowned, thin-branched, bark thick, rough scaly, light reddish-brown, young twigs thickly tomentose, becoming red-brown and glabrous by fall, winter buds yellow pubescent; leaflets 7—13, lanceolate, somewhat sickle-shape, thin, but tough, 7—12 cm long, yellow-green beneath, pubescent, finely serrate; fruit oblong to obovoid, somewhat 4 winged, more or less yellow lepidote; nut oblong-ovoid, folded, angular, acute at both ends, 4 sided at obtuse angles, red-brown, very thin-shelled, kernel very bitter. SM 170; SS 719 (= *C. buckleyi* [Durand] Ashe; *C. texana* Schneid. non Buckl.). Texas; along the Brazos River in low spots. 1862. z9

C. myristiciformis (Michx. f.) Nutt. Nutmeg Hickory. Tree, 25(40) m high, bark dark brown, fragmented (small, tight plates), young twigs yellow or brown scaly, dark brown in the 2nd year; leaflets 5—11, oval-lanceolate, nearly sessile, pubescent beneath and silver-white (important for identification!), 8—12 cm long; fruit ovate, singular, to 4 cm long, shell splitting almost to the base; nut ovate, red-brown, furrowed like nutmeg, thick shelled, kernel sweet. SS 342; SM 173. S. Atlantic coast of the USA, to Mexico. 1911. Beautiful foliage tree. z9

C. ovalis (Wangenh.) Sarg. Red Hickory. Very similar to *C. glabra*; tall tree, to 30 m, young twigs "scabby" and pubescent, later glabrous; leaves with 5—7 leaflets, these lanceolate, oblanceolate to obovate, some 7 cm long, terminal leaflet to 15 cm, all finely serrate and finely pubescent, scabby like the young twigs; fruits unusually variable, resembling those of *C. glabra*, but sweet and edible (the latter bitter and harsh tasting). SM 183; BC 827 (= *C. microcarpa* Nutt. p.p.). Eastern USA, from New York to Georgia. z6

C. ovata (Mill.) K. Koch. Shagbark Hickory. tree, 20—30(40) m high, crown narrow oblong, bark peeling in strips (shorter than those of *C. laciniosa*), young twigs more scaly, soon becoming glabrous, light brown; leaflets 5, elliptic-lanceolate, 10—15 cm long, acuminate, serrate and densely ciliate, glandular and pubescent beneath when young, fall color an attractive gold-yellow; fruits globose, 3—6 cm long, thick outer shell, splitting to the base; nut ellipsoid, white, 4 sided, thin-shelled, kernel sweet. SHD 68; EH 173; SM 174 (=

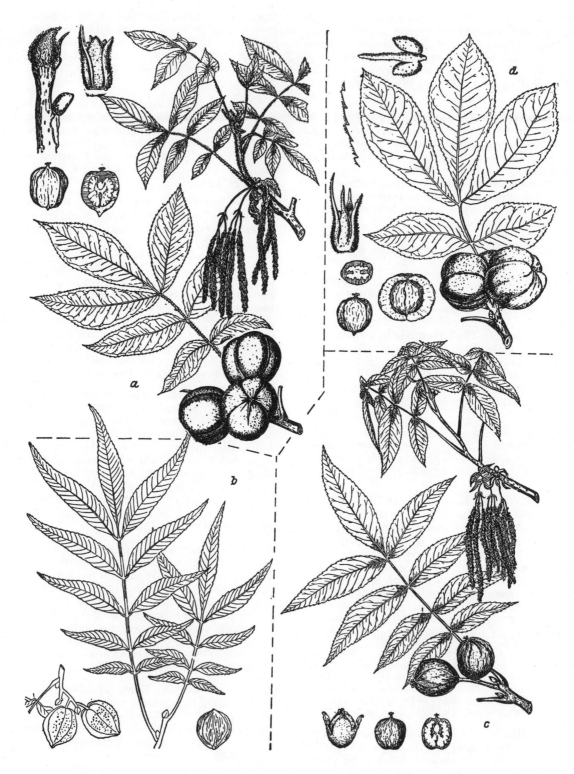

Fig. 200. **Carya** a. *C. tomentosa*, Mockernut; b. *C. aquatica*; c. *C. cordiformis*, Bitternut;
d. *C. ovata*, Shagbark (from Sargent, Illinck)

C. alba Nutt. non K. Koch). E. USA. 1629. Very valuable tree; the wood and fruits both having economic uses; the Indians once made a sugar from the sap. Hickory wood is especially desirable for smoking meats. Ⓕ Germany (early trials). z5 Plate 98; Fig. 200. ⌀

C. pallida (Ashe). Engl. & Graebn. Sand Hickory. Tall tree, bark very coarsely furrowed (on poor soils), but smooth on more fertile soils, young twigs purple brown; leaflets 7(9), oblong-lanceolate, 8−12 cm long, finely serrate, light green above, silver-white scaly beneath and silvery pubescent when young (important for identification!), leaf rachis stellate pubescent; fruits rounded, 2−3 cm long, outer shell thin, eventually splitting open to the base; nuts whitish, flat, thin shelled. SM 180; GF 10: 305; KTF 29. USA, Alabama and Tennessee. 1898. z6

C. texana Buckley non DC. Black Hickory. Tree, 10−15 m high, dark bark, furrowed, young twigs rust-brown pubescent; leaflets usually 7, lanceolate, 10−15 cm long, venation pubescent beneath, petioles of the younger leaves shaggy pubescent; fruits rounded, 3.5 cm long, shell splitting open to the base; nuts acute, 4 sided above the middle, red-brown, kernel sweet. SM 188 to 190 (= *C. villosa* [Sarg.] Schneid.; *C. arkansana*

Sarg.). USA, Texas to Arkansas. 1909. z6

C. tomentosa Nutt. Mockernut. Tree, 25−30 m high, bark furrowed with flattened ridges, young twigs tomentose, becoming glabrous in fall, terminal buds to 2 cm long; leaflets 7−9, oblong, acuminate, 8−18 cm long, tapering to the base, serrate, glandular and tomentose beneath, rachis and petiole tomentose; fruits globose to pear-shape, 3−5 cm long, outer shell very thick; nut somewhat flattened angular, 3 cm long, light brown, thick shelled, kernel sweet. HHD 72; SM 178 (= *C. alba* [Mill.] K. Koch non Nutt.). E. USA. 1766. The most valuable species of *Carya* for its widely usable wood. z5 Fig. 200. ⌀

All species make very attractive park trees, some interesting for their notably exfoliating bark (*C. laciniosa* and *C. ovata*), others with attractive foliage or gold-yellow fall color (*C. ovata* and *tomentosa*). All are quite valuable lumber trees. *Carya* species are all quite winter hardy, but young plants are occasionally damaged by a late frost. Transplanting is somewhat difficult because of the fleshy tap root. Prefer a good fertile soil.

Soil Nomenclature from Little, E. L.: Check List of native and naturalized Trees of the United States; Washington, D.C. 1953 ● Sargent, C. S.: Notes on North American Trees. II. *Carya*; in Bot. Gaz. **66**, 229−258, 1918.

CARYOPTERIS Bge. — Blue Spirea — VERBENACEAE

Deciduous subshrubs or shrubs; twigs glabrous to gray tomentose; leaves opposite, entire to toothed; flowers in small axillary "false-umbels"; corolla blue or red, tube short, limb with 5 lobes; calyx campanulate, deeply 5 lobed, becoming larger after the blooming period; stamens 4, widely protruding; fruit a capsule, shorter than the calyx. — 15 species in E. Asia.

Key to the Mentioned Species

Leaf margins always entire:
    C. mongholica
Leaf margins partly entire, partly with some large teeth:
    C. × *clandonensis*
Leaf margins always serrate, 2−7 cm long:
    C. incana
As above, but only 1.5−2.5 cm long:
    C. glutinosa

Caryopteris × **clandonensis** Simmonds (*C. incana* × *C. mongholica*). A small group of hybrids, having the form and character of the cultivar 'Arthur Simmonds'.

'Arthur Simmonds' (A. Simmonds 1930). Shrub, to 1 m high and wide, densely branched, twigs gray, with fine and short pubescence; leaves oblong-lanceolate, 5−8 cm long, acuminate, partly entire, partly coarsely dentate, with 1−4 teeth on either side, deep green above, glossy, gray-green beneath, short pubescent; buds deep violet-blue, flowers to 20 in axillary and terminal, branched clusters, dark blue, August−September. BMns 75. Developed by A. Simmonds, West Clandon, England. Very useful for late summer flowers. z8 Plate 99. ✧

'Ferndown' (Stewarts). Shrub, some 0.5−0.7 m high, quite

bushy, twigs reddish-brown, short pubescent; leaves lanceolate, 5−7 cm long, entire or occasionally with a solitary tooth, deep green above, blue-green beneath; flowers dark violet, 6−12 in axillary, stalked clusters, buds darker, September−October, latest flowering variety. Introduced to the trade by Stewarts Nurseries, Ferndown, Dorset, England in 1958.

'Heavenly Blue'. American selection, very similar to 'Arthur Simmonds', but growth more compact and narrowly upright. Introduced by Wayside Gardens, Mentor, Ohio. ✧

'Kew Blue' (Kew Gardens 1945). Seedling of 'Arthur Simmonds' with darker flowers.

C. glutinosa Rehd. Shrub, similar to *C. mongholica*, but to 1.5 m high; leaves short petioled, lanceolate, 1.5−2.5 cm long, thick, entire, margin rolled inward, dark green above and viscid, white tomentose beneath and with distinct, dark venation; flowers blue, abundant. NW. China. 1933. z8

C. incana (Houttuyn) Miq. Shrub, 1(2) m high, twigs, leaves and inflorescence short gray tomentose; leaves oblong to ovate, 2−7 cm long, acute or blunt tipped, coarsely serrate, dull green above, pubescent; flowers violet-blue, buds lighter, in dense cymes, August to September. BM 6799; ICS 5164; LWT 331 (= *C. mastacanthus* Schau.; *C. sinensis* Dipp.; *C. tangutica* Maxim.). E. China, Japan. 1844. z6 Plate 99. ✧

Including several garden varieties:

'Candida' (before 1941). Flowers whitish, not as attractive and less hardy than the type. USA.

'Nana' and **'Superba'**. 2 more garden forms from the USA. Before 1941. Not grown in Europe.

Many authors consider *C. tangutica* to be a separate species for its smaller leaves, more obtuse toothed margin and less divided 'corona' (crown). Its retention as a separate species is, however, not totally justifiable.

C. mongholica Bge. Shrub, 30–70 cm high, twigs gray pubescent; leaves narrow linear-lanceolate, entire, margin rolled inward, 2.5–4 cm long, pubescent on both sides, especially beneath; flowers 6–9 in axillary, stalked clusters, July–August; corona with 4 small and 1 large points or tips, all very fimbriate. BM 9219; ICS 5166. Mongolia, N. China. 1844. Short lived shrub. z8

All the mentioned species are quite valuable as late summer and fall flowering shrubs. Often freezes back in winter but this is of little consequence since the plant flowers on the current year's wood. Prefers sun and a fertile, alkaline soil.

Lit. P'ei, Ch.: The Verbenaceae of China; in Mem. Sci. Soc. China, 3/1/1932.

CASSIA L. — Senna — LEGUMINOSAE

Shrubs, trees or herbs with alternate, even pinnate leaves; flowers regular (not papilionaceous), without nectar; 5 equal calyx teeth, usually longer than the tube; petals 5, flared; stamens 5–10, frequently uneven and often with some anthers abortive; pods flat or rod-like, with numerous seeds. — Some 500–600 species in the warmer regions, only a few in the cooler climates. Only relatively few species grown in gardens. *C. acutifolia* Del. in Egypt and *C. angustifolia* in NW. India are cultivated for "Senna leaves".

Cassia alata L. Shrub, to 2.5 m, with thick, pithy twigs; leaves 45–55 cm long, with 8–14 pairs of leaflets, these oblong, 5–15 cm long, base rounded to cordate, with 12–15 paired veins, stipules thorny and persistent; flowers in 30–50 cm long, axillary and terminal racemes, gold-yellow, December; pods 15–25 cm long, 2 cm wide, winged. BM 6425. Tropical America. 1731. Used as a pharmaceutical in the treatment of skin rashes. ⓕ Tropics. z9

C. artemisioides Gaudich. ex DC. Silver Cassia. Bushy shrub, 1.5–3 m high, twigs and leaves gray silky pubescent; leaflets in 3–7 pairs, narrow-linear, 6–25 mm long, cylindrical; flowers in thick, axillary racemes near the branch tips, 5–8 flowers each, corona gold-yellow, 2–2.5 cm wide, flowers abundantly; pods flat, 5–7 cm long. BMns 599; MCL 41. Australia. z9

C. corymbosa Lam. Shrub, 1–1.5 m high; leaflets 4 or 6, lanceolate to oblong-ovate, 2–4 cm long, tapering to the base or round; flowers gold-yelow, petals rather cup-shaped; in axillary and terminal corymbs, August. BM 633; HTS 122 (= *C. floribunda* Hort.). Northern Argentina. z8 ⊕

C. didymobotrya Forsk. Shrub to small tree, 1.5–3 m high, narrowly upright, young twigs and leaves finely pubescent; leaves 15–35 cm long, with 4–18 leaflet pairs, these oval-oblong to more lanceolate, rounded apex, 2.5–6 cm long, 1.5–2 cm wide, deep green, flow-ers in narrowly upright, 15–30 cm long, slender racemes, gold-yellow and black-brown, summer. Tropical Africa. Common in the gardens of the Mediterranean region. z9 Plate 93.

C. fistula L. This tree, often used as a street tree in the tropics and referred to as "Golden Rain", produces a chambered pod often sold in health food stores as "Manna". The fruits contain a sticky, dark brown, sweet pith of platelets. BIT 3. Occasionally cultivated as a greenhouse plant. ⓕ India, Phillipines. z9

C. laevigata Willd. Upright, glabrous shrub, to 1.5 m; leaflets in 2–4 pairs, oval-lanceolate, 3.5–7 cm long, 1.5–2.5 cm wide, acuminate, base rounded; flowers 6–8 in long stalked, axillary and terminal clusters, corolla 2.5–3 cm wide, petals yellow, obovate, con-cave; pods cylindrical, 5–7 cm long, July. Tropical America, but also planted in Australia and Africa. z9

C. marylandica L. Subshrub, twigs pithy, upright, 0.5–1 m high, dying back to the woody rhizomes each year; leaves 15–25 cm long, leaflets 12–20, oblong to oval, with small apical tips, 2.5–4 cm long, blue-green beneath; flowers in axillary racemes at the branch tips, often grouped in panicles, gold-yellow, dark red an-thers, July–September; pods linear, flat. HM 1294. SE. USA. 1723. Prefers a moist soil. z7 Plate 93. ⊕

C. tomentosa L.f. Shrub, 2–3 m high, twigs and espe-cially the leaf undersides white tomentose; leaves 7–11 cm long, with 6–8 pairs of leaflets, these narrow oval-oblong, 2–3 cm long, 1.2–1.5 cm wide, base oblique; flowers 2–8 in axillary and terminal racemes, corolla 3 cm wide, gold-yellow. HTS 123. Tropical Asia. 1822. z9

C. corymbosa and *C. marylandica* are easily cultivated; both species are attractive summer-flowering shrubs. The former species is, however, not tolerant of frost, the latter will with-stand a frost if it is covered and cut back in the fall. All the other species require a frost free climate.

CASSINIA R. Br. — COMPOSITAE

Evergreen shrubs with "heather-like" appearance; leaves alternate, linear, densely spaced, entire; flowers in numerous small heads, grouped in corymbs; singu-lar flowers usually bisexual or sometimes also pistil-late, without ray florets; calyx surrounded by colorful, membranous sepals; fruit with a bristly pappus. — 28 species in S. Africa, Australia and New Zealand.

Cassinia fulvida Hook. f. Shrub, upright, very densely branched, 1 (1.5) m high, young twigs viscid, yellowish pubescent; leaves narrow oblong-obovate, 4–8 mm long, 2 mm wide, margin somewhat rolled inward, dark green above, glabrous, somewhat viscid, yellow tomentose beneath; flowers small, white, very numer-ous, in 3–7 cm wide, terminal corymbs, July. SL 115 (=

Diplopappus chrysophyllus Koehne). New Zealand, in the mountains to 1200 m. z7 Plate 95. # ∅

C. leptophylla (Forst. f.) R. Br. Shrub, upright, 1 m high, twigs not viscid, densely gray pubescent; leaves linear, somewhat widened at the apex, 3—4 mm long, 1 mm wide, deep green above, white or yellow tomentose beneath; flowers in 3—5 cm wide corymbs, August—September. New Zealand. 1821. Very similar to *C. fulvida*, but generally more gray-white. z8 # ∅

C. retorta A. Cunn. ex DC. Shrub, 1 m high or somewhat taller, twigs stiff, white tomentose; leaves narrow oblong to narrow obovate, usually sessile, reflexed, 3—5 mm long, glabrous above, densely white tomentose beneath; flowers white, numerous heads in 8—12 mm wide corymbs, 6—20 together, July—August. New Zealand, sand dunes of the North Island. z8 # ∅

C. vauvilliersii Hook. f. Shrub, strict upright, 0.5—1.5 m high, growth less dense than the very similar *C. fulvida*, twigs yellowish or whitish tomentose; leaves 6—8 mm long, linear-obovate, rounded at the apex, glabrous above, dark green, somewhat viscid; flowers white, in 2—5 cm wide, rounded corymbs, July—August. SFP 146; LNz 184; BMns 549. New Zealand. z8 # ∅

var.**albida** Kirk. Twigs and leaves white tomentose; leaves linear-spathulate, eventually glabrous above. New Zealand. Plate 95.

var. **pallida** Allan. Twigs and leaves greenish-yellow tomentose; leaves some 10 × 3 mm, narrow oblong-spathulate. New Zealand.

Interesting shrubs but of little ornamental value. Suitable only for the mildest climates or for the greenhouse. The hardiest and most common species is *C. fulvida*.

CASSIOPE D. Don — ERICACEAE

Evergreen dwarf shrubs often forming mats; leaves usually 4 ranked and imbricate, very tiny, furrowed on the dorsal side, entire or ciliate; flowers solitary, axillary or terminal, campanulate to broad cup form, corolla with 4—5 upright or reflexed lobes; stamens 8—10, anthers opening by a large pore, with a large awn on the dorsal side; style thickened at the base; ovaries 4—5 chambered; fruit a globose capsule. — Some 12 species in the northern temperate zones and in the Himalayas; most species in cultivation.

Cassiope ericoides (Pall.) D. Don. Evergreen, dwarf shrublets, heather-like, with numerous erect branches; leaves small, oval-oblong without a membranous margin, very finely ciliate, furrowed on the underside; flowers small, corolla 4 lobed. Siberia. Introduced in England around 1965. z2

C. fastigiata (Wall.) D. Don. Shrub, 15—25 cm high in its native habitat, densely bushy, erect branching, dense foliage 4 ranked, twigs 4 sided, hidden by the foliage; leaves sessile, lanceolate, dark green, 3—4 mm long; limb silvery membranous and finely ciliate; flowers solitary, axillary, on 6—8 mm long, finely pubescent stalks; corolla campanulate, 8 mm wide, white, April—May, lobes reflexed; calyx lobes narrow lanceolate. BM 4796; HAL 197; ICS 4292; BS 1: 32. Himalaya. 1849. One of the most beautiful species, although seldom true in cultivation. z4 Fig. 202. # ✧

C. hypnoides (L.) D. Don. Procumbent, very small, moss-like cushion plants in rock fissures, 2—5 cm high, branchlets very dense with linear, needle-like, 2—3 cm long, alternately arranged, erect leaves, dark green, quite glabrous; flowers solitary, on reddish, 2 cm long stalks, nodding, campanulate, white, 8 mm long, with 5 deep, rounded lobes; calyx red, sepals triangular. PAr 338; NF 6: 66. N. Europe, N. Asia, N. America. z2 Plate 99; Fig. 201. #

C. lycopodioides (Pall.) D. Don. Shrublets, 3—5 cm high, twigs 2 mm wide, procumbent, very densely branched and mat-like, becoming 30—80 cm wide, twigs very thin, glabrous; leaves 4 ranked, densely imbricate, oval-lanceolate, entire, 2 mm long, with whitish membranous limb, keeled on the bottom side and glabrous, upper surface concave and bluish; flowers solitary, axillary, campanulate, white, 8 mm long, nodding, on a filamentous 2 cm long stalk, May—June. NF 7: 267; BMns 298; BS 1: 31. Alaska to Kamchatka; Higher mountains of Japan. Leaves coloring a coppery brown in fall. z3 # ∅

'**Major**'. Larger in all parts, 7—8 cm high; flowers more tubular-campanulate. JRHS 66: 278; GC 139: 484 (= *C. rigida* Wada). NE. Asia.

C. mertensiana (Bong.) D. Don. 20—30 cm high, twigs 4 mm wide; resembling *C. tetragona*, but with leaves not so tightly appressed, not pubescent, not furrowed on the dorsal side, 4 ranked, strongly keeled beneath, oblong, 4 mm long; flowers singular, axillary, nodding on 12 mm long stalks, corolla campanulate, white, with reflexed lobes; stamens very short, filament white, anthers brown; sepals ovate, reddish, April. RWF 268; NF 10: 233. Alaska to California. 1885. Rather variable. z5 Plate 100. #

Fig. 201. *Cassiope hypnoides*, natural size (from Dippel, altered; the original illustration erroneously showed the flowers opening upward)

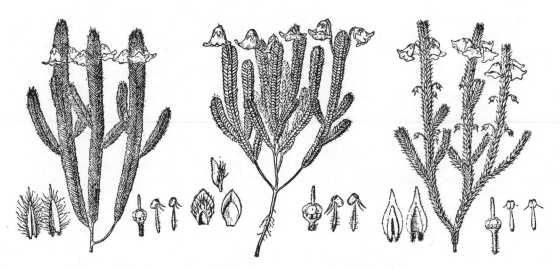

Fig. 202. From left to right: *Cassiope wardii*; *C. myosuroides*; *C. fastigiata* (from ICS)

ssp. **gracilis** Piper. Shorter than the species, 7–10 cm high, twigs darker; flowers larger, calyx and flower stalks red (at least on cultivated plants), May. USA; Montana, Oregon, in the mountains. More easily cultivated and blooming better than the species.

C. myosuroides W. W. Sm. Growth mat-like; leaves small, imbricate, swollen at the base, with a broad membranous limb, ciliate. Upper Burma and W. Yunnan. Collected by Kingdon Ward (Nr. 1788), also by Forrest but as yet not in cultivation. z6 Fig. 202.

C. redowskii G. Don. Not completely known; leaves very numerous, dark green, with darker limb, a conical cavity inside, not recognizable from the outside; for this reason of botanical interest, but otherwise of little garden merit; flowers 4 lobed. Siberia. z2

C. saximontana Small. Dwarf shrublet, 10–20 cm high, branches ascending, scale leaves 4 ranked, densely grooved beneath; flowers small, on short stalks, scarcely reaching beyond the branch tips, May–June. BM 3181 (as *Andromeda tetragona*). N. America, Rocky Mountains, from Alberta to Alaska. Long confused with *C. tetragona*, but distinctly differing in the much smaller flowers with very short stalks. z3

C. selaginoides Hook. f. & Thoms. Shrublet, densely bushy, twigs distinctively long, to 25 cm high; leaves densely imbricate, 4 ranked, appressed, lanceolate, furrowed on the dorsal side, with small bristles on the tip (important for identification!); 3 mm long; flowers usually solitary on each branch, on 2–2.5 cm long, thin stalks, ovate-campanulate, white or slightly reddish, lobes triangular, somewhat erect, April–May; calyx lobes lanceolate, green. FIO 2. Himalaya, W. China. 1920. z4 #

'**Nana**'. Only 2–3 cm high; flowers more ovate. BM 9003 (b).

C. stelleriana (Pall.) DC. Creeping, dense mat-like, seldom over 10 cm high, twigs wiry, rooting all along the stem; leaves 3 mm long, not appressed, rather protruding (important for identification!), obtuse linear; flowers terminal, solitary, on filamentous, finely pubescent stalks, nodding; corolla campanulate, deeply cleft, with 4 lobes, some 8 mm long and wide, cream-white, often with a trace of pink, April–May; stamens 8; calyx red, lobes ovate (= *Harrimanella stelleriana* Cov.). NW.–N. America, NE. Asia, often in large masses in the high mountains. Rare in cultivation. z4 #

C. tetragona (L.) DC. Shrub, to 30 cm high, usually lower growing, narrowly upright, branching often procumbent at first; leaves 4 ranked, densely appressed, tough leathery, ovate, 3 sided, 3–5 mm long, distinctly furrowed on the dorsal side (important for identification!); flowers solitary, axillary, on short stalks, nodding, April–May; corolla campanulate, 6 mm long, white, occasionally somewhat pink, with 4–5 lobes; calyx lobes oval-oblong, reddish. BM 3181; BB 2762. N. America, N. Scandinavia, Siberia, very common in the mountains. 1810. z3 Plate 100. # ✥

C. wardii Marquand. To 30 cm high, main branches procumbent, secondary branches ascending; leaves 8 mm thick, densely imbricate, lanceolate, 5 mm long, dorsal side distinctly furrowed, limb densely fimbriate-ciliate (important for identification!); flowers singular, axillary, nodding, on small stalks; corolla broadly campanulate, 8 mm long, white, reddish inside at the base; calyx lobes oblong, reddish at the tip, May. BMns 151; ICS 4294; JRHS 87: 76. SE. Tibet. 1938. Considered the most beautiful of the genus. z4 Fig. 202. # ✥

Hybrids

Numerous hybrids are in cultivation, all developed in England; they are generally easy to cultivate and more vigorous than the wild species.

'**Badenoch**' (J. Drake) (= *C. lycopodioides* × *C. fastigiata*). Loose growing, nest forming, twigs thin, to 10 cm high; flowers on filamentous, thin twigs.

'Edinburgh' (Bot. Gard. Edinburgh, around 1950). The parents now known for sure, probably *C. fastigiata* × *C. saximontana*, very similar in appearance to the latter, but grows more vigorously, 25—30 cm high; leaves deep green, branch tips light green; flowers very short stalked, about 12 densely arranged at the branch tips, pure white, 7 mm wide, calyx green, sepals with reddish apex. JRHS 1958: 40.

'George Taylor' (R. B. Cooke) (= *C. wardii* × *C. fastigiata*). Resembling *C. wardii*, but more open growing; leaves very fimbriate-ciliate. First found among the parents in the wild by Sir George Taylor, and later developed by Cooke.

'Kathleen Dryden' (Mrs. Dryden) (= *C. lycopodioides* × *C. fastigiata*). Twigs horizontally spreading; flowers abundant, hanging perpendicular to the branches. Vigorous.

'Medusa' (E. B. Anderson) (= *C. fastigiata* × *C. lycopodioides*). More similar in growth to *C. lycopodioides*, but less compact, more vigorous; leaf margins finely fimbriate; flowers large, with reddish stalks and dark red calyx lobes.

'Muirhead' (R. B. Cooke, before 1953) (= *C. wardii* × *C. lycopodioides*). Broad and low, branches rooting; leaves small, margin fimbriate (like those of *C. wardii*), with short furrows on the dorsal side; flowers very abundantly, flower size intermediate between the parents. Developed by R. B. Cooke, Corbidge, England.

'Randle Cooke' (= *C. fastigiata* × *C. lycopodioides*). Broad and open growing, but only 15 cm high; leaves short furrowed, margin fimbriate; flowers rather large, on short, pubescent stalks.

All species somewhat difficult to cultivate, with the exception of *C. tetragona*; preferring lime free, peaty soil, sufficiently moist. The moss-like *C. hypnoides* is very difficult to cultivate preferring rock fissures on a northern exposure.

Lit. Good, R. D. O.: The genera Phyllodoce and Cassiope; in Jour. Bot. (London) **64**, 1—10, 1926 ● Lilley, S. E.: The genus *Cassiope*; in Bull. Alp. Gard. Soc., 72—87. ● Lilley, S. E.: *Cassiopes*;in Jour. RHS 1965: 302 ● Kummert, F.: Maigloeckchenheide — *Cassiope*; Erwerbsgaertner 1972: 43—44.

CASTANEA Mill. — Chestnut — FAGACEAE

Deciduous trees with grooved, oak-like bark; terminal buds absent; leaves alternate, 2 ranked, toothed; flowers monoecious; male flowers in erect or ascending, cylindrical catkins, female flowers unattractive,usually at the base of the male catkins, rarely in separate catkins; fruit a large nut, in a dense, prickly hull, surrounding a brown leathery shell. — 12 species in the temperate zones of the Northern Hemisphere.

Castanea × alabamensis Ashe (*C. alnifolia*? × *C. dentata*). Von Camus, l.c., also considered a possible hybrid of *C. dentata* × *C. alnifolia* var. *floridana*. Not in cultivation.

C. alnifolia Nutt. Creeping dwarf shrub, 0.2—0.5 m high, forming wide columns; leaves oval-oblong, obtuse, 5—15 cm long, dentate, dark green and glabrous above, yellow-brown short tomentose or pubescent beneath, with 12—16 vein pairs; fruits similar to those of *C. pumila*, but the calyx cup with fewer and shorter prickles, with only 1 nut. CCh 6—8 (= *C. nana* Muhl.). Southeastern USA. Very easily distinguished but nonetheless often confused with *C. pumila*. z6

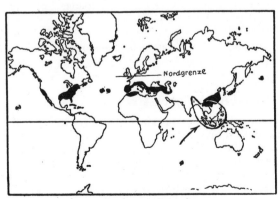
Fig.203. Range of *Castanea* and *Castanopsis* (arrow)

C. crenata S. & Z. Japanese Chestnut. Often shrubby, occasionally also a small tree, to 9 m high, resembling *C. sativa*, twigs likewise pubescent at first, but soon becoming glabrous; although with leaves crenate-serrate, 8—16 cm long, usually tomentose and glandular scaly beneath or also glabrous, oblong-lanceolate, usually long acuminate; fruits with 2—3 nuts, 2.5 cm wide, prickles glabrous. EH 237; CCh 10—12; KIF 1: 41 (= *C. japonica* Bl.). Japan. 1876. Fruits earlier than *C. sativa*, fruit valuable and of economic importance in Japan. ⑫ Italy, Japan (for erosion control). z6 Plate 102. ∅ ✕

C. dentata (Marsh.) Borkh. American Chestnut. Tree, to 30 m, crown not as broad as *C. sativa*, young twigs and winter buds glabrous; leaves oblong-lanceolate, coarsely serrate, 12—24 long, bases regularly cuneate, always glabrous; fruits to 6 cm wide, nuts 2—3 in a hull, tasty. BB 1226; GTP 152; EH 202 (= *C. americana* Raf.). N. America. 1800. Very popular in America but largely destroyed by the Chestnut Blight. z5 Plate 101, 103. ∅ ⚭ ✕

C. henryi (Skan) Rehd. Tree, 18—25 m high, twigs glabrous; leaves oval-oblong to lanceolate, long acuminate, bristly dentate, 8—16 cm long, lighter beneath, quite glabrous, with 12—20 paired veins; fruit with only 1 nut, oval-rounded, acute tipped, 2 cm long, prickles of the pericarp somewhat pubescent. CCh 20; FIO 112 (= *C. fargesii* Dode; *C. vilmoriniana* Dode). Middle and W. China. 1900. ⑫ E. China. z6 Plate 101.

C. mollissima Bl. Chinese Chestnut. Tree, 12—20 m high, occasionally shrubby, branches short pubescent, with long erect pubescence on the young twigs; leaves eliptic-oblong, acuminate with a short tip, 8—15 cm long, base rounded, gray or whitish tomentose beneath or nearly glabrous; fruits quite variable in size, 3—6 cm wide, with 2—3 nuts; prickles of the pericarp softly pubescent. LF 87; CCh 13—14; FIO 112 (= *C. bungeana* Bl.; *C. duclouxii* Dode; *C. hupehensis* Dode). N.

and Central China. Of great economic importance in China for its fruits, also in Europe and N. America for its resistance to the Chestnut Blight (*Endothia parasitica*). Ⓕ China; USA. z5 Plate 101. ∅ ⚭ ✕

C. × neglecta Dode (*C. dentata × C. pumila*). Shrubby, very similar to *C. pumila*, but with leaves less pubescent; fruits larger. BD 1908: 143. Found in the wild in N. Carolina. Considered a possible form of *C. pumila* by Ferdinand. z5

C. ozarkensis Ashe. Closely related to *C. pumila*, but a tree, to 20 m high; leaves much larger, 15—20 cm long, coarsely dentate, white tomentose beneath, very rarely glabrous; fruits 3 cm thick, very dense prickles, nut 1.5 cm long. CCh 74 (= *C. arkansana* Ashe). S. USA. 1891. z6

C. pumila (L.) Mill. Chinquapin. Tree, to 15 m, frequently only shrubby, stoloniferous, twigs remaining short tomentose, red-brown; leaves eliptic-oblong, coarsely serrate or bristly dentate, 7—12 cm long, white tomentose beneath; pretty white male flower catkins in June—July; fruits 3 cm thick, with only 1 nut, long rounded, acuminate, 2.5 cm long, kernel sweet. BB 1227; BS 1: 531; GSP 108. Eastern N. America. 1699. z5 Plate 101, 103.

C. sativa Mill. Sweet, Spanish Chestnut. Broad crowned tree, to 30 cm high, trunk with distinctly spiralling bark, young twigs tomentose at first, soon becoming glabrous, red-brown; leaves oblong-lanceolate, 12 to 20 cm long, deep green above and glossy, at first stellate tomentose beneath, but soon becoming glabrous, coarsely serrate; male flower catkins greenish white, long, May; fruit 5—6 cm wide, with 2—3 nuts, usually at the branch tips, very tasty. HM 488; EH 232 (= *C. vesca* Gaertn.). Asia Minor, S. Europe, N. Africa; in cultivation for centuries, especially in S. Europe where it is grown for its fruit and wood. Ⓕ SW. Germany, Bulgaria, Italy, Romania, Yugoslavia. z6

Including many cultivars:

'Argenteovariegata'. Periclinal chimera; leaves often somewhat deformed, margin more or less white variegated, often narrow, often incised to the midrib. NDJ 1955: 58 fig. 4a; BS 1:34 (= 'Argenteovariegata'; 'Argenteomarginata'). 1864. Very attractive foliage. ∅

'Asplenifolia'. Leaves of various forms from irregular, deeply incised acute teeth on large blades, to somewhat linear-lanceolate, 12 mm wide leaves, the latter form normally found at the tips of summer branches (=

'Comptoniifolia'; 'Heterophylla'; 'Salicifolia'). Before 1838. Very conspicuous, attractive form. ∅

'Aureomaculata'. Leaves with wide yellow and greenish-yellow patches in the middle. Known since 1862.

'Cochleata'. Dwarf habit; leaves smaller than those of the type, more densely arranged, concave or convex, irregular margin (= 'Bullata'; 'Monstosa'). Known since 1836.

'Fastigiata'. Grows narrowly columnar. Before 1866.

'Glabra'. Large leaved, tough, dark green, glossy, eventually quite glabrous. Since 1836.

'Laciniata'. Margin teeth long and drawn out, filamentous. Different from 'Asplenifolia'.

'Pendula'. Branches umbrella-like, pendulous. Found in Holland (around 1943) and Japan (1919).

'Pendulifolia'. Leaves hanging vertically, 20—30 cm long, 5—9 cm wide. ∅

'Prolifera'. Lush growing; leaves large, long, narrow, glossy above, somewhat tough, the youngest leaves densely gray-white tomentose beneath (= 'Discolor'). Before 1872. ∅

'Purpurea'. Leaves very large, to 15 cm wide, purple in spring, fall color coppery-red. Before 1909. ∅

'Pyramidalis'. Growth conical, narrow (= 'Holdtii'). Before 1914. Not to be confused with 'Fastigiata'.

'Variegata'. Yellow variegated margin, partly variegated in patches (= 'Aureovariegata'). Before 1755.

In the interest of conserving space, the large-fruited cultivars will not be covered here; they may be found in other works covering fruit and nut trees.

C. seguinii Dode. Tall shrub or tree, to 10 m, twigs short pubescent; leaves elliptic-oblong to lanceolate, acuminate, 6 to 15 cm long, base rounded to nearly cordate, coarsely dentate, green and glandular scaly beneath, with 12—16 paired veins; fruits normally with 3, occasionally 5—7 nuts. CCh 13, 15—17 (= *C. davidii* Dode). E. and Middle China. 1853 and 1907. z6

All species prefer a deep, heavy or sandy soil, not very alkaline. They will tolerate extreme dryness, wilting only in very hot dry summers. The fruits ripen only in warm locations.

Unfortunately, the chestnuts of the USA were nearly devastated in the eary 1900's by an epidemic of Chestnut Blight (*Endothia parasitica*). This same pathogen found its way onto the European continent in 1937 in S. Switzerland.

Lit. Camus, A.: Les Chataigniers; monographie des genres *Castanea* et *Castanopsis*; 1 Vol., 100 Pl., Paris 1929.

CASTANOPSIS (D. Don) Spach) — FAGACEAE

Evergreen trees and shrubs, intermediate between *Castanea* and *Quercus*; scaly bark; leaves 2 ranked or spirally arranged, entire or serrate, leathery; staminate flowers in erect spikes; calyx 5—6 parted, stamens 10—12; pistillate flowers in especially short spikes; fruit, a nut ripening in the 2nd year, usually 3 in a prickly hull. — Some 120 spcies in subtropical S. and E. Asia, of those, 30 in China.

Castanopsis chinensis Hance. Tall tree, 15—18 m high, bark dark gray, grooved, twigs dark gray, densely covered with white lenticels; leaves elliptic, 8 cm long, 3 cm wide, long acuminate, sparsely serrate on the apical half, basal half usually entire, thick, leathery, glossy, bluish beneath, petiole 1.5—2 cm, glabrous; fruit clusters 10 cm long, fruits densely covered with branched prickles, greenish-brown, somewhat pubescent; male inflorescences rather short, yellowish-green at the tips of the young twigs. ICS 840. China; Yunnan, Kwangtung, 1000–1300 m. z9

C. chrysophylla see: **Chrysolepis chrysophylla** (Hook.) Hjelmqvist

C. concolor Rehd. & Wils. Tree, 10–20 m high, bark dark gray, finely grooved, twigs glabrous, rough, dark brown, dense with rounded, whitish lenticels; leaves oblanceolate to oval-elliptic, tough leathery, to 7 cm long and 3.8 cm wide, long acuminate, cuneate at the base, irregularly serrate on the apical blade half, basal half entire, both sides bluish-green, petiole 8–15 mm long, glabrous; fruit cluster 6 cm long, rachis glabrous, fruits nearly globose, irregularly 2–3 lobed, 3 cm thick; male inflorescence 8–10 cm long, very fragrant. China; Yunnan, Szechwan, 2000–2600 m. In cultivation only at Caerhays Castle, Cornwall, Eng. z8

C. cuspidata (Thunb.) Schottky. Tree, to 15 m, branches wide and attractively pendant, dark gray bark, smooth or quite shallowly grooved; leaves ovate to oblong, 5–8 cm long, 2–4 cm wide, apex long drawn out, obtuse, base rounded to cuneate, dark green and glossy above, fine scales beneath, metallic brown to nearly white, thick, tough, entire; fruit clusters 5–7 cm long, with 6–10 fruits, globose at first, but always ovate when ripe, 1.5 cm long and 1 cm thick, pubescent, but without prickles. KIF 1:42. Japan; very rare in China. 1879. Valuable forest tree in Japan. z8

C. delavayi Franch. Tree, to 15 m, bark dark gray, twigs gray stellate tomentose in spring, soon becoming glabrous and gray-brown; leaves elliptic or more obovate, base cuneate, 5–12 cm long, margin wavy and

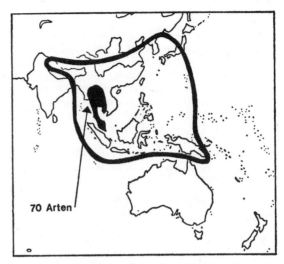

Fig. 204. Range of the genus *Castanopsis* (excluding California)

irregularly coarsely dentate, with 6–8 vein pairs, silver-gray or whitish beneath; male catkins yellow, slender, 10–18 cm long; fruits 6–10 together, on a 10–12 cm long rachis, globose, 12 mm thick, with 1 nut, pericarp with short stiff prickles. ICS 834. China; Szechwan, Yunnan, 1300–3000 m. 1924. z8

Cultivation possible only in the mildest regions.

Lit. Lee, S. C., Forest Bot. of China — 32 species described in detail; 27 species are illustrated and described (in Chinese) in the Iconographia Cormophyt. Sinic. (I), 822–848.

CASUARNIA L. — Australian Pine — CASUARINACEAE

Evergreen trees and shrubs; twigs thin, filamentous, foliage similar to *Equisetum*; "leaves" reduced to pointed scales, fused at the base to form a short sheath surrounding the stem at the nodes; the number of connate scales between 4–16 (important for identification!); flowers mono- and dioecious, the male in cylindrical spikes, with a small perianth, the female in small, rounded cones, without a perianth; fruit a globose to cylindrical or ovate, woody cone. — 45 species in Australia, New Caledonia and E. India.

Casuarina equisetifolia L. Tree, to 25 m high, very fast growing, twigs thin, nodding, light green; internodes 6 mm long; sheaths with 7(6–8) teeth; cones short stalked, 12 mm wide, conical, scales ovate, smooth. N. Australia, Queensland. z8 Plate 93. # Ø

C. nana Sieb. Shrub, 1.5–1.8 m high, densely branched, dioecious, twigs short, cylindrical, sheaths with 5 teeth; male flower spikes slender, 6–12 mm long; fruit cones sessile, various in form, from nearly globose and 8 mm thick to oblong-cylindrical and to 18 mm long. Australia; NS. Wales. Cultivated in England. z8 #

C. stricta Dry. Small tree, 6–9 m high, twigs erect, later nodding, dense, dark green, thin, glabrous; internodes 12 mm long or more; sheaths usually with 7 teeth, these oval-lanceolate, appressed; cones rounded to ovate, 2.5–5 cm long (= *C. quadrivalvis* Labill.). Australia, Tasmania. 1812. z8 # Ø

C. torulosa Dry. Tree, to 15 m and higher, corky bark, curling on older branches and stems, twigs erect; sheaths with 4 short, triangular, appressed teeth, dioecious; cones globose; 2 cm wide (= *C. tenuissima* Sieb.). Australia. z8 # Ø

The species mentioned should only be considered for planting in frost free areas and otherwise over-wintered in a cool greenhouse.

Lit. Treub, M.: Sur les Casuarinacées et leur place dans le système naturel; in Ann. Jard. Bot. Buitenzorg **10**, 145–231, 1891.

CATALPA Scop. — BIGNONIACEAE

Deciduous trees; leaves opposite or in whorls of 3, usually very large, entire or 3 lobed, often with red glandular patches in the vein axils beneath; flowers in terminal panicles or racemes; calyx closed when young, then opening irregularly or 2 lobed; corolla tube oblique campanuate, 2 lobed, with 2 small lobes above and 3 smaller ones beneath, limb sinuate-crispate; fertile stamens 2, curved, with outspread anthers; pistil 2 lobed at the tip; fruit a very long, bi-valved, tubular capsule, with numerous, flat seeds, with hair fascicles at either end. — 11 species in N. America, Cuba, SW. China and Tibet.

Catalpa bignonioides Walt. Tree, to 15 m high, short trunk, bark light brown, thin; leaves cordate-ovate, short acuminate, 10—20 cm long, normally entire, rarely with 1—2 small side lobes, dark green above, more or less thick, short, soft pubescence beneath, light green, crushed leaves have an unpleasant smell (important for identification!); flowers in 15—20 cm long, many flowered, branched panicles; corolla pure white, 4—5 cm long and wide, throat with yellow stripes and many purple spots, June—July; fruit capsules to 35 cm long, 6—8 mm thick, thin walled. BM 1094; BB 3367; GTP 336 (= *C. syringaefolia* Sims). S. USA, Virginia. 1726. z5 Plate 104, 105; Fig. 206. 207. ⊕ ⌀ ⌀

'Aurea'. Leaves gold-yellow in spring, becoming light green during summer. Before 1877. Plate 106. ⌀

'Koehnei'. Leaves green in the middle, margin yellowish-green or yellow, veins green. Gw 1915: 445. Before 1903. Plate 106. ⌀

'Nana'. Densely branched, flat rounded form, but nearly always top grafted on a standard; leaves much smaller than the species, only slightly pubescent beneath; flowers not observed. Originated around 1850 in the Masson Nursery, France. Plate 104. ⌀

'Rehderi'. Tree-like; leaves nearly triangular, youngest often elliptic-ovate, always with 1—2 side lobes, these caudate tipped, leaf petiole usually longer than the midrib, 13—15 cm long. Candollea 1952: p. 260. A specimen may be found in the Pruhonice Arboretum near Prague, Czechoslovakia.

C. bungei C. A. Mey. Small tree, leaves triangular-ovate, to 15 cm long, acuminate, entire, base more or less cuneate, glabrous beneath or with insignificantly pubescent venation; inflorescence with only 3—12 flowers, July; corolla 3—3.5 cm long, pale pink to white, purple spots inside; fruit capsule 30—50(100!) cm long. LF 268. N. China. 1877. Very rare in cultivation and usually confused with *C. ovata* or *C. bignonioides* 'Nana'; flowers frequently erroneously described as "greenish-yellow". Ⓕ N. China. z6 Fig. 207.

var. **heterophylla** C. A. Mey. Like the species, but with the leaves only occasionally entire, usually irregularly toothed or lobed, quite glabrous; flowers less numerous and in smaller clusters.

C. × erubescens Carr. (*C. bignonioides* × *C. ovata*). In-cluded here are several hybrids originating in cultivation. The type is described by Carrière in the Revue Horticole, 1869, but it is probably not in the trade (= *C. hybrida* Spaeth; *C. teasii* Dode).

The following forms are included:

'Adina'. Flowers more or less double resulting from the petaloid staminodes surrounding the stamens. Only twice observed in 1947 in the Parc de Buttes, Chaumont, France; 1948 in Pilsen, Czech.).

'Hybrida'. This form was made available by Spaeth, Berlin, in 1898; black-red new growth, later becoming generally dark green; flowers 3 cm wide, tube somewhat swollen, with oblique, 2 lobed limb, white, throat violet punctate and yellow striped, in loose, erect panicles, July—August (= *C. hybrida atropurpurea* Spaeth). This clone is probably identical with 'J. C. Teas.'.

'Japonica'. Leaves triangular to cordate, larger than those of the type, partly entire, partly with 1—2 lobes, usually glossy green above; flowers in large bouquets, corolla white, otherwise like the type (= *C. japonica* Dode). Apparently originating in Japan and presumably a cross of *C. bignonioides* × *C. ovata* 'Flavescens'. Around 1907.

'J. C. Teas'. New growth purple; leaves broad ovate or slightly 3 lobed, to 30 cm long, cordate, softly pubescent beneath; flowers white, with yellow patches and fine purple spots, the spots smaller than those of *C. bignonioides*, but more numerous, late July—August. Raised from seed by J. C. Teas of Bayville, Indiana, USA around 1874. Very strong grower, leaves occasionally to 60 cm long; flower panicles of 300 blooms have been observed.

'Purpurea'. Leaves nearly black-red at bud break, 8 cm long, often with lobes on the apical half of the blade; flowers white, 3 cm long. Candollea 1952: p. 265. Originated before 1886 by A. Waterer in England.

C. fargesii Bur. Tree, to 20 m high, branches stellate pubescent; leaves ovate, 8—14 cm long, apex long, drawn out, base rounded to cordate, sparsely yellowish tomentose above, densely so beneath, margin on young plants 3 lobed; flowers in mock umbels of 7—10, June; corolla 3.5 cm long, pink, inside brown and yel-

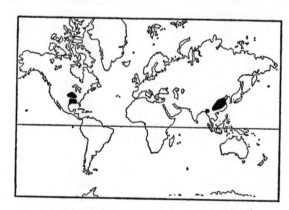

Fig. 205. Range of the genus *Catalpa* (from Pacelt). In the American region with *C. speciosa* above and *C. bignonioides* beneath; in the Asiatic region, *C. tibetica*

low spotted; fruit capsules 30—50 cm long, thin (= *C. vestita* Diels). W. China; Hupeh, Szechwan. 1900. Ⓕ China; Yunnan. z6 Fig. 206.

f. **duclouxii** (Dode) Gilmour. Tree, leaves more acute-ovate, 3 lobed on young plants, 10—20 cm long, apex long and drawn out, glabrous on both sides, reddish spots in the vein axils beneath; flowers in flat mock umbels, corolla violet-purple, 3.5 cm long; fruit capsules 60—80 cm long. LF 269; BM 9458 (= *C. duclouxii* Dode; *C. sutchuenensis* Dode). W. China, growing the type species. 1900. Fig. 206.

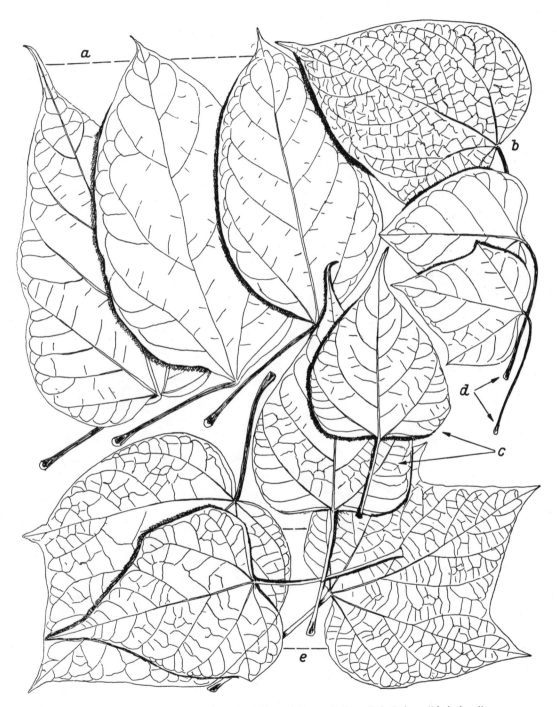

Fig. 206. **Catalpa.** a. *C. speciosa*; b. *C. bignonioides*; c. *C. fargesii*; d. *C. fargesii* f. *duclouxii*; e. *C. ovata* (Original)

C. × galleana Dode (*C. ovata* × *C. speciosa*). Tree, leaves cordate, often elliptic-ovate when young, quite variable, short acuminate, base truncate, cordate or cuneate, occasionally with 1–2 small side lobes, 8–10 cm long, petiole 4–7 cm long; flowers very similar to *C. speciosa*. Candollea 1952; 269. First observed in 1907. A specimen stands in Pilsen, Czechoslovakia.

C. ovata. G. Don. Tree, to 10 m high, broad crowned, twigs glabrous, rarely slightly pubescent; leaves wide cordate-ovate, 10–25 cm long, abruptly acuminate, usually 3(5) lobed, rich green above, lighter beneath with pubescent venation, red glandular spots in the vein axils; flowers in 10–25 cm long panicles; corolla dull white, yellow inside with purple spots and stripes, 2.5 cm wide, limb crispate, July; fruit capsules 20–30 cm long, 8 mm thick. BM 6611; LF 270 (= *C. kaempferi* S. & Z.; *C. henryi* Dode). China, in the mountains to 2500 m. 1849. z5 Fig. 206, 207.

'Flavescens'. Leaves somewhat smaller, lighter; flowers smaller than the species, corolla totally yellowish, otherwise like the species. Origin unknown. Appeared in the Botanic Garden of Geneva, Switzerland before 1863.

C. speciosa Warder. Tree, to 30 m high, crown slender conical, bark red-brown, thick, deeply furrowed; leaves cordate-ovate, 15–30 cm long, long acuminate, dark green and glabrous above, dense pubescence beneath, crushed leaves not scented (important ·for identification!);· flowers few, in 13–15 cm long, erect panicles, fragrant, June (3 weeks earlier than *C. bignonioides*); calyx 2 lobed, corolla 5 cm wide, white, with 2 yellow stripes in the throat and very small purple spots; fruits few, 20–40 cm long, 1.5 cm thick, thick walled. RH 1895: 136; BB 3368; NBB 3: 254 (= *C. cordifolia* Jaume). USA, forest tree of the Wabash Valley; common in Illinois and Indiana. 1754. Valued for its lumber. Prefers sandy soil; very frost tolerant. Much more attractive and hardy than *C. bignonioides* but less common in international garden culture. Ⓕ New Zealand; earlier also in W. Germany. z5 Fig. 206, 207. ⊕ ∅

'Albovariegata'. Leaves irregularly large yellow or whitish spotted (= *C. bignonioides* 'Variegata'). Before 1894. Of little garden merit. ∅

'Pulverulenta'. Leaves finely and densely white punctate. Introduced by B. Paul & Son, England in 1908. ∅

Fig. 207. **Catalpa.** a. *C. bignonioides*, inflorescence, flower (in front view and cross section). seed; b. *C. ovata*, inflorescence; c. *C. bunggei*, part of an inflorescence; d. *C. speciosa*, inflorescence and d₁ seed (from Sargent, Schumann, Lavallée, Bureau)

C. tibetica Forrest. Shrub, leaves like those of *C. ovata*, glabrous above, softly pubescent beneath; flowers like *C. ovata*, but 2.5 cm long or somewhat longer; calyx 8–9 mm long; fruits 13 to 18 cm long, to 13 mm wide. Tibet; Salween River, Tsarong. Known since 1921, but as yet not in cultivation. z5

Good, winter-hardy trees for specimen planting in open park areas; soil sandy to clay, preferably somewhat moist. After slow establishment, a fast growing tree. *C. speciosa* is worthy of greater use in Europe for its quality of sparse fruit production. Young plants of all the species should be protected from a late frost.

CAVENDISHIA Lindl. — ERICACEAE

Evergreen shrubs or trees; leaves alternate, leathery, entire, glabrous, short petioled; flowers attractive, in axillary or terminal racemes or corymbs, stalked; calyx hemispherical or short campanulate, with short, 5 lobed or toothed limb; corolla tubular, limb 5 toothed, teeth valvate, stamens 10. — Some 100 species in tropical America.

Cavendishia acuminata (Hook.) Benth. Shrub, 1 m high, branches nodding, occasionally somewhat pubescent, new growth pink, later deep green; leaves ovate to oblong or lanceolate, apex long and drawn out, base rounded, 5–7 cm long, petiole very short and thick; flower bright red, 2 cm long, lobe green in short racemes, surrounded by large, scarlet red bracts, November. BM 5752; DRHS 421 (as *Thibaudia acuminata*). Andes of Columbia and Ecuador. 1868. z8 # ⊕

Culture somewhat like that of *Agapetes*; for moist, shady areas in very mild climates.

CEANOTHUS L. — RHAMNACEAE

Deciduous or evergreen shrubs, often also trees in their native habitats; leaves alternate or opposite, pinnate or tri-veined, margin serrate or entire; flowers small, 5 parted, in sessile umbels, grouped into large racemes or panicles; style branched at the apex; fruits fleshy at first, later dry, 3 parted schizocarp, eventually breaking down into 3 dehiscent nutlets. — 55 species, mostly in western N. America, mainly in the coastal areas, south to Mexico and Guatemala.

Section 1: **Euceanothus** McMinn

Leaves alternate; fruits lacking small horns, but often with combs or keels on the dorsal side of each locule; stipules thin and abscising early; stomates on the leaf underside never in sunken cavities;
    Leaves evergreen;
        Flowers white:
            C. incana, velutinus
        Flowers blue:
            C. arboreus, cyaneus, dentatus, foliosus, griseus, impressus, lobbianus, mendocinensis, papillosus, sorediatus, thyrsiflorus, veitchianus
    Leaves deciduous;
        Flowers white:
            C. americanus, fendleri, integerrimus, ovatus, parvifolius, sanguineus
        Flowers blue:
            C. coeruleus, delilianus (Hybrids)
        Flowers pink:
            C. pallidus (Hybrids)

Section 2: **Cerastes** McMinn
Leaves opposite; fruit normally with small apical or sub-apical horns; stipules usually persistent, thick, corky; stomates in sunken cavities on the leaf undersides;
    Leaves evergreen;
        Flowers white:
            C. cuneatus, megacarpus
        Flowers blue:
            C. divergens, gloriosus, jepsonii, prostratus, rigidus, purpureus

Fig. 208. *Ceanothus americanus* (from Lauche)

Ceanothus americanus L. Deciduous shrub, to 1 m high, twigs thin, erect, finely pubescent when young, reddish or brownish; leaves ovate-oblong, 3—10 cm long, acute, base occasionally somewhat cordate, finely serrate, light green above, somewhat pubescent beneath; flowers white, in large terminal and axillary panicles, July—fall, on the current year's wood. BM 1479. E. and Middle USA; dry forests and hills. 1713. Quite hardy, useful plant. z5 Fig. 208. ✥

C. arboreus Greene. Growth tree-like, to 9 m, or a rounded shrub on a short thick stem, 3—5 m, bark flaking, young branches densely pubescent; leaves alternate, ovate to broad elliptic, base rounded to slightly cordate, short acuminate, shallowly dentate, each tooth with a gland, 4—10 cm long, 2.5—6 cm wide, dark green above with fine pubescence, light gray tomentose beneath, distinctly 3 veined; flowers small, pale gray, in conical, axillary, to 10 cm long and 5 cm wide panicles, May—July. California. z8

'Trewithen Blue'. Selection with darker blue flowers. Found in Trewithen Garden, near Truro, SW. England. Before 1967.

C. coeruleus Lag. Deciduous shrub, 1 m high, twigs dense gray-yellow tomentose or softly pubescent; leaves usually narrow-oblong, seldom ovate, finely serrate, base rounded, 3—7 cm long, apexes obtuse to acute, both sides densely pubescent at first, eventually only on underside; flower light blue, in 5—6 cm long panicles, July—October. BR 291; DRHS 422 (= *C. azureus* Desf.). Mexico. 1818. z9 Fig. 211.

Fig. 209. **Ceanothus** (most actual size, the fruits enlarged 2×). a. *C. impressus;* b. *C. dentatus;* c. *C. purpureus;* d. *C. cuneatus;* e. *C. prostratus;* f. *C. rigidus* (from McMinn)

The species somewhat unusual in cultivation, but valuable for hybridizing purposes; this is a parent of 'Gloire de Versailles'.

C. cuneatus (Hook.) Nutt. Evergreen shrub, 1 m tall, twigs pubescent when young; leaves opposite, obovate, entire, 15–25 mm long, apex rounded, dull gray-green, pubescent at first; flowers dull white, occasionally with blue tones, May. MCea 81. California. 1848. A vigorous weed in its habitat. z7? Fig. 209. #

C. cyaneus Eastw. Evergreen shrub, tree-like in its native habitat, twigs angular, glabrous; leaves alternate, palmate venation, 2.5–5 cm long, ovate-elliptic, glandular toothed, glossy green above, dull green and glabrous beneath; flowers in cylindrical, 5–10 cm long panicles, light or dark blue, June. MCea 4, 5, 55. California. 1925. z8 Fig. 211. #

C. × delilianus Spach. (*C. americanus × C. coeruleus*). Young twigs finely pubescent; leaves elliptic to ovate-oblong, 4–8 cm long, acuminate, dark green above, pubescent to tomentose beneath; flowers from light to dark blue (according to cultivar), in large terminal and axillary panicles, July–October; rachis of inflorescence pubescent (= *C. arnouldii* Carr.).

In addition, the following blue flowered huybrids, all developed in France before 1890:

'Bijou'. Blue-lilac.

'Blue Céleste'. Panicles wide and compact, sky blue.

'Charles Détriché'. (Chenault). Heliotrope-violet, HCC 636.

'Ciel de Provence'. Deep blue. ⊕

'Distinction' (Lemoine). White with soft blue.

'Gloire de Plantières' (Simon-Lois Frères). Low growing, dark blue, July–October. ⊕

'Gloire de Versailles' (Dauvesse). Strong grower, flowers abundantly, dark blue, in large panicles, HCC 738/2, July–October. Before 1891. ⊕

'Henry Défosse'. Grows to a medium size; flowers in large bouquets, dark blue.

'Indigo' (Chenault). Deep indigo blue, HCC 738/2. Darkest blue cultivar, not very vigorous, somewhat tender, protected sites preferable. ⊕

'Léon Simon' (Simon-Louis Frères). Panicles long, light blue. ⊕

'Pinguet-Guidon'. Lavender colored.

'Saphir'. Steel blue.

'Sceptre d'Azur'. Strong grower, dark blue.

'Sirius'. Metallic blue.

'Topaze' (Lemoine). Soft indigo blue, HCC 636/1, July–September; leaves much like those of 'Indigo', but growing much more vigorously. ⊕

'Victor Jouin' (Simon-Louis Frères). Twigs very dark; flowers light blue.

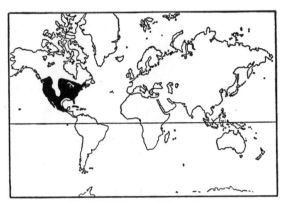

Fig. 210. Range of *Ceanothus*

C. dentatus Torr. & Gray. Evergreen shrub, 1 m high, twigs not angular, finely pubescent; leaves alternate, obovate to oval, 1–2.5 cm long, margin along both sides curled under (leaves therefore appearing rectangular), glandular dentate, light green above, densely pubescent beneath and gray-green; flowers very numerous, in 1–3 cm long, cylindrical or rounded panicles, blue, May. MCea 6, 72. California. 1848. z8 Fig. 209. # ⊕

'Floribundus'. Leaves 1 cm wide or more, less curled margins; flowers in dense clusters, numerous, on short stalks. ⊕

'Microphyllus. Leaves less than 6 mm wide, axillary veins not distinguishable, margin entire. Transition form of *C. papillosus*.

C. divergens Parry. Closely related to *C. purpureus*, but more open growing; leaf margins less distinctly sinuate; branches sparse, wide spreading close to the ground; flowers dark blue in racemes, April. California. z8

C. fendleri Gray. Shrub, to 1 m high, but usually prostrate, twigs ascending, thorny, young branches rounded, thorny, finely tomentose; leaves elliptic, 1–2.5 cm long, light green, gray-green tomentose beneath, entire to finely crenate; flowers white, occasionally with lilac tones, in clusters on short side branches, grouped in terminal panicles, June–July. BM 9264; MCea 57. W. USA. Hardy. z6 Fig. 211. ⊕

C. foliosus Parry. Low shrub, to 80 cm, or also procumbent, branches thin, pubescent; leaves elliptic to ovate or oblong, 5 to 15 mm long, glossy dark green above, glandular dentate, venation pubescent beneath; flowers in globose, 12 mm wide heads, grouped 1–4 on short terminal stalks, blue, May. BM 9540. California. z8

'Russellianus'. Cultivar of *C. × lobbianus*, with equally vigorous habit, but with very small, glossy leaves and long stalked, small inflorescences in spring. z8

Fig. 211. **Ceanothus** (most actual size, fruits enlarged 2×). a. *C. fendleri*; b. *C. parvifolius*; c. *S. sanguineus*; d. *C. ovatus*; e. *C. velutinus*; f. *C. coeruleus*; g. *C. thyrsiflorus*; h. *C. griseus*; i. *C. cyaneus* (from McMinn)

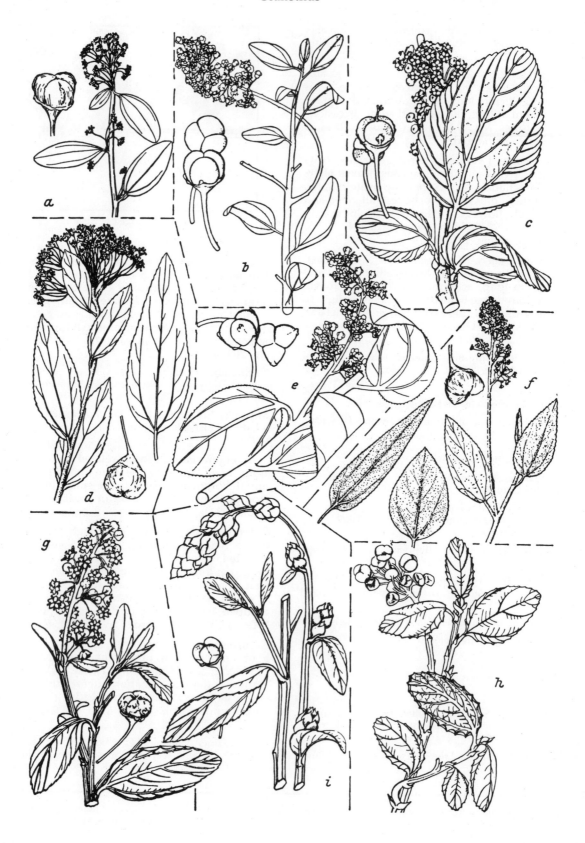

'**Southmead**'. Cultivar of *C.* × *lobbianus*; shrub, medium sized, growth very dense; leaves small, oblong, deep green, glossy; flowers an intense blue, May—June. Breeder: Capt. C. K. Mooney. Before 1964. z8

C. gloriosus J. T. Howell. Evergreen, procumbent shrub, to 30 cm high and 3—4 m wide, with long, thick, red-brown branches; leaves opposite, 1.5—4 cm long, to 2.5 cm wide, elliptic to oblong, rounded, thick and leathery, deep green above, lighter beneath, margin densely dentate, occasionally also entire; flowers deep blue or purple, in umbels, on short, thick stalks, April—May. California; along the coast. z8 #

C. griseus (Trel.) McMinn. Tall shrub, resembling *C. thyriflorus*, but with leaves broadly ovate to rounded, obtuse, silky pubescent beneath, usually sinuate between the margin teeth; flowers violet blue (on the wild species; although light blue in culture in England), March—May. MCea 68 (= *C. thyrsiflorus* var. *griseus* Trel.). California. z8

C. impressus Trel. Shrub, 0.3—1 m high, broad and densely branched; leaves elliptic to nearly round, evergreen, 6—12 mm long, all venation distinctly visible as grooves above, blade therefore rugose, dark green, margin rolled inward, crenate, occasionally somewhat glandular; flowers blue, in simple 12—25 mm long clusters, July (March—April in its habitat). Mcea 71. California; Santa Barbara County. Beautiful shrub, blooms as 2 year seedling. z7? Plate 107; Fig. 209. # ⊕

var. **nipomensis** McMinn. Shrub, to 6 m wide, 0.5—2 m high; leaves 2—2.5 cm long, usually yellow-green, venation only slightly indented above, margin not so distinctly curled; flowers 3—4 weeks earlier. MCea 12, 13. California, Nipomo Mesa. # ⊕

C.incanus Torr. & Gray. Evergreen shrub, 2—3 m high, short thorny twigs, white pruinose; leaves alternate, ovate to broad elliptic, 2—5 cm long, rounded at both ends or with slightly cordate base, dull gray-green above, lighter and nearly glabrous beneath, entire to somewhat dentate, 3 veined; flowers white, in branched, 2.5—7 cm long fascicles, May. California. z8 #

C. integerrimus Hook. & Arn. Deciduous to evergreen shrub, to 3 m high or higher, twigs thin, pubescent to glabrous; leaves alternate, variable in form, from oblong or elliptic to ovate and lanceolate, 2.5—7.5 cm long, acute or obtuse, base rounded, glabrous above or somewhat pubescent, normally pubescent beneath, especially on the venation, entire or somewhat dentate near the apex, usually veined, but also with pinnate venation; flowers variable, from white to light blue, in compound panicles, 7—15 cm long, grouped in large terminal, 25—35 long panicles, June. BM 7640. California. 1853. z8

C. jepsonii Greene. Very closely related to *C. purpureus* and with *Ilex*-like leaves; the main difference is in the seed capsule, the valves of *C. purpureus* are horned at the apex, while those of *C. jepsonii* have a ridge and

wrinkle running to the base; flowers of the species, blue or violet, often also white. California. z8

C. × **lobbianus** (Hook). McMinn (Natural hybrid of ? *C. dentatus* × *C. griseus* [Trel.] McMinn). Shrub, 1 m high, erect, densely branched, young twigs green, softly pubescent; leaves evergreen, 2—2.5 cm long, elliptic, obtuse, leathery, 3 veined, somewhat pubescent above and deep green, lighter and pubescent beneath, margin always somewhat inward curling, dentate, teeth erect and with a gland at the tip; flowers dark blue, in capitate racemes, axillary at the branch tips, stalk pubescent. MCea 99. California, Monterey. z8? # ⊕

C. megacarpus Nutt. Evergreen shrub, to 3 m high, twigs thin, finely pubescent at first; leaves alternate, obovate to elliptic, entire, apex rounded but notched, base rounded, 1.5—3 cm long, glabrous above, fine, dense pubescence beneath, with many, distinct, parallel veins, petiole 3 mm; flowers white, 5 mm wide, in small, 12 mm wide umbels on short stalks, March to May; fruit to nearly 1 cm wide, with a distinct border and a few horns. California. z7 #

C. × **mendocinensis** McMinn. Natural hybrid between *C. velutinus* var. *laevigatus* and *C. thyrsiflorus*; leaves evergreen, ovate, to 6 cm long and 2.5 cm wide, dark green above and glossy, blue-green beneath, 3 veined; flowers light blue or more lilac, in nearly sessile umbels, these grouped in 5—10 cm long panicles; rachis and side branches glabrous. California; Mendocino County. z8 #

C. ovatus Desf. Upright shrub, 1 m high, young twigs somewhat glandular and pubescent; leaves narrow-elliptic, 2—6 cm long, obtuse, finely crenate, glossy above, lighter and glabrous beneath; flowers white, more attractive than those of *C. americanus*, June. MCea 43. E and Middle USA. Winter hardiness about that of *C. americanus*. z5 Fig. 211. ⊕

C. × **pallidus** Lindl. (= ? *C. delilianus* × *C. ovatus*). Here belong the pink to white flowering garden varieties. Most developed in France before 1900.

The following are the most popular cultivars:

'**Albert Pittet**'. Light pink.

'**Albus Plenus**' (Simon-Louis Frères). Buds white, flowers white, double. Occasionally found in English gardens. ⊕

'**Carmen**'. Pink.

'**Cérès**' (Lemoine). Flowers in large panicles, pink-red. July—October. ⊕

'**Cigale**'. Lilac.

'**Coquetterie**'. Carmine-pink.

'**Felibre**'. Lilac-pink.

'**Gladiateur**'. Pink.

'**Ibis Rose**'. Pink.

'**Le Géant**'. White, flower stalk reddish.

'**Marie Simon**' (Simon-Louis Frères). Low, pink, HCC 627/3, July—September. One of the best pink cultivars. ⊕

'Mme Furtado'. Pink-lilac.

'Perle Rose; (Lemoine). Soft strawberry pink, July—October. Unfortunately, does not thrive in many soil types. ⊕

'Plenus'. Buds pink, flowers white, double.

'Président Reveil'. Soft pink, flowers in lage bouquets.

'Richesse'. Pink.

'Vesta'. Pink.

'Virginal' (Lemoine). Pure white.

C. papillosus Torr. & Gray. Evergreen shrub, to 3 m high, twigs rod-like, densely pubescent; leaves alternate, pinnately veined, 1.5 to 5 cm long, 3—12 mm wide, narrow-oblong, glandular toothed, glossy green above and with numerous dots (papillae); flowers in terminal and axillary, 3—4 cm long racemes, soft blue, May. BM 4815. California. 1850. z8

C. parvifolius (Wats.) Trel. Deciduous to evergreen shrub, 0.5—1 m high, young twigs thin, glabrous; leaves alternate, oblong, rounded, 12—25 mm long, entire, glabrous or nearly so; flowers in 2.5—5 cm long panicles, light or dark blue, June—July. MCea 48, 51. USA, mountains in Utah, Nevada, Colorado. z6—7 Fig. 211.

C. prostratus Benth. Evergreen, mat-form, creeping shrub, to 2.5 m wide, young twigs pubescent; leaves opposite, tough and stiff, nearly *Ilex*-like, thorny toothed, 1—2.5 cm long, glossy; flowers lavender-blue (to white), grouped 12—20 in 2.5 cm wide clusters on the ends of short branches, April—June; fruits bright red, very ornamental. NF 2: 268; MCea 22, 97. USA, California to Washington. z7 Fig. 209. # ⊕

C. purpureus Jepson. Like a dwarf *Ilex* in appearance; shrub, evergreen, erect, sparse, 1 m high, twigs reddish; leaves *Ilex*-like, 2.5 cm long, tough leathery, margin sinuate and scabrous toothed; flowers large, purple, in dense, wide racemes, April. BMns 37; MCea 23, 94. California. 1934. z8 Fig. 209. # ⊕

C. rigidus Nutt. Evergreen shrub, 0.3—0.5 m high, twice as wide, young twigs stiff, erect, brown, pubescent; leaves opposite, obovate, 6—12 mm long, coarsely dentate to entire, deep green above, gray-green and pubescent beneath; flowers deep lilac-blue, in 1.5 cm wide, axillary clusters on the previous year's wood, April—June, fragrant, very abundant. BM 4664; DRHS 423; MCea 26, 27, 91. California. 1847. z8 Fig. 209. # ⊕

'Pallens'. Leaves more coarsely dentate, glossier; flowers in longer stalked clusters. BS 1: 389. Prettier than the species. # ⊕

C. sanguineus Pursh. Deciduous shrub, to 3 m high, young twigs reddish, glabrous; leaves alternate, oval to ovate, 1—3 veined, 3—7 cm long, obtuse, base rounded to cordate, obtuse toothed; flowers white, in 5—12 cm long, 3—8 cm wide panicles on short branches of the previous year's wood. z7 Fig. 211.

C. sorediatus Hook. & Arn. Dense, evergreen shrub, 1—2.5 m high or more, branches sparse, erect, gray-

green or purple, long haired, rather thorny; leaves alternate, 3 veined, elliptic to ovate, acute, to 2.5 cm long, dark green and glossy above, with long appressed pubescence beneath, especially on the venation, margin glandular dentate; flowers light or dark blue, in small dense clusters, May and in fall. California. z8 #

C. thyrsiflorus Esch. Evergreen shrub, a tree in its native habitat, to 7 m high, young twigs angular, glabrous to somewhat pubescent; leaves alternate, 3 veined, ovate, 2—4 cm long, glandular dentate, glabrous above and glossy, glabrous beneath or pubescent on the venation; flowers light blue, in rounded, stalked, axillary, 3—7 cm long panicles, May—June, very abundant. MCea 33, 67. California, coastal areas. z8 Plate 73; Fig. 211. # ⊕

C. × veitchianus Hook. (= *C. rigidus* × *C. griseus*). Evergreen shrub, tall, young twigs somewhat angular, pubescent; leaves obovate, pinnate venation, 1—2 cm long, glossy green above, gray-green and pubescent beneath; flowers dark blue, in long, loose, capitate clusters, May—June. BM 5127; MCea 34, 100. California. 1853. Presumably a natural hybrid. z8 # ⊕

C. velutinus Dougl. Evergreen shrub, to 3 m high, occasionally tree-like in its habitat; leaves alternate, 3 veined, rounded ovate, 2—8 cm long, obtuse, base slightly cordate, margin finely glandular dentate, very glossy above, light green and finely pubescent beneath; flowers white, in stiff, axillary, pubescent panicles, 7—12 cm long, June—July. BM 5165; MCea 40. California. z8 Fig. 211. #

var. **laevigatus** (Hook.) Torr. & Gray. Leaves light green, very glossy, rather glabrous beneath; inflorescence smaller, October. MCea 41. California. z8 #

Evergreen *Ceanothus* Hybrids

'A. T. Johnson'. Flowers abundantly, intense blue, spring and fall. Originated before 1930. For protected areas. z8 #

'Autumnal Blue' (*C. thyrsiflorus* × ?). Shrub, to 1.5 m; leaves large, elliptic, very glossy, distinctly 3 veined; flowers soft blue in large panicles, late summer and fall. Developed by Burkwood & Skipwith. Probably the hardiest evergreen form. z6—7 #

'Burkwoodii' (*C.* 'Floribundus' × *C.* 'Indigo'). Shrub, 1.5 m high, foliage very dense; leaves elliptic, rounded at both ends, 1.5—3 cm long, dentate, dark green above, glossy, glabrous, gray and pubescent beneath; flowers a good blue, in 3—6 cm long panicles, May—October. Developed by Burkwood & Skipwith, Kingston-on-Thames, England. Before 1930. z8 #

'Burtonensis' (? *C. impressus* × *C. thyrsiflorus*). Natural hybrid, parents not definitely credited; very similar to *C. impressus* in appearance, but with leaves usually circular and very glossy; flowers blue. Found, 1941 in Burton Mesa, California. Cultivated in Wisley Gardens, England. z8 #

'Cascade'. Very similar to *C. thyrsiflorus*, and probably a form thereof; tall (to 8 m along sheltering walls in England!), branches broadly arching; leaves narrow, glossy green; flowers light blue, in cylindrical, loose, 8 cm long panicles, several grouped together. Developed by Jackman, Woking, Surrey,

England. Before 1946. z8 #

'Delight' (*C. papillosus* × *C. rigidus*). Tall; leaves light green, very glossy; flowers a strong blue, in long panicles, May. Breeder: Burkwood & Skipwith. Before 1931. One of the hardiest forms. z8 #

'Dignity'. Rather similar to 'Delight'; flowers clear blue, in large bouquets, in both spring and fall. #

'Edinburgh' (*C. griseus* × ?). Tall shrub, 2−3 m, very densely branched, twigs very long; leaves olive-green; flowers an intensive blue, May−June (= *C.* 'Edinensis'). Found about 1934 in the Edinburgh Botanic Garden among seedlings of *C. austromontanus*. z8 #

'Italian Skies' (*C. foliosus* × ?). Low growing, to 1 m high and 2 m wide; leaves similar to those of the mother plant, but flowers in dense, conical panicles, 5−7 cm long, bright blue. Breeder: E. B. Anderson. 1957. z8 #

'La Primavera' (*C. cyaneus* × ?). Shrub, 1−2 m, resembling *C. cyaneus*, but flowering earlier (April) and very abundantly. Selected in 1935 as a seedling of *C. cyaneus* in Santa Barbara, California. z8 #

'La Purisima' (*C. roweanus* × *C. impressus*). To 70 cm high; leaves narrow-elliptic, 2.5 cm long, intermediate between the parents in form; flowers a good strong blue, in small panicles, but numerous, March−April. Originated in 1938 in Santa Barbara and La Purisima Mission at the same time. z8 #

'Mountain Haze'. Developed from seedling of 'La Primavera' in 1948 by Lammerts. z8 #

'Sierra Blue'. Seedling of 'La Primavera', 1948, also by Lammerts. z8 #

'Treasure Island' (*C. arboreus* × *C. thyrsiflorus*). Growth very vigorous; flowers deep blue. Originated before 1940 in California and very popular there. z8 #

Only a few species suitable for the cooler temperate zones. Most should be considered only for gardens in the milder regions. Highly regarded for their beautiful blue flowers in summer. Many species make excellent subjects to espalier on a sheltered wall.

Lit. Suessenbugh, K.: *Ceanothus* (Rhamnaceae); in Engler-Prantl, **20d**, 72−82, 1953 ● McMinn, H.E.: A systematic study of the genus *Ceanothus*; Santa Barabara 1942 (here abbreviated MCea).

CEDRELA P. Browne — MELIACEAE

Deciduous or evergreen trees; leaves alternate, pinnate, without stipules, all leaflets usually of similar form; flowers small, whitish, greenish or reddish, in large panicles; calyx 5 toothed, petals 5; stamens 5; fruit a small woody, dehiscent capsule; seeds winged at the apex. — 18 species in tropical America, SE. Asia to southern Australia.

Cedrela sinensis Juss. Deciduous tree resembling *Ailanthus*, 12−15 m high in European gardens, young twigs thick, pubescent, bark distinctly split, peeling in strips, leaves 40−60 cm long, rachis yellow-green, finely pubescent, leaflets 20−26, opposite, ovate-lanceolate, long acuminate, 5−12 cm long, nearly entire, with some widely spaced, indistinct teeth, base rounded, occasionally somewhat oblique, lighter beneath, finely pubescent at first, eventually nearly totally glabrous, yellow fall color, terminal leaflet usually not developed; flowers in pyramidal, lpendulous, 50−70 cm long panicles, petals white to greenish-white, June−July; fruit capsules 3 cm long, woody, opening by 5 valves on the apical half. LF 195−196 (= *Toona sinensis* [Juss.] Roem; *Ailanthus flavescens* Carr.). China. 1862. Ⓕ China. Plate 110. ∅

The tree is valued in China not only for its yellow-brown, red striped, aromatic wod, but also for the young shoots which are cooked as a vegetable. The leaves and flowers emit a slight fragrance resembling leeks when crushed.

Lit. Harms, H.: Zur Kenntnis des Chinesischen Surenbaumes; in Mitt. DDG 1940, 183−188.

CELASTRUS L. — Bittersweet — CELASTRACEAE

Deciduous, rarely evergreen, usually twining shrubs; twigs with solid or chambered pith; leaves alternate, serrate or crenate; flowers polygamous-dioecious, small, whitish-green, 5 parted, in axillary or terminal panicles; calyx 5 parted; petals erect; ovary with 2−4 locules; fruits dehiscing with 3 valves, 1−2 seeds in each valve, these surrounded by a carmine-red aril. — 30 species, most in E. and S. Asia, also in America, Madagascar and on the Fiji Islands.

Key to the most important species (from Rehder)

Flowers in terminal panicles;
  Young twigs rod-like, pith solid, leaves 5−10 cm long:
    C. scandens
  Young twigs angular, pith chambered, leaves 10−18 cm long:
    C. angulata

Flowers in axillary cymes, often partly grouped in panicles;
  Leaves blue-green beneath; flowers partly in panicles:
    C. hypoleuca
  Leaves green beneath;
    ×Stipules abscising; leaves 5−12 cm long;
      ★ Cymes partly arranged in terminal panicles; leaves scabrous above, reticulate venation beneath; chambered pith:
        C. rugosa
      ★★ Cymes all axillary, occasionally grouped on short, leafless side branches;
        + Young twigs with chambered pith:
          C. loeseneri
        ++ Young twigs with solid pith:
          C. orbiculata
    ×× Stipules persistent, thorned, hook-like; leaves 2−6 cm long, thin petioled:
      C. flagellaris

Celastrus angulatus Maxim. Twining to 7 m high, growth luxuriant, twigs angular, purple-brown, with chambered pith; leaves broad ovate, 10—18 cm long, 8—14 cm wide, short acuminate, crenate, glabrous; flowers greenish, in terminal, 10—15 cm long, pendulous panicles, June; seeds orange with a red aril (= *C. latifolius* Hemsl.). NW. and Central China. 1900. Very ornamental with its large leaves and abundant pendulous fruits in fall. Hardy. Plants dioecious (important when planting for fruit!). z5 Plate 107; Fig. 213. ∅ ⚭

C. dependens Wall. Resembles *C. scandens*. Young twigs with distinct lenticels and brown, partly absent pith; leaves oblong, abruptly long acuminate, 8—12 cm long, finely crenate, glossy above, petiole 5—10 mm long; flowers in 8—17 cm long panicles (= *C. paniculatus* Willd.). Himalaya to SW. China. 1934. z8 Fig. 212.

C. flagellaris Rupr. Twining to 8 m high, young twigs hollow, red-brown, with hook-like, thorned, persistent stipules; leaves broad ovate, 3—5 cm long, abruptly acuminate, finely serrate, light green; flowers 1—3 in axillary, sessile cymes, June; fruit yellow-green, aril orange-red. Manchuria, Korea. 1857. z5

C. gemmatus Loes. Resembles *C. orbiculatus*; winter buds oval-conical 10—12 mm long (important for identification!); leaves elliptic, 5—11 cm long, abruptly acuminate, finely serrate or crenate, glossy green above, fine reticulate venation beneath; flowers in short stalked corymbs; fruits 1 cm wide. Middle and W. China. 1907. z7

C. glaucophyllus Rehd. & Wils. Climbing to 10 m high, rather glabrous, young twigs purple in the 2nd year, chambered pith; leaves elliptic-obovate, 5—10 cm long, acuminate, tapering to the base, sparsely crenate, dull bluish-green above, blue-green beneath; flowers green, small, indistinct, few in the leaf axils and in short, terminal racemes; fruits ovate at first, 1 cm long, yellow, stalk 1 cm. W. China. 1908. z8 ∅

C. hookeri Prain. Twining to 6 m high, young twigs reddish pubescent, but becoming more or less glabrous by fall; leaves elliptic to ovate, coarsely dentate, base rounded or broad cuneate, apex slender, midrib and major veins pubescent beneath, petiole 3—7 cm long; flowers inconspicuous, in short stalked, axillary clusters, stamen filaments glabrous; fruit orange, 6 mm long, abundant fruits persisting into the new year, seed hull red. Himalaya; China. 1908. Quite hardy, strong growing, cultivated in Kew Gardens, London. z6

C. hypoleucus (Oliv.) Loes. Twining to 5 m high, young twigs pruinose, glabrous; leaves oblong-elliptic, short acuminate, 6—14 cm long, sparsely fine serrate, dark green above, bluish-white beneath (important for identification!); flowers in loose terminal panicles to 12 cm long, June; fruits coloring yellow very late (= *C. hypoglaucus* Hemsl.). China; Hupeh, Szechwan. 1900. z8 Fig. 213. ∅ ⚭

C. loeseneri Rehd. & Wils. Twining to 6 m high, with

Fig. 212. *Celastrus dependens* (from Dippel)

numerous, long young twigs, these glabrous, reddish brown, somewhat punctate, chambered pith; leaves oval to broad ovate to elliptic-lanceolate, 5—11 cm long, acuminate, sparsely crenate, thick, dark green above, lighter beneath; flowers greenish-white, small, only a few grouped in short stalked, axillary cymes, seldom in terminal racemes; fruits yellow, 8 mm thick, aril red. GC 90: Pl. 196. Middle China. 1907. Hardy and attractive, but it is not yet clear as to whether the true species is in cultivation. z6 ⚭

C. orbiculatus Thunb. Twining to 12 m high, twigs rod-like, pith solid and white; leaves oval-rounded to circular, 5—10 cm long, abruptly short acuminate, crenate, light green on both sides; flowers pale green, in short, axillary cymes, June; fruits deep yellow, aril red, very ornamental from October to December. BM 9394; DL 2: 230. 1870. Best known species. Hardy. z5 Plate 108; Fig. 213, 214. ∅ ⚭

var. **punctatus** (Thunb.) Rehd. Not as vigorous; leaves smaller, elliptic-ovate to elliptic-oblong. SH 2: 117 k—l (= *C. punctatus* Thunb.).

C. rosthornianus Loes. Twining to 5 m high, young twigs exceptionally thin, chambered pith; leaves oval-lanceolate, 4—8 cm long, acute, finely dentate, very glossy; fruits barely pea-sized, usually only 2—3 in small, but numerous cymes in the leaf axils; fruits orange-yellow, aril red. W. China. 1910. Hardy. z5 ⚭

C. rugosus Rehd. & Wils. Twining to 6 m high, young twigs angular or striated, pith chambered, glabrous, densely punctate; leaves ovate to oblong, 5—13 cm long, short acuminate, somewhat rugose and rough above, venation eventually reticulate beneath, venation glabrous or pubescent, petiole 1—1.5 cm long; flowers small, greenish, few in axillary cymes or short,

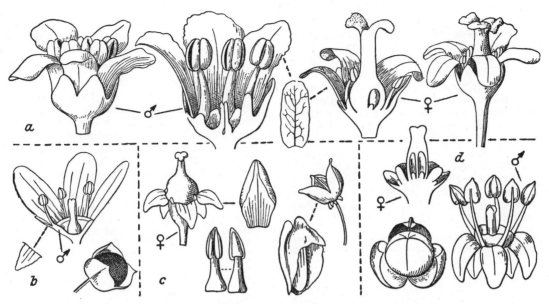

Fig. 213. **Celastrus**, flowers, flower parts and fruits. a. *C. orbiculatus*; b. *C. scandens*; c. *C. hypoleucus*; d. *C. angulatus* (from Hemsley, Koehne, Oliver, Sargent)

terminal racemes; fruits orange-yellow, aril red, fruits abundantly. W. China. 1908. z6 ⚥

C. scandens L. Twining to 7 m high, twigs rod-like rounded, glabrous, with solid, white pith; leaves ovate-oblong, acuminate, 5–10 cm long, serrate, base broadly cuneate, glabrous flowers in terminal (important for identification!), 5–10 cm long panicles; fruits globose, pea-sized, yellow, aril carmine-red. BB 2370;

BC 855. E. USA, in thickets along river banks. Hardy and attractive; the fruits are poisonous to humans, likewise the leaves to horses. z3 Fig. 213, 214. ⚥

Attractive, usually winter hardy vines for the large garden; leaves a good gold yellow in fall, fruits yellow at first, then opening to show the orange-red seed, persisting late into the winter. Easily cultivated in any soil, sun or semishade. Be aware that many species are dioecious and require both sexes for fruit production.

Fig. 214. Left *Celastrus scandens*; right *C. orbiculatus*

CELTIS L. — Hackberry — ULMACEAE

Deciduous trees, occasionally shrubs; also many evergreen species in the tropics; leaves 3 veined at the base, entire or serrate, veins straight at first, suddenly bending before reaching the margin; flowers inconspicuous, monoecious or polygamous; male flowers in small fascicles near the base of the current year's growth, calyx deeply 5 lobed, stamens 5, the calyx lobes opposite one another, ovaries absent; female flowers solitary or paired in the upper leaf axils on the same branch, with or without stamens, ovary unilocular, style very short, stigma split, with 2 widespread, reflexed arms; fruit a globose drupe, surrounded by a thin, sweet flesh, seed thick walled, pitted, seldom smooth. — 80 species, most in the tropics, the others in the northern temperate zones.

The mentioned species belong collectively to the Section *Euceltis*. These approximately 30 species are very difficult to distinguish because of the many varieties and natural hybrids. A monograph of the genus has yet to be done.

Celtis australis L. Tree, to 25 m high, crown often attractively wide-spreading, trunk gray, smooth, nearly beech-like, young twigs pubescent; leaves elliptic-oblong, long acuminate to caudate apex, 5—15 cm long, scabrous serrate, rough and dark green above, gray-green above, and softly pubescent beneath (!); fruit dark red, sweet, 1.2 cm thick, seed pitted, stalk to 3 cm long. HM 497. S. Europe, N. Africa, W. Asia. 1796. z6 ⓕ Italy, Yugoslavia, Tunisia, Kashmir. Plate 109. ∅

Good street tree for the city; slow growing when young, can be damaged by early frosts. Produces a hard wood for manufacturing uses. The tough branches were once used as whip handles.

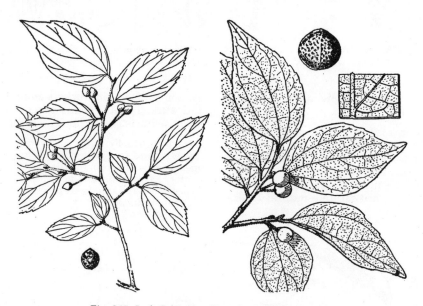

Fig. 215. Left *Celtis biondii*; right *C. labilis* (from ICS)

C. biondii Pamp. Shrub or small tree, 6—9 m high, bark gray, smooth, twigs thin, glabrous and dark green, reticulate venation beneath, acuminate, usually rounded only on the apical half, somewhat pubescent above at first, later crenate-serrate, the oblique base is cuneate, glabrous; leaves ovate to ovate-oblong, 5—10 cm, yellow-green, petiole 3—8 mm long; fruits orange, in groups of 1—3, 6 mm thick, seed finely furrowed, stalk 1—1.5 cm long. Central China. 1894. Hardy. z5 Plate 109; Fig. 215. ∅

var. **cavalieriei** Schneid. Current year's shoots gray-brown, finely punctate, usually red-brown pubescent when young; leaves tough, leathery, ovate-oblong, to 6 cm long, silky pubescent on both sides, petiole 5 mm long, yellow pubescent; fruit stalk 1.5—2 cm long (= *C. cavalieriei* Lév.). W. China.

var. **heterophylla** Schneid. Leaves very tough, obovate-obcordate, with a caudate tip protruding from the middle, tip entire, leaves two ranked, becoming smaller toward the branch tip (= *C. bungeana* var. *heterophylla* Lév.). China, Fukien; S. Korea. Cultivated in the Dortmund Botanic Garden, W. Germany, since 1965 and quite winter hardY. Fig. 216.

C. bungeana Bl. Tree, to 15 m, crown rounded to flat, bark smooth, light gray, young twigs finely pubescent at first, later becoming glabrous; leaves oval-oblong, 4—8 cm long, margin crenate on the apical half, glossy green above, glabrous on both sides, glossy beneath; fruits black, ovate, 7 mm thick, seed smooth, white, stalk 1.5 cm long. LF 108; NK 19: 17 (= *C. davidiana* Carr.). Central and N. China, Manchuria, Korea. 1868. Hardy. Rarely true in cultivation. z5

Fig. 216. *Celtis biondii* var. *heterophylla* (Original)

C. caucasica Willd. Tree, medium sized, crown bushy, stem gray, young twigs pubescent; leaves oblique obovate to ovate-lanceolate, acuminate, coarsely dentate, 3—8 cm long, rough bristly above when young, later less rough, underside at first softly pubescent, eventually glabrous except on the veins, petiole 6—12 mm long; fruits yellow to red-brown, 8 mm thick, stalk 1.5—2.5 cm long. Caucasus, Asia Minor, Afghanistan. 1884. Hardy. z6 Plate 109.

C. cerasifera Schneid. Slender, narrow crowned tree, 10 m high or more, bark smooth, nearly white, young twigs thin, gray-brown, glabrous; leaves tough, ovate to elliptic-oblong, 6—10 cm long, acuminate, base rounded to nearly cordate, simple and coarsely crenate margin, both sides glabrous, somewhat dark glossy green above, lighter beneath, petiole 1—1.5 cm long; fruits globose, 1.2 cm thick, black, solitary, axillary, stalk 2—3 cm long, seed shallowly pitted, with a flat, sharp tip. Middle China. 1907. Hardy. z6

C. douglasii Planch. Tree, 5—10 m high, crown round, young twigs pubescent; leaves usually oblong-ovate to broad ovate, 4—7 cm long, base somewhat cordate, sharply serrate to nearly entire, distinctly acuminate, glossy above and somewhat rough, dull yellow-green beneath, glabrous, petiole around 1 cm long; fruits brownish, rounded, 8 mm thick, stalk some 2 cm long. SM 292 (= *C. rugulosa* Rydb.). SE. USA. 1898. Hardy. z6

C. glabrata Planch. Small tree or shrub, crown round, young twigs finely pubescent, but quickly becoming glabrous and light brown; leaves oblique ovate, 3—7 cm long, acuminate, coarsely serrate nearly to the base, teeth curved inward (important for identification!), dark green above and scabrous with small warts, lighter and glabrous beneath (!) except for tiny bristles on the venation; fruits rounded, red-brown, 4 mm thick, petiole 1—2.5 cm long. EH 267. Caucasus, Asia Minor. 1870. Hardy. z6 Fig. 217.

C. jessoensis Koidz. Tree, to 20 m, young twigs pubescent; leaves ovate to ovate-oblong, long acuminate, 5—10 cm long, sharply serrate nearly to the rounded base, dark green above, whitish beneath or gray-green, venation somewhat pubescent or glabrous, petiole 6—10 mm long; fruits 8 mm thick, black, stalk 2 cm long, seed pitted. NK 19: 18. Korea, Japan. 1892. Hardy. z6 Plate 109.

C. julianae Schneid. Beautiful tree, 20—25 m high, straight trunked, bark smooth, light gray, branches stiff, crown round, young twigs dense yellow-brown silky pubescent, densely covered with red-brown flower buds in winter; leaves obovate, 11 cm long, 8 cm wide, long acuminate, base cuneate or oblique, usually crenate toothed margin on the apical half, somewhat glossy and glabrous above, dense orange-yellow pubescent beneath (important for identification!), leathery tough, petiole 2—3 cm long; fruits orange, oval-rounded, some 1.2 cm thick, seed pit white, finely pitted. Central China. 1907. Hardy. Easily recognized by the conspicuous leaves. ∅

Fig. 217. *Celtis glabrata* (from Dippel)

C. koraiensis Nakai. Tree, to 12 m high, bark dark gray, twigs brown, usually glabrous; leaves broad-oval, to 15 cm long and 11 cm wide, abruptly short acuminate, coarsely serrate, dull green above and glabrous, venation somewhat pubescent beneath; fruits orange, oblong-rounded, 1 cm long, stalk to 2 cm long. NK 19: 21. Korea, Manchuria, N. China. 1923. Very attractive, easily recognizable, good winter hardy species. z5 Plate 109. ⊘

C. labilis Schneid. Tree, 10–15 m high, bark smooth and light gray, young twigs yellowish and densely pubescent; leaves ovate to lanceolate, short acuminate, base oblique-rounded, 6–9 cm long, dark glossy green above, coarsely serrate nearly to the base, somewhat pubescent, lighter beneath, not glossy, silky pubescent, leathery tough, petiole 3–4 mm long, densely pubescent; fruits usually grouped 2–3, orange, rounded, 8 mm thick, stalk 8 mm long, pubescent; the short fruiting twigs abscising when ripe (important for identification!). Middle China. Hardy at Kew Gardens, London. z6 Fig. 215.

C. laevigata Willd. Tree, 10–30 m high, broad rounded crown, branches nodding, bark light gray, usually densely covered with corky warts, young twigs pubescent at first, later glabrous; leaves oval-oblong, long acuminate, 5–10 cm long, usually completely entire (important for identification!) or with only a few teeth, base broadly cuneate, thin; fruits rounded, 6 mm thick, orange at first, later purple-black, stalk 1–2 cm long. BB 1256; NBB 2: 51; SM 295 (= *C. mississippiensis* Bosc.; *C. berlandieri* Klotsch). S. USA. 1811. z6 Fig. 218.

var. **smallii** (Beadle) Sarg. Tree, to 10 m high; leaves sharply serrate (= *C. smallii* Beadle). SE. USA. 1909.

var. **texana** (Scheele) Sarg. Twigs usually pubescent; leaves ovate to lanceolate, 4–7 cm long, much tougher, often pubescent on the venation beneath. SM 297 (= *C. texana* Scheele). S. USA. 1922.

C. lindheimeri Engelm. Tree, to 8 m high, young twigs pubescent; leaves ovate to oval-oblong, obtuse or acute, base truncate to somewhat cordate, nearly symmetrical, margin coarsely serrate, 5–7 cm long, dark green and rough above, gray-green beneath, densely pubescent; fruits light brown, 8 mm thick, rounded, stalk pubescent, 12 mm long, stiff (= *C. helleri* Small). Texas. z7

C. occidentalis L. Medium sized tree, occasionally over 25 m high, broad crowned, branches somewhat nodding, bark gray, thick, deeply furrowed, young twigs more or less pubescent; leaves oblique acute-ovate, 5–12 cm long, margin sharply serrate at least on the apical blade half, glossy green above, smooth, faintly pubescent on the venation beneath, gold-yellow in fall, petiole 1 cm long; fruits orange to dark purple, 7–10 mm thick, seed pitted, stalk 2 cm long. BB 1255; Rho. Pl. 1907–08 (1948); SS 317. N. America. Attractive tree, hardy, fast growing when young, very useful street tree if space is available for the broad crown. Very resistant to disease and insect problems. ⓕ Yugoslavia. z2 Plate 109. ⊘

Fig. 218. *Celtis laevigata* (from Garden and Forest)

var. **canina** (Raf.) Sarg. Leaves narrower, oblong-ovate, 8–14 cm long, long acuminate, glabrous beneath or somewhat pubescent on the venation and light green, petiole to 1.8 cm long. SM 290 (= *C. canina* Raf.). 1898.

var. **cordata** (Pers.) Willd. Twigs pubescent; leaves oblong-ovate, 9–15 cm long, usually cordate at the base, tough, scabrous above, venation pubescent beneath. RM 128; SM 291 (= var. *crassifolia* [Lam.] Gray; var *audibertiana* [Spach.] K. Koch; *C. audibertiana* Spach.) S. USA. 1825.

var. **pumila** Muhl. Shrub, to 4 m or lower, twigs finely pubescent; leaves oval-oblong, 3–8 cm long, acute, somewhat rough above or quite smooth, lighter beneath, glabrous, young leaves pubescent on both sides; fruits orange-reddish, 8 m thick, seed slightly pitted. GF 3: 41 (= *C. pumila* Pursh). Central and S. USA.

According to research by Fernald and Schubert, the plant normally listed as "*C. pumila*" is actually *C. tenuifolia* Nutt.; therefore *C. pumila* Pursh is only a variety of *C. occidentalis*, as it is listed above.

C. reticulata Torr. Small tree, often shrubby, twigs densely pubescent when young; leaves ovate, 3–7 cm long, acute, base oblique, margin sharply serrate on young plants, nearly always entire on older plants or with few teeth, rough above, dark green and somewhat rugose, distinct reticulate venation beneath, somewhat pubescent, leathery; fruits orange-red, 1 cm thick, stalk 1 cm long, pubescent. SPa 152; MS 72. SW. USA. 1828. Easily distinguished by the distinct reticulate venation on the leaf undersides. z6 Plate 108. ⊘

C. sinensis Pers. Tree, to 15 m high, bark gray and smooth, young twigs red-brown, densely punctate, somewhat brownish pubescent; leaves quite various in form and size, oblong to ovate, 5—8 cm long, short acuminate, obtuse toothed on the apical half, dark glossy green above, lighter beneath, reticulate venation, leathery tough, thick, glabrous on both sides, petiole 1 cm long; fruits solitary, dark orange, 1 cm thick, seed pitted and ribbed. LF 109 (= *C. willdenowiana* Schultes; *C. japonica* Planch.). E. China, Japan, Korea. 1892. z6 Plate 109.

C. tenuifolia Nutt. Shrub or tree, to 5 m; leaves lanceolate, 4—8 cm long, long acuminate, entire or occasionally with a few short teeth, base broad cuneate to rounded, both sides glabrous or nearly so; fruits dark orange, 5—9 mm thick, stalk usually 8 mm long, seed shallow and indistinctly pitted. NBB 2: 51; Rho. 1948: 160 (= *C. georgiana* Small; *C. pumila* var. *georgiana* [Small] Sarg.). SE. USA. z6

C. tournefortii Lam. Small tree, 3—6 m high, often only a shrub, young twigs glabrous; leaves acute ovate, 3—7 cm long, base rounded to cordate, obtusely dentate, bluish-green or gray-green (important for identification!), occasionally somewhat pubescent; fruits orange-yellow, 8 mm thick, stalk 1 cm long (= *C. aspera* Stev.; *C. orientalis* Mill. non L.). SE. Europe, Asia Minor. 1739. z7 Plate 109.

Good street and park trees, often with picturesque crowns and attractive fall foliage; fruits and flowers not conspicuous. Prefers a deep fertile soil, but will succeed on gravelly, sterile soil. Very resistant to disease and insects and therefore, often substituted for Elm.

CEPHALANTHUS L. — Buttonbush — RUBIACEAE

Deciduous or evergreens shrubs or small trees; leaves opposite or in whorls of 3—4, short petioled, oblong to lanceolate; flowers rather small, grouped in globose heads; corolla tubular, 5 lobed, stamens 5, style simple, prominent; fruits composed of 2 small nutlets. — 17 species in Asia, Africa and N. America, with only the following found in cultivation.

Cephalanthus occidentalis L. Deciduous, bushy shrub, to 2 m high; leaves opposite or in whorls of 3, elliptic-lanceolate, 6—15 cm long, acuminate, margins entire, glossy green above, lighter beneath, thinly pubescent; flowers yellowish-white, small, in 2.5 cm wide globose heads, July—August. BB 3403; SPa 206; GSP 443. N. America. 1735. Hardy. z6—10. Fig. 219. **m** ⊕

f. **angustifolia** André. Leaves oblong-lanceolate, 6—8 cm long, 1.5—2 cm wide, in whorls of 3.

var. **pubescens** Raf. Young twigs and leaf undersides softly pubescent. More susceptible to frost damage than the species.

Pretty shrubs for full sun, preferably in moist to swampy soils; otherwise without cultural preference.

Fig. 219. *Cephalanthus occidentalis*

CERATONIA L. — Carob — LEGUMINOSAE

Evergreen tree; leaves alternate, even pinnate, leathery tough, glossy; flowers in axillary, erect racemes or catkin-like inflorescences, often on older wood; corolla absent; male flowers with 5 long filaments, female with short stalked ovaries; fruit a 10—20 cm long, 3 cm wide pod with soft, sweet, later hardening pulp; seeds numerous, flat, glossy brown. — 1 species in the Eastern Mediterranean region.

Ceratonia siliqua L. Walnut-like tree with a broad crown (in plantations seldom over 4 m high and wide), foliage dense; leaves 10—20 cm long, leaflets 6—12, obovate-rounded or oval, 3—7 cm long, of little note, May—September; fruits black-brown, ripening in fall. HM 1295. The fruits are used as feed for livestock in S. Europe, especially for horses. z8 Ⓕ Iran.

Widely planted in the Mediterranean countries where many cultivars have been developed, such as: 'Melas', 'Costolates', 'Lindas' and 'Sonaglina' in Spain; 'Sicilian Carob', 'Honey-Carob' and 'Massa' in Italy; and in Greece, 'Cipro'.

Often found in botanic gardens of frost free regions.

CERATOSTIGMA Bge. — PLUMBAGINACEAE

Deciduous shrubs or subshrubs; leaves alternate, ciliate, undivided; flowers in terminal and axillary heads; corolla salverform with a long tube; pistil thin, with 5 styles.— 8 species in China, Himalaya and Middle America.

Ceratostigma griffithii C. B. Clarke. Low, evergreen shrublet, densely branched, young twigs with forward pointing bristles; leaves alternate, obovate, short acuminate, 1.5—3 cm long, 0.5—1.5 cm wide, dull green, purple margin, both sides with appressed bristly hairs, underside also with fine scales, margin bristly ciliate; flowers in terminal fascicles, corolla clear blue, calyx tubular, 1 cm long, bristly, with 5 awn-shaped teeth, August—October. NF 228. E. Himalaya; Yunnan. z9 Fig. 220. # ✧

C. minus Prain. Deciduous shrub, 40—80 cm high; leaves obovate, rounded or obtuse at the apex, 2—3.5 cm long, base tapering to a short petiole, glabrous or nearly so above, appressed bristly and somewhat scaly beneath, margin bristly ciliate; flowers densely arranged in terminal and axillary clusters, opening one after the other, light blue, calyx carmine, August—October (= *C. polhillii* Bulley.) W. China; Yunnan. Similar to *C. willmottianum*, but smaller in all parts and differing in leaf form. z8 Fig. 221. ✧

C. plumbaginoides Bge. Subshrub with creeping habit, 30—40 cm high, twigs angular, somewhat bristly pubescent, reddish, many branched; leaves obovate, nearly sessile, 4 cm long, deep green, entire, finely ciliate, red-brown in fall; flowers deep blue, in dense, terminal and axillary heads, September—October. BMns 210; FS 307 (= *Plumbago larpentae* Lindl.). N. China. 1846. z7 Fig. 220. ○ ✧

Fig. 221. *Ceratostigma minus* (from ICS)

C. willmottianum Stapf. Deciduous shrub, to 1 m high, often lower, usually much branched, twigs angular, usually reddish, bristly; leaves rhombic to obovate, sessile, to 5 cm long, ciliate, both sides strigose (and therefore somewhat gray-green); flowers in terminal and axillary clusters, an attractive blue, opening one after the other from July—October, tube pink-red, anthers lilac. BM 8591. W. China. Often freezing back, but recovering well if placed in a protected location. z7 Fig. 220. ○ ✧

For sunny areas in the rock garden; sandy-clay soil.

Fig. 220. From left to right: *Ceratostigma plumbaginoides*; *C. griffithii*; *C. willmottianum* (from ICS)

CERCIDIPHYLLUM S. & Z. — Katsuratree — CERCIDIPHYLLACEAE

Deciduous trees having opposite, sometimes alternate leaves with palmate venation and crenate margins; flowers inconspicuous, without a perianth, dioecious; male flowers with 16—35 uneven stamens, female flowers with 3—5 long styles; fruit a small, dehiscent pod having a more or less curved apex, with many small winged seeds. — 2 species in E. Asia.

Cercidiphyllum japonicum S. & Z. An imposing tree in its habitat, to 30 m high, normally a multistemmed tree, in cultivation only half as high or lower, bark deeply furrowed, peeling in long strips, crown broadly pyramidal, young twigs red-brown, glossy, glabrous, new growth violet-red; leaves ovate to broad rounded, base usually more or less cordate, 6 cm long, crenate margin, bluish-green above, whitish blue-green beneath; flowers appearing just before the leaves, carmine-red, April—May; fruits 15—20 mm long, indistinctly curved at the tip, with a short stalk, seed brown. DB 1953: 117; SL 140. Japan. 1864. Quite Hardy. z5 Plate 110. ⌀

'Pendulum'. Very rare form with long arching, pendulous branches, habit somewhat like that of weeping willow (= *C. japonicum* f. *pendulum* [Miyoshi] Ohwi). In culture for over 300 years at a Buddist Temple on Honshu Island, Japan and considered a natural monument. In Japanese nursery trade at the Yokohama Nursery Co. Plate 85.

var. **sinense** Rehd. & Wils. Tree, taller, normally single stemmed; leaf petiole shorter (to 2 cm long), leaves somewhat pubescent on the veneation beneath; fruit pods shorter, 1—1.5 cm long, generally tapering to the apex. Central and W. China. 1907. z6—7

C. magnificum (Nakai) Nakai. Small tree, normally single stemmed, bark smoother, branches always with small, spur-like twigs (like *C. japonicum*); leaves usually larger, to 10 cm long, more rounded, tougher, more deeply cordate at the base, the basal lobes often overlapping; leaf petioles 2 cm long; fruits somewhat thicker, pod walls tougher, apex curved into a semicircle, seed yellowish-white. Bot. Tidskr. 51: 213—216 (= *C. japonicum* var. *magnificum* Nakai). Japan; Mt. Maeshirane and Konsei Toge. Quite hardy. z6 Plate 110. ⌀

Beautiful park trees with attractive yellow, orange-red or salmon fall foliage; leaves give off a very strong gingerbread scent just before abscising in the fall. The latter species is more frequently planted in European gardens but not often recognized. They prefer semishade and dislike dry soils.

Lit. Harms, H.: Zur Kenntnis der Gattung *Cercidiphyllum*; in Mitt. DDG 1917 ● Lindquist, B.: Notes on *Cercidiphyllum magnificum*; in Botanisk Tidskrift **51**, 212—219, 1954.

CERCIDIUM Tul. — LEGUMINOSAE

Small trees or shrubs with green bark; leaves alternate, bipinnate; flowers yellow, bisexual, nearly regular, in axillary racemes; calyx campanuate, the 5 lobes reflexed; petals obovate, clawed; stamens 10, filament pubescent near the base; ovaries superior, unilocular; fruit a linear or oblong, flattened or cylindrical pod. — 10 species, in the SW. USA to Mexico and NW. South America.

Cercidium floridum Benth. Palo Verde. Large shrub to small tree, 4—10 m high, branches and twigs thin, yellowish-green and with short thorns, foliage gray, leafless for most of the year; leaves normally with 2 pinnae, seldom with 4—6, each pinna with 2—4 pairs of leaflets, these elliptic, 3—10 mm long; flowers yellow, 2 cm wide, in axillary, 5—10 cm long racemes, April to July; pods oblong, thick, somewhat flattened, 5—10 cm long, usually connected by a filamentous 'string'. MS 254. USA: Colorado, deserts to Mexico. Desert plant. z9 Fig. 222. ⊕

Requires no cultural attention other than long periods of heat and dryness. Attractive in flower but otherwise without ornamental value.

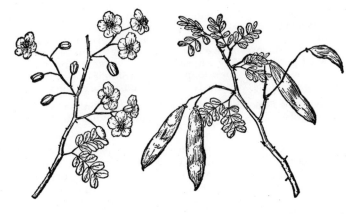

Fig. 222. *Cercidium floridium* (from Sargent)

CERCIS L. — Redbud — LEGUMINOSAE

Deciduous trees or shrubs; leaves alternate, simple, undivided, usually kidney-shaped, occasionally somewhat 2 lobed; flowers in fascicles or racemes, often appearng on old wood (occasionally on the main stem), before the leaves, in April to May; flowers with 5 petals,

10 distinct stamens; ovaries short stalked; fruit an oblong, flat, compressed pod, dehiscing by 2 valves, narrowly winged on the ventral seam; several smooth, flat seeds in each pod. — 7 species in N. America and from S. Europe to E. Asia.

Cercis canadensis L. Tree, to 12 m high, crown broad and round; leaves broadly rounded, 7–12 cm long, abruptly short acuminate, glossy above, somewhat pubescent beneath, often only in the vein axils, blade base at petiole a wide, flattened sinus; flowers clustered 4–8, about 1 cm long, light pink, April–May; pods 6–8 cm long. BB 2033; GTP 251; SS 133. N. America, understory tree in the forests and river valleys from New Jersey to Florida. Before 1903. Not indigenous to Canada as might be inferred from the Latin name. z5 Plate 110, 111; Fig. 224.⊕

'Alba'. Flowers pure white.

'Flame'. Growth more narrowly upright; flowers larger than the species, frequently with several (nonfunctional) pistils and stamens and to 20 petals per bloom, these clustered, color like the species. Found in the wild in 1905, but not introduced to the trade until 1965 by the Louis Gerardi Nursery, R. F. D. 1, O'Fallon, Ill. USA. ⊕

'Forest Pansy'. Foliage remains dark red the entire season. In culture in the U. S. National Arboretum, Washington, D.C. ⊕ ⌀

'Plena'. Flowers pink, somewhat double.⊕

'Royal White'. Flowers pure white, somewhat larger and flowering earlier than the usual 'Alba'; growth more compact; leaf base wide angled. Introduced 1950 by the Louis Gerardi Nursery, O'Fallon, Ill. USA.⊕

'Silver Cloud'. Leaves with silver-white border and mottling, especialy in semishaded locations; only a few flowers. Selected by Th. R. Klein, Yellow-Dell Nursery, Crestwood, Kentucky, USA. 1964. ⊕

var. **texensis** (S. Wats.) Hopkins. Usually a tall shrub, seldom a small tree, always with multiple stems from the base, often only 1–2 m high; leaves kidney-shaped, eventually dark green and glossy above, lighter beneath, glabrous to somewhat pubescent, 5–7 cm wide; flowers in clusters or small racemes; pods 5–10 cm long. GF 4: 448; SM 458 (= *C. texensis* Sarg.; *C. nitida* Greene). Texas, Colorado, in the mountains.⊕

'Wither's Pink Charm'. Flowers pink. Found in the mountains of Virginia, USA around 1930 and introduced by D. D. Wither.⊕

C. chinensis Bge. Tall, bushy shrub, also tree-like in its native habitat, branches and twigs ascending; leaves rounded, 7–12 cm long and nearly as wide, abruptly acuminate, rather leathery, base deeply cordate, glossy above, young leaves also glossy beneath, leaf margins distinctly white, knobby; flowers violet-red, 5–8 together, 1.5–2 cm long, May; pods 7–12 cm long. LF 175; BC 883; FS 849 (= *C. japonica* Planch.). Central China. z6 Plate 73, 110; Fig. 224. ⊕

C. griffithii Boiss. Very similar to *C. siliquastrum*, mainly differing in the fruit. Afghanistan. z6 Fig. 224.

C. occidentalis Torr. Normally a shrub, usually 1–2 m high in its habitat, forming dense clumps with many stems, occasionally tree-like, then single stemmed; leaves kidney-shaped, 4–7 cm wide, wider than long, emarginate at the apex with small (usually abscising later) tips, blue-green above, dull base more or less deeply cordate, light bluish-green beneath; flowers pink, 5–6 in small fascicles on the previous year's

wood, 1–1.5 cm long, usually short stalked, April–May; pods 5–8 cm long, abundant fruiting. SPa 172 (= *C. californica* Torr.). California. z8 Fig. 224. ⊕

C. racemosa Oliv. Shrub or small tree, young twigs more or less pubescent; leaves broadly ovate, 6–10 cm long, fresh green above, pubescent beneath, eventually gray pruinose, tough, base cordate; flowers light pink, in 4–10 cm long racemes with 10–30 flowers, pendulous, May. BM 9316. Central China. 1907. Very conspicuous with the large, pendulous inflorescences on old wood. Most beautiful species in the genus. z7? Plate 73, 110; Fig. 224.⊕

C. reniformis Engelm. Small tree, closely related to *C. occidentalis*; leaves broadly ovate to kidney-shaped, often wider than long, 5–7 cm wide, rather tough, leathery, softly pubescent beneath; flowers pink, 12 mm long, often in racemes; fruits 5–10 cm long. Texas, New Mexico. z8 Fig. 224.⊕

'Oklahoma'. Leaves more densely arranged, tough, glossy; flowers quite purple-red, flowers abundantly even on young plants. Introduced by Warren & Son Nursery, Oklahoma City, Oklahoma, USA, 1965.⊕

C. siliquastrum L. Tree, to 10 m high, young twigs red-brown; leaves quite glabrous, kidney-shaped, rounded, obtuse, without tips, base broadly cordate, usually with 7 veins, leaf margin not stiff, bluish-green above and not glossy; flowers purple-pink, 3–6 in fascicles, often appearing on older stems, stalk 2–2.5 cm long, before foliate bud break; pods 9–10 cm long, 2.5 cm wide. HM 1295; BM 1138. S. Europe. Before 1600. (Especially tender when young.) z6 Plate 111; Fig. 223, 224. ⊕

'Alba'. Flowers white; leaves lighter green.

'Bodnant'. Clone with especially deep purple flowers. In cultivation in England before 1944. (Hillier 1975). ⊕

'Variegated'. Leaves white and green variegated.

The hardiest species is *C. canadensis*; *C. siliquastrum* freezes back somewhat as a young plant, but not when mature. All species prefer a fertile, not too dry, alkaline soil. Fall color usually a good gold-yellow. The flowers very interesting in that they appear on older trunks.

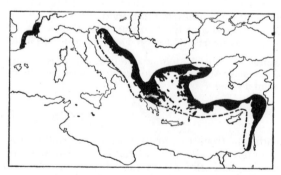

Fig. 223. Range of *Cercis siliquatrum*
(from Rickli)

Plate 97

Carya glabra, Pignut,
in its native habitat in Mississippi, U.S.A.
Photo: US Forest Service

Carya laciniosa,
multistemmed, with typical bark
Photo: US Forest Service

Carya cordiformis, Bitternut,
in Michigan, U.S.A.
Photo: US Forest Service

Carya cordiformis,
stem with typical bark, in North Carolina, U.S.A.
Photo: US Forest Service

Plate 98

Carya ovata
in Corrick's Ford near Parsons, West Virginia, U.S.A.
Photo: US Forest Service

Carya ovata, Shagbark,
stem with typical bark
Photo: US Forest Service

Carya ovata — fruit in the Arboretum Banska Stiavnica, Czechoslovakia

Photo: Dr. Pilát, Prague

Plate 99

Caryopteris incana
Photo: Archivbild

Caryopteris clandonensis 'Arthur Simmonds'
Photo: Archivbild

Cassiope hypnoides in its habitat in the mountains at 900 m
Photo: T. Lagerberg (Archiv Svenska Turistfoereningen)

Plate 100

Cassiope mertensiana in Mount Rainier National Park, Washington, U.S.A.
Photo: Brockman, U.S.A.

Cassiope tetragona   Photo: C. R. Jelitto

Plate 101

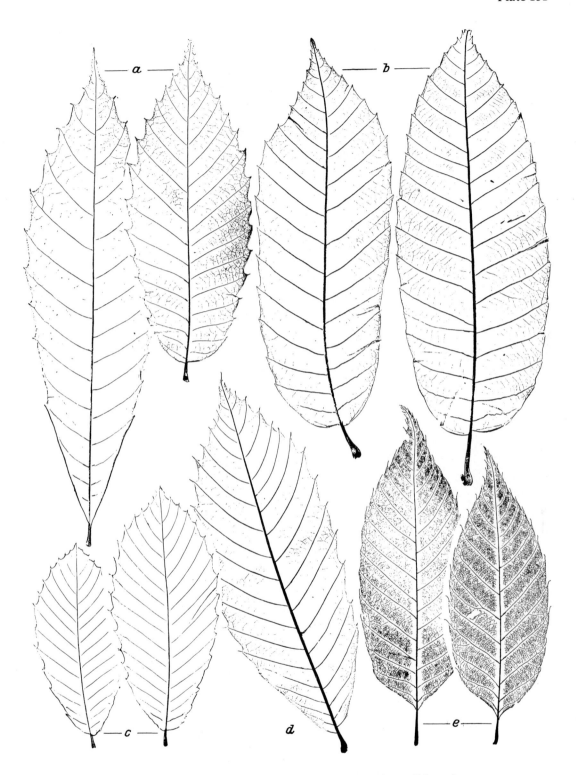

a. *C. dentata*; b. *C. mollissima*; c. *C. pumila*; d. *C. sativa*; e. *C. henryi*

Plate 102

Castanea crenata in flower in Japan   Photo: Dr. Watari, Tokyo

Castanea crenata with young fruits in Japan   Photo: Dr. Watari, Tokyo

Plate 103

Castanea dentata, full of fruits, in its native habitat in Tennessee, USA

Photo: US Forest Service

Castanea pumila, Chinquapin, in its natural range in Harlan County, Kentucky, USA

Photo: US Forest Service

Plate 104

Catalpa bignonioides, inflorescence,
in the Dortmund Botanic Garden, W. Germany

Catalpa bignonioides, inflorescence
Photo: US Forest Service

Callicarpa japonica in fruit
Photo: W. Schact

Catalpa bignonioides 'Nana'
in the Dortmund Botanic Garden, W. Germany

Plate 105

Catalpa bignonioides as a street tree in Maryland, U.S.A.

Photo: US Forest Service

Plate 106

Catalpa bignonioides 'Koehnei' in the Dortmund Botanic Garden, W. Germany

Catalpa bignonioides 'Aurea' in the Dortmund Botanic Garden, W. Germany

Plate 107

Ceonothus impressus in Birr Castle Park, Ireland (4 × 4)

Celastrus angulatus, with fruit cluster, in the Les Barres Arboretum, France

Plate 108

Celastrus orbiculatus, right, fruiting twig enlarged, in the Dortmund Botanic Garden, W. Germany

Celtis reticulata, fruiting twig   Photo: US Forest Service

Plate 109

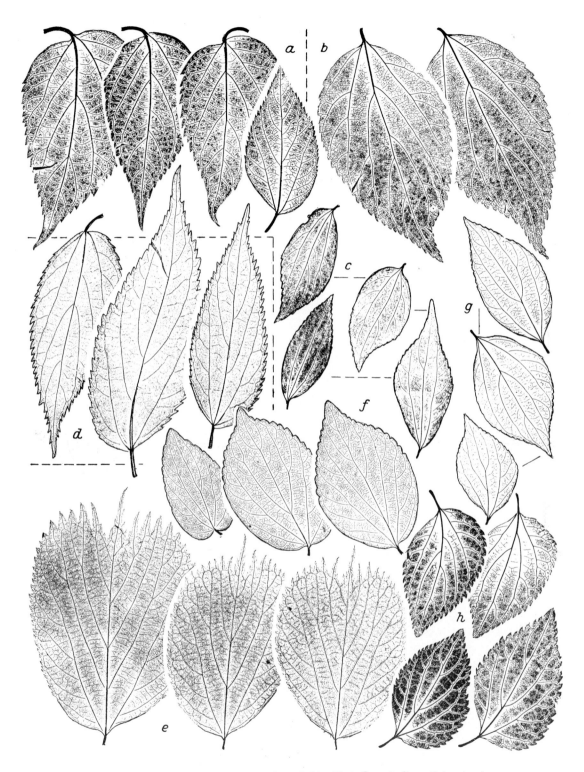

Celtis a. *C. occidentalis*; b. *C. jessoensis*; c. *C. biondii*; d. *C. australis*; e. *C. koraiensis*;
f. *C. tournefortii*; g. *C. sinensis*; h. *C. caucasica*

Plate 110

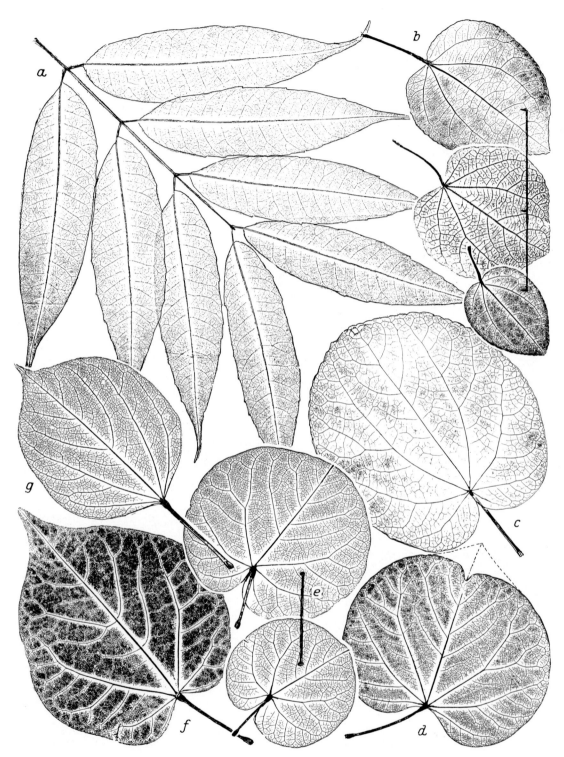

Cedrela a. *C. sinensis*, apical leaf half. — **Cercidiphyllum.** b. *C. japonicum*; c. *C. magnificum*. — **Cercis.** d. *C. canadensis*, this leaf is not very typical, more common form shown in outline; e. *C. siliquastrum*; f. *C. chinensis*; g. *C. racemosa*

Plate 111

Cercis canadensis in its native range in Louisiana, USA
Photo: US Forest Service

Chaenomeles cathayensis var. *wilsonii*
in the Dortmund Botanic Garden, W. Germany

Cercis siliquastrum, flowering branch   Photo: J. R. Jelitto

Plate 112

Chaenomeles japonica, flowering branch   Archive Deutsche Baumschule

Chaenomeles japonica, fruiting branch   Archive Deutsche Baumschule

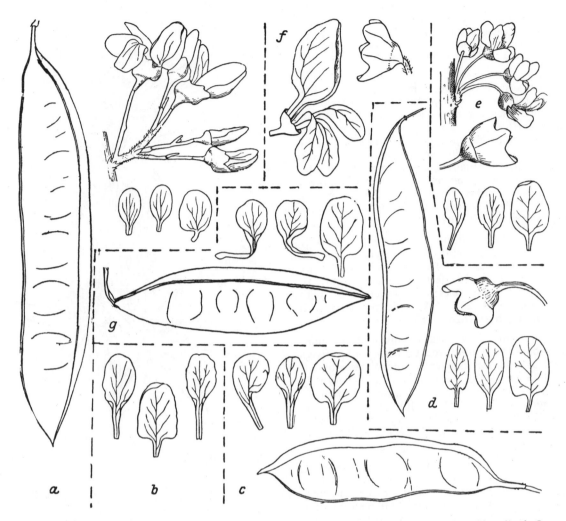

Fig. 224. **Cercis**, flowers, flower parts and fruit. a. *C. siliquastrum*; b. *C. reniformis*; c. *C. occidentalis*; d. *C. chinensis*; e. *C. canadensis*; f. *C. racemosa*; g. *C. griffithii* (from Baillon, Oliver, Sargent, Schneider)

CERCOCARPUS H. B. K. — ROSACEAE

Evergreen or semi-evergreen shrubs or small trees; leaves alternate, usually clustered, entire or dentate; flowers inconspicuous, whitish-yellow, without petals, 1—10 axillary between the leaf clusters; calyx tubular, abruptly broadening cup-shaped, with 5 lobes; unilocular ovary, enclosed by the calyx tube; style long, pinnate, very prominent; fruit a small nutlet with a long feathery tail. — Some 20 species in western N. America.

Cercocarpus argenteus Rydb. Shrub, 2—3 m high, bark gray; leaves oblanceolate to obovate, 2—4 cm long, obtuse at the apex, seldom rounded, crenate on the apical margin, silvery-white beneath, teeth ovate, obtuse; sepals 8—10 mm long, silky pubescent, June—July. Colorado, Texas, on hills and mountains. Hardy. z5? ⚭

C. betuloides Nutt. A collective species recently divided into the following 3 varieties:

var. **betuloides** Little. Shrub or small tree, to 7 m high, sparsely branched, bark thick, persistent, young twigs softly pubescent; leaves obovate, 1—3 cm long, toothed at the apex, dull green above and somewhat pubescent at first, softly pubescent beneath and distinctly veined; flowers 2—3 in clusters, May; fruit tail 5—10 cm long, silver-white, attractive. MS 228 (= *C. douglasii* Rydb.; *C. parviflorus* Nutt. p. p.). USA, Oregon to Mexico. z7 ⚭

var. **blancheae** (Schneid.). Littl. Large shrub or small tree, 2—6 m high; leaves broad elliptic, 3—5 cm long, tough-leathery, dark green and glabrous above, lighter beneath and nearly glabrous; flowering period March—April (= *C. alnifolius* Rydb.). S. California. z9 ⚭

var. **traskiae** (Eastw.) Dunkle. Tree, to 7 m high, young twigs reddish-brown, hairy; leaves oval to rounded, 3—5 cm long, margin of older leaves distinctly rolled inward, dark green above, white tomentose beneath. SPa 157; MS 233; SM 418 (= *C. traskiae* Eastw.). California, Santa Catalina, Santa Cruz. Rare. z9 ⚭

C. breviflorus A. Gray. Tree, with a long stem, 6—7 m high, branches erect, crown narrow and irregular, young twigs thickly tomentose, becoming glabrous and red-brown after 2—3 years; leaves oblong-obovate, usually rounded at the apex, generally tapering to the base, apical half usually somewhat dentate and sinuate, tough, eventually gray-green above, lighter beneath and densely pubescent on the venation; flowering time March—May; fruits with a 2.5—3 cm long feathery tail. SM 421. Arizona and Texas to N. Mexico, usually in the mountains, over 1500 m. z8 ⚭

C. intricatus S. Wats. Shrub, to 1.5 m high, sparsely branched, young twigs stiff, dark brown, pubescent; leaves linear-lanceolate, 1—4 cm long, margin entire and clearly rolled inward, dark green above, gray tomentose beneath; calyx bristly pubescent; fruit with 2.5—5 cm long tail. MS 230. USA, in the canyons and on the hills from Utah to Arizona. z5 ⚭

C. ledifolius Nutt. Tree, occasionally to 12 m high, aromatic, bark furrowed, red-brown, young twigs pubescent at first; leaves narrow lanceolate to oblanceolate, 1—3 cm long, 5—10 mm wide, eventually glossy green and glabrous above, gray or brown tomentose beneath; flowers May to July; fruit tail 5—7 cm long. SPa 158; MS 229; SM 420 (= *C. hypoleucus* Rydb.). W. USA, from Washington to New Mexico. Hardy. z6 Fig. 225. ⚭

C. montanus Raf. Shrub, 1—2 m high, twigs pubescent; leaves broad oval, 2—5 cm long, coarsely dentate, pubescent above, tomentose beneath, calyx 1 cm long, pubescent; flowers May to July; fruit tail 6—8 cm long. SPa 159 (= *C. parvifolius* Nutt. p. p.). W. USA, California to Washington; hills and mountain areas. z6 Fig. 226. ⚭

The mentioned species have only slight ornamental value. Attractive when covered with the silver-white feathery tails. All species prefer a sandy-clay soil in full sun.

Lit. Martin, F. L.: A revision of *Cercocarpus;* in Brittonia 1950, 91—111 ● Francey, P.: Monographie du genre *Cestrum*; in Candollea **6**, 46—398, 1935; 7, 192, 1936.

CESTRUM L. — SOLANACEAE

Evergreen or deciduous shrubs; leaves alternate, simple, entire; flowers usually in axillary and terminal racemes; calyx campanulate, with 5 small lobes; corolla tubular, limb 5 lobed; fruit a juicy berry. — Over 200 species in tropical and subtropical America, south of Mexico.

Cestrum aurantiacum Lindl. Nearly evergreen shrub, to 2 m high, with glabrous twigs; leaves ovate, 5—9 cm long and half as wide; flowers in terminal and axillary racemes, grouped in conical, 10 cm wide panicles;

Fig. 225. *Cercocarpus ledifolius* (from Hooker)

Fig. 226. *Cercocarpus montanus* (from Sudworth)

corolla tubular, 2 cm long, 1 cm wide (distinguished by the reflexed lobes), flowering in summer. BIC 115. Guatemala. z8

C. elegans (Brongn.) Schlect. Evergreen, tall growing, open, well-branched shrub, to 3 m high, twigs elegantly nodding, softly pubescent; leaves lanceolate, entire, 7—10 cm long, acuminate, base rounded to somewhat cordate, dull green, softly pubescent; flowers in dense, pendulous, compound panicles, 10 cm long at the branch tips; corolla tube-form, widening toward the limb, purple-red, 2.5 cm long, the 5 limb tips inflexed, flowering all summer, long flowering period in the greenhouse; fruit a globose, juicy, 1.5 cm wide, dark red berry. BM 5659; DRHS 443 (= *C. purpureum* [Lindl.] Standley; *Habrothamnus elegans* Brogn.). Mexico. 1840. z8 Plate 74. # ✧

var. **longiflorum** Francey. Flowers over 2.5 cm long.

var. **smithii** (Hort.) Bailey. Flowers pink. BMns 249.

C. fasciculatum (Schlect.) Miers. Evergreen, thinly branched shrub, 1.5—2.5 m; leaves oval-lanceolate, 7—12 cm long and half as wide; flowers in dense terminal fascicles, 5—7 cm wide; corolla more pitcher-shaped, dark carmine pink, 2 cm long, softly pubescent outside (!). BM 4183. Mexico. 1843. Often confused with *C. elegans*, but flowering earlier and the bright red flowers pubescent ouside. z8

C. 'Newellii' (Newell). Garden origin; parents either *C. elegans* or *C. fasciculatum*. Corolla urceolate, intense carmine, more intensely colored than the alleged parents, 2.5 cm long, 8 mm wide at the narrow limbed throat. GC 136: 112 (= *Habrothamnus newelli* Veitch.) Developed around 1880 by a Mr. Newell in Downham Market, Norfolk, England. z8

C. parqui L'Hér. Deciduous shrub, 2.5—3 m high, branches and leaves glabrous; leaves lanceolate to oval-

Fig. 227. *Cestrum parqui* (from Wettstein)

lanceolate, tapering to both ends, 5—12 cm long, petiole 12 mm long; flowers in terminal panicles, 10—15 cm long, yellowish-green, fragrant, June—July; corolla tubular, 2 cm long, limb 1 cm wide; fruit ovate, 1 cm long, violet-brown. BM 1770. Chile. Excellent greenhouse plant especially for the very fragrant flowers. z8 Fig. 227. ✧

The mentioned species need good, fertile soil, and protected locations in the warmer regions. Best over-wintered in a cool greenhouse in the cooler temperate zones.

Lit. Francey. P.: Monographie de genre *Cestrum* L.; in Candollea 1935, 46—398; 1936, 1—132.

CHAENOMELES Lindl. — Flowering Quince — ROSACEAE

Deciduous shrubs with more or less thorny branches; leaves alternate, crenate or serrate; stipules usually large, stalked, persistent; flowers solitary or several together; calyx and corolla 5 parted, stamens 20—50, in one or more whorls; styles 5, connate at the base; fruit a fragrant pome, with 5 chambered seed compartment, seeds not slimy. — 4 species in E. Asia.

Chaenomeles × californica Clarke ex Weber (*C. cathayensis × C. superba*). A group of hybrids; shrubs, most to 1.8 m high, armed with thorny short branches, young twigs sparsely pubescent, 2nd year twigs with a few warts; leaves lanceolate, often light brown tomentose beneath when young, dentate margin intermediate between the parents; flowers large, most pink or carmine-pink, often a combination of the two; fruits medium size to large, egg, apple or orange shaped. The first hybrids were selected by A. B. Clarke in 1938 and brought into the trade in 1939 as "Cathayensis Hybrids"; in 1940 he changed the name

to that given above. z6 ✧ ⚭

See cultivar list at the end of this section.

C. cathayensis (Hemsl.) Schneid. Upright shrub, 2—2.5 m high, branches covered with many short, thorny secondary branches; leaves elliptic-lanceolate, finely and sharply serrate, 3—10 cm long, midrib beneath pubescent at first; flowers white, usually 2—3 together, March—April, style shaggy pubescent at the base; fruits ovate, 10—15 cm long, heavy, usually dull green, hard and bitter (nevertheless economically useful!). RH 1924: Pl. 20. Central China. z6—7 Fig. 228. ✧ ⚭

var. **wilsonii** Bean. To 3 m (6 m in ideal conditions) high; leaves short brown haired beneath; flowers salmon-pink, but not attractive; fruits likewise very large, hardy and green. JRHS 1910: 9—10 (= *Cydonia mallardii* Hort.). 1910. Plate 111. ✧

C. × clarkiana Weber (*C. cathayensis × C. japonica*). Low shrub, mature height not yet known, branches erect-

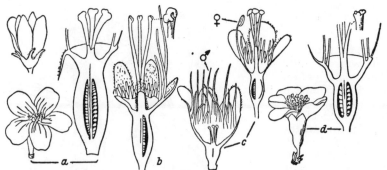

Fig. 228. **Chaenomeles**—flowers. a. (*Pseudocydonia sinensis*); b. *C. cathayensis*; c. *C. japonica*; d. *C. speciosa* (from Hemsley, Koehne, Schneider

spreading, densely covered with short thorny side branches, more numerous and longer than those of *C. japonica*, thinner than those of *C. cathayensis*, young twigs pubescent, slight fine wartiness in the 2nd year; leaves and margins intermediate between the parents; flowers large, light to darker pink; fruits medium sized, apple or orange shaped.

'Cynthia' and 'Minerva' were the first two cultivars selected by W. B. Clarke; called the "Miniature Cathayensis Hybrids"

C. japonica (Thunb.) Lindl. Japanese Flowering Quince. Dense, low shrub, to 1 m high and wide, twigs thorny, short coarse tomentose when young; leaves broad ovate, 3–5 cm long, usually obtuse, coarsely crenate, glabrous; flowers brick-red, 3 cm wide, 2–4 together, March–April; fruit yellowish-green, rounded, 4–5 cm thick, usually with several deep furrows, very aromatic. BM 6780 (= *Cydonia maulei* Moore). Japan. 1874. Introduced from Japan by Messrs. Maule, Bristol, England. z5 Plate 112; Fig. 228. ⊕ ⚭

f. **alba** (Nakai) Ohwi. Flowers white. Not to be confused with the garden variety 'Alba'.

var. **alpina**. Growth flat along the ground; leaves only 1–2 cm long, nearly circular. The typical form is not present in European culture since the seed collected by Sargent from plants in the mountains of Japan seem to give up their dwarf character when grown in culture. These were brought into the trade by Lemoine as *Cydonia sargentii*.

C. sinensis see: **Pseudocydonia sinensis**

C. speciosa (Sweet) Nakai. Erect, often dense, bushy or also an open growing shrub, branches sprawling, glabrous, thorny, young twigs glabrous; leaves oval-oblong, acute, sharply serrate, glossy above; flowers solitary or grouped, on older wood, scarlet-red, 3–4 cm wide, March–April; fruits long-rounded, 4(–6) cm long, yellow-green, often somewhat reddish, fragrant. Rh 1876: 330 (= *C. lagenaria* [Loisel.] Koidz.; *C. japonica* Spach non Lindl.; *Cydonia japonica* Loisel.). China, Japan. 1796. z5 Plate 113; Fig. 228. ⊕ ⚭

Including many garden forms; see cultivar list.

For further study of the complicated nomenclature of this often confused species; see Stearn in Dict. RHS, Suppl., 1956.

C. × superba (Frahm) Rehd. (*C. japonica* × *C. speciosa*).

Shrubs, usually 1.2–1.5 m high, densely branched, twigs erect, with thin, thorny short side branches, young twigs short, rough tomentose, fine warts in the 2nd year, the thickness of the layer of tomentum is quite variable; leaves intermediate between the parents in form, size and margin, but more similar to *C. japonica*; flowers medium sized, white, pink, orange or red; fruits usually apple-shaped, larger than *C. japonica* and ripening somewhat later. z5 ⊕ ⚭

The first cultivar of this species was developed around 1900 by O. Froebel in Zurich, Switzerland; described by Frahm in Gartenwelt as *C. maulei* var. *superba* in 1898; and finally in 1920, classed as the type of the new hybrids. For further cultivars, see the list.

C. × vilmoriniana Weber (*C. cathayensis* × *C. speciosa*). Shrub, 2–2.5 m high, branches stiff like *C. cathayensis*, but more numerous, also with strong, thorny side branches, young twig glabrous or sparsely pubescent, fully glabrous in the 2nd year; leaves elliptic to ovate, slightly brownish tomentose beneath when young, margin sharply serrate, teeth usually drawn out to a short awn-like tip; flowers large, white, with traces of pink like *C. cathayensis*; fruits few, ovate, 8 cm long, ripening late. Named for Philippe De Vilmorin, developer of the first cultivar of this group ('Vedrariensis'). z6 ⊕ ⚭

Hybridization. In the middle of the 19th century, V. Lemoine of France was busy developing new cultivars, presumably by selection. Around the turn of the century, O. Froebel, Zurich, began crossing *C. japonica* and *C. speciosa*; some of his hybrids have been assigned Latin varietal names. After 1920, W. B. Clarke of San Jose, California, USA, began his hybridizing. Many of his hybrids are widely used today. He crossed *C. cathayensis* with *C. superba*, which until then had been an untried combination. In recent years some hybrids have come into the trade from K. Verboom, of Boskoop, Holland.

Outline of *Chaenomeles* cultivars

In this list, the species of origin are abbreviated as follows: (cal) = *californica*; (clar) = *clarkiana*; (jap) = *japonica*; (spec) = *speciosa*; (sup) = *superba*; (vil) = *vilmoriniana*.

'**Abricot**' (Lemoine 1908, *sup*). Low growing, compact; flowers semidouble, orange-red.

'**Afterglow**' (Clarke 1947; *vil*). The type of the *Vilmoriniana* group; leaves long and narrow; flowers white, semidouble, spent flowers with a slight trace of lilac-pink; fruits ovate, somewhat ribbed. US Pl. Pat. No. 847.

'Alba' (Froebel 1899; *sup*). Low; flowers cream-white, simple (= *Cydonia japonica maulei alba* Froebel).

'Apple Blossom' (Clarke 1937); *spec*). Flowers white, with pink and yellowish tones, simple to semidouble; fruits ovate to apple-shaped.

'Atrococcinea Plena' (Van Houtte 1969; *spec*). Tall growing, new growth dark brown; flowers dark scarlet, slightly double; fruits apple-shaped, slightly ribbed.

'Atrosanguinea' (Moerloose, before 1856; *spec*). Flowers blood-red, simple. Not the same as 'Simonii'.

'Aurora' (Origin unknown, before 1868; *spec*). Tall growing; flowers pink, with yellow overtones, simple; fruits large, orange.

'Baltzii' (Spaeth 1887; *spec*). Open growing; flowers carmine-pink, simple, to 5 cm wide;' fruits apple-shaped.

'Boule de Feu' (Barbier, around 1916; *sup*). To 2 m high, very thorny; flowers carmine-red, flat, very abundant, well distributed over the plant, flowering very early.

'Brilliant' (Leonard, Ohio, 1939; *spec*). Flowers vary from light to dark pink, simple. That grown under this name in the Dutch nurseries is not the same plant; this plant has large, dark red flowers, abundant, but susceptible to apple scab.

'Candida' (Origin unknown, before 1868; *spec*). Flowers pure white (not yellowish!), simple; fruits apple-shaped.

'Cardinal' (Clarke 1947; *cal*). Flowers deep red, simple.

'Cardinalis' (Moerloose 1856; *spec*). Growth broad and low, unattractive; flowers a bright dark scarlet, simple to double, often hidden by the leaves; fruits apple-shaped. RH 1885: 225.

'Carl Ramcke' (Timm 1949; *sup*). Growth wide, seldom over 1 m high, new growth brown; flowers bright vermillion red, very numerous. Breeder: Carl Ramcke, Hamburg, W. Germany. 1924. Often offered as a seedling in the trade. Plate 114.

'Choshan' see: **'Yaegaki'.**

'Coquelicot' (Lemoine, before 1950; *sup*). Flowers bright orange-red with some pink, simple, very abundant.

'Contorta' (Coming from Japan, imported to the USA in 1929 and distributed from there; *spec*). Branches and twigs erratically twisted; flowers white, fading to pink. The Japanese name is 'Rinho'.

'Coral Beauty' (Clarke 1949; *sup*). Twigs nearly completely thornless, growth broader than high; flowers salmon- to coral-pink, simple. US Pl. Pat. No. 252. Seedling of 'Candida'.

'Clementine' (Experiment Station at Boskoop, Holland, 1965; *sup*). Growth bushy and wide, to 1.5 m high; flowers orange-red, globose, flowers abundantly.

'Corallina' (Clarke 1934; *sup*). Flowers orange, simple; fruits small, apple-shaped. Most of the *californica*-group have come from crosses of this cultivar with *C. cathayensis.*

'Coral Glow' see: **Corallina.**

'Coral Sea' (Clarke 1943; sup). Medium grower; leaves narrow, tough; flowers salmon to coral-pink, to 4 cm wide,

simple, flowers for a very long time; fruits orange-shaped.

'Crimson and Gold' (Clarke 1939; *sup*). Only 1 m high, becoming very wide, dense foliage; flowers dark red, simple, early, with conspicuous gold-yellow anthers; fruits abundantly, fruits apple-shaped. Originated from 'Naranja' (*sup*) × 'Sanguinea' (*sup*).

'Cynthia' (Clarke 1947; *clar*). Flowers light and dark pink, simple; fruit orange-shaped.

'Dwarf Coral' (Clarke, around 1946; *sup*). Growth broad, bushy; flowers orange, simple, rather hidden in the foliage.

'Dwarf Poppy Red' (Clarke 1946; *jap*). Poppy-red, flat, open, simple, large flowered.

'Early Apple Blossom' (Clarke 1940; *sup*). Flowers light and deep pink, early, simple; fruits irregularly apple-shaped.

'Early Orange' (Clarke 1942; *sup*). Grows to medium size; flowers orange, semidouble, early, flowers in November–December in California, USA.

'Ecarlate' (Barbier 1913; *sup*). Flowers scarlet-red, simple. Originated from a cross of 'Baltzii' and 'Maulei'.

'Elly Mossel' (J. Mossel 1950; *sup*). grows to medium height; flowers fire-red, large, flat, simple; fruits apple-shaped. Resembling 'Fascination'.

'Enchantress' (Clarke 1940; *cal*). Branches stiffly upright, covered with stiff, thorny, short twigs; leaves like those of *C. carhayensis*; flowers large, pink, opening without uniform color, often hidden under the foliage.

'Ernst Finken' ((Loebner, before 1939; *sup*). Shrub, to 2 m high and wide; flowers arranged singly, fire-red, very large. Gw 1952: 137. Breeder: Max Loebner, Friesdorf, W. Germany. Brought into the trade by H. Finken of Rodenkirchen near Cologne, W. Germany. 1952.

'Etna' (K. Verboom, before 1953; *sup*). Flowers scarlet-red, flat, simple; fruits apple-shaped. Resembles 'Hollandia'.

'Falconnet Charlet' (Pépinière Falconnet, before 1900; *spec*). Strong grower; flowers light with traces of dark pink, semidouble; fruits large, apple-shaped. The name is often misspelled; selected in the Pépinière Falconnet Thoissey, France.

'Fascination' (J. Mossel 1954; *sup*). Grows to medium height and width, many branches spreading horizontally; leaves resembling those of *C. speciosa*; flowers deep scarlet-red, very large, flat, well distributed; fruits apple-shaped.

'Fire' (Clarke 1944; *cal*). Very strong grower; flowers bright red, large, flowering in 3 periods, one after the other; fruits ovate.

'Fire Dance' (Verboom 1953; *sup*). Grows to medium height and breadth; flowers bright red, very large, opening flat, flowers abundantly; fruits apple- or pear-shaped.

'Gaujardii' (Moerloose, before 1860; *spec*). Flowers salmon to coral-pink, simple, few; fruits small, apple-shaped, somewhat ribbed.

'Grandiflora' (Van Houtte 1869; *spec*). Strong grower, sprawling, flowers white, pink and yellowish toned, simple to somewhat semidouble; fruits ovate, large (= *Cydonia japonica grandiflora* Van Houtte).

'Grandiflora Perfecta' (Froebel 1900; *sup*). Flowers vermillion-red, simple to semidouble (= *Cydonia maulei grandiflora perfecta* Olbrich).

'Grandiflora Rosea' (Froebel 1900; *sup*). Flowers light cream-yellow to soft pink, simple (= *Cydonia maulei grandiflora rosea* Olbrich).

'Grenade' (Lemoine 1908; *sup*). Flowers orange-red, simple to semidouble, globose; fruits small, globose.

'Hollandia' (K. Verboom 1953; *sup*). Of medium height, bushy, to around 1.5 m; flowers along the branches to the tips, large flowers, scarlet-red, flat, simple; fruits apple-shaped.

'Incendie' (Lemoine 1912; *sup*). Low growing; leaves deep green, tips red-brown; flowers scarlet-red, semidouble; fruits apple-shaped. Difficult to cultivate.

'Jet Trail' (Templeton 1961; *sup*). Low growing; flowers pure white, simple, flat; fruits ovate.

'Juliet' (Clarke 1940; *sup*). Flowers salmon- to coral-pink, simple; fruits ovate.

'Kermesina' (Spaeth 1915; *spec*). Growth narrowly upright; flowers pink-carmine (= *Cydonia japonica kermesina* Spaeth).

'Kermesina Semiplena' (Spaeth 1890; *spec*). Flowers salmon-pink, semidouble; fruits ovate, small, somewhat ribbed.

'Knap Hill Radiance' (Knap Hill, before 1948; *spec*). Strong grower; flowers large, geranium-red, to 6 cm wide.

'Knap Hill Scarlet' (A. Waterer, before 1891; *sup*). Compact habit, poor grower; flowers tangerine-red, very large and numerous; fruits small, strongly ribbed. Difficult to cultivate.

'Mallardii' (Mallard, before 1857; *spec*). Flowers pink-red in the middle, margin white, simple.

'Marmorata' (Spaeth, before 1887; *spec*). Flowers white and pink marbled; fruits apple-shaped (= *Cydonia japonica marmorata* Spaeth).

'Masterpiece' (Clarke 1940; *cal*). Flowers pink-red, simple, numerous, unusually early; fruits large, ovate.

'Minerva' (Vilmorin 1921; *vil*). Upright habit; leaves short and broad; flowers white, pink toned, simple; fruits obovoid.

'Moerloosei' (Moerloose, before 1856; *spec*). Tall growing; flowers white, pink striped, unnattractive color, few flowers.

'Mount Everest' (Clarke 1940; *vil*). Leaves long and narrow; flowers large, white, older flowers with traces of lilac-pink, simple; fruits ovate.

'Mount Shasta' (Clarke 1949; *sup*). Buds a light lilac-pink, opening pure white, some petals with a soft pink margin.

'Naranja' (Clarke, before 1934; *sup*). Quite low and dense; flowers orange with pink-red, simple; fruits ovate.

'Nasturtium' (Clarke 1950; *cal*). Strong upright grower, foliage appearing just after the flowers; flowers 'lobster' red, to 5 cm wide, simple.

'Nicoline' (Doorenbos, before 1954; *sup*). Grows very wide, and to 1 m high, if tied up when young; flowers large, carmine-red, simple to semidouble, flowers very abundantly; fruits ovate, somewhat ribbed.

'Nivalis' (Lemoine 1881; *spec*). Strong grower, upright, to 2 m; flowers pure white, simple, medium sized, flowering

more heavily at the branch tips; fruits apple-shaped.

'Nivea Extus Coccinea' (Van Houtte, before 1867; *spec*). Flowers white inside, outer petals dark pink, simple.

'Orange' (Lemoine 1908; *sup*). Flowers red-orange, semidouble.

'Orange Beauty' (Boskoop, before 1954; *jap*). Flowers orange, simple, but usually hidden beneath the foliage.

'Perfecta' (Origin unknown, before 1905; *sup*). Flowers cream-white with pink, yellowish and greenish to pink-red, simple; fruit small, apple-shaped. First distributed by Spaeth(see also 'Grandiflora Perfecta').

'Phyllis Moore' (Knap Hill, before 1930; *spec*). Growth habit not particularly attractive, flat; flowers light and dark pink, semidouble; fruits ovate, distinctly ribbed.

'Pink Beauty' (Clarke 1941; *cal*). Flowers soft pink with darker traces, flowering in 3 periods; fruits orange-shaped.

'Pink Lady' (Clarke 1946; *sup*). Flowers dark pink, simple; fruits apple-shaped.

'Red Chief' (Clarke 1953; *sup*). Upright habit, flowers dark pink, double, but an unattractive flower form.

'Red Ruffles' (Clarke 1951; *spec*). Upright habit, branches almost totally thornless; flowers large, pure red, simple, petals overlapping. US Pl. Pat. No. 941.

'Rosea Plena' (Froebel 1878; *spec*). Flowers pink to coral-pink, semidouble; fruits ovate, ribbed (= *Cydonia japonica rosea plena* Hort.; not synonymous with 'Falconnet Charlet').

'Rosemary' (Clarke 1940; *cal*). Flowers light to dark pink, simple, medium-late; fruits ovate.

'Rosy Morn' (Clarke 1951; *cal*). Grows to medium-height, bushy; flowers soft carmine to porcelain-pink, single, very large, flowers abundantly, long flowering period.

'Rowallane' (Armitage Moore 1920; *sup*). Broad spreading to nearly decumbent habit, 70–100 cm high; flowers light scarlet-red, single, more abundant at the branch tips, 3.5 cm wide, flowers abundantly; fruits apple- to egg-shaped. JRHS 1958: 136.

Roxana Foster' (Clarke 1951; *sup*). Low growing; flowers orange-red, single.

'Rubrifolia' (Spaeth 1887; *sup*). New growth a bright brown-red; flowers coral-pink.

'Ruby Glow' (Clarke 1947; *sup*). Grows strongly upright, with few thorns; flowers red, single; fruits large, ovate.

'Sanguinea Semiplena' (Spaeth, before 1905; *spec*). Leaves light green; flowers scarlet-red, lightly double; fruits small, apple-shaped.

'Sargentii' (Lemoine 1899; *jap*). Lower growing than the typical *C. japonica*; flowers salmon-pink to orange, simple. Grown from seed collected in the mountains of Japan by C. S. Sargent, 1892.

'Simonii' (Simon-Louis, before 1882; *spec*). Low grower, scarcely 1 m high; leaves small; flowers dark velvet-red, semidouble or single, well distributed. Still, one of the best forms. Plate 74.

'Snow' (Clarke 1945; *spec*). Flowers large, white, simple, not abundant; fruits apple-shaped.

'Spitfire' (Wayside Gardens 1949; *spec*). Narrow upright habit, nearly columnar; flowers carmine-red, simple, abundant; fruits apple-shaped, ribbed. US Pl. Pat. No. 830.

'Stanford Red' (Clarke 1940; *sup*). Growth broad and low, branches spreading nearly horizontally; flowers tomato-red, simple, flat; fruits small, ovate.

'Sunset Glow' (Clarke 1940; *cal*). Resembles 'Rosemary', but a darker pink, especially on old blossoms, often with a few late opening flowers.

'Texas Scarlet' (Clarke 1951; *sup*). Bushy, low growing branches nearly thornless; flowers scarlet-red, large, flat, simple; fruits apple-shaped.

'Tricolor' (In culture since 1887, first distributed by Parsons, USA; *jap*). Leaves pink and white variegated; flowers salmon-pink.

'Umbilicata' (Introduced by Von Siebold before 1847 from Japan; *spec*). Strong grower, upright, to 2 m; flowers medium sized, cherry-pink, simple, somewhat hidden by the leaves; fruits apple-shaped and with a hilum scar. FS 510—512.

'Vedrariensis' (Vilmorin 1921; *vil*). Leaves short and wide; flowers white, going to pink, simple; fruits obovoid (= *C. hybrida vedrariensis* Lemoine).

'Verboom's Vermilion' see: **'Etna'**.

'Vermilion' (Barbier 1913; *sup*). Bushy, half as tall as the species; flowers vermillion-orange, simple, abundant; fruits apple-shaped.

'Versicolor' (Osborn?, before 1870; *spec*). Flowers white, pink and salmon colored; fruits ovate.

'Versicolor Lutescens' (Leroy 1865; *spec*). Flowers salmon-pink with orange-red, simple; fruits irregularly obovoid.

'Vesuvius' (Verboom 1953; *sup*). Flowers scarlet-red, large, single; fruits apple-shaped.

'Yaegaki' (Wada 1936; *sup*). Flowers orange-apricot colored, semidouble.

All require sunny areas in good garden soil. The more tender Californian hybrids require winter protection such as espaliered on a south wall. Prune carefully as the flowers are produced on the previous year's wood. Good for forcing or as cut flowers.

Lit. Weber, C.: Cultivars in the genus *Chaenomeles*; in Arnoldia **23**, 17—25, 1963; the best, most complete work on the subject ● An older variety list is presented in the Revue Horticole 1886, 182 ● The nursery of Simon Louis Frères in Metz, France listed 40 named varieties in their catalogue in 1869 ● For information on the use of *Chaenomeles* as cut flowers, refer to a report by the Horticultural Institute (Gartenbaulehranstalt) Friesdorf, near Bonn, W. Germany.

CHAMAEBATIA Benth. — ROSACEAE

Semi-evergreen, erect, small shrub; leaves alternate, 3(−4) pinnate, fine textured, fern-like, aromatic; flowers in terminal, sparsely flowered panicled cymes; receptacle flat, dish-formed; sepals 5; valvate; petals 5, projecting outward; stamens very numerous; carpels only 1, fruit leathery, single seeded, indehiscent. — 2 species in California.

Chamaebatia australis Abrams. Shrub, to 2 m high, woody; leaves only bipinnate (by exception, 3 pinnate), lanceolate in outline, 3.5—8 cm long; leaflets on the last pinna 1—3(5) together; flowers like those of *C. foliolosa*, with calyx and petals smaller, stamens less numerous, ovaries pubescent. MS 183. California, widespread as a groundcover in the pine forests of the Sierra Nevada. z8

C. foliolosa Benth. Shrub, 20—60 cm high, leaves, young branches and flower stalks gray, pubescent with stalked glands; leaves obovate in outline, 3.5—5.5(−10) cm long, normally 3(4) pinnate; leaflets on the last pinna 4—5(8) together; flowers 1.5—2 cm wide, white, in terminal corymbose panicles, June—July, ovaries pubescent. BM 5171; MS 182. California. 1855. z8 Fig. 229. ○ Ø

Attractive, uncommon, aromatic shrubs for protected areas in the rock garden; need full sun and winter protection.

Fig. 229. *Chamaebatia foliolosa* (from Dippel)

CHAMAEBATIARIA (Porter) Maxim. — ROSACEAE

Very closely related to *Chamaebatia*, but with leaves only bipinnate or with pinna only deeply lobed; sepals erect, stamens 60; fruit composed of 5 leathery follicles, surrounded by the calyx; each capsule with several seeds. — 1 species in the USA.

Chamaebatiaria millefolium (Torr.) Maxim. Deciduous shrubs, aromatic, open growing, heavily branched, 0.5–1 m (rarely to 1.5 m) high, twigs glandular and stellate pubescent; leaves alternate, short petioled, oblong-lanceolate, 2–7 cm long, finely bipinnate or with pinna deeply incised, the 'lobes' very tiny, glandular pubescent; flowers white, in terminal, leafy, tomentose-glandular, 8–15 cm long panicles, July–August. MS 181; MG 1908: 208 (= *Spiraea millefolium* Torr.). California to Utah, on gravelly slopes and ravines; not unusual in its habitat. 1880. Fig. 230. ⌀

Cultivated like Chamaebatia.

CHAMAECISTUS see: **LOISELEURIA**

CHAMAECYTISUS Link see: **CYTISUS**

Chamaecytisus	= **Cytisus**
— *albus* (Hacq.) Rothm. 1944	— **albus** Hacq.
— *austriacus* (L.) Link 1831	— **austriacus** L.
— *ciliatus*	— **ciliatus**
— *glaber* (L. fil.) Rothm. 1944	— **elongatus** W. & K.
— *heuffelli*	— **amstriacus**
— *hirsutus* (L.) Link 1831	— **hirsutus** L.
— *purpureus* (Scop.) Link 1831	— **purpureus** Scop.
— *ratisbonensis* (Schaeffer) Rothm. 1944	— **ratisbonensis** Schaeff.

Fig. 230. *Chamaebatiaria millefolium* (from Garden and Forest)

— *rochelii*	— **rochelii**
— *supinus* (L.) Link 1831	— **supinus** L.
— *tommasinii*	— **tommasinii**

CHAMAEDAPHNE Moench — ERICACEAE

Low evergreen shrub; leaves small, alternate, simple; flowers facing to one side, in terminal, leafy nodding racemes; calyx small, 5 parted, brown scales; corolla urceolate-oblong, 5 lobed, with 5 enclosed stamens, anthers drawn out into long tubes, without appendages; fruit an appressed, 5 chambered capsule, with several seeds in each chamber. — Only 1 species in the northern temperate regions.

Chamaedaphne calyculata (L.) Moench. Widely disseminated shrub, dense, usually not over 50 cm high, branches broadly arching; leaves short petioled, ovate, leathery, 1–5 cm long, obtuse, margin inflexed, dull green above, yellowish-green to rust-brown and scaly beneath; flowers at the branch tips in 4–12 cm long, nodding racemes, April–May; corolla white, urceolate-oblong. HM 2269; HF 2035; MB 1286 (= *Andromeda calyculata* L.; *Lyonia calyculata* Reichenb.). N. Europe, N. Asia, N. America, in peat bogs. z2 Plate 115. # **H** ⊕

'Angustifolia'. Leaves narrow-lanceolate, margin wavy.

'Nana'. Dwarf form, smaller in all respects, only 20 to 30 cm high, very dense, branches arranged more horizontally.

Culture somewhat like *Rhododendron*; for mass planting in parks in suitable conditions or also as a specimen plant in a small garden.

Differing from *Leucothoe* in th scaly undersides of the leaves, from *Lyonia* in the overlapping sepals and from both of these in the hidden prophylls.

A typical plant of the northern peat bogs, very often the dominant species especially in coastal areas. Distributed in the Baltic region, Lappland, Finland, N. Asia, and the high plains of Siberia, in open forests of *Picea obovata* and *Larix dahurica*.

CHAMAELAUCIUM Desf. — MYRTACEAE

Evergreen, heather-like shrub, or occasionally a small tree; leaves opposite, sometimes scattered, small, very narrow, sessile; flowers terminal or axillary; calyx lobes and petals 5, stamens 10, alternating with 10 staminodes, grouped in a ring. — 12 species in W. Australia.

Chamaelaucium uncinatum Schau. Small evergreen shrub, 1 m high, occasionally a small tree (to 6 m) in its native habitat, branches very thin, erect, glabrous; leaves opposite, linear, 1.5—3 cm long, 2 mm wide, curled into a hook at the apex; flowers in small clusters of 2—4, sometimes grouped in larger 8—15 cm wide corymbs, calyx thick, cupola-shaped, petals broad rounded, white, pink, or lilac, 3—6 mm wide. April. BM 9233. W. Australia. 1926. z9

Cultural requirements like the Australian *Acacia* species; to be treated as a greenhouse plant in temperate zones.

CHAMAEROPS L. — PALMACEAE

Monotypic genus; low, variable palm with fan-shaped, semicircular, terminal leaves; leaf rays narrow, split twice, blade somewhat bluish-green; petiole sharply thorny; inflorescence axillary; fruits olive-like in appearance, usually single seeded. — Well established in the Mediterranean region from Spain to Sicily and Morocco to Algeria.

Chamaerops humilis L. Dwarf Palm. Evergreen palm, either with numerous short stems and usually not over 1—2 m tall, or single stemmed (as an older plant) and 3—5(7) m tall, trunk covered with the old leaf sheaths; leaves terminal, stiff, blade nearly circular, 50—60 cm long, gray or bluish green, without a midrib, divided into numerous segments cleft to the base, petiole 75—100 cm long, thorned; flowers yellow, fruits reddish. BM 2152; Gs 125: 77. Habitat as in genus description. 1731. z8 Plate 114. # ○

The species contains many garden forms which will not be described here.

Sunny areas; prefers frequent watering but good drainage;

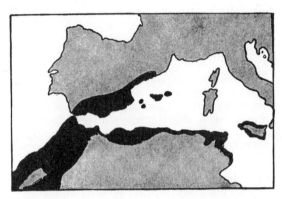

Fig. 231. Range of *Chamaerops* (from Gessner)

usually over-wintered in a cool greenhouse in the temperate zones.

Lit. Gessner, F.: Die Verbreitung der Zwergpalme in Europe, in *Mitt.* DDG 1933, 96—100, with plates.

CHILIOTRICHUM Cass. — COMPOSITAE

Evergreen shrubs, closely related to *Olearia* and similar in appearance; leaves alternate, narrow, entire, pubescent beneath; flower heads medium size, long stalked; ray florets white or violet, in a circle, female; disk florets all bisexual and infertile; involucre campanulate with imbricately arranged bracts; receptacle flat or convex, distinguishing character from *Olearia*; pappus with 2 or 3 rings of erect bristles. — 2 or 3 species in S. America.

Chiliotrichum diffusum (Forst.) O. Kuntze. Evergreen shrub, 30—90 cm high in its habitat, to 2 m wide, young branches frequently erect, white tomentose; leaves alternate, densely arranged, linear, 2—5 cm long, 2—4 mm wide, flat or with inflexed margin, gray tomentose when young, especially beneath, later becoming glabrous and green above, brown tomentose beneath, midrib distinctly depressed; flower heads 2.5—5 cm wide, terminal, solitary on 5—10 cm long stalks, with 12 white, linear ray florets, disk florets yellow. HI 485 (= *C. amelloides* DC.; *C. rosmarinifolium* Lessing). S. America, from the Andes in Chile and Argentina to the Straight of Magellan. 1927. z8 # ⊙

For sunny, but very protected areas; hardier and more attractive than most *Olearia* species. Cultivated in England by Hillier.

CHILOPSIS D. Don — Desert Willow — BIGNONIACEAE

Monotypic genus, very closely related to *Catalpa*, but evergreen, leaves alternate, lanceolate; flowers more trumpet-like, the limb lobes crenate; stamens 5, with one rudimentary; fruit a long, thin capsule, opening by 2 narrow, dehiscent valves when ripe. — 1 species in Mexico.

Chilopsis linearis (Cav.) Sweet. In its habitat a 2.5—5
m tall, erect, branched shrub or small tree, branches
densely tomentose in the first year, yellowish or
brown and glabrous in the second year; leaves evergreen, 10—15(30) cm long, elliptic-lanceolate, tapering to both ends, glabrous, leathery; flowers in terminal racemes; corolla 3.5 cm long and nearly as wide,
lilac, yellow speckled throat, May; fruits 15—30 cm
long. SW. USA, N. Mexico. River banks and low areas
in the desert, usually in dry gravelly areas. 1825. z8
Fig. 232. # ⊕

'Alba'. Like the species, but with white flowers.

Over-wintering in a cool greenhouse advisable in the temperate zones.

Lit. Fosberg, F. R.: Varieties of the Desert Willow, *Chilopsis
linearis*; in Madrono **3**, 363—366, 1936.

CHIMAPHILA Pursh. — PYROLACEAE

Low, usually creeping, evergreen subshrubs; leaves
alternate or whorled; flowers in pendulous, terminal
umbels; calyx 5 parted; petals 5, stamens 10; ovaries 5
chambered; style short, thick, with a wide 5 pointed
stigma; fruit a 5 chambered capsule, dehiscing from
bottom to top. — 7 species in the northern temperate
zones.

Chimaphila maculata (L.) Pursh. Shrublet, 10 cm
high, twigs glabrous or finely pubescent; leaves usually in whorls of 3, ovate to lanceolate, 2.5—5 cm long,
acuminate, base rounded, serrate, white colored
along the venation; flowers in umbels grouped 2—5,
white or pink, July. BB 2737. Eastern N. America.
1759. z5 Fig. 233. # H ◑ ⊕

C. menziesii (D. Don) Spreng. 7—20 cm high; leaves
alternate or in whorls of 3, 2—4 cm long, ovate to
lanceolate, tapering to the base, whitish along the
veins; flowers in umbels of 1—3, white, 12 mm wide,
June. BM 987. Western N. America. z6 Fig. 233. # H
◑ ⊕

C. umbellata (L.) W. Barton. 20 cm high; leaves in
whorls of 3—6, oblong-obovate, obtuse, 1.5—6 cm
long, sharply serrate, bright green above, glossy,
tough; flowers 3—6 in umbels, greenish-white to light
pink, July—August. NF 4: 247; RFW 273. Eastern N.

Fig. 232. *Chilopsis linearis*, flowering branch,
fruit capsule and seed (from Sudworth)

America, N. and Middle Europe, N. Asia, Japan. 1762.
z6 Fig. 233. # H ◑ ⊕

var. **cisatlantica** Blake. Leaves acute and with small thorny
tips. RMi 333 (= *C. corymbosa* Blake). Eastern N. America.

var. **occidentalis** (Rydb.) Blake. Leaves longer than those of
the species; inflorescence more racemose than umbellate (=
C. occidentalis Rydb.). Western N. America.

All species prefer a loose, humus soil, well drained, in
shade or semishade. *C. umbellata* grows wild in dry Oak and
Pine forests. These plants have medicinal uses for rheu-
matism, fever and as diuretics.

CHIMONANTHUS Lindl. — CALYCANTHACEAE

Deciduous or evergreen shrubs; leaves opposite, simple, entire; flowers short stalked, axillary; sepals and
petals not differentiated, numerous; stamens 5 to 6;
fruit a capsule, compressed at the apical end. — 3
species in China.

Chimonanthus praecox (L.) Link. Deciduous shrub,
in cold climates 1—2 m high, to 3—4 m in warmer
regions, branches gray-green at first, later brown;
leaves oval-elliptic to oval-lanceolate, 7—20 cm long,
3—7 cm wide, light glossy green, glabrous above,
lighter beneath with pubescent venation; flowers on
the 2nd year wood, 2.5 cm wide, outer petals bright
yellow, inner petals brown-yellow to purple, very
fragrant, January—March, depending on the weather;
fruit elliptic, 4 cm long. BMns 184 (= *Calycanthus
praecox* L.; *Chimonanthus fragrans* Lindl.; *Meratia
praecox* Rehd. & Wils.). China. 1766. z7 Fig. 234. ⊕

Including the following cultivars:

'Concolor'. Flowers 2.6 cm wide, outer sepals outspread,
oblong, somewhat inflexed, 2 cm long, 7 mm wide, light

yellow, inner sepals also light yellow, inner petals 7 mm long, light yellow. BMns 184 (4) (= var. *luteus*). Very fragrant. ⊕

'Grandiflorus'. Flowers 2.3 cm wide, outer sepals erect, narrow oblanceolate-oblong, 2 cm long, light yellow, inner petals 1.2 cm long, distinctly purple striped and bordered. BMns 184 (3). Slightly fragrant. ⊕

'Luteo-grandiflorus'. Flowers nearly 3 cm wide, sepals ovate, broadly campanulate, solid waxy yellow, May. GC 1957: 18. Japanese garden form, as yet not well known in the West; however one of the most beautiful in Japan. ⊕

'Parviflorus'. Flowers 1 cm wide, outer sepals erect, oblong, 1.2 cm long, 3 mm wide, rolled inward, almost entire length very light yellowish-white, inner sepals red striped, inner petals 4 mm long, purple spotted and bordered. Bmns 184 (4). ⊕

'Patens'. Flowers 2.4 cm wide, outer sepals nearly erect, oblanceolate, 1.8 cm long, yellowish-white, inner ones with purple margin and stripes, inner petals with purple margins. BMns 184 (1). ⊕

C. nitens Oliv. Evergreen shrub; leaves elliptic-lanceolate, long acuminate, 7—10 cm long, 3—4 cm wide, base rounded; flowers solitary, axillary, white, petals long acuminate. IH 1600. China; Tchang. Found in 1887, but not yet in cultivation. z8 # ⊕

C. yunnanensis W. W. Sm. Found by G. Forrest in the Sungkwei Valley, China at the 2000—2300 m range. Not in cultivation as yet.

Beautiful winter flowering shrub, but blooming only in protected areas where it develops into an attractive plant. Flowers especially well in hot, dry summers, no particular soil preference.

Lit. Turrill, W. B.: *Chimonanthus praecox*; in Bot. Mag. ns. Plate 184 with 8 pages of text.

CHIOGENES Salisb. — ERICACEAE

Monotypic genus; evergreen, procumbent shrublets with filamentous, creeping branches; leaves alternate, small, entire; flowers small, singular, urceolate, 4 parted; stamens 8, enclosed; anthers drawn out to a point, opening by a slit; ovaries half inferior, upper portion surrounded by the calyx lobes; style filamentous; fruit a globose, many seeded berry, ringed with calyx lobes beneath the apex. — 1 species in N. America and Japan.

Chiogenes hispidula (L.) Torr. & Gray. Evergreen, fast growing dwarf shrub, somewhat resembling *Thymus* in appearance; branches rough hairy; leaves oval-rounded, 4—10 mm long, 2 ranked, somewhat inflexed; flowers urceolate-campanulate, white, 4 mm long, solitary, axillary, May—June; fruit a white, 6 mm thick, rough hairy, many seeded berry. BB 2798; GSP 411. Northern N. America, Japan. 1815. z6 Fig. 235. # ⊕

Cultivated like *Vaccinium*; lime free soil, humus, moist, protected from the midday sun. Only recommended for collectors.

Fig. 233 **Chimaphila** a. *C. umbellata; b. C. maculata; c. C. menziesii.* S = Stamens, Sa = Seed (from Drude, Hooker, Bot. Mag.)

Fig. 234. *Chimonanthus praecox* (from Bot. Mag.)

CHIONANTHUS L. — White Fringe Tree — OLEACEAE

Deciduous shrubs, also occasionally tree-like in its habitat; leaves opposite, entire; flowers dioecious, white, in loose, branched panicles at the branch tips of the previous year; calyx 4 lobed; petals 4, very narrow, connate only at the base; stamens 2, very short; fruit a single seeded, blue-black drupe. — One species each in N. America and China.

Chionanthus retusus Lindl. & Paxt. Shrub, 2–3 m high, occasionally a small tree in its habitat, young twigs softly pubescent; leaves elliptic or ovate, 4–10 cm long, bright green above, densely white pubescent beneath, entire, but also often finely serrate on young plants (important for identification!); flowers white, in erect panicles, at the base of the young twigs, June; fruits blue, ovate, 12 mm long. NK 10: 1; LF 263; GF 7: 327 (= *C. chinensis* Maxim.). Korea, Japan. 1845. Hardy, but rare. z6–8 Fig. 236. ⊕

C. virginicus L. Tall shrub to small tree; leaves usually oval-oblong, 8–20 cm long (large leaves especially when grafted on *Fraxinus ornus* which is often done in Europe), dark green and glossy above, pubescent venation beneath, yellow fall foliage; flowers white, fragrant, in pendulous panicles to 20 cm long, June; fruit ovate, blue-black, 16 mm long. GF 7: 325; NBB 3: 53. Eastern USA. 1736. z3–9 ⊕

In addition, the following varieties:

'Angustifolius'. Leaves narrow-oblong to lanceolate.

'Latifolius'. Leaves large, oval to broad-obovate, to 15 cm long, 6–8 cm wide, short pubescent beneath (= *C. montanus* Pursh). z7

var. maritimus Pursh. Leaves oblong to broadly elliptic, softly pubescent beneath, also somewhat pubescent and, therefore, dull green above; flower panicles very loose (= var. *pubescens* Dipp.).

Thrives in any good garden soil, does especially well in moist, loam soil; full sun. Makes a good specimen plant. Quite winter hardy.

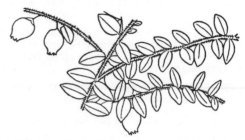

Fig. 235. *Chiogenes hispidula* (from Michaux)

Fig. 236. *Chionanthus retusus* (from Lindley)

CHLORANTHUS Sw. — CHLORANTHACEAE

Aromatic shrubs or perennials; leaves evergreen, opposite or in whorls of 3–4, petiolate, serrate, pinnate venation; flowers in terminal, sometimes branched spikes; flowers small, without a distinct perianth, sessile, stamens 3, connate and also fused to the ovary forming a 3 lobed structure; fruit a small, nearly globose drupe. — Over 10 species in S. and E. Asia.

Chloranthus glaber Makino. Evergreen shrub, 30–90 cm high, branches wide spreading, somewhat swollen at the nodes; leaves opposite, leathery, ovate to slightly elliptic, 5–10 cm long, acute, scabrous toothed, base rounded, glossy green above, short stalked; flowers small, greenish-yellow, without sepals and petals, in small, terminal spikes, June; fruits globose, fleshy, 6 mm thick, red berries. HKS 24 (= *C. brachystachys* Bl.). Japan, China, India, Malaysia,

widespread in dense, shady forests. z9 #

C. spicatus (Thunb.) Makino. Small, glabrous shrub, densely branched, branches ascending; leaves opposite, oval-oblong or slightly elliptic, 4–8 cm long, 2.5–4 cm wide, rather obtuse, shallowly wavy dentate, petiole 5–12 mm long; flowers in terminal, stalked spikes. China; in cultivation in Japan for a long time. z9 #

Only for frost free regions in moist, warm areas.

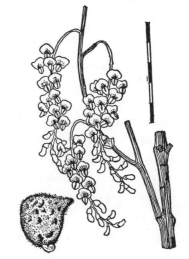

CHOISYA H. B. K. — Mexican Orange — RUTACEAE

Evergreen shrub, aromatic, often distinctly glandular; leaves opposite or nearly so, palmate, 3–12 parted; flowers in terminal or axillary panicles or solitary in the leaf axils; sepals 4 or usually 5; petals 4 or usually 5, large, white, glabrous; stamens 10; ovaries pubescent, with a 5 lobed stigma; fruit a 5 parted capsule. — 7 species in Mexico and in the Southern USA, with only the following in cultivation.

Choisya ternata H. B. K. Evergreen shrub, dense foliage, to 2m high; leaves trifoliate, leathery, leaflets oblong, translucent punctate, aromatic; flowers white, 3 cm wide, grouped 3–6 in cymes, scented much like oranges, May to June. BS 1: 609. Mexico; found there for centuries in cultivation, but only rarely in the wild. 1866. z8 Plate 115, 118. # ⊕ ∅

CHORDOSPARTIUM Cheesem. — LEGUMINOSAE

Nearly leafless shrub, similar to *Carmichaelia* and *Notospartium*; otherwise as follows. — 1 species in New Zealand, but very rare and diminishing in numbers.

Chordospartium stevensonii Cheesem. Only a small shrub in Europe, a leafless weeping willow in appearance, 3 m high; branches glabrous, striped, thin; leaves only found on young plants and only for a few months, small; flowers purple, standard petal striped, in 2–7 cm long, dense pendulous racemes, May–July; fruits 5 mm long, single seeded. BM 9654; MNZ 2. New Zealand, S. Island. 1923. z8 Fig. 237. ⊕

Fig. 237. *Chordospartium stevensonii* (from Adams)

In colder regions a worthwhile greenhouse plant; can be forced into flower every 2 months by drying and then regular watering. Prefers a fertile soil. A gorgeous flowering shrub in milder climates.

Lit. Muller, C. H.: A revision of *Choisya*; in American Midland Naturalist, 1940, 729–742; with illustrations of all species.

CHORISIA Kunth. — BOMBACEAE

Tall tropical tree with dense, prickly bark; leaves palmate, with 5–7 entire or toothed leaflets; flowers attractive, reddish, calyx cupola-shaped, irregularly 2–5 lobed, petals 5, linear or oblong, axillary or terminal; stamens connate forming 2 columns, the outer being shorter and having sterile anthers; ovary 5 chambered; fruit a pear-shaped capsule with many seeds, these having long silky hairs. — 5 species in tropical S. America; the seed hairs are used to stuff pillows, etc.

Chorisia speciosa St. Hil. Deciduous tree, trunk becoming thick, club-shaped with age, bark green, densely covered with stout, large, conical prickles; leaves long petioled, palmately compound, with 5–7 stalked leaflets, these lanceolate, acute, dentate; flowers solitary in the leaf axils, 10 cm wide, yellowish to reddish, brown striped at the base, ouside pubescent; calyx glossy outside, silky pubescent inside, stamen column very long, nearly as long as the petals, white, flowering in fall and winter while in a leafless state. MCL 17. Brazil. 1888. Found in frost free regions. z9 Plate 114.

CHOSENIA Nakai — SALICACEAE

Deciduous tree, very closely related to *Salix*, but differing in the presence of 2 styles, both split (*Salix* has only 1 style); female catkins pendulous (those of *Salix* are erect); stamens adnate to the bracts (those of *Salix* are distinct); flowers without nectar glands (*salix* has 1–2 glands); fruit capsule bivalved. — 1 species in NE. Asia.

Chosenia bracteosa (Trautv.) Nakai. Tree, to 20(30) m, branches erect, young twigs pruinose, glabrous; leaves oblong-lanceolate, 5–8 cm long, acuminate, indistinctly serrate to nearly entire, base cuneate, pruinose, glabrous, wtih many secondary veins; catkins 1.5–2.5 cm long, with 3–5 leaflike bracts at the base. NK 18: 3–5; TM 17 (= *C. macrolepis* [Turcz.] Komar.; *Salix bracteosa* Trautv.). NE. Asia. 1906. Hardy. Rarely found in cultivation (Botanic Gardens of Bothenburg, Sweden and Dortmund, W. Ger.). Plate 117. z6

Only of botanical interest; cultivated like *Salix* and *Populus*.

CHRONANTHUS

Chronanthus biflorus see: **Cytisus fontanesii**

CHRYSANTHEMUM L. — COMPOSITAE

Annual, perennial or subshrubs, not dealt with in this work except for:

Chrysanthemum frutescens L. Glabrous subshrub, many branched, foliage very dense, 50—75 cm high; leaves pinnately cleft, with few, linear, somewhat toothed lobes, slightly fleshy; flower heads numerous, large, white, blooming sequentially the entire summer in full sun, also flowering in winter in the greenhouse. PBI 2: 576 (= *Pyrethrum frutescens* Willd.). Canary Islands. z8 ⊕

Including also the following cultivars:

'Coronation'. White.

'Etoile d'Or'. Light yellow, very large flowered.

'Maja Bofinger'. White, large flowered.

'Mrs. Saunders'. White, double.

'Silver Leaf'. White, large flowered, foliage silver-gray.

Normally used in mass plantings, winter protection or overwintering in a cool greenhouse advisable for young plants.

CHRYSOLEPIS Hjelmqvist — FAGACEAE

Evergreen shrub or trees; leaves alternate, simple; flowers unisexual, male and female flowers always found on the same spike (on separate spikes with *Castanopsis*); calyx 5 to 7 parted; fruit a globose, densely prickly, small nut with 5 valves, these at all times distinct (not connate), with 2 additional walls inside separating the 3 seeds. — 2 species in California. Both species have been removed from the genus *Castanopsis* and given their own generic name.

Chrysolepis chrysophylla (Hook.) Hjelmq. Branches ocher-brown to gold-yellow, remaining scaly; leaves ovate-oblong, tapering to both ends, 5—14 cm long, leathery tough, dark glossy green above, gold-yellow scaly beneath; fruit 2.5 cm thick, hull very densely covered with stout prickles. SP 121 to 122 (= *Castanopsis chrysophylla* [Hook.] DC.). California. 1848. z8 Plate 116; Fig. 238. # ⊘

var. **minor** (Benth.) A. DC. Only shrubby; leaves smaller. NH 1955; 207. #

'Obovata'. Small shrub; leaves obovate, ovate to nearly circular, always rounded at the apex, 2—2.5 cm long, yellow beneath when young. Grown from N. American seed sown by T. Smith & Son, Newry, County Down, Ireland, 1914. Rare. z8 Plate 116. #

CHRYSOTHAMNUS Nutt. — COMPOSITAE

Shrubs and subshrubs, all parts glabrous to tomentose, often resinous and aromatic; leaves simple, alternate, entire; flowers in heads, seldom solitary,

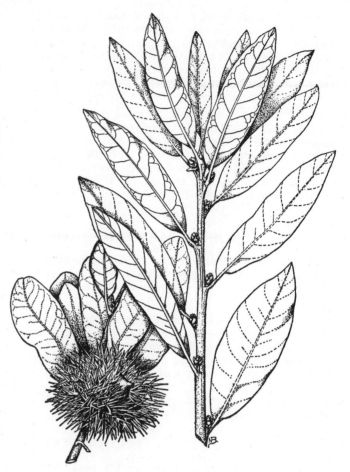

Fig. 238. *Chrysolepis chrysophylla*, sterile branch and short branch with fruit (from Sudworth)

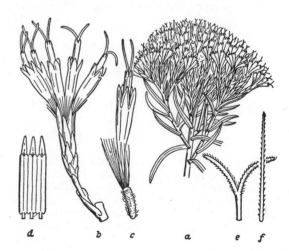

Fig. 239. *Chrysothamnus graveolens*. a. inflorescence, b. flower heads, c. single bloom, d. stamens, e. style with stigma, f. awn (from Bot. Mag.)

mostly grouped in panicles or cymes; ray florets absent; blades of the perianth arranged in more or less distinctly horizontal rows. — 12 species in W. North America (including *Bigelowia* DC.).

Chrysothamnus graveolens (Nutt). Greene. Evergreen, 1—2 m tall shrub, densely branched, young branches white and pubescent; aromatic when crushed; leaves clustered, linear, 3—7 cm long, acuminate, glabrous; flower heads bright yellow, usually in groups of 5, in flat, terminal corymbs to 10 cm wide, September—October. Bm 8255 (= *Bigelowia graveolens* Gray). Western N. America. Blooming shrub with abundant flowers for very dry locations. z8 Fig. 239. # ⊕

C. nauseosus (Pall.) Britt. Shrub, from 0.30 to 2 m high, with several erect stems originating at the base and flexible, moderately leafy side branches, these densely covered with a gray-green to whitish tomentum; leaves nearly filamentous to broadly linear, 2—6 cm long, more or less finely tomentose; flowers usually grouped 5—6 in terminal, rounded cymes, these occasionally compound, involucre usually with 20—25 scales, without herbaceous tips, September—October; fruits 5 sided, glabrous to dense shaggy pubescent. MS 706; MCL 177. California, mainly in the desert areas, but also found on the coast and in the mountains. Can be subdivided into 9 geographical varieties. z9 ⊕

Lit. McMinn: Ill. Man. Cal. Shrubs, 580—589, with 8 illustrations (foremost work) ● Hall, H. M.: *Chrysothamnus nauseosus* and its varieties; in Univ. Calif. Publ. Bull. **7**, 159—181.

CHUNIODENDRON Hu — MELIACEAE

A little known genus with 2 species in SW. China, presumably not yet introduced.

Chuniodendron spicatum Hu is illustrated in JRHS 1938, Pl. 104, but without text; leaves pinnate; flowers unattractive, in loose spikes 15 cm long; fruit a globose, red drupe, 1 cm thick.

CHUSQUEA Kunth — GRAMINEAE

Genus of shrubby, tree-like and climbing bamboos; leaves evergreen; flowers in terminal racemes or panicles, bisexual; stamens 3, styles 2. — 70 species on the high plains of S. America.

Chusquea culeou Desv. Halme 3(5—7) m high, tough, glabrous, black, solid stems, sheaths white, side branches erect, thin, very numerous, clustered at the nodes; leaves linear, narrow acuminate, tough, finely dentate, 3—7 cm long, with 5 paired veins, secondary venation reticulate. CBa 56. Chile; Patagonia. 1926. Wintering well at Wisley and colder parts of England, presumably hardier than first thought. z7? Plate 118.

Cultivated like bamboo.

CINNAMOMUM Schaeffer — Camphor Tree — LAURACEAE

Evergreen trees and shrubs; leaves usually opposite, thick, 3 veined or with pinnate venation, very aromatic (as is the wood); flowers usually complete, with 12 stamens, 3 of which are sterile; corolla short, with 6, generally even lobes; fruit a small, single seeded berry, surrounded by the cup-shaped corolla. — Around 250 species in E. Asia and Indomalaysia.

Cinnamomum camphora (L.) Presl. 1825. Camphor Tree. Densely crowned tree, to 12 m high, base generally very broad; leaves alternate, ovate-elliptic, long acuminate, rather thin, 6—12 cm long and half as wide, smooth and glossy, very aromatic when crushed, most with 3—4 paired veins, the lowest pair very distinct, petiole 2—3 cm long, young leaves reddish; flowers small, yellowish- to greenish-white, in axillary panicles 5—7 cm long, spring; fruit about pea-sized. Bm 2658; LWT 75; KIF 1—67. China, Japan. 1727. The wood is of economic importance in the production of camphor. z9 Ⓕ S. China, S. Japan, Taiwan, Ceylon, E. Africa. Plate 115; Fig. 241. # ⌀

C. glanduliferum (Wall.) Meissn. Large tree, 20—25 m

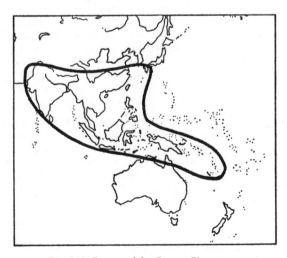

Fig. 240. Range of the Genus *Cinnamomum* (from Berry)

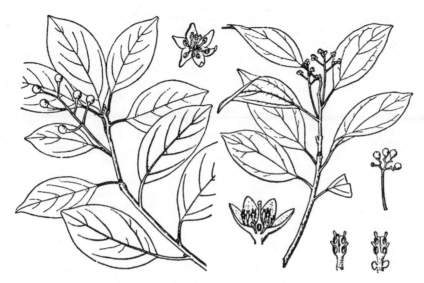

Fig. 241. Left *Cinnamomum glanduliferum*, right *C. camphora* (from ICS)

high, broad crowned, smooth bark, branches thin, greenish-brown, glabrous; leaves oblong-ovate, to 9 cm long and 5 cm wide, short acuminate, base broadly cuneate, entire, glossy green above, bluish beneath, glabrous on both sides, thick, leathery, petiole 2—3 cm; flowers yellowish-green, small, but in large panicles, sepals 6, with dense silky white pubescence; fruit globose, 5 mm thick. China. Not uncommon in the Mediterranean region. z9 ⓕ E. Himalaya. Plate 117; Fig. 241. # ⌀

C. japonicum Sieb. ex Nees. Medium sized tree, with thin, glabrous branches; leaves very thin, oval-oblong to oval-lanceolate, 6—9 cm long, 2.5—3.5 cm wide, acute, base obtuse, 3 veined, glabrous, petiole 8—12 mm long; flowers in axillary or terminal cymes, 3 cm long and glabrous, June; fruit oblong, 1 cm long. KIF 2: 23. Japan, Korea. z8 # ⌀

C. zeylanicum Bl. The true Cinnamon-tree, a tropical plant omitted from this work. #

The first two species are planted in Southern England, but more frequently in the Mediterranean region. *C. glanduliferum* is frequently found as a street tree in the eastern Black Sea region (Suchumi, Batumi, Sotchi).

CISSUS L. — VITACEAE

Evergreen or deciduous vines, usually with tendrils, some species with succulent stems and roots for survival in the desert; very similar to *Vitis*, but differing in the 4 parted flowers, the unfolding corolla (not formed like a cap), 4 parted disc, and dry (inedible) fruit with 1 (rarely 2) seeds; leaves simple, 3 parted or palmately cleft; flowers small, greenish, yellow or reddish, in corymbs. — Some 350 species in the tropics, some subtropical, only a few in cultivation.

Cissus antarctica Vent. Evergreen vine, branches with tendrils, pubescent; leaves simple, petiolate, ovate to oblong, usually long acuminate, 7—10 cm long, 3—5 cm wide, base somewhat cordate, entire or sinuate to irregularly dentate, rather tough and leathery; flowers few in axillary fascicles, green, pubescent, July; fruit a small globose berry. BM 2488 (as *Vitis antarctica*). Australia. 1790. Popular plant, but found in the landscape only in frost free regions. z8 # ⌀

C. striata Ruiz & Pav. Low, evergreen vine, climbing with tendrils; branches thin, angular, striped, pubescent with dense foliage; leaves palmately compound, with 5 leaflets, these nearly sessile, on a common, 2—3 cm long petiole, obovate to oblanceolate, 1.5—3 cm long, 6—15 mm wide, leathery, coarsely dentate on the apical half, each tooth with a small gland, both sides dark green and glabrous; flowers green, in small corymbs; fruits numerous, purple-red, about the size of small currants, fruits abundantly. Chile, S. Brazil. Planted in open areas only in the milder regions. z8 # ⌀ ⚭

CISTUS L. — CISTACEAE

Low, evergreen shrubs; branches usually shaggy-glandular pubescent, often aromatic; leaves opposite, entire; flowers attractive, white to purple, often with a basal spot on the petals, in terminal or axillary cymes at the branch tips; petals 5, sepals 3 or 5; fruit a 5 or 10 valved capsule. — 20 species in the Mediterranean region.

Plate 113

Chaenomeles speciosa, flowering branch   Archive Deutsche Baumschule

Chaenomeles speciosa, fruiting branch   Archive Deutsche Baumschule

Plate 114

Chaenomeles supeba ('Carl Ramcke'), fruits
Photo: J. Timm & Co.

Chorisia speciosa
in a park in Granada, Spain

Chamaerops humilis in its native habitat near Arta, Mallorca, Spain,
with *Rubus* and *Asphodelus microcarpus*

Plate 115

Chamaedaphne calyculata
Photo: Otto, Wolbeck

Choisya ternata, Lismore Castle, Ireland;
for growth habit see plate 118

Cinnamomum camphora in the Kirstenbosch Botanical Garden, Cape Town, S. Africa

Plate 116

Chrysolepis chrysophylla var. *obovata* in the Royal Botanic Garden, Edinburgh, Scotland

Chrysolepis chrysophylla in the Royal Botanic Garden, Ediburgh

Plate 117

Cinnamomum glanduliferum
in front of a hotel in Locarno, Tessin, Switzerland

Chosenia bracteosa
in the Dortmund Botanic Garden, W. Germany

Citrus reticulata
in the Brissago Botanic Garden, Tessin, Switzerland

Citrus limetta, Sweet Lemon,
in a garden on Mallorca, Spain

Plate 118

Cistus albidus
in the Dortmund Botanic Garden, W. Germany

Chusquea culeou
in Wisley Gardens, England

Choisya ternata
in Taranto, Pallanza, Italy

Plate 119

Clematus rehderiana
in Kew Gardens, London, England

Clematis heracleifolia
in the Copenhagen Botanic Garden, Denmark

Clematis veitchiana

Photo: J. E. Downward

Plate 120

Clematis orientalis 'Orange Peel'
Photo: J. E. Downward

Clematis napaulensis
Photo: J. E. Downward

Clematis jackmanii
in the Oslo Botanic Garden, Norway

Clematis montana var. *rubens*
in the Berlin Botanic Garden, W. Germany

Plate 121

Clematis alpina   Photo: Wilh. Schact, Muenchen

Clematis macropetala
in the Edinburgh Botanic Garden, Scotland

Clematis afoliata
in the Edinburgh Botanic Garden

Plate 122

Clematis armandii 'Snowdrift'   Photo: J. E. Downward

Clematis chrysocoma var. *sericea* in Birr Castle, Ireland

Plate 123

Clematis durandii in the Dortmund Botanic Garden, W. Germany

Clematis gouriana   Photo: J. E. Downward

Plate 124

Clethra acuminata
in the Dortmund Botanic Garden, W. Germany

Clethra fargesii
in the Dortmund Botanic Garden

Clematis 'Nelly Moser'

Archivbild

Plate 125

Corylus avellana 'Contorta'

Cotinus coggyria

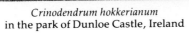

Crinodendrum hokkerianum
in the park of Dunloe Castle, Ireland

Cotoneaster watereri 'Cornubia'

Plate 126

Cyrilla racemiflora
in the Villa Taranto Garden, Italy, in fall color

Cytisus scoparius 'Luna'

Cytisus scoparius 'Palette'

Cytisus demissus
in the Edinburgh Botanic Garden, Scotland

Plate 127

Datura suaveolens,
Pink, flowering form

Datura sanguinea,
Yellow flowering form on Mainau Island, W. Germany

Dendromecon rigida
in Kew Gardens, England

Desfontainia spinosa
in an English park

Plate 128

Decaisnea fargesii,
fruit

Dombeya wallichii
in a Spanish garden

Doxantha unguis-cati
in a Spanish garden

Daphne collina
in an English garden

Key to the most important species and hybrids
(from Bean, expanded)

+ Flowers white (pure white or with spots); sepals 3;
    Flowers solitary, leaves nearly sessile, sepals scaly:
        C. landanifer
    Flowers in clusters, leaves short stalked, sepals scaly and pubescent:
        C. cyprius
    Flowers in clusters, leaves petiolate, sepals pubescent:
        C. laurifolius

++ Flowers white; sepals 5, cordate;
    Leaves 3 veined, sessile:
        C. hirsutus
    Leaves to 10 cm long, long petioled:
        C. populifolius
    Leaves to 5 cm long, petiolate, pinnate venation:
        C. salvifolius
    Leaves stellate pubesent, margin wavy, dull green:
        C. hybridus
    Leaves stellate pubescent, gray woolly beneath:
        C. florentinus

+++ Flowers white, sepals 5, ovate; leaves 3 veined, sessile;
    Leaves not wider than 1.5 cm:
        C. monspeliensis
    Leaves to 2 cm wide, petals with red spots:
        C. lusitanicus

☆ Flowers monochrome, reddish, without spots;
    Leaves 3 veined, margin smooth, flowers long stalked:
        C. albidus
    Leaves 3 veined, margin wavy, flowers short stalked:
        C. crispus
    Leaves with pinnate venation, stellate pubescent on both sides:
        C. creticus

☆☆ Flowers reddish, petals with darker spots;
    Leaves lanceolate, gray-green beneath:
        C. purpureus

Cistus — see × **Halimiocistus**

Cistus × aguilarii Pau. (*C.ladanifer* × *C. populifolius*). Natural hybrid; leaves lanceolate, to 10 cm long, bright green above, lighter beneath, 3 veined with distinct reticulate venation, margin dense wavy, petiole short. BC 30; JRHS 1931:77. Iberian Peninsula and Morocco. z8 # ☉

C. albidus L. Compact shrub, seldom 1 m high, all parts with dense white stellate pubescence; leaves sessile, oval to oblong, to 5 cm long, rounded or obtuse, base 3 veined, distinct reticulate venation beneath; flowers light lilac-pink, with a yellow spot at the base of the petals, 5–6 cm wide, grouped 3–5 together, June, sepals 5, broad ovate. SW. Mediterranean region. 1640. BCi 4; PMe 99. z8 Plate 118; Fig. 242. # ☉

The specific epithet *albidus* (= whitish) refers to the whitish underside of the leaves; the flowers are lilac-pink.

f. **albus** (warb.) Dansereau. Flowers pure white. JRHS 1830: 5. Occasionally found in the wild with the species.

C. algarvensis see: **Halimium ocymoides**

C. alyssoides see: **Halimium allyssoides**

C. atriplicifolius see: **Halimium atriplicifolium**

C. × canescens Sweet. (*C. albidus* × *C. villosus*). Growth habit like that of *C. albidus*, but more green, not so densely stellate pubescent; leaves narrower, more acute, margin wavy; flowers more numerous, sepals like those of *C. albidus*. SC 45. Algeria. z8 # ☉

C. clusii Dun. Shrub, only around 20 cm high, branches thin, pubescent; leaves linear, 2.5 cm long, only 3–4 mm wide, usually obtuse, margin involute, both sides pubescent; flowers white, light yellow in the middle, 2.5 cm wide, usually 3–5 in terminal or axillary clusters, sepals 3–5, ovate. SC 32; DRHS 493 (= *C. rosmarinifolius* Pourr. p. p.); PSw 30. SW. Europe. Flowers abundantly, low growing species. z8 # ☉

C. × corbariensis Pourr. (*C. populifolius* × *C. salvifolius*). Shrub, dense, bushy, 0.5 m high, but often wider than tall, branches glabrous or finely pubescent; leaves ovate, acute, 2–5 cm long, 1–2.5 cm wide, base cordate or rounded, margin wavy and finely dentate, each tooth with a tiny cluster of hairs, venation reticulate, dull dark green above, lighter beneath, both sides with stellate pubescence, petiole 6–12 mm long; flowers white, with a yellow spot at the base of the petals, 3.5 cm wide, terminal on short side branches, solitary or in groups of 3, outer sepals cordate, June. BCi 35; JRHS 1931: 74. S. France; Corbieres. Mountains. One of the hardiest species. z8 # ☉

C. creticus L. Shrub, 0.5–1 m high, compact and densely branched, young branches long haired or stellate pubescent (or also glandular, especially on Crete and in the eastern Mediterranean region); leaves quite variable in form, from ovate to obovate, apex acute to rounded, tapering at the base to a short, wide, flat petiole with generally swollen base and more or less connate to the opposite petiole base, both sides pubescent, more pronounced on the underside, venation concave, margin often wavy; flowers purple to pink, petal base yellowish, 5–6 cm wide, in clusters of 3–5 at the branch tips, flower stalk and calyx with similar pubescence to the leaves, sepals broad ovate, with fine tips. BS 1: 619; JRHS 1930: 7; PEu 77; PMe 100 (= *C. villosus* L.; *C. incanus* auct. non L.; *C. polymorphus* Willk.). Mediterranean region. 1650. Differing from *C. albidus* and *C. crispus* in the pinnate venation of the leaves, while the latter have 3 parallel veins. Extraordinarily variable species. z8 Fig. 242. # ☉

C. (Crispal) 'Anne Palmer' (*C. crispus* × *C. palhinhae*). Flowers very large, clear pink, cup-shaped, petals quite prominent. JRHS 1960: 39. Breeder: C. Ingram, Benenden, England. Before 1960. z8 # ☉

C. crispus L. Shrub, compact, densely branched, 50 cm high, young branches with long white pubescence;

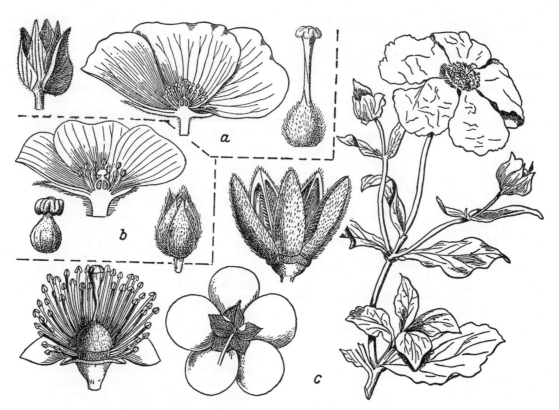

Fig. 242. **Cistus** a. *C. albidus*; b. *C. monspeliensis*; c. *C. creticus*
(from Grosser, Willkomm, Bot. Mag.)

leaves sessile, lanceolate to oval, 2–4 cm long, base 3 veined, densely stellate pubescent, margin wavy, both sides with venation indented and, therefore, rugose, gray-green; flowers purple-red, 3 cm wide, flower stalk very distinctly pubescent, in terminal, nearly sessile clusters, June. BM 9306; Bi 5; PMe 106. SW. Europe, N. Africa. 1656. z8 # ☉

'Sunset'. Selection with carmine-pink flowers. HTS 147.

C. × cyprius Lam. (*C. landanifer* × *C. laurifolius*). Bushy shrub, 1–2 m high in its native habitat, branches viscid, aromatic; leaves oblong-lanceolate, 3–10 cm long, tapering to the apex, margin wavy, cuneate at the base, 3 veined, dark gray-green above, gray pubescent beneath, both sides sticky; flowers white with a carmine basal spot, 7 cm wide, 3–6 in long stalked clusters (important for identification!), sepals 3, June. Bm 112 (as *C. landaniferus*); BCi 31 (= *C. grandiflorus* Tausch.). Origin unknown. In cultivation before 1800. z8 # ☉

C. × florentinus Lam. (*C. monspeliensis* × *C. salvifolius*). Shrub, 0.5(1) m high, densely branched, not viscid, young twigs stellate pubescent at first; leaves oval-lanceolate, 2.5–3 cm long, acute, margin wavy, dull green above, rough, reticulate venation beneath, venation pinnately branched, gray woolly when young; flowers 2–4 on a stalk, white with a yellow basal spot, 3.5–5 cm wide, flowers very abundantly, sepals 5,

pubescent, ovate, base cordate, June. SC 59; DRHS 492; BCi 27–28. Found as a natural hybrid in S. Europe and Algeria. z8 # ☉

Cistus formosus see: **Halimium lasianthum**

C. glaucus Pourret (*C. laurifolius* × *C. monspeliensis*). Shrub, to 1 m high, branches thin and white pubescent; leaves linear-oblong, 2.5–5 cm long, tapering to both ends, viscid above, pubescent beneath; flowers pure white (without spots), 4–5 cm wide, several in terminal and axillary clusters, petals 2 cm long. S. France, E. Pyrenees. z8 # ☉

C. × hetieri Verguin (*C. landanifer* × *C. laurifolius* × *C. monspelliensis*). Grows 1 m high; leaves lanceolate, margin wavy, pale gray-green above, somewhat rugose; flowers pure white or also spotted. z8 # ☉

C. hirsutus Lam. Shrub, densely branched, to 70 cm high, branches dense and short pubescent, interspersed with many long, white hairs; leaves sessile, ovate-oblong, obtuse, base rounded and 3 veined, 3–5 cm long, long white pubescent above, stellate pubescent beneath; flowers white, with yellow basal spots, 3 cm wide, in terminal clusters, sepals 5, the outer ones cordate, 2 cm long, the inner ones smaller, all white pubescent. SC 19; BCi 8. Spain, Portugal, France. 1650. z8 # ☉

C. × hybridus Pourret (*C. populifolius* × *C. salvifolius*. Shrub, very bushy, 0.4—0.7 m high, young twigs only sparsely pubescent; leaves 2.5—5 cm long, ovate, base rounded or cordate, margin wavy, finely dentate, each tooth tipped with a fine cluster of hairs, dark green above, lighter beneath, both sides stellate pubescent; flowers white, with yellow basal spots, 1—3 on a stalk, June, buds carmine-pink, sepals cordate. SC 8 (= *C. corbariensis* Pourret). S. France. A. natural hybrid first discovered in the Corbières region. Much hardier than most of the other species and hybrids. z7? # ✿

C. ladanifer L. Shrub, to 1.5 m high, young branches viscid; leaves linear-lanceolate, nearly sessile, 4—8 cm long, glabrous above, viscid, gray pubescent beneath; flowers singular on short side branches, white with red-brown basal spots, 7 to 10 cm wide, sepals 3, large, yellow, concave scaly, June—July. SC 1; JRHS 1952: 107; BCi 13—14; PMe 104. SW. Europe, N. Africa. 1629. Well known but delicate species. z8 Plate 3. # ✿

C. laurifolius L. Shrub, 1—2 m high, young twigs pubescent and viscid; leaves oval-oblong, petioled, 4—7 cm long, dark green above, glabrous, viscid, gray tomentose beneath; flowers white with yellow basal spot, 5—7 cm wide, grouped 3—8 together, fragrant, July—August. SC 52; BCi 16; PSw 30. SW. Europe. 1731. Most popular and hardiest species. z8 # ✿

C. × laxus Ait. f. (*C. hirsutus* × *C. populifolius*). Shrub with open habit, to about 1 m high, branches short tomentose interpersed with long hairs; leaves short petioled, ovate-lanceolate, 5—10 cm long, 3 veined at the base, both sides pubescent when young, petiole viscid; flowers white with yellow center, 5 cm wide, in axillary, long stalked fascicles, stalk pubescent, sepals 5, cordate, very pubescent, June. SC 12; JRHS 1930: 12. Known since 1656. z8 # ✿

C. libanotis L. Very similar to *C. clusii*, but with inflorescence glabrous, sepals reddish. BCi 18 (= *C. bourgeanus* Coss.). Only in S. Portugal (Algarve) and S. Spain, from the Portugese border to Cádiz. z8 # ✿

C. × loretii Rouy & Fouc. (*C. landanifer* × *C. monspeliensis*). Upright shrub, 1 m high; leaves linear-lanceolate, intermediate in form between the parents; flowers resembling those of *C. monspeliensis*, 2.5 cm wide, white, but with smaller, darker yellow spots. France, Algeria. Not to be confused with *C. loretii* Hort.! z8 # ✿

C. × lusitanicus Maund (non Mill.). Shrub, 30—60 cm high, branches viscid; leaves sessile, oblong to lanceolate, 3—6 cm long, 3 veined, dull green above and nearly glabrous; reticulate venation beneath and somewhat stellate pubescent; flowers 3—5 in terminal fascicles, short stalked, 6—7 cm wide, white, with a pink basal spot, June to July, sepals 4—5, broad ovate, outside stellate pubescent. JRHS 1930: 9. z8 # ✿

var. **decumbens** Maund. Grows wider; leaves oblong-lanceolate, smooth above, glossy; flowers with distinct carmine-red spot: DRHS 492; BM 8480 (as *C. loretii*); JRHS 130: 8, 14 (= *C. loretii* Hort. nn Rouy & Fouc.). z8 # ✿

C. monspeliensis L. Shrub, 0.5—1(1.5) m high, branches pubescent, viscid when young; leaves nearly sessile, lanceolate to nearly linear, 3 veined, 2—5 cm long, margin involute, dark green and rugose above, gray beneath, stellate pubescent, venation pubescent on both sides; flowers 3—10 in dense, long stalked cymes, white, 2.5 cm wide, June—July, sepals 5, ovate, very pubescent. SC 27; BCi 9; PEu 77. SW. Europe. 1650. z8 Fig. 242. # ✿

C. × nigricans Pourr. (presumably *C. monspeliensis* × *C. populifolius*). Leaves lanceolate, base tapering to a short petiole, glabrous above, with concave reticulate venation; flowers 3—6 in corymbs, flower stalk short pubescent, but interspersed with long hairs, sepals elliptic, base cordate. JRHS 1931: 76. z8 # ✿

C. × obtusifolius Sweet (*C. hirsutus* × *C. salvifolius*). Shrub, 40—60 cm high, branches thin, gray stellate pubescent; leaves usually sessile, ovate to oblong, obtuse, tapering to the base, margin somewhat involute, rough above, both sides gray-green and stellate pubescent, especially beneath; flowers white, with a yellow basal spot, 3 cm wide, several in cymes, sepals green, cordate, outer ones smaller, short and sparsely pubescent. SC 42; BCi 34. Grows wild in Portugal. 1827. z7 # ✿

C. palhinhai Ingram. Shrub, 40—60 cm high, wider than tall, foliage very dense, branches glabrous; leaves nearly sessile, obovate, obtuse, tapering to the base, 4—5 cm long, pinnate venation, deep green above, white tomentose beneath; flowers solitary, pure white, 7—10 cm wide, May—June, sepals 3, densely ciliate. BMns 157; PSw 31. Portugal. 1939. One of the most beautiful species; similar to *C. ladanifer*. z7? # ✿

C. parviflorus Lam. Shrub, to 1 m high, compact, young branches pubescent; leaves ovate, apex acute to rounded, to 6 cm long and 3 cm wide, with winged petiole, gray-green above, more green beneath, both sides pubescent, 3 veined from the base, with secondary reticulate venation concave; flowers pure pink, 2.5 cm wide, in terminal and axillary heads, petals triangular-ovate, not covering the inflorescence, sepals 5, pubescent, stigma large, nearly sessile (= *C. complicatus* Lam.). E. Mediterrfanean region. z8 # ✿

C. × platysepalus Sweet (*C. hirsutus* × *C. monspeliensis*). Shrub, 50—70 cm high, branches white pubescent; leaves sessile, 3 veined, ovate-lanceolate, 3—5 cm long, nearly glabrous except for the pubescent venation beneath; flowers 4—5 cm wide, white with yellow patch at the petal base, grouped 3—4 in cymes, June, sepals cordate, margin not inflexed, loosely pubescent as is the flower stalk. SC 47; JRHS 1930: 13. 1827. z8 # ✿

C. populifolius L. Shrub, 0.7(2) m high, strong grower, branches finely pubescent and viscid; leaves long petioled, ovate, long acuminate, base deeply cordate, 5—9 cm long, glabrous, reticulate venation beneath, petiole somewhat pubescent; flowers grouped 2—5, white, with a yellow basal spot, 5 cm wide, in June, on older wood, sepals 5, the outer ones cordate, 2 cm long, the inner ones smaller. SC 23; DRHS 492; BCi 15; PMe 107 (= *C. cordifolius* Mill.). SW. Europe. 1656. z8 # ⊕

C. × pulverulentus Pourret (*C. albidus* × *C. crispus*). Low shrub, 50–70 cm high, densely branched; leaves oblong, 3–5 cm long, wavy, but the higher leaves nearly or totally entire on the margin, gray pubescent; flowers short stalked, 5 cm wide, purple, sepals oval-lanceolate. BCi 20; JRHS 1931: 73 (= *C. delilei* Burnat). SW. Europe, occurring in the wild. 1929. z8 # ⊕

C. × purpureus Lam. (*C. ladanifer* × *C. villosus*). Rounded shrub, 0.5–1 m high and wide, young branches pubescent and resinous; leaves nearly sessile, oblong-lanceolate, 3 veined at the base, otherwise with pinnate venation, 3–5 cm long, dull gray-green above, venation concave, lighter and stellate pubescent beneath; flowers usually 3 in terminal cymes, pink with a dark red basal spot, 5–7 cm wide, sepals ovate, stellate pubescent, June. BR 408; JRHS 1930: 6. Before 1790. z8 # ⊕

Including the following garden forms;

'Brilliancy'. An intense dark pink with deep brown spots. HTS 144.

'Doris Hibberson'. Light pink, flowers very abundantly. MCL 67.

C. revolii see: × **Halimium revolii**

C. salvifolius L. Shrub, 0.5 m high, dense, young branches stellate pubescent; leaves short petioled, oval-oblong, 2–4 cm long, rugose above, gray-green, lighter beneath, both sides dense stellate pubescent; flowers white with a yellow spot, 3–4 cm wide, June, solitary or 3 together, sepals 5, the outer ones cordate. SC 54; HM 2026; BCi 10–12; PMe 102. S. Europe, Mediterranean coast, widely disseminated. 1548. z8 Fig. 243. # ⊕

C. 'Silver Pink' (Hillier) (*C. laurifolius* × *C. villosus*). Low shrub, 30–50 cm·high, very bushy; leaves tough, lanceolate, dark green above, gray-green beneath, 3–7 cm long; flowers a pure silvery-pink, 7 cm wide, usually several together, June—July. HTS 145. Developed by Hillier, Winchester, England around 1916. z8 # ⊕

C. × skanbergii Lojacono-Pojero (*C. monspeliensis* × *C. parviflorus*). Shrub, 0.7–1 m high, branches thin, white pubescent; leaves linear-lanceolate to oblanceolate, nearly sessile, 3 veined at the base, 2.5–5 cm long, stellate and silky pubescent beneath; flowers 6 together in terminal and axillary cymes, light pink, petals obcordate (important for identification!), June—July. BM 9514. Greece. z8 # ⊕

C. symphytifolius Lam. Loose growing shrub, 0.6–1.8 m high, young branches sparsely covered with long hairs; leaves oblong to slightly elliptic, 4–10 cm long, 1.5–6 cm wide, acute, tapering to a short petiole at the base, dark green with scattered pubescence above, to-

mentose beneath, margin flat or wavy; flowers purple-pink, to 5 cm wide or somewhat larger, grouped 2–9 in pubescent panicles, sepals 5, especially pubescent at the base, style to 2.5 cm long, always longer than the stamen filament. FS 1501 (= *C. vaginatus* Ait.). Canary Islands. z8 # ⊕

C. verguinii Coste & Soulié. (*C. ladanifer* × *C. salvifolius*). Shrub, upright, somewhat viscid; leaves short petioled, lanceolate, nearly glabrous or whitish pubescent beneath, venation reticulate, 3 veined at the base; flowers solitary on tomentose stalks, white with brown spots, 4–5 cm wide, sepals 4–5, somewhat ciliate. JRHS 1952: 106; BCi 32. Growing wild in S. France and Spain. z8 # ⊕

All species require warm spots in full sun and tolerate the severest droughts without harm. A few species will survive the winter in protected areas (e.g. *C. laurifolius*, *C. hybridus*), while the others should be over-wintered in a cool greenhouse. The beautiful flowers never last longer than a day and most only a few hours in the morning, but new flowers appear successively.

Lit. Bolanos, M. M., & E. G. Lopez: Jarales y Jaras; Cistologia Hispanica. 228 pp. 51 photos, 36 plates, many range maps. Madrid 1949 ● The work "Cistaceas Espanolas" from E. Guinea (187 pp., many ills., Madrid 1954) covering the other Cistaceae outside the genus *Cistus* ● Dansereau, P. M.: Monographie du genre *Cistus*; in Boissiera 1939, **1** to 90 (a recent monograph surpassing those of Grosser) ● Gard, M.: Atlas d'Hybrides artificiels obtenus par E. Bornet à Antibes; 41 plates, 5 in color. Paris 1933 ● Grosser, W.: Cistaceae; in Engler, Pflanzenreich, IV, 193, 10–32 (*Cistus*), 1903 ● Sweet, R.: Cistineae; 112 color plates, London, 1825–1830; valuable work for its plates ● Warbug, E. F.: A preliminary study of the genus *Cistus*; in Jour. Roy. Hort. Soc. **55**, 1–52, 1930 ● Warburg, E. F.: *Cistus* Hybrids; in Jour. Roy. Hort. Soc. **51**, 217–224, 1931.

Fig. 243 *Cistus salvifolius* (from Reichenbach)

× **CITROFORTUNELLA** J. Ingram & H. E. Moore — RUTACEAE

Hybrids between *Citrus* L. and *Fortunella* Swingle. — So far the following 3 hybrids are known:

× **Citrofortunella floridana** J. Ingram & H. E. Moore (*Citrus aurantifoia* × *Fortunella japonica*). Evergreen tree, leaves composed of only one simple leaflet, dark green above, lighter beneath; flowers white or slightly reddish; fruits ovate to rounded, light yellow, fruit pulp light yellow, with 6—9 segments, usually with 1 seed in each segment. 1923. # ⊕ ⚭

× **C. mitis** (Blanco) J. Ingram & H. E. Moore (*Citrus reticulata* × *Fortunella* spec. [*F. margarita*?]). Calamondin. Small, evergreen tree, very dense crown, branches with few or without very short thorns; leaves

with 1 leaflet, broad ovate, petiole with a narrow wing; fruits small, globose to flat-globose, 2.5—3.5 cm at the branch tips, orange-colored, peel loose, pulp very sour (= *Citrus mitis* Blanco; *C. microcarpa* Bge.). Philippines. 1837. z9 # ⊕ ⚭

× **S. swinglei** J. Ingram & H. E. Moore. Evergreen tree, leaves with a single leaflet, lanceolate; flower buds pink; fruits obovoid to ovate or flat-globose, light yellow with lighter colored pulp, 7—8 segments. 1923. z9 # ⊕ ⚭

Lit. Nomenclatural Notes for Hortus Third; Rutaceae (John Ingram & H. E. Moore Jr., in Baileya **19**, 169—171, 1975).

× **CITRONCIRUS** J. Ingram & H. E. Moore — RUTACEAE

Hybrids between *Citrus* L. and *Poncirus* Rafinesque. — To date only the following hybrid known:

× **Citroncirus webberi** J. Ingram & H. E. Moore. Evergreen or semi-deciduous shrub, broad, strong grower, branches with long thorns; leaves with 3 or only 1 leaflet, large, petiole narrow winged; flowers to 6 cm

wide, white, fragrant; fruits globose, 5—6 cm thick, orange or yellow, fruit pulp sour and bitter (= *Citrus sinensis* × *Poncirus trifoliata*). Garden origin 1897. In cultivation in S. England. z8 # ⊕ ⚭

Lit. Same as × *Citrofortunella*.

CITRUS L. — CITRUS — RUTACEAE

Evergreen, small trees or shrubs with axillary thorns; leaves simple, glandular punctate, petiole narrow or broad winged; flowers usually in clusters, white, fragrant, often pink in bud; petals 5 (occasionally 4 or 6), fleshy, strap-like, not claw-like at the base, imbricate, stamen filaments numerous, 15 to 60, but usually 20—40; ovaries 8—15 chambered; fruit a globose or flat-round "berry" (more botanically correct, "hesperidium"). — 12 species in S. China, SE. Asia, Indomalaysia, but widely cultivated in the Mediterranean region, southern USA, S. America and other warm climates.

There is some disagreement regarding the *Citrus* nomenclature; the following outline is generally consistent with that used by Swingle.

Key to the Species
(From Swingle, in Bailey; somewhat altered)

1. Petiole nearly as broad winged and large as the leaf blade; seed very large and thick; fruits rough, ovate, lemon-yellow when ripe; flowers solitary.
   C. ichangensis
   Petiole narrow or broad winged, but always much smaller than the leaf blade; seed small or medium size; flowers usually in clusters 2

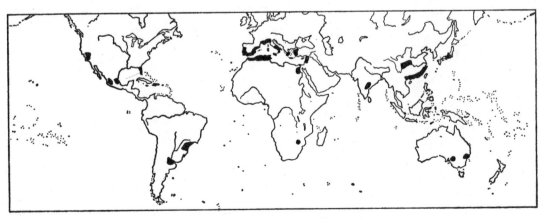

Fig. 244. *Citrus* Range in cultivation (from Schutt 1972)

2. Petiole and leaf blade not distinctly separated, oblong, serrate, petiole not winged; flower buds reddish; fruit peel very thick, fragrant, pulp sour:
   C. medica
   Petiole and leaf blade distinctly separate, crenate; peel thin or moderately thick   3

3. Buds reddish outside; petiole only very narrowly winged, leaves crenate; fruits ellipsoid with a small or large protruding apical tip:
   C. limon
   Buds white, petiole narrow or broad winged   4

4. Fruits ellipsoid, often somewhat glandular-punctate, only 2.5—3.5 cm long, greenish-yellow when ripe, thin rind, smooth; petiole narrow, winged, leaves small, pale green above, crenate, more or less glandular punctate; thorns short, but very sharp:
   C. aurantifolia
   Fruits globose or flat-globose, seldom ellipsoid to slightly pear-shaped, never glandular punctate,

   orange colored or, if yellow, a very large fruit with a thick rind   5

5. Fruit very large and heavy, ripening pale yellow, young branches pubescent, petiole broad winged:
   C. maxima, C. paradisi
   Fruit medium sized or small, orange or orange-900 yellow   6

6. Interior of fruit full, rind thin, fruit pulp sweet, petiole slightly winged:
   C. sinensis
   Interior of fruit with a cavity when fully ripe, rind loose or somewhat tight, pulp sour and petioles broad winged   7

7. Rind tight; petiole broad winged, pulp sour:
   C. auranticum
   Rind loose; petiole only narrowly winged or somewhat ribbed   8

8. Fruits solitary at the branch tips, small, with 7—10

Fig. 245. **Citrus** a. *C. sinensis*; b. *C. aurantium*; c. *C. maxima*; d. *C. medica*; e. *C. medica* 'Sacrodactylis'; f. *C. limon* (from ICS)

segments, fruit pulp very sour; leaves light green beneath:
> (× *Citrofortunella mitis*)
> Fruits in the leaf axils; with 8—15 segments, fruit pulp sweet; leaves dark green beneath:
> *C. reticulata*

Citrus aurantifolia (Christm.) Swingle. Lime. Small tree, 3—5 m high, irregularly branched, thorns short, stiff, very sharp; leaves small, 5—7 cm long, elliptic-ovate, crenate, rather bright green, petiole distinct, but narrow winged; flowers small, white in bud, few in axillary clusters, petals white on both sides; fruits small, ovate, 3—6 cm wide, yellow-green when ripe, rind distinctly glandular punctate, very thin, fruit pulp abundant, very sour. BM 6745 (= *Limonia aurantifolia* Christm.; *C. limetta* auct. non Risso). Tropical Asia. Widely cultivated in the West Indies; exceptionally susceptible to frost damage. 1648. z9 # ⊕ ⌘

C. aurantium L. Bitter Orange. Small tree, round crowned, regularly branched, 5 m high or more, branches with long, curved but blunt tipped thorns; leaves elliptic, acute, base more or less keeled, 7—10 cm long, petiole broad winged; flowers solitary or in axillary clusters, white in bud, petals later white on both sides, very fragrant; fruits globose or somewhat flattened, 5—7 cm wide, interior with a cavity when fully ripe, fruit pulp sour. BC 976; ICS 2846 (= *C. bigaradia* Risso). Found in the wild in Himalaya (south slopes), Malaysia, E. Africa; cultivated throughout the Mediterranean region (provides an ether extract, and used in the preparation of orange marmalade) and in S. Asia. 1595. Relatively frost tolerant. Not grafted, rather grown from seed. Often also planted as a street and park tree in the Mediterranean region. z9 Fig. 245. # ⊕ ⌘ ✕

C. ichangensis Swingle. Small tree, 1—10 m high in its habitat, thorns long and thin; leaves narrow, oval-lanceolate, 6—12 cm long, 1.5—2 cm wide, the winged leaf petiole usually larger and broader than the leaf blade; flowers white; fruits lemon-shaped, 7—10 cm long, with a short, broad pronounced tip, ringed with a circular furrow, fruit pulp sour, but flavorful, seeds very large and thick, to 2 cm long. BC 978. SW. China, in the mountains at 1000—1600 m. The hardiest species of the genus; cultivated in England (Hillier). z8 # ⊕ ⌘

C. limetta Risso. Sweet Lemon. Small tree; leaves acute ovate, 8—10 cm long, petiole short, not winged or only slightly so; fruits lemon-shaped, light yellow, with a 2 cm wide, hemispherical, protruding tip, pulp sweet/sour, but not sweet. Occasionally found in gardens of the Mediterranean region. z9 Plate 117. # ✕

C. limon (L.) Burm. Lemon. Small tree, 2—7 m high, branches long and irregular with short, thick, stiff thorns; leaves oblong-ovate, acute, flat toothed, petiole short, not winged or only very narrowly so, but distinctly separated from the blade; flowers solitary or in small clusters in the leaf axils, appearing the whole year, reddish in bud, petals white above, reddish beneath; fruits lemon-shaped, with short, broad, pro-

truding tips, 7—15 cm long and 5—7 cm wide, with 8—10 segments, lemon-yellow when ripe, rind glandular punctate, often more or less rough, medium thick, fruit pulp abundant, very sour. ICS 2845; BC 974 (= *C. limonia* Osbeck; *C. limonium* Risso; *C. medica* var. *limon* L.). Asia. 1648. z9 Fig. 245. # ⊕ ⌘ ✕

C. maxima (Burm.) Merr. Shaddock, Pummelo. Large, round crowned tree, regularly branched, thorns (when present) thin, blunt and bowed, young twigs pubescent; leaves large, ovate-elliptic, acute, base rounded, dark green above, pubescent beneath, petioles broad winged and more or less cordate; flowers axillary, solitary or in small clusters, white in bud, petals also white on both sides; fruit very large, globose, broad globose or broad pear-shaped, 10—15 cm wide and becoming 3kg in weight, rind thick, light lemon-yellow when ripe, seeds large, flat, numerous, rugose. BC 975; ICS 2848 (= *C. grandis* Osbeck; *C. decumana* L.). Originating in Polynesia. 1722. z9 Fig. 245. # ⊕ ⌘ ✕

C. medica L. Citron. Shrub or small tree, 4—5 m high, branches long, irregular, with short, thick, stiff thorns; leaves oblong, 10—18 cm long, obtuse, toothed, petiole not winged and not separated from the blade; flowers large, usually reddish in bud, usually in terminal panicles or also in axillary clusters, petals large, white above, reddish-purple beneath; fruit large, ellipsoid to oblong, 15—30 cm long and 10—15 cm wide, with apex obtuse, often with a rough rind, lemon-yellow when ripe, very thick, fragrant, fruit pulp white, usually sour. ICS 2843. Originating in Asia; cultivated today in the East Indies and the Mediterranean region, but mainly on Corsica. The 2.5kg heavy fruits are harvested unripe, and the very thick rind candied to produce a confection. z9 Fig. 245. # ⊕ ⌘ ✕

Included here is the var. **sacrodactylis** (Nooten) Swingle. Finger-Orange or Buddhafinger, the fruits of which have the segments separated down to half their length and protruding distinctly, like fingers; fruits very fragrant and much valued in Japan and China. ICS 2844; BC 973. z9 Fig. 245. # ⊕ ⌘ ✕

C. paradisi Macf. Grapefruit. Very similar to *C. maxima*, but the branches thinner and not pubescent; leaves totally glabrous beneath, petiole broad winged; fruits smaller, more juicy, yellow to slightly orange (according to cultivar), rind thin, fruit pulp light yellow to reddish, very juicy. China; cultivated today primarily in the USA and Israel. z9 # ⊕ ⌘ ✕

C. reticulata Blanco. Mandarin. Shrub to small tree, branches thin; leaves ovate, petiole only narrowly winged; fruits flat, rounded, yellow-orange or red-orange, rind easily peeled, fruit pulp very sweet and aromatic, with small seeds. ICS 2851 (*C. nobilis* André non Lour.). SE. Asia; cultivated in the Mediterranean region, East Asia, India, USA and S. America. z9 Plate 117. # ⊕ ⌘ ✕

Also included here are the **Clementines**, a self-sterile form, therefore seedless, ripening already in October-December; cultivated primarily in N. Africa. The **Tangerines** also belong to this group, distinguished by the large fruits, broad ovate leaves and reddish fruits.

C. sinensis (L.) Pers. Orange. Tree, 8–13 m, round crowned, regularly branched, thorns thin (when present), rather blunt and bowed; leaves medium sized, acute, base round, petiole narrow winged, distinctly separated from the blade and branch; flowers medium sized, white in bud, petals white, on both sides, very fragrant; fruit globose to somewhat ellipsoid, usually with 10–12 segments, fruit pulp abundant, sweet, orange, rind varying in thickness according to cultivar. BC 977; ICS 2847. China. 1595. Cultivated worldwide, especially in the USA, also in Brazil, Japan, Spain and Italy. z9 Fig. 245. #⊕ ⌀ ✗

C. wilsonii Tanaka. Tree in its habitat, 9–11 m high, thorny, glabrous; leaves elliptic-oblong, 8–25 mm long, 5–15 mm wide, apex long acuminate or somewhat rounded, entire or somewhat wavy dentate, base broad cuneate, petiole obcordate winged, 3–8 mm long; flowers solitary or fascicled, occasionally in short racemes, calyx cup-shaped, with 5 triangular lobes, petals obovate-oblong, with elevated venation; stamens numerous, filaments connate; fruits globose, with thick, rough rind. ICS 2849. China; cultivated in the Yangtse Valley. z9 Fig 246. #

Much literature is available on *Citrus* cultivation to which the reader is referred.

Lit. Swingle, W. T.: *Citrus* L.; in C. S. Sargent, Plantae

Fig. 246. *Citrus wilsonii* (from ICS)

Wilsonianae, II, 141–149, 1916 ● Swingle, W. T.: *Citrus*; in L. H. Bailey, Standard Cyclopedia of Horticulture, 799–785, 1950 ● Schuett, P.: Weltwirtschaftspflanzen; Berlin 1972 ● Tanaka, T.: Species problem in *Citrus*; Revisio Aurantiacearum IX: 1–152; 1954.

CLADOTHAMNUS Bong. — ERICACEAE

Monotypic genus. Deciduous shrubs, winter buds with 2–3 scales, leaves alternate, nearly sessile; flowers terminal, regular, normally solitary, nodding; sepals 5, narrow oblong, green; petals 5, oblong, pink; stamens 10; anthers opening by a short slit; style thin, shorter than the petals; fruit a 5–6 chambered, many seeded capsule. — 1 species in NW. America.

Cladothamnus pyrolaeflorus Bong. Deciduous shrub, densely upright branched, 1(3) m high, branches red-brown, angular, glabrous; leaves nearly sessile, oval-oblong, 3–6 cm long, entire with a small tip; flowers solitary, petals pink, yellow tipped, some 2 cm wide, June. GF 10: 216; DL 1: 436; BM 8353. Alaska to Oregon. 1910. Quite hardy but rare in cultivation. z5 Fig. 247. **H**

CLADRASTIS Raf. - Yellow-wood — LEGUMINOSAE

Deciduous trees or shrubs; branches break easily; leaves alternate, unevenly pinnate; leaflets either few and large or numerous and smaller; flowers white or light pink, in terminal and axillary panicled racemes, pendulous or erect; stamens distinct or nearly so; ovaries sessile or stalked; fruit a linear, flat compressed, leathery or thin pod. — 4 species in N. America and E. Asia.

Cladrastis lutea (Michx. f.) K. Koch. Tree, 5 to 10 m high, usually becoming multistemmed just above the ground, broad crowned, branches somewhat nodding, bark smooth, wood yellow; leaflets 7–9, ovate-elliptic,

Fig. 247. *Cladothamnus pirolaeflorus* (from Bong.)

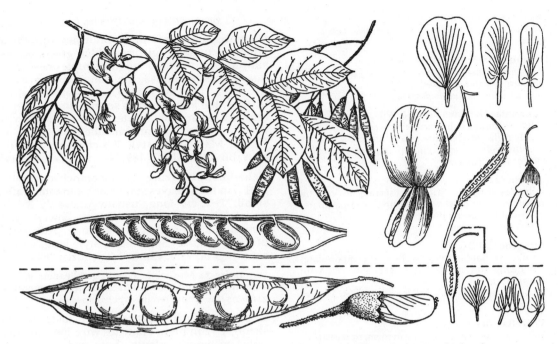

Fig. 248. **Cladrastis.** Above *C. lutea*, below *C. platycarpa* (from Sargent and others)

glabrous, light green, gold-yellow in fall; flowers white, in 20—40 cm long, pendulous racemes, somewhat fragrant, May—June. SS 119—120; BB 2046; HM 1303; BM 7767 (= *C. tinctoria* Raf.; *Virgil lutea* Michx. f.). SE. USA. 1812. Quite hardy and wonderful flowering tree. z3 Fig. 248. ⊕ ⌀

'Rosea'. Flowers like that of the species, but light pink. The parent plant may be found at the Perkins Institute for the Blind, Cambridge, Mass., USA. ⊕ ⌀

C. platycarpa (Maxim.) Makino. Tall tree, branches glabrous; leaflets 7—15, ovate to lanceolate, 5—10 cm long, acuminate, green beneath, reticulate venation, appressed pubescence, with stipules; flowers in erect (important for identification!), 15 cm long racemes, white with a yellow basal spot, June; pod 5 cm long, winged all around. KIF 1: 76. Japan. 1919. Easily identified by the small stipule on each individual leaflet. z7 Fig. 248. ⊕

C. sinensis Hemsl. Tree, to 15 m high; leaflets normally

9—13 (important for identification!), oblong-lanceolate, 5—10 cm long, gray-green beneath, rachis pubescent; flowers reddish-white, in erect (important for identification!) panicles, June—July; pod 3—6 cm long, glabrous, not winged. BM 9040; BS 1:48; LF 181. Central and W. China. 1901. Hardy. z6 ⊕

C. wilsonii Takeda. Tree, to 10 m, young branches reddish-gray, tips of the current year's growth always somewhat expanded, brown pubescent and with many lenticels; leaflets 7—9, oblong-ovate, 7 cm long, glossy dark green above with concave venation, bluish with pubescent venation beneath, petiole 10 mm long, dense yellow-brown pubescent; flowers white, in terminal panicled racemes, 12—18 cm long; pod straight, flat, very thin, with 1—6 seeds. LF 182. Central China. 1907. Hardy. z6 ⊕

Beautiful for large parks and gardens; requires a fertile soil. Somewhat susceptible to frost damage when young, although quite hardy later.

CLEMATIS L. — RANUNCULACEAE

Deciduous or evergreen, usually high climbing vines or erect subshrubs or perennials; leaves opposite, simple, trifoliate or pinnate, leaf petiole often twisted; flowers campanulate to disc form, solitary or in panicles; sepals 4 or more, resembling the petals; fruits usually in silky pubescent seed heads of single seeds with hairy styles. — 250 species in nearly all parts of the world.

In cultivation, the large flowering cultivars are more important than the wild species; please refer to the list on p. 379.

Outline of the genus *Clematis* including a summary of the mentioned species

Section I. *Viorna* (Reichenb.) Prantl
    Flowers never fully open, usually campanulate, tubular or urceolate; sepals usually 4, reflexed at the tips; stamens erect, usually pubescent;

Series 1. **Crispae** Prantl
    Leaves or leaflets entire; flowers solitary or grouped 2—3; stamen filaments pubescent; subshrubs:
        C. adisonii, albicoma, crispa, divaricata, douglasii, fre-

monti, fusca, integrifolia, ochroleuca, pitcheri, pratti, pseudococcinea, reticulata, scottii, texensis, versicolor, viorna

Series 2. Tubulosae (Decne.) Rehd. & Wils.
Non climbing subshrub; leaves trifoliate, leaflets serrate; flowers tubular, reflexed:
    C. heracleifoia, ranunculoides, stans

Series 3. Connatae (Koehne) Rehd. & Wils.
Vines; leaves simple or bipinnate; flowers tubular; sepals slightly reflexed at the tips; stamens pubescent:
    C. aethusifolia, buchananiana, connata, lasiandra, rehdereana, veitchiana

Series 4. Cirrhosae Prantl
Vines; leaves simple or trifoliate, serrate; flowers on the previous year's wood, nodding, campanulate, with an involucre under the sepals:
    C. cirrhosa, napaulensis

Section II. Atragene (L.) DC.
Leaves trifoliate or doubly trifoliate; flowers campanulate, solitary, nodding, on the previous year's wood, with petaloid staminodes:
    C. alpina, koreana, macropetala, occidentalis, pseudo-alpina

Section II. Viticella (Moench) DC.
Strong growing vine; leaves varying in form; flowers 1–3, broadly campanulate or disc form, large; sepals 4–8; stamens glabrous:
    C. campaniflora, durandii, eriostemon, florida, francofurtensis, guascoi, jackmanii, lanuginosa, lawsoniana, patens, viticella

Section IV. Flammula DC.
Usually a high climbing shrub; leaves simple to bipinnate; flowers white, pink or yellow, sepals valvate, usually with a narrow limb; stamens protruding; nectaries absent;

Series 1. Montanae (Schneid.) Rehd.
Woody climber; leaves trifoliate or pinnate, leaflets serrate; flowers attractive, white or pink, appearing on older wood:
    C. barbellata, chrysocoma, gracilifolia, montana, vedrariensis

Series 2. Rectae Prantl
Upright perennials or climbers; leaves simple to bipinnate; flowers usually white, on young branches in terminal and axillary panicles; sepals with a narrow limb:
    C. apiifolia, armandii, aromatica, chinensis, delavayi, dioscoreifolia, fargesii, fasciculiflora, finetiana, flammula, fruticosa, jeuneiana, maximowicziana, meyeniana, pierotii, quinquefoliolata, recta, songarica, uncinata

Series 3. Hexapetalea
Woody climbing vines; leaves evergreen; sepals usually 6. Only hardy in mild climates:
    C. afoliata, colensoi, paniculata

Series 4. Vitalbae Prantl
Woody climbing shrubs; leaves always compound; flowers bisexual or dioecious, white, small:
    C. brevicaudata, grata, jouiniana, ligusticifolia, virginiana, vitalba

Series 5. Orientales Prantl
Woody climbing vines; leaves trifoliate or simple to bipinnate; flowers yellow, usually solitary:

C. glauca, orientalis, serratifolia, tangutica

Clematis addisonii Britt. Branches upright at first, later procumbent, glabrous, blue-green; leaves partly simple, partly compound, the simple ones broad ovate, nearly sessile, obtuse, the compound leaves developing later, usually with 4, occasionally with 6 oval leaflets, the lower leaflets several times larger than the others; flowers solitary, terminal and axillary, purple, nodding, sepals ovate, inclined together, apex reflexed, May–June, style 2.5 cm long, brown pubescent. BB 1587; NBB 2: 189. N. Carolina to Georgia. z6

C. aethusifolia Trucz. Thinly branched, climbing vine 1–1.5 m high; leaves simple or bipinnate, leaflets 5–9, small, 1–2 cm long, usually unevenly 3 lobed and deeply incised, bright green; flowers yellowish, campanulate, nodding, 1.5 cm long, axillary in groups of 1–3, August–September, style long, white pubescent. ICS 1479. N. China, Manchuria. 1855. z5?

var. **latisecta** Maxim. Leaves larger, leaflets to 4 cm long, lobes more round to oval. BM 6542. More frequently found in gardens than the often mislabeled species.

C. afoliata Buch. Erratically branched, nearly leafless shrub, 1–2 m high, branches wire-like, striped; leaves only on young plants, later reduced to only the petioles, occasionally with 3 tiny leaflets; flowers greenish-white, 2 cm wide, with 4 tubular-campanulate inward leaning sepals, fragrant, May. NF 11: 134; BM 8686; BS 1: Pl. 21. New Zealand. z8 Plate 121.

C. albicoma Wherry. Resembling *C. ochroleuca*, but branching narrowly upright, 30–60 cm high, pubescent when young, eventually glabrous; leaves ovate, entire, 4–5 cm long, eventually with distinct reticulate venation and glabrous; flowers solitary at the branch tips, purple, nodding, campanulate, apex reflexed, May–June; seed 'tail' 2.5 to 3 cm long, short white pubescent. BB 1589; NBB 2: 186 (= *C. ovata* sensu Brit. & Br.). NE. USA. z5

C. alpina (L.) Mill. Climbing to 2 m high; leaves usually doubly trifoliate (or simply trifoliate on a form of var. *ochotensis*), leaflets lanceolate to oblong-lanceolate or narrow ovate; sepals 3.5–6 cm long, sterile staminodes always present, narrow or broad spathulate.

Including 3 Varieties:

var. **alpina**. Leaves regularly finely serrate; sepals usually violet-blue, seldom light blue, reddish-violet or white, oblong-lanceolate, long acuminate, outer staminodes broad spathulate, the upper portion circular, often surpassing the fertile stamens in length, apex usually rounded, occasionally obtuse. HM Pl. 114. Alps, from SE. France to Austria, Apennines, Carpathians and the Northern Balkan Mountains. z5 Plate 121. ⊕

var. **sibirica** (L.) Schneid. Leaflets coarser and more irregularly serrate than those of var. *alpina*; sepals white, seldom with slight blue tones, elliptic-lanceolate, long acuminate, outer staminodes spathulate, narrower than var. *alpina* and more densely pubescent, not completely covering the fertile stamens, generally blunt tipped. BM 1951; GFl 1870: Pl. 6; MCL 57 (= *C. sibirica* [L.] Mill.). From N. Norway and Finland to E. Siberia, middle Urals and Manchuria. z2 ⊕

Fig. 249. From left to right: *Clematis armandii*; *C. chrysosoma*; *C. montana* (from ICS)

var. **ochotensis** (Pall.) S. Wats. Leaves and leaflets nearly like those of var. *sibirica*; sepals violet-blue, more acute, staminodes narrow to broad spathulate, densely pubescent, apexes usually rounded. MF 1655 (= *C. ochotensis* [Pall.] Poir.; *C. platysepala* [Trautv. & Mey.] Hand.-Mazz.). Korea and Japan, E. Siberia, Sachalin and Kamchatka. Fig. 256. z5 ⊕

Also includes the following cultivars:

'Bluebell' (Jackman 1956). Blue, very similar to 'Pamela Jackman', but surpassed by the latter. ⊕

'Columbine' (Markham, around 1937). Flowers a soft lavender-blue, sepals very long and acute, inclined inward in a campanulate form. LLC 92. ⊕

'Francis Rivis' (C. Morris 1966). Sepals to 5 cm long and 2 cm wide, ovate, deep blue, staminodes 1.5 cm long, 2–3 mm wide. JRHS 1966: 181 (= *C. alpina thibetica* Hort.). Belongs to var. *ochotensis*. ⊕

'Gravetye Form' (Markham 1935). Selection from var. *sibirica* with much larger, cream-yellow flowers, flowers very early, March. ⊕

'Pamela Jackman' (Jackman 1960). Flowers to 7 cm wide, deep azure-blue, staminodes also bluish, sepals 4.5 cm long, 1.5 cm wide. ⊕

'Pauline' (Washfield Nurseries 1970). Dark blue. ⊕

'Ruby' (Markham 1937). Amethyst-lilac, staminodes white, unfortunately the flowers are mostly hidden by the foliage. ⊕

Since the botanical classification of the cultivars is occasionally confused, see also the cultivars of *C. macropetala*.

C. apiifolia DC. Shrub, climbing to 3 m high; leaves usually trifoliate or pinnate with 5 leaflets, these broad ovate to more lanceolate, deeply incised and often 3 lobed; flowers white, small, 1.5 cm wide, in axillary panicles, September–October, sepals pubescent on both sides. NF 1: 108; ICS 1501; MJ 1650. Central China, Japan. 1869. Similar to *C. vitalba*, but without attractive fruit clusters and more difficult to grow. z7

C. armandii Franch. Evergreen vine, climbing to 5 m high; leaves trifoliate, oblong-lanceolate, 8–12 cm long, tough leathery, glossy above; flowers white, 3–6 cm wide, in axillary cymes on the previous year's wood, March–April, sepals 4–6. BM 8587; LLC 93. Central and W. China. 1907. Gorgeous evergreen climber for very mild areas. z8 Fig. 249. # ⊕ ∅

'Apple Blossom'. Leaves bronze-green, especially when young; flowers light pink. # ⊕ ∅

'Snowdrift'. Leaves dark green, leaflets long acuminate; flowers pure white, larger and more numerous than on the species (Jackman's catalogue). Plate 122. # ∅

C. × aromatica Lenné & Koch (*C. flammula* × *C. integrifolia*). Subshrub, erect, 0.5–2 m high, not climbing; leaves simple, trilobed to pinnate, leaflets ovate to broad oval, entire, 2.5–3 cm long, glabrous; flowers dark violet, 4 cm wide, fragrant, long stalked, in loose, terminal cymes, July–fall, sepals 4, stamen filaments pubescent at the tips, white or yellow. LCl 9 (= *C. "coerulea odorata"* Hort.). 1845. Very attractive, hardy plant. z6 ⊕

C. barbellata Edgew. Vine, branches glabrous or nearly so, cylindrical; leaves trifoliate, leaflets oval-lanceolate, abundantly lobed and irregularly sharply serrate; flowers solitary, axillary, stalks shorter than the leaf petioles at first, sepals 2.5 cm long, lanceolate, pubescent, dull purple, somewhat outspread, May–June. FS 956. W. Himalaya, 2600–4000 m (in cultivation at the Edinburgh Botanic Garden.) z6 ⊕

Much like *C. montana* in appearance but differing in the flower color.

C. brevicaudata DC. Strong growing and high climbing; closely related to *C. vitalba*, but with much smaller fruits; less bipinnate, pinnae with 5–7 leaflets (the lower ones with 3), occasionally also only 3 lobed, leaflets 3–7 cm long, oval-oblong, coarsely dentate or occasionally entire, glabrous or pubescent; flowers white, to 2 cm wide, in axillary cymes, grouped into large, terminal panicles, July–August; fruits with short, feathery 'tails', heads 3 cm wide. GF 5: 139; ICS 1504; MJ 1651. Manchuria to W. China. z5

C. buchananiana DC. Strong growing, pubescent; closely related to *C. rehderiana*, but with leaflets normally 5, occasionally 3 or 7, coarsely dentate, occasionally slightly 3 lobed; flowers 2–3 cm long, tubular, in panicles, sepals tomentose and ribbed outside, inside finely pubescent. Himalaya. z6

C. campaniflora Brot. Climbing subshrub, appearing somewhat like a weak growing *C. viticella*, climbing 2(5) m high, branches very thin; leaves bipinnate or doubly trifoliate, leaflets simple or lobed; flowers more shell-like (not campanulate), solitary or grouped, but generally distributed over the entire plant, white, violet traces, sepals 4, 1 cm long, obovate, abruptly acuminate, stamen filaments nearly glabrous, style glabrous or tomentose, June–July, fragrant. LCl 8. Portugal. 1820. Hardy and attractive. z6 Fig. 257. ⊕

C. chinensis Osbeck. Strong growing, high climbing, branches furrowed, glabrous except for the pubescent nodes; leaves pinnate, leaflets 5, ovate, base usually cordate, 3–5 veined, 3–6 cm long, nearly completely glabrous beneath; flowers white, resembling *C. vitalba*, sepals 4, very narrow, margins pubescent, style pubescent, 2.5–3 cm long, September–October. ICS 1491. China. 1900. Best in warm locations because it blooms late. z6

C. chrysocoma Franch. Growth either shrubby or climbing to 2 m high, branches, leaves and flower stalks dense yellowish pubescent; leaves trifoliate, leaflets variable, broad ovate to narrow-obovate, 3–6 cm long, lobed or coarsely dentate; flowers resembling those of *C. montana*, but appearing over 2–3 periods one after the other, appearing first in June on older wood, then in August–September on young branches, sepals 4, elliptic, white with a trace of pink, outside dense silky pubescent. BM 8395; LCC 72; ICS 1498. China, Yunnan. Around 1900. z7 Fig. 249. ⊕

Best known is the var. **sericea** (Franch.) Schneid. Growing to 6 m high; leaves trifoliate, leaflets ovate, coarsely serrate, 2.5–7 cm long, yellowish silky pubescent beneath (important for identification!); flowers pure white, grouped 1–2 axillary on older wood, May, 5–6 cm wide, sepals outside yellowish silky pubescent, obovate. BS 1: Pl. 25; MCL 100 (= *C. spooneri* Rehd. & Wils.). China. 1909. Exceptionally popular in England and much hardier than the species. z6 Plate 122. ⊕

C. cirrhose L. Evergreen, climbing to 3 m high, young twigs silky pubescent; leaves simple, ovate, 2–4 cm long, coarsely crenate to 3 lobed, very glossy above; flowers yellowish-white, broadly campanulate, 3–5 cm wide, 1–2 axillary, January–March, sepals softly pubescent ouside, originating from a cuplike involucre, like var. *balearica*. BM 1070; DRHS 500. Spain, Algeria, Palestine. 1590. z8 # ⊕

var. **balearica** (Rich.) Willk. & Lange. Leaves nearly fern-like,

finely divided, the larger leaflets deeply and doubly serrate, the smaller ones 3–5 lobed, the smallest ones only linear, dark green in summer, bronze-purple in winter, leaves of the non-blooming branches more distinctly divided than those of the flowering branches; flowers campanulate, yellowish-white, inside brown-red spotted, solitary, January–March, often blooming in late fall, involucre under the sepals composed of 2 connate bracts, as in the species. Bm 959 (= *C. balearica* Rich.; *C. calyciona* Ait.). Corsica, Balearic Islands. 1783. z8 # ⊕

C. colensoi Hook. f. Tall growing, evergreen climber, branches thin, much branched, somewhat pubescent when young; leaves triangular in outline, 7 cm long, 8 cm wide, eventually also trifoliate, leaflets pinnate or pinnatisect, the lobes generally rounded at the apex; flowers in the leaf axils, grouped 10 together, greenish (important for identification!), sepals usually 6, narrow lanceolate, both sides dense silky pubescent, May–June. BMns 250. New Zealand. Cultivated in England. z8 # ⊕

C. connata DC. Climbing to 8 m high, branches glabrous; leaves pinnate, leaflets 3–7, oval-oblong, 5–12 cm long, regularly coarsely dentate or 1–3 lobed; flowers campanulate, nodding, 2 cm long, light yellow tips reflexed, in 8–12 cm long panicles, sepals 4, both sides short pubescent, August–October; styles with feathery 'tails'. SW. China, Himalaya. z6

C. crispa L. Climbing shrub, 1(2) m high, branches generally dying back to the ground annually; leaves simple, pinnately divided or trifoliate, leaflets oval-lanceolate, entire or lobed, 4–8 cm long; flowers solitary, terminal, long stalked, nodding, campanulate, red-violet, 2–4 cm long, scent like oranges, June to September, sepals with a whitish, wavy margin, bases arranged in campanulate fashion, apexes flared wide; styles only slightly feathery. BB 1583; RFW 128; LCl 13 (= *C. simsii* Sweet). Eastern N. America. 1726. z6 Fig. 257.

'**Distorta**'. Like the species, but with sepals loosely curved. LCl 11 (= *C. distorta* Lav.).

C. delavayi Franch. Erect shrub, to 1.5 m high, resembling a white flowering *Potentilla* more than a *Clematis*; leaves pinnate, 3–10 cm long, leaflets sessile, ovate, only 1–2 cm long, dark green above, silvery-white beneath and densely silky pubescent; flowers grouped 3–6 in terminal cymes, white, 2–3 cm wide, sepals 4–6, obovate, outside densely pubescent, July–August. Mot 6; ICS 1488. China. 1908. Hardy. z5

C. dioscoreifolia (Lév. & Vaniot) Rehd. The species is seldom found in cultivation and distinguished from its better known varieties in the usually ovate leaflets, cordate at the base and rounded at the apex, often emarginate on flowering branches, often also thickish; sepals wider, ovate-oblong. Korea. 1911. var. *robusta*, see: *C. maximowicziana*.

C. × divaricata Jacq. (*C. ? integrifolia × C. viorna*). Shrub, upright, not climbing; leaves pinnate or simple and irregularly, deeply lobed, leaflets 3–7, sessile, of-

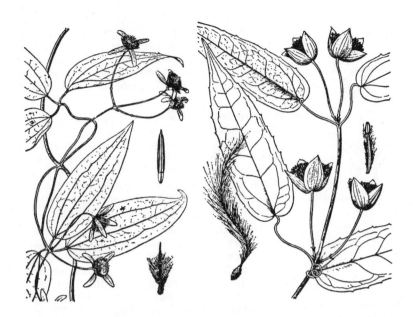

Fig. 250. Left *Clematis
finetiana*, right *C. henryi*
(from ICS)

ten decurrent, glabrous beneath; flowers nodding, campanulate, reddish-lilac, 2.5 cm long, short stalked, sepals widespread, apical half with a marginal limb, styles feathery, June–July. Gw 1910: 562 (= *C. integrifolia* pinnata Hort.). Before 1805. Hardy. z6

C. douglasii Hook. Similar in appearance to *C. integrifolia*, 0.5 m high, branches and flower stalks angular and furrowed; leaves bipinnate or doubly trifoliate, leaflet narrow-linear to lanceolate; flowers standing above the foliage, solitary, terminal, tubular or campanulate, 2.5 cm long, deep purple, sepals 4, oblong, reflexed, lighter outside, May. N. America. 1881. Hardy. z6

C. × durandii Durand. (= *C. jackmanii* × *C. integrifolia*). Shrub, erect, not climbing, 1.2–1.8 m high; leaves simple, ovate, 8–12 cm long, petiole 2–5 cm long; flowers usually in 3's, dark violet-blue, 8–12 dcm wide, sepals 4(6), widespread or reflexed, obovate, limb somewhat undulate, stamen filaments pubescent, with shaggy tips, June–September. Gw 17: 108. Before 1870. Attractive; often used for forcing. Hardy. z6–7 Plate 123. ⊕

'Pallida'. Flowers lighter, pink toned. MCl 7. Very pretty. ⊕

C. × eriostemon Dcne. (*C. integrifolia* × *C. viticella*). Shrubby, to 3 m high, branches ornamental, striped, brown, glabrous or somewhat pubescent, with foliage extending to the ground; leaves pinnate, usually with 7 leaflets, these elliptic, entire, acute, terminal leaflets usually somewhat lobed, dark green, petiole 2–4 cm; flowers in terminal groups of 1–3, flowers abundantly, with 4 sepals, these spathulate, with small tips, 4 cm long and 2.5 cm wide, distinctly 3 veined, dark violet to bluish, in a rather flattened arrangement, tips reflexed, summer; seeds resembling those of *C. viticella*, but with a hairy 'tail' 2–3 cm long. LCl 12; Mot 7 (not

typical!). Originated in France around 1830, hybridizer unknown. z5-6

Including 3 cultivars:

'Bergeronii'. To 3 m high, branches striped, finely pubescent; leaves tougher than the type, leaflets usually broad oval, stalked, the lowest pair being asymmetrical, very large, nearly sessile; flowers terminal and axillary, grouped 1–3, nearly campanulate, sepals spathulate-cuneate, to 3 cm long, 15 mm wide, violet-pink; fruit clusters nearly globular, 3–5 cm wide, seed with a long hairy 'tail'. LCl 10 (= *C. bergeronii* Lav.). Origin unknown. 1884. ⊕

'Hendersonii'. To 2.5 m high, branches thin, dying back to the ground in winter, resembling *C. viticella* in appearance, but not climbing; flowers and fruits resembling *C. integrifolia*, sepals purple-blue, flowers 5–6 cm wide, very abundant, somewhat fragrant, July–September. Bredder, Henderson, St. John's Wood, England. Around 1830. Long cultivated and valued in England, a perennial. ⊕

'Intermedia'. Very similar to 'Hendersonii', but the branches stouter and shorter; flowers bear more resemblance to *C. integrifolia*, bluer. ⊕

C. fargesii Franch. Climbing to 6 m high; leaves bipinnate, with 5–7 leaflets, these 2–5 cm long, ovate, deeply serrate or lobed, somewhat silky pubescent; flowers pure white, grouped 1–3 on 7–18 cm long stalks, sepals usually 6, outside yellowish, pubescent, June to September. BM 8702 (as *C. fargesii* var. *souliei*, closely resemblig the species). China. 1911. z6 ⊕

C. fasciculiflora Franch. Evergreen, climbing to 6 m high, resembling *C. armandii*; leaflets 3, oval-oblong, 4–10 cm long; flowers yellowish-white, outside woolly pubescent, in dense, axillary clusters on 1–2 cm long, common stalk, anthers much shorter than the filaments; fruits glabrous. SW. China. 1910. z8 # ⊕

C. finetiana Lév. & Vaniot. Semi-evergreen vine,

Fig. 251. *Clematis fusca* (from Lavallee)

climbing to 4 m high, branches glabrous; leaflets 3, on 7 cm long stalks, narrow ovate, 3–7 cm long, acute, entire, base cordate or round, 3 veined, thin, leather-like; flowers 3 in axillary cymes, with small, lanceolate bracts, sepals whitish inside, greenish outside, nearly glabrous, 1.5 cm long, June. BM 8655; ICS 1495 (= *C. pavoliniana* Pamp.). China. 1908. z8 Fig. 250 #

C. flammula L. Climbing 2–5 m high, often only a subshrub; leaves usually bipinnate, pinna trifoliate, leaflets usually ovate, 2–5 cm long, entire or lobed, fresh green; flowers white, 2–3 cm wide, scent like bitter almonds, in many flowered panicles, sepals 4, obtuse, otherwise like *C. recta*, August–October; fruits rounded at the base. HM 665; HF 986; MCL 76. Mediterranean region to Persia (Iran). 1590. z7 ✥

C. florida Thunb. Climbing to 4 m high, often semi-evergreen; leaves usually doubly trifoliate, leaflets ovate, 2–5 cm long, entire or with 1–2 lobes or teeth; flowers solitary, axillary, yellowish-white, ventral side greenish striped, 5–8 cm wide, flat, sepals 4–8, June–July. BM 834. China, probably also Japan. 1776. The species is generally used for hybridizing and not often found in cultivation. The hybrids are better performers and more winter hardy. z7 Fig. 252. ✥

'Sieboldii'. Sepals usually 6, white, many anthers becoming purple colored staminodes, only half as large as the sepals, arranged in rosettes. FS 487; MCl 77 (= var. *bicolor* Lind.). Especially attractive. z7 ✥

C. × francofurtensis Rinz (*C. florida* × *C. viticella*). Vine, similar to *C. viticella*; leaves bipinnate, leaflets ovate, acute, somewhat pubescent beneath; flowers large, sepals 4–6, purple, inside nearly pure white, venation distinctly reticulate, anthers violet. FS 487; LCl 6 (= *C. venosa* [Carr.] K. Koch; *C. florida* venosa Lav.). 1860. Not to be confused with *C. guascoi* Lem.! z6 ✥

C. fremontii Wats. A perennial, 0.3 to 0.5 m high,

usually somewhat branched, long haired especially at the nodes; leaves simple, ovate, 3–10 cm long, tough, entire, sessile, with distinct reticulate venaton; flowers solitary, terminal, nodding, 2.5 cm long, sepals 4, purple, thick, apexes reflexed, margin tomentose, July–August. BB 1590; NBB 2:186; GF 3: 381. NW. America. z5?

C. fruticosa Turcz. Closely related to *C. recta*; subshrub, 50 cm high, densely branched, branches brown; leaves lanceolate, entire or deeply dentate, dark green, glabrous; flowers grouped 1–4, sepals 4, widespread, yellow, 2 cm long, August (= *C. recta* f. *fruticosa* O. Ktze.). Central Asia to Mongolia and China, W. Szechwan, 3000 m high in the mountains in dry spots. Hardy and very attractive. z4 Plate 75, 130; Fig. 255

C. fusca Turcz. Subshrub, climbing 2(3) m high, young branches finely pubescent, angular; leaves pinnate, 15–20 cm long, leaflets 5–7, terminal leaflet often absent, ovate, 3–6 cm long, acute, glabrous or pubescent beneath; flowers solitary, nodding, urceolate, outside dense red-brown pubescent, violet inside, sepals reflexed at the apex, June–August. LCl 20; ICS 1470. NE. Asia. Attractive and hardy. 1860. z5 Fig. 251. ✥

var. **violacea** Maxim. Flowers violet; less pubescent. GF 13: 455. Manchuria.

C. glauca Willd. Climbing to 2.5(–4) m high, branches glabrous, thin; leaves pinnate or bipinnate, leaflets elliptic to lanceolate, 2–5 cm long, blue-green on both sides, 2–3 lobed; flowers yellow, 4 cm wide, grouped 1(2) on 3–8 cm long stalks, axillary, August–September, sepals elliptic, broadly campanulate at first, eventually widely spread, but not reflexed, both sides glabrous (important for identification!). RH 1890: W. China to Siberia. 1752. Hardy. z4 ✥ ⚭

Much confused with *C. orientalis*, but easily differentiated:
C. glauca: Sepals glabrous on both sides, broadly campanulate, eventually widely spread, but not reflexed.
C. orientalis: Sepals usually pubescent on both sides, broadly campanulate, eventually distinctly backward curving.

Both with attractive fruits.

var. **akebioides** (Maxim.) Rehd. & Wils. Stoloniferous; leaves ovate to ovate-lanceolate, 2–3 lobed and irregularly crenate; flowers yellow with bronze-brown middle. W. China. 1904.

f. **phaeantha** Rehd. A form of the above; flowers a dull violet outside. 1918.

C. gouriana Roxb. Similar to *C. vitalba*, but with 5–7 leaflets, these oval-oblong, 3–8 cm long, long acuminate, often entire, base normally nearly cordate, petiolules 5–10 mm long; flowers white, 1.5–2 cm wide. Himalaya, China. 1901. z6 Plate 123.

C. gracilifolia Rehd. & Wils. Climbing to 4 m high, branches striped, gray, with appressed pubescence when young; leaves pinnate, leaflets 5–7, nearly sessile, 1–2 cm long, acute, 3 lobed or with a few large teeth, sparsely pubescent; flowers in clusters of 1–4 in the leaf axils, white, 3–4 cm wide, on 3–5 cm long, pubescent stalks, June. W. China. 1910. Very similar to *C. montana*, but more ornamental. Hardy. z5 ⊕

C. grata Wall. Very similar to *C. vitalba*, also high climbing, but with leaves pubescent on both sides (or only beneath), young branches pubescent; leaves pinnate, leaflets usually 5, broad ovate, 3–6 cm long, coarsely and deeply dentate; flowers white, 2 cm wide, in dense terminal and axillary panicles, sepals densely pubescent ouside, glabrous inside, buds obovoid, September to October, styles long, feathery. Himalaya. Existence in cultivation doubtful. See also *C. jouiniana*. ⊕ ⚭

var. **argentilucida** (Lév. & Vaniot) Rehd. Growth stronger, reaching 5–7 m high in a single year under favorable conditions, apex silvery pubescent; leaflets often only 3, large than those of the species, 5–9 cm long, with a few large teeth, eventually glabrous above; flowers in 25–30 cm long panicles on the previous year's wood, May–June, fragrant, white (= var. *grandidentata* Rehd. & Wils.). Central and W. China. 1907. Hardy and very attractive. ⊕ ⚭

C. × guascoi Lem. (*C. patens* × *C. viticella*). High climbing vine, young branches pubescent; leaflets usually 5, glabrous or nearly so; flowers solitary, to 8 cm wide, with 4–6 obovate, 3 veined, violet-red sepals, these tomentose outside, styles pubescent. LCl 7 (= *C. francofurtensis* Lav. non Rinz). Before 1857. z6 ⊕

Included here are several large flowering cultivars, although seldom found in cultivation today, i.e.: **'Minos'**, blue with a trace of carmine-red; **'Albert Victor'**, lavender-blue with a lighter limb; **'Fair Rosamond'**, pink-white; **'Maiden Blush'**, bluish-white; **'The Queen'**, bluish-lilac.

C. henryi Oliv. Vine, 2–4 m high; leaves simple, oval-oblong, long acuminate, 10–12 cm long, base flattened cordate, margin with tiny, sparsely arranged teeth, veins 5, petiole 3–5 cm long; flowers usually solitary axillary, sepals 4, oblong-elliptic, acute, 2.5–3 cm long, brownish outside, otherwise light pink, stamens nearly as long as the sepals, filaments very pubescent, February. HI 1819. China; Hupeh, Ichang. z6 Fig. 250.

C. heracleifolia DC. Bushy subshrub, 70 cm high, woody only at the base, branching rigidly upright, somewhat pubescent; leaves trifoliate, broad ovate, 6–15 cm long, scabrous and coarsely serrate or dentate or slightly lobed, base broad cuneate, lightly pubescent; flowers polygamous, fascicled, tubular, resembling a hyacinth, 2–2.5 cm long, pale blue, outside pubescent, sepals reflexed at the apex, August–September. BM 4269 and 6801; ICS 1469 (= *C. tubulosa* Turcz.). E. China. 1837. z5 Plate 119; Fig. 255. ⊕ ∅

var. **davidiana** (Verlot) Hemsl. To 1 m high, branches striped; leaves tough; flowers in dense, axillary fascicles, sepals tubular only at the base, wide spreading at the apex (not reflexed, like the type), indigo-blue, fragrant, dioecious. LLC 84–85 (= *C. davidiana* Hemsl.). China. 1864. Much prettier than the species. z5 ⊕ ∅

var. **ichangensis** Rehd. & Wils. Leaflets rounded at the base, pubescent on both sides, especially dense beneath, flowers densely silvery pubescent outside, dark blue inside. Central and N. China. 1908. ⊕ ∅

C. indivisa Willd. see: *C. paniculata* Gmelin. non Thunb.

C. integrifolia L. Subshrub or only a perennial, 80–100 cm high; leaves broad ovate to lanceolate, undivided, 6–10 cm long, entire, both sides green, thinly pubescent beneath; flowers solitary, terminal, flat, spreading, sepals 4, seldom 3 or 5, short or long acuminate, margin often sinuate, outside either gray tomentose or glabrous and then more lilac, inside purple to dark blue, often somewhat inflexed, June–August. HM 666; HF 984. SE. Europe to W. Asia. Prefers a moist soil. z6 ⊕

'Alba'. Flowers white.

C. × jackmanii Moore (*C. lanuginosa* × *C. viticella*). Vine, climbing 3–4 m high; leaves simple to trifoliate, leaflets broad ovate, 10–12 cm long, dark green above, glabrous, lighter beneath, lightly pubescent; flowers usually in groups of 3, numerous at the ends of the current year's wood, July–October, sepals 4–6, obovate, violet-purple, flat spreading, stalk 10–14 cm long. FS 1628; RH 1868: 390. HYbrid crossed by Jackman in Woking, England in 1858. z6 Plate 120. ⊕

One of the most beautiful, hardy climbing vines. Including a long list of cultivars; see the list at the end of this section.

C. × jeuneiana Symons-Jeune. (*C. armandii* × *C. finetiana*). Evergreen, resembling *C. armandii*, strong grower; leaves nearly like those of *C. armandii*; flowers in cymes, 3–5 axillary, often to 30 flowers at a leaf axil, sepals usually 5 or 6, white, silvery-pink beneath. Developed by Symons-Jeune in England around 1916. z8 # ⊕

C. jouianiana Schneid. (*C. heracliefolia* × *C. vitalba*). Subshrub, climbing 3–4 m high; leaflets 3–5, ovate, 5–10 cm long, coarsely dentate, weakly pubescent, form intermediate between the parents; flowers 3 cm wide, in large, terminal and axillary panicles at the branch tips, white at first, turning to pale lilac, sepals linear, wide spreading, slightly reflexed, slightly fragrant, August–September. BS 1: 447; LCC 85. Before 1900. z5

Including the following seedling selections (presumably from Simon Louis):

'Campanile'. 75 cm high; flowers numerous, good fragrance, light blue, sepals half tubular. Very attractive form. ⊕

'Côte d'Azur'. Growth taller and more open than 'Campanile'; leaves glossier; flowers deep azure-blue. MCl 87.

'Oiseau Blue'. Growth tall and open, resembles 'Côte d'Azur', but with leaves much smaller; flowers lilac-pink. ⊕

'Praecox'. Very strong grower; flowers hyacinth-like, light blue, appearing in August to October. ⊕

C. koreana Komar. Closely related to *C. verticillata*, but not climbing, rather growing along the ground; leaflets 3, long acuminate, 4–8 cm long, coarsely dentate, ovate and slightly cordate at the base, often 3 lobed or 3 parted; flowers dull violet, 2.5–3.5 cm long, sepals elliptic-lanceolate, staminodes spathulate in form, 2 cm long, June–August. Korea. 1920. Hardy. z6 ⊕

Fig. 252. **Clematis.** a. *C. lanuginosa*; b. *C. patens*; c. *C. florida* (from Lavallée)

f. **lutea** Rehd. Flowers yellow. Gs. 9: 285. Plate 74.

C. lanuginosa Lincl. Climbing to 2 m, occasionally higher, branches pubescent; leaves simple or trifoliate, tough, dense white hairy beneath, ovate to oval-lanceolate, 6—12 cm long; flower stalk and buds very woolly pubescent, flowers solitary or grouped 2—3 in cymes, opening one after the other, 10—20 cm wide (the largest flowers of the entire genus), white to soft lilac, July—September, sepals 6—8, elliptic, over-lapping, woolly pubescent outside. LCl 1; FS 811; LLC 16. China. 1850. Hardy. z6 Fig. 252. ⊕

Many hybrids though the species is seldom found in cultivation. For cultivars see the list at the end of this section.

C. lasiandra Maxim. Climbing to 4 m high, young branches somewhat viscid; leaves bipinnate, leaflets 3—7, ovate to oval-lanceolate, usually trifoliate to 3 lobed, 3—8 cm long, scabrous serrate, usually glabrous or sparsely pubescent, bright green; flowers grouped 1—3 axillary on 3—7 cm long stalks, campanulate, whitish with a trace of violet, sepals with reflexed tips, rather glabrous outside, stamen filaments nearly as long as the sepals, densely pubescent, style feathery, August—October. ICS 1478. Central and W. China. 1900. Hardy. z6

C. × lawsoniana Moore & Jackm. (*C. lanuginosa* × *C. patens*). Climbing to 2 m high, woody; leaves trifoliate; flowers large, long stalked, sepals 6—8, elliptic, violet-red, darker veined, overlapping, style feathery. Before 1872. z6 ⊕

With many cultivars; see the list at the end of this section.

C. ligusticifolia Nutt. Climbing to 6 m high; leaves pinnate, leaflets 5—7, ovate to lanceolate, 3—7 cm long, long acuminate, base cuneate, coarsely dentate and often 3 lobed, tough, yellow-green, somewhat bristly haired or glabrous; flowers dioecious, otherwise nearly like those of *C. vitalba*, 2 cm wide, white, August—September; seed heads dense feathery, grouped in large clusters. BB 1583; MS 108. N. America. 1880. Hardy. z6 ⊗

C. macropetala Ledeb. Climbing, but only to around 1 m high, woody, branches angular, pubescent at first; leaves usually twice trifoliate, the 9 leaflets ovate to lanceolate, 2—3.5 cm long, coarsely dentate or some-what lobed, glabrous beneath; flowers solitary, nod-ding, 5—10 cm wide, sepals 4, blue to violet, staminodes very numerous, in several rows, lanceo-late, violet-blue, becoming smaller and lighter toward the center, May—June. NF 3: 34; BM 9142. N. China, Manchuria, Siberia. 1912. One of the best species for the rock garden. Quite hardy. z5—6 Plate 121. ⊕

With a few cultivars:

'Ballet Blanc' (J. Jefferies & Son 1951). Seedling of 'Maidwell Hall', also white; flower somewhat smaller, but very densely double. ⊕

'Maidwell Hall' (Jackman 1956). Flowers nodding, semidou-ble, pure lavender-blue, 4—5 cm wide (= *C. macropetala* 'Lagoon'). ⊕

Fig. 253. *Clematis maximowicziana* (from GF)

'Markham's Pink' (Markham 1935). Sepals a strong purple-pink with a faint lilac limb, staminodes greenish-white (= *C. macropetala* 'Markhamii' Markham). ⊕

'Rodklokke' (A. Olsen, before 1959). Pink-red. ⊕

'White Moth' (Jackman 155). Flowers nodding, pure white, sepals acute. Not a cultivar of *C. alpina* var. *sibirica* as previously thought. ⊕

The cultivars 'Blue Bird', 'Rosy O'Grady' and 'White Swan' which are frequently categorized here are in reality interspecific hybrids. Please see list at the end of this section.

C. maximowicziana Franch.& Sav. Cimbing to 10 m high; leaves trifoliate or pinnate, leaflets 3–5, ovate, entire, 3–10 cm long, quite glabrous; flowers white, fragrant (somewhat like *Crataegus*), 3 cm wide, in many-flowered panicles, September–October, sepals 4, linear; fruit seldom develops (in the N. European climate). RH 1902: 86 (= *C. paniculata* Thunb.; *C. dioscoreifolia* var. *robusta* [Carr.] Rehd.). Japan. 1864. Generally quite winter hardy, late blooming, beautiful. z6 Fig. 253. ⊕

C. meyeniana Walp. Evergreen climber, to 5 m high or more, branches wire-like, reddish, glabrous; leaves trifoliate, leaflets broad ovate to lanceolate, base cordate, tough, leathery; flowers numerous, in large, loose panicles, sepals 4, white, 12 mm long, 5–12 cm long, distinctly 3 veined, entire, narrow-oblong, limb woolly, anthers gold-yellow, May. BM 7897; ICS 1494; BS 1: 23. SE. China. 1820. Resembling *C. armandii*, but with smaller flowers. z8 #

C. montana Buch.-Ham. Climbing to 8 m high, very strong grower, young branches somewhat pubescent only at first, soon becoming quite glabrous; leaves trifoliate, leaflets short stalked, ovate, usually deeply dentate, 3–10 cm long, glabrous, leaf petiole 5–9 cm long; flowers white, 5 cm wide, grouped 1–5 in axillary clusters, sepals 4, elliptic, outspread, somewhat fragrant, May. LCl 22; BS Pl. 24. Cenral and W. China, Himalaya. 1831. One of the most abundantly flowering and hardiest species. z5–6 Fig. 249.

Including several varieties:

'Alexander'. Flowers cream-white, good fragrance. Brought from N. India by R. D. Alexander. ⊕

'Elizabeth'. Lilke var. *rubens*, but fragrant, more intensely pink and with larger flowers (*C. montana rubens* 'Scented Form'). Much valued in England. (Jackman, 1958). ⊕

f. grandiflora (Hook). Rehd. Flowers white, to 8 cm wide, May–June. BM 4061. Very strong grower. ⊕

'Lilacina' (Lemoine). Flowers lilac. Originating from a cross between f. *grandiflora* and var. *rubens*. 1910. ⊕

'Perfecta' (Lemoine). Branches dark red-brown; flowers 8 cm wide, white with a trace of soft lilac-pink. Gs 1922: 97; 1920: 3. Also a cross of f. *grandiflora* × var. *rubens*. Very strong grower. ⊕

'Pink Perfection'. An English selection of var. *rubens*, especially deep pink. ⊕

f. platypetala Rehd. & Wils. A form of *C. wilsonii*, with wider obovate sepals and flowering in May. China. ⊕

var. rubens O. Kuntze. Leaves purple, especially in spring, later becoming bronze-green; flowers pink-red, 5–6 cm wide, flowers somewhat later than the others. BS 1: Pl. 24. China. 1900. Camillo Schneider maintains that the true Chinese form has dark red flowers and is no longer in cultivation. Plate 120. ⊕

'Superba' (Jackman). Flowers white, somewhat larger than those of the species. Allegedly var. *rubens* × 'Mrs. Geo. Jackman'. Strong grower. ⊕

'Tetrarose' (Boskoop Research Station 1960). Leaflets with 2–3 lobes and coarsely serrate; flowers lilac-pink to 8 cm wide, sepals broad elliptic, apex often somewhat emarginate, filaments white, anthers light yellow, flowers very abundantly. Tetraploid; originated with a colchicine treatment of seedlings of *C. montana* var. *rubens*. Strong grower. ⊕

'Undulata' (M. Krause) (f. *grandiflora* × var. *rubens*). Leaves very similar to var. *rubens*; flowers white, with a trace of light violet-pink, sepals reflexed, anthers yellowish-white, flowers very abundantly, May. Very strong grower.

var. wilsonii Sprague. Leaflets ovate, venation pubescent beneath; flowers white, 6–8 cm wide, sepals obovate, outside pubescent, July–August (!!). BM 8365. 1910? Hardy.

C. nannophylla Maxim. Deciduous shrub, dense and erect, about 1 m high and wide, young branches slender, striped, with appressed gray pubescence; leaves quite variable, 2–6 cm long, ornamentally 3 lobed or deeply pinnatisect, each section narrow and sharply acuminate, glabrous or nearly so; flowers usually solitary, occasionally in 3's at the branch tips, 2–3 cm wide, the sepals ovate to elliptic, 8–12 mm wide, brown with a broad yellow margin (!), style clusters to 2.5 cm wide. BM 9641; ICS 1487. China; Kansu. 1915. ⊕

Found in very dry areas. Existence in cultivation today uncertain. z7 ⊕

C. napaulensis DC. Evergreen vine, to 7 m high in its native habitat, young branches gray, furrowed; leaflets 3 or 5, oval-lanceolate, 3−8 cm long, entire or 3 lobed, glabrous, thin, terminal leaflet larger than the others; flowers grouped 6−8 in axillary clusters, narrowly campanulate, cream-yellow, 2.5 cm long, sepals 4, silky pubescent, stamens as long as the sepals, anthers purple, December to March. BM 9037 (= *C. forrestii* W. W. Sm.). SW. China, N. India. Quite rare, but in cultivation in England. z8 Plate 120. # ⊕

C. ochroleuca Ait. Only 50 cm high, subshrub, closely related to *C. integrifolia*; leaves simple, ovate; flowers solitary, erect, campanulate, 2 cm long, sepals 4, inside whitish, outside yellow, occasionally somewhat reddish, May to June. BB 1558; NBB 2: 186. Eastern N. America. 1767. On dry soil. Hardy. z6

C. occidentalis (Hornem.) DC. Climbing to 2 m high, young branches somewhat furrowed, glabrous, nodes distinctly thickened with age; leaves usually 4 to a node, each being trifoliate, leaflets ovate, 5−7 cm long, entire or coarsely dentate, cordate base; flowers solitary, blue or purple, nodding at first, 5−8 cm wide when fully developed, sepals 4, lanceolate, thin, margin and venation pubescent, staminodes narrow, spathulate, May−June; fruits 3 cm long, feathery. BB 1592; 65; NBB 2: 185; GSP 128 (= *C. verticillaris* DC.). N. America. 1797. Hardy, but quite rare in cultivation. z6 Fig. 257. ⊗

C. orientalis L. Climbing 3−5 m high, branches thin, striped, quite glabrous; leaves 15−20 cm long, pinnate to bipinnate, the lower pinnae often trifoliate, leaflets bluish-green, ovate to lanceolate, 2−5 cm long, lobed or large toothed, glabrous or with tiny hairs; flowers solitary or only a few together, 3−5 cm wide, yellow, stalk 4−10 cm long, sepals 4, elliptic, acute, very thick and fleshy, August−September; seed heads with feathery styles. JRHS 151: 75. Himalaya. z6 ⊕⊗

There exists in the trade a plant called **'Orange Peel'**, an, as yet, invalidly named *Clematis*, closely related to *C. orientalis*; to 4 m high; leaves blue-green; flowers deep yellow, eventually orange-yellow, sepals thick and fleshy ("like orange peels"), stamens brown. LLC 80. Collected in Tibet by Ludlow, Sherriff and Elliott in 1947 and distributed in England as "Nr. 13342". Especially valuable for its late flowers, September−October. z6 Plate 120. ⊕

C. paniculata Gmel. Evergreen, tall growing species; overtaking large trees in its native habitat, branches furrowed and softly pubescent; leaflets 3, ovate, 5−8 cm long, entire or occasionally somewhat lobed; flowers dioecious, male flowers larger than the female, 5 to 7 cm wide, whitish-yellow, in loose, axillary panicles to 30 cm long, anthers pink, filaments yellow, May−June. BM 4398; MNZ 4; NF 11: 38 (= *C. indivisa* Willd.). New Zealand. 1840. Gorgeous species. z8 ⊕ ∅

var. **lobata** Hook. with lobed leaves, hardier and withstands winter in the open in S. England. ⊕

C. paniculata Thunb. non Gmel., refer to **C. maximowicziana.**

(This species was for a time referred to as *C. dioscoreifolia* var. *robusta* [Carr.] Rehd., also as *C. flammula* var. *robusta* Carr.)

C. patens Morr. & Decne. Climbing to 2(4) m high; leaves trifoliate or pinnate, leaflets 3−5, oval-lanceolate, 4−10 cm long, entire, acute, somewhat pubescent beneath; flowers terminal, solitary on side branches, violet, 10−15 cm wide, sepals 6−8, flower stalks without bracts (important, *C. florida* has 2 bracts), May−summer; seed heads feathery. Japan. LCl 2−3, BR 1955; LLC 16. z6 Fig. 252. ⊕

'Fortunei'. Flowers 8−12 cm wide, milk-white, eventually turning pink, double, solitary on the tips of the young branches, June—July. FS 1533. Around 1860. Fig. 242. ⊕

'Standishii'. Leaves trifoliate; flowrs light blue-lilac, with a metallic brilliance, center reddish-lilac, 12−14 cm wide (= *C. standishii* Van Houtte). ⊕

For the numerous garden varieties, see listing at the end of this section.

C. petriei Allan. Thinly branched vine, climbing over shrubs, young branches pubescent, bi- to tripinnate; the leaflets ovate to oblong, 1−3 cm long, 0.5−2 cm wide, obtuse, entire or with 1−2 blunt teeth, leathery tough; flowers solitary or a few in small panicles, axillary, sepals 6−8, oval-oblong, pubescent, yellowish-green (!), 2 cm long, October−November. MNZ 3. New Zealand, South Island. z8 ⊕

Fig. 254. *Clematis patens* 'Fortunei' (from Flore des Serres)

Fig. 255. From left to right: *Clematis fruticosa*; *C. songarica*; *C. heracleifolia* (from ICS)

C. pitcheri Torr. & Gray. High climbing, young branches pubescent; leaflets 6—8, ovate, 3—7 cm long, reticulate venation beneath, terminal leaflet generally reduced to the midrib and twining; flowers solitary, urceolate, long stalked, purple, outside pubescent, June—July; seed heads not feathery. BB 1585; NBB 2: 187 (= *C. simsii* Sweet, sensu Brit. & Br. non Sweet). SE. USA. 1878. z7

C. pratti Hemsl. Climbing to 3 m high, woody, glabrous; leaves trifoliate, leaflets oval-oblong, 2 to 3.5 cm long, entire, blue-green beneath; flowers solitary, axillary, long stalked, tubular, 2 cm long, bright yellow; seed heads feathery. W. China. 1908. Hardy and very beautiful, but rare. z6 ✧ ☙

C. pseudoapina (Ktze.) J. M. Coulter & A. Nelson. Vine, climbing over thickets; leaves bi- to trifoliate, leaflets lanceolate to oval-lanceolate, acuminate, 2—4 cm long, deeply serrate or 2—3 lobed, glabrous beneath; flowers very similar to *C. alpina*, but with staminodes less numerous and with rudimentary anthers at the tips, sepals 4, lanceolate, purple or blue, seldom white, 3 to 5 cm long, April—June; seed heads 3—4 cm long, feathery. SH 1: 186c (= *C. alpina* var. *occidentalis* Gray). S. USA. 1916. Hardy. ✧

C. × psuedococcinia Schneid. (*C. jackmanii* × *C. texensis*). To 3 m high, perennial, similar to *C. texensis*, although with flowers campanulate, sepals 4—6, July—September.

Including a few hybrids from Jackman:

'Admiration'. Sepals salmon-pink, violet limbed, white inside. ✧

'Countess of Onslow'. Flowers more tubular, violet-purple, with a red mid-line on the ventral side to the base. ✧

'Duchess of Albany'. Cherry-pink, more brown in the center, with white stripes on the ventral side. Gn 52: Pl. 304. ✧

'Duchess of York'. Pink, with a darker middle band outside. Gn 52: Pl. 304. ✧

'Grace Darling'. Soft carmine-pink, flowers very abundantly. ✧

C. quinquefoliolata Hutchins. Evergreen, strong grower, high climbing, branches finely pubescent and striped; leaflets 5, lanceolate, 5—10 cm long; flowers 3—7 in axillary cymes, sepals milk-white, 4 or 6, narrow oblong, pubescent on the ventral side and especially along the margin, stamens very numerous, anthers yellow, August—September; fruits yellow-brown feathery. China. 1900. Similar to *C. armandii*, but with 5 leaflets. z8 #

C. ranunculoides Franch. Erect perennial, 0.5 m high or climbing to 2 m, branches purple-red, pubescent, striped, angular; leaves quite variable, trifoliate or pinnate with 5 leaflets or simple and 3 lobed, leaflets (or blade) rounded obovate or ovate, coarsely dentate, 3—5 cm long; flowers axillary and terminal, solitary or few in groups, sepals 4, purple to pink, wide spreading and reflexed, pubescent. BM 9329; NF 2: 118. China. 1906. z6 Fig. 256.

C. recta L. Shrub, erect, not climbing, 1—1.5 m high, densely branched, glabrous; leaves pinnate, to 15 cm long, leaflets 5 to 7, oval-lanceolate, acute, entire, stalked, 3—5 cm long; flowers white, numerous in terminal panicles, fragrant, June—July. HM 666; LLC 81. S. and Middle Europe. 1597. z7 ✧

'Grandiflora'. Flowers larger, more numerous. Better than the species in all regards. ✧

'Plena'. Flowers double. Very nice. ✧

'Purpurea'. Branches and leaves bronze-red to a dull green-red; flowers white. ✧

C. rehderiana Craib. Very strong grower, climbing to 7 m high, branches pubescent and angular; leaves pinnate, leaflets 7—9, broad ovate, 4—8 cm long, coarsely dentate, often 3 lobed, base somewhat cordate, venation indented above, both sides pubescent; flowers campanulate, nodding, to 1.5 cm long, light yellow, several in 8—12 cm long, erect, pubescent panicles, sepals somewhat reflexed at the apex, inside not pubescent, fragrant, bracts ovate to elliptic, occasionally deeply 3 lobed (!!), August—October. LLC 73; BMns 523. W. China. 1898. Hardy. z6 Plate 119. ✥

C. reticulata Walt. Climbing to 3 m high, woody, branches thin; leaflets 3—7, broad ovate to more lanceolate, 3—7 cm long, acute, somewhat leathery, with reticulate venation beneath and somewhat pubescent; flowers solitary in the leaf axils, campanulate, nodding, 2 cm long, outside gray-yellow and pubescent, inside lilac, sepals somewhat reflexed at the apex, June—July; seed heads feathery. BM 6574; LCl 16. Southeast USA. Before 1884. Hardy. z6

C. scottii Porter. Shrubby perennial, 0.5 m high, erect, long pubescent when young; leaves petiolate, the upper ones pinnate to bipinnate, leaflets lanceolate, entire or with some teeth, lower leaves often simple and pinnatisect; flowers solitary, terminal and axillary, long stalked, nodding, campanulate, purple, 2.5 cm long, May—June, sepals thick, ovate, outside pubescent. BB 1591 (= *C. douglasii* var. *scottii* Coutler). Central USA. Hardy. z6

C. serratifolia Rehd. Climbing to 3 m high, branches furrowed; leaves twice trifoliate, leaflets oval-lanceolate, long acuminate, sharply serrate, often 2—3 lobed, bright green, 3—6 cm long; flowers axillary, grouped 1—3 on 4—6 cm long stalks, yellow, nodding, somewhat fragrant, sepals 2—2.5 cm long, outside glabrous, inside somewhat shaggy pubescent, broadly campanulate at first, later wide spreading, stamen filaments purple, August—September; fruits long feathery. Korea. 1918. Similar to *C. tangutica*, but with smaller flowers. Hardy. z6

C. songarica Bge. Erect, to 1.5 m high, perennial, glabrous; leaves simple, lanceolate to linear, 3—8 cm long, entire to coarsely dentate, blue-green, glabrous, wtih 3 distinct veins; flowers yellowish—white, 2—2.5 cm wide, 1—2 terminal or axillary, nodding, sepals pubescent outside, inside glabrous, August—September; seed heads feathery. ICS 1486 (= *C. gebleriana* Bong.). Korea. Hardy. Similar to *C. orientalis*,. but leaves not pinnate. z6 Fig. 255. ✥

C. spooneri Rehd. & Wils. — **C. chrysocoma** var. **sericea** Schneid.

C. stans S. & Z. Shrub, or subshrub, growing to 2 m high, branches gray-white pubescent; leaves rather broad, variable in form and margin; sepals white and tomentose outside, inside more or less blue, 1 cm long. BM 6810; MF 1655. Japan. Easily distinguished from the smaller *C. heracleifolia* by the generally terminal flower panicles. z6 ∅

C. tangutica (Maxim). Korsh. Climbing to 3 m high, branches pubescent when young; leaves pinnate to bipinnate, bright green, leaflets oblong to lanceolate, 3—8 cm long, irregularly dentate, the teeth directed outward (important for identification!); flowers gold-yellow, usually solitary, on 8—15 cm long, pubescent stalks, erect, the flowers nodding, to 8 cm wide, sepals 4, oval-lanceolate, 3—4 cm long, broad campanulate at first, eventually wide spreading, June—fall; seed heads feathery. BM 7710; Gs 193: 195; LLC 77 (= *C. eriopoda* Koehne). Mongolia, NW. China. 1898. Best yellow species. Hardy. z6 Fig. 256. ✥ ⚭

var. **obtusiuscula** Rehd. & Wils. Branches more woolly pubescent; leaflets smaller, less serrate; sepals smaller, 3 cm long, obtuse-elliptic. ✥ ⚭

C. texensis Buckl. Climbing to 2 m high, subshrub or perennial, branches brown-red, nearly totally glabrous; leaves pinnate, leaflets 4 to 8, tough, rather bluish-green, cordate-round, with small thorny tips,

Fig. 256. From left to right: *Clematis tangutica; C. ranunculoides; C. alpina* var. *ochotensis* (from ICS)

Fig. 257. **Clematis** a. *C. viorna*; b. *C. viticella*; c. *C. crispa*; d. *C. campaniflora*; 3. *C. occidentalis*
(from Dippel, Lauche, Lavallee, Spr. & Gray)

3−8 cm long, terminal leaflet developing into a tendril; flowers solitary, urceolate, scarlet-red or carmine, 2−3 cm long, July−September; fruits with feathery styles. LCl 19; MCl 110; BM 6594 (= *C. coccinea* Engelm.). Texas. Around 1878. Very attractive, popular, but relatively rare species. z5 ⊕

'Major'. Flowers 1−1.5 cm wide, 2−3 cm long, outside scarlet-red, inside white to yellowish, sepals very thick. ⊕

'Parviflora'. Sepals to 2 cm long, to 1 cm wide, less thick, both sides scarlet-red.

See also the garden hybrids under *C. pseudococcinea*.

C. × triternata DC. (*C. flammula* × *C. viticella*). Climbing to 4 m high, branches woody; leaves simple or bipinnate, leaflets entire; flowers 3 cm wide, lilac, in terminal panicles, sepals often 6, style pubescent (= *C. × violacea* A. DC. f.). Originated before 1840. Hardy. z6

'Rubro-marginata'. Like the species, but with the white sepals also having violet-red margins, August−fall, flowers abundantly (= *C. flammula rubro-marginata* Cripps). Before 1883. ⊕

C. uncinata Champ. Semi-evergreen, high climbing; leaves pinnate to twice trifoliate, leaflets linear-lanceolate to oval-round, margins entire, 3−10 cm long, acute, blue-green beneath, 3−5 veined; flowers in terminal and axillary panicles, 2.5 cm wide, white, fragrant, the inflorescences to 30 cm wide, June−July; seed heads glabrous. BM 8633; ICS 1493. Central China. 1901. z6

C. × vedrariensis Vilm. (*C. chrysocoma* × *C. montana* var. *rubens*). Very similar to *C. montana* var. *rubens*, but with sepals broad elliptic, lilac or pink, flowers 5−6 cm wide; strong grower to 5 m high, young branches pubescent; leaves trifoliate, leaflets ovate, 2.5−6 cm long, often 3 lobed, coarsely dentate and densely pubescent, May (= *C. verrierensis* Gard. Chron.). Developed before 1912 by Vilmorin in France. z6 ⊕

'Rosea'. Flowers larger than species, 8−10 cm wide, light pink. RH 1917: Pl. 214 (= *C. spooneri* 'Rosea' Vilm.). 1917. ⊕

C. veitchiana Craib. Climbing to 3 m high; similar to *C. rehderiana*, but with leaves bipinnate and more deeply incised; leaflets 7−9, most trifoliate or 3 lobed, ovate to oval-lanceolate, 3−6 cm long, silky pubescent beneath, often over 20 leaflets to a leaf; flowers campanulate, yellowish-white, slightly fragrant, in panicles, September−October. W. China. 1904. Plate 119. ⊕

Occasionally included with *C. rehderiana*, but differing in the finer foliage, smaller flowers (although similar in form and color), and the awl-shaped bracts.

C. versicolor Small. Shoots climbing, glabrous, bluish; leaflets usually in 4 pairs, leathery tough, glabrous, blue-green, oval-oblong, 4—6 cm long, base cordate, entire, often 2—3 lobed, very strong reticulate venation beneath; flowers purple, campanulate, apexes reflexed, sepals 4, glabrous on both sides, only the margin densely pubescent, styles long, feathery, June—July. NBB 2: 187; NH 1934: 88 (= *C. troutbeckiana* Spingarn). S. USA, in dry forests. Hardy. z6

C. virginiana L. Climbing 3—5 m high, young branches usually furrowed and glabrous; leaves nearly always with 3, occasionally 5 leaflets, these ovate, 5—9 cm long, coarsely dentate; flowers usually dioecious, white, 2—3 cm wide, in many flowered, axillary panicles, sepals spathulate, pubescent outside, style feathery, August—September. NBB 2: 185; BB 1582. Eastern N. America. 1730. Occasionally freezes back, but regenerates well. Resembles *C. vitalba*, but with 3 leaflets. z6 ⊗

C. viorna L. Shrub or subshrub, climbing to 3 m high; leaflets 5—7, ovate to elliptic-lanceolate, 3—7 cm long, dark green, usually glabrous, entire or somewhat lobed; flowers solitary, nodding, urceolate, violet or dull purple, margin more gray-white pubescent, apex reflexed, May—July; fruits brownish feathery. LCl 17; BB 1586. Eastern N. America. 1730. z7 Fig. 257.

C. vitalba L. Climbing to 10 m high, fast growing and quickly covering large areas, older stems up to 3 cm thick, young branches furrowed and pubescent; leaves pinnate, leaflets usually 5, the lower pair sometimes also trifoliate, coarsely dentate or entire; flowers white, 2 cm wide, slightly fragrant in terminal and axillary panicles, sepals densely pubescent outside, July—September; fruit styles long, dense feathery and very ornamental for the entire winter. HF 987; HM Pl. 117. Europe, Orient, Caucasus. In culture for centuries, but because of its rapid growth only suitable for large areas. Common understock for some grafted varieties. Likes alkaline soil. ℗ Austria. (for screening) z5 ✧ ⊗

C. viticella L. Climbing to 4 m high, ornamental, branches furrowed, finely pubescent when young; leaves pinnate, leaflets 5—7, broad elliptic to narrow lanceolate, entire to 3 lobed; flowers in groups of 1—3, purple-pink to violet, 3—5 cm wide, sepals 4, obovate, in a flat spray radially, glabrous or pubescent, limb usually somewhat crispate, June—August; fruits with short, glabrous styles. HM 668; BM 565; HF 988; LCl 7. S. Europe to Asia Minor. 1569. z6 Fig. 257. ✧

Including many garden varieties:

f. **albiflora** (O. Kuntze.) Rehd. Flowrs pure white. Occurring in the wild with the species.

'Coerulea'. Flowers blue-violet.

'Marmorata' (Jackman). Flowers rather small, sepals 4, gray-blue, more darkly veined. FS 2050.

'Nana'. Bushy, not climbing, only 1 m high, otherwise like the species. 1869.

'Plena'. Flowers double, blue-violet. 1774.

'Purpurea'. Flowers purple-red.

'Rubra Grandiflora'. Flowers larger than those of the species, carmine-red. with 6 sepals. FS 2053.

For the large blooming hybrids, please see the following list.

List of the Large Flowering Clematis-Hybrids

The so-called 'large blooming' *Clematis* are a result of crosses between relatively few species, namely *C. viticella, florida, patens, lanuginosa, texensis* and the hybrids of *C. jackmanii*. Most of the hybridizing work was done between the years 1860—1880. About 500 hybrids have been developed but many are no longer in existence. Of these, about 100 originated from Jackman (Woking, England), 70 from Lemoine (Nancy, France), 60 from Ch. Noble (Sunningdale, England) and 50 from Cripps (Tunbridge, Wells, England).

While the *Clemtis* work is but a small part of gardening history, a thorough discussion of the peak period of activity, to 1877, may be found in Moore & Jackman (pp. 7—20).

The following firms have introduced from 10—20 hybrids into the trade:

France: Carre (Troyes), Christen (Versailles), Dauvesse (Orléans), Morel (Lyon), Moser (Versailles) and Simon-Louis Frères (Metz).

Scotland: Anderson-Henry (Edinburgh).

Germany: Goos & Koenemann (Niederwalluf, after 1900).

The following breeders have developed a few hybrids. Here again, France far outranks the other countries:

France: Boisselot (Nantes), Baron-Veillard; Bonamy Frères (Toulouse), Briolay-Griffon (Orléans), Desfossé (Orléans), Gégu (Angers), Gerbeaux (Nancy), Contier; Grange (Orléans), Jamain (Orléans), Leroy (Angers), Modeste-Guérin (Paris) and Paillat (Chatenay).

England: Baker & Son (Bagshot), Cobbell, Markham (Gravetye), Henderson (London), Pennell (Lincoln), Smith & Sons (Worcester).

Germany: Spaeth (Berlin), Rinz (Frankfurt/Main) and Heinemann (Erfurt).

Belgium: Spae.

Switzerland: Froebel (Zurich).

Holland: M. Koster and Swijnenburg (both Boskoop).

Canada: F. L. Skinner (Manitoba).

Sweden: Magnus Johnson; T. Lundell.

Plant Descriptions

The most complete and detailed descriptions are to be found in T. Moore & G. Jackman, no less than 248 hybrids on 54 pages in small type, although this work includes only those plants developed through 1887. Notably shorter are the lists of C. Lloyd (16 pp.) and J. Fisk (13 pp.). The 'Check-List' by Spingarn is by far the most comprehensive list with around 500 cultivars. Included is everything developed through 1934, although the descriptions are very brief with only one line given to each.

In the following list, the group name, the hybridizer and the year developed, if known, are given after the plant name. The group classification is based on the following simple outline developed by Moore & Jackman:

☆ Flowers on the previous year's wood;
　　Flowers in spring:
　　　patens-group
　　Flowers in summer:
　　　florida-group
☆ ☆ Flowers on the current year's (also young) wood;
　　Flowers appearing consecutively, loosely arranged, very large flowers:
　　　lanuginosa-group
　　Flowers appearing one after the other, more abundantly, not so large as the above:
　　　viticella-group
　　Flowers in masses, usually 4 sepals, 8—14 cm wide:
　　　jackmanii-group

'Abendstern' (*vit.* Goos & Koenemann). Wine-red, medium sized, anthers yellowish, July—September. Improved 'Kermesina'.

'Abundance' (*vit.* Jackman). Purple, darker veined, anthers cream-white, 5 cm wide, 4—5 sepals, nodding, flowers abundantly, June—August.

'Alba Luxurians' (*vit.* Veitch). Flowers 4—6 cm wide, 4 sepals, most deformed, white with green tips, July—September.

'Aurora' (*flor.* Noble, before 1877). Flowers medium sized, sepals lanceolate, pink-lilac with darker center, semidouble, with a cluster of small, white staminodes, anthers carmine, May—June.

'Bagatelle' (*pat.*). Light violet with a darker middle stripe, anthers dark brown. Very attractive.

'Barbara Dibley' (*pat.* Jackman 1949). Strong violet with a darker middle stripe, anthers cream-yellow, May—June. LLC 1. Similar to 'Nelly Moser', but blooms more abundantly.

'Barbara Jackman' (*pat.* Jackman). Flowers to 15 cm wide, with 5—6 sepals, widely overlapping, sharply acuminate, dark violet with a magenta middle stripe, opening to lilac except for the middle stripe, anthers cream-white, May—June. LLC 21.

'Beauty of Worcester' (*lan.* Smith). Flowers single or double, blue-violet, anthers white, May—August. Weak grower.

'Belle Nantaise' (*lan.* Boisselot). Large flowers, sepals long, acute, lavender colored, anthers whitish, July—October. LLC 6.

'Belle of Woking' (*flor.* Jackman, before 1877). densely double, with about 8 rings of sepals in rosette form, bluish-lilac to silver-gray, May—June. NH 1935: 74. Weak grower.

'Blue Belle' (*lan.*). Flowers very large, nearly black-blue, July—August. Easily the darkest hybrid of all.

'Blue Bird' (*macropetala* × *alpina* var. *sibirica*, Skinner 1970). Semidouble, 7 cm wide, purple-blue.

'Blue Gem' (*lan.* Jackman, before 1877). Flowers very large, to 20 cm wide, 8 sepals, ovate, much overlapped, sky-blue, older flowers soft lilac, anthers deep purple. Always highly prized.

'Cassiopeia' (M. Johnson 1952). Flowers star shaped, 14—16 cm wide, white, 6 sepals, anthers purple-red, filaments greenish, June—July.

'Corona' (T. Lundell 1972). Flowers 12—14 cm wide, with 6 sepals, a bright velvety purple-red, anthers purple-red, filaments white, June—July.

'Comtesse de Bouchaud' (*jack.* Morel). Strong grower; flowers disc-shaped, soft silky pink with a trace of lilac, June—August. MCl 78; JRHS 1946: 128. The title "Bouchard" is incorrect.

'Countess of Lovelace' (*pat.* Jackman 1876). Flowers double, sepals densely overlapping in 6—7 series, 15 cm wide, blue-lilac, becoming lighter with time, fall flowers single, May—June and fall. LLC 45.

'Crimson King' (*lan.* Jackman 1916). Wine red, with 2 lighter stripes on the ventral side, anthers brown, July—August. Prefers semishade.

'Daniel Deronda' (*pat.* Nobel). First flowers double, later only single, purple-blue, anthers yellow, June—September.

'Duchess of Edinburgh' (*flor.* Jackman, before 1877). Strong grower; leaves trifoliate; flowers 10 cm wide, double in rosettes, sepals in 10—11 rings, pure white, fragrant, anthers brown, May—June. One of the best white types.

'Duchess of Sutherland' (*vit.* Jackman). Petunia-red with a darker middle stripe, frequently also double, July—August.

'Duke of Edinburgh' (*pat.* Cripps 1877). Flowers medium sized, with 6 acute sepals, violet-purple with reddish trace, anthers red-brown, July—August. (Cripps had a *jackmanii* type by the same name aound 1877 but it is no longer available; see Moore & Jackman, p. 84.)

'Edouard Desfossé' (*pat.* Desfossé 1880). Very large flowers, violet, middle stripe darker, anthers dark brown, May—June.

'Elfenreigen' (Goos & Koenemann, before 1933). Lilac-pink to carmine. Gs 1933: 103.

'Elsa Spaeth' (*lan.* Spaeth 1891). Medium size flowers, sepals acute, dark blue, August—September, strong bloomer. Cultivated and valued in England.

'Ernest Markham' (*vit.* Jackman, around 1937). Large flowers, sepals overlapped, dark violet-red with velvety sheen, flowers abundantly, July—September.

'Etoile de Malicorne' (*pat.* A. Girault). Flowers 15—20 cm wide, sepals very wide, lavender-blue with a purple-pink middle stripe, anthers brownish, May and August—September. A novelty.

'Etoile Violette' (*jack.* Morel). Medium-sized, sepals a dark violet with carmine-red middle stripe, anthers yellowish, flowers abundantly, June—September.

'Fair Rosamond' (*pat.* Jackman 1874). Flowers to 15 cm wide, with 8 sepals, somewhat overlapped, soft bluish-white with a narrow, wine-red middle stripe, fragrant, flowers abundantly, lush growing, May—June. FS 2342.

'Fairy Queen' (*lan.* Cripps 1887). Flowers to 20 cm wide, flesh pink with a darker midstripe, June to August.

'Francofurtensis' (*vit.* × *pat.* Rinz, before 1877). Strong grower; 8 cm wide, the 6 petals spathulate, violet. LCl 7b.

'Gipsy Queen' (*jack.* Cripps 1877). Sepals 6, dark purple with 3 reddish stripes, with 3 whitish stripes on the ventral side, July—October. Gs 1938: 204.

'Gluecksstern' (Goos & Koenemann). Dark lavender-blue, anthers white.

'**Hagley Hybrid**' (*jack.* Percy Picton 1956). Sepals usually 6, finely acuminate, lilac-pink, becoming lighter as they age, anthers dark brown, flowers very abundantly, June–September. LLC 60. Only growing to about 2 m high.

'**Henryi**' (*lan.* Anderson-Henry). Very robust grower; very large flowers, 6–8 sepals, acuminate, white, anthers dark brown, May and August–September.

'**Horn of Plenty**' (K. Maarse Dzn. Jr. 1962). Flowers with 8 sepals, wide and overlapping, soft purple-blue, anthers brown, May–June. Gw 1967: 256.

Huldine' (*vit.* Morel). Flowers white, translucent, lilac on the ventral side, flowers abundantly, July–September. MCl 112.

'**jackmanii**', see main entry in species list.

jackmanii '**Alba**' (*jack.* Noble, before 1877). Sepals elliptic-lanceolate, on younger wood white and with 4–6 sepals, on older wood bluish-white and with 8 petals, anthers brown, May–June and September. LLC 29.

jackmanii '**Superba**' (*jack.*). Differing from the species in the wider sepals and darker, purple-violet color, July–August. Gs 1938: 14; LLC 45.

'**John Gould Veitch**' (*flor.* 1862 introduced by Fortune from Japan). Flowers 10–12 cm wide, double in rosette form, with 6–8 series of sepals, labender-blue, June. MJCl 7; FS 1875 (= *C. fortunei coerulea* Standish). Overshadowed by the generally superior 'Countess of Lovelace'.

'**Kathleen Wheeler**' (Pennell). Flowers with 8 sepals, purple-violet, anthers gold-yellow, June–September. A novelty plant.

'**Kermesina**' (*vit.* Lemoine). Usually 6 sepals, medium sized, dark wine-red. Gn 39: 30. Popular old cultivar, still found in cultivation.

'**Lady Betty Balfour**' (*vit.* Jackman 1913). Strong grower; flowers deep velvety-purple, anthers yellow, August–October. Flowers poorly in some years, needs full sun.

'**Lady Caroline Nevill**' (*lan.* Cripps 1871). Flowers at first very large and often semidouble, later smaller and single, with 6–8 sepals, to 17 cm wide, pale lilac with a darker middle stripe, June–July. Gn 46: 33; JRHS 1946: 130.

'**Lady Londesborough**' (*pat.* Noble, before 1877). Flowers 12–15 cm wide, with 8 sepals, soft lilac at first, later silvery-gray, anthers dark brown. Flowers well.

'**Lady Northcliffe**' (*lan.* Jackman). Dark blue with a reddish cast, anthers white, May–June and August–September. NH 1935: 71; MCl 55; LLC 21.

'**Lasurstern**' (*pat.* Goos & Koenemann 1905). Very large flowers, sepals narrow and tapering to an acute apex, margins sinuate, dark purple-blue, anthers yellowish-white, May–June and fall. Gs 1926: 172; LLC 17.

'**Lincoln Star**' (*lan.* Pennell). Medium sized, sepals acute, purple-pink, anthers brown, May–June.

'**Marcel Moser**' (*pat.* Moser 1896). Sepals long acuminate, violet-lilac with a darker middle stripe, ventral side dark pink, May–June. Gs 1938: 264; LLC 36. Always a good variety but not superior to 'Nelly Moser'.

'**Maerchenfee**' (Goos & Koenemann). Carmine-pink.

'**Marie Boisselot**' (*lan.* Boisselot). Leaves simple to trifoliate, large, wide, dark green, somewhat tough, venation distinct,

indented; flowers 20 cm wide, petals seldom more than 6, pure white, overlapping, flat, somewhat transculcent, young anthers a clear light yellow. (Not identical to 'Mme Le Coultré.)

'**Miss Bateman**' (*pat.* Noble, before 1877). Medium sized, stellate form, 8 broad elliptic sepals, white, anthers red-brown, somewhat fragrant, May–June. NH 1937: LLC 29.

'**Miss Crawshay**' (*pat.* Jackman, before 1877). Flowers 12–13 cm wide, usually with 8 sepals, also with 12 in 2 series, obtuse elliptic-oblong, pink-lilac with darker middle stripe, June–August. LLC 53.

'**Mme Baron-Veillard**' (*jack.* Baron-Veillard 1885). Pale lilac-pink, July–September. Very strong grower.

'**Mme Edouard André**' (*jack.* Baron-Veillard 1892). Sepals acuminate, medium sized, dark reddish-purple, anthers light yellow, July–August.

'**Mme Grangé**' (*vit.* Grangé 1873). Sepal margins always rolled inward, never totally open and showing the pink underside, inside a bronze-purple with a deep brown mid-stripe, July–September. RH 1877: 150 (= *C. lanuginosa purpurea* Grangé).

'**Mme Le Coultre**' (*lan.*). Leaves large and wide, simple to trifoliate, rahter light green, not tough, venation distinct; flowers 20 cm wide, with 6–8(9) petals, pure white to nearly cream-white, seldom overlapping, margins often reflexed downward, not translucent, young anthers bright yellow to light brown. (Not identical to 'Marie Boisselot'.)

'**Mrs. Cholmondeley**' (*jack.* Noble, before 1877). Flowers to 20 cm wide, sepals 6, elliptic, narrow, soft lavender-blue, anthers brown, exceptionally abundant flowering, May–August.

'**Mrs. George Jackman**' (*pat.* Jackman, before 1877). Sepals elliptic, overlapping, white, cream-white on the ventral side, anthers brown (distinguishing it from the very similar 'Marie Boisselot'). Gn 16: 128; MCl 99.

'**Mrs. Hope**' (*lan.* Jackman). Flowers 15–17 cm wide, sepals wide and overlapping, clear lavender-blue, not fading, anthers purple-brown, May to June and August–September. Occasionally confused in the trade with 'Blue Gem' and 'William Kennett'.

'**Mrs. N. Thompson**' (*pat.* Pennell). Dark violet with a red midstripe, May–June and September. A novelty plant.

'**Mrs. Oud**' (= 'Mevr. Oud'; *lan.* Maarse 1957). Leaves usually trifoliate, sepals large, wide and overlapping, white, anthers brown, May–June. Gw 1967: 256. Poor grower.

'**Mrs. P. T. James**' (from the USA). Densely double, sepals rather regular and flatly arranged, narrowing in the middle, acuminate (much more acute than the similar 'Vyvyan Pennell'), violet, anthers yellow. US Pl. Pat. 2094.

'**Mrs. Wasscher**' (*lan.* Maarse 1961). Flowers very large, to 20 cm wide, with 7–8 sepals, light lavender with a darker mid-stripe, anthers purple. Novelty.

'**Nelly Koster**' (*pat.* Koster & Zonen). Flowers pearl-white. MCl 88.

'**Nelly Moser**' (*lan.* Moser 1897). Soft lilac-pink with a red midstripe, darker ventral side, May–June and September. JRHS 1946: 127; MCl 88; LLC 33. Best planted in semishade to prevent fading of the blooms. Plate 124.

'Neodynamia' (M. Johnson 1957). Jackmanii-type, with 4–6 sepals, purple-violet, anthers dark purple-red, filaments greenish, flowers very abundantly, July–September.

'Nordstern' (Goos & Koenemann). Violet-lilac to lavender-blue. Gs 1933: 131.

'Ordensstern' (Goos & Koenemann). Dark cornflower (centaurea)-blue. Gs 1938: 264.

'Perle d'Azur' (*jack*. Morel 1885). Light blue, otherwise very similar to 'Comtesse de Bouchard', June–August, flowers abundantly. NH 1934: 75; LLC 28.

'Phoenix' (M. Johnson 1958). Flowers 16–18 cm wide, with 8 sepals, blue-violet with a purple-red midstripe, anthers purple-red, filaments and stigmas white, July–August.

'Polarlicht' (Goos & Koenemann). Light blue.

'President' (*pat*. Noble, before 1877). Flowers 15 cm wide, 8 sepals, widest on the basal end, violet. Ventral side lighter and striped, June–July and October. Gs 133: 102 (= 'The President').

'Prins Hendrik (*lan*. P. Goedt, Boskoop 1908). Very large flowers, margin of the sepals sinuate, soft lilac, June and August–September. LLC 37. Good for forcing but somewhat difficult in culture.

'Proteus' (*flor*. Noble, before 1877). Large flowers, sepals elliptic, flowers double, although single on younger wood, lilac-pink, anthers light yellow, May–June. LLC 17. (First introduced under the name 'The Premier'.)

'Regenbogen' (Goos & Koenemann). Carmine-violet, anthers white.

'Rosy O'Grady' (*macropetala* × *alpina*, Skinner 1967). Flowers semidouble, stellate form, 7 cm, pink.

'Rouge Cardinal' (*pat*. Girault). Flowers 15–20 cm wide, usually with 6 sepals, rounded at the apex with a small tip, opening a velvety purple-red, later becoming purple, dense whitish pubescent on the ventral side, anthers reddish at first, later whitish, May–June and August–October.

'Royal Velours' (*vit*.). Flowers velvety purple, flowers very abundantly, July–September.

'Serenata' (Lundell, Sweden). Flowers stellate form, 6 sepals, purple-red, anthers gold-yellow, May–June. Novelty.

'Sir Garnet Wolseley' (*pat*. Jackman, before 1877). Flowers 12 cm wide, 8 sepals, bluish with a bronze cast, with a plum-blue middle stripe, anthers dark purple, May–June.

'Souvenir de J. L. Delbard'. Large flowers, 8 sepals, elliptic, obtuse, with a small apical tip, pink-lilac with a darker midstripe, anthers brown. Novelty plant.

'Star of India' (*jack*. Cripps, before 1877). Flowers 12 cm wide, sepals 4–6, purple, later violet-purple with a reddish midstripe, July–August. IH 1871: Pl. 50.

'Sternenwunder' (Goos & Koenemann). Cornflower-blue, anthers white-gray.

'The President'. Refer to **'President'**.

'Titania' (M. Johnson 1952). Flowers 20–22 cm wide, with 6–8 white sepals, often slightly reddish at the base, anthers dark purple-red, July–September.

'Ulrique' (M. Johnson 1952). Very large flowers, purple-pink, anthers purple-red, July–September.

'Venosa' (*vit*. Krampen? Wilke?, before 1860; alleged hybrid with *C. patens*). Flowers medium sized, reddish-purple, prominently veined. FS 1364 (= *C. viticella* venosa Hort.).

'Victoria' (*jack*. Cripps, before 1877). Flowers with 6 petals, obovate, purple-pink, paling, anthers brown, July–September, flowers abundantly. LLC 7. Strong grower.

'Ville de Lyon' (*vit*. Morel 1899). Flowers medium size, sepals wide, rounded, overlapping, deep carmine-red, limb somewhat darker than the middle, anthers yellowish, May–September. RH 1899: 184; Gs 1938: LLC 4; MCl 111.

'Ville de Paris' (*lan*. Christen 1885). Very large flowers, white to soft lilac, reddish ventral side. RH 1885: 133; Gs 1938: 264.

'Voluceau' (Girault). Flowers violet-purple, similar to 'Rouge Cardinal', but with older flowers distinctly more purple, anthers yellow at first, later whitish. Novelty.

'Vyvyan Pennll' (*pat*. Pennell). Flowers medium sized, very densely double and abundant, lilac-blue, with traces of purple and carmine in the center, sinuate margin, single, lighter flowers also appearing in the fall, anthers light yellow. As yet the best double flowered cultivar. Plate 75.

'Wallufer Rebe' (Goos & Koenemann). Wine-red, semi-double.

'W. E. Gladstone; (*lan*. Noble). Very large blooms, lilac, with darker middle stripe, anthers purple, June to September, but some years flowers poorly. LLC 61.

'White Swan' (*macropetala* × *alpina* var. *sibirica*, Skinner 1967). Flowers not double, pure white, to 12 cm wide.

'William Kennett' (*lan*. Cobbett, before 1877). Flowers 15–17 cm wide, 8 sepals, overlapping, margin sinuate, dark lilac with darker midstripe, anthers purple, May–August.

'Xerxes' (*jack*. Noble, before 1877). Large flowers, 6 sepals, violet with purple midstripe.

'Zauberstern' (Goos & Koenemann). Lilac-pink. Gs 1929: 153.

All *Clematis* prefer a semishaded location, at least at midday. They especially need a deep, cool topsoil, unheated by the sun. A fertile, humus soil with occasional fertilization is helpful. There are *'Clematis'* diseases that will suddenly kill a plant in midseason; effective counter measures have yet to be developed.

Lit. Boucher, G., & S. Mottet: Les Clématites, chèvrefeuilles, Bignones, Glycines, Aristoloches et Passiflores; 160 pp., 30 ill. Paris 1898. Contains descriptions of most of the French hybrids through 1898 ● Erickson, R. O.: Taxonomy of *Clematis* section Viorna; Ann. Mo. Bot. Gard. 1943, 1–62 ● Fisk, J.: Success with *Clematis*; 83 pp. Edinburgh 1962; 8 Pl. ● Kuntze, O.: Monogr. *Clematis*; in Verh. Bot. Ver. Brandenburg 1885, 83–202; with 1 ill. ● Jouin, E.: Die in Deutschland kultivierten, winterharten *Clematis*; in Jahrb. DDG 1907, 228–238 ● Lavallée: Les Clématites à grandes fleurs; Paris 1884, with many large plates ● Lloyd, C.: *Clematis*; 112 pp., 37 Pl. London 1965 ● Markham, E.: The Large and Small Flowered *Clematis* and Their Culture in the Open Air; 3. ed. London 1951, 124 pp. ● Moore, T., & G. Jackman: The *Clematis* as a Garden Flower; new edition, London 1877; 134 pp., 17 Pl. ● Pringle, J. S.: The cultivated taxa of *Clematis* sec. Atragene; in Baileya **19**, 49–90, 1973 ● Spingarn: The Large-flowered *Clematis* Hybrids; in Nat. Hort. Magazine 1935, 64–94 ● Fisk, I.: The Queen of Climbers; 88 pp., 43 color ill. Westleton 1975.

CLEMATOCLETHRA Maxim. — ACTINIDIACEAE

Deciduous twining vines, closely related to *Actinidia*, but easily distinguished by the 10 stamens and 1 pistil; winter buds distinct, branches with solid pith; leaves simple, alternate, finely dentate, without stipules; flowers in axillary racemes or panicles, sepals and petals 5 each; fruit a fleshy berry. — 10 species in China.

Clematoclethra actinoides Maxim. Twining to 10 m high or more, branches glabrous; leaves oval-oblong, 3–8 cm long, base rounded to somewhat cordate, finely dentate, glabrous except for tufts of hair in the vein axils beneath; flowers grouped in 3's, often also solitary, white, June; fruits black. BM 9439; DRHS 503. W. China. 1908. Hardy. z6 Plate 131; Fig. 258.

C. hemsleyi Baill. High twining, young parts tomentose, but soon becoming glabrous; leaves ovate, long acuminate, 5–10 cm long, fine glandular dentate, thin, base sometimes cordate, venation beneath brown pubescent, petiole 4–8 cm long; flowers grouped 8–12 together, in long stalked clusters, June; fruits black. SH 2: 609. China, Hupeh. z7 Fig. 258.

C. integrifolia Maxim. Twining to 5 m high, branches nearly glabrous; leaves oval-oblong, 4–7 cm long, base round, bristly dentate, glabrous beneath, blue-green; flowers solitary or in small clusters, small, white, fragrant, July; fruits black. Margin without actual teeth, simple dense and fine bristly (important for identification!). China, Kansu. 1908. z6

C. lasioclada Maxim. Twining 4 m high; branches pubescent; leaves ovate, 5–10 cm long, long acuminate, base round to cordate, bristly dentate, midrib above pubescent, venation beneath sparsely pubescent and lighter green; flowers 12 mm wide, 2–7 in axillary

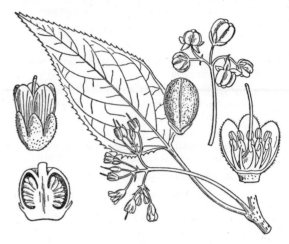

Fig. 258. *Clematoclethra hemsleyi*.
Fruit cluster above right (from Hemsley)

clusters, these shorter than the leaves; fruits 8 mm thick, black. ICS 3421. W. China. 1908. Plate 131. z6

C. scandens Maxim. Twining to 5 m high, branches densely brown bristly, leaves oblong to oval-lanceolate, 5–12 cm long, long acuminate, base round or tapering, margin somewhat bristly dentate, midrib above pubescent, likewise the venation beneath, petiole bristly; flowers grouped 3–6 in small, axillary cymes, June; fruits red. ICS 3420. W. China. 1908. z6 Plate 131.

Generally very hardy in England, unpretentious, preferring a fertile organic soil, otherwise cultivated like *Actinidia*.

CLERODENDRUM L. — VERBENACEAE

Small deciduous trees or shrubs, also vines; leaves simple, opposite, very unpleasant odor when crushed; flowers tubular, fragrant, usually in terminal umbels, limb 5 parted, stamen filaments often protrude wildly; calyx persistent, campanulate at first or inflated; fruit a fleshy, round, 4 seeded, light colored berry. — Over 150 species in the tropics and subtropics, of which a large group are grown as greenhouse plants, but only 2 species as landscape plants, in the temperate zone.

Clerodendrum bungei Steud. Shrub, to 2 m high, all parts unpleasant smelling, branches soon becoming glabrous; leaves broadly cordate-ovate, 10–20 cm long, coarsely dentate, pubescent beneath; flowers pink, 1.5 cm wide, fragrant, in 10–15 cm wide, capitate cymes, calyx reddish, August–September. BM 4880 (as *C. foetidum*); FS 863; JRHS 69: 29 (= *C. foettidum* Bge.). China. 1844. z7 Plate 74, 130. ⊕ ∅

C. trichotomum Thunb. Upright, tree-like shrub to 8 m high, branches short pubescent at first, very pithy; leaves ovate to elliptic, acuminate, 10–20 cm wide, entire or very finely crenate, dark green and softly pubescent on both sides; flowers white with reddish calyx, fragrant, 3 cm wide, in long stalked, 20 cm wide cymes, August–September; fruits blue, later becoming black, connate to the wide, red, fleshy calyx. BM 6561; BC 996; KIF 2:69 (= *C. serotinum* Carr.). Japan, E. China. 1800. z6 Plate 38. ⊕ ∅

var. **fargesii** (Dode) Rehd. Strong grower, very dense foliage, branches with narrow pith, nearly glabrous; leaves somewhat smaller, light green, new growth reddish, less pubescent; flowers white, calyx green (not red); fruits light blue, calyx lobe eventually pink. RH 1911: 522; HTS 149 (= *C. fargesii* Dode). China. 1898. Hardier than the species, but less ornamental value. z5? ∅

Pretty, but somewhat touchy shrubs with attractive foliage, flowers and fruit, however unpleasant odor when handled.

CLETHRA L. — Summersweet - CLETHRACEAE

Deciduous shrubs or also evergreen trees, branches stellate pubescent; leaves alternate, undivided, usually serrate; flowers white, in panicles or racemes, with persistent, 5 toothed calyx, petals 5, flared outward, stamens 10, style long, with 3 stigmas; fruit a 3 valved capsule with numerous fine seeds. — 30 species in the tropics and subtropics, of which only a few are in cultivation and winter hardy.

Clethra acuminata Michx. Shrub, to 3 m (to 6 m in its native habitat), young branches finely pubescent; leaves clustered at the branch tips, ovate-oblong, 7—14 cm long, long acuminate, pubescent beneath, at least on the venation; flowers in terminal, densely pubescent racemes, 5—20 cm long, petals white, erect, 8 mm long, calyx ribbed, stamen filaments pubescent, July—August. BB 2727; BC 1427; NBB 3:1; GSP 363. SE. USA, mountain forests. z6 Plate 124; Fig. 261. ✿

C. alnifolia L. Shrub, to 3 m high, growth narrowly upright, branches softly pubescent when young; leaves obovate, 4—10 cm long, short acuminate, sharply serrate, glabrous on both sides, with 7—10 vein pairs; flowers in 5—15 cm long, erect, pubescent racemes, fragrant, July—September. BB 2724; GSP 360; NBB 3: 1. Eastern N. America, in swamps and moist forests. z3—9 Plate 129, 131; Fig. 261. ✿

'Paniculata'. Strong grower; flowers in terminal panicles (not racemes!), much more attractive, as beautiful as *C. tomentosa* (= *C. paniculata* Ait.). Completely winter hardy. Introduced in England, 1770, but not a species, rather a clone of *C. alnifolia* and regarded as the best type for the landscape.

'Rosea'. Buds pink, flowers light pink, flowers somewhat less abundantly. Am. Nurseryman 1951; 3: 59. 1908. ✿

C. arborea Ait. Dense evergreen shrub or small tree, young branches rust-brown pubescent; leaves oblong, tapering at both ends, 8—12 cm long, serrate, glabrous

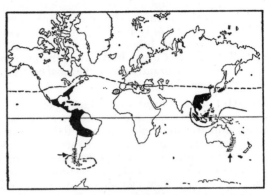

Fig. 259. Range map of *Clethra*; arrows, *Eucryphia*.
——— Southern limit of *Empetrum nigrum*, beneath, range of *E. rubrum*

above, rust-brown pubescent beneath; flowers in 15 cm long, nodding, brown pubescent panicles, white, August—October. Bm 1057; NF 4: 268; Pl. 54; HTS 148. Madeira, understory plant in the mountain forests. z8 Fig. 261. #

C. barbinervis S. & Z. Shrub, to 10 m high in its native habitat, much lower in cultivation, branches red-brown, smooth; leaves obovate, clustered at the branch tips, 6—12 cm long, with 10—15 paired veins, sharply serrate, both sides pubescent at first, eventually only on the venation beneath; flowers in 10—15 cm long, rather dense, terminal panicles, calyx and pistil pubescent, stamen filament glabrous, July—September. SH 2: 308 h—l; ICS 3968. Japan. 1870. Attractive species. z6 Plate 129, 131; Fig. 261, 262. ✿

C. delavayi Franch. Deciduous shrub, in its habitat to 10 m high, young branches stellate pubescent; leaves ovate-lanceolate, long acuminate, 5—15 cm long,

Fig. 260. From left to right: *Clethra delavayi*; *C. monostachya*; *C. fargesii* (from ICS)

serrate, softly pubescent beneath; flowers in terminal, 10—15 cm long, erect or horizontal, one-sided racemes, calyx lobes gray tomentose, becoming pink after the petals fall, stamens only half as long as the petals, somewhat pubescent, July—August. BS 1: Pl. 27; BM 8970; ICS 3964. W. China. 1884. After the evergreen species *C. arborea*, without a doubt the most beautiful of the genus. z7—8 Plate 131; Fig. 260. ⊕

C. fargesii Franch. Shrub, to 4 m high, glabrous, very similar to *C. barbinervis*, but the leaves are widest at midleaf, and the undersides remian densely tomentose; flowers in clusters of terminal racemes, to 25 cm long, fragrant, inflorescence and stalk densely tomentose, sepals lanceolate and long acuminate (on *C. barbinervis* round), style glabrous, July—August. ICS 3969. Central China. 1900 Hardy. z6 Plate 124, 131; Fig. 260. ⊕

C. monostachya Rehd. & Wils. Deciduous shrub or small tree, 2—8 m high; leaves elliptic or oval-elliptic, very rarely lanceolate, 7—13 cm long, 2.5—5.5 cm wide, long acuminate at both ends, sharply serrate, with 16—21 vein pairs, both sides glabrous, with axillary pubescence beneath, petiole 1—2.5 cm long; flowers in unbranched (!) racemes, 7—18 cm long, rachis densely brown pubescent, petals 5—6 mm long, with papillae outside, filaments and style pubescent; July—August. BM 8970 (as *C. delavayi*); ICS 3963. China; Yunnan, Sikang, Szechwan, in mountain thickets, 1700—2800 m. z6 Differing from *C. fargesii* in the very long, unbranched racemes, from *C. barbinervis* by the leaves being generally widest in the middle. Fig. 260.

C. tomentosa lam. Shrub, to 3 m high, young branches densely gray tometose; leaves similar to those of *C. alnifolia*, but tomentose beneath, serrate on the apical half, entire plant appearing gray; flowers a better white than those of *C. alnifolia*, blooming a month later, style pubescent. BM 3743; GF 4: 65; BC 998; BS 1: 672 (= *C. alnifolia* var. *tomentosa* Michx.). Southeastern N. America. 1731. z6—7 Plate 131. ⊕

Most species prefer a protected area in open forest, somewhat like *Azalea* culture.

Lit. Britton, N.L.: *Clethra*; in N. Amer. Flora **29**, 3—9, 1914 ● Hu. S.-Y. A revision of the genus *Clethra* in China; in Journ. Arnold Arbor. **41**, 164—190, 1960 (15 species are described) ● Preston, F. G.: The genus *Clethra*; in JRHS 1949, 245—247 ● Sleumer, H.: *Clethra*; in Englers Botan. Jahrb. **87**, 36—175.

CLEYERA Thunb. — THEACEAE

Evergreen shrubs; leaves alternate, leathery tough, stalked, undivided; flowers bisexual, solitary or in fascicles, usually axillary, rather small; calyx 5 parted, petals 5, with numerous stamens attached to the base of the petals; fruit more or less fleshy. — 1 species from Himalaya to Japan, 16 species from Mexico and Panama to the W. Indies. Very closely related to *Eurya*, which is, however, dioecious.

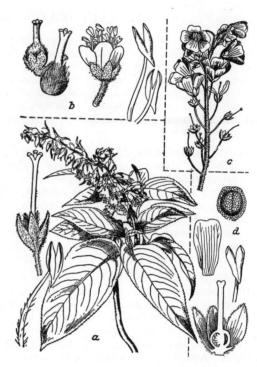

Fig. 261. **Clethra** a. *C. acuminata*; b. *C. barbinervis*; c. *C. arborea*; d. *C. alnifolia* (from Loddiges, Drude, Koehne)

Fig. 262. *Cleathra barbinervis* (from ICS)

Cleyera japonica Thunb. Evergreen shrub; branches sparse and open, leaves narrow oblong to oval-oblong, 7—10 cm long, 2—4 cm wide, entire, acute, dark green and glossy above, lighter beneath, petiole to 2 cm long; flowers grouped 1—3, axillary, white, later becoming yellowish, sepals ovate, 3 mm long, ciliate, petals rather thick, narrow oblong, 8—10 mm long, anthers white, June—July; fruit a pea-sized, eventually black berry. ICS 3462 (= *C. ochnacea* DC.). Japan, Korea and China to Nepal. z8

The plants found in cultivation in England are of the following varieties:

var. **japonica**. Leaves relatively small, usually only 5—7 cm long and 2—3 cm wide, petiole 6—8 mm long; flower stalk 6—10 mm long, calyx smaller (= *C. japonica* var. *kaempferiana* [DC.] Sealy; *C. ochnacea* var. *kaempferiana* DC.). Japan. z8 # Ø

var. **wallichiana** (DC.) Sealy. Leaves longer, 6—9 cm long, 3—4 cm wide, petiole 8—10 mm long; flower stalk 12—25 mm long, calyx larger. BM 9606; HAl 36. China, Nepal. z8 # Ø

'Tricolor'. Small shrub; leaves elliptic to linear—lanceolate, 10—12 cm long, margin light green and gold-yellow, gray-green and cream-white parallel striped, also pink-red toned when young; flowers pale yellow, 1—2 in the leaf axils. BM 7434 (= *C. fortunei* Hook. f.). Exported from Japan by R. Fortune around 1860. z8 Plate 130. # Ø

Culture somewhat like *Rhododendron*, but recommended only for very mild areas.

Lit. Kobuski, C.E.: Studies in the Theaceae. II. *Cleyera*; in Jour. Arnold Arb. **18**, 118—129, 1937.

CLIANTHUS Banks & Soland. — LEGUMINOSAE

Evergreen shrub with long, ascending branches; leaves alternate, pinnate, unpaired, entire; flowers large, red or 2—3 colored, standard petal reflexed, keel beak-like and bowed downward, wings quite small and narrow; calyx campanulate, with 5 nearly evenly long teeth; fruit an inflated pod. — 4 species in Australia, New Zealand, Indochina and the Phillipines. Only 2 species in cultivation.

Clianthus puniceus Banks & Soland. Evergreen shrub, to 5 m high both in its habitat and in cultivation in very mild areas, branches long woody, climbing, young branches finely pubescent; leaves 7—15 cm long, odd pinnate, leaflets 13—25, oblong, 1—3 cm long, dark green and glabrous above, finely appressed pubescence beneath; flowers 6—15 in pendulous racemes, scarlet-red, June—fall; fruits 5—7 cm long. BM 3584; LNz 77; HTS 152; MNZ 5; DRHS 507. New Zealand, North Island. 1831. z8 Plate 75; Fig. 263. # ✧

'Albus'. Flowers cream-white, less abundantly flowering. MNZ 6. Not as attractive.

'Magnificus'. Leaflets larger, to 3 cm long; flowers smaller

Fig. 263. *Clianthus puniceus*

than the species, but darker red and with dark spot on the standard petal base. # ✧

'Roseus'. Flowers dark carmine-pink. MNZ 7.

Very beautiful plants, but useful only in the very mildest areas, otherwise to be over-wintered in a cool greenhouse.

CLIFTONIA Banks ex Gaertn. f. — CYRILLACEAE

Evergreen shrubs, open branched, occasionally a small tree, rare in cultivation; leaves alternate, short petioled, without stipules, entire; flowers in terminal panicles, with 5—8 sepals and petals, the filaments flattened at the basal end; ovaries superior, 3—4 chambered, with a 3—4 lobed, nearly sessile stigma; fruit not dehiscent, ovate, with 3—4 wings and as many seeds. — Only 1 species. Closely related to *Cyrilla*.

Cliftonia monophylla (Lam.) Sarg. Only a small shrub in European gardens but under favorable conditions in its habitat, a small to medium sized tree; leaves oblong-lanceolate, 4—5 cm long, obtuse, base cuneate, dark green above; flowers in 3—6 cm long racemes, white, fragrant, with 5 obovate petals, calyx small, green, 10 stamens (*Cyrilla* has 5!), February—March; fruits winged and resembling those of buckwheat, 6 mm long. BM 1625; SS 2: 52; KTF 127 (= *C. ligustrina* [Willd.] Spreng.; *Ptelea monophylla* Lam.). SE. USA. Around 1814. z8 #

Soil preference somewhat like that of *Rhododendron*; a light soil with peat and sand, but very tender!

CLYTOSTOMA Miers — BIGNONIACEAE

Evergreen vine, climbing by means of tendrils; leaves opposite, with 1 pair of opposing, short stalked leaflets, the rachis elongated into a thin, simple tendril, these also occasionally absent; flowers in 2's and axil-lary or terminal and in panicles; calyx campanulate, with 5 small or awl-shaped (subulate) teeth, corolla funnelform-campanulate, the limb lobes imbricate, stamens 4; ovaries conical, warty, 2 chambered, with ovules in 2 rows; fruit a compressed, prickly capsule with numerous seeds, each nearly encircled by a wing. — 12 species in tropical America.

Clytostoma callistegioides Bur. & Schum. High climbing vines; leaflets elliptic-oblong, 7—8 cm long, acuminate, margin sinuate, glabrous, glossy above, venation reticulate beneath; flowers in 2's, calyx campanulate, with awl-shaped teeth, corolla pale purple, striped, 7 cm long, tube yellowish with purple stripes, limb 5—7 cm wide, the lobes outspread, broad ovate, obtuse, undulate, April—June. FS 907; BR 28: 45; BM 3888; MCL 107 (= *Bignonia callistegioides* Cham.; *B. speciosa* Graham; *B. picta* Lindl.). S. Brazil, Argentina. z10 # ☺

C. purpureum Rehd. High climbing vine; leaflets occasionally in 3's, oval-oblong or obovate-oblong, short acuminate, fresh green above, lighter beneath, entire or occasionally toothed, about 7—8 cm long; flowers in 2's axillary or also in clusters, calyx tubular-campanulate, with short, triangular teeth, corolla lilac with a white eye, a rather slender, 2.5 cm long tube, lobes ovate and outspread. BM 5800; DRHS 510 (= *C. binatum*; *Bignonia purpurea* Lodd.). Uruguay. 1898. z10 # ☺

Grown outdoors only in completely frost free areas, otherwise under glass. Culture like that of *Bignonia*.

CNEORUM L. — CNEORACEAE

Low, evergreen shrub; leaves alternate, without stipules, leathery, narrow, with oil cells in the leaves and on the bark; flowers solitary in the leaf axils or in groups, regularly arranged; calyx usually 3—(occasionally 4) parted, corolla likewise; stamens and carpels 3—4; fruits small, drupe-like aggregates dividing into 3 parts. — 2 species in the Mediterranean region and on the Canary Islands.

Cneorum pulverulentum Vent. Small, evergreen shrub, 0.3—1.5 m high, young branches and leaves with a dense, appressed fine gray pubescence; leaves linear to oblanceolate, 2.5—7 cm long, rounded at the apex; flowers light yellow, solitary in the leaf axils of the upper leaves; fruits usually 2—3, gray, globose. BFCa 38 and 191 (= *Neochamaelea pulverulenta* [Vent.] Erdtm.). Canary Islands. z9 #

C. tricoccum L. Small shrub, narrowly upright, 30—50 cm high, branches thin, forked, gray-green; leaves linear to oblanceolate, 3—5 cm long, rounded at the apex; flowers yellow, inconspicuous, few on the branch tips, May—June; fruits red-brown. Mediterranean region. 1793. z8 Plate 131. #

Found in most botanic gardns.

COCCULUS DC. — MENISPERMACEAE

Deciduous or evergreen, usually twining vines or shrubs; leaves alternate, simple, usually rounded or lobed, palmately veined, without stipules; flowers in axillary panicles, racemes or cymes, with 6 petals and 6 stamens (the closely related genus *Menispermum* has 6—8 petals and 12—24 stamens); fruit a generally curved drupe. — 11 species in the tropics and subtropics.

Cocculus carolinus (L.) DC. Deciduous vine, twining to 3—4 m high, branches pubescent; leaves ovate to cordate, 3—7 veined, 5—10 cm long, often indistinctly lobed, blue-green beneath, pubescent, glabrous above and glossy green; flowers white, inconspicuous, July; fruits red, globose, pea-size. BB 1648; DL 3: 47. South-eastern USA. 1759. z7 Plate 132; Fig. 264. ∅ ⚭

C. laurifolius DC. Evergreen shrub or small tree; leaves lanceolate, 10—15 cm long, 3—5 cm wide, acuminate, distinctly 3 veined, dark green and glossy; flowers small, in 3 to 10 cm long, axillary panicles; fruits black, like small peas. Himalaya. Very attractive for the warmer temperate regions. z8 Fig. 132. # ∅ ⚭

C. trilobus (Thunb.) DC. Twining to 4 m high, branches pubescent; leaves ovate, undivided or 3 lobed, 4—9 cm long, middle lobe elongated, both sides pubescent, green foliage persistent; flowers inconspicuous, in axillary cymes, June—August; fruits black-

Fig. 264. *Cocculus carolinus*. Right female flower, left 2 male flowers (from Gay, Baillon)

blue, pruinose. BS 1: 470; BM 8489 (= *C. thunbergii* DC.; *Cebatha orbiculata* Ktze). Japan, China, Philippines. Hardiest species. z7 ∅ ⚭

Culture and uses like that of *Menispermum*; which see.

CODIAEUM A. Juss. — EUPHORBIACEAE

Evergreen shrubs, leaves alternate, leathery and rather thick, glabrous, with a milky sap; flowers monoecious, in slender, axillary racemes, male flowers with 3–6(usually 5) relfexed sepals, 5 scale-like petals, smaller than the sepals; 20–30 stamens; female flowers without petals, with 5 sepals, ovaries 3 chambered, with a seed compartment in each chamber. — Around 15 species in Malaysia, Polynesia and N. Australia, but only 1 species in common cultivation.

Codiaeum variegatum (L.) A. Juss "Croton". Of this species, only the var. *pictum* (Lodd.) Hook. has any garden significance; leaves ovate to linear, entire or lobed, variegated, especially with red, yellow and mixed tones. — A long cultivar list may be found in Bailey, Stand. Cycloped. Hortic.: 815–819. z9 # ∅

Planted as an ornamental shrub in the frost free Mediterranean region, and in S. Africa as a hedging plant. Otherwise useful only as a greenhouse plant.

COLEOGYNE Torr. - ROSACEAE

Monotpyic genus; deciduous shrub, branches opposite and thorned; leaves simple, opposite, small, entire; flowers solitary, sepals 4, persistent, petals absent, stamens 20–40, style attached to the side of the unilocular ovary, long haired at the base; fruit a small, glabrous drupe. — 1 species in Colorado, USA.

Coleogyne ramosissima Torr. Deciduous shrub, very thick, sparse branches, thorned, 0.3–1.5 m high, bark ash-gray, later black; leaves clustered at the branch tips, linear to spathulate, 6–12 mm long, entire, flat above, with 2–4 furrows beneath, stipules very small, persistent; flowers solitary, 1 cm wide, yellowish to brownish, at the tips of short side branches, March–May. MS 202. SW. USA, on the desert frines. z7 **d s** ○

Cultural preferences unknown.

COLEONEMA Bartl. & Wendl. — RUTACEAE

Small evergreen shrubs, leaves alternate, linear to filamentous, glandular punctate; flowers solitary axillary, calyx 5 parted, petals 5, channelled beneath; 10 stamens, of which 5 are fertile, the other 5 are hidden in the grooves of the petals; fruit an aggregate capsule of 5 parts, each with a small "horn" — 5 species in S. Africa, SW. Cape Province.

Coleonema album (Thunb.) Bartl. & Wendl. Small, very densely branched shrub, 60–80 cm high; leaves very densely packed, linear, 6–12 mm long, 1–2 mm wide, acute, finely dentate, with 2 or more rows of glandular dots beneath, aromatic; flowers solitary in the upper leaf axils, 8 mm wide, white, petals spathulate, April. RCA 26; EKW 362 (= *Diosma album* Thunb.).

S. Africa. 1798. z9 Plate 130.

For landscape use only in the mildest areas.

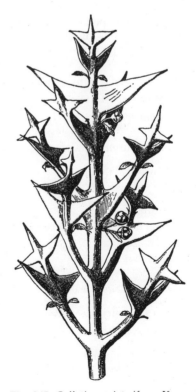

COLLETIA Comm. — RHAMNACEAE

Leafless or nearly leafless thorny shrub, branches decussate, sometimes thick and flattened, not cross-furrowed or pinnate; leaves (if present) very small, opposite, normally found only on small seedlings and quickly abscising; flowers solitary or in fascicles, appearing under the thorns, calyx campanulate or tubular, 4–6 parted, petals absent, stamens 4–6; fruit a 3 parted capsule. — 17 species in S. America, outside of the tropics.

Colletia armata Miers. Shrub, 2 m high; the younger, pubescent branches armed with slender, cylindrical, sparse thorns, all decussate, the thorns about 1 to 3 m long, sharp acuminate; leaves elliptic, 1 cm long (usually absent); flowers waxy-white, tubular, 3 mm long, grouped 1–3 together, fragrant, August–

Fig. 265. *Colletia cruciata* (from Kerner)

September. BMns 586 (= *C. valdiviana* Phil.). Chile. 1862. Pretty. z8 **d** ○

'**Rosea**'. Flowers with a trace of pink-red, very abundant, even on very small plants.

C. cruciata Gill. & Hook. Shrub, to 3 m high, very stiff, with 2 types of thorns: flat, triangular branch thorns, and ones that are thinner and more rounded, all blue-green and opposite; flowers yellowish-white, greenish at the base, small, flowering in fall and winter, but only flowering well after a warm summer, scented like almonds. HM 1883; BM 5033; FS 1451. Uruguay. 1824. z8

Fig. 265. **d** ○

C. infausta N. E. Br, Shrub, to 2.5 m high, the younger parts actually only awl-shaped thorns like those of *C. armata*, but glabrous; leaves (when present) 6−8 mm long; flowers dull white, with traces of red, 6 mm long, the lobes reflexed, anthers only half protruding, April −June. BM 3644 (as *C. horrida*). Chile. 1833. z8

Very interesting shrubs, notable for their curious appearance. Hardy in mild areas. Found in most botanic gardens.

COLQUIHOUNIA Wall. — LABIATAE

Evergreen shrubs, branches soft, erect or twining; leaves large, opposite, petioled, crenate; flowers few in axillary whorls or in terminal racemes or spikes; corolla tube curved, throat inflated. — 6 species in Asia, E. Himalaya, SW. China.

Colquhounia coccinea Wall. Shrub, 2 m high, branches semiwoody, 4 sided, softly pubescent; leaves elliptic-lanceolate to cordate, 7−15 cm long, crenate, gray-white tomentose beneath; flowers 3−5 in axillary, short whorls, scarlet-red and yellow, corolla 2.5 cm long, tubular, 2 lobed, lower lobe further 3 lobed, upper lobe directed upward, August−October. BM 4514; SNp 123; BMns 115. Himalaya. z8 Ⓕ Himalaya (for erosion control). # ✿ ∅

var. **vestita** (Wall.) Prain. Lower growing, entire plant densely woolly, otherwise like the species. Himalaya, dry areas. z8 Plate 131. # ✿ ∅

COLUTEA L. — LEGUMINOSAE

Deciduous, non-thorny shrub with patchy or peeling bark; leaves odd pinnate, leaflets entire, stipules small; flowers yellow to red-brown, in few flowered, axillary, long stalked racemes; pods stalked, membranous-inflated, bi-valved, dehiscing at the tip, or not. — 27 species, from M. Europe eastward to SW. China and NW. Africa.

(Those species not found in cultivation have been omitted.)

Key to the Most Important Species (from Browicz)

1.   Flowers usually yellow   3
    Flowers more or less reddish or coppery   2

2. (1) Fruits typically curving upward at the tips:
    C. orientalis
    Fruits not curved at the tip:
    C. × media

3. (1) Keel terminating beak-like:
    C. nepalensis
    Keel round at the tip, without a beak   4

4. (3) Incisions between the calyx teeth acute:
    C. melanocalyx
    Incisions between the calyx teeth rounded   5

5. (4) Leaves with 2−3 pairs of leaflets:
    C. persica
    Leaves with 3−7 pairs of leaflets   6

6. (5) Wings longer than the keel, with spurs:
    C. cilicica
    Wings as long or shorter than the keel, occasionally somewhat longer, but then without spurs:
    C. arborescens

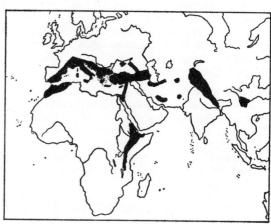

Fig. 266. Range of the genus *Colutea*
(from Browicz)

Colutea arborescens L. Shrub, 2−3 m high and wide, young branches pubescent; leaflets 9−13, obovate-elliptic, 1.5−3 cm long, slightly emarginate and with fine thorny tips, lighter beneath, thinly pubescent; flowers yellow, 2 cm long, 6−8 in racemes, wings as long or longer than the keel, June−August; pod inflated, greenish, large, glabrous, not dehiscent. BM 81; HM 1499; HF 2423. S. Europe, N. Africa. 1570. Ⓕ USSR (for erosion control). z6 Fig. 267. **S** ✿ ⚭

f. **brevialata** (Lange) Browicz. Only about 1 m high; leaflets usually 11, much smaller; flowers 2−6 in racemes, yellow, wing petals of the 1−1.5 cm long flowers much shorter than

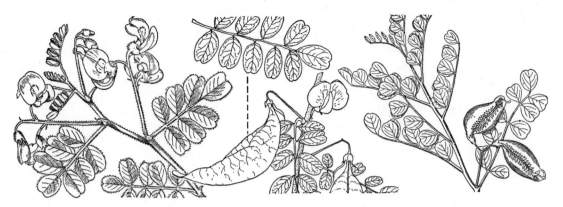

Fig. 267. **Colutea.** From left to right, *C. media*, *C. arborescens*, *C. orientalis* (from Schmidt, Watson, D. B.)

the keel; pods narrower. SH 2:53 k−m, 54q (= *C. brevialata* Lange). S. France. **S**

'Bullata'. Dwarf form; leaflets 5−7, obovate to nearly circular, ached somewhat spoon-like, 1−1.5 cm long, Before 1902.

'Crispa'. Low form; leaflets sinuate on the margin, otherwise like the species. Before 1864.

C. cilicica Boiss. & Balansa. Very similar in growth habit to *C. arborescens*; leaflets 9−13, but not emarginate, bluish beneath and not pubescent; flowers 3−5 in racemes, yellow, more clustered at the branch tips, wings longer than the keel (important for identification!), calyx not tomentose, June−July. SH 2: 54 h−k, 55 a−e; Browicz, Pl. 3 (= *C. longialata* Koehne). Asia Minor, Crimea, Caucasus. Hardy. z6 **S** ○

C. gracilis Freyn & Sintenis. Shrub, to 3 m high, young branches pubescent; leaflets 7−9, obovate, only 4−8 mm long, thickish, indistinctly veined, with appressed pubescence beneath; flowers yellow, 1−4 in racemes, keel not beaked, calyx with appressed dark pubescence; pods 3−4 cm long, dehiscing at the tip. SH 2: 51 i−k, 57 a−e; SL 156; Browicz, Pl. 12. Transcaspian. 1911. z6 **S** ○

C. istria Mill. Shrub, 1 m high; leaflets 9−13 (occasionally to 19), obovate, to 1 cm long, with appressed pubescence; flowers brownish-yellow, 2 cm long, 1−4 in racemes, standard 1.5 cm wide, wings as long as the keel, June to August; pods 5 cm long. SH 2:53 e−i, 54p; Browicz, Pl. 11 (= *C. halepica* Lam.; *C. pocockii* Ait.). SE. Turkey to Sinai. 1752. z7−8 ○

C. × media Willd. (*C. arborescens × C. orientalis*). Similar to *C. arborescens*, but with brown or deep orange flowers; leaves blue-green, leaflets 11−13, obovate, 1.5−2.5 cm long, pubescent beneath; pods 6−7 cm long, always closed at the tip, June to July. DL 3: 273; SH 2: 53 t−x. Known before 1790. Often found with *C. arborescens* in cultivation. z6 Fig. 267. ⊕ ⚭

C. melanocalyx Boiss. & Heldr. Very similar to *C. arborescens*, mainly differing in the longer calyx (1 cm long, more tubular, brown tomentose); leaflets 7−11, more pubescent beneath; flowers yellow, wings some-

what longer than the keel, July−September; pod about 5 cm long. SH 2: 54 l−m, 55 f−i; Browicz, Pl. 5. Turkey, in the mountains. z7

C. nepalensis Sims. Shrub, to 3 m high, young branches loosely white pubescent, later becoming glabrous; leaves 4−8 cm long, with 3−5 pairs of leaflets, these elliptic to obovate, to 10 mm long and 7−8 mm wide; flowers yellow, often somewhat reddish, to 22 mm long, keel with distinct, 2−3 mm long, upward bowed beak, calyx broadly campanulate, to 8 mm long, with acute teeth, inside black pubescent; pods 4−6 cm long and 2−2.5 cm wide, rounded above, with short tips, June−July. Browicz, Pl. 25; BM 2622. Afghanistan, Pakistan, Kashmir, N. India, Nepal, in the mountains to 4000 m. z6

C. orientalis Mill. Shrub, to 2 m high, young branches pubescent; leaflets 7−11, thickish, blue-green on both sides, 8−15 mm long, somewhat pubescent beneath when young; flowers reddish-brown or orange, 2−5 in racemes, June−September, wings shorter than the keel, calyx somewhat pubescent; pods to 4 cm long, light violet-purple, dehiscing at the tip. HF 2424; DL 3: 274; Browicz, Pl. 17. Caucasus. 1710. z7 Fig. 267. **S** ○ ⚭

C. persica Boiss. Shrub, 1.5−2 m high; similar to *C. gracilis*, but with young branches glabrous; leaflets 5−7, thick, bluish, obovate, 8−15 mm long; flowers 2 cm long, 3−5 together, pure yellow, wings longer than the keel, July—August, calyx funnelform, with 5 sharp teeth, somewhat pubescent; pods to 5 cm long, glabrous, dehiscing at the tip. SH 2: 55 o−q, 56 g−h; Browicz, Pl. 13. Iran. 1902. Used in Persia (Iran) for wicker work; probably not to be found in cultivation. z7 **S** ○

var. **buhsei** Boiss. Flowers and leaves somewhat larger; pods somewhat appressed pubescent. Browicz, Pl. 20. 1925. **S** ○

Unpretentious ornamental shrubs for light, alkaline soil, fast growing, with no disease problems, easy to grow.

Lit. Browicz, K.: The genus *Colutea* L.; in Monogr. Botan. **14**, 1−135; 28 plates Warsaw 1963.

COMPTONIA L'Hér. — MYRICACEAE

Deciduous shrubs, closely related to *Myrica*, but differing in the fern-like incised leaves and stipules. — 1 species in N. America.

Comptonia peregrina (L.). Coult. Densely branched shrub, 0.5—1 m high, all parts aromatic, branches pubescent, red-brown at first, brittle; leaves alternate, oblong-linear, 5—12 cm long, 1—1.5 cm wide, deeply pinnatisect; fruits appearing like small acaena burrs from the awl-shaped bracts; flowers inconspicuous. BB

1162; GSP 93; RMi 94; Rho 40: 415 (= var. *tomentosa* Chevalier). E. Canada to SE. USA. 1714. z2 Plate 131. **S** ○ ∅

var. **asplenifolia** (L.) Fern. Branches with finer pubesence; leaves smaller, glabrous or nearly so. Rho 40: 415. Coast of Long Island to Virginia. Plate 131. **S** ○ ∅

Found on dry, sterile, sandy soil in its habitat. Generally only in botanic gardens but quite hardy and attractive.

CONVOLVULUS L. — CONVOLVULACEAE

Annuals or perennials, only rarely shrubby or semi-shrubby; branches procumbent or twining or erect; leaves alternate, entire, toothed or lobed; flowers funnelform. — 250 species in the temperate and subtropical zones.

Convolvulus canariensis L. Twining vine, woody at least on the lower portion; leaes oval-oblong, 4—9 cm long, densely pubescent, venation elevated on the underside; flowers in axillary cymes with 7—9 flowers, sepals densely pubescent, corolla light blue. Canary Islands, common in the forest. z9

C. cneorum L. Silver-gray subshrub, 20—60 cm high, foliage dense; leaves evergreen, lanceolate, silvery, 2—5 cm long; flowers funnelform, light pink, in small umbels at the branch tips, opening one after the other, May. BM 459. S. Europe. 1640. z8 Fig. 268. # ∅

Very attractive small shrub for the rock garden, needs a very warm, sunny location. Keep dry and protected from frost in the winter.

C. floridius L. f. Shrub, 2—4 m; leaves oblong-linear or oblong, seldom spathulate, 2—14 cm long, short and densely pubescent; flowers in terminal panicles, many flowered, corolla white or light pink, 1 cm wide. BFCa 217; KGC 44. Canary Islands, frequently found in low spots and also in gardens. z9

C. oleifolius Desr. var. *pumilis* Pamp. Subshrub, foliage dense, flowering branches to 15 cm high, densely branched; leaves narrow oblanceolate, gradually becoming cuneate at the base, without a petiole, 1—3.2 cm long, 3.5—7 mm wide, with dense appressed silvery pubescence on both sides; sepals broad ovate, 6 mm long, corolla funnelform, 2.7 cm wide, soft pink, with 5 darker lines. BMns 324. Cypress, N. Africa. z9

C. scoparius L. f. Shrub, 1 m or taller; leaves linear-filamentous, abscising quickly, 0.5—5 cm long, short pubescent or also glandular; flowers 5—6 terminal or axillary, corolla white or pink. BFCa 221. Canary Islands, rather common. z9

Fig. 268. *Convolvulus cneorum* (from Bot. Mag.)

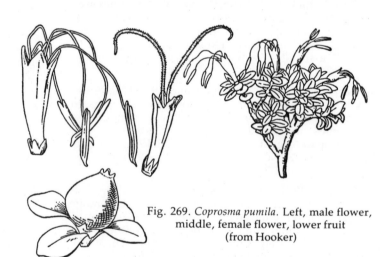

Fig. 269. *Coprosma pumila*. Left, male flower, middle, female flower, lower fruit (from Hooker)

COPROSMA Forst. — RUBIACEAE

Evergreen shrubs or small trees, leaves opposite, each species being quite distinctive in size (from a few mil-

limeters to 20 cm); flowers dioecious, neither attractive nor ornamental, solitary and a few in fascicles, calyx

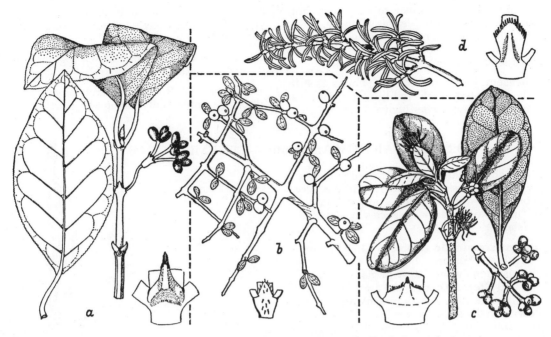

Fig. 270. **Coprosma** a. *C. cunninghamii*; b. *C. rigida*; c. *C. lucida*; d. *C. pseudocuneata*
(from Adams)

with 4–5 teeth, corolla funnelform to campanulate, 4–5 parted, stamens 4–5, filaments long, threadlike, anthers hanging from the tips; fruit a fleshy, ovate to round drupe. — About 90 species in New Zealand, Tasmania to New Guinea. ⚭

Coprosma acerosa Cunn. Evergreen, low shrub, mostly procumbent, occasionally about 1 m high, branches wiry and tangled, finely pubescent at first; leaves linear, in opposing pairs or fascicled, 6–18 mm long; flowers conspicuous; fruits globose, 6 mm thick, translucent light blue. New Zealand. Good in the rockery for its fruit. z8 #

var. **brunnea** Kir. Shoots brown, shorter; leaves spaced farther apart (= *C. brunnea* [Kirk.] Chesem.). Interesting in the garden for the brown leaf color. z8 # ∅

C. cunninghamii Hook. f. (perhaps *C. propinqua* × *C. robusta*). Shrub, 1.5–3 m high; leaves 1.5–5 cm long, 3–6 mm wide, acute or obtuse; flowers in unstalked clusters, grouped 2–12 together on short, thick branchlets, inconspicuous; fruits light yellow, 6 mm. New Zealand. z8 Fig. 270. #⚭

C. lucida Forst. Shrub, 1–4 m high, abundantly branched; leaves 5–12 cm long, elliptic-obovate, apex obtuse, leathery tough, very glossy; fruits 8–12 mm long, oblong, orange-red, very attractive. LNz 160. New Zealand. z8 Fig. 270. #⚭ ∅

C. nitida Hook. f. Densely branched shrub, to 2 m, or lower in high altitudes in its habitat, branches stiff, more or less glabrous; leaves oblong-elliptic to lanceolate, 4–20 mm long, leathery, glossy, densely ar-

ranged; flowers at the ends of short branches, dioecious; fruits red or orange. BMns 88. Tasmania; Victoria. z8 #⚭

C. parviflora Hook. F. Broad growing shrub; leaves opposite, circular to obovate, 7–12 mm long, 4–6 mm wide, leathery, with lighter reticulte venation above; fruits dark purple or white, globose, transparent, 5 mm thick. MNZ 7; JRHS 70: 110. New Zealand; quite rare in cultivation. z8 #⚭

C. petriei Cheesem. Dwarf shrub with mat-like habit, only a few centimeters high; leaves narrow obovate, more or less pubescent, 3–6 mm long; flowers solitary, only a few millimeters long, tubular; fruits 3–6 mm wide, globose, dark purple to violet, very attractive. New Zealand. z7 #⚭

C. propinqua A. Cunn. Shrub to small tree, branches opposite, often at right angles to the stem, very thin, finely pubescent at first; leaves opposite or in opposing clusters, 8–15 mm long, 2–3 mm wide, linear to oblong; flowers inconspicuous, solitary or 2–4 axillary; fruits usually light blue, translucent, globose, 7 mm. BM 9286. New Zealand. z8 #⚭

C. pseudocumeata W. R. B. Oliver. Wide growing shrub, to 3 m in its habitat, but often to only 50 cm, branches short, thick, somewhat 4 sided; leaves on short branches, fascicled, cuneate or narrow obovate, 15–20 mm long, 2–6 mm wide, thick, leathery, dark green above, lighter beneath; fruits scarlet-red, oblong, 5–6 mm long. PRP 23. New Zealand, in the mountains, frequently near the timber line and very attractive in fruit. z8 Fig. 270. #⚭

C. pumila Hook. f. Very similar to *C. petriei*, but branches and leaves glabrous; leaves leathery, light green, 3—8 mm long, margin thickened; flowers greenish-white; fruits red to orange (= *C. repens* Hook. f.). New Zealand. z8 Fig. 269. # ⚭

C. rigida Cheesem. Erect shrub, 2(5) m, branches stiff and sparsely arranged, bark red-brown, branches wiry, somewhat glossy; leaves obovate-oblong, 1—2 cm long, 3—9 mm wide, thick, leathery; fruits orange-yellow to white, obovoid, 4—6 mm long. New Zealand. z8 Fig. 270.

All species only for the mildest regions, needs a cool protected area.

Lit. Oliver, W. R. B.: The genus *Coprosma*; 207 pp., 67 illus., 59 plates; Bull. Bishop Museum, Honolulu 1935.

CORALLOSPARTIUM Armstrong — LEGUMIONOSAE

Nearly leaflesss shrub with deeply furrowed branches; very similar to *Carmichaelia*, but differing in the very thick, erect branches and the bivalved pod without the thickened, frame-like border. — 1 species in New Zealand, South Island.

Corallospartium crassicaule (Hook. f.) J. B. Armst. Stiff, erect shrub, 1—2 m, branches thick, more or less cylindrical or also somewhat flat, with many, parallel, deep furrows and alternate nodes, to 1 cm wide; leaves small, but rarely seen, circular on young plants, oblong with age; flowers in dense clusters of 8—20, petiole and calyx densely pubescent, the 6—8 mm long papilionaceous corolla dull cream-white; pod 6—7 mm long, with 1 seed. MNZ 9. New Zealand (in cultivation at Malahide, Ireland). Fig. 271.

var. **racemosum** Kirk. Branches only 4 mm thick, less stiff, with fewer furrows; calyx teeth acute, flowers less numerous in the clusters or also in racemes (= *C. racemosum* [Kirk] Cockayne & Allan). z8

Easily cultivated in dry, well drained soil, in mild climates.

Fig. 271. *Corallospartium crassicaule* (from Adams)

CORDYLINE Comm. ex Juss. - AGAVACEAE

Evergreen trees or shrubs with single or multiple stems and with long, narrow leaves clustered at the branch tips; flowers white, in branched panicles; corolla 6 parted, stamens 6, stigma 3 lobed; fruit a fleshy, globose, 3 seeded berry. — About 15 species in New Zealand, Australia and S. America.

Cordyline australis Hook. Tree, to 12 m, either with an unbranched trunk or multistemmed just above the ground and then branched (as in Plate 145); leaves 30—90 cm long, 2.5—6 cm wide, stout, acuminate; flowers in 50—100 cm long, much branched panicles, cream-white, fragrant, anthers yellow, May; fruits white or bluish, globose, 6 mm thick. LNz 28; BM 5636. New Zealand. 1823. z8 # ✧ Ø

Also in cultivation, the following forms:

'**Aureostriata**'. Leaves with several yellow longitudinal stripes. 1843. Especially attractive. # Ø

'**Lineata**'. Leaves wider than those of the species, the sheath-like leaf base purple. # Ø

'**Purpurea**'. Not uniform, many plants more or less brownish colored, others more purple, leaf base and midrib beneath purple (= 'Atropurpurea'). # Ø

'**Veitchii**'. Leaf base and midrib beneath carmine. # Ø

C. banksii Hook. f. Shrub, occasionally branched, otherwise forming a rosette branching from the ground, stems 1—3 m long; leaves numerous, erect, apexes nodding, 0.7—1.5 m long, 4—8 cm wide at the middle, linear-lanceolate, long acuminate, with 4—8 distinct veins on either side of the midrib, the other veins much thicker, primary veins green, red or yellow, midrib thick, rather flat above, but elevated semicircular beneath, petiole 30—60 cm long, deeply furrowed above, half-round beneath; flowers white, in 50—120 cm long, erect or somewhat pendulous, loose, many-branched panicles, the individual flowers white, only 1.2 cm long; fruit white, globose, 1.2 mm thick. New Zealand. z9 # Ø

'**Purpurea**' (Duncan & Davies). Leaves bronze-purple. Originated in cultire, about 1945. #

C. baueri Hook. f. Tree-like, single stemmed, 1.5 to 3 m high, with a crest of 35—60 cm long leaves, these sword-like, tapering to the base, with a wide midrib and veins of similar form; flowers white, about 1 cm wide, sessile, fragrant, in large panicles above the foliage. BM 2835 (as *Dracaena australis*). Norfolk Island. Around 1820. Easily distinguished from *C. australis* by the shorter, wider and uniformly veined leaves. z9 # Ø

C. indivisa (Forst. f.) Steud. Single stemmed, 3–6 m high, stem densely covered with ring-like leaf scars, crest 1.8–2.5 m wide, composed of numerous, densely arranged leaves; leaves 0.7–1.5 m long and 12–18 cm wide, with long, drawn out tips, very tough and leathery, with distinct yellow and red patterned midvein

and green longitudinal ribs, bluish-green beneath; flowers in pendulous, 60–120 cm long panicles, the individual flowers about 1 cm wide, white with a trace of pink or lilac; fruit a globose, 8 mm thick berry with black seeds. BM 9096. New Zealand, first introduced into England around 1850, rather rare in cultivation but extremely ornamental. z9 Plate 143. # Ø

The plant often found in gardens under this name is usually *C. australis*, or at least, not *C. indivisa*.

Some large specimens may be found in Western Europe along the Atlantic coast and in the Mediterranean region, always in frost free climates.

COREMA D. Don. — EMPETRACEAE

Small, evergreen shrubs, heather-like in appearance; leaves small, linear, usually in whorls of 3, flowers in terminal fascicles (difering from *Empetrum*); fruit a berry with 3 seeds. — 2 species in Spain, Portugal and eastern N. America.

Corema album (L.) D. Don. Shrub, 25–50 cm high, upright, heather-like, young branches densely pubescent; leaves narrow linear, 6–9 mm long, obtuse, margin inflexed leaving only a thin slit visible on the dorsal side, soon glabrous, dark green, in whorls of 3; flowers inconspicuous; fruits white, 6 mm thick. SH

2:92 a–f. Spain, Portugal. 1774. z8 # Ø

C. conradii (Torr.) Loud. Shrub, heather-like, bushy, broader growth habit, young branches nearly totally glabrous; leaves narrow linear, 3–6 mm long, obtuse, margin involute, usually in whorls of 3, very densely arranged, dark green; flowers in terminal heads, inconspicuous, the male flowers have purple-brown stamens, April; fruits quite small, dry when ripe. BB 2344. Eastern N. America. 1841. Hardy. z6 # Ø

Like *Empetrum* in appearance, with somewhat larger leaves, fruits and flowers on the branch tips.

CORIARIA L. — CORIARIACEAE

Deciduous shrubs, subshrubs or perennials with angular branches; leaves opposite or in whorls, simple, entire, distichous; flowers monoecious or bisexual, in racemes, 5 parted, with 10 stamens; fruit berry-like, poisonous, with 5 seeds, enclosed within the fleshy, persistent, enlarged, and colored petals. — About 15 species in the Mediterranean region, India, China, Japan, New Zealand and temperate S. America.

Coriaria japonica Gray. Shrub, to 1 m high; leaves ovate-lanceolate, 3–10 cm long, bright green, 3 veined; flowers axillary, on older wood, May; fruits flat-globose, bright red at first, later violet-black. BM 7509; DRHS 545; BC 1057. Japan. 1893. z7 Plate 133.

C. myrtifolia L. To 3 m high in its habitat, growth wide, branches angular; leaves ovate, 3–6 cm long, acute, tough, bright green above, more gray-green beneath; fruits greenish at first, later black. Lauche, Dendrologi: 175. Mediterranean region. 1629. Poisonous to man and livestock, once used for tanning and to produce a black dye, particularly in France. z7–8 Ⓕ S. Europe (screening). Fig. 273.

C. nepalensis Wall. Deciduous shrub, widely branching; leaves ovate to oblong, 7–10 cm long on the long branches, much smaller on the short branches, distinctly 3 veined, glabrous, entire, base somewhat cordate; flowers on the previous year's wood in 5 cm

long, cylindrical racemes, greenish-yellow, the petals becoming fleshy at fruiting and purple-black. HAl 72c. Himalaya, Upper Burma. Only for the warmest areas. z9

C. sinica Maxim. Deciduous shrub, broad and open growing, to 2 m high in European cultivation, to 4 m high in its habitat, branches 4 sided, warty; leaves elliptic to ovate, quite short acuminate, nearly sessile, base rounded, 3 veined, 3–8 cm long; anthers red and somewhat ornamental; fruits in axillary, 3–5 cm long racemes, black. China. 1907. Of slight garden merit.

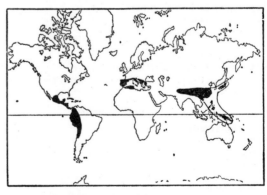

Fig. 272. Range of the genus *Coriaria*

C. terminalis Hemsl. To 1 m high, young branches finely scabrous; leaves broad ovate to ovate-lanceolate, 3—7 cm long, abruptly acuminate; flowers in 15—20 cm long, terminal racemes, June; fruits black. W. China. 1908. z7 ⚭

f. **fructo-rubro** Hemsl. Fruits 'currant' red, translucent. Cultivated by Hillier.

var. **xanthocarpa** Rehd. & Wils. Fruits translucent, yellow. BM 8325; MD 1897: Pl. 1. Sikkim. More frequently found in cultivation than the species and also hardier. z7 ⚭

C. thymifolia Humboldt. Subshrub or more perennial-like, but the rhizomes becoming woody, to 1 m high, branches outspread, 4 sided, somewhat pubescent; leaves ovate, 1—1.5 cm long, very narrow and densely spaced along the branches; flowers in 15—20 cm long, terminal racemes, frequently unisexual, dark brown, petals later becoming fleshy and black. Mexico to Peru. It is not yet certain whether this species occurs in New Zealand; Allan includes this plant in the *C. lurida* complex. z8 Plate 133.

All these species thrive on well drained soils, preferably in warm, protected areas; a protective covering is advisable in the winter. The branches may freeze back to the ground in winter but regrowth is good the following spring.

Fig. 273. *Coriaria myrtifolia* (from Lauche)

CORNUS L. — Dogwood — CORNACEAE

Deciduous shrubs, occasionally also trees; leaves opposite, (except on *C. alternifolia* and *C. controversa*), entire, usually pubescent; flowers small, 4 parted, in terminal cymes without bracts or in capitate umbels with 4 or 6 bracts; fruit a berry-like, white, blue, red or black drupe. — About 40 species in the northern temperate zone.

Since the genus *Cornus* is so various, individual species are often singled out as new genera. The traditional genus has been retained in this book; an outline of the new genera is as follows:

Cornus L.
    4 species in Europe
Afrocrania (Harms) Hutch.
    1 species in tropical Africa
Benthamidia Spach
    3 species in N. and C. America
Chamaepericlymenum Hill
    2 circumpolar species
Dendrobenthamia Hutch. (*Cynoxylon*)
    12 species in Himalaya and E. Asia
Swida Opiz (= *Thelycrania* [Dumort.] Fourr.)
    36 species in the northern temperate zone, 3 in Mexico and 1 in the N. Andres.

Outline of the Genus

Section **Thelycrania** (C. A. Mey.) Endl.
    Flowers in short panicles or cymes, without a bract-perianth;
        ● Leaves alternate:
            C. alternifolia, controversa
        ●● Leaves opposite:
            C. alba, amomum, amoldiana, australis, baileyi,
bretschneideri, coreana, drummondii, globrata, hessei, macrophylla, obliqua, oblonga, paucinervis, pumila, racemosa, rugosa, sanguinea, slavinii, stolonifera, stricta, walteri

Section **Macrocarpium** Spach
    Flowers yellow, in umbels with a small bracteate perianth, appearing before the leaves; fruits oblong:
        C. chinensis, mas, officinalis, sessilis

Section **Cynoxylon** Raf.
    Flowers greenish-yellow, in dense umbels, surrounded by very large, white or reddish, petal-like bracts; fruits capitate, dense, but not connate;
        C. florida, nuttallii

Section **Benthamia** (Lindl.) Benth. & Hook.
    Like the above section, but fruits connate in a fleshy head:
        C. kousa, capitata

Section **Arctocrania** Endl.
    Perennials; flowers in capitate umbels, surrounded by 4 bracts:
        C. suecica, canadensis

Cornus alba L. Shrub, to 3 m high, branches narrowly upright, not creeping, always without stolons, red and pruinose when young; leaves ovate-elliptic, acute, 4—8 cm long, bright green above, scattered pubescent, bluish beneath, usually with 6 vein pairs; flowers yellowish-white, in 3—5 cm wide cymes, May—June; fruits a dirty white to light blue, ellipsoid, taller than wide, flattened on both ends. NK 16: Pl. 78; DB 1955: 10 (= *C. tatarica* Mill.). Siberia to Manchuria and N. Korea. 1741. z2 Fig. 274. ∅ ⚭

'Argentomarginata'. Leaves regular, broad white margins, fall coloring carmine-red (= 'Variegata'). Before 1800. Plate 134. ∅

'Behnschii'. Leaves reddish and white marbled, but rather inconsistent. Originated in the nursery of R. Behnsch, in Duerrgoy near Breslau (now Wroclaw, Poland). Before 1898.

'Gouchaultii' (Gouchault). Good grower; leaves with a pink border at first, often partly white, middle pink and green, later becoming green with yellow spots. ∅

'Kesselringii'. Branches deep black-brown, new growth dark brown; leaves later brownish-green. Originated from seed of 'Sibirica' in the Petersburg Botanic Garden, Russia, 1905. ∅

'Rosenthalii' (Rosenthal). Leaves large, with a wide gold-yellow border, gray-green in the center. Brought into the trade by the Rosenthal nursery of Albern near Vienna, Austria before 1896. ∅

'Sibirica'. Somewhat weaker grower than the species, branches with a light coral-red bark; leaves more broadly oval (= C. tatarica var. sibirica Koehne). Before 1830. ∅

'Sibirica Variegata'. Leaves larger than those of 'Argenteo-marginata', often irregular and somewhat stunted, more gray-green, margin narrow white (= 'Elegantissima'). Before 1867. Rather common. Plate 139. ∅

'Spaethii' (Spaeth). Weak grower, compact; leaves bronze-yellow at first, later with a broad gold-yellow margin, sometimes totally gold-yellow, heat tolerant. Spaeth, Berlin. 1884. (in the trade 1889). ∅

C. alternifolia L. Tall shrub, occasionally also a small tree, to 8 m high, branches arranged in horizontal tiers, bark a glossy purple-brown, young branches not pruinose, green, glabrous; leaves ovate-elliptic, clustered at the branch tips, 6−12 cm long, glossy dark green above, nearly glabrous, bluish beneath, with pubescence irregularly appressed in various directions, and 5−6 vein pairs; flowers small, white, in 5 cm wide cymes, May−June; fruits blue-black, pruinose, stalk red. BB 2720; GTP 312; NBB 2: 644. Eastern N. America. 1760. Likes moist areas. z3 Plate 138; Fig. 274.

'Argentea' (Temple & Beard, USA). Leaves white variegated; easily distinguished from the white variegated form of C. controversa in the cuneate leaf blade base. Around 1900. Plate 76. ∅

C. amomum L. Shrub, to 4 m high, branches purple-brown, erect, pith brown; leaves ovate-elliptic, to 12 cm long, dull green above, lighter beneath and with 4−7 red-brown pubescent vein pairs; flowers yellowish-white, in 4−6 cm wide, arched cymes, May−June; fruits gray-blue, rounded. BB 2714; GSP 350; NBB 2:644. Eastern N. America, in moist forests and along streams. 1683. Widely used as an understock for grafting some species. Plate 137. z6 ∅

C. × arnoldiana Rehd. (C. obliqua × C. racemosa). Differing from C. obliqua in its more upright growth habit, branches thinner, turning gray in the 2nd year; inflorescence less pubescent; fruits white to light blue, seed less furrowed. ST 2: Pl. 40. Before 1900. Plate 138. z4

C. aspera see: **C. bretschneideri**

C. asperifolia see: **C. drummondii**

C. australis C. A. Mey. Very similar to C. sanguinea, but with leaves more ovate, 8 cm long, both sides densely pubescent at first, later both sides with appressed pubescence, rough beneath, with 3−4 vein pairs; style clavate (club-shaped); fruits 5−6 mm thick. SH 2:299c. Asia Minor, around the Black and Caspian Seas. z7 Plate 138.

var. **koenigii** (Schneid.) Leaves large, on flowering branches to 13 cm long, petiole 1−2 cm long; fruits 8−10 mm thick. SH 2: 299d (= C. koenigii Schneid.). Transcaucasia. 1912.

C. baileyi Coult. & Evans. Shrub, upright, to 2.5 m high, without stolons, branches short woolly pubescent, red-brown in winter, pith white, wide; leaves oval-lanceolate, 5−12 cm long, bluish and woolly pubescent beneath; flowers small, in pubescent, 3−5

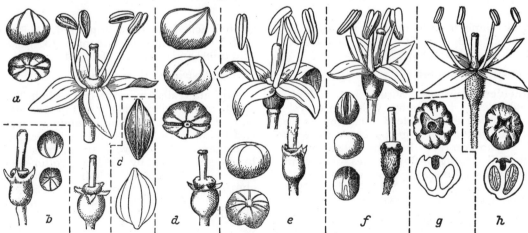

Fig. 274.**Cornus** (single flowers, staminate and pistillate flowers, fruit as seen from several sides). a. C. stolonifera; b. C. racemosa; c. C. alba; d. C. baileyi; e. C. stricta; f. C. drummondii; g. C. alternifolia; h. C. controversa (from Koehne, Wangerin)

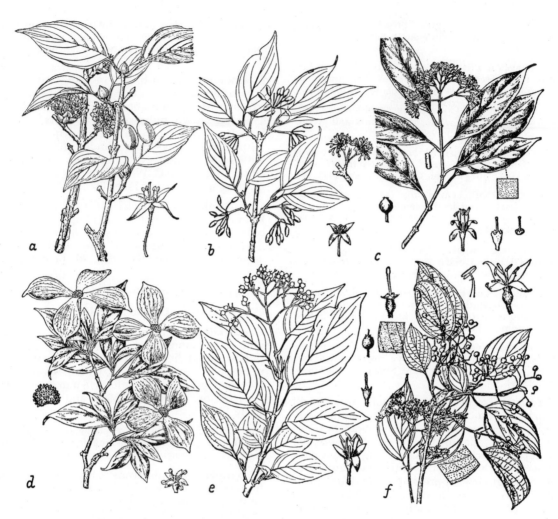

Fig. 275. **Cornus** a. *C. officinalis*; b. *C. chinensis*; c. *C. oblonga*; d. *C. capitata*;
e. *C. macrophylla*; f. *C. walteri* (from ICS)

cm wide cymes, June; fruits 8 mm thick, round, wider than long, white. BB 2716; BC 1065; GSP 348. N. America. 1892. z5 Plate 137; Fig. 274.

C. brachypoda see: **C. controversa**

C. bretschneideri L. Henry. Shrub, 3–4 m high, branches pubescent when young, yellowish or yellowish-red in winter; leaves ovate, 5–10 cm long, long acuminate, dull green above, gray-green with loose appressed pubescence beneath, somewhat rough, with 5–7 vein pairs; flowers cream-white, in 5–10 cm wide cymes, June, style shorter than the petals; fruits blue-black, 6 mm thick. SH 2: 298d; ICS 3937 (= *C. aspera* Wanger.). N. China. 1887 z5

C. canadensis L. A perennial, 10–20 cm high, all the leaves in whorls at the branch tips (important distinction from the very similar *C. suecica*); leaves ovate, 2–4 cm long, with 2–3 paired veins; flowers greenish-red, in small, terminal conical heads, surrounded by 4 large,

white bracts, June; fruits bright red. BM 880; RFW 250; NBB 2: 643. N. America. Greenland to Alaska, in moist, acid forest and moor. z2 Plate 134.

C. candidissima see: **C. racemosa**

C. capitata Wall. An evergreen tree in its habitat, a tall shrub in the milder parts of Europe; leaves ovate-lanceolate, 7–12 cm long, acuminate, tapering to a short petiole, dull gray-green, with dense appressed pubescence; flowers very small, in small, terminal heads, surrounded by 4–6 large, sulfur-yellow bracts, June–July; fruits strawberry-like, fleshy, carmine, 2.5 cm thick, favorite food of birds, October. LF 249; BM 4641; FS 739; SNp 72 (= *Benthamia fragifera* Lindl.). Himalaya. 1825. z8 Plate 75, 138, 140; Fig. 275. # ✧ ⊘ ⚭

C. chinensis Wanger. Closely related to *C. mas* and *C. officinalis*; tree, 8–10 m high or taller; leaves elliptic-ovate, long acuminate, base rounded, in general to 14 cm long and 7 cm wide (although a specimen in a cool greenhouse at Savill Garden, Windsor Great Park, England has leaves about 30 cm long), with 6−7 veins on both sides, bright green above, whitish pubescent beneath; flowers sulfur-yellow, in large, sessile fascicles, appearing before the leaves, March−April; fruits black. ICS 3941; BS 1: 59; JRHS 87: 72. Central and S. China, Szechwan, over a broad range. Known since 1901, but only introduced into cultivation in England around 1950. z8−9 Fig. 275.

C. circinata see: **C. rugosa**

C. controversa Hemsl. Very similar to *C. alternifolia*, but much taller, normally tree-like, to 15 m, branches also tiered, brown, pruinose (important for identification!); leaves broad elliptic, short acuminate, 7−15 cm long, with 6−9 vein pairs, pubescent beneath, hairs all facing in one direction; flowers in flat, 10−15 cm wide cymes, June; fruits blue-black, 6 mm thick. BM 8464; NK 16: 15; KIF 1: 94 (= *C. brachypoda* K. Koch non C. A. Mey.; *C. macrophylla* Koehne non Wall.). Japan, China. 1880. z5−6 Plate 138; Fig. 274. ∅

'Variegata' (Barbier). Leaves white bordered. Introduced by Barbier to the trade in 1896. Beautiful planted as a specimen; frequently found in French and Italian parks. The most splendid specimen in Europe is in the park of Dunloe Castle, near Killarney, Ireland, about 8 m high and 10 m wide, quite regular in its broad conical habit. Plate 76. ∅

C. coreana Wanger. Tree, to 20 m, closely related to *C. walteri*, bark deeply furrowed and broken into square plates, young branches reddish; leaves elliptic, base round cuneate to round; petiole 1−2 cm long; inflorescence 7−8 cm wide; fruits 5 mm thick. NK 16: Pl. 27. Korea. z6 Plate 140. Fig. 274.

C. drummondii C. A. Mey. Upright shrub, to 6m high, branches rough hairy, pith brown, narrow; leaves oval-elliptic, acuminate, 4−10 cm long, rough above, densely gray tomentose beneath; flowers yellowish-white, in loose, to 8 cm wide cymes, June−July; fruits white, globose, 5−6 mm thick, seed globose. BB 2715 (as *C. asperifolia*) (= *C. asperifolia* auct.). Eastern USA, from Virginia to Florida and Texas, usually in moist forests and thickets. 1836. Having only slight garden merit. Ⓕ USA (in windbreaks and screens). z7

C. 'Eddie's White Wonder' (Eddie, around 1966). *C. nuttallii* × *C. florida*. Small tree or tall shrub, with a dominant single stem, branches rather horizontally spreading and short; leaves like those of *C. nuttallii*, coloring orange, brown and red in fall; inflorescence with 4 large, white bracts, nearly circular to broad obovate, overlapping, occasionally also with 5−6 bracts, inflorescence (with 4 bracts) 10−12 cm wide, flowers very abundantly. Breeder H. M. Eddie & Sons, Vancouver, B.C., Canada. Cold hardiness to −10°C, probably tolerating even colder temperatures for short periods of time. Plate 132. ✧

C. femina see: **C. stricta**

C. florida L. Common White Dogwood. Tree to 10 m high or a broad branched, dense shrub; young branches green and soon becoming glabrous, brown and often pruinose in winter; leaves ovate to broad ovate, 7−15 cm long, dull green above, whitish beneath, the 6−7 paired veins pubescent, fall foliage a good scarlet-red to violet; flowers small, indistinct, greenish, 12 mm wide heads, but surrounded by 4 white, obovate, emarginate bracts to 4 cm long, May; fruits ovate, scarlet-red, 1 cm long, with persistent calyx. BB 2712; NBB 2: 643; DB 1951: 206. N. America, in moist and dry forests. Ⓕ USA (in green belts). z5−6 Plate 135, 136; Fig. 276. ✧ ∅

Of over 30 cultivars the following are some of the most important found in American nurseries:

'Cherokee Chief' (US Pl. Pat. 1710). Bracts dark red, the young growth an attractive light red. Introduced by Ike Hawkersmith, Winchester, Tenn., USA in 1958. ✧

'Cherokee Princess;'. Growth narrowly upright, good grower; flowers on young plants, flowers 10−12 cm wide. Originated by C. W. Highdon, Kentucky, USA but introduced by Hawkersmith.✧

'De Kalb Red' (US Pl. Pat. 965). Semi-dwarf; bracts an intense dark wine-red. Breeder, De Kalb Nurseries, Norristown, Penn. USA 1950.✧

'Fastigiata' Growth especially narrow and upright. Originated 1910 inthe Arnold Arboretum.✧

'First Lady' (US Pl. Pat. 2916). Young leaves yellow and green, in fall the green turns a chestnut brown, the yellow becomes pink tinted; flowers white. ✧

'Gigantea'. Inflorescence measures 15 cm wide over the bracts. Originated 1932 on the Phipps Estate, Long Island, N.Y., USA. ✧

'Pendula'. Branches rather stiffly pendulous. Selected in 1887 in Vienna, Austria from material sent from New Jersey, USA.✧

'Pluribracteata'. With 6−8 bracts, sticking together at the tips forming a "crown", white (= var. *urbiniana* [Rose] Wanger.?). Originated before 1914 in Orange County, N. Carolina, USA. Plate 135. ✧

'Prosser Red'. Poor grower; flowers carmine-red (not pink), few flowers on younger plants. Selected 1914 by Bruce Howel, Knoxville, Tenn., USA.✧

'Pygmy'. Dwarf habit, 8 year old plants are scarcely 1 m high; flowers white, abundant, but the bracts are small. Found in the Riverside Nursery by Leon Hawkersmith.✧

'Rainbow' (US Pl. Pat. 2743). Large white bracts; bicolored yellow-green leaves, fall color scarlet-red. Introduced 1967 by J. D. Schmidt, Troutdale, Ore., USA. ✧

f. **rubra** (West.) Schnelle. Bracts light or dark pink or red. In cultivation since at least 1770; found in 1731 by the botanist Marc Catesby. This is the wild form frequently found in nurseries, but much surpassed by the clones with larger bracts. Plate 76. ✧

'Welchii'. Leaves irregularly white variegated, green and pink, but also often deformed. DB 1955: 220 (as "Willsii"). Disseminated from the Cole Nursery, Painesville, Ohio, USA, since 1937.✧ ∅

Fig. 276. *Cornus florida* (from Baillon)

'White Cloud' Foliage bronze; flowers especially abundantly, white. Grown since 1946 by the Wayside Nursery, Mentor, Ohio, USA. ⊕

'Xanthocarpa'. Leaves light green; fruits yellow. Selected in 1919 from material grown in Saluda, N. Carolina, USA. ⊕

C. glabrata Benth. Shrub, to 4 m high, branches slender, nodding, red-brown, soon glabrous; leaves narrow-elliptic, acuminate, 3—8 cm long, both sides glossy bright green, with 3—4 vein pairs; flowers white, in 3 cm wide cymes, June; fruits 5—6 mm thick, white to light blue. SH 2: 269 g—h. Western N. America. 1894. z6

C. gracilis see: **C. racemosa**

C. hemsleyi Schneid. & Wanger. Shrub or also small tree, branches pubescent, later red; leaves oval-rounded, 5—7 cm long, short acuminate, gray-white beneath, with dense appressed pubescence, 6—8 brown pubescent vein pairs (important for identification!); flowers small, in 5—7 cm wide cymes, anthers blue, July; fruits globose, black-blue, 6 mm thick. Sh 2: 296 m—n. China. 1908. z6 Plate 138.

C. hessei Koehne. Shrub, only 50 cm high; leaves narrow-elliptic, to 3 cm long, blackish-green, dark violet in fall; flowers in 3—4 cm wide cymes, June—August; fruits bluish-white, pea-size, seed wider than long. Sh 2: 294 k—l. Origin unknown, probably NE. Asia. Closely related to *C. alba*. z5 ∅

C. kousa (Buerg.) Tall shrub or tree to 7 m, branches erect, soon becoming glabrous; leaves ovate-elliptic, acuminate, 5—9 cm long, base cuneate, margin usually sinuate, dark green above, blue-green beneath, with large, brown axillary tufts, scarlet-red in fall; flowers in very small, dense heads, surrounded by 4 acute-ovate, 3—5 cm long bracts, June; fruits pink-red, strawberry-like, globose, 2 cm thick, fleshy, on 4—6 cm long stalks. Add 2: 43; DB 1951: 212 (*Benthamia japonica* S. & Z.).

Japan, Korea. 1875. Flowers 2 weeks after the similar *C. florida*. z5—6 Plate 139; Fig. 277. ⊕ ∅ ⚭

var. **chinensis** Osborn. Usually tree-like, taller than the Japanese type, some fine, as well as some thick branched types in cultivation; leaves light green, seldom sinuate, veins yellowish, more pubescent beneath; bracts to 6 cm long, wider at the base and overlapping. BM 8833; DB 1952: 76; ICS 3945. China. 1907. z5—6 Plate 139. ⊕ ∅ ⚭

'Milky Way'. Especially attractive form, selected by Wayside Gardens, Mentor, Ohio, USA, 1961. ⊕

'Rubra'. Bracts carmine-pink. Originated in 1950 in the Hohman nursery at Kingsville, Md. (USA); also later found in Japan by Creech. ⊕

'Xanthocarpa'. Fruits yellow. Found in Holland. ⊕ ⚭

C. macrophylla Wall. Tall shrub, or a multistemmed tree to 15 m high in its habitat, branches yellowish or reddish; leaves elliptic-ovate to elliptic-oblong, 10—16 cm long, long acuminate, dark green above, glabrous, bluish beneath, appressed pubescent, with 6—8 vein pairs; flowers yellowish-white, in 8—15 cm wide, rounded, panicle-like cymes, July—August; fruits blue-black, globose, 6 mm thick. BM 8261; LF 251; ST 1: 41; ICS 3931 (= *C. brachypoda* C. A. Mey. non K. Koch non Miq.). Japan, China, Himalaya. 1827. z6 Plate 138; Fig. 275. ⊕ ∅

C. mas L. Cornelian Cherry. Shrub, to 5 m high and wide, occasionally a small tree, young branches greenish pubescent, later glabrous; leaves ovate-elliptic, acute, 4—10 cm long, glossy above, both sides with appressed pubescence, 3 to 5 vein pairs; flowers gold-yellow, in small umbels, with yellow subtending leaf before the normal foliage, flowering on older wood, February—April; fruits red, oblong, 2 cm long, glossy, edible but sour. HF 2705; HM Pl. 204. Middle and Southern Europe, Asia Minor, Armenia, Caucasus; in dry deciduous forests and brushlands. Cultivated for centuries; valued hedge shrub. Ⓕ Czechoslovakia (in screens and windbreaks). z5 ⊕ ⚭

'Alba'. Fruits nearly white.

'Aurea'. Leaves yellow; fruits red (grown by Hillier). ∅

'Elegantissima'. Leaves partly broad yellow or pink margined, partly all yellow (= f. *aureomarginata* Schelle).

'Flava'. Fruits yellow (= f. *xanthocarpa* Bean). ∅

'Macrocarpa. Fruits larger than those of the species, pear-shaped. Cultivated on the Balkan Peninsula and in Caucasia (around Tiflis!). ⚭

'Nana'. Growth dwarf and rounded.

'Pyramidalis'. Growth narrowly upright, branches only slightly outspread. Only plant observed by the author is in the Alpine Botanic Garden in Frohnleiten, Steiermark, Austria; 1972, 2 m high. Plate 140.

f. **sphaerocarpa** Cretzoiu. Fruits globose, not oblong. Romania.

'Variegata'. Leaves regularly with a wide white border (= var. *argenteomarginata* Schelle). ∅

'Violaceae'. Fruits violet-red. Before 1865. Rare. ⚭

The Cornelian Cherry Dogwood is still cultivated in some parts of Europe for its fruits. In Turkey it is used to make sherbert, in Russia it is made into preserves. The fruits contain sugar but they have a tangy taste.

C. nuttallii Audubon. Tall shrub, a 25 m tree in its native habitat; leaves elliptic-ovate to obovate, short acuminate, 8—12 cm long, both sides pubescent only when young, later becoming completely glabrous, with 5—6 paired veins; flowers very small, in hemispherical heads, surrounded usually by 6 (occasionally 4 or 8) yellowish-white, 4—6 cm long bracts, later somewhat pink toned, May; fruits ellipsoid, 1 cm long, orange-red. BM 8311; SPa 197; SS 112. Western N. America. 1835. Hardy. Most attractive species of the entire genus. Plate 76, 137, 138; z7 Fig. 277. ⊕

'Eddiei'. Leaves on new growth green, later sulfur-yellow spotted. Found in the wild near Vancouver, 1925. ⊕ ⌗

'Gold Spot'. Leaves yellow variegated. American selection. Around 1965 (?). Without particular garden merit.

'North Star'. American selection with narrow, long, not overlapping bracts. Less attractive than the species (grown by Hillier).

C. oblonga Wall. Evergreen shrub, 3—6 m high, young branches angular and distinctly yellow-brown pubescent; leaves opposite, narrow elliptic, acuminate, base cuneate, 3—12 cm long, 1.2—3.5 cm wide, dark green above, glossy and appressed pubescent, dull gray beneath and softly pubescent, especially on the 5—6 veins on either side of the yellow-brown pubescent midrib; flowers in terminal, conical panicles, 7 cm long and equally wide, fragrant, the individual flowers white, only 4 mm wide, October—November; fruits ovate, 8 mm long, black. ICS 3932. Himalaya, Khasi Hills, China, Szechwan, Yunnan. 1818. Very rare in cultivation. z9 Fig. 275.

C. obliqua Raf. Very similar to *C. amomum*, open growing, branches more olive-green; leaves oval-elliptic to oblong, acuminate, 5—8 cm long, pendulous, dull green above, whitish beneath, venation brownish pubescent; flowers white, in 4 to 5 cm wide, gray shaggy pubescent corymbs, June—July; fruits dull blue, seed furrowed. MS 438; GSP 348 (= *C. purpusii* Koehne). NE. USA. 1888. z4 Plate 137.

C. officinalis S. & Z. Very similar to *C. mas*, but more tree-like in a favorable climate, otherwise a tall shrub; leaves oval-elliptic, acuminate, 5—12 cm long, dull green above, somewhat pubescent, light green beneath, 6—7 vein pairs with distinct brown pubescent tufts in the axils (especially noticeable in summer), fall foliage a bright red-brown; flowers yellow, as on *C. mas*, but somewhat larger and 1—2 weeks earlier, March—April; fruits scarlet red, 1.5 cm long. KO 176; ICS 3940. Japan. 1877. z6 Plate 138; Fig. 275. ⊕ ⌗

C. paniculata see: **C. racemosa**

C. paucinervis Hance. Shrub, to 3 m high, branches angular, pubescent at first; leaves elliptic or oblong-obovate to elliptic-lanceolate, 4—10 cm long, equally tapering at both ends, deep green above, lighter beneath, both sides thinly pubescent, with 2—4 vein pairs; flowers in dense, long stalked, 6—8 cm wide cymes, July—August; fruits black, globose, 5—6 mm wide. Bm 9157; EP IV 229: 18 a—e; ICS 3934. Middle China. 1907. z5? Easily recognized by the narrow leaves with few veins.

C. pumila Koehne. Shrub, to 2 m high, densely branched, slow growing, internodes very short; leaves packed at the branch tips, broadly ovate, 4—8 cm long, dark green above, lighter beneath, appressed pubescent, with 4—5 vein pairs; flowers in long stalked

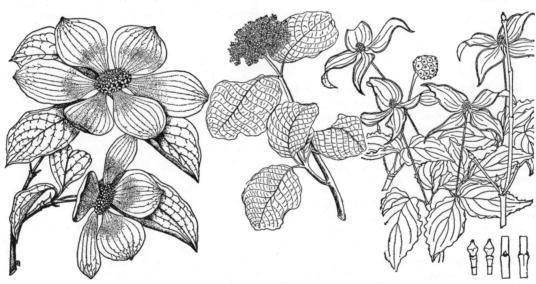

Fig. **Cornus.** Left *C. nuttallii*; middle *C. rugosa*; right *C. kousa* (from Sudworth, L'Heritier and D. B.)

cymes, white, style clavate, July; fruits black. SH 2: 298 i–k, 301 e–f. Origin unknown. In cultivation since 1890. Rare! z5? Plate 138.

C. purpusii see: **C. obliqua**

C. racemosa Lam. Shrub, to 5 m high, usually lower, branches gray, pith white to light brown; leaves elliptic, long acuminate, dull green, bluish beneath, finely appressed pubescent, 5–10 cm long, with 3–4 vein pairs; flowers white, in arched, loose umbellate panicles, June–July; fruits white, pea-size, seed red, wider than long. BB 2718; GSP 354; EP IV 229: 15 (= *C. gracilis* Koehne; *C. paniculata* L'Hér.; *C. candidissima* Marsh.). Eastern USA. 1758. z5 Fig. 274. ⊕ ⚭

C. rugosa Lam. Upright shrub, to 3 m high, branches warty, green at first, then purple, pith white; leaves broad oval, 5–12 cm long, short acuminate, dull green, gray tomentose beneath; flowers in 5–7 cm wide, arched cymes, May–June; fruits pale blue, pea-size, seed rounded. BB 2713; GSP 352 (= *C. circinata* L'Hér.). Eastern N. America. 1784. Noted for its round leaves. z5 Plate 138; Fig. 277. ⌀

C. sanguinea L. Shrub, to 4 m high, branches dull brownish green, reddish on the sunny side; leaves more or less broad elliptic, acuminate, 4–10 cm long, with 3–5 vein pairs, light green beneath, both sides with a thin scattered pubescence, red in fall; flowers in dense pubescent cymes, whitish, very fragrant, May–June; fruits globose, black-blue with whitish dots. HF 2704; HM Pl. 204. Europe; in thickets, meadows, riverbanks, dry slopes and moors, on alkaline or acidic soils. In cultivation for centuries. Ⓕ Czechoslovakia, Romania (in screens). z5 Plate 138. ⌀

'Compressa'. Dwarf form, scarcely 1 m high, erect, very densely branched; small leaved. DB 1964: 175. Selected by Magyar at the School of Horticulture in Budapest, Hungary and still growing there today.

'Mietzschii' (Schwer.). Leaves densely white marbled, blood-red in fall with pink markings. Before 1896. ⌀

'Variegata'. Leaves yellow and white variegated. ⌀

'Viridissima'. Branches and fruits green.

C. sessilis Torr. Shrub, 2–3 m high, branches thinly pubescent; leaves ovate-elliptic, 5–7 cm long, light green above, glabrous, loose appressed pubescence beneath; flowers few in sessile umbels, small, gold-yellow, surrounded by yellow bracts (quickly abscising), before the petals appear, April; fruits ovate to oval, 1.5 cm long, red at first, then black, glossy. MS 436. California. Very similar to *C. mas.* z7–8

C. × slavinii Rehd. (*C. rugosa* × *C. stolonifera*). Growth like *C. stolonifera*, but more upright, young branches reddish like *C. rugosa*; leaves intermediate; fruits bluish, seldom white. Before 1910. z4 Plate 138.

C. stolonifera Michx. Shrub, scarcely over 2 m high, branches procumbent, bowed, often rooting, dark red; leaves lanceolate to elliptic or ovate, acuminate, 5–10 cm long, dark green above, blue-green beneath, with

5–7 veins, glabrous or nearly so; flowers in 3–5 cm wide cymes, yellowish-white, May–June; fruits white, 7–9 mm wide, seed as long as wide, base round. BB 2717; NBB 2: 645; GSP 340. Eastern N. America. Well known and common but often mistakenly labeled shrub. z2 Plate 137; Fig. 274. ⌀ ⚭

'Flaveramea' (Spaeth). Branches with bright green-yellow young bark. Introduced by Spaeth of Berlin, 1899.

var. **coloradensis** (Koehne) Schneid. Branches brownish, bowed and nodding; leaves narrower; fruits bluish-white, seed longer than wide. N. America.

'Kelsey'. Dwaf type to only 75 cm high, spreading growth habit, roots easily. Am. Nurs. (11/15/1959): 11. Good groundcover.

var. **nitida** (Koehne) Schneid. Branches remaining green in winter; leaves very glossy above, with 6–8 vein pairs.

C. stricta Lam. Shrub, to 5 m high, narrowly upright, branches purple-brown, pith white, narrow; leaves oval-elliptic to oval-lanceolate, acuminate, 3–7 cm long, both sides light green with appressed pubescence; flowers white, in 3–6 cm wide cymes, May–June, anthers light blue; fruits light blue, rounded, 5 mm thick. BB 2719 (= *C. femina* Mill.). Western N. America. Plate 140. z6 Fig. 274. ⊕ ⚭

C. suecica L. Perennial, only 10–15 cm high, leaves with a few opposite leaf pairs (not in a whorl at the tips, as on *C. canadensis*); flowers inconspicuous, blood-red, surrounded by 4 white, 1 cm long bracts, June–July; fruits scarlet red; fall foliage bright red. BB 2711; HM 2598; NBB 2: 643. N. Europe to N. Japan, Northern N. America, among dwarf shrubs in heaths, open thickets and forests. z2

C. tatarica see: **C. alba**

C. walteri Wanger. Tree, 10–12 m, somewhat related to *C. sanguinea*, young branches soon becoming glabrous, green-yellow to reddish; leaves elliptic, 10–12 cm long, acuminate, cuneate at the base, appressed pubescent on both sides, denser beneath, with 4–5 vein pairs; flowers in 5–7 cm wide cymes in June; fruits rounded, 6–7 mm thick, black. SL 202; ICS 3935 (= *C. wilsoniana* Schneid. non Wanger). Central China. 1907. One of the few trees of the genus. z6 Plate 137; Fig. 275.

Most of the species are satisfied with any soil type; somewhat more particular are the "large flowering" types (horticulturally speaking, not botanically!), like *C. florida, C. kousa* and *C. nuttallii,* which prefer a fertile, organic soil. Most appreciate frequent watering, but some will also withstand much dryness.

Lit. Hara, Hirishi: The nomenclature of the Flowering Dogwood and its allies; in Jour. Arnold Arboretum 1948, 111–115 ● Howard, R. A.: Registration of cultivar names in *Cornus*; in Arnoldia 1961, 9–18 ● Koehne, E.: Die Sektion *Microcarpium* der Gattung *Cornus*; in Mitt. DDG 1903, 23–46 ● Wangerin, W.: Cornaceae; in Engler, Pflanzenreich **41** (IV), 229), 43–92, 1910 ● Pojarkova, A. I.: Cornaceae; in Flora SSSR, vol. 17 (1951), a summary.

Fig. 278. From left to right: *Corokia cotoneaster*; *C. virgata* 'Cheesemanii'; *C. macrocarpa* and *C. buddleoides* (from Adams)

COROKIA Cunn. — CORNACEAE

Evergreen shrubs, bark often black, branches twisted; leaves alternate or fascicled, stalked, entire; flowers small, yellow, calyx tubular, limb 5 lobed, petals 5, stellate spreading, linear; stamens 5; fruit a small, oblong drupe, with persistent calyx. — 5 species in New Zealand, Chatham Islands.

Corokia buddleioides A. Cunn. Shrub, 2 m high, branches long, thin, gray tomentose; leaves linear-lanceolate, 3–12 cm long, tapering to both ends, glossy green above, silvery tomentose beneath; flowers in 3–5 cm long, terminal panicles on small side branches, May; fruits rounded, black-red, 8 mm thick. BM 9019. New Zealand, N. Island. z8 Fig. 278. #⌀⚭

var. **linearis** Cheesem. Leaves linear-lanceolate, 4.5 to 8 cm long, 4–6 mm wide. New Zealand. z8

C. cotoneaster Raoul. Shrub, to 2m high, densely branched, branches growing erratically through each other, twisted, white tomentose at first, later becoming brownish, foliage sparse and open; leaves spathulate to oval rounded, 1–2 cm long, dark green above, white tomentose beneath; flowers yellow, fragrant, from 1 to 4 at the ends of short side branches, May–June; fruits red, globose, 8 mm thick. BM 8425; DRHS 548. New Zealand. 1875. Grown in Europe primarily as a potted plant. z8 Fig. 278, 279. #⌖⚭

C. macrocarpa T. Kirk. Shrub, to 5m high, young branches somewhat stiff, silvery tomentose (likewise the leaf undersides and petiole); leaves narrow-ovate to oblong-lanceolate, 5–10 cm long, tapering to both ends, leathery; flowers 3–8 in axillary racemes, yellow, stellate, June; fruits 1 cm long, oblong, orange. BM 9168; DRHS 548. Chatham Islands. 1916. z8 Fig. 278. #⚭

C. × virgata (Turrill) Metcalf. (*C. buddleioides × C. cotoneaster*). Shrub, to 2 m high, branches undulated, but not erratically twisted (like *C. cotoneaster*), white tomentose when young; leaves oblanceolate to somewhat spathulate, 3–30 mm long, glossy green above, white beneath; flowers yellow, usually 3 toward the branch tips, May; fruits orange-yellow, ovate. BM 8466. New Zealand. 1907. z8 Plate 131. #⚙⌀

'Cheesemanii' A transition form, upright, branches dense, more or less undulated; leaves oblanceolate to elliptic-oblong, quite variable, 2–4.5 cm long, 1–10 mm wide, deep green above, glossy; fruits red (= *C. cotoneaster* 'Erecta'; *C. cheesemanii* H. Carse). z8 Fig. 278.

Including a long list of cultivars such as; 'Bronze King', 'Bronze Lady', 'Bronze Knight', 'Red Wonder', 'Yellow Wonder' among others, all cultivated by Duncan & Davies, described by Metcalf in MNZ.

Survive the winter in only the mildest regions of the temperate zone, otherwise must be grown in a cool greenhouse.

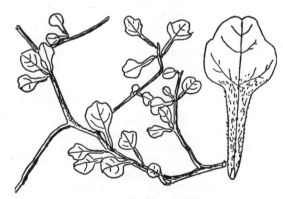

Fig. 279. *Corokia cotoneaster*. Nearly actual size, leaf enlarged.

CORONILLA L. — Crownvetch — LEGUMINOSAE

Shrubs or perennials, usually glabrous, occasionally silky pubescent; leaves alternate, odd pinnate; leaflets numerous, blue-green, small; flowers yellow, in long stalked, axillary umbels; calyx short campanulate, with nearly equally long teeth, standard nearly circular, keel curved inward, wing obovate; pod cylindrical or rectangular or somewhat compressed, oblong segments. — About 20 species in Middle and S. Europe, the Orient, N. Africa.

Coronilla emerus L. Deciduous shrub, 1—2 m high, branches ornamentally nodding, rod-like, angular, glabrous; leaves alternate, pinnate, 2 ranked, 2.5—6 cm long, usually composed of 7—9 leaflets, these obovate, 1—2 cm long, light green, somewhat pubescent only when young; flowers normally in groups of 3, in the leaf axils, on 2.5—5 cm long stalks, yellow, 2 cm long, standard with a red-brown midstripe on the dorsal side, petal claws longer than the calyx, May—July; pods 5 cm long, very thin, cylindrical, somewhat segmented. BM 445; HM Pl. 168. M. and S. Europe, especially common in thickets on the French and Italian Riviera. z6—7 Fig. 280. ✤

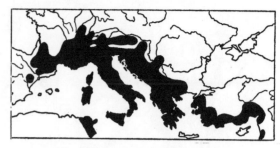

Fig. 281 Range of *Cornilla emerus*

C. glauca L. Evergreen, dense, rounded shrub, 1—2 m high, glabrous; leaves distinctly blue-green, pinnate, 2.5—3 cm long, with 5—7 leaflets, these obovate, apex rounded or somewhat indented, tapering to the base, 6—15 mm long, sessile or short petioled; flowers gold-yellow, in dense umbellate fascicles on 2.5 to 5 cm long stalks, very fragrant, but only during the day, not at night, flowers very abundantly, April—June. Bm 13; PSw 23. S. Europe. 1722. z9 # ✤

C. juncea L. Shrub, to 1m high, sparsely branched, branches gray-green, nearly reed-like in appearance, undulated; leaves only 1.5 cm long, with 3—7 tiny, narrow leaflets; flowers yellow, 8 mm long, 6—12 in globose, axillary umbels on thin, 2.5—5 cm long stalks, March—June; pods very thin, somewhat rectangular and bowed, 2.5 cm long. PMe 71. S. Europe. 1656. z9 ✤

C. valentina L. Evergreen shrub, 1 m high, glabrous; leaves pinnate, 3—5 cm long, usually with 7—11 leaflets, these obovate, truncate at the apex, 6—18 mm long, bright green above, bluish beneath, stipules rounded-kidney shaped (!!), 6—12 mm wide; flowers in umbellate fascicles in groups of 10—14, on 7 cm long stalks, flowers abundant, fragrant, May—July; pods slender, bowed, constricted, 2.5—3 cm long. Bm 185. Mediterranean region, from Spain to Dalmatia. 1596. z9 # ✤

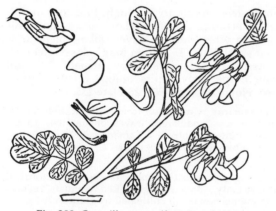

Fig. 280. *Coronilla emerus* (from Lauche)

ssp. **emeroides** (Boiss. & Sprun) Hayek. Very familiar to the species, but usually with only 7 leaflets, terminal leaflet somewhat larger; flowers in umbels usually 5 (2—8) together, petals yellow, often somewhat reddish at the apex, the umbels longer stalked, March to May; pods pendulous, 5—10 cm long, straight, with 7—10 constricted areas. PMe 68. European and Asiatic Mediterranean region. z8 ✤

All species prefer full sun and light soils, although they also do well in rock crags and against sunny stone walls; often overgrazed by wildlife in winter or freeze back. Otherwise trouble free, serviceable and attractive plants.

CORREA Andr. — RUTACEAE

Evergreen shrubs or small trees, usually densely and stellate tomentose-pubesent; leaves opposite, stalked, entire, translucent punctate; flowers 1—3 in the leaf axils or terminal, pendulous, attractive, white, green, yellow or red; calyx cup-shaped, with 4 teeth, corolla tubular, from 4 connate petals, separated however at the apexes, stamens 8, exserted. — 11 species in temperate Australia.

Correa alba Andr. Shrub, to 2 m, growing rather stiffly upright, young branches and leaf undersides densely tomentose and with gray or brown stellate hairs; leaves obovate, elliptic to nearly circular, 1—3 cm long, leathery, somewhat rough above, white tomentose beneath and stellate pubescent; flowers solitary or in groups of 2—3, at the ends of short branches, white, corolla campanulate, but eventually with the 4 petals distinct, oblong-lanceolate, 10—15 mm long, thick, outside stellate pubescent, April—June. EKW 363; BR 515. S. Australia, Tasmania. 1793. Does not bloom abundantly. z8 ⊕

C. backhousiana Hook. Shrub, to 4 m high in its habitat, densely branched, young branches thin, gray-brown, densely stellate pubescent; leaves broad elliptic, obtuse, 1.5—3 cm long, tough and leathery, usually quite glossy and smooth above, densely red-brown tomentose and stellate pubescent beneath, somewhat cordate, petiole 5—8 mm long; flowers 1—3 at the ends of short side branches, petals greenish-white or somewhat yellowish, rather thick, stellate pubescent outside, fused into a 2.5 cm long tube, but distinct at the base, with 4 lobes at the apex, stamens scarcely protruding, 4 stamens situated opposite the petals with wide filaments and flattened bases (!!), style glabrous, April—May. Bm 289; HI 2. Tasmania. z8 # ⊕

C. decumbens F. v. Muell. Low shrub, branches tomentose; leaves narrow-oblong, obtuse, 1.5—3.5 cm long, 3—6 mm wide, glabrous above and furrowed, tomentose beneath, edge slightly inflexed; flowers solitary, terminal, erect, on short stalks, petals 25 mm long, red, stamens protrude markedly, calyx with 4 short and 4 long teeth. BMns 538. Tasmania. z8 # ⊕

C. × harrisii Paxt. (*C. reflexa* ×?). Small shrub, very similar to *C. reflexa*, flowers early, flowers scarlet-pink, 2.5 cm long. # ⊕

C. lawrenciana Hook. Slender shrub, 1—4 m high in its habitat, young branches scabby tomentose; leaves elliptic-oblong to somewhat lanceolate, 1.5—4 cm long, obtuse, 0.5—1.5 cm wide, although occasionally to 9 cm long, leathery tough, glabrous above, densely tomentose beneath with gray or brown hairs; flowers axillary and terminal, 1—3 on short stalks, pendulous, calyx stellate pubescent, petals greenish-yellow, thick, stellate pubescent outside, tube 1.5—2.5 cm long, the ptals only distinct at the base and the apex, with 4 straight, short lobes, stamens protruding, all the filaments equal, style glabrous, May. HI 3 (= *C. ferruginea* Benth.). Tasmania, Victoria. 1836. z8 # ⊕

C. reflexa (Labill.) Vent. Stiff, upright shrub, 1—3 m high in its habitat, branches and leaf undersides stellate pubescent; leaves oval-cordate to oval-oblong, obtuse, 1.5 cm long, 0.5—2.5 cm wide, blade often reflexed downward, green and somewhat rough above, loosely tomentose with gray or brown hairs beneath; flowers 1—3, at the ends of short side branches, most pendulous, often with 2 bracts, calyx campanulate, tomentose, with or without 4 tiny teeth, petals yellowish-red or yellowish-green, rather thick, stellate pubescent outside, the tube 2 to 3.5 cm long, distinct at the base, with 4 erect lobes at the apex, stamens 8, the 4 opposite the petals with wide filaments and flattened bases, style swollen and stellate pubescent at the base. HTS 158; FS 1144 (as *C. cardinalis*); BM 4912 (as *C. cardinalis*) (= *C. speciosa* Ait. var. *normalis* Benth.; *C. cardinalis* F. v. Muell.). Tasmania, S. Australia. 1804. Widely disseminated and quite variable. z8 # ⊕

Also having some varieties, like *pulchella* (BM 29; HTS 158) with soft pink flowers and *bicolor* (FS 12), while *virens* is included in the species.

The mentioned species are cultivated in the landscape in England and the Mediterranean region, otherwise grown in botanic gardens as an easily cultivated, attractive flowering cool greenhouse plant.

CORYLOPSIS S. & Z. — HAMAMELIDACEAE

Deciduous shrubs with soft-stellate pubescent branches; leaves alternate, petioled, broad ovate to rounded-cordate, oblique, serrate, stipules large, quickly abscising; flowers appearing before the leaves, in axillary, pendulous racemes, enveloped in small, yellow, cup-shaped subtending bracts, calyx tube and ovary adnate, limb 5 parted, petals 5, obovate-spathulate, stamens 5; fruit a 2 chambered, 2 pointed capsule; seeds black. — About 20 species in Japan, China, Himalaya.

Corylopsis glabrescens Franch. & Sav. Large shrub; leaves ovate, 5—10 cm long, 3—7 cm wide, short dentate, teeth distinctly bristly acuminate, glabrous above, blue-green beneath and sparsely stellate pubescent when young, abruptly acuminate, base slightly cordate, veins appressed pubescent when young; flowers yellow, 15 mm long, stamens half as long as the petals, anthers purple, April. MJ 1431 (= *C. kesakii* auct. jap. non. S. & Z.). Japan, Kyushu, in the mountains. 1916. z6 ⊕

C. gotoana Makina. Tall shrub to small tree, 5 m; leaves usually obovate, occasionally obovate-oval-rounded, young leaves with scattered, appressed pubescence, blue-green beneath with appressed pubescence on the venation, stellate pubescent when young, later becoming glabrous, margin dentate with quite small bristly teeth; flowers yellow, 10 mm long, stamens about as long as the petals, anthers purple, April. Japan; Honshu, Shikoku, Kyushu, in the mountains but quite rare. z6 ⊕

C. griffithii Hemsl. Tall shrub, branches densely pubescent; leaves cordate-ovate, 7—12 cm long, 3—10 cm wide, acuminate, toothed, softly pubescent beneath; racemes to 6 cm long, bracts small, both sides pubescent, the lowest glabrous outside; flowers sulfur-yellow, petals outspread, stamens and styles much shorter than the petals, February—March. Bm 6779; HI 2820 (= *C. himilayana* Bot. Mag.). Himalaya. 1879. Similar to *C. spicata*, but with larger leaves and flowers. z8 ⊕

C. pauciflora S. & Z. Shrub, to 2m high, finely branched, branches very dense and glabrous, new growth red-brown; leaves cordate-ovate, acute, 2.5—7

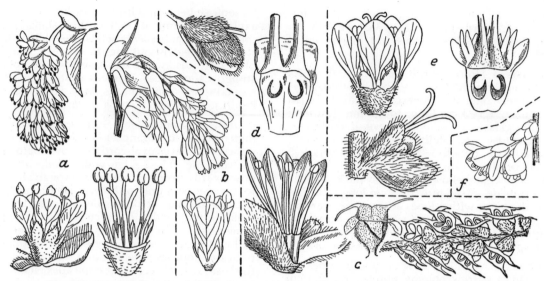

Fig. 282. **Corylopsis** a. *C. veitchiana*; b. *C. spicata*; c. same, fruits; d. *C. wilsonii*; e. *C. sinensis*; f. *C. pauciflora* (from Hemsley, Bot. Mag., Lauche) (the individual flowers 5−6× actual size)

cm long, sparsely dentate, bluish−green beneath, lightly pubescent; flowers soft yellow, campanulate, grouped 2−3 in about 2 cm long, numerous racemes, calyx and bracts glabrous on the ventral side, March−April. BM 7736; LWT 96; KIF 4: 8; DB 1951: 95. Japan. 1874. Most abundantly flowering species. z6 Fig. 282. ⊕

C. platypetala Rehd. & Wils. Shrub, 2.5 to 3.5 m high, branches glabrous, but glandular punctate, violet-red at first; leaves ovate to rounded, base cordate, short acuminate, bristly dentate, glabrous, 5−10 cm long; flowers in 3−5 cm long racemes, pale yellow, fragrant, petals kidney-shaped, 3−4 mm long, April. GC 1934: 176. Central China. 1907. z6 Plate 144. ⊕

var. **levis** Rehd. & Wils. Young twigs and leaf petioles without glands, otherwise like the species. RH 1916: 16. ⊕

C. sinensis Hemsl. Shrub, also tree-like in its habitat, young branches softly pubescent; leaves obovate to obovate-oblong, 5−10 cm long, base cordate, blue-green beneath and softly pubescent; flowers lemon-yellow, 12−18 in 3−5 cm long racemes, fragrant, petals ovate, 8 mm long, anthers yellow (important for identification!), bracts large, pubescent, April. GC 39 (1906): 18; ICS 2057; HI 2820. Central and West China. 1901. z7 Fig. 282. ⊕

C. spicata S. & Z. Shrub, to 2 m high, young branches, leaf petioles and blade undersides pubescent; leaves ovate, abruptly short acuminate, 5−10 cm long, finely bristly dentate, blue-green beneath; flowers 6−12 in 3−4 cm long racemes, light yellow, fragrant, anthers purple, bracts glabrous outside, April. BM 5458; DB 1951: 93; FS 2135. Japan. 1863. z6 Plate 141; Fig. 282. ⊕

C. veitchiana Bean. Shrub, to 2 m high, branches reddish, nearly glabrous; leaves ovate, 5−12 cm long, glabrous, reddish beneath when young, eventually becoming glabrous and green; flowers 10−15 in 2−3 cm long, dense racemes, pale yellow, fragrant, petals

spathulate arched, anthers red-brown, April; calyx, fruit and bracts (except the bases) pubescent. BM 8349; BS 1: 721. China, W. Hupeh. 1900. Flowers often damaged by late frost. z7 Fig. 282. ⊕

C. willmottiae Rehd. & Wils. Strong growing shrub, to 4 m high, branches long, glabrous; leaves ovate to obovate, 3−8 cm long, acuminate, sparsely dentate with prickly tips, pale or blue-green beneath, softly pubescent; flowers to 20 in 5−7 cm long racemes, light yellow, fragrant, petals spathulate to kidney-shaped, anthers yellow, March−April; calyx and fruit glabrous. BMns 438; ICS 2058. China; W. Szechwan. 1908. z6 Plate 143.

'Spring Purple'. Selection with beautiful purple-violet new growth (Hillier 1973).

C. wilsonii Hemsl. Shrub or small tree, branches stellate pubescent; leaves cordate-ovate to obovate, 7−12 cm long, abruptly slender acuminate, bristly dentate, blue-green and eventually totally glabrous beneath; flower light yellow, in 5−7 cm long racemes, bracts densely silky pubescent on both sides, March−April. LF 156; HI 2819. Central China. 1900. z6 Fig. 282. ⊕

C. yunnanensis Diels. Shrub or small tree, young branches glabrous, reddish; leaves rounded to ovate or obovate, base cordate, short acuminate, 3−7 cm long, quite finely dentate, rather blue-green beneath and somewhat pubescent; flowers more orange-yellow (important for identification!), in dense, 2.5−3.5 cm long racemes, petals rounded, 6 mm long, April. ICS 2056. W. China. z5 ⊕

Best for semishady locations, in humus soil; need protection from spring frosts when in bloom; all species very effective for early spring flowers.

Lit. Tong, Kol-Yang: A Study of the Hamamelidaceae Family with Special Consideration to the Organization and Historical Development of *Corylopsis*; in Bull. Dept. Biol. Sun Yatsen Univ. **2**, 1−72, 1931.

Plate 129

Clethra barbinervis in Japan   Photo: Dr. Watari, Tokyo

Clethra alnifolia in the Dortmund Botanic Garden, W. Germany

Plate 130

Clematis fruticosa in the Nikita Botanic Garden,
Yalta, USSR

Clerodendrum bungei
in the Bern Botanic Garden, Switzerland

Cleyera japonica 'Tricolor'
in the Villa Taranto Gardens, Pallanza, Italy

Coleonema album
in its native habitat in South Africa

Plate 131

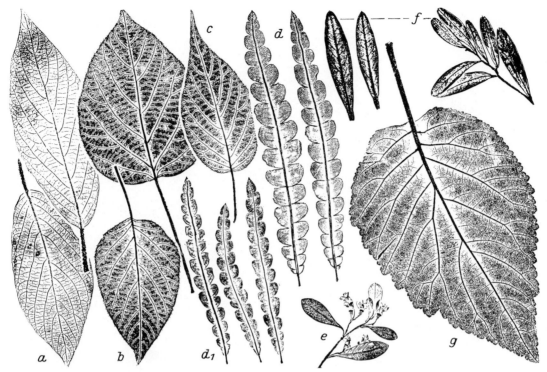

Clemotoclethra. a. *C. scandens*; b. *C. lasioclada*; c. *C. actinidioides*. — **Comptonia.** d. *C. peregrina*; d1 *C. peregrina* var. *asplenifolia*. — **Corokia.** e. *C. birgata*. — **Cneorum.** f. *C. tricoccum*. — **Colquhounia.** g. *C. coccinea* var. *vestita* (all leaves collected from wild plants in their habitat)

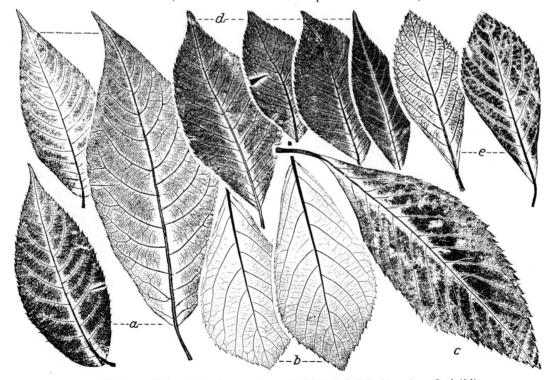

Clethra. a. *C. fargesii*; b. *C. tomentosa*; c. *C. delavayi*; d. *C. barbinervis*; e. *C. alnifolia* (all leaves collected from wild plants in their habitat)

Plate 132

Cocculus laurifolius
in the Marimurtra Garden, Blanes, Spain

Cocculus carolinus
in the National Arboretum, Les Barres, France

Colquhounia coccinea var. **vestita**
in the Taranto Garden, Pallanza, N. Italy

Cornus 'Eddie's White Wonder'
in the nursery of R. Minier, Angers, France

Plate 133

Coriaria japonica, fruit clusters, in Japan   Photo:Dr. Watari, Tokyo

Coriaria japonica,
flowering in the Zurich Botanic Garden, Switzerland

Coriaria thymifolia
in the Malahide Castle Gardens, Ire.

Plate 134

Cornus alba 'Argenteomarginata'
in Kolding, Den.

Cornus canadensis in flower
in the Mount Rainer National Park, USA
Photo: Brockman, Washington

Cornus canadensis in front in Mount Rainier National Park
Photo: Brockman, Washington

Plate 135

Cornus florida, flowering branch in Washington, D.C., USA
Photo: US Forest Service

Cornus florida 'Pluribracteata; in Taranto, Pallanza, Italy

Plate 136

Cornus florida in full bloom in a park in Washington, D.C., USA   Photo: US Forest Service

Plate 137

Cornus nuttallii in Taranto, Pallanza, Italy

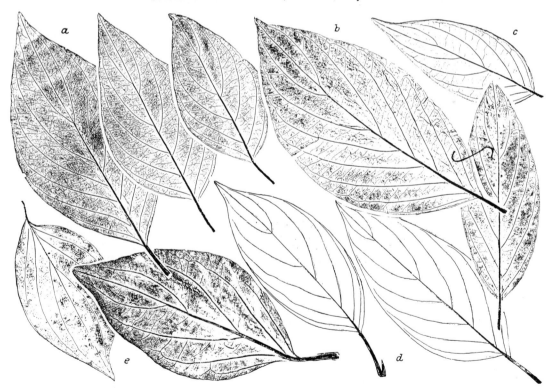

Cornus. a. *C. stolonifera*; b. *C. baileyi*; c. *C. obliqua*; d. *C. amomum*; c. *C. walteri*
(leaves collected from plants in their habitat)

Plate 138

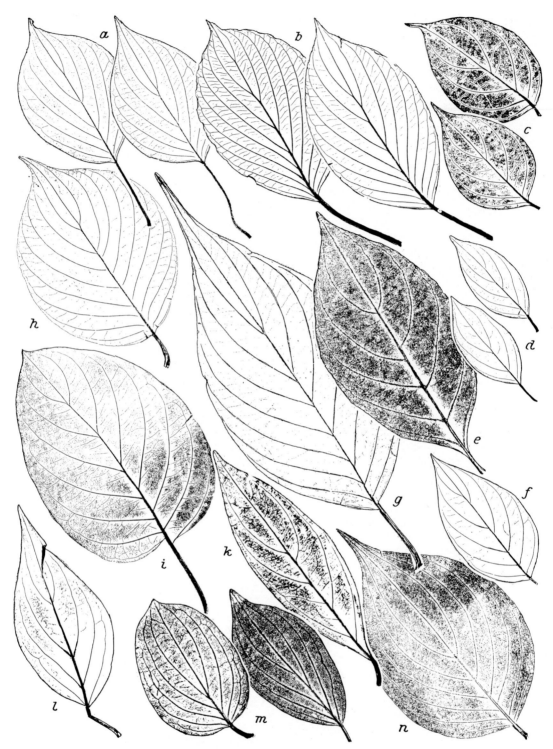

Cornus. a. *C. alternifolia*; b. *C. controversa*; c. *C. pumila*; d. *C. arnoldiana*; e. *C. nuttallii*; f. *C. slavinii*; g. *C. macrophylla*; h. *C. rugosa*; i. *C. hemsleyi*; k. *C. capitata*; l. *C. sanguinea*; m. *C. australis*, n. *C. officinalis* (leaves taken from plants in cultivation, except i, l, m)

Plate 139

Cornus alba 'Sibirica Variegata' in Kolding, Den.

Cornus kousa var. *chinensis*
in the Dortmund Botanic Garden, W. Germany

Cornus kousa
in the Dortmund Botanic Garden, W. Germany

Plate 140

Cornus stricta
in the Dortmund Botanic Garden, W. Germany

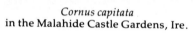

Cornus capitata
in the Malahide Castle Gardens, Ire.

Cornus coreana
in the Arnold Arboretum, USA

Cornus mas 'Pyramidalis'
in the alpine garden, Frohnleiten, Steiermark, Austria

Plate 141

Corylopsis platypetala, just before blooming
in the Wageningen Arboretum, Holland

Corylus avellana 'Contorta' with hoarfrost
at the Dortmund Botanic Garden, W. Germany

Corylopsis spicata in bloom, at the Dortmund Botanic Garden

Plate 142

Corylus sieboldiana in fruit, in Japan   Photo: Dr. Watari, Tokyo

Corylus heterophylla in fruit, in Japan   Photo: Dr. Watari, Tokyo

Plate 143

Corylopsis willmottiae
Photo: W. Berndt

Cordyline indivisa
in Castlewellan Park, N. Ireland

Corylus avellana 'Pendula' in Killesberg Park, Stuttgart, W. Germany

Plate 144

Cotinus coggygria, in fruit, at the Les Barres Arboretum, France

Cotinus coggygria in the Dortmund Botanic Garden, W. Germany

CORYLUS L. — Filbert, Hazelnut — CORYLACEAE

Tall deciduous shrubs, occasionally trees; leaves 2 ranked, alternate, usually doubly serrate; male catkins naked in winter; the bud-form female flowers have only the red stigmas prominent; fruit a nut surrounded by a 2 bladed tubular hull more or less shredded at the apex. — About 15 species in Europe, N. America and N. Asia, notable for their edible fruits and as ornamental shrubs.

Corylus americana Marsh. Shrub, to 3 m high, young branches glandular pubescent; leaves broad-ovate, short acuminate, irregularly doubly serrate, 6—12 cm long, softly pubescent beneath; catkins 4—7 cm long; fruits 2—6, cup-shaped hull twice as long as the nut, often glandular pubescent. BB 1209; GSP 98; GoeH 71 (= *C. calyculata* Dipp.; *C. humilis* Willd.). Canada, Eastern USA. 1798. Only of slight ornamental value. z5 Fig. 285.

C. avellana L. Hazelnut. Shrub, to 5m high, branches glandular pubescent; leaves rounded-broad ovate, abruptly acuminate, 5—10 cm long, doubly serrate to weakly lobed, with 6—7 vein pairs; flower catkins 3—6 cm long; fruits 1—4, hull shorter than the length of the nut, lobes toothed. HW 2: 28; HM Pl. 84. Europe. In cultivation for centuries. Ⓕ Austria, W. Germany (for green screens). z5 Fig. 285. ◐ ⚭

The species includes many fruit varieties which will not be covered here (please see Lit.).

'Aurea'. Gold Hazel. Weaker growing than the species, branches orange in winter; leaves yellow, later yellowish green. GoeH 8. Before 1864. ⌀

'Contorta'. Growth upright, weak, branches twisting in corkscrew fashion; leaves partly crispate and involute. Found 1863 in Frocester, England. Plate 125, 141.

'Funduk'. Leaves with a dark brown spot in the middle, especially visible after the new growth. Apparently found in Turkey but also in Holland (from Biejerinck).

'Fuscorubra'. Red Leaves Forest Hazel. Weak grower; leaves red-brown, dark red only in spring. GoeH 4. Before 1887. Not as attractive as *C. maxima* 'Purpurea'. ⌀

'Glomerata'. Fruits 7—10 together, often small fruited. Before 1789.

'Heterophylla'. Leaves more ovate, narrower than those of the species, more pubescent, deeply incised. GoeH 5 (= f. *laciniata*; f. *urticaefolia*; f. *quercifolia* Hort.). Before 1825. ⌀

'Pendula'. Branches erect at first, then pendant in a short arch. GoeH 7; Gw 2: 13. From France. Known since 1867. Plate 143.

'Piliciensis'. Leaves 7—8 cm long, 6—7 cm wide, gray tomentose beneath; cup-shaped hull shorter than the obovoid, short beaked, small fruit. Found in Hungary. Before 1891.

'Microphylla'. Weaker growing than the species; leaves rounded-elliptic to oval-elliptic, 3—5 cm long, 2÷4 cm wide, short petiolate, indistinctly doubly or simply serrate; internodes short. DB 1955: 144. Found by P. Thyssen near Siegburg, W. Ger. 1955.

'Variegata'. Leaves partly yellow-white bordered, partly yellow-white speckled. ⌀

'Zimmermanii'. Leaves connate at the base, trumpet form inflexed. Found 1864 by Zimmermann in Menden near Iserlohn, W. Berlin. ⌀

C. californica (A. DC.) Rose. Californian Hazel. Very closely related to *C. cornuta*, but with leaf blade underside more pubescent; cup-shaped hull somewhat shorter and wider, only slightly longer than the nut. EP IV 61: 14d; NDJ 17: 9; MS 49 (= *C. rostrata* var. *californica* A. DC.). W. USA. 1910. z7

C. chinensis Franch. Tree, to 40 m in its habitat, branches brown and glandular pubescent; leaves ovate, acute, 10—18 cm long, base obliquely cordate, evenly simply serrate, glabrous above, pubescent on the approximately 13 vein pairs beneath; fruits 4—6 together, cup-shaped hull striped, finely pubescent to glabrous, narrowing tube-like over the nut, toothed at the apex. SH 2: 560c, 561d; NDJ 17: 8; ICS 794. China, Yunnan. 1900. The most beautiful species of the entire genus. z6? ⌀

C. colurna L. Turkish Filbert. Tree, to over 20 m high, crown attractively pyramidal, bark gray-white, rough, corky, young branches glandular pubescent; leaves broad ovate, cordate at the base, 8—12 cm long, double

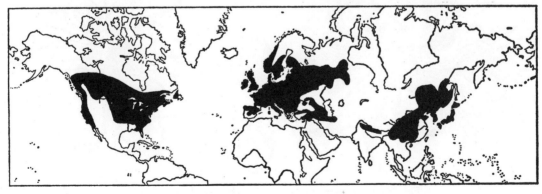

Fig. 283. Range of the Genus *Corylus*

serrate or small lobed, dark green, venation pubescent beneath; male catkins short. DB 1955: 144. Found by P. Thyssen near Siegburg, W. Germany. 1955.to 12 cm long; fruits in ball-like clusters, nut to 2 cm long, flat, very thick shelled, but edible, surrounded by a deeply parted, glandular hull. FS 2223; BM 9469. SE. Europe, Asia Minor. 1582. Valuable street and park tree. z5 Fig. 284. 285. ⊘ ⌾

C. × colurnoides Schneid. (*C. avellana × C. colurna*). Growth shrubby or also a tree (20 m high in the Muenster Botanic Garden, W. Germany), bark less corky, more split, somewhat peeling on young plants; leaves wider, similar to those of *C. colurna*, but more scabrous serrate; fruit hull deeply incised, partly connate, glandular-bristly, nut broad ovate, hilum smaller, nut very good tasting. SH 1:83r; NDJ 17: 7; GoeH 74 (= *C. intermedia Lodd.*).Before 1835. z5 Fig. 284. ⊘

C. cornuta Marsh. Shrub, to 3 m high, branches softly pubescent; leaves ovate to obovate, acuminate, finely serrate and slightly lobed, 4–10 cm long, petiole only 6–12 mm long; fruits grouped1–2, hull tightly appressed to the nut, drawn out to a narrow, 3–4 cm long tube past the nut, densely bristly. BB 1210; GSP 101; GF 8: 345 (= *C. rostrata* Ait.). East and Middle N. America. 1745. z5 Fig. 285 ⊘

C. ferox Wall. Tree, 8–10 m high, bark gray, branches with large lenticels, pubescent when young; leaves obovate, base round to ovate, 8–12 cm long, 3–4 cm wide, irregularly doubly serrate; fruits grouped several together, in 5–8 cm thick clusters, the cup-shaped hull densely prickly ouside (like *Castanea*). EP IV 61: 13; NDJ 17: 6; HAL 28c; ICS 789. Himalaya; Nepal, Sikkim. z7? Fig. 286.

C. heterophylla Fisch. ex Trautv. Shrub, to 4 m high, branches glandular pubescent; leaves oval-rounded, abruptly acuminate (important for identification!) (of-ten flattened at the apex to emarginate, but still with a small tip in the middle), irregularly serrate and small lobed, 5–10 cm long, glabrous above, venation beneath pubescent; fruits grouped 1–3, cup-shaped hull somewhat longer than the nut, striped, velvety pubescent, glandular bristly at the base. EP IV 61: 14b; KO 95; ICS 791. Japan, China. Around 1882. Similar to *C. avellana*, but more lobed; of only slight ornamental merit. Ⓕ Korea. z6 Plate 142; Fig. 285. ⊘

var. **sutchensis** Franch. Leaves less truncate at the apex, usually glabrous beneath; fruit hull often shorter than the nut, lobes often toothed. ICS 792. Middle and W. China. 1909.

var. **yunnanensis** Franch. Leaves dense and softly pubescent beneath, leaf petioles and young branches glandular bristly. ICS 793 (= *C. yunnanensis* [Franch.] A. Camus). SW. China. 1910.

C. jacquemontii Decne. Similar to *C. colurna*, new growth appears 2 weeks earlier; tree, 10–12 m high, growth habit the same as *C. colurna*, but with obovate leaves, 15–20 cm long, shallowly lobed and scabrous toothed; fruit hull like that of *colurna*, but without the glandular hairs. NDJ 17:6; BMns 391. NW. Himalaya; Kumaun, Nepal. 1898. z5

C. maxima Mill. Filbert. Tall shrub, resembling *C. avellana*, but with young twigs gray, glandular bristly; leaves wider, slightly lobed, with 7–8 vein pairs; catkins longer, 5–7 cm long; fruit hull tubular and closed, twice as long as the nut. HW 2:30; GoeH 55 to 64 (= *C. tubulosa* Willd.). SE. Europe, Asia Minor. In cultivation for centuries and grown in many cultivars. z5 ⊘ ⌾

'Purpurea'. The true, deep black-red leaved "Purple Filbert", which holds its color throughout the summer; the catkins are also red. BMns 268 (= var. *atropurpurea* Bean). ⊘

'Rubra'. Red Filbert. Leaves a normal green; but the fruit kernels have a red skin. ⌾

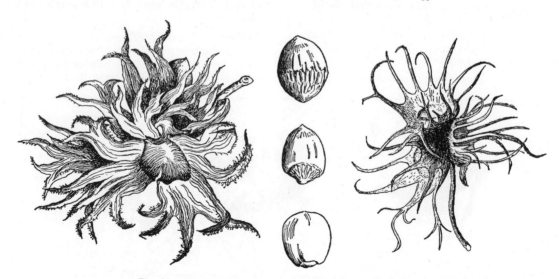

Fig. 284. **Corylus** fruits. Left and middle above *C. colurna*; beneath and right *C. colurnoides*; lowest nut *C. avellana* (from E. Jahn)

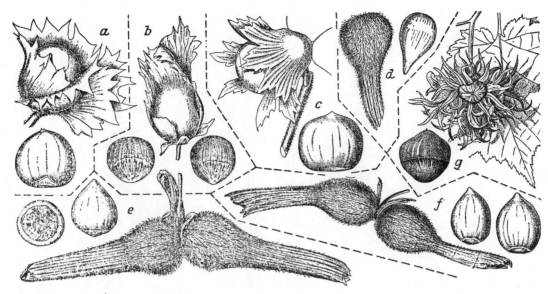

Fig. 285. **Corylus** fruits. a. *C. hetyerophylla*; b. *C. americana*; c. *C. avellana*; d. *C. sieboldiana*; e. *C. sieboldiana* var. *mandschurica*; f. *C. cornuta*; g. *C. colurna* (from Baillon, Hempel & Wilhelm, Schneider, Shirasawa)

C. sieboldiana Bl. Shrub, to 5 m high, branches pubescent; leaves elliptic-oblong, 5—10 cm long, doubly serrate, often with a red-brown patch in the middle, petiole 1.5—2 cm long; fruit hull covering the nut and extending in a narrow tube, fruits grouped 1—3; anthers reddish. KIF 3: 7; KO 96; NDJ 17: 8 (= *C. rostrata* var. *sieboldiana* [Bl.] Maxim.) Japan. 1904. z6 Plate 142; Fig. 285. ⊗

var. **mandschurica** (Maxim. & Rupr.) Schneid. leaves more cordate, coarsely serrate and lobed, petiole to 2.5 cm long; fruit hull longer and wider, stiffly pubescent. BM 8623; NDJ 17: 8; ICS 795 (= *C. mandschurica* Maxim. & Rupr.) NE. Asia to N. Japan. 1882. Fig. 285.

C. tibetica Batal. Large shrub, to 8 m high, branches glabrous, brown, with lenticels; leaves broad-ovate, glabrous except for the venation beneath, 5—12 cm long, acuminate, sharply serrate, petiole to 2.5 cm long; nuts grouped 3—6 together, as prickly as *Castanea* fruits. RH 1910: 204; NDJ 17: 6; ICS 790 (= *C. ferox* var.

thibetica [Batal.] Franch.). China. 1901. z5 Fig. 286.

C. × vilmorinii Rehd. (*C. chinensis* × *C. avellana*). Growth habit resembles *C. chienesis*, but with leaves smaller and less cordate; cup-shaped fruit hull covering the nut and only slightly drawn together, occasionally split to the base on one side, nut large, shell thin. NDJ 17: 9. Before 1911. z5

For large areas most species will do best in shade or semishade and on cool, fertile soil.

Lit. Biejerinck, W.: Het geslacht *Corylus* en de verspeiding van de soorten en vormen; in Jaarb. Ned. Dendrol. Ver. **17**, 67—107 (1949; Lit. index of 48 works) ● Goeschke, E.: Die Hazel nuss, ihre Arten und ihre Kultur; Berlin 1887, 100pp. of text and 78 plates; the best work covering the Hazelnuts ● Kasapligil, B.: A Bibliography on *Corylus* (*Betulaceae*) with Annotations; in Ann. Rep. North. Nut Growers Assn. 1972, 107—162; contains 550 titles, 9 plates and an index to all the botanic names ● Winkler, H.: *Corylus*; in Engler, Pflanzenreich, IV, **61**, 44—56, 1904.

CORYNOCARPUS R. J. & G. Forst. — CORYNOCARPACEAE

Evergreen trees or shrubs with rounded branches; leaves alternate, short stalked, entire, oblong to obovate; flowers small, in terminal panicles, sepals and petals 5 each, stamens 5, alternating with 5 staminodes; fruit an oblong or more globose, fleshy drupe. — 4—5 species in New Guinea, New Zealand and the neighboring islands.

Corynocarpus laevigatus R. J. & G. Forst. Evergreen tree, to 20 m high in its habitat, only a tall shrub in European cultivation; leaves elliptic or more oblong, to 20 cm long, entire, thick, leathery, dark green, short

petiolate; flowers white, small, 4 mm large, in 10—20 cm long, erect, stiff, branched panicles; drupes obovoid, 2.5—3 cm long, orange, flesh edible, but the seeds bitter and very poisonous, it is eaten however by the native peoples with special handling. BM 4379; KF 88. New Zealand. 1823. z9 # ⊗

Normal garden soil is sufficient, but the plant requires a frost free climate or cool greenhouse.

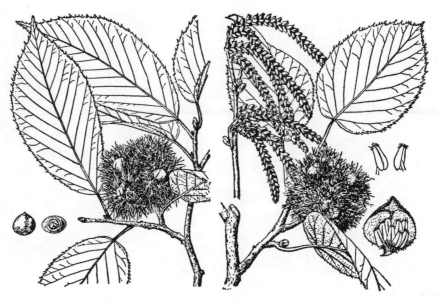

Fig. 286. Left *Corylus ferox*; right *C. tibetica* (from ICS)

COTINUS Mill. — Smoketree — ANACARDIACEAE

Tall, deciduous shrubs with yellow wood, without milky sap, sap very aromatic leaves simple (important distinction from *Rhus*), long petioled; flowers polygamous or dioecious, yellow, in very large, terminal panicles; fruit stalks covered with long, erect hairs; fruit a small, oblique drupe. — 1 species in N. America and 1 in S. Europe to Middle Asia.

Cotinus coggyria Scop. Shrub, 2—3(5) m high, pith brown; leaves elliptic to oblong-obovate, 3—8 cm long, base rounded to truncate, bright green, coloring a beautiful orange in fall, petiole 2—4 cm long; flowers small, usually infertile, in 15—20 cm long panicles, with long, green to somewhat reddish fruit stalks, covered with long, erect hairs, June—July. HM 1821; DB 1954: 307 (= *Rhus cotinus* L.). S. Europe to Central China and NW. Himalaya. 1656. Ⓕ USSR (in screen plantings). z5 Plate 125. 144. ⊘ ⚭

Following are a few cultivars. (At the Academy of Horticulture in Budapest, Hungary a 10-year test was done on *Cotinus* and selections made for fall color. Many colors were selected from lemon-yellow to scarlet-red but these have presumably not been introduced into the trade.)

'Flame'. English selection with bright orange-red fall color. ⊘ ⚭

'Notcutt's Variety' (Notcutt 1911). Selected from 'Rubrifolius'; leaves dark purple-brown; inflorescence purple-pink. One of the most beautiful forms in England, but seldom used elsewhere. ⊘ ✧

'Pendulous'. Branches weeping; leaves green. Before 1871.

'Purpureus'. Leaves green, fruit clusters carmine-pink pubescent. In cultivation before 1871. ⊘ ⚭

'Red Beauty' (Gebr. Boer, Boskoop). Strong grower and rather broad, well branched; leaves large, bright purple-red at first, later more dark red on both sides. A large-leaved form, lighter than 'Royal Purple', holds its color to leaf fall. ⊘ ⚭

'Royal Purple'. (Kromhout & Co., Boskoop). Leaf color an intensive scarlet-red. Thus far the most frequently grown red leaved form. ⊘ ⚭

'Rubrifolius'. Leaves dark red, but later becoming partly green, especially on the inside of the plant; flowers somewhat reddish; fruit clusters pink-red pubescent (= "Foliis Purpureis" hort.) Before 1930. Long surpassed by modern selections and seldom found in cultivation. ⊘ ⚭

C. obovatus Raf. Grows more tree-like, not unusual to 6—10 m high, inner bark white, but changing to orange when exposed to the air; leaves broad elliptic, always truncate at the base, 6—12 cm long, the younger leaves often purple spotted, petiole red, fall color a bright orange; fruit clusters only about 10 cm long, otherwise like *C. coggygria*. NBB 2: 497 (= *C. americanus* Nutt., *Rhus cotinoides* Nutt.). N. America, Tennessee to Alabama and Texas. z4? 1882. ⊘ ✧

Both species very attractive shrubs as specimens, interesting for their fruiting effect and bright fall color; thriving in any good garden soil, but preferring a warm, sunny location.

Lit. Domokos, J.: Consistent fall coloration as cultivar qualities; in Kertészeti Evkoenyv, **25**, 179—180, 1961 (in Hungarian).

COTONEASTER Ehrh. — ROSACEAE

Deciduous or evergreen, thornless shrubs, also tree-like in mild areas; leaves alternate, simple, entire; stipules narrow; flowers solitary or several to many flowers in corymbs, usually white, seldom light pink; sepals 5, petals 5, erect or outspread; stamens 15 to 20; styles 2–5, occasionally only 1; carpels distinct on the ventral side (nearest the style), but connate on the ventral side to half the length of the calyx tube, the apex of the carpel always remains distinct (also distinctly separate on the fully developed fruit); fruit a small, red or black pome with 2–5 seeds. — About 50 species in Europe, N. Africa, Eastern Asia, Siberia and Himalaya, but not Japan.

Outline of the Genus

Section 1. **Orthopetalum** Koehne

Petals upright, becoming reddish especially on the base, glabrous; styles 1–5, the ovaries joined below the apex;

☆ Fruits red (black-red on *C. nitens*);
  ● Leaves glabrous or somewhat pubescent beneath, 5–30 mm long; flowers usually 1–4; branches with strigose pubescence;
    1. Growth prostate:
       C. adpressus, 'Hessei', *horizontalis, praecox, splendens*,

    2. Growth erect:
       C. apiculatis, distichus, divaricatus, harry-smithii, nitens, rubens, simonsii

  ● ● Leaves tomentose or pubescent beneath; flowers grouped 2 to many together; branches with appressed shaggy pubescence;

    1. Calyx glabrous or only slightly pubescent:
       C. integerrimus, roseus, uniflorus

    2. Calyx dense pubescent or tomentose; leaves pubescent above, dull green:
       C. acuminatus, amoenus, bullatus, dielsianus, franchetii, nebrodensis, newryensis, nitidifolius, obscurus, sikangensis, sternianus, wardii, zabelii

☆ ☆ Fruits black (brown-red on *C. ignavus*);
       C. acutifolius, ambiguus, foveolatus, ignavus, lucidus, moupinensis, niger

Section 2. **Chaenopetalum** Koehne

Petals radiating outward, white, very rarely reddish; styles 1–2, the ovary joined at the apex;

☆ Flowers many in corymbs; growth erect:
  ● Leaves deciduous; green to gray-green, without papillae beneath; anthers yellow:
       C. affinis, cooperi, crispii, frigidus, hebephyllus, hupehensis, insignis, multiflorus, racemiflorus, watereri

  ● ● Leaves evergreen or wintergreen, tough to leather-like, anthers reddish:
       C. glabratus, glaucophyllus, harrovianus, henryanus, lacteus, pannosus, rhytidophyllus, rugosus, salicifolius, turbinatus

☆ ☆Flowers 1–3, growth prostrate or creeping; leaves evergreen;

  ● Leaves green to blue-green beneath, 1–3 cm long, without papillae beneath, soon becoming glabrous:
       C. dammeri

  ● ● Leaves blue-green beneath, papillate (except *C. buxifolius*), smaller than 1.5 cm:
       C. buxifolius, congestus, conspicuus, microphyllus, rotundifolius

Outline of the botanical classification of the *Cotoneaster* Cultivars

(Synonyms in normal type)

'Aldenhamensis'	— *watereri*
'Avondrood'	— *salicifolius* 'Repens'
'Blackburn'	— *apiculatus*
'Boer'	— *praecox*
'Calocarpus'	— *racemiflorus*
'Cochleatus'	— *microphyllus*
'Coral Beauty'	— *dammeri*
'Coralle'	— *horizontalis*
'Cornubia'	— *watereri*
'Decorus'	— *conspicuus*
'Dortmund'	— *salicifolius* 'Repens'
'Eichholz'	— *dammeri*
'Exburiensis'	— *watereri*
'Firebrand'	— *bullatus*
'Firebird'	— *bullatus*
'Glabratus'	— *watereri*
"Gloire de Versailles"	— *franchetii*
'Gnom'	— *salicifolius*
'Gracia'	— *salicifolius* × *horizontalis*
'Herbstfeuer'	— *salicifolius*
"hybridus pendulus"	— *watereri* 'Pendulus'
'Inchmery'	— *watereri*
'John Waterer'	— *watereri*
'Juergl'	— *dammeri*
'Klampen'	— *salicifolius*
'Little Gem'	— *adpressus*
melanotrochus	— *microphyllus*
'Minipolster'	— *dammeri*
'Nan Shan'	— *praecox*
'Notcutt's Var.'	— *frigidus*
'Parkteppich'	— *salicifolius*
'Pendulus'	— *watereri*
'Perkeo'	— *salicifolius*
'Pink Champagne'	— *watereri*
'Repens'	— *salicifolius*
'Robusta'	— *horizontalis*
'Rothschildianus'	— *watereri*
'Royal Beauty'	— *dammeri*, 'Coral Beauty'
'Royal Carpet'	— *dammeri* 'Coral Beauty'
'Ruby'	— *rotundifolius*
'Sabrina'	— *splendens*
'Saldam'	— *salicifolius*
'Salmon Spray'	— *watereri*
'Saxatilis'	— *horizontalis*
'Skogholm'	— *dammeri*
'Smaragdpolster'	— *dammeri*
'St. Monica'	— *watereri*
'Streibs Findling'	— *dammeri*
'Valkenburg'	— *salicifolius* × *horizontalis*
'Vicaryi'	— *watereri*

Cotoneaster acuminatus Lindl. Deciduous shrub, to 4 m high, young branches densely pubescent; leaves oval-elliptic, acuminate, 3—6 cm long, dull green above, pubescent at first, lighter and denser beneath, eventually becoming glabrous; flowers reddish, 2—5 in short, pubescent cymes, May; fruits light red, 8—10 mm long, pubescent on the apex. SH 1: 418 r—s, 419i; ICS 2117 (= *C. nepalensis* André; *C. roylei* Hort.). Himalaya. 1820. Fruits few, much used but not as attractive as *C. dielsianus* or *divaricatus*. z5

C. acutifolius Turcz. To 3 m high, broad growing, branches pubescent, later red-brown; leaves ovate to elliptic, 2—5 cm long, dull green above, somewhat pubescent at first, lighter and more sparse beneath; flowers reddish, 2—5 in short, pubescent cymes, May—June; fruits black, elliptic, 1 cm long, with 2 seeds, dehiscing in September. SH 1: 421 a—b, 422 b—h; ICS 2121 (= *C. pekinensis* Zabel). N. China. 1883. Ornamental merit slight, but good for hedges. z5 Fig. 288. See also: *C. lucidus*

var. **villosulus** Rehd. & Wils. Leaves larger, densely shaggy pubescent beneath; fruits likewise somewhat pubescent. Central and W. China.

C. adpressus Bois. Deciduous shrub, procumbent, scarcely 25 cm high, branches creeping, internodes very short; leaves broad ovate with small tips, 5—15 mm long, margin wavy, dull green above, ciliate when young; flowers 1—2, reddish, nearly sessile, June; fruits oval-rounded, red, with 2 seeds, but only a few fruits. SH 1: 418 k—m, 419e; ICS 2131. W. China. 1895. z5 Plate 150, 152; Fig. 289. Ø

'Little Gem' (Verboom). Growth weaker, more cushion form; leaves without much fall coloration; does not fruit. Chance seedling; originated at K. Verboom in Boskoop, Holland. Before 1946.

var. *praecox* see: **C. praecox**

C. affinis Lindl. Deciduous shrub, to 5 m tall in mild areas, branches erect to outspread, pubescent at first, later becoming glabrous, brown; leaves usually 2 ranked, obovate, obtuse with small tips, 3—9 cm long, dull green above, gray tomentose beneath, later glabrous and bluish-green, with 5—7 vein pairs; flowers 15—30 in 3—5 cm wide umbellate planicles, axils hairy tomentose, May; fruits nearly globose, dark red-brown to nearly black, 6—8 mm thick. Sh 1: 426 b—e, 427 d—f. W. Himalaya; Nepal to Kashmir. 1822. z6—7 Fig. 287. Ø ⚭

var. **baccillaris** (Lindl.) Schneid. To 5m high, occasionally also a tree; leaves wider, smaller, 3—6 cm long, usually rounded at the apex, usually glabrous beneath; inflorescence downy pubescent (not tomentose), flowers 10—25 together, May—June; fruits dark brown-red to black, 5—6 mm thick. BR 1229; FS 338 (= *C. comptus* Lem.). In the range of the species. Very attractive shrub. z6—7 Fig. 287. Ø ⚭

C. ambiguus Rehd. & Wils. Deciduous shrub, very similar to *C. acutifolius*, to 2 m high, young branches pubescent; leaves usually ovate, finely acuminate, 2.5—5 cm long, densely pubescent beneath; flowers 5—10 together, white turning red, calyx nearly gla-

brous, June; fruits glossy black, globose, 8—12 mm thick, with 2—5 (usually 3) seeds. BM 9106; ICS 2122. W. and SW. China. 1903. z5

C. amoenus Wils. Evergreen or wintergreen shrub, erect, scarcely over 1.5 m high, very similar to *C. franchetii*, but more upright, denser and bushier, branches more upright, internodes shorter; leaves ovate, 1—2 cm long, glossy dark green above, gray tomentose beneath; flowers 4—14 together, white, reddish, June; fruits globose, light red, 5—6 mm thick, with 2—3 seeds, long persistent. GC 51 (1912): 2. Middle China. 1904. z6 Plate 148. #

C. apiculatus Rehd. & Wils. Deciduous shrub, to 2 m high, resembling *C. horizontalis*, but irregularly branched, not 2 ranked, young branches yellow-gray strigose pubescent at first; leavse obovate-rounded, thin, 1—1.5 cm wide, acuminate, ciliate; flowers usually singular, nearly sessile, pink, June; fruits scarlet-red, globose, 8—10 mm thick, with 3 seeds. ICS 2130. W. China. 1901. z5

'Blackburn'. American selection; growth very compact and dense; fruits somewhat larger, more numerous, scarlet-red. Morton Arboretum, USA. ⚭

C. applanatus see: **C. dielsianus**

C. bullatus Bois. Deciduous shrub, to 3 m high, growth broad and open, young branches pubescent; leaves acute oval-oblong, 3—7 cm long, dark green and rugose above, gray-green and pubescent beneath; flowers reddish, 3—7, May to June, very abundant; fruits light red, globose, 7—8 mm thick, with 4 or 5 seeds, August—October. BM 8284 (as *C. moupinensis*); ICS 2118. W. China. 1898. Very hardy, abundant fruiting, good flowering, but often attacked by aphids. z5 Plate 146; Fig. 290. ⚭

'Firebird' (W. J. Hooftman 1959). Shrub, to 3 m high; leaves 3 by 6 cm, dull green above and somewhat convex, with dense whitish pubescence beneath; fruits short teardrop shape, to 9 by 12 mm, bright red, 1—2 together, but densely arranged along shorter side banches, September—January (= 'Firebrand' W. J. Hooftman; *C.* 'Firebird' F. J. Grootendorst & Zn.). Selected by C. Verboom (W. J. Hooftman Co.), Boskoop in 1950, but possibly *C. bullatus* × *C. franchetii*. Plate 147.

var. **floribundus** Rehd. & Wils. Leaf stalks shorter, 1.5—2.5 cm long; inflorescence many flowered, with 15 to 30 flowers; fruits larger, 8—10 mm thick. BM 8284 (as *C. moupinensis* var. *floribundus*). W. China. More attractive than the species.. ⊕ ⚭

var. **macrophyllus** Rehd. & Wils. Shrub, to 5 m high; leaves 5—15 cm long, to 8 cm wide, apical veins very indented, with 8—10 vein pairs, petiole 2 mm long; inflorescence 5—8 cm wide, flowers to 30 together; fruits 7—9 mm thick, with 5 seeds. W. China. Uncommonly large leaved for a *Cotoneaster*. Plate 149. Ø ⚭

C. buxifolius Wall. ex Lindl. Evergreen shrub, much branched, sprawling, upright, to 1.8 m high, young branches tomentose; leaves spirally arranged, elliptic to obovate, 5—15 mm long, obtuse or acute, young leaves pubescent above, later becoming glabrous and dark green, white woolly beneath, tomentose, margin

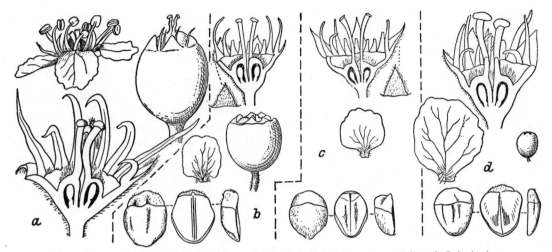

Fig. 287. **Cotoneaster** a. *C. affinis* var. *bacillaris*; b. *C. affinis*; c. *C. buxifolius*; d. *C. insignis*
(from Schneider, Koehne)

somewhat inflexed; flowers 2−4, on short side branches, white, petals outspread, calyx and stalk, tomentose; fruits red, globose, 5−6 mm thick, with few hairs, seeds 2. ICS 2129. Southeast India; Nilgiri Mountains. Presumably not in cultivation; cultivated plants by this name are probably always *C. rotundifolius*. z7 Fig. 287. #

f. vellaceus Franch. Growth procumbent; very similar to 'Cochleatus', leaves with both sides pubescent at first, leathery, usually obovate, 5−10 mm long, margin not or only slightly revolute, densely gray-white tomentose beneath and papillate; flowers usually solitary, petals white, outspread. SW. China; Szechwan, Yunnan. Rather rare in cultivation. #

C. comptus see: **C. affinis** and **C. frigidus**

C. congestus Baker. Dwarf growing, hugging the ground, to 70 cm high with age, densely compact; leaves evergreen, obovate, 6−12 mm long, dull green above, whitish beneath, quickly becoming completely glabrous; flowers solitary, whitish pink, 6 mm wide, June; fruits light red, 6 mm thick, usually with 2 seeds (= *C. pyrenaicus* Hort.; *C. mircophyllus* var. *glacialis* Hook.). Himalaya. 1868. z6 # ∅

C. conspicuus Marquand. Evergreen, 1−2 m high shrub, branches fine, nodding; leaves spirally arranged, usually oblong-elliptic, 7−10 mm (to 20 mm on long branches) long, usually obtuse and with small tips, dark green above, dull, appressed pubescent beneath; flower solitary, but very numerous, small, white, May; fruits light orange-red, globose, about 9 mm long, usually with 2 seeds, fruits abundantly. Bm 9554. SE. Tibet. 1934. z6 # ∅ ✧ ⊗

'Decorus'. Growth mat-like or with branches short bowed, rooting, foliage dense, flowers and fruits abundantly; otherwise like the species (= *C. conspicuus* var. *decorus* Russel). Plate 145. # ∅ ✧ ⊗

'Nanus'. Described by Klotz as intermediate between the previous 2 plants; branches stiff, outspread, foliage dense. From the Peking Botanic Garden.

C. cooperi Marquand. Deciduous shrub, about 2.5 m high, growth open, branches tomentose at first, soon becoming glabrous; leaves lanceolate, acuminate, 3−8 cm long, glabrous above, white tomentose beneath at first, soon becoming glabrous and bluish, flowers white, in numerous, 3 cm wide clusters, axils pubescent, June; fruits teardrop shape, 1 cm long, black-red, with 2 seeds. Himalaya; Bhutan. 1915. Seldom true in the garden. z7−8

var. **microcarpus** Marquand. Branches thin, long arching; fruits more rounded, 7 mm long, purple-red. BM 9478. Bhutan. 1914.

C. × crispii Exell (*C. frigidus* × *C. pannosus*). Tall shrub, deciduous; leaves like those of *C. pannosus*, but 3−5 cm long, thinner, short loose tomentum beneath; fruits like those of *C. frigidus*, broad ellipsoid, 5 mm long, light red. Originated by Waterer, Sons and Crisp Ltd., England, 1928. z6

C. dammeri Schneid. Evergreen, creeping shrub, growth tight along the ground, branches rooting; leaves 2-ranked, leathery smooth, dull, elliptic to obovate-oblong, 2−3(5) cm long, round or obtuse at the apex, occasionally emarginate, usually with a small apical tip; flowers usually solitary or also in 2's, white, short stalked (important for identification!), anthers reddish; fruits light red, globose, 7 mm thick, usually with 5 seeds. NF 1: 176; ICS 2127 (= *C. humifusus* Duthie). Central China; Hupeh. 1900. Hardy and attractive. z5 Plate 150. 152. # ∅ ⊗

Including many cultivars, of which 'Skogholm' is the most common in nurseries.

'Coral Beauty'. (Hoogendoorn 1967). Low growing, branches spreading, resembles 'Skogholm', but remains lower and fruits very abundantly; fruits orange-red. Good winter hardiness. 'Royal Beauty' (1968) and 'Royal Carpet' (1970), both from the Darthuizer Nursery, Holland, are practically the same. # ∅ ⊗

'Eichholz' (H. Simon 1965). Presumably *C. dammeri* × *C.*

microphyllus 'Cochleatus'; very good groundcover, grows quickly, to 25 cm high, branches brown; leaves 1.5–2 cm long, fresh green, roots easily at the branch tips; fruits regularly, but not abundantly, carmine, large. Breeder: Dr. Hans Simon, 8772 Markheidenfeld, W. Germany. # ⌀

'Juergl' (K. H. Juergl 1959). Probably *C. dammeri × C. rotundifolius*, but not with *C. congestus*; low growing, not over 50 cm high, branches wide spreading-nodding, red-brown; leaves elliptic, obtuse, 9 by 15 mm, glossy green above, lighter beneath and eventually glabrous; fruits to 6 by 9 mm in size, light red, 1–2 together, fruits abundantly, with 2–3 seeds. Very similar to *C. dammeri* 'Skogholm', but fruits more abundantly. # ⌀

'Major'. Growth somewhat stronger than the species; leaves somewhat larger, 2.5–3.5 cm, some leaves turning orange-yellow in November (!). Often found in the nursery under the false name, "*C. dammeri radicans*". Very valuable type. More winter hardy than *C. dammeri*. # ⌀

'Minipolster; (Joh. Hachmann 1967) (= *C. dammeri* 'Major × 'Coral Beauty'). Weak grower, developing into a dense round cushion shape, like an evergreen *C. adpressus*. # ⌀

var. **radicans** Dammer. Leaves 1–1.5 cm long, ovate to obovate, usually obtuse at the apex and often emarginate, glossier above, petiole to 8 mm long; flowers 1–3, petiole 5–15 mm long (important for identification!). China; W. Szechwan. 1908. Hardy. Often confused. Plate 152. # ⌀

'Skogholm'. Possibly a hybrid with *C. rotundifolius* Wall. Shrub, to 60 cm high, but 2–3 m wide, branches long arching, roots lightly at the branch tips (if they touch the ground); leaves loosely arranged, elliptic, 1.5 × 3 cm large, rounded at both ends, dull glossy green above, not rugose; flowers grouped 2–6, 8 mm wide; fruits not numerous, dull red, 4–6 mm wide, with 3–4 seeds. Selected from a seedling of *C. dammeri* in 1941 by O. Goeransson, Skogholmens Nursery in Hindby near Malmoe, Sweden, but only introduced to the nursery trade in 1950. Very popular cultivar in Europe. Plate 147, 152. # ⌀

A white variegated form was exhibited by Boot & Co., Boskoop at the "Flora Nova" in 1965, but it has yet to reach the nursery trade. # ⌀

'Smaragdpolster' (J. Hachmann 1976) (= *C. dammeri* 'Major' × 'Coral Beauty'). Growth like 'Coral Beauty', but somewhat more compact, better branched, dark green leaves, semi-deciduous (!), also better fruiting. Breeder: Johannes Hachmann, 2202 Barmstedt, W. Germany. # ⌀

'Streibs Findling." A small-leaved selection; leaves broad elliptic, 8–15 mm long. Introduced around 1960 by W. Bofinger, 7121 Pleidesheim near Marbach, W. Germany. Excellent, flat growing groundcover. Plate 147. # ⌀

C. dielsianus Pritz. Deciduous, occasionally semi-deciduous shrub, to 2 m high, branches bowed outward, densely pubescent when young; leves oval-rounded tough, 1–2.5 cm long, dark green above, somewhat pubescent, dense, yellowish tomentose beneath, distinctly veined; flowers 3–7 in pubescent corymbs, petals erect, pink or white with red, June; fruits red, glossy, globose, 6 mm thick, several or singular, with 3–5 seeds. Sh 1: 418 a–b; ICS 2125 (= *C. applanatus* Duthie). China; Szechwan, Yunnan. 1908. Very diverse species. Hady. z5 Fig. 291. ✧ ⌀ ⌀

var. **elegans** Rehd. & Wils. More or less semi-deciduous; leaves thinner, smaller, only to 1.5 cm long, distinctly glabrous above, somewhat glossy; fruits lighter red, somewhat pubescent. China; Szechwan. ⌀ ⌀

var. **major** Rehd. & Wils. Leaves larger than those of the species, to 3.5 cm long and 2.5 cm wide, thinner; inflorescence loose, longer stalked. W. China. ⌀ ⌀

C. distichus Lange. Semi-deciduous or deciduous shrub, growth narrowly upright, but wide branched, branches 2 ranked, resembling *C. horizontalis*; leaves rather rounded, 1–1.5 cm wide, tough, dark green, more or less glabrous; flowers light pink, solitary, short stalked, May–June; fruits around 1 cm long, pear-shaped, scarlet-red, persisting to January / February. Bm 8010 (= *C. rotundifolius* Baker non Wall.). Himalaya. 1857. Not superior to *C. horizonatlis*. z7 Fig. 291.

var. **tongolensis** Schneid. Leaves thin woolly above, densely brown woolly beneath. China; W. Szechwan.

C. divaricatus Rehd. & Wils. Deciduous shrub, to 2 m high, erect, branches wide-spreading; leaves elliptic, 1–2.5 cm long, apex elliptic, glossy dark green above, lighter beneath, somewhat pubescent, often scarlet-red in fall; flowers 2–4 on small side branches, petals erect, white, base reddish, June; fruits elliptic, 8 mm long, deep red, most with 2 seeds, persisting to October. ICS 2133. China. 1904. Hardy. One of the best fruiting types. z5 Plate 151. ⌀

C. fontanesii see: **C. racemiflorus**

C. foveolatus Rehd. & Wils. Deciduous shrub, erect, about 3 m high, branches outspread, 2 ranked, yellowish pubescent when young, later glabrous and red-brown; leaves elliptic to oval-oblong, acuminate, 3.5–8 cm long, dull glazed above, venation indented, tomentose beneath, orange and red in fall; flowers 3–6 in pubescent cymes, petals erect, white and pink, June; fruits black, globose, 7–8 mm thick, with 3–4 seeds. ICS 2120. Central China; Hupeh. 1907. Hardy; resembling *C. moupinensis*, but with leaves less rugose. z5 Plate 149. ⌀

C. franchetii Bois. Semi-deciduous or evergreen shrub in mild areas, 1–2(3) m high, branches attractively nodding, tomentose at first, later brown; leaves mostly 2 ranked, oval-elliptic to broad lanceolate, 2–3.5 cm long, venation indented above, with a dull glaze, yellowish tomentose beneath; flowers usually grouped 5–15, axils tomentose, petals erect, white to pink, June; fruits orange-red, oblong, with 3 seeds, persisting very long. BM 8571; RH 1907: 256. SW. China; Szechwan, Yunnan; Upper Burma. 1895. Variable in cultivation. z6 Plate 149; Fig. 290. ⌀ ⌀

var. **cinerascens** Rehd. Growth taller, to 4 m; leaves to 4 cm long, underside looser and more gray or greenish tomentose; inflorescence larger, with up to 30 flowers, on about 5 cm long side branches. W. China; Szechwan, Yunnan. ⌀

var. **sternianus** Turrill. Semi-deciduous shrub, about 2–3 m high, somewhat stiff, branches more open-spreading, tomentose at first; leaves usually 2 ranked, tough, elliptic, acuminate, 2.5–3.5 cm long, dark green above and glabrous,

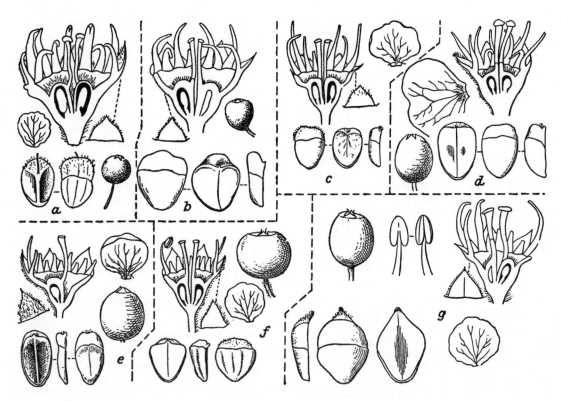

Fig. 289. **Cotoneaster** a. *C. horizontalis*; b. *C. horizontalis* 'Ascendes'; c. *C. horizontalis* var. *perpusillus*;
d. *C. horizontalis* 'Saxatilis'; e. *C. adpressus*; f. *C. praecox*

dense, white, shaggy pubescent beneath; flowers grouped 7–15, petals white, very reddish in the apical half, erect, May–June; fruits usually oblong-rounded, 8–10 mm long, in dense, short stalked clusters, light red, most with 3 seeds. BMns 130 (= *C. sternianus* [Turrill] Boom; *C. wardii* Hort. non W. W. Sm.; *C.* 'Gloire de Versailles' Hesse). SE. Tibet, N. Burma. 1913.

C. frigidus Wall. Deciduous to semi-deciduous shrub, to 5 m (tree-like in mild areas), branches widely arching, pubescent when young, soon becoming glabrous; leaves on erect branches, spiralling, otherwise 2 ranked, thin leathery, 6–12 cm long, 2.5–5 cm wide, elliptic to oblanceolate, obtuse, with small tips, dark green above, smooth, glabrous, dull glazed, underside gray tomentose at first or hairy, often becoming glabrous; flowers 20–40 in umbellate panicles on short side branches, axils tomentose at first, petals white, erect, June; fruits light red (important for identification!), persisting to about Christmas, 5 mm thick, with 2 seeds. BR 1229 (= *C. comptus* Hort.; *C. nepalensis* Hort.). Himalaya; Nepal, Sikkim. 1824. z7 Plate 149; Fig. 288. ⌀ ⚭

'Notcutt's Var.' Leaves larger, bright green above, often reddish beneath in winter. Introduced to the trade by Notcutt from England. ⌀ ⚭

'Pendulus'. Branches very pendulous. Selected 1924, in England as a seedling. Seed came from Darjeeling, India. Not to be confused with *C. watereri* 'Pendulus.'

'Xanthocarpus'. Fruits yellow to cream white. From England. Before 1914. z7 Plate 149.

C. glabratus Rehd. & Wils. Evergreen, upright shrub, 3–5 m high, branches wide spreading, young branches lightly pubescent, but quickly becoming glabrous; leaves leathery, lanceolate to oblanceolate, 5–10 cm long, light green above, glabrous, finely rugose, slightly pubescent on the 7–10 vein pairs beneath, otherwise glabrous; flowers many in 4 cm wide umbellate panicles, petals white, outspread, June–July; fruits light red, globose, 5 mm thick, with 2 seeds. W. China. 1908. Seldom true in cultivation; not to be confused with *C. watereri* 'Glabratus'. z6–7 #

C. glaucophyllus Franch. Evergreen shrub, 2–4 m high; leaves ovate, tapering to both ends, 3 cm long, leathery tough, glabrous above, pale green, bluish-white beneath, soon becoming glabrous, with 7–8 vein pairs; flowers small, white, many in about 2.5 cm wide inflorescences, axils loose pubescent, June; fruits ovate, orange, 6–7 mm large, with 2–3 seeds. ICS 2211. China. Often confused in cultivation wtih f. *serotinus*. z6–7 Fig. 288. # ⌀

f. **serotinus** (Hutchins.) Stapf. Growth stiffer, branches nodding; leaves elliptic-lanceolate to obovate, acuminate at both ends, with 5–9 vein pairs, dull glazed and dark green above, glabrous, underside densely shaggy pubescent at first, later nearly glabrous and gray-green; flowers to 40 together, not apearing until the end of July (important for identification!); fruits 6 mm thick, light red, rounded, coloring late, December–February. BM 8854 (= *C. serotinus* Hutchins.). W. China, Yunnan. #

var. **vestitus** W. W. Sm. Axils and leaf undersides densely tomentose; inflorescences smaller, flowers less numerous, calyx densely tomentose at first. W. China; Yunnan. #

C. "Gloire de Versailles". Introduced 1950 by Herm. A. Hesse, Vienna, Austria, not France, as presumed by Klotz (1957, p. 950).

C. harrovianus Wils. Evergreen shrub, growth habit like *C. salicifolius*, but leaves more like *C. pannosus*; about 1.5 m high, often wider than tall; leaves oval to obovate, 2.5–6 cm long, glossy deep green above, yellow-brown pubescent beneath, dense and shaggy, eventually glabrous, tough; flowers white, numerous in dense, 3 cm wide umbellate panicles, June; fruits dark red, dull glazed, 7 mm thick, globose, with 2 seeds. W. China, Yunnan. 1899. Very attractive fruiting species. z7 Fig. 291. # ✧

C. harrysmithii Flinck & Hylmoe. Deciduous shrub, 1–2 m high, side branches always horizontal, young branches gray-yellow pubescent, later becoming glabrous; leaves 2 ranked, elliptic to more ovate, acute, 17–19 mm long, 8–9 mm wide, base rounded, remaining loosely pubescent above, hairs wavy, with long gray-white hairs beneath; flowers usually 3 on short side branches, petals erect, pink-red with wide, white limb; fruits erect, ovate, 6–7 mm long, brownish black to black, with 2–3 seeds. Bot. Not. 115: 32 (Pl.). W. China. Closely related to *C. nitens*, but with branches all on an even plane, leaves acute elliptic and softly pubescent on both sides. z6

C. hebephyllus Diels. Deciduous, tall shrub, occasionally tree-like; leaves oval to circular, 2–4 cm long, glabrous above, blue-green beneath, dense gray shaggy at first, later glabrous, thin leathery; flowers 5–15 on short side branches, petals white, outspread, antehrs violet, late May; fruits dark red, ovate, 8 mm long, usually with 2 seeds. ICS 2114. W. China, Yunnan. 1910. z6 Fig. 291.

var. **monopyrenus** W. W. Sm. Fruits brown-red, to 10 cm long and 8 mm thick, with 2 nutlets, one of these compressed and seedless. BM 9389. W. China; Yunnan.

C. henryanus (Schneid.) Rehd. & Wils. Semi-deciduous (evergreen in mild areas) shrub, to 4 m high, branches broadly arching, pubescent; leaves oblong-lanceolate, leathery, 4.5–11 cm long, 1.5–3.5 cm wide, caudate at both ends, at first thinly pubescent and rugose above, eventually only on the venation, underside gray tomentose or eventually glabrous and blue-green to the 9–12 vein pairs; flowers white, many in 3–5 cm wide umbellate panicles, June; fruits dark red, ovate, 6 mm long, with 2–3 seeds, ripening in October. Rh 1919: 264; SH 1: 426g. Central China, Hupeh, Szechwan. 1901. Often falsely labelled in the garden! Plants by this name are usually *C. salicifolius*. z7 Plate 149. ✧ ∅ ⚬

C. × 'Hessei' (Hesse). Deciduous shrub, growth weak, to 60 cm high, irregularly branched, branches bowed; leaves round to broad elliptic, 7–15 mm long, thin, dark green above and glabrous, lighter beneath and eventually glabrous or nearly so; flowers normally solitary, petals erect, reddish, May; fruits light red, nearly globose, 6–7 mm thick, with 2–3 seeds, October. Originated by H. A. Hesse, Weener, W. Germany, before 1933; parentage unknown, probably *C. horizontalis* × *praecox*. Plate 152.

C. horizontalis Decne. Semi-evergreen or deciduous shrub, low growing, scarcely over 40 cm high, often several times as wide, branches horizontal and 2 ranked; leaves nearly circular, with a small tip, 5–12 mm long, dark green above, glossy, lighter beneath and strigose, coloring orange and scarlet in fall; flowers 1–2, short stalked, petals erect, reddish or white, June; fruits light red, obovoid, 5 mm long, usually with 3 seeds. HM 1018. W. China; Szechwan. 1879. z5–6 Fig. 289. ∅ ⚬

'Ascendens'. Growth more upright than the species; leaves 12–16 mm long, 7–10 mm wide, ovate, acuminate; fruits oblong, blood-red (= *C. horizontalis fructu-sanguineo* Spaeth). Often erroneously labeled "perpusilla". Fig. 289.

var. **perpusillus** Schneid. Lower than the species, densely branched, branches shorter and more bowed; leaves densely arranged, smaller, 6–8 mm long, margin often somewhat sinuate; flowers smaller; fruits elliptic, 5–6 mm long, usually with 3 seeds. SH 1: 419e. Central China; Hupeh, Shansi, Szechwan. 1906. Plate 157; Fig. 289.

'Robusta' (Vuyk van Nes 1954). Very strong growing shrub, broad, upright, side branches more or less on a single plane, later nodding, a plant in Boskoop after 8 years 2 m wide and 1.2 m high; leaves ovate, to 20 mm long, 15 mm wide, fall color an intense red, persisting to December; fruits light red, very numerous along the branches on older plants (= *C. horizontalis* 'Coralle' Hesse 1961; *C. horizontalis* 'Rotundifolius' Hort.). Discovered by Tips, Herk de Stad, Belgium, but disseminated by Vuyk Van Nes.

'Saxatilis' (Hesse). Weak growing selection with exceptionally regular (fishbone-like!), 2 ranked branch arragement, branches lying flat on the ground; leaves somewhat smaller than those of the species. Introduced by H. A. Hesse, Weener, Plate 145; Fig. 289. ∅ ⚬

'Variegatus'. Growth weak; leaves white variegated, more undulate. First described in England, 1922. ∅

var. **wilsonii** Havemeyer ex Wils. Growth 1–2 m high, branches wide and upright; leaves larger than on the species; fruits darker red, to 6 mm thick, abscising in October, few fruits produced on young plants, better fruiting with age (= *C. wilsonii* Hort. non Nakai). Before 1917.

C. horizontalis male × *C. salicifolia* var. *flocossa* female see: **C. salicifolia** male × **C. horizontalis** female

C. humifusus see: **C. dammeri**

C. hupehensis Rehd. & Wils. Deciduous shrub, to 2 m high, growth wide and nodding, branches pubescent at first, then brown; leaves elliptic, 2–3.5 cm long, tough, bright green and glabrous above, underside thinly gray tomentose, fall color yellow; flowers 6–12

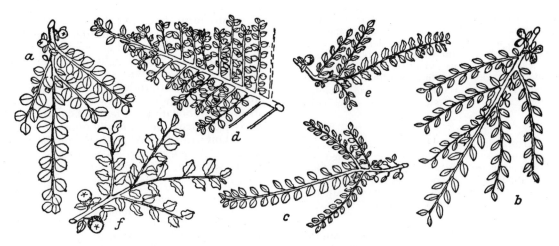

Fig. 289. **Cotoneaster** a. *C. horizontalis*; b. *C. horizontalis* 'Ascendens'; c. *C. horizontalis* var. *perpusillus*; d. *C. horizontalis* 'Saxatilis'; e. *C. adpressus*; f. *C. praecox*

in shaggy pubescent corymbs, May; fruits a bright red, globose, 8–12 mm thick, with 2 seeds. BMns 245; ICS 2116. China; Szechwan to Kiangsi. 1907. Variable species between *C. multiflorus* and *C. racemiflorus*. z5 ⚭

C. ignavus Wolf. Deciduous shrub, closely related to *C. niger*; growth stiff, upright, to 2 m high, young branches gray tomentose at first, then becoming glabrous; leaves spirally arranged, ovate, 2.5 to 4.5 cm long, dull green above, whitish-green beneath, pubescent; flowers 8–13 in loose umbellate panicles, petals tilting diagonally upwards (important for identification!), pink, May; fruit dark brown-red, elliptic, to 8 mm long, with 2–3 seeds. E. Turkestan, Tientsin. 1907. Leaves orange-red in fall. z6 ∅

C. insignis Pojark. Deciduous to semi-deciduous shrub, upright, to 6 m high, branches outspread, gray tomentose when young, later glabrous and brown; leaves usually 2 ranked, tough, broad elliptic to broad obovate or nearly circular, 2–5 cm long, 1.5–4.5 cm wide, usually obtuse, dull green above, gray to yellowish tomentose beneath, eventually rather glabrous, petiole 4–7 mm long; flowers 5–20 in dense umbellate panicles, petals white, outspread, May; fruits black, bluish pruinose, nearly globose, 7–9 mm thick, with 1–2 seeds. Central Asia; Iran, Afghanistan, Turkestan. Often found in the garden under the name "*C. lindleyi*". z6 Plate 149; Fig. 287. ∅ ⚭

C. integerrimus Med. Deciduous shrub, of many forms, scarcely over 1.5 m high, sprawling to procumbent, branches appressed woolly pubescent, later becoming glabrous, light gray-green and tomentose beneath; flowers 2–4 in nodding corymbs, petals erect, white and reddish, May; fruits bright red, 6 mm thick, rounded, usually with 2–3 seeds. HM Pl. 145 (= *C. vulgaris* Lindl.). S, SE and Middle Europe. Of little merit for garden use. Plate 146, 149; Fig. 290. z6

C. lacteus W. W. Sm. Evergreen shrub, to 3 m high and wide, branches drooping, woolly tomentose at first;

leaves usually 2 ranked, tough, leathery, 3–8 cm long, broad elliptic to lanceolate, usually obtuse, a dull glazed dark green above, with 7–10 indented vein pairs, underside white at first, later yellowish tomentose, more glabrous and gray in the 2nd year; flowers numerous (to 70), in 4–6 cm wide umbellate panicles terminal on short side branches, petals milk-white, outspread, anthers pink, June; fruits red, ovate, 6 mm long, usually with 2 seeds, persistent. BM 9454; NF 3:4. W. China; Yunnan. 1913. z7 Fig. 291. # ∅ ⚭

C. laxiflorus see: **C. niger**

C. lindleyi Steud. = *C. insignis* Pojark. Please refer to the explanation in Klotz, pp. 961–962.

C. lucidus Schlechtd. Deciduous shrub, upright, to 3 m high, young branches pubescent; leaves usually 2 ranked, acute ovate, 2–7 cm long, glossy green above, whitish-green pubescent beneath, often eventually glabrous; flowers 3–12 in terminal or axillary cymes, petals erect, white with reddish tones, May–June; fruits black, ovate, not pruinose, usually with 3 seeds. SH 1: 421c, 432 a–c (= *C. acutifolius* Lindl. non Turcz.). Central Asia; Baikal region. 1840. Very hardy; especially as a hedging plant, but otherwise of little garden worth; fruits abscising early. z3 Plate 146; Fig. 290.

C. melanocarpus see: **C. niger** Fries.

C. microphyllus Wall. Evergreen, procumbent shrub, occasionally to 1 m high, densely branched; leaves oblong-obovate, 5–8 mm long, rounded to emarginate at the apex, glossy dark green above, glabrous, margins revolute, papillate beneath, whitish, pubescent or glabrous; flowers 1(2), short stalkd, at the ends of short side branches, petals white, radiating outward, May; fruits globose, red, 6 mm thick, with 2 seeds. BR 1114; ICS 2128. Himalaya; Nepal, Sikkim to Kashmir; SW. China, Yunnan. 1824. Slightly glabrous as an older plant. Often incorrecntly labeled in cultivation as *C. rotundifolius* Lindl. z6 ⓕ Himalaya (for erosion control). # ∅

'Cochleatus'. Growth procumbent or bowed downward, branches occasionally rooting; leaves spirally arranged, elliptic to obovate, 5–10 mm long, glossy dark green above, white pubescent breneath; flowers usually solitary on short side branches, white, petals outspread, May–June; fruits 5–6 mm thick, red, globose, with 2 seeds (= *C. microphyllus melanotrichus* Hort., non Hand. Mazz.). Those plants in culture today can be considered a clone, as suggested by Boom. # Ø

f. **thymifolius** (Lindl.) Koehne. Growth very compact, branches outspread, densely branched; leaves densely spiralled, oblong to obovate, 4–15 mm long, rounded at the apex or also emarginate, glossy dark green above, white to gray pubescent beneath; flowers 1–4 together, petals somewhat reddish; fruits red, globose, 5 mm thick, only a few plants fruit. HM 1018g. Himalaya; Sikkim to Kashmir. 1852. z7 Plate 148. # Ø

C. moupinensis Franch. Deciduous shrub, sprawling, to 5 m high, branches slender, often nodding, densely downly pubescent at first, soon becoming glabrous and glossy; leaves elliptic-oblong, acuminate, 4–10 cm long, glossy dark green above, somewhat rugose, light gray-green beneath, tomentose, fall color dark brown; flowers 10–25 in small umbellate panicles, petals erect, white, with a reddish trace, June; fruits black, nearly globose, 6–8 mm long, with 4–5 seeds. ICS 2119. China; Szechwan, Yunnan. 1907. Hardy; tolerates shade. Similar to *C. bullatus*, but with black fruits. z5

C. multiflorus Bge. Deciduous shrub, 3(4) m high, branches slender, often nodding, downy pubescent at first, then red-brown and glossy; leaves broad ovate to elliptic, 2–5 cm long, bright green above, light gray-green beneath, tomentose at first, soon becoming glabrous, apex rounded to somewhat emarginate, midrib on the underside usually reddish; flowers 6–20 in erect umbellate panicles, petals white, outspread, early June; fruits red, usually obovate, 6–9 mm long, abundant fruiting in August–September. BS 1: 66; ICS 2112 (= *C. reflexa* carr.). Caucasus to E. Asia. 1837. Quite variable, hardy and attractive species. z3 Fig. 288, 291. ⊕ ⚭

var. **calocarpus** Rehd. & Wils. Leaves larger and narrower, 3–4.5 cm long; more floriferous and with more flowers in an inflorescence; fruits 10 to 12 mm thick, numerous. W. China. 1900. More attractive than the species. Fall color yellow. ⊕ ⚭

'Calocarpus' Hort. The plant by this name in European nurseries and gardens (and presumably elsewhere) is actually *C. racemiflorus* var. *songoricus*!

var. **granatensis** (Boiss.) Wenz. Like the species, but growing somewhat taller; leaves at first more densely pubescent beneath; inflorescences longer, looser, axils pubescent. Spain; Sierra Nevada.

C. nanchuanicus see: **C. praecox**

C. nebrodensis (Guss.) K. Koch. Deciduous shrub,

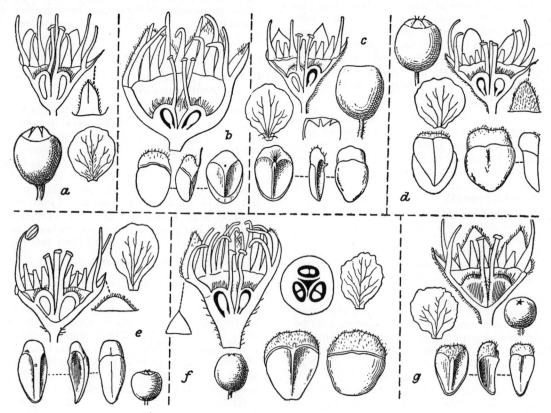

Fig. 290. **Cotoneaster** a. *C. roseus*; b. *C. integgerimus*; c. *D. franchetii*; d. *C. zabelii*; e. *C. bullatus*; f. *C. lucidus*; g. *C. nebrodensis* (from Schneider, Koehne)

Fig. 291. **Cotoneaster** a. *C. lacteus*; b. *C. deilsianus*; c. *C. harrovianus*; d. *C. multiflorus*; e. *C. racemiflorus* var. *soongoricuis*; f. *C. racemiflorus* var. *royleanus*; g. *C. distichus*; h. *C. nitens*; i. *C. hebephyllus*; k. *C. racemiflorus* var. *veitchii*

0.6−2 m high, resembles *C. integerrimus*, but in all parts larger and more pubescent; branches tomentose, glabrous and brown in the 2nd year; leaves broad elliptic to oval, 3−6 cm long, obtuse, dull green above, densely light gray tomentose beneath; flowers 3−12 in nodding corymbs, calyx and flower stalks white tomentose, petals erect, outside usually reddish, May−June; fruits bright red, nearly globose, 7 to 8 mm thick, somewhat pubescent, erect, with 3−5 seeds. HM Pl. 145 (= *C. tomentosus* [Ait.] Lindl.). S. Europe, Balkan Peninsula, in the mountains. 1759. z6 Fig. 290.

C. nepalensis see: **C. acuminatus** and **C. frigidus**

C. × newryensis Lemoine (? *C. franchetii* × *C. simonii*). Shrub, deciduous to semi-evergreen, branches outspread to nodding; leaves usually 2 ranked, rough, usually elliptic, acute to obtuse, 2−4 cm long, dark green and glabrous above, gray-green and shaggy pubescent beneath; flowers in dense umbellate panicles; fruits red. Introduced to the trade before 1933 by Lemoine.

C. niger (Thunb.) Fries. Deciduous shrub, growth broad and upright, 0.5−2 m high, branches sprawling or nodding, gray shaggy pubescent at first, later glossy red-brown; leaves usually 2 ranked, broad oval-oblong, obtuse or acute, 2−5 cm long, dull dark green above, densely gray shaggy beneath, becoming somewhat glabrous; flowers 2−12 in loose, slightly pubescent, nodding corymbs, May−June, petals erect, reddish or white with reddish trace; fruits black-red,

usually blue pruinose, oval-rounded, 6−9 mm long, with 2−3 seeds. HM 1019; ICS 2126 (= *C. melanocarpus* Lodd.). E. Europe to W. Asia; E. Mongolia. 1826. z5 Plate 149; Fig. 288.

var. **commixtus** Schneid. Leaves more ovate; flowers grouped 8−15. BM 3519 (as *C. laxiflorus sensu* Hook.).

var. **latiflorus** (Lindl.) Schneid. Leaves larger; flowers grouped 20−40 in pendulous corymbs; conspicuous for the large inflorescences. BM 1229 + 1305 (= *C. laxiflorus* Lindl.)⊕

C. nitens Rehd. & Wils. Deciduous shrub, dense, upright, to 2.5 m high, branches nodding at first, eventually sprawling; leaves usually 2 ranked, round-ovate, acute, to 2 cm long, glossy dark green above, lighter beneath, soon becoming quite glabrous; flowers 2−6 (usually 3) mostly along the branches, petals erect, pink, or white with red, May−June; fruits rounded, red at first, turning black-red (October), 6−8 mm thick, usually with 2 seeds. W. China, Szechwan. 1910. z6 Fig. 291.⊕

C. nitidifolius Marquand. Deciduous shrub, dense, upright, similar to *C. acuminatus*, but with leaves very glossy above, 4−6 cm long, oval-lanceolate, base obtuse, glabrous above, underside densely pubescent at first, later more sparse, petiole 2−3 mm long; flowers grouped 3−10, petals erect, white, June; fruits rounded, 5−6 mm thick, brown-red to dark red, usually with 2 seeds. SW. China; Yunnan. 1924. z6

C. obscurus Rehd.& Wils. Deciduous shrub, to 3 m

high, branches sprawling, long, nodding, pubescent, eventually red-brown and glabrous; leaves oval-elliptic, acuminate, 2–4 cm long, dull green above, thinly pubescent, gray-yellow tomentose beneath, 5–7 vein pairs, these elevated; flowers 3–7(10) in short, densely pubescent umbellate panicles, petals erect, white or (usually) with a trace of pink, early June; fruits teardrop shape, dark red to brown red, 7–9 mm long, with 3–4 seeds. China; Szechwan, Hupeh. z5?

var. **cornifolius** Rehd. & Wils. Leaves larger, 4 to 7 cm long with 5–7 vein pairs, distinctly indented above, loose pubescence beneath; fruits to 10 mm long, black-red, usually with 5 achenes. W. China, Szechwan.

C. pannosus Franch. Semi-evergreen shrub, to 2 m high, branches arching, densely pubescent at first; leaves 2 ranked, leathery, elliptic, with prickly tips, 1–2.5 cm long, dull green and glabrous above, gray tomentose beneath, with 4–6 vein pairs; flowers 6–20 in dense, nearly hemispherical corymbs, June; petals white, outspread; fruits rounded, 6–8 mm long, dull light red, with 2 seeds. Bm 8594; NF 3: 5; GC 132: 9. SW. China. 1888. Resembles *C. racemiflorus.* z6 Fig. 288.

C. pekinensis see: **C. acutifolius**

C. praecox Vilmorin-Andrieux. Deciduous shrub, to 50 cm high, branches arching outward to 1 m to creeping, brownish above, green beneath; leaves ovate, 1 to 2.5 cm long, margin very sinuate, dark green above, light green beneath, coloring red in fall but quickly abscising; flowers 1–2(3), usually sessile in the leaf axils, large, petals erect, pink, May; fruits globose, 8–12 mm thick, usually with 2 seeds, coloring in August, abscising as soon as September. Gs 16: 37; Gw 33: 584 (= *C. adpressus* var. *praecox* [Vilm.] Bois. & Berth.; C. Nan Shan Vilm.; *C. nanchuanicus* Rgl.). W. China, Szechwan, Nan-Shan Mts. 1504. z5 Fig. 289.⊕ ⊗

'Boer' (Boer). Dutch selection; branches more ascending, not curved downward, otherwise little difference. Brought into the trade by Jan Boer & Zoon, Boskoop. Around 1950. ⊕ ⊗

C. racemiflorus (Desf.) K. Koch. Deciduous shrub, to 2.5 m high, branches wide, noding, gray tomentose at first; leaves elliptic, 1.5–3 cm long, dull green above, light gray or whitish tomentose beneath; flowers white, 8 mm wide, 3–12 on tomentose, stalked cymes, petals outspread, May–June; fruits light red, globose, 7–9 mm thick, with 2 seeds (= *C. fontanesii* Spach). N. Africa, W. Asia to Turkestan. 1829. Quite variable species. z3 Fig. 288. ⊕ ⊗

var. **nummalaria** (Fisch. & Mey.) Dipp. Lower growing, scarcely over 1.5 m high, branches shorter; leaves smaller, more rounded, 15–25 mm long, loosely pubescent above; inflorescence smaller, with only 2–7 flowers; fruits usually 7–8 mm thick. Caucasus, Western Asia to W. Himalaya.

var. **royleanus** Dipp. Low shrub; leaves round to broad obovate, apex rounded to emarginate, 8–20 mm long; flowers grouped 3–6. Himalaya. Fig. 291.

var. **songoricus** (Rgl. & Herd.) Schneid. To 2 m high, similar to *C. multiflorus*, branches long, arching; leaves usually 2

ranked, tough, ovate, usually obtuse, 25–35 mm long, gray-green, pubescent at first, usually soon becoming rather glabrous; flowers 3–12 in loose, erect inflorescences; fruits red, 7–10 mm long, October. SH 1: 424i; ICS 2115. Dsungarei, W. Himalaya to NE. China. Fruits abundantly and much prized. This plant is often found in nurseries and gardens under the name "*C. multiflorus* 'Calocarpus' ". Fig. 291. ⊕ ⊗

var. **veitchii** Rehd. & Wils. Similar to *C. racemiflorus*; shrub, to 2 m high, branches wide spreading; leaves elliptic, acute, 2–3.5 cm long, soon becoming glabrous above, gray tomentose beneath; flowers large, 3–10 in dense inflorescences, flowers solitary, 12–15 mm wide (important for identification!); fruits dark red, globose, 10 mm thick, with 1(2) seeds. China; Hupeh. Very attractive, but rarely true in cultivation. Fig. 291. ⊕ ⊗

C. reflexa see: **C. multiflorus**

C. rhytidophyllus Rehd. & Wils. Evergreen or semi-deciduous shrub, to 2 m high, branches widely arching, tomentose at first; leaves usually 2 ranked, oval-oblong to lanceolate, 3–8 cm long, with 5–10 vein pairs, very rugose above, dense yellowish or whitish woolly beneath, petiole 2–4 mm long; flowers 10–15 in about 3 cm wide umbellate panicles, petals outspread, white, June; fruits orange-red, pear-shaped, densely pubescent at first, 6mm long, with 3–4 seeds. W. China, Szechwan. 1908. Similar to *C. henryanus* and *C. rugosus.* z7 Plate 149. # ∅

C. roseus Edgew. Deciduous upright shrub, 2–3 m high, branches thin, nodding, white pubescent at first, but soon becoming glabrous; leaves usually 2 ranked, thin, elliptic to ovate, 2–6 cm long, dull green above and pubescent at first, gray-green beneath and also at first pubescent, later pruinose; flowers 3–9 in glabrous corymbs, petals erect-outspread, white with a trace of red, June; fruits rounded, 7 mm long, red, usually with 2 seeds. Sh 1: 423r, 424n. NW. Himalaya, Afghanistan. Frequently found in cultivation. z6 Fig. 290. ⊕ ⊗

C. rotundifolius Wall. Evergreen, upright shrub, to 4 m high in its native habitat; occasionally wider than tall, branches wide spreading, curved, densely covered with short branches, with yellowish strigose pubescence when young; leaves spirally arranged (important for identification!), thick and leathery, broad elliptic to obovate, 8–20 mm long, round or obtuse, with small tips, dark green, dull glazed, blue-green beneath, somewhat pubescent; flowers 1–3 on short side branches, petals outspread, white, June; fruits red, globose, 7–9 mm thick, with 2 seeds. Himalaya. 1825. Occasionally found in cultivation, but usually under the name "*C. buxifolius*". z6–7 See also: *C. distichous.* #

'Ruby'. To 1 m high, branches outspread, glabrous; leaves oval, 8–15 mm long, obtuse or with small tips, base acute to round, glossy dark green above, light green to bluish-green beneath, later often with reddish midvein, blade with scattered white pubescence, edge somewhat involute; flowers solitary, white, 1 cm wide (= *C. rubens* Hort. non Rehd. & Wils.; *C. microphyllus* 'Ruby' Boom). Disseminated in recent years from European nurseries as "*C. rubens*".

C. roylei see: **C. acuminatus**

C. rubens W. W. Sm. Deciduous or semi-deciduous shrub, 0.5–1 m high, irregularly branched, wide growing, young branches densely pubescent, soon becoming glabrous; leaves 2 ranked and spiralled, tough, circular to broad elliptic, 8–20 mm long, rounded at both ends, yellowish to whitish tomentose beneath; flowers solitary, petals red, erect, June; fruits obovoid, 8–9 mm long, red, with 3 seeds. China, Yunnan. Nearly always erroneously labelled. Plants in cultivation by this name are evergreen and have white flowers. z7 See also: *C. rotundifolius* 'Ruby'.

C. rugosus Printz. Evergreen or semi-deciduous shrub, branches widely arching, yellowish floccose-tomentose at first, glabrous and brown in the 2nd year; leaves similar to *C. salicifolius*; but usually 2 ranked, elliptic-lanceolate, 4–7.5 cm long, to 3.5 cm wide, acute at both ends, with 8–11 vein pairs, much more rugose above, deep green, dense yellowish floccose-tomentose, soon becoming glabrous; flowers in 5–6 cm wide umbellate panicles, petals white, outspread, June; fruits red, oval-rounded, 6 mm long, with 2 seeds. BM 8694 (= *C. salicifolius* var. *rugosus* [Pritz.] Rehd. & Wils.). China, E. Szechwan, W. Hupeh. z6 # ⌀

C. 'Sabrina' see: **C. splendens**

C. salicifolius Franch. Evergreen or semi-deciduous shrub, 4–6 m tall in its native habitat, branches long arching, strigose pubescent at first; leaves 2 ranked and spirally arranged, narrow lanceolate, 4–8 cm long, 1–2 cm wide, acute, margin revolute, dark green above, with 5–12 indented vein pairs, most rather rugose, at first white floccose-tomentose beneath, soon becoming more or less glabrous, venation reddish; flowers many in 3–4 cm wide, pubescent umbellate panicles, petals white, outspread, anthers red, June; fruits globose, red, 4–6 mm thick, with 2–3 seeds. BM 8999; ICS 2110. W. China, Szechwan. Good identifying characters are the revolute leaf tips and margins, otherwise the species is quite variable. z5 # ⌀ ⚭

var. **floccosus** Rehd. & Wils. Branches widely arching; leaves more lanceolate or oblong, larger than those of the species, with 7–14 vein pairs, edge more or less involute, underside floccose-tomentose at first, soon becoming glabrous; fruits 6 mm long, with 3 seeds. Gs 14: 25; GC 71: 114. 1908. Quite variable. Plate 149. # ⌀ ⚭

'Gnom' (Juergl). Evergreen shrub, procumbent, growth wide, nearly mat-like, very slow growing, long internodes; leaves oblong, about 2 cm long, 5 mm wide, obtuse at both ends, with 4–6 vein pairs; fruits 3–6 in loose fascicles, light red, 3–4 mm thick. Originated around 1938 by K. H. Juergl, near Cologne, W. Germany from seed of a flat growing *C. salicifolius* seedlings, introduced 1955. Plate 152. # ⌀ ⚭

'Herbstfeuer' (H. Bruns). Growth broadly procumbent, branches lying on the ground, partly rooting; leaves oval, 4–6 cm long, leathery, usually acute on both ends, dark green and glossy above, somewhat rugose, glabrous, blue-green and papillate beneath, eventually only the midrib pubescent, with 7–9 vein pairs, coloring to purple-red, November; flowers grouped 5–12; fruits light red, usually with 4 seeds. Developed around 1930 by H. Bruns, Wester-

stede, W. Germany from seed. Not very good as a ground-cover since the shoots are sparsely branched. ⌀ ⚭

'Klampen' (Harald Oltmanns, 2913 Klampen near Westerstede, 1963). Evergreen, branches partly lying along the ground, partly ascending; leaves large, deep green, strikingly red petioles; fruits bright red, numerous. Very fast growing form; presumably a seedling from *C. salicifolius* var. *floccosus*. #

'Parkteppich' (Hachmann). Like 'Gnom', but the leaves normally somewhat larger, on long branches to 25–30 mm long and 7–10 mm wide, rounded at both ends; fruits 6–10 in dense inflorescences, light red, with 3–4 seeds. Introduced to the trade in 1957 by J. Hachmann, Barmstedt (Holstein) W. Germany, but cultivated since 1950. Plate 151. # ⌀ ⚭

'Perkeo' (Hesse). Dwarf form of *C. salicifolius*, only 1 m high, densely branched, branches nodding; leaves somewhat smaller. Introduced to the trade in 1952 by H. A. Hesse, Weener, W. Germany. # ⌀

'Repens' (Haalboom 1948). Shrub, procumbent, branches not rooting, green at first, later dark brown, with few, distinct lenticels; leaves 25–35 mm in size, long oval, glossy dark green above, bluish beneath, covered with papillae, pubescent at first, later rather glabrous, petiole 4 mm long; flowers grouped 3–10; fruit to 6 together, 5–7 mm wide, light red, with 4–5 seeds. Dfl 3: 26 (= *C. salicifolius* 'Avodrood' Haalboom; *C. salicifolius* 'Dortmund'). Developed from seed of *C. salicifolius floccosus* by W. Haalboom of Driebergen, Holland; brought into the trade in 1948. Plate 152.

'Saldam' (J. Timm & Co. 1954). In growth habit and foliage scarcely distinguishable from 'Herbstfeuer', but leaves somewhat lighter green and dull, only a few leaves turning red in fall. Originated as a seedling at Timm & Co., Elmshorn, W. Germany before 1945, but not introduced to the trade until 1954. #

C. salicifolius var. *floccosus* female × *C. horizontalis* male. A small group of hybrids containing 2 Dutch selections:

'Gracia' (Boskoop Experiment Station 1961). Deciduous shrub, broad and flat growing, not over 60 cm high, branches ornamentally arching; leaves glossy green, somewhat rugose, similar to those of *C. horizontalis*, but somewhat coarser, coloring a dull red in November, persisting to December; fruitless. Somewhat tender in cold winer. z6–7

'Valkenburg' (Boskoop Experiment Station 1961). Semi-deciduous shrub, to 1.7 m high, growth dense and wide, branches arching; leaves glossy green, without fall coloration, remaining green over winter and abscising in spring; also fruitless. Dfl 1: 35.

C. *serotinus* see: **C. glaucophyllus**

C. sikangensis Flinck & Hylmoe. Deciduous shrub, closely related *C. obscurus* and *C. bullatus*, 2–3 m high, growth narrowly upright, branches dense, yellowish-white, rough hairy at first, glabrous after a year; leaves leathery tough, oval-elliptic, acuminate, 2–5 cm long, 1–2.5 cm wide, base obtuse to acute, dark green above, blistered (like *C. bullatus*), glossy, whitish-yellow to yellowish-brown tomentose beneath, with 4–5 veins on either blade half; flowers 3–6 together (to 12 on plants in cultivation), erect, calyx yellowish-white pubescent, petals erect, curved inward, with a greenish-brown, wide middle stripe; fruits teardrop shape, 1 cm long, glossy reddish-orange. Bot. Not. 115: 377 (Pl.). China; W. Szechwan. In the Botanic Garden of Upsala, Sweden before 1937, extremely winter hardy and with considerable garden merit. z5

C. simonsii Baker. Deciduous to semi-deciduous shrub, narrowly upright, straggly branched, 1.5−3 m high, young branches yellowish pubescent, glabrous and brown in the 2nd year; leaves thin, elliptic to obovate, 1.5−3 cm long, deep green above, glossy, light green beneath, somewhat pubescent; flowers grouped 2−5, petals erect, white with reddish traces, May−June; fruits elliptic, coral-red, 8−9 mm long, with 3−4 seeds. Gs 1933: 24; SH 1: 418 n−o, 419f. Himalaya, Khasi Hills (India). 1865. z6 ⌀ ⌘

C. splendens Flinck & Hylmoe. Deciduous shrub, growth wide, related to *C. dielsianus*, 1(2) m high, branches ascending or somewhat procumbent, side branches 2 ranked; leaves broad ovate or elliptic to nearly circular, acute, base rounded, usually 16−18 mm long, 13−15 mm wide, slightly glossy above, light green and persistently pubescent, white tomentose beneath; flowers usually in 3's, erect on tiny branchlets, petals erect, circular, red, with pink limb; fruits obovoid, 9−11 mm long, 8−10 mm wide, orange-red, usually with 4 seeds. Bot. Not. 117: 126 (Pl.) W. China; Sikang. 1934 (Upsala). z5 Plate 151.

The plant named **C. 'Sabrina'** in cultivation was found as a seedling in the garden of Norman Hadden, Porlock, England before 1950 and described as a hybrid between *C. horizontalis* and *C. pannosus*, but later designated as *C. horizontalis* × *C. franchetii*. Seedlings of this cross seem to be quite consistent and hardly distinguishable from *C. splendens*. (*Sabrina* is the Latin term for the Bristol Canal). Plate 152.

C. sternianus see: **C. franchetii**

C. tomentosus see: **C. nebrodensis**

C. turbinatus Craib. Evergreen shrub, 2−3 m high, narrowly upright, branches nodding, somewhat tomentose at first; leaves mostly 2 ranked, thin leathery, elliptic-lanceolate, 2−6 cm long, acute or obtuse, dull dark green above, glabrous, persistently white tomentose beneath, with 6−8 vein pairs; flowers in about 5 cm wide umbellate panicles with very many (to 75) flowers, anthers pink, petals white, outspread, July; fruits light red, teardrop shape, 4−5 mm long, loosely pubescent. BM 8546. W. and Central China. 1910. Pretty in flower, less so in fruit. z7 # ⌀ ⌘

C. uniflorus Bge. Deciduous shrub, similar to *C. integerrimus*, but only 0.5 m high, often spreading along the ground or also upright, branches pubescent, soon becoming glabrous; leaves thin, elliptic, usually obtuse, seldom round or acute, 1−3 cm long, dark green above, glabrous, underside short-haired at first, later glabrous and blue-green; flowers solitary, on small branches, nodding, petals erect, greenish or reddish white, May−June; fruits purple-red, globose, 6−7 mm thick, with 3−4 seeds. Central Asia, Altai Mts., Tientsin. z5

C. vulgaris see: **C. integerrimus**

C. wardii W. W. Sm. Evergreen shrub, to 3 m high, closely related to *C. franchetii*, but with young shoots white tomentose; leaves ovate, 2.5−4.5 cm long, leathery, glossy above, dark green, rugose, eventually becoming glabrous, dense silvery-white tomentose beneath, venation elevated; flowers grouped 10−15, on tomentose branches, petals erect, white with reddish traces, June; fruits orange-red, obovoid, to 8 mm long, usually with 2 seeds, October. SE. Tibet. 1913. Very attractive, but rarely true in cultivation. z6 See also: *C. franchetii*. # ⌀ ⌘

C. × watereri Excell. (Hybrids between *C. frigidus* with *C. salicifolius* and *rugosus*). Evergreen, or more commonly semi-deciduous shrub, strong grower, tall or sometimes procumbent; see the following outline.

    * Growth strongly upright:
        'Cornubia', 'St. Monica' 'Salmon Spray', 'Vicaryi'

    ** Growth with arching branch habit:
        'Aldenhamensis', 'Exburiensis', 'Glabratus', 'Inchmery', 'John Waterer', 'Pink Champagne', 'Rothschildeanus'

    *** Growth weak, branches procumbent or distinctly pendulous:
        'Pendulus'

'Aldenhamensis' (Gibbs). Growth narrowly upright, about 3 m high, branches nodding, dark brown, with many, light lenticels; leaves oblong-lanceolate, 4−7 cm long, 1.2−1.8 cm wide, acute at both ends, very rugose above, leathery, persistent long haired beneath; flowers in rather small corymbs; fruits purple-red, persisting for a long time, 5−7 mm thick, with 2 seeds (= *C. frigidus aldenhamensis* Gibbs; *C. aldenhamensis* Gibbs). Developed by Gibbs, Aldenham, England before 1934. ⌀ ⌘

'Cornubia' (Rothschild). Tall shrub, also tree-like in mild areas, branches ascending diagonally, dark brown with many white lenticels; leaves 7−10 cm long, 2.5−4 cm wide, dull green, slightly rugose, somewhat acuminate, eventually nearly totally glabrous beneath; fruits abundant, bright red, nearly globose, 7−9 mm thick, with 2−3 seeds, long persistent. GC 132: 101 Originated around 1930 by L. Rothschild, Exbury, England. Plate 125. ⌀ ⌘

'Exburiensis' (Rothschild) (*C. frigiduis* 'Xanthocarpus' × *C. salicifolius*). Strong grower, stem erect, branches green at first (important for identification!), eventually brownish and then densely white punctate; leaves 8−12 cm long, 2−3 cm wide, glossy light green above, very rugose, slightly pubescent beneath; fruits yellowish (not gold-yellow). Originated around 1930 by L. Rothschild. See also 'Rothschildianus'. Plate 149. ⌀ ⌘

'Glabratus'. Strong grower, branches somewhat nodding; similar to 'Watereri', but with leaves somewhat smaller, the fruits smaller and dull red. GC 132: 106. Known in England before 1951, but not the same as *C. glabratus* Rehd. & Wils. ⌀ ⌘

'Inchmery'. Tall shrub or tree-like, resembling *C. frigidus* in general appearance; fruits yellow at first, later salmon-pink. Cultivated by Hillier 1971.

'John Waterer' (Waterer & Crisp). The type of this group. Strong grower, branches nodding, dark brown, with only a few lenticels; leaves 7−10 cm long, 2.5−5 cm wide, dull green above, slightly rugose, underside pubescent at first, later glabrous, obtuse or acute; fruits numerous, in wide inflorescences, light red and glossy, 8−9 mm thick, usually with 2 seeds. GC 1928, I: 21; BMns 282 (= C. *watereri* Exell). Originated around 1920 by Waterer Sons & Crisp in Bagshot, England. Plate 149. ∅ ⚭

'Pendulus'. Branches long, more or less lying on the ground, fast grower, ocasionally rooting, often grown on a vertical standard, then the branches are very pendulous, branches brown, green at the tip; leaves 4−7 cm long, 1.5−2.5 cm wide, somewhat glossy and smooth above, lighter beneath, fall foliage yellow; flowers in small corymbs; fruits very numerous, globose, red, 6−8 mm thick, with 2−3 seeds. (= C. "*hybrida pendula*" Hort.). Origin unknown but presumably in England, about 20 years ago. Not to be confused with C. *frigidus* 'Pendulus'. Plate 149, 151. ∅ ⚭

'Pink Champagne'. Tall, strong growing shrub, branches arching downward; leaves narrow; fruits small, but very numerous, yellow at first, then with a trace of pink. Cultivated by Hillier 1971.

'Rothschildianus' (Rothschild). Scarcely distguishable from 'Exburiensis' and originating from the same cross, fruits however gold-yellow; but only of slight ornamental merit. The plant cultivated by this name in Holland is always 'Exburiensis'. ∅

'Salmon Spray' (Hillier). Medium size shrub, very similar to C. *henryanus*, but the abundant fruits salmon-red. Cultivated by Hillier, 1971.

'St. Monica (Bauer). Especially strong grower; leaves elliptic-oblong, 10−15 cm long; fruits red, in large, nodding bouquets. Originated before 1945 by Dr. Bauer, St. Monica House, Bristol, England. z7 Plate 149. ∅ ⚭

'Vicaryi' (Gibbs). Growth strongly upright, branches glossy dark brown, with many lenticels; leaves to 10 cm long, to 3.5 cm wide, green and somewhat rugose above, persistent long haired beneath, often with red midrib in winter; fruits rather small, purple-red. Originated around 1920 in Aldenham House, England. ∅ ⚭

C. *wilsonii* see: **C. horizontalis**

C. zabelii Schneid. Deciduous shrub, 2−3 m high, branches thin, ornamentally nodding, densely pubescent; leaves oval-elliptic, obtuse, 1.5−3 cm long, dull green above, loosely pubescent, densely gray-yellow tomentose beneath; flowers 3−10 in pubescent, loose corymbs, petals erect, reddish or white with a trace of red, May−June; fruits light red, globose, pubescent, 7−8 mm thick, with 2 seeds. Sh 1: 420 f−h, 422 i−k; ICS 2124. China. 1907. z5 Fig. 290. ∅ ⚭

var. **miniatus** Rehd. & Wils. Leaves yellow before falling; fruits smaller, more light orange. China, Hupeh.

The *Cotoneaster* species are very valuable plant materials for the garden designer, the genus contains a large number of species, ornamental for their attractive foliage, abundant flowers, but especially for their bright red (sometimes black) fruits. The low types should be considered for the rock garden, the strong growing types for the park. All species prefer full sun and a fertile, humus soil. C. *dammeri* has generally proved to be an excellent groundcover. The tall evergreen types require protection from hard frosts.

Lit. Boom, B. B.: Benaming, geschiedenis en kenmerken van een aantal houtachtige planten; in Jaarb. **21**, Ned Dendrol. Ver., 104−114, 1959 ● Browicz, K.: Species of the genus *Cotoneaster* Ehr. in Poland; in the Kornickie Arboretum **4**, 5−108, 1959 ● Flinck, K. E. & B. Hylmoe: *Cotoneaster Harrysmithii*, a new species from Western China; in Bot. Not. **115**, 29−34, 1962 ● Flinck, K. E., & B. Hylmoe: On two recently described species of *Cotoneaster* of Northwestern Europe; in Bot. Not. **115**, 343−350, 1962 ● Flinck, K. E., & B. Hylmoe: *Cotoneaster sikangensis*, a new species from Western China; in Bot. Not. **115**, 375−384, 1962 ● Flinck, K. E., & B. Hylmoe: *Cotoneaster splendens*, a new species from Western China; in Bot. Not. **117**, 124−132, 1964 ● Flinck, K. E., & B. Hylmoe: A list of series and species in the genus *Cotoneaster*; in Bot. Not. **119**, 445−463, 1966 ● Flinck, K. E., & B. Hylmoe: *Cotoneaster* i svensk odling; in Lustgarden 1966−67, 5−10 ● Hensen, K. J. W., Het geslacht *Cotoneaster*; in Dendroflora **3**, 17−27, 1966 ● Hurusawa, I., S. Kawakame & Y. Ito: Revisio generis *Cotoneaster* quod species in Horto Botanico Koishikawaensi cultas; in Inform. Ann. Hort. Bot. Fac. Sci. Univ. Tokyo 1967, 1−24 ● Klotz, G.: Uebersicht ueber die in culture befindlichen *Cotoneaster* — Arten und formen; in Wiss. Z. Univ. Halle, Math.-Nat. 1957, 945−982 (alphabetical listing) ● Klotz, G.: Neue oder kritische *Cotoneaster*-Arten; (I) ibid. **12**, 753−768, 1963; (II) **12**, 769−786, 1963; (III−IV) **15**, 529−544, 1966; (V) **17**, 333−339, 1968; (VI) **21**, 969−977, 1972; (VII) **21**, 979−1021, 1972 ● Sax, Mrs. H. J.: Polyploidy and apomicts in *Cotoneaster*; in Jour. Arnold Arb. **35**, 334−365, 1954 ● Yue, T. T.: *Cotoneasters* from the Eastern Himalaya; in Bull. Brit, Mus. (Nat. Hist.), Bot. I, 125−141, 1954, with 2 Pl. ● Zeilinga, A. E.: Polyploidy in *Cotoneaster*; in Bot. Not. **117**, 262−278, 1964.

COWANIA D. Don — ROSACEAE

Evergreen shrubs; leaves alternate, leathery tough, lobed or pinnatisect, glandular punctate, margin usually involute, finely tomentose beneath; flowers solitary, terminal on short branches, rose-shaped, with 5 sepals and petals each, stamens numerous; styles 4−12, on 1 species only 1−3, distinct, sessile, densely pubescent; stigma on the fruit elongated to a feathery 'tail'. — 4−5 species in Mexico and SW. USA.

Cowania plicata D. Don. Stiff shrub, about 1.5 m high, branches reddish, glandular and woolly; leaves obovate, 8−15 mm long, pinnatisect, with 5−9 lobes, with stalked glands, white tomentose beneath; flowers rose-like, 3 cm wide, pink-red, June; the feathery fruit 'tail' 3 cm long. NF 5: 56; BM 8889; DRHS 564. New Mexico, SW. USA, usually on alkaline soils. 1830. z8 # ⊕

C. stansburiana Torr. Evergreen, very rigid, aromatic shrub, about 1−2 m high, light colored bark on the branches, cracked or rough barked, young branches reddish-brown, glandular; leaves obovate, 8−15 mm long, with 3−5 lobes, these linear, margins involute, glandular above, white tomentose beneath; flowers white to light yellow, 2 cm wide, July; feathery appendage 2.5−5 cm long. MS 226−227 (= C. *mexicana* A. Gray). Mexico, SW. USA; dry hills. z8 Fig. 292. # ⊕

Only recommended for collectors; ornamental value slight.

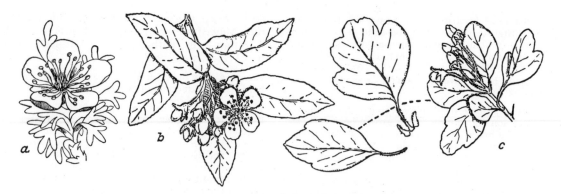

Fig. 292. a. *Cowania stansburiana*; b. *Crataegomespilus dardarii*; c. *C. dardarii* var. '*Asnieresii*'
(from Don and D.B.)

CRATAEGOMESPILUS Simon-Louis — ROSACEAE

Deciduous shrubs; originated as a grafted hybrid between *Crataegus* and *Mespilus*. Differing from *Mespilus* in the smaller flowers, several clustered at the branch tips, the 14—18 stamens and 2—3 seeds, seeds not viable; differing from *Crataegus* in the *Mespilus*-type fruits.

Crataegomespilus + dardarii Simon-Louis (*C. monogyna* + *M. germanica*). Similar to *Mespilus germanica*, but with thorny twigs; leaves narrowly oblong-elliptic, to 15 cm long, dark green, lighter and woolly beneath, dark yellow and red in fall; flowers 1.5 cm wide, grouped 5—8, stamens 15—20, May; fruit a small, to 2 cm wide medlar fruit. BM 1: 761. Originated around 1895 at the graft union of a very old *Mespilus* which was grafted onto *Crataegus monogyna*, in the Dardar Garden, Bronvaux near Metz, France. It is not uncommon to find new shoots reverting back to either of the parents. Fig. 292.

'Asnieresii'. Originating from the same plant but more similar to *Crataegus*, branches pubescent, thorny; leaves broad ovate, finely serrate, with 1—2 lobes on either side; flowers grouped 3—12, only 1 cm wide, stamens 20, styles 1—2; May; fruits globose, 1 cm thick, like that of *Crataegus*, but brownish and somewhat glossy (= 'Jules d'Asnières'). Fig. 292.

'Jouinii'. Originating from the same plant, in appearance like the above, but earlier flowering and totally sterile. This form is scarcely known. See MG 1912: 100.

C. grandiflora and *C. gillottii*, see: × **Crataemespilus**

Lit. Bornmueller: Ueber Rueckschlagsbildungen an *Crataegomespilus*; in Jahrb. DDG 1932, 75—87, with ill.

CRATAEGUS L. — Hawthorn — ROSACEAE

Deciduous shrubs or trees, with or without thorns; leaves alternate, simple, pinnatisect or pinnate, never entire, otherwise crenate, dentate or lobed; flowers in umbellate panicles, seldom solitary; stamens usually about 20, occasionally only 10, rarely (if some are connate) only 5; styles 1—5, distinct or connate; carpels 1—5, with chambers of varying sizes, 2 seeds in each carpel, 1 sessile, fertile, and 1 stalked, infertile, or the latter absent. The seeds (nutlets) become stone hard and embedded within the recaptacle in such a way that a wide or very narrow apical tip remains open. Fruits apple-like, red, yellow, black and bluish. — N. America, Asia, Europe.

The North American botanists have described over 1100 species, nearly all native to the eastern half of the continent; Sargent alone has named over 700! In recent years this number has been considerably reduced with many synonyms being eliminated. There are today between 100—200 actual species recognized in N. America.

The L. Spaeth Nursery, Berlin, has collected 377 species and varieties of *Crataegus* in cultivation from the Arnold Arboretum and The Hague, Holland. (S. G. A. Doorenbos).

Considering the number of species in this genus with little horticultural importance, only the better known and more frequently planted species will be dealt with. A key or outline to the genus will not be included here since the distinguishing characters are so minute. Should the reader seek further detail on *Crataegus*, he will find an abundant supply of literature on the subject.

Crataegus altaica (Loud.) Lge. Small, straggly tree, thorns few, stout, about 2 cm long; leaves ovate, deeply lobed and scabrous serrate, bright green; flowers in loose umbellate panicles, May; fruits 8—10 mm thick, globose, yellow. ICS 2142. Central Asia. 1838. z5 Plate 153.

C. aprica Beadle. Shrub or small tree, to 6 m high, branches outspread and undulate, thorns straight, slender, 2—3.5 cm long; leaves broad ovate to elliptic, acute to rounded, 2—3.5 cm long, base cuneate, usually serrate and often slightly lobed on the apical half, teeth glandular at the tips, tough, pubescent when young, later glabrous; flowers grouped 3—6, 1.8 cm wide, in pubescent, small corymbs, sepals glandular serrate, stamens 10, anthers yellow, May; fruits globose, dull orange-red, 1.2 cm thick, with 3–5 seeds, October. SS 698. SE. USA. 1876. Belongs to the *Flavae* series, but more ornamental than *C. flava*. z6 ⊛

C. arkansana Sarg. Now included with *C. mollis* and not especially characteristic.

C. arnoldiana Sarg. Small tree, 7–10 m high, branches stiff, thorny, shaggy pubescent at first; leaves broad ovate, base rounded or truncated, 4–5 cm long, with 3–5 points on either side, small, scabrous serrate lobes, leaves much larger on long shoots; flowers 2 cm wide, many in loose, pubescent corymbs, stamens 10, anthers light yellow, May; fruits round, light carmine, slightly punctate, shaggy pubescent on both ends, 1.5 cm thick, pulp thick and soft, seeds 3–4. BC 1098; NBB 373. Northeastern USA. z5 ⊕ ⊛

C. azarolus L. Small tree, branches pubescent, often thornless; leaves oval-rhombic, cuneate, 3–7 cm long, deep 3–5 lobed, both sides pubescent at first, eventually glossy green above, gray-green beneath, pubescent; flowers few in tomentose umbellate panicles, May; fruits globose, 2 cm thick, yellow to orange, tastes like an apple. RH 1856: 441. S. Europe, N. Africa, W. Asia. 1640. z6 Plate 152.

var. **sinaica** (Boiss.) Lange. Differing in the mature height, usually not over 2–5 m, branches with exceptionally stout thorns; leaves like the type, but green and glabrous, the inflorescence likewise, leaves occasionally entire, but usually slightly 3 lobed; flowers 5–8, with 1–2 styles, March–May; fruits ellipsoid, 6–7 mm long, 4–5 mm wide, reddish. Nouv. Fl. Liban et Syrie, Pl. 77 (= *C. sinaica* Boiss.). Sinai. 1822. z7?

C. brachyacantha Sarg. & Engelm. Tree, to 15 m, the curved thorns only 8–15 mm long, leaves obovate-oblong to elliptic, acute or occasionally obtuse, cuneate, 2–5 cm long, crenate, seldom somewhat lobed, pubescent above when young, but later becoming glabrous and glossy; flowers many in glabrous corymbs, 8 mm wide, spent flowers turning orange (!) stamens 15–20; fruits nearly globose, dark blue (!) and pruinose, 1 cm thick, with 3–5 seeds, August. SS 177. USA; Texas to Louisiana. 1900. z8?

C. calpodendron (Ehrh.) Med. To 6 m, branches erect, thornless or short thorned; leaves elliptic-oblong, 5–12 cm long, serrate, often slightly lobed, dull green above but eventually glabrous, pubescent beneath; flowers many in 6–12 cm wide umbellate panicles, June; fruits elliptic, yellow-red, 1 cm long, fleshy BC 1101; BB 2002; NBB 375 (= *C. tomentosa* Duroi). Ontario to Central USA. z2 Plate 153; Fig. 293. ⊕

C. carrierei see: **C. × lavellei**

C. celsiana see: **C. × dippeliana**

C. chlorosarca Maxim. Pyramidal growing small tree, young branches thinly pubescent at first, dark red, thorns 10–12 mm long, straight; leaves triangular to broad ovate, short acuminate, 5–9 cm long, with 3–5 pairs of short, wide, unevenly serrate lobes, both sides pubescent at first, eventually glabrous above; flowers 1

cm wide, in 4–7 cm wide umbellate panicles, May; fruits black, pulp green. DL 3: 219. Manchuria. 1870. z5 Plate 153; Fig. 293.

C. chrysocarpa Ashe. To 6 m high, densely branched, thorns slender; leaves elliptic-rounded, 3–5 cm long, rather coarse doubly serrate, with 3–4 short, scabrous lobe pairs; flowers 2 cm wide, sepals and bracts glandular serrate, May; fruits globose, red, pulp yellow, sweet, September. NBB 355 (= *C. rotundifolia* Moench). Northeastern North America, in thickets and rocky areas along river banks. 1906. z5

var. **phoenicea** E. J. Palmer. Young branches and inflorescences quite glabrous; leaves pubescent only on the venation beneath; fruits 1–1.2 cm thick, dark red, glossy. BR 1957 (= *C. rotundifolia* Moench non Lam.; *C. coccinea* var. *rotundifolia* [Moench] Sarg.). E. USA. 1737. Please refer to the notes for *C. coccinea*.

C. coccinea L. This description must be omitted, since the herbarium material collected by Linnaeus actually included 2 species, *C. intricata* and *C. pedicellata*. Furthermore, the nursery trade cultivates many species under the above name, such as *C. mollis*, *C. ellwangeriana*, *C. holmesiana*, *C. chrysocarpa* var. *phoenicea*, etc.

C. coccinoides Ashe. Small tree, thorns straight, 3–5 cm long; leaves red on the new growth, dull gray above, underside brownish at first, truncate at the base, orange-red in fall; flowers 5–7, 2 cm wide, stamens 20, anthers pink, May; fruits nearly globose, dark carmine, glossy, early October. BC 1099; NBB 373. Central USA. In thickets on alkaline soil. 1883. z5 ⊕ ∅ ⊛

C. collina Chapm. Shrub to small tree, occasionally to 8 m high, branches wide spreading with stout thorns, also found on the stem; leaves obovate to elliptic, acute, base broadly cuneate, irregular and often doubly serrate, eventually yellow-green above, lighter and glabrous beneath to the midrib; inflorescence long haired, calyx lobes glandular ciliate, anthers yellow, May; fruits nearly globose, dull red, about 1 cm long, with yellow, mealy pulp and usually 5 seeds, October. SS 654. C. and E. USA. 1889. z4

C. crus-galli L. Cockspur Hawthorn. To 10 m high, growth wide, flat crowned, vase-shaped, thorns slender, to 8 cm long, straight; leaves reversed oval-oblong, cuneate at the base, apex rounded, 2–8 cm long, smooth, leathery, orange-red in fall; flowers to 1.5 cm wide, May–June; fruits dull red, persisting for some time, pulp red. SS 178; BB 1991; NBB 345. Eastern USA. Forest fringes and meadows. z5 Plate 158. ⊕ ∅ ⊛

'Pyracanthifolia'. Growth wide, horizontal branching, with thorns; leaves more spathulate; stamens 8–10, styles 1–2. SS 637. 1879.

'Salicifolia'. Horizontal branching, with only a few thorns, brown; leaves more lanceolate, thinner; stamens 15–20, styles usually 3–4 (= *C. linearis* Ser.).

C. cuneata Sieb. Shrub, to 1.5 m, densely branched, thorns slender, 5–8 mm long; leaves obovate, generally tapering to the petiole, 2–6 cm long, incised and

Fig. 293. Left *Crataegus cuneata*; middle *C. calpodendron*; right *C. chlorosarca*
(from Dippel, G. & F.)

irregularly serrate, often 3 lobed at the apex, glabrous above, loosely pubescent beneath; flowers few in pubescent umbellate panicles, stamens 20, May—June; fruits globose, red. ICS 2139. Japan, China. 1880. z6 Fig. 293.

C. dahurica Koehne. Small tree or shrub, branches dark brown, with 4 cm long thorns; leafing out very early, leaves oval-rhombic to elliptic, 2—5 cm long, acute lobed, deep green, bright red-brown in fall; flowers in glabrous, loose umbellate panicles, late April to early May; fruits globose, 8 mm thick, light brown. SE. Siberia. z5 Plate 153.

C. × dippeliana Lge. (? *C. punctata × tanacetifolia*). Shrub or small tree, resembling *C. tanacetifolia*, but with lobes only going to the middle of the leaf blade, lobes acute, serrate, pubescent on both sides, denser beneath; inflorescences dense, calyx and flower stalks pubescent, stamens about 20, anthers red, June; fruits globose, 1.5 cm thick, yellow, red to dull red. DH 3: 452 (= *C. celsiana* Dipp. non Bosc). Originated in the Lee nursery in Hammersmith, England around 1830. z5

C. douglasii Lindl. To 12 m high, branches often pendulous, thorns stout, 3 cm long, not numerous; leaves broad oval-oblong, 3—8 cm long, serrate and slightly lobed, eventually dark green and glossy above, only the midrib pubescent beneath, otherwise glabrous; flowers 1 cm wide, grouped 10—20 in glabrous umbellate panicles, 20 stamens, May; fruits short elliptic, deep wine-red at first, then black, glossy, ripening in August, abscising quickly, sweet, well liked by birds. MS 222; SS 175; NBB 375. Western N. America, groves and gravelly streams. z5 Fig. 294.

C. dsungarica Zab. Resembles *C. altaica*; but with leaves oval-rhombic to broad ovate, 3—8 cm long, deep lobed, with 2—4 pairs of sparsely dentate lobes, glabrous; inflorescence loose, glabrous; fruits black-brown. SE. Siberia, N. China. z5 1885.

C. × durobrivensis Sarg. Probably *C. pruinosa × suborbiculata*. To 6 m high, leaves ovate to oval in outline, large, base broad cuneate, dark yellowish-green, venation slightly indented above; flowers 2 cm wide, several grouped together, in glabrous corymbs, stamens 20, anthers red, May; fruits rounded, 1.5 cm thick, pulp mealy, seeds 5. USA, New York. z5 1901.

C. ellwangeriana Sarg. Having few thorns when older; leaves oblong-oval, with short, acute lobes, tough and firm, rough above due to short appressed pubescence, underside shaggy pubescent only when young; flowers many, to 2 cm wide, with 10 stamens; fruits oblong, to 1.5 cm thick, bright red, thick and fleshy. BMns 105 (= *C. pedicellata* var. *ellwangeriana* [Sarg.] Eggl.). Eastern USA. z5

C. flabellata (Bosc) K. Koch. Shrub, to 6 m, thorns slightly curved, 4—10 cm long; leaves broad ovate, 3—7 cm long, doubly serrate and very sharply lobed, lightly shaggy above, eventually glabrous and rough, venation beneath shaggy pubescent at first; flowers 1.5—2 cm wide, sepals serrate, stamens 10—20, May; fruits rounded, carmine, 1 cm thick, becoming mealy textured after some time. NBB 361. Eastern N. America, thickets, forests. z5 Plate 153.

C. flava Ait. Small, wide spreading, slow growing shrub, thorns few, to 1.5 cm long; leaves broad rounded, cuneate, slightly lobed, fine crenate, to 2.5 cm long, light green, tough, with large, rounded stipules; flowers 1 cm wide, in few flowered umbellate panicles, June; fruits light green, oblong to pear-shaped, 1 cm thick, pulp thick and dry. BB 2003; NBB 351. Southeastern USA, forests, hills in sandy soil. z6 Fig. 295.

C. fontanesiana (Spach) Steud. Few thorns, to 4 cm long; leaves elliptic-lanceolate, not so tough as those of *C. crus-galli*, leaf petiole somewhat pubescent; flowers with 16—18 stamens, anthers yellow; fruits rounded to elliptic, red or green with red, pulp thin and dry, seeds 2−3. NBB 349. Eastern N. America.

C. × grignonensis Mouillef. (*C. grus-galli* × *C. pubescens*). Medium sized, vase-shaped, nearly thornless shrub; leaves ovate, base cuneate, with 2−4 pairs of short, crenate lobes, short pubescent, persisting for some time, often to January; flowers in small umbellate panicles, May−June; fruits to 1.5 cm long, brown-red, with gray spots. Originated 1873 in Frankfurt, W. Germany. Fig. 296. z5

C. heldreichii Boiss. Very similar tro *C. orientalis*, but smaller, thorns 1 cm long.; leaves 1.5−3 cm long, lobes rounded and entire, dull green above, light green beneath; flowers small, in erect umbellate panicles, June; fruits pea-size, red. Greece. z6?

C. henryi Dunn. Shrub or also a tree, 5−7 m high, completely thornless (!); stipules semi-cordate, 12 mm long, serrate, leaves oval-lanceolate to narrow-elliptic, on flowering branches unlobed and finely serrate, on vegetative shoots occasionally 3 lobed, coarse and doubly serrate, with appressed short pubescence above when young, later dark green and glossy, usually only the distinct venation pubescent beneath, 3−7 cm long, 1.5−3 cm wide on the flowering branches, otherwise 2 cm longer; flowers cream-white, in small umbellate panicles, stalk glabrous; fruits globose, 1.2 cm thick, dull red, with 5 seeds. China, Yunnan. 1909. (Kew) z7?

C. heterophylla Fluegge. Shrub or small, round crowned, very dense tree, to 5 m, thornless or with only a few thorns, young branches completely glabrous; leaves in 2 forms (hence the name!), diamond-shaped with entire base on the vegetative shoots, apical half sharply acuminate, deeply lobed (like that of *C. monogyna*), the lobes sharp and irregularly serrate, 3−7 cm long, 3−6 cm wide, petiole 12−18 mm long, much smaller on flowering branches, oblong, obovate or elliptic, occasionally entire or with some teeth at the

Fig. 295. *Crataegus flava* (from Bot. Reg.)

apex, the uppermost leaves occasionally distinctly 3 lobed at the apex, 2.5−3 cm long, 8−18 wide, all glossy green and glabrous, with coarsely serrate stipules only on the vegetative shoots; flowers white, 1.8 cm wide, in 5−7cm wide corymbs, stamens 15−20, style 1, May−June; fruits slender elliptic, 12−15 mm long, bright red. BR 1161. Armenia. 1816. z6

C. holmesiana Ashe. Tree-like shrub, occasionally to 10 m high, crown not dense, conical, branches ascending, with thin thorns; leaves ovate-oblong, with 4−6 lobes on either side, sharply serrate to the base, thin, but firm, yellow-green above, glabrous beneath; flowers many in glabrous corymbs, anthers red, stamens 10; fruits light red, oblong, about 1 cm thick, seeds 3, pulp usually dry or mealy. NBB 367; SS 676. Eastern N. America, in thickets and forest fringes, usually on moist soils. z5 Plate 153.

C. intricata Lge. Shrub, 1−3 m, branches with 2−4 cm long, curved thorns; leaves oval-elliptic, short and acutely lobed, doubly serrate, bright green above, glabrous; inflorescence somewhat pubescent, calyx lobes glandular serrate, anthers yellow; fruits globose to oval, dull red-brown, October−November. NBB 355. Northeastern USA. z5 Plate 152.

C. jackii Sarg. Small, tree-like shrub, to about 3 m high; leaves oval elliptic to broad ovate, scabrous serrate, with shallow, indistinct lobes, base truncate to broad cuneate, 2.5−3 cm long; flowers grouped 5−10, anthers yellow; fruits dull red, juicy, broad ellipsoid to slightly ovate, about 12 mm long, with 2−3 seeds. Canada; S. Quebec. z4

C. jonesiae Sarg. Tall shrub or small tree, to 6 m high, young branches pubescent, later glossy orange-brown, with 5−7 cm long thorns; leaves broad elliptic to obo-

Fig. 294. *Crataegus douglasii* (from Sudworth)

vate, to 10 cm long, base cuneate, scabrous serrate above the middle and with acute lobes, glossy dark green above, pubescent beneath at least when young; flowers to 2.5 cm wide (!), anthers 10, pink; fruits bright red, juicy, 15 mm thick, with 2–3 seeds. NE. N. America. 1901? z5

C. korolkowii see: **C. pinnatifida** and **C. wattiana**

C. laciniata Urcia see: **C. orientalis** Bieb.

C. laevigata (Poir.) DC. Shrub or small tree, 2–5 m, thorns 2.5 cm long, branches becoming glabrous; leaves obovate, 3(5) lobed, obtusely serrate, base usu- ally cuneate, light green beneath, stipules acuminate, unevenly serrate; inflorescence glabrous, flowers in umbellate panicles, white to pink, 15–18 mm wide, May–June; fruits ovate-globose, 2(1–3) seeds (= *C. oxtcantha* L. emend. Jacq.; *C. oxycanthoides* Thuill.). Europe, N. Africa. Cultivated for ages, but in hedges and gardens often confused with *C. monogyna* and *C. × media*. ⓕ India. z6

Including 2 ssp:

ssp. **laevigata**. Leaves 15–35 mm long, vein axils without hair fascicles beneath; sepals appressed to the fruit, about as long as wide; fruits 8–10 mm long (= *C. oxycantha* L. ssp. *oxycantha*). In mountains and plains.

ssp. **palmstruchii** (Lindm.) Franco. Leaves 3–5 cm long, un- dersides with hair fascicles in the vein axils beneath; sepals erect to horizontally arranged, nearly twice as long as wide; fruit 10 to 12 mm long (= *C. palmstruchii* Lindm.). Mountains and plains.

Exact range of both ssp. not yet known.

In addition there are many cultivars for which it has not yet been decided whether they belong to *C. laevigata* or *C. mo- nogyna*; here the former has been retained.

'Aurea'. Fruits yellow (= *C.oxycantha aurea* Hort.).

'Auriculata'. Leaves rather large, 3–5 cm long, ovate, stipules stalked, large, uneven-sided half moon shape, outer margin unevenly deep crenate; fruits deep red, normally with 2 seeds.

'Candidoplena'. Flowers double, remaining pure white until faded. Known since 1894, but first disseminated by L. Spaeth, Berlin, 1911. The best of the double white forms. ✪

'François Rigaud'. Branches with yellow bark; fruits yellow.

'Gireoudii' (Spaeth). Spring growth normal, dark green, later growth with small, pink and white marbled leaves. Found around 1890, introduced to the trade in 1899 by Spaeth. ∅

'Masekii' (Masek). Flowers a pretty soft pink, on a white base, somewhat lighter on old blooms. Introduced to the trade in 1899 by Spaeth, Berlin.

'Mutabilis'. Flowers double, opening soft pink, but quickly turning a dirty white. Presumably found in the wild in Eng- land around 1800.

'Paul's Scarlet' (Paul). The "true Red Hawthorne"; flowers bright crimson. FS 1509 (= *C. monogyna paulii* Hort.). Originated as a sport on 'Rubra Plena' by Ch. Boyd, near Waltham Cross, in England; brought into the trade by Wil-

Fig. 296. *Crataegus grignonensis* (from Nose)

liam Paul, Waltham Cross, 1866. Constantly reverting back to the parent tree and therefore when planted with 'Rubra Plena', the flowers will never be solid colored. ✪

'Plena'. Flowers double, white, fading to pale pink. FS 1509. Cultivated since 1770. Well known and widely planted cultivar.

'Punicea'. Flowers simple, 2 cm wide, crimson red, white in the center. FS 1509 (all flowers with 1 style). ✪

'Rosea'. Flowers simple, light pink, white in the center. Cultivated before 1796. Rare.

'Rubra Plena'. Flowers double, carmine-pink. FS 1509. 'Paul's Scarlet' originated from this cultivar by a mutation. ✪

C. × lavallei Herincq ex Lav. (*C. stipulacea× C. crus- galli*). Originated around 1870 in the Segrez Ar- boretum, France, and depicted in 1880 by Herincq in Lavallee, in the Segrez Arb. Icon, 21, Plate 7. Whether or not this plant is as yet propagated and disseminated is unknown. In 1883 Vauvel announced in the Revue Horticole, Paris, a new species, originated from seed of *C. mexicana* (= *C. stipulaceae*) around 1870 in the Jardin des Plantes, Paris and given the name *C. carrieri*. Later the two species proved to be so similar that they could not be considered botanically separate. *C. × lavallei* had yellow anthers, *C. carrierei* on the other hand was pink toned. Since the former is not found in cultivation, the name of the latter is retained as a clone. z5 ∅ ⚥

'Carrierei'. To 7 m high, thorns to 5 cm long; leaves elliptic- oblong, acute, base cuneate, 5–10 cm long, unevenly serrate, thinly pubescent beneath; flowers 2 cm wide, anthers 5–10 pink; fruits elliptic, 16–18 mm thick, orange-red, persisting for some time. DB 1952: 39; RH 1883: 108 (= *C. carrierei* Vauvel). ∅ ⚥

C. macrancantha Lodd. see: **C. succulenta** var. **macracantha**

C. maximowoczii Schneid. Closely related to *C. san-guinea*, but with leaves more deeply lobed, shaggy pubescent beneath, likewise the inflorescence. SH 1: 437 a to b, 438 a–c; ICS 2141 (= *C. sanguinea* var. *villosa* Maxim.). NE. Asia. 1904. z5?

C. × media Bechst.(*C. monogyna* ssp. *nordica* × *C. laevigata* ssp. *laevigata*). Frequently found in the same areas as the parents (also in hedges); leaves similar to *C. laevigata*, but the 3 lobes acute or acuminate, more sawtooth-crenate; inflorescence and flowers glabrous, styles 1–2, occasionally also Y-shaped connate; sepals somewhat longer than wide, more or less appressed to the fruits, hypanthium rough haired; fruits nearly globose, with 1–2 seeds. z5

C. mollis (Torr. & Gray) Scheele. To 10 m high, crown wide, thorns short, straight; leaves wide ovate, 6–10 cm long, sharply doubly serrate, with 4–5 pairs of short, sharp lobes, at first densely pubescent beneath, eventually only on the venation; flowers to 2.5 cm wide, inflorescences finely tomentose, with 20 stamens, April–May; fruits pear-shaped, scarlet-red, usually pubescent on both ends, pulp mealy, abscising early. SS 659; BB 2001; NBB 371. Ohio to Kansas, light forests, especially on fertile soils. 1853. z5 Plate 153. ⊕ Ø ⚭

C. monogyna Jacq. Tall shrub or occasionally tree-like, 2–5(10) m high, with 2–2.5 cm long thorns, branches glabrous or pubescent; leaves broad-ovate to diamond-shaped, 3–7 lobed, deeply incised (!) ¾ of the way to the midrib, often whitish-green beneath and usually pubescent, lobes round and obtuse or acute, stipules entire (!), leaf petiole often pubescent; flowers in um-bellate panicles, white, 8–15 mm wide, sepals oblong (!), May–June; fruits ovate–globose or more ellipsoid, with 1 seed. Quite variable. ⊕ Austria, Denmark, (windbreaks). z5

Growing among the parent plants, the following subspecies:

ssp. **azarella** (Griseb.) Franco. Branches and young leaves densely downy pubescent; leaves deeply 3–5–7 lobed, to 3 cm long, light green beneath, petiole 4–13 mm long, hypanthium rough hairy; fruits brownish-red, nearly glo-bose. Spain to the Balkans and Russia; Continental Mediterranean.

ssp. **brevispina** (G. Kunze). Franco. Leaves 3–5 lobed, leath-ery, to 3 cm long, bluish-green beneath, not pubescent, petiole 3–15 mm long, hypanthium usually glabrous (very seldom rough hairy); fruits bright red, globose. Iberian Peninsula to Sardinia; Western Mediterranean region.

ssp. **monogyna**. Leaves deeply 3 lobed, to 3.5 cm long, light green beneath, not pubescent, petiole 0.5 to 1.5 cm long, hypanthium glabrous or with solitary scattered hairs; fruits dark red, globose to cup-shaped. From France to the Car-pathians and W. Yugoslavia; hedges and underbrush.

ssp. **nordica** Franco. Leaves 3–5–7 lobed, to 5 cm long, grayish beneath, not pubescent, petiole 2–2.5 cm long, hypanthium rough haired; fruit dark red, nearly globose. N. and C. Europe, subatlantic (northern) flatlands; extension of range into the mountains not adequately known.

Included here are numerous cultivars which are often incor-rectly labeled in the garden and actually belong to *C. laevigata*. The *monogyna* types always have only 1 pistil and therefore only 1 stone in the fruit.

'Aurea'. Fruit yellow. ⚭

'Bicolor (Gumpper). Flowers simple, white, margin wide pink-red. FS 1651 (= *C. monogyna gumperi* Voss). Brought into the trade around 1860 by P. J. Gumpper of Stuttgart, W. Germany.

'Biflora'. Flowers around Christmas time, depending upon the weather, and again in May; leaves also open early, gray tomentose beneath; fruits darker than those of the type (= *C. monogyna praecox* Bean). Found in England before 1770 and known as the 'Glastonbury Thorn'. z7 ⊕

'Compacta' (Spaeth). Growth wide and compact, branches short, thick, thornless; flowers not numerous (= *C. monogyna inermis compacta* Spaeth; *C. monogyna compacta* Spaeth). Brought into the trade in 1907 by Spaeth, Berlin. Differing from 'Inermis'.

var. **eriocarpa** Dipp. Fruits dark red, woolly pubescent when young. Found around Breslau, (now Wroclaw), Poland.

'Ferox'. Branches usually sprawling outward, with numer-ous and stout thorns arranged in fascicles; flowers smaller than those of the species. FS 1468 (= 'Horrida'). Known since 1859 in France.

'Fissa'. Limbs and branches outspread, nodding on older plants; leaves to 7 cm long and wide, most incised to the midrib with wide sinuses between the doubly serrate lobes. Ø

'Flexuosa'. Branches bent and often twisting spirally (= *C. monogyna tortuosa* Hort.). Known before 1838 in England.

'Granatensis'. Branches pendulous, with only a few thorns. From Spain.

'Inermis'. Growth dense and compact, branches diagonally ascending; leaves, flowers and fruit lke the type. American Nurseryman: 11/1/1959 (cover). Before 1900.

'Kermesina Plena' = **C. laevigata** 'Paul's Scarlet'.

'Lutescens'. Leaves yellow-green.

f. **microphylla** Chenev. Leaves very small. Found in Switzer-land, along the Tessin River and in Wallis.

'Pendula'. Limbs and branches pendulous. Including 'Reginae', from a garden near Edinburgh, Scotland, where, allegedly, Queen Mary often sat.

'Pteridifolia'. Leaves wide fan-shaped and incised, the lobes with densely crispate margins. FS 2076 (= *C. monogyna filicifolia* Hort.). Known before 1838 in England. Ø

'Rosea'. Flowers simple, pink. Often erroneously labelled in gardens.

'Semperflorens'. Dense and bushy, very slow growing, branches thin; leaves 1.5–2.5 cm long; flowering several times between May and August (= *C. monogyna bruanti* Hort.). Originated by Bruant, Poitiers, France, before 1894.

'Stricta'. Growth columnar and densely upright, several me-ters high (= *C. monogyna fastigiata* and *pyramidalis* Hort.).

'Variegata'. Leaves white variegated.

C. × mordenensis Boom (*C. laevigata* female × *C. suc-culenta* male). Differing from *C. laevigata* in the larger leaves and flowers, from *C. succulenta* by the shorter thorns, more deeply incised, smoother leaves, the glabrous inflorescences and sepals without glands.

Only the following clones are known:

'Toba' (Morden Farm Exp.) (*C. laevigata* 'Paul's Scarlet × *C. succulenta*). Large shrub or also a tree, thorns about 1.5 cm long, thicker than those of *C. laevigata*; leaves 5−7 cm long, petiole 2 cm long, with 3 finely serrate lobes on either side, glossy green above, lighter beneath; flowers 2 cm wide, in about 5 cm wide corymbs, with 25−30 petals, white at first, later becoming pink, styles 2−3, often connate; fruits red. Developed at the Morden Experiment Farm, Manitoba, Canada, 1935. ⊕

'Snowbird'. A seedling from 'Toba'; small tree or tall shrub, upright; leaves deep green, glossy, partly lobed, partly almost entire; flowers white, double; fruits globose, carmine, 1 cm thick, but with few fruits. Disseminated by F. Fopma, Boskoop.

C. nigra Waldst. & Kit. Hungarian Hawthorn. To 7 m high, branches tomentose at first, thornless or with few short thorns; leaves triangular or ovate, 4−9 cm long, with 7−11 scabrous serrate lobes, dull green above, light green beneath and densely pubescent; flowers 2 cm wide, in dense, wide umbellate panicles, fading to purple-pink, May−June; fruits pea-size, black, glossy, soft. SE. Europe. 1808. z6 Plate 153.

C. nitida (Engelm.) Sarg. To 7 m, often nearly totally thornless, crown rounded; leaves elliptic-oblong, 2−8 cm long, coarsely serrate to slightly lobed, orange and red in fall; fruits ovate, dull brick-red, pruinose. SS 703; NBB 349 (possibly *C. viridis* × *C. crus-galli*). Ohio to Missouri and Arkansas. 1883. z5 ⌀ ⌀

C. orientalis Pall. Tree, to 7 m, growth straggly, short branches developing into thorns, tomentose; leaves to 5 cm long, deeply lobed, dark gray-green above, pubescent, gray tomentose beneath; flowers 1.5 cm wide, to 10 flowers in dense, white tomentose umbellate panicles, June; fruits globose, 1.5 cm thick, orange-red, pubescent. BM 2314; HF 2527. SE. Europe, W. Asia. 1810. z6 Plate 154. ⌀ ⌀

var. **sanguinea** (Schrad.) Loud. Leaves less pubescent; fruits smaller, deep red. SE. Europe. 1810. ⌀

C. oxycantha see: **C. laevigata**

C. oxycanthoides see: **C. laevigata**

C. palmstruchii see: **C. laevigata**

C. pedicellata Sarg. To 7 m, thinly branched, thorns straight to slightly bowed, 3−5 mm long; leaves broadly ovate, broad cuneate or truncate, 5−10 cm long, coarsely and often doubly serrate, with 4−5 short lobe pairs on the apical blade half, dark green above, rough, eventually glabrous beneath; inflorescence shaggy, flowers 1.5−2 cm wide, anthers pink, May; fruits pear-shaped, glossy scarlet, pulp mealy, September. NBB 367 (= *C. coccinea* L. pp.; *C. robesoniana* Sarg.). Eastern USA. z5 Plate 152. See also: *C. ellwangeriana*. ⌀

C. persistens Sarg. Tall shrub, or small tree, 3−4 m,

branches wide spreading, with many thick, to 5 cm long thorns; leaves lanceolate to oblong-obovate, long acuminate, base cuneate, coarsely serrate on the apical half, eventually glabrous above, dark green and glossy and persisting green deep into the winter; flowers about 2 cm wide, with 20 white anthers, May; fruits ovate, carmine-red, not glossy, nearly 1.5 cm thick, pulp thick, mealy, 2−3 seeds. ST 190. Originated in the Arnold Arboretum, perhaps a *C. crus-galli* hybrid, exact parentage unknown. Greatly valued for its semi-deciduous foliage and equally persistent fruits. z5

C. pentagyna Waldst. & Kit. To 5 m high, young branches pubescent, with few, 1 cm long thorns; leaves rhombic-broad ovate, 2−6 cm long, with 3−7 unevenly serrate lobes, deep green, lighter and short pubescent beneath, long petioled, gold-yellow in fall; flowers 1.5 cm wide, in loose, 4−7 cm wide, gray shaggy umbellate panicles, June; fruits oblong, deep purple-red. RH 1901: 310. SE. Europe. Caucasus, Persia. 1822. z6 Plate 153.

C. phaenopyrum (L.f.) Med. To 10 m high; thorns to 7 cm long; leaves nearly triangular, 3−7 cm long, sharply serrate, 3−5 lobed, light green above, glossy, paler beneath; flowers, many in umbellate panicles, 1.2 cm wide, anthers pink, May−June; fruits flattened globose, 8 mm thick, scarlet, glossy. SS 186; BB 1994; NBB 345; HH 296 (= *C. populifolia* Walt.). Virginia to Alabama. 1738. z5 Plate 153. ⊕ ⌀ ⌀

'Fastigiata'. Like the species, but growth more columnar. ⊕ ⌀ ⌀

C. pinnatifida Bge. Tree, to 6 m, branches glabrous, thorns not numerous, to 1 cm long; leaves angular ovate, 5−10 cm long, 5−9 feathery lobes, dark green above, lighter beneath, glossy on both sides, yellow in fall, quickly abscising; flowers 1.5 cm wide, few in loose umbellate panicles, May; fruits globose to short oval, bright red, finely punctate, on 2 cm long, thin stalks. BC 1104; LF 164; ICS 2137. NE. Asia. 1860. Ⓕ China, forestation of sandy soil. z6 Fig. 297. ⌀ ⌀

Fig. 297. *Crataegus pinnatifida* (from Dippel)

var. **major** N. E. Br. Leaves larger, less deeply lobed, tougher; fruits larger, to 2.5 cm thick, glossy deep red (= *C. korolkowii* Schneid.). N. China. 1880. Grown on a large scale in N. China for edible fruit. ∅ ⊗ ✕

C. populifolia see: **C. phaenopyrum**

C. pruinosa (Wendl.) K. Koch. To 6 m, stout thorned; leaves oval-elliptic, 3−5 cm long, irregularly and often doubly serrate, new growth red, later blue-green, glabrous; flowers 22.5 cm wide, stamens 20, anthers reddish, May; fruits globose, 1 cm thick, blue-green until nearly fully ripe, eventually dark red, pulp yellow, sweet, October. SS 648; NBB 365. Northeastern N. America. 1823. z5 ⊕ ∅ ⊗

C. × **prunifolia** (Poir.) Pers. (? *C. crus-galli* × *C. macracantha*). Shrub or small tree, thorns to 4 cm long, slightly bowed; leaves broad elliptic, to 8 cm long, scabrous serrate, glossy dark green, lighter beneath, yellow and red in fall; flowers in dense, pubescent, many flowered umbellate panicles, May−June; fruits globose, to 1.5 cm thick, abscising early, scarlet-red (= *C. crus-galli* var. *splendens* Ait. f.). Origin unknown. Cultivated in Germany since 1783. Ⓕ Germany (Holstein). z5 Plate 153.

C. pubescens Steud. f. **stipulacea** (Loud). Stapf. Shrubby in European culture, few thorns; leaves elliptic-cuneate to oblong-lanceolate, 4−8 cm long, crenate, dark green above, tomentose beneath; flowers 6−12, to 2 cm wide, March; fruits dull orange-red, thick, juicy, edible. BM 8589 (= *C. stipulacea* Loud.; *C. mexicana* DC.). Mexico. 1824. The species, *C. pubescens* Steud. is not in cultivation, according to Rehder.

C. punctata Jacq. Tree-like, branches stiff and horizontally spreading, short thorned to thornless; leaves obovate, 5−10 cm long, irregularly serrate, shaggy pubescent beneath; flowers numerous, 1.5−2 cm wide, stamens 20, anthers pink, styles 2−5; fruits round, cherry size, yellow-red, light spotted, mealy, abscising early. SS 184; BB 1993; NBB 349. Eastern N. America. 1746. ⊗

'**Aurea**'. Fruits yellow, anthers also usually yellow. Found in the northern range of the species. 1789. Best yellow fruiting variety. ⊗

C. robesoniana see: **C. pedicallata**

C. rotundifolia see: **C. chrysocarpa**

C. saligna Greene. To 6 m high, branches ornamentally nodding, bright brown-red, thorns 2−3 cm long; leaves narrow, elliptic, to 7 cm long, crenate, light green, orange and brown in fall; flowers small, June; fruits pea-size, wine-red at first, eventually blue-black, glossy. SS 636. Colorado. z4

C. sanguinea Pall. To 7 m high, branches glossy purple-brown, thorns not numerous, stout, 3 cm long; leaves oval-rhombic to broad ovate, 5−8 cm long, with 2−3 pairs of short, scabrous to doubly serrate lobes, tough, dark green above, light gray-green beneath, pubescent; flowers in small umbellate panicles, May; fruits over 1 cm thick, bright red, ripening in August and translucent. E. Siberia. 1822. z4 ⊗

C. sinica see: **C. azarolus**

C. sorbifolia Lge. (*C. laevigata* × ?). Medium sized shrub, thorns 1 cm long; leaves oval-elliptic with short, obtuse, crenate lobes, to 8 cm long, glossy dark green above, light green beneath and short pubesent, persisting well into fall; flowers to 12 in umbellate panicles, May−June; fruits oblong, scarlet-red. Origin unknown. z5

C. spathulata Michx. Shrub or tree, to 8 m, thorns to 3 cm long or totally absent; leaves oval-rhombic, apex often 3−5 lobed, 1−4 cm long, crenate; flowers many in glabrous umbellate panicles, May—June; fruits scarlet-red, globose. 4−5 mm thick, October. BB 1992; NBB 345. Virginia to Texas. z7 Plate 152.

C. stppulaceae see: **C. pubescens**

C. submollis Sarg. Large shrub or tree, 8−10 m high, branches thorny, with long pubescence at first; leaves ovate to oval, 4−8 cm long, base abruptly truncated or also round to cordate on long shoots, with 4−5 coarsely serrate, shallow lobes on either side, densely pubescent above, tomentose beneath, eventually glabrous above, underside remaining somewhat pubescent, thin, but tough, deep green above; flowers about 2 cm wide, many in loose, tomentose corymbs, stamens 10, anthers white to yellow, calyx tomentose, sepals with red stalked glands; fruits obovoid to pear-shaped, 1 cm thick, light red, remaining lightly pubescent, pulp dry, seeds 5. NBB 371; GC 134: 73. Northeast N. America. Forested hills, moist and fertile soil. 1850. z5

C. succulenta Link. To 5m, straggly, branches red-brown with numerous, stout 7 cm long thorns; leaves cuneate-broad oval, 5 to 8 cm long, coarsely and doubly serrate, glossy above, eventually glabrous beneath; flowers many, in pubescent umbellate panicles, stamens 20, anthers pink, seldom white, May; fruits globose, 1 cm thick, glossy scarlet. NBB 375. Eastern N. America. z4 ⊗

var. **macracantha** (Lodd.) Eggl. Not easily distinguished from the species; thorns more numerous, 7−8 cm long; stamens about 10, anthers white or light yellow, rarely pink; fruits scarcely 1 cm thick, becoming soft very late (= *C. macracantha* Lodd.). Eastern N. America. 1819. ⊗

C. tanacetifolia (Lam.) Pers. Shrub or small tree, branches upright, tomentose at first; leaves oval-rhombic, 2.5 cm long, pinnately cleft, with 5−7 narrow, glandular serrate lobes, both sides shaggy pubescent, stipules very large, bowed; flowers 2−2.5 cm wide, 4−8 in tomentose umbellate panicles, May−June; fruits orange-yellow, 2−2.5 cm thick. BR 1884. W. Asia. 1789. z6 Plate 153. ∅ ⊗

C. tomentosa L. It appears impossible to verify this species, therefore Palmer (in Jour. Arnold Arb. **19**, 287−289, 1938) has omitted this name and substituted *C. calpodendron* in its place.

C. triflora Chapm. Shrub, to 7m; leaves oval-elliptic, 2−7 cm long, serrate, short lobed, pubescent; flowers usually in 3's, pubescent, 2−3 cm wide, stamens 20, anthers yellow; fruits globose, 1−1.5 cm thick, pubescent, red, September−October. Alabama. z7

C. uniflora Muenchh. Straggly shrub, to 3m, thorns thin, to 4 cm long; leaves cuneate-obovate, 4 cm long, finely crenate, pubescent above at first, eventually glabrous on both sides; flowers usually solitary or in 3's, nearly sessile, 1.5 cm wide, May−June; fruits globose, yellowish-green. SS 191; BB 2004; NBB 345. Eastern USA. z5 Fig. 298.

C. viridis L. To 12 m, branches spreading, thorns thin; leaves obovate-oblong, 2−6 cm long, serrate; fruits nearly globose, bright red to orange, persisting well into the winter. BB 1996; NBB 349; HKH 290. Eastern USA. 1853. z5 ⊕ ⚭

C. wattiana Hemsl. & Lace. Small tree, resembling *C. sanguinea*; young branches red-brown, thornless or with short thorns; leaves ovate, acute, 5−9 cm long, glabrous, petiole thin, with 3−5 lobes on either side; stamens 15−20, anthers whitish; fruits rounded, 1 cm thick, orange-yellow, fleshy, August. Bm 8818; RH 1901: 308 (= *C. korolkowii* L. Henry). Altai Mountains to Beluchistan (Central Asia). 1888. z5 ⚭

C. wilsonii Sarg. To 6 m high; similar to *C. calpodendron*; leaves ovate to obovate, eventually glossy above, sparsely shaggy pubescent beneath; fruits elliptic, 1 cm long, red. ICS 2140. Central China. z6

The Hawthorns are easily cultivated preferring a fertile, not too light, clay or alkaline soil in sunny locations. The flowers and fruits are especially abundant in dry soils, but the foliage will abscise early in the fall which detracts from the many species having good fall color.

Very few nurseries carry a large number of species but most will have a few of the more popular species and varieties.

Lit. Palmer, E. J.: The *Crataegus* problem; Journ. Arnold Arboretum **13**, 342−362, 1932 ● Britton, N. L., & A. Brown: An illustrated Flora of the Northern United States, Canada, and the British possessions; Ed. 2, 3 vols., ill. 1913 (*Cratae-*

Fig. 298. *Crataegus uniflora* (from Watson)

gus in vol. 2, 294−321, Revised by W. W. Eggleston) ● Coker, W. C., & H. R. Totten: Trees of the Southeastern States; Ed. 3, 1937 (*Crataegus* pp. 210−242, ill.) ● Deam, C. C.: Flora of Indiana; 1940 (*Crataegus* pp. 535−555, Revised by E. J. palmer) ● Gleason, H. A.: New Britton and Brown Illustr. Flora of the Northeastern States of America and Canada; 3 vols. ill. 1952 (*Crataegus* in vol. 2, 338−375, revised by E. J. Palmer) ● Laughlin, K.: Manual of the hawthorns of Cook and Du Page Counties of Illinois; ill. 1956; including supplements in 1958 and 1959 ● Palmer, E. J.: Synopsis of the North American Crataegi; Journ. Arnold Arboretum **6**, 5−128, 1925 ● Little, L. E.: Check List of the Trees of the United States; ed. **2**, *Crataegus* pp. 124−168, 1953 ● Penzes, A.: Galagonya-Tanulmanyok (*Crataegus* Studies); Ann, Acad. Hort. Viticult. Budapest **18**, 107−137, ill., 1956 ● Sargent, C. S.: Manual of the trees of North America (exclusive of Mexico); Ed. **2**, reprinted 1933; *Crataegus* pp. 397−549, 1913.

× CRATAEMESPILUS G. Camus — ROSACEAE

Hyrids between the genera *Crataegus* and *Mespilus*, originated through normal fruiting, not by grafting, vegetative means or Chimeras. Both hybrids to date appear somewhere between the parents. They must, however, by the rules of nomenclature, be considered a separate genus.

× **Crataemespilus gillotii** Beck & Reinchenb. (*Crataegus monogyna* × *Mespilus germanica*). Very similar to *C. grandiflora*, but with leaves lobed, not serrate; flowers smaller, with 2 styles. Originated around 1890 in France. z6

× **C. grandiflora** G. Camus (*Crataegus laevigata* × *Mespilus germanica*). Tall shrub or also a small tree, crown foliage dense, branches pubescent; leaves ovate to obovate, 3−7 cm long, unevenly serrate, lightly lobed in the upper 1/3, pubescent beneath, an attractive brown and yellow in fall; flowers 2−3 together, abundantly flowering, white, to 2.5 cm wide, May−June; fruits like small *Mespilus* fruits, to 1.5 cm wide, brown, pubescent, edible, taste like medlars. BM 3442 (as *Mespilus lobata*) (= *Mespilus grandiflora* Smith; *Crataegus grandiflora* K. Koch). Found in the wild in France around 1800. Pretty tree. Plate 152. z6

Lit. see: *Crataegomespilus*.

CRINODENDRON Molina — ELAEOCARPACEAE

Evergreen trees; leaves alternate or opposite, simple, short stalked, serrate, tough; flowers usually solitary, seldom 2 in a leaf axil, cup- or urn-shaped, white or red, pendulous on long flower stalks, petals 5, somewhat fleshy, usually with 3 teeth at the apex; stamens 15—20; fruit a leathery capsule. — 2 species in Chile, 1 in Argentina.

Crinodendron hookerianum Gay. 3—9 m high in its habitat, usually multistemmed; leaves narrow elliptic, 5—10 cm long, leathery, serrate, deep green above, venation pubescent beneath; flowers urn-shaped, carmine-red, about 2 cm long, flower stalk also carmine-red, 5 cm long, May. BM 7160; BS 1: 791; PFC 82 (= *C. lanceolatum* Miq.; *Tricuspidaria lanceolata* Miq.). Chile. 1848. Wonderful plant in bloom, covered with red lantern-shaped flowers. z8 Plate 125, 154. # ✧

'Album'. Flowers white, otherwise like the type.

C. patagua Molina. Large, evergreen shrub in the conservatory, a tall tree in its habitat; leaves elliptic to narrow obovate, 3—7 cm long, tough, serrate, glabrous; flowers cup-shaped, white, petals not drawn together at the tips, flowering in fall or winter. BM 8115 (= *C. dependens* [Ruiz & Pav.] Ktze.; *Tricuspidaria dependens* Ruiz & Pav.). Chile. Not as beautiful as the former species, and blooms less abundantly. 1901. z7 # ✧

Gorgeous shrubs for areas with scarce or only slight frost. Prefers a humus, fertile, moist soil.

CROTON

Croton japonicum see: **Mallotus japonicus**

CUDRANIA Trécul — MORACEAE

Deciduous or evergreen trees or shrubs; branches thorny; leaves alternate, with a straight thorn in each leaf axil; flowers insignificant, in small, globose heads; fruits grouped into a globose aggregate. — 4 species in E. Asia, Australia, New Caledonia.

Cudrania tricuspidata (Carr.) Bureau. Deciduous tree, to 8 m high, branches lightly striped, olive-brownish, buds red-brown; leaves often somewhat 3 lobed at the apex, base broad rounded, 5—8 cm long, deep green; flowers in globose, green, 8 mm wide heads, without bracts, but the individual flowers with very small, fleshy bracts, adnate to an orange-yellow, glossy, hard fruit about 2.5 cm thick. RH 1872: 56; BS 1: 795; HI 1792; ICS 199 (= *Vaniera tricuspidata* Hu). Central China. 1862. z6—7 Plate 154. ⚭

Cultivation of this species like that of *Morus*.

CUNONIA L. — CUNONIACEAE

Evergreen tree; leaves opposite, odd pinnate or trifoliate, thick and leathery, petiolate, hidden between the elliptic stipules when in bud, stipules later abscising; flowers in compound, spike-form, axillary racemes, the individual flowers very small, with 5 petals and 10 stamens flattened at the base, fruit a leather beaked capsule. — 1 species in S. Africa, 14 species in New Caledonia.

Cunonia capensis L. A large shrub or tree in its native habitat, to 15 m; leaves pinnate, leaflets 5—7, lanceolate, 5—10 cm long, scabrous serrate; flowers white, in opposite, spike-form racemes, August. PBl: 782; BM 8504. S. Africa, Cape Province and Natal, in moist areas. 1816. z9 Plate 154. # ✧

For light humus soil in frost free regions.

CYATHEA Sm. — Tree Fern — CYATHEACEAE

Tree fern with erect, thick stem, scaly at the apex; leaves large, doubly or very distinctly pinnate, usually thin, leather-like, venation open; sori (fruiting bodies) on the dorsal venation or in the vein axils; indusium primarily covering the sori, complete and globose (on *C. arborea* and *dealbata*) or stunted and composed only of a basal scale (*C. capensis*) or also completely lacking (*C. australis*). — Over 600 species in the Tropics and subtropics, encompassing the earlier genera *Alsophila* and *Hemitelia*.

Only a few species will be covered, those found in the gardens of mild areas in the British Isles and Ireland or in the Mediterranean region. In the northern temperate regions only suitable as a greenhouse plant or occasionally seen outside in summer.

Cyathea arborea (L.) Sm. Stem becoming tall; leaves pendulous, doubly pinnate, rather tough, leaf petioles thornless, brown to black, likewise the rachis, pinnae 12—20 cm long, sessile, oblong-lanceolate, leaflets deeply incised and scabrous serrate, oblong and somewhat sickle-shaped; sori on the basal half of the leaflet lobes; indusium hard, in the form of a flat scale, pesisting after the spores have fallen. Brazil, Antilles. 1793. The first known tree-fern. z9 ⊘

C. australis (R. Br.) Domin. Stem to 20 m high; leaves double and on the lower portions triple pinnate, pale green beneath, somewhat pubescent on the venation with blistery scales, soft or leathery (varying according to location), leaflets 8—10 cm long, lobes linear to lanceolate, the basal portions distinctly cleft to the midrib, the upper portions flowing one into the other, the spore bearing leaflets entire or somewhat crenate, the sterile ones frequently serrate, venation of the fertile lobes usually simple forked, that of the sterile lobes usually branched in multiples; sori small, numerous, in 2 rows, quite regular on many plants, on others found only at the base of the lobes. LF 8: 63 (= *Alsophila australis* R. Br.). Australia, Tasmania. 1833. z8 ∅

C. capensis (L. f.) Sm. Slender stem, to 4 m high; often with many adventitious pinnae on the petiole base, these completely different from the actual pinnae, very narrow, translucent, soft, leaves 3-pinnate, frequently thornless, 2—3 m long, 0.5—1 m wide, leaflets with densely arranged, lanceolate, acute, sickle-shaped and scabrous serrate lobes, venation simple, occasionally forked; usually only 1 sorus on the base of the lobes; indusium very small, ciliate. LF 8: 62; PBl (1.) 1: 8 (= *Hemitelia capensis* [L. f.] R. Br.) S. Africa. z8 ∅

C. dealbata (G. Forst.) Sw. Silver Tree-fern. Stem to 12 m high, thornless; leaf rachis and midribs rust-brown tomentose, petioles rust-brown woolly when young, leaves doubly to 3-pinnate, in a flat spray, to 4 m long, dark green and glabrous above, bluish-white pruinose beneath, leaflet lobes densely arranged, oblong, scabrous serrate; sori numerous, often only on the basal half of the leaflet lobes; indusium irregularly split. DRHS 603; LF 8: 58. New Zealand. z8 Plate 158. ∅

While *C. dealbata* prefers a somewhat dry location, as in its habitat, all the other species will thrive better in moist, warm, protected areas. Cultivated in the gardens of S. England, Southern USA, W. Scotland, S. Ireland and in the Mediterranean region.

CYATHODES Labill. — EPACRIDACEAE

Evergreen shrubs, nearly heather-like; leaves small; flowers small, petiole with numerous scales or small bracts; calyx 5 lobed, corolla with tubular base and 5 lobed erect limb; stamens 5; fruit a berry-like drupe with 3—5 seeds.— 15 species in Australia, Tasmania and Polynesia.

The species described here will not need to be classified under *Leucopogon*, as explained by H. H. Allan (Fl. N. Zeal. I, 513, 1961).

Cyathodes colensoi Hook. f. Rather strong growing shrublet, about 20 cm wide, branches procumbent or ascending, branches more or less erect; leaves sessile, glabrous, narrow oblong, 5—9 mm long, 1—2 mm wide, margin thickened, ciliate, blue-green beneath, with 3—5 distinct veins; flowers 3—5 in short, erect racemes, corolla tips densely pubescent above; fruits white or pink to carmine, globose, 4—5 mm thick (= *Leucopogon colensoi* Hook. f.). New Zealand. z8 # ⊕ ⊛

C. fraseri (A. Cunn.) Allan. Shrub, low or procumbent, about 15 cm high, but much wider, branches procumbent-ascending, densely arranged, densely pubescent when young; leaves imbricately arranged, erect, tightly appressed, nearly sessile, leathery tough, obovate-oblong, 4—9 mm long, 1—2 mm wide, margin membranous, finely ciliate, apexes 2 mm long, prickly (!); flowers solitary, axillary, white, corolla lobes densely pubescent above; fruits orange to yellow, somewhat broad-oblong, 8—9 mm long. PRP 59 (= *Leucopogon fraseri* A. Cunn.). New Zealand. z8 # ⊕ ⊛

C. juniperina (J. R. & G. Forst.) Druce. Upright or also a wide shrub, 1—2 m high (to 5 m in its habitat), bark black, branches erect; leaves leather-like, linear, 6—15 mm long, 0.5—1 mm wide, blue-green beneath, margin somewhat involute and finely ciliate, with prickly, 1 mm long tips; flowers whitish-green, only 3 mm long, solitary, axillary, corolla lobes usually glabrous above; fruits white to carmine or purple, globose, 4—7 mm thick (= *C. acerosa* [Gaertn.] R. Br.; *C. articulata* Co.; *Leucopogon forsteri* A. Rich.). New Zealand, Australia, Tasmania. z8 # ⊕ ⊛

C. robusta Hook. f. Shrub, similar to *C. juniperina*, but much stronger growing, 1—2 m, to 5 m in its habitat; leaves stiff and leathery, 12—20 mm long, 3—7 mm wide, with 5—11 veins above, linear, obtuse at the tips (!); flowers solitary, axillary, 3 mm long, stalks with many, imbricately overlapping bracts; fruits red, globose, 7—12 mm thick. Chatham Island. z8 # ⊕ ⊛

Suitable for the rock garden in mild areas; prefer a lime free soil, like the *Ericaceae*.

CYCAS L. — CYCAS — CYCADACEAE

Growth like palms or tree-ferns, stem woody, usually not branched, densely covered with scales and persistent petiole bases; leaves large, rolled up like fiddle-heads when young, usually arranged nearly in whorls and developing equally on all sides; pinnae one ribbed, linear, without side veins; plants dioecious with flowers in large, terminal cones. — 20 species in tropical Asia, Africa, Australia and Polynesia.

Cycas circinalis L. Becoming 2—3 m high in cultivation, stem cylindrical; leaves to 2 m long or longer, erect when young, becoming reflexed with age, leaf petioles rounded beneath, nearly triangular above, thornless at the base or nearly to the middle, with 2 ranked thorns further up, with 50—60 pinnae on either side, these narrow-lanceolate, straight or sickle-shaped, drawn out into an occasionally prickly tip, flat or somewhat revolute, nodding, about 25 cm long, 1.5 cm wide, rather densely arranged, green or bluish-green reddish-brown pubescent when young. BM 2826; NH 38: 16; BC Pl. 33. East Indies. 1800. Very handsome species; cultivated in many botanic gardens. z8 Plate 155. # ∅

C. revoluta Thunb. Stem cylindrical, to 3 m high, occasionally forked; leaves 0.5—2 m long, deep green, leaflets narrow linear, margin revolute, very densely arranged, becoming smaller toward the base of the leaf, eventually thorny, petiole somewhat 4 sided. BM 2963/64. China, E. Indies. Suitable for outdoors only in the mildest areas, especially z8. Plate 155. # ∅

CYDONIA Mill. — Quince — ROSACEAE

Deciduous shrub or small tree, without thorns; leaves entire; flowers solitary, white, stamens 20 or more, anthers yellow; carpels 5, completely enclosed within the receptacle (hypanthium); styles 5, distinct, but with a wide section constructed from the swollen upper margin of the receptacle; each locule with numerous ovules; fruit pulp always with gritty cells. — 1 species.

Cydonia see: **Chaenomeles**

C. oblonga Mill. Quince. Thornless shrub, to 6 m high and often equally wide or tree-like, young branches white-gray tomentose; leaves rounded-oval, deep green above, gray tomentose beneath, 5—10 cm long, fall color yellow, petiole 1—1.5 cm long; flowers appearing after the leaves, usually solitary, terminal, white with darker veins to soft pink, May—June; fruit apple- or pear-shaped, yellow, finely tomentose, eventually glabrous, aromatic. Native habitat is Transcaucasia, Persia (Iran), Turkestan, Saudi Arabia, widely disseminated today as a fruit tree. Plate 155. z5 ⊗ ✂

For culture and varieties, please see; Fruit—Lit.; Krussmann: Die Quitten; Aachen 1951, 28 pp., 5 Pl.

CYRILLA Gard. — CYRILLACEAE

Monotypic genus; deciduous shrub (evergreen tree in very mild areas), branches glabrous; leaves short petioled, alternate; flowers very small, but many in axillary racemes, each flower with 5 stamens, these shorter than the petals; fruit a small, dehiscent capsule. — 1 species, from Eastern N. America to the W. Indies.

Cyrilla racemiflora L. A deciduous shrub in cooler climates, about 1 m high; leaves oblanceolate to obovate, 4—10 cm long, glossy green above, lighter beneath, venation reticulate, orange-red fall foliage; flowers white, 5 mm long, many in 8—15 cm long racemes, several clustered at the base of the previous year's wood, June—July. BM 2456; BB 2355; KTF 129. Native habitat as above. 1765. z6 Plate 126. ∅

The small leaved type found in N. Florida with only 1.8—3.5 cm long by 6—12 mm wide leaves, and 3—8 cm long flower racemes is occasionally classified as *C. paviflora.* KTF 128.

CYTISUS L. — Broom — LEGUMINOSAE

Deciduous or evergreen, thornless shrubs, occasionally small trees; leaves trifoliate, occasionally simple, often very small to nearly absent; flowers yellow or white, occasionally red, in terminal racemes or heads or axillary; calyx bilabiate, petals distinct, keel petal obtuse, stamens connate, style bowed inward; pods linear-oblong, flat, dehiscent, 2 to several seeded. — About 70 species in Central Europe and the Mediterranean region.

In Flora Europaea, Vol. 2 (1968) the genus is subdivided into the following subgenera; *Lembotropis* Griseb. (1 species), *Cytisus* L. (25 species), *Chamaecytisus* Link (35 species), *Chronanthus* (DC.) K. Koch and *Teline* Medicus (2 species). In this work, however, the previously accepted classification system will be maintained.

Outline of the Genus

● Calyx campanulate, about as long as wide; branches grooved or angular;

Section 1. **Teline** Benth & Hook.
Flowers in mock racemes or heads; leaves trifoliate; calyx deeply 3 lobed, upper lobe deeply split, lower lobe somewhat less deeply 3 cleft:
C. canariensis, linifolius, maderensis, monspessulanus, × *spachianus, stenopetalus*

Section 2. **Sarothamnus** (Wimm.) Benth. & Hook.
Flowers axillary along the branches, usually solitary, 2—2.5 cm long; style longer than the keel petal, spirally curving:
C. grandiflorus, ingramii, scoparius

Section 3. **Corothamnus** (Koch) Nyman
Procumbent shrub, leaves simple; flowers small, along branches, calyx short bilabiate, stamens of uneven size, style shorter than the keel petal, slightly curved:
C. decubens, diffusus, procumbens

Section 4. **Trianthocytisus** Griseb.
Like the above Section, but with leaves trifoliate;

flowers solitary or few axillary; calyx short campanulate, short toothed:
C. ardoinii, beanii, emeriflorus, kewensis

Section 5. **Spartothamnus** (Webb.) Schneid.
Branches resembling those of *Ephedra*, leaves single to trifoliate, the apical leaves simple; flowers white or yellow, 1—5 axillary; calyx short bilabiate:
C. dallimorei, filipes, multiflorus, praecox, purgans, supranubius

Section 6. **Phyllocytisus** Koch
Leaves trifoliate; flowers in terminal racemes; calyx campanulate, short bilabiate; keel petal distinctly bowed, terminating in short beak; pods sessile or very short stalked:
C. nigricans, sessilifolius

●● Calyx tubular, much longer than wide; leaves always trifoliate; branches cylindrical, never striped;

Section 7. **Tubocytisus** DC.
Leaves trifoliate; flowers in terminal or axillary, few flowered, fascicled racemes; calyx tubular, upper lobe 2 toothed or 2 cleft, lower lobe 3 toothed or undivided; pods nearly always sessile:
C. albus, austriacus, ciliatus, demissus, elongatus, hirsutus, palmensis, proliferus, purpureus, ratisbonensis, rochelii, supinus, tommasinii, versicolor

Section 8. **Argyrocytisus** Maire
Tall, *Laburnum*-like shrub, but with all parts silver-gray pubescent; flowers in erect racemes:
C. battgandieri

Cytisus adami see: + **Laburnocytisius**

C. albus Hacq. Upright shrub, about 30 cm high, branches usually appressed pubescent, green at first, then brown-green; leves trifoliate, narrow elliptic, 1.5 cm long, light green above, gray-green beneath, pubescent; flowers white or yellowish, 3—6 in terminal heads, June—July. BM 8693 (= *C. leucanthus* Waldst. & Kit.; *C. leucanthus* var. *schipkaensis* Dipp.). Hungary, W. Germany (Siebenbuergen, Bulgaria. 1806. z6 Fig. 300. See also: *C. multiflorus*

C. alpinus see: **Laburnum alpinum**

C. alschiengeri see: **Laburnum anagyroides** var. **alschingeri**

C. ardoinii Fourn. Procumbent shrub, 10—20 cm high, flat globose, young branches octagonal, pubescent, striped; leaves trifoliate, obovate-oblong, 8 mm long, both sides long haired, especially when young; flowers 1—3, axillary, at the branch tips, gold-yellow, April—May, calyx long haired, also the generally 2 seeded pod. GC 127: 16. S. France, maritime Alps, but exceptionally rare in the wild. 1866. z7 Fig. 301.⊕

C. austriacus L. Upright shrub, 30—100 cm high, although often also procumbent, entire plant appressed pubescent; leaves trifoliate, narrow elliptic, 10—30 mm long, both sides with persistent pubescence; flowers yellow,' in terminal heads, standard petal pubescent outside, calyx with erect (!) pubescence, July—August. HM 1321; HF 2312 (= *C. canescens*

Presl). Central and SE. Europe to the Caucasus z6 Fig. 300. ⊕

var. **heuffelii** (Griseb. & Schenk) Schneid. This variety normally represents the species in gardens; shrub, upright or with branches also drooping, with gray appressed pubescence; leaflets 1.2 to 1.8 cm long, 3 mm wide, linear-oblong to more obovate, appressed pubescent beneath, eventually glabrous above; flowers in terminal heads on the current year's wood, yellow, petals narrow, calyx very pubescent; pods 2.5 cm long, gray silky pubescent (= *Chamaecytisus heuffelii* [Griseb. & Schenk] Rothm.). Hungary, Romania.

C. battandieri Maire. Strong growing, upright shrub, in mild areas to 3—5 m high and wide, entire plant dense silver-gray pubescent (like a silver-gray *Laburnum* with erect inflorescences); leaves trifoliate, leaflets oval-elliptic, 4—7 cm long; flowers gold-yellow, pleasantly fragrant, many dense, 5—15 cm long, erect racemes, straight, 5 cm long. Bm 9528. Morocco, Atlas Mountains. 1922. z7—8 Fig. 299.⊕ ⊘

Including the variety 'Yellow Tail' (Hillier).

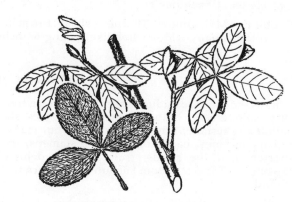

Fig. 299. *Cytisus battandieri*

C. × beanii Nichols. (*C. ardoinii* × *C. purgans*). Shrub, to 40 cm high, branches procumbent-ascending; leaves simple, linear, 12 mm long, pubescent; flowers axillary, grouped 1—3, deep yellow, calyx campanulate, more or less pubescent, May. BS 1: Pl. 75; BMns 366. Originated in Kew Gardens, 1900. z6 ⊕

C. canariensis (L.) O. Ktze. Evergreen, densely branched shrub, about 1.5 m high, young branches with appressed pubescence; leaves trifoliate, the basal leaflets stalked, the apical leaf sessile, obovate-oblong, apex rounded, 6—12 mm long, appressed silky pubescent; flowers in short, terminal, fragrant yellow racemes on the ends of the young branches, calyx campanulate, appressed silky pubescent, May—July. KGC 21; BFCa 29 (= *Genista canariensis* L.). Canary Islands. z8 # ⊕

var. **ramosissimus** (Poir.) Briq. Leaves smaller, glabrous above; racemes shorter and more numeruos. BR 217 (= *Genista fragrans* Hort.). Frequently cultivated as a pot plant. z8

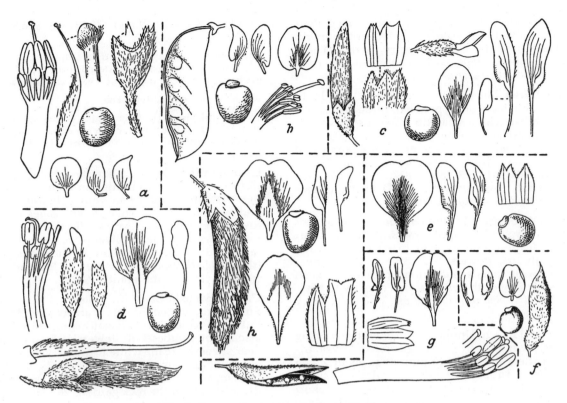

Fig. 300. **Cytisus** a. *C. nigricans*; b. *C. sessilifolius*; c. *C. albus*;
d. *C. ratisbonensis*; e. *C. purpureus*; f. *C. purgans*; g. *C. au-*
striacus; h. *C. supinus* (from Schneider, Ulbrich)

C. canescens see: **C. austriacus**

C. capitatus see: **C. supinus**

C. ciliatus Wahlenb. Shrub, to 1 m, branches usually
erect or ascending, seldom procumbent, erect pubescent or shaggy; leaflets obovate to elliptic, 2–3 cm
long, 1–1.5 cm wide, glabrous above to pubescent,
erect pubescence beneath; calyx with erect pubescence or shaggy, corolla yellow, standard petal with
or without brown spot; pods 2–4 cm long, pubescent
on the seam, otherwise glabrous or also densely
pubescent (= *Chamaecytisus ciliatus* [Wahlenb.]
Rothm.). Eastern Central Europe and the Balkans.
Similar to *C. hirsutum*, but with larger leaves. z6 ✿

C. × dallimorei Rolfe. (*C. multiflorus* × *C. scoparius*
'Andreanus'). Habit and appearance like *C. scoparius*,
but shorter; leaves usually trifoliate, leaflets sessile,
elliptic to oblanceolate, pubescent at first; flowers
1–2, lilac-pink, wings carmine-red, calyx brown,
somewhat pubescent, May; pods 2.5 cm long, pubescent on the margin. Bm 8482; GC 51; 198. Originated
in Kew Gardens. 1900. z7 ✿

C. decumbens (Durand) Spach. Procumbent shrub, to
20 cm high, branches pentagonal, pubescent when
young; leaves simple, sessile, oblong, 8–20 mm long,
densely pubescent beneath, less so above; flowers

grouped 1–3, gold-yellow, calyx campanulate,
pubescent, May to June; pods 2 cm long, pubescent,
with 3–4 seeds. BM 8230 (= *C.prostratus* Simonkai). S.
Europe. 1775. One of the best dwarf species. z6 Plate
157; Fig. 301. ✿

C. demissus Boiss. Low, wide shrub, scarcely higher
than 10 cm, branches very thin, with dense and loose
gray pubescence; leaves light green, trifoliate, leaflets
elliptic, rounded or obovate, 6–12 mm long, 2–4 mm
wide, especially pubescent beneath; flowers yellow,
in clusters of 2–3 in the upper leaf axils, 18–30 mm
long, standard circular, 12 mm wide, apex incised,
keel red-brown, calyx tubular, 12–15 mm long,
pubescent, May (= *C. hirsutus* var. *demissus* [Boiss.]
Halacsy). Greece; NE. Asia Minor. z6 Plate 126. ✿

C. diffusus (Willd.) Vis. Procumbent, thinly
branched shrub, branches ascending, glabrous or
pubescent; leaves simple, oblong lanceolate, 1 cm
long, glabrous or pubescent; flowers grouped 1–3,
axillary, yellow, banner petal not emarginate, flower
stalk 3 times as long as the calyx, May–June; pods
very pubescent. HF 2295. Lorraine (W. Germany) to
Austria on gravelly mountain slopes. z5

C. elongatus Waldst.& Kit. Upright shrub, branches
appressed pubescent, twigs very long, cylindrical and

densely covered with flowers, grouped 3—4 together, distinctly stalked, flat yellow with red-brown markings, May—June. BR 1191. Hungary, Serbia (Yugoslavia), in forests. 1804. Often cultivated under the name *C. ratisbonensis*. z6 ⊕

C. emeriflorus Reichenb. Shrub, 30—70 cm high, rounded habit; leaves long petioled, trifoliate, leaflets oblong, obtuse with a small tip, glabrous above, appressed pubescent beneath; flowers grouped 1—2—4, axillary, gold-yellow, calyx campanulate, appressed pubescent, May—June; pods smooth, about 2.5 cm long. BM 8201; HF 2310; BS 1: 817 (= *C. glabrescens* Sart.). Ticino (Switzerland) and Dalmatia (Yugoslavia). 1890. Rare in cultivation. z6 Fig. 301.

C. filipes Webb. Small shrub with densely arranged, thin, wiry, bowed, striped branches; leaves short petioled, leaflets oblanceolate to narrow obovate, nearly glabrous; flowers 1—2 axillary, pure white, fragrant, wing petals much longer than the keel, flower stalk longer than the calyx, February to May. BFCa 171 (= *Spartocytisus filipes* Webb). Canary Islands. z9 ⊕

C. fontanesii Spach. Upright shrub or with ascending branches, twigs 5—10 sided, glabrous; leaves trifoliate, leaflets linear, 6—12 mm long, about 2 mm wide, short and appressed pubescent; flowers usually grouped 2—4 on the current year's branch tips, short stalked, corolla cordate, 8—12 mm, keel petal nearly equally long, gold-yellow, calyx membranous, 3 mm long, May; the spent corolla enveloping the 1—1.5 cm long pod. VG 44 (= *Spartium biflorum* Desf.: *Chronanthus biflorus* [Desf.] Frodin & Heywood). E. and S. Spain; Balearic Islands, in thickets. z8 ⊕

C. fragrens see: **C. supranubius**

C. glabrescens see: **C. emeriflorus**

C. grandiflorus (Brot.) DC. Deciduous shrub, 2—2.5 m high, like *C. scoparius* in appearance, but with young branches and leaves silver-gray pubescent; leaves usually with 3 leaflets, or with only 1, elliptic, obovate or awl-shaped, 6—12 mm long; flowers 1—2, on the previous year's wood, gold-yellow, standard about 18 mm wide, keel 2.5 cm long, calyx dome-shaped, glabrous to slightly pubescent, 4 mm long, May; pods straight or somewhat bowed, 2—4.5 cm long, about 1 cm wide, densely covered with long white hairs. VG 50 (= *Spartium grandiflorum* Brot.; *Genista grandiflora* [Brot.] Spach). S. Spain, S. and Middle Portugal. 1816, 1837. z8 ⊕

C. hirsutus L. Shrub with quite variable growth habit, 30—100 cm high, branches and twigs often prostrate, older plants usually upright, vegetative branches, leaves and calyx with erect rough hairs; leaves trifoliate, leaflets obovate, 2 cm long, pubescent on both sides; flowers all axillary, grouped 1—3, gold-yellow, banner reddish-brown in the middle, flower stalks always without bracts, May—July; pods linear to somewhat sickle-shaped, rough haired, 3—4 cm long.

HM 1323; BM 6819; PEu 51; HF 2315. S. and SE. Europe to the Caucasus. z6 ⊕

var. **alpestris** Arcang. Alpine dwarf form; growth prostrate, branches twisted, leaves clustered at the branch tips; flowers usually at the branch tips (= var. *polytrichus* Briq.). ⊕

var. *demissus* see: **C. demissus**

var. **hirsutissimus** (K. Koch) Boiss. Strong grower, about 1 m high, narrowly upright, branches densely shaggy; leaves more densely pubescent; otherwise like the species. S. Europe.

C. ingramii Blakelock. Densely leaved, twiggy, upright shrub, 1.5—1.8 m high in its habitat, branches densely pubescent when young; becoming angular and with few hairs when older; leaves simple, the lower ones trifoliate, leaflets elliptic-oblong, 1—2 cm long, margin distinctly silver pubescent; flowers solitary, axillary, large, yellow outside, inside white. BMns 211. N. Spain. Found by C. Ingram, 1936. Attractive, flowers abundantly. ⊕

C. × kewensis Bean (*C. ardoinii* × *C. multiflorus*). Small, procumbent shrub, scarcely over 30 cm high, but much wider; leaves usually trifoliate, occasionally also simple, pubescent; flowers 1—3 on the previous year's wood, cream-white to sulfur-yellow, standard petal about 12 mm wide, May. BS 1: 74; BMns 299. Developed in Kew Gardens, 1891. Very beautiful dwarf shrub for the rock garden. z6 Plate 156. ⊕

C. laburnum see: **Laburnum anagyroides**

C. leucanthus see: **C. albus** and **C. rochelii**

C. linifolius (L.) Lam. Evergreen or semi-deciduous shrub, to 3 m high, branches upright, appressed silky pubescent, leaves nearly sessile, leaflets linear or more lanceolate, acute, 1—2.5 cm long, glabrous above, appressed silky pubescent beneath, margin somewhat involuted; flowers in short, compact terminal racemes, gold-yellow, standard petal silky pubescent (glabrous on *C. monspessulanus*!), 10—18 mm long, wide ovate, April—June. BFCa 167; VG 35; BM 442 (= *Teline linifolius* [L.] Webb & Berth.). Spain, N. Africa, Canary Islands, in thickets; dislikes alkaline soil. z9 # ⊕

C. lobelii see: **C. sessilifolius**

C. maderensis Masf. Evergreen shrub, also a small tree in its habitat, to 6 m high, branches stiff, knotty, young branches brownish or silvery pubescent; leaves densely arranged, rather long petioled, trifoliate, leaflets oblong-obovate to more lanceolate, acute, silky pubescent on both sides or glabrous above, 6—9 mm long; flowers in rather compact, terminal racemes on the current year's wood, 6—12 flowers in a raceme, gold-yellow, fragrant, standard glabrous, keel dense silky pubescent, calyx campanulate, dense shaggy, May—June; pods 2.5 cm long, flat, pubescent (= *Teline maderensis* Webb). Madeira Islands. z9 # ⊕

var. **magnifoliosus** Briq. Leaves larger, 1.5—3 cm long; racemes with 10—20 flowers. BR 26: 23 (as *Genista bracteolata*). Madeira Islands. z9 # ⊕

Plate 145

Cotoneaster conspicuus 'Decorus'
in the Copenhagen Botanic Garden, Denmark.

Cordylnie australis
in Bell Park, Fota Island, Ireland

Cotoneaster horizontalis 'Saxatilis' in the Dortmund Botanic Garden, W. Germany

Plate 146

Cotoneaster integerrimus, fruits
Photo: Dr. Pilat, Prag

Cotoneaster lucidus, fruits
Photo: Dr. Pilat, Prag

Cotoneaster bullatus in the Malonya Arboretum, Czechoslovakia   Photo: Dr. Pilat, Prag

Plate 147

Cotoneaster bullatus 'Firebird'
Plant Propaganda Holland

Cotoneaster dammeri 'Skogholm'
in Westfalenpark, Dortmund, W. Germany

Cotoneaster dammeri 'Streibs Findling' in the Dortmund Botanic Garden

Plate 148

Cotoneaster microphyllus var. *thymifolius*
in a park in Orleans, France

Cotoneaster amoernus
in the Tbilisi Botanic Garden

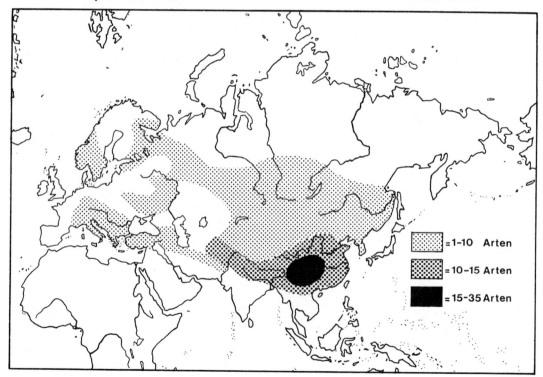

=1–10 Arten

=10–15 Arten

=15–35 Arten

Range of the genus *Cotoneaster*
(*Arten = species +*) after Browicz

Plate 149

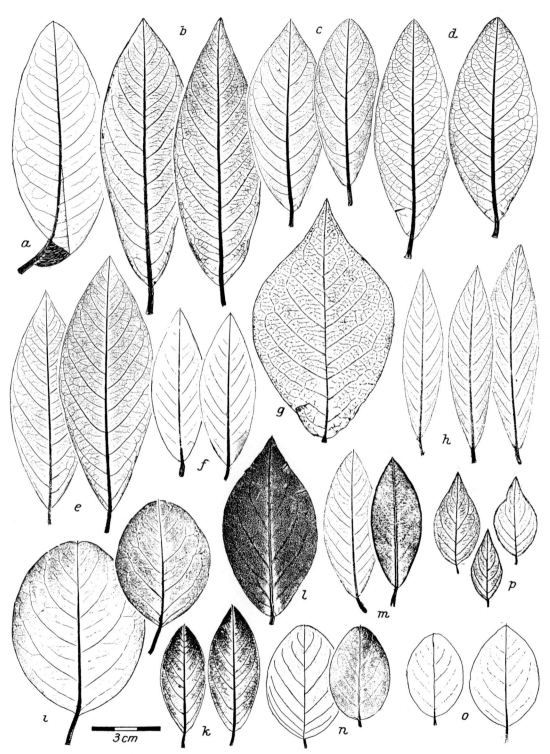

Cotoneaster. a. *C. frigidus*; b. *C. henryanus*; c. *C. watereri* 'John Waterer'; d. *C. grigidus* 'Xanthocarpus'; e. *C. watereri* 'St. Monica'; f. *C. watereri* 'Exburiensis'; g. *C. bullatus* var. *macrophyllus*; h. *C. salicifolius* var. *floccosus*; i. *C. insignis*; k. *C. watereri* 'Pendulus'; l. *C. foveolatus*; m. *C. rhytidophyllus*; n. *C. niger*; o. *C. integerrimus*; p. *C. franchetii* (leaves taken from cultivated plants)

Plate 150

Cotoneaster adpressus with haorfrost
Archivild

Cotoneaster dammeri
in the Dortmund Botanic Garden, W. Germany

Cotoneaster dammeri in the Dortmund Botanic Garden
Archivbild

Plate 151

Cotoneaster divaricatus
in the Kolding Botanic Garden, Denmark

Cotoneaster splendens
in the Flinck Garden, Bjuv, Sweden

Cotoneaster salicifolius 'Parkteppich'
in Westfalenpark, Dortmund, W. Germany

Cotoneaster watereri 'Pendulus'
in the Dortmund Botanic Garden

Plate 152

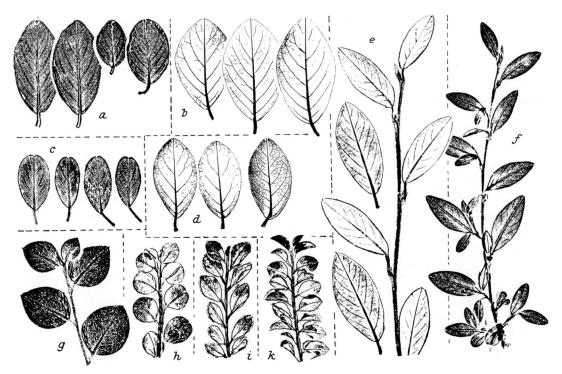

Cotoneaster (leaves slightly reduced in size). a. *C. dammeri* (the true species from China); b. *C. dammeri* (from culture); c. *C. dammeri* var. *radicans* (from a plant in China); d. *C. dammeri* 'Skogholm'; e. *C. salicifolius* 'Repens'; f. *C. salicifolius* 'Gnom'; g. *C. Sabrina*; h. *C.* 'Hessei'; i. *C. adpressus*; k. *C. horizontalis* var. *perpusillus*

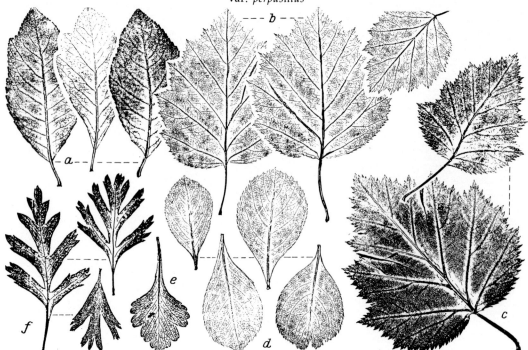

Crataemespilus. a. *C. grandiflora.* — **Crataegus.** b. *C. pedicellata* (typical); c. *C. intricata*; d. *C. crus-galli*; e. *C. spathulata*; f. *C. azarolus* (b, c, d, and e. collected from wild plants in the USA)

Plate 153

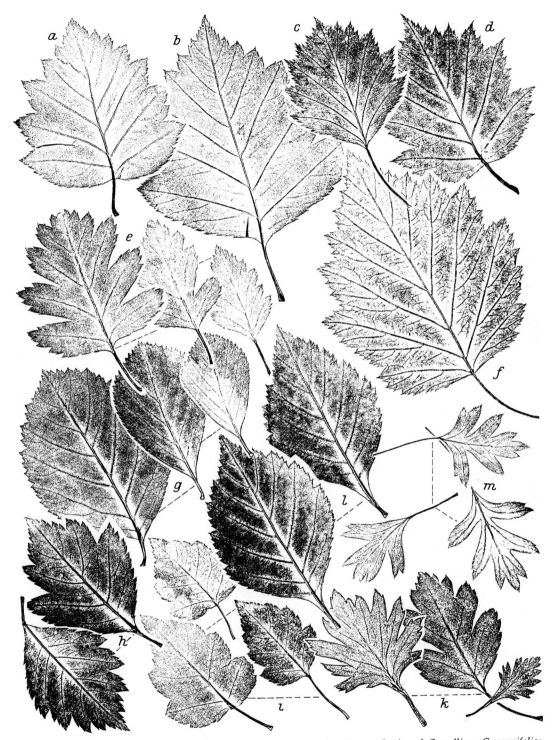

Crataegus. a. *C. altaica*; b. *C. chlorosarca*; c. *C. flabellata*; d. *C. holmesiana*; e. *C. nigra*; f. *C. mollis*; g. *C. prunifolia*; h. *C. dahurica*; i. *C. phaenopyrum*; k. *C. tanacetifolia*; l. *C. calpodendron*; m. *C pentagyna*

Plate 154

Crataegus orientalis
in the Thiensen Arboretum in Ellerhoop
near Elmshorn, W. Germany

Cudriania tricuspidata
in the Mlynany Botanic Garden, Czechoslovakia

Cunonia capensis
in the Stellenbosch Botanic Garden, So. Africa

Crinodendron hookerianum
in a park in western Ire.

Plate 155

Cycas revoluta
in the Coimbra Botanic Garden, Portugal

Cycas revoluta, fruit cluster, in the Jardin
Les Cedres, St. Jean-Cap Ferrat, France

Cycas circinalis
in the Hamburg Botanic Garden, W. Germany

Cydonia oblonga

Plate 156

Cytisus supinus
in the Dortmund Botanic Garden, W. Germany

Cytisus supinus, close-up,
in the Dortmund Botanic Garden

Cytisus kewensis in Kew Gardens, London, England

Plate 157

Dais cotinifolia in the Public Garden for Forestry and the Lumber Industry in Reinbek, near Hamburg, W. Germany

Cytisus procumbens
in the Edinburgh Botanic Garden, Scotland

Cytisus decumbens
in an alpine garden at Wuerm, near Pforsheim, W. Germany

Cytisus purgans
in the Dortmund Botanic Garden

Cytisus versicolor
in the Edinburgh Botanic Garden

Plate 158

Daphne pontica
in the Hillier Arboretum, England

Daphne tangutica
in the Copenhagen Botanic Garden, Denmark

Cyathea dealbata in a park in southern Ire.   Photo: Dr. Th. Oudemans

Plate 159

Daphne arbuscula in a private garden in Renton, Scotland

Daphne retusa in Pygmy Pinetum in Devizes, Engl.

Plate 160

Daphne giraldii
in the Berlin Botanic Garden, W. Germany
Photo: C. R. Jelitto

Daphne gnidium
in its native habitat in Setubal, Port.

Daphne gnidium in its native habitat in Setubal, Port.

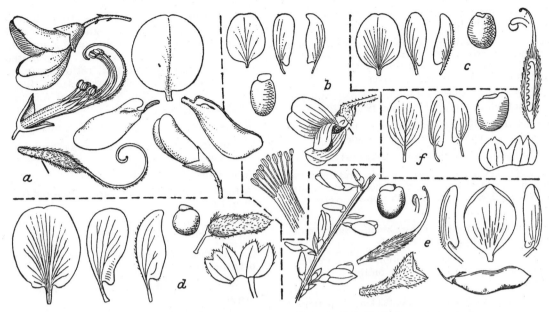

Fig. 301. **Cytisus** a. *C. scoparius*; b. *C. decumbens*; c. *C. pro-cumbens*; d. *C. ardoinii*; e. *C. multiflorus*; f. *C. emerifloris* (from Schneider, Ulbrich)

C. monspessulanus L. Evergreen shrub, densely branched, to 2.5 m high, young branches furrowed and pubescent; leaves petiolate, trifoliate, leaflets broad obovate, obtuse with erect tip or also incised at the tip, glabrous above, pubescent beneath, 12–20 mm long; flowers in small racemes or umbel-like clusters of 3–9 at the tips of the current year's branches, standard yellow, broad elliptic, keel nearly glabrous, calyx campanulate, pubescent, April–June; pods 2–3 cm long, pubescent or somewhat scaly, straight or bowed. BM 8685; SDK 4: 15; VG 34 (= *Genista candicans* L.; *Teline monspessulana* [L.] K. Koch). S. Europe, from Portugal to Dalmatia (Yugoslavia), Greece and Asia Minor. z9 # ⊕

C. multiflorus (Ait.) Sweet. Spanish Broom. Tall shrub, 2–3 m high in its habitat, branches rod-like, striped, pubescent when young; leaves at the branch tips, simple, otherwise trifoliate, linear-oblong, about 1 cm long, thin silky pubescent; flowers 1–3, pure white, abundant and very attractive; pods appressed pubescent, May–June. BM 8693; PSw 16; VG 47 (= *C. albus* Link non Hacq.). Spain, N. Africa. Gorgeous, but unfortunately a tender shrub z7 Fig. 301. ⊕

'Durus'. An especially winter hardy race. Much cultivated in French gardens. z6

'Pallidus'. Flowers yellowish.

'Toome's Variety'. Flowers white, with a trace of soft pink; appearing very early. In English gardens. z8 ⊕

C. nigricans L. Upright shrub, 0.5–2 m high, branches rod-like, appressed pubescent; leaves petiolate, trifoliate, leaflets oblong-obovate, 1.5–2.5 cm long, glabrous above, appressed pubescent beneath; flowers yellow, in 8–20 cm long, silky pubescent, leafless, terminal racemes, June–July; pods appressed rough pubescent. BM 8479; HM 2308; BS 1: 822; PEu 51. Central Europe, N. Italy. z6 Fig. 300.

C. palmensis (Christ) Hutchins. Evergreen, open shrub, branches long, thin, softly pubescent; leaves trifoliate, leaflets narrow elliptic to oblanceolate, 2–3.5 cm long, 4–10 mm wide, with a small tuft of hair at the apex, glabrous above, with fine soft pubescence beneath (not silky!), quite short stalked, leaf petiole 1.5–2.5 cm long; flowers white, 2–4 in axillary clusters, 2 cm long, calyx with triangular-lanceolate lobes, densely pubescent like the flower stalk, February-April; pods 3 cm long, 1 cm wide, seed black, glossy(= *C. proliferus* var. *palmensis* Christ). Canary Islands, but only on La Palma, where it is also used as fodder for livestock. z9 # ⊕

C. × praecox Bean (*C. multiflorus* × *C. purgans*). "Warminster Broom". Bushy, dense shrub, 0.7–1.5 (to 3) m high, branches often somewhat nodding, gray-green, long rod-like; leaves usually simple, lanceolate to linear-spathulate, 8–20 mm long, silky pubescent; flowers 1–2, along the entire twig, very fragrant, cream-white, April–May. Originated in 1867 by Wheeler in Warminister, England. z7 ⊕

'Albus' (Th. Smith). Growth weak, branches more pendulous; flowers white. Originated before 1911. ⊕

'Allgold' (A. G. Brand, Boskoop 1963). Growth like the species; flowers pure yellow, fading somewhat lighter. ⊕

'Frisia' (Boskoop Experiment Station 1963). Growth tall and wide, like a small flowering 'Donard Seedling'; standard lilac-white, carmine-pink outside, wings brown-yellow, keel cream-yellow with lilac. z6−7 ⊕

'Goldspeer' (G. Arends 1955). Growth somewhat weaker than the species; flowers somewhat smaller, but deep yellow and very numerous (= 'Gold Spear'; 'Canary Bird'). Originated from a back cross with *C. purgans*. ⊕

'Hollandia' (Boskoop Experiment Station). Flowers purple-red, keel cream-white bordered. Around 1950.

'Kathleen Ferrier' (Nijveldt). Habit very ornamental; flowers cream-yellow, somewhat darker than the species. ⊕

'Luteus'. Dwarf form; flowers yellow. Before 1911. ⊕

'Osbornii'. Flowers like *C. praecox*, in color and form, but appearing in late May−early June, without a strong fragrance. Originated in Kew Gardens. Probably a hybrid of *C. dallimorei?*

'Sneeuwwitje' (Nijveldt). Habit more broadly bushy, more ornamental, lower; flowers pure white. ⊕

'Zeelandia' (Boskoop Experiment Station). Flowers cream-white, wings and standard petals lilac on the dorsal side. Around 1950.

The latter 2 cultivars originated at the Boskoop Experiment Station by crossing *C. praecox* × *C. dallimorei*; the branches are greener than those of *C. praecox*, they are bushier and hardier than *C. dallimorei*, the flowers appear somewhat later than *C. praecox*.

'Zitronenregen' (K. Foerster). Habit somewhat more compact than *C. praecox*, to 1.5 m; flowers pure yellow, very abundant. Presumably *C. praecox* × *C. beanii*. ⊕

C. procumbens (Willd.) Spreng. Procumbent shrub, very similar to *C. decumbens*, but 30−60 cm high, leaves petiolate, entire plant appressed pubescent; leaves simple, oblong-obovate, obtuse, nearly glabrous above; flowers 1−3, axillary, yellow, calyx campanulate, pubescent, May−July; pods about 2.5 cm long. HM 1345; BR 1150. SE. Europe. z6 Plate 157; Fig. 301.

C. proliferus L. f. Escabon. Evergreen shrub, 3−5 m high, open growing, branches long, thin, softly pubescent; leaves trifoliate, leaflets linear, silky pubescent beneath (not softly pubescent like *C. palmensis!*); flowers white, 2.5 cm long, in clusters of 4−7, axillary, near the tips of short, leafy twigs, calyx funnelform, with narrow, triangular teeth, densely pubescent, April. BFCa 28; 170; KGC 23. Canary Islands, but only wild on Tenerife and Gomera; used there as livestock fodder. Ⓕ Australia, in windbreak plantings. z9 # ⊕

var. *palmensis* see: **C. palmensis**

C. purgans (L.) Spach. Dense, strongly branched, upright shrub, 0.2—1 m high, branches stiff, striped, pubescent when young; leaves simple, sessile, lanceolate, 8−12 mm long, usually abscising early, somewhat silky pubescent; flowers 1−2, axillary, gold-yellow, petals glabrous, all of equal length, calyx campanulate, persistent, distinctly 2 lobed, April−June; young pods with appressed soft pubescence. BM 7618; VG 46. Spain, S. France, N. Africa. z6 Plate 157; Fig. 300. ⊕

C. purpureus Scop. Shrub, to 60 cm high, procumbent-erect, branches glabrous, rod-like, green; leaves trifoliate, leaflets obovate, glabrous, often also ciliate, 1−2.5 cm long; flowers 1−3, situated along the entire branch, purple-red, rather large, stalk short, calyx tubular, somewhat pubescent, June−July. HF 2316; BM 1176; PEu 51. Central and SE. Europe. 1792. z6 Fig. 300. ⊕

'Albocarneus'. Flowers light pink. Before 1840.

f. **albus** (Sweet) Zab. Flowers white. Found in the wild in Tirol. Before 1838.

'Amsaticus'. Flowers bluish-red.

'Atropurpureus'. Flowers dark purple-red (= f. *incarnatus* Dipp.). ⊕

'Erectus'. Growth narrowly upright, otherwise like the species. Before 1840.

C. racemosus Marnock see: **C. maderensis** var. **magnifoliosus**

C. racemosus Nichols. non Marnock see: **C. × spachianus**

C. ratisbonensis Schaeff. Variable shrub, growth either creeping and procumbent or also 1(2) m high, branched with appressed silky pubescence, cylindrical; leaves trifoliate, petiole 2 cm long, leaflets obovate, 2−3.5 cm long, glabrous above, soft silky pubescent beneath; flowers axillary, 2−4, yellow with brown markings, calyx tube-form, appressed pubescent, May−June. HM Pl. 159; HF 2314. Germany to W. Siberia and the Caucasus. 1800. z5 Fig. 300.

C. rochelii Griseb. & Schenk. Deciduous shrub, 1 m high, branches upright, cylindrical, very hairy; leaves trifoliate, leaflets oblong-lanceolate or more oblanceolate, 1−3 cm long, 2−9 mm wide, terminating in a short tip or pubescent tuft, appressed pubescent on both sides; flowers 2 cm long, clustered near the tips of leafy twigs, light yellow, brown spotted, calyx and pods very pubescent, standard pubescent outside, calyx tubular, June−July (= *Chamaecytisus rochelii* [Wierzb.] Rothm; *Cytisus leucanthus* ssp. *obscurus* [Rochel] Hayek). Bulgaria and E. Yugoslavia to the Ukraine. z6 ⊕

C. scoparius (L.) Link. Erect shrub, 0.5−2 m high, branches rod-like, angular, deep green, pubescent when young; leaves trifoliate, often simple at the branch tips, oblanceolate, somewhat appressed pubescent, 1−2 cm long; flowers 1−2, axillary large, gold-yellow, standard circular, 2 cm wide, May−June; pods narrow oblong, 4−5 cm long, glabrous, margin pubescent. HF 2294; HM Pl. 160; VG 49 (= *Spartium scoparius* L.; *Sarothamnus scoparius* Wimm.). Central and S. Europe. Cultivated for ages. z6 Fig. 301. ⊕

Included here is a large number of cultivars.

The hybridizing has been done principally in England, W. Germany, Ireland and Holland. The following nurseries have been the most important breeders:

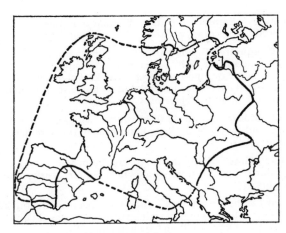

Fig. 302. range of *Cytisus scoparius*

Reinhold Arnold, Alveslohe (Holstein). W. Germany.

Burkwood & Skipwith, Kingston on Thames, England.

Donard Nurseries, Newcastle, Co. Down, N. Ireland.

Sydney B. Mitchell, San José, California (the hybrids, such as 'California'. 'Borsch's Prostrate', 'Pomona', 'St. Mary's', 'San Francisco', 'Stanford', all originated around 1934, but are generally not found in European cultivation; described by Wyman in Amer. Nurseryman 6/1/1963, pp. 75—77).

Smith & Sons, Darley Dale, Matlock, England.

Th. Smith, Daisy Hill Nurseries, Newry, N. Ireland.

Underwood Nurseries, Hookstone, Woking, England.

Watson's Nurseries, Killiney, Co. Dublin, Ireland.

K. Wezelenburg & Zonen, Hazerswoude, Holland.

The earliest hybridizing is considered to have begun in 1884 when E. André of Normandy, France found a plant with flowers deep brown and yellow colored ('Andreanus'). About 15 years later this plant was crossed with *C. multiflorus*, resulting in *C. dallimorei*. Around the turn of the century many crosses were made, as well as seedling selections, giving rise to numerous new cultivars.

Cultivars and Hybrids

This list contains the true *C. scoparius* descendants (with yellow to brown, one or bicolored flowers) as well as the crosses with *C. multiflorus* (with carmine-red, pink-red, salmon colored and whitish flowers), which actually could be classified as *C. dallimorei* types. The following list compiled by color groups will greatly ease identification.

1. Cream-yellow to sulfur-yellow toned
   'Cornish Cream', 'Cornish Cream Improved', 'Den Ouden's Cream', 'Moonlight; (= 'Sulphureus' and 'Pallidus')

2. Gold-yellow, monochrome or with 2 yellow tones
   'Dukaat', 'Golden Cascade', 'Golden Sunlight', 'Luna', 'Newry Gold', 'Plenus', 'Prostratus', 'Pyramidalis', 'Variegatus'

3. Yellow with brown spots
   'Andreanus', 'Andreanus Splendens', 'Brightness', 'Butterfly', 'Dragonfly', 'Firefly', 'Fulgens', 'Mayfly'

4. Standard petal yellowish and lilac, wings and keel pink and red
   'Bumble Bee', 'Daisy Hill', 'Daisy Hill Splendens', 'Donard Seedling', 'Eastern Queen', 'Eileen', 'Geoffrey Skipwith', 'Gloria', 'Goldfinch', 'Hookstone', 'La Coquette', 'Lilac Time', 'Lord Lambourne', Mrs. Norman Henry', 'Newry Seedling', 'Palette', 'Queen Mary', 'Slieve Donard'

5. Monochrome red to deep brown
   'Burkwoodii', 'Darley Dale Red', 'Donard Gem', 'Dorothy Walpole', 'Hookstone Purple', 'Johnson's Crimson', 'Jubilee', "Killiney Burgundy', 'Killiney Red', 'Maroon', 'Peter Pan', 'Roter Favorit', 'Ruby', 'Windelsham Ruby'

6. Otherwise bi-colored types
   'C. E. Pearson', 'Criterion', 'Diana', 'Enchantress', 'Erlkoenig', 'Fairy Queen', 'Garden Magic', 'Hibernia', 'Killiney Bicolour', 'Killiney Salmon', 'Lady Moore', 'Maria Burkwood', 'Mrs. W. A. Slocock', 'Plantagenet', 'Radiance, 'Redstart', 'Red Wings'

'Andreanus'. Flowers gold-yellow, wings red-brown. Found in the wild in Normandy, France around 1884.

'Andreanus Splendens'. Branches widely arching; standard petal gold-yellow, wings velvety red, keel yellow, large flowers appearing about 10 days later than the otherwise similar 'Andreanus' and 'Firefly' (= 'Splendens'). ⊕

'Brightness'. Standard deep yellow, dorsal side more bronze, wings brown.

'Bumble Bee' (Und.). Standard cream-white, wings dark carmine.

'Burkwoodii' (Burkw.). Strong grower, branches light green; standard carmine-red, wings red-brown with a narrow gold border. Improved from 'Dorothy Walpole'. ⊕

'Butterfly' (Smith). Compact grower; standard deep yellow, wings yellow with a little light brown.

'C. E. Pearson' (Wats.). Standard orange, dorsal side reddish, wings red-brown, keel yellow. Surpassed by 'Goldfinch'.

'Cornish Cream' Standard whitish, wings and keel cream-yellow. Originated in Cornwall, England.

'Cornish Cream Improved' (Burkw.). As above but growth more narrowly upright. ⊕

'Criterion' (Burkw.). Strong grower; standard salmon-red, wings orange, large flowers. ⊕

'Daisy Hill' (Smith). Standard pure yellow, wings reddish, margin cream-yellow. Old cultivar.

'Daisy Hill Splendens' (Smith). Standard cream-yellow, wings a good red (= 'Newryensis'). ⊕

'Darley Dale Red' (Smith). Standard cream-white, dull carmine-red outside, wings dark brown-red to deep carmine-red, keel carmine with small yellow tips. Surpassed by 'Roter Favorit'.

'Den Ouden's Cream' (Den Ouden, Boskoop). Cream-yellow.

'Diana' (Burkw.). Low; standard ivory-white, keel likewise, wings gold-yellow.

'Donard Gem' (Donard). Ornamental; dark pink-red, flowers abundantly.

'Donard Seedling' (Donard). Standard gray-white, dorsal side lilac, wings lilac with bronze and yellow spots; dull colored.

'Dorothy Walpole' (Wats.). Standard velvety carmine, wings red-brown. Surpassed by 'Burkwoodii'.

'Dragonfly' (Smith). Compact grower; standard deep yellow, wings brown, hanging loosely, keel pure yellow.

'Dukaat' (Boskoop Experiment Station 1965). Dwarf, only about 50 cm, dense and stiffly upright; large flowers, standard light yellow, wings dark yellow, keel light yellow. Occasionally reverting back to the species with long branches which must be removed. F2—Selection of *C. praecox* × 'Burkwoodii'. ✧

'Eastern Queen' (Und.). Standard amber-yellow, wings deep red.

'Eileen' (Und.). Branches long nodding; standard whitish-yellow, large, wings pink-red.

'Enchantress' (Burkw.). Strong grower; flowers pink, red striped.

'Erlkoenig' (Julius Stahl, Rellingen). Selection from the 'Andreanus' seedlings, red-brown and yellow.

'Fairy Queen' (Burks.). Standard pale lilac, wings brown; early.

'Firefly' (Smith, around 1906). Standard yellow, wings yellow with brown spots; similar to 'Andreanus', but growth more upright. Old cultivar.

'Fulgens'. Standard amber-orange, dorsal side bronze, wings deep brown; late. Poor grower. ✧

'Garden Magic' (Burkw.). Upright growth; flowers mahogany-red and purple; late.

'Geoffrey Skipwith' (Burkw.). Ornamental habit, small flowers, standard dark lilac, wings red, fading to lilac; very early.

'Gloria'. Flowers dark pink, with light pink.

'Golden Cascade' (Smith). Standard and keel light yellow, wings dark yellow. Surpassed by 'Luna'.

'Golden Sunlight' (Wezelenb. 1929). Weak grower; monochrome light yellow, very large flowers. ✧

'Goldfinch' (Burkw.). Low grower and wide, foliage dense; standard yellow, dorsal side pink, wings dark red, keel gold-yellow. ✧

'Hibernia' (Wats.). Flowers crimson-orange. Obsolete.

'Hookstone' (Und.). Standard lilac, wings orange.

'Hookstone Purple' (Und.). Flowers large, monochrome purple, fading lighter.

'Johnson's Crimson' (Wats.). Ornamental growth habit, branches long arching; pure carmine and deep pink.

'Jubilee' (Smith & Sons). Standard carmine, wings bright red with some yellow, buds ilac.

'Killiney Bicolour' (Wats.). Standard pure yellow, wings deep orange.

'Killiney Burgundy' (Wats.). Monochrome burgundy-red.

'Killiney Red' (Wats.). Low; monochrome bright red. ✧

'Killiney Salmon' (Wats). Standard reddish salmon colored, wings orange. ✧

'La Couquette' (P. Lombarts 1965). Strong upright grower, tall; standard whitish, carmine-lilac outside, wings deep yellow with orange-brown stripes, keel light yellow. F2 seedlings from *C. praecox* 'Hollandia', but with no similarity in growth habit to *C. praecox*. ✧

'Lady Moore'. Standard light yellow, wings fire-red, very long and outspread, keel light brown. Seldom true to name. z7 ✧

'Lilac Time'. Growth compact, branches gray-green; standard lilac, wings somewhat lighter, early, small flowers.

'Lord Lambourne' (Wats.). Standard cream-white, outside somewhat lilac, wings carmine with a narrow gold border, keel light yellow. Seldom true to name. z7

'Luna' (R. Arnold, 1959). Strong grower, broad upright; standard light yellow, wings dark yellow, keel light yellow; large flowers, 10 days earlier than 'Golden Cascade. Plate 126. ✧

'Maria Burkwood'. Strong grower; standard carmine-red, wings coppery-brown; large flowers. ✧

'Maroon'. Wide growth; flowers monochrome deep brown.

'Mayfly (Smith). Standard yellow, wings yellow with a brown spot, somewhat lighter than 'Andreanus'.

'Moonlight'. Nodding growth habit; cream-white, large flowers (= 'Pallidus'; 'Sulphureus'). ✧

'Mrs. Norman Henry' (Burkw.). Habit ornamental; flowers soft lilac-pink, small, but very abundant.

'Mrs. W. A. Slocock' (Slocock). Standard deep purple, wings dark red with yellow.

'Newry Gold' (Smith). Growth narrowly upright; gold-yellow. Darkest cultivar. ✧

'Newry Seedling' (Smith). Standard light yellow, wings dull red-brown, large flowers, late. ✧

'Palette' (R. Arnold 1959). Strong grower, broad upright; standard yellow and white, outside light carmine-lilac, wings pure velvety red, keel yellow with lilac tones. Better than the similar 'C. E. Pearson'. Plate 126. ✧

'Peter Pan' (Burkw.). Flowers deep red, like 'Dorothy Walpole', but weaker grower, wide, only 30 cm high. ✧

'Plantagenet' (Burkw.). Standard pink-red wings light yellow. Resembles 'Garden Magic', but 2 weeks earlier.

'Plenus'. Flowers gold-yellow, double, small. Rare.

'Prostratus'. Growth procumbent; flowers gold-yellow, occasionally also somewhat reddish (= 'Pendulus').

'Pyramidalis' (Nijveldt 1959). Habit narrowly upright; flowers gold-yellow, very large (= 'Strictus'). ✧

'Queen Mary'. Standard cream-white, wings and keel brown.

'Radiance' (Burkw.). Compact growth; standard ivory-white, wings brown, keel white; strikingly colored. The title 'Radiant' is incorrect.

'Redstart' (Burkw.). Flowers salmon-red and cream yellow.

'**Red Wings**' (De Jong, Boskoop 1953). Standard and wings carmine-red, keel lilac. ✧

Roter Favorit' (R. Arnold, around 1959). Growth rather broad and high, branches stiff; standard light carmine-red above, outside carmine, wings deep velvety red, keel light carmine (= 'Red Favorite'). Flowers larger, if not quite so attractive as the otherwise similar 'Killiney Red'. ✧

'**Slieve Donard**' (Donard). Flowers light and dark pink.

'**Variegatus**'. Leaves white bordered, more gray-green.

'**Windlesham Ruby**'. Branches narrowly upright; flowers large, red. Breeder: L. R. Russel, Windlesham, Surrey, England. ✧

C. sessilifolius L. Shrub, upright, bushy, about 1m high, occasionally to 2 m, branches long, green, reddish when young, glabrous; leaves trifoliate, usually sessile on flowering branches, otherwise petiolate, leaflets obovate, light green, 8—20 mm long, glabrous; flowers 4—12, in erect terminal racemes, light yellow, flower stalk with 2—3 bracts, May—June; pods glabrous, curved at the base. BM 255; HM 1320; HF 2309; PEu 51; GV 43. S. Europe, N. Africa. 1864. z7 Fig. 300.

f. **leucanthus** (Dipp.) Zab. Flowers yellowish-white (= *C. lobelii* Tausch).

C. × spachianus Webb. (*C. stenopetalus × C. canariensis*). Evergreen shrub, 3—6 m high in its habitat (and in SW. England), very lush and dense foliage, young branches pubescent and somewhat channeled; leaves trifoliate, leaflets obovate, 1—2 cm long, usually rounded at the apex, base cuneate, nearly sessile, leaf petiole 6 mm long, dark green above and glabrous, with appressed silky pubescence beneath; flowers bright gold-yellow, in slender, 5—10 cm long racemes, rachis pubescent, corolla about 12 mm long, calyx with 5 awl-shaped teeth, with 2 larger than the others, all glossy pubescent, flower stalk 2 mm long, January—April; BM 4195 (= *C. racemosus* Nichols non Marnock). Around 1850. Often seen as a pot plant, but also as a cool greenhouse plant because of the early and long flowering period. z9 # ✧

'**Elegans**'. Strong grower; leaves larger, 4—5 cm long, more gray-green; the single flowers likewise larger, appearing in spring. Origin unknown but usually classified under *C. × spachianus*. Must be propagated by grafting on the latter. z8 ✧

'**Everestianus**'. Low grower; flowers darker yellow. RR 1873: 390 (= *C. everestianus* Carr.). Before 1862. z8 ✧

C. stenopetalus (Webb) Christ. Very similar to *C. maderensis* but the pubescence is silvery-gray (not brownish); shrub, to 6m high in its habitat; leaves trifoliate and petiolate, leaflets elliptic to lanceolate, 3— 18 mm wide, glabrous above or loose silky pubescent; flowers 10—26 in terminal racemes, yellow, standard more or less glabrous; pods narrow oblong, dense shaggy pubescent. BMns 327; BFCa 30; 168 (= *Teline stenopetala* Webb & Berth.). Canary Islands; La Palma, Hierro and Gomera. z9 # ✧

C. supinus L. Shrub, upright, rounded occasionally procumbent, about 0.5—1 m high and wide, branches narrowly upright or outspread with long and erect pubescence; leaves trifoliate, leaflets oblong-elliptic, obtuse, 2—2.5 cm long, more densely pubescent beneath; flowers in terminal heads, dull yellow, fading to brownish, flowers very abundantly, June—August; pods pubescent. HM 1321; HF 2313; VG 42 (= *C. capitatus* Scop.). Central and S. Europe. 1755. Valuable summer bloomer. z7 Plate 156; Fig. 300. ✧

C. supranubius (L. f.). O. Kuntze. Stiff, upright shrub with thick, blue-green, pruinose branches, pubescent at first, soon becoming glabrous, 2—3m high; leaves trifoliate, nearly sessile, leaflets linear, 4—8 mm long, 2—3 mm wide; flowers in dense fascicles at the ends of the previous year's branches, milk-white, pink toned, fragrant, calyx and stalk pubescent, calyx as long or shorter than the stalk, May. BM 8509; BFCa 172 (= *Spartocytisus supranubius* Webb & Berth.; *Spartium supranubius* L. f.; *Cytisus fragrans* Lam.). Canary Islands; Teneriffe and La Palma, in the mountains at 1700—2200 m. z9 ✧

C. tenera see: **Genista tenera**

C. tommasinii Vis. Deciduous shrub, upright, to about 50 cm, young branches very thin, appressed pubescent; leaves trifoliate, leaflets elliptic-lanceolate, 1.2—2.5 cm long, 2—6 mm wide, short acuminate, generally tapering to the base, middle leaflet usually obovate, with fine appressed pubesence beneath when young; flowers short stalked in terminal umbels, yellow, the solitary flowers appearing very narrow with the long, tubular, pubescent calyx (= *Chamaecytisus tommasinii* [Vis.] Rothm.). W. Yugoslavia and N. Albania, in the mountains, especially in the area around Kotor. z7 ✧

C. × versicolor (Kirchn.) Dipp. (*C. hirsutus × C. purpureus*). About 0.5 m high, growth broad or upright, branches long rod-like, somewhat shaggy pubescent; leaves trifoliate, leaflets obovate, appearing with the flowers, pubescent beneath, margin ciliate, about 2.5 cm long; flowers multicolored, standard usually whitish, wings yellowish, keel lilac-pink, grouped 1—3 together, May—June; pods pubescent. Originated around 1860. More attractive than *C. elongatus*. z6 Plate 157. ✧

'**Hillieri**' (Hillier 1933) (*C. versicolor × C. hirsutus* var. *hirsutissimus*). Low shrub, branches bowed outward; flowers large, yellow, with shades of light brown, later becoming more pink, May—June. ✧

C. × watererii see: **Laburnum watererii**

All the *Cytisus* species prefer full sun, southern exposures if possible, and light sandy to gravelly soils; they require however, a natural to acid soil to prevent yellowing and eventual death. It is sometimes advisable to cut them back after the flowering period.

Lit. Briquet, J.: Études sur les Cytises des Alpes Maritimes, comprenant un examen des affinités et une révision générale du genre *Cytisus*; 1894 ● Ulbrich, Benennung und Formenkreis von *C. scoparius*; in Mit. DDG 1921, 129—137 ●

Van de Laar, H.: *Cytisus* en *Genista*; in Dendroflora 8, 3—18, 1971; test reports with evaluations ● Vicioso, C.: Genisteas Espanolas II, 1—104; 26 Pl. in Bol. Inst. Forest. Invest. Exp. Madrid 72, 1955 ● Wyman, D.: Easy to grow, Brooms add color to any Garden; in American Nurseryman 6/1/1963, 9, 69—78.

DABOECIA D. Don. — ERICACEAE

Evergreen, ornamental, heather-like shrubs; leaves small, petiolate, densely arranged, sticky pubescent; flowers in long, terminal spikes in leaf axils at the ends of leafy twigs; corolla convex ovate, abscising, limb with reflexed lobes; calyx persistent, deep 4 lobed, stamens 8, enclosed, filaments flat, anthers narrow spear-shaped, pollen sacs drawn out to tubular ends; ovaries with 4 locules; fruit an oblong, ovate, 4 valved, many seeded capsule; seed rounded, densely warty. — In the coastal heath areas from Ireland to Portugal and in the Azores.

Although the genus is named for the Irish Saint Dabeoc and "Dabeocia" the correct spelling, the above given name will be retained by rules of priority.

Daboecia azorica Tutin & Warburg. Growth cushion-like, 15—20 cm high, branches erect at first, later procumbent; leaves more involuted than *D. cantabrica*, hairy above, white tomentose beneath; flowers ruby-red, in erect, very glandular racemes of 4—10 together, corolla oval-round, June—July. BMns 46; GC 133: 10. Mountains of Pico Island (the Azores), around 1000 m. 1929. z7—8 Fig. 303. # ⊕

D. cantabrica (Huds.) K. Koch. Procumbent, twiggy shrub, 25—30 cm high, occasionally somewhat taller, branches red-brown, glandular pubescent; leaves alternate, oval-oblong, 1 cm long, margin somewhat involuted, dark green and glossy above, white tomentose beneath; flowers in 10 cm long, loose racemes at the branch tips, corolla to 12 mm long, convex-cylindrical, purple, limb reflexed, July—September. HM 2638. Ireland to N. Spain. 1800. z6 Fig. 304. # ⊕

Mentioned here are only the most important of approximately 20 cultivars:

'Alba'. Growth more erect, to about 50 cm; leaves in long spikes protruding beyond the foliage, May—October. JRHS 67: 115. Found around 1820 in the Connemara region of Ireland.

'Alba Globosa'. To 50 cm high; flowers larger than 'Alba' and more globose, a very pure white, June—October. ⊕

'Atropurpurea' see: **'Purpurea'.**

'Bicolor'. To 50 cm high, young branches light green; leaves a fresh green; flowers sometimes purple, sometimes white, sometimes striped half and half on the same plant, June—October. (According to Jackman this plant will not thrive in soils with high iron content.) ⊕

'Hookstone Purple'. To 50 cm, strong grower; flowers an intense purple, larger than those of the species. ⊕

'Porter's Variety'. Only 30 cm high, compact, erect; flowers dark carmine, July—September. Requires much water in the growth period, otherwise flowers poorly.

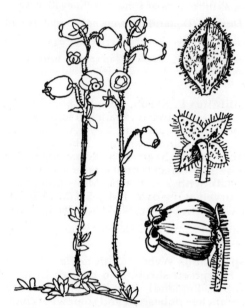

Fig. 303. *Daboecia azorica* (from Bot. Mag.)

Fig. 304. *Daboecia cantabrica* (from Dippel)

'Praegerae'. Low growing, to about 30 cm, quite dense, growth weak; flowers salmon-pink, without any purple tones in large, somewhat bowed spikes, July—September. Found in Connemara, Ireland by the wife of the botanist, Praeger. 1932. More tender than the other forms. z7—8. ⊕

'Purpurea'. About 50 cm high; leaves very dark green; flowers an intense purple, above the foliage, June—October (= 'Atropurpurea').

'Rosea'. 40—50 cm high; flowers pure pink, June—October (= 'Pallida').

'William Buchanan' (Possibly *D. azorica* × *C. cantabrica*).

Low, only about 20—25 cm high, but 40 cm wide; leaves glossy dark green; flowers carmine-pink, uninterrupted from June—October. Originated in the garden of W. Buchanan of Bearsden near Glasgow, Scotland. Before 1968. ⊕

Cultivated like *Erica*; in lime free, cool, moist soil; light winter protection is advised.

DAIS Royen ex L. — THYMELAEACEAE

Deciduous shrubs; leaves opposite, often clustered at the tips of the branches; flowers in terminal heads; corolla tube cylindrical, frequently bowed, stamens 10, in 2 circles of varying length, with only the longer or all exserted, styles also exserted. — 2 species in S. Africa and Madagascar, but only the following in culture.

Dais cotinifolia L. Deciduous shrub, 2—3 m high, in its habitat occasionally a small tree; leaves opposite or also alternate, elliptic, ovate or obovate, 3—7 cm long, 2—5 cm wide, acute on both ends, entire, bluish-green, glabrous, petiole 3 mm; flowers in erect, terminal umbels, 3—7 cm wide on thin, 4—5 cm long stalks, with about 15 individual flowers, these 15 mm wide, with 5 corolla lobes, soft lilac, tube 1.5 cm long,

fragrant, June—July. Bm 147; GC 127: 47; HTS 178. S. Africa. 1776. z9 Plate 157. ⊕

Beautiful shrub for a frost free climate; otherwise to be over-wintered in a cool greenhouse.

DANAE Med. — RUSCACEAE

Monotypic genus; erect, evergreen, many branched shrub; with cladodes for leaves; true leaves very small, scale-like; flowers bisexual, in terminal racemes; fruit a 1—3 seeded berry.— Syria to Persia.

Danae racemosa (L.) Moench. Evergreen, glabrous shrub, superficially resembling a bamboo or *Ruscus*, 0.5—1 m high; cladodes lanceolate, acuminate, short stalked, 6—10 cm long, both sides very glossy; flowers white, inconspicuous, June—July; fruits red, pea-size (= *Ruscus racemosa* L.). Transcaucasus, N. Persia, N. Syria. z7 Fig. 305. # ∅ ⌘

Fig. 305. *Danae racemosa*

DAPHNE L. — THYMELAEACEAE

Evergreen or deciduous shrubs; leaves alternate, occasionally opposite, short petioled, entire; flowers with simple perianth, colored, very fragrant, in terminal or axillary umbels, calyx tubular, with 4 erect lobes, stamens 8—10, in 2 rows (one over the other inside the tube), style very short or absent, stigma capitate, large; fruit a single seeded, fleshy or leathery drupe. — About 70 species in Europe, N. Africa, temperate and subtropical Asia, Australia and islands in the Pacific.

Outline of the Genus
(from Domke altered)

Section I. **Daphnanthes** C. A. Mey.
Leaves usually leathery and persisting several years, seldom abscising annually; flowers generally in terminal heads or racemes on the main branches, occasionally axillary on short branchs at the same time; main shoot

usually much forked or as a 'false axis' (composed of several year's growth and appearing as one shoot), seldom a single dominant stem;

Subsection 1. **Daphnanthoides**
Leaves usually leathery, nearly without exception persisting years, not punctate; main shoot annually terminating in a flower head, usually with bracts at the base;
a) Leaves tough, leathery; base of the inflorescence usually in a direct line with the main axis:
D. *acutiloba, bholua, japonica, odora, papyracea, sureil*
b) Leaves semi-leathery; base of inflorescence usually at sharp angle to the side:
D. × *mantensiana, retusa, tangutica*

Subsection 2. **Alpinae**
Leaves always abscising annually; main shoot annually terminating in a bractless flower head or remain-

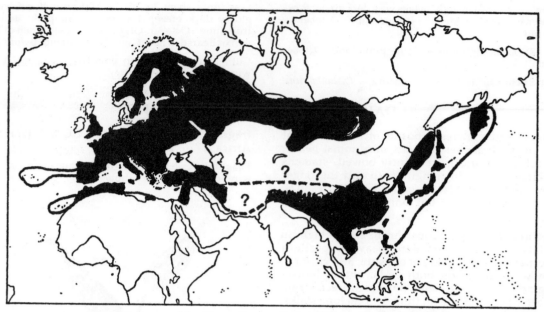

Fig. 306. Range of the Genus *Daphne* (from Domke, somewhat altered)

ing vegetative with inflorescences at the ends of short branches; main shoot developing into a multibranched or single branched cyme or racemose inflorescence:

> D. altaica, × burkwoodii, caucasica, giraldii, longilobata, sophia

Subsection 3.   Pseudo-mezereum

Leaves always abscising annually (often appearing after the flowers); main shoot annually terminating in a bractless flower head, never growing on vegatatively; main shoot always developing into a single branched cyme:

> D. kamtschatica, pseudo-mesereum

Subsection 4.   Oleoides

Leaves nearly always leathery and persisting several years, underside usually punctate; flower heads, racemes or panicles always without bracts; usually cymose (single or multibranched);

a) Flowers in heads, these eventually becoming racemose; evergreen:

> D. jasminea, kiusiana, kosaninii, oleoides

deciduous:

> D. alpina

b) Flowers in racemes or panicles:

> D. gnidioides, gnidium

Subsection 5.   Collinae

Leaves always leathery, underside not punctate; heads terminal and usually also axillary with large, silky pubescent bracts; branching usually cymose (single to multibranched);

a) Never with bracts between the individual flowers of the capitate inflorescence; calyx tube densely pubescent:

> D. collina, × hybrida, × neopolitana, sericea

b) Frequently with bracts between the flowers in the capitate inflorescence; calyx tube only sparsely pubescent:

> D. blagayana

Subsection 6.   Cneorum

Leaves leathery or semi-leathery, but always persisting for several years, weakly punctate beneath; flowers heads terminal, with narrow, membranous or leaf-like, glabrous or sparsely pubescent bracts; usually cymose branched (multi to single forked):

> D. arbuscula, cneorum, julia, petraea, striata, × thauma aurantiaca,

Section II   Laureola Spach

Leaves usually leathery and persisting for several years; flowers in racemes or heads in the leaf axils of the terminal growth; main axis always dominant throughout;

a) Leaves multi-annual:

> D. × houtteana, laureola, pontica

b) Leaves annual:

> D. glomerata

Section III.   Mezereum Spach.

Leaves annual; flowers in few flowered heads in the axils of the next-to-last growth; main axis always dominant:

> D. mezereum

Section IV.   Genkwa Benth. & Hook.

Leaves opposite, annual, appearing before the flowers; flowers axillary:

> D. genkwa

Daphne acutiloba Rehd. Evergreen, stocky shrub, 0.7—1.5 m high, young branches more or less erect bristly pubescent; leaves lanceolate to oblanceolate, acute at both ends, 5—10 cm long, glabrous, leathery; flowers greenish-white, calyx glabrous, lobes narrow elliptic, nearly without fragrance, 6 or more in stalked cymes, appearing in July (!); fruits red, attractive. ICS 3626. China; Hupeh, Szechwan. 1908. Very attractive. z6 #

D. alpina L. Deciduous, procumbent, 15—30 cm high shrub, branches pubescent; leaves scattered, clustered at the branch tips, elliptic-obovate, 1–4 cm long, gray-green, both sides pubescent, especially beneath; flowers white, fragrant, calyx pubescent outside, lobes acute lanceolate, 6–10 in terminal heads, May–June; fruits oblong, red. HM 2131; HF 978. S. Europe, mountains from the Pyrenees to N. Serbia, Asia Minor, N. Africa, in gravel and rock cracks; likes limestone. 1759. z5 Fig. 307.⊕

D. altaica Pall. Deciduous shrub, 30–75 cm high, branches glabrous; leaves narrow oblong, 3–6 cm long, dull green above, bluish beneath, glabrous; flower white, somewhat fragrant, calyx exterior slightly downy pubescent, 6–10 in terminal heads, May–June; fruits yellow-red, ovaries glabrous. BM 7388 (= *D. caucasica*); DL 3: 100. Altai Mountains, Dzungaria (W. China). 1796. z5 Plate 162.

var. *longilobata* see: **D. longilobata**

D. arbuscula Celak. Evergreen, procumbent shrub, resembling *D. cneorum*, but differing in the leaves clustered at the branch tips and with involuted margins, about 2 cm long; 15 mm long flowers, finely appressed pubescent outside, pink, with ovate-oblong lobes, from spring to autumn. HM 2139; JRHS 78: Pl. 3. Slovakia, N. Carpathians, Mount Murany. Before 1915. Prefers a light soil. z6 Plate 25. #⊕

D. aurantiaca Diels. Evergreen shrub, open growth, irregular, 50–120 cm high, branches glabrous; leaves oval, obovate to oblong, 1.5–2 cm long, acute, tapering to the base, curved, glabrous, somewhat bluish beneath; flowers orange-yellow, 2–4 in the leaf axils at the branch tips, calyx narrow, lobes broad ovate, very fragrant, May. BM 9313; ICS 3628. SW. China, Lichiang. 1910. Quite rare in cultivation. z6 # **A** ⊕

D. bholua Buch.-Ham. Evergreen shrub, often deciduous in cultivation, nearly 2 m high in its habitat, lower in cultivation, 'long-leggy', bark papery; leaves lanceolate to oblanceolate 5–10 cm long, apex obtuse acuminate, margin sinuate to indistinctly glandular dentate; flowers purple, fragrant, 3 or more in terminal and axillary fascicles, calyx silky pubescent outside, limb white with lilac-pink, nearly 2 cm wide, January–March; fruits ovate, black. BS 2: Pl. 2; SNp 134; HAL 80 (= *D. cannabina* Wall. pp.). Nepal, Bhutan, Assam, Sikkim. z8 # ⊕

D. blagayana Frey. Evergreen, procumbent shrublet, erratic growth habit, branches glabrous; leaves clustered at the branch tips, obovate-oblong, 3–4 cm long, glabrous; flowers yellowish-white, very fragrant, 10–20 in terminal heads, April—May, calyx tube 1.5 cm long, slightly pubescent outside; fruits reddish-white. BM 7579; HF 979; HM 2140; FS 2313. S. Austria and Yugoslavia, in light deciduous and coniferous forests. 1875. Avoid limestone! z6 Plate 161; Fig. 307. # **H ◑** ⊕

D. × burkwoodii Turrill (*D. caucasica* × *D. cneorum*). Deciduous shrub, 0.5–0.7 m high, dense and bushy, upright; leaves narrow oblong to oblanceolate, to 3 cm long and 7.5 mm wide, apiculate at the apex, deep green, persistent for some time; flowers white, eventually pale pink, very numerous, in large, terminal clusters, May—June, very fragrant, BMns 55. Originated before 1935 by R. Aireton, Longfleet Nurseries, Poole, Dorset, England; introduced into the trade by Burkwood & Skipwith. z6 Plate 161. ⊕

'Somerset'. Only slightly different; larger in all respects, 1.5–1.8 m; leaves oblanceolate, to 4 cm long, 12 mm wide, apex obtuse or mucronulate; corolla tube purple-pink, lobes

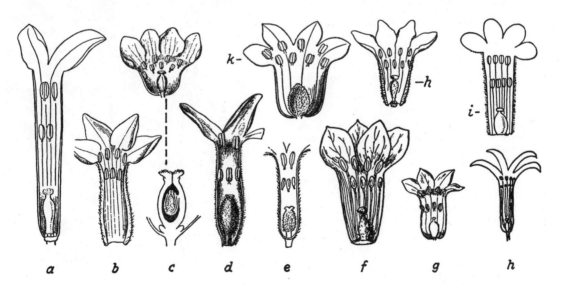

Fig. 307. **Daphne.** Flowers in longitudinal section, enlarged. a. *D. striata*; b. *D. blagayana*; c. *D. mezereum*; d. *D. alpina*; e. *D. cneorum*; f. *D. genkwa*; g. *D. laureola*; h. *D. pontica*; i. *D. petraea*; h. (left of i.) *D. caucasica*; k. *D. collina* (from Sibthorp, Ratzeburg, Jaub. & Spach, Bot. Mag., Jaquin, Reichenbach)

light pink. Bay 11: 1. Developed by Alfred Burkwood; introduced by Scott & Co.

'**Variegata'.** Leaves white bordered. HTS 180.

D. buxifolia see: **D. oleoides**

D. cannabina see: **D. bholua**

D. caucasica Pall. Deciduous shrub, to 1 m high; leaves lanceolate, 3−5 cm long, tough, blue-green beneath; flowers white, 5−20 in terminal heads, fragrant, May−June, calyx tube silky pubescent outside, ovaries slightly downy pubescent. BM 7388; DL: 101. Caucasus, Asia Minor. 1893. z6 Plate 161; Fig. 307.⊕

D. cneorum L. Garland Flower. Evergreen, procumbent, shrub to about 30 cm tall (usually lower), young branches pubescent; leaves packed at the branch tips, lanceolate, 1−2 cm long, with small tips, dark green above, blue-green beneath, glabrous; flowers carmine-pink, grouped 6−8 in terminal heads, very fragrant, calx lobes ovate, obtuse, May−June, often with sparse flowers again from August−September; fruits yellow-brown. BM 313; HM Pl. 187; HF 982. Mountains in Middle and S. Europe, on rocky, dry, chalky soil. 1752. z5 Fig. 307, 308. #⊕

For further information on the ecology and geography of this species, please refer to Ruffier-Lanche.

'**Alba'** Growth quite wide, low, cushion form; flowers waxy white. Found by Correvon in the Jura Mountains (France & Switzerland). White flowering form of 'Pygmaea'.

f. **arbusculoides** Tuzson. Growth more upright; leaf margins involute. W. Hungary, SE. Austrai, N. Yugoslavia, only on acid soils. Known since 1911. Presence in cultivation is not known.

'**Eximia'.** All parts only a third the size of the species; buds carmine, flowers deep pink. JRHS 86: 149.⊕

'**Major'.** To 30 cm high; flowers larger. Not as attractive as 'Eximia'.

var. **pygmaea** Stoder. In all parts smaller than the species; corolla tube rugose outside, flowering branches more or less lying flat on the ground, blooms well; Alps; also in the maritime Alps of SE. France. ⊕

'**Variegata'.** Leaves white variegated.

var. **verlotii** Meissn. Leaves linear-lanceolate, to 2.5 cm long; inflorescence loose, calyx tube longer, calyx lobes narrower than the species. SE. France. Found around Grenoble by Verlot in 1856.

D. collina Smith. Evergreen shrub, to 1 m high in its habitat, branches shaggy pubescent; leaves obovate oblong, 3−4 cm long; flowers 1 cm wide, purple, grouped 10−15 in heads, fragrant, May−June. BM 428; JRHS 82: 96. Italy, Asia Minor. 1752. z8 Plate 128; Fig. 307, 310. #⊕

var. *neopolitana* see: **D. neopolitana**

D. dauphinii see: **D. × hybrida**

D. delphinii see: **D. × hybrida**

D. fioniana see: **D. neopolitana**

D. genkwa S. & Z. Deciduous shrub, to 1 m high and wide in its habitat, densely branched, branches silky pubescent; leaves opposite (important for identification!), elliptic-oblong, 3−5 cm long, venation pubescent beneath; flowers axillary, violet, grouped 3−7 in short stalked fascicles, appearing before the leaves, April−May. FS 208; NK 17: 12; JRHS 87: 153; BMns 360. China, Korea; frequently planted in Japan. 1843. The most beautiful species of the genus. z6 Plate 162; Fig. 307. H◐⊕

D. fortunei not as wide as a typical plant of the above species, with somewhat larger flowers. Pl. 627.

D. giradlii Nitsche. Deciduous shrub, to 50 cm high, quite glabrous; leaves sessile, oblanceolate, 3−6 cm long, obtuse or acute, with small tips at the apex; flowers gold-yellow, 3−8 in terminal heads, small, glabrous, calyx lobes outspread, May; fruits red. BM 8732; ICS 3631. NW. China, Kansu, Shansi. 1911. z3 Plate 160.⊕

D. glomerata Lam. Evergreen dwarf shrub about 25 cm high; leaves densely clustered at the branch tips, obovate-oblong to lanceolate, 2.5−4 cm long, generally tapering to the base, glabrous and glossy; flowers 2−6 in axillary racemes, light pink, calyx, 12 mm long, glabrous, 12 mm wide at the limb, June−July; fruits pink. SH 2: 267. Asia Minor, Caucasus, Transcaucasus. Very rare in cultivation. z6 Fig. 309. #⊕

D. gnidioides Jaub. & Spach. Upright, evergreen shrub with thick, long, erect branches, young branches brown pubescent; leaves oblong-lanceolate,

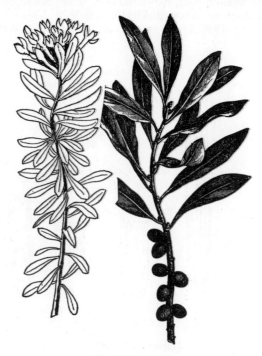

Fig. 308. **Daphne**
Left *D. cneorum*, right *D. mezereum* (from Kern)

Fig. 309. *Daphne glomerata* (from Jaub.)

long acuminate and pungent, erect, sessile, blue-green, 2.5—4 cm long, 5—7 mm wide, tough and leathery; flowers pink, 5—8 in terminal heads and also grouped 2—3 in the axils of the upper leaves (!). Eastern Aegean region and S. Anatolia (Turkey). Known since 1850. z8 #

D. gnidium L. Deciduous, upright shrub, 0.5—1 m high, branches brown, pubescent when young, foliage dense, along the entire length; leaves lanceolate, 2.5—5 cm long, glabrous, sharply acuminate; flowers white to a weak pink, few in terminal fascicles, July—September; fruits small, red. HM 2125; PSw 27. S. Europe, Asia Minor, N. Africa. 1797. z8 Plate 160.

D. × houtteana Lindl. & Paxt. (*D. laureola × D. mezereum*). Growth habit and flowers similar to *D. mezereum*, but leaves tougher, nearly leathery and semi-evergreen, blackish-red (!); flowers lilac-red, grouped 2—5 in fascicles, April. FS 592 (= *D. mezereum atropurpurea* Dipp.). Before 1850. z6 ⊕

D. × hybrida Cov. (*D. collina × D. odora*). Evergreen, bushy shrub, 0.7—1 m high; leaves ovate to oblong, 3—7 cm long, acute, glabrous and glossy above, venation finely pubescent beneath; flowers purple-red, very fragrant, 8—15 in terminal heads, good fragrance, calyx tube pubescent outside, September—October. BR 1177; BMns 320 (= *D. dauphinii* Hort.; *D. delphinii* Hort.). Before 1827. z6 Fig. 310. # ⊕

D. japonica S. & Z. Evergreen shrub, 1.5 m high in its habitat, branches glabrous, usually in whorls; leaves oblong-lanceolate, 3—7 cm long or longer, apex obtuse, glabrous, glossy above; flowers 8—12 in axillary and (!) terminal fascicles, outside usually purple-pink, inside white, glabrous, calyx lobes ovate, fragrant, November-January. NF 9: 274. Japan, China. Resembling *D. odora*, but seldom found in cultivation and with a differently arranged inflorescence. z8 # ⊕

D. jasminea Sibth. & Sm. Small evergreen shrublet, to 30 cm, much branched, branches short, twisted, procumbent or ascending, with many elevated leaf scars, young branches glabrous; leaves oblong-obovate, mucronate, 8—11 mm long, 1.5—3 mm wide, glabrous; flowers in terminal fascicles of 2—3, surrounded by very small, distinctly pubescent, abscis-

ing bracts, corolla tube purple outside, opening white, very fragrant, sepals triangular, acute. SE. Greece. Cultivated in England. Not identical with *D. jasminea* Griseb. and *D. oleoides* var. *jasminea* Meissn. z9 # ⊕

D. jezoensis see: **D. kamtschatica**

D. julia Kozo-Polianski. Evergreen shrub, very closely related to *D. cneorum*, similarly low growing, but stiffly erect and very wide growing; leaves narrower than *D. cneorum*; flowers to 25 in dense heads. Found only in a very precisely defined area NW to SW of Woronesch (which is abut 400 km south of Moscow), in low rolling steppes on alkaline soil (!). Introduced into England 1960. z6 #

D. kamtsachatica Maxim. Deciduous shrub, low, to 40 cm high, densely branched; leaves oblong-lanceolate, acute; flowers yellow, in axillary fascicles. NE. Asia. As yet not in cultivation. z6

var. **jezoensis** (Maxim.) Ohwi. Evergreen shrub, about 0.5 m high, erect; leaves oblong-obovate, 3—7 cm long, obtuse, tapering to the base; flowers yellow, in axillary clusters, calyx lobes acute ovate, fragrant, March—April. BMns 613 (= *D. jezoensis* Maxim.). Japan. #

D. kosaninii (Stoyanov) Stoyanov. Very closely related to *D. oleoides*, but taller, bark reddish, leaves smaller, flowers deep pink, sepals shorter. SW. Bulgaria, in the mountains. Possibly a hybrid between *D. oleoides* and *D. cneorum*. #

D. kiusiana Miq. Evergreen shrub, very closely related to *D. odora*, but smaller in all respects; leaves alternate, oblong, tapering to the base, 7—12 cm long; flowers several in densely compact heads, white, corolla tube 6 mm long, finely pubescent outside, April (= *D. odora* var. *kiusiana* [Miq.] Keissler). S. Japan. z8 #

D. laureola L. Evergreen, upright shrub, 0.5—1 m high, quite glabrous; leaves oblanceolate, 5—8 cm long, dark green and glossy above, somewhat lighter beneath; flowers yellowish-green, 5—10 in sessile to short stalked racemes, slightly fragrant, March—May; fruits ovate, blue-black. HM 2126; HF 977; PEu 74. W. to SE. Europe, Sicily, Corsica, N. Africa, Azores. 1561. z7 Plate 162; Fig. 307. # ⊕ ∅

ssp. **philippi** (Gren. & Godr.) Rouy. Procumbent, 20—40 cm high; leaves smaller than those of the species, yellow-green, but outside often somewhat violet, April—May. PSw 26 (= *D. philippi* Gren. & Godr.). Pyrenees. 1894. z7

D. laureola var. *philippi × D. cneorum* see: **D. 'Rosetii'**

D. longilobata (Lecomte) Turrill. Very closely related to *D. altaica*, but with evergreen leaves, young leaves especially pubescent at the tips; shrub to 1.5 m high, branches light green with fine pubescence, especially dense on the younger parts; leaves narrow oblanceolate to linear-elliptic, 5—9 cm long, 1.2—1.7 cm wide, acute; flowers 4—6 at the branch tips, yellowish-white, the 4 lanceolate lobes each 7 mm long; fruit broad ellipsoid, 1 cm thick, scarlet-red. BMns 344; ICS 3627 (= *D. altaica* var. *longilobata* Lecomte). SE. Tibet; China, Yunnan. 1947. z6 #

D. × mantensiana T. M. C. Taylor & F. Vrugtman (*D. burkwoodii* × *D. retusa*). Evergreen shrub, to 70 cm high, densely branched, young branches with dense and fine frizzy hair; leaves oblong to narrow obovate, 3–3.5 cm long, generally tapering to the base, shallow, but distinctly emarginate, tiny white punctate beneath; flowers 3 or more in terminal fascicles, very fragrant, purple outside, inside white with a purple tone, calyx tube 7 mm long, softly pubescent, calyx lobes oval-lanceolate, flowering from spring to fall; fruits as yet unknown. Brought into the trade in 1953 by Mantens Nursery, White Rock, B.C., Canada. z6 # ✧

'Manten'. The original clone.

D. mazelii see: **D. odora**

D. mezereum L. Deciduous shrub, about 1 m high, branches thick, glabrous, very flexible; leaves thin, oblong-lanceolate, 3–8 cm long, bright green, gray-green beneath, often clustered at the branch tips; flowers pale carmine-red to purple-pink, usually 3 in sessile clusters along the branches, very fragrant, March–April; fruits red, poisonous. HM Pl. 187; HF 976; BMns 272; GPN 596–597. Europe, Asia Minor, Caucasus, Siberia. 1561. z5 Fig. 307, 308. ✧

Including the following varieties and cultivars:

f. **alba** (West.) Schelle. Growth usually narrowly upright, branches thicker; leaves lighter green; flower cream-white; fruits light yellow. Found in the wild and comes true from seed. ✧

'Autumnalis'. Flowers about like the species, but appearing in October and lasting to February. Must be grafted; fruitless. ✧

'Bowles' White' (E. A. Bowles 1947). Presumably developed from seed of 'Paul's White'; fruits yellow. Even so it generally comes true from seed; pure white.

'Grandiflora'. Shrub, to 2 high; flowers larger and darker, often appearing in October (= f. *maxima* Hort.). Several selections have been developed in Boskoop, Holland, such as 'Jongenburger', 'Kromhout', 'Lapidoth', 'Lutterveld', 'Wezelenburg'. All have been surpassed by 'Rubra Select', introduced in 1953. ✧

'Paul's White' (Paul). Flowers pure white; rather true from seed. Known since 1910, probably no longer cultivated. ✧

'Plena'. Flowers double. Only a white one is known.

'Ruby Glow'; (J. van Klaveren WZ). Growth broad and upright; flowers dark violet-red (HCC 031/1), very large, numerous. This is not a clone, rather a population of seedlings, from which the darkest and largest flowering plants have been selected. ✧

'Variegata'. Leaves white variegated. Before 1865.

D. × neopolitana Lodd. Evergreen shrub, bushy, upright, 0.5–0.7 m high, branches pubescent; leaves oblanceolate, 2–4 cm long, obtuse or acute, glabrous and glossy above, bluish and somewhat pubescent at the base beneath; flowers pink-lilac, in terminal heads, calyx white pubescent outside, March–June. BS 2:16; BR 822 (= *D. collina* var. *neapolitana* [Lodd.] Lindl.; *D. fioniana* Hort.). Often grown as a pot plant, also tolerates alkaline soils. z8 # ✧

The botanical origin is as yet unclear; it is either a natural hybrid between *C. cneorum* and *D. oleoides* or *D. collina*, or a variety of *D. collina*.

D. odora Thunb. Evergreen shrub, to 2 m high in its habitat, upright, branches smooth; leaves oblong-lanceolate, 5–8 cm long, acute, glabrous, densely arranged; flowers around 10 together in terminal (!, see *D. japonica*), 1.5 cm wide heads, calyx tube white,

Fig. 310. **Daphne.** Left *D. hybrida*; middle *D. odora*; right *D. collina* (from Paxton, Bot. Reg.)

often turning reddish outside, silky pubescent, very strong fragrance, January—March. BM 1587; SH 2: 269a; HTS 183. China, Japan. 1771. Once used as a pot plant, still recommended today. z8 Fig. 310. # ⊕

'Alba'. Flowers white. ⊕.

'Aureo-marginata'. Leaves quite narrow, yellowish-white bordered. Much more common than the green leaved type. z8 Plate 162.

var. *Kiusiana* see: **D. kiusiana**

'Mazelii'. Only slightly different from the species in habit, foliage and flower, although the latter not only terminal, but also in axillary clusters along the branches, from November on, flowering throughout the winter (= *D. mazelii* Carr.) Introduced from Japan around 1866 by E. A. Mazel of Montsauve, France, very rare in cultivation today. z8 # ⊕

'Rose Queen'. Leaves totally green; flowers dark pink-red, in dense heads. z8 ⊕

D. oleoides Schreb. Evergreen, upright shrub, much branched, to 0.7 m high in its habitat, 30 cm high in cultivation, branches gray pubescent when young; leaves oblanceolate, 2—3 cm long, acute, tapering to the base, underside silky pubescent at first, later more or less punctate, smooth above; flowers 3—6 in terminal heads, always white (not pink, as stated by Rehder & Bean), pubescent outside, fragrant, calyx lobes ovate to lanceolate, acute; fruits red, small. NF 10: 225 (= *D. buxifolia* Vahl). SE. Spain to Asia Minor, Afghanistan, Himalaya. 1815. Plants with reddish flowers are normally not true. z8 # ⊕

D. papyracea Wall. ex Steud. Evergreen, upright shrub, closely related to *D. bholua*, to 3 m high in its habitat, bark paper-like, young branches bristly pubescent, brown; leaves elliptic to oblanceolate, obtuse at the apex (!), 10—15 cm long, 1.5—3 cm wide, rather glabrous; flowers, around 12 in terminal clusters, white and without fragrance (!), bud scales persistent, flowering from January on; fruits red, obovate. ICS 3633. N. India, Nepal; Assam. z8 # ⊕

D. petraea Leybold. Dwarf evergreen shrub, to 15 cm high, much branched, branches somewhat pubescent; leaves clustered, sessile, lineal-spathulate, 8—12 mm long, glabrous, leathery; flowers pink, 2—3 or more, pubescent, fragrant, June. HM 2138 (= *D. rupestris* Facchini). S. Tyrol, on vertical rock walls in narrow cracks. 1894. Needs abundant moisture. z6 Fig. 307, 311. # ⊕

'Grandiflora'. Plants somewhat stronger growing; flowers somewhat larger, intensely colored. NF 7: 93. ⊕

D. philippi see: **D. laureola**

D. pontica L. Evergreen shrub, to 80 cm high, branches glabrous; leaves lanceolate-elliptic to obovate, 2.5—7 cm long, acute, tapering to the base, leathery, glossy green, short stalked; flowers usually 2 on a common stalk, greenish-yellow, in the leaf axils of the upper leaves, fragrant, May. BS 2: 20; BM 1282. Asia Minor. 1752. Dislikes alkalinity! z6 Plate 158; Fig. 307. # **H ◐** ⊕

Fig. 311. *Daphne petraea* (from Reichenbach)

D. pseudo-mezereum Gray. Deciduous shrub, usually somewhat procumbent; leaves oblanceolate, 5—7 cm long, obtuse or acute, becoming narrower at the base, short stalked, glabrous; flowers in axillary clusters with the leaves, greenish- or yellowish-white, calyx tube glabrous, without fragrance, March—April; fruits red. Central Japan. 1905. z6 ⊕

D. retusa Hemsl. Evergreen shrub, densely branched, about 0.7 m high, young branches yellow-green with strigose pubescence; flowers in dense, terminal heads to 7 cm wide, calyx tube purple-pink outside, white with a trace of pink inside, May—June; fruits red. ICS 3634; BM 8430. W. China. 1901. Unpretentious, easily cultivated species, however it dislikes alkalinity! z6 Plate 158, 159. # ⊕

D. 'Rosetii' (*D. laureola* ssp. *philippi* × *D. cneorum*). Natural hybrid; growth dense and rather globose, to 0.6 m high, branches more woody than on the ssp. *philippi* and light brown; leaves narrow oblanceolate, intermediate between the parents, 1.5—3 cm long, acute, arranged very tightly on the stem, sessile or short petioled; flowers dull brown-pink. Found in the Pyrenees by M. Rosset, Head Gardener at Correvon, Geneva. 1927. (The spelling ''Rosettii'' is incorrect.)

D. sericea Vahl. Small evergreen shrub, 0.2 to 0.4 m high, young branches silky pubescent or glabrous; leaves lanceolate to more spathulate, 1—3 cm long, acute or obtuse, glossy and smooth above, silky pubescent beneath; flowers 3—8 in terminal heads, pink-red, calyx tube silky pubescent, calyx lobes broad ovate, May—June. Eastern Mediterranean region. Seldom seen in cultivation but very attractive. z8 # ⊕

D. sophia Kalenichenko. Deciduous shrub, to 60 cm high, branches thin; leaves obovate-oblong, 2.5–7 cm long, with small tips, tapering to the base, smooth and rather glossy above, blue-green beneath; flowers 6–15 in terminal clusters with bracts, white to yellowish, fragrant, calyx with scattered, white hairs, lobes acute ovate, May–June; fruits red. Central Russia. 1895. Difficult to cultivate. z5

D. striata Tratt. Dwarf evergreen shrublet, usually quite procumbent, very similar to *D. cneorum*, but differing in the open habit and the calyx tube which is glabrous outside, carmine-pink colored and usually lightly striped; flowers 8–12 in heads, June to July. HM 2137; HF 981. W. Alps to the Carpathian Mountains. 1827. Very difficult to cultivate. z5 Fig. 307. # ✿

'Alba'. Flowers white, otherwise like the species. Very rare and difficult in cultivation.

D. sureil Smith & Cave. Deciduous to semi-deciduous shrub, upright, to nearly 2 m high in its habitat, young branches densely white tomentose, bark later becoming smooth, brown; leaves lanceolate to oblong, 5–7 cm long, long acuminate, tapering to the base, underside tomentose when young or also glabrous; flowers 10–20 in loose, terminal and axillary heads, greenish, later white, fragrant, pubescent outside; fruits orange-red. BM 9297; HAL 102. Himalaya, Sikkim, S. Assam. 1925. Rare in cultivation. z8 ✿

D. tangutica Maxim. Evergreen shrub, about 1 m high, young branches thick, gray bristly pubescent at first; leaves elliptic-oblong, 3–8 cm long, glabrous, rather glossy above; flowers in terminal heads to 5 cm wide, purple-pink outside, inside lighter, fragrant, stigma soft pubescent, March–April; fruits red. BM 8855; JRHS 78: Pl. 5; ICS 3635 (= *D. wilsonii* Rehd.). China, Kansu. z6 Plate 164. # ✿

Known in 2 forms:

a) Flowers purple-pink, leaves dark green (Farrer No. 271);

b) Flowers cream-white, leaves pale green. Rare in cultivation (Farrer No. 535).

D. × thauma Farr. (*D. petraea* × *D. striata*). Natural hybrid. Low shrublet, evergreen; leaves linear-lanceolate to oblanceolate, glabrous; flowers in terminal heads, bright purple-pink, resembling *D. striata*. GC 52: 22 (1912). S. Tyrol, found on Cima Tombea. 1910. Very rare. #

D. wilsonii see: **D. tangutica**

The cultivation of the most popular species (*D. mezereum, burkwoodii, laureola, retusa*, etc.) is not difficult; the others are however, generally more touchy and must be carefully tended in a rock garden or "alpine house". Nearly all the European species prefer humus, alkaline soil and abundant moisture, winter as well as summer; but many also thrive in lime free soil. The more tender species often bloom in winter and have very fragrant flowers.

Lit. Amsler, A. M.: *Daphen*; in Journ. RHS **78**, 5–18, 1953 ● Domke, W.: Untersuchungen ueber die systematische und geographische Gliederung der Thymelaeaceen nebst einer Neubeschreibung ihrer Gattungen; in Bibl. Bot. **27**, III, 1–151; 7 plates, 5 maps; Stuttgart 1934 ● Hodgkin, E.: Daphnes; in Jour. RHS **86**, 481–488, 1961 ● Von Keissler, K.: Die Arten der Gattung *Daphne* aus der Sektion *Daphnanthes*; in Bot. Jahrb. 1898, 29–125 ● Mol. J. L.: *Daphne*; in Jaarb. Ned. Dendr. Ver. **19**, 53 to 70, 1953 ● Nitsche, W.: Beitraege zur Kenntnis der Gattung *Daphne*; 1907 ● Ruffier-Lanche, R.: Some variations of *Daphne cneorum*; in Bull. Alp. Gard. Soc. **26**, 65–68, 1958 ● Stenzel, A.: Immergruene *Daphne*-Arten; in Jahrb. D. Rhod. Ges. 1939, 25–32 ● Taylor, T. M. C., & F. Vrugtman: *Daphne × mantensiana* cv. 'Manten' — validation of the name of a hybrid; Baileya **12**, 39–42, 1964 ● Vrugtman, F.: Origin of *Daphne × burkwoodii* and cv. 'Somerset', a source of confusion; Baileya **11**, 1–3, 1963.

DAPHNIPHYLLUM Bl. — DAPHNIPHYLLACEAE

Evergreen shrubs or small trees; leaves alternate, long petioled, simple, pinnate venation, usually blue-green beneath, without stipules; flowers dioecious, without petals, in axillary racemes; male flowers with 5–18 stamens; fruit a single seeded drupe. — 25 species in tropical Asia.

Daphniphyllum humile Maxim. Broad shrub, densely branched, 30–50 cm high; leaves elliptic to obovate, 5–12 cm long, glossy green above, blue-green beneath; flowers inconspicuous. SH 2:37g (= *D. jezoense* Bean; *D. macropodum* var. *humile* [Maxim.] Rosenth.). Japan, Yezo. 1879. Groundcover for mild areas. z8 Plate 163. # ◐

D. macropodum Miq. Tall shrub, also a tree in its habitat, to 15 m, very densely branched, young branches thick, blue-green to reddish; leaves oblong, 8–20 cm long, new growth light green, later deep green above, bluish-white beneath, petiole and midrib red, with 12–17 vein pairs; flowers greenish, May–June; fruits black, 1 cm long. KIF 3: 32 (= *C. glaucescens* Hort. non Bl.). Japan, Korea, China. 1879. Looks like a large leaved *Rhododendron*, but without the attractive flowers. z7 Plate 163. # ∅

'Variegatum'. Leaves with irregularly wide cream-yellow markings, occasionally to the midrib. Very pretty, but somewhat more difficult to grow than the species. z8 Plate 163. # ∅

f. **viridipes** Ohwi. Leaf petioles always green, not red. Japan. z7 # ∅

Attractive shrubs of *Rhododendron*-like appearance, but flowers not particularly attractive; *D. macropodum* in a wooded area of the Dortmund Botanic Garden with no winter protection has thus far not sustained any frost damage. Cultivated like *Rhododendron*.

DASYLIRION Zucc. — AGAVACEAE

Evergreen plants, closely related to *Nolina*; stem upright or ascending, thick and stout; leaves very long, narrow lanceolate, flat or slightly concave, dentate; flowers dioecious, small, campanulate, in very dense, narrow, about 1.5 mm long panicles on a 2—3 m tall shaft; fruit a triangular, 1 chambered capsule; seeds globose to ovate. — 18 species in the dry areas of SW. USA and Mexico.

Key to the Mentioned Species

Leaves flat and prickly on the margin;
    Leaves brown and shredded at the apex;
        Leaves green:
            D. acrotrichum
        Leaves gray-green:
            D. serratifolium
    Leaves not shredded at the tips;
        D. glauchophyllum
Leaves more or less 4 sided in cross section, margin not prickly, without shredded tips:
    D. longissimum

Dasylirion acrotrichum Zucc. Stem short and thick, to 1 m or more; leaves very numerous, in a dense cluster, green, linear, drooping, to 1m long and 1 m wide, margins densely covered with small, somewhat forward-curving prickles, sharp and brown at the tips, leaf apex shredded; inflorescence 2—4 m high, flowers white; fruit capsule rounded-cordate. BM 5030; FS 1448 (= *C. gracile* Planch.). Mexico. 1851. The most frequently cultivated species. z9 # ⟡ ∅

D. glaucophyllum Hook. Developing a stem; leaves in dense rosettes, bluish-green, to over 1 m long, 12 mm wide, margins with fine, yellowish sharp prickles; flowers yellowish-white, inflorescence 3—5 m high; fruit ellipsoid. BM 5041. Eastern Middle Mexico. 1858. z9 # ⟡

D. longissimum Lem. Stem thick, 1 m high, old stems to 2 m high; leaves very numerous, dull green, 1.2—1.8 m long, generally acuminate, 6 mm wide, radiating in all directions and therefore developing into a regular, globose plant, upper and undersides nearly angular convex, 4 sided in cross section; inflorescence 2—4 m high; fruit 6—9 mm long, slightly notched. BM 7749; GF 1887: 280; PBl 1:307 (= *D. quadrangulatum* S. Wats.). E. Mexico. 1887. z9 # ⟡ ∅

D. serratifolium (Karw. ex Schult. f.) Zucc. Stem short and thick; leaves 0.7—1 m long, about 2.5 cm wide, rough, shredded at the apex, margins with many large prickles about 2 cm apart, finely dentate in between; flowers white, in very dense, about 30 cm long panicles (= *D. laxiflorum* Baker). SE. Mexico. z9 Plate 164. # ∅

Easily cultivated plants for dry areas, the flowers less attractive than those of Yucca; will tolerate some frost if in dry soils.

DATURA L. — SOLANACEAE

Annual plants or perennials, shrubs or small trees; leaves alternate, large, simple, entire or wavy dentate; flowers large, solitary, erect or pendulous, usually white, but also more or less lilac, occasionally red or yellow, funnelform, throat broad, usually very fragrant; calyx usually 5 toothed, with persistent margin or totally abscising or splitting open lengthwise; stamens 5; fruit a large, 2 chambered capsule, usually thorny or prickly, dry and dehiscing with 4 valves at the apex or also fleshy and irregularly dehiscing. — About 25 species in the warmer regions of the earth, the 10 species of the subgenus *Brugmansia* Pers. are indigenous to tropical America. Many perennial types are confused in cutivation and unfortunately, also in the botanical literature, although they are easily distinguished by flower and, as mentioned here, by the form of the calyx. All species poisonous.

Key to the Mentioned Species

Calyx sheathlike; the only lobe with or without a long horn-like tip;
    Corolla white;
        Calyx persistent, surrounding the ripe fruit; corolla limb without open sinuses between the lobes;
            D. candida
        Calyx completely abscising, the horn-like tips quite short; corolla limb with open sinuses between the lobes
           Leaves entire, glabrous, flowers not over 17 cm long, calyx without horn-like tips:
            D. arborea
            Leaves angular lobed, pubescent; the horn-like tips of the calyx nearly as long as the corolla:
            D. cornigera
    Corolla orange:
        D. rosei
Calyx tube form; with two or more distinct teeth;
    Calyx persistent; fruits ovate; flowers reddish and yellow:
        D. sanguinea
    Calyx completely abscising; fruits spindle form; flowers white (some cultivars also pink):
        D. suaveolens
    Calyx abscising; fruit acute ovate; flowers orange-yellow:
        D. aurea

Datura arborea L. Shrub or small tree, 3—6 m high; leaves acute ovate, entire, glabrous; flowers white, not over 17 cm long, corolla limb with sinuses open and incised between lobes, musk scented, calyx sheathlike, without horn-like drawn out tip, completely abscising, petiole pubescent; fruits ovate. NH 1966: 380; Bai 4: 8. Andes of Peru and Chile. 1813. Rare in cultivation and usually confused with *D. suaveolens* or other species. z9 ⟡

Presumably included here is a form present in cultivation with 20—30 cm long, gold-yellow flowers, calyx sectioned, more than half as long as the corolla, totally abscising. RH

1908: 302 (as *D. aurea*). Plate 127.

D. aurea (Lagerheim) Saff. Shrub or small tree, to 6 m, young branches light green, with white erect pubescence; leaves broad elliptic, 20–50 cm long, 12–25 cm wide, margins sinuate, blue-green beneath, venation glandular; flowers pendulous, tubular-funnelform, 18–23 cm long, light green outside, with traces of orange and green stripes, limb a good orange inside, the nearly semicircular lobes with a 5–7 cm long, caudate-like tip, calyx tubular, with 5 ovate, erect, 2 cm long teeth, abscising; fruits narrow ovate, acute, 6–11 cm long, 2.5–4 cm wide, yellowish-brown. BMns 484. Columbia. z9 ⊕

D. candida (Pers.) Saff. Flowers white, 20 cm long, hanging vertically, corolla limb without open sinuses and not incised between the lobes, the caudate tip usually curled into a ring on the upper side, calyx persistent, sectioned, surrounding the ripe fruit, anthers distinct, stalk pubescent; fruit cylindrical. NH 1966: 382; Bai 4: 9 (= *Brugmansia candida* Pers.). Peru, Chile. z9 Fig. 312. ⊕

D. cornigera Hook. Shrub, to 3 m, white pubescent; leaves usually clustered at the branch tips, ovate, long acuminate, angular lobed, pubescent; flowers pendulous, funnelform, striped, white, very fragrant at night, limb outspread, lobes drawn out to a long erect or reflexed apex, calyx sectioned, the horn-like tips often nearly as long as the corolla tube. NH 1966: 381; DRHS 641; BM 4252. Mexico. z9 ⊕

Frequently found in cultivation, often with 2 or 3 corollas inside one another (= *D. cornigera* 'Knightii').

D. rosei Saff. Young branches with erect white hairs; leaves with dense, soft pubescence, margins angular dentate; flowers tubular, 15–20 cm long, pubescent outside, limb red, tube orange to yellow-orange outside, green along the veins, calyx sectioned, with only 1 lobe, terminated in a small, horn-like tip, persistent. Bai 4: 1. Ecuador. The epithet *rosei* honors the botanist J. N. Rose. z9 ⊕

D. sanguinea Ruiz & Pav. Shrub, 1.5–2.5 m high; leaves usually clustered at the branch tips, oval-lanceolate, to 15 cm long, entire and undulate or somewhat sinuate; flowers tubular, to 25 cm long, pendulous, glabrous, orange-red and yellow, without fragrance, yellow along the corolla veins, calyx ovate, somewhat inflated, persistent, with 2 or more distinct teeth; fruits ovate, smooth. FS 1883; NH 1966: 385; 386; Bai 4: 10. Peru. z9 Plate 164; Fig. 312. ⊕

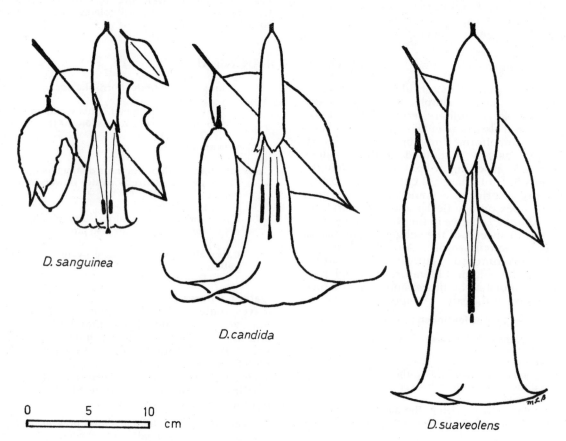

D. sanguinea

D. candida

D. suaveolens

0 5 10 cm

Fig. 312. *Datura*. Flowers, leaves and (left) a fruit (from M. L. Bristol)

D. suaveolens Humb. & Bonpl. Angels Trumpet. Shrub, 3—4 m high; leaves oval-oblong, entire, 6—12 cm long, base somewhat asymmetrical; flowers white, nodding, to 30 cm long, very fragrant at night, calyx inflated, completely abscising, with 5 short, triangular, 1—2 cm long teeth, anthers clinging together (!), fruit spindle-shaped, 12 cm long when ripe, 2 cm thick, brown and dry, on a 7 cm long stalk. NH 1966: 374; PBl 2: 492. Central and S. America. z9 Fig. 312.

Also in culture are some flesh toned forms such as 'Grand Marnier', 'California Peach' and as yet unnamed seed-lings. Plate 127. ⊕

The *Datura* are strong growing plants requiring a fertile, humus soil, abundant moisture and some protection; frequently found in the Mediterranean region, otherwise as a greenhouse plant which is set outside in the summer.

Lit. Avery, Satin & Rietsema: The genus *Datura*; New York 1959 ● De Wolf, D. P.: Notes on cultivated Solanaceae, (2) *Datura*; in Baileya 4, 12—23, 1959 ● Menninger, E. A.: *Datura* species in Florida gardens; in Am. Hort. Mag. 1966, 375—387.

DAVIDIA Baill. — DAVIDIACAE

Deciduous trees with large winter buds; leaves alternate, long petioled, simple, without stipules; flowers in dense heads, composed of numerous male and one bisexual flower; surrounded at the base by 2 large, white involucral leaves; fruit a nearly walnut-like, long stalked drupe with 3—5 seeds. — 1 species in W. China.

Davidia involucrata Baill. In its habitat a 20 m tall tree of nearly *Linden*-like appearance, stem with dominant central leader, branches thick, glabrous, winter buds large; leaves broad ovate, 8—14 cm long, base cordate, dentate, glossy and glabrous above, densely gray tomentose beneath (important!), petiole 4—5 cm long, red; flower heads about 2 cm wide, surrounded by 2 opposite, uneven size, 8—16 cm long, pendulous, yellowish-white involucral leaves, May—June; fruits ellipsoid, about 2.5 cm long, leather-brown, with a wide, scarlet-red ring on the basal end. DB 1950: 58; 1953: 34; FIO 19. W. China. 1904. z6 Plate 164. ⊕ ∅ ⚭

var. **laeta** (Dode) Kruessm. Like the species, but with leaves quite glabrous beneath, glossy and yellow-green, petiole red, branches green, new growth brownish; fruits more globose (GC 131: 34, fruits). Hupeh, Szechwan. 1903. Not unusual in European gardens. ⚭

var. **vilmoriniana** (Dode) Wanger. Leaves like the species, but quite glabrous beneath, bluish-green, petiole green, branches olive-brown; fruits only 3 cm long, without the red ring at the basal end. BM 8432; DB 1953: FIO 16. Szechwan. 1900. In cultivation, plants labeled as the species are nearly always this variety. ⊕ ∅ ⚭

Prefers a fertile, not too dry soil, protected area, thrives in an organic forest soil.

Lit Cocker, H.: *Davidia*; in Gard. Chron. 1953, II, 226.

DECAISNEA Hook. f. & Thoms. — LARDIZABALACEAE

Deciduous, upright shrubs with thick branches; leaves alternate, odd pinnate, leaflets entire; flowers long stalked in long, pendulous panicles on the ends of side branches; sepals 6, petal-like, stamens 6, styles 3, distinct; fruit a long, thick, soft, nearly sausage-like follicle with numerous seeds bedded in a whitish fruit pulp. — 2 species in E. Asia.

Decaisnea fargesii Franch. Shrub, to 5 m high, in European cultivation only half as high, upright, sparsely branched, branches thick, glabrous, blue pruinose, winter buds large; leaves 50—80 cm long, with 13—25 leaflets, these opposite, ovate, long acuminate, 6—14 cm long, deep green above, blue-green beneath; flowers greenish, sepals inclined together in campanulate fashion, 2—3 cm long, in 20 cm long, pendulous panicles, June; fruits like small sausages, 5—10 cm long, usually 3 together, blue, white pruinose. BM 7848; FIO 60. W. China. 1897. The fruits are allegedly eaten in China. z6 Plate 128, 165.

D. insignis Hook. f. & Thoms. Only slightly different from the previous species in all parts; fruits though are yellow, thicker, curved, edible. BM 6731; FS 1335. E. Himalaya. z8

Warm climate, protection from cold wind, fertile soil and constant supply of moisture are the cultural requirements.

DECODON J. F. Gmel. — Water Willow — LYTHRACEAE

Deciduous subshrub; leaves in whorls or opposite, entire; flowers in axillary cymes; calyx broad campanulate, 5—7 veined; stamens usually 10, alternately long and short; style filamentous; fruit a small, globose capsule. — 1 species.

Decodon verticillatus (L.) Ell. A subshrub from the swamps, branches 0.5—2 m high, 4 or 6 sided, glabrous or finely pubescent; leaves lanceolate, 5—12 cm long, acute at both ends, glabrous above, somewhat pubescent beneath; flowers purple-pink, petals cuneate, 12 mm long, surpassed by the filaments, July—September. BB 2: 3003 (= *Nesaea verticillata* H. B. K.; *Lythrum verticillatum* L.). Eastern USA, in swamps. z5 ⊕

Only recommended for swampy areas in a large garden; branch tips will root upon contact with the ground.

DECUMARIA L. — HYDRANGEACAE

Deciduous to evergreen climbing shrubs, similar to *Hydrangea*, but with all the flowers alike and fertile; leaves simple, opposite, petiolate, stellate pubescent, margins serrate, without stipules; flower small, white, in umbellate panicles, sepals and petals 7—10 each, stamens 20—30, style connate, fruit a several seeded capsule. — 2 species in N. America and China.

Decumaria barbara L. High climbing, branches pubescent; leaves ovate, 5—12 cm long, short acuminate, glabrous or somewhat pubescent at first, somewhat serrate toward the apex; flowers white, fragrant, in terminal, 5—7 cm wide umbellate panicles, May—June. BB 2: 233; SL 182. Southeast USA. 1785. z7 Plate 165; Fig. 313.

D. sinensis Oliv. Climbing, to only 4 m, branches pubescent when young; leaves occasionally evergreen, 3—7 cm long, obovate to rounded, obtuse, occasionally somewhat serrate, dull green; flowers white, in terminal or axillary, 3—8 cm wide umbellate

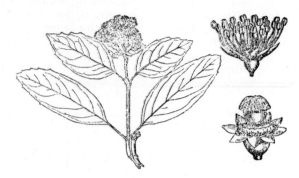

Fig. 313. *Decumaria barbara*. Right, individual flowers with and without stamens respectively (from Dippel, Engler)

panicles, May, BM 9429. Central China, z8

Need a protected area, preferably on a south facing wall or in the forest; humus soil, fertile and moist.

DELONIX Raf. — LEGUMINOSAE

Deciduous or evergreen trees, thornless; leaves bipinnate, leaflets numerous, small, stipules very small; bracts small, abscising; flowers large and attractive, scarlet-red or white, in corymbs at the branch tips; calyx lobes valvate; petals 5, long claw-like, circular; stamens 10, distinct; pods long and flat, hard. — 3 species in tropical Africa and Madagascar. The following species is planted as an ornamental worldwide in the tropics.

Delonix regia (Bojer) Raf. "Flamboyant". Deciduous tree, 12—15 m high, crown flat and very wide; leaves bipinnate, to 50 cm long, with 11—18 paired pinnae, each with 20—30 pairs of small, oblong, 5—10 mm long and 2—3 mm wide leaflets, leaves falling in February—March, new growth appears in May; flow-

ers in large corymbs, the individual flowers about 10 cm wide, petals 5, nearly spathulate and very long "clawed", 4 of these scarlet-red, the 5th (standard petal) white and red patterned, margin finely crispate, flowers from the end of May throughout the summer, calyx with 5 narrow sepals, red inside, outside green, stamens 10, with long, red filaments, style green; pods 30—50 cm long, 5 cm wide, green at first and flexible, later brown and stiff, persisting for some time. BM 2884 (as *Poinciana regia*); PCa 96; HKT 37; BIT 10 (= *Poinciana regia* Bojer). Madagascar. One of the most popular ornamental trees of the subtropics and tropics. z9 Plate 165. ⊕

Lit. Blatter, Millard & Stearn: Some beautiful Indian trees; 1955; pp. 52—57, with color plates.

DENDROMECON Benth. — PAPAVERACEAE

Polymorphic genus, separated by many authors into about 20 species; evergreen, sparsely branched shrubs with alternate, entire, tough leaves; flowers *Papaver*-like, yellow; petals 4, large, sepals 2, stamens numerous, short; fruit an oblong, bowed capsule. — 2 species in California.

Dendromecon hardfordii Kell. Upright, globose, evergreen shrub, 2—6 m high, branches also sometimes drooping; leaves crowded along the stem, elliptic-oval-oblong, 3—10 cm long, 1.5—4 cm wide, round above, dark green; flowers yellow, 7 cm wide, solitary at the tips of short side branches, like *D. rigida*, but on short stalks. MS 126 (= *D. rigida* var. *harfordii* [Kell.] K. Brandeg.). California, but only on the islands of Santa Cruz and Santa Rosa. 1933. z9 # ⊕

var. **rhamnoides** (Greene) Munz. Leaves not so densely arranged as those of the species, to 12 cm long, distinctly blue-green, sharp acuminate at the apex; flowers lighter yellow. JRHS 80: 231. Found with the species. 1963. z9 # ⊕

D. ridiga Benth. Sparse, 0.5—2 m tall shrub, bark yellowish-white, branches stiff, foliage dense; leaves linear-lanceolate to elliptic, 2.5—10 cm long, fine reticulate venation, tough, thick, blue-green, entire (although finely dentate under the magnifying glass); flowers gold-yellow, 5—7 cm wide, stalked, fragrant, April—June; fruit capsule 5—10 cm long. BM 5134; FS 1411; MS 125; BS 2: Pl. 7; MCL 180. California; in the dry Chaparral. 1854. z8 Plate 127, 166; Fig. 314. # ⊕ ∅

Dry, very warm locations in sandy soil.

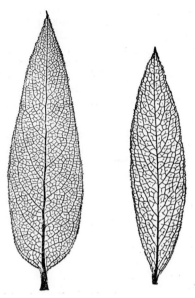

Fig. 314. *Dendromecon rigida*
(Natural pressing; original)

DENDROPANAX Dcne. & Planch. — ARALIACEAE

Thornless evergreen trees or shrubs; leaves alternate, simple and entire or 3−5 lobed, stipules small, hidden by the leaf petiole or adnate to the back side of the petiole or totally absent; flowers in simple or branched umbels, bisexual, seldom polygamous; petals rather thick; fruit globose, somewhat fleshy and juicy, seeds large, flat or nearly triangular. — 75 species in the subtropics and tropics, but only the following usually found in cultivation.

Dendropanax japonicus (Junghuhn) Seem. Evergreen small tree, branches green, rather thick; leaves quite variable in form and size, on young plants often partly 3 or 5 lobed and the base broad truncate, on older plants usually elliptic to ovate or rhombic, base broad cuneate, entire, tough and leathery, glossy dark green, the lobed leaves to 20 × 15 cm in size, the simple leaves only 5−12 × 3−7 cm; flowers inconspicuous, 3−5 in terminal umbels, long stalked, August; fruits ellipsoid, black, furrowed, to 1 cm long. KIF 2: 66 (= *D. trifidus* [Thunb.] Makino). Japan, China and Khasi Hills (India). z9 # ∅

Cultivated in open areas as with *Fatsia*.

DESFONTAINIA Ruiz & Pav. — DESFONTAINIACEAE

Evergreen shrubs of *Ilex*-like appearance; leaves opposite, petiolate, very thorny dentate; flowers solitary, terminal or axillary, pendulous, corolla funnelform, long, calyx small, 5 parted; stamens 5, inserted under the throat; ovaries 5 chambered; fruit a globose berry, surrounded by the persistent calyx. — 5 species in S. America.

The systematic relationship of the genus is not yet fully clear: Engler, Syllabus (1964), placed it in its own family, Hutchinson classified it under the *Potaliaceae*, while previously it had been generally considered to be in the *Loganiaceae*.

Desfontainia spinosa Ruiz & Pav. Evergreen shrub, much like *Ilex aquifolium* in appearance, but denser, 1−2 m high; leaves opposite, oval-ovate, dentate (*Ilex*-like), 2.5−4 cm long, deep green and glossy above; flowers 4 cm long, scarlet red. FS 938; HI 33; HTS 179; BM 4781. Chile, Andes, Patagonia. 1834. z8 Plate 127; Fig. 315. # ⊕ ∅

'Harold Coomber' Flowers to 5 cm long, more vermilion-red. Originated by Mr. Messel, Nymans, Handcross, England. Before 1955. ⊕

Fig. 315. *Desfontainia spinosa*
(from Hooker, altered)

Requires protected sites, humus soil, moist and semishady; keeps roots cool.

DESMODIUM Desv. — LEGUMINOSAE

Deciduous shrubs or perennials; leaves odd pinnate, with 3−5, very rarely only 1 large leaflet, hanging limp at night; flowers small, in axillary or terminal racemes or panicles, usually purple; calyx top-shaped or campanulate, more or less 2 lobed; standard petal oblong to rounded, wings appressed to the keel petal, upper stamens distinct at the base, style curved inward; fruit a segmented pod, breaking apart when ripe (important to distinguish from *Lespedeza*). — About 450 species in the tropics and subtropics.

Desmodium floribundum (D. Don) Sweet. Shrub, to 1.5 m high; leaflets of varying size, terminal leaflet rhombic-elliptic, 5—7 cm long, tapering to the base and abruptly rounded, side leaflets much smaller, base round, dark green and glabrous above, gray beneath, appressed pubescent and with reticulate venation; flowers purple-pink in large, terminal panicles, October; pod 1—2 cm long, with 3—5 seeds. BM 2960; BR 967. China, Himalaya. 1908. z8. ✥

D. penduliflorum see: **Laburnum thunbergii, Lespedioza thunbergii**

D. praestans Forrest. Shrub, 3—4 m high, young branches softly pubescent; leaves usually with only 1 leaflet, these broad ovate, rounded at the apex, base truncate, 10—20 cm long, 8—15 cm wide, the trifoliate leaves have the middle leaflet the same size and form as the single leaflet leaves, while the side leaflets are much smaller, light green above, gray-green beneath, soft pubescent; flowers purple-pink, in pubescent, terminal, 40 cm long, dense panicles, September to frost. BMns 407; JRHS 68: 36. SW. China; Yunnan, Szechwan. 1914. Distinctly different from the other species in the large, single leaflet leaves. z9 Plate 165.✥

D. spicatum Rehd. Loosely branched shrub, about 1.5 m high, branches striped, pubescent, leaflets 3, the terminal leaflet obovate-rounded, to 5 cm long, the side leaflets smaller, obliquely ovate, all with dense gray tomentum beneath; flowers carmine-pink, in about 15 cm long, terminal spikes and in whorls of 6—8, September—October; pods to 5 cm long, bowed, with 4—6 seeds. BM 8805 (as *D. cinerascens*); SDK 4: 22. China. z6 ✥

D. tiliifolium (D. Don). G. Don. Subshrub, growing from the roots each year, branches 0.7—1.5 m high; leaflets 3, terminal leaflet broad obovate, 5—10 cm long, the side leaflets smaller, ovate; flowers pale lilac to dark pink, in 20—30 cm long panicles, August—October; pods 5—7 cm long, with 6—9 seeds. SH 2: 68 a—f. Himalaya. 1879. z6 ⓕ Himalaya, as groundcover. ✥

Pretty, late bloomer, but little known; for sunny areas in a light, well drained soil; needs protection in winter.

DEUTZIA Thunb. — PHILADELPHACEAE

Deciduous shrubs with rod-like, opposite branches; leaves opposite, ovate to lanceolate, crenate or serrate, more or less rough from stellate, appressed pubescence; flowers axillary or terminal, usually cymose or racemose, occasionally solitary, white to pink; calyx campanulate, 5 lobed; petals 5, valvate or imbricate in the bud stage; stamens 10, occasionally 12—15, filaments flat, awl-shaped or usually widened, 2 notched, ovaries inferior, 3—4 (rarely 5) chambered; styles 3—4, long, thickened at the apex; fruit globose, 3—5 chambered, eventually dehiscing at the chamber walls (loculicidal) into several parts. — About 50 species in the Himalayas, E. Asia, Phillipines and Mexico.

The positive identification of *Deutzia* is very difficult. While the characteristically formed filaments are often used, one must frequently count (by magnifying glass) the rays on the stellate pubescence. An exceptionally thorough key has been compiled by T. I. Zaikonnikova but it is complex and the nomenclature does not conform to that used in this work.

The numerous garden varieties all come from V. Lemoine of Nancy, France, and were introduced into the trade between 1885 and 1930. The following wild species (and later his own hybrids) were used by Lemoine in his hybridizing work: *D. discolor, longifolia, parviflora, purpurascens, scabra, setchuensis* with var. *corymbiflora, sieboldiana* and *vilmoriniae*; possibly also *D. mollis*.

Outline of the Genus

Section I. **Eudeutzia** Engl.
Petals valvate while in bud;

Series 1. **Latisepalae** (Schneid.) Rehd.
Flowers in panicles; calyx teeth shorter than the tube; petals more or less erect; filaments with short teeth or awl-shaped:

D. × *candelabrum, chunii, gracilis,* × *magnifica, maximowicziana,* **ningpoensis,** × *scabra, schneideriana, sieboldiana*

Series 2. **Cymosae** Rehd.
Flowers few in loose corymbs or cymes; calyx lobes broad triangular; filaments with large teeth, protruding past the anthers on the inner stamens:
D. monbeigii, setchuenensis

Series 3. **Stenosepalae** Schneid.
Flowers in corymbs; calyx lobes as long as the tube or longer; teeth of the inner stamens frequently reaching past the anthers:
D. albidia, discolor, × *elegantissima,* × *excellens, globosa, glomeruliflora,* × 'Hillieri', × *hybrida, longifolia, purpurescens, reflexa, rehderiana, staminae, vilmoriniae*

Series 4. **Grandiflora** Bge.
Flowers grouped 1—3 together; calyx lobes narrow lanceolate; filaments with long, curving teeth:
D. grandiflora

Series 5. **Coreanae** Rehd.
Flowers solitary, from axillary, leafless buds on the previous year's wood:
D. coreana

Section II. **Mesodeutzia** Schneid.
Petals imbricate, overlapping; filaments awl-shaped or toothed:
D. × *candida, compacta, corymbosa, hookerana,* × *kalmiiflora,* × *lemoinei,* × *maliflora, mollis,* × *myriantha, parviflora, rubens,* × *wilsonii*

Deutzia albida Batal. Shrub, 3—4 m high in its habitat, bushy, young branches glabrous or thin stellate pubescent; leaves ovate-lanceolate, 5—10 cm long, long acuminate, fine toothed, base round, although cuneate on the flowering branches, dark green above

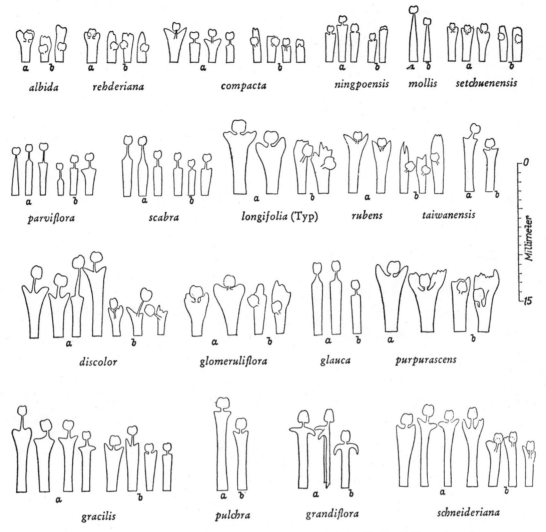

albida   rehderiana   compacta   ningpoensis   mollis   setchuenensis

parviflora   scabra   longifolia (Typ)   rubens   taiwanensis

discolor   glomeruliflora   glauca   purpurascens

gracilis   pulchra   grandiflora   schneideriana

Fig. 316. *Deutzia*. Anthers (a = outer, b = inner) (compiled by Zaikonnikova)

with scattered, 5−6 rayed stellate pubescence, nearly white beneath with very dense stellate pubescence, veins bristly pubescent; flowers pure white, 1−1.3 cm wide, in 5−7 cm wide cymes, anthers brownish-yellow, filaments with 2 large teeth, June. NW. China, Kansu. 1885. Presumably not in cultivation. z5 Plate 170; Fig. 316. ⊕

D. amurensis (Reg.) Airy Shaw see: **D. parviflora** var. **amurensis**

D. × **candelabrum** (Lemoine) Rehd. (*D. gracilis* × *D. sieboldiana*). Growth wide, branches slender, nodding, gray-brown; leaves oval-lanceolate, light green, 6−7 cm long, somewhat rugose and finely scabrous above, with 3−5 rayed stellate pubescence beneath; flowers 2 cm wide, cream-white, in about 6−8 cm long, many flowered panicles, May−June. Lemoine 1907. z6 ⊕

The common English spelling "candelabra" is erroneous; Lemline and Rehder both specify "candelabrum".

'Erecta' (Lemoine 1908). Growth upright; leaves dark green; flowers somewhat smaller, pure white, in medium-sized, pyramidal panicles. ⊕

'Fastuosa' (Lemoine 1906). Hardly differing from the species, but growth upright, not nodding. ⊕

D. × **candida** (Lemoine) Rehd. (*D. lemoinei* × *D. sieboldiana*). Growth upright; leaves oval-oblong, 4−6 cm long, light green, finely serrate, finely scabrous above, scattered stellate pubescence beneath; flowers 2 cm wide, pure white, star-like in form, in loose, upright, ornamental panicled cymes, June. MG 1907: 376 (= *D. discolor candida* Lemoine). Lemoine 1910. z6 ⊕

D. × **carnea** (Lemoine) Rehd. (*D. rosea* 'Grandiflora' × *D. sieboldiana*). Lower, erect shrub, branches brown; leaves oblong, acuminate, 3−5 cm long, serrate, both

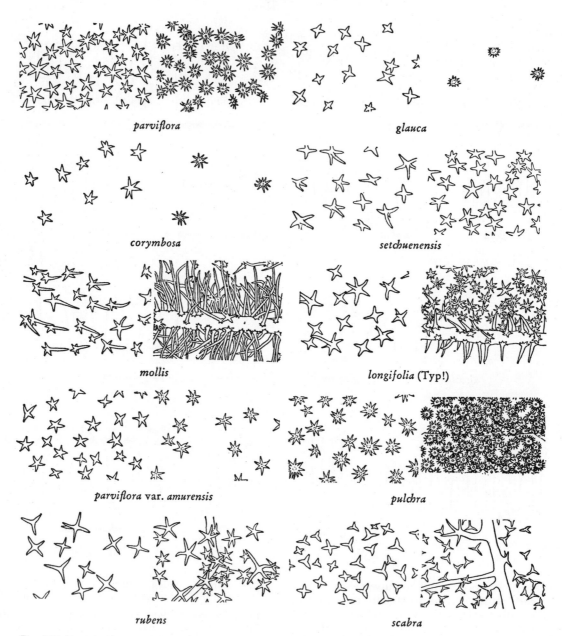

parviflora　　　　　　　　　　　　　*glauca*

corymbosa　　　　　　　　　　　　*setchuenensis*

mollis　　　　　　　　　　　　*longifolia* (Typ!)

parviflora var. *amurensis*　　　　　　　*pulchra*

rubens　　　　　　　　　　　　*scabra*

Fig. 317. *Deutzia*. Forms of the stellate pubescence (left, on the upper leaf surface; right, beneath the leaf blade) (compiled by Zaikonnikova)

sides with 4−6 stellate hairs; flowers nearly 2 cm wide, white inside, outside with a trace of pink, in loose, erect panicles, sepals triangular, reddish (= *D. discolor carnea* Lemoine). Lemoine 1907. z6 ⊕

Including the following cultivars:

'**Densiflora**' (Lemoine 1908). Flowers rather large, milk-white, petals lanceolate, buds pink. ⊕

'**Lactea**' (Lemoine 1907). Similar to the species, but with narrower leaves, light green; flowers milk-white, in rather large panicles. ⊕

'**Stellata**' (Lemoine 1906). Flowers whitish-pink, or carmine-pink, petals narrow, outspread. Plate 166. ⊕

D. chunii Hu. Shrub, to 2 m high; leaves oblong lanceolate, sparsely and finely serrate, with sparse stellate pubescence only above; flowers in to 8 cm long panicles, petals ovate-oblong, 6 mm long, flowers late, early July. CIS 71. E. China. 1935. Still rather rare in cultivation, but quite hardy. z6 Plate 168, 172. ⊕ Ø

D. compacta Craib. Shrub, to 1.5 m high, densely bushy, branches quickly glabrous; leaves usually broad lanceolate, drawn out from the middle to the apex, 5–6 cm long, base rounded, finely serrate, dull green above, gray-green beneath from usually 5–8 rayed,uneven sized stellate hairs, 5–7 vein pairs; flowers dense in about 5 cm wide cymes, petals pure white, rounded, buds pink, calyx lobes broad ovate, filaments toothed, July. BM 8795. China. 1910. z6 Fig. 316.

'Lavender Time'. Flowers lilac at first, later becoming somewhat lighter. Found in the wild. Very beautiful. (Hillier). ⊕

D. coreana Lév. Shrub, to 2 m high, current year's wood rough from small warty growth; leaves elliptic-lanceolate, lighter green beneath, serrate to doubly serrate, both sides with scattered, 4–6 rayed stellate hairs; flowers white, solitary from axillary, leafless buds on the previous year's wood. NK 15: 16. Korea. 1917. z6 Plate 170. ⊕

D. corymbiflora see: **D. setchuenensis**

D. corymbosa R. Br. Shrub, about 2m high, branches glabrous, bark brown, peeling; leaves ovate, long acuminate, 4–6(10) cm long, serrate, teeth directed inward, both sides bright green, dense with 5–6 rayed stellate hairs above, scattered 8–12 rayed stellate pubescence beneath; flowers white, to 1.5 cm wide, in 4–6 cm wide, pyramidal corymbs, petals oval-rounded, anthers large, yellow, filaments large toothed, June. BR 265. W. Himalaya. 1830. z8 Fig. 317, 319. See also: *D. setchuenensis*. ⊕

D. crenata see: **D. × magnifica** and **D. scabra**

D. discolor Hemsl. Shrub, to 1.5 m high, branches red-brown, bark peeling; leaves oblong-lanceolate, 3–7 cm long, to 10 cm on long branches, finely serrate, finely scabrous above, whitish beneath, stellate pubescence with 10–15 rays, but only half the size of those on the upper side; flowers 2 cm wide, white, occasionally somewhat pink on the outside, usually in very loose, seldom dense, nearly hemispherical, wide umbellate panicles, filaments above the teeth elongated into an anther "stalk", often as long as half the filament, calyx and flower stalk dense stellate pubescent, June. CIS 226; ICS 1932. Central and W. China. 1901. z5 Plate 168, 170; Fig. 316. See also: *D. × rosea*. ⊕

var. *candida* see: **D. × candida**
var. *carnea* see: **D. × carnea**
var. *elegantissima* see: **D. × elegantissima**

'Major' (Veitch). Growth upright; leaves stellate pubescent beneath (the often confused *D. longifolia* has both stellate hairs and simple hairs); flowers larger, to 3 cm wide, normally somewhat pink outside. BS 2: 37; NH 30: 99; MG 1913: 9. 1901.

var. *purpurascens* see: **D. purpurascens**

D. × elegantissima (Lemoine) Rehd. (*D. purpurascens* × *D. sieboldiana*). Growth upright, to 2 m high, branches slender; leaves oval-oblong, 5–8 cm long, short acuminate, irregular serrate, dull green, rugose, sparse 4–6 rayed stellate pubescence beneath; flowers 2 cm wide, white, with a trace of pink, stronger

pink outside, in many flowered, loose, erect, axillary cymes, June. NH 30: 99 (= *D. discolor elegantissima* Lemoine). z6 Plate 172.

Including the following cultivars:

'Arcuata' (Lemoine 1908). Flowers large, pure white, buds light pink, petals rounded, 8–10 in small cymes, but in large numbers along the nodding branches. ⊕

'Conspicua' (Lemoine). Branches long arching; flowers glossy white, buds pink, in rounded cymes. ⊕

'Elegantissima' (Lemoine 1909). The type of this cross.

'Fasciculata' (Lemoine 1911). Flowers flat, white inside, a trace of soft pink, pink outside. ⊕

'Rosalind' (Slieve Donard Nursery, before 1962). Growth 1–1.5 m high; flowers dark carmine-pink. ⊕

D. × excellens (Lemoine) Rehd. (*D. rosea* 'Grandiflora' × *D. vilmoriniae*). Shrub with upright, slender branches; leaves oval-oblong, 3–6 cm long, to 9 cm on long shoots, acuminate, base round, finely scabrous above, gray-white with red pubescence beneath, serrate; flowers pure white, 2 cm wide, in loose, 4–6 cm wide cymes, calyx teeth lanceolate, filaments with large, erect teeth. Lemoine 1910. z6 ∅

D. globosa Duthie. Small shrub, branches red-brown, bark peeling; leaves oval-lanceolate to elliptic, 5–9 cm long, blunt acuminate, dentate, rough stellate pubescence above, whitish stellate pubescent beneath; flowers yellowish-white, 1.5 cm wide, in dense, nearly globose umbellate panicles, calyx teeth narrow triangular, as long as the calyx tube, June–July. Central China. Without particular ornamental value. z6

D. glomeruliflora Franch. Shrub, to 1.8 m high, branches long rod-like, nodding, gray stellate pubescent at first, then with red-brown bark, peeling; leaves oval-lanceolate to lanceolate, long acuminate, 3–6 cm long, to 8 cm on long shoots, rugose, serrate, rough above, stellate hairs with 3–4 rays, dull green, light gray-green beneath, dense, soft pubescence with 4–5 rayed stellate hairs; flowers white to cream-white, 1.5–2 cm wide, petals broad elliptic, filaments much widened and with large wide teeth, umbellate panicles rather small, but numerous along the previous year's branches, June. CIS 224; ICS 1934. W. China. 1908. Plate 170; Fig. 316. z5 ⊕

D. gracilis S. & Z. Low shrub, seldom taller than 70 cm, growth narrowly upright; leaves oblong lanceolate, 3–6 cm long, long acuminate, light green, with scattered stellate pubescence above, glabrous beneath; flowers 1.5–2 cm wide, pure white, in 4–9 cm long, upright panicles or racemes, May–June. FS 611; DB 1952: 242. Japan. z5 Plate 167, 170; Fig. 316. See also: *D. × rosea*. ⊕

'Marmorata'. Leaves yellow speckled. ∅

D. grandiflora Bge. Shrub, to 1.5 m high, somewhat sparse, young branches with dense stellate pubescence; leaves ovate, acuminate, 3–6 cm long, uneven dentate, base round, dark green and rough stellate pubescent above, densely white tomentose and reticulate venation beneath; flowers 1—3 on short side branches, pure white, 2.5—3 cm wide, filaments with 2 long, narrow, reflexed teeth, April—May. CIS 228; ICS 1935. China. 1910. Blooms the earliest of the genus but with only a few flowers. z6 Fig. 316. ⊕

D. × 'Hillieri' (Hillier) (*D. longifolia* 'Veitchii' × *D. setchuensis* var. *corymbiflora*). Beautiful ornamental shrub, buds purple, opening pink, becoming white, 20—30 in dense corymbs, June—July. ⊕

D. hookerana (Schneid.) Airy Shaw. Very closely related to *D. corymbosa*; leaves however with much denser 4—8 rayed stellate hairs beneath, and numerous 4—6 rayed stellate hairs above, ovate, 3—5 cm long, 1.3—1.8 cm wide; flowers pure white, in dense corymbs, all stamen filaments distincty toothed, late June (= *D. corymbosa* var. *hookerana* Schneid.). Nepal to W. China. z5 ⊕

D. × hybrida Lemoine (*D. discolor* × *D. longifolia*). Uprght shrub, 1—1.5 m high; leaves oblong-ovate, 6—8(10) cm long, serrate; flowers large, mallow-pink, opening wide, limb generally somewhat lighter, petals slightly crispate on the margin, anthers a conspicuous yellow, filaments toothed, June. NH 30: 87. z6

In addition, the following cultivars:

'Contraste' (Lemoine 1928). Branches more pendulous; flowers very large, mallow-pink, outside with a darker midstripe, petals very crispate. One of the largest flowered types. ⊕

'Joconde' (Lemoine). Leaves long acuminate, finely serrate; flowers pale lilac, nearly white inside, petals with narrow purple stripes on the dorsal side, obovate. NH 30: 91. ⊕

'Magicien' (Lemoine 1927). Leaves elliptic, long acuminate; flowers nearly like those of 'Contraste', but a darker pink on the dorsal side, limb white, crispate. NH 30: 88. Plate 167, 168. ⊕

'Mont Rose' (Lemoine 1925). The type of the cross. For description see *D.* × *hybrida*. Plate 167, 168. ⊕

'Perle Rose' (Lemoine 1936). Flowers mallow-pink, smaller than those of the other cultivars, but more numerous and lasting longer. NH 30: 89. Plate 168. ⊕

'Pink Pompon' (Slieve Donard Nursery). Buds carmine outside, opening to a strong pink, in very dense, hemispherical corymbs. Around 1965 (?). ⊕

D. hypoglacua see: **D. rubens**

D. hypoleuca see: **D. maximowicziana**

D. × kalmiiflora Lemoine (*D. parviflora* × *D. purpurascens*). Shrub, about 1.5 m high, growth loose, branches arching; leaves oval-oblong to oval-lanceolate, 3—6 cm long, finely serrate, light green and stellate pubescent beneath, base broad cuneate; flowers white inside with a trace of pink, a good pink outside, petals rounded and sinuate, 5—12 in upright umbellate panicles. MG 1913: 25. Lemoine 1900. ⊕

D. × lemoinei Lemoine ex Bois. (*D. gracilis* × *D. parviflora*). Small shrub, to 1 m high, bushy, upright, young branches glabrous, later with browner, peeling bark; leaves lanceolate, 3—6 cm long, to 8 cm on long shoots, rugose, serrate, both sides green, acuminate; flowers to 2 cm wide, white, in 3—8 cm long, erect umbellate panicles, June, flowers very abundantly. z5

Including the following cultivars:

'Avalanche' (Lemoine 1904). Presumably a back cross of *D.* 'Lemoine' with *D. gracilis*. Leaves dark green, small; flowers pure white, in small, dense corymbs on drooping branches, larger than those of the species, very abundant (= *D. maliflora* Rehd. 'Avalanche'). ⊕

'Boule de neige' (Lemoine 1899). Inflorescence globose, dense, flowers large, cream-white, anthers and disc a bright yellow. ⊕

'Compacta' (Lemoine 1897). More compact than the species; flowers smaller, flat spreading, snow-white, inflorescences only medium sized, very numerous. ⊕

'Lemoinei (Lemoine 1891). The type of the cross. GF 9: 285. For description, see above. Also valued for forcing, better than *D. gracilis*. ⊕

D. longiflora Franch. Upright shrub, 1 to 2 m high, bark gray-brown, peeling, young branches densely pubescent; leaves narrow lanceolate, long acuminate, 5—8 cm long, 10—15 cm long on long shoots, finely dentate, tough, rough stellate pubescent above, dense gray-white stellate pubescent beneath, also with erect pubescence on the venation, stellate hairs with 8—12 rays; flowers white inside, bright purple-red outside, 2 cm wide, petals oval-oblong, the longer filaments with 2 large teeth, the shorter linear-lanceolate, cymes loose or compact, inflorescences shorter and wider than on *D. scabra*, filaments with ascending teeth, June. BM 8493; CIS 227; ICS 1933. China, Szechwan. 1905. z6 Plate 168; Fig. 316. 317. ⊕ ⊘

'Elegans'. Branches slender, drooping; flowers 2 cm wide, purple-pink outside, in loose inflorescences. 1906.

var. **farreri** Airy-Shaw. Flowers white, 2.5 cm wide, with 4—5 styles, occasionally with 3. BM 9532. Closely related to *D. albida*.

'Veitchii' (Veitch 1912). Flowers darker purple-pink, inflorescences larger and denser. NH 30: 85; MG 1913: 17. ⊕ ⊘

D. × magnifica Rehd. (*D. scabra* × *D. vilmorianiae*). Growth strong, upright shrub, stout branches, bark brown; leaves oblong-lanceolate, 4—6 cm long, to 14 cm on long shoots, margins finely crenate, rough, bright green above, gray-green beneath, with 10—15 rayed stellate pubescence; flowers 2.5 cm wide, pure white, either simple or double in rosette form according to cultivar, in 4—8 cm long, dense, rounded, umbellate panicles, calyx teeth as long as the tube, styles usually 4, June. DB 1950: 162 (= *D. crenata magnifica* Lemoine). z6 ⊕

Including the following cultivars:

'Azaleaeflora' Lemoine 1920). Flowers opening wide, simple, alabaster-white, erect, very early. ✧

'Eburnea' (Lemoine 1912). Flowers simple, campanulate, in loose panicles, styles 4. Plate 169. ✧

'Eminens' (Lemoine 1927). Tall plant; flowers simple, petals glossy white, horizontally spread, inflorescences pyramidal. ✧

'Erecta' (Lemoine 1912). Flowers simple, milk-white, in long, pyramidal, erect panicles, styles 3. Plate 169. ✧

'Formosa' (Lemoine 1912). Flowers double, large, petals curved inward and somewhat crispate. NH 30: 95 ✧

'Latiflora' (Lemoine 1910). Flowers simple, pure white, to 3 cm wide, 15—20 in erect umbellate panicles, petals outspread. Plate 168, 169. ✧

'Longipetala' Lemoine). Growth upright; leaves small and narrow; flowers pure white, in dense umbellate panicles, petals very narrow and long, margin crispate.

'Macrothyrsa' (Lemoine 1918). Tall plant; flowers pure white, in large umbellate panicles along the entire branch. ✧

'Magnifica' (Lemoine 1909). The type of this cross; leaves very similar to those of *D. scabra*, but the flowers in shorter, wider, denser panicles. Otherwise see above. ✧

'Mirabilis' (Lemoine). Flowers milky-white, simple, in very large, erect panicles.✧

'Staphyleoides' (Lemoine). Flowers large, simple, white, petals long, reflexed, therefore somewhat resembling *Staphylea*.✧

'Superba' (Lemoine 1912). Leaves without simple hairs beneath; flowers large, simple, styles 3—4, calyx teeth as long or somewhat longer than the receptacle. ✧

'Suspensa' (Lemoine). Flowers simple, pure white, in numerous, densely arranged pendulous umbellate panicles, abundant. NH 30: 97. ✧

D. × maliflora Rehd. (*D. lemoinei* × *D. purpurascens*). Small, upright shrub, branches long rod-like; leaves oval-oblong, 3—4 cm long, rugose, finely serrate, green beneath with scattered stellate pubescence; flowers 2 cm wide, bright reddish outside, white in-

Fig. 318. *Deutzia parviflora* (from Maxim.)

side, in dense, rounded, 3—6 cm long umbellate panicles along the entire branch, May—June (= *D. myriantha* 'Fleur de Pommier'). Lemone 1905. z6 ✧

'Avalanche' see: **D. lemoinei**.

'Boule Rose' (Lemoine 1904). Rounded shrub, to 1 m high; flowers white, pink margined, outside with pink tones, flowers very abundantly. Plate 166. ✧

'Fleur de Pommier' (Lemoine 1905). The type of this cross; for description see above (= *D. myriantha* 'Fleur de Pommier' Lemoine).

D. maximowicziana Makino. Shrub, 1—1.5 m high, branches brown, thin, stellate tomentose; leaves narrow oblanceolate, long acuminate, base cuneate, indistinctly toothed, 3—8 cm long, densely white tomentose beneath; flowers white, 2 cm wide, in erect 5—7 cm long panicles, terminal on small side branches, petals oblong, May (= *D. hypoleuca* Maxim.). Japan. 1915. z6 Plate 170. ✧

D. mollis Duthie. Shrub, 1.5—2 m high, strong growing, upright, branches stellate pubescent at first, later red-brown; leaves elliptic-lanceolate to ovate, obtuse, 4—8 cm long, 10—12 cm on long shoots, unevenly dentate, rough above from 3—4 rayed stellate pubescence, dense gray-green soft pubescence beneath; flowers 1 cm wide, white or slight reddish toned, in wide, flat cymes, petals rounded, filaments without teeth, June. BS 2: 42; CIS 230; BM 8559. China; Hupeh. 1901. z6 Plate 168; Fig. 316, 317.

D. monbeigii W. W. Sm. Shrub, 1—1.5 m high, branches slender, red-brown, densely stellate tomentose; leaves oval-lanceolate, 4—4.5 cm long, margins with many, small, hard teeth, base cuneate, tough, dark green above with 5—8 rayed stellate hairs, underside white and densely covered with 15 rayed stellate hairs; flowers white, 7—12 in loose, long stalked umbellate panicles, petals 1 cm long, calyx teeth triangular, late May to June. BMns 123. China, NW. Yunnan. 1921. z6 ✧

D. × myriantha Lemoine (*D. parviflora* × *D. setchuenensis*). Upright shrub, 1 m high; leaves oblong-lanceolate, 7—10 cm long, finely serrate, both sides finely scabrous, dark green above, with 5—6 rayed stellate hairs beneath; flowers white, 2 cm wide, in loose, large umbellate panicles, June. Lemoine 1904. Those cultivars once included here are now found under *D. maliflora*. z5 ✧

D. ningpoensis Rehd. Tall shrub; leaves oval-oblong, 8—12 cm long, 2.5—3.5 cm wide, very long acuminate, sparsely dentate to nearly entire, whitish beneath, base usually broad cuneate to rounded, petiole 1—3 mm long; flowers white, in 12 cm long panicles, petals oblong, only 5—8 mm long. CIS 222; ICS 1930. E. China. 1937. z6 Plate 168, 172; Fig. 316. ✧

D. parviflora Bge. Shrub, to 1 m high, branches with loose stellate pubescence; leaves oval-lanceolate, 3—6 cm long, unevenly serrate, teeth erect, dull green above with scattered stellate pubescence, light green

Fig. 319. **Deutzia** Left *D. corymbosa;* middle *D. sieboldiana;* right *D. staminea*
(from Royle, Dippel, Sieb, & Zucc.)

and usually smooth beneath; flowers white, 1.2 cm wide, in 5−7 cm wide umbellate panicles, filaments without teeth, June. NK 15: 20; CIS 232; ICS 1923. China, Manchuria. 1883. z5 Plate 170; Fig. 316, 317, 318.

The plant by this name in gardens is nearly always var. *amurensis.*

var. **amurensis** Rgl. Leaves more ovate, upper surface with 4−5 rayed stellate hairs, light green beneath, without simple, erect pubescence on the midrib beneath; loose inflorescences. NK 15: 20; GF 1: 361 (= *D. amurensis* [Rgl.] Airy Shaw; *D. parviflora* Hort. non Bge.). Korea, Manchuria. 1862. Fig. 317.

'Museai' (Lemoine). Stronger growing than the species, to 2 m high, upright; leaves oblong-lanceolate, 12−15 cm long, dark green; flowers cream-white, in dense, convex corymbs. ⊕

D. pulchra Vidal. Shrub, to 2 m or taller, branches with fine stellate pubescence, bark eventually peeling and brownish-orange; leaves narrow ovate to lanceolate, 3−10 cm long, sparsely and finely toothed, both sides stellate pubescent, denser beneath, petiole 6−15 mm long; flowers in 5−10(20) cm long, pendulous panicles, white, reddish outside, May, petals narrow oblong, acuminate, about 12 mm long, filaments with erect wings at the apex. BM 8962; GC 1950 (II): 110, LWT 89; LT 352. Philippines, Formosa (Taiwan). One of the most beautiful species. z6 Fig. 316, 317. ⊕

D. purpurascens (L. Henry) Rehd. Shrub, 1(2) m high, branches slender, nodding, bark brown, peeling; leaves ovate to oval-lanceolate, unevenly dentate to crenate, base broad cuneate to rounded, 4−6 cm long, both sides green and with 5−7 rayed stellate hairs (the similar *D. discolor* has 10−15 rays!); flowers white inside, turning bright red outside, 2 cm wide,

petals obovate, erect, 5−10 in rounded corymbs, filaments on the longer stamens with 2 large, wide teeth, May−June. BM 7708; NF 4: 103; NF 6: 106 (= *D. discolor* var. *purpurascens* L. Henry). W. China. 1888. z6 Fig. 316. ⊕

D. reflexa Duthie. Shrub, 0.7 m high, braches thin, smooth; leaves oblong-lanceolate, acuminate, toothed, 5−7 cm long, with scattered rough stellate pubescence above, dense whitish stellate pubescence beneath with simple hairs along the midrib (like *D. vilmoriniae*); flowers white, 1.6 cm wide, in dense, about 5−6 cm wide umbellate panicles, petal margins reflexed (!), filaments very much widened, with 2 short teeth, petal limb reflexed, calyx teeth triangular-lanceolate, June−July. China. 1901. z6

D. rehderiana Schneid. Shrub, to 1.5 m high, bushy, branches densely stellate pubescent; leaves ovate to oval-lanceolate, 1.5−3 cm long, base round, finely dentate, dull green above and rough, both sides stellate pubescent; flowers white, 2.5 cm wide, 3−5 on the terminals of short side branches, April−May. China. 1913. z6 Plate 168; Fig. 316.

D. × rosea (Lemoine) Rehd. (*D. gracilis* × *D. purpurascens*). Bushy habit, compact, about 1 m high, bark brown, peeling; leaves oval-oblong to lanceolate, serrate, with scattered, 4−6 rayed stellate pubescence above; flowers opening campanulate, to 2 cm wide, reddish outside, white inside, in short, wide panicles, calyx teeth lanceolate, June. z6 Plate 170, 171. ⊕

'Campanulata' (Lemoine 1889). Bushy habit, branches upturned-nodding; leaves oval-lanceolate, bright green, rugose, 7−10 cm long; flowers deep shell-like, to 2.5 cm wide, pure white, stalk and calyx purple-brown, calyx teeth lanceolate, panicles dense, rounded, June. BK 5:58 (= *D.*

gracilis campanulata Lemoine). ⊕

'Carminea' (Lemoine 1900). Habit broadly arching; flowers 2 cm wide, white inside, outside carmine-pink, sepals triangular, reddish, in dense, oblong panicles (= *D. gracilis carminea* Lemoine). ⊕

'Eximia' (Lemoine 1901). Flowers white inside, outside light pink, in erect panicles, filaments short, distinctly toothed, sepals reddish, triangular (= *D. gracilis eximia* Lemoine). ⊕

'Floribunda' ((Lemoine 1901). Upright habit, dense; flowers 2 cm wide, white inside, outside carmine-pink toned, in dense, rounded panicles, sepals triangular, reddish (= *D. discolor floribunda* Lemoine).

'Grandiflora' (Lemoine 1899). Growth strongly upright, branches long, arching; flowers to 3 cm wide, white inside, light carmine-pink outside, in loose panicles covering the entire branch (= *D. discolor grandiflora* Lemoine). ⊕

'Multiflora' (Lemoine 1903). Flowers white, sepals lanceolate (= *D. gracilis multiflora* Lemoine).

'Rosea' (Lemoine 1898). The type of the cross; otherwise as described above (= *D. gracilis rosea* Lemoine). That illustrated in BMns 189 is presumably 'Carminea'.

'Venusta' (Lemoine 1898). Flowers large, white, sepals green, triangular (= *D. discolor venusta* Lemoine).

D. rubens Rehd. Shrub, to 2 m high, red-brown bark, peeling in the 2nd year, young branches glabrous; leaves oval-oblong to lanceolate, 3—5 to 9 cm long, serrate, sparse with 4 rayed stellate pubescence above, rugose and dark green, blue-green beneath and quite loose or also dense with 3—6 rayed hairs; flowers white, to 2 cm wide, many in 4—10 cm wide, hemispherical umbellate panicles, filaments arranged together in tube form, anthers gold-yellow, June. BM 9362; CIS 233; ICS 1925. China; Hupeh, Shansi. 1910. z6 Plate 170; Fig. 316, 317.

D. scabra Thunb. Tall shrub, 2.5—3 m high, growth narrowly strict upright, densely branched, bark red-brown, peeling in later years, young branches stellate pubescent; leaves ovate to oval-oblong, 5—10 cm long, 10—14 cm on long shoots, crenate, dark green, both sides rough from 10—15 rayed stellate pubescence; flowers white, 1.5—2 cm wide, in narrow, erect, stellate haired panicles, petals oblong, rather erect, filaments toothed beneath the apex, outer stamens as long as the petals, styles usually 3, calyx teeth triangular, abscising at fruiting time, June—July. BM 3838; ICS 1928; CIS 220 (= *D. crenata* S. & Z.). Japan, China. 1822. z6 Plate 171; Fig. 316, 317.

There is some disagreement among botanists as to which species should bear the name *D. scabra*. The species considered to be *D. scabra* by Siebold in 1835 was later named *D. sieboldiana* by Maximowicz in 1867, and the above described species was called *D. crenata*. In this work the most common nomenclature from the USA and W. Europe has been retained.

Here are the many cultivars included:

'Angustifolia'. Leaves oblong-ovate to lanceolate; only the inflorescence having stellate pubescence, without simple hairs. 1856.

'Candidissima' (Froebel). Growth narrowly upright; flowers densely double, outside pure white, rosette form, to 2.5 cm wide, soft reddish traces while in bud only. FS 1850 (= *D. scabra* var. *alboplena* Schneid.). 1868. Plate 171. ⊕

'Codsall Pink'. Strong grower, somewhat vase-like; flowers mallow-pink, double, in erect panicles, very abundant, June—July.

'Marmorata'. Leaves yellow-white marbled and with 2 or 3 shades of green. 1900.

'Macropetala'. Flowers very large, pure white, petals to 15 mm long.

'Plena'. Flowers densely double, outside pink. FS 1799; NH 30: 94 (= *D. crenata plena* Lemoine; *D. crenata purpurata plena* Hort.). Introduced from Japan, 1861. ⊕

'Pride of Rochester' (Ellwanger & Barry, USA). Growth upright, slightly nodding; leaves horizontally arranged, on the long shoots somewhat bullate; flowers densely double, petals very narrow, white inside, outside slightly pink striped. ⊕

'Punctata'. Leaves quite finely white dotted. 1894.

'Watereri'. Flowers simple, white inside, outside pink-red toned. GC 39: 340 (= *D. crenata punicea* Schneid.). 1877.

D. schneideriana Rehd. Shrub, to 2 m high, bark brown, peeling with age; leaves elliptic to oblong-lanceolate, acuminate, 3—7 cm long, serrate, dull green, with 5—6 rayed stellate pubescence above, underside white to gray from many rayed stellate pubescence, venation with simple hairs; flowers white, in broadly pyramidal, loose panicles, 6—9 cm long, petals oblong, 10 mm long, filaments distinctly toothed, styles usually 3, June. NH 30: 124; ICS 1931; CIS 221. China; W. Hupeh. 1907. z6 Fig. 316.

var. **laxiflora** Rehd. Bark light brown; leaves oval-oblong, 9—12 cm long, green beneath, stellate pubescent; flowers milk-white, in broad conical, loose inflorescences, petals 12—14 mm long. Central China. 1901.

D. setchuenensis Franch. Shrub, to 2 m high, branches with brown, late peeling bark; leaves lanceolate, 2—4 cm long, to 8 cm on long shoots, finely scabrous and with simple hairs above, underside gray-green with 6 rayed stellate pubescence; flowers white, 1 cm wide, with erect elliptic petals, few to many flowers in loose corymbs, styles 3, short, filaments with wide, ascending teeth, June—July. ICS 1926; BS 2: Pl. 9; BM 2855 (= *D. corymbiflora erecta* Lemoine). Central to W. China. 1893. Much less frequently found in cultivation than the variety since it has smaller inflorescences, leaves likewise smaller and more narrow. Fig. 316, 317. z6

var. **corymbiflora** (Lemoine) Rehd. Leaves larger and wider, 3—11 cm long, 1.5—3 cm wide, dull green above, rough with stellate pubescence, gray and densely pubescent beneath; flowers larger, to 1.5 cm wide, star-shaped, corymbs to 10 cm wide. MG 1913: 9; BM 8255 (as *D. setchuenensis*); SH 1: 42r (as *D. corymbiflora*) (= *D. corymbiflora* Lemoine; *D. corymbosa* André non Royle). 1895. Plate 169, 170. ⊕

D. sieboldiana Maxim. Open growing, shrub, graceful habit, to 1 m tall, bark brown, peeling, young branches stellate pubescent; leaves acute-ovate, 3–6 cm long, 7–9 cm on long shoots, rugose above, dull green, sharply dentate, both sides with 3–5 rayed stellate hairs, subtending leaf pair under the inflorescence cordate and sessile; flowers 1.5 cm wide, white, in dense, 7 cm long, upright, stellate pubescent panicles, flower stalk with stellate pubescence and simple bristly hairs, filaments without teeth, June–July. BS 2: 49 (= *D. scabra* S. & Z. non Thunb.). Japan. 1890. z6 Plate 168; Fig. 319.⊕

var. **dippeliana** Schneid. Leaves smaller and wider; inflorescense looser, flower stalks with only stellate pubescence, filaments totally without teeth. Japan. 1875.

D. staminea R. BR. Shrub, to about 1 m high, branches with rough stellate pubescence; leaves ovate, long acuminate, 3–6 cm long, base usually round, margin unevenly dentate, dull green above and scabrous, gray and dense stellate pubescent beneath; flowers white, 1.5 cm wide, in about 5 cm wide corymbs, June. BR 33: 13; SNp 57. Himalaya. 1841. Very rare in cultivation, plants usually found by this name are the following variety. z8 Plate 170; Fig. 319. ⊕

var. **brunoniana** Hook. f. & Thoms. Leaves less pubescent; flowers larger, filaments with 2 large teeth, style longer than the stamens. BR 26: 5. z7

D. taiwanensis (Maxim.) Schneid. Shrub, upright, to 1.5 m high, branches slender, pubescent; leaves ovate to oval-lanceolate, 5–10 cm long, finely dentate, with 3–5 rayed stellate pubescence above, 4–5 rayed beneath, petiole 3–8 mm long; flowers white in narrow, 9–15 cm long, terminal panicles on leafy branches, petals 1 cm long, calyx with short, triangular teeth, stellate pubescent, filaments with triangular teeth under the anthers. Taiwan. 1918. z7 Plate 170, 172; Fig. 316.⊕

D. vilmoriniae Lemoine. Fast growing shrub, about 1.5 m high, erect-nodding habit, bark brown and glossy, scattered pubescent at first, later exfoliating; leaves ovate to oblong, 3–6(8) cm long, sharply dentate, dull green above with loose stellate pubescence, underside gray with 9–12 rayed stellate pubescence, venation with simple hairs (like *D. reflexa*); flowers pure white, 2 cm wide, in loose, axillary cymes, petiole 1 cm long, filaments toothed, calyx lobes linear-lanceolate, reflexed, June. RH 1905: 266; CIS 225. Central China. 1897. Plate 170. ⊕

D. × wilsonii Duthie (*D. ? discolor* × *D. mollis*). To 2 m high, strong growing, branches with red-brown, exfoliating bark; leaves elliptic, to oblong-lanceolate, 7–11 cm long, short acuminate, base round, upper surface rough with 4–10 rayed stellate hairs, stellate pubescent beneath intermixed with long, simple hairs, gray; flowers 2 cm wide, petals flat outspread, obovate, margin somewhat involuted, wings on the filaments widest at the middle, becoming narrower at both ends, with small teeth at the apex, June. BM 8033; NH 30: 93; MB 1913: 27. Central China. 1901. Natural hybrid. Closely related to *D. discolor*, but with filaments not or indistinctly toothed and with calyx teeth shorter and wider. One of the most beautiful white flowering *Deutzias*. z6 Plate 168.

All species prefer a fertile, clay soil, sufficient moisture and full sun; only a few species are tender in a frost (*D. staminea, corymbosa* etc.); older branches should be removed. The Deutzias are some of the most beautiful flowering shrubs for the garden.

Lit. Bean, W. J.: *Deutzias*; in New Flora and Silva **4**, 103–111, m. Taf. ● Fox, H. M.: Victor Lemoine and the *Deutzias*; in Nat. Hort. Mag. **30**, 83–100, 1951 ● Lemoine, E.: Monographie horticole du genre *Deutzia*; in Jour. Soc. Nat. Hort. **3**, 298, 1902 ● Rehder, A.: Die Gattung *Deutzia*; in Moellers Deut. Gaert. Z. 1913, 7–9, 15–17, 25–26 ● Schneider, C. K.: Beitrag zur Kenntnis der Gattung *Deutzia*; in Mitt. Dtsch. Dendrol. Ges 1904, 296–312 ● Zaikonnikova, T. I.: Deitsii — Dekorativnie Kustarniki: Monografia roda *Deutzia* Thunb.; Leningrad 1966; englische Uebersetzung des Schluessels von H. K. Airy Shaw in Baileya **19**, 133 – 143, 1975.

DIAPENSIA L. — DIAPENSIACEAE

Evergreen, cushion-like dwarf shrub with more or less rosette form, small leaves; flowers solitary, terminal, on short stalks; corolla cupulate with 5 wide lobes, calyx lobes somewhat overlapping; stamens 5, stigma 3 lobed; fruit a 3 chambered, 3 valved, loculicidal, many seeded capsule. — 4 species in the higher mountains of N. Europe, N. America, NW. Asia, Himalaya.

Diapensia lapponica L. Carpet-like growth, 2–8 cm high, cushion very tough and firm; leaves spathulate, 6–12 mm long, imbricately arranged, yellow-green, dull, leathery tough; flowers white, on about a 2–3 cm long stalk, April–May. BM 1108; GPN 672; PEu 87. N. America, NW. Asia, N. Europe, in the high mountains. z1 Plate 175. #

var. **obovata** F. Schmidt. 1–3 cm high; leaves more obovate, 7–15 mm long, 3–5 mm wide; flowering period June–July. Sachalin, Kuril Islands, Kamchatka, Alaska and Eastern N. America.

The Chinese species is rarely found in cultivation; here are references to illustrations: *Diapensia himalaica* Hook. f. & Thoms. (ICS 3955); *D. purpurea* Diels (ICS 3956); *D. bulleyana* Forrest (ICS 3957) and *D. wardii* W. E. Evans (JRHS 1950: 48).

The Diapensias are rarely seen in cultivation, since they are difficult to maintain; they require, like *Loiseleuria*, a windswept, open area.

DICHOTOMANTHES Kurz — ROSACEAE

Monotypic genus very closely related to *Cotoneaster*, differing mainly in the dry fruit capsules. For other differences see the description of the species.

Dichotomanthes tristaniicarpa Kurz. Tall, evergreen shrub or also a small tree, young branches dense white woolly; leaves alternate, elliptic, acute, cuneate at the base, margins entire, 3—10 cm long, 1.5—3 cm wide, dark green above and somewhat glossy, silky pubescent beneath, stipules thread-like, abscising early, petiole to 1 cm; flowers white, small, 6 mm wide, in terminal corymbs, 5 cm wide, petals 5, stamens 15—20, glabrous, calyx 5 lobed, woolly outside, June; fruit a dry, oblong, 6 mm long capsule, nearly totally surrounded by the calyx which later becomes fleshy. ICS 2362. China; Yunnan. 1917. Of only slight garden merit, but botanically interesting. Long cultivated in England. z8 Fig. 320. #

Fig. 320. *Dichotomanthes tristaniicarpa* (from ICS)

DICKSONIA L'Hér. — CYATHEACEAE

Tree fern with a tall, bristly, thick stem; leaves (fronds) large, rough, tripinnate, somewhat narrower toward the base; pinnae or secondary leaflets of various shapes; petiole on the fertile fronds shortened or absent; sori arranged along the margins, indusium bivalvate, outer valve produced by a modified, concave tooth of the leaf blade, inner valve is the actual indusium. — About 30 species in Malaysia (in the mountains), Australia, New Caledonia, New Zealand, in tropical America and on St. Helena Island. Cultivated in the open landscape only in the mildest areas of Europe and then only the following species.

Dicksonia antarctica Labill. Stem thick, black to black-brown, 8—10 m high in its habitat, in Europe scarcely over 3—4 m high; leaves (fronds) broad oval, to 2 m long, tripinnate, green beneath, rachis slightly pubescent; sori numerous, to 2 mm wide. LNH 249. Australia, Tasmania. 1786. z8 Plate 174. #∅

Will succeed outdoors only in very mild areas; otherwise must be over wintered in a cool greenhouse; needs abundant moisture and winter temperatures no less than 8—12°C.

DICTAMNUS

Dictamnus capenstris see: **Calodendrum capense**

DIERVILLA Mill. — CAPRIFOLIACEAE

Deciduous shrub, low; leaves opposite, sessile or short petiolate, simple; flowers on the current year's wood; corolla tubular, narrow, nearly 2 lobed, upper incision deeper than the 2 lower ones, about 1 cm long; stamens distinct; fruit a 2-chambered capsule, seeds without wings. — 3 species in N. America.

Diervilla lonicera Mill. Shrub, to 1 m high, stoloniferous, entire plant glabrous, branches cylindrical; leaves oblong-lanceolate to oval-lanceolate, 4—10 cm long, serrate and ciliate, distinctly petioled; flowers greenish-yellow, usually in 3's axillary and 5's terminal, June—July. BM 1796; GSP 445; NBB 2: 296 (= *D. canadensis* Willd.). Eastern N. America, on dry, gravelly soil. 1720. z4 Fig. 321.

D. rivularis Gatt. Shrub, to 1 m high, branches rod-like, densely pubescent; leaves ovate to oblong-lanceolate, 5—7 cm long, acuminate, nearly sessile, pubescent on both sides; flowers lemon-yellow, often turning reddish, in many flowered cymes grouped into terminal panicles, corolla lobes nearly as long as the corolla tube, July—August. GC 38: 339. Eastern N. America, on cool, moist soil. 1898. z5 Fig. 321.

D. sessilifolia Buckl. Shrub, to 1 m, very similar to *D. rivularis*, but with young branches 4 sided, pubescent at the nodes; leaves sessile, 5—15 cm long, glabrous except for the pubescent midrib, ovate-lanceolate, generally tapered, tough, corolla sulfur-yellow, corolla lobes shorter than the corolla tube, June—August. GC42: 247. N. America. 1844. z5 Fig. 321.

D. × splendens (Carr.) Kirchn. (*D. lonicera × D. ses-*

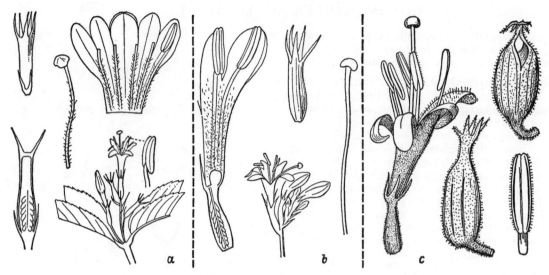

Fig. 321. *Diervilla* a. *D. lonicera*; b. *D. sessilifolia*; c. *D. rivularis*.
Details of flowers and fruit (from Koehne and C. Schneider)

silifolia). Resembles *D. sessilifolia*, but leaves short petiolate, venation green beneath. Cultivated since 1853, but origin unknown.

Easly cultivated plants for semishaded areas, either moist or dry soil; good understory plant in wooded areas.

DILLENIA

Dillenia speciosa see: **Hibbertia scandens**

DIMORPHOTHECA

Dimorphotheca ecklonis see: **Osteospermum ecklonis**

DIOSPYROS L. — Persimmon — EBENACEAE

Deciduous or evergreen trees and shrubs; leaves alternate, occasionally nearly opposite, simple; flowers mon- or dioecious, seldom bisexual or polygamous, the male flowers usually grouped in terminal or axillary clusters, the female solitary; calyx persistent, 3—7 parted; corolla inconspicuous, regular, 3—7 lobed, leathery; stamens 6—14; styles usually split; ovaries 3 to many chambered; fruit a juicy or dry berry. — About 500 species in the tropics and subtropics.

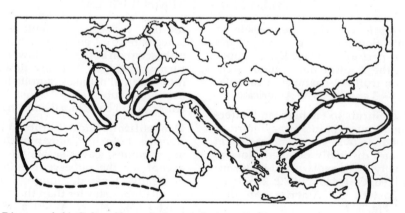

Fig. 322. *Diospyros kaki*. Cultural boundaries as a fruit tree in Europe, ——— indicates sporadic use (from Jaeger)

Diospyros armata Hemsl. Tall, evergreen tree in its habitat, branches pubescent at first, soon becoming glabrous and gray, occasionally terminating in a thorn; leaves elliptic, 2–5 cm long, acute or obtuse, base cuneate, tough, deep green and glossy above, with translucent spots beneath; flowers white, fragrant, in short racemes; fruits yellow, 1.5 cm wide, bristly. China; W. Hupeh. z8 #

D. kaki L. "Kaki" (jap.) Round crowned tree, 6–12 m high, branches brownish pubescent; leaves oval-elliptic, 6–18 cm long, dark green above, glossy, glabrous, pubescent beneath; flowers yellowish-white, 3 cm wide, June; fruits ovate, 3–7 cm long, orange to gold-brown, short stalked, with large, persistent calyx at the base, August–November. LF 253; BC 1273 (= *D. chinensis* Bl.; *D. schitse* Bge.). Japan, China. 1796. Frequently planted as a fruit tree in China, Japan and S. Europe and available in many cultivars. z6 Plate 173.⚥ ✗

var. **silvestris** Mak. Tree to 18 m high; female flowers smaller; ovaries densely pubescent, fruits smaller. China, Szechwan, Hupeh, Yunnan. The wild type.⚥ ✗

Of about 20 cultivars, those most commonly found in S. European culture are presented here:

'Costata'. Tree with fast growing, upright habit; fruits medium sized, slightly 4 sided, conical, with a small tip, 6 cm high, 5 cm wide, salmon-yellow, fruit pulp light yellow, very tasty when ripe. IH 18: Pl. 131 (= *D. kaki* var. *costata* [Carr.] André). Prolific fruiter, but also very ornamental. ⚥ ✗

'Hachiya'. Fruit very large, broad conical, with short tip, to 8 cm long and 7 cm thick, rind deep orange-red, translucent, occasionally with few dark patches and rings at the apex, fruit pulp orange-yellow, with seeds, very sweet when ripe, very sour and astringent if not ripe. The best and most beautiful cultivar in Italy and also California, but fruit production is minimal. Fig. 323.⚥ ✗

In Italian nurseries there are about 10 cultivars in cultivation; among them are 'Lycopersicum', like a very large tomato, squat rounded, orange-red, with very large sepals; and 'Mazelii' (E. A. Mazel, Montsauve, France), fruits large, orange-like, with 8 flattened furrows, leaves ovate, often with a slightly cordate base. RH 1874: 70 (= *D. kaki* var. *mazelii* [Carr.] Moullef.).

As a matter of historical record, 2 French cultivars (surely selected seedlings) are possibly still to be found in cultivation in S. France.

'Wieseneri'. Only shrubby; fruits very abundantly, fruits medium sized, broad ovate with small, sharp tips, orange-red when ripe, very sweet tasting. Breeder, M. Wiesener, Fontenay-aux-Roses. Before 1890.

'Sahutii'. Broadly conical, about 6.5 cm wide, 6 cm high, with a warty thickening at the apex, rind translucent gold-orange. Breeder, F. Sahut, Montpellier. Before 1890.

D. lotus L. Lotus Plant, Date Plum. Deciduous tree, 12–15 m high, young branches brownish pubescent, crown rounded, larger branches gray, pubescent; leaves elliptic-oblong, acute, 6–12 cm long, both sides pubescent at first, eventually only pubescent on

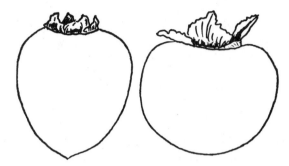

Fig. 323. Fruits from cultivars of *Diospyros kaki*. left 'Hachiya', right 'Lycopersicum' (Original). 1/2 actual size

the venation beneath, leathery tough; flowers solitary, axillary, yellowish, June; fruits orange-shaped, 1.5–2 cm wide, yellow or reddish, blue pruinose, stale tasting. LF 254; HM 2892 (= *D. japonica* S. & Z.). Manchuria to Yunnan, found both in the wild and in cultivation. 1597. Hardy. Ⓕ SW. Transcaucasia. z5 Plate 173. ⚥

D. morrisiana Hance. Small evergreen tree or large shrub, young branches with fine gray pubescence; leaves leathery tough, narrow-elliptic to oblong, 6–9 cm long, 2–3.5 cm wide, short acuminate, with obtuse apex, base long and narrowly attenuate, dark green above, new leaves brownish beneath with appressed pubescence; flowers short stalked, white, calyx lobes triangular, brown pubescent, June; fruits globose, yellow, to 2 cm thick, edible. KHT 38; KIF 2: 73. SE. China, Hong Kong, Formosa, Japan. z9

D. sinensis Hemsl. Shrub, 1.5–3 m high, bark gray, rough, branches with erect, sharp thorns, young branches thin, gray silky pubescent; leaves elliptic oblong, 3–6 cm long, 1–2 cm wide, acute at both ends, glossy green above, lighter beneath, margin crenate; flowers white, fragrant, solitary; fruits globose, 2 cm thick, yellow. Central to S. China. 1907. z8 ⚥

D. virginiana L. Persimmon. Deciduous tree, to 20 m high in ints habitat, round crowned, branches glabrous, outspread to nodding; leaves oval-elliptic, acute, 6–12 cm long, deep outspread to nodding; leaves oval-elliptic, acute, 6–12 cm long, deep green above and glossy, lighter beneath and glabrous except for the midrib; male flowers grouped 1–3, female solitary, greenish-yellow, June; fruits 2.5–3 cm wide (also larger on the cultivars), orange, eventually sweet, edible. BB 2831; GTP 320. Eastern N. America. 1699. Hardy. z5 Plate 173. ⚥

Many cultivars have been derived from this species which will not be covered here. For more information, please refer to Bailey.

var. **pubescens** (Pursh) Rehd. Branches and leaf undersides densely pubescent. 1889.

var. **platycarpa** Sarg. Leaves broader, base round to cordate; fruits flat rounded, 4–7 cm wide, Missouri to Arkansas. 1904.

D. virginiana is quite hardy, the others can be grown only in mild areas; prefer a deep fertile soil in a warm, protected area.

Lit. Bailey, L. H.: Persimmon; in Standard Cyclopedia of Horticulture (1950), 2556–2560; with 20 cultivar descriptions and 15 fruit illustrations ● Camp, A.F., & H. H. Mowry: The cultivated Persimmon (*Diospyros kaki*) in Florida; Bull. **124** Agr. Ext. Serv. Gainesville, Florida, 1948; 32 pp. with detailed cultivar descriptions ● Hume, H. H.: A kaki classification; in Jour. heredity **5**, 400–406, 1914.

DIOSMA

Diosma album see: **Coleonema album**

DIOSTEA Miers — VERBENACEAE

Deciduous shrubs or small trees, closely related to *Lippia*, but differing in habit, in the thin, green branches, branches with very long, hollow, cylindrical internodes; leaves opposite. — 3 species in S. America.

Diostea juncea (Gill. & Hook.) Miers. Deciduous, slender, reedlike branching shrub, 4–6 m high, young branches thin, with scattered pubescence when young, later becoming glabrous; the few leaves opposite, often spaced 5 cm apart, sessile, oval-oblong, thick, 1 to 1.8 cm long, 3–4 mm wide, triangular serrate, slightly pubescent; flowers tubular, tapering to the base, 8 mm long, pale lilac, with 5 small, round lobes, in small, 2.5 cm long spikes, June. BM 7695; BS 2:58 (= *Verbena juncea* Gill. & Hook.; *Baillonia juncea* [Gill. & Hook] Briq.) Chile and Argentina; Andes. 1890. Presumably quite hardy. ⊕

Not especially attractive, but easy to cultivate; good background plant for its long bare branches.

DIPELTA Maxim. — CAPRIFOLIACEAE

Deciduous shrubs, very similar to *Weigela* in appearance, but with different fruits and smaller flowers; leaves opposite, simple, short petioled; flowers tubular-campanulate, 2–8 in fascicles, pink or yellow outside, white and yellow inside; fruit a dry capsule surrounded by a widened, peltate bract. — 4 species in Middle and W. China.

Dipelta elegans Batal. From E. Kansu is presumably not yet in cultivation.

D. floribunda Maxim. Shrub, to 5 m high, usually only half as large in cultivation, multistemmed, stems with long shredding bark, yellow-brown, young branches glandular pubescent; leaves oval to elliptic-

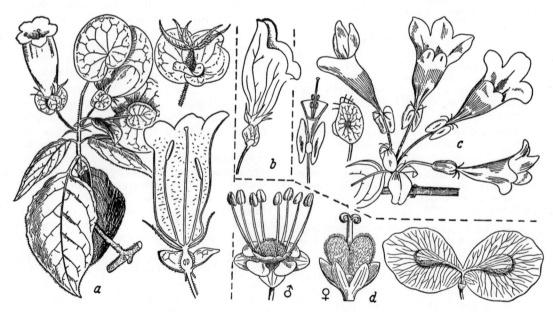

Fig. 324. **Dipelta.** a. *D. ventricosa*; b. *D. yunnanensis*; c. *D. floribunda*. **Dipteronia** d. *D. sinensis*, flowers and double fruit (from Gard. Chron., Rev. Hort., Oliver)

Plate 161

Daphne burkwoodii   *Daphne caucasica*

Daphne blagayana
(all 3 photos from the Berlin Bot. Garden, West Germany. C. R. Jellitto)

Plate 162

Daphne laureola
Photo: C. R. Jelitto

Daphne odora 'Aureomarginata'
in Killerton Park, England

Daphne genkwa
in the Berlin-Dahlem Botanic Garden
Photo: C. R. Jelitto

Daphne altaica
Photo: C. R. Jelitto

Plate 163

Daphniphyllum macropodum
on Garnish Island, Ireland

Daphniphyllum macropodum 'Variegatum'
in Wakehurst, England

Daphniphyllum macropodum
in the Taranto Garden, Pallanza, Italy

Daphniphyllum macropodum var. *humile*
in Japan

Plate 164

Daphne retusa in the Berlin Botanic Garden
Photo: C. R. Jelitto

Dasylirion serratifolium
in the Marimurtra Garden, Blanes, Spain

Davidia involucrata
in Kew Gardens, London, England

Datura sanguinea
in La Mortola, Italy

Plate 165

Desmodium spicatum
in the Glasnevin Botanical Garden, Dublin, Ireland

Decaisnea fargesii, with fruits
in Charlottenlund, Denmark

Decumaria barbara
in the Wageningen Arboretum, Holland

Delonix regia, a street tree
in Nelspruit, Transvaal, S. Africa

Plate 166

Deutzia carnea 'Stellata'
in the Glasnevin Botanical Garden, Dublin, Ireland

Deutzia maliflora 'Boule Rose'
in the Spaeth Arboretum, Berlin

Dendromecon rigida in Wisley Gardens, England

Plate 167

Deutzia gracilis
Photo: Dr. Pilat, Prague

Deutzia hybrida 'Mont Rose'
in the Kurpark, Kissingen, W. Germany

Deutzia hybrida 'Magicien' in the Dortmund Botanic Garden

Plate 168

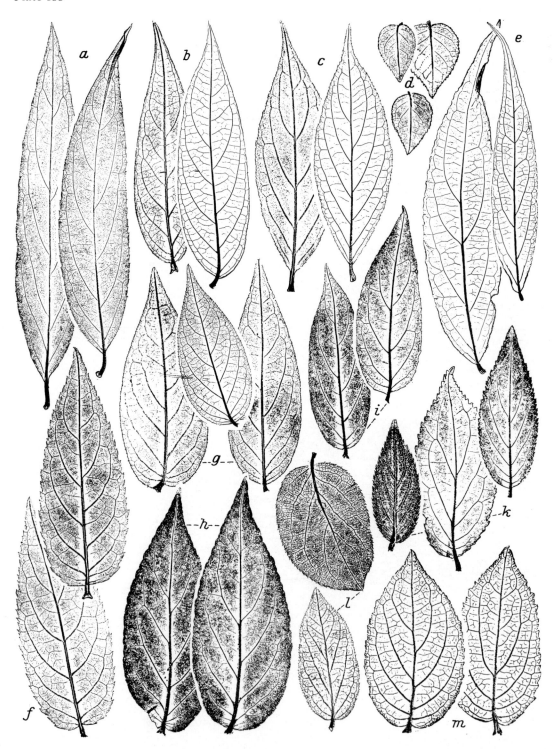

Deutzia a. *D. longifolia*; b. *D. ningpoensis*; c. *D. hybrida* 'Magicien'; d. *D. rehderiana*; e. *D. chunii*; f. *D. discolor*; g. *D. wilsonii*; h. *D. magnifica* 'Latifolia'; i. *D. hybrida* 'Perle Rose'; k. *D. hybrida* 'Mont Rose'; l. *D. mollis*; m. *D. sieboldiana* (Most of the leaves collected from the wild)

Plate 169

Deutzia magnifica 'Erecta'

Deutzia magnifica 'Eburnea'
(both photos in the Dort. Bot. Garden)

Deutzia magnifica 'Latiflora'
from Spaeth, Berlin

Deutzia setchuenensis var. *corymbiflora*
in the Malahide Castle Park, Ireland

Plate 170

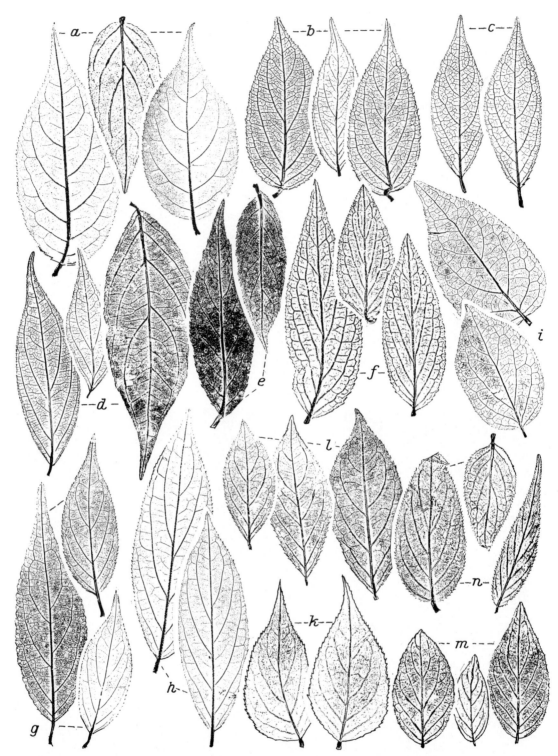

Deutzia a. *D. setchuenensis corymbiflora*; b. *D. taiwanensis*; c. *D. gracilis*; d. *D. maximowicziana*; e. *D. rubens*; f. *D. discolor*; g. *D. rosea*; h. *D. vilmoriniae*; i. *D. parviflora*; k. *D. staminea*; 1. *D. coreana*; m. *D. albida*; n. *D. glomeruliflora* (2 types) (most leaves collected from the wild)

Plate 171

Deutzia scabra 'Candidissima'
in the Dortmund Botanic Garden

Deutzia rosea
in the Glasnevin Botanic Garden, Dublin, Ireland

Deutzia scabra in its native habitat in Japan (enlarged)

Photo: Dr. Watari, Tokyo

Plate 172

Deutzia elegantissima
from L. Spaeth, Berlin

Deutzia ningpoensis
in the Dortmund Botanic Garden

Deutzia chunii
in the Dortmund Botanic Garden

Deutzia taiwanensis
in the Dortmund Botanic Garden

Plate 173

Diospyros kaki, young fruits
Photo: Dr. Watari, Tokyo

Diospyros kaki, whitish flowers
Photo: Dr. Watari, Tokyo

Diospyros lotus, ripe fruits
Photo: Dr. Watari, Tokyo

Diospyros virginiana with fruits
on the Mainau Island, W. Germany

Plate 174

Dipteronia sinensis
in the Copenhagen Botanic Garden, Denmark

Dipelta floribunda
in the Stadtpark, Lugano, Switzerland

Dickonia antarctica, surviving in the open
in Logan, West Scotland

Discaria toumatou
in Kew Gardens, England

Plate 175

Drimys winteri var. *latifolia*
in the Bell Park, Fota Island, Ireland

Diapensia lapponica, from North Norway
an imported plant in Berlin
Photo: C. R. Jelitto

Disanthus cercidfolius in the Villa Taranto Park, Pallaza, Italy

Plate 176

Drimys winteri var. *andina*
in the Hillier Arboretum in England

Drimys lanceolata
in the Borde Hill Park, England

Dracophyllum paludosum
in the Castelwellan Park, N. Ireland

Drypis spinosa
in the Lausanne, Switzerland

lanceolate 5—10 cm long, long acuminate, sparsely dentate only on the long shoots, soon glabrous; flowers in terminal and axillary clusters, nodding, fragrant, corolla 3.5 cm long, light pink outside, orange-yellow and white inside, May—June; fruit bract attached in the middle of the blade. BM 8310; BS 1: 630. Central China. 1902. Hardy. z6 Plate 174; Fig. 324.⊕⊗

D. ventricosa Hemsl. Shrub, to 5 m, much smaller in cultivation, branches softly pubescent; leaves as the previous species but somewhat narrower, longer acuminate, dentate, densely pubescent on the venation beneath, corolla campanulate, 3 cm long, oblique at the base, purple ouside, lighter pink and orange inside, June—July; bracts about 2 cm wide, auriculate,

attached at the base. BS 2: 59; BM 8294. W. China. z6 Fig. 324. ⊕ ⊗

D. yunnanensis Franch. Shrub, to 2 m, usually smaller, young branches 4 sided, finely pubescent; leaves oval-lanceolate, long acuminate, 5—12 cm long, entire, midrib pubescent beneath; flowers grouped 1—4 at the ends of small side branches, corolla 2—2.5 cm long, tubular at the base, limb composed of 5 round lobes, outside yellow with some pink, inside orange, May; fruit bracts cordate. RH 1891: China, Yunnan. 1910. z7 Fig. 324. ⊕ ⊗

Cultural requirements like those of *Weigela*; normal garden soil, sunny location, but somewhat more tender as a young plant.

DIPLACUS Nutt. see: **Mimulus L.**

Many botanists classify the shrubby species of the genus *Mimulus* in a separate genus, *Diplacus*, while

only the perennial and annual species remain in the *Mimulus*.

DIPLOPAPPUS

Diplopappus chrysophyllus see: **Cassinia fulvida**

D. ericoides see: **Haplopappus ericoides**

DIPTERONIA Oliv. — ACERACEAE

Deciduous trees; leaves opposite, pinnate, leaflets 7—15, serrate; flowers in erect, terminal panicles; sepals longer than the short petals; stamens usually 8; fruits composed of 2 nutlets, connate at the base, totally encircled by a wing. — 2 species in China.

Dipteronia sinensis Oliv. Tree, often only a small shrub in cultivation, buds densely pubescent; leaves

20—30 cm long, with 7—13 leaflets, coarse and irregularly dentate; flowers greenish, very small, in erect panicles, June; fruits in large fascicles, pale red. EP IV, 163: 2; FIO 142; CIS 36. Central China; Hupeh, Szechwan. Around 1900. z7 Plate 174; Fig. 324. ∅ ⊗

Needs a good garden soil, somewhat protected location; interesting for its foliage.

DIRCA L. — Leatherwood — THYMELAEACEAE

Deciduous shrubs; branches very flexible; leaf buds hidden in the petiole base until leaf drop, without a terminal bud; leaves alternate, thin; flowers without petals, 2—3 in axillaryfascicles on the previous year's wood, receptacle narrow funnel-form, distinctly 4 lobed; stamens 8, filamentous, markedly exserted; fruit a small drupe. — 2 species in N. America.

Dirca palustris L. Multistemmed or also single, 1—2 m tall shrub, branches smooth, yellowish, with very tough bark; leaves broad elliptic, entire, 3—7 cm long, light green, bluish beneath and somewhat pubescent at first; flowers small, light yellow, numerous, March—May; fruits ellipsoid, greenish or reddish. BB 2535; NBB 2: 572. Eastern USA. z5 Fig. 325. ⊕

For cool, moist organic soil, semishade, likes peat. The flowers are damaged by frost. The branches were once used by the Indians in wickerwork and the bark for bow strings.

Lit. Choquette, L.: Le Bois de Plomb, *Dirca palustris* L.; 93 pp., Paris 1926 ● Vogelmann, H.: A comparison of *Dirca palustris* and *D. occidentalis*; in Asa Gray Bull. **2**, 77—82, 1953.

Fig. 325. *Dirca palustris*, branch and singular flowers (from Guimpel, Gilg)

DISANTHUS Maxim — HAMAMELIDACEAE

Monotypic genus. Deciduous shrub; leaves alternate, venation palmate, long stalked, with small, quickly abscising stipules; flowers in 2 flowered heads at the leaf axils, calyx 5 parted, petals 5, narrow lanceolate, erect; stamens 5; fruit a many seeded capsule with 2 lobed tip. — Habitat China and Japan.

Disanthus cercidifolius Maxim. Deciduous shrub, dense, 2(4) m tall, branches with lenticels; leaves ovate, base cordate, 5—12 cm long and wide, bluish-green above, lighter beneath, tough, carmine-red to orange in fall, wonderful fall color; flowers similar to those of *Hamamelis*, violet-purple, October; fruit ripens in fall of the second year. BM 8716; MD 1900: 1. Mountains in Japan and China. z6 Plate 175; Fig. 326. Ø

Cultural requirements like those of *Hamamelis*; needs a protected area.

DISCARIA Hook. — RHAMNACEAE

Thorny shrub, resembling *Colletia*, but easily distinguished by the long, thin, opposite thorns, the stipules connected by a thin line (totally absent on *Colletia*), and the small, opposite leaves; flowers small, numerous, campanulate, in axillary fascicles, 4—5 parted, petals often absent; stigma often 3 lobed; fruit a 3 parted capsule. — 10 species in S. America, 1 each in Australia and New Zealand.

Discaria discolor Dusen. Thorny shrub, to 1 m high and twice as wide, all parts glabrous; leaves opposite, elliptic to obovate, rounded at the apex, tapering to the base, entire to slightly dentate, 5—18 mm long; flowers 2—3, in axillary, short stalked fascicles, white, fragrant, calyx without petals, May—June, flowers very abundantly (= *Colletia discolor* Hook.). Andes of Argentina and Patagonia. 1927. z8 ☺

D. serratifolia (Vent.) Benth. & Hook. Thorny shrub, also a small tree in its habitat, branches slender, pendulous, thorns about 2 cm long; leaves opposite, 1.2—2.5 cm long, ovate-oblong, crenate, glossy green above, polished appearance, less glossy beneath; flowers in large numbers in clusters on short branches of the previous year's wood, petals absent, calyx greenish-white, limb with 5 triangular lobes, fragrant, June. Chile, Patagonia. 1842. z8 ☺

D. toumatou Raoul. "Wild Irishman" (British common name). Thorny shrub, also a small tree in its native habitat, branches long, very thin, exceptionally stout thorny, thorns 2.5—4 cm long, stiff, very sharp, opposite and at right angles from the branch, not developed on young seedlings; leaves 8—20 mm long, only on young plants and current year's growth, generally abscising; flowers very numerous, together with the leaves at the base of the thorns, greenish-white, May. BS 1: 636; LNz 254. New Zealand, both islands. 1875. z8 Plate 174.

Dry, sunny areas; only for the collector; only attractive when in flower.

Lit. Cockayne: On the significance of the spines of *Discaria toumatou*; in New Phytolog., London, 1904, no. 4.

DISTICTIS Mart. ex Meissn. — BIGNONIACEAE

Evergreen high climbing vines with twisting stems; leaves opposite, with 2 or 3 leaflets, often the terminal leaf is modified into a simple or 3 branched tendril; flowers large, in dense, terminal panicles; calyx tubular-campanulate, truncate, often jagged, corolla funnelform-campanulate, tough, with a broad limb, stamens enclosed; fruit a smooth capsule, seeds in several rows. — 4 species in Mexico and the West Indies.

Distictis laxiflora (DC.) Greenm. Evergreen, high climber, gray tomentose, with simple hairs, tendrils 3 parted; leaflets 2—3, ovate or elliptic, obtuse or also acute, 3—5 cm long, entire; corolla finely tomentose outside, 5—8 cm long, 3—6 cm wide over the limb, purple, fading lighter to white, yellow throat, fragrant, April—July; fruit capsule oblong-elliptic, 7—9 cm long, 4 cm wide (= *D. cinerea* Greenm.). Mexico. z9 # ☺

In addition there is the selection 'Mrs. Rivers', flowers more deeply purple-violet, glossier leaves. MCL 110 (= *Distictis* 'Riversii'). US Plant Pat. Nr. 554.

One of the most beautiful evergreen climbers, but only for the mildest regions.

DISTYLIUM S. & Z. — HAMAMELIDACEAE

Evergreen trees or shrubs; leaves alternate, simple, ovate to lanceolate, usually entire, leathery; flowers in loose or dense, axillary spikes or racemes of male and bisexual flowers, without petals. — 6 species (according to Harms, 8) in the Indo-Malaysian and warmer East Asiatic region.

Distylium racemosum S. & Z. Evergreen shrub, a large tree in Japan; leaves lanceolate to elliptic, entire, 3—7 cm long, tough and leathery; flowers stellate pubescent, in 2—4 cm long, axillary spikes, conspicuous for the long, red anthers, March—April; fruit a woody, 2 pointed capsule. LF 154; BM 9501; GC 136: 46. Japan; mountain forests. z7 Fig. 326. # Ø

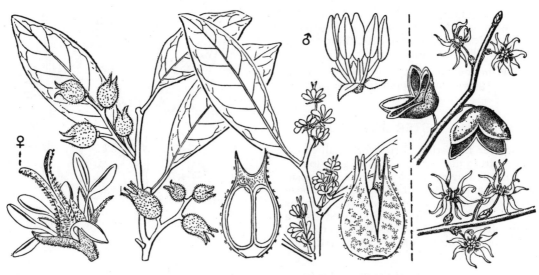

Fig. 326. Left *Distylium racemosum*. Right *Disanthus cercidifolius*.
Branches with flowers and fruits (from Lauche, Harms)

Thrives on a sandy-humus soil, but best grown as a hardy cool-greenhouse plant. Plants in cultivation have larger leaves than those found in the wild (The Botanic Garden at Tuebingen, W. Germany, near Stuttgart, has a plant in the landscape 2 m high).

Lit. Walker, E. H.: A revision of *Distylium* and *Sycopsis*; Jour. Arnold Arb. **25**, 319—341, 1944.

DOCYNIA Decne. — ROSCEAE

Evergreen shrubs, very similar to *Cydonia* (*Docynia* is an anagram of *Cydonia*), but differing in the evergreen leaves and styles connate at the base; flowers grouped 2—5, petals 5, styles 5; fruit quince-like, with persistent, very dense woolly calyx. — 5 species in China, East Indies and Vietnam.

Docynia delavaya (Franch.) Schneid. Evergreen shrub, also a tree in its habitat, to 7 m high, wide habit, young branches pubescent, later red-brown and glabrous to black, occasionally also somewhat thorny; leaves oval-lanceolate, 3—7 cm long, acute, entire, densely tomentose beneath, the 1—1.5 cm long petiole is likewise tomentose; flowers sessile, like apple flowers, pink-white, 2—4 in sessile umbels, fragance like *Crataegus* flowers, April—May; fruits like small apples, 3 cm wide, yellow, pubescent. RH 1918: 45—47 (= *Pirus delavayi* Franch.). China; Yunnan.

1890. Occasionally planted on the French Riviera. z8 # ✿ ⊘ ✿

D. indica Dcne. Small tree, 3—5 m high, short branches frequently thorned, young branches and leaf undersides densely white woolly, later more or less glabrous; leaves on the long shoots lobed to pinnatisect, also on young plants, on older plants and flower branches lanceolate, nearly entire or indistinctly serrate, 5—7 cm long, petiole 1—1.5 cm; flowers grouped 1—3, axillary, white, calyx gray-yellow tomentose, May; fruit oval-rounded, 4—5 cm long, yellow, with persistent, crowned with reflexed sepals, these eventually breaking off, edible. Brandis, *Indian Trees*, Fig. 124. SH 402—403 (= *D. griffithiana* Dcne; *Pyrus indica* Wall.). E. Himalaya, from Sikkim to Manipur, in the mountains to 2000m. z8 Fig. 327. ⊘ ✿

DODONAEA Mill. — SAPINDACEAE

Evergreen or deciduous trees and shrubs; leaves alternate, without stipules, simple or pinnate; flowers unisexual, dioecious, occasionally also bisexual, regular; sepals 3—7, imbricate, petals absent; stamens usually 8(5—10), with very short filaments; ovaries round, usually (but not always) 3 chambered, usually 2 seeds per locule. — About 60 species, most in Australia, some in Africa, Hawaii and N. America.

Dodonaea triquetra Andr. Upright shrub, young branches flattened or very angular; leavs oval-elliptic to oblong-lanceolate, long acuminate, to 10 cm long, entire or nearly so; flowers in short, compact, oblong panicles or racemes, sepals tiny; fruit capsules like those of *D. viscosa*. Australia. z9

D. viscosa (L.) Jacq. Evergreen shrub, to 5m; leaves simple, very viscid, oblong, acuminate, yellow-green, entire, both sides resinous punctate; flowers in short, axillary and terminal racemes, greenish, sepals ovate; capsule to 2 cm long, broad 3 winged, incised at the apex, base more or less cordate. KF 17. Tropics of Australia, S. Africa, Mexico and USA (Florida and Arizona). Before 1800. z9 Fig. 328. #

Cultivated in loam soil; for frost free climates or over-wintering in a cool greenhouse; tolerates dryness, salty sea breezes and wind.

DOMBEYA Cav. — STERCULIACEAE

Evergreen, winter flowering shrubs or small trees, leaves large, alternate, often cordate and lobed, palmate venation; flowers pink or white, in loose, axillary or terminal cymes, umbels or dense globose heads; calyx 5 parted, persistent, petals 5, stamens 15—20, of those 5 sterile, the others fused into a cupule or tube; fruit a capsule — 50 species in tropical Africa, and about 300 more in Madagascar and Mascarene Islands.

Dombeya calantha Schum. Broad shrub, 3—4 m high, but also to 6 m; leaves very large, to 30 cm long, 3—5 lobed, coarsely dentate, base cordate, pubescent above, tomentose beneath, long petioled; flowers in pink "balls", 4 cm wide, above the foliage. BM 8424. Tropical Africa. One of the best species. z9 # ✧

D. × cayeuxii Hort. (*D. mastersii × D. wallichii*). Only about 3 m high; leaves cordate, often also 3 lobed, dentate, large, dark green above, lighter beneath, reticulate venation, petioles 10—15 cm long; flowers pink, with fine dark veins, in axillary, many flowered, pendulous, globose umbels, January.RH 1897; BMns 473. Developed by H. M. Cayeux in the Lisbon Botanic

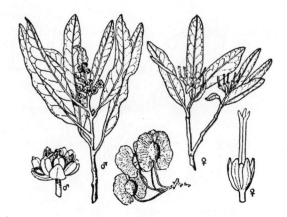

Fig. 328. *Dodonaea viscosa* (from Adams)

Garden, Portugal. z8 # ✧

D. wallichii Benth. & Hook. To 9 m high; leaves large, cordate, angular lobed, rough, stipules leaf-like; flowers lilac-pink, in large, pendulous balls, on long, thin, pubescent stalks, occasionally somewhat hidden under the foliage, February—April. EKW 383 (= *Astrapaea wallichii* Lindl.). Madagascar. 1820. z9 Plate 128. # ✧

Illustrations of other species: *D. ameliae* (FS 605); *D. cacuminum* (MCL 18); *D. viburnifolia* (FS 626).

All species very fast growing, needing a good, fertile soil, protection, frost free location, a very impressive plant.

Fig. 327. Left *Dorycnium suffruiticosum* (from Schneider).
Right *Docynia indica* (from Chaudin [altered] and Schneider)

DORYCNIUM Mill. — LEGUMINOSAE

Perennials or small shrubs; leaves 5 parted (actually only 3 parted, but the stipules are of equal form and size to the leaflets); flowers in axillary heads; calyx campanulate, with 5 equal or unequal teeth; corolla white or pink, with an obtuse, dark red or black keel petal; pods oblong or ovate. — 15 species in the Mediterranean region, but only 2 are commonly found in cultivation.

Dorycnium hirsutum (L.) Ser. Subshrub, 20—50 cm, usually shaggy pubescent; leaves with or without very short rachis, leaflets oblong-obovate, 7—25 × 3—8 mm; flower head with 4—10 flowers, on 3—5 cm long stalks, in the leaf axils at the branch tips, the solitary flowers about 2 cm long, white, occasionally turning pink, calyx teeth uneven, June—September; pods 6—12 mm long, oval-oblong. Meditteranean region and S. Portugal. 1683. z8 ⊕

D. suffruticosum Vill. Shrub, 10—50 cm high, branches with appressed pubescence; leaves without a rachis, leaflets linear to obovate-oblong, leaflets of the upper leaves 6—12 × 2—3 mm; flower head with 5—15 flowers, stalks usually shorter than the calyx tube, these with 5 uneven sized teeth, corolla only about 6 mm long, pink-white, June—September. SDK 4:15 (= *D. pentaphyllum* Scop.). SW. Europe to S. Italy. z8 Fig. 327. ⊕

Best cultivated on a sandy-loam soil in a sunny, dry area; both mentioned species flower abundantly and are most attractive.

DOXANTHA Miers — BIGNONIACEAE

Evergreen, climbing vines; leaves opposite, 1—3 parted and with terminal, 3 parted, claw-like tendrils; flowers solitary or in short panicles; calyx truncate, margin uniform or lobed, corolla funnelform, attractive, stamens enclosed; ovaries somewhat 4 sided, with many locules; fruit capsule linear, seeds with membranous wings. — 2 species in tropical America.

Doxantha unguis-cati (L.) Rehd. Evergreen vine, climbing to 10 m high, branches smooth; leaflets oval-oblong to elliptic, 3—6 cm long; flowers in fascicles on 1—3 cm long, thin stalks, calyx 1—1.5 cm long, greenish, corolla 8—9 cm long, yellow, with orange lines in the throat, 6—10 cm wide over the erect lobes, nearly *Allamanda*-like, April to July; fruit capsule 30—40 cm long, 1 cm thick, seeds 2—3 cm long, winged. BR 26:45; MCL 109 (= *Bignonia unguis-cati* L.). Argentina. Tolerates temperature to 0°C in the open landscape. z8 Plate 128. # ⊕

Cultivated like *Campsis*; in good soil this plant will develop into a gorgeous specimen, in the greenhouse it needs a well ventilated location.

DRACAENA Vand. ex L. — AGAVACEAE

Evergreen shrubs or trees, without creeping rhizomes; leaves lanceolate or oblanceolate, often bowed-erect; flowers in panicles, occasionally in dense, sessile heads or oblong spikes, whitish, corolla campanulate or plate-like, with 6 erect lobes; stamens 6; fruit a 3 chambered berry. — About 150 species in the warmer regions of the world.

Differing from the similar genus *Cordyline* in the larger flowers and single seed in each chamber (instead of many).

Dracaena darco L. Dracena. Tree, to 18 m high, crown branched and becoming very broad; leaves very numerous, densely packed, sword-form, erect, the outer ones reflexed, 45—60 cm long, 3—4 cm wide, scarcely tapering to the base, generally tapering to the apex, blue-green; flowers greenish-white, very small, in large panicles, May—August; fruits globose, orange, 1 cm. KGC 6; BM 4571. Canary Islands. 1640. Found in most botanic gardens. z8 #

The oldest tree of this species stood in Orotava until it was unfortunately lost in 1868; its age was estimated to have been around 6000 years. The largest specimen today is in Icod (Teneriffe) and is estimated to be about 2000 years old; illustrated in MD 1930, Pl. 54.

Lit. Mengel, P. F.: *Dracaena draco* L.: der Drachenbaum; Mitt. Dtsch. Dendr. Ges. 1930, 351—535, with plates.

DRACOPHYLLUM Labill. — EPACRIDACEAE

Somewhat resembling *Dracaena*, evergreen shrubs or rarely small trees in their native habitat; leaves often lanceolate or grass-like in appearance, long acuminate, stem clasping; flowers in terminal racemes or spikes; corolla cylindrical or campanulate, limb with 5 lobes, anthers 5, sessile, adnate to the corolla throat; fruit a chambered dehiscent capsule. — About 30 species in Australia, New Caledonia and New Zealand.

For positive identification the sheath-like leaf base and the leaf apex must be closely observed; for the New Zealand species, please refer to the descriptions in H. H. Allan, Fl. NZ I, Fig. 21 and 22.

Dracophyllum paludosum Cockayne. Shrub, broad and upright, to 2 m, stem thin, with nearly black bark, branches thin, densely arranged, bark reddish-brown; leaves nearly filamentous, 30—40 × 1.5 mm, margins finely ciliate; flowers solitary or 3—4 in 2 cm long racemes, corolla nearly campanulate, 3–4 mm long, limb tips white, fragrant, June. JRHS 37:60 (= *D. scoparium* var. *paludosum* Cockayne). Chatham Island. z8 Plate 176. #

Rather rare in cultivation.

Lit. Oliver, W. R. B.: A revision of the genus *Dracophyllum*; Transact. N. Z. Inst. **59**, 678–714, 1929 ● Supplement: T. R. S. N. Z. **80**, 1–17, 1952.

DRIMYS Forst. — WINTERACEAE

Evergreen shrubs or trees; bark aromatic; leaves alternate, translucent punctate, entire, glabrous; flowers axillary and terminal; sepals and petals distinctly differentiated, sepals adnate to a bud scale, tearing apart at bud break and abscising; petals 6 to many, attractive, white, yellowish to pink, in 2 or more whorls; stamens numerous; stigma sessile; fruit many seeded. — About 36 species in S. America, Australia, New Zealand and Borneo.

Drimys lanceolata (Poir.) Baill. Shrubby, in its habitat (and also in milder climates) to 4.5 m high; leaves oblong lanceolate, obtuse, 3–7 cm long, young branches and leaf petioles red; flowers very numerous, dioecious, in terminal and axillary clusters, petals 6(8), white, linear, April. BR 1845; BS 2:69 (= *D. aromatica* [R. Br.] F. v. Muell.). Australia, Tasmania. All parts of the plant carry the pungent scent of pepper. z8 Plate 176. # ✧

D. winteri J. R. & G. Forst. Shrubby in European cultivation, tree-like in its habitat, quite glabrous, young branches reddish; leaves oblong, 12–20 cm long, obtuse, dull green above, blue-green beneath and finely punctate; flowers ivory-white, star-shaped, 4 cm wide, scented like Jasmine, grouped 7–8 in long stalked umbels, May to June. HuF 1: 3, BS 2: Pl. 12; PFC 199; EKW 400. S. America, Middle Chile to Tierra Del Fuego. z8 # ✧ ∅

Over its large range, the following geographical varieties can be distinguished:

var. **andina** Reiche. Dwarf form, to only about 1 m high, but much wider, very slow growing (a 40 year old plant in Nymans, England is 1.5 m high and 3.5 m wide), flowering on 30 cm high plants; leaves obovate, 10–12 cm long, 4–5 cm wide, obtuse, petiole 1–2 cm. Andes, near Llolli, on the border between Chile and Argentina, at 1300 m. 1926. z7? Plate 176. ✧

var. **chilensis** (DC.) A. Gray. Leaves 8–12 cm long, narrow oblong to oblong-lanceolate, rounded at the apex, deep green above, bluish beneath; inflorescence a compound umbel of 4–5 umbels with 4–7 flowers each. BMns 200. Middle Chile. ✧ ∅

var. **latifolia** Miers. Shrub, to 5 m high, branches thicker, green; leaves under the inflorescences about 12 cm long, usually oblanceolate, 4–7 cm wide; flowers normally 20–30 in simple umbels. Not uncommon in S. English and Irish parks. z8 Plate 175. ✧ ∅

var. **winteri**. The type of this species; leaves clustered at the branch tips; inflorescences normally with single flowered stalks, seldom with umbels, flowers with 5–7 petals (= *D. winteri* var. *D. punctata* [Lam.] DC.; *D. punctata* Lam.). Chile, south of 42° S. Latitude (which is south of Valdivia) ✧

Beautiful, tall shrubs with pretty flowers, only for the landscape in warmer climates.

Lit. Smith, A. C.: The American species of *Drimys*; in Jour. Arnold Arb. 1943, 1–33 ● Vine, W.: The Winteraceae of the Old World. I; *Pseudowintera* and *Drimys*, morphology and taxonomy; in Blumea, 225–354, 1970; 34 ills.

DRYANDRA R. Br.— PROTEACEAE

Evergreen shrubs; leaves alternate, nearly always pinnatisect or pinnately lobed; flowers orange or yellow, in dense terminal or axillary heads, surrounded at the base by a dense involucre of numerous, imbricate bracts; perianth slender, erect, tubular at the base, divide at the apex into 4 narrow-linear segments, wider at the tip, concave at the point where the sessile anthers are connected; style erect, thin, often reaching beyond the anthers. — 50 species in W. Australia; at one time very popular in European gardens.

Dryandra formosa R. Br. Shrub, 1–3 m high, branches softly pubescent; leaves 10–20 cm long, 1–1.5 cm wide, divided into triangular lobes from the midrib out on both sides, dark green above, pubescent beneath; flowers orange-yellow, in about 6–7 cm wide heads, terminal, fragrant, perianth 2–2.5 cm long, glabrous at the base, apex silky pubescent, the corolla lobes pubescent, fragrant, May. BM 4102; HTS 188. W. Australia, on sandy and gravelly hills. z9 # ✧

D. longifolia R. Br. Tall shrub, branches pubescent; leaves 15–30 cm long, 0.8–1.2 cm wide, pinnatisect and regularly lobed, lobes triangular, acute, 12 mm wide, gray pubescent beneath; flowers in terminal heads, the 4–5 cm wide and high, yellow, perianth 3.5 cm long, the 4 corolla lobes pubescent, February–July. BM 1582. W. Australia. 1805. z9 # ✧

D. nobilis Lindl. Shrub, about 2m high, branches thick, woolly pubescent; leaves 12–25 cm long, 1–2 cm wide, pinnatisect, glabrous above, white pubescence beneath; flowers in 5–7 cm wide, terminal heads, yellow, perianth 3.5 cm long, pubescent, style 5 cm long, May. BM 4633; HTS 189; EWA 121. W. Australia. z9 # ✧

Cultivated like *Banksia*.

DRYAS L. — ROSACEAE

Evergreen, creeping dwarf shrubs, wide dense mat-like habit; leaves alternate, simple and stalked, more or less leathery, rugose above and usually white beneath; flowers solitary on long stalks, usually bisexual, calyx shell-form to campanulate, with 7−10 lobes; petals 7−10, larger than the calyx lobes, white to yellowish; fruits like those of *Clematis*, with long feathery tail-like appendage. — 3 species in the mountains of the Northern Hemisphere (divided nto 18 species by Juzepczuk)

Dryas drummondii Richards. Leaves elliptic to obovate, 1−3 cm long, light green above, dull, pubescent or glabrous, white tomentose beneath, coarsely crenate, base acute, apex rounded; flower stalk 5−20 cm long, flowers yellow, nodding, usually do not open fully, calyx somewhat tomentose and with black glandular pubescence inside and out (important), June−August. RWF 175−165; BB 1951; BM 2972. N. America, high mountains. Garden merit slight because the flowers do not open completely. z3 # ✧

D. octopetala L. Growth procumbent mat-like; leaves oblong-elliptic to ovate, 6−25 mm long, round or obtuse at both ends, dull green above, glabrous, silvery-white tomentose beneath, margin coarse round crenate, widest in the middle; flower stalk 5−20 cm long, tomentose more or less black pubescent, flowers white, wide spreading, petals elliptic to obovate, 1−1.5 cm long, calyx tomentose and black pubescent inside and out, June−August. BB 1949; PAr 265; FFA 13; GPN 480−482. Circumpoplar in the high mountains of the Northern Hemisphere. z2 # ✧

Variable species, separated into many geographical races:

ssp. **octopetala.** Leaves 2−3 cm long, rather coarsely crenate, glabrous above or somewhat pubescent (= ssp. *chamaedryfolia* [Crantz] Gams). The type in the European mountains. ✧

var. **asiatica** (Nakai) Nakai. Leaves shorter, wider and more obtuse than the type. TAP 189; ICS 2298 (= *D. tschonoskii* Juzep.). Mountains of Japan and Korea.

var. **collina** Schmid. Flower stalk to 40 cm high. Fruilian Alps.

var. **integrifolia** (Vahl) Hook. f. Leaves very small, lanceolate to elliptic, 6−25 mm long, apex acute, base round to cordate. Margin involute, entire, very glossy above, widest at the base. BB 1950; PAr 265 (= *D. integrifolia* Vahl; *D. tenella* Pursh). Labrador, Greenland.

var. **vestita** Beck. Leaves with upper surface also more or less tomentose (= var. *lanata* Kern; f. *argentea* [Blytt] Hult.). East Alps.

D. × suendermannii Kellerer (*D. drummondii × D. octopetala*). Resembles *D. octopetala*, but flowers yellowish in bud, then opening white, nodding. Developed by Suendermann, Lindau (Bodensee). Around 1925. z3 # ✧

D. tomentosa Farr. Very similar to *D. drummondii*, but with upper leaf surface also gray tomentose, obovate to elliptic; flowers yellow, sepals without glands (= *D. drummondii* var. *tomentosa* [Farr] Williams). N. America, Rocky Mountains; Canada. z2 # ✧

Easily cultivated alpine plants for full sun and good, alkaline soil.

Lit. Porsild, A. E.: The genus *Dryas* in North America; in The Canadian Field-Naturalist **61**, 175 to 192, 1947; with several range maps and 2 plates; 14 species described.

DRYPIS L. — CARYOPHYLLACEAE

Monotypic genus, closely related to *Silene*, but the fruit capsules opening irregularly, instead of toothed. Otherwise see the following description of the species.

Drypis spinosa L. Small, bushy, glabrous subshrub, 8−15 cm high, branches 4 sided, strongly branched; leaves opposite, awl-shaped, 12 mm long, stiff and with prickly tips, glossy green; flowers in terminal, capitate umbels, pale pink or white, the individual flowers 12 mm wide, the 5 petals very narrow and deeply incised, stamens 5, June−July; fruit an obovoid capsule, dehiscing on the total circumference. BM 2216; HM 579. West Mediterranean region, from Italy to Greece, on gravelly slopes, especially near the sea. 1775. Interesting but only of slight garden merit. z7 Plate 176.

Cultivated in sandy, dry soil in full sun.

DURANTA L. — VERBENACEAE

Evergreen, tropical trees and shrubs; leaves opposite

Fig. 329. *Duranta repens* (from ICS)

or in whorls, entire or toothed; flowers rather small, either in long terminal or short axillary panicles; corolla tube cylindrical, with erect, 5 lobed limb; stamens 4, of these 2 longer, 2 shorter; fruit a juicy drupe, with 8 seeds, surrounded by the enlarged calyx. — 36 species in the tropics, S. America and the W. Indies.

Duranta plumieri Jacq. Evergreen shrub, 1.5—5 m, branches with or without thorns, 4 sided, leaves obovate, oblong, ovate or elliptic, usually entire, 1—5 cm long, tapering into a short petiole; flowers in racemes, grouped into loose, 15 cm long panicles, pendulous, blue, August; fruit yellow, juicy, to 1 cm thick, enveloped in the enlarged calyx with a curved beaked tip. BM 1759 (as *D. spinosa* L.). Mexico to Brazil, W. Indies, frequently found in the gardens of the tropics and subtropics. z9 Fig. 329. # ✿ ⚭

Also available in forms with white flowers and white variegated leaves.